☞ From Ireland 2003

POSTCARDS FROM

P9-EMD-967

Located on the south shore of Galway Bay, Dunguaire Castle was erected in the 16th century by the O'Heynes family and was later the country retreat of Oliver St. John Gogarty, Irish surgeon, author, poet, and wit. It boasts an amazing view of the nearby Burren and Galway Bay, and hosts a summertime medieval banquet with a literary-themed show. See chapter 11. © Greg Gawlowski/Lonely Planet Images.

The Carrick-A-Rede rope bridge in Larrybane, county Antrim, spans a chasm 18m (60 ft.) wide and 24m (80 ft.) above the sea between the mainland and a small island. Local fishermen put up the bridge each spring to allow access to the island's salmon fishery, and visitors can head across for a thrilling walk. See chapter 15. © David W. Hamilton/The Image Bank.

One of the best preserved of all ancient Irish structures, Staigue Fort, along the Ring of Kerry, is constructed of rough stones without mortar of any kind. The walls are 4m (13 ft.) thick at the base, and the diameter is about 27m (90 ft.). Not much is known of its history, but experts think it probably dates from around 1000 B.C. See chapter 9. © Richard Cummins Photography.

A traditional thatch-roof cottage in Ballbriggan, county Dublin. © *Richard Cummins Photography.*

The oldest university in Ireland, Trinity College is located on a picturesque site just south of the River Liffey in Dublin. Visitors flock here to see the Book of Kells, a magnificently illuminated manuscript of the four Gospels. See chapter 4.
© *Catherine Karnow Photography.*

Shops, fast-food restaurants, and movie theaters now rim O'Connell Street, once the fashionable and historic focal point of Dublin. The wide, sweeping thoroughfare still sports a few great landmarks, such as the General Post Office and the Gresham Hotel. See chapter 4. © *Catherine Karnow Photography.*

Established by an act of Parliament in 1854, Ireland's National Gallery in Dublin houses one of Europe's finest collections of paintings, drawings, miniatures, prints, sculptures, and objets d'art. See chapter 4. © *Dave Bartruff Photography.*

Thatch-roof cottages were the traditional dwellings of Irish farmers, though today most have traded up to modern bungalows and two-story homes. Even so, you can still see many inhabited cottages throughout the country and can rent one yourself as self-catering accommodations. See chapter 2. © Kelly/Mooney Photography.

Throughout Ireland, pubs are some of the best places to hear traditional Irish music. See chapter 1 for a list of Frommer's favorite Irish pubs. © Kevin Galvin Photography.

A Celtic cross marks a grave at Kilmalooda Church, Timoleague, county Cork. In earlier times, large versions known as high crosses were status symbols for monasteries and were sometimes covered with biblical scenes. They can be seen all over the country, with some standout examples in county Meath. See chapter 5. © *Richard Cummins Photography*.

Often called the eighth wonder of the world, the Giant's Causeway, Bushmills, county Antrim, consists of roughly 40,000 tightly packed basalt columns that extend for 4.8km (3 miles) along the coast. Scientists believe they were formed 60 or 70 million years ago by volcanic eruptions and cooling lava. Legend, on the other hand, says the rock formation was the work of giants. See chapter 15. © *Tom Till Photography.*

A New Star-Rating System & Other Exciting News from Frommer's!

In our continuing effort to publish the savviest, most up-to-date, and most appealing travel guides available, we've added some great new features.

Frommer's guides now include a new **star-rating system.** Every hotel, restaurant, and attraction is rated from 0 to 3 stars to help you set priorities and organize your time.

We've also added **seven brand-new features** that point you to the great deals, in-the-know advice, and unique experiences that separate travelers from tourists. Throughout the guide, look for:

Finds	Special finds—those places only insiders know about
Fun Fact	Fun facts—details that make travelers more informed and their trips more fun
Kids	Best bets for kids—advice for the whole family
Moments	Special moments—those experiences that memories are made of
Overrated	Places or experiences not worth your time or money
Tips	Insider tips—some great ways to save time and money
Value	Great values—where to get the best deals

We've also added a **"What's New"** section in every guide—a timely crash course in what's hot and what's not in every destination we cover.

Here's what the critics say about Frommer's:

"Amazingly easy to use. Very portable, very complete."
—*Booklist*

"Detailed, accurate, and easy-to-read information for all price ranges."
—*Glamour Magazine*

"Hotel information is close to encyclopedic."
—*Des Moines Sunday Register*

"Frommer's Guides have a way of giving you a real feel for a place."
—*Knight Ridder Newspapers*

Frommer's®

Ireland
2003

by Suzanne Rowan Kelleher

WILEY
Wiley Publishing, Inc.

About the Author

Suzanne Rowan Kelleher is a freelance travel writer and the former Europe Editor of *Travel Holiday* magazine. She has traveled extensively in Ireland, is married to an Irishman, and currently lives in county Dublin.

Published by:

Wiley Publishing, Inc.

909 Third Ave.
New York, NY 10022

ISBN 0-7645-6681-4
ISSN 1534-5947

Editor: Christine Ryan
Production Editor: Tammy Ahrens
Cartographer: Nick Trotter
Photo Editor: Richard Fox
Production by Wiley Indianapolis Composition Services

Front cover photo: Blarney Castle, county Cork

For information on our other products and services or to obtain technical support, please contact our Customer Care Department within the U.S. at 800-762-2974, outside the U.S. at 317-572-3993 or fax 317-572-4002.

Wiley also publishes its books in a variety of electronic formats. Some content that appears in print may not be available in electronic formats.

Manufactured in the United States of America

5 4 3 2

Contents

Appendix: Ireland in Depth   559

Index   573

List of Maps

An Invitation to the Reader

In researching this book, we discovered many wonderful places—hotels, restaurants, shops, and more. We're sure you'll find others. Please tell us about them, so we can share the information with your fellow travelers in upcoming editions. If you were disappointed with a recommendation, we'd love to know that, too. Please write to:

Frommer's Ireland 2003
Wiley Publishing, Inc. • 909 Third Ave. • New York, NY 10022

An Additional Note

Please be advised that travel information is subject to change at any time—and this is especially true of prices. We therefore suggest that you write or call ahead for confirmation when making your travel plans. The authors, editors, and publisher cannot be held responsible for the experiences of readers while traveling. Your safety is important to us, however, so we encourage you to stay alert and be aware of your surroundings. Keep a close eye on cameras, purses, and wallets, all favorite targets of thieves and pickpockets.

New! Frommer's Star Ratings & Icons

Every hotel, restaurant, and attraction listing in this guide has been ranked for quality, value, service, amenities, and special features using a star-rating scale. In country, state, and regional guides, we also rate towns and regions to help you narrow down your choices and budget your time accordingly. Hotels and restaurants in the Very Expensive and Expensive categories are rated on a scale of one (highly recommended) to three stars (exceptional). Those in the Moderate and Inexpensive categories rate from zero (recommended) to two stars (very highly recommended). Attractions, towns, and regions are rated according to the following scale: zero stars (recommended), one star (highly recommended), two stars (very highly recommended), and three stars (must-see).

In addition to the rating system, we also use seven icons to highlight insider information, useful tips, special bargains, hidden gems, memorable experiences, kid-friendly venues, places to avoid, and other useful information:

Finds *Fun Fact* *Kids* *Moments* *Overrated* *Tips* *Value*

The following abbreviations are used for credit cards:

AE American Express	DISC Discover	V Visa
DC Diners Club	MC MasterCard	

FROMMERS.COM

Now that you have the guidebook to a great trip, visit our website at **www.frommers.com** for travel information on nearly 2,500 destinations. With features updated regularly, we give you instant access to the most current trip-planning information available. At Frommers.com, you'll also find the best prices on airfares, accommodations, and car rentals—and you can even book travel online through our travel booking partners. At Frommers.com, you'll also find the following:

- Online updates to our most popular guidebooks
- Vacation sweepstakes and contest giveaways
- Newsletter highlighting the hottest travel trends
- Online travel message boards with featured travel discussions

What's New in Ireland

If you're looking for somewhere less discovered—in search of the Great Irish Destination for the upcoming years—point your compass north. Should you be the outdoorsy type and crave unspoiled wilderness and pubs that feature excellent traditional music, head to the **Inishowen Peninsula,** in county Donegal (see chapter 13); if you're yearning for a healthy dose of culture, head to the historic walls of **Derry City,** county Derry, in Northern Ireland (see chapter 15). Both are destined to be huge tourist haunts, so go now, before the word gets out.

Of course, Ireland's major tourist destinations—Dublin, Cork, Connemara, the Ring of Kerry, and so on—deserve your attention as well. And, though its hospitality remains constant, Ireland is always in a constant state of flux. Here are some of the more notable developments for the year.

PLANNING YOUR TRIP No doubt the biggest practical change returning travelers to Ireland will notice in 2003 is that the **euro** has become the country's national currency. The changeover from Irish punt to euro happened relatively quickly and painlessly last year. Northern Ireland, as part of the United Kingdom, continues to use the British pound as its currency.

If you're thinking of renting short-term, self-catered accommodation in Ireland, there's no better time to go. One of our favorite organizations, the **Irish Landmark Trust (ILT; © 01/670-4733),** has added several wonderful new properties to its impressive stable. This organization's mission is to rescue historic but neglected properties all over the island and restore them into fabulous hideaways, complete with period furnishings. When Ireland's lighthouses were automated in the late 1970s and early 1980s, most of the lightkeepers' houses were left unattended. The ILT has recently bought and restored several properties, including the **Galley Head Lightkeeper's House,** in county Cork (see chapter 8) and the **Loop Head Lightkeeper's House,** in county Clare (see chapter 10), and turned them into stunning getaways with spectacular views. An added bonus: As a not-for-profit institution, the ILT's prices are hard to beat.

The year 2002 was another dismal one for Ireland's tourist industry. After being hit by falling tourism in 2001 following the foot-and-mouth epidemic that afflicted Britain and other European countries, the tragedy of September 11, 2001, made many travelers even more skittish about voyaging abroad. The fact that you're reading this book suggests that you plan to travel to Ireland in the near future, and the Irish hospitality industry will no doubt outdo itself to make your stay a warm and welcoming one.

DUBLIN Where to Stay Though the economy has slowed in the past year or so, Dublin continues to be a fast-growing, trendy destination, with a skyline full of cranes to prove it. The capital is still sprouting new hotels at breakneck speed—fortunately, catering to all budgets. This influx of additional accommodation should help keep hotel prices at bay.

Thankfully, Dublin's upward mobility hasn't meant becoming overrun by big chain hotels. One of our favorite new entries to this year's guide is **Browne's Townhouse** (© 01/638-3939), a sumptuously restored Georgian townhouse with an unbeatable location on St. Stephen's Green. It gets our vote for the city's best boutique hotel. See p. 104.

Shopping Hoping to bring home some chic souvenirs? As we mentioned last year, the hippest new shopping destination continues to be the up-and-coming **Old City** neighborhood, just west of Temple Bar. The area is centered on the pedestrianized Cow's Lane and is particularly good for fashion and smart, craft-based housewares.

OUT FROM CORK **Where to Stay** One of our favorite foodie B&Bs, **Lettercollum House** (© 023/46251), in Timoleague, West Cork, is again offering bed-and-breakfast for more-than-reasonable prices, and you can also still dine at the award-winning restaurant. See p. 308.

NORTHERN IRELAND **Where to Stay** Belfast is buzzing! As the city prepares its bid to be the European Capital of Culture 2008, hip new hotels and eateries are popping up like daisies. Case in point is **TENsq** (© 028/9024-1001), as stylish a boutique hotel as you'll find anywhere. It's Belfast's first Pudong-style hotel, and it delivers Asian luxury, elegant minimalism, and a white-hot restaurant and bar. See p. 507.

Where to Dine Belfast's dining scene is exploding with exciting new places to eat. Try **Restaurant Michael Deane** (© 028/9033-1134) for Michelin-star winning fusion cooking (p. 508); **Ginger** (© 028/9049-3143) for memorable modern cuisine in a minimalist setting (p. 508); and **Le Tavole** (© 028/9066-3211) for a great neighborhood joint dishing up down-to-earth Mediterranean cooking (p. 508).

The Best of Ireland

"The modern American tourist," wrote historian Daniel J. Boorstin, "has come to expect both more strangeness and more familiarity than the world naturally offers." That said, Ireland continues to offer more than its share of both.

At first glance, Ireland presents a familiar face to American visitors. The language is the same, only more lyrical, the faces are familiar, the food recognizable, the stout legendary. Many visitors, notably Irish Americans, experience their arrival as a kind of homecoming. It takes a while for this experience to wear off. When it does, the other face of Ireland shows itself, and this is when the country becomes truly exciting.

Ireland is a place of profound contradiction and complexity. For one thing, it is at the same time both ancient and adolescent. It's as young as it is old.

Ireland's age is obvious to anyone with a car. Within a half day's drive of downtown Dublin lie Neolithic tombs, Bronze Age forts, early Christian monastic sites, Viking walls, and Georgian estates—enough antiquity to make your head spin, all in plain sight. Centuries-old castles are as commonplace in Ireland as Wal-Mart stores are in the United States. The Irish past doesn't exist just in books; it's in the backyard. A shovel, digging for peat or potatoes, may well strike a 5,000-year-old grave. Thousands of unexcavated ancient sites litter the countryside. Any visitor to Ireland who ventures beyond its shops and pubs will soon be struck by how the country revels in its age.

What is less obvious is how new Ireland is as a nation. The Republic of Ireland, with its own constitution and currency, is barely 50 years old. Mary McAleese, the current president of Ireland, is only the eighth person to hold that office. In political age, Ireland, for all its antiquity, is a mere pup. Like any adolescent, it's doing many things for the first time, and at least a few of its contradictions make sense when you keep that fact in mind. Compounding Ireland's youth as a nation is the youth of its people. Roughly half of the population is under 25, and nearly a quarter is under 15. This means that, in many homes, those who once fought for Irish independence are living under the same roof with those who have never known anything else. In these same homes, the gap between generations is often seismic. It is indeed curious that in a country where what happened 1,000 years ago reads like yesterday's news, it is common to feel old and outnumbered at 30.

Ireland's past has been remarkably tumultuous, inspiring a tradition of courage, humor, and creativity. Change is nothing new to the island, yet the rate and scale of the changes occurring in Ireland today are without precedent. And that's where the contradictions become so endearing, like the old farmer in a tweed cap who is afraid of computers but rings his bookmaker on a cellphone. Like the publican progressive enough to have a website but traditional enough to not like seeing a woman drinking from a pint glass. (Older folks often tsk-tsk that "Ladies should drink from half-pint glasses.") Like the grocer-cum-post

Ireland

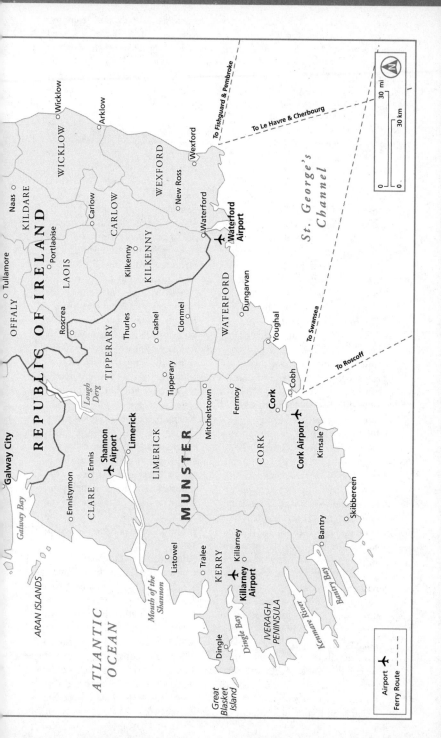

office, or better still, the grocer-cum-hardware store-cum-pub, both common entities in many a rural town. Like the national weather forecasts, which, even with the help of a gazillion satellites, still manage to appear so off-the-cuff and informal. One Nostradamus-like radio weatherman actually offered this by way of a forecast: "It's dry and clear across most of the country, and let's hope it stays that way." The magic of today's Ireland lies in these daily slices of life. Take the time to let them wash over you.

1 The Best Picture-Postcard Towns

- **Dalkey** (county Dublin): This charming south-coast suburb of Dublin enjoys both easy access to the city and freedom from its snarls and frenzy. It has a castle, an island, a mountaintop folly, and a few parks, all in ample miniature. With all the fine and simple restaurants and pubs and shops anyone needs for a brief visit or a long stay, Dalkey is a tempting town to settle into. See chapter 4.
- **Carlingford** (county Louth): What a pleasant surprise, up in lackluster Louth: A charming, tiny medieval village with castle ruins right on the bay, excellent eateries, and pedestrian-friendly lanes filled with colorful shops, cafes, and pubs. See chapter 5.
- **Inistioge** (county Kilkenny): Nestled in the Nore River Valley, cupped in the soft palm of rounded hills, this idyllic river-front village with two spacious greens and a collection of pleasant cafes and pubs is among the most photographed Irish towns. It also attracts hosts of anglers, because fish invariably show good taste and love this place. See chapter 6.
- **Kilkenny** (county Kilkenny): Slightly larger than a small town but terribly picture-postcard nonetheless, Kilkenny may offer the best surviving Irish example of a medieval town. Its walls, the splendidly restored castle, and the renowned design center housed in the castle stables draw visitors from Ireland and abroad. Kilkenny,

however, is no museum. Many regard it as perhaps the most attractive large town in Ireland. See chapter 6.
- **Kinsale** (county Cork): Kinsale's narrow streets all lead to the sea, dropping steeply from the hills that rim the beautiful harbor. This is undoubtedly one of Ireland's most picturesque towns, but the myriad visitors who crowd the streets every summer attest to the fact that the secret is out. The walk from Kinsale through Scilly to Charles Fort and Frower Point is breathtaking. Kinsale has the added benefit of being a foodie town, with no shortage of good restaurants. See chapter 8.
- **Kenmare** (county Kerry): If you're driving the Ring of Kerry, this is the most charming base camp you could wish for. The "little nest" has a blessed location at the mouth of the River Roughty on Kenmare Bay, and is loaded to the gills with flower boxes, enchanting shops, and places to eat. See chapter 9.
- **Adare** (county Limerick): Like a perfect little medieval town plucked from a children's book, Adare is a bastion of thatched cottages, black-and-white timbered houses, lichen-covered churches, and romantic ruins, all strewn along the banks of the River Maigue. And it's got two of the best hotels and one of the best restaurants in Ireland, to boot. See chapter 10.

- **Westport** (county Mayo): It's never a surprise in Ireland when someone says Westport is his favorite town—it's small and bursting. Someday it might explode into a city, but for now Westport remains a hyperactive town that somehow manages to be as friendly and welcoming as a village. See chapter 13.

2 The Best Natural Wonders

- **The Slieve Bloom Environmental Park** (county Laois): Slieve Bloom, Ireland's largest and most unspoiled blanket bog, has been described as a "scenic bulge" rising gently above the midland's peat fields. Its beauty—gentle slopes, glens, rivers, waterfalls, and boglands—is subtle rather than dramatic, but it is comparatively untouched. You can have it more or less to yourself, apart from its deer, foxes, and badgers, and an occasional marten or otter. See the box "Beyond the Pale in County Laois" in chapter 5.

- **MacGillycuddy's Reeks** (county Kerry): One of several mountain ranges on the Iveragh Peninsula, MacGillycuddy's Reeks boasts the highest mountain in Ireland, Carrantuohill (1,361m/3,404 ft.). Whether gazed at from afar or explored up close on foot, the Reeks are among Ireland's greatest spectacles. See "Outdoor Pursuits," under "Killarney," in chapter 9.

- **The Burren** (county Clare): The Burren—from the Irish *Boireann,* meaning "a rocky place"—is one of the strangest landscapes you're ever likely to see: a vast limestone grassland, spread with a quilt of wildflowers from as far afield as the Mediterranean, the Alps, and the Arctic. Its inhabitants include the pine marten and nearly every species of butterfly found in Ireland. See "The Burren," under "County Clare," in chapter 10.

- **Cliffs of Moher** (county Clare): Rising from Hag's Head to the south, these magnificent sea cliffs reach their full height of 228m (760 ft.) just north of O'Brien's Tower. The views of the open sea, of the distant Aran Islands, and of the Twelve Bens of Connemara (see below) are spectacular. A walk south along the cliff edge at sunset makes a perfect end to any day. See p. 376.

- **Croagh Patrick** (county Mayo): Rising steeply 750m (2,500 ft.) above the coast, Croagh Patrick is Ireland's holiest mountain, to which the saint is said to have retreated in penance. The place is biblically imposing. Traditionally, barefoot pilgrims climb it on the last Sunday of July, but in recent years, hundreds of Nike-shod tourists have been making the ascent daily. The view from above can be breathtaking or nonexistent—the summit is often wrapped in clouds, adding to its mystery. See "County Mayo" in chapter 13.

- **The Twelve Bens** (county Galway): Amid Connemara's central mountains, bogs, and lakes rises a rugged range known as the Twelve Bens, crowning a landscape that is among the most spectacular in Ireland. Some of the peaks are bare and rocky, others clothed in peat. The loftiest, Benbaun, in Connemara National Park, reaches a height of 719m (2,395 ft.). See p. 409 for more information on visiting the park.

- **Slieve League** (county Donegal): The Slieve League peninsula stretches for 48km (30 miles) into the Atlantic and is 19km (12 miles) across at its widest point. Its wonderfully pigmented bluffs are the highest sea cliffs in Europe, and can be gazed at from Carrigan Head or walked along, if you dare. From below or from above, Slieve League serves up some of the most dazzling sights in Ireland. See "Northern Donegal Bay," under "The Donegal Bay Coast," in chapter 13.

- **The Giant's Causeway** (county Antrim): In case you lose count, roughly 40,000 tightly packed, mostly hexagonal basalt columns form the giant Finn McCool's path from the Antrim headland into the sea toward the Scottish island of Staffa. This volcanic wonder, formed 60 million years ago, can be marveled at from a distance or negotiated cautiously on foot. See p. 521.

3 The Best Castles

- **Trim Castle** (county Meath): Trim, also called King John's Castle, newly restored as a "preserved ruin," is the most massive and important Anglo-Norman castle in Ireland. It proved all but impregnable for over 4 centuries (late 12th to mid-17th), suffering only one siege during that entire period. In fact, until it collapsed sometime in the 17th century, it never underwent any significant alteration. For anyone with imagination, Trim is a virtual gateway into medieval Ireland. See p. 200.
- **Cahir Castle** (county Tipperary): One of the largest of Ireland's medieval fortresses, this castle is in an extraordinary state of preservation. Tours explain some fascinating features of the military architecture, and then you're free to roam through a maze of tiny chambers, spiral staircases, and dizzying battlements. See p. 238.
- **Kilkenny Castle** (county Kilkenny): Although parts of the castle date from the 13th century, the existing structure has the feel of an 18th-century palace. There have been many modifications since

medieval times, including the addition of beautiful landscaping around the castle. See p. 250.

- **Blarney Castle** (county Cork): Despite the mobs of tourists who besiege the castle daily, this majestic tower house is worth a visit. While you're there, check out the Badger Cave and dungeons at the tower's base, as well as the serpentine paths that wind through the castle gardens, in a picturesque rocky glen. Need we mention the stone? You sidle in under the upper wall with your head hanging over a 10-story drop. You kiss it. It's a thing people do. See p. 274.
- **Charles Fort** (county Cork): On a promontory in stunning Kinsale Harbor, the fort's massive walls enclose a complex array of buildings in varying states of repair. At the entrance you're handed a map and left on your own to explore, discover, and almost certainly get lost in the maze of courtyards, passages, walls, and barracks. See p. 282.
- **Bunratty Castle** and Folk Park (county Clare): The castle has been restored and filled with a

Impressions

. . . we are a very perverse, complex people. It's what makes us lovable. We're banking heavily that God has a sense of humor.

—Jim Murray, *Los Angeles Times,* 1976

curious assortment of medieval furnishings, giving the modern-day visitor a glimpse into the life of its past inhabitants. This is the first stop for many arrivals from Shannon, so expect crowds. See p. 365.

- **Doe Castle** (county Donegal): Location, location, location. This tower house is surrounded on three sides by the waters of Sheep Haven Bay and on the fourth by a moat carved into the bedrock that forms its foundation. With its remote seaside setting and sweeping views of the nearby hills, this is one of the most beautifully situated castles in Ireland. See p. 461.

- **Carrickfergus Castle** (county Antrim): This fortress on the bank of Belfast Lough is the best-preserved Norman castle in Ireland. It consists of an imposing tower house and a high wall punctuated by corner towers. See p. 511.

- **Dunluce Castle** (county Antrim): The castle ruins surmount a razor-sharp promontory jutting into the sea. This was no doubt a highly defensible setting, and the castle wasn't abandoned until a large section collapsed and fell into the breakers one day in 1639. See p. 520.

4 The Best of Ancient Ireland

- **Newgrange** (county Meath): Poised atop a low hill north of the River Boyne, Newgrange is the centerpiece of a dramatic megalithic cemetery dating from more than 5,000 years ago. The massive, heart-shaped mound and passage tomb were constructed, it seems, as a communal vault to house cremated remains. The tomb's passage is so perfectly aligned with the equinoctial sunrise that the central chamber, deep within the mound, is marvelously illuminated at the winter solstice. See p. 199.

- **Hill of Tara** (county Meath): Of ritual significance from the Stone Age to the Christian period, Tara has seen it all and kept it all a secret. This was the traditional center and seat of Ireland's high kings, who could look out from here and survey their realm. Although the Tara hill is only 154m (512 ft.) above sea level, from here you can see each of Ireland's four Celtic provinces on a clear day. The site is mostly unexcavated, and tells its story in

whispers. It's a place to be walked slowly, with an imagination steeped in Ireland's past. See p. 198.

- **Loughcrew** (county Meath): At this little-known site, not far from Newgrange, a series of cruciform passage tombs crown two hills. On the east hill, a guide unlocks the door to one of the domed tombs, answering your questions with a personal touch not possible at the larger, more popular sites. More rewarding, however, is a hike up the west hill to a second, more solitary series of tombs where the connections to be made between ruin and imaginative reconstruction are your own. See p. 199.

- **Lough Gur** (county Limerick): This lakefront site will convince you that the Neolithic farmers of Ireland had an estimable sense of real estate. Inhabited for more than 4,000 years, the ancient farming settlement offers a number of prehistoric remains. The most impressive of these is the largest surviving stone circle in

Ireland, made up of 113 stones. See p. 360.

- **Dún Aengus** (county Galway): No one knows who built this massive stone fort, or when. The eminent archaeologist George Petrie called Dún Aengus "the most magnificent barbaric monument in Europe." Facing the sea, where its three stone rings meet steep 90m (300-ft.) cliffs, Dún Aengus still stands guard today over the southern coast of the island of Inishmore, the largest of the Arans. See "Side Trips from Galway City" in chapter 11.

- **Carrowmore and Carrowkeel** (county Sligo): These two megalithic cities of the dead (Europe's largest) on the Coolera Peninsula may have once contained more than 200 passage tombs. The two together—one in the valley and the other atop a nearby mountain—convey an unequaled sense of the scale and wonder of the ancient megalithic peoples' reverence for the dead. Carrowmore is well presented and interpreted, while Carrowkeel is left to itself and to those who seek it out. See "Exploring the Surrounding Countryside" under "Sligo & Yeats Country" in chapter 13.

- **Navan Fort** (county Antrim): There is now little to see of this place's past greatness, though it was once the ritual and royal seat of Ulster. Thankfully, the interpretive center here is nothing short of remarkable, and it offers a great introduction to the myth and archaeology of the fort, known in Irish as *Emain Macha*. See p. 519.

5 Remnants of the Golden Age: The Best Early Christian Ruins

- **Glendalough** (county Wicklow): Nestled in "the glen of the two lakes," this important monastic settlement was founded in the 6th century by St. Kevin, who was looking for tranquil seclusion. Its setting is disarmingly scenic, exactly the opposite of the harsh environment you'd expect ascetic medieval monks to have sought out. Although quite remote, Glendalough suffered numerous assaults from the Vikings and the English, and eventually dwindled into insignificance. Today its picturesque ruins collude with the countryside to create one of the loveliest spots in Ireland. See p. 176.

- **Jerpoint Abbey** (county Kilkenny): Jerpoint is perhaps the finest representative of the many Cistercian abbeys whose ruins dot the Irish landscape. What draws visitors are the splendid cloister, the most richly carved in Ireland, and the impressive tomb sculptures. The abbey's tower is the tallest of its kind in Ireland. See p. 252.

- **The Rock of Cashel** (county Tipperary): In name and appearance, "the Rock" suggests a citadel, a place more familiar with power than with prayer. In fact, Cashel (or *Caiseal*) means "fortress," and so it was. The rock is a huge outcropping—or rather *up*cropping—of limestone topped with some of the most spectacular ruins in Ireland, including what was formerly the country's finest Romanesque chapel. This was the seat of clerics and kings, a center to rival Tara. Now, however, the two sites vie only for tourists. See p. 238.

- **Skellig Michael** (county Kerry): Thirteen kilometers (8 miles) offshore of the Iveragh Peninsula, rising sharply 214m (714 ft.) out of the Atlantic, is a stunning crag of rock dedicated to the Archangel Michael. In flight from the world, early Irish monks in pursuit of "white martyrdom" chose this spot to build their austere hermitage. Today, the journey to Skellig, across choppy seas, and the arduous climb to its summit are challenging and unforgettable. See "The Skellig Islands," under "The Iveragh Peninsula," in chapter 9.

- **Inishmurray** (county Sligo): This uninhabited island nearly 6.5km (4 miles) off the Sligo coast is home to a most striking monastic complex, surrounded by what appear to be the walls of an even more ancient stone fort. Despite its remoteness, the Vikings sought out this outpost of peace-seeking monks for destruction in 807.

Today its circular ruins and the surrounding sea present a stunning sight, well worth the effort required to reach the shores. See "Exploring the Surrounding Countryside," under "Sligo & Yeats Country," in chapter 13.

- **Clonmacnois** (county Offaly): This was once one of Ireland's most important religious, artistic, and literary centers, a place of pilgrimage and high culture. Founded in the mid–5th century at the axis of the River Shannon and the medieval east-west thoroughfare known as the Eiscir Riada, Clonmacnois thrived for centuries until its prime riverfront location brought repeated raids that nearly proved its undoing. Even in ruins, Clonmacnois remains a place of peculiar beauty and serenity. See p. 482.

6 The Best Literary Spots

- **Glasnevin Cemetery** (county Dublin): Besides being the setting for part of the sixth episode of *Ulysses,* this is the resting place of James Joyce's parents and several other members of his family. The English-born poet Gerard Manley Hopkins is buried here, in the Jesuit plot. Maud Gonne, the Irish nationalist and longtime Dublin resident who is said to have inspired Yeats's play *Cathleen ní Houlihan,* is buried in the Republican plot. See p. #133.
- **Newman House** (county Dublin): Cardinal John Henry Newman was the first rector of the Catholic University in Dublin, which was housed in two buildings on St. Stephen's Green in the center of the city's south side. He worked in that capacity from 1852 until his retirement in 1859. The Catholic University later became

University College Dublin, where Gerard Manley Hopkins began teaching in 1884, as a professor of Greek; after 5 years of teaching here, Hopkins died at the age of 44. James Joyce studied here from 1899 to 1902. See p. 136.

- **North Dublin:** The streets north of the Liffey are home to many of the characters in James Joyce's stories and novels; Joyce lived in this part of Dublin and had a special affinity for it. Much has changed since his time, and Bloom's house at 7 Eccles St. has been replaced by a new wing of the Mater Private Hospital. Still, many mementos of the city as it was in 1904 survive. Tours of the area begin at the James Joyce Centre (p. 137). See chapter 4.
- **St. Patrick's Cathedral** (county Dublin): Jonathan Swift was born

in Dublin in 1667, and entered Trinity College in his 15th year. He later became dean of St. Patrick's Cathedral, and is buried alongside Hester Johnson (Stella) in the cathedral's south aisle. See p. 130.

- **The Aran Islands:** John Millington Synge set his play *Riders to the Sea* on Inishmaan, and wrote an account of life on the islands, titled simply *The Aran Islands.* Liam O'Flaherty, known for his novel *Famine,* is from the island of Inishmore. See "Side Trips from Galway City" in chapter 11.

- **County Sligo:** It seems at times that every hill, house, and lake in the county is signposted in recognition of some relation to W. B. Yeats. The poet's writing was shaped by the landscape, mythology, and people of this region. Many of Sligo's natural and historic monuments—including Lough Gill, Glencar Lake, Ben Bulben Mountain, and Maeve's tomb atop Knocknarea Mountain—appear in Yeats's poetry. There are also several museums housing first editions, photographs, and other memorabilia, and Yeats's grave is in Drumcliff. See chapter 13.

7 The Best Gardens

- **Powerscourt Gardens** (county Wicklow): One of the most grandiose of Irish gardens, set amid the natural splendor of the northern Wicklow Hills. Only 19km (12 miles) from Dublin, the gardens and nearby waterfall make a great day's outing, and a welcome respite from the noise and congestion of the city. See p. 178.

- **Japanese Gardens** (county Kildare): On the grounds of the National Stud, this is considered the only authentic Japanese garden in Ireland, and one of the finest in Europe. A Japanese specialist planned the structure and symbolism, and most of the plants and stones were imported from Japan. See p. 192.

- **Creagh Gardens** (county Cork): Meandering paths lead the visitor past a sequence of exquisite vistas, with many hidden corners to explore. The garden is on a beautiful estuary. See p. 295.

- **Ilnacullin** (county Cork): A ferry conveys visitors from a lovely, rhododendron-rimmed bay in the town of Glengarriff to Garinish Island, the unlikely site of a fine Italianate garden. The formal garden, with the Casita at its center, is linked to a "wild garden" that showcases a collection of rhododendrons, azaleas, and rare trees. See p. 295.

- **Glenveagh National Park** (county Donegal): The gardens and castle are located in a barren, beautiful valley high in the hills of Donegal, along the banks of Lough Veagh. The park contains a statuary garden, a walled garden, and a rhododendron-lined path that leads to a stunning vista overlooking castle and lake. See p. 461.

- **Mount Stewart Gardens** (county Down): Built upon an elaborate plan, the Mount Stewart house has several small gardens of distinctive character. The Ards Peninsula provides a climate conducive to cultivating many subtropical species. The statuary, topiary, and planting designs reflect a touch of whimsy. See p. 513.

8 The Best Attractions for the Whole Family

- **The Ark: A Cultural Centre for Children** (Dublin): The Ark provides a unique chance for kids to have hands-on exposure to art, music, and theater in workshop sessions with artists. There are also excellent theater productions for families. See p. 139.
- **Dublin's Viking Adventure** (Dublin): This is a fun learning experience. Kids travel back in time to be part of Viking life with "real Vikings" working and interacting in a model Norse town. It's on the site where the Vikings made their home in Dublin. See p. 139.
- **Dublin Zoo in the Phoenix Park** (Dublin): Kids love this nearly 24-hectare (60-acre) zoo, with its array of creatures, animal-petting corner, and train ride. The surrounding park has room to run, picnic, and explore for hours (or days!). See p. 140.
- **Irish National Heritage Park** (county Wexford): Nearly 9,000 years of Irish history come alive here in ways that will fascinate visitors of all ages. The whole family will be captivated by the story of ancient Ireland, from its first inhabitants to its Norman conquerors. See p. 210.
- **Muckross House & Gardens** (Killarney, county Kerry): This stunning Victorian mansion with its exquisite gardens is also home to skilled artisans at work. Nearby are a series of reconstructed traditional farms, with animals and docents, providing a gateway to rural Ireland as it was for centuries. See p. 325.
- **Fungie the Dolphin Tours** (Dingle, county Kerry): Every day, fishing boats ferry visitors out into the nearby waters to see Fungie, the friendliest dolphin you're ever likely to meet. Fungie really does swim up to the boat, and the boatmen stay out long enough for ample sightings. You can also arrange an early-morning dolphin swim. See p. 337.
- **Bunratty Castle and Folk Park** (county Clare): Kids are enthralled by this great restored medieval castle and re-created 19th-century village. It's complete with a school and loaded with active craftspeople. See p. 365.
- **Marble Arch Caves** (Marlbank, county Fermanagh): Adventurous families are guided by boat through well-lit underground waterways to explore caves and view amazing stone formations. See p. 554.

9 The Best Active Vacations

- **Sailing Ireland's West Coast:** Spectacular coastal scenery, interesting harbor towns, and an abundance of islands make the West Coast a delight for cruising sailors. See "Sailing" in chapter 3.
- **Horseback Riding in the Galtee Mountains:** The gentle contours of Tipperary's Galty Mountains offer the perfect scenic backdrop for trail riding. You'll be provided with all you need for a horse-riding holiday at Bansha House, a commodious B&B with access to an excellent nearby equestrian program. See p. 243.
- **Sea Kayaking in West Cork:** In Castletownbere on the dramatic and rugged Beara Peninsula, Beara Outdoor Pursuits specializes in

accompanied trips out and around Bere Island and as far as Glengariff. You can play it as safe or as rough as you want. See p. 299.

- **Bicycling in the Southwest:** The peninsulas and islands of Cork and Kerry are perfect for cycling, with light traffic and an abundance of beautiful places to visit. Roycroft's Stores in Skibbereen, county Cork, rent bikes that are a notch above the usual rental

equipment. See the "Sports & Outdoor Pursuits" sections in chapters 8 and 9.

- **Walking the Donegal Coast:** The cliff-rimmed headlands of Donegal are the most spectacular in Ireland, and the best way to explore them is on foot. Among the finest walks are Slieve League, Glen Head, and Horn Head. See "The Donegal Bay Coast" in chapter 13.

10 The Best Luxury Accommodations

- **The Morrison** (Dublin; ✆ 01/ 887-2400): This stunning minimalist hotel is the best thing to hit the central Northside in years. John Rocha's design uses clean lines and quality, natural elements to evoke a very sensuous, luxurious feeling of space and relaxation. Halo, the atrium-style main restaurant, is one of the most talked-about, exciting eateries in town. See p. 110.

- **Marlfield House** (county Wexford; ✆ 800/323-5463 in the U.S., or 055/21124): This grand 1820 house, amid mature gardens and woods, is one of Ireland's most elegant and comfortable guest mansions. Equally renowned is the cuisine, served in the dining room or the conservatory. Amenities abound. See p. 219.

- **Waterford Castle** (county Waterford; ✆ 051/878203): An oasis of elegance and tranquility circled by the River Suir, this island retreat offers both grandeur and informality, along with shoreline walks, a championship golf course, exquisite cuisine, and warm genuine hospitality. See p. 231.

- **Sheen Falls Lodge** (county Kerry; ✆ 800/537-8483 in the U.S., or 064/41600): This salubrious resort sits beside a natural waterfall on 120 hectares (300 acres) of

lawns and semitropical gardens where the River Sheen meets the Kenmare Bay estuary. Of the graceful public rooms, don't miss the wonderful 1,000-volume library, whose green leather sofas and floor-to-ceiling tomes evoke a fine gentlemen's club. Each guest room overlooks the falls (stunning when floodlit at night) or the bay. See p. 317.

- **Ashford Castle** (county Mayo; ✆ 800/346-7007 in the U.S., or 092/46003): *Accommodations* is an understatement for the degree of luxury and elegance you'll find at this castle on the north shore of Lough Corrib—just ask Pierce Brosnan, who held his wedding reception there in 2001. Its magnificent grounds comprise 140 hectares (350 acres) of park and woods and a golf course. Its two restaurants, the Connaught Room and the George V Room, will likely leave you unmotivated to leave the grounds. See p. 428.

- **Delphi Lodge** (county Galway; ✆ 095/42222): This was once the country hideaway for the marquis of Sligo, and now it can be yours, too. Inside, the emphasis is on clean, bright simplicity in perfect taste; the grounds and environs are among the most beautiful in Ireland. *Tranquillity, comfort,* and *fishing* are the operative words here. You will want to stay longer than you'd planned—and by renting one of the cottages for a week or more, you can make the indulgence more affordable. See p. 418.

- **TENsq** (county Antrim; ✆ **028/9024-1001**): This funky boutique hotel overflows with Asian luxury. Low-level beds with white comforters and dark headboards lie on cream coir carpet. Armoires, shutters, and double doors are all inlaid with white opal glass. The overall feel is one of luxurious, elegant minimalism. Don't miss a meal at Porcelain, the hotel's excellent, cutting-edge Asian fusion restaurant. See p. 507.

11 The Best Moderately Priced Accommodations

- **Lorum Old Rectory** (county Carlow; ✆ **0503/75282**): Hospitality is one of those intangibles that no one is able to define in advance but which everyone knows when they've found it. A venerably warm and gracious home, exquisite meals, a lovely setting, and a style that puts its guests in rare form and humor make this place one of Ireland's best. See p. 185.

- **Buggy's Glencairn Inn** (county Waterford; ✆ **058/56232**): Ken and Cathleen Buggy have an incredible talent for getting the details right. Their guest rooms are chock-full of covetable auction finds, the beds are like something out of a fairy tale, and the restaurant is a foodie's destination in itself. See p. 232.

- **Barnabrow Country House** (county Cork; ✆ **021/465-2534**): This completely original, highly romantic, and incredibly stylish place to stay lies in the rolling hills of East Cork. Guest rooms are exceptionally beautiful and feature a wonderful collection of African furniture and crafts. Kids are able to roam freely, and there are plenty of tame animals to meet and pet—donkeys, ducks, hens, geese, sheep, goats—plus a playground for letting off steam. See p. 292.

- **Bruckless House** (county Donegal; ✆ **073/37071**): This mid-18th-century farmhouse, restored with impeccable taste, has many charms, including award-winning gardens and a stable of Connemara ponies. Spacious, welcoming, and comfortable, Bruckless House feels like home (or better) after only a very short time. See p. 458.

- **Rhu-Gorse** (county Donegal; ✆ **073/21685**): The views of Lough Eske from this eminently comfortable modern guesthouse are not to be believed. If you have the makings of a convert to Donegal, it will happen here. See p. 450.

- **Glencarne House** (county Leitrim; ✆ **079/67013**): This attentively restored late-Georgian house on a 40-hectare (100-acre) working farm offers a rare quality of hospitality and charm to midland lake region visitors. Lovely, spacious rooms, chiropractic beds, gracious hosts, and award-winning breakfasts are yours for surprisingly affordable rates. Dinners are a high point, so there's no need to venture out once you've settled in. See p. 490.

- **Ross Castle and House** (county Cavan; ✆ **049/854-0237**): A tower room in a centrally heated haunted castle—with the longest bathtub I've ever seen—awaits you at Ross Castle. It won't take too big a bite out of your wallet, either. It might not be elegance, but it is unquestionably memorable. Warm, comfortable Ross Castle and nearby Ross House are great places to relax beside Lough Sheelin, a noteworthy source of trout and pike. See p. 490.

- **Slieve Croob Inn** (county Down; ℰ **028/4377-1412**): Whether you want to drop anchor and set up a home away from home in a self-catering cottage or just spend a night in a magically stunning landscape, it doesn't get much better than this perfectly tasteful hideaway in the magical Mournes. See p. 532.

- **The Saddlers House & the Merchant's House** (county Derry; ℰ **028/7126-9691** for Saddlers House, 028/7126-4223 for Old Rectory): Compared to the Merchant's House, the Saddlers House is modest. Its rooms are clean and spare, decorated with the simplicity that its merchant origins seem to demand. The Merchant House is more elegant, and beautifully restored. Both houses, run by the inimitable Joan Pyne, are a brief stroll from the center of Derry. See p. 543.

12 The Best Restaurants

- **Peacock Alley** (Dublin; ℰ **01/478-7015**): You'll find Ireland's most daring and talented chef ensconced (with his Michelin stars) in the Fitzwilliam Hotel. Expect complex, creative, nirvana-inducing food and a big bill. See p. 116.

- **Blair's Cove** (county Cork; ℰ **027/61127**): Blair's Cove House is one of the most idyllic and romantic spots in Ireland to enjoy an unforgettable meal. You can also spend a week, if you can't pull yourselves away. This is one of the finest restaurants on the isle, in a part of Ireland to which you're all too likely to become attached. See p. 306.

- **The Wild Geese** (county Limerick; ℰ **061/396451**). After spending years making other people's restaurants absolutely fabulous, owner-chef David Foley created a gem in one of the prettiest towns in Ireland. The cooking is complex, flavorful, and refined, yet always restrained. Expect great desserts, impeccable service, and a buzzing atmosphere. See p. 361.

- **Moran's Oyster Cottage** (county Galway; ℰ **091/796113**): A short drive from Galway center, this seafood mecca is worth the drive from Dublin. For six generations, the Morans have focused on what they know and do best—seafood and nothing but, all day every day. You may not find better oysters and wild salmon anywhere, and surely not at this price. See p. 402.

- **Cromleach Lodge** (county Sligo; ℰ **071/65155**): In this lovely country house with panoramic views of Lough Arrow and environs, Christy and Moira Tighe have created a culinary destination with few peers. The menu, Irish in focus, changes daily and never fails to delight. The eight-course gourmet menu is the ultimate indulgence. See p. 440.

- **The Corncrake** (county Donegal; ℰ **077/74534**): Such a judicious blend of fresh ingredients and culinary imagination is a rare treat. The nettle soup, roast lamb, and desserts of Noreen Lynch and Brid McCartney warrant a detour to the town of Carndonagh, where the living room of a small row house has been transformed into an extraordinary restaurant. See p. 470.

- **The Narrows** (county Down; ℂ **028/4272-8148**). Who'd have thought that the sleepy little waterside hamlet of Portaferry would have a restaurant like this? Danny Millar is one of the hottest young chefs on this island—just ask *Food & Wine* magazine—and his complex-yet-earthy cooking is worth going out of your way for. See p. 515.

13 The Best Pubs

- **Abbey Tavern** (county Dublin): A short distance from Dublin center, the Abbey Tavern is the perfect place to recover and refuel after exploring Howth Head, Ireland's Eye, and the attractive fishing and yachting village of Howth on the northern tip of Dublin Bay. The Abbey is known far and wide for its ballads as well as its brew. See p. 159.
- **Brazen Head** (county Dublin): Nearly qualifying as one of Ireland's ancient sites, the Brazen Head, commissioned by Charles II, is more than 300 years old, but its stout is as fresh as it comes. Among its illustrious alumni are Wolfe Tone, Daniel O'Connell, and Robert Emmet, who planned the Dublin rising of 1803 under the Head's low timbers. In fact, he was hanged not far from here when everything went wrong. See p. 155.
- **The Long Valley** (county Cork): For anyone who knows and loves Cork, this is a place of pilgrimage. One endless, low-slung room with a bar running its full length, doors taken from an ocean liner, barmen in white butcher's coats, and a selection of delectable sandwiches. A little slice of heaven. See p. 277.
- **McGann's** (county Clare): Doolin, a dot of a town on the Clare Coast, is a magnet for traditional Irish musicians—and is consequently a wonderful spot to hear impromptu sessions of Irish music. Gus O'Connor's, down the road, is more famous (but also thicker with tourists); McGann's remains the genuine article without the hype. See p. 381.
- **Moran's Oyster Cottage** (county Galway): Famed for its seafood, this centuries-old thatched-cottage pub on the weir also draws a perfect pint. This may well be the oyster capital of Ireland. It's 19km (12 miles) out of Galway and well worth the drive—or the walk, for that matter. See p. 402.
- **Smuggler's Creek** (county Donegal): This place is worth a stop if only for its spectacular cliff-top views of Donegal Bay. Stone walls, beamed ceilings, open fires, excellent fare, and the brew that's true are among the charms proprietor Conor Britton has on tap. See p. 454.
- **Crown Liquor Saloon** (county Antrim): This National Trust pub, across from the Grand Opera House in Belfast, is a Victorian gem. Your mouth will drop open at its antique publican splendor even before you lift your first pint. See p. 509.

14 The Best Websites

- **Irelandhotels.com** (www.ireland hotels.com): What catapults this accommodations database ahead of the raft of hotel-finding sites is its "search by facility" function. Gotta have a gym? Need to find a babysitter? Want an in-room modem dataport for checking your e-mail? No problem. Just plug in your requirements and it will spit out a list of hotels and guesthouses that fit the bill.

- **Ireland Consolidated** (www. irelandconsolidated.com): One of the best bucket shops specializing in Ireland, it offers unsold tickets on major airlines at well below published rates. The downside is that while you can view the great fares online, you still have to contact the company by phone to seal the deal.
- **Irish Tourist Board** (www.ireland. travel.ie): Bord Failte's site is both easy to navigate and extremely informative. An excellent place to start gathering ideas for your trip.
- **AA Roadwatch** (www.aaroad watch.ie): Planning on driving in Ireland? The route-planning feature of the Irish Automobile Association's site is brilliantly simple. Plug in your starting point and destination, and you'll get a very detailed set of directions on how to get from A to B. You can even tell the database to avoid motorways and toll roads, if you so desire.

- **Entertainment Ireland** (www. entertainment.ie): This handy, exhaustive, searchable database includes just about every event going on in Ireland, from museum exhibitions to rock concerts to hot new plays to nightclub theme nights. And there are well-written reviews of them all, to boot.
- **Irish Family History Foundation** (www.irishroots.net): This brand-new, comprehensive genealogy resource contains documentation from all 32 counties on the island. Much of the archived information is free for your perusal, and you can also avail of researchers to do the work for you.
- **Newshound** (www.nuzhound. com): Hands down, the best singular resource for keeping up to date on Northern Ireland. It's a searchable library of news articles about developments in the North, including a terrific timeline of key events in "the Troubles." In addition, there's a vast array of articles on the Republic, including travel and dining reviews.

2

Planning Your Trip to Ireland

Chances are that you've been looking forward to this trip to Ireland for some time. You've probably set aside a significant amount of hard-earned cash, taken time off from work, school, or other commitments, and now want to make the most of your holiday. So where do you start?

The aim of this chapter is to provide you with the information you need to make sound decisions when planning your trip: When should you go? How will you get there? Should you book a tour or travel independently? What should you pack? How much will it cost? You'll find all the necessary resources, along with addresses, phone numbers, and websites here.

1 The Lay of the Land

The island of Ireland is comprised of the Republic of Ireland and Northern Ireland, with the Atlantic Ocean off its western shores and the Irish Sea to the east. Well over 3,228km (2,000 miles) of ocean separate it from Newfoundland, but it is close enough to Great Britain that, on a clear day, you can glimpse the northern Welsh coast. Dublin, the capital city of the Republic, shares nearly the same latitude as Edmonton, Alberta, and Bremen, Germany, yet distinguishes itself by its palm trees and bougainvillea. We can thank the Gulf Stream, originating in the Caribbean and sending its warm currents northward, for Ireland's mild disposition. Yet both the Atlantic and the Irish Sea have notorious tempers— something you'll want to remember if you plan to tour the coast.

With a landmass of approximately 84,434 sq. km (32,600 sq. miles), the island is roughly the same size as the state of Maine. In rounded figures, it is at most 484km (300 miles) north to south, and 274km (170 miles) east to west. No point in Ireland is farther than 113km (70 miles) from one of its encircling waters: the Atlantic Ocean,

the Irish Sea, or the St. George and North channels. It may seem strange, but in the past, the Irish rarely saw their offshore waters as a resource. Traditionally, the Irish disliked eating fish and avoided learning to swim. The sea was to be feared. It was perilous to cross, and, worse, its waves brought invaders, one after another.

The country's topography is unusual. Instead of its shores sloping to the sea and its interior rising to mountain peaks, the reverse is the case. Shaped like a saucer, Ireland's twisted, 3,228km (2,000-mile) coastline is, with a few notable exceptions, a breachless bulwark of rugged hills and low mountains, with sea cliffs to the west. Its interior is generally a flat to rolling limestone plain made up of fertile farmland and raised bogs. Ireland's longest and greatest river is the Shannon, flowing 371km (230 miles) south and west across the midlands from its source in the Cuileagh Mountains of county Cavan to its estuary in county Limerick. The island's largest lake, Lough Neagh, occupies 396 sq. km (153 sq. miles) of counties Antrim and Armagh in the north.

Technically speaking, Ireland has no mountains, only hills—its highest peak, Carantuohill in county Kerry, reaches to only about 1,020m (3,400 ft.). Most of its heights, whether mountains or hills, were rounded off and smoothed into graceful slopes tens of thousands of years ago by receding glaciers.

One of Europe's least densely populated countries (third behind Finland and Sweden), Ireland is commonly described as unspoiled, even "untouched." Not so. Ireland was once almost entirely forested but—like Scotland—was almost completely cleared under British rule to provide timber for English shipbuilders. Only about 1% of the hardwood forests have survived and Ireland has imported virtually all of its wood for the past 200 years. Relatively recently, there has been a concerted effort to plant pine forests and the government has created 60 forest parks around the island. In addition, six national parks are open to the public: Connemara National Park in county Galway, Glenveagh National Park in county Donegal, Killarney National Park in county Kerry, Wicklow Mountains National Park in county Wicklow, Burren National Park in county Clare, and Mayo National Park in county Mayo.

Moreover, many prehistoric bogs and limestone plains have remained virtually untouched for centuries and the predominance of small-scale mixed agriculture has long contributed to the preservation of an unusually wide range of flora and fauna in the Irish countryside, with the notable and famous exception of snakes and other reptiles. As it happens, Mother Nature, not St. Patrick, deserves credit for Ireland's "snakelessness"—all she gave to the island, herpetologically speaking, is one lonely type of common lizard, featured several years ago on a 32p postage stamp.

2 The Regions in Brief

Ireland is a land divided many different ways, all of which are significant in finding your course through its history, along its roads, and amid its people.

The island is divided into two major political units—Northern Ireland, which along with Great Britain forms the United Kingdom, and the Republic of Ireland. Of the 32 counties in Ireland, 26 are in the Republic. Of the four historic provinces, three and part of the fourth are in the Republic.

The line partitioning the land and people of Ireland into two separate entities became an official boundary in 1922, when the Republic became a free state. For some Irish on both sides of the border, the division of the island remains a matter of dispute. But in simplest practical terms, for the tourist, the line between north and south represents a national border.

Still very much alive on the maps and in the minds of the Irish, however, is another, much older, Gaelic set of divisions corresponding to the four points of the compass. In this early scheme of things, Ulster is north, Leinster is east, Munster is south, Connaught is west. The traditional center of Ireland is the hill of Uisneach in county Westmeath.

Next, there are the **counties.** This is most important because it is how the Irish themselves think and talk. These are the "states" of Ireland, from which individuals and families hail, with which citizens identify (as in "He's a Corkman married to a Donegal girl"). Each county is the butt of the next's jokes ("A Dublinman, a Meath man, and a Kildare man walk into a pub . . ."), and they all tangle in fierce athletic contests in the pursuit of national titles in Gaelic football and hurling.

The island's 32 counties, grouped under the four traditional provinces of Ireland cited above, are listed here:

In Ulster (to the north): Cavan, Donegal, and Monaghan in the Republic; Antrim, Armagh, Derry, Down, Fermanagh, and Tyrone in Northern Ireland.

In Munster (to the south): Clare, Cork, Kerry, Limerick, Tipperary, and Waterford.

In Leinster (to the east): Dublin, Carlow, Kildare, Kilkenny, Laois, Longford, Louth, Meath, Offaly, Westmeath, Wexford, and Wicklow.

In Connaught (to the west): Sligo, Mayo, Galway, Roscommon, and Leitrim.

Lastly, in practical terms for the tourist, Ireland may be divided into **regions:** the southeast, the southwest, the west, the northwest, the midlands, and Northern Ireland. These, with several specific cities and their environs—Dublin, Cork, and Galway—make up the principal areas of interest for Ireland's visitors and serve to structure the information in this guide.

DUBLIN & ENVIRONS With 40% of the Republic's population living within 97km (61 miles) of Dublin, the capital is a hotbed for profound, high-speed changes that are transforming Ireland into a prosperous, venturesome European country. What was old and venerable in the city remains so, though it now shares space with an all-out 20- and 30-something Irish renaissance. There's something here for everyone. Within an hour or slightly more north and south of Dublin—by car or public transportation—lie a handful of engaging coastal towns, the barren beauty of the Wicklow Mountains, some of the most important prehistoric and early Christian ruins of Europe in county Meath, Kildare's thoroughbred country, and the stately mansions and lush gardens of county Wicklow.

THE SOUTHEAST Boasting the best (warmest and driest) weather in Ireland, the southeast coast is often one alternative to a pub for getting out of the rain. Besides its weather, the southeast offers sandy beaches, Waterford's city walls and crystal works, Kilkenny and Cahir castles, the Rock of Cashel, the Irish National Heritage Park at Ferrycarig, and Ireland's largest bird sanctuary, on the Saltee Islands.

CORK & ENVIRONS Cork, Ireland's second city in size, is Dublin's rival in sport and stout. It feels more like a buzzy university town than a city, and provides a congenial gateway to the south and west of Ireland, which many consider Ireland's Oz, the ultimate destination. Within arm's reach of Cork are the truly impressive Blarney Castle (with its less impressive stone), the culinary and scenic delights of Kinsale, the Dromberg Stone Circle, Sherkin and Clear islands, and Mizen Head. Also in this region is the spectacular landscape of West Cork, one of the truly gorgeous pockets of Ireland.

THE SOUTHWEST The mountains and seascapes of the southwest, the wettest corner of Ireland, make the same point as Seattle: There are more important things in life than staying dry. The once-remote splendors of county Kerry have long ceased to be a secret, so at least during high season, visitors must be prepared to share the view. Some highlights of this region are the Dingle Peninsula, the Skellig and the Blaskett islands, Staigue Fort, the truly lovely town of Kenmare, Tralee and its annual international and folk festivals, and dazzling views of sea, shore, and mountains—a new one, it seems, at every bend in the road. Killarney was put on the map by its surrounding natural beauty—serene lakes, mountain peaks (the tallest in Ireland), and the ever-present sea—and is now synonymous with souvenir shops and tour buses. The "Ring of Kerry" (less glamorously known as N70 and N71), a 178km (110-mile) circuit of the Iveragh Peninsula, is the most visited attraction in Ireland next to the Book of Kells. That's both a recommendation and a warning. Nearby, Killarney National Park—10,000 hectares (25,000 acres) of mountains, woodlands, waterfalls, and wildlife—provides a dramatic haven from tour buses and the din of massed camera shutters clicking away.

THE WEST The west of Ireland, once a land of last resort, today offers a first taste of Ireland's beauty and striking diversity for those who fly into Shannon Airport. County Limerick boasts a number of historic sites, from the Stone Age center at Lough Gur to an array of impressive castles. They include Knappogue, Bunratty, King John's, Ashrod, and (just over the county line in Galway) Dunguaire. County Clare's natural offerings, the 210m (700-ft.) Cliffs of Moher and the lunarlike limestone plateau of the Burren, are unforgettable. Farther up the coast to the north, past Galway, lies county Mayo, home of the stunningly set town of Westport on Clew Bay. Nearby, 750m (2,500 ft.) up stands Croagh Patrick, a place of pilgrimage for centuries. Another, more recent pilgrimage site is the shrine of Knock, with its massive basilica. Also nearby, off the Connemara and southern Mayo coasts, is a string of islands—including Inishbofin, Inishturk, and Clare—that are well worth the crossing. Achill Island, Ireland's largest, is a favored vacation spot and is accessible by car.

GALWAY & ENVIRONS Galway just may be the perfect small city. It is without a doubt the most vibrant, colorful, buzzy place in Ireland—a youthful, prospering port and university city, and the self-acclaimed arts capital of Ireland with theater, music, dance, and a vibrant street life to prove it. There's nothing sleepy about Galway.

And if that's not enough reason to point your compass west, Galway is the gateway to Connemara, one of the most moody, melancholy, magical landscapes in the world. Must-sees in this beautifully desolate part of the world include the Twelve Bens, Kylemore Abbey, a 1,600 hectare (4,000-acre) national park, and the area's charming "capital," the town of Clifden. Offshore lie the legendary Aran Islands—Inishmore, Inishmaan, and Inisheer—further studies in irresistible desolation.

THE NORTHWEST In Ireland, it's easy to become convinced that isolated austerity is beautiful, and nowhere is this more true than Donegal, with its 323km (200 miles) of drenched, jagged coastline that, if you don't mind the cold, offers some of the finest surfing in the world. Inland, the Deeryveagh Mountains and Glenveagh National Park offer as much wilderness as can be found anywhere in Ireland. County Sligo contains the greatest concentration of megalithic sites in Ireland: the stone circles, passage tombs, dolmens, and cairns of, most notably, Carrowmore, Knocknarea, and Carrowkeel. This region was also inspiration for much of the poetry of W. B. Yeats, the poet laureate of Sligo. Nearby, Leitrim's unspoiled lakes are a favorite retreat, particularly for anglers.

THE MIDLANDS The lush center of Ireland, bisected by the mighty but lazy Shannon, is a land of pastures, rivers, lakes, woods, and gentle mountain slopes, an antidote to the barren beauty of Connemara and a retreat, in high season, from the throngs of tourists who crowd the coasts. The midlands have no cities, and their towns are not their attractions; the shores and waters of the Shannon and Lough Derg and of their many lesser cousins provide much of the lure. Outdoor pursuits—cycling, boating, fishing, trekking, and hunting—are the heart of the matter here. The midlands also offer visits to some remarkable sites, such as Birr Castle and its splendid gardens, and Clonmacnois, now the stunning ruins of a famous Irish monastic center.

NORTHERN IRELAND Across the border, in a corner of both Ireland and the United Kingdom, Northern Ireland's six counties are well worth exploring. The stunning Antrim coast (particularly between Ballycastle and Cushendum), the 40,000 black basalt columns of the Giant's Causeway, and the luring nine Glens of Antrim are perhaps the greatest draw for sightseers. Written in a minor key is the loveliness of the Fermanagh Lake District to the south, while county Down with its Mourne Mountains marks the sunniest and driest spot in the North. The city walls of Derry, Carrickfergus Castle, Belfast's "Golden Mile," and Navan Fort (or Emain Macha, the royal center of Ulster for 800 years) are just a sampling of what the North has to offer.

3 Visitor Information

To get your planning under way, contact the following offices of the Irish Tourist Board and the Northern Ireland Tourist Board. They are eager to answer your questions, and have bags of genuinely helpful information, mostly free of charge.

After you've perused the brochures, surf the Web to scoop up even more information.

IN THE UNITED STATES
- **Irish Tourist Board,** 345 Park Ave., New York, NY 10154 (© **800/223-6470** in the U.S., or 212/418-0800; fax 212/371-9052; www.tourismireland.com).
- **Northern Ireland Tourist Board,** 551 Fifth Ave., Suite 701, New York, NY 10176 (© **800/326-0036** in the U.S., or 212/922-0101; fax 212/922-0099; www.discovernorthernireland.com).

IN CANADA
- **Irish Tourist Board,** 2 Bloor St. W., Suite 1501, Toronto, ON M4W 3E2 (© **800/223-6470;** fax 416/929-6783).
- **Northern Ireland Tourist Board,** 2 Bloor St. W., Suite 1501, Toronto, ON M4W 3E2 (© **800/576-8174** or 416/925-6368; fax 416/925-6033; infocanada@nitb.com).

IN THE UNITED KINGDOM
- **Irish Tourist Board/Bord Fáilte,** 150 New Bond St., London W1Y 0AQ (© **020/7493-3201;** fax 020/7493-9065; www.tourism ireland.com).
- **Northern Ireland Tourist Board,** 24 Haymarket, London SW1 4DG (© **020/7766-9920;** fax 020/7766-9929; infogb@nitb.com).

IN AUSTRALIA
- **All Ireland Tourism** (Republic and Northern Ireland), 36 Carrington St., 5th Level, Sydney, NSW 2000 (© **02/9299-6177;** fax 02/9299-6323).

IN NEW ZEALAND
- **Irish Tourist Board,** Dingwall Building, 2nd Floor, 87 Queen St., Auckland (© **0064-9-379-8720;** fax 0064-9-302-2420).

IN IRELAND
- **Irish Tourist Board/Bord Fáilte,** Baggot Street Bridge, Dublin 2 (© **1850-230330;** fax 01/602-4100; www.ireland.travel.ie).

- **Northern Ireland Tourist Board,** 16 Nassau St., Dublin 2 (© 01/ 679-1977; fax 01/679-1863; info dublin@nitb.com).

IN NORTHERN IRELAND
- **Irish Tourist Board,** 53 Castle St., Belfast BT1 1GH (© 028/ 9032-7888; fax 028/9024-0201).

- **Northern Ireland Tourist Board,** St. Anne's Court, 59 North St., Belfast BT1 1NB (© 028/9023-1221; fax 028/9024-0960; www. discovernorthernireland.com).

4 Entry Requirements & Customs

ENTRY REQUIREMENTS
For citizens of the United States, Canada, Australia, and New Zealand entering the Republic of Ireland for a stay of up to 3 months, no visa is necessary, but a valid passport is required.

Citizens of the United Kingdom, when traveling on flights originating in Britain, do not need to show passports to enter Ireland (though they do need some form of identification). Nationals of the United Kingdom and colonies who were not born in Great Britain or Northern Ireland must have a valid passport or national identity document.

For entry into Northern Ireland, the same conditions apply.

CUSTOMS
WHAT YOU CAN BRING TO IRELAND
Like all the European Union (EU) member states, Ireland and Northern Ireland customs are mainly concerned with two categories of goods: (1) items bought duty-paid and value-added-tax-paid (VAT-paid) in other EU countries and (2) goods bought under duty-free and VAT-free allowances at duty-free shops.

The first case normally applies to Irish citizens, visitors from Britain, and travelers from other EU countries. If the goods are for personal use, you won't need to pay additional duty or VAT. The limits for goods in this category are 800 cigarettes, 10 liters of spirits, 45 liters of wine, and 55 liters of beer.

The second category pertains primarily to overseas visitors, such as U.S. and Canadian citizens. The limit on duty-free and VAT-free items that may be brought into the EU for personal use: 200 cigarettes, 1 liter of liquor, 2 liters of wine, and other goods (including beer) not exceeding the value of €150 ($134) per adult. There are no restrictions on bringing currency into Ireland.

Regardless of whether you arrive in the Republic or Northern Ireland, the customs system is the same, operating on a Green, Red, and Blue Channel format. If you're coming from the United States or another non-EU country, use the Green Channel if you don't exceed the duty-free allowances and the Red Channel if you have extra goods to declare. If you are like most visitors, bringing in only your own clothes and personal effects, use the Green Channel. The Blue Channel is exclusively for use by passengers entering Ireland from other EU countries.

In addition to your luggage, you may bring in sports equipment for your own recreational use or electronic equipment for your own business or professional use while in Ireland. Prohibited goods include firearms, ammunition, and explosives; narcotics; meat, poultry, plants, and their byproducts; and domestic animals from outside the United Kingdom.

WHAT YOU CAN BRING HOME
On board the flight back to the United States, you'll be given a

customs declaration to fill out. Be sure to pack the goods you'll declare separately and have your sales receipts handy. Returning **U.S. citizens** who have been away for 48 hours or more are allowed to bring back, once every 30 days, $400 worth of merchandise duty-free. You'll be charged a flat rate of 5% duty on the next $1,000 worth of purchases. On gifts, the duty-free limit is $100. You cannot bring fresh foodstuffs into the United States; tinned foods are allowed. For more information, write the **U.S. Customs Service,** 1300 Pennsylvania Ave. NW, Room 54D, Washington, DC 20229, to request the free pamphlet *Know Before You Go.* It's also available on the Web at www.customs.gov/travel/travel.htm.

Citizens of the United Kingdom who are returning from a European Community (EC) country will go through a separate Customs Exit (the Blue Channel) for EC travelers. In essence, there is no limit on what you can import from an EC country, as long as the items are for personal use. But be aware that if you exceed the government's guidance levels, you may be asked to prove that the goods are for your own use. Guidance levels on goods bought in the EC for your own use are 800 cigarettes, 200 cigars, 1 kilogram smoking tobacco, 10 liters of spirits, 90 liters of wine (of which not more than 60 liters can be sparkling wine), and 110 liters of beer. For more information, contact **HM Customs & Excise,** Passenger Enquiry Point, 2nd Floor Wayfarer House, Great South West Road, Feltham, Middlesex TW14 8NP (✆ **020/8910-3744,** or 44/181-910-3744 from outside the U.K.; www.hmce.gov.uk).

For a clear summary of **Canadian** rules, write for the booklet *I Declare,* issued by **Revenue Canada,** 2265 St. Laurent Blvd., Ottawa K1G 4KE (✆ **506/636-5064;** www.ccra-adrc.gc.ca).

Australians can obtain a helpful brochure, *Know Before You Go,* available from Australian consulates or Customs offices. For more information, contact **Australian Customs Services,** GPO Box 8, Sydney NSW 2001 (✆ **02/9213-2000;** www.customs.gov.au).

New Zealand citizens should obtain a free pamphlet available at New Zealand consulates and Customs offices: *New Zealand Customs Guide for Travelers,* Notice no. 4. For more information, contact **New Zealand Customs,** 50 Anzac Ave., P.O. Box 29, Auckland (✆ **09/359-6655;** www.customs.govt.nz).

5 Money

CASH/CURRENCY

The Republic of Ireland has adopted the single European currency known as the **euro.** In this volume, the € sign symbolizes the euro. In converting prices into U.S. dollars, we used the rates €1 = $.89.

Euro notes come in denominations of €5, €10, €20, €50, €100, €200, and €500. The euro is divided into 100 cents; coins come in denominations of €2, €1, 50¢, 20¢, 10¢, 5¢, 2¢, and 1¢. It may seem awkward, particularly for Americans, but the terms "euro" and "cent" are never pluralized. That is, €50.25 is spoken as "50 euro, 25 cent."

So far, the United Kingdom has resisted the euro and retained its traditional currency, the **pound sterling,** which continues to trade independently on the world currency market. Northern Ireland, as part of the United Kingdom, uses the British pound. In this volume, the £ sign symbolizes the British pound. The

> **Tips Avoiding Bank Fees**
>
> Remember that each time you withdraw cash from an ATM, your bank will likely slap you with a fee of between $4 and $8 (check how much your bank charges before leaving home). Rather than taking out small denominations again and again, it makes sense to take out larger amounts every 2 to 3 days. Not only will this keep you from racking up fees, but you won't waste time in lines waiting for a free machine.

British pound is not legal tender in the Republic, and neither the Irish punt nor the euro is legal tender in the North. In converting prices for this guide, we used the rate £1 = $1.42.

The British currency used in Northern Ireland has notes in denominations of £5, £10, £20, £50, and £100. Coins are issued in £1, 50p, 20p, 10p, 5p, 2p, and 1p denominations.

Note: The values of the euro and the British pound fluctuate daily, so it is best to begin checking exchange rates well in advance of your visit to gain a sense of their recent range.

CREDIT CARDS

Leading international credit cards such as Visa (also known as Visa/Barclay), MasterCard (also known as Access or Eurocard), American Express, Carte Blanche, and Diners Club are readily accepted throughout all 32 counties. Most establishments display on their windows the logos of the credit cards they accept. Note that MasterCard and Visa are far more widely accepted than American Express, and Diners Club is accepted at only very upscale restaurants and hotels.

However handy it is to make purchases with credit, note that many banks add a service charge (sometimes as high as 3%) to all transactions made in a foreign currency; check with your card's issuer before you leave to avoid a nasty surprise when you get your bill.

ATMS

Repeat this until it sticks: The best way to get cash is with your bank card

in an automated teller machine (ATM). Any town large enough to have a bank branch (all but the smallest villages) will have an ATM linked to a network that includes your home bank. **Cirrus** (© **800/424-7787;** www.mastercard.com) and **PLUS** (© **800/843-7587;** www.visa.com) are the two most popular networks. Using ATMs gets you the best possible exchange rate because Cirrus and PLUS let you take advantage of their high-volume wholesale exchange rate, which leaves all other players—traveler's checks, exchange bureaus, and credit cards—in the dust. Use the toll-free numbers to locate ATMs in your destination.

Most Irish and Northern Irish ATMs accept PINs of four to six digits. One hiccup, however, is that they often don't have alphanumeric keypads. So to withdraw cash using your bank card, your PIN must be made up of just numbers. If your PIN features letters (STAN37), use a telephone dial to figure out the numeric equivalents (or better yet, memorize it before you get to Ireland).

Traveler's checks are something of an anachronism from the days before the ATM made cash accessible at any time, but some travelers still like the perceived security of the tried-and-true. You can get them at almost any bank, for a small service charge. American Express traveler's checks are also available over the phone by calling © **800/221-7282** or 800/721-9768, or you can purchase checks online at www.americanexpress.com. Amex gold or platinum cardholders can avoid paying the fee by ordering over the telephone; platinum cardholders can also purchase checks fee-free in person at Amex Travel Service locations. American Automobile Association members can obtain checks with no fee at most AAA offices.

6 When to Go

CLIMATE

To get a feel for just how hilarious Irish weather is, just tune into one of the TV or radio weather forecasts. Nowhere else will you hear the phrase, "Today we can expect showers, followed by periods of rain." Categorizing rain is an art form in Ireland. First you have "soft rain," which is like being spritzed by a spray bottle. Then you have "spitting," just a few random drops that don't even leave the ground wet. Next come "showers," brief intervals of rain that last only a few minutes—often while the sun is shining. The Irish don't consider it to be true rain unless it's steady and ongoing enough to warrant an umbrella. In a downpour, you may hear someone complain that it's "lashing," "bucketing," or "pelting."

The only thing consistent about Irish weather is its changeability, with the best of times and the worst of times often only hours, or minutes, apart. There's a saying that in Ireland you get "all four seasons in one day," which means you could start your day in heavenly, summery sunshine, get caught in a brief springlike downpour by lunchtime, go through an autumnal, dry but windy spell in midafternoon, and need a sweater as a wintry evening chill sets in. In other words, when packing, think *layers* for any time of year.

On the upside, the Irish climate is responsible for those 40 shades of green you'll encounter on your travels. And there's nothing like coming across a rainbow over the peat fields of Connemara or the Wicklow Gap.

In Ireland, the thermometers, gratefully, are a lot less busy than the barometers. Temperatures are mild and fluctuate within what any New Englander would call "spring." The generally coldest months, January and February, bring frosts but seldom snow, and the warmest months, July and August, rarely become truly hot. Remember, the Irish consider any temperature over 68°F (20°C) to be "roasting," and 34°F (1°C) is truly "freezing." Both are unusual, but funny things happen. On occasion, summer days can get positively scorching, and last winter, Ireland got hit with several harsh cold snaps that brought not only snow but gale-force winds of 70 mph. For a complete online guide to Irish weather, including year-round averages, daily updates, and a weather cam of Dublin's city center, consult **www.ireland.com/weather**.

Average Monthly Temperatures in Dublin

	Jan	Feb	Mar	Apr	May	June	July	Aug	Sept	Oct	Nov	Dec
Temp (°F)	36–46	37–48	37–49	38–52	42–57	46–62	51–66	50–65	48–62	44–56	39–49	38–47
Temp (°C)	2–8	3–9	3–9	3–11	6–14	8–17	11–19	10–18	9–17	7–13	4–9	3–8

HIGH & LOW SEASONS

Apart from climatic considerations, there's the matter of cost and crowds. How much these go up and down in the course of the year depends on where you're headed. On the one hand, there's Dublin, which gets tourists year-round and doesn't really

---

Impressions

Ireland has one of the world's heaviest rainfalls. If you see an Irishman with a tan, it's rust.

—Dave Allen, Irish comedian (b. 1936)

---

have a low season. It's always fairly crowded, and hotel prices never truly plummet. On the other hand, places such as Inishowen or Cape Clear are very affected by seasonal tourism fluctuations.

A few generalizations, however, might be helpful.

In summer, transatlantic airfares, car-rental rates, and hotel prices are at their highest and crowds at their most intense. But the days are brilliantly long (6am sunrises and 10pm sunsets), the weather is warmest, and every sightseeing attraction and B&B is open.

In winter, you can get rock-bottom prices on airfare, especially if you book a package through a good travel agent or Aer Lingus (see "Getting There," later in this chapter). If your destination is Dublin, the weather will not likely be a defining factor, since so much of Dublin's lure dwells indoors. But elsewhere in Ireland, winter means that you'll be more limited in your lodging and sightseeing choices.

All things considered, best of all are the hedge months—April, May, and mid-September through October—when you're most likely to get simultaneously lucky with weather, crowds, and prices.

HOLIDAYS

The Republic observes the following national holidays: New Year's Day (Jan 1), St. Patrick's Day (Mar 17), Easter Monday (variable), May Day (May 1), first Monday in June and August (Summer Bank Holidays), last Monday in October (Autumn Bank Holiday), Christmas (Dec 25), and St. Stephen's Day (Dec 26). Good Friday

(the Fri before Easter) is mostly observed, but not statutory.

In the North, the schedule of holidays is the same as in the Republic, with some exceptions: the North's Summer Bank Holidays fall on the last Monday of May and August; the Battle of the Boyne is celebrated on Orangeman's Day (July 12); and Boxing Day (Dec 26) follows Christmas.

In both Ireland and Northern Ireland, holidays that fall on weekends are celebrated the following Monday.

IRELAND CALENDAR OF EVENTS

This sampling of events is drawn from 2002 schedules. Be sure to consult the calendars available from the tourist boards of Ireland and of Northern Ireland for 2003; they're usually released in January. The most up-to-date listings of events can be found at **www.ireland.travel.ie** and **www. entertainment.ie** (for Ireland), **www. eventguide.ie** and **www.visitdublin.com** (for Dublin).

January

Funderland. Royal Dublin Society, Ballsbridge, Dublin 4. An annual indoor funfair, complete with white-knuckle rides, carnival stalls, and family entertainment (© 061/ 419988; info@funfair.ie). December 26 to January 13.

January Sales. The best blowout sale in Ireland lasts all month long, with deep savings of up to 70% at practically every department store, shop, and boutique in Ireland and Northern Ireland.

Unfringed 2002. Belltable Arts Centre and various venues in Limerick. This annual theater festival features a wide array of mainstream to avant-garde productions (© **061/ 211258;** fax 061/418552; www. commerce.ie/belltable). January 23 to February 3.

Yeats Winter School. Sligo Park Hotel, Sligo Town. This event offers a weekend of relaxation, lectures, and a tour of Yeats Country (© **071/42693;** fax 071/42780; www.yeats-sligo.com). January 25 to 27.

February

Six Nations Rugby Tournament. Lansdowne Road, Ballsbridge, county Dublin. This annual international tourney features Ireland, England, Scotland, Wales, France, and Italy. It's a brilliant atmosphere, be it at Lansdowne Road or a neighborhood pub. Contact Irish Rugby Football Union, 62 Lansdowne Rd., Dublin 4 (© **01/668-4601;** fax 01/660-5640). Alternate Saturdays, early February to April.

Antiques and Collectibles Fair. Newman House, 85 St. Stephen's Green, Dublin 2. About 60 dealers sell small pieces and collectors' items (© and fax **01/670-8295;** antiques fairsireland@esatclear.ie). Four consecutive Sundays in February.

All Ireland Dancing Championships. West County Hotel, Ennis, county Clare. Winners here automatically go on to the World Dancing Championship (© **01/ 475-2220;** fax 01/475-1053; cirg@ tinet.ie). February 3 to 9.

March

Bridge House Irish Festival. Bridge House Hotel and Leisure Centre, Tullamore, county Offaly. Ireland's biggest indoor festival celebrates good Irish food, song, and dance. There's free entertainment featuring national and international acts (© **506/22000;** fax 506/ 25690; www.bridgehouse.com). March 10 to 18.

St. Patrick's Dublin Festival. It's a massive 4-day fest that's open, free, and accessible to everyone. Street theater, carnival acts, sports, music, fireworks, and other festivities culminate in Ireland's grandest parade, with marching bands, drill teams, floats, and delegations from around the world (© **01/676-3205;** fax 01/676-3208; www.stpatricksday. ie). March 15 to 18.

St. Patrick's Day Parades. In celebration of Ireland's patron saint. All over Ireland, North and South. March 17.

Samhlaíocht Chiarrai/Kerry Arts Festival. A spring festival of music, drama, film, dance, literature, craft, and visual art (© **066/712-9934;** fax 066/712-0934; samhlaiocht@ indigo.ie). March 29 to April 1.

April

32nd Pan Celtic Festival. Kilkenny, county Kilkenny. For 5 days, the wider Celtic family (including Cornwall, Isle of Man, Scotland, Wales, and Brittany) unites for culture, song, dance, sports, and parades with marching bands and pipers. Lots of fringe events, from nature walks to poetry readings (© **056/51500;** panceltic@eircom. net). April 2 to 7.

World Irish Dancing Championships. Ennis, county Clare. The premier international competition in Irish dancing, it features more than 4,000 contenders from as far as New Zealand (© **01/475-2220;** fax 01/475-1053; cirg@tinet.ie). April 6 to 14.

Dublin Film Festival. Irish Film Centre, Temple Bar, Dublin 2 and various cinemas in Dublin. More than 100 films are featured, with screenings of the best in Irish and world cinema, plus seminars and lectures on filmmaking (© **01/ 679-2937;** fax 01/679-2939; dff@ iol.ie). April 20 to 29.

May

County Wicklow Gardens Festival. In the county known as the "garden of Ireland," stately heritage properties and gardens open their gates to visitors on selected dates. Contact Wicklow County Tourism (© **0404/66058**; fax 0404/66057; www.wicklow.ie). May 1 to May 31.

Diversions Temple Bar. Dublin 2. This is an all-free, all-outdoor, all-ages cultural program, featuring a combination of day and night performances in dance, film, theater, music, and visual arts. Beginning in May, the Diversions program includes live music, open-air films, and a circus (© **01/677-2255**; fax 01/677-2525; www.temple-bar.ie). May to September.

Belfast City Marathon. An epic, 42km (26.2-mile) race of 6,000 international runners through the city. Start and finish at Maysfield Leisure Centre (© **028/9027-0345**). May 6.

May Day Races. Down Royal Racecourse, Maze, Lisburn, county Antrim. One of the major events on the horse-racing calendar (© **028/9262-1256**; www.downroyal.com). May 7.

Murphy's International Mussel Fair. Bantry, county Cork. Free mussels are served in all bars and restaurants, and there are free, open-air concerts at Wolfe Tone Square (© **027/50360**; fax 027/50438; www.bantrymusselfair.ie). May 9 to 12.

Murphy's Cat Laughs Comedy Festival. Various venues in Kilkenny Town. An international festival of stand-up comedy whose past performers include North America's Bill Murray, George Wendt, and Emo Phillips, and Ireland's Ardal O'Hanlon (© **056/63416**; fax 056/63679; www.the catlaughs.com). May 20 to June 17.

June

Waterford Maritime Festival. Quays of Waterford City. The highlight of this 4-day celebration over June bank holiday weekend is an international round-trip powerboat race from Waterford to Swansea, Wales. Other events include close-to-shore kayak races, open-air concerts, and family entertainment. Representatives from Irish, British, French, Dutch naval fleets in Waterford Harbor (© **051/304114**). May 31 to June 2.

AIB Music Festival in Great Irish Houses. Various venues throughout counties Dublin, Wicklow, and Kildare. This 10-day festival of classical music performed by leading Irish and world-renowned international artists is intimately set in the receiving rooms of stately buildings and mansions (© **01/278-1528**; fax 01/278-1529). June 7 to 17.

Bloomsday Festival. Various venues in Dublin. This unique day of festivity commemorates 24 hours in the life of Leopold Bloom, the central character of James Joyce's *Ulysses*. Every aspect of the city, including the menus at restaurants and pubs, seeks to duplicate the aromas, sights, sounds, and tastes of Dublin on June 16, 1904. Special ceremonies are held at the James Joyce Tower and Museum, and there are guided walks of Joycean sights. Contact the James Joyce Centre, 35 N. Great George's St., Dublin 1 (© **01/878-8547**; fax 01/878-8488; www.jamesjoyce.ie). June 12 to 17.

Cork Midsummer Arts Festival. Emmet Place, Cork City. The program includes musical performances, traditional Irish ceili bands, and always has a very strong literary content. Bonfire nights are particularly popular (© **021/4550946**; fax 021/4501124; www.corkfestival. ie). June 19 to July 1.

Murphy's Irish Open Golf Championship. The venue for this tournament changes each year. In 2002 it was held at Fota Island Golf Club, Kinsale, county Cork. Ireland's premier international golf event, it's televised to more than 90 countries and features the world's top players. For information surf over to **www.murphysirishopen. ie**; for tickets, **www.ticketmaster. ie**. June 27 to 30.

Budweiser Irish Derby. The Curragh, county Kildare. It's one of the richest horse races in Europe, and widely accepted as the definitive European middle-distance classic. This is Ireland's version of the Kentucky Derby or Royal Ascot and is a fashionable gathering (*hint:* jackets for men, hats for ladies) of racing fans from all over the world (© **045/441205;** fax 045/441442). *Note:* It's a good idea to prebook tickets at **www.curragh.ie**. June 28 to July 1.

July

Battle of the Boyne Commemoration. Belfast and other cities. This annual event, often called Orangeman's Day, recalls the historic battle between two 17th-century kings. It's a national day of parades and celebration by Protestants all over Northern Ireland. Contact the House of Orange, 65 Dublin Rd., Belfast BT2 7HE (© **028/9032-2801**). July 12.

Galway Arts Festival and Races. Galway City and Racecourse. This 2-week fest is a shining star on the Irish arts scene, featuring international theater, big-top concerts, literary evenings, street shows, arts, parades, music, and more. The famous Galway Races follows, with 5 more days of racing and merriment, music, and song (© **091/ 566577;** fax 091/562655; www. galwayartsfestival.ie). Festival July 16 to 28; Races July 29 to August 3.

Lughnasa Fair. Carrickfergus Castle, county Antrim. A spectacular revival with a 12th-century Norman castle and its grounds, this event features people in period costumes, medieval games, traditional food, entertainment, and crafts (© **028/4336-6455**). July 28.

August

Kerrygold Horse Show. RDS Showgrounds, Ballsbridge, Dublin 4. This is the most important equestrian and social event on the Irish national calendar. Aside from the dressage and jumping competitions each day, highlights include a fashionable ladies' day (don't forget your hat!), formal hunt balls each evening, and the awarding of the Aga Khan Trophy and the Nation's Cup (© **01/668-0866;** fax 01/660-4014; www.rds.ie). August 7 to 11.

Puck Fair. Killorglin, county Kerry. One of Ireland's oldest festivals. Each year the residents of this tiny Ring of Kerry town capture a wild goat and enthrone it as "king" over 3 days of merrymaking that include open-air concerts, traditional horse fairs, parades, and fireworks (© and fax **066/976-2366;** www.puckfair. ie). August 10 to 12.

Kilkenny Arts Festival. Kilkenny Town. This weeklong event has it all, from classical and traditional music to plays, one-person shows, readings, films, poetry, and visual arts exhibitions (© **056/52175;** fax 056/51704; www.kilkennyarts.ie). August 9 to 18.

Rose of Tralee International Festival. Tralee, county Kerry. A galalike atmosphere prevails at this 5-day event, with a full program of concerts, street entertainment, horse races, and a beauty and talent pageant leading up to the televised selection of the "Rose of Tralee" (© **066/ 712-1322;** fax 066/22654; www. roseoftralee.ie). August 23 to 27.

September

Lisdoonvarna Matchmaking Festival. Lisdoonvarna, county Clare. Still the biggest and best singles' event after all these years. A traditional "bachelor" festival carries on in the lovely spa town of Lisdoonvarna, with lots of wonderful music and dance (✆ **065/7074005;** fax 065/7074406; www.matchmaker ireland.com). August 30 to September 6.

National Heritage Week. More than 400 events are held throughout the country—walks, lectures, exhibitions, music recitals, and more (✆ **01/647-2455;** www.heritage ireland.ie). September 1 to 8.

All-Ireland Hurling and Gaelic Football Finals. Croke Park, Dublin 3. The finals of Ireland's most beloved sports, hurling and Gaelic football, are Ireland's equivalent of the Superbowl. If you can't be at Croke Park, experience this in the full bonhomie of a pub. Tickets can be obtained through Ticketmaster at www.ticketmaster.ie (✆ **01/836-3222;** fax 01/836-6420). Hurling Final September 8; Gaelic Football Final September 22.

Fleadh Cheoil na hEireann. Listowel, county Kerry. Ireland's premier summer festival of traditional music, with competitions held to select the all-Ireland champions in all categories of instruments and singing (✆ **01/280-0295;** fax 01/ 280-3759; www.comhaltas.com). September 23 to 27.

Galway International Oyster Festival. Galway and environs. Find out why London's *Sunday Times* put it on its "Top 12 World's Best Event List." First held in 1954, this event attracts oyster aficionados from all over the globe. Highlights include the World Oyster-Opening Championship, a golf tournament, a

yacht race, an art exhibition, a gala banquet, traditional music and song, and lots of oyster eating (✆ **091/522066;** fax 091/527282; www.galwayoysterfest.com). September 26 to 29.

Irish Antique Dealers' Fair. RDS Showgrounds, Ballsbridge, Dublin 4. Ireland's premier annual antiques fair, with hundreds of dealers from all over the island (✆ **01/285-9294**). September 25 to 29.

October

Dublin Theatre Festival. Theaters throughout Dublin. Europe's largest theater-dedicated event showcases new plays by every major Irish company (including the Abbey and the Gate) and presents a range of productions from abroad (✆ **01/677-8439;** fax 01/679-7709; www.iftn.ie/dublinfestival). October 1 to 29.

Kinsale International Gourmet Festival. Kinsale, county Cork. The foodie capital of Ireland hosts this well-respected annual fest, featuring special menus in all the restaurants and plenty of star chefs in town from abroad (✆ **021/477-4026;** fax 021/477-4438). October 10 to 13.

Murphy's Cork International Film Festival. Cinemas throughout Cork. Ireland's oldest and biggest film festival offers a plethora of international features, documentaries, short films, and special programs (✆ **021/427-1711;** fax 021/427-5945; www.corkfilmfest. org). October 6 to 13.

Baboró International Arts Festival for Children. Galway. A brilliant, fun-filled, educational festival geared to kids 3 to 12 years old, with age-appropriate theater, music, dance, museum exhibitions, and literary events (✆ **091/ 509705;** fax 091/562655; www. baboro.ie). October 15 to 20.

Wexford Festival Opera. Theatre Royal, Wexford City. Simply like no other (stuffy) opera festival, this one positively brims over with sheer good fun. For more than 50 years, this event has been highly acclaimed for its productions of lesser-known 18th- and 19th-century operatic masterpieces, plus classical music concerts, recitals, and more. If for nothing else, come for the jubilant atmosphere in this pretty coastal town (② **053/22400;** fax 053/ 424289; www.wexfordopera.com). October 17 to November 3.

Guinness Cork Jazz Festival. Cork City. Ireland's number-two city stages a first-rate festival of jazz, with an international lineup of live acts playing in hotels, concert halls, and pubs (meanwhile, not to be outdone, nearby Kinsale plays host to its own, concurrent fringe jazz festival) (② **021/427-8979;** fax 021/427-0463; www.corkjazz festival.com). October 25 to 28.

Belfast Festival at Queens. Queens University, Belfast. The island's largest arts festival attracts enormous crowds each year for its stellar program of drama, opera, music, and film events in and around Queens University (② **028/ 9066-7687;** fax 028/9066-5577;

www.belfastfestival.com). There's also a concurrent fringe festival in the Cathedral Quarter (② **028/ 9027-0466**). October 25 to November 10.

Dublin City Marathon. More than 5,000 runners from both sides of the Atlantic and the Irish Sea participate in this popular run through the streets of the capital (② **01/626-3746;** www.dublincity marathon.ie). October 28.

December

Limerick Christmas Racing Festival. Limerick Racecourse, Greenpark, Limerick. This festival features 3 days of holiday horse racing (② **061/229377;** fax 061/ 227644). December 26 to 28.

Woodford Mummers Feile. Woodford, county Galway. This festival offers traditional music, song, dance, and mime performed by mummers in period costume (② **0509/49248**). December 26 to 27.

Leopardstown National Hunt Festival. Leopardstown Racecourse, Foxrock, Dublin 18. This festival offers 3 days of winter racing for thoroughbreds (② **01/289-2888;** fax 01/289-2634; www.leopards town.com). December 26 to 29.

7 Health & Insurance

STAYING HEALTHY

As a rule, no health documents are required to enter Ireland or Northern Ireland from the United States, Canada, the United Kingdom, Australia, New Zealand, or most other countries. If, however, you have visited areas in the previous 14 days where a contagious disease is prevalent, proof of immunization may be required.

If you have a condition that could require emergency care but might

not be readily recognizable, consider joining **Medic Alert** (② 800/432-5378; www.medicalert.org). It provides ID tags, cards, and a 24-hour emergency information hot line. If you are diabetic, the **American Diabetes Association** (② 800/342-2383; www.diabetes.org) offers plenty of good advice for traveling with diabetes.

If you require the services of a physician, dentist, or other health professional during your stay in Ireland, your accommodations host may be in the best position to recommend someone local. Otherwise, contact the **consulate** of your home country (see "Fast Facts: Ireland," later in this chapter) or the **Irish Medical Council,** Lynn House, Portabello Court, Lower Rathmines Road, Dublin 6 (© **01/496-5588**), for a referral.

INSURANCE
TRAVEL INSURANCE AT A GLANCE

Check your existing insurance policies before you buy travel insurance to cover trip cancellation, lost luggage, medical expenses, or car-rental insurance. You're likely to have partial or complete coverage. But if you need some, ask your travel agent about a comprehensive package. The cost of travel insurance varies widely, depending on the cost and length of your trip, your age and overall health, and the type of trip you're taking.

Keep in mind that in the aftermath of the September 11, 2001, terrorist attacks, a number of airlines, cruise lines, and tour operators are no longer covered by insurers. *The bottom line:* Always, always check the fine print before you sign on; more and more policies have built-in exclusions and restrictions that may leave you out in the cold if something does go awry.

For information, contact one of the following popular insurers:

- **Access America** (© **800/284-8300**); www.accessamerica.com)
- **Travel Guard International** (© **800/826-1300;** www.travelguard.com)
- **Travel Insured International** (© **800/243-3174;** www.travelinsured.com)
- **Travelex Insurance Services** (© **800/228-9792;** www.travelexinsurance.com)

TRIP-CANCELLATION INSURANCE (TCI)

There are three major types of trip-cancellation insurance—one, in the event that you prepay a cruise or tour that gets cancelled, and you can't get your money back; a second when you or someone in your family gets sick or dies, and you can't travel (but beware that you may not be covered for a preexisting condition); and a third, when bad weather makes travel impossible. Some insurers provide coverage for events like jury duty; natural disasters close to home, like floods or fire; even the loss of a job. A few have added provisions for cancellations due to terrorist activities. Always check the fine print before signing on, and don't buy trip-cancellation insurance from the tour operator that may be responsible for the cancellation; buy it only from a reputable travel insurance agency. Don't overbuy. You won't be reimbursed for more than the cost of your trip.

MEDICAL INSURANCE

Most health insurance policies cover you if you get sick away from home—but check, particularly if you're insured by an HMO. With the exception of certain HMOs and Medicare/Medicaid, your medical insurance should cover medical treatment—even hospital care—overseas. However, most out-of-country hospitals make you pay your bills up front, and send you a refund after you've returned home and filed the necessary paperwork. Members of **Blue Cross/Blue Shield** can now use their cards at select hospitals in most major cities worldwide (© **800/810-BLUE** or www.bluecares.com for a list of hospitals).

Some credit cards (American Express and certain gold and platinum Visa and MasterCards, for example) offer automatic flight insurance against death or dismemberment in case of an airplane crash if you charged the cost of your ticket.

If you require additional insurance, try one of the following companies:

- **MEDEX International,** 9515 Deereco Rd., Timonium, MD 21093-5375 (📞 **888/MEDEX-00** or 410/453-6300; fax 410/453-6301; www.medexassist.com)
- **Travel Assistance International** (📞 **800/821-2828;** www.travel assistance.com), 9200 Keystone Crossing, Suite 300, Indianapolis, IN 46240 (for general information on services, call the company's Worldwide Assistance Services, Inc., at 📞 **800/777-8710**).

The cost of travel medical insurance varies widely. Check your existing policies before you buy additional coverage. Also, check to see if your medical insurance covers you for emergency medical evacuation: If you have to buy a one-way same-day ticket home and forfeit your nonrefundable round-trip ticket, you may be out big bucks.

LOST-LUGGAGE INSURANCE

On international flights (including U.S. portions of international trips), baggage coverage is limited to approximately $9.07 per pound, up to approximately $635 per checked bag. If you plan to check items more valuable than the standard liability, you may purchase "excess valuation" coverage from the airline, up to $5,000. Be sure to take any valuables or irreplaceable items with you in your carry-on luggage. If you file a lost-luggage claim, be prepared to answer detailed questions about the contents of your baggage, and be sure to file a claim immediately, as most airlines enforce a 21-day deadline. Before you leave home, compile an inventory of all packed items and a rough estimate of the total value to ensure you're properly compensated if your luggage is lost. You will only be reimbursed for what you lost, no more. Once you've filed a complaint, persist in securing your reimbursement; there are no laws governing the length of time it takes for a carrier to reimburse you.

Lost luggage may also be covered by your homeowner's or renter's policy. Many platinum and gold credit cards cover you as well. If you choose to purchase additional lost-luggage insurance, be sure not to buy more than you need. Buy in advance from the insurer or a trusted agent (prices will be much higher at the airport).

CAR-RENTAL INSURANCE (LOSS/DAMAGE WAIVER OR COLLISION DAMAGE WAIVER)

Even if you hold a private auto insurance policy, you probably are not covered abroad for loss or damage to the car, or liability in case a passenger is injured. The credit card you used to rent the car may provide some coverage, but many cards have restrictions on coverage in Ireland.

Before you purchase insurance, check your own auto insurance policy, the rental company policy, and your credit card coverage for the extent of coverage: Is your destination covered? Are other drivers covered? How much liability is covered if a passenger is injured? (If you rely on your credit card for coverage, you may want to bring a second credit card with you, as damages may be charged to your card and you may find yourself stranded with no money.) For more information on renting a car in Ireland, see "Getting Around," later in this chapter.

8 Tips for Travelers with Special Needs

FOR TRAVELERS WITH DISABILITIES

A disability shouldn't stop anyone from traveling. There are more resources out there than ever before.

You can join the **Society for Accessible Travel and Hospitality** (SATH; ℂ 212/447-7284; fax 212/725-8253; www.sath.org) to gain access to their vast network of connections in the travel industry. Membership requires a tax-deductible contribution of $45 annually for adults, $30 for seniors and students.

Finding accessible lodging can be tricky in Ireland. Unfortunately, many of the older hotels, small guesthouses, and landmark buildings still have steps both outside and within. The **National Rehabilitation Board of Ireland,** 24/25 Clyde Rd., Ballsbridge, Dublin 4 (ℂ 01/608-0400), publishes several guides, the best of which is *Guide to Accessible Accommodations in Ireland.*

Travelers with vision impairments should contact the **American Foundation for the Blind** (ℂ 800/232-5463) for information on traveling with Seeing Eye dogs.

The **Irish Wheelchair Association,** 24 Blackheath Dr., Clontarf, Dublin 3 (ℂ 01/833-8241; www.iwa.ie), loans free wheelchairs to travelers in Ireland. A donation is appreciated. Branch offices are at Parnell Street, Kilkenny (ℂ 056/62775); White Street, Cork (ℂ 021/966354); Henry Street, Limerick (ℂ 061/313691); and Dominick Street, Galway (ℂ 091/771550), as well as in a range of smaller towns. If you plan to travel by train in Ireland, be sure to check out Iarnrod Eireann's website (**www.irishrail.ie**), which includes services for travelers with disabilities. A Mobility Impaired Liaison Officer (ℂ 01/703-2634) can arrange assistance for disabled travelers if given 24-hour notice prior to the departure time.

For advice on travel to Northern Ireland, contact **Disability Action,** Portside Business Park, 189 Airport Rd. West, Belfast BT3 9ED (ℂ 028/9029-7880; www.disabilityaction.org). The Northern Ireland Tourist Board also publishes a helpful annual *Information Guide to Accessible Accommodation,* available from any of its offices worldwide.

FOR SENIORS

One of the benefits of age is that travel often costs less. Always bring a photo ID, especially if you've kept your youthful glow. Also mention the fact that you're a senior when you first make your travel reservations, since many airlines and hotels offer discount programs for senior travelers.

For an annual fee of just $12.50, members of the **AARP** (ℂ 800/424-3410; www.aarp.com/memberguide/privileges) get discounts on hotels, airfares, and car rentals.

Seniors, known in Ireland and Northern Ireland as OAPs (old age pensioners), enjoy a variety of discounts and privileges. Native OAPs ride the public transport system free of charge, but the privilege does not extend to tourists. Visiting seniors can avail themselves of other discounts, however, particularly on admission to attractions and theaters. Always ask about a senior discount if special rates are not posted.

The Irish Tourist Board publishes a list of reduced-rate hotel packages for seniors, *Golden Holidays/For the Over 55s.* These packages are usually available during the hedge months, from March to June and September to November.

Some tour operators in the United States give notable senior discounts. **CIE Tours International** (ℂ 800/243-8687 or 973/292-3438; www.cietours.com), which specializes in Ireland and Northern Ireland, gives a

Moments Summer School

Got a yearning for learning? Choose from a raft of short summer courses on Irish history and culture.

Get in on the secrets of Ireland's most famous chef, Darina Allen, at **Ballymaloe Cookery School,** in Shanagarry, county Cork (© **021/465-2531;** fax 021/465-2021; www.cookingisfun.ie).

Spend a week in Glencolmcille, county Donegal, studying the Irish Gaelic language, set dancing, archaeology, Celtic pottery, or tapestry weaving at **Oideas Gael** (© **073/30248;** fax 073/30348; www.oideas-gael.com).

Discover the four greatest Irish playwrights—Synge, O'Casey, Beckett, and Friel—in a 3-week course with the **Irish Theatre Summer School** and the **Gaiety School of Acting** at University College Dublin. Contact the North American Institute for Study Abroad (© **570/275-5099;** fax 570/275-1644; www.naisa.com).

For more on summer study in Ireland, contact the Irish Tourist Office (see "Visitor Information," earlier in this chapter).

$75 discount to travelers age 55 and up who book early on selected departures of regular tour programs. In addition, **SAGA Tours** (© **800/343-0273** or 617/262-2262) operates tours to Ireland specifically geared to seniors or anyone over 50. **Elderhostel** (© **877/426-8056;** www.elderhostel.org) offers a range of educational travel programs for seniors.

FOR STUDENTS, TEACHERS & YOUTH

With almost half its population under age 25, Ireland is geared to students, whether you're planning to study or are just passing through.

An excellent source book that will help you explore the opportunities for study in Ireland is *The Transitions Abroad Alternative Travel Directory,* published by Transitions Abroad (**www.transitionsabroad.com**) and available in bookstores.

Ireland in general is extremely student-friendly. Most attractions have a reduced student-rate admission charge, with the presentation of a valid student ID card. A range of travel discounts are available to students, teachers (at any grade level, kindergarten through university), and youths (age 12–25). For further information on international student, teacher, and youth ID cards and fares, call **Council Travel** (© **800/226-8624;** www.counciltravel.com), which operates more than 40 offices in the United States and works through a network of world affiliates. In Canada, **Travel CUTS,** 200 Ronson St., Suite 320, Toronto, ON M9W 5Z9 (© **800/667-2887** or 416/614-2887; www.travelcuts.com), offers similar services for students. **USIT/Campus Travel,** 52 Grosvenor Gardens, London SW1W 0AG (© **0870/240-1010;** www.usitcampus.co.uk), opposite Victoria Station, is Britain's leading specialist in student and youth travel.

In Ireland, Council Travel's affiliate is **USIT, the Irish Student Travel Service,** 19 Aston Quay, Dublin 2 (© **01/679-8833;** www.usitnow.ie). In Northern Ireland, contact USIT in the Sountain Centre, College Street,

Belfast BT1 6ET (© **028/9032-4073**), or at Queens University Travel, Student Union Building, University Road, Belfast BT7 1PE (© **028/9024-1830**). In the United States, USIT is at 891 Amsterdam Ave., New York, NY 10025 (© **212/663-5435**).

U.S. firms offering educational travel programs to Ireland include **Academic Travel Abroad** (© **800/556-7896** or 202/785-9000; www.academic-travel.com), **North American Institute for Study Abroad** (© **570/275-5099** or 570/275-1644; www.naisa.com), and **Irish American Cultural Institute** (© **800/232-3746** or 973/605-1991; www.irishaci.org).

FOR FAMILIES

So you're bringing the kids to Ireland. You'll all have a fantastic time, especially if you realize that traveling with kids—like doing anything with kids—requires a bit of extra planning. And the best way to raise your kids' enthusiasm is to involve them in the decision-making process. So pore over brochures and maps together. Perhaps each family member can choose one or two "must" destinations or activities.

Use the time leading up to the trip to rent some movies set in Ireland—for younger kids and preteens, *Into the West, Waking Ned Devine,* and *The Secret of Roan Inish* are delightful and packed with picture-postcard views. Encourage your kids to read books set in Ireland. Favorites include *O'Sullivan Stew,* by Hudson Talbott (for 4–8-year-olds); and *A Wizard Abroad,* by Diane Duane (for 9–12-year-olds). Teenagers can discover a classic by James Joyce, Brendan Behan, or Sean O'Casey, or try out the king of contemporary Irish writing, Roddy Doyle.

Your first goal will be to find truly child-friendly places to stay. Hotels that *say* they welcome small children and hotels that really provide for them are, sadly, not always the same. To sort the wheat from the chaff, the most helpful website is **www.irelandhotels.com**, for its no-nonsense "detailed search" facility. Just check the options that are important to you: Kids' meals? Pool? Outdoor playground? Babysitting service? Supervised playroom? The site churns out a list of hotels and guesthouses that have exactly what you need.

If your kids are under the age of 6, consider staying a few days to a week in one place with a farm stay or a self-catered vacation home. It's a lot more relaxing to have a home base and make day trips from there than to have to pack and unpack daily to stick to an on-the-go itinerary. Another plus is that your children may have the opportunity to meet and make friends with local kids. The information provided in the section "From Cottages to Castles: Putting a Roof over Your Head," later in this chapter, will be helpful in pursuing farmhouse accommodations and self-catering options.

If given 24-hour advance notice, most airlines can arrange for a special children's menu. If you're renting a car, be sure to reserve car seats if your kids are small—don't assume that the car-rental companies will have extras on hand. Throughout the island, entrance fees and tickets on public transportation are often reduced by at least half for children under 12. Family rates for parents with children are also commonplace. In this guide, a "family" rate, unless otherwise stated, is for two adults with two children. Additional increments are often charged for larger families. Aside from all-too-familiar fast-food fare, many hotels and restaurants offer children's menus. Some hotels, guesthouses, and B&Bs provide babysitting, and others can arrange it. Let hotels know in advance if you'll need a baby crib or any other equipment. See the "Fast Facts" feature for each major city for listings of drugstores and other crucial health information. An especially helpful general source for planning an overseas family trip is *Take Your Kids to Europe,* by Cynthia W. Harriman, available at bookstores or at www. amazon.com.

FOR GAY & LESBIAN TRAVELERS

Gay Ireland has rapidly come out of the closet since homosexuality became legal in the North in 1982 and in the Republic in July 1993. Although the gay and lesbian community has received increasing support over the past several years, some of (mainly rural) Ireland continues to discourage its gay population. In cities such as Dublin, Cork, and Galway, however, gay and lesbian visitors can find enthusiastic support.

The most essential publication is *Gay Community News,* a monthly free newspaper of comprehensive Irish gay-related information, available in gay venues and bookshops. *In Dublin,* the city's leading event listings guide, dedicates several pages to gay events, current club information, AIDS and health information resources, accommodations options, and helpful organizations.

The most comprehensive websites for gay organizations, events, issues, and information are **Gay Ireland Online** (www.gay-ireland.com) and **Outhouse** (www.outhouse.ie).

The following organizations and help lines are staffed by knowledgeable and friendly people:

- **Outhouse Community & Resource Centre**, 105 Capel St., Dublin 1 (© **01/873-4932;** fax 01/873-4933; www.outhouse.ie), available Monday to Friday 10am to 5pm.

- **National Lesbian and Gay Federation (NLGF),** 6 S. William St., Dublin 2 (© **01/670-6377;** fax 01/679-1603; http://homepage. eircom.net/~nlgf), available Monday to Friday noon to 6pm.

- **Gay Switchboard Dublin,** Carmichael House, North Brunswick Street, Dublin 7 (© **01/872-1055;** fax 01/873-5737; gsd@iol.ie), Monday to Friday 8 to 10pm and Saturday 3:30 to 6pm.

- **Lesbian Line Dublin** (© 01/ **872-9911**), Thursday 7 to 9pm.

- **LOT (Lesbians Organizing Together),** the umbrella group of the lesbian community, 5 Capel St., Dublin 1 (© and fax **01/872-7770**), accommodates drop-ins Mondays to Thursdays 10am to 6pm and Fridays 10am to 4pm. LOT also sponsors LEA/Lesbian Education Awareness (© and fax **01/872-0460**; leanow@indigo.ie).

- **AIDS Helpline Dublin** (© 01/ **872-4277**), run Monday to Friday 9am to 7pm and Saturday 3 to 5pm, offers assistance with HIV/AIDS prevention, testing, and treatment.

Gay and lesbian travelers seeking information and assistance on travel abroad might want to consult the **International Gay and Lesbian Travel Association (IGLTA),** 52 W. Oakland Park Blvd. #237, Wilton Manors, FL 33311 (© **800/448-8550** or 954/776-2626; fax 954/776-3303; www.iglta.org).

General gay and lesbian travel agencies include **Above and Beyond Tours** (© **800/397-2681;** www.above beyondtours.com).

9 Getting There

BY PLANE

About half of all visitors from North America arrive in Ireland on direct transatlantic flights to Dublin Airport, Shannon Airport, or Belfast International Airport. The other half fly first

> **Tips Backtracking to Ireland**
>
> Your favorite airline doesn't fly to Ireland? Many travelers opt to fly to Britain and backtrack into Ireland (see "From Britain," below). Carriers serving Britain from the United States include **American Airlines** (© 800/433-7300; www.aa.com), **British Airways** (© 800/247-9297; www.british-airways.com), **Continental Airlines** (© 800/231-0856; www.continental.com), **Delta Airlines** (© 800/241-4141; www.delta.com), **Northwest Airlines** (© 800/447-4747; www.nwa.com), **United** (© 800/241-6522; www.ual.com), and **Virgin Atlantic Airways** (© 800/862-8621; www.virgin-atlantic.com).

into Britain or Europe, then "backtrack" into Ireland by air or sea. In the Republic, there are seven smaller regional airports, all of which (except Knock) offer service to Dublin and several of which receive some European traffic. They are Cork, Donegal, Galway, Kerry, Knock, Sligo, and Waterford. In Northern Ireland, the secondary airports are Belfast City Airport and Derry City Airport. Services and schedules are always subject to change, so be sure to consult your preferred airline or travel agent as soon as you begin to sketch your itinerary. The routes and carriers listed below are provided to suggest the range of possibilities for air travel to Ireland.

FROM THE UNITED STATES

The Irish national carrier, **Aer Lingus** (© 800/474-7424; www.aerlingus.com) is the traditional leader in providing transatlantic flights to Ireland, with scheduled, nonstop flights from New York (JFK), Boston, Chicago, Los Angeles, and Baltimore to Dublin, Shannon, and Belfast International Airports. From there, you can connect to Ireland's regional airports. *Note:* Aer Lingus offers a wide range of excellent-value packages that bundle your flight with a rental car and/or accommodation. These aren't tours—you still travel independently once you get to Ireland—but by booking all the elements at once rather than separately, your savings can be significant.

As you'd expect, the discounts are deepest in the winter months.

Delta Airlines (© 800/241-4141; www.delta.com) flies directly from Atlanta and New York (JFK) to Dublin and Shannon. **Continental Airlines** (© 800/231-0856; www.continental.com) offers nonstop service to Dublin and Shannon from its Newark hub. **America Trans Air** (© 800/435-9282; www.ata.ie) offers chartered flights from New York (JFK) and Boston to Dublin and Shannon. And finally, **Royal Jordanian Airlines** (© 800/223-0474 or 212/949/0050; www.rja.com.jo) flies directly from Chicago to Shannon.

You can often save big by booking your air tickets through a consolidator (aka bucket shop) who works with the airlines to sell off their unsold air tickets at a cut price. **Ireland Consolidated** (© 212/661-1999; www.irelandconsolidated.com) sells tickets to Ireland on regular Delta, British Airways, and Continental flights. **Evergreen Holidays** (© 800/443-0070) offers air travel on the Boston-to-Shannon route.

FROM BRITAIN

The London-Dublin and London-Shannon routes are two of the busiest flight paths in Europe, and competition is stiff—which means that you can often get a fantastic deal. The most hilarious round of airline jousting occurred a couple of years ago, when Virgin Express offered free round-trip flights from London to Shannon to anyone surnamed Ryan. Ryanair, which dominates the market for cheap flights between Ireland and Britain, retaliated by offering a free round-trip flight on the same route to anyone with the surname Ryan, plus a free ticket for a traveling companion. The punch line: A spokeswoman for Ryanair said they had considered offering free flights to virgins but thought it would be easier to identify passengers by surname.

The following carriers offer direct flights from London: **Aer Lingus** (© 800/474-7424 in the U.S.; 020/8899-4747 in Britain); British Airways' short-flight sister, **City Flyer Express** (© 0345/222111; www.british-airways.com); **Lufthansa** (© 800/645-3880 in the U.S.; www.lufthansa.co.uk), **British Midland** (© 800/788-0555 in the U.S. or 0870/607-0555 in Britain; www.ifly britishmidland.com). Two low-cost airlines making the London-Dublin hop are **CityJet** (© 0345/445588 in Britain) and **Ryanair** (© 0541/569569 in Britain; www.ryanair.com). The budget-minded **Virgin Express** (© 01293/747747; www.virgin-atlantic.com) flies from London Gatwick to Shannon.

In addition to the London-Dublin and London-Shannon routes, the aforementioned carriers make direct flights from more than 20 other British cities to Dublin, Cork, Shannon, Galway, and other regional Irish airports.

Belfast has two airports, **Belfast International Airport** (© 028/9448-4848; www.bial.co.uk) and **Belfast City Airport** (© 028/9093-9093; www.belfastcityairport.com). Airlines flying directly from Britain to Belfast include **British Airways** (© 0345/222111; www.british-airways.com), **Virgin Express** (© 01293/747747;

www.virgin-atlantic.com), and **Jersey European** (© 0990/676676).

FROM THE CONTINENT

Major direct flights into Dublin from the Continent include service from Amsterdam on **KLM** (© 800/374-7747 in the U.S.; www.klm.com); Madrid and Barcelona on **Iberia** (© 800/772-4642 in the U.S.; www.iberia.com); Brussels on **Sabena** (© 800/952-2000 in the U.S.; www.sabena.com); Copenhagen on **Aer Lingus** and SAS (© 800/221-2350 in the U.S.; www.scandinavian.net); Frankfurt on **Aer Lingus** and **Lufthansa** (© 800/645-3880 in the U.S.; www.lufthansa.com); Paris on **Aer Lingus** and **Air France** (© 800/237-2747 in the U.S.; www.airfrance.com); Prague on **CSA Czech Airlines** (© 212/765-6588 in the U.S.; www.csa.cz); and Rome on **Aer Lingus.**

Quite recently, **Cork Airport** (© 021/431-3131; www.cork-airport.com) passed Shannon to become the second-ranked airport in Ireland, though it offers no nonstop transatlantic service. **Aer Lingus, British Airways, KLM,** and **Ryanair** are among the airlines flying into Cork from Great Britain and the Continent (see above for their contact info). Direct service to Shannon from the Continent includes **Aer Lingus** from Düsseldorf, Frankfurt, Paris, and Zurich and **Virgin Express** from Brussels.

FLY FOR LESS: TIPS FOR GETTING THE BEST AIRFARES

- **Book early.** Booking your ticket at least 14 days in advance will almost always get you a lower fare. Be sure you understand cancellation and refund policies before you buy.
- **Travel Midweek.** Flying Tuesday to Thursday is cheaper than flying

on weekend days. An added bonus: Midweek transatlantic flights are often half empty, allowing you to stretch out across extra seats. Ahhhh, nice.

- **Stay over Saturday.** To exclude business travelers from the cheapest fares, most airlines offer lower rates for trips that include at least one Saturday night. So don't book a 6-night trip where you arrive on Sunday and depart for home the following Saturday, or you'll pay more than you have to.
- **Use a consolidator.** Also known as a bucket shop, a consolidator is a gold mine for low fares, often below the airlines' discounted rates. There's nothing shady about them—basically, they're just wholesalers that buy in bulk and pass some of the savings on to you. Some of the most reliable consolidators include **Cheap Tickets** (© 800/377-1000; www.cheaptickets.com), **Payless Travel** (© 202/822-8018; www.paylessairfares.com), **Council Travel** (© 800/226-8624; www.counciltravel.com), **STA Travel** (© 800/781-4040; www.statravel.com), **Lowestfare.com** (© 888/278-8830; www.lowestfare.com), **Cheap Seats** (© 800/451-7200; www.cheapseatstravel.com), and **1-800-FLY-CHEAP** (www.flycheap.com).
- **Surf the Internet.** This is the hot way to buy air tickets, though it's still best to compare your findings with the research of a dedicated travel agent. See "Planning Your Trip Online," below.
- **Make a bid.** You can also bid for seats on your desired flight with travel auctioneers such as **Priceline** (www.priceline.com). In some cases—though very rarely—winning bids are as low as $5.
- Consider a **charter flight.** They're often dirt cheap, but the down-

sides are that they offer fewer frills, offer fewer flights per week, and their tickets are ordinarily nonrefundable. From the United States, **Sceptre Charters** (© 800/221-0924 or 516/255-9800) operates the largest and most reliable charter program to Ireland. It sells tickets on America Trans Air flights to Shannon from Boston, Philadelphia, Chicago, and Los Angeles. Several companies in Canada operate charter flights from Toronto to Ireland, including **Signature Vacations** (© 800/268-7063 in Canada, or 800/268-1105 in the U.S.), **Air Transat Holidays** (© 800/587-2672 in Canada, or 514/987-1550), and **Regent Holidays** (© 800/387-4860 in Canada, or 905/673-3343).

BY FERRY

If you're traveling to Ireland from Britain or the Continent, especially if you're behind the wheel of a car, ferries can get you there. The Irish Sea has a reputation for making seafarers woozy, however, so it's always a good idea to consider an over-the-counter pill or patch to guard against seasickness. (Be sure to take any pills *before* you set out; once you're under way, it's generally too late.)

Several car and passenger ferries offer reasonably comfortable furnishings, cabin berths (for longer crossings), restaurants, duty-free shopping, and lounges.

Prices fluctuate seasonally and depend on your route, your time of travel, and whether you are on foot or in a car. It's best to check with your travel agent for up-to-date details, but just to give you an idea, the lowest one-way adult fare in high season on the cruise ferry from Holyhead to Dublin is €28 ($25). Add your car, and the grand total will be €185 ($165). The websites given below have regularly updated schedules and prices.

FROM BRITAIN

Irish Ferries (www.irishferries.ie) operates from Holyhead, Wales, to Dublin, and from Pembroke, Wales, to Rosslare, county Wexford. For reservations, call **Scots-American Travel** (© 561/563-2856 in the U.S.; info@scotsamerican.com) or **Irish Ferries** (© 08705/171717 in the U.K. or 01/638-3333 in Ireland). **Stena Line** (© 888/274-8724 in the U.S. or 01233/647022 in Britain; www.stenaline.com) sails from Holyhead to Dun Laoghaire, 13km (8 miles) south of Dublin; from Fishguard, Wales, to Rosslare; and from Stranraer, Scotland, to Belfast, Northern Ireland. **Brittany Ferries** (© 021/427-7801 in Cork; www.brittany-ferries.com) operates from Holyhead to Dublin; from Fishguard and Pembroke to Rosslare; and from Stranraer to Belfast. **Swansea/Cork Ferries** (© 011792/456116 in Britain; www.swansea-cork.ie) links Swansea, Wales, to Ringaskiddy, just outside Cork City, county Cork. **P&O European Ferries** operates from Liverpool to Dublin and from Cairnryan, Scotland, to Larne, county Antrim, Northern Ireland. For reservations, call Scots-American Travel (© 561/563-2856 in the U.S. or 01/638-3333 in Ireland; www.poferries.com). **Norse** Merchant Ferries (© 0870/6004321 in Britain or 01/819-2999 in Ireland; www.norsemerchant.com) sails from Liverpool to both Dublin and Belfast. **Seacat Scotland Ltd.** (© 800/551743 in Britain or 01/874-1231 in Ireland; www.seacat.co.uk) operates ferries from Liverpool to Dublin, and from Heysham and Troon, both in Scotland, to Belfast.

FROM CONTINENTAL EUROPE

Irish Ferries sails from Roscoff and Cherbourg, France, to Rosslare. For reservations, call Scots-American Travel (© 561/563-2856 in the U.S.; info@scotsamerican.com) or **Irish Ferries** (© 08705/171717 in the U.K. or 01/638-3333 in Ireland). **P&O European Ferries** operates from Cherbourg, France, to Rosslare. For reservations, call Scots-American Travel (© 561/563-2856 in the U.S. or 01/638-3333 in Ireland; www.poferries.com). **Brittany Ferries** (© 021/427-7801 in Cork; www.brittany-ferries.com) connects Roscoff, France, to Cork.

Note to Eurailpass holders: Because Irish Ferries is a member of the Eurail system, you can travel free between Rosslare and Roscoff or Cherbourg.

10 Planning Your Trip Online

Researching and booking your trip online can save time and money. Then again, it may not. It is simply not true that you always get the best deal online. Most booking engines do not include schedules and prices for budget airlines, and from time to time you'll get a better last-minute price by calling the airline directly, so it's best to call the airline to see if you can do better before booking online.

On the plus side, Internet users today can tap into the same travel-planning databases that were once accessible only to travel agents—and do it at the same speed. Sites such as **Frommers.com**, **Travelocity.com**, **Expedia.com**, and **Orbitz.com** allow consumers to comparison shop for airfares, access special bargains, book flights, and reserve hotel rooms and rental cars.

But don't fire your travel agent just yet. Although online booking sites offer tips and hard data to help you bargain shop, they cannot endow you with the hard-earned experience that makes a seasoned, reliable travel agent an invaluable resource, even in the Internet age. And for consumers with

Frommers.com: The Complete Travel Resource

For an excellent travel-planning resource, we highly recommend **Frommers. com** (www.frommers.com). We're a little biased, of course, but we guarantee that you'll find the travel tips, reviews, monthly vacation giveaways, and online-booking capabilities thoroughly indispensable. Among the special features are our popular **Message Boards,** where Frommer's readers post queries and share advice (sometimes even our authors show up to answer questions); **Frommers.com Newsletter,** for the latest travel bargains and inside travel secrets; and Frommer's **Destinations Section,** where you'll get expert travel tips, hotel and dining recommendations, and advice on the sights to see for more than 2,500 destinations around the globe. When your research is done, the **Online Reservation System** (www. frommers.com/booktravelnow) takes you to Frommer's favorite sites for booking your vacation at affordable prices.

a complex itinerary, a trusty travel agent is still the best way to arrange the most direct flights to and from the best airports.

Still, there's no denying the Internet's emergence as a powerful tool in researching and plotting travel time. The benefits of researching your trip online can be well worth the effort.

Last-minute specials, such as weekend deals or Internet-only fares, are offered by airlines to fill empty seats. Most of these are announced on Tuesday or Wednesday and must be purchased online. They are only valid for travel that weekend, but some can be booked weeks or months in advance. Sign up for weekly e-mail alerts at airline websites or check megasites that compile comprehensive lists of last-minute specials, such as **Smarter Living** (www.smarterliving. com) or **WebFlyer** (www.webflyer. com).

Some sites, such as Expedia.com, will send you **e-mail notification** when a cheap fare becomes available to your favorite destination. Some will also tell you when fares to a particular destination are lowest.

TRAVEL PLANNING & BOOKING SITES

Keep in mind that because several airlines are no longer willing to pay

commissions on tickets sold by online travel agencies, these agencies may either add a $10 surcharge to your bill if you book on that carrier—or neglect to offer those carriers' schedules.

The list of sites below is selective, not comprehensive. Some sites will have evolved or disappeared by the time you read this.

- **Travelocity** (www.travelocity.com or www.frommers.travelocity. com) and **Expedia** (www.expedia. com) are among the most popular sites, each offering an excellent range of options. Travelers search by destination, dates, and cost.
- **Orbitz** (www.orbitz.com) is a popular site launched by United, Delta, Northwest, American, and Continental airlines. (Stay tuned: At press time, travel-agency associations were waging an antitrust battle against this site.)
- **Qixo** (www.qixo.com) is another powerful search engine that allows you to search for flights and accommodations from some 20 airline and travel-planning sites (such as Travelocity) at once. Qixo sorts results by price.
- **Priceline** (www.priceline.com) lets you "name your price" for airline tickets, hotel rooms, and rental cars. For airline tickets, you

can't say what time you want to fly—you have to accept any flight between 6am and 10pm on the dates you've selected, and you may have to make one or more stopovers. Tickets are nonrefundable, and no frequent-flyer miles are awarded.

SMART E-SHOPPING

The savvy traveler is armed with insider information. Here are a few tips to help you navigate the Internet successfully and safely.

- **Know when sales start.** Last-minute deals may vanish in minutes. If you have a favorite booking site or airline, find out when last-minute deals are released to the public. (For example, Southwest's specials are posted every Tues at 12:01am central time.)
- **Shop around.** If you're looking for bargains, compare prices on different sites and airlines—and against a travel agent's best fare. Try a range of times and alternative airports before you make a purchase.
- **Stay secure.** Book only through secure sites (some airline sites are not secure). Look for a key icon (Netscape) or a padlock (Internet Explorer) at the bottom of your Web browser before you enter credit card information or other personal data.
- **Avoid online auctions.** Sites that auction airline tickets and frequent-flier miles are the number-one

perpetrators of Internet fraud, according to the National Consumers League.
- **Maintain a paper trail.** If you book an E-ticket, print out a confirmation, or write down your confirmation number, and keep it safe and accessible—or your trip could be a virtual one!

ONLINE TRAVELER'S TOOLBOX

Veteran travelers usually carry some essential items to make their trips easier. Following is a selection of online tools to bookmark and use.

- **Visa ATM Locator** (www.visa. com) or **MasterCard ATM Locator** (www.mastercard.com). Find ATMs in hundreds of cities in the United States and around the world.
- **Intellicast** (www.intellicast.com). Find weather forecasts for all 50 states and for cities around the world. *Note:* Temperatures are in Celsius for many international destinations.
- **Cybercafes.com** (www.cyber cafes.com) or **Net Café Guide** (www.netcafeguide.com/map index.htm). Locate Internet cafes at hundreds of locations around the globe. Catch up on your e-mail and log on to the Web for a few dollars per hour.
- **Universal Currency Converter** (www.xe.net/currency). See what your dollar or pound is worth in more than 100 other countries.

11 Getting Around

BY PLANE

Because Ireland is such a small country, it's unlikely you'll be flying from place to place. If you do require an air transfer, however, **Aer Lingus** (© 01/ 705-3333; www.aerlingus.com) operates daily scheduled flights linking Dublin with Cork, Galway, Kerry, Knock, Shannon, Sligo, and Belfast.

BY TRAIN

Iarnrod Eireann (toll-free © 1850/ 366222 or 01/836-6222; www.irish rail.ie) operates the train services in

Value Money-Saving Rail & Bus Passes

For extensive travel by public transport, you can save money by purchasing a rail/bus pass or a rail-only pass. The options include the following:

- **Eurailpass:** Of the dozens of different Eurailpasses available, some are valid for unlimited rail travel in 17 European countries—but none include Britain or Northern Ireland. Other passes let you save money by selecting fewer countries. In the Irish Republic, the Eurailpass is good for travel on trains, Expressway coaches, and the Irish Continental Lines ferries between France and Ireland. For passes that let you travel throughout continental Europe and the Republic of Ireland, first-class passes begin at $588 for 15 consecutive days of travel; youth passes (passengers must be under 26 years old) begin at $414 for 15 consecutive days of travel in second class. The pass must be purchased 21 days before departure for Europe by a non–European Union resident. For further details or for purchase, call **Rail Pass Express** (© 800/722-7151; www.eurail.com). It's also available from **Council Travel** (© 800/2COUNCIL; www.council travel.com) and other travel agents. You can also find more information online at www.eurail.com.
- **BritRail Pass + Ireland:** Includes all rail travel throughout the United Kingdom and Ireland, including a round-trip ferry crossing on Stena Line. A pass good for any 5 days unlimited travel within a 30-day period costs $529 first class, $399 second class; 10 days unlimited travel within a 30-day period costs $749 first class, $569 second class. It must be purchased before departure for Ireland or the United Kingdom. Available from **BritRail** (© 800/BRITRAIL, or 800/555-2748 in Canada; www.britrail.net).
- **Emerald Card:** Valid for second-class rail and bus service throughout Ireland and Northern Ireland, the pass costs $316 for 15 days of travel within a 30-day period, or $182 for 8 days of travel within a 15-day period. You must purchase a voucher 21 days before departure for Ireland, available from **CIE Tours International** (© 800/243-8687, 973/292-3438 in the U.S., or 800/387-2667 in Canada; www. cietours.com). Once in Ireland, you then exchange the voucher for your pass.
- **Irish Explorer:** For use only in the Republic of Ireland, this pass is good for either 8 days of combined rail and bus services for $158 or 5 days of rail only for $106. It's available from **CIE Tours International.**
- **Irish Rover:** For use in the Republic of Ireland and Northern Ireland, this pass entitles you to 5 days of rail travel within a 15-day period for $132. It's available from **CIE Tours International.**

Ireland. With the exception of flying, train travel is the fastest way to get around the country. Most lines radiate from Dublin to other principal cities and towns. From Dublin, the journey time to Cork is 3 hours; to Belfast, 2 hours; to Galway, 3 hours; to Limerick, 2¼ hours; to Killarney, 4 hours; to

Irish Rail Routes

North
Channel

ATLANTIC
OCEAN

Portrush
Ballycastle
Coleraine
Larne
Harbour
Derry   Ballymoney
Larne   Whitehead
Carrickfergus
Antrim   Bangor
Belfast York
Road
Lurgan   **BELFAST
CENTRAL**
Enniskillen   Portadown   Lisburn

Ballina   Sligo   Collooney
Foxford   Ballymote   Boyle   Carrick-on-
Shannon   Newry
Castlebar   Dromod   Dundalk
**MANULLA
JUNCTION**   Ballyhaunis   Longford
Westport   Claremorris   Mostrim
Castlerea   Roscommon   Mullingar   Enfield   Malahide
Tuam   Woodlawn   Athlone   Clara   Maynooth
Athenry   Ballinasloe   Tullamore   Kildare
Galway   Attymon   **PORTARLINGTON**   Dublin
Portlaoise   Newbridge   Heuston
Ennistymon   Roscrea   Portlaoise   Athy
Cloughjordan   Carlow
Ennis   Nenagh   Temple-   **BALLYBROPHY**   Muine
Birdhill   more   Kilkenny   Bheag
Limerick   Castle-   Thurles   Thomastown
connell   Enniscorthy
LIMERICK   JUNCTION   Clonmel   Campile
Listowel   Charleville   Tipperary   Cahir   Wexford
Tralee   Rathmore   Carrick-on-Suir   **WATERFORD**   Rosslare Strand
Farranfore   **MALLOW**   Rosslare
Killarney   Banteer   Ballycullane   Harbour
Millstreet   Cork   Fota   Bridgetown
Cobh   Wellington
Bridge

Drogheda
Mosney
Balbriggan
Skerries
Dublin
Connolly
DUBLIN
Dublin
Pearse
Bray   Dun
Laoghaire
Greystones
Wicklow
Rathdrum
Arklow
Gorey

Irish
Sea

ARAN ISLANDS

Mouth of the
Shannon

St. George's
Channel

0   30 mi
0   30 km
N

Ticket Talk

When buying travel tickets—air, ferry, train—ask for either a "single" (one-way) or a "return" (round-trip).

Sligo, 3¼ hours; and to Waterford, 2¾ hours.

Iarnrod Eireann/Irish Rail also offers an enticing array of weekend to weeklong holiday packages or **Rail-Breaks** to practically every corner of Ireland, North as well as South.

In addition to the Irish Rail service between Dublin and Belfast, **Northern Ireland Railways** (© **888/ BRITRAIL** or 028/9089-9411; www.nirailways.co.uk) operates routes from Belfast that include Coleraine and Derry; and suburban routes from Belfast to Portadown, Bangor, and Larne.

BY BUS

Bus Eireann (© 01/830-2222; www.buseireann.ie) operates an extensive system of express bus service, as well as local service to nearly every town in Ireland. Express routes include Dublin to Donegal (4¼ hr.), Killarney to Limerick (2½ hr.), Limerick to Galway (2 hr.), and Limerick to Cork (2 hr.). The Bus Eireann website provides the latest timetables and fares for bus service throughout Ireland. Bus travel is usually affordable, reliable, and comfortable.

Ulsterbus (© 028/9033-3000; www.translink.co.uk) runs virtually all bus service in and between 21 localities in Northern Ireland. The same organization runs the Belfast city service, called **Citybus.**

BY CAR

Although Ireland offers an extensive network of public transportation, there are big advantages to having your own car. Mainly, you'll be unhampered by imposed schedules and have the freedom to explore anywhere serendipity leads you—a real plus in a country like Ireland, where small-town doings can be the highlight of your day, or entire trip. In a nutshell, if you want to see the "real Ireland" outside the major cities, you'll want a car.

The disadvantages of having a car begin with the cost of rental and continue with each refueling. In high season, weekly rental rates on a compact vehicle begin at around $275 (if you've shopped around) and ascend steeply—but it's at the pump that you're likely to go into shock. Irish gas prices can be triple what you pay in the United States. The consolation is that Ireland is relatively small, so distances are comparatively short.

Another potential pitfall is that rental cars in Ireland are almost always equipped with standard transmissions—you can rent an automatic, but it will cost substantially more. Driving on the left side of the road and shifting gears with your left hand can take some getting used to. Then consider that another fact of life in Ireland is cramped roads. Even the major Irish motorways are surprisingly narrow, with lanes made to order for what many Americans would regard as miniature cars—just the kind you'll wish you had rented once you're under way. Off the motorways, it's rare to find a road with a hard shoulder—leaving precious little maneuvering space when a bus or truck is coming from the opposite direction. So think small when you pick out your rental car. The choice is yours: between room in the car and room on the road.

Unless your stay in Ireland extends beyond 6 months, your own valid U.S. or Canadian driver's license (provided you've had it for at least 6 months) is

Major Irish Bus Routes

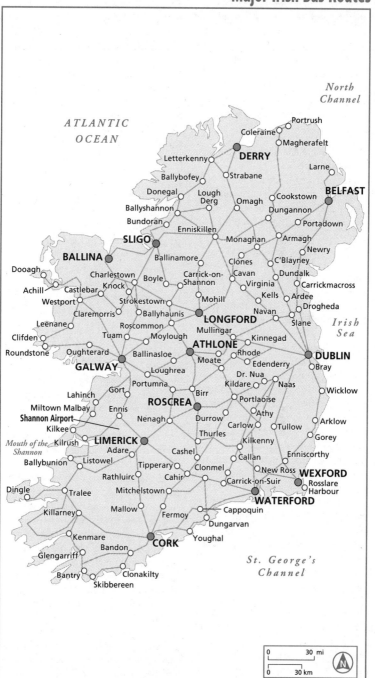

Portrush

Coleraine
Magherafelt
DERRY
Letterkenny
Larne
Ballybofey
Strabane
BELFAST
Donegal
Lough
Derg
Omagh
Cookstown
Ballyshannon
Dungannon
Bundoran
Portadown
Enniskillen
Monaghan
Armagh
SLIGO
Ballinamore
Clones
C'Blayney
Newry
BALLINA
Ballymote
Cavan
Dundalk
Dooagh
Charlestown
Boyle
Carrick-on-
Shannon
Virginia
Carrickmacross
Achill
Castlebar
Knock
Mohill
Kells
Ardee
Westport
Strokestown
Navan
Drogheda
Claremorris
Ballyhaunis
LONGFORD
Slane
Leenane
Roscommon
Mullingar
Clifden
Tuam
Moylough
ATHLONE
Kinnegad
DUBLIN
Roundstone
Oughterard
Ballinasloe
Moate
Rhode
Bray
GALWAY
Loughrea
Edenderry
Dr. Nua
Gort
Portumna
Kildare
Naas
Wicklow
Lahinch
Birr
Portlaoise
Miltown Malbay
Ennis
ROSCREA
Athy
Arklow
Shannon Airport
Nenagh
Durrow
Carlow
Tullow
Gorey
Kilkee
Thurles
Kilrush
LIMERICK
Cashel
Kilkenny
Enniscorthy
Ballybunion
Adare
Listowel
Callan
WEXFORD
Dingle
Rathluirc
Tipperary
Clonmel
New Ross
Rosslare
Harbour
Tralee
Cahir
Carrick-on-Suir
Mitchelstown
WATERFORD
Killarney
Mallow
Fermoy
Cappoquin
Kenmare
Dungarvan
Bandon
Youghal
CORK
Glengarriff
Bantry
Clonakilty
Skibbereen

ATLANTIC
OCEAN

North
Channel

Irish
Sea

St. George's
Channel

Mouth of the
Shannon

0   30 mi

0   30 km

all you need to drive in Ireland. Rules and restrictions for car rental vary slightly and correspond roughly to those in the United States.

Note: Double check your credit card's policy on picking up the insurance on rental cars. Almost none of the American-issued cards—including gold cards—cover the collision damage waiver (CDW) on car rentals in Ireland anymore.

DRIVING LAWS, TIPS & CAUTIONS

Highway safety has become a critical national issue in Ireland during the past several years. The number of highway fatalities is shocking for such a small nation, and Ireland is ranked as the second-most-dangerous country in Europe in which to drive (second only to Greece and twice as dangerous as its next "competitor").

In light of Ireland's unfortunate highway statistics, every possible precaution is in order. Try to avoid driving late at night, after dark, and around pub closing time; get off the road when driving conditions are compromised by rain, fog, or excessive holiday traffic; and don't drive alone. Getting used to left-side driving, left-handed stick shift (almost all rental cars have standard transmissions), narrow roads, and a new landscape are enough for the driver to manage, not to mention having to find his or her way to a destination. Consider driving only an hour or two on the day you arrive, just far enough to get to a nearby hotel or bed-and-breakfast and to get a feel for the roads.

Irish drivers tend to drive annoyingly faster than the speed limits of 112kmph (67 mph) on the motorways and 100kmph (60 mph) on open, nonurban roads. Meanwhile, traffic in Dublin provides its own frustration. Don't even think about renting a car for your time in Dublin. The pace of traffic in the capital's city center is now officially down to 8kmph

(about 5 mph), against an average of 15kmph (9 mph) in most other European capitals. When you figure in all the one-way streets and shameful lack of parking, you're much better off on foot.

"Roundabouts" (what Americans call traffic circles or rotaries) are found on all major and minor motorways and take a little getting used to. Remember always to yield to traffic on the right as you approach a roundabout and follow the traffic to the left.

One signal that could be particularly misleading to U.S. drivers is a flashing yellow light at a pedestrian traffic light. This almost always follows a red light and it means yield to pedestrians, then proceed when the crossing is clear.

There are relatively few types of roads in the Republic. **National** (N) roads link major cities on the island. Though these are the equivalent of U.S. highways, they are rarely more than two lanes in each direction and many pass directly through towns, making cross-country trips longer than you'd expect. **Regional** (R) roads have one lane of traffic traveling in each direction, and generally link smaller cities and towns. Lastly, there are the rural or unclassified roads, often the most scenic back roads. These can be poorly signposted.

In the North, there are two **Major Motorways** (M), equivalent to interstates, as well as a network of lesser A- and B-level roads. Speed limits are posted. In general, the limit for urban areas is 46kmph (29 mph), for open but undivided highways 95kmph (59 mph), and for major motorways 110kmph (68 mph).

The enforcement of speed limits is becoming increasingly stringent, and Irish roads have some built-in enforcers. Roads are often slick, with many bends and rises, any one of which can present a sheep or other four-legged pedestrian on very short notice. The low density of traffic on some of Ireland's roads can promote the deadly fantasy that you have the road to yourself. Don't wait to be contradicted.

Both the North and the Republic have appropriately severe laws against drunk driving, and they will gladly enforce them. Both countries also enforce the mandatory use of seat belts in the front seat, and the North extends that to rear-seat passengers. Additionally, it is against the law in the Republic for any child under 12 to sit in the front seat.

RENTALS

Try to make car-rental arrangements well in advance of your departure. Leaving such arrangements until the last minute—or, worse, until your arrival in Ireland—can mean you wind up either walking or wishing you were. Ireland is a small country, and in high season, it can completely run out of rental cars—but before it does, it runs out of *affordable* rental cars. Discounts are common in the off-season, of course, but it's also possible to negotiate a decent deal for July and August, if you put in enough time and effort.

Major international car-rental firms are represented at airports and cities throughout Ireland and Northern Ireland. They include **Alamo-Treaty** (© 800/522-9696 in the U.S.; www. goalamo.com), **Auto-Europe** (© 800/223-5555 in the U.S.; www.auto europe.com), **Avis** (© 800/331-1084 in the U.S.; www.avis.com), **Budget** (© 800/472-3325 in the U.S.; https://rent.drivebudget.com), **Hertz** (© 800/838-0826 in the U.S.; www. hertz.com), **Murrays Europcar** (© 800/800-6000 in the U.S.; www. europcar.ie), **National** (© 800/227-7368 in the U.S.; www.nationalcar. com), and **Payless/Bunratty** (© 800/729-5377 in the U.S.; www.payless carrental.com). It's best to shop around, because it is impossible to know who'll be offering the best rate for your travel needs, although Budget and Hertz seem consistently quite competitive.

Auto Europe (© **800/223-5555;** fax 207/828-1177; www.autoeurope. com) offers superior rates and service on overseas rentals and long-term leases. Their agreements are clear, straightforward, and all-inclusive. Better yet, they can beat any bona fide offer from another company; ask for the "Beat Rate Desk." Another well-established firm offering good deals on long-term leases and rentals is **Europe by Car** (© **800/223-1516;** www.europebycar.com).

In addition, a variety of Irish-based companies have desks at the major airports and full-service offices in city or town locations. The leader among the Irish-based firms is **Dan Dooley/Kenning Rent-a-Car** (© **800/331-9301** in the U.S.; www.dan-dooley.ie).

When comparing prices, always ask if the quoted rate includes the 12.5% government tax (VAT), the €15 ($13) airport pickup fee (assuming you pick up your car right upon arrival), CDW (collision damage waiver), or theft insurance. If you have your own auto insurance, you may be covered; check your existing policy before you pay for additional coverage you may not need. If you rent a car in the Republic, it is best to return it to the Republic, and if you rent it in the North, return it in the North (most firms charge extra for cross-border drop-offs).

A sticky—and expensive—caveat about car rentals: If you rent with a credit card that claims to provide free protection, be sure to call your card's customer service line to make certain there are no restrictions on that coverage in Ireland. Visa *does not* offer insurance protection for car rentals in Ireland. And MasterCard and American Express—even gold cards—have recently limited their protection on Irish rentals. Be certain that your information is current. Always confirm the details of your coverage when you charge your car rental to your credit card. If you are renting a car in the Republic and taking it into the North (or vice versa), be sure to ask the car-rental firm if the CDW and theft insurance covers cross-border transport. If not, you may be required to buy extra insurance.

PARKING

Rule Number 1: Not to beat a dead horse, but you're better off without a car in Dublin. Traffic, a shortage of parking places, and one-way streets conspire to make you regret having wheels. Cork is nearly as bad.

Rule Number 2: Never park in bus lanes or next to a curb with double yellow lines. Dublin, in particular, cracks down hard on offenders by clamping or towing delinquent cars. It will cost you €85 ($76) to have your car unclamped, or a whopping €165 ($147) to reclaim a towed car—so be extra vigilant.

Some small cities and most towns still have free street parking, but in larger cities such as Dublin and Cork you're forced to buy a "parking disc" or use a parking lot or garage. "Disc parking" works like this: You buy a paper disc (available in most newsagents, many hotels, and in all the tourist offices) and display it on your windshield for the time you are parked in a disc-appointed space. In Dublin, a five-pack of discs currently costs €6.35 ($5.65); each disc has a maximum of 3 hours of parking.

Multistory car parks in central Dublin average €2 ($1.80) per hour and €20 ($18) for 24 hours. Night rates run €6 to €9 ($5.35–$8) per hour. In central Dublin, you'll find car parks on Kildare Street, Lower Abbey Street, Marlborough Street, and St. Stephen's Green West, among other locations.

In Belfast and other large cities in the North, certain security measures are in place. Control zone signs indicate that no unattended vehicle can be left there at any time. That means if you are a single traveler, you cannot leave your car; if you are a twosome, one person must remain in the car while it's parked. Also, unlocked cars anywhere in the North are subject to a fine, for security reasons.

BY TAXI & HACKNEY

Taxis and hackneys look very much alike. Both drive you where you ask them to, and the drivers collect a fee at the end and are quite likely to entertain you with stories. There are some significant differences, however. Hackneys are not allowed to wait at taxi "ranks" or display a sign atop their cars; they don't use meters; and they are not regulated by any municipal or state agency. In other words, they are private individuals doing business as drivers for hire. They agree with you on a fare, which could be more or less than the regulated fee a taxi would charge. Both taxis and hackneys advertise in the classifieds or "Golden Pages."

BY CHAUFFERED CAR

If cost is no concern, or if you can't shake the fear of the left lane, you might want to consider being chauffeured in style. The fleets of such services usually begin at ground level with a basic Mercedes sedan and stretch from there. If you're interested, contact **Carey Limousine International** (© **800/336-4646;** www.careyint.com), whose 8-hour daily rate is currently around €525 ($467). We recommend Bord Fáilte–approved **Dave Sullivan Chauffeur Drive Limited** (© **01/820-1076;** fax 01/820-6333; www.chauffeur.ie), with offices in Dublin and Shannon. A typical 8-hour fee for two people in and around Dublin will run about €420 ($374).

For larger parties, Chrysler Voyagers are available.

BY FERRY

The coast of Ireland is not so razor-straight as, say, the borders of Kansas. A number of passenger and car ferries cut across the wider bays, shaving hours off land-only driving times. Ferries operate between Tarbert, county Kerry, and Killimer, county Clare; Passage East, county Waterford, and Ballyhack, county Wexford; and Glenbrook, east of Cork City, and Carrigaloe, outside of Cobh. For details, see chapter 10 (particularly the section on county Clare); chapter 6, and chapter 7.

Additionally, because Ireland includes a number of must-see islands, getting around includes getting on a boat now and then. Some boats, including all major ferries, have official licenses and offer regular scheduled service. Sometimes, however, making a crossing is a matter of staring out across a body of water to where you want to be and asking someone with a boat to take you there. Both methods work. To supplement the boat listings in this guide, you might want to request a copy of Information Sheet 50C—*Island Boat/Air Services*—from the Irish Tourist Board.

12 From Cottages to Castles: Putting a Roof Over Your Head

In Ireland, a man's (or woman's) home is often quite literally a castle, and some castles take in guests, becoming homes away from homes for visitors. In fact, Ireland offers a remarkable array of accommodations, some quite affordable and others outrageously lavish. There is something for everyone, from families on a budget to lovers on the splurge of a lifetime. Here's a sketch of what's out there.

HOTELS & GUESTHOUSES

Be Our Guest, a comprehensive guide to the hotels, country houses, castles, and inns of Ireland, is published by the Irish Hotel Federation and is available from the Irish Tourist Board. It's also online at **www.beourguest.ie**, which is a particularly handy, searchable site. Hotels and guesthouses, depending on their size and scope, offer a good deal more than a bed and a meal—everything from nightclubs to children's playrooms to golf courses. Some were historic buildings in a former life and others have been elegant hotels from birth, but there are plenty that are nondescript. If you're traveling with a well-padded wallet, **Ireland's**

Blue Book (www.irelands-blue-book. com) is a collection of upscale manor house hotels and castles.

The governments of the Republic and of the North inspect and rate all approved hotels and guesthouses. In the Republic, hotels can aspire to five stars, but guesthouses can reach no higher than four. In the North, hotels receive one to four stars, and guesthouses are either grade A or grade B.

In this guide, however, we use our own system of zero to three stars for rating places to stay, based on quality of amenities, atmosphere, and the most elusive, overall value for money. Cost is only a factor in as much as it affects value. For example, an expensive hotel may rate only one star while a moderately-priced guesthouse rates two stars if the guesthouse delivers an exceptional experience for the money you'll spend. See "Where to Stay" sections throughout this book for recommendations.

BED & BREAKFASTS

Throughout Ireland, in cities and countryside, a huge number of private homes are open to lodgers, by the night or longer. A warm bed and a substantial Irish breakfast can be expected, and other meals are negotiable. While most B&Bs are regulated and inspected by Tourism Quality Services (look for the shamrock seal of approval), approximately 12,000 premises are under no external supervision. Regulated or not, they are all different, as are your hosts. (*Note:* Establishments without governmental supervision or approval are not necessarily inferior to those stamped with the green shamrock. Approval involves an annual fee, as well as specific restrictions that some proprietors prefer not to embrace.)

For a modest fee, the Irish Tourist Board will send you a detailed listing of roughly 2,000 approved B&Bs, complete with a color photo of each. Or, you can follow the recommendations in this book. Needless to say, you receive the personal touch when you stay in someone's home, and more often than not, this is a real bonus. For anyone on a budget who is touring the country and spending only a night or two in each location, B&Bs are often hard to beat.

In high season, it's a good idea to make your reservation at least 24 hours in advance; your room will ordinarily be held until 6pm. The cost for a room with private bathroom is roughly €18 to €30 ($16–$27) per person, per night. *Note:* More and more B&Bs accept credit cards, but some still do not.

In the North, the Northern Ireland Tourist Board inspects each of its recommended B&Bs annually. Its *Information Guide to Bed & Breakfast* is available free from the NITB. The NITB also sells a useful comprehensive annual listing titled *Where to Stay in Northern Ireland.*

THE HIDDEN IRELAND

The Hidden Ireland is essentially a collection of very upscale B&Bs— think *Town & Country* with a brogue. These are private houses offering visitors the opportunity to sample Irish country life at its very best, in a style not usually experienced by the ordinary tourist. The properties include some of Ireland's oldest and grandest buildings, many of particular architectural merit and character. A B&B for two people generally runs €115 to €210 ($102–$187). To explore this option, contact The Hidden Ireland, P.O. Box 31, Westport, Co. Mayo (© **800/688-0299** in the U.S., or 01/662-7166; fax 01/662-7144; www. hidden-ireland.com).

FARMHOUSE ACCOMMODATIONS

Many of Ireland's small, family-run farms open their doors to visitors, offering an attractive alternative to hotels, guesthouses, and more standard B&B homes, particularly for families with small children. The **Irish Farm Holidays Association** (www. irishfarmholidays.com) produces an annual guide to farmhouse accommodations throughout the country. It is available from the Irish Tourist Board.

Farm holidays can take various forms, from one-night-at-a-time bed-and-breakfasts to extended self-catering rentals. Many of the farmhouse accommodations offer half board. That is, in addition to breakfast, you

Spa Vacations

If healing, renewal, and healthful relaxation are a central goal of your vacation, you might consider one of the centers, spas, or retreats approved by the **Health Farms of Ireland Association.** For a brochure, contact (© **091/790606**; fax 091/790837; www.healthfarmsofireland.com).

Moments **Keys to the Castle**

Dream of spending your vacation like a king or queen? Two companies specialize in self-catering accommodation in Ireland's historic and architecturally significant properties—including elegant Georgian manor houses, stately country mansions, lighthouses, and castles. The **Irish Landmark Trust,** 25 Eustace St., Dublin 2 (© **01/670-4733;** fax 01/670-4887; www.irishlandmark.com), rescues historic but neglected properties all over the island and restores them into fabulous hideaways, complete with period furnishings. It's a not-for-profit institution, so prices are hard to beat. **Elegant Ireland,** 15 Harcourt St., Dublin 2 (© **01/475-1632;** fax 01/475-1012; www.elegant.ie), can put you up in anything from an upscale seaside bungalow to a medieval castle that sleeps 20. As most properties are privately owned, they are priced according to what the market will bear. Bargains are harder to come by, and deals are more likely in the off-season.

can also have high tea or a full supper—but at an extra cost. Some farmhouses are everything you could dream of—full working family farms in untouched, often spectacular surroundings—while others stretch the meaning of *farm* to include country houses with a garden and a dog nearby, or guesthouses that are more "lodging with greenery" than "farm with lodging."

SELF-CATERING

If you want to stay a while and establish a base, you might want to consider renting an apartment, town house, cottage, or castle. Self-catering is a huge business in Ireland, and the range of available accommodations is startling. The minimum rental period is usually 1 week, although shorter periods are sometimes negotiable off-season. For families or small groups, you can usually get the best bargains with self-catering options.

In high season, in both the Republic and the North, a cottage sleeping seven could cost anywhere from $250 to more than $1,500 per week. While this guide does not focus on self-catering, you will find a scattering of specific recommendations in the chapters that follow. Both the Irish

Tourist Board and the Northern Ireland Tourist Board prepare helpful annual guides to self-catering.

Several recommended self-catering companies offer especially attractive accommodations throughout Ireland, mostly along the coasts. One is **Trident Holiday Homes,** 15 Irishtown Rd., Irishtown, Dublin 4 (© **01/668-3534;** fax 01/660-6465; www.thh.ie). For alluring seaside properties in west county Cork, try **Cashelfean Holiday Houses,** Durrus, county Cork (© **027/62000;** fax 027/62012; www.cashelfean.com). In the west of Ireland, from Kerry to Connemara, a selection of traditional Irish cottages, fully equipped to meet modern expectations, is offered by **Rent an Irish Cottage PLC.,** 85 O'Connell St., Limerick, county Limerick (© **061/411109;** fax 061/314821; www.rentacottage.ie). If you're interested in sampling the rural lifestyle, there's **Irish Country Holidays,** Discovery Centre, Rearcross, county Tipperary (© **062/79330;** fax 062/79331; www.country-holidays.ie), with properties all over Ireland.

Finally, for self-catering in any of Northern Ireland's areas of outstanding natural beauty, there is one surefire recommendation: **Rural Cottage Holidays Ltd.,** St. Anne's Ct., 59 North St., Belfast BT1 1NB (✆ **028/ 9024-1100;** fax 028/9024-1100; www.ruralcottageholidays.com). Founded in 1994 by the Northern Irish Tourist Board, Rural Cottage Holidays has restored and refurbished more than 30 traditional homes of character and charm, and done so with remarkable care and style. Each of these gems is in an area of special beauty and interest and is hosted by a nearby local family.

YOUTH HOSTELS

Ordinarily, youth hostels fall beyond the scope of what we recommend in this book. You should be aware, however, that some Irish hostels are broadening their scope and redesigning their accommodations to welcome travelers of all ages, as well as families. Some of these, although they cost a fraction of even a modest bed-and-breakfast, provide remarkably appealing accommodations. In fact, with sufficient notice, the Irish Youth Hostel Association is able to rent some entire hostels to clubs or groups at remarkably reasonable rates.

An Óige, the Irish Youth Hostel Association, 61 Mountjoy St., Dublin 7 (✆ **01/830-4555;** fax 01/830-5808; www.irelandyha.org), is the place to begin your planning. At one time, anyone showing up at an Irish Youth Hostel in a car was turned away. But that was then. The net has widened

considerably. These places are sometimes hard to get to and very hard to leave. Most often located in drop-dead-beautiful spots and housed in former residences of real character, several hostels in particular offer private rooms for couples and families, some with private bathrooms. Before you dismiss this option, explore the website and see if you can believe the views and the prices.

The corresponding organization in the North, whose hostels are maintained to a very high standard, is **YHANI** (Youth Hostels Association of Northern Ireland), 22–32 Donegall Rd., Belfast BT12 5JN (✆ **028/9032-4733;** fax 028/90439699; www.hini.org.uk). When you come across related references to **HINI** (Hostelling International Northern Ireland), don't be confused. It's another name for the same organization.

BOTTOM LINE ON BEDS

RATES Room charges quoted in this guide include 12.5% government tax (VAT) in the Republic of Ireland and 17.5% VAT in Northern Ireland. They do not (unless otherwise noted) include service charges, which are usually between 10% and 15%. Most hotels and guesthouses automatically add the service charge onto your final bill, although in recent years many family-run or limited-service places have begun the practice of not charging for service, leaving it as an option

---

Tips Think Green

ECEAT, the European Centre for Eco Agro Tourism, was established in 1993 to foster small-scale, sustainable green tourism throughout Europe. Their guides currently offer 1,200 select sites—farms, natural campsites, guesthouses, and small hotels in 21 countries—committed to the preservation of natural and cultural landscapes. Look for a copy of *The Green Holiday Guides: Great Britain and Ireland* in bookstores, or contact the Ireland coordinator, Margaret Hedge, Triskel Flower Farm, Cloonagh, Beltra, Co. Sligo (✆ **071/66714**).

for the guest. Home-style B&Bs do not ordinarily charge for service.

The price categories used throughout this guide indicate the cost of a double room for two per night, including tax but not service charges:

Very Expensive: €253 ($225) and up

Expensive: €180–€253 ($160–$225)

Moderate: €101–€180 ($90–$160)

Inexpensive: Under €101 ($90)

Note: Many accommodations span more than one of these categories, and in those cases, we've done our best to assign each to the category that best represents its characteristic rates in high season.

Ordinarily, the Irish cite the per-person price of a double room—a policy not followed in this guide, which for the sake of uniform comparison assumes double occupancy. Most accommodations make adjustments for children. Children staying in their parents' room are usually charged at 20% to 50% of the adult rate. If you're traveling on your own, there is most often a supplemental charge for single occupancy of a double room.

THREE WAYS TO SAVE

- **Book from home.** If your desired hotel has a toll-free number in the United States, get a quote and compare it to what the hotel's front desk offers. Nine times out of 10, the toll-free number's rate will be substantially lower than those offered at the door.
- **Haggle.** If you have a talent for haggling, room prices in hotels— especially privately owned hotels in the off-season—are often negotiable. Your best bet is to politely ask, "Is that your best rate?" or, "Can you do a little bit better?"
- **Use a Consolidator.** Just like with airfares, you can often save money on hotel accommodation if you go through a middleman. On the Web, try **www.hotelsireland.net**

for savings of up to 50% on rack rates (published rates) for two- to five-star hotels across Ireland.

TERMINOLOGY The Irish use the phrase "en suite" to indicate a room with private bathroom. A "double" has a double bed, and a "twin" has two single beds. An "orthopedic" bed has an extrafirm mattress. Queen- and king-size beds are not common except in large, deluxe hotels.

RESERVATIONS It usually pays to book in advance before you leave home. Many hotels can be booked through toll-free numbers in the United States, and the quoted prices offered can be appreciably (as much as 40%) lower than those offered at the door. For properties that do not have a U.S. reservation number, the fastest way to reserve is by telephone, fax, or e-mail. Fax and e-mail are advisable, because they give you a written confirmation. You can then follow up by sending a deposit check (usually the equivalent of 1 night's room rate) or by giving your credit-card number.

If you arrive in Ireland without a reservation, the staff members at the tourist offices throughout the Republic and Northern Ireland will gladly find you a room using a computerized reservation service known as **Gulliver.** In Ireland or Northern Ireland, you can also call the Gulliver line directly (© **00800/668-668-66**). This is a nationwide and cross-border "freephone" facility for credit-card bookings, operated daily 8am to 11pm. Gulliver is also accessible from the United States (© **011-800/668-668-66**) and on the Web at **www.gulliver.ie**.

QUALITY & VALUE Despite the various systems of approval, regulation, and rating, accommodations in Ireland are quite uneven in quality and cost. Often these variations are due to location; a wonderful, budget

B&B in an isolated area of countryside can be dirt cheap, whereas a mediocre guesthouse in Dublin or Cork can cost a comparative ransom.

If possible, always ask to see your room before committing yourself to a stay. In any given lodging, the size and quality of the rooms can vary considerably, often without any corresponding variation in cost. This is particularly true of single rooms, which can approach boarding-house standards even in a semiluxurious hotel. Don't be discouraged by this, but know what you're getting into so you're not disappointed. If you have complaints, state them at once and unambiguously—doing so may bring an immediate resolution (perhaps a lower rate or a better room).

Note: Many lodgings close for a few days or more on and around Christmas, even when they announce that they are open year-round. If you plan to visit Ireland during the Christmas holidays, double-check that the hotels, restaurants, and attractions you're counting on will be open. In this guide, what is true on Sundays is nearly always true on bank holidays. And be aware that only the most expensive hotels have air-conditioning—but there are only a handful of days a year when you would want it.

13 Tips on Restaurants & Pubs

RESTAURANTS

Ireland has an admirable range of restaurants in all price categories. The settings range from old-world hotel dining rooms, country mansions, and castles to skylit terraces, shop-front bistros, riverside cottages, thatched-roof pubs, and converted chapels. Best of all, there is a new appreciation for creative cooking in Ireland, with an emphasis on ingredients that are fresh (often organic), varied, and delicious (see the appendix, "Ireland in Depth.").

Before you book a table, here are a few things you should know:

RESERVATIONS Except for self-service eateries, informal cafes, and some popular seafood spots, most restaurants encourage reservations. The more expensive restaurants absolutely require reservations because there is little turnover—once a table is booked, it is yours for the whole lunch period or for the evening until closing. In the most popular eateries, seatings for Friday and Saturday nights (and Sun lunch) are often booked a week or more in advance, so have a few options in mind if you're booking at the last minute and want to try out the hot spots in town.

Here's a tip for those who don't mind dining early: If you stop into or phone a restaurant and find that it is booked from 8 or 8:30pm onward, ask if you can dine early (at 6:30 or 7pm), with a promise to leave by 8pm. You will sometimes get a table. Quite a few restaurants are experimenting with lower-priced early-bird and pretheater menus to attract people for early evening seating.

TABLE D'HOTE OR A LA CARTE

Some restaurants offer two menus: *table d'hôte,* a fixed-price three- or four-course lunch or dinner with a variety of choices; and *a la carte,* a menu offering a wide choice of individually priced appetizers (starters), soups, main courses, salads or vegetables, and desserts (sweets).

With the former, you pay the set price whether you take each course or not. If you do take each course, the total price offers very good value. With the latter, you choose what you want and pay accordingly. If you are a salad-and-entree person, then a la carte will probably work out to be less

Value Dining Bargains

If you want to try a top-rated restaurant but can't afford dinner, have your main meal there in the middle of the day by trying the table d'hôte set lunch menu. You'll experience the same great cuisine at half the price of a nighttime meal

Some restaurants offer a fixed-price three-course tourist menu during certain hours and days. These menus offer limited choices, but are usually lower in price than the restaurant's regular table d'hôte menu. Look for a tourist menu with a green Irish chef symbol in the window, listing the choices and the hours when the prices are in effect.

expensive; if you want all the courses and the trimmings, stick with the table d'hôte.

As a final suggestion, try an inexpensive lunch of pub grub. Pub grub is usually a lot better than its name suggests; the menu usually includes sandwiches, stews, quiches, and salads. In recent years, many pubs have converted or expanded into restaurants, serving excellent, unpretentious meals at prices to which you can lift a pint.

PRICES Meal prices at restaurants include a 12.5% VAT in the Republic of Ireland and a 17.5% VAT in Northern Ireland, but the service charge is extra. In perhaps half of all restaurants, a set service charge is added automatically; it can range from 10% to 15%. In the remaining restaurants, it is now the custom not to add any service charge, leaving the tip to your discretion. This can be confusing for a visitor, but each restaurant normally prints its policy on the menu. If it is not clear, ask.

When no service charge is added, tip up to 15% depending on the quality of the service. If 10% to 12.5% has already been added to your bill, leave an appropriate amount that will total 15% if service has been satisfactory.

The price categories used in this book are based on the price of a complete dinner (or lunch, if dinner is not served) for one person, including tax

and tip, but not wine or alcoholic beverages:

Very Expensive: €56 ($50) and up

Expensive: €34–€56 ($30–$50)

Moderate: €17–34 ($15–$30)

Inexpensive: Under €17 ($15)

DINING TIPS Don't be surprised if you are not ushered to your table as soon as you arrive at a restaurant. This is not a delaying tactic—many of the better dining rooms carry on the old custom of seating you in a lounge or bar area while you sip an aperitif and peruse the menu. Your waiter then comes to discuss the choices and to take your order. You are not called to the table until the first course is about to be served.

Happily, for those fond of a beer with a meal, Ireland recently relaxed its liquor laws. Restaurants are now permitted to serve beer with meals (previously they could only serve wine).

PUBS

The pub continues to be a mainstay of Irish social life. With more than 10,000 specimens throughout the country, there are pubs in every city, town, and hamlet, on every street and at every turn. Everyone has a "local"—a favorite pub near home—where he or she goes for a drink and some conversation. But there is a big distinction between the way the Irish use their pubs and the way, say, the French use cafes. Whereas the French hang out in cafes day or night, a recent study conducted by the Vintners' Federation of Ireland revealed that 80% of drinkers do not go to the pub until after 9pm.

The origin of pubs reaches back several centuries to a time when neighbors would gather in a kitchen to talk and maybe sample some home brew. As a certain spot grew popular, word spread and people came from all directions, always assured of a warm welcome. Such places gradually became known as public houses—"pubs," for short. In time, the name of the person who tended a public house was mounted over the doorway, and many pubs still bear a family or proprietor's name, such as Davy Byrnes, Doheny and Nesbitt, or W. Ryan. A good percentage of these have been in the same family for generations. Although they might have added televisions, pool tables, dartboards, or nightly music sessions, their primary purpose is still to be a stage for conversation and a warm spot to down a pint.

PUB HOURS The Republic of Ireland's drinking hours were extended in the year 2000, a mere 2 centuries after they were introduced. Hours are 10:30am to 11.30pm Monday to Wednesday; 10:30am to 12.30am Thursday to Saturday; and 12:30pm to 11pm Sunday (pubs previously had to close between 2–4pm). After normal drinking hours, there are always nightclubs and discos, which close at 3am.

You'll notice that when the dreaded "closing time" comes, nobody clears out of the pub. That's because the term is a misnomer. The "closing time" is actually the time when the barmen must stop serving alcohol, so expect to hear a shout for "Last orders!" Anyone who wants to order his or her last drink does so, and the bars don't actually shut their doors until up to an hour later.

In the North, pubs are open year-round from 11:30am to 11pm Monday to Saturday, and 12:30 to 2pm and 7 to 10pm on Sunday.

14 Tips on Sightseeing & Shopping

SIGHTSEEING DISCOUNTS

Sightseeing on a budget? You can stretch a dollar (or a pound) by saving on admission charges at major attractions.

In the Republic, a **Heritage Card** entitles you to unlimited admission to the more than 65 attractions all over Ireland operated by Dúchas, the Heritage Service. These include castles, stately homes, historic monuments, national parks, and more. The card costs €19 ($17) for adults, €13 ($12) for seniors, €7.60 ($6.75) for children and students, and €46 ($41) for a family. There are three ways to get the card: You can buy it at any of the participating attractions; you can purchase it by phone (© **1800-600601,** toll-free in Ireland, or 01/647-2461)

with your Visa or MasterCard; or you can order it on the Web at **www.heritageireland.ie.** If you plan to do serious sightseeing, this is a wise purchase. It's far more pleasant to pick up one of these cards the first time you visit a Heritage site than to realize a week later how much you would have saved if you had.

Detailed information about National Trust attractions in Northern Ireland is available from the Northern Ireland Tourist Board.

VAT REFUNDS

First, the bad news: In Ireland, almost all consumer products are subject to value-added tax—better known as VAT—of 21% on the net price of goods, which is roughly 17% of the

Tips Closing Times

At many sights and attractions, new visitors are not admitted 30 minutes prior to the stated closing time. So don't plan to slip into a museum or castle at 4:40pm when it officially closes at 5pm.

selling price. Now, the good news: If you're not a citizen of an EU country, you are entitled to this money back.

The first thing you should know is that VAT is a "hidden tax"—it's already added into the purchase price of any items you see in shops. (The two notable exceptions: no VAT on books and no VAT on children's clothing and footwear).

There are two ways to get your money back.

Global Refund (© 800/566-9828; www.globalrefund.ie) is the world's largest private company offering VAT refunds, with more than 5,000 stores in Ireland displaying "Tax Free for Tourists" stickers in their front windows. Unlike all other EU countries, Ireland requires no minimum purchase in a single store. The system works like this:

Step 1: Collect refund checks at every store where you make a purchase.

Step 2: Fill in the blanks (name, address, passport number, and so on) on the checks, noting whether you'd like your refund in cash or credit card.

Step 3: Hand in your completed checks to the VAT-refund desk at the airport just before departing Ireland. The VAT desk is in the departures hall at Dublin airport and in the arrivals hall at Shannon airport. If you're running late at the airport, you can have the checks stamped by customs and mail them to Global Refund in an international prepaid envelope. Finally, if you forget to get your checks stamped at Customs, all is

not lost. Just get them stamped by either a notary public, justice of the peace, or a police officer (with a badge number) in your home country, and mail them back.

What if the shop isn't part of the Global Refund network? For a **store refund,** get a full receipt at the time of purchase that shows the shop's name, address, and VAT paid. (Customs does not accept generic cash-register tally slips.) Save your receipts until you're ready to depart Ireland, then go to the Customs Office at the airport or ferry port to have your receipts stamped and your goods inspected. A passport and other forms of identification (a driver's license, for example) may be required. Then send your stamped receipts back to the store where you made the purchase, which will then issue a VAT refund check to you by mail to your home address. Most stores deduct a small handling fee for this service.

AVOIDING THE VAT HASSLE
Don't want to fill out those forms? Hate the thought of lining up at the airport refund desk? There are three ways to pay no VAT from the beginning.

• **Mail your purchases home.** Arrange for the store to ship your purchases home, and the VAT will be subtracted at the point of sale. You save having to fill out those forms, and you don't have to lug around your stuff. But you still have to pay shipping costs, which may outweigh any hassle you save.

• **Buy at the airport.** When returning home from Ireland, non-EU citizens are entitled to shop in the duty-free shops at Shannon and Dublin Airports. If you're flying on Aer Lingus, you can also shop onboard at the airline's "Duty-Free Sky Shop." These shops offer prices that are free of duty or tax. There are no forms to fill out and no lines to reclaim money. The main drawback is the very limited variety of goods compared to the shops around Ireland.

- **Support a good cause.** Ireland's nonprofit organizations that sell goods operate as charitable trusts and are not subject to VAT, so all their prices are VAT-free. Check out **Oxfam** shops (www.oxfam ireland.org) for pottery and other trendy housewares.

15 Tracing Your Irish Roots

Whether your name is Kelly or Klein, you might have some ancestral ties with Ireland—about 40 million Americans do. If you are planning to visit Ireland to trace your roots, you'll enjoy the greatest success if you do some planning. The more information you can gather about your family before your visit, the easier it will be to find your ancestral home or even a distant cousin once you arrive.

One of the best places to start is the **Church of Latter Day Saints,** in Salt Lake City, Utah (© **801-240-2331;** fax 801-240-5551; www.familysearch. org), keepers of the world's largest family history library. For archives of ancestors who were born, died, or were married in the United States, check out the searchable databases of the **National Archives and Records Administration** (www.nara.gov). Other excellent, searchable online genealogy aids include www.ancestry. com and www.geneaology.com.

Getting specific to Ireland, the principal online resources for any search should be the **Irish National Archives** (www.nationalarchives.ie/ geneaology.html), which holds online searchable databases of Ireland's vital records. In addition, the Irish Tourist Board publishes a book called *Tracing Your Ancestors in Ireland,* which outlines the range of resources for genealogical research in Dublin, as well as throughout the island, and helps you get started. It's free of charge at any Irish Tourist Board office.

A brand-new, excellent genealogy resource covering all 32 counties on the island is the **Irish Family History Foundation**'s new website at www. irishroots.net. Much of the archived information is free for your perusal, or you can hire researchers to do the work for you. Initial searches cost €75 ($67) and comprehensive family searches cost €250 ($223).

In Ireland, you can do the research and footwork yourself, or you can use the services of a commercial agency. One of the best firms is **Hibernian Research Co.,** P.O. Box 3097, Dublin 6 (© **01/496-6522;** fax 01/497-3011). The researchers, all trained by the Chief Herald of Ireland, have a combined total of more than 100 years' professional experience in working on all aspects of family histories. Among the cases that Hibernian Research handled were U.S. President Ronald Reagan, Canadian Prime Minister Brian Mulrooney, and Ireland's former president, Mary Robinson. **ENECLANN,** Trinity College Enterprise Centre, Pearse St., Dublin 2 (© **01/671-0338;** fax 01/671-0281; www.eneclann.ie), is an award-winning company specializing in historical and heritage records. Rates run from €175 ($156) for a 3-hour exploratory search up to €435 ($387) for an 8-hour advanced search.

If you prefer to do the digging yourself, Dublin City is the location for all the Republic of Ireland's centralized genealogical records, and

Belfast is the place to go for Ulster ancestral hunts. Here are the major sources of information:

The Manuscripts Reading Room in the **National Library,** Kildare Street, Dublin 2 (℗ **01/603-0200;** fax 01/676-6690; www.nli.ie) has an extensive collection of pre-1880 Catholic records of baptisms, births, and marriages. Its other genealogical material includes trade directories, journals of historical and archaeological societies, local histories, and newspapers. In addition, the library has a comprehensive indexing system that enables you to identify the material you need to consult.

As mentioned above, **The National Archives,** Bishop Street, Dublin 8 (℗ **01/407-2300;** fax 01/407-2333; www.nationalarchives.ie) is a key resource. Until 1988, it was known as the Public Record Office. A fire severely damaged this facility in the early 1920s, and many valuable source documents were lost. However, numerous records rich in genealogical interest are still available. They include *Griffith's Primary Valuation of Ireland, 1848–63,* which records the names of all those owning or occupying land or property in Ireland at the time; the complete national census of 1901 to 1911; and tithe listings, indexes to wills, administrations, licenses, and marriage bonds. In addition, there is also an ever-expanding collection of Church of Ireland Parish Registers on microfilm. You'll also find partial surviving census returns for the 19th

century, reports and records relating to the period of the 1798 rebellion, crime and convict records, and details of those sentenced to transportation to Australia. There is no fee for conducting personal searches for family history and genealogy in the archives, and an instruction booklet is provided to get you started. There is a fee for photocopies. The National Archives reading room is open Monday to Friday, 10am to 5pm.

The Genealogical Office, Kildare Street, Dublin (℗ **01/603-0311;** fax 01/662-1062), attached to the National Library, incorporates the office of the Chief Herald and operates a specialist consultation service on how to trace your ancestry. The library no longer offers an in-house researcher, but its Web page (www.nli.ie/fr_offi.htm) lists dozens of professional researchers who can be hired for a fee.

The General Register Office, Joyce House, 8/11 Lombard St. E., Dublin 2 (℗ **01/635-4000;** www.groireland.ie), is the central repository for records relating to births, deaths, and marriages in the Republic (Catholic marriages from Jan 1, 1864; all other marriages from Apr 1, 1845). Full birth, death, or marriage certificates each cost €7 ($6.20). General searches cost €15 ($14). The office is open weekdays from 9:30am to 12:30pm and 2:15 to 4:30pm.

The Registry of Deeds, Kings Inns, Henrietta Street, Dublin 1 (℗ **01/670-7500;** fax 01/804-8406;

Planning an Irish Wedding

For those with Irish roots, getting married on the auld sod has become an extremely popular, romantic way to kick off your new life together. The basic requirements for getting married in Ireland can be found on the Dublin info page on the U.S. Embassy website at **www.usembassy.ie/consulate/marriage.html.** For help finding the perfect church, reception hall, florist, and band, visit **www.wedding-ireland.com** or **www.weddings online.ie.**

www.irlgov.ie/landreg), has records that date from 1708 and relate to all the usual transactions affecting property—notably leases, mortgages, and settlements—and some wills. The fee of €13 ($12) per day includes instructions on how to handle the indexes.

North of the border, **The Public Record Office of Northern Ireland,** 66 Balmoral Ave., Belfast BT9 6NY (© **028/9025-1318;** fax 028/9025-5999; http://proni.nics.gov.uk), has most of the surviving official records of Northern Ireland. They include tithe and valuation records from the 1820s and 1830s, copies of wills from 1858 for Ulster, the records of many landed estates in Ulster, and copies of most pre-1900 registers of baptisms, marriages, and burial papers for all denominations in Ulster. The office is open weekdays 9:15am to 4:45pm (until 8:45pm on Thurs, closed for 2 weeks in late Nov).The website has a useful section entitled "How to Trace Your Family Tree," accessible through the "Frequently Asked Questions" rubric.

For post-1900 birth, marriage, and death certificates, contact the General Register Office Northern Ireland, Oxford House, 49-55 Chichester St., Belfast BT1 4HC (© **028/1232-251318**).

16 Suggested Itineraries

To make the rounds of Ireland, North and South, you'll need at least 2 weeks—or, better, 3 weeks. With even a week, however, you can convince yourself and others you've been there.

Here are a few recommended itineraries, with the number of days suggested for each city or touring center indicated in parentheses. Each tour starts or finishes near Shannon or Dublin, the two main arrival and departure points. You can ask your travel agent to design a trip based on your interests or on the amount of time you can spend.

1 Week—Southern Coast: Clare (1), Kerry (2), Cork (2); Wexford (1), Dublin (1).

1 Week—Main Highlights: Galway (1), Clare (1), Kerry (1), Cork (1), Waterford (1), Dublin (2).

1 Week—East Coast: Dublin (3), Wicklow Mountains (1), Kilkenny (1), Waterford (1), Wexford (1).

1 Week—West Coast: Sligo, Mayo, and Connemara (2), Galway (2), Clare (1), Kerry (2).

1 Week—The Northwest: Galway (2), Sligo, Mayo, and Connemara (2), Donegal (2), Clare (1).

1 Week—The North: Newcastle (1), Belfast (2), Antrim Coast (2), Derry (1), Enniskillen (1).

2 Weeks: The Coastal Circuit: Shannon (1); Kerry (2); West Cork (1); Cork City (1); Dublin (2); Belfast (2); Donegal (2); Sligo, Mayo, and Connemara (2), Galway (1).

3 Weeks—The Complete Tour: Clare (1), Kerry (2), Cork (2), Kilkenny (1), Waterford or Wexford (1), Dublin (3), Belfast (2), Portrush (1), Derry or Enniskillen (1), Donegal (2), Sligo, Mayo, and Connemara (3), Galway (2).

All of the above itineraries describe circles, which are not for everyone. When time is scarce, many people prefer to settle into one place for a week and reach out from there. This is the "hub" plan, a viable alternative to the 7-day dash. If it's your first time in Ireland, Dublin, Cork, and Galway make great hubs. Don't feel like you have to see all three of those cities in the same trip. In fact, choosing one city and its surrounding regions is probably the most enjoyable option, as it allows you to take advantage of the city's amenities and also spend time in the

---

Tips **Navigator Par Excellence**

One nifty little travel aid is the "Route Planning" facility offered by Ireland's **AA Roadwatch** (www.aaroadwatch.ie). You simply plug in your starting point and destination, with as many places in between that you'd like to visit. You can also avoid the rush or save money by specifying that you'd like to "avoid motorways" or "avoid toll roads," respectively. The route planner then spits out a detailed itinerary that anyone can follow.

---

countryside and seaside. Whether you decide to tour or to stay put might depend on whether you're primarily in search of sights or a sense of place.

You'll see more sights while moving around, but you'll likely feel like you got to know Ireland if you give yourself time to simply observe and reflect.

17 Recommended Reading

FICTION

If you're especially ambitious, you could bite off James Joyce's *Ulysses* (Random House, 1986), a classic to be certain, but one that's so dense with insider lexicon that you'd also better pack *Cliffs Notes*. Better yet, try *Ulysses Annotated* (University of California Press, 1989), which helps explain Joyce's puns, foreign expressions, and Dublin vernacular. Or dive into the plays of Brendan Behan with *Behan Complete Plays* (Methuen, 2001).

The current king of Irish contemporary writing is Roddy Doyle, and any of his novels makes for excellent entertainment. There's The Barrytown Trilogy, which includes *The Commitments*, *The Snapper*, and *The Van* (Penguin, 1995); the Booker prize-winning *Paddy Clarke Ha Ha Ha* (Penguin, 1995); and *A Star Called Henry* (Penguin, 2000).

An excellent companion for any book-loving traveler is *For the Love of Ireland: A Literary Companion for Readers and Travelers* (Ballantine, 2001), an anthology of more than 60 writings by over 40 top-notch authors that's chock-a-block with geographic, sociological, literary, and cultural richness. Contributors include James Joyce, Roddy Doyle, Samuel Beckett, W. B. Yeats, Edna O'Brien, Seamus Heaney and Frank McCourt. The book suggests excursions in 16 counties and includes pertinent travel details, such as the current schedule for the ferry that Sean O'Faolain described 50 years ago in *An Irish Journey*.

POETRY

If you like poetry, you've come to the right country. In the past two centuries, Ireland has produced arguably the best stable of poets in the world. Start with *Collected Poems* by Patrick Kavanagh (W. W. Norton, 1973), Nobel-prize winning Seamus Heaney's *Opened Ground: Selected Poems 1966–1996* (Farrar, Strauss & Giroux, 1999), and, of course, *The Collected Poems of W. B. Yeats* (Scribner, 1996), by the famous honorary Irish poet.

AUTOBIOGRAPHY

Many are familiar with *Angela's Ashes* (Simon & Schuster, 1996), Frank McCourt's award-winning childhood memoir of growing up in Limerick in the 1940s and 1950s. It's a poignant, heartbreaking, but often hilarious account of a family's struggle through alcoholism and poverty in Ireland, and one that will resonate with you long after you put it down. It was, however, received with mixed reaction by the citizens of Limerick because it portrayed their hometown in a very unfavorable light. Rest assured that the Limerick of today is a far more prosperous, hospitable place.

For a humorous travelogue of one man's meanderings around Ireland, don't miss *McCarthy's Bar: A Journey of Discovery in the West of Ireland* by BBC writer and performer Pete McCarthy (St. Martin's, 2001). McCarthy's knack for affectionately retelling a hearty, side-splitting yarn rivals that of essayists like P. J. O'Rourke, Peter Mayle, and Bill Bryson. Small wonder that it was a number-one bestseller in Ireland.

HISTORY

How the Irish Saved Civilization (Anchor, 1996), by Thomas Cahill, tells of a crucial window in European history after the fall of the Roman Empire. When Europeans languished, Irish scholars were instrumental in saving literature, especially the Gospel, and became not only the conservators of civilization, but also the shapers of the medieval mind, putting their unique stamp on Western culture.

Two excellent books by Tim Pat Coogan, *The Irish Civil War* (Seven Dials, 2001), and *The Troubles: Ireland's Ordeal 1966–1996 and the Search for Peace* (National Book Network, 1997), are essential reading for anyone wanting to understand the complexities of 21st-century Ireland.

 FAST FACTS: Ireland

American Express The only American Express offices in Ireland are in Dublin at 41 Nassau St. (✆ 01/617-5597) and Killarney on East Avenue Road (✆ 066/35722). There are no longer offices in the North. In an emergency, traveler's checks can be reported lost or stolen by dialing collect (to the U.S.) ✆ 00-1-336-333-3211.

Business Hours **Banks** are open 10am to 4pm Monday to Wednesday and Friday, and 10am to 5pm Thursday.

Post offices (known as **An Post**) in city centers are open from 9am to 5:30pm Monday to Friday and 9am to 1:30pm Saturday. The GPO on O'Connell Street is open 8am to 8pm Monday to Saturday, and 10:30am to 6:30pm Sunday (for stamps only). Post offices in small towns often close for lunch from 1 to 2:30pm.

Museums and sights are generally open 10am to 5pm Tuesday to Saturday, and 2 to 5pm Sunday.

Shops generally open 9am to 6pm, Monday to Friday with late opening on Thursdays until 7 or 8pm. In Dublin's city center most department stores and many shops are open 12 to 6pm Sundays.

In **Northern Ireland**, bank hours are Monday to Friday 9:30pm to 4.30pm. Post Offices are open 9:30am to 5:30pm Monday to Friday and Saturday 9am to 1pm. Some in smaller towns close for an hour at lunch time. Shopping hours are much the same as in the Republic with some smaller shops closing for an hour at lunch time.

Currency Exchange Currency-exchange services, signposted as BUREAU DE CHANGE, are in all banks and at many branches of the Irish post-office system, known as **An Post**. A bureau de change operates daily during flight arrival and departure times at Dublin airport; a foreign currency note-exchanger machine is also available on a 24-hour basis in the upstairs level of the main arrivals hall. Many hotels and travel agencies offer currency exchange services, although the best rate of exchange is usually given by ATMs and credit cards for purchases.

Dentists For listings, look under "Dental Surgeons" in the Golden Pages (yellow pages) of the Irish telephone book or in the Yellow Pages of the Northern Ireland telephone book—or better yet, ask your innkeeper for advice. Expect to pay up front. In Dublin, the American Embassy (see "Embassies," below) can provide a list of dentists in the city and surrounding areas.

Doctors If you need to see a physician, most hotels and guesthouses will contact a doctor for you. (You will also find referral services for the greater Dublin area listed in "Fast Facts: Dublin" in chapter 4.) Otherwise, consult the Golden Pages of the Irish telephone book or the Yellow Pages of the Northern Ireland telephone book. As with dentists, expect to pay for treatment up front and be reimbursed after the fact by your insurance company. In Dublin, the American Embassy (see "Embassies," below) can provide a list of doctors in the city and surrounding areas.

Drugstores Drugstores are called "chemist shops" and are found in every city, town, and village. Look under "Chemists—Pharmaceutical" in the Golden Pages of the Irish telephone book or "Chemists—Dispensing" in the Yellow Pages of the Northern Ireland telephone book.

Electricity The Irish electric system operates on 220 volts with a plug bearing three rectangular prongs. The Northern Irish system operates on 250 volts. To use standard American 110 volt appliances, you'll need both a transformer and a plug adapter. Most new laptops have built-in transformers, but some do not, so beware. Attempting to use only a plug adapter is a sure way to fry your appliance or, worse, cause a fire.

Embassies/Consulates The **American Embassy** is at 42 Elgin Rd., Ballsbridge, Dublin 4 (© 01/668-8777); the **Canadian Embassy** at 65/68 St. Stephen's Green, Dublin 2 (© 01/678-1988); the **British Embassy** at 29 Merrion Rd., Dublin 2 (© 01/269-5211); and the **Australian Embassy** at Fitzwilton House, Wilton Terrace, Dublin 2 (© 01/676-1517). In addition, there is an **American Consulate** at 14 Queen St., Belfast BT1 6EQ (© 028/9032-8239).

Emergencies For the **Garda** (police), fire, or other emergencies, dial © **999.**

Internet Access Public access terminals are no longer hard to find in Ireland; they're now in shopping malls, hotels, and even hostels, especially in the larger towns and more tourist-centered areas. Virtually every town with a public library offers free Internet access, though you may have to call ahead to reserve time on a PC. (For a list of public libraries in Ireland, visit **www.libdex.com/country/Ireland.html**.) Additionally, there are an increasing number of Internet cafes sprouting up across the island. We list many of these in the chapters that follow.

Language See the "Language" section in the appendix, "Ireland in Depth."

Liquor Laws Individuals must be age 18 or over to be served alcoholic beverages in Ireland. For pub hours, see "Tips on Restaurants & Pubs," earlier in this chapter. Restaurants with liquor licenses are permitted to serve alcohol during the hours when meals are served. Hotels and guesthouses with licenses can serve during normal hours to the public; overnight guests, referred to as "residents," can be served after closing hours. Alcoholic beverages by the bottle can be purchased at liquor stores, at pubs displaying "off-license" signs, and at most supermarkets.

Ireland has very severe laws and penalties regarding driving while intoxicated, so don't even think about it.

Mail In Ireland, mailboxes are painted green with the word POST on top. In Northern Ireland, they are painted red with a royal coat of arms symbol. From the Republic, an airmail letter or postcard to the United States or Canada, not exceeding 25 grams, costs €.57 (51¢) and takes 5 to 7 days to arrive. Prestamped aerogrammes or air letters are also €.57. From Northern Ireland to the United States or Canada, airmail letters cost 39p (55¢) and postcards 34p (48¢). Delivery takes about 5 days to a week.

Police In the Republic of Ireland, a law enforcement officer is called a **Garda,** a member of the *Garda Siochana* (guardian of the peace); in the plural, it's *Gardai* (pronounced *gar*-dee) or simply "the Guards." Dial ⓒ **999** to reach the Gardai in an emergency. Except for special detachments, Irish police are unarmed and wear dark blue uniforms. In Northern Ireland, you can also reach the police by dialing ⓒ **999.**

Restrooms Public restrooms are usually simply called "toilets," or are marked with international symbols. In the Republic of Ireland, some of the older ones still carry the Gaelic words *Fir* (Men) and *Mna* (Women). Among the newest and best-kept rest rooms are those found at shopping malls and at multistory parking lots. Some cost €.15 (15¢) to enter. Free restrooms are available to customers of sightseeing attractions, museums, hotels, restaurants, pubs, shops, theaters, and department stores. Most of the newer gas stations have public toilets, and some even have baby-changing facilities.

Safety The Republic of Ireland has enjoyed a traditionally low crime rate, particularly when it comes to violent crime. Those days are not entirely over, but they do regrettably seem to be passing, especially in the cities. By U.S. standards, Ireland is still very safe, but not safe enough to warrant carelessness. Travelers should take normal precautions to protect their belongings from theft and themselves from harm.

In recent years, the larger cities have been prey to pickpockets, purse-snatchers, car thieves, and drug traffickers. To alert visitors to potential dangers, the Garda Siochana publishes a small leaflet, *A Short Guide to Tourist Security,* which is available at tourist offices and other public places. The booklet advises you not to carry large amounts of money or important documents like your passport or airline tickets when strolling around. Leave them in a safe-deposit box at your hotel. Do not leave cars unlocked or cameras, binoculars, or other expensive equipment unattended. Be alert and aware of your surroundings, and do not wander in lonely areas alone at night. And take special care if you'll be out in Dublin when the pubs and nightclubs close for the night. Ask at your hotel about which areas are safe and which are not, and when.

In the north of Ireland, safety is a somewhat greater concern because of the political unrest that has prevailed there for the past 30 years. Violence seems to have diminished somewhat since the Good Friday Agreement was instituted, but short flare-ups are common. Before traveling to Northern Ireland, contact the U.S. State Department and the Northern Ireland Tourist Board to obtain the latest safety recommendations. The **U.S. Department of State 24-hour hot line** (© 202/647-5225) provides travel warnings and security recommendations, as well as emergency assistance.

Taxes As in many European countries, sales tax is called VAT (value-added tax) and is often already included in the price quoted to you or shown on price tags. In the Republic, VAT rates vary—for hotels, restaurants, and car rentals, it is 12.5%; for souvenirs and gifts, it is 21%. In Northern Ireland, the VAT is 17.5% across the board. VAT charged on services such as hotel stays, meals, car rentals, and entertainment cannot be refunded to visitors, but the VAT on products such as souvenirs is refundable. For full details on VAT refunds for purchases, see "VAT Refunds," under "Tips on Sightseeing & Shopping," earlier in this chapter.

Telephone In the Republic, the telephone system is known as Eircom; in Northern Ireland, it's British Telecom. Phone numbers in Ireland are currently in flux, as digits are added to accommodate expanded service. Every effort has been made to ensure that the numbers and information in this guide are accurate at the time of writing. If you have difficulty reaching a party, the Irish toll-free number for directory assistance is © **11811.** From the United States, the (toll) number to call is © **00353-91-770220.**

Local calls from a phone booth require a Callcard (in the Republic) or Phonecard (in the North). Both are prepaid computerized cards that you insert into the phone instead of coins. They can be purchased in a range of denominations at phone company offices, post offices, and many retail outlets (such as newsstands). There's a local and international phone center at the General Post Office on O'Connell Street.

Overseas calls from Ireland can be quite costly, whether you use a local Phonecard or your own calling card. If you think you will want to call home regularly while in Ireland, you may want to open an account with **Swiftcall** (toll-free in Ireland © **1800/929932;** www.swiftcall.com). Its rates represent a considerable savings, not only from Ireland to the United States but vice versa (handy for planning your trip as well as keeping in touch afterward). **International WORLDLINK** (© **800/864-8000** in the U.S., or 1800/551514 in Ireland) offers an array of additional services for overseas travelers—such as toll-free voice-mail boxes, fax mail, and news services—which can be crucial for keeping in touch when you don't know where or when you can be reached.

To place a call from your home country to Ireland, dial the international access code (011 in the U.S., 0011 in Australia, 0170 in New Zealand, 00 in the U.K.), plus the country code (**353** for the Republic, **44** for the North), and finally the number, remembering to omit the initial 0, which is for use only within Ireland (for example, to call the county Kerry number 066/00000 from the United States, you'd dial 011-353-66/00000).

To place a direct international call from Ireland, dial the international access code (**00**) plus the country code (U.S. and Canada 1, the U.K. 44, Australia 61, New Zealand 64), the area or city code, and the number. For example, to call the U.S. number (212/000-0000) you'd dial (00-1-212/000-0000). The toll-free international access code for **AT&T** is ① 1-800-550-000; for **Sprint** it's ① 1-800-552-001; and for **MCI** it's ① 1-800-55-1001. *Note:* To dial direct to Northern Ireland from the Republic, simply replace the 028 prefix with 048.

Time Ireland follows Greenwich Mean Time (1 hr. earlier than Central European Time) from November to March, and British Standard Time (the same as Central European Time) from April to October. Ireland is 5 hours ahead of the eastern United States (when it's noon in New York, it's 5pm in Ireland).

Ireland's latitude makes for longer days and shorter nights in the summer, and the reverse in the winter. In June, there is bright sun until 11pm, but in December, it is truly dark at 4pm.

Tipping Most hotels and guesthouses add a service charge to the bill, usually 12.5% to 15%, although some smaller places add only 10% or nothing at all. Always check to see what amount, if any, has been added to your bill. If it is 12.5% to 15%, and you feel this is sufficient, then there is no need for more gratuities. However, if a smaller amount has been added or if staff members have provided exceptional service, it is appropriate to give additional cash gratuities. For porters or bellhops, tip €1 (90¢) per piece of luggage. For taxi drivers, hairdressers, and other providers of service, tip as you would at home, an average of 10% to 15%.

For restaurants, the policy is usually printed on the menu—either a gratuity of 10% to 15% is automatically added to your bill or it's left up to you. Always ask if you are in doubt. As a rule, bartenders do not expect a tip, except when table service is provided.

Water Tap water throughout the island of Ireland is generally safe. If you prefer bottled water, it is readily available at all hotels, guesthouses, restaurants, and pubs.

Yellow Pages The classified section of telephone books in the Republic of Ireland is called the **Golden Pages** (www.goldenpages.ie). In the North, it's called the **Yellow Pages.**

3

Ireland Outdoors

Imagine an island where foxes and hares are spotted within city limits, otters swim in city rivers, roadsides are speckled with Mediterranean, Caribbean, and Arctic wildflowers, and sea lions are common sights on suburban beaches. Imagine being able to walk for hours along a coastal headland without meeting another human being. This is Ireland—a largely unspoiled utopia for nature and nature-lovers. About a third of Ireland's 3.7 million residents live in Dublin or the surrounding areas. Apart from a few other cities, the rest of the population is thinly settled on the island, putting very few demands on the environment. The result is remarkably intact bird and wildlife habitats.

Every corner of Ireland is packed with opportunities for outdoor pursuits. Think of the Irish as the Mediterraneans of the north. Like the Greeks and southern Italians, they love the outdoors and spend as much of their time in it as possible. So what if it rains—that doesn't stop the Irish from doing anything they want, when they want, from golfing to hiking (called hillwalking here) to fishing to windsurfing to cycling. "But 'tis only rain," they say. And they're right.

1 Bicycling

Bicycling is a wonderful way to see the Irish landscape in its many forms, from barren bogland to crashing surf to inland lakes. The distances are quite manageable, and in a week or two on a bike, you can travel through several of the regions described in this guide or explore one in greater detail. Accommodations in the form of hostels, B&Bs, and hotels are abundantly available for touring cyclists who don't want to deal with the extra weight of a tent and sleeping bag.

Even if you're not game to undertake a full-fledged bike tour, day trips on two wheels can be a great way to stretch your legs after spending too much time in the car. Rentals are available in most towns that cater in any way to tourists.

Roads in Ireland are categorized as M (Motorway), N (National), or R (Regional); some still bear the older T (Trunk) and L (Link) designations. For reasons of scenery as well as safety, you probably want to avoid the busier roads. The R and L roads are always suitable for cycling, as are the N roads in outlying areas where there isn't too much traffic. The biggest disadvantage of the smaller roads in remote areas is that they are often not signposted, so you should have a good map and compass to be sure of your way. In some areas of the west and northwest, *only* the N roads are consistently signposted.

If you're going to hook up with a cycling outfitter (see below), you probably won't need to bring your own gear. But if you're planning on going it alone, ask your airline how much it will cost to stow your bike in the baggage hold; some carriers charge around $75, while others will take bikes free if they're properly packed and are taking the place of one of your allowable checked bags.

Even if you'll be renting a bike, you'll still want to consider bringing a few of your own items. Helmets are only sporadically available, and your chances of finding one that fits are poor; so, bring one if you care about your head. The panniers (saddlebags) offered for rental are often on the flimsy side. If you have cycling shoes and good pedals, you can easily attach them to the rental bike and make your trip immeasurably more enjoyable. With advance notice, most rental shops can outfit a bike with toe clips, bar ends, and water-bottle cages; an advance booking can also improve your chances of reserving the right size bike. Many rental outfits can also arrange a one-way rental over a short distance (up to 161km/100 miles or so). The national companies, such as Raleigh Rent-A-Bike and Rent-A-Bike Ireland (see below), are set up for one-way rentals throughout the country.

Anyone cycling in Ireland should be prepared for two inevitable obstacles to progress: wind and hills. Outside the midlands, there are hills just about everywhere, and those on the back roads can have thigh-burning steep grades. Road engineering is rather primitive—instead of having switchbacks on a steep slope, roads often climb by the most direct route.

Cyclists have long favored the coastal roads of the southwest, west, and northwest. The quiet roads and rugged scenery of the Beara Peninsula (see chapter 8) make it perfect for a cycling tour, along with the nearby Dingle Peninsula (see chapter 9). The spectacular Iveragh Peninsula (see chapter 9) is okay for cycling if you don't mind dodging tour buses on the renowned "Ring of Kerry" road. Donegal (see chapter 13) is one of the hilliest regions and rewards the energetic cyclist with some of the country's most spectacular coastal and mountain scenery.

Also ideal for cycling are Ireland's many islands; you can bring your bike on all passenger ferries, often for no extra charge, and discover roads with little or no traffic. Some of the best islands with accommodations are Cape Clear, county Cork (see chapter 8); Great Blasket Island, county Kerry (see chapter 9); the Aran Islands, county Galway (see chapter 11); and Achill and Clare Islands, county Mayo (see chapter 13).

BICYCLING OUTFITTERS & RESOURCES

If you're booking from the United States, **Backroads** (② **800/GO-ACTIVE** or 510/527-1555; www.backroads.com) and **VBT** (② **800/BIKE-TOUR;** www.vbt.com) are two well-regarded companies offering all-inclusive bicycle itineraries in Ireland—bikes, gear, luggage transportation via a support van, good food, and accommodations in local inns and hotels of character—everything bundled into one price.

> **Biking Tip**
> If you'll be biking in the west, plan your route from south to north—the same direction as the prevailing winds.

If you want to design your own itinerary and bike independently, several rental agencies with depots nationwide permit one-way rental. They include **Raleigh Rent-A-Bike** (Ireland's largest), Raleigh House, Kylemore Road, Dublin 10 (② **01/626-1333;** www.iol.ie/raleigh); and **Rent-A-Bike Ireland,** 1 Patrick St., Limerick, Co. Limerick (② **061/416983;** www.irelandrentabike.com). Mountain and cross-country bike rental rates average €13 ($12) per day, €51 ($45) per week. The one-way drop-off fee averages €19 ($17).

If you want your cycling trip to be orchestrated and outfitted by affable experts on the ground, consider **Irish Cycling Safaris** (② **01/260-0749;** fax

---

Impressions

To know fully even one field or one lane is a lifetime's experience. In the world of poetic experience it is depth that counts and not width. A gap in a hedge, a smooth rock surfacing a narrow lane, a view of a woody meadow, the stream at the junction of four small fields—these are as much as a man can fully experience.

—Patrick Kavanagh, poet (1904–67)

01/706-1168; www.cyclingsafaris.com). It's run by Eamon Ryan and family, who offer trips to practically every part of Ireland suitable for two wheels.

For independent cycling adventures in the southeast of Ireland, contact **Celtic Cycling,** Lorum Old Rectory, Bagenalstown, county Carlow (© **0503/75282;** fax 0503/75455; www.celticcycling.com). On the opposite side of the island, **Irish Cycling Tours** (© **095/42302;** fax 095/42314; www.irishcyclingtours. com) offers guided and self-guided tours in the west—specifically Kerry and Connemara—for everyone from honeymooners to families to seniors to singles.

2 Walking

Hiking is a relatively new sport in Ireland, but one that is growing incredibly fast. Since 1982, the network of long-distance, marked trails has grown from one to 25, covering some 2,414km (1,500 miles). The first to open was the **Wicklow Way,** which begins just outside Dublin and proceeds through rugged hills and serene pastures on its 132km (82-mile) course. Others include the **South Leinster Way,** the **Beara Peninsula** (see chapter 8), the **Kerry Way** (see chapter 9), the **Dingle Way** (see chapter 9), and the **Ulster Way** (see chapter 15). Most trails are routed so that meals and accommodations—whether in B&Bs, hostels, or hotels—are never more than a day's walk apart. The routes are generally uncrowded, and you tend to meet a lot of locals walking just part of the distance.

Though the long-distance routes are the best-marked trails in Ireland, the signposting is surprisingly random and inadequate, and a map is an absolute necessity. Markers are frequently miles apart and often seem to be lacking at crucial crossroads. Because trees on Irish hillsides rarely impede visibility, a post or cairn on each summit usually indicates the way between two peaks. A compass becomes crucial when a fog blows in and all landmarks quickly disappear. *Be warned:* This can happen quite unexpectedly, and the safest strategy when you can't see your way is to stay exactly where you are until the fog clears.

The walks listed in this guide are on clearly marked trails whenever possible, and if sections are without markings, that is indicated. We can't give you all the information you need for the walks, of course, so you should consult the local tourist office for advice before setting out.

For inland hill walking, try the Wicklow Way (see chapter 5), the Blackstairs Mountains (see chapter 6), the Galtee Mountains (see chapter 6), or Glenveagh National Park (see chapter 13). For coastal walks, the best-known kind in this island country, try the Beara Peninsula (see chapter 8), the Iveragh Peninsula (see chapter 9), the Dingle Peninsula (see chapter 9), the Western Way in Connemara (see chapter 12), and the Donegal Bay Coast (see chapter 13).

National Parks

Ireland's six **national parks** offer up some of most spectacular scenery and best walking in the country, and all have free admission. They are:

The Burren National Park, Mullaghmore, county Clare (http://home page.tinet.ie/~knp/burren), is one of the most fascinating regions in western Europe—a series of limestone beds eroded during the Ice Age to form a barren, lunarlike landscape. The Burren is of particular interest to botanists, since it's the only place in the world where Arctic, Mediterranean, and Alpine species of wildflowers grow side-by-side in the fissures of the rock.

Connemara National Park, Letterfrack, county Galway (http://home page.tinet.ie/~knp/connemara/index.htm), is a rugged, heather-clad landscape of blanket bog and wet heath, encompassing some of the Twelve Ben mountain range. There are nature trails with accompanying map/booklets (guided walks are available in summer) and a visitor center at Letterfrack.

Glenveagh National Park, near Gweedore, county Donegal (http://homepage.tinet.ie/~knp/glenveagh), is Ireland's largest national park and also its remotest wilderness—103,600 sq. km (40,000 sq. miles) of mountains, lakes, and natural woodlands that are home to the largest population of red deer in Ireland. From the visitor center, you can grab a ride on a minibus along the shores of Lough Veagh to Glenveagh Castle, notable for its outstanding gardens. There's also a self-guided nature trail and a summer program of guided walks.

Killarney National Park, Killarney, county Kerry (http://homepage. tinet.ie/~knp/intro), contains nearly 64,750 sq. km (25,000 sq. miles) of spectacular lake and mountain scenery. There are four self-guided trails, a visitor's center with a restaurant/coffee shop, and two small lodges with tearooms.

Mayo National Park, Ballycroy, county Mayo (http://homepage. tinet.ie/~knp/mayo/index.htm), is the newest of the parks, centered in the Owenduff-Nephinbeg area. It features some of the best Atlantic bog landscapes in Europe. Along with a visitor's center in Ballycroy, there are nature trails galore.

Wicklow Mountains National Park, Glendalough, county Wicklow (http://homepage.tinet.ie/~knp/wicklow/index.htm), is the only park of the six that's not on the west coast. At over 129,500 sq. km (50,000 sq. miles), it contains some of the most picturesque woodlands, moors, and mountains in Ireland, and includes the Glendalough monastic site and the Glenealo Valley. There is a park information office at the Upper Lake, near the Glendalough car park.

In addition to national parks, there are 12 **forest reserve parks,** several of which were former private estates. Among the most enchanting is Lough Key Forest Park in county Roscommon, which features a bog-garden, fairy bridge, old estate chapel, viewing tower and wishing chair, and archaeological and historical monuments. Contact the Irish Tourist Board for more information on Ireland's park system.

For more detailed information on the long-distance marked trails, visit **Walking Ireland** at **www.irishwaymarkedways.ie**. Before leaving home, you can order maps and guidebooks, including details of available accommodation en route, from **East West Mapping** (© and fax **054/77835;** http://homepage.tinet. ie/~eastwest). In Ireland, you can buy maps and guidebooks in local bookshops and outdoor gear shops. Most guides can also be obtained from **An Óige,** the Irish Youth Hostel Association, 61 Mountjoy St., Dublin 1 (© **01/830-4555**), or in the North from **YHANI,** Northern Ireland's Youth Hostel Association, 22 Donegal Rd., Belfast BT12 5JN (© **028/9032-4733**).

Ordnance survey maps are available in several scales; the most helpful to the walker is the 1:50,000, or 1¼ inches to 1 mile, scale. This series is currently available for all of Northern Ireland and a limited number of locations in the Republic. The ½-inch-to-1-mile series covers the whole country in 25 maps, and local maps are available in most shops. They indicate roads, major trails, and historic monuments in some detail. Although they are on too small a scale for walkers, they are all that is available in many areas. For ordnance survey maps, contact **Ordnance Survey Service,** Phoenix Park, Dublin 8 (© **01/802-5300**), or **Ordnance Survey of Northern Ireland,** Colby House, Stranmillis Court, Belfast BT9 5BJ (© **028/9066-1244;** www.ordsvy.gov.uk/getamap). The Irish Tourist Board's booklet *Walking Ireland* and the Northern Ireland Tourist Board's *An Information Guide to Walking* are both very helpful. Other excellent resources include *Best Irish Walks,* edited by Joss Lynam (Passport Books, 1995); and *Irish Long Distance Walks: A Guide to the Waymarked Trails,* by Michael Fewer (Gill and Macmillan, 1993).

Hidden Trails (© **888/9-TRAILS;** www.hiddentrails.com) offers 7-day guided and self-guided hiking tours of six regions in Ireland, including the Wicklow Mountains, West Cork, the Burren, and Connemara. The tours are graded "easy," "moderate," or "challenging," and include lodging, meals (breakfast, picnic lunch, and dinner), and luggage transport to and from the trailheads. Rates average $395 per person, double occupancy, for 1 week.

In the west of Ireland, you have a wide selection of guided walks in the Burren, from 1 day to a week or more. Contact **Burren Walking Holidays,** with the Carrigann Hotel (see chapter 10), Lisdoonvarna (© **065/707-4036;** fax 065/707-4567). In the southwest, contact **SouthWest Walks Ireland,** 40 Ashe St., Tralee, county Kerry (© **066/712-8733;** fax 066/712-8762; www.south westwalksireland.com). For a full walking holiday package to county Kerry or county Clare and Connemara, consult **BCT Scenic Walking,** 227 North El Camino Real, Encinitas, CA 92024 (© **800/473-1210;** www.bctwalk.com).

On the Northern Ireland Tourist Board's website (**www.discovernorthern ireland.com**), click the "Activities" rubric to reach a walking and hiking page that lists self-guided tours, 14 short hikes along the Ulster Way, and names and addresses of organizations offering guided walks throughout the North.

3 Bird-Watching

Ireland is of great interest to birders primarily because of its position on the migration routes of many passerines and seabirds, which find the isle a convenient stopping point on their Atlantic journeys. Opportunities for birding abound, particularly in the 71 **National Nature Reserves.** The network of reserves covers woodlands, boglands, grasslands, sand dune systems, bird sanctuaries, coastal heathlands, and marine areas.

Most of the important seabird nesting colonies are on the west coast, the westernmost promontory of Europe; exceptions are Lambey Island, near Dublin, and Great Saltee in county Wexford. Sandy beaches and tidal flats on the east and west coasts are nesting grounds for large populations of winter waders and smaller, isolated tern colonies. In the North, the largest seabird colony is on Rathlin Island, off the North Antrim coast.

Until recently, rural Ireland was home to large numbers of a small bird known as the corncrake (*Crex crex*), whose unusual cry during breeding season was a common feature of the early summer night. Sadly, the introduction of heavy machinery for cutting silage has destroyed the protective high-grass environment in which the mother corncrake lays her eggs. (The period for cutting silage coincides with the corncrake breeding period.) Ireland now has only a few areas where the corncrake still breeds. One is the **Shannon Callows** , where the bird's cry can often be heard after night's quiet replaces the noises of the day.

In the **winter,** Ireland's lakes and wetlands serve as a wintering ground for great numbers of wildfowl from the Arctic and northern Europe. From Greenland, Iceland, and Canada come waders such as knot, golden plover, and black-tailed godwit, flocks of brent, barnacle, and white-fronted geese, and thousands of whooper swans. Every year as many as 10,000 Greenland white-fronted geese winter on the north shores of Wexford Harbor, making it a mecca for birders. Flooded fields, or "callows," provide habitats for wigeons, whooping swans, and plover; the callows of the Shannon and the Blackwater are especially popular with birders. One of the best winter bird-watching sites is the Wexford Wildfowl Reserve (see chapter 6).

From March onwards, mild **spring** weather invites Irish birds to begin nesting early and their songs fill the woods and hedgerows. The arrival of migrants from Africa can be observed in April and May all along the south coast. Rathlin Island Reserve (see chapter 15), home to Northern Ireland's largest seabird colony, is best visited in May and June.

Summer is the time to head to the west of Ireland, where seaside cliffs are an ideal place for large sea bird colonies such as puffins and gannets. Some of the best summer birding sites are Great Saltee Island (see chapter 6), Cape Clear Island (see chapter 8), the Skellig Islands (see chapter 9), and Loop Head (see chapter 10).

Autumn is a particularly attractive time for bird-watchers in Ireland, when many rare American waders—mainly sandpipers and plovers—arrive when blown across the Atlantic. A spectacular avian event is the annual fall migration of brent geese. On the shores of Strangford Lough in county Down—Europe's premier brent-watching site—you might see as many as 3,000 on a single day.

BIRD-WATCHING RESOURCES

One of the best sources of information is the **Irish Bird Watching Home Page** (**www.geocities.com/RainForest/2801**), which features links on birding events, sites, and news.

Birdwatch Ireland, Ruttledge House, 8 Longford Place, Monkstown, county Dublin (© 01/280-4322; www.birdwatchireland.ie), is an organization devoted to bird conservation in the Republic of Ireland. An equivalent organization in Northern Ireland is **The Royal Society for the Protection of Birds,** Belvoir Park Forest, Belfast BT8 7QT (© 028/9049-1547). The umbrella organization for birding in the North is **Birdwatch Northern Ireland,** 12 Belvoir Close, Belfast BT8 7PL (© 028/9069-3232; fax 028/9064-4681; www.birdwatch-ni.co.uk).

Wexford Wildfowl Reserve, North Slob, Wexford (© **053/23129;** fax 053/ 24785; cjwilson@esat.clear.ie), has a visitor center with information on local bird-watching sites. The reserve's full-time warden, Chris Wilson, can direct you to other places corresponding to your areas of interest.

The **Altamount Gardens,** Tullow, county Wicklow (© **0503/59128**), offers weekend courses in ornithology. See chapter 5 for more information.

On **Cape Clear Island,** there is a bird observatory at the North Harbour, with a warden in residence from March to November, and accommodations for bird-watchers. To arrange a stay, write **Kieran Grace,** 84 Dorney Court, Shankhill, county Dublin. **Ciarán O'Driscoll** (© **028/39153**), who operates a B&B on the island, also runs boat trips for bird-watchers around the island, and has a keen eye for vagrants and rarities.

Northern Ireland has two first-class nature centers for bird enthusiasts, both ideal for families. **Castle Espie,** Ballydrain Road, Comber, county Down BT23 6EA (© **028/9187-4146**), is home to Ireland's largest collection of ducks, geese, and swans. The **Lough Neagh Discovery Centre,** Craigavon, county Armagh (© **028/3832-2205**), is in the outstanding Oxford Island National Nature Reserve. For all-inclusive bird-watching packages in the North, contact **Murphy's Wildlife Tours,** 12 Belvoir Close, Belfast BT8 7PL (© **028/9069-3232;** fax 028/9064-4681).

4 Golf

Golf is the single biggest sporting attraction in Ireland, with over 204,000 visitors traveling to Ireland specifically to play golf. Boasting 384 courses—including scores of championship courses—the island has devoted a greater percentage of its soil to the game than any other country in the world. The Irish landscape and climate, like those of Scotland, seem almost to have been custom-designed to offer some of the most scenic links, the fairest fairways, the greenest greens, and the most dramatic traps you'll ever encounter. And there is never a shortage of 19th holes. In short, Ireland is for the golfer a place of pilgrimage.

Golfing in Ireland is not confined to those with an Olympian income. Membership fees do not require mortgages, and greens fees for walk-ins are often quite modest, especially on weekdays and at off-peak hours.

See "Outdoor Pursuits" in the chapters that follow for a recommended selection of Ireland's top courses.

GOLF RESOURCES

The **Irish Tourist Board** has a dedicated golf website with numerous links and contacts at **www.golf.travel.ie**.

Specialty Ireland, Castlemeadows, Murrintown, county Wexford (© **053/ 39962;** fax 053/39977; www.specialtyireland.com), can customize your itinerary to include any of 27 championship clubs and more than 400 other courses on the island. You can find out detailed information on 105 of Ireland's courses by searching the database at **www.golfcourse.com**.

A host of U.S. companies offer package golf tours. Among them are **Atlantic golf** (© **800/542-6224** or 203/454-1086; fax 203/454-8840; www.atlantic golf.com); **Emerald Isle Golf Tours** (© **800/446-8845** or 847/446-7885; fax 847/446-2248; www.emeraldislegolftours.com); **Golf International** (© **800/ 833-1389** or 212/986-9176; fax 212/986-3720; www.golfinternational.com); and **Wide World of Golf** (© **800/214-4653** or 831/625-9671; www.wide worldofgolf.com).

5 Horseback Riding

Ireland is a horse-loving country, with a plethora of stables and equestrian centers offering trail rides and instruction. The **Association of Irish Riding Establishments (AIRE)** is the regulatory body that accredits stables, ensuring adequate safety standards and instructor competence. Riding prices range from €13 ($12) to €32 ($28) per hour; expect to pay €19 ($17) on average. A list of accredited stables throughout the country is available from the Irish Tourist Board.

A great variety of riding options can be found to suit different interests and levels of experience. Pony trekking caters primarily to beginners, and you don't need experience. Trail riding over longer distances requires the ability to trot for extended periods, and can be quite exhausting for the novice. Riding establishments also commonly offer such advanced options as jumping and dressage, and some have enclosed arenas—an attractive option on rainy days. Several establishments have accommodations and offer packages that include meals, lodging, and riding. Post-to-post trail riding allows a rider to stay at different lodgings each night, riding on trails all day. Not all stables can accommodate young children, but some make a point of being open to riders of all ages.

County Kildare is the epicenter of Irish horse country. The **Irish National Stud** and the **Curragh** are hubs of thoroughbred breeding and racing, and there are many fine stables nearby (see chapter 5). The hills and valleys of county Wicklow (see chapter 5) have a number of fine riding establishments, as do counties Wexford and Tipperary (see chapter 6), Galway (see chapter 12), and the Northwest (see chapter 13).

RIDING RESOURCES

The **Irish Tourist Board** has a dedicated horseback riding website with numerous links and contacts at www.equestrian.travel.ie.

Equestrian Holidays Ireland (www.ehi.ie) is a collection of some 37 riding centers, each registered with the Association of Irish Riding Establishments, offering a wide variety of accommodations and riding holiday experiences. EHI properties include **Horetown Equestrian Centre,** Foulksmills, county Wexford (© **051/565786**); **Dingle Horse Riding,** Ballinabula, Dingle (© **066/915-2199;** www.dinglehorseriding.com); and **Drumindoo Stud & Equestrian Centre,** Knockranny, Westport, county Mayo (© **098/25616**).

If you don't want to dedicate your entire trip to riding, many equestrian centers let you ride for the day or just a few hours; you can search by county at **www.react.ie/activities/horseriding.htm.**

6 Fishing

What makes Ireland such a great fishing destination? First, there's lots of water: a coastline of more than 5,603km (3,472 miles), a plethora of lakes and ponds, and countless creeks, rills, streams, and rivers. Next, Ireland's temperate climate and low pollution encourage a high fish population. And finally, low human density has put little pressure on that population. All in all, Ireland is perhaps the best place to fish for salmon, sea trout, and brown trout in all of Europe.

The sport of catching those fish—referred to by the Irish as angling—has a cherished tradition. Many festivals and competitions celebrating the many forms of this sport are held between March and September; for dates and locations, contact the Irish Tourist Board (you have to sign up well in advance to participate in most of the competitions). Among the festivals are Killybegs International Fishing Festival and the Baltimore Angling Festival in July, and the Cobh Sea Angling Festival in September.

In the west and northwest, Killybegs (see chapter 13) is a center for sea angling, while loughs Corrib, Conn, and Mask (see chapters 12 and 13) offer much to entice the freshwater angler. The Killarney area (see chapter 9) is a popular angling destination, as are the Blackwater River near Cork (see chapter 7) and Kinsale (see chapter 8) for sea angling. Also consider the Shannon River and its lakes, especially Lough Derg (see chapter 14).

FISHING RESOURCES

Fishing seasons are as follows: salmon, January 1 to September 30; brown trout, February 15 to October 12; sea trout, June 1 to September 30; course fishing and sea angling, all year. A license is only required for salmon and sea trout angling; the cost is €4 ($3.55) for 1 day, €13 ($12) for 21 days, €32, ($28) annually. For all private salmon and sea trout fisheries, a permit is required in addition to the license. Prices vary greatly, from €6 to €190, ($5.35–$169) per rod per day, although most permits run €25 to €32 ($22–$28).

The Irish Tourist Board has websites dedicated to fishing at www.angling.travel.ie. A helpful brochure, *Angling in Ireland,* detailing what fish can be caught where, is available from the **Central Fisheries Board,** Balnagowan House, Mobhi Boreen, Glasnevin, Dublin 9 (℗ **01/837-9206;** fax 01/836-0060). Another helpful resource, *The Angler's Guide,* is published by the Irish Tourist Board. Permits, licenses, and specific information can be obtained from local outfitters or the Central Fisheries Board.

Many hotels have exclusive access to lakes and ponds, and will rent boats, gear, and *ghillies* (fishing guides) to their guests. Nearly two dozen such hotels have gotten together to form **The Great Fishing Houses of Ireland** (www. irelandfishing.com). Examples include Adare Manor in Limerick (see chapter 10); Ballynahinch Castle in county Galway (see chapter 12); and Newport House Hotel and Enniscoe House, both in Mayo (see chapter 13).

In Northern Ireland, you must get a rod license from the **Fisheries Conservancy Board,** 1 Mahon Rd., Portadown, Craigavon, county Armagh (℗ **028/ 3833-4666),** or in the Derry area from the **Foyle Fisheries Commission,** 8 Victoria Rd., Derry BT47 2AB (℗ **028/7134-2100**). A permit may also be required; information can be obtained from local outfitters or the **Department of Culture, Arts and Leisure,** Interpoint Centre, York Street, Belfast BT4 3PW (℗ **028/9052-3434;** fax 028/9052-3121). A rod license costs £10 ($14) for 8 days; permits run £9 ($13) a day or £45 ($65) for 8 days. You can find a wealth of information and contacts in *An Information Guide to Game Fishing,* available from any office of the Northern Ireland Tourist Board.

7 Kayaking

Known as "canoeing" in Ireland, this sport enjoys considerable popularity. And no wonder, considering the island's 4,830km (3,000 miles) of coastline, plus its numerous lakes and rivers.

In particular, the coastline provides year-round, superb sea kayaking waters, some of which are remote, with spectacular scenery. In a sea kayak, the wonders of the Irish coast can be investigated at close hand. You'll find caves and tiny inlets, out-of-the-way cliffs and reefs inhabited by abundant seabirds, colorful crustaceans, seals, and the occasional dolphin. Many islands are within easy

Angling for Trout & Salmon

Yeats imagined his ideal fisherman "climbing up to a place / where stone is dark under froth," and vividly pictured "the down-turn of his wrist / when the flies drop in the stream." Anglers visiting Ireland are free to do so, because they don't need a license to take brown trout, and many a small stream or mountain tarn offers free fishing. Generally you do not need to ask permission to walk across a couple of fields to reach a suitable fishing place. Ask locals where the best places to fish are. Also, the better known lakes will have boats and guides available. Be sure to check with the local tourist office or tackle dealer before dropping your line. Unless you're staying at a fishing lodge that provides gear, you'll need to bring rods, reels, and waders with you. Suitable flies can always be bought locally. Catch and release is not widely practiced, but on most club waters an angler will be limited to the amount and size of fish.

If your quest is for larger brown trout, head for the bigger lakes where the underlying rock is limestone rather than granite. Oughterard in county Galway, Ballinrobe in county Mayo, and Pontoon in county Mayo are good centers for Lough Carrib, Lough Mask, and Lough Conn, respectively. No permit is required, but you need to hire a boat and an experienced boatman. May and June are the best months to fish there, as they are for the great midland lakes that can easily be reached from Mullingar in county Westmeath. The lakes around Ennis in county Clare fish well in March or April. Excellent brown trout fishing can also be had in the rivers of county Cork and county Tipperary, where you usually have to apply to the local angling club for a visitor's ticket.

Many rivers and lakes hold good stocks of salmon and sea trout. A license (obtained locally) is required, and advance booking is a virtual necessity for the more famous locations, such as the Salmon Weir pool in Galway City and the Ridge pool in Ballina. Sea trout run from late June to August. There are two main salmon runs: the spring run of older, bigger fish and the "grilse" run in June and July. Opening and closing dates vary from river to river, but most waters are open from March to September. Serious anglers reserve accommodations by the week in centers like Waterville in county Kerry and Newport in county Mayo. If you are touring by car, it is always worth inquiring locally. Day tickets are often available from hotels or angling clubs.

Two excellent books by Peter O'Reilly, *Trout and Salmon Rivers of Ireland* (3rd edition, 1995) and *Trout and Salmon Loughs of Ireland* (1987), give full coverage of the waters available.

—J. V. Luce, Royal Irish Academy and Trinity College, Dublin

Dr. Luce, an avid world-traveled angler, learned the art from his father, A. A. Luce, former chaplain and professor of philosophy at Trinity and author of a noted book on Irish angling, titled *Fishing and Thinking.*

reach of the mainland, and with experience and good conditions, a sea kayaker can reach any of Ireland's island outposts.

A number of adventure centers offer kayaking lessons, and a few schools are devoted solely to kayaking. Some of them will rent equipment as long as you can demonstrate adequate proficiency—call ahead to make arrangements if that is what you plan to do. For those new to the sport or unfamiliar with the Irish coast, a guided excursion is the best option.

The deeply indented coast of West Cork (see chapter 8) and Kerry (see chapter 9) is a sea kayaker's paradise, with clear water, cliffs rising to dizzying heights, and rocky shorelines so full of caves in some places that they seem hollow. The west coast of Ireland (see chapters 10 and 13) offers many tiny islands and remote spots to explore.

Canoeing can be enjoyed by the young and old, timid and daring. If you're looking for white water, visit in winter, when frequent rains fill the rivers enough for good paddling. By early summer, most white-water streams are reduced to a trickle. One exception is the Liffey, which is dam-controlled and has some minor rapids upstream from Dublin that are sometimes passable during the summer months.

KAYAKING RESOURCES

A rich source for the latest information on kayaking throughout Ireland can be found on the Web, at the official website of the **Irish Canoe Union:** www.irish canoeunion.ie.

Kayaking vacations are also available at **Delphi Adventure Center,** Leenane, county Galway (© **095/42307;** fax 095/42303; see chapter 12), and **National Mountain and Whitewater Centre,** Ashford, county Wicklow (© **0404/40169;** www.tiglin.com; see chapter 5).

8 Sailing

Whether by cruising from port to port or dinghy sailing on the lakes, many regions of Ireland can best be experienced from the water. The elaborately indented coastline offers a plethora of safe havens for overnight stops—there are more than 140 between Cork Harbor and the Dingle Peninsula alone. This region of West Cork and Kerry is the most popular coastline for cruising, and several companies offer yacht charters.

Some of the harbors in the southwest that are most popular with sailors include Cork, Kinsale, Glandore, Baltimore, and Bantry. On the **west coast,** Killary Harbour, Westport, and Sligo have sailing clubs and are in areas of great beauty. There are also several sailing clubs and yacht charter companies in the Dublin area.

SAILING RESOURCES

Sailing schools hold courses for sailors at all levels of experience, and sometimes offer day sailing as well. Ireland also has more than 120 yacht and sailing clubs along the coast and lakes. The best sources for information are: the Irish Tourist Board; the **Irish Sailing Association,** 3 Park Rd., Dun Laoghaire, county Dublin (© **01/280-0239;** fax 01/280-7558; www.sailing.ie); and the *Irish Cruising Club Sailing Directions,* which is a publication that gives information on harbors, port facilities, tides, and other topics of interest. It's available in bookshops or through Mrs. B. McGonagle, "The Tansey," Baily, county Dublin (© **01/322823).**

The **International Sailing Association** is an excellent resource for finding a sailing school; you can find links to members at www.sailingschools.org/ireland.htm. **Sailing Holidays in Ireland** (www.sailingireland.com) lists many sailing schools and yacht charter companies throughout the Republic. One of the best-known schools, **Glenans Irish Sailing Club,** 28 Merrion Sq., Dublin 2 (© 01/661-1481; fax 01/676-4249; www.glenans-ireland.com), has two locations in West Cork and one in Mayo, and offers classes at all levels (see chapter 8). Day sailing is available during the summer at the West Cork location.

Sail Ireland Charters, Trident Hotel Marina, Kinsale, county Cork (© 021/477-2927; fax 021/774170; www.sailireland.com; see chapter 8) is the largest charter firm in Ireland, and also offer sailing holidays. Yacht charters are also available at **Sporting Tours Ireland,** 71 Main St., Kinsale, county Cork (© and fax 021/774727); **Shannon Sailing Ltd.,** New Harbor, Dromineer, Nenagh, county Tipperary (© 067/24499); and **Dingle Sea Ventures,** Dingle, county Kerry (© 066/915-2244; www.charterireland.com). Hobie Cat sailing can be arranged at the **Little Killary Adventure Centre,** Salruck, Renvyle, county Galway (© 095/43411).

In addition, innumerable sailing trips are offered on Ireland's coasts, rivers, and lakes. For a selection of the best, see "Outdoor Pursuits" in the destination chapters that follow.

9 Diving

With visibility averaging 15m (49 ft.) and occasionally reaching 29m (98 ft.), and many wrecks to explore, the west coast of Ireland is a great place for divers—in fact, it offers some of the best scuba diving in Europe.

The Irish dive season generally starts in March and ends in October, although specific dates depend on your comfort zone. Outside these months, weather and ocean conditions could make jumping into the sea unappealing for some. The PADI open-water diver certification is the minimum requirement for all dives; most schools also offer introductory dives for novices.

The rocky coast of West Cork and Kerry is great for diving, with centers in Baltimore (see chapter 8) and Dingle (see chapter 9). On the west coast there are many great locations, one of which is the deep, sheltered Killary Harbour. Northern Ireland offers many interesting dives, with more than 400 named wrecks off the coast and many in the Irish Sea and in Belfast Lough.

DIVING RESOURCES

The **Irish Underwater Council** (CFT, or Comhairle Fo-Thuinn), 78A Patrick St., Dun Laoghaire, county Dublin (© 01/284-4601; fax 01/284-4602; www.scubaireland.com), is an association of more than 70 Irish diving clubs. It operates under the aegis of the CMAS (Confederation Mondiale des Activites Subaquatiques), the world diving federation. Its website lists information on diving and snorkeling, dive centers, and dive hotels (no pun intended) throughout the Republic and publishes the *CFT Guide to Dive Sites* and other information on exploring the Emerald Isle's emerald waters.

The **UK Diving** website, **www.ukdiving.co.uk,** features information on diving in the North, including a wreck database you can access either through a conventional listing or by pinpointing on a map. Wrecks are marked as red dots, which can be clicked on to find more information.

Irish dive centers and schools include **The National Diving School,** Malahide, county Dublin (© 01/845-2000; www.nds.ie); **Oceantec Adventures,** Dun

Laoghaire, county Dublin (℗ **01/280-1083;** www.oceatecadventures.com); **Baltimore Diving & Watersport Centre,** Baltimore, county Cork (℗ and fax **028/20300;** http://diving.foundmark.com); and **Scubadive West,** Renvyle, county Galway (℗ **095/43922;** fax 095/43923; www.scubadivewest.com).

10 Windsurfing

Windsurfing has become a very popular sport in Ireland, and some spots play host to vast flotillas of colorful sails and wet-suited windsurfers when conditions are good. Some of the best locations are in remote areas of the west coast, and those spots are rarely crowded. Windsurfing schools with boards for rent can be found in most regions of the country, with the greatest concentration on the southeast and southwest coasts.

In Dublin, the most popular spot is Dollymount Beach; Salthill, behind Dun Laoghaire Harbour, is another good choice. In the southeast, try Brittas Bay (county Wicklow), Cahore (county Wexford), and Rosslare (county Wexford). Dunmore East (county Waterford), Dungarvan (county Waterford), and Cobh (county Cork) are good in the south. The most challenging waves and winds are in the west, at Brandon Bay on the Dingle Peninsula, Roundstone in Galway, Achill Island in Mayo, and Magheroarty and Rossnowlagh in Donegal.

Because even skilled windsurfers spend a sizable portion of their time in the water, the water quality is surely a concern. The good news is that nearly 90% of Ireland's beaches surpass EU voluntary guideline levels. Ireland has 27 designated European Union "Blue Flag" beaches and marinas, and Northern Ireland has 12. Keep your eyes peeled for a blue flag bearing a circular logo and the current year to be assured of the highest standard in water quality. To find a complete listing or to check out a particular beach in advance, go to **www.blue flag.org**.

WINDSURFING RESOURCES

Equipment rental and lessons are widely available on Ireland's coasts and lakes. To find a windsurfing center in a particular county, search the database at **www.react.ie/activities/windsurfing.htm**. Also try the following centers: the **Surfdock Centre,** Grand Canal Dock Yard, Ringsend, Dublin 4 (℗ **01/668-3945;** fax 01/668-1215; www.surfdock.ie); the **Dunmore East Adventure Centre,** Dunmore East, county Waterford (℗ **051/383783;** fax 051/383786); **Oysterhaven Windsurfing Centre,** Oysterhaven, Kinsale, county Cork (℗ **021/770738;** fax 021/770776); **Cappanalea Outdoor Education Centre,** Oulagh West, Caragh Lake, county Kerry (℗ **066/69244**); and, in the North, the **Ardclinis Activity Center,** High Street, Cushendall, county Antrim (℗ and fax **028/2177-1340**).

4

Dublin

It's nearly impossible for first-time visitors to appreciate just how fast Dublin is moving. Native "Dubs," however, who left years ago and returned to the "Celtic Tiger" economy, can't believe their eyes. Their beloved—if slightly down-at-the-heels—hometown has metamorphosed into a bastion of trendy coffee shops and juice bars, fusion-cuisine restaurants, minimalist interiors, designer boutiques, and Mercedes-Benz and BMW dealerships. Greater Dublin is the O'Camelot of one of the fastest-growing economies in Europe. Make no mistake: Despite last year's global economic slowdown, there's plenty of money being made—and spent—here.

What's amazing is not that Dublin has gotten so hot, but that it's happened so quickly. In 1997, *Fortune* magazine named Dublin the number-one European city in which to do business—an accolade fueled, no doubt, by its reputation as the "Silicon Valley" of Europe and strategic Euro-headquarters for such computer giants as Microsoft, Dell, Intel, and Sun Microsystems. Then, in 1998, Dublin became the fifth-most-visited city in Europe—nudging ahead of such tourist powerhouses as Rome and Amsterdam. More recently, in 2000, an annual survey of world cities conducted by William M. Mercer Ltd. ranked Dublin among the world's top-10 most livable cities—above New York, Boston, and Washington, D.C. The word has gotten out: For work or play, Dublin is the place to be. Meanwhile, Dublin certainly gets the glamour vote as Europe's trendiest, coolest city. Sightings of Gwyneth Paltrow, Brad Pitt, Julia Roberts, Winona Ryder, the Spice Girls, and Naomi Campbell have become so commonplace that locals barely blink an eye. (The Irish polite indifference to celebrity is a slice of nirvana for privacy-loving stars.)

How times have changed. Twenty years ago most visitors to Ireland either bypassed Dublin altogether or made a mad dash from the ferry to the train station, determined to spend their first night beyond the pale. Now the opposite is the case. Dublin's centripetal force attracts millions of visitors a year and holds them. The time has passed when aspiring Irish artists owed it to themselves to emigrate. Today, they dig in. If Joyce and Beckett and Wilde could see Dublin today, they'd be back. Dublin is simply contagious, and its addictive quality isn't in the Guinness. It's where it's always been, in the people.

Dublin, like most ancient cities, lies sprawled along a river. The Liffey has divided Dublin into north and south for more than 1,000 years. Neither as romantic as the Seine nor as mighty as the Mississippi, the Liffey is just there, old and polluted, with walls to sit on or lean against when your legs give out. Still, it is and always has been the center of things here, and it does make for a pretty picture on a good day. Despite all the changes, the Liffey continues to divide the town as it once divided Viking from Celt and Norman from Norse.

So far, the buzzing, prosperous hub of Dublin lies mostly south of the Liffey. The area containing most of the best hotels, restaurants, shops, and sights is a small, well-defined compound that can be easily walked in a half hour. It comprises a large part of Dublin 2 (the postal code for each neighborhood is listed in "The Neighborhoods in Brief," later in this chapter), beginning with the Georgian elegance of St. Stephen's Green, moving toward the river via bustling Grafton Street, heading farther north and west through the trendy cafe scene of Temple Bar, and even farther

west to the capital's hippest new shopping district, known as "Old City."

That said, a visit confined to this small pocket of Dublin is not a true visit to Dublin. An hour's walk from the top of Grafton Street, across the Liffey, up O'Connell Street, and farther into north Dublin is a walk through time and, simultaneously, a glimpse of some of the pieces that must eventually fit together. Explore, get a haircut (in a barbershop, not a salon), get lost and ask directions, and you may uncover a time capsule from the Dublin of a century ago—or was it only a generation?

1 Orientation

Dublin is 222km (138 miles) northeast of Shannon Airport, 258km (160 miles) northeast of Cork, 167km (104 miles) south of Belfast, 309km (192 miles) northeast of Killarney, 219km (136 miles) east of Galway, 237km (147 miles) southeast of Derry, and 142km (88 miles) north of Wexford.

ARRIVING

BY PLANE   Aer Lingus, Ireland's national airline, operates regularly scheduled flights into Dublin International Airport from Chicago, Boston, Los Angeles, Baltimore, and New York's JFK. **Delta Airlines** flies to Dublin from Atlanta and New York; and **Continental Airlines** flies to Dublin from Newark. Charters also operate from a number of U.S. and Canadian cities. You can also fly from the United States to London or other European cities and backtrack to Dublin (see "Getting There" in chapter 2).

Dublin International Airport (© 01/814-1111; www.dublin-airport.com) is 11km (7 miles) north of the city center. A Travel Information Desk located in the Arrivals Concourse provides information on public bus and rail services throughout the country.

An excellent airport-to-city bus service called **AirCoach** operates 24 hours a day, making runs at 15-minute intervals. AirCoach runs direct from the airport to Dublin's city center and south side, servicing O'Connell Street, St. Stephen's Green, Fitzwilliam Square, Merrion Square, Ballsbridge, and Donnybrook—that is, all the key hotel and business districts. The one-way fare is €5 ($4.45); you buy your ticket from the driver. Although AirCoach is more expensive than the Dublin Bus (see below), it is also faster because it makes fewer intermediary stops and it brings you right into the hotel districts. To confirm AirCoach departures and arrivals, call © 01/844-7118 or find it on the Web at **www.aircoach.ie**.

If you need to connect with the Irish bus or rail service, the **Airlink Express Coach** (© 01/873-4222) provides express coach service from the airport into the city's central bus station, **Busaras,** on Store Street, and on to the two main rail stations, **Connolly** and **Heuston.** Service runs daily from 7am until 11pm (8:30pm Sun), with departures every 20 to 30 minutes. One-way fare is €4.50 ($4) for adults and €2 ($1.80) for children under age 12.

Finally, **Dublin Bus** (© 01/873-4222; www.dublinbus.ie) service runs between the airport and the city center between 6am and 11:30pm. The one-way trip

Dublin Orientation

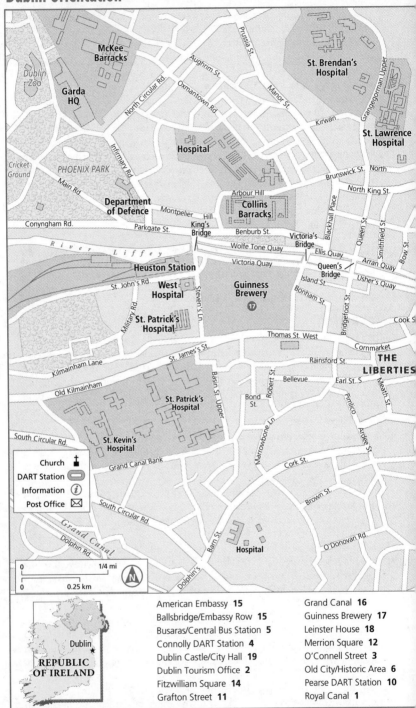

McKee Barracks

Garda HQ

Dublin Zoo

Prussia St.

Aughrim St.

Oxmantown Rd.

North Circular Rd.

Manor St.

St. Brendan's Hospital

Grangegorman Upper

Kirwan

St. Lawrence Hospital

Cricket Ground

PHOENIX PARK

Infirmary Rd.

Main Rd.

Hospital

Brunswick St. North

North King St.

Department of Defence

Montpelier Hill

Arbour Hill

Collins Barracks

Blackhall Place

Queen St.

Smithfield St.

Conyngham Rd.

Parkgate St.

King's Bridge

Benburb St.

Victoria's Bridge

Ellis Quay

Arran Quay

Bow St.

River Liffey

Wolfe Tone Quay

Victoria Quay

Queen's Bridge

Usher's Quay

Heuston Station

St. John's Rd.

West Hospital

Steven's Ln.

Guinness Brewery ⑰

Island St.

Bonham St.

Bridgefoot St.

Cook S

St. Patrick's Hospital

Military Rd.

Thomas St. West

Cornmarket

THE LIBERTIES

Kilmainham Lane

St. James's St.

Rainsford St.

Old Kilmainham

Basin St. Upper

Robert St.

Bellevue

Earl St. S.

Meath St.

St. Patrick's Hospital

Bond St.

Pimlico

Ardee St.

South Circular Rd.

St. Kevin's Hospital

Marrowbone Ln.

Cork St.

Grand Canal Bank

South Circular Rd

Brown St.

Grand Canal

Dolphin Rd.

Barn St.

Dolphin's

Hospital

O'Donovan Rd.

Church ✝
DART Station ⬭
Information ⓘ
Post Office ✉

0 — 1/4 mi
0 — 0.25 km

Ⓝ

Dublin ★

REPUBLIC OF IRELAND

American Embassy **15**
Ballsbridge/Embassy Row **15**
Busaras/Central Bus Station **5**
Connolly DART Station **4**
Dublin Castle/City Hall **19**
Dublin Tourism Office **2**
Fitzwilliam Square **14**
Grafton Street **11**

Grand Canal **16**
Guinness Brewery **17**
Leinster House **18**
Merrion Square **12**
O'Connell Street **3**
Old City/Historic Area **6**
Pearse DART Station **10**
Royal Canal **1**

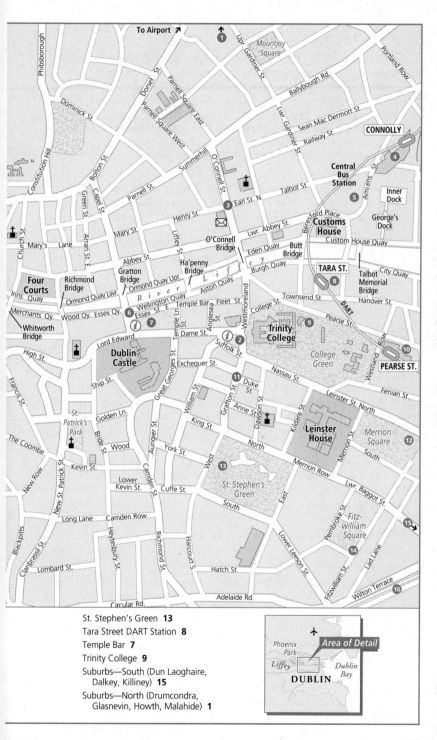

Finds **The Bird's-Eye View**

To start out with the big picture and to get your bearings once and for all, make your way to the **Old Jameson Distillery** (see "Seeing the Sights," later in this chapter) and ascend, via glass elevator, to the observation chamber atop "The Chimney." In a city without skyscrapers, this is your best 360° vantage point on Greater (and smaller) Dublin. The trip to the top costs €6.35 ($5.65) for adults, €5 ($4.45) for seniors and students, €4.50 ($4) for children, and €19 ($17) for a family. Open daily 10am to 6pm.

---

takes about 30 minutes, and the fare is €1.45 ($1.30). The 16, 16A, 16B, 16C, 33, 41, 41a, 41b, and 41c all serve the city center from Dublin Airport. Consult the Travel Information Desk located in the Arrivals Concourse to figure out which bus will bring you closest to your hotel.

For speed and ease—especially if you have a lot of luggage—a **taxi** is the best way to get directly to your hotel or guesthouse. Depending on your destination in Dublin, fares average between €13 and €19 ($12–$17). Surcharges include €.50 (45¢) for each additional passenger and for each piece of luggage. Depending on traffic, a cab should take between 20 to 45 minutes to get into the city center. A 10% tip is standard. Taxis are lined up at a first-come, first-served taxi stand outside the arrivals terminal.

Major international and local car-rental companies operate desks at Dublin Airport. For a list of companies, see "Getting Around," below.

BY FERRY Passenger and car ferries from Britain arrive at the **Dublin Ferryport** (© 01/855-2222), on the eastern end of the North Docks, and at the **Dun Laoghaire Ferryport.** Call **Irish Ferries** (© 01/661-0511; www.irishferries.ie) for bookings and information. There is bus and taxi service from both ports.

BY TRAIN Irish Rail (© 01/836-6222; www.irishrail.ie) operates daily train service to Dublin from Belfast, Northern Ireland, and all major cities in the Irish Republic, including Cork, Galway, Limerick, Killarney, Sligo, Wexford, and Waterford. Trains from the south, west, and southwest arrive at **Heuston Station,** Kingsbridge, off St. John's Road; from the north and northwest at **Connolly Station,** Amiens Street; and from the southeast at **Pearse Station,** Westland Row, Tara Street.

BY BUS Bus Eireann (© 01/836-6111; www.buseireann.ie) operates daily express coach and local bus service from all major cities and towns in Ireland into Dublin's central bus station, **Busaras,** Store Street.

BY CAR If you are arriving by car from other parts of Ireland or on a car ferry from Britain, all main roads lead into the heart of Dublin and are well signposted to An Lar (City Centre). To bypass the city center, the East Link (toll bridge €1.05/95¢) and West Link are signposted, and M50 circuits the city on three sides.

VISITOR INFORMATION

Dublin Tourism operates six walk-in visitor centers in greater Dublin that are open every day except Christmas. The principal center is on Suffolk Street, Dublin 2, open from June to August Monday to Saturday from 9am to 8:30pm, Sunday and Bank Holidays 10:30am to 2:30pm, and the rest of the year Monday to Saturday 9am to 5:30pm, Sunday and bank holidays 10:30am to 3pm.

The Suffolk Street office includes a currency exchange counter, a car-rental counter, an accommodation reservations service, bus and rail information desks, a gift shop, and a cafe. For accommodation reservations throughout Ireland by credit card, contact Dublin Tourism at (℮ **01/605-7700;** www.visitdublin.com).

The five other centers are in the **Arrivals Hall** of Dublin Airport; **Exclusively Irish,** O'Connell Street, Dublin 1; **Baggot Street Bridge,** Baggot Street, Dublin 2; **The Square Towncentre,** Tallaght, Dublin 24; and the new ferry terminal, **Dun Laoghaire Harbor** (all telephone inquiries should be directed to the number listed above). All centers are open year-round with at least the following hours: Monday to Friday 9am to 5:30pm and Saturday 9am to 1pm.

For information on Ireland outside of Dublin, call **Bord Fáilte** (℮ **1850/ 230330** in Ireland; www.travel.ireland.ie).

In addition, an independent center offers details on concerts, exhibits, and other goings-on in the **Temple Bar** neighborhood at 18 Eustace St., Temple Bar, Dublin 2 (℮ **01/671-5717;** www.temple-bar.ie), open year-round Monday to Friday 9:30am to 5:30pm, and Saturday 10am to 5:30pm.

At any of these centers you can pick up the free *Tourism News;* or the free *Event Guide,* a biweekly entertainment guide, online at **www.eventguide.ie.** *In Dublin,* a biweekly arts-and-entertainment magazine selling for €3.70 ($3.30), is available at most newsstands.

CITY LAYOUT

Compared to other European capitals, Dublin is a relatively small metropolis and easily traversed. The city center—identified in Irish on bus destination signs as AN LAR—is bisected by the River Liffey flowing west to east into Dublin Bay. Canals ring the city center: The Royal Canal forms a skirt through the north half, and the Grand Canal the south half. True Dubliners, it is said, live between the two canals.

Northside suburbs include Drumcondra, Glasnevin, Howth, Clontarf, and Malahide. Southside suburbs include Ballsbridge, Blackrock, Dun Laoghaire, Dalkey, Killiney, Rathgar, and Rathmines.

MAIN ARTERIES, STREETS & SQUARES   The focal point of Dublin is the **River Liffey,** with 16 bridges connecting its north and south banks. The most famous of these, **O'Connell Bridge,** was originally made of rope and could only carry one man and a donkey at a time. It was replaced with a wooden structure in 1801. The current concrete bridge was built in 1863 and is the only traffic-carrying bridge in Europe that is wider than it is long. The newest bridge, the **Millenium Bridge**, is a footbridge erected in 1999, linking Temple Bar with the Northside.

On the north side of the river, the main thoroughfare is **O'Connell Street,** a wide, two-way avenue that starts at the riverside quays and runs north to

⌒ **Fun Fact**   **A Toll Tale**

Built in 1816 as one of the earliest cast-iron bridges in Britain and Ireland, the graceful pedestrians-only Ha'penny Bridge (pronounced *Hay*-penny) is the most beloved of Dublin bridges. Though officially named the Liffey Bridge, it's far better known by the toll that was initially charged to cross it: half a penny. The turnstiles were removed in 1919, when passage was declared free to the public.

Parnell Square. Enhanced by statues, trees, and a modern fountain, the O'Connell Street of earlier days was the glamorous shopping drag of the city. It is still important today, although neither as fashionable nor as safe as it used to be. Work is under way, however, to give the north side of the Liffey a mighty makeover and make it once again a focus of attention.

On the south side of the Liffey, **Grafton Street** is Dublin's main shopping street. It is home to Ireland's most exclusive department store, Brown Thomas, and has clearly bent over backward in recent years to attract and please tourists—though cynics point out, quite rightly, that much of its "Irishness" has been displaced in recent years by British chain shops. Narrow and restricted to pedestrians, Grafton Street is the center of Dublin's commercial district, surrounded by a maze of small streets and lanes that boast a terrific variety of shops, restaurants, and hotels. At the south end of Grafton Street is **St. Stephen's Green,** the city's most beloved park and an urban oasis ringed by rows of historic Georgian townhouses, fine hotels, and restaurants.

At the north end of Grafton Street, **Nassau Street** rims the south side of **Trinity College.** The street is noted for its fine shops and because it leads to **Merrion Square,** another fashionable Georgian park surrounded by historic brick-front townhouses. Merrion Square is also adjacent to Leinster House, the Irish House of Parliament, the National Gallery, and the National Museum.

In the older section of the city, **High Street** is the gateway to medieval and Viking Dublin, from the city's two medieval cathedrals to the old city walls and nearby Dublin Castle. The other noteworthy street in the older part of the city is **Francis Street,** Dublin's antique row.

THE NEIGHBORHOODS IN BRIEF

Trinity College Area On the south side of the River Liffey, the Trinity College complex is a 42-acre center of academia in the heart of the city, surrounded by fine bookstores and shops. This area lies in the Dublin 2 postal code.

Temple Bar Wedged between Trinity College and the Old City, this section took off in the 1990s and was transformed into the city's cultural and entertainment hub. As Dublin's self-proclaimed Left Bank, Temple Bar offers a vibrant array of cafes, unique shops, art galleries, recording studios, theaters, trendy restaurants, and atmospheric pubs. This is largely the stomping ground of young tourists (it's a huge stag night destination on weekends), and it's easy to feel over the hill if you're over 25. Still, it's fun and buzzy. This area lies in the Dublin 2 and Dublin 8 postal codes.

Old City Dating from Viking and medieval times, the cobblestone enclave of the historic Old City includes Dublin Castle, the remnants of the city's original walls, and the city's two main cathedrals, Christ Church and St. Patrick's. In the past few years, Old City has rocketed on to the map as a hip shopping destination, particularly for fashion (designer boutiques, eyewear) and stylish, craft-based housewares. The area encompasses the Dublin 8 and 2 zones.

Liberties The adjacent Liberties district, just west of High Street, takes its name from the fact that the people who lived here long ago were exempt from the local jurisdiction within the city walls. Although it prospered in its early days, the Liberties fell on hard times in the 17th and 18th centuries and is only now feeling a touch of urban renewal. Highlights range from the Guinness Brewery and Royal Hospital to the original Cornmarket area. Most of this area lies in the Dublin 8 zone.

St. Stephen's Green/Grafton Street Area A magnet for visitors, this district is home to some of the city's finest hotels, restaurants, and shops. There are some stunning residential townhouses near the Green, but this is primarily a business and shopping neighborhood. It is part of the Dublin 2 zone.

Fitzwilliam & Merrion Square These two little square parks are surrounded by fashionable brick-faced Georgian town houses, each with a distinctive and colorful doorway. Some of Dublin's most famous citizens once resided here; today many of the houses are offices for doctors, lawyers, government offices, and other professionals. This area is part of the Dublin 2 zone.

Ballsbridge/Embassy Row Immediately south of the Grand Canal, this is Dublin's most prestigious suburb, yet it is within walking distance of downtown. Although primarily a residential area, it is also the home of some leading hotels, restaurants, and embassies, including that of the United States. There are plenty of upscale hotels in this part of town, as well as very good B&Bs. This area is part of the Dublin 4 zone.

O'Connell Street (North of the Liffey) Once a fashionable and historic focal point, this area has lost much of its charm and importance in recent years but could be poised to rebound with the arrival of the Northside's first designer hotel, the Morrison. Shops, fast-food restaurants, and movie theaters rim the wide, sweeping thoroughfare, where you'll find a few great landmarks like the General Post Office and the Gresham Hotel. Within walking distance of O'Connell Street are four theaters, plus the Catholic Pro-Cathedral, the Moore Street open markets, the Henry Street pedestrian shopping area, the new Financial Services Centre, the ILAC Centre, the Jervis Shopping Centre, and the Central Bus Station. Most of this area lies in the Dublin 1 postal code.

2 Getting Around

Getting around Dublin is not at all daunting. Public transportation is good and getting better, taxis are plentiful and reasonably priced, and there are always your own two feet. Central Dublin is quite walkable. In fact, with its current traffic and parking problems, it's a city where the foot is mightier than the wheel. If you can avoid it, don't rent a car while you're in the city.

BY BUS Dublin Bus operates a fleet of green double-decker buses, single-deck buses, and minibuses (called "imps") throughout the city and its suburbs. Most buses originate on or near O'Connell Street, Abbey Street, and Eden Quay on the north side, and at Aston Quay, College Street, and Fleet Street on the south side. Bus stops are located every 2 or 3 blocks. Destinations and bus numbers are posted above the front windows; buses destined for the city center are marked with the Irish Gaelic words AN LAR.

Bus service runs daily throughout the city, starting at 6am (10am on Sun), with the last bus at 11:30pm. On Thursday, Friday, and Saturday nights, Nitelink service runs from the city center to the suburbs from midnight to 3am. Buses operate every 10 to 15 minutes for most runs; schedules are posted on revolving notice boards at each bus stop.

Inner-city fares are calculated based on distances traveled. The minimum fare is €.75 (65¢); the maximum fare is €1.65 ($1.45). The Nitelink fare is a flat €4 ($3.55). Buy your tickets from the driver as you enter the bus; exact change is welcomed but not required. Notes of €5 or higher may not be accepted. Discounted 1-day, 3-day, and 4-day passes are available. The 1-day bus-only pass costs €4.50 ($4); The 3-day pass costs €8.80 ($7.85); and the 5-day pass goes for €13.90 ($12). For more information, contact **Dublin Bus,** 59 Upper O'Connell St., Dublin 1 (✆ **01/872-1000;** www.dublinbus.ie).

BY DART   While Dublin has no subway in the strict sense, there is an electric rapid-transit train, known as the **DART** (Dublin Area Rapid Transit). It travels mostly at ground level or on elevated tracks, linking the city-center stations at **Connolly Station, Tara Street, Pearse Street,** and **Amiens Street** with suburbs and seaside communities as far as Balbriggan to the north and Greystones to the south. Service operates roughly every 10 to 20 minutes Monday to Saturday from 7am to midnight and Sunday from 9:30am to 11pm. The minimum fare is €.90 (80¢). One-day and 10-journey passes, as well as student and family tickets, are available at reduced rates. For further information, contact **DART,** Pearse Station, Dublin 2 (✆ **1850/366222** in Ireland, or 01/836-6222; www. irishrail.ie).

BY TRAM   The newest addition to Dublin's public transportation network is set to be the sleek light-rail tram known as **LUAS,** due for completion in 2003. Traveling at a maximum speed of 70kmph (45 mph) and departing every 5 minutes in peak hours, LUAS aims to appease Dublin's congestion problems and bring the city's transportation into the 21st century. Three lines will link the city center at **Connolly Station** and **St. Stephen's Green** with the suburbs of Tallaght in the southwest and Dundrum and Sandyford to the south. Fares were not yet set as of press time. For further information, contact **LUAS** (✆ **01/ 703-2029;** www.luas.ie).

ON FOOT   Small and compact, Dublin is ideal for walking, as long as you remember to look right and then left (in the direction opposite your instincts) for oncoming traffic before crossing the street, and to obey traffic signals. Each traffic light has timed "walk–don't walk" signals for pedestrians. Pedestrians have the right of way at specially marked, zebra-striped crossings; as a warning, there are usually two flashing lights at these intersections. For some walking-tour suggestions, see "Seeing the Sights," later in this chapter.

BY TAXI   The Dublin taxi market currently suffers from chronic excess demand, with long lines for taxis and little new supply since 1978. The government's initial overtures to deregulate and allow more cabs into the market resulted in massive taxi strikes and mayhem in the city for several weeks in late 2000 and early 2001. More cabs should eventually make the situation better, but for now it can be extremely difficult to catch a cab in the city center—especially at night on a weekend.

It's very difficult to hail a taxi on the street; instead, they line up at ranks. Ranks are located outside all of the leading hotels, at bus and train stations, and on prime thoroughfares such as Upper O'Connell Street, College Green, and the north side of St. Stephen's Green near the Shelbourne Hotel.

You can also phone for a taxi. Some of the companies that operate a 24-hour radio-call service are **Co-Op** (✆ **01/676-6666**), **Shamrock Radio Cabs** (✆ **01/855-5444**), and **VIP Taxis** (✆ **01/478-3333**). If you need a wake-up call, VIP offers that service, along with especially courteous dependability.

Dublin Area Rapid Transit (DART) Routes

Taxi rates are fixed by law and posted in each vehicle. A 2002 survey found the following to be typical travel costs in the city center: A 3.25km (2-mile) journey costs €4.95 ($4.40) by day and €6.85 ($6.10) at night; an 8km (5-mile) journey runs €10 ($8.90) by day and €12.25 ($10.90) at night; and a 16km (10-mile) journey costs €16.25 ($14.45) by day and €21.25 ($18.90) at night. There's an additional charge for each extra passenger and for each suitcase of €.50 (45¢). And it costs an extra €1.50 ($1.35) for a dispatched pickup. *Be warned:* Some hotel staff members will tack on as much as €4 ($3.55) for calling you a cab, although this practice violates city taxi regulations.

BY CAR   Unless you plan to do a lot of driving from Dublin to neighboring counties, it's not practical or affordable to rent a car. In fact, getting around the city and its environs is much easier without a car.

If you must drive in Dublin, remember to keep to the *left-hand side of the road,* and don't drive in bus lanes. The speed limit within the city is 46kmph (30 mph), and seat belts must be worn at all times by driver and passengers.

Most major international **car-rental firms** are represented in Dublin, as are many Irish-based companies. They have desks at the airport, full-service offices downtown, or both. The rates vary greatly according to company, season, type of car, and duration of rental. In high season, the average weekly cost of a car, from subcompact standard to full-size automatic, ranges from €200 to €1,525 ($178–$1,357); you'll be much better off if you've made your car-rental arrangements well in advance from home. (Also see "By Car" under "Getting Around" in chapter 2.)

International firms represented in Dublin include **Avis,** 1 Hanover St. E., Dublin 1 and at Dublin Airport (© **01/605-7500**); **Budget,** in Dublin (© **01/ 837-9611**), and at Dublin Airport (© **01/844-5919**); **Dan Dooley Rent-a-Car,** 42 Westland Row, Dublin 2 (© **01/677-2723**), and at Dublin Airport (© **01/844-5156**); **Hertz,** 149 Upper Leeson St., Dublin 4 (© **01/660-2255**), and at Dublin Airport (© **01/844-5466**); and **Murray's Europcar,** Baggot Street Bridge, Dublin 4 (© **01/614-2800**), and at Dublin Airport (© **01/ 812-0410**).

During normal business hours, free parking on Dublin streets is nonexistent. Never park in bus lanes or along a curb with double yellow lines. City officials will either clamp or tow errant vehicles. To get your car declamped, the fee is €85 ($76); if your car is towed away, it costs €165 ($147) to reclaim it.

Throughout Dublin, you'll find multibay meters and "pay and display" **disc parking.** In Dublin, a five-pack of discs costs €6.35 ($5.65). Each ticket is good for a maximum of 3 hours. The most reliable and safest places to park are surface parking lots and multistory car parks in central locations such as Kildare Street, Lower Abbey Street, Marlborough Street, and St. Stephen's Green West. Expect to pay €1.90 ($1.70) per hour and €19 ($17) for 24 hours. Night rates run €6.35 to €9 ($5.65–$8) per hour. The bottom line here is that you're better off without a car in Dublin. The city is aggressively discouraging cars for commuters, much less for tourists.

BY BICYCLE   The steady flow of Dublin traffic rushing down one-way streets may be a little intimidating for most cyclists, but there are many opportunities for more relaxed pedaling in residential areas and suburbs, along the seafront, and around Phoenix Park. The Dublin Tourism office can supply you with bicycle touring information and suggested routes.

Bicycle rental averages €13 ($12) per day, €50 ($45) per week, with a €65 ($58) deposit. In the downtown area, bicycles can be rented from **Raleigh Ireland,** Kylemore Road, Dublin 10 (© **01/626-1333;** Raleigh@iol.ie).

 ## FAST FACTS: Dublin

For countrywide information, see "Fast Facts: Ireland" in chapter 2.

Airport See "Orientation," earlier in this chapter.

American Express **American Express International,** 41 Nassau St., Dublin 2 (© **01/679-9000**), is a full-service travel agency that also offers currency exchange, traveler's checks, and (for members) mail-holding. It is opposite Trinity College, just off College Green, and is open Monday to Saturday 9am to 5pm. American Express also has a desk at the **Dublin Tourism Office** on Suffolk Street (© **01/605-7709**). In an emergency, traveler's checks can be reported lost or stolen by dialing toll-free in Ireland © **1800/282728.**

Banks Nearly all banks are open Monday to Friday 10am to 4pm (to 5pm Thurs) and have ATMs that accept Cirrus network cards as well as MasterCard and Visa. Convenient locations include the **Bank of Ireland,** at 28 O'Connell Street, Dublin 1, and 34 College Green, Dublin 2; and the **Allied Irish Bank,** at 64 Grafton St., Dublin 2; 37 O'Connell St., Dublin 1; and 12 St. Stephen's Green, Dublin 2.

Business Hours **Banks** are open 10am to 4pm, Monday to Wednesday and Friday; and 10am to 5pm Thursday. **Post Offices** (known as **An Post**) are open from 9am to 5:30pm Monday to Friday and 9am to 1:30pm Saturday. The GPO on O'Connell Street is open 8am to 8pm Monday to Saturday, and 10:30am to 6:30pm Sunday (for stamps only). **Museums and Sights** are generally open 10am to 5pm Tuesday to Saturday, and 2pm to 5pm Sunday. **Shops** generally open 9am to 6pm Monday to Friday, with late opening on Thursdays until 7 or 8pm. In the city center most department stores and many shops are open noon to 6pm Sundays.

Currency Exchange Currency-exchange services, signposted as BUREAU DE CHANGE, are in all banks and at many branches of the Irish post office system, known as **An Post.** A bureau de change operates daily during flight arrival and departure times at Dublin airport; a foreign currency note-exchanger machine is also available on a 24-hour basis in the main arrivals hall. Some hotels and travel agencies offer bureau de change services, although the best rate of exchange is usually when you use your bank card at an ATM.

Dentist For dental emergencies, contact the Eastern Health Board Headquarters, Dr. Steevens Hospital, Dublin 8 (© **01/679-0700**), or try **Molesworth Clinic,** 2 Molesworth Place, Dublin 2 (© **01/661-5544**). See also "Dental Surgeons" in the Golden Pages (yellow pages) of the telephone book. The American Embassy (see "Embassies," below) can provide a list of dentists in the city and surrounding areas. Expect to be charged up front for services.

Doctor If you need to see a physician, most hotels and guesthouses will contact a house doctor for you. Otherwise, you can call either the **Eastern Health Board Headquarters,** Dr. Steevens Hospital, Dublin 8 (© **01/679-0700**); or the **Irish Medical Organization,** 10 Fitzwilliam Place, Dublin 2 (© **01/676-7273**), 9:15am to 5:15pm for a referral. As with dentists, expect to pay for treatment up front and be reimbursed after the fact by your insurance company. The American Embassy (see "Embassies," below) can provide a list of doctors in the city and surrounding areas.

Embassies/Consulates The **American Embassy** is at 42 Elgin Rd., Ballsbridge, Dublin 4 (© **01/668-8777**); the **Canadian Embassy** at 65/68 St. Stephen's Green, Dublin 2 (© **01/417-4100**); the **British Embassy** at 29 Merrion Rd., Dublin 2 (© **01/205-3700**); and the **Australian Embassy** at Fitzwilton House, Wilton Terrace, Dublin 2 (© **01/676-1517**). In addition, there is an **American Consulate** at 14 Queen St., Belfast BT1 6EQ (© **028/9032-8239**).

Emergencies For police, fire, or other emergencies, dial © **999.**

Gay & Lesbian Resources Contact the **Gay Switchboard Dublin,** Carmichael House, North Brunswick Street, Dublin 7 (© **01/872-1055**; fax 01/873-5737; gsd@iol.ie); the **National Lesbian and Gay Federation (NLGF),** 6 South William St., Dublin 2 (© **01/671-0939**; fax 01/679-1603); or the **LOT (Lesbians Organizing Together),** 5 Capel St., Dublin 1 (© **01/872-7770**). For fuller listings see "Tips for Travelers with Special Needs" in chapter 2.

Hospitals For emergency care, two of the most modern are **St. Vincent's University Hospital,** Elm Park (© **01/269-4533**), on the south side of the city; and **Beaumont Hospital,** Beaumont (© **01/837-7755**), on the north side.

Hot Lines In Ireland, hot lines are called "helplines." For **emergencies, police, or fire,** dial **999; Aids Helpline** (© **01/872-4277**), Monday to Friday from 7am to 9pm and Saturday from 3 to 5pm; **Alcoholics Anonymous** (© **01/453-8998** and after hours 01/679-5967); **Asthma Line** (© **1850/445-464**); **Narcotics Anonymous** (© **01/830-0944**); **Rape Crisis Centre** (© **01/661-4911**) and **FreeFone** (© **1800/778-888**), after 5:30pm and weekends (© **01/661-4564**); and **Samaritans** (© **01/872-7700** and 1850/609-090).

Information For directory assistance, dial © **11811.** For visitor information offices, see "Orientation," earlier in this chapter.

Internet Access In cybersavvy Dublin, public access terminals are no longer hard to find, appearing in shopping malls, hotels, and hostels throughout the city center. Like all of Dublin's public libraries, the **Central Library,** in the ILAC Centre, off Henry Street, Dublin 1 (© **01/873-4333**), has a bank of PCs with free Internet access. One of the most convenient and comfortable of the many cybercafes in town is Betacafe@Arthouse, Curved Street, Dublin 2 (© **01/605-6800**; www.arthouse.ie), located above the Multimedia Centre for the Arts, in Temple Bar. Fifteen minutes online will set you back €2 ($1.80). It's open Monday to

Friday 9:15am to 5:30pm, Saturday 9:15am to 2pm. Also in Temple Bar is the **Cyberia Cafe,** Temple Lane South, Dublin 2 (*©* **01/679-7607;** www.cyberia.ie), where 15 minutes online costs €2 ($1.80), or €1.60 ($1.40) for students. It's open Monday to Thursday 10am to 10pm and Friday and Saturday 10am to 2pm. At both the **Central Cybercafe,** 6 Grafton St., Dublin 2 (*©* **677-8298**), and **Planet Cyber Café,** 13 St. Andrews St., Dublin 2 (*©* **01/670-5183**), 30 minutes online costs €3.50 ($3.10).

Magazines The leading magazines for upcoming events and happenings are *In Dublin* (€4/$3.55), published every 2 weeks; and the free biweekly *Event Guide* (**www.eventguide.ie**). The *Event Guide,* which contains up-to-date listings of events throughout Ireland, with a focus on Dublin, is widely available. *Where: Dublin,* published bimonthly, is aimed specifically at tourists and visitors and is a useful one-stop source for shopping, dining, and entertainment. It's free at the more exclusive hotels.

Pharmacies Centrally located drugstores, known locally as pharmacies or chemist shops, include **Hamilton Long & Co.,** 5 Lower O'Connell St. (*©* **01/874-8456**), and **Dame Street Pharmacy,** 16 Dame St., Dublin 2 (*©* **01/670-4523**). A late-night chemist shop is **Byrne's Pharmacy,** 4 Merrion Rd., Dublin 4 (*©* **01/668-3287**). It closes at 9pm on weekdays, 6pm on Saturday, and 1pm on Sunday.

Police Dial *©* **999** in an emergency. The metropolitan headquarters for the **Dublin Garda Siochana** (Police) is in Phoenix Park, Dublin 8 (*©* **01/666-0000**).

Post Office The **General Post Office (GPO)** is located on O'Connell Street, Dublin 1 (*©* **01/705-7000**). Hours are Monday to Saturday 8am to 8pm, Sunday and holidays 10:30am to 6:30pm. Branch offices, identified by the sign OIFIG AN POST/POST OFFICE, are open Monday to Saturday only, 9am to 6pm.

Weather Phone *©* **1550/122112,** or check the Web at **www.ireland. com/weather**.

Yellow Pages The classified section of the telephone book is called the Golden Pages (**www.goldenpages.ie**).

3 Where to Stay

From legendary old-world landmarks to sleek high-rises, Dublin offers a great diversity of places to stay. Although prices are rising, even travelers on a moderate budget, with enough advance planning, should be able to find comfortable, attractive accommodations. Dublin is sprouting new hotels at a somewhat alarming rate—more than 20 in the past handful of years—to meet an ever-accelerating demand. It's also a decidedly upmarket demand—the number of luxury hotels has risen by 36% since 1995. Fortunately, a concerted effort is being made to assure that the new hotels represent the economic diversity of Dublin's visitors, from millionaires to money-savers.

The Irish Tourist Board implements a grading system consistent with those of other European countries and international standards, ranking hotels with one to five stars. While this system is helpful as a guideline of the comfort level you

Dublin Accommodations

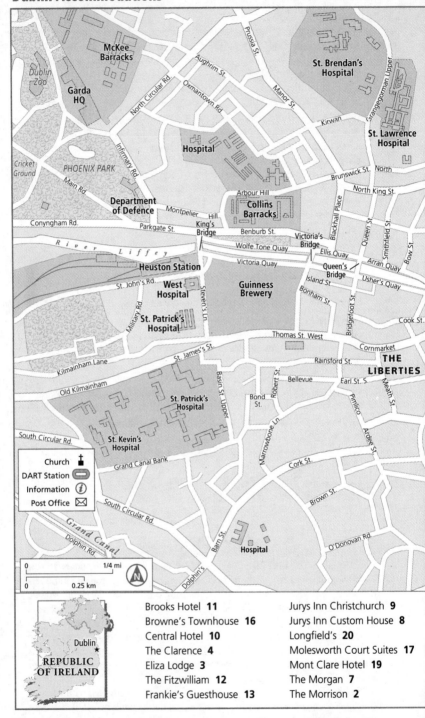

Brooks Hotel **11**
Browne's Townhouse **16**
Central Hotel **10**
The Clarence **4**
Eliza Lodge **3**
The Fitzwilliam **12**
Frankie's Guesthouse **13**

Jurys Inn Christchurch **9**
Jurys Inn Custom House **8**
Longfield's **20**
Molesworth Court Suites **17**
Mont Clare Hotel **19**
The Morgan **7**
The Morrison **2**

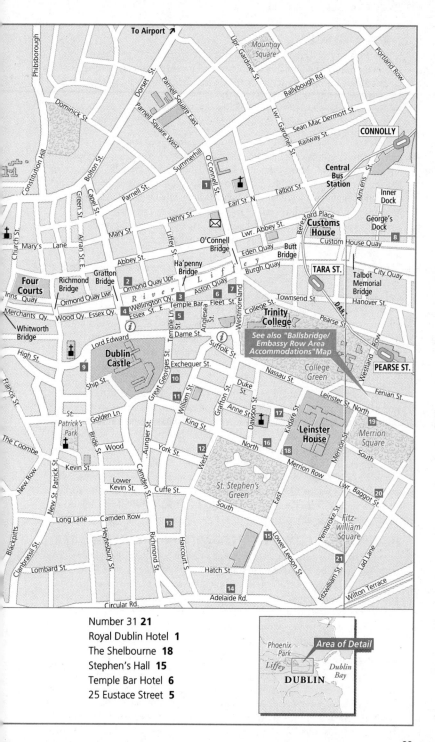

Number 31 **21**
Royal Dublin Hotel **1**
The Shelbourne **18**
Stephen's Hall **15**
Temple Bar Hotel **6**
25 Eustace Street **5**

A Parking Note

The majority of Dublin hotels do not offer parking; if you have a car, you'll have to find (and pay for) street parking. In this section, we've provided parking information only for the few hotels that do offer parking arrangements or discounts for guests.

---

can expect, it is based strictly on facilities and amenities and fails to take into consideration atmosphere, decor, charm, friendly owners, or an especially appealing breakfast. Moreover, some hotels are ungraded—usually because they are brand-new or they simply choose to remain out of the system. For example, the Clarence Hotel, owned by members of the band U2, is ungraded (presumably out of preference) but certainly falls into the luxury category.

In this guide, we give each hotel zero to three stars, based on overall value for money. As a result, a fine, but expensive hotel may get one star, while an excellent budget choice may get two.

In general, rates for Dublin hotels do not vary as greatly with the seasons as they do in the countryside. Some hotels charge slightly higher prices during special events, such as the Dublin Horse Show. For the best deals, try to reserve a room over a weekend, and ask if there is a reduction or a weekend package in effect. Some Dublin hotels cut their rates by as much as 50% on Friday and Saturday nights, when business traffic is low. Just to complicate matters, other hotels, especially in the off-season, offer midweek specials.

It usually pays to book hotels well in advance. Many hotels can be booked through toll-free numbers in the United States, and the quoted prices offered can be appreciably (as much as 40%) lower than those offered at the door. For properties that do not have a U.S. reservation number, the fastest way to reserve is by telephone, fax, or e-mail. If you arrive in Ireland without a reservation, the staff members at the tourist offices throughout the Republic and Northern Ireland will gladly find you a room using a computerized reservation service known as **Gulliver.** In Ireland or Northern Ireland, you can also call the Gulliver line directly (© **00800/668-668-66**). This is a nationwide and cross-border "freephone" facility for credit-card bookings, operated daily 8am to 11pm. Gulliver is also accessible from the United States (© **011-800/668-668-66**) and on the Web at **www.gulliver.ie.**

HISTORIC OLD CITY & TEMPLE BAR/TRINITY COLLEGE AREA

Temple Bar is the youngest, most vibrant niche in a young, vibrant town. Stay here and you'll be on the doorstep of practically anywhere you'd want to go. That said, it can get woefully noisy at night, so request a room on a top floor if you want some shut-eye.

If you've got more dash than cash, head just west of Temple Bar to Old City. You'll be in one of the up-and-coming pockets of town, but hoteliers haven't yet started jacking up their rates to reflect the area's newfound popularity.

VERY EXPENSIVE

The Clarence ★★★   So what if the place is partly owned by members of the rock band U2? Don't dismiss it as a glitzy, see-and-be-seen haunt for celebrities (Jack Nicholson, Gwyneth Paltrow, and Mick Jagger are fans)—the Clarence is one of the finest and truly stylish hotels in Dublin. Situated beside the Liffey in Temple Bar, this mid-19th-century, Regency-style hotel was totally overhauled in 1996 to offer larger rooms and luxurious suites. In the process it traded antique charm for contemporary elegance. Each room features a rich color—crimson, royal blue, eggplant, chocolate, or gold—against cream walls and light Shaker-style oak furniture, including exceptionally firm beds. Twin rooms are available but most doubles feature king-size beds. Suites and deluxe rooms have balconies, some overlooking the Liffey. The Clarence's elegant Tea Room restaurant (p. 114), in what was once the ballroom, is one of the best places in town to dine on contemporary Irish cuisine. For drinks and lighter fare there's the Octagon Bar and after hours there's The Kitchen, one of the city's most glamorous nightspots (p. 157).

6/8 Wellington Quay, Dublin 2. 🕻 **01/670-9000.** Fax 01/407-0820. www.theclarence.ie. 50 units. €285–€305 ($254–$271) double; €590 ($525) 1-bedroom suite; €720 ($641) 2-bedroom suite. Full Irish breakfast €20 ($18). AE, DC, MC, V. Valet parking/service (fee charged). Bus: 51B, 51C, 68, 69, or 79. **Amenities:** Restaurant (eclectic Continental); bar; after-hours nightclub; concierge; salon; room service; babysitting; laundry/dry cleaning; nonsmoking rooms; foreign-currency exchange; video library. *In room:* A/C, TV/VCR, dataport, minibar, hair dryer, safe.

MODERATE

Eliza Lodge ⭐   A new entry this year, the spanking-new Eliza Lodge sits right beside the Liffey and embodies all the exuberance and zest of Temple Bar. If The Morgan is booked, this place gives the Temple Bar Hotel competition as the second-best, moderately-priced choice. Rooms are very attractive, done up in neutral creams and blond woods, with big floor-to-ceiling windows—the better to take in the riverside vistas. At the top end, executive rooms have Jacuzzi tubs and mod, round bay windows perched over the quay. But better value are the smaller penthouse doubles, which have balconies overlooking the river and are a comparative steal at €165 to €190 ($147–$169).

23 Wellington Quay, Dublin 2. 🕻 **01/671-8044.** Fax 01/671-8362. www.dublinlodge.com. 18 units. €152–€228 ($135–$203) double. AE, MC, V. Bus: 51B, 51C, 68, 69, or 79. **Amenities:** Restaurant; bar; nonsmoking rooms. *In room:* A/C, TV, tea/coffeemaker, hair dryer, iron.

The Morgan ⭐⭐   If you love Temple Bar but can't afford to stay at the Clarence, this is a fabulous consolation prize. In just a few short years, this stylized little boutique hotel has developed a cult following among folks in fashion and music. Rooms are airy and minimalist, featuring light beechwood furnishings and crisp, white bedspreads against creamy neutral tones, with a smattering of modern artworks adding visual punch. The overall effect is understated elegance, with a modern, luxurious twist. But the attraction here goes beyond mere good looks. Every detail—from the classy cutlery to the way the staff is unobtrusively attentive—hits just the right note. Though it sounds like a contradiction in terms, this place manages to be both trendy and a classic at the same time.

10 Fleet St., Dublin 2. 🕻 **01/679-3939.** Fax 01/679-3946. www.themorgan.com. 61 units. €126–€241 ($112–$214) double. AE, DC, MC, V. Bus: 78A or 78B. **Amenities:** Cafe; bar; fitness center; room service; aromatherapy/masseuse; babysitting; laundry/dry cleaning; nonsmoking rooms; video/CD library. *In room:* TV/VCR, CD player, dataport, tea/coffeemaker, iron, garment press, safe, voice mail.

Temple Bar Hotel ⭐   It's twice as big and half as stylish as the Morgan, but still a solid pick if the Morgan is sold out. Opened in 1993, the five-story hotel

---

⸜Fun Fact⸝   What's in a Name?

The "bar" in Temple Bar has nothing to do with a pub or the law. It is the old Irish word for a riverside path.

was developed from a former bank building with great care taken to preserve the brick facade and Victorian mansard roof. The Art Deco lobby features a cast-iron fireplace and plenty of greenery. Guest rooms feature traditional mahogany furnishings and an autumnal russet-and-green color palette, with a very comfortable level of amenities. The double-size orthopedic beds are blissfully firm, though they make the rooms fairly cramped. The hotel has a skylit, garden-style Terrace Restaurant serving light fare (sandwiches and pasta) and an Old Dublin–theme pub, Buskers.

Fleet St., Temple Bar, Dublin 2. © 800/44-UTELL in the U.S., or 01/677-3333. Fax 01/677-3088. www.tower hotelgroup.ie. 130 units. €130–€185 ($116–$165) double. Rates include full Irish breakfast. AE, DC, MC, V. Discounted parking available in nearby car park. DART: Tara St. Bus: 78A or 78B. **Amenities:** Restaurant (light fare); bar; access to a nearby health club; concierge; room service; babysitting; nonsmoking rooms; foreign-currency exchange. *In room:* TV, minibar, tea/coffeemaker, hair dryer, garment press.

INEXPENSIVE

Jurys Inn Christchurch ★ *Value* A good location in Old City, facing Christ Church cathedral, makes this a solid choice in the budget category. Totally refurbished in 1998, the rooms are larger than you'd expect and bright, though the decor has the same floral bedspreads and framed watercolors as every other chain hotel you've ever visited. Make your reservations early and request a fifth-floor room facing west for a memorable view of Christ Church. *Tip:* Rooms 501, 507, and 419 are especially spacious.

Christ Church Place, Dublin 8. © 800/44-UTELL in the U.S., or 01/454-0000. Fax 01/454-0012. www.jurys. com. 182 units. €96 ($85) double. Breakfast €8 ($7.10). Service charge included. AE, MC, V. Discounted parking available at adjacent lot. Bus: 21A, 50, 50A, 78, 78A, or 78B. **Amenities:** Restaurant (Continental); pub; babysitting; laundry/dry cleaning; nonsmoking rooms. *In room:* A/C, TV, coffeemaker, hair dryer.

SELF-CATERING

25 Eustace Street *Finds* This wonderfully restored Georgian town house, dating from 1720, has an enviable location smack in the heart of Temple Bar. It is a showcase property for the Irish Landmark Trust, whose mission is to rescue neglected historic buildings and restore them. And that it does with aplomb. 25 Eustace Street is the only property that the ILT lets out for fewer than three nights, and it is truly a privilege to stay here for even one night. The house has been faithfully reinstated to the gracious, slightly sober atmosphere of a house of its period, with a superb timber paneled staircase, fireplaces in every room, mainly mahogany furniture, and brass beds. You have the run of three entire floors of the house, including a huge drawing room with a baby grand piano, dining room, equipped galley kitchen, and three bedrooms (a double, a twin, and a triple). There are two bathrooms, one of which is enormous with an extraroomy cast-iron claw-foot tub placed dead center. Bookshelves and deep windowsills have been thoughtfully stocked with classics by Irish novelists. Like all ILT properties, there is no TV. (To have it any other way would seem a callous intrusion.) All this, and Temple Bar at your doorstep.

Service Charges

A reminder: Unless otherwise noted, room rates don't include service charges (usually 10%–15% of your bill).

---

25 Eustace St., Dublin 2. Contact the Irish Landmark Trust © **01/670-4733.** Fax 01/670-4887. landmark@iol.ie. €255 ($227) per night or €1,143 ($1,017) per week. **Amenities:** Full kitchen. *In room:* No phone.

ST. STEPHEN'S GREEN/GRAFTON STREET AREA

Location, location, location: The area around St. Stephen's Green is the epicenter of the city's shopping and sightseeing. So what's not to love? Prepare to pay more for less here.

VERY EXPENSIVE

The Fitzwilliam Hotel ★★★   Take an unbeatable location with stunning views over the Green, a Michelin-starred restaurant, and an ultracool, contemporary design by Terence Conran, and you have the makings of the Fitzwilliam. Conran has a knack for easy-going sophistication, using clean lines and only a few neutral colors (white, beige, gray) throughout the public rooms and guest rooms. Every detail echoes the theme of understated luxury—even the staff uniforms are custom-made by Irish designers Marc O'Neill and Cuan Hanly. Rooms are beautifully appointed and very relaxing. Dublin's best restaurant, the Michelin-starred Peacock Alley (p. 116), is downstairs, and you can also have a meal at the stylish Inn on the Green bar. If staying somewhere fashionable is important to you, this gets the nod over the Shelbourne.

109 St. Stephen's Green, Dublin 2. ℂ 01/478-7000. Fax 01/478-7878. www.fitzwilliam-hotel.com. 130 units. €292–€356 ($260–$317) double. AE, DC, MC, V. DART: Pearse. Bus: 10, 11A, 11B, 13, or 20B. **Amenities:** Restaurant (Mediterranean/fusion); bar; roof garden; concierge; room service; babysitting; laundry/dry cleaning; nonsmoking rooms; foreign-currency exchange. *In room:* A/C, TV/VCR, CD player, fax, dataport, minibar, tea/coffeemaker, hair dryer, garment press, voice mail.

The Shelbourne ★★★   While the Fitzwilliam is all about cutting-edge style, the Shelbourne is all about tradition. This is Dublin's answer to the Grand Hotel, and nothing—not even getting swallowed up by the Meridien Group—has changed its status. Founded in 1824, it has played a significant role in Irish history—the constitution was drafted here in 1922, in room 112. The Shelbourne often plays host to international leaders, movie stars, and literary giants. Guest rooms vary in size, but all offer up-to-date comforts and are beautifully appointed with antiques and period pieces. Ask for one that overlooks bucolic St. Stephen's Green. The public areas, replete with glowing fireplaces, Waterford chandeliers, and original artworks, are popular rendezvous spots for Dublin's movers and shakers. (Indeed, the Horseshoe Bar remains the preferred watering hole for sealing deals over a pint of Guinness.) The spanking-new fitness center is state-of-the-art, and service is impeccable. Needless to say, you don't stay here just for the beds, but for a slice of Irish heritage.

27 St. Stephen's Green, Dublin 2. ℂ 800/225-5843 in the U.S., or 01/663-4500. Fax 01/661-6006. www. shelbourne.ie. 190 units. €235–€260 ($209–$231) double. AE, DC, MC, V. Limited free parking. DART: Pearse. Bus: 10, 11A, 11B, 13, or 20B. **Amenities:** 2 restaurants (Continental, modern Irish); 2 bars; tearoom; fitness center; concierge; room service; babysitting; laundry/dry cleaning; barber shop; foreign-currency exchange; safe-deposit boxes; video library. *In room:* A/C, TV, radio, dataport, minibar.

EXPENSIVE

Brooks Hotel ★   If you love the neighborhood but can't afford the Shelbourne or the Fitzwilliam (see above), this 6-year-old hotel offers excellent services and doesn't scrimp on the in-room creature comforts. Every room has a king-size orthopedic bed, handmade oak furniture from Galway, and a bold but tasteful color scheme. (We're not kidding: The hotel's facade is awash in lilac.) The bathrooms have blissfully powerful showers. Superior and executive rooms (still significantly cheaper than a standard double at the Shelbourne or Fitzwilliam) are extra spacious and have VCRs and antique radios. The oak-paneled drawing room is a restful oasis for tea or sherry while you peruse the *Irish Times.*

59–62 Drury St., Dublin 2. ⓒ **01/670-4000.** Fax 01/670-4455. www.sinnotthotels.com/brooks. 75 units. €235–€260 ($209–$231) double. No service charge. AE, DC, MC, V. Discounted overnight parking at adjacent car park. DART: Tara St. or Pearse. Bus: 10, 11A, 11B, 13, 14, 15, 15A, 15B, 20B, or 46A. **Amenities:** Restaurant (international); bar; concierge; secretarial services; room service; babysitting; laundry/dry cleaning; nonsmoking floors; foreign-currency exchange; video library. *In room:* A/C, TV, VCR (in superior rooms and up), fax, dataport, minibar, hair dryer, iron, garment press, safe.

Browne's Townhouse ⚘⚘   If you love luxury but hate big chain hotels, look no further than this sumptuously restored Georgian townhouse with an unbeatable location on St. Stephen's Green—and our favorite of this year's new entries. Originally a gentleman's club, it was converted in 2000 into one of the city's best boutique hotels and has been chalking up awards and accolades ever since. Downstairs is all Georgian splendor: comfy wingback chairs, rich upholsteries, ornate ceiling plasterwork. The dozen guest rooms come in all shapes and sizes, but all are sumptuously decorated with period furnishings, four-poster king-size beds (some of them 8 ft. wide!), marble bathrooms, and unique architectural details. When you book, voice your decor preferences; rooms vary drastically according to masculine, feminine, classic, or elaborate tastes. If you splurge on the Thomas Leighton suite, you'll sleep on a magnificent king-size mahogany Murphy bed that once belonged to Marilyn Monroe. Downstairs, the elegant brasserie serves up excellent traditional French fare.

22 St. Stephen's Green, Dublin 2. ⓒ **01/638-3939.** Fax 01/638-3900. www.brownesdublin.com. 12 units. €205–€235 ($182–$209) double. No service charge. Rates include full breakfast. MC, V. DART: Pearse. Bus: 10, 11A, 11B, 13, or 20B. **Amenities:** Restaurant (French). *In room:* A/C, TV, fax, dataport, tea/coffeemaker, hair dryer.

Stephen's Hall ⚘ *Value*   How suite it is. Wonderfully situated on the southeast corner of St. Stephen's Green in a handsome Georgian town house, this all-suite hotel offers great value for families, visitors who plan an extended stay, or folks who want to entertain or do their own cooking. Each suite is tastefully decorated and contains a sitting room, dining area, fully-equipped kitchenette, bathroom, and bedroom. The luxury penthouse suites, on the upper floors, offer great views of the city. Ground-level townhouse suites have private entrances. An added bonus: Morels, one of Dublin's best restaurants—a Michelin award-winner, no less—is in the basement.

14–18 Lower Leeson St., Dublin 2. ⓒ **800/223-6510** in the U.S., or 01/638-1111. Fax 01/638-1122. www.premgroup.ie. 37 units. €150–€355 ($134–$316) 1-bedroom suite. No service charge. Full breakfast €13 ($12). AE, DC, MC, V. Free parking. DART: Pearse. Bus: 11, 11A, 11B, 13, 13A, or 13B. **Amenities:** Restaurant (Continental); bar; access to nearby health club; concierge; babysitting; nonsmoking floor; safe-deposit boxes; video library. *In room:* TV, CD player, fax, dataport.

MODERATE

Central Hotel ⚘   Between Grafton Street and Dublin Castle, this century-old five-story hotel is now part of the Best Western chain. The public areas retain a Victorian atmosphere, enhanced by an impressive collection of contemporary Irish art. Guest rooms are high-ceilinged, with cheerful and colorful fabrics, and sturdy, Irish-made furnishings. The tucked-away Library Bar is a cozy haven for a drink and a moment's calm.

1–5 Exchequer St. (at the corner of Great Georges St.), Dublin 2. ⓒ **800/780-1234** in the U.S., or 01/679-7302. Fax 01/679-7303. www.centralhotel.ie. 70 units. €133–€200 ($118–$178) double. Rates include full Irish breakfast and service charge. AE, DC, MC, V. Discounted parking in nearby public lot. Bus: 22A. **Amenities:** Restaurant (Irish/Continental); bar; lounge; room service; nonsmoking rooms. *In room:* TV, minibar, tea/coffeemaker, hair dryer, iron, garment press, voice mail.

Molesworth Court Suites ⋒   Hate hotels? Then consider an apartment. Tucked away behind Mansion House, Molesworth Courts is no more than 5 minutes on foot to Stephens Green and yet is country quiet. These tastefully-decorated, comfortable apartments offer everything you need to set up your own base in Dublin, whether for a night or a month. They all have small balconies, and the bi-level penthouses have spacious verandas. The staff here goes the extra mile to be helpful, and there's daily maid service. The internal phone system provides you with a private extension and your own voice mail. If, despite the fact that you have your own kitchen, you want to let others do your cooking, you can order out from any of the roughly 25 local restaurants listed in the *Restaurant Express* menu booklet lying only an arm's reach from the couch.

Schoolhouse Lane (off Molesworth St.), Dublin 2. ℂ **01/676-4799.** Fax 01/676-4982. www.molesworth court.ie. 12 units. €160 ($142) 1-bedroom apt, €200 ($178) 2-bedroom apt. Nonrefundable booking deposit of €100 ($89) due 4 weeks before arrival. AE, MC, V. DART: Pearse. Bus: 10, 11A, 11B, 13, or 20B. **Amenities:** Laundry. *In room:* TV.

Number 31 ⋒⋒   A discreet plaque at an elegant gated entrance in the heart of Georgian Dublin is your only clue that what lies beyond is an award-winning town-house B&B. The house is actually two beautifully renovated architectural show houses—it's the former home of Sam Stephenson, Ireland's best-known modern architect—featuring a fabulous sunken fireside seating area with mosaic tiles in the main lounge. In the main house, rooms vary from grand, high-ceilinged affairs to cozier nests. The smaller coach house has lower ceilings, but some rooms have their own patios. All the rooms are a triumph of quiet, good taste, decorated with fine fabrics against a cream backdrop. Breakfast is truly magnificent—think mushroom frittatas, cranberry bread, and scrumptious little potato cakes.

31 Leeson Close, Lower Leeson St., Dublin 2. ℂ **01/676-5011.** Fax 01/676-2929. www.number31.ie. 20 units (all with bathroom). €114–€178 ($101–$158) double. Rates include breakfast. AE, MC, V. Discounted adjacent parking. Bus: 11, 11A, 11B, 13, 13A, or 13B. **Amenities:** Bar; lounge. *In room:* TV, hair dryer.

INEXPENSIVE

Frankie's Guesthouse ⋒   Billed as Dublin's only guesthouse exclusively for lesbians and gays, Frankie's is a charming, mews-style building with a wonderful address on a quiet street in the heart of Georgian Dublin. Set on a quiet back street, the house has a Mediterranean feel, with fresh whitewashed rooms and simple furnishings. Book well in advance, especially for a weekend stay.

8 Camden Place, Dublin 2. ℂ and fax **01/478-3087.** www.frankiesguesthouse.com. 12 units, 5 with private bathroom. €90–€95 ($80–$85) double with private bathroom; €75–€80 ($67–$71) double with shared bathroom. Rates include breakfast. AE, MC, V. Bus: 16, 16A, 16C, 19A, 22, or 22A. **Amenities:** Sauna; TV lounge; roof terrace. *In room:* TV, tea/coffeemaker.

FITZWILLIAM SQUARE/MERRION SQUARE AREA

This Georgian neighborhood feels a lot like the nearby St. Stephen's Green area, but its streets are less busy and commercialized. Fitzwilliam Square and Merrion Square are each little square parks surrounded by Georgian town houses with colorful doors. Some of Dublin's most famous citizens once resided here; today many of the houses are offices for doctors, lawyers, government officials, and other professionals. This area is only a few minutes on foot from St. Stephen's Green and Grafton Street, but accommodations tend to be considerably less pricey.

EXPENSIVE

Longfield's ⋒⋒   Created from two 18th-century Georgian town houses, this award-winning hotel is a small, elegant alternative to the large upscale hotels in this area. The hotel is named after Richard Longfield (also known as Viscount Longueville), who originally owned this site and was a member of the Irish Parliament 2 centuries ago. Totally restored and recently refurbished, it combines Georgian decor and reproduction-period furnishings of dark woods and brass trim. The standard-size rooms are on the small side; the best doubles feature four-poster beds. Like the eye of a storm, Longfield's is centrally located yet remarkably quiet, an elegant yet unpretentious getaway 5 minutes' walk from St. Stephen's Green. The restaurant, simply known as Number 10, is beloved by foodies.

10 Lower Fitzwilliam St., Dublin 2. ✆ **01/676-1367.** Fax 01/676-1542. www.longfields.ie. 26 units. €190–€230 ($169–$205) double. No service charge. Rates include full breakfast. AE, DC, MC, V. No parking available. DART: Pearse. Bus: 10. **Amenities:** Restaurant (international); concierge; room service; babysitting; laundry/dry cleaning; foreign-currency exchange. In room: TV, clock radio, hair dryer.

MODERATE

Kilronan House ⋒⋒   This extremely comfortable B&B is set on a peaceful, leafy road just 5 minutes' walk from St. Stephen's Green. Much of the Georgian character remains, such as the ceiling cornicing, hardwood parquet floors, and the fine staircase. The sitting room on the ground floor is particularly intimate, with a fire glowing through the cold months of the year. The rooms are brightly inviting in white and yellow, and those facing the front have commodious bay windows. There's no elevator, so consider requesting a room on a lower floor. The front rooms, facing Adelaide Street, are also preferable to those in back, which face onto office buildings and a parking lot. Breakfast here is especially good, featuring homemade breads.

70 Adelaide Rd., Dublin 2. ✆ **01/475-5266.** Fax 01/478-2841. www.dublinn.com/kilronan.htm. 15 units, 13 with private bathroom (shower only). €152 ($135) double. Rates include full breakfast. AE, MC, V. Free private parking. Bus: 14, 15, 19, 20, or 46A. In room: TV, tea/coffeemaker, hair dryer.

Mont Clare Hotel ⋒   Overlooking the northwest corner of Merrion Square, this vintage six-story brick-faced hotel recently underwent a thorough restoration. It has a typical Georgian facade, matched inside by period furnishings of dark woods and polished brass. The smallish guest rooms were completely refurbished in 1998 and given a brighter, more contemporary feel.

Merrion Sq., Dublin 2. ✆ **800/569-9983** in the U.S., or 01/607-3800. Fax 01/661-5663. www.montclarehotel.ie. 80 units. €148–€205 ($132–$182) double. AE, DC, MC, V. Free valet parking. DART: Pearse. Bus: 5, 7A, or 8. **Amenities:** Restaurant (international); bar; access to nearby fitness center; concierge; room service; babysitting; laundry/dry cleaning; nonsmoking floor. In room: A/C, TV, minibar, tea/coffeemaker, hair dryer, garment press, safe.

BALLSBRIDGE/EMBASSY ROW AREA

Visitors want to stay here for the same reason Dubliners want to live here: quality of life. It's the most prestigious part of town, known for its embassies, tree-lined streets, and historic buildings. If you're coming to Dublin specifically for a conference at the RDS show grounds or a match at the Lansdowne Rugby Ground, this neighborhood will put you right in the thick of things. The downside is that it's a good 20- to 30-minute walk to get into the city's best sightseeing and shopping areas.

VERY EXPENSIVE

Berkeley Court ⋒   The first Irish member of Leading Hotels of the World, the Berkeley Court (pronounced *Bark*-lay) has a distinguished address near the American Embassy. A favorite haunt of diplomats and international business leaders, the hotel is known for its posh gold-and-blue lobby decorated with fine

Ballsbridge/Embassy Row Area Accommodations

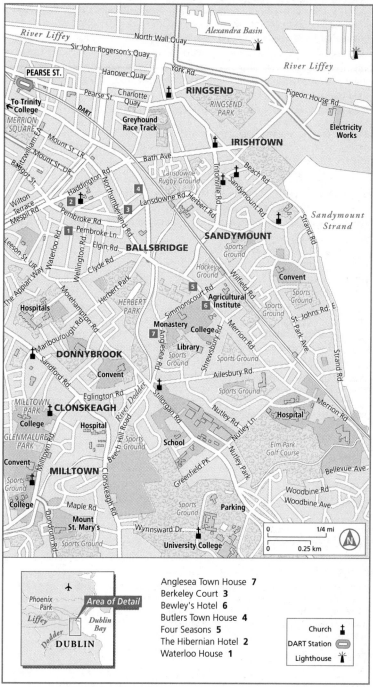

Anglesea Town House 7
Berkeley Court 3
Bewley's Hotel 6
Butlers Town House 4
Four Seasons 5
The Hibernian Hotel 2
Waterloo House 1

Church ✝
DART Station ⊜
Lighthouse ⚓

antiques, original paintings, mirrored columns, and Irish-made carpets and furnishings. The guest rooms aim to convey an air of elegance, but some visitors might find them overly busy and fussy—think patterned wallpaper, patterned bedspreads, and still more patterns on the carpet. Nevertheless, they are decked out in designer fabrics, firm half-canopy beds, dark woods, and bathrooms fitted with marble accoutrements. The well-tended grounds were once part of the Botanic Gardens of University College.

Lansdowne Rd., Ballsbridge, Dublin 4. ℂ **800/44-UTELL** in the U.S., or 01/660-1711. Fax 01/661-7238. www.jurys.com. 188 units. €300–€345 ($267–$307) double. AE, DC, MC, V. Free valet parking. DART: Lansdowne Rd. Bus: 7, 8, or 45. **Amenities:** 2 restaurants (Continental, bistro); bar; lounge; small health club; concierge; salon; room service; laundry service; nonsmoking rooms; foreign-currency exchange. *In room:* TV, radio, dataport, minibar, hair dryer, garment press, safe, voice mail.

Four Seasons 🏵🏵 *Kids* The 2-year-old drop-dead gorgeous Four Seasons hiked up its prices by a whopping 50% after its successful first year—so don't look for any sweet deals here. Still, if money is no object, the Four Seasons blows Dublin's other luxury hotels out of the water in terms of services and leisure facilities. The health club is state-of-the-art, and the spa treatments top-flight (some, like massage, are available in your room). The indoor pool and whirlpool complex overlooks a sunken garden—just one small example of how beauty is worked into the overall design of the hotel. The public rooms and guest rooms share a smart and very plush look, thanks to liberal use of natural elements and fine fabrics. This is an absolutely fabulous place for families. Not only are there complimentary cribs, child-proof bedrooms, and a babysitting service, but there is also a menu of children's activities to keep the kids occupied while you have a romantic meal, grab a massage, or just kick back for some quiet meditation (the better to prepare yourself for the bill).

Simmonscourt Rd., Ballsbridge, Dublin 4. ℂ **800/819-5053** in the U.S., or 01/665-4000. Fax 01/665-4099. www.fourseasons.com. 259 units. €375–€495 ($334–$441) double. AE, DC, MC, V. Valet parking. DART: Sandymount (5-min. walk). Bus: 7, 7A, 7X, 8, or 45. **Amenities:** 2 restaurants (modern Continental, cafe); bar; lobby lounge; indoor pool; whirlpool; health club/spa; children's programs; concierge; room service; babysitting; laundry/dry cleaning; nonsmoking rooms. *In room:* TV/VCR, radio, CD player available, dataport, minibar, hair dryer, safe, voice mail.

EXPENSIVE

The Hibernian Hotel 🏵🏵 This grand, restored Victorian hotel manages to exude both the elegance of a graceful townhouse and the warmth of a fine country inn. The prestigious Small Luxury Hotels of the World named it Hotel of the Year in 1997. Antiques, graceful pillars, and floral arrangements fill the public areas. The guest rooms, of varying size and layout, are individually decorated in keeping with the Victorian period, with quality furnishings, rich fabrics, and specially commissioned paintings of Dublin and wildlife scenes. Unlike some converted 19th-century buildings, it has an elevator.

Eastmoreland Place, Ballsbridge, Dublin 4. ℂ **800/525-4800** in the U.S., or 01/668-7666. Fax 01/660-2655. www.hibernianhotel.com. 40 units. €190–€215 ($169–$191); €241 ($214) suite. No service charge. AE, DC, MC, V. Free valet parking. Bus: 10. **Amenities:** Restaurant (Irish/Continental); bar; access to nearby health club (extra fee); concierge; room service; babysitting; laundry/dry cleaning; nonsmoking floor. *In room:* TV, tea/coffeemaker, hair dryer, garment press.

MODERATE

Anglesea Town House 🏵 Everyone who stays at this 1903 Edwardian-style B&B raves on and on about the same thing: the extraordinary breakfasts served by Helen Kirrane. Start with freshly squeezed orange juice. Then perhaps have a bit of homemade fruit compote or fresh yogurt and baked fruit. Next it's

Helen's wonderful homemade baked cereals or porridge ("homemade" is a big thing with Helen), then tuck into your main meal: Perhaps bacon, eggs, and sausages? Or how about a smoked salmon omelet? And naturally there's always a dessert (the profiteroles are divine) and gallons of brewed coffee. The place is full of old-world comforts—rocking chairs, settees, a sun deck, and lots of flowering plants—and guest rooms are pretty and very comfortable. But it's the breakfasts that you'll remember long after you leave Dublin.

63 Anglesea Rd., Ballsbridge, Dublin 4. ☎ 01/668-3877. Fax 01/668-3461. 7 units. €115 ($102) double. No service charge. Rates include full breakfast. AE, MC, V. DART: Lansdowne Rd. Bus: 10, 46A, 46B, 63, or 84. **Amenities:** Babysitting. *In room:* TV, hair dryer.

Butlers Town House ★★ *Value*   This beautifully restored and expanded Victorian townhouse B&B feels like a gracious family home into which you are lucky enough to be welcomed. The atmosphere is semiformal yet invitingly elegant, class without the starched collar. Rooms are richly furnished with four-poster or half-tester beds, using top-quality fabrics and an eye for blending rich colors. It's hard to elude comfort here—the sheets are of two-fold Egyptian cotton, the shower's water pressure is heavenly, and staff is especially solicitous. The gem here, in our opinion, is the Glendalough Room, with its lovely bay window and small library; it requires early booking. The hotel offers free tea and coffee all day. Breakfast, afternoon tea, and high tea are served in the atrium dining room.

44 Lansdowne Rd., Ballsbridge, Dublin 4. ☎ 800/44-UTELL in the U.S., or 01/667-4022. Fax 01/667-3960. www.butlers-hotel.com. 20 units. €140–€190 ($125–$169) double. Rates include full breakfast. AE, DC, MC, V. Closed Dec 23–Jan 8. DART: Lansdowne Rd. Bus: 7, 7A, 8, or 45. **Amenities:** Breakfast room; room service; babysitting; laundry/dry cleaning. *In room:* A/C, TV, dataport, hair dryer.

Waterloo House ★   Waterloo House (actually not one, but two Georgian townhouses) is one of the most popular B&Bs in Dublin. Perhaps it's because Evelyn Corcoran and her staff take such good care of you, in a friendly but unobtrusive way. The place is charming in an old-world kind of way, with classical music wafting through the lobby, and the elegant, high-ceilinged drawing room looking like a parlor out of an Agatha Christie novel. Guest rooms are comfortable and large (some have two double beds) but it's hard to decide whether the decor, featuring red-patterned carpet and box-pleated bedspreads, is a look that's reassuringly traditional, or merely dated. The varied breakfast menu is a high point. This is a nonsmoking house.

8–10 Waterloo Rd., Ballsbridge, Dublin 4. ☎ 01/660-1888. Fax 01/667-1955. www.waterloohouse.ie. 17 units. €74–€164 ($66–$146) double. Rates include full breakfast. MC, V. Closed Christmas week. Free car parking. DART: Lansdowne Rd. Bus: 5, 7, or 8. **Amenities:** Breakfast room. *In room:* TV, tea/coffeemaker, hair dryer, garment press.

INEXPENSIVE

Bewley's Hotel ★   The new Bewley's Hotel occupies what was once a 19th-century brick Masonic school building adjacent to the RDS show grounds and next to the British Embassy. A new wing harmonizes well with the old structure, and is indistinguishable on the interior. Public lounges and reception areas are spacious and appointed with mahogany wainscoting, marble paneling, and polished bronze. Rooms, too, are spacious and well furnished—each has a writing desk, an armchair, and either one king-size bed or a double and a twin bed. The studios have a bedroom with a double bed, plus an additional room with a foldout couch, a table (seats six), a pull-out kitchenette/bar hidden in a cabinet, and an additional bathroom (shower only). The basement restaurant (O'Connell's) is run by the

Allen family of Ballymaloe fame, and offers very good food at reasonable prices; there's also an informal Bewley's tearoom. The hotel is an excellent value for families and groups; the big downside is its location outside the city center.

Merrion Rd., Ballsbridge, Dublin 4. ℭ 01/668-1111. Fax: 01/668-1999. www.bewleyshotels.com. 220 units. €99 ($88) double. Rates includes service charge and taxes. AE, DC, MC, V. DART: Sandymount (5-min. walk). Bus: 7, 7A, 7X, 8, or 45. **Amenities:** Restaurant (Irish/Continental); tearoom. *In room:* TV, dataport, kitchenette, tea/coffeemaker, hair dryer, garment press, safe.

O'CONNELL STREET AREA/NORTH OF THE LIFFEY

While not generally as chic or salubrious as the South of the Liffey, the Northside is going through a spurt of rejuvenation, most visible through the arrival of the Morrison Hotel, below. The big upside to staying here is that, while it's very central and within walking distance of all the major sights and shops, hotel rates tend to be lower than they are just across the bridge.

VERY EXPENSIVE

The Morrison ★★★   Just when it seemed that everything chic and hip happened south of the Liffey, the Hong Kong–born, Irish designer John Rocha opened the Morrison and suddenly, the central Northside doesn't look so shabby after all. This stunning, contemporary hotel is located a 5-minute walk from O'Connell Street and directly across the river from Temple Bar. Rocha's design uses clean lines and quality, natural elements to evoke a very sensuous, luxurious feeling of space and relaxation. Guest rooms are minimalist but don't feel cold the way minimalism can, undoubtedly because Rocha has used a palette of neutral colors such as cream, chocolate, and black. Halo, the atrium-style main restaurant, is one of the most talked-about, exciting eateries in town. The upshot: The Morrison is every bit as stylish as the Clarence (Temple Bar) and the Fitzwilliam (St. Stephen's Green), with the sky-high rates to prove it.

Lower Ormond Quay, Dublin 1. ℭ **01/887-2400.** Fax 01/878-3185. www.morrisonhotel.ie. 93 units. €270–€445 ($240–$396) double. AE, DC, MC, V. DART: Connolly. Bus: 70 or 80. **Amenities:** 2 restaurants (fusion, Asian); 2 bars; concierge; room service; babysitting; dry cleaning; video/CD library. *In room:* A/C, CD player, dataport, minibar, hair dryer, safe, voice mail.

MODERATE

Royal Dublin Hotel ★   Romantically floodlit at night, this five-story hotel is near Parnell Square at the north end of Dublin's main thoroughfare, within walking distance of all the main theaters and Northside attractions. The contemporary skylit lobby lies adjacent to lounge areas that were part of the original 1752 building. These Georgian-style rooms are elegant, with high molded ceilings, ornate cornices, crystal chandeliers, gilt-edged mirrors, and open fireplaces. Guest rooms are contemporary, featuring light woods, bold, checked bedspreads, and bay windows that extend over the busy street below. *Warning:* The price for a double room doubles in the summer to an outrageous €350 ($312), so save this for off-season trips.

40 Upper O'Connell St., Dublin 1. ℭ **800/528-1234** in the U.S., or 01/873-3666. Fax 01/873-3120. www. royaldublin.com. 120 units. €175–€350 ($156–$312) double. Rates include full Irish breakfast, service charge, and VAT. AE, DC, MC, V. Free parking. DART: Connolly. Bus: 36A, 40A, 40B, 40C, or 51A. **Amenities:** Restaurant (brasserie); bar; lounge; concierge; car-rental desk; room service; babysitting; laundry; foreign-currency exchange. *In room:* TV, radio, tea/coffeemaker, hair dryer.

INEXPENSIVE

Jurys Inn Custom House ★★ (Value   Ensconced in the grandiose new financial services district and facing the quays, this Jurys Inn follows the successful formula of affordable comfort without frills. Single rooms have a double bed and a pullout sofa, while double rooms offer both a double and a twin bed. Twenty-two especially spacious rooms, if available, cost nothing extra. Rooms facing the quays also enjoy vistas of the Dublin hills, but those facing the financial district are quieter. As occupancy runs at 100% from May to September and at roughly 95% for the rest of the year, be sure to book well in advance.

Custom House Quay, Dublin 1. © **800/44-UTELL** in the U.S., or 01/607-5000. Fax 01/829-0400. www. jurys.com. 239 units. €96 ($85) double. Rates include service charge. Full Irish breakfast €8 ($7.10). AE, DC, MC, V. Discounted parking available at adjacent lot. DART: Tara Street. Bus: 27A, 27B, or 53A. **Amenities:** Restaurant (Continental); bar; laundry/dry cleaning; nonsmoking rooms. *In room:* TV, dataport, tea/ coffeemaker, hair dryer.

4 Where to Dine

You're here. You're famished. Where do you go? A formal, old-world hotel dining room? Perhaps a casual bistro or wine bar? Ethnic cuisine, maybe? Dublin has the goods, across a wide range of price categories. Expect generally higher prices than you'd pay for comparable fare in a comparable U.S. city. (Hey, Dublin's hip—you always pay for hip.) As befits a European capital, there's plenty of Continental cuisine, with a particular leaning toward French and Italian influences. But there's also a lot of exciting fusion cooking going on here these days, and chefs make excellent use of the wondrous Irish produce available at their doorsteps.

HISTORIC OLD CITY/LIBERTIES AREA
MODERATE

Lord Edward ⚐ SEAFOOD   Established in 1890 and situated in the heart of the Old City opposite Christ Church Cathedral, this cozy upstairs dining room claims to be Dublin's oldest seafood restaurant. A dozen preparations of sole, including au gratin and Veronique, are served; there are many variations of prawns, from thermidor to Provençal; and fresh lobster is prepared au naturel or in sauces. Fresh fish—from salmon and sea trout to plaice and turbot—is served grilled, fried, meunière, or poached. Vegetarian dishes are also available. At lunch, light snacks and simpler fare are served in the bar.

23 Christ Church Place, Dublin 8. © **01/454-2420.** Reservations required. Main courses €13–€19 ($12–$17); fixed-price dinner €25 ($22). AE, DC, MC, V. Mon–Fri noon–10:45pm; Sat 6–10:45pm. Closed Dec 24–Jan 3. Bus: 50, 54A, 56A, 65, 65A, 77, 77A, 123, or 150.

INEXPENSIVE

Govinda's VEGETARIAN   The motto here is healthy square meals on square plates for very good prices. The meals are generous, belly-warming concoctions of vegetables, cheese, rice, and pasta. Every day, two main courses are offered cafeteria-style. One is always East Indian, and the other a simple, plainly-flavored staple such as lasagna or macaroni and cheese. Veggie burgers are also prepared to order. All are accompanied by a choice of two salads and can be enjoyed unaccompanied by smoke—the restaurant is nonsmoking throughout. Desserts are healthy and huge, like a rich wedge of carob cake with a dollop of cream or homemade ice cream.

4 Aungier St., Dublin 2. © **01/475-0309.** Main courses €6.25 ($5.55); soup and freshly baked bread €2.25 ($2). MC, V. Mon–Sat noon–9pm. Closed Dec 24–Jan 2. Bus: 16, 16A, 19, or 22.

Leo Burdock's ⚐ FISH AND CHIPS   Every visitor should go to a Dublin takeout "chipper" at least once, and you might as well do it at the best in town. Established in 1913 across from Christchurch, this quintessential Irish takeout shop remains a cherished Dublin institution, despite a devastating fire in 1998.

Dublin Dining

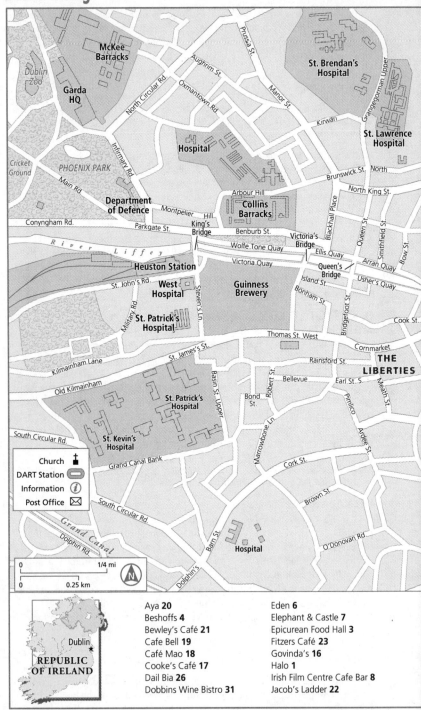

Aya **20**
Beshoffs **4**
Bewley's Café **21**
Cafe Bell **19**
Café Mao **18**
Cooke's Café **17**
Dail Bia **26**
Dobbins Wine Bistro **31**

Eden **6**
Elephant & Castle **7**
Epicurean Food Hall **3**
Fitzers Café **23**
Govinda's **16**
Halo **1**
Irish Film Centre Cafe Bar **8**
Jacob's Ladder **22**

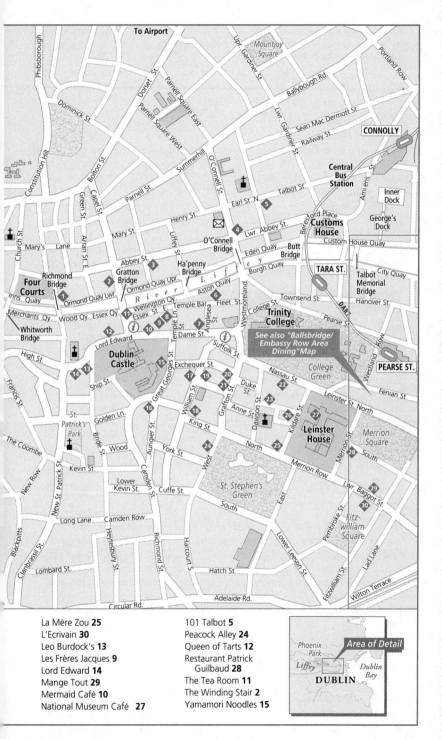

See also "Ballsbridge/Embassy Row Area Dining" Map

La Mère Zou **25**
L'Ecrivain **30**
Leo Burdock's **13**
Les Frères Jacques **9**
Lord Edward **14**
Mange Tout **29**
Mermaid Café **10**
National Museum Café **27**

101 Talbot **5**
Peacock Alley **24**
Queen of Tarts **12**
Restaurant Patrick Guilbaud **28**
The Tea Room **11**
The Winding Stair **2**
Yamamori Noodles **15**

Rebuilt from the ground up, Burdock's is back. Cabinet ministers, university students, and businesspeople alike can be found in the queue. They're waiting for fish bought fresh that morning and those good Irish potatoes, both cooked in "drippings" (none of that modern cooking oil!). There's no seating, but you can sit on a nearby bench or stroll down to the park at St. Patrick's Cathedral.

2 Werburgh St., Dublin 8. © **01/454-0306.** Main courses €3.25–€6 ($2.90–$5.35). No credit cards. Mon–Sat noon–midnight; Sun 4pm–midnight. Bus: 21A, 50, 50A, 78, 78A, or 78B.

Queen of Tarts ★★ TEA SHOP This tiny tearoom is David to the Goliath of Irish tearooms (Bewley's, see below). It's earned a reputation for the best cheap, home-cooked meals in town. Start with a gourmet sandwich, Greek salad, or savory tart of ham and spinach or cheddar cheese and chives. Then follow it up with the flaky sweetness of warm almond cranberry or blackberry pie. The scones here are tender and light, dusted with powdered sugar and accompanied by a little pot of fruit jam. The restaurant is small, smoke-free, and full of delicious aromas.

4 Corkhill, Dublin 2. © **01/670-7499.** Soup and fresh bread €3 ($2.65), sandwiches and savory tarts €4–€5 ($3.55–$4.45), baked goods and cakes €.65–€3.85 (60¢–$3.45). No credit cards. Mon–Fri 7:30am–7pm; Sat 9am–6pm; Sun 10am–6pm. Bus: Any city-center bus.

TEMPLE BAR/TRINITY COLLEGE AREA
EXPENSIVE

Jacob's Ladder ★★★ (Value) MODERN IRISH When a talented, confident chef knows what to do with the exceptional quality of Irish produce, the results can be superb. Inspired cooking by chef-owner Adrian Roche and a stylish dining room with great views over Trinity College make this one of the most consistently packed places in town. Roche's forte is taking old Irish stalwarts and updating them into sublime signature dishes. His Dublin Coddle is a soupy seafood stew of onions, potatoes, mussels, clams, Dublin bay prawns, salmon, carrots, and turnips. He serves his excellent braised wood pigeon with colcannon—an old Irish favorite of potatoes and cabbage mashed together with plenty of butter—that is fluffier and more refined here than perhaps anywhere else on the island. Service is terrific and you get great value for your money.

4–5 Nassau St., Dublin 2. © **01/670-3865.** Reservations required. Main courses €17–€24 ($15–$21); Early bird menu 6–7pm €18 ($16); fixed-price dinner €32 ($28). AE, DC, MC, V. Mon–Fri 12:30–2:30pm; Mon–Thurs 7:15–10:30pm; Fri–Sat 7:15–11pm. Closed Dec 24–Jan 4. DART: Pearse. Bus: 7, 8, 10, 11, or 46A.

Les Frères Jacques ★★ FRENCH/SEAFOOD The business crowd loves this friendly, upmarket French restaurant, which brings a touch of haute cuisine to the lower edge of the trendy Temple Bar district. The dining room evokes old Paris, with its dark green and cream backdrop. The menu offers such entrees as Daube of beef with root vegetables, rabbit lasagna with Madeira sauce, and rosette of spring lamb in meat juice sabayon and tomato coulis with crispy potato straws. Chef Darragh Kavanagh is particularly talented with seafood and shellfish dishes, such as grilled black sole with lemon and parsley butter and grilled lobster flamed in whiskey.

74 Dame St., Dublin 2. © **01/679-4555.** Reservations recommended. Main courses avg. €23 ($20). AE, DC, MC, V. Mon–Fri 12:30–2:30pm; Mon–Thurs 7:15–10:30pm; Fri–Sat 7:15–11pm. Closed Dec 24–Jan 4. Bus: 50, 50A, 54, 56, or 77.

The Tea Room ★★★ INTERNATIONAL This ultrasmart restaurant, ensconced in the very hip Clarence hotel, is virtually guaranteed to deliver one of your best meals in Ireland. This gorgeous dining room's soaring yet understated lines are the perfect backdrop for Antony Ely's complex but controlled cooking. A classic such as beef filet with red wine jus is downright zingy when served with arugula on a Dijon-infused potato-and-onion mash. Likewise, the saucisson of salmon becomes up-to-date and elegant astride teeny risoni pasta and chive dressing. Desserts, such as the caramelized peach with rice pudding pie, are heaven-sent.

In the Clarence, 6/8 Wellington Quay, Dublin 2. ✆ **01/670-9000.** Reservations required. Main courses €17–€24 ($15–$21). AE, MC, V. Mon–Fri 12:30–2:00pm; Mon–Sun 6:30–9:45pm. Bus: 51B, 51C, 68, 69, or 79.

MODERATE

Eden ✿✿ INTERNATIONAL/MEDITERRANEAN This is one of Temple Bar's hippest eateries, a cool minimalist dining room with an open-plan kitchen and a vista overlooking Meeting House Square. Eleanor Walsh is one of Ireland's most exciting young chefs, and here she offers a delicious menu of well-thought-out food at reasonable prices. Her food is influenced by the global village but she has a special penchant for Mediterranean flavors—her fresh hake comes served with black olives, sun-dried tomatoes, arugula (called rocket in Ireland), and pesto. On a cold day, opt for an updated Irish favorite such as a paper-thin smoked loin of pork (called kassler here) laid over an apple mash with port-infused gravy. Desserts are worth saving room for. The fixed-price lunch is a particularly good value.

Meeting House Sq. (entrance on Sycamore St.), Dublin 2. ✆ **01/670-5372.** Main courses €15–€22 ($13–$20). Fixed-price lunch menu €18 ($16). AE, DC, MC, V. Daily 12:30–3pm, 6–10:30pm. Bus: 51B, 51C, 68, 69, or 79.

Elephant & Castle ✿✿ AMERICAN You'd be forgiven for thinking you could find this kind of food—burgers, chicken wings, omelets—at any old Yankee-style joint, but give it a chance and you won't be disappointed: Liz Mee does these stalwarts better than just about any cook in town. Her chicken wings are the best in Dublin, her burgers are out of this world, and her omelets are "spot on," as the Irish would say. It's a buzzing, immensely popular place for breakfast, brunch, lunch, afternoon nibble, dinner, or late dinner.

18 Temple Bar, Dublin 2. ✆ **01/679-3121.** Main courses €8–€23 ($7.10–$20). AE, MC, V. Mon–Sat 8am–11:30pm; Sun noon–11:30pm. Bus: 51B, 51C, 68, 69, or 79.

Mermaid Café ✿✿✿ INTERNATIONAL The Mermaid Café—known to locals as simply the Mermaid—has attained cult status in Dublin. Like a certain mild-mannered reporter for the *Daily Planet,* this could be something very ordinary. But it's not. Ben Gorman's cooking is consistently remarkable—think classic cooking with a fresh, eclectic twist. The combination of ingredients and the blending of spices are, on paper, boldly inventive, yet the resulting dishes are subtle and harmonious. As a starter, the beet, quail egg, and baby spinach salad offers a good launch without threatening your appetite, though the paprika smoked chicken with avocado and cilantro (especially when combined with the dangerously appealing assortment of freshly baked breads) may leave you with the will but not the way for the generous entrees soon to emerge from the kitchen. The New England crab cakes, grilled swordfish with mango relish, roast duck breast on curried noodles, and chargrilled monkfish are all flawlessly prepared and quite memorable. On top of all that, the wine list is one of the best in Ireland and the desserts—especially the pecan pie—are divine.

70 Dame St., Dublin 2. ✆ **01/670-8236.** Reservations required. Dinner main courses €15–€25 ($13–$22). Sun brunch €8–€11 ($7.10–$9.80). MC, V. Mon–Sat 12:30–2:30pm and 6–10:30pm; Sun brunch 12:30–3:30pm and dinner 6–9pm. Bus: 50, 50A, 54, 56A, 77, 77A, or 77B.

Yamamori Noodles ★★ JAPANESE   If you're still skeptical about Japanese cuisine, Yamamori will make you an instant believer. In a pop, casual, and exuberant atmosphere, you may just be startled by how good the food is here. The splendid menu is a who's who of Japanese cuisine, and the prices range from budget to splurge. Regardless of the bottom line, however, everyone goes away feeling full and feted. On a raw, drizzly Dublin day, the chile chicken ramen is a pot of bliss, while the Yamamori Yaki Soba offers, in a mound of wok-fried noodles, a well-rewarded treasure hunt for prawns, squid, chicken, and roast pork. Vegetarians aren't overlooked and the selective international wine list is well priced and well chosen. The lunch specials are outstanding. Even at 9:30pm on a Monday night, this place is jammed, not by tourists but by local Dubs, which tells you how good the food is.

71–2 S. Great George's St., Dublin 2. ☏ 01/475-5001. Reservations only for parties of 4 or more persons. Main courses €9–€13 ($8–$12). MC, V. Sun–Wed 12:30–11pm; Thurs–Sat 12:30–11:30pm. Bus: 50, 50A, 54, 56, or 77.

INEXPENSIVE

Irish Film Centre Cafe Bar ★ IRISH/INTERNATIONAL   One of the most popular drinking spots in Temple Bar, the hip Cafe Bar (in the lobby of the city's coolest place to grab a movie) features an excellent, affordable menu that changes daily. A vegetarian and Middle Eastern menu is available for both lunch and dinner. The weekend entertainment usually includes music or comedy.

6 Eustace St., Temple Bar, Dublin 2. ☏ 01/677-8788. Lunch and dinner €6–€10 ($5.35–$8.90). MC, V. Mon–Fri 12:30–3pm; Sat–Sun 1–3pm; daily 6–9pm. Bus: 21A, 78A, or 78B.

ST. STEPHEN'S GREEN/GRAFTON STREET AREA
VERY EXPENSIVE

Peacock Alley ★★ MODERN EUROPEAN   Whether you think him an *enfant terrible* or a genius (or both), there is no doubt about young Conrad Gallagher's immense talent and daring. After training with the top kitchens in Paris and London, he returned to Dublin to become Ireland's most outrageous celebrity chef, so nobody is surprised that the Alley is the most talked-about, lauded restaurant in Dublin. Housed in Terence Conran's supercool Fitzwilliam Hotel, the dining room exudes Conran's sleek, elegant style, while the food is equally stylish and extremely memorable—an ever-changing symphony of complex tastes and textures that earned him stars from the folks at Michelin. The one rain cloud over this parade is the fear that Gallagher could become a victim of his own success, which he is busy parlaying into a string of other restaurant ventures and a cooking school. If distractions take him out of the Alley kitchen on a regular basis, the food will most certainly become less spectacular. But at least for now, go, indulge, and enjoy.

In the Fitzwilliam Hotel, 109 St. Stephen's Green, Dublin 2. ☏ 01/478-7015. Reservations required. Lunch avg. €30 ($27), dinner avg. €70 ($62). AE, DC, MC, V. Mon–Sat 12:30–2:30pm and 6:30–10:30pm. AE, DC, MC, V. DART: Pearse. Bus: 10, 11A, 11B, 13, or 20B.

EXPENSIVE/MODERATE

Aya @ Brown Thomas ★★★ JAPANESE   This buzzy, fashionable new annex to Dublin's poshest department store (actually, it's just across the street on Clarendon St.) took off like a skyrocket and is very much the good-time destination of the moment. Yes, the conveyor belt sushi bar has finally arrived, and Dubliners may never be the same. The good news is that, beyond the trendiness, the food here is damn good. Lunch offers all the classics—tempura, gyosa, toritatsuta, and, of course, plenty of sushi—while the dinner menu expands to include yakitori, steaks, and noodle salads. Come for dinner Sunday through Tuesday for the Sushi55 special: all you can eat, including one complimentary drink, for €24 ($21).

49–52 Clarendon St., Dublin 2. ℭ **01/677-1544.** Reservations recommended for dinner. Lunch avg. €11 ($9.80), dinner avg. €32 ($28). AE, DC, MC, V. Mon–Sat 10:30am–11pm; Sun noon–10pm. DART: Tara St. Bus: 16A, 19A, 22A, 55, or 83.

Cooke's Café 🦝🦝 MODERN CLASSIC   Named for owner and chef Johnny Cooke, this shop-front restaurant is a longtime Dublin favorite. The food is all about classic dishes executed with just the right amount of originality. Specialties include a fabulous black bean soup; grilled duck with pancetta, Marsala balsamic sauce, and wilted endive; sautéed brill and Dover sole with capers and croutons; and baked grouper with a ragout of mussels, clams, artichokes, and tomatoes. The open kitchen and murals dominate the cafe, and on weekend evenings, they open the upstairs Rhino Room, where there's a terrific New York–grill atmosphere. In fine weather, you can sit outside on the terrace.

14 S. William St., Dublin 2. ℭ **01/679-0536.** Reservations required. Fixed-price lunch menu €19 ($17); early-bird menu (6–7pm) €19 ($17); dinner main courses €19–€28 ($17–$25). AE, DC, MC, V. Daily 12:30–3pm; Mon–Sat 6–11pm; Sun 6–10pm. DART: Tara St. Bus: 16A, 19A, 22A, 55, or 83.

La Mère Zou 🦝 FRENCH   Imagine a country house in Provence where you could get superb Gallic cooking *en famille.* Chef-proprietor Eric Tydgadt has created a warm, comfortable Mediterranean ambience in which to savor his fresh French country specialties. The emphasis is on perfectly cooked food accompanied by persuasive but "unarmed" sauces served in an unpretentious manner. Mussels are a house specialty, with an array of poultry, seafood, lamb, and game offerings. The quality of ingredients and attention to enhancing the flavor of all dishes is consistent from appetizers to dessert. The excellent wine list favors the French, but also includes several €13 ($12) house wines.

22 St. Steven's Green, Dublin 2. ℭ **01/661-6669.** Reservations recommended. Fixed-price lunch €15 ($13); early-bird dinner menu €19 ($17); dinner main courses €14–€23 ($12–$20). AE, DC, MC, V. Mon–Fri 12:30–2:30pm; Mon–Thurs 6–10:30pm; Fri–Sat 6–11pm; Sun 6–9:30pm. DART: Pearse. Bus: 10, 11A, 11B, 13, or 20B.

MODERATE

Café Mao 🦝🦝🦝 ASIAN   Dubliners have beaten a path to this place since it opened a few years back, and it's already become something of an icon. This is where to go when you feel like Asian cooking laced with a fun and exhilarating attitude. An exposed kitchen lines an entire wall, and the rest of the space is wide open—fantastic for people-watching on weekends. The menu reads like a "best of Asia": Thai fish cakes, nasi goreng, chicken hoi sin, salmon ramen. Everything is well prepared and delicious, so you can't go wrong.

2 Chatham Row, Dublin 2. ℭ **01/670-4899.** Reservations recommended. Main courses €10–€15 ($8.90–$13). AE, MC, V. Mon–Thurs noon–11pm; Fri–Sat noon–11:30pm; Sun noon–10pm. DART: Pearse. Bus: 10, 11A, 11B, 13, or 20B.

Fitzers Café 🦝 INTERNATIONAL   This is one branch of a chain of winning cafes that serve up excellent, up-to-date, and reasonably priced food. Nestled on a street known for its bookshops, this bright, airy Irish-style bistro has a multi-windowed facade and modern decor. Choices range from chicken breast with hot chile cream sauce or brochette of lamb tandoori with mild curry sauce to gratin of smoked cod. There are also tempting vegetarian dishes made from organic produce. Fitzers has two other Dublin locations: just a few blocks away at the National Gallery, Merrion Square West (ℭ **01/661-4496**) and at Temple

Tips Picnic, Anyone?

The parks of Dublin offer plenty of sylvan settings for a picnic lunch; so feel free to park it on a bench, or pick a grassy patch and spread a blanket. In particular, try **St. Stephen's Green** at lunchtime (in the summer there are open-air band concerts), the **Phoenix Park,** and **Merrion Square.** You can also take a ride on the DART to the suburbs of **Dun Laoghaire, Dalkey, Killiney,** and **Bray** (to the south) or **Howth** (to the north) and picnic along a bay-front pier or promenade.

In recent years, some fine delicatessens and gourmet food shops—ideal for picnic fare—have sprung up. For the best selection of fixings, try any of the following: **Gruel,** 69 Dame St., Dublin 2 (© **01/670-8236),** has a cult following for its hot roasted gourmet sandwiches that change daily. **Gallic Kitchen,** 49 Francis St., Dublin 8 (© **01/454-4912),** has gourmet prepared food to go, from salmon en croûte to pastries filled with meats or vegetables, patés, quiches, sausage rolls, and homemade pies, breads, and cakes. **Magills Delicatessen,** 14 Clarendon St., Dublin 2 (© **01/671-3830),** offers Asian and Continental delicacies, meats, cheeses, spices, and salads. For a fine selection of Irish cheeses, luncheon meat, and other delicacies, seek out **Sheridan's Cheesemongers,** 11 S. Anne St., Dublin 2 (© **01/679-3143),** perhaps the best of Dublin's cheese emporiums, or the **Big Cheese Company,** 14/15 Trinity St. (© **01/671-1399).**

Bar Square (© **01/679-0440).** As with all chains, consistency is the operative word—the same menu, the same decor theme, and the same good service at each location.

51 Dawson St., Dublin 2. © **01/677-1155.** Dinner main courses €13–€20 ($12–$18). AE, DC, MC, V. Daily 12:30–11pm. Closed Dec 24–27 and Good Friday. DART: Pearse. Bus: 10, 11A, 11B, 13, or 20B.

INEXPENSIVE

Bewley's Café *(Overrated* TRADITIONAL CAFE/TEAROOM Bewley's, a three-story landmark on Grafton Street, has been around forever (more specifically, since 1840) and is so ingrained in the Irish identity that you have to wonder whether people go out of habit rather than desire. Not that the place isn't busy. It's always bustling with the clink of teapots and hum of customers, but the atmosphere is somehow listless rather than buzzy. The interior is a traditional, mellow, mix of dark wood, amber glass, and deep red velvet banquettes—a look that would be deemed welcoming if the food was great. Unfortunately, the scones, pies, and cakes are surprisingly mediocre, and the sandwiches, pasta dishes, sausages, chips, and casseroles are no better.

Most Bewley's establishments are self-service cafeterias, but Bewley's of Grafton Street also has several full-service tearooms. Go once, because Bewley's is a quintessential hit of real Dublin, and the people-watching is good. But go only once, and stick to coffee and tea.

78/79 Grafton St., Dublin 2. © **01/677-6761.** Homemade soup €3 ($2.65); main courses €3.85–€9 ($3.45–$8); lunch specials from €6.50 ($5.80). Dinner main courses from €15 ($13). AE, DC, MC, V. Sun–Thurs 7:30am–11pm; Fri–Sat 7:30am–1am (continuous service for breakfast, hot food, and snacks). Bus: Any city-center bus.

America Online Keyword: Travel
Booked seat 6A, open return.
Rented red 4-wheel drive.
Reserved cabin, no running water.
Discovered space.

Book your air, hotel, and transportation all in one place.

Hotel or hostel? Cruise or canoe? Car? Plane? Camel? Wherever you're going, visit Yahoo! Travel and get total control over your arrangements. Even choose your seat assignment. So. One hump or two? travel.yahoo.com

YAHOO!
Travel

Cafe Bell ⚑ *(Value* IRISH/SELF-SERVICE   In the cobbled courtyard of early-19th-century St. Teresa's Church, this serene little place is one of a handful of dining options springing up in historic or ecclesiastical surroundings. With high ceilings and an old-world decor, Cafe Bell is a welcome contrast to the bustle of Grafton Street a block away and Powerscourt Town House Centre across the street. The menu changes daily but usually includes very good homemade soups, sandwiches, salads, quiches, lasagna, sausage rolls, hot scones, and other baked goods.

St. Teresa's Courtyard, Clarendon St., Dublin 2. ℂ **01/677-7645.** All items €2.50–€6.35 ($2.25–$5.65). No credit cards. Mon–Sat 9am–5:30pm. Bus: 16, 16A, 19, 19A, 22A, 55, or 83.

FITZWILLIAM SQUARE/MERRION SQUARE AREA
VERY EXPENSIVE

Restaurant Patrick Guilbaud ⚑⚑⚑ FRENCH   Ireland's most award-winning restaurant (including two Michelin stars) is ensconced in elegant quarters at the Merrion Hotel. The menu features such dishes as roasted West Cork turbot, honey-roasted quail, wild sea bass with ragout of mussels, and pan-fried fois gras with marinated red cabbage in a raspberry vinaigrette. If you're undecided, order the scrumptious ravioli of lobster with coconut cream, and finish with the *assiette gourmande au chocolat* (five small hot and cold chocolate desserts).

In the Merrion Hotel, 21 Upper Merrion St., Dublin 2. ℂ **01/676-4192.** Reservations required. Fixed-price lunch €25 ($22); main courses from €36 ($32). AE, DC, MC, V. Tues–Sat 12:30–2pm and 7:30–10:15pm. DART: Westland Row. Bus: 10, 11A, 11B, 13, or 20B.

EXPENSIVE

L'Ecrivain ⚑⚑⚑ FRENCH   This is one of Dublin's truly exceptional restaurants, from start to finish. The atmosphere is relaxed, welcoming, and unpretentious, and chef Derry Clarke's food is extraordinary. You can dine on the garden terrace, weather permitting, or in the newly renovated dining rooms. Each course seems to receive the same devoted attention, and most consist of traditional "best of Irish" ingredients, prepared without dense sauces. The seared sea trout with sweet potato purée and the entrecôte with caramelized onion are perfectly prepared and elegantly presented. The desserts are creations of a talented pastry chef. The crème brûlée here may be the best outside of France.

109 Lower Baggot St., Dublin 2. ℂ **01/661-1919.** Reservations required Fixed-price 3-course lunch €22 ($20). Fixed-price 4-course dinner €42 ($37). Main courses €23–€28 ($20–$25). AE, DC, MC, V. Mon–Fri 12:30–2pm; Mon–Thurs 6:30–10:30pm; Fri–Sat 7–11pm. Bus: 10.

Mange Tout ⚑⚑ MODERN EUROPEAN   At the junction of Baggot Street and Fitzwilliam Place, in the basement of a fine Georgian building, hides this intimate little restaurant. Humble as it appears, this is one of Dublin's best, run by the very gifted chef-owner Brian Beattie. The menu can seem a shopping list of unlikely ingredients, but these are dishes that work. Grilled chicken that comes astride sautéed beans and pine nuts. Scallops that blend marvelously with marinated cucumber, crème fraîche, and chile oil. And who would have thought crabmeat could be so delicious with beet? Service is very good and you get what you pay for.

112 Lower Baggot St., Dublin 2. ℂ **01/676-7866.** Reservations recommended. Main courses €15–€23 ($13–$20). AE, MC, V. Tues–Fri 12:30–2:15pm; Tues–Sat 7–11pm. Bus: 10.

MODERATE

Dobbins Wine Bistro ⚑⚑ BISTRO   Almost hidden in a lane between Upper and Lower Mount Streets, this hip, friendly bistro is a haven for inventive Continental cuisine. The menu changes often, but usually includes such items as duckling with orange and port sauce; steamed *paupiette* of black sole with salmon, crab, and prawn filling; panfried veal kidneys in pastry; and filet of beef topped with crispy herb bread crumbs with shallot and Madeira sauce. You'll have a choice of sitting in the bistro, with checkered tablecloths and sawdust on the floor, or on the atrium patio.

15 Stephen's Lane (off Upper Mount St.), Dublin 2. ℂ **01/676-4670.** Reservations recommended. Dinner main courses €14–€23 ($12–$20). AE, DC, MC, V. Mon–Fri 12:30–2:30pm; Tues–Sat 7:30–10:30pm. DART: Pearse. Bus: 5, 7A, 8, 46, or 84.

INEXPENSIVE

Dail Bia ★★ Ⓥ𝘢𝘭𝘶𝘦 MODERN IRISH   The name is Irish for "Food Parliament," a wink at its proximity to the Irish Parliament headquarters down the road. It's also home to one of the greatest cheap lunches in town, so work it into your itinerary when you visit the nearby National Museum or National Gallery. Sinead Flanagan cooks up Irish traditional dishes with a twist—nothing hokey, just down-to-earth, honest comfort food in an uncluttered, minimalist chic setting. Start with one of the fresh, homemade soups, then dive into the cockles and mussels or the beef-and-Guinness pie. Everything is delicious, and everything comes at rock-bottom prices.

46 Kildare St., Dublin 2. ℂ **01/670-6079.** Main courses €6–€10 ($5.35–$8.90). MC, V. Mon–Fri 8am–7pm; Sat 9am–5pm. Bus: 7, 7A, 8, 10, 11, or 13.

National Museum Café ★ CAFETERIA   This is a great place to step out of the rain, warm yourself, and then wander among the nation's treasures. The cafe is informal but has a certain elegance, thanks to an elaborate mosaic floor, enameled fireplace, marble tabletops, chandelier, and tall windows that look across a cobbled yard toward the National Library. Everything is made fresh: beef salad, chicken salad, quiche, an abundance of pastries. The soup of the day is often vegetarian, and quite good. Admission to the museum is free, so you can visit at your own pace, as often as your curiosity (or appetite) demands.

National Museum of Ireland, Kildare St., Dublin 2. ℂ **01/662-1269.** Soup €2.50 ($2.25), lunch main courses under €8 ($7.10). MC, V. Tues–Sat 10am–5pm; Sun 2–5pm. Bus: 7, 7A, 8, 10, 11, or 13.

BALLSBRIDGE/EMBASSY ROW AREA
VERY EXPENSIVE

Le Coq Hardi ★★★ FRENCH   In a society obsessed with discovering the next big thing, this 20-year-old plush, gentlemen's club–style restaurant continues to rank at the top of its class. Award-winning chef John Howard is a maestro with the classics, such as quail with foie gras, spring lamb with *pommes boulangères*, king scallops served with bacon, *darne* (steak) of Irish wild salmon on fresh spinach leaves, and filet of prime beef flamed in Irish whiskey. The 700-bin wine cellar is the best in Dublin, boasting a complete collection of Château Mouton Rothschild, dating from 1945 to the present.

35 Pembroke Rd., Ballsbridge, Dublin 4. ℂ **01/668-9070.** Reservations required. Lunch avg. €40 ($36); dinner avg. €58 ($52). AE, MC, V. Mon–Fri 12:30–2:30pm; Mon–Sat 7–10:45pm. DART: Lansdowne Rd. Bus: 18, 46, 63, or 84.

MODERATE

Dish ★★ INTERNATIONAL   Maybe it should call itself New Dish. After being a popular Temple Bar eatery for years, Dish moved last year to these Ballsbridge digs and instantly became a huge hit, all over again. The chic, contemporary surroundings work well with the ambitious, eclectic cooking that awaits you. Chef Gerard Foote believes in organic, fresh ingredients and is a master at combining unlikely flavors and coming up with tantalizing results. The griddled scallops with mousseline potatoes and garlic butter is perfect, as is the grilled

Ballsbridge/Embassy Row Area Dining

Dish **1**
La Finezza **4**
Le Coq Hardi **2**
Roly's Bistro **3**

Church †
DART Station ⬭
Lighthouse ☀

salmon with avocado, papaya and tequila-lime dressing. The desserts—including a meltaway vanilla panna cotta and amaretti chocolate cheesecake—are nothing short of sensational.

146 Upper Leeson St., Dublin 4. ℂ 01/671-1249. Reservations recommended. Fixed-price lunch €15 ($13); dinner main courses €10–€23 ($8.90–$20). AE, DC, MC, V. Daily 12:30–11:30pm. DART: Tara St. Bus: 21A, 46A, 46B, 51B, 51C, 68, 69, or 86.

La Finezza ⭐ ITALIAN/MEDITERRANEAN Since its opening a few years back, La Finezza has garnered a number of awards, including restaurant of the year. Its candlelit mirrored-gallery decor is quite tasteful. The menu is imaginative and ambitious—perhaps overly so for a purist's palate. Panfried lamb cutlets and fresh pepper and black-bean mousse are simply exquisite. The presentation is delightful, and the service superb.

Over Kiely's, Donnybrook Rd. (N11), Donnybrook, Dublin 4. ℂ 01/283-7166. Reservations recommended. Early-bird menu (5:30–7pm) €17 ($15). Main courses €12–€24 ($11–$21). AE, MC, V. Mon–Sat 5–11pm; Sun 4–9:30pm. Bus: 10, 46A, or 46B.

Roly's Bistro ⭐⭐ IRISH/INTERNATIONAL Opened in 1992, this two-story shop-front restaurant quickly became an institution. The recent departure of Roly Saul, who pioneered the venture, spurred former head chef Colin O'Daly to step up as owner. Even with the changes, the Roly's magic is still palpable. The new head chef, Paul Cartwright, cooks the same kind of excellent, tummy-warming food you never get tired of: confit of duck with garlic mash, roasted venison, chicken-and-bean sprout spring roll, panfried Dublin Bay prawns, game pie with chestnuts, wild mushroom risotto. The main dining room, with a bright and airy decor and lots of windows, can be noisy when the house is full, but the nonsmoking section has a quiet enclave of booths laid out in an Orient Express style for those who prefer a quiet tête-à-tête. An excellent array of international wines is offered, starting at €14 ($12) a bottle.

7 Ballsbridge Terrace, Dublin 4. ℂ 01/668-2611. Reservations required. Main courses €15–€19 ($13–$17). Set-price lunch €17 ($15). AE, DC, MC, V. Daily noon–3pm and 6–10pm. DART to Lansdowne Rd. Station. Bus: 5, 6, 7, 8, 18, or 45.

O'CONNELL STREET AREA/NORTH OF THE LIFFEY
EXPENSIVE

Halo ⭐⭐ FRENCH/FUSION This is easily the hippest, hottest, coolest, most stylish place to eat in Dublin—so book your table before you leave home. The pity is that it's the kind of self-conscious, cigar-smoking hipness that is so annoying—especially when chef Jean-Michel Poulot's cooking is fabulous enough to warrant a ban on such crassness. The food is all about French fusion—snazzy, mind-blowing combinations of taste and texture that manage to be elegant instead of just far-flung. Consider the curried king scallops with lime potato, fennel, mizuna, and ginger vinaigrette. Or the baked goat's cheese wrapped in Parma ham with mizuna salad. Eating at Halo is an intense experience for all of your senses, and one that should be savored.

Morrison Hotel, Ormond Quay, Dublin 1. ℂ 01/878-2999. Reservations required. Lunch avg. €24 ($21), dinner avg. €48 ($43). AE, MC, V. Daily 12:30–2pm and 7–10:30pm. DART: Connolly. Bus: 70 or 80.

MODERATE

101 Talbot ⭐⭐ INTERNATIONAL This modest, friendly, second-floor eatery over a camping shop is a bright beacon of great cooking in a neighborhood that's otherwise culinarily challenged. The menu features light, healthy foods, with a strong emphasis on vegetarian dishes. Main dishes include seared filet of tuna with mango cardamom salsa, roast duck breast with plum and ginger sauce, Halloumi cheese and mushroom brochette served with couscous and raita, and a blue cheese and pistachio cream sauce on pasta. The dinner menu changes weekly. The dining room is bright and casually funky, with contemporary Irish art on display, big windows, yellow rag-rolled walls, ash-topped tables, and newspapers to read. Espresso and cappuccino are always available, and there is a full bar. The restaurant is convenient to the Abbey Theatre.

101 Talbot St. (at Talbot Lane near Marlborough St.), Dublin 1. ℂ **01/874-5011.** Reservations recommended. Main courses €13–€18 ($12–$16). AE, MC, V. Tues–Sat 5–11pm. DART: Connolly. Bus: 27A, 31A, 31B, 32A, 32B, 42B, 42C, 43, or 44A.

INEXPENSIVE

Beshoffs ⭐ FISH AND CHIPS   The Beshoff name is synonymous with fresh fish in Dublin. Ivan Beshoff emigrated here from Odessa, Russia, in 1913 and started a fish business that developed into this top-notch fish-and-chips eatery. Recently renovated in Victorian style, it has an informal atmosphere and a simple self-service menu. Crisp chips are served with a choice of fresh fish, from the original recipe of cod to classier variations using salmon, shark, prawns, and other local sea fare—some days as many as 20 varieties. The potatoes are grown on a 300-acre farm in Tipperary and freshly cut each day. A second shop is just south of the Liffey at 14 Westmoreland St., Dublin 2 (ℂ **01/677-8026**).

6 Upper O'Connell St., Dublin 1. ℂ **01/872-4400.** All items €2.50–€6.50 ($2.25–$5.80). No credit cards. Mon–Sat 10am–9pm; Sun noon–9pm. DART: Tara St. Bus: Any city-center bus.

Epicurean Food Hall ⭐⭐ GOURMET FOOD COURT   This wonderful food hall houses a wide variety of artisan produce, delicious local Irish delicacies, and regional specialties. Favorites include: Caviston's, Dublin's premier deli, for smoked salmon and seafood; Itsabagel, for its delicious bagels, imported from H&H Bagels in New York City; Crème de la Crème, for its French-style pastries and cakes; Missy and Mandy's, for its American-style ice cream; Nectar, for its plethora of healthy juice drinks; and Aroma Bistro for Italian paninis. There is limited seating but this place gets uncomfortably jammed during lunchtime midweek, so go midmorning or afternoon.

Middle Abbey St., Dublin 1. No phone. All items €2–€12 ($1.80–$11). No credit cards. Mon–Sat 10am–6pm. Bus: 70 or 80.

The Winding Stair ⭐ HEALTH   Retreat from the bustle of the north side's busy quays into this darling bookshop's self-service cafe, and indulge in a snack while browsing for secondhand gems. There are three floors—one smoke-free, and each chock-full of used books (from novels, plays, and poetry to history, art, music, and sports) connected by a winding 18th-century staircase. (There's also an elevator available.) Tall, wide windows provide expansive views of the Ha'penny Bridge and River Liffey. The food is simple and healthy—sandwiches made with additive-free meats or fruits (such as banana and honey), organic salads, homemade soups, and natural juices. Evening events include poetry readings and recitals.

40 Lower Ormond Quay, Dublin 1. ℂ **01/873-3292.** All items €1.90–€5 ($1.70–$4.45). AE, MC, V. Mon–Sat 10am–6pm; Sun 1–6pm. Bus: 70 or 80.

5 Seeing the Sights

Dublin is a city of many moods and landscapes. There are medieval churches and imposing castles, graceful Georgian squares and lantern-lit lanes, broad boulevards and crowded bridges, picturesque parks and pedestrian walkways,

Dublin Attractions

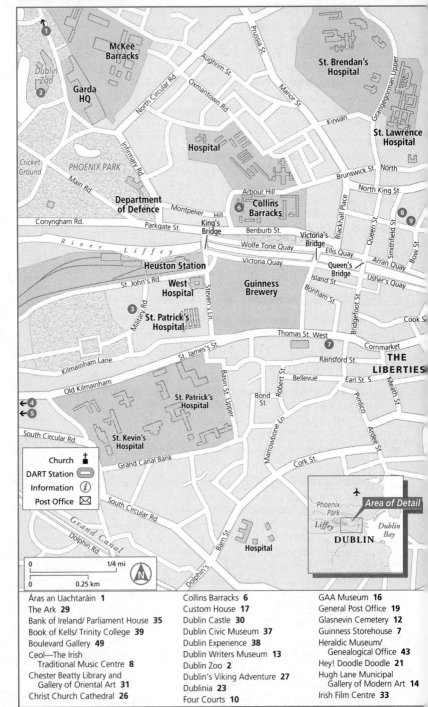

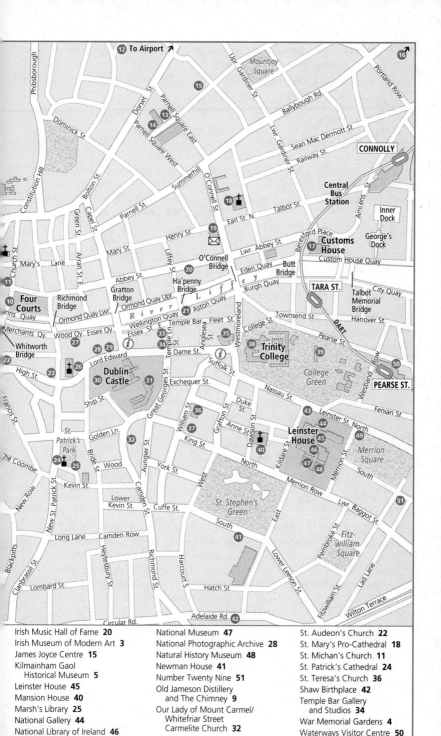

intriguing museums and markets, gardens and galleries, and—if you have any energy left after all that—electric nightlife. Enjoy!

THE TOP ATTRACTIONS

Áras an Uachtaráin (The Irish White House) ⚸ Áras an Uachtaráin (Irish for "House of the President") was once the Viceregal Lodge, the summer retreat of the British viceroy, whose ordinary digs were in Dublin Castle. From what were never humble beginnings, the original 1751 country house was expanded several times, gradually accumulating splendor. President Mary McAleese recently opened her home to visitors; guided tours originate at the Phoenix Park Visitors Centre every Saturday. After an introductory historical film, a bus brings visitors to and from Áras an Uachtaráin. The focus of the tour is the state reception rooms. The entire tour lasts 1 hour. Only 525 tickets are given out, first-come, first-served; arrive before 1:30pm, especially in summer.

Note: For security reasons, no backpacks, travel bags, strollers, buggies, cameras, or mobile phones are allowed on the tour. No smoking, eating, or drinking are permitted, and no visitor toilets are available once the tour begins.

In Phoenix Park, Dublin 7. ✆ **01/670-9155.** Free admission. Sat 9:40am–4:20pm. Closed Dec 24–26. Same-day tickets issued at Phoenix Park Visitors Centre (see below). Bus: 10, 37, or 39.

The Book of Kells ⚸⚸⚸ The jewel in Ireland's tourism crown is the Book of Kells, a magnificent manuscript of the four Gospels, around A.D. 800, with elaborate scripting and illumination. This famous treasure and other early Christian manuscripts are on permanent public view at Trinity College, in the Colonnades, an exhibition area on the ground floor of the Old Library. Also housed in the Old Library is the **Dublin Experience** (see separate listing under "More Attractions," later in this chapter), an excellent multimedia introduction to the history and people of Dublin. The oldest university in Ireland, Trinity was founded in 1592 by Queen Elizabeth I. It occupies a beautiful 16-hectare (40-acre) site just south of the River Liffey, with cobbled squares, gardens, a picturesque quadrangle, and buildings dating from the 17th to the 20th centuries.

College Green, Dublin 2. ✆ **01/608-2320.** www.tcd.ie/library/kells.htm. Free admission to college grounds. €6 ($5.35) adults, €5 ($4.45) seniors/students, €11 ($9.80) families, free for children under 12. Combination tickets for the Library and Dublin Experience also available. Mon–Sat 9:30am–5pm; Sun noon–4:30pm (opens at 9:30am June–Sept).

Ceol—The Irish Traditional Music Centre ⚸⚸ Ceol means "music" in Irish, and this is a must for any lover of Irish traditional music and dance, or for anyone else wondering just what all the fuss is about. No matter how much you think you know, you'll learn something more here that will deepen your appreciation of one of Ireland's most profound legacies. The beautifully designed ultra-high-tech center offers a plethora of interactive audiovisual displays and videos presenting the basic ingredients of Irish traditional music—song, dance, story, and instruments. A dazzling diversity of riches is packed into a relatively small space here. The climax of Ceol is the extraordinary film, shown in the 180° wide-screen main auditorium, titled *The Music of the People,* which is reason enough for going well out of your way to pay Ceol a visit. Plan on at least a couple of hours here. Some visitors, intending to spend an hour, make it a day without realizing it.

Smithfield Village, Dublin 7. ✆ **01/817-3820.** www.ceol.ie. €6.50 ($5.80) adults, €5 ($4.45) seniors and students, €4.50 ($4) children, €19 ($17) family. Mon–Sat 10am–6pm; Sun 11am–6pm (last film 45 min. before closing). Bus: 25, 25A, 67, 67A, 68, 69, 79, or 90.

Christ Church Cathedral ⚸⚸ Standing on high ground in the oldest part of the city, this cathedral is one of Dublin's finest historic buildings. It dates from

The Book of Kells

The Book of Kells is a large-format illuminated manuscript of the four Gospels in Latin, dated on comparative grounds to about A.D. 800. It's impossible to be more precise about its date because some leaves from the end of the book, where such information was normally recorded, are missing. It is the most majestic work of art to survive from the early centuries of Celtic Christianity, and has often been described as "the most beautiful book in the world." A team of talented scribes and artists working in a monastic scriptorium produced the book.

Its fascination derives from the dignified but elusive character of its main motifs, and the astonishing variety and complexity of the linear ornamentation that adorns every one of its 680 pages. Its creators managed to combine new artistic influences from Eastern Christendom with the traditional interlace patterning of Celtic metalwork to produce what Gerald of Wales, a 13th-century chronicler, called "the work not of men, but of angels." The message sometimes may not be easy to read, but everyone can admire the elegant precision of the standard script, the subtlety of the color harmonies, and the exuberant vitality of the human and animal ornamentation.

The book was certainly in the possession of the Columban monastery of Kells, a town in county Meath, during most of the Middle Ages. The Annals of Ulster record its theft from the western sacristy of the stone-built monastic church in 1007, and relate that it was recovered 2 to 3 months later from "under the sod," without the jewel-encrusted silver shrine in which such prestigious books were kept. Whether it was originally created in Kells remains an unresolved question. Some authorities think that it might have been begun, if not completed, in the great monastery founded by St. Columba himself (in about 561) on the island of Iona off the west coast of Scotland. Iona had a famous scriptorium and remained the headquarters of the Columban monastic system until the early years of the 9th century. It then became an untenable location because of repeated Viking raids, and in 807 a remnant of the monastic community retreated to the Irish mainland to build a new headquarters at Kells. It has been suggested that the great Gospel book that we call "of Kells" may have been started on Iona, possibly to mark the bicentenary of St. Columba's death in 797, and later transferred to Kells for completion. But it is also possible to argue that the work was entirely done in Kells, and that its object was to equip the monastery with a great new book to stand on the high altar of the new foundation.

In the medieval period, the book was (wrongly) regarded as the work of St. Columba himself and was known as the "great Gospel book of Colum Cille" (Colum of the Churches). The designation "Book of Kells" seems to have originated with the famous biblical scholar James Ussher, who made a study of its original Latin text in the 1620s. The gift shop in the Colonnades of the Old Library in Trinity College stocks a large selection of illustrative materials relating to the Book of Kells.

—J. V. Luce, Trinity College and the Royal Irish Academy

1038, when Sitric, Danish king of Dublin, built the first wooden Christ Church here. In 1171, the original simple foundation was extended into a cruciform and rebuilt in stone by Strongbow. The present structure dates mainly from 1871 to 1878, when a huge restoration took place. Highlights of the interior include magnificent stonework and graceful pointed arches, with delicately chiseled supporting columns. This is the mother church for the diocese of Dublin and Glendalough of the Church of Ireland. The new Treasury in the crypt is now open to the public, and you can hear new bells pealing in the belfry.

Christ Church Place, Dublin 8. © 01/677-8099. cccdub@indigo.ie. Suggested donation €3 ($2.65) adults, €1.50 ($1.35) students and children under 15. Daily 10am–5:30pm. Closed Dec 26. Bus: 21A, 50, 50A, 78, 78A, or 78B.

Collins Barracks   Officially part of the National Museum, Collins Barracks is the oldest military barracks in Europe. Even if it were empty, it would be well worth a visit for the structure itself, a splendidly restored early-18th-century masterwork by Colonel Thomas Burgh, Ireland's Chief Engineer and Surveyor General under Queen Anne. The collection housed here focuses on the decorative arts. Most notable is the extraordinary display of Irish silver and furniture. Until the acquisition of this vast space, only a fraction of the National Museum's collection could be displayed, but that is changing, and more and more treasures find their way here. It is a prime site for touring exhibitions, so consult *The Event Guide* for details. There is also a cafe and gift shop on the premises.

Benburb St., Dublin 7. © 01/677-7444. Free admission. Tours (hours vary) €1.50 ($1.35) adults, free for seniors and children. Tues–Sat 10am–5pm; Sun 2–5pm. Bus: 34, 70, or 80.

Dublin Castle ★★   Built between 1208 and 1220, this complex represents some of the oldest surviving architecture in the city. It was the center of British power in Ireland for more than 7 centuries, until the new Irish government took it over in 1922. Film buffs might recognize the castle's courtyard as a setting in the Neil Jordan film *Michael Collins.* Highlights include the 13th-century Record Tower; the State Apartments, once the residence of English viceroys; and the Chapel Royal, a 19th-century Gothic building with particularly fine plaster decoration and carved oak gallery fronts and fittings. The newest developments are the Undercroft, an excavated site on the grounds where an early Viking fortress stood, and the Treasury, built between 1712 and 1715 and believed to be the oldest surviving office building in Ireland. Also here are a craft shop, heritage center, and restaurant.

Palace St. (off Dame St.), Dublin 2. © 01/677-7129. dublincastle@eircom.net. Admission €4 ($3.55) adults, €3 ($2.65) seniors and students, €1.50 ($1.35) children under 12. No credit cards. Mon–Fri 10am–5pm; Sat–Sun and holidays 2–5pm. Guided tours every 20–25 min. Bus: 50, 50A, 54, 56A, 77, 77A, or 77B.

Dublin Writers Museum ★★   Housed in a stunning 18th-century Georgian mansion with splendid plasterwork and stained glass, the museum is itself an impressive reminder of the grandeur of the Irish literary tradition. A fine collection of personal manuscripts and mementos that belonged to Yeats, Joyce, Beckett, Behan, Shaw, Wilde, Swift, and Sheridan are among the items that celebrate the written word. One of the museum's rooms is devoted to children's literature.

18–19 Parnell Sq. N., Dublin 1. © 01/475-0854. Admission €4 ($3.55) adults, €3.50 ($3.10) seniors/students, €2 ($1.80) ages 3–11, €11 ($9.80) families (2 adults and up to 4 children). AE, DC, MC, V. Mon–Sat 10am–5pm (6pm June–Aug); Sun and holidays 11am–5pm. DART to Connolly Station. Bus: 11, 13, 16, 16A, 22, or 22A.

Dublinia ★   What was Dublin like in medieval times? This historically accurate presentation of the Old City from 1170 to 1540 is re-created through a series of theme exhibits, spectacles, and experiences. Highlights include an illu-minated Medieval Maze, complete with visual effects, background sounds, and aromas that lead you on a journey through time from the arrival of the Anglo-Normans in 1170 to the closure of the monasteries in the 1530s. Another segment depicts everyday life in medieval Dublin with a diorama, as well as a prototype of a 13th-century quay along the banks of the Liffey. A new addition is the medieval Fayre, displaying the wares of merchants from all over Europe. You can try on a flattering new robe, or, if you're feeling vulnerable, stop in at the armorer's and be fitted for chain mail.

St. Michael's Hill, Christ Church, Dublin 8. ℭ 01/679-4611. www.dublinia.ie. Admission €5 ($4.45) adults, €3.80 ($3.40) seniors, students, and children, €13 ($12) family. AE, MC, V. Apr–Sept daily 10am–5pm; Oct–Mar Mon–Sat 11am–4pm, Sun 10am–4:30pm. Bus: 50, 78A, or 123.

Hugh Lane Municipal Gallery of Modern Art ✯

Housed in a finely restored 18th-century building known as Charlemont House, this gallery is sit-uated next to the Dublin Writers Museum. It is named after Hugh Lane, an Irish art connoisseur who was killed during the sinking of the *Lusitania* in 1915 and who willed his collection (including works by Courbet, Manet, Monet, and Corot) to be shared between the government of Ireland and the National Gallery of London. With the Lane collection as its nucleus, this gallery also contains paintings from the Impressionist and post-Impressionist traditions, sculptures by Rodin, stained glass, and works by modern Irish artists. In 2001 the museum opened the studio of Irish painter Francis Bacon; it was moved piece by piece from Bacon's original studio and reconstructed at the museum. The bookshop is considered the best art bookshop in the city.

Parnell Sq. N., Dublin 1. ℭ 01/874-1903. Fax 01/872-2182. www.hughlane.ie. Free admission to museum; Francis Bacon studio €6 ($5.35). MC, V. Tues–Thurs 9:30am–6pm; Fri–Sat 9:30am–5pm; Sun 11am–5pm. DART to Connolly or Tara stations. Bus: 3, 10, 11, 13, 16, or 19.

Kilmainham Gaol Historical Museum ✯

This is a key sight for anyone interested in Ireland's struggle for independence from British rule. Within these walls political prisoners were incarcerated, tortured, and killed from 1796 until 1924, when President Eamon de Valera left as its final prisoner. To walk along these corridors, through the exercise yard, or into the main compound is a mov-ing experience that lingers hauntingly in the memory. *Note:* The **War Memor-ial Gardens** (ℭ 01/677-0236), along the banks of the Liffey, are a 5-minute walk from Kilmainham Gaol. The gardens were designed by the famous British architect Sir Edwin Lutyens (1869–1944), who completed a number of com-missions for Irish houses and gardens. The gardens are fairly well maintained, and continue to present a moving testimony to Ireland's war dead. They are open weekdays 8am to dark, Saturday 10am to dark.

Kilmainham, Dublin 8. ℭ 01/453-5984. www.heritageireland.ie. Guided tour €4.50 ($4) adults, €3.25 ($2.90) seniors, €2 ($1.80) children, €10 ($8.90) family. AE, MC, V. Apr–Sept daily 9:30am–4:45pm; Oct–Mar Mon–Fri 9:30am–4pm, Sun 10am–4:45pm. Bus: 51B, 78A, or 79 at O'Connell Bridge.

National Gallery of Ireland ✯✯✯

This museum houses Ireland's national art collection, as well as a superb European collection of art spanning from the 14th to the 20th centuries. Every major European school of painting is represented, including fine selections by Italian Renaissance artists (especially Caravaggio's *The Taking of Christ*), French Impressionists, and Dutch 17th-century masters. The highlight of the Irish collection is the room dedicated to the mesmerizing works of Jack B. Yeats, brother of the poet W. B. Yeats. All public areas are wheelchair acces-sible. The museum has a fine gallery shop and an excellent self-service restaurant.

Merrion Sq. W., Dublin 2. ⒸⒸ **01/661-5133.** Fax 01/661-5372. www.nationalgallery.ie. Free admission. Mon–Sat 9:30am–5:30pm; Thurs 9:30am–8:30pm; Sun noon–5pm. Free guided tours (meet in the Shaw Room) Sat 3pm, Sun 2, 3, and 4pm. Closed Good Friday and Dec. 24–26. DART: Pearse. Bus: 5, 6, 7, 7A, 8, 10, 44, 47, 47B, 48A, or 62.

National Museum ★★★ Established in 1890, this museum is a reflection of Ireland's heritage from 2000 B.C. to the present. It is the home of many of the country's greatest historical finds, including the Treasury exhibit, which toured the United States and Europe in the 1970s with the Ardagh Chalice, Tara Brooch, and Cross of Cong. Other highlights range from the artifacts from the Wood Quay excavations of the Old Dublin Settlements to "Ór," an extensive exhibition of Irish Bronze Age gold ornaments dating from 2200 to 700 B.C. The museum has a shop and a cafe. *Note:* The National Museum encompasses two other attractions, Collins Barracks and the Natural History Museum; see their separate listings.

Kildare St. and Merrion St., Dublin 2. ⒸⒸ **01/677-7444.** Free admission. Tours (hours vary) €1.50 ($1.35) adults, free for seniors and children. MC, V. Tues–Sat 10am–5pm; Sun 2–5pm. DART: Pearse. Bus: 7, 7A, 8, 10, 11, or 13.

Phoenix Park ★★ *Kids* Just 3.2km (2 miles) west of the city center, the Phoenix Park, the largest urban park in Europe, is the playground of Dublin. A network of roads and quiet pedestrian walkways traverses its 704 hectares (1,760 acres), which are informally landscaped with ornamental gardens and nature trails. Avenues of trees, including oak, beech, pine, chestnut, and lime, separate broad expanses of grassland. The homes of the Irish president (see above) and the U.S. ambassador are on the grounds, as is the Dublin Zoo (see "Especially for Kids," later in this chapter). Livestock graze peacefully on pasturelands, deer roam the forested areas, and horses romp on polo fields. The new Phoenix Park Visitor Centre, adjacent to Ashtown Castle, offers exhibitions and an audiovisual presentation on the park's history. The cafe/restaurant is open 10am to 5pm weekdays, 10am to 6pm weekends. Free car parking is adjacent to the center.

Phoenix Park, Dublin 8. ⒸⒸ **01/677-0095.** www.heritageireland.ie. Visitor Centre: Admission €2.50 ($2.25) adults, €1.90 ($1.70) seniors, €1.30 ($1.15) students and children, €6.35 ($5.65) families. June–Sept 10am–6pm (call for off-season hours). Bus: 37, 38, or 39.

St. Patrick's Cathedral ★ It is said that St. Patrick baptized converts on this site, and consequently a church has stood here since A.D. 450, making it the oldest Christian site in Dublin. The present cathedral dates from 1190, but because of a fire and 14th-century rebuilding, not much of the original foundation remains. It is mainly early English in style, with a square medieval tower that houses the largest ringing peal bells in Ireland, and an 18th-century spire. The 90m-long (300-ft.) interior makes it the longest church in the country. St. Patrick's is closely associated with Jonathan Swift, who was dean from 1713 to 1745 and whose tomb lies in the south aisle. Others memorialized within the cathedral include Turlough O'Carolan, a blind harpist and composer and the last of the great Irish bards; Michael William Balfe, the composer; and Douglas Hyde, the first president of Ireland. St. Patrick's is the national cathedral of the Church of Ireland.

21–50 Patrick's Close, Patrick St., Dublin 8. ⒸⒸ **01/475-4817.** Fax 01/454-6374. www.stpatrickscathedral.ie. Admission €3.50 ($3.10) adults, €2.50 ($2.25) students and seniors, €8 ($7.10) family. MC, V. Mon–Fri 9am–6pm year-round; Nov–Feb Sat 9am–5pm and Sun 9am–3pm. Closed except for services Dec 24–26 and Jan 1. Bus: 65, 65B, 50, 50A, 54, 54A, 56A, or 77.

MORE ATTRACTIONS
ART GALLERIES & ART MUSEUMS

Boulevard Gallery   The fence around Merrion Square doubles as a display railing on summer weekends for an outdoor display of local art similar to those you'll find in Greenwich Village or Montmartre. Permits are given to local artists only for the sale of their own work, so this is a chance to meet an artist as well as to browse or buy.

Merrion Sq. W., Dublin 2. Free admission. May–Sept Sat–Sun 10:30am–6pm. DART: Pearse. Bus: 5, 7A, 8, 46, or 62.

Irish Film Centre ✪   This art house film institute is a hip hangout in Dublin's artsy Temple Bar district. The Irish Film Centre houses two cinemas, the Irish Film Archive, a library, a bookshop and cafe, and eight film-related organizations. Free screenings of *Flashback,* a history of Irish film since 1896, start at noon Wednesday to Sunday from June to mid-September. Follow with lunch in the cafe for a perfect midday outing.

6 Eustace St., Dublin 2. ✆ **01/679-5744**, or 01/679-3477 for cinema box office. Free admission; cinema tickets €4–€6 ($3.55–$5.35) Centre open daily 10am–11pm; cinemas daily 2–11pm; cinema box office daily 1:30–9pm. Bus: 21A, 78A, or 78B.

Irish Music Hall of Fame ✪   The draw here is the exhaustive collection of memorabilia—much of it exclusive—chronicling the history of Irish music, from traditional and folk through pop, rock, and dance. There's loads of great stuff about U2, Van Morrison, Christy Moore, the Chieftains, the Dubliners, Thin Lizzy, Bob Geldof, Enya, the Cranberries, Sinéad O'Connor, and right up to BoyZone, Westlife, and Samantha Mumba.

57 Middle Abbey St., Dublin 1. Free admission. Daily 10am–5:30pm. DART: Connolly. Bus: 25, 26, 34, 37, 38A, 39A, 39B, 66A, or 67A.

Irish Museum of Modern Art (IMMA) ✪   Housed in the splendidly restored 17th-century edifice known as the Royal Hospital, IMMA is a showcase of Irish and international art from the latter half of the 20th century. The buildings and grounds also provide a venue for theatrical and musical events, overlapping the visual and performing arts. The galleries contain the work of Irish and international artists from the small but impressive permanent collection, with numerous temporary exhibitions. There's even a drawing room, where kids and parents can record their impressions of the museum with the crayons provided. The formal gardens, an important early feature of this magnificent structure, have been restored and are open to the public during museum hours. In 2000, a series of new galleries opened in the restored Deputy Master's House, in the northeast corner of the Royal Hospital site.

Military Rd., Kilmainham. ✆ **01/612-9900**. www.modernart.ie. Free admission. Tues–Sat 10am–5:30pm; Sun noon–5:30pm. Bus: 79 or 90.

Temple Bar Gallery and Studios   Founded in 1983 in the heart of Dublin's "Left Bank," this is one of the largest studio and gallery complexes in Europe. More than 30 Irish artists work here at a variety of contemporary visual arts, including sculpture, painting, printing, and photography. Only the gallery section is open to the public, but you can make an appointment in advance to view individual artists at work.

5–9 Temple Bar, Dublin 2. ✆ **01/671-0073**. Fax 01/677-7527. Free admission. Tues–Wed 11am–6pm; Thurs 11am–7pm; Sun 2–6pm. Bus: 21A, 46A, 46B, 51B, 51C, 68, 69, or 86.

BREWERIES/DISTILLERIES

Guinness Storehouse 🎯   Founded in 1759, the Guinness Brewery is one of the world's largest breweries, producing a distinctive dark stout, famous for its thick, creamy head. Although tours of the brewery itself are no longer allowed, visitors are welcome to explore the adjacent Guinness Hopstore, a converted 19th-century four-story building. It houses the World of Guinness Exhibition, an audiovisual presentation showing how the stout is made; the Cooperage Gallery, displaying one of the finest collections of tools in Europe; the Gilroy Gallery, dedicated to the graphic design work of John Gilroy; and last but not least a bar where visitors can sample a glass of the famous brew. The brewery recently became home to the largest glass of stout in the world, roughly 60m (200 ft.) tall, whose head is in fact an observatory restaurant offering spectacular views of the city.

St. James's Gate, Dublin 8. ℂ 01/408-4800. www.guinness.com. Admission €12 ($11) adults, €5 ($4.45) seniors and students, €2.50 ($2.23) children under 12, €26 ($23) family. AE, MC, V. Mon–Sat 9:30am–5pm. Guided tours every ½ hour. Bus: 51B, 78A, or 123.

The Old Jameson Distillery 🎯   This museum illustrates the history of Irish whiskey, known in Irish as *uisce beatha* (the water of life). Housed in a former distillery warehouse, it consists of a short introductory audiovisual presentation, an exhibition area, and a whiskey-making demonstration. At the end of the tour, visitors can sample whiskey at an in-house pub, where an array of fixed-price menus (for lunch, tea, or dinner) is available. A new added attraction here at Smithfield Village is **"The Chimney,"** a ride to the top of a 56m (185-ft.) brick chimney built in 1895 and converted to support an observation chamber from which you'll enjoy unparalleled views of the city.

Bow St., Smithfield Village, Dublin 7. ℂ 01/807-2355. Admission €5 ($4.45) adults, €4 ($3.55) students and seniors, €2 ($1.80) children, €13 ($12) family. Daily 9:30am–6pm (last tour at 5pm). Chimney ascent €6.50 ($5.80) adults, €5 ($4.45) seniors and students, €4.50 ($4) children, €19 ($17) family. Mon–Sat 10am–6pm; Sun 11am–7pm. Bus: 67, 67A, 68, 69, 79, or 90.

CATHEDRALS & CHURCHES

St. Patrick's Cathedral and Christ Church Cathedral are listed above, under "The Top Attractions."

Our Lady of Mount Carmel/Whitefriar Street Carmelite Church   One of the city's largest churches, this edifice was built between 1825 and 1827 on the site of a pre-Reformation Carmelite priory (1539) and an earlier Carmelite abbey (13th c.). It has since been extended, with a new entrance from Aungier Street. This is a favorite place of pilgrimage, especially on February 14, because the body of St. Valentine is enshrined here (Pope Gregory XVI presented it to the church in 1836). The other highlight is the 15th-century black oak Madonna, Our Lady of Dublin.

56 Aungier St., Dublin 2. ℂ 01/475-8821. Free admission. Mon and Wed–Fri 8am–6:30pm; Sat 8am–7pm; Sun 8am–7:30pm; Tues 8am–9:30pm. Bus: 16, 16A, 19, 19A, 122, 155, or 83.

St. Audeon's Church   Situated next to the only remaining gate of the Old City walls (dating from 1214), this church is said to be the only surviving medieval parish in Dublin. Although it is partly in ruins, significant parts have survived, including the west doorway, which dates from 1190, and the 13th-century nave. In addition, the 17th-century bell tower houses three bells cast in 1423, making them the oldest in Ireland. It's a Church of Ireland property, but nearby is another St. Audeon's Church, this one Catholic and dating from 1846. It was in the latter church that Father Flash Kavanagh used to say the world's fastest mass so that his congregation was out in time for the football matches.

Since 1999, entrance to the ancient church is through the new visitor center. The center's exhibition, relating the history of St. Audeon's, is self-guided, while visits to the church itself are by guided tour only.

Cornmarket (off High St.), Dublin 8. ℭ **01/677-0088.** Admission and tour €2 ($1.80) adults, €1.50 ($1.35) seniors, €.75 (65¢) children and students, €5 ($4.45) families. June–Sept daily 9:30am–5:30pm. Last admission 45 min. prior to closing. Bus: 21A, 78A, or 78B.

St. Mary's Pro-Cathedral Because Dublin's two main cathedrals (Christ Church and St. Patrick's) belong to the Protestant Church of Ireland, St. Mary's is the closest the Catholics get to having their own. Tucked into a corner of a rather-unimpressive back street, it is in the heart of the city's north side and is considered the main Catholic parish church of the city center. Built between 1815 and 1825, it is of the Greek Revival Doric style, providing a distinct contrast to the Gothic Revival look of most other churches of the period. The exterior portico is modeled on the Temple of Theseus in Athens, with six Doric columns, while the Renaissance-style interior is patterned after the Church of St. Philip de Reule of Paris. The church is noted for its Palestrina Choir, which sings a Latin Mass every Sunday at 11am.

Cathedral and Marlborough sts., Dublin 1. ℭ **01/874-5441.** Free admission. Mon–Fri 8am–6pm; Sat –Sun 8am–7pm. DART: Connolly. Bus: 28, 29A, 30, 31A, 31B, 32A, 32B, or 44A.

St. Michan's Church Built on the site of an early Danish chapel (1095), this 17th-century edifice claims to be the only parish church on the north side of the Liffey surviving from a Viking foundation. Now under the Church of Ireland banner, it has some fine interior woodwork and an organ (dated 1724) on which Handel is said to have played his *Messiah*. The church was completely and beautifully restored in 1998. A unique (and, let it be noted, most macabre) feature of this church is the underground burial vault. Because of the dry atmosphere, bodies have lain for centuries without showing signs of decomposition. The church is wheelchair accessible, but the vaults are not.

Church St., Dublin 7. ℭ **01/872-4154.** Free admission. Guided tour of church and vaults €2.50 ($2.25) adults, €2 ($1.80) seniors and students, €.65 (60¢) children under 12. Nov–Feb Mon–Fri 12:30–2:30pm, Sat 10am–1pm; Mar–Oct Mon–Fri 10am–12:45pm and 2–4:45pm, Sat 10am–1pm. Bus: 134 (from Abbey St.).

St. Teresa's Church The foundation stone was laid in 1793, and the church was opened in 1810 by the Discalced Carmelite Fathers. After continuous enlargement, it reached its present form in 1876. This was the first post–Penal Law church to be legally and openly erected in Dublin, following the Catholic Relief Act of 1793. Among the artistic highlights are John Hogan's *Dead Christ*, a sculpture displayed beneath the altar, and Phyllis Burke's seven beautiful stained-glass windows.

Clarendon St., Dublin 2. ℭ **01/671-8466.** Free admission; donations welcome. Daily 8am–8pm or longer. Bus: 16, 16A, 19, 19A, 22, 22A, 55, or 83.

A CEMETERY

Glasnevin Cemetery ★★ Situated north of the city center, the Irish National Cemetery was founded in 1832 and covers more than 50 hectares (124 acres). Most people buried here were ordinary citizens (especially poignant are the sections dedicated to children who died young), but there are also many famous names on the headstones. They range from former Irish presidents such as Eamon de Valera and Sean T. O'Kelly to other political heroes such as Michael Collins, Daniel O'Connell, Roger Casement, and Charles Stewart Parnell. Literary figures also have their place here, including poet Gerard Manley Hopkins and writers Christy Brown and Brendan Behan. Though open to all, this is primarily a Catholic burial ground, with many Celtic crosses. A heritage map, on sale in the flower shop at the entrance, serves as a guide to who's buried where, or you can take a free 2-hour guided tour.

Finglas Rd., Dublin 11. ℂ **01/830-1133.** Free admission. Daily 8am–4pm. Free guided tours Wed and Fri 2:30pm from main gate. Map: €3.25 ($2.90). Bus: 19, 19A, 40, 40A, 40B, or 40C.

MORE HISTORIC BUILDINGS

Although it's not open to the public, one building whose exterior is worth a look is **Mansion House,** Dawson Street, Dublin 2 (ℂ **01/676-1845**). Built by Joshua Dawson, the Queen Anne–style building has been the official residence of Dublin's lord mayors since 1715. Here the first Dáil Éireann (House of Representatives) assembled, in 1919, to adopt Ireland's Declaration of Independence and ratify the Proclamation of the Irish Republic by the insurgents of 1916. Ride the DART to Pearse, or take bus no. 10, 11A, 11B, 13, or 20B.

Bank of Ireland Centre/Parliament House ⭐   Although it's now a busy bank, this building was erected in 1729 to house the Irish Parliament. It became superfluous when the British and Irish Parliaments were merged in London. In fact, the Irish Parliament voted itself out of existence, becoming the only recorded parliament in history to do so. Highlights include the windowless front portico, built to avoid distractions from the outside when Parliament was in session, and the unique House of Lords chamber. The room is famed for its Irish oak woodwork, 18th-century tapestries, golden mace, and a sparkling Irish crystal chandelier of 1,233 pieces, dating from 1765.

This is also the home of the **Bank of Ireland Arts Centre,** which plays host to an impressive program of art exhibitions, concerts, and poetry readings. Entry to readings, lunchtime recitals, and exhibitions is free. Another attraction in the bank center is the **Story of Banking,** an interactive museum offering a glimpse of the history of banking and of Ireland more generally over the past 2 centuries. It's open Tuesday to Friday 10am to 4pm; admission is €2 ($1.80) for adults, €1.50 ($1.35) students.

2 College Green, Dublin 2. ℂ **01/661-5933,** ext. 2265. Free admission. Mon–Wed and Fri 10am–4pm; Thurs 10am–5pm. Guided 45-min. tours of House of Lords chamber Tues 10:30am, 11:30am, and 1:45pm (except holidays). DART: Tara St. Bus: Any city-center bus.

Custom House   The Custom House, which sits prominently on the Liffey's north bank, is one of Dublin's finest Georgian buildings. Designed by James Gandon and completed in 1791, it is beautifully proportioned, with a long classical facade of graceful pavilions, arcades, and columns, and a central dome topped by a 5m (16-ft.) statue of Commerce. The 14 keystones over the doors and windows are known as the Riverine Heads, because they represent the Atlantic Ocean and the 13 principal rivers of Ireland. Although burned to a shell in 1921, the building has been masterfully restored and its bright Portland stone recently cleaned. The new visitor center's exhibitions and audiovisual presentation unfold the remarkable history of the structure from its creation by James Gandon to its reconstruction after the War of Independence.

Custom House Quay, Dublin 1. ℂ **01/878-7760.** €1.25 ($1.10) adults, €4 ($3.55) family. Mid-Mar to Oct Mon–Fri 10am–12:30pm, Sat–Sun 2–5pm; Nov to mid-Mar Wed–Fri 10am–12:30pm, Sun 2–5pm. DART: Tara St.

Four Courts   Home to the Irish law courts since 1796, this fine 18th-century building overlooks the north bank of the Liffey on Dublin's west side. With a sprawling 132m (440-ft.) facade, it was designed by James Gandon and is distinguished by its graceful Corinthian columns, massive dome (192m/64 ft. in

(*Fun Fact* **Monumental Humor**

Dublin boasts countless public monuments, some modest, others boldly evident. The Irish make a sport of naming them, giving their irrepressible wit and ridicule yet another outlet. A sampler:

Anna Livia, Joyce's mythical personification of the River Liffey, may be found cast in bronze on O'Connell Street across from the General Post Office. Reclining in a pool of streaming water, Anna has been renamed by locals "the floozie in the Jacuzzi."

Sweet **Molly Malone,** another figment of Irish imagination—inspiring poetry, song, and most recently sculpture—appears complete with her flower cart, all larger than life, at the intersection of Nassau and Grafton streets, across from the Trinity College Provost's house. Ms. Malone's plunging neckline may explain why she is known as "the tart with the cart."

Just around the corner from Molly on Dame Street stands another sculpture, a silent frenzy of **trumpeters** and streaming columns of water, proclaiming "You're a nation again"—popularly transliterated as "urination again."

Then there's Dublin's testimonial to arguably Ireland's greatest patriot and Dublin's most eminent native son, **Theobald Wolfe Tone.** Born at 44 Stafford St. in 1763 and graduated from Trinity College, Tone went on to spark a revolutionary fervor among the Irish. His timeless contribution to Ireland and the world is commemorated in a semicircular assemblage of rough-hewn columns on the north side of Stephen's Green—better known as "Tonehenge."

Across the Liffey, on Dublin's north side, are two theaters, the Gate and the Abbey, that have set the standard for Irish theater in this century. The Gate was founded by and flourished for decades under Michael MacLiammoir and Hilton Edwards, a respected gay couple. The Abbey, for its part, gained a reputation for stage-Irish productions served up for overseas tourists. Their stature makes them not immune from but prey to Irish irreverence—they were collectively known as "Sodom and Begorrah."

Finally, the city's newest monument is the **Spire of Dublin,** a 120m-high (394 ft.) conical spire made of stainless steel. The new spire is hoped to reflect Dublin of the 21st century and replaces Nelson's Pillar, which was erected by the British during colonial times. Work was still ongoing as of press time, inspiring one radio DJ to quip that the city council should leave the spire unfinished so that everyone could call it what it really was: "the Pointless."

diameter), and exterior statues of Justice, Mercy, Wisdom, and Moses (sculpted by Edward Smyth). The building was severely burned during the Irish Civil War of 1922, but has been artfully restored. The public is admitted only when court is in session, so phone in advance.

Inns Quay, Dublin 8. © **01/872-5555**. Free admission. Mon–Fri 11am–1pm and 2–4pm, but only if court is in session. Bus: 34, 70, or 80.

General Post Office (GPO) ✛   With a facade of Ionic columns and Greco-Roman pilasters 60m (200 ft.) long and 17m (56 ft.) high, this is more than a post office; it is the symbol of Irish freedom. Built between 1815 and 1818, it was the main stronghold of the Irish Volunteers in 1916. Set afire, the building was gutted and abandoned after the surrender and execution of many of the Irish rebel leaders. It reopened as a post office in 1929 after the formation of the Irish Free State. In memory of the building's dramatic role in Irish history, an impressive bronze statue of Cuchulainn, the legendary Irish hero, is on display. Look closely at the pillars outside—you can still see bullet holes from the siege.

O'Connell St., Dublin 1. ☎ 01/705-8833. www.anpost.ie. Free admission. Mon–Sat 8am–8pm; Sun 10:30am–6:30pm. DART: Connolly. Bus: 25, 26, 34, 37, 38A, 39A, 39B, 66A, or 67A.

Leinster House   Dating from 1745 and originally known as Kildare House, this building is said to have been the model for Irish-born architect James Hoban's design for the White House in Washington, D.C. It was sold in 1815 to the Royal Dublin Society, which developed it as a cultural center. The National Museum, Library, and Gallery all surround it. In 1924, however, it took on a new role when the Irish Free State government acquired it as a parliament house. Since then, it has been the meeting place for the Dáil Éireann (Irish House of Representatives) and Seanad Éireann (Irish Senate), which together constitute the Oireachtas (National Parliament). Tickets for a guided tour when the Dáil is in session (Oct–May, Tues–Thurs) must be arranged in advance from the Public Relations Office (☎ **01/618-3066**).

Kildare St. and Merrion Sq., Dublin 2. ☎ 01/618-3000. Free admission. By appointment only, Oct–May Mon and Fri 10am–4:30pm. DART: Pearse. Bus: 5, 7A, or 8.

Newman House ✛   In the heart of Dublin on the south side of St. Stephen's Green, this is the historic seat of the Catholic University of Ireland. Named for Cardinal John Henry Newman, the 19th-century writer and theologian and first rector of the university, it consists of two of the finest Georgian town houses in Dublin. They date from 1740 and are decorated with outstanding Palladian and rococo plasterwork, marble tiled floors, and wainscot paneling. No. 85 has been magnificently restored to its original splendor. *Note:* Every other Sunday, Newman House hosts an antiques and collectibles fair, where dealers from throughout Ireland sell a wide range of items, including silver, rare books, paintings and prints, coins, stamps, and so forth.

85–86 St. Stephen's Green, Dublin 2. ☎ 01/706-7422. Fax 01/706-7211. Guided tours €4 ($3.55) adults, €2.50 ($2.25) seniors, students, and children under 12. June–Aug Tues–Fri noon–5pm, Sat 2–5pm, Sun 11am–2pm; Oct–May by appointment only. Bus: 10, 11, 13, 14, 14A, 15A, or 15B.

LIBRARIES

Chester Beatty Library and Gallery of Oriental Art ✛   Bequeathed to the Irish nation in 1956 by Sir Alfred Chester Beatty, this extraordinary collection contains approximately 22,000 manuscripts, rare books, miniature paintings, and objects from Western, Middle Eastern, and Far Eastern cultures. There are more than 270 copies of the Koran to be found here, and the library has especially impressive biblical and early Christian manuscripts. There's a gift shop on the premises.

Clock Tower Building. Dublin Castle, Dublin 2. ☎ 01/407-0750. info@cbl.ie. Free admission. Tues–Fri 10am–5pm; Sat 11am–5pm; Sun 1–5pm. Free guided tours Wed and Sat 2:30pm. DART: Sandymount. Bus: 5, 6, 6A, 7A, 8, 10, 46, 46A, 46B, or 64.

Marsh's Library   This is Ireland's oldest public library, founded in 1701 by Narcissus Marsh, Archbishop of Dublin. It is a repository of more than 25,000 scholarly volumes, chiefly on theology, medicine, ancient history, maps, Hebrew, Syriac, Greek, Latin, and French literature. In his capacity as dean of St. Patrick's Cathedral, Jonathan Swift was a governor of Marsh's Library. The interior—a magnificent example of a 17th-century scholar's library—has remained very much the same for 3 centuries. Special exhibits are designed and mounted annually.

St. Patrick's Close, Upper Kevin St., Dublin 8. ☎ 01/454-3511. www.kst.dit.ie/marsh. Donation of €1.25 ($1.10) requested, free for children. Mon and Wed–Fri 10am–12:45pm and 2–5pm; Sat 10:30am–12:45pm. Bus: 50, 54A, or 56A.

National Library of Ireland   If you're coming to Ireland to research your roots, this library should be one of your first stops (along with the Heraldic Museum; see below). It has thousands of volumes and records that yield ancestral information. Opened at this location in 1890, this is the principal library of Irish studies. It's particularly noted for its collection of first editions and the papers of Irish writers and political figures, such as W. B. Yeats, Daniel O'Connell, and Patrick Pearse. It also has an unrivaled collection of maps of Ireland.

Kildare St., Dublin 2. ☎ 01/603-0200. Fax 01/676-6690. www.nli.ie. Free admission. Mon–Wed 10am–9pm; Thurs–Fri 10am–5pm; Sat 10am–1pm. DART: Pearse. Bus: 10, 11A, 11B, 13, or 20B.

National Photographic Archive   The newest member of the Temple Bar cultural complex, the National Photographic Archive houses the extensive (more than 300,000 items) photo collection of the National Library, and serves as its photo exhibition space. In addition to the exhibition area, there are a library and a small gift shop. Admission to the reading room is by appointment.

Meeting House Sq., Temple Bar, Dublin 2. ☎ 01/603-0200. photoarchive@nli.ie. Free admission. Mon–Fri 10am–5pm. DART: Tara St. Bus: 21A, 46A, 46B, 51B, 51C, 68, 69, or 86.

LITERARY LANDMARKS

See also "Libraries," above, and the listing for the Dublin Writers Museum, under "The Top Attractions," earlier in this section. You might also be interested in the James Joyce Museum, in nearby Sandycove; it's described in section 10, "Side Trips from Dublin."

James Joyce Centre ⚅   Near Parnell Square and the Dublin Writers Museum, the Joyce center is in a restored 1784 Georgian town house, once the home of Denis J. Maginni, a dancing instructor who appears briefly in *Ulysses*. The Ulysses Portrait Gallery on the second floor has a fascinating collection of photographs and drawings of characters from *Ulysses* who had a life outside the novel. The recently opened Paul Leon Exhibition Room holds the table and writing table used by Joyce in Paris when he was working on *Finnegan's Wake*. The room is named after Paul Leon, an academic who aided Joyce in literary, business, and domestic affairs and salvaged many of the author's papers after Joyce and his family left Paris. There are talks and audiovisual presentations daily. Guided walking tours through the neighborhood streets of "Joyce Country" in Dublin's north inner city are offered daily.

35 N. Great George's St., Dublin 1. ☎ 01/878-8547. www.jamesjoyce.ie. Admission €3.50 ($3.10) adults, €2.50 ($2.25) seniors and students, €1 (90¢) children, €8 ($7.10) family. Separate fees for walking tours and events. AE, MC, V. Mon–Sat 9:30am–5pm; Sun 12:30–5pm. Closed Dec 24–26. DART: Connolly. Bus: 3, 10, 11, 11A, 13, 16, 16A, 19, 19A, 22, or 22A.

Shaw Birthplace   This simple two-story terraced house, built in 1838, was the birthplace in 1856 of George Bernard Shaw, one of Dublin's three winners of the Nobel Prize for Literature. Recently restored, it has been furnished in Victorian style to re-create the atmosphere of Shaw's early days. Rooms on view are the kitchen, the maid's room, the nursery, the drawing room, and a couple of bedrooms, including young Bernard's. The house is off South Circular Road, a 15-minute walk from St. Stephen's Green.

33 Synge St., Dublin 2. ✆ 01/475-0854. Admission €3.50 ($3.10) adults, €3 ($2.65) seniors and students, €2 ($1.80) children, €10 ($8.90) family. Discounted combination ticket with Dublin Writers Museum and James Joyce Museum available. May–Oct Mon–Sat 10am–5pm, Sun 11am–5pm. Closed Nov–Apr. Bus: 16, 16, 19, or 22.

MORE MUSEUMS

See also "Art Galleries & Art Museums," earlier in this chapter. The National Gallery, the National Museum, the Dublin Writers Museum, and Kilmainham Gaol Historical Museum are all listed earlier in this section, in "The Top Attractions."

Dublin Civic Museum   In the old City Assembly House, a fine 18th-century Georgian structure next to the Powerscourt Townhouse Centre, this museum focuses on the history of the Dublin area from medieval to modern times. In addition to old street signs, maps, and prints, you can see Viking artifacts, wooden water mains, coal covers—and even the head from the statue of Lord Nelson, which stood in O'Connell Street until it was blown up in 1965. Exhibits change three or four times a year.

58 S. William St., Dublin 2. ✆ 01/679-4260. Free admission. Tues–Sat 10am–6pm; Sun 11am–2pm. Bus: 10, 11, or 13.

GAA Museum   On the grounds of Croke Park, principal stadium of the Gaelic Athletic Association, this museum dramatically presents the athletic heritage of Ireland. The Gaelic Games (Gaelic football, hurling, handball, and camogie) have long been contested on an annual basis between teams representing the various regions of Ireland. Test your skills with interactive exhibits, and peruse the extensive video archive of football finals dating back to 1931. The 12-minute film *A Sunday in September* captures admirably the hysteria of the final match. Note that the museum is open only to new stand ticket holders on match days.

Croke Park, Dublin 3. ✆ 01/855-8176. Fax 01/855-8104. www.gaa.ie. Admission €5 ($4.45) adults, €3.50 ($3.10) students, €3 ($2.65) children, €13 ($12) families. May–Sept daily 9:30am–5pm; Oct–Apr Tues–Sat 10am–5pm, Sun noon–5pm. Bus: 3, 11, 11A, 16, 16A, 51A, or 123.

Heraldic Museum/Genealogical Office   The only one of its kind in the world, this museum focuses on the uses of heraldry. Exhibits include shields, banners, coins, paintings, porcelain, and stamps depicting coats of arms. In-house searches by the office researcher are billed at the rate of €56 ($50) per hour. This is the ideal place to start researching your roots.

2 Kildare St., Dublin 2. ✆ 01/603-0200. Fax 01/662-1062. Free admission. Mon–Wed 10am–8:30pm; Thurs–Fri 10am–4:30pm; Sat 10am–12:30pm. DART: Pearse. Bus: 5, 7A, 8, 9, 10, 14, or 15.

Natural History Museum   A division of the National Museum of Ireland, the recently renovated Natural History Museum is considered one of the finest traditional Victorian-style museums in the world. In addition to presenting the zoological history of Ireland, it contains examples of major animal groups from around the world, including many that are rare or extinct. The Blaschka glass models of marine animals are a big attraction.

Merrion St., Dublin 2. ✆ 01/677-7444. Free admission. Tues–Sat 10am–5pm; Sun 2–5pm. DART: Pearse. Bus: 7, 7A, 8, or 13A.

Number Twenty Nine   This unique museum is in the heart of one of Dublin's fashionable Georgian streets. The restored four-story town house is designed to reflect the lifestyle of a middle-class Georgian family during the heyday period from 1790 to 1820. The exhibition ranges from artifacts and artwork of the time to carpets, curtains, decorations, plasterwork, and bell pulls. The nursery holds dolls and toys of the era.

29 Lower Fitzwilliam St., Dublin 2. ✆ **01/702-6165.** Admission €3 ($2.65) adults, €1.25 ($1.10) seniors and students, free for children under 16. MC, V. Tues–Sat 10am–5pm; Sun 2–5pm. Closed 2 weeks before Christmas. DART: Pearse. Bus: 7, 8, 10, or 45.

Waterways Visitor Centre Heading south from Dublin on the DART, you may notice the tiny Waterways Visitor Centre, a brilliant white cube floating on the Grand Canal Basin amidst massive derelict brick warehouses. This intriguing modern building is home to a fascinating exhibit describing the history of Ireland's inland waterways, a network of canals connecting Dublin westward and northward to the Shannon watershed. The center's shiny white exterior gives way inside to the subdued tones of Irish oak wall panels and a hardwood ship's floor. A series of exhibits describe aspects of canal design, and several interactive models attempt to demonstrate dynamically the daily operations of the canals. No longer used for transporting goods, the canals of Ireland are now popular with boaters and hikers, and there's some information here for those interested in these activities.

Grand Canal Quay, Ringsend Rd., Dublin 2. ✆ **01/677-7510.** Admission €2.50 ($2.25) adults, €1.90 ($1.70) seniors, €1.20 ($1.05) children and students, €6 ($5.35) families. No credit cards. June–Sept daily 9:30am–5:30pm; Oct–May Wed–Sun 12:30–5pm. DART: Pearse. Bus: 1 or 3.

A SIGHT & SOUND SHOW

Dublin Experience ★★ An ideal orientation for first-time visitors to the Irish capital, this 45-minute multimedia sight-and-sound show traces the history of Dublin from the earliest times to the present. It takes place in the Davis Theater of Trinity College, on Nassau Street.

Trinity College, Davis Theatre, Dublin 2. ✆ **01/608-1688.** €4 ($3.55) adults, €3.25 ($2.90) seniors and students, €2 ($1.80) children, €8 ($7.10) family. Daily late May to early Oct, hourly shows 10am–5pm. DART: Tara St. Bus: 5, 7A, 8, 15A, 15B, 15C, 46, 55, 62, 63, 83, or 84.

ESPECIALLY FOR KIDS

The Ark: A Cultural Centre for Children ★★★ *Kids* If you've got kids, make this place a top priority on your itinerary. Every year, more than 20,000 children visit this unique cultural center where they are the makers, thinkers, doers, listeners, and watchers. Age-specific programs are geared to small groups of kids from 3 to 13 years old. There are organized minicourses (1–2 hr. long) designed around themes in music, visual arts, and theater, as well as workshops in photography, instrument making, and the art of architecture. The custom-designed arts center has three modern floors that house a theater, a gallery, and a workshop for hands-on learning sessions. The wonderful semicircular theater can be configured to open onto either of the other spaces, or outdoors onto Meeting House Square. Weekdays are often booked for school groups, but Saturdays (and sometimes Sun) are kept open for families. Check the current themes and schedule, and book accordingly.

Eustace St., Temple Bar, Dublin 2. ✆ **01/670-7788.** Fax 01/670-7758. www.ark.ie. Individual activities €3–€5 ($2.65–$4.45). Daily 10am–4pm. Closed mid-Aug to mid-Sept. DART: Tara St. Bus: 51, 51B, 37, or 39.

Dublin's Viking Adventure ★ *Kids* Much like Colonial Williamsburg does, this popular attraction brings you back in time with the help of actors playing citizens of Viking-era Dublin. The "Vikings" who populate the village create a lively, authentic atmosphere in their period houses and detailed costumes. The

(Kids) Family Favorites

There is so much for families to see and do in Dublin that it's hard to know where to begin, but here are a few child- and parent-tested favorites:

Dublin's parks give families on the go a respite from the city's ruckus. In **Merrion Square** and **St. Stephen's Green** you will find lawns for picnicking, ducks for feeding, playgrounds for swinging, and gardens for viewing. Horse-loving youngsters will especially enjoy taking a family carriage tour around the parks (see "Organized Tours," below).

West of Dublin's city center, the vast **Phoenix Park** entices visitors and locals alike (see "The Top Attractions," earlier in this section). Phoenix Park is home to the **Dublin Zoo** (see below), myriad trails, amazing trees, sports fields, playgrounds, and herds of lovely free-roaming deer. You will discover mansions, castles, and many secret gardens. Ice-cream vendors and teahouses spring up in all the right places to keep you going. Those weary of walking can take a trail ride through the park thanks to the nearby **Ashtown Riding Stables** (see section 6, "The Great Outdoors").

If a day with Vikings appeals to your family, don't miss **Dublin's Viking Adventure** (see below) or the lively **Viking Splash Tour** in a reconditioned World War II amphibious "Duck" vehicle. You'll see Dublin from land and water with a Viking tour guide who will keep the whole family dry and well entertained (see "Organized Tours," below).

Interactive creative activities for families can be found in the **Temple Bar** area. **The Ark** (see above) offers unique arts classes and cultural experiences for children, while **Hey! Doodle Doodle** (see below) is a paint-it-yourself pottery studio for the whole family. The entire family will enjoy the popular **ESB Sunday Circus** held in Meeting House Square directly behind The Ark in Temple Bar. These captivating theater, puppet, dance, music, and circus events are all free but do require that you pick up tickets for the show from 2pm on the show day at the Essex Street entrance to Meeting House Square. Performance times vary from 2 to 4pm on Sundays from May to August, and the schedule

townspeople engage in the activities of daily life in the Wood Quay area along the Liffey, while you watch and interact with them.

Temple Bar (enter from Essex St.), Dublin 8. © 01/679-6040. Fax 01/679-6033. Admission €6 ($5.35) adults, €5 ($4.45) seniors and students, €4 ($3.55) children, €18, ($16) family. AE, MC, V. Mar–Oct Tues–Sat 10am–4:30pm; Nov–Feb Tues–Sat 10am–1pm and 2–4:30pm. DART: Tara St., then no. 90 bus. Bus: 51, 51B, 79, or 90.

Dublin Zoo *(Kids)* Established in 1830, this is the third-oldest zoo in the world (after those in London and Paris), nestled in the city's largest playground, the Phoenix Park, about 3.2km (2 miles) west of the city center. In the past few years, the zoo has doubled in size to about 24 hectares (60 acres) and provides a naturally landscaped habitat for more than 235 species of wild animals and of events can be found through Temple Bar Properties, 18 Eustace St., Temple Bar, Dublin 2 (© **01/677-2255**), or the Cultureline (© **01/671-5717**).

Day excursions out of town are great fun, especially when there are beaches to run on and treasures to discover. North of the city is the **Malahide Castle Demesne** (see "Dublin's Northern Suburbs" under "Side Trips from Dublin," later in this chapter). This great estate features not only the beautiful **Malahide Castle** but also the fascinating **Fry Model Railway** exhibit, a display of exquisite antique dollhouses and toys at **Tara's Palace,** acres of parkland, playgrounds, and picnic areas.

The towns south of Dublin are best explored by DART light rail from the city center. You might stop in Monkstown to see a puppet show at the famous **Lambert Puppet Theatre and Museum** (see below), or, if the kids need a little seaside adventure, go on a few more stops to the charming heritage village of Dalkey. **The Ferryman** of Coliemore Harbor (see "Dublin's Southern Suburbs" under "Side Trips from Dublin," later in this chapter), just a 10-minute walk from the train, can take the family out to explore **Dalkey Island** and return you to shore. After your adventure, you can reward your daring with a creamy soft-serve ice-cream cone in the village. The park at the top of **Dalkey Hill** offers a memorable view of the town and bay beyond.

One stop after Dalkey on the DART lies the long pebbled beach of **Killiney.** This is just the place to find the perfect stone for your family collection or to take a beachcombing stroll along the strand. Farther on down the line is the seaside resort town of **Bray.** Irish water creatures, from starfish to sharks, can be found in the **National Sea Life Centre** (see chapter 5, section 1, on county Wicklow, for a full listing). Along with the aquarium, Bray also sports arcades, games, and other family amusements along its boardwalk. If you get to Bray with energy and daylight to spare, the hike up **Bray Head** will give you a spectacular view of the Dublin coastline. In season, the purple heather and yellow gorse are stunning, and you might see rabbits inquiring around the bushes.

tropical birds. Highlights for youngsters include the Children's Pets' Corner and a train ride around the zoo. New additions to the zoo, part of a $24 million redevelopment, are the "Fringes of the Arctic" exhibition, the "World of Primates," the "World of Cats," and the "City Farm and Pets Corner." There are playgrounds interspersed throughout the zoo, and there are also several restaurants, coffee shops, and gift shops.

Phoenix Park, Dublin 8. © **01/677-1425.** www.dublinzoo.ie. Admission €9 ($8) adults, €5.75 ($5.10) seniors and children 3–16, free for children under 3, €27–€34 ($24–$30) family, depending on number of children. V. Summer Mon–Sat 9:30am–6pm, Sun 10:30am–6pm. Bus: 10, 25, or 26.

Hey! Doodle Doodle ★★ (Kids (Finds   If your child likes arts and crafts, make a point of stopping into Temple Bar's paint-it-yourself ceramics studio. Kids of all ages can choose from a wide range of white ready-to-paint pieces—including mugs, plates, wine coolers, pasta dishes, cups and dinnerware—and personalize each with their own artwork. Paints, stencils, stamps and inspiration are all provided along with a little instruction for novices. The finished pieces are kiln-fired and ready to pick up a few days later (so it makes sense to visit on one of your first days in town). All paints are nontoxic, and the pottery is all dishwasher proof. Painting time is charged per hour with a minimum time of 1 hour. Items start at €8 ($7.10). Discounts are available for groups.

14 Crown Alley, Dublin 2. ℂ 01/672-7382. www.heydoodledoodle.com. Mon–Sat 11am–6pm. DART: Tara St. Bus: 51, 51B, 37, or 39.

Lambert Puppet Theatre and Museum *Kids*   Founded by master ventriloquist Eugene Lambert, this 300-seat suburban theater presents puppet shows designed to delight audiences both young and young at heart. During intermission, you can browse in the puppet museum or look for a take-home puppet in the shop.

5 Clifden Lane, Monkstown, county Dublin. ℂ 01/280-0974. www.lambertpuppettheatre.com. No box office; call for same-day reservations. Admission €7 ($6.25). Shows Sat–Sun 3:30pm. DART: Salthill. Bus: 7, 7A, or 8.

ORGANIZED TOURS
BUS TOURS
The city bus company, **Dublin Bus** (ℂ 01/873-4222; www.dublinbus.ie), operates four different tours, all of which depart from the Dublin Bus office at 59 Upper O'Connell St., Dublin 1. Free pickup from many hotels is available for morning tours. You can buy your ticket from the bus driver or book in advance at the Dublin Bus office or at the Dublin Tourism ticket desk on Suffolk Street.

The 75-minute guided **Dublin City Tour** operates on a hop-on, hop-off basis, connecting 10 major points of interest, including museums, art galleries, churches and cathedrals, libraries, and historic sites. Rates are €9 ($8) adults, €5 ($4.45) children under 14, €15 ($13) for a family of four. Daily from 9:30am to 6:30pm.

The 2-hour-15-minute **Dublin Ghost Bus** is an evening tour, departing Tuesday to Friday at 8pm and Saturday to Sunday at 7 and 9:30pm. The tour highlights Dublin's troubled history of felons, fiends, and phantoms. You'll see haunted houses, learn of Dracula's Dublin origins, and even get a crash course in body snatching. Fares are €15 ($14); adults and children over 14 only.

The 3-hour **Coast and Castle Tour** departs daily at 10am, traveling up the north coast to Malahide and Howth. Fares, which include free admission to Malahide Castle are €15 ($14) adults, €8 ($7.10) children under 14.

The 3-hour-45-minute **South Coast Tour** departs daily at 11am and 2pm, traveling south through the seaside town of Dun Laoghaire, through the upscale "Irish Riviera" villages of Dalkey and Killiney, and farther south to visit the Avoca Handweavers in county Wicklow. Fares are €15 ($14) for adults, €8 ($7.10) children under 14.

Gray Line (ℂ 01/605-7705; www.guidefriday.com), the world's largest sightseeing organization, operates its own hop-on, hop-off city tour, covering all the same major sights as the Dublin Bus's Dublin City Tour. The tours are identical, so there's no reason to pay more for Gray Line.

The first tours leave at 10am from 14 Upper O'Connell St., and at 10am from the Dublin Tourism Center on Suffolk Street, Dublin 2, and run every 10

Kids **Horse-Drawn Carriage Tours**

You can tour Dublin in style in a handsomely outfitted horse-drawn carriage with a driver who will comment on the sights as you travel the city's streets and squares. To arrange a ride, consult one of the drivers stationed with carriages at the Grafton Street side of St. Stephen's Green. Rides range from a short swing around the Green to an extensive half-hour Georgian tour or an hour-long Old City tour. It's slightly touristy, but kids (and romantics) love it.

Rides are available on a first-come, first-served basis from approximately April to October (weather permitting), and will run you between €13 and €50 ($12–$45) for one to four passengers, depending on duration of ride.

---

to 15 minutes thereafter. The last departures are 4pm from Suffolk Street, 4:30pm from O'Connell Street. You can also join the tour at any of a number of pickup points along the route and buy your ticket from the driver. Gray Line's Dublin city tour costs €11 ($10) adults, €10 ($9.20) seniors and students, €4 ($3.55) children, €27 ($24) family.

Gray Line also offers a range of full-day excursions from Dublin to such nearby sights as Glendalough, Newgrange, and Powerscourt. Adult fares for their other tours range from €19 to €34 ($17–$30).

HELICOPTER TOURS

Want a bird's-eye view of Dublin's fair city? **First Flight Aviation Ltd.,** Dublin, Helicopter Centre NSC, Cloghran, county Dublin (© **01/890-0222;** www.firstflight.ie), offers 20-minute helicopter tours over the center city, with more distant views of Dublin Bay and the north and south coastlines. The cost is from €127 ($113) per person.

LAND & WATER TOURS

The immensely-popular, 2-year-old **Viking Splash Tour** ★★ (© **01/855-3000;** www.vikingsplashtours.com) is an especially fun way to see Dublin. Aboard a reconditioned World War II amphibious landing craft, or "duck," this tour starts on land (from Bull Alley St. beside St. Patrick's Cathedral) and eventually splashes into the Grand Canal. Passengers wear horned Viking helmets (a reference to the original settlers of the Dublin area) and are encouraged to issue war cries at appropriate moments. One of the ducks even has bullet holes as evidence of its military service. Tours depart roughly every half hour Monday to Saturday 10am to 5pm and Sunday 11am to 6:30pm and last an hour and 15 minutes. It costs €13.50 ($12) for adults, €7.50 ($6.70) for children under 12, and €45 ($40) for a family of five. To book with a credit card by phone, call **086/828-3773.**

WALKING TOURS

Small and compact, Dublin lends itself to walking tours. If you prefer to set off on your own, the **Dublin Tourism Office,** St. Andrew's Church, Suffolk Street, Dublin 2, has been stellar in the development of self-guided walking tours around Dublin. To date, four tourist trails have been mapped out and signposted throughout the city: Old City, Georgian Heritage, Cultural Heritage, and Rock 'n Stroll/Music Theme. For each trail, the tourist office has produced a handy booklet that maps out the route and provides commentary about each place along the trail.

If you like some guidance, some historical background, or just some company, you might want to consider one of the following options.

Historical Walking Tours of Dublin ☆☆ *Value* This award-winning outfit has recently expanded its repertoire to include six terrific introductory walks, all 2-hour primers on Dublin's historic landmarks, from medieval walls and Viking remains around Wood Quay to Christ Church, to the architectural splendors of Georgian Dublin, to highlights of Irish history. All guides are history graduates of Trinity College, and participants are encouraged to ask questions. Tours assemble just inside the front gate of Trinity College; no reservations are needed.

From Trinity College. ✆ **01/878-0227.** www.historicalinsights.ie. Tickets €7.50 ($6.70) adults, €5 ($4.45) seniors and students. May–Sept Mon–Fri 11am and 3pm, Sun 11am, noon, 3pm; Oct–Apr Fri–Sun noon.

Literary Pub Crawl Walking in the footsteps of Joyce, Behan, Beckett, Shaw, Kavanagh, and other Irish literary greats, this guided tour, winner of the "Living Dublin Award," visits a number of Dublin's most famous pubs with literary connections. Actors provide humorous performances and commentary between stops. Throughout the night, there is a Literary Quiz with prizes for the winners. The tour assembles nightly at 7:30pm and Sundays at noon, upstairs at the Duke Pub on Duke Street (off Grafton St.).

37 Exchequer St., Dublin 2. ✆ **01/670-5602.** Tickets €8 ($7.10) per person.

Traditional Irish Musical Pub Crawl This tour explores and samples the traditional music scene, and the price includes a songbook. Two professional musicians, who sing as you make your way from one famous pub to another in Temple Bar, lead the tour. The evening is touristy but the music is good and thankfully free from clichés. It lasts 2½ hours. The "crawl" better describes the way back to your hotel.

Leaves from Oliver St. John Gogarty pub and restaurant, 57/58 Fleet St. (at Anglesea St.), Temple Bar. ✆ **01/478-0193.** Tickets €8 ($7.10) adults, €6 ($5.35) students and seniors. Mid-May to Oct daily 7:30pm; Nov and Feb to mid-May Fri–Sat 7:30pm. Tickets on sale at 7pm or in advance from Dublin Tourist Office.

Walk Macabre The Trapeze Theatre Company offers this 90-minute walk past the homes of famous writers around Merrion Square, St. Stephen's Green and Merrion Row, while reconstructing old scenes of murder and intrigue. The tour includes reenactments from some of the darker pages of Yeats, Joyce, Bram Stoker, and Oscar Wilde. This one would be rated "R" for violent imagery, so it's not for children or light sleepers. Advance booking is essential. Tours leave from the main gates of St. Stephen's Green, opposite Planet Hollywood.

Bookings: ✆ **087/677-1512** or 087/271-1346. Tickets €8 ($7.10) per person. Daily 7:30pm.

The Zosimus Experience ☆ This is the latest rage on the walking tour circuit. Its creators call it a "cocktail mix" of ghosts, murderous tales, horror stories, humor, circus, history, street theater, and whatever's left, all within the precincts of medieval Dublin. With the blind and aging Zosimus as your storyteller, you help guide him down the ascetic alleyways. It's essential to book in advance, when you'll receive the where (outside the pedestrian gate of Dublin Castle, opposite the Olympia Theatre) and the when (time varies according to nightfall). The experience lasts approximately 1½ hours.

28 Fitzwilliam Lane, Dublin 2. ✆ **01/661-8646.** www.zozimus.com. €8 ($7.10) per person. Daily at nightfall, by appointment.

BICYCLE TOURS

Dublin Bike Tours   Riding a bike in Dublin isn't recommended. Traffic is very heavy, the streets are narrow, and pedestrians crowd every corner. But if you're determined to take to the streets on wheels, Dublin Bike Tours does an excellent job at showing you another facet of the city along mostly quieter back streets at a relaxed pace. The 3-hour standard Dublin bike tour is broken by frequent stops, including one for refreshments. If you insist on setting out on your own, you can rent bikes and all the gear, from helmets to baby seats, here as well.

Lord Edward St., Dublin 2. © **01/679-0899.** Fax 01/679-6504. www.dublinbiketours.com. €19 ($17), including bike, tour guide, and insurance. Apr 1–Oct 31, Sat 6am, Sat–Sun 10am, daily 2pm. All tours start at gate of Christ Church Cathedral, opposite the Lord Edward pub. Arrive 15 min. early.

6 The Great Outdoors

BEACHES   Dublin has a good selection of fine beaches accessible by either city bus or DART, since the tramway follows the coast from Howth, north of the city, to Bray, south of the city in county Wicklow. Some popular beaches include **Dollymount,** 5.6km (3½ miles) away; **Sutton,** 11km (7 miles) away; **Howth,** 15km (9 miles) away; and **Portmarnock** and **Malahide,** each 11km (7 miles) away. In addition, the southern suburb of **Dun Laoghaire,** 11km (7 miles) away, offers a beach (at Sandycove) and a long bay-front promenade that's ideal for strolling in the sea air. For more details, inquire at the Dublin Tourism Office.

BIRD-WATCHING   The many estuaries, salt marshes, sand flats, and islands near Dublin Bay provide a varied habitat for a number of species. **Rockabill Island,** off the coast at Skerries, is home to an important colony of roseate terns; there is no public access to the island, but the birds can be seen from the shore. **Rogerstown and Malahide estuaries,** on the north side of Dublin, are wintering grounds for large numbers of brent geese, ducks, and waders. **Sandymount Strand** on Dublin's south side has a vast intertidal zone; around dusk in July and August you can often see large numbers of terns, including visiting roseate terns from Rockabill Island.

But for top birding and convenient location, your all-around best bet is a bird sanctuary called Bull Island, also known as the **North Bull,** which lies just north of Dublin city harbor. Actually, it's a misnomer—not an island, but rather a 3km (2-mile) spit of land connected to the mainland by a bridge. It comprises dunes, a salt marsh, and extensive intertidal flats on the side facing the mainland. Because of this unique environment, the North Bull attracts thousands of seabirds—nearly 200 different species have been recorded, and up to 40,000 birds shelter and nest here. In winter, these figures are boosted by tens of thousands of visiting migrants from the arctic circle, as well as North American spoonbills, little egrets, and sandpipers. Together, they all make a delightfully deafening racket. A visitor center is open daily 10:15am to 4:30pm.

DIVING   **Oceantec Adventures** in Dun Laoghaire (© **01/280-1083;** toll-free within Ireland 1800/272822) offers a five-star PADI diving school and arranges dive vacations on the west coast. Also check out the **National Diving School,** 8 St. James Terrace, Malahide, county Dublin (© **01/845-2000;** www.nds.ie).

FISHING   The greater Dublin area offers a wide range of opportunities for freshwater angling on local rivers, reservoirs, and fisheries. A day's catch might include perch, rudd, pike, salmon, sea trout, brown trout, or freshwater eel. The

Irish Tourist Board operates a good website dedicated to fishing (**www. angling.travel.ie**); just run the search engine for county Dublin and out will pop possibilities ranging from angling for brown trout with the River Dodder Anglers' Club (© **01/298-2112**) in southwest county Dublin to sea fishing on Charles Weston's 11m (35-ft.) ketch (© **01/843-6239**) off the shores of Malahide, just north of the city. In addition, the **Dublin Angling Initiative,** Balnagowan, Mobhi Boreen, Glasnevin, Dublin 9 (© **01/837-9209**), offers a guide—the *Dublin Freshwater Angling Guide,* available for €1.50 ($1.35)—to tell you everything you'll need to know about local fishing.

GOLF Dublin is one of the world's great golfing capitals. A quarter of Ireland's courses—including 5 of the top 10—lie within an hour's drive of the city. Visitors are welcome, but be sure to phone ahead and make a reservation. The following four courses—two parkland and two links—are among the best 18-hole courses in the Dublin area.

Elm Park Golf Club ⚘, Nutley Lane, Donnybrook, Dublin 4 (© **01/269-3438**), is in the residential, privileged south side of Dublin. The beautifully manicured parkland par-69 course is especially popular with visitors because it is within 5.6km (3½ miles) of the city center and close to the Jurys, Berkeley Court, and Four Seasons hotels. Greens fees are €70 ($62) on weekdays, €85 ($76) on weekends.

Portmarnock Golf Club ⚘⚘⚘, Portmarnock, county Dublin (© **01/846-2968**; www.portmarnockgolfclub.ie), is one of the finest links courses in Europe, not to mention Ireland. The course is located 16km (10 miles) from the city center on Dublin's north side, on a spit of land between the Irish Sea and a tidal inlet. Opened in 1894, the par-72 championship course has been the scene of leading tournaments, including the Dunlop Masters (1959, 1965), Canada Cup (1960), Alcan (1970), St. Andrews Trophy (1968), and many an Irish Open. Greens fees are €127 ($113) on weekdays, €158 ($141) on weekends.

Royal Dublin Golf Club ⚘⚘, Bull Island, Dollymount, Dublin 3 (© **01/833-6346**; www.theroyaldublingolfclub.com), is often compared to St. Andrews. The century-old par-73 championship seaside links is on an island in Dublin Bay, 4.8km (3 miles) northeast of the city center. Like Portmarnock, it has been rated among the world's top courses and has played host to several Irish Opens. The home base of Ireland's legendary champion Christy O'Connor, Sr., the Royal Dublin is well known for its fine bunkers, close lies, and subtle trappings. Greens fees are €100 ($89) on Monday to Thursday, €115 ($102) Friday to Sunday.

St. Margaret's Golf Club ⚘, Skephubble, St. Margaret's, county Dublin (© **01/864-0400**; www.st-margarets.net), is a stunning, par-72 parkland course 4.8km (3 miles) west of Dublin Airport. Though one of Dublin's newest championship golf venues, St. Margaret's has already hosted three international tournaments, including the Irish Open. Greens fees are €60 ($53) Monday to Wednesday, €70 ($62) Thursday and Friday, and €75 ($67) on weekends.

HORSEBACK RIDING For equestrian enthusiasts of any experience level, almost a dozen riding stables are within easy reach. Prices average about €25 ($22) an hour, with or without instruction. Many stables offer guided trail riding, as well as courses in show jumping, dressage, prehunting, eventing, and cross-country riding. For trail riding through Phoenix Park, **Ashtown Riding Stables** (© **01/838-3807**) is ideal. They're located in the village of Ashtown, adjoining the park and only 10 minutes by car or bus (nos. 37, 38, 39, or 70) from the city center. Among the other riding centers within easy reach of downtown Dublin are **Calliaghstown Riding Centre,** Calliaghstown, Rathcoole, county Dublin (✆ **01/458-9236**); and **Carrickmines Equestrian Centre,** Glenamuck Road, Foxrock, Dublin 18 (✆ **01/295-5990**).

WALKING   For casual walking, the Royal Canal and Grand Canal, which skirt the north and south city centers, respectively, are ideal for seeing both the city and neighboring areas. Both have been restored as marked trails for serious walkers, so you can't get lost. And because they stick to the towpaths of the canals, they are flat and easy. Moreover, both routes pass through a range of small towns and villages that can be used as starting or stopping points. For more information, contact the Waterways Service at **Duchas The Heritage Service** (✆ **01/647-6000**).

The walk from Bray (the southern terminus of the DART) to Greystones along the rocky promontory of **Bray Head** is a great excursion, with beautiful views back toward Killiney Bay, Dalkey Island, and Bray. It's readily accessible from Dublin. Follow the beachside promenade south through town; at the outskirts of town the promenade turns left and up, beginning the ascent of Bray Head. Shortly after the ascent begins, a trail branches to the left—this is the cliff-side walk, which continues another 5.6km (3½ miles) along the coast to Greystones. From the center of Greystones, a train will take you back to Bray. This is an easy walk, about 2 hours each way.

Dalkey Hill and **Killiney Hill** drop steeply into the sea, and command great views of Killiney Bay, Bray Head, and Sugarloaf Mountain. To get there, leave the Dalkey DART station, head into the center of Dalkey and then south on Dalkey Avenue (at the post office). About half a mile from the post office, you'll pass a road ascending through fields on your left—this is the entrance to the Dalkey Hill Park. From the parking lot, climb a series of steps to the top of Dalkey Hill; from here you can see the expanse of the bay, the Wicklow Hills in the distance, and the obelisk topping nearby Killiney Hill. If you continue on to the obelisk, there is a trail leading from there down on the seaward side to Vico Road, another lovely place for a seaside walk. It's about half a mile from the parking lot to Killiney Hill.

WATERSPORTS   Certified level-one and level-two instruction and equipment rental for three watersports—kayaking, sailing, and windsurfing—are available at the **Surfdock Centre,** Grand Canal Dock Yard, Ringsend, Dublin 4 (✆ **01/668-3945;** fax 01/668-1215; www.surfdock.ie). The center has 17 hectares (42 acres) of enclosed fresh water for its courses. It's open from June to September.

7 Spectator Sports

GAELIC SPORTS   If your schedule permits, try to get to a **Gaelic football** or **hurling** match—the only indigenously Irish games and two of the fastest moving sports in the world. Gaelic football is vaguely a cross between soccer and American football; you can move the ball with either your hands or feet. **Hurling** is a lightning-speed game in which 30 men use heavy sticks to fling a hard leather ball called a *sliotar*—think field hockey meets lacrosse. Both amateur sports are played every weekend throughout the summer at various local fields, culminating in September with the **All-Ireland Finals,** the Irish version of the Super Bowl. For schedules and admission fees, phone the **Gaelic Athletic Association,** Croke Park, Jones Road, Dublin 3 (✆ **01/836-3222;** www.gaa.ie).

GREYHOUND RACING   Watching these lean, swift canines is one of the leading spectator sports in the Dublin area. Races are held throughout the year at **Shelbourne Park Greyhound Stadium,** Southlotts Road, Dublin 4 (© 01/ 668-3502), and **Harold's Cross Stadium,** 151 Harold's Cross Rd., Dublin 6 (© 01/497-1081). For a complete schedule and details for races throughout Ireland, contact **Bord na gCon** (the Greyhound Board), Limerick (© 061/315-788; www.igb.ie).

HORSE RACING   The closest racecourse to the city center is the **Leopardstown Race Course,** off the Stillorgan road (N11), Foxrock, Dublin 18 (© 01/ 289-2888; www.leopardstown.com). This modern facility with all-weather glass-enclosed spectator stands is 9.7km (6 miles) south of the city center. Racing meets—mainly steeplechases, but also a few flats—are scheduled throughout the year, two or three times a month.

POLO   With the Dublin Mountains as a backdrop, polo is played from May to mid-September on the green fields of Phoenix Park, on Dublin's west side. Matches take place on Wednesday evenings and Saturday and Sunday afternoons. Admission is free. For full details, contact the **All Ireland Polo Club,** Phoenix Park, Dublin 8 (© 01/677-6248), or check the sports pages of the newspapers.

8 Shopping

Ireland is known the world over for its handmade products and fine craftsmanship, and Dublin is a one-stop source for the country's best wares. Also, due to Ireland's wholehearted membership in the European Union, Irish shops are brimming with imported goods from the Continent. In broad terms (though, obviously, there are exceptions) most of the trendy shops and upscale designer stores are located south of the Liffey, while north of the Liffey is a bit more downscale and serviceable.

Generally, Dublin shops are open from 9am to 6pm Monday to Saturday, and Thursday until 9pm. Many of the larger shops also have Sunday hours from noon to 6pm.

The hub of shopping south of the Liffey is **Grafton Street,** crowned by the city's most fashionable department store, Brown Thomas (known simply as BT), and most exclusive jeweler, Weirs. Sadly, many Irish specialty shops on Grafton Street have been displaced over the years by British chain shops (Principles, Jigsaw, Monsoon, Oasis, A–Wear, Next, Boots, Mothercare) so that it now resembles the average High Street in England. Since it's pedestrianized, Grafton Street tends to have a festive atmosphere thanks to street performers and sidewalk artists. But you'll find better shopping on the smaller streets radiating out from Grafton—Duke, Dawson, Nassau, and Wicklow—which have more Irish shops that specialize in small books, handcrafts, jewelry, gifts, and clothing.

A 2-minute walk toward the river brings you to **Temple Bar,** the hub of Dublin's colorful bohemian district and the setting for art and music shops, vintage clothing stores, and a host of other increasingly fine and interesting boutiques, cafes, and restaurants.

Major department stores include **Arnotts,** 12 Henry St., Dublin 1 (© 01/ 805-0400); the most exclusive of them all, **Brown Thomas,** 15–20 Grafton St., Dublin 2 (© 01/605-6666); and **Clerys,** Lower O'Connell Street, Dublin 1 (© 01/878-6000).

Dublin also has several clusters of shops in **multistory malls** or ground-level arcades, ideal for indoor shopping on rainy days. These include the **ILAC Centre,** off Henry Street, Dublin 1; the **Jervis Shopping Centre,** off Henry Street,

---

Tips **New Kid on the Block: The Old City**

Shoppers take note: Dublin's latest "it" shopping district is **Old City**, located just west of Temple Bar and roughly comprising the area between Castle Street and Fishamble Street. Though still under development, there's already a good mix of hip fashion, modern interior design, crafts, and leisure shops, as well as a bakery, Internet cafe, and a hair salon. The center of the action is a cobbled, pedestrianized street called Cow's Lane, which links Lord Edward Street with Essex Street West. Granted, the name may not immediately conjure up a cool image, but it's become a destination in itself for stylemongers who like to get their retail therapy away from the crush of Grafton and Henry Streets. On Cow's Lane, don't miss **Whichcraft** (see "Craft Emporiums," below), contemporary pieces for the home at **2cooldesign,** postwar home accessories from **20th Century Furniture,** and the latest looks in glasses at the swish London eyewear outlet **Kirk Originals.**

North of the Liffey, the **O'Connell Street** area is the main inner-city shopping nucleus, along with its nearby offshoots—Abbey Street for crafts, Moore Street for its open-air market, and most notably, Henry Street, a pedestrian-only strip of chain stores, department stores, and indoor malls such as the ILAC Centre and the Jervis Shopping Centre.

Dublin 1; **Royal Hibernian Way,** 49/50 Dawson St., Dublin 2; and **Powerscourt Townhouse,** where Grafton Street meets St. Stephen's Green, Dublin 2.

ART

Combridge Fine Arts   In business for more than 100 years, this shop features works by modern Irish artists as well as quality reproductions of classic Irish art. 17 S. William St., Dublin 2. ✆ **01/677-4652.** DART: Pearse. Bus: 15A, 15B, 15C, 55, or 83.

Davis Gallery   One block north of the Liffey, this shop offers a wide selection of Irish watercolors and oil paintings, with emphasis on Dublin scenes, wildlife, and flora. 11 Capel St., Dublin 1. ✆ **01/872-6969.** Bus: 34, 70, or 80.

M. Kennedy and Sons Ltd   If you are looking for a souvenir that reflects Irish art, try this interesting shop, established more than 100 years ago. It's a treasure trove of books on Irish artists and works, and it stocks a lovely selection of fine-art greeting cards, postcards, and bookmarks. There are all types of artists' supplies as well, and an excellent art gallery on the upstairs level. 12 Harcourt St., Dublin 2. ✆ **01/475-1749.** Bus: 62.

BOOKS

Greene's Bookshop Ltd   Established in 1843, this shop near Trinity College is one of Dublin's treasures for scholarly bibliophiles. It's chock-full of new and secondhand books on every topic from religion to the modern novel. The catalog of Irish-interest books is issued five to six times a year. 16 Clare St., Dublin 2. ✆ **01/676-2554.** DART: Pearse. Bus: 5, 7A, 8, or 62.

CERAMICS

Louis Mulcahy   The ceramic creations of Louis Mulcahey are internationally renowned. For years he has been exporting his work throughout Ireland and the rest of the world from his studio on the Dingle Peninsula. This modest new shop across from the Shelbourne Hotel gives him a base in Dublin. In addition to pottery, he designs furniture, lighting, and hand-painted silk and cotton lampshades. 51c Dawson St., Dublin 2. © 01/670-9311. DART: Pearse. Bus: 10, 11A, 11B, 13, or 20B.

CHINA & CRYSTAL

If you're specifically looking for Waterford Crystal, don't bother shopping around because it has fixed pricing. You'll find the best selections at **Brown Thomas** (Grafton St., Dublin 2), **Weirs** (Grafton St., Dublin 2), and **House of Ireland** (Nassau St., Dublin 2). If brand names aren't important, check out other native crystal makers, including Galway, Tipperary, Cavan, and Tyrone. Don't forget to get your cash-back forms if you want to reclaim the VAT (see chapter 2, "Shopping," for more information on VAT reclamation).

The China Showrooms   Established in 1939, this is Ireland's oldest china and crystal shop in continuous operation. It's a one-stop source for fine china such as Belleek, Aynsley, Royal Doulton, and Rosenthal; hand-cut crystal from Waterford, Tipperary, and Tyrone; and handmade Irish pottery. Worldwide shipping is available. 32/33 Abbey St., Dublin 1. © 01/878-6211. www.chinashowrooms.ie. DART: Connolly. Bus: 27B or 53A.

Dublin Crystal Glass Company   This is Dublin's own distinctive hand-cut crystal business, founded in 1764 and revived in 1968. Visitors are welcome to browse in the factory shop and see the glass being made and engraved. Brookfield Terrace, Carysfort Ave., Blackrock, county Dublin. © 01/288-7932. www.dublincrystal.ie. DART: Blackrock. Bus: 114.

CRAFT EMPORIUMS

Craft Centre of Ireland   Perched on the top floor of a popular shopping mall, this place offers an exquisite collection of ceramics, wood turning, glassware, and more—all by top Irish artisans. Unit 214 (top floor), St. Stephen's Green Centre, Dublin 2. © 01/475-4526. All cross-city buses.

Powerscourt Townhouse Centre   Housed in a restored 1774 town house, this four-story complex consists of a central skylit courtyard and more than 60 boutiques, craft shops, art galleries, snack bars, wine bars, and restaurants. The wares include all kinds of crafts, antiques, paintings, prints, ceramics, leather work, jewelry, clothing, hand-dipped chocolates, and farmhouse cheeses. 59 S. William St., Dublin 2. © 01/679-4144. Bus: 10, 11A, 11B, 13, 16A, 19A, 20B, 22A, 55, or 83.

Tower Design Centre   Alongside the Grand Canal, this beautifully restored 1862 sugar refinery now houses a nest of craft workshops where you can watch the artisans at work. The merchandise ranges from fine-art greeting cards and hand-marbled stationery to pewter, ceramics, pottery, knitwear, hand-painted silks, copper-plate etchings, all-wool wall hangings, silver and gold Celtic jewelry, and heraldic gifts. Pearse St. (off Grand Canal Quay), Dublin 2. © 01/677-5655. Limited free parking. DART: Pearse. Bus: 2 or 3.

Whichcraft   If you're serious about taking home quality, contemporary Irish crafts, this is an essential stop for finding out what the best contemporary artisans from all over Ireland are doing. All kinds of crafts are represented, from wooden bowls to basketry to rocking horses to pottery to jewelry to ironmongery to batiks. There's a second Whichcraft shop on Cow's Lane in the burgeoning Old City. 5 Castlegate, Lord Edward St., Dublin 2. © 01/670-9371. Bus: 50, 54A, 56A, 65, 65A, 77, 77A, 123, or 150.

FASHION
See also "Knitwear," below.

MEN'S
Alias Tom   This was Dublin's best small, men's designer shop until BT2 opened. The emphasis is Italian (Gucci, Prada, Armani), but the range covers other chic designers from the rest of Europe and America. Prices are exorbitant. Duke House, Duke St., Dublin 2 ✆ 01/671 5443. DART: Pearse. Bus: 10, 11A, 11B, 13, or 20B.

BT2   This new offshoot of Brown Thomas, located across the street on Grafton, is the best shop in Dublin for the hippest designer labels for both men and women. The look is sportier, more casual, and geared to the younger, hopelessly cool set. The prices are nearly as crazy as in BT. Grafton St., Dublin 2 ✆ 01/ 605-6666. All cross-city buses.

Kevin & Howlin   Open for more than a half century, this is the best place in town for hand-woven Donegal tweed garments. The selection includes suits, overcoats, jackets, scarves, vests, and myriad hats—everything from Patch caps and Gatsby fedoras to Sherlock Holmes–style deerstalkers and the ubiquitous Paddy hats. 31 Nassau St., Dublin 2. ✆ 01/677-0257. DART: Pearse. Bus: 7, 8, 10, 11, or 46A.

Louis Copeland and Sons   Behind a distinctive old-world shop front, this is where well-dressed insiders, from Pierce Brosnan to the Prime Minister Bertie Ahern, buy their suits. Louis Copeland is a tailor known for high-quality work in made-to-measure suits, but also carries ready-to-wear men's suits, coats, and shirts. The look here is conservative and classic, not trendy. Branches at 30 Pembroke St., Dublin 2 (✆ 01/661-0110), and 18 Wicklow St., Dublin 2 (✆ 01/677-7038). 39–41 Capel St., Dublin 1. ✆ 01/872-1600. Bus: 34, 70, or 80.

WOMEN'S
BT2   Brown Thomas's new sister shop, located right across the street, is the best place in town for A-list designer labels. BT2 targets a younger, but no less label-conscious, crowd than BT—think style-obsessed Trustifarians and yuppies and you've got the clientele in a nutshell. Grafton St., Dublin 2. ✆ 01/605-6666. All cross-city buses.

Claire Garvey   The brightest luminary in Old City is a 34-year-old Dublin native with a talent for creating romantic, dramatic, and feminine clothing with Celtic flair. A favorite designer of Irish divas Enya and Sinead O'Connor, Garvey transforms hand-dyed velvet and silk into sumptuous garments that beg to be worn on special occasions. Her one-of-a-kind bijou handbags are a white-hot fashion accessory. 6 Cow's Lane, Old City, Dublin 8. ✆ 01/671-7287. Bus: 50, 54A, 56A, 65, 65A, 77, 77A, 123, or 150.

Design Centre   This is the city's best one-stop shop if you want to find all of Ireland's hottest contemporary designers—including Louise Kennedy, Mary Gregory, Karen Millen, and Sharon Hoey—under one roof. Prices are generally high, but there are good bargains to be had during sale seasons and on the seconds rack. Powerscourt Townhouse, Dublin 2. ✆ 01/679-4144. DART: Pearse. Bus: 10, 11A, 11B, 13, or 20B.

Jenny Vander   This is where actresses and supermodels come to find extraordinary and stylish antique clothing. There's plenty of jeweled frocks, vintage day wear and stunning costume jewelry filling the clothing racks and display cases. Overall, it's a fabulous place to shop for one-of-a-kind pieces. 20 Georges St. Arcade, South Great Georges St., Dublin 2. ✆ 01/677-0406. DART: Pearse. Bus: 10, 11A, 11B, 13, or 20B.

Louise Kennedy   This glamorous and sophisticated designer is a longtime favorite of Meryl Streep, British first lady Cherie Blair, and Carol Vorderman, and recently Dublin native and popstress/actress/model Samantha Mumba has signed on to be the body and face of Kennedy's sumptuous collection. Her elegant showroom carries her clothing, accessories, and home collections, as well as Philip Treacy hats, Lulu Guinness handbags, Lindley furniture, and other items of perfect taste. 56 Merrion Square, Dublin 2. ℂ **01/662-0056.** DART: Pearse. Bus: 5, 7A, or 8.

GIFTS & IRISH KEEPSAKES

House of Ireland   This shop opposite Trinity College is a happy blend of European and Irish products, from Waterford and Belleek to Wedgwood and Lladró. It also carries high-quality tweeds, linens, knitwear, Celtic jewelry, mohair capes, shawls, kilts, blankets, and dolls. 37–38 Nassau St., Dublin 2. ℂ **01/ 677-7473.** www.hoi.ie. DART: Pearse. Bus: 5, 7A, 15A, 15B, 46, 55, 62, 63, 83, or 84.

The Kilkenny Shop   A sister operation of the Blarney Woollen Mills (see "Knitwear," below), this modern multilevel shop is also a showplace for original Irish designs and quality products, including pottery, glass, candles, woolens, pipes, knitwear, jewelry, books, and prints. The pleasant cafe is ideal for coffee and pastries or a light lunch. 6–10 Nassau St., Dublin 2. ℂ **01/677-7066.** DART: Pearse. Bus: 5, 7A, 15A, 15B, 46, 55, 62, 63, 83, or 84.

HERALDRY

Heraldic Artists   For more than 20 years, this shop has been known for helping visitors locate their family roots. In addition to tracing surnames, it sells all the usual heraldic items, from family crest parchments, scrolls, and mahogany wall plaques, to books on researching ancestry. 3 Nassau St., Dublin 2. ℂ **01/679-7020.** www.roots.ie. DART: Pearse. Bus: 5, 7A, 8, 15A, 15B, 46, 55, 62, 63, 83, or 84.

House of Names   As its name implies, this company offers a wide selection of Irish, British, and European family names affixed—along with their attendant crests and mottoes—to plaques, shields, parchments, jewelry, glassware, and sweaters. 26 Nassau St., Dublin 2. ℂ **01/679-7287.** DART: Pearse. Bus: 5, 7A, 8, 15A, 15B, 46, 55, 62, 63, 83, or 84.

JEWELRY

DESIGNyard   The ground-floor studio of this beautiful emporium showcases exquisite, often affordable work from the very best contemporary Irish jewelry designers. Upstairs in the same building, the Crafts Council Gallery displays and sells Irish-made crafts, including furniture, ceramics, glass, lighting, and textiles. All exhibited pieces are for sale, and you may also make an appointment to commission an original work of Irish applied art and design. 12 E. Essex St., Temple Bar, Dublin 2. ℂ **01/677-8453.** DART: Tara St. Bus: 21A, 46A, 46B, 51B, 51C, 68, 69, or 86.

The Steensons   Bill and Christina Steenson, based in Northern Ireland, have long been two of the most celebrated goldsmiths on the island. This, their first shop in the Republic, opened in November 1999 and was an immediate success—no wonder, as their workmanship and design are exquisite. The focus here is on contemporary Irish design, though roughly 20% of their inventory comes from other European sources, especially Germany. 16 S. Frederick St., Dublin 2. ℂ and fax **01/672-7007.** DART: Pearse. Bus: 5, 7A, 15A, 15B, 46, 55, 62, 63, 83, or 84.

Weir and Sons   Established in 1869, this is the granddaddy of Dublin's fine jewelry shops. It sells new and antique jewelry as well as silver, china, and crystal. There is a second branch at the ILAC Centre, Henry Street (© **01/872-9588**). 96 Grafton St., Dublin 2. © **01/677-9678**. DART: Pearse. Bus: 10, 11A, 11B, 13, or 20B.

KNITWEAR

Blarney Woollen Mills This branch of the highly successful Cork-based enterprise stands opposite the south side of Trinity College. Known for its competitive prices, it stocks a wide range of woolen knitwear made at the home base in Blarney, as well as Irish-made crystal, china, pottery, and souvenirs. Always check the label or ask a sales assistant to verify whether a sweater is hand-knit or made by machine. 21–23 Nassau St., Dublin 2. © **01/671-0068**. DART: Pearse. Bus: 5, 7A, 8, 15A, 15B, 46, 55, 62, 63, 83, or 84.

Brown Thomas This is the only place in town to find Dubliner Lainey Keogh's creative and sensuous knitwear—a far cry from the chunky Aran sweaters you see everywhere else. The creator of what *Vogue* magazine calls "amazingly organic knitwear" had her first, rapturously received show in 1997, and has been a staple in the closets of Hollywood celebrities such as Demi Moore and Isabella Rosselini ever since. She works mostly with cashmere and her pieces are predominantly made by expert hand-knitters, so prices are high. Grafton St., Dublin 2. © **01/605-6666**. All cross-city buses.

Dublin Woollen Mills Since 1888, this shop has been a leading source of Aran sweaters, vests, hats, jackets, and scarves, as well as lamb's-wool sweaters, kilts, ponchos, and tweeds at competitive prices. As at Blarney Woollen Mills, always verify whether a sweater is hand-knit. The shop is on the north side of the River Liffey next to the Halfpenny Bridge. There is a 5% discount for those with current international student cards. 41–42 Lower Ormond Quay, Dublin 1. © **01/677-0301**. Bus: 70 or 80.

Monaghan's Established in 1960 and operated by two generations of the Monaghan family, this store is a prime source of cashmere sweaters for men and women. It boasts the best selection of colors, sizes, and styles anywhere in Ireland. Other items include traditional Aran knits, lamb's wool, crochet, and Shetland wool products. There's another store at 4/5 Royal Hibernian Way, off Dawson Street (© **01/679-4451**). 15/17 Grafton Arcade, Grafton St., Dublin 2. © **01/677-0823**. DART: Pearse. Bus: 10, 11A, 11B, 13, or 20B.

MARKETS

Blackrock Market More than 60 vendors run stalls that offer everything from gourmet cheese to vintage clothing in an indoor/outdoor setting. As at most markets, prices range from very reasonable to highway robbery. Open Saturday from 11am to 5:30pm and Sunday from noon to 5:30pm, including holidays. 19a Main St., Blackrock. © **01/283-3522**. DART: Blackrock. Bus: 5, 7, 7A, 8, 17, 45, or 114.

Book Market Temple Bar This weekend market has enough of everything to make for excellent browsing—old and new titles, classics and contemporary novels, science fiction and mysteries, serious biographies, and pulp fiction. Open Saturday and Sunday only, from 11am to 4pm. Temple Bar Square, Dublin 2. No phone. Bus: 50, 50A, 54, 56, or 77.

Food Market Temple Bar Like Moore Street, this is another great picnic shopping spot. Everything here is organic, from fruits and veggies to a delicious selection of homemade cheeses, chutneys, breads, and jams. Open Saturday and Sunday only, from 10 am to 5pm. Meeting House Square, Dublin 2. No phone. Bus: 50, 50A, 54, 56, or 77.

Moore Street Market For a walk into the past, the Moore Street Market is full of street-side barrow vendors plus plenty of local color and chatter. It's the city's principal open-air fruit, flower, fish, and vegetable market and a great stop for stocking up on picnic provisions. Open daily from 10am to 4pm. Moore St., Dublin 1. No phone. DART: Connolly. Bus: 25, 34, 37, 38A, 66A, or 67A.

Mother Red Caps Market In the heart of Old Dublin, this enclosed market calls itself the "mother of all markets." The stalls offer the usual garage-sale junk mixed in with the occasional treasure (some more in hiding than others), including antiques, used books and coins, silver, handcrafts, leather products, knitwear, music tapes, and furniture. There's even a fortuneteller! The pickings can be hit or miss, but do make a point of popping by the Ryefield Foods stall (farm-made cheeses, baked goods, marmalades, and jams). Open Friday to Sunday only, from 10am to 5:30pm. Back Lane (off High St.), Dublin 8. ℂ 01/453-8306. Bus: 21A, 78A, or 78B.

TRADITIONAL IRISH MUSIC

The Celtic Note Second only to Claddagh Records, this is a terrific source of recorded Irish music in Dublin. The staff is experienced and helpful, and you can listen to a CD before purchasing it. You'll pay full price here, but you're likely to find what you're looking for. 14–15 Nassau St., Dublin 2. ℂ 01/670-4157. www.celticnote.ie. DART: Pearse. Bus: 5, 7A, 15A, 15B, 46, 55, 62, 63, 83, or 84.

Claddagh Records Renowned among insiders in traditional Irish music circles, this is where to find "the genuine article" in traditional music and perhaps discover a new favorite. Not only is the staff knowledgeable and enthusiastic about turning you on to new artists, but they're able to tell you which venues and pubs are hosting the best sessions of live traditional music that week. Dame St., Dublin 2. ℂ 01/677-8943. www.claddaghrecords.com. Bus: 50, 50A, 54, 56, or 77.

9 Dublin After Dark

A more appropriate title for this section might be "Dublin Almost Dark," because during high season, Dublin's nightlife takes place mostly in daylight. Situated roughly 53° north of the equator, Dublin in June gets really dark only as the pubs are closing. Night, then, is just a state of mind.

One general fact to keep in mind concerning Dublin's nightlife is that there are very few fixed points. Apart from a handful of established institutions, venues come and go, change character, open their doors to ballet one night and cabaret the next. *In Dublin* and *The Event Guide* offer the most thorough and up-to-date listings. They can be found on almost any magazine stand.

The award-winning website of the *Irish Times* (**www.ireland.com**) offers a "what's on" daily guide to cinema, theater, music, and whatever else you're up for. The **Dublin Events Guide,** at www.dublinevents.com, also provides a comprehensive listing of the week's entertainment possibilities. *Time Out* now covers Dublin as well; check their website at **www.timeout.com/Dublin.**

Advance bookings for most large concerts, plays, and so forth can be made through **Ticketmaster Ireland** (ℂ 01/677-9409; www.ticketmaster.ie), with ticket centers in most HMV stores, as well as at the Dublin Tourism Centre, Suffolk Street, Dublin 2.

THE PUB SCENE

The mainstay of Dublin social life is unquestionably the pub. More than 1,000 specimens spread throughout the city, on every street, at every turn. In *Ulysses,* James Joyce referred to the puzzle of trying to cross Dublin without passing a pub; his characters quickly abandoned the quest as fruitless, preferring to sample a few in their path. You will need no assistance finding a pub, but here are recommendations of some of the city's most distinctive.

PUBS FOR CONVERSATION & ATMOSPHERE

Brazen Head Sure it's touristy, but it's an institution. This brass-filled, lantern-lit pub claims to be the city's oldest, and it might very well be, considering that it was licensed in 1661 and occupies the site of an even earlier tavern dating from 1198. Nestled on the south bank of the River Liffey, it is at the end of a cobblestone courtyard and was once the meeting place of Irish freedom fighters such as Robert Emmet and Wolfe Tone. A full a la carte menu is offered. 20 Lower Bridge St., Dublin 8. ℂ 01/679-5186.

Davy Byrnes Referred to as a "moral pub" by James Joyce in *Ulysses,* this imbibers' landmark has drawn poets, writers, and literature lovers ever since. It dates from 1873, when Davy Byrnes first opened the doors. He presided for more than 50 years, and visitors can still see his likeness on one of the turn-of-the-20th-century murals hanging over the bar. 21 Duke St. (off Grafton St.), Dublin 2. ℂ 01/677-5217.

Doheny and Nesbitt The locals call this Victorian-style pub simply "Nesbitt's." The place houses two fine old "snugs"—small rooms behind the main bar where women could have a drink out of the sight of men in days of old—and a restaurant. 5 Lower Baggot St., Dublin 2. ℂ 01/676-2945.

J. W. Ryan This Victorian gem also houses a fine gourmet restaurant. You'll see some of Dublin's best traditional pub features, including a metal ceiling, a domed skylight, beveled mirrors, etched glass, brass lamp holders, a mahogany bar, and four old-style snugs. It's on the north side of the Liffey, near Phoenix Park. 28 Parkgate St., Dublin 7. ℂ 01/677-6097.

The Long Hall This is one of the city's most photographed pubs, with a beautiful Victorian decor of filigree-edged mirrors, polished dark woods, and traditional snugs. The hand-carved bar is said to be the longest counter in the city. 51 S. Great George's St., Dublin 2. ℂ 01/475-1590.

Neary's Adjacent to the back door of the Gaiety Theatre, this celebrated enclave is a favorite with stage folk and theatergoers. Its trademarks are the pink-and-gray marble bar and the brass hands that support the globe lanterns adorning the entrance. 1 Chatham St., Dublin 2. ℂ 01/677-7371.

Palace Bar This old charmer is decorated with local memorabilia, cartoons, and paintings that tell the story of Dublin through the years. 21 Fleet St., Dublin 2. ℂ 01/677-9290.

River Club Converted from an old merchant's warehouse, this wine bar–cum–supper club combines soaring ceilings, an enviable position overlooking the river, and contemporary furnishings for an overall feeling of easygoing sophistication. It's a favorite of Ireland's film glitterati for a late drink, so don't be surprised to spy author-screenwriter Roddy Doyle, Pierce Brosnan, or director Jim Sheridan. Ha'penny Theatre, 48 Wellington Quay, Dublin 2. ℂ 01/677-2382.

Searsons This formerly down-at-its-heels rugby pub underwent a face-lift and has a new lease on life, thanks to hordes of Ballsbridge hipsters who pack the place every night. 42 Upper Baggot St., Dublin 4. ℂ 01/660-0330.

Stag's Head   Mounted stags' heads and eight stag-themed stained-glass windows dominate the decor, and there are wrought-iron chandeliers, polished Aberdeen granite, old barrels, skylights, and ceiling-high mirrors. Look for the stag sign inlaid into the sidewalk. This place is a classic. 1 Dame Court (off Dame St.), Dublin 2. ℂ 01/679-3701.

PUBS FOR TRADITIONAL & FOLK MUSIC

The Castle Inn   Situated between Dublin Castle and Christ Church Cathedral, this recently rejuvenated bilevel pub exudes an "old city" atmosphere. It has stone walls, flagstone steps, suits of armor, big stone fireplaces, beamed ceilings, and lots of early Dublin memorabilia. From May to September, it is also the setting for an Irish ceili (traditional music and dance session) and banquet. Christchurch Place, Dublin 8. ℂ 01/475-1122.

Chief O'Neill's   One of the city's best haunts for gimmick-free traditional music, in the hotel of the same name. Smithfield Village, Dublin 7. ℂ 01/817-3838. www.chiefoneills.com. Bus: 25, 25A, 66, 67, or 90.

Flannery's Temple Bar   In the heart of the trendy Temple Bar district on the corner of Temple Lane, this small three-room pub was established in 1840. The decor is an interesting mix of crackling fireplaces, globe ceiling lights, old pictures on the walls, and shelves filled with local memorabilia. There's live Irish music daily. 47/48 Temple Bar. ℂ 01/497-4766.

Kitty O'Shea's   Just south of the Grand Canal, this popular pub is named after the sweetheart of 19th-century Irish statesman Charles Stewart Parnell. The decor reflects the Parnell era, with ornate oak paneling, stained-glass windows, old political posters, cozy alcoves, and brass railings. Traditional Irish music is on tap most every night. 23–25 Upper Grand Canal St., Dublin 4. ℂ 01/660-9965.

Mother Red Caps Tavern   A former shoe factory in the heart of the Liberties section of the city, this large two-story pub exudes Old Dublin atmosphere. It has eclectic mahogany and stripped pine furnishings, antiques and curios on the shelves, and walls lined with old paintings and 19th-century newspaper clippings. On Sundays, there is usually a midday session of traditional Irish music; everyone is invited to bring an instrument and join in. On many nights, there is traditional music on an informal basis or in a concert setting upstairs. Back Lane, Dublin 8. ℂ 01/454-4655. No cover except for concerts.

O'Donoghue's *Overrated*   Tucked between St. Stephen's Green and Merrion Street, this much-touristed, smoke-filled enclave is widely heralded as the granddaddy of traditional music pubs. A spontaneous session is likely to erupt at almost any time of the day or night. 15 Merrion Row, Dublin 2. ℂ 01/661-4303.

Oliver St. John Gogarty   Situated in the heart of Temple Bar and named for one of Ireland's literary greats, this pub has an inviting old-world atmosphere, with shelves of empty bottles, stacks of dusty books, a horseshoe-shaped bar, and old barrels for seats. There are traditional music sessions most every night from 9 to 11pm, as well as Saturday at 4:30pm, and Sunday from noon to 2pm. 57/58 Fleet St., Dublin 2. ℂ 01/671-1822.

LATE-NIGHT PUBS

If you're still going strong when the pubs shut down (11pm in winter, 11:30pm in summer), you might want to crawl to a "late-night pub"—one with a loophole allowing it to remain open after hours. Late-nighters for the 18-to-25 set include **Hogans,** 35 S. Great George's St., Dublin 2 (ℂ **01/677-5904**), and the

Club mono (see "Smaller Concert Venues," later in this chapter). After-hours pubs that attract the young and hip but are still congenial for those over 25 include Whelans, 25 Wexford St., Dublin 2 (© 01/478-0766), and the second-oldest pub in Dublin, the Bleeding Horse, 24–25 Camden St., Dublin 2 (© 01/475-2705). For the over-30 late crowd, try: Break for the Border, Lower Steven's Street, Dublin 2 (© 01/478-0300); Bad Bob's Backstage Bar, East Essex Street, Dublin 2 (© 01/677-5482); Major Tom's, South King Street, Dublin 2 (© 01/478-3266); and Sinnotts, South King Street, Dublin 2 (© 01/478-4698).

THE CLUB & MUSIC SCENE

Dublin's club and music scene is confoundingly complex and volatile. Jazz, blues, folk, country, traditional, rock, and comedy move from venue to venue, night by night. The same club could be a gay fetish scene one night and a techno-pop dance hall the next, so you have to stay on your toes to find what you want. The first rule is to get the very latest listings and see what's on and where (see the introduction to "Dublin After Dark" for a couple of suggested resources). Keeping all this in mind, a few low-risk generalizations might prove helpful to give you a sense of what to expect.

One fact unlikely to change is that the after-hours scene in Dublin is definitively young, averaging about 25. The hottest clubs have a "strict" (read unfriendly) door policy of admitting only "regulars." It helps if you're a celebrity or a supermodel—or just look like one. But barring that, your chances of getting past the door increase if you go in smallish groups and wear your hippest clothes and your coolest attitude.

Most trendy clubs have DJs or live music, with the current genre of choice being "rave" and the drug of choice being ecstasy, among even the youngest clubgoers. Clubbers on "E" don't drink anything but water, which they must consume in great quantities. Cover charges tend to fluctuate not only from place to place, but from night to night and from person to person (some people can't buy their way in, while others glide in gratis). Cover charges range from nominal to €15 ($13).

HIPPER THAN THOU

Wear your designer duds and a big attitude to these cutting-edge clubs, where Europe's best DJs are the prime entertainers:

The Kitchen   In the basement of the Clarence hotel in the heart of the Temple Bar district, this is one of Dublin's hottest, hippest, coolest nightclubs, partly owned by the rock group U2. The DJs are all fabulous, whether dishing up progressive house, drum and bass, trance, or techno (check listings magazines to find out the specialty on any given night). Open Wednesday to Sunday from 11pm to 2am. 6/8 Wellington Quay, Dublin 2. © 01/677-6635.

Lillie's Bordello   Open 10 years and still the hippest of them all, Lillie's breaks the rule that you've got to be new to be hot. Paintings of nudes hanging on whorehouse-red walls is the look that's made Lillie's a surprisingly unraunchy icon of kitsch. There's a well-deserved reputation for posers and boy band celebrities, and the door policy can best be described as callous, except for Sundays. If you don't feel like dancing, head for "The Library," whose floor-to-ceiling bookcases and well-worn leather Chesterfields evoke a Victorian gentlemen's club. Open daily from 11pm to 3am. Adam Court, off Grafton St., Dublin 2. © 01/ 679-9204. Daily 11pm–3am.

Tips   **Late-Night Bites**

Although Dublin is keeping later and later hours, it is still nearly impossible to find anything approaching 24-hour dining. One place that comes close is the **Coffee Dock at Jurys Hotel,** Ballsbridge, Dublin 4 (© **01/660-5000**). It's open Monday 7am to 4:30am, Tuesday to Saturday 6am to 4:30am, Sunday 6am to 10:30pm. **Bewley's,** 78/79 Grafton St., Dublin 2 (© **01/677-6761**), is open until 1am on Friday and Saturday. **Juice,** 73–83 S. Great George's St., Dublin 2 (© **01/475-7856**), serves a limited menu Friday and Saturday until 4am.

PoD   The "Place of Dance" is run by John Reynolds (nephew of the former prime minister of Ireland, Albert Reynolds) and has won the "European nightclub of the year" award, as well as a European design award for its colorful Barcelona-inspired decor. It's as loud as it is dazzling to behold. Open Wednesday to Saturday from 11pm until at least 2am. 35 Harcourt St., Dublin 2. © **01/478-0166.** www.pod.ie.

Renards   This quasi-jazz club is the see-and-be-seen choice of the glam set. Regulars include Bono of U2, the actor Gabriel Byrne, and the Corrs, while out-of-towners like Mick Jagger pop in when they're in town. The look is modern (think glass and chrome) on all three floors: the upstairs piano bar with its small tables and comfy armchairs; the bustling ground-floor cafe-bar; and the basement Plus club, which pulls in the crowd with live music—everything from acid jazz to Latin beats—Sunday to Thursday. Renards is open nightly from 11pm to 3am. 23–25 Frederick St. South, Dublin 2. © **01/677-5876.**

Rí-Rá   The name means "uproar" in Irish. Though trendy, Rí-Rá has a friendlier door policy than most of its competition, so this may be the place to try first. Open nightly from 11:30pm to 4am or later. 1 Exchequer St., Dublin 2. © **01/677-4835.**

Spy Club   Fashionable 30-somethings love this new lounge bar, where the emphasis is off dance and firmly on socializing. The look begins with a classical, 18th-century town house with mile-high, corniced ceilings. Next, add Greco-Roman friezes and pared-down, contemporary furnishings. Need more drama? The VIP room's focal point is a photo of a woman in the buff riding a tiger pelt—an in-your-face wink at the Celtic tiger. Sunday is gay night. Open nightly from 7pm to 3am. Powerscourt Townhouse; South William St., Dublin 2. No phone.

KINDER & GENTLER CLUBS

These established clubs, while they attract young singles and couples, have friendly door policies and are places where people of almost any age and ilk are likely to feel comfortable.

Annabel's   Just south of the Lower Leeson Street nightclub strip, this club is one of the longest lasting in town. It welcomes a mix of tourists and locals of all ages with a disco party atmosphere. Open Tuesday to Saturday from 10pm to 2am. Burlington hotel, Upper Leeson St., Dublin 4. © **01/660-5222.**

Club M   In the basement of Blooms hotel, in the trendy Temple Bar district close to Trinity College, this club boasts Ireland's largest laser lighting system. It offers DJ-driven dance or live music for the over-23 age bracket. Open Tuesday to Sunday from 11pm to 2am. Blooms hotel, Anglesea St., Dublin 2. © **01/671-5622.**

COMEDY CLUBS

The Irish comedy circuit is relatively new and quite popular. The timing, wit, and twist of mind required for comedy seems to me so native to the Irish that it's difficult to draw a line between those who practice comedy for a living and those who practice it as a way of life. You'll find both in the flourishing Dublin comedy clubs. Besides the favorite clubs listed below, **Vicar Street** (see "Smaller Concert Venues," below) tends to get many of the international comics who happen to be in town. As always, check the latest listings magazines for details. Admission ranges from €5 ($4.45) to €20 ($18) depending on the act and the night.

Ha'Penny Laugh Comedy Club　The former plays host to some of Ireland's funniest people, many of whom are in theater. The Battle of the Axe is a weekly show in which comedians, singers, songwriters, musicians, actors, and whoever storm the open mike in pursuit of the Lucky Duck Award. Ha'penny Bridge Inn, Merchant's Arch, Wellington Quay, Dublin 2. © 01/677-0616.

Murphy's International Comedy Club　A very small, packed venue, full of enthusiastic exchange. This is up-close, in-your-face improv, with nowhere to hide, so stake out your turf early. International Bar, 23 Wicklow St., Dublin 2. © 01/ 677-9250.

Murphy's Laughter Lounge　This 400-seat comedy venue is the current prime-time king of the Irish comedy circuit. It attracts the most popular stand-ups on the Irish scene as well as top international acts. Middle Abbey St., Dublin 1. © 1-800/COMEDY.

DINNER SHOWS & TRADITIONAL IRISH ENTERTAINMENT

These shows are outside the city center and aimed at tourists, although locals also attend and enjoy them.

Abbey Tavern　After you've ordered an a la carte dinner, the show—authentic Irish ballad music, with its blend of fiddles, pipes, tin whistles, and spoons— costs an extra €4.50 ($4). The price of a full dinner and show averages €38–€45 ($34–$40). The box office is open Monday to Saturday from 9am to 5pm. Dinner is at 7pm, and shows start at 9pm. There are shows nightly in the summer; in the off-season, call ahead to find out which nights shows will be offered. Abbey Rd., Howth, county Dublin. © 01/839-0307.

Culturlann Na hÉireann　This is the home of Comhaltas Ceoltoiri Éireann, an Irish cultural organization that has been the prime mover in encouraging a renewed appreciation of and interest in Irish traditional music. The year-round entertainment programs include old-fashioned ceili dances (Fri 9pm–midnight) and informal music sessions (Fri–Sat 9:30–11:30pm). From mid-June to early September, there's an authentic fully costumed show featuring traditional music, song, and dance (Mon–Thurs 9–10:30pm). No reservations are necessary for any of the events. 32 Belgrave Sq., Monkstown, county Dublin. © 01/280-0295. www. comhaltas.com. Tickets for ceilis €6 ($5.35); informal music €2 ($1.80); stage show €8 ($7.10). DART: Monkstown. Bus: 7, 7A, or 8.

Jurys Irish Cabaret　Ireland's longest-running show (more than 30 years) offers a unique mix. You'll see and hear traditional Irish and international music, rousing ballads and Broadway classics, toe-tapping set dancing and graceful ballet, humorous monologues and telling recitations, plus audience participation. The show takes place May through October, Tuesday to Sunday. Dinner is served at 7:15pm; the show starts at 8pm. In Jurys Hotel and Towers, Pembroke Rd.,

Ballsbridge, Dublin 4. ⓒ **01/660-5000.** Tickets €50 ($45). AE, DC, MC, V. Free parking. DART: Lansdowne Rd. Bus: 5, 7, 7A, or 8.

THE GAY & LESBIAN SCENE

New gay and lesbian bars, clubs, and venues appear monthly, it seems, and many clubs and organizations, such as the Irish Film Centre, have special gay events or evenings once a week to once a month. The social scene ranges from quiet pub conversation and dancing to fetish nights and hilarious contests. Cover charges range from €5 to €15 ($4.45–$13), depending on the club or venue, with discounts for students and seniors.

Check the *Gay Community News, In Dublin,* or *The Event Guide* to find out what's going on in town. The most comprehensive websites for gay organizations, events, issues, and information are **Gay Ireland Online** (www.gay-ireland.com), **Outhouse** (www.outhouse.ie; click on the "Ireland's Pink Pages" link), and **Dublin's Queer Guide** (www.dublinqueer.com). Folks on the help lines **Lesbians Organizing Together** (ⓒ **01/872-7770)** and **Gay Switchboard Dublin** (ⓒ **01/872-1055),** are also extremely helpful in directing you to activities of particular interest. (See "Tips for Travelers with Special Needs," in chapter 2, for details on many of these resources.)

The Front Lounge   This Temple Bar hangout is one of the coolest, chicest pubs in Dublin, with every drink under the sun, and great big loungey couches to chill in. Go early, get a nice seat, and relax with a G and T. The crowd is mixed, but definitely more gay than straight. Every Tuesday night, there's a cabaret hosted by a drag queen—one of the most popular gay nights out in Dublin. 32 Parliament St., Dublin 2. ⓒ 01/670-4112. Mon–Sat 11:30am–11:30pm; Sun 4–11:30pm. Bus 54, 65.

The George   The George is Dublin's largest gay bar, covering two floors where both the decor and clientele can be described as camp. Theme nights include "Carwash," a 1970s disco night every Thursday, and bingo in the bar Sundays at 5pm. 89 S. Great George's St., Dublin 2. ⓒ 01/478-2983. Daily 12:30–11pm; Wed–Sun 12:30pm–2:30am. Admission for theme nights, usually 10pm–2am, €6.50 ($5.80). DART: Tara St. Bus: 22A.

Out on the Liffey   This relaxed, friendly pub caters to a balance of gays and lesbians (except for Sat, which is men only) and serves up pub food with good conversation. In 1998, "Out" expanded to include a happening late-night venue, Oscar's, where you can dance (or drink) until you drop. 27 Upper Ormond Quay, Dublin 1. ⓒ 01/872-2480. DART: Tara St. Walk up the Liffey and cross at Parliament Bridge. Bus: 34, 70, or 80.

Stonewallz   On Saturday nights, this place turns into one of Dublin's most popular women-only clubs, offering three floors of music, each with its own DJ and music style. Molloy's Bar, High St. (beside Christchurch), Dublin 8. ⓒ 01/872-7770. Admission €5 ($4.45). No credit cards. Sat 8:30pm–2am. Bus: 21A, 50, 50A, 78, 78A, or 78B.

THE PERFORMING ARTS
THEATER

Dublin has a venerable and vital theatrical tradition, in which imagination and talent have consistently outstripped funding. Apart from some mammoth shows at the Point, production budgets and ticket prices remain modest, even minuscule, compared with those in New York or any other major U.S. city. With the exception of a handful of houses that offer a more or less uninterrupted flow of productions, most theaters mount shows only as they find the funds and opportunity to do so. A few venerable (or at least well-established) theaters offer serious drama more or less regularly.

The online booking site Ticketmaster (**www.ticketmaster.ie**) is an excellent place to get a quick look at what's playing where and also buy tickets. In addition to the major theaters listed below, other venues present fewer, although on occasion quite impressive, productions. They also book music and dance performances. They include the **Focus Theatre,** 6 Pembroke Place, off Pembroke Street, Dublin 2 (© **01/676-3071**); the **Gaiety Theatre,** South King Street, Dublin 2 (© **01/677-1717**); the **Olympia,** 72 Dame St., Dublin 2 (© **01/677-7744**); the **Players,** Trinity College, Dublin 2 (© **01/677-3370,** ext. 1239); **Project: Dublin,** 39 East Essex St., Dublin 2 (© **01/679-6622**); and the **Tivoli,** 135–138 Francis St., opposite Iveagh Market, Dublin 8 (© **01/454-4472**).

Abbey Theatre   For more than 90 years, the Abbey has been the national theater of Ireland. The original theater, destroyed by fire in 1951, was replaced in 1966 by the current functional, although uninspired, 600-seat house. The Abbey's artistic reputation in Ireland has risen and fallen many times, but is reasonably strong at present. Lower Abbey St., Dublin 1. © 01/878-7222. www.abbeytheatre.ie. Box office Mon–Sat 10:30am–7pm; shows Mon–Sat 8pm, Sat 2:30pm. Tickets €15–€26 ($13–$23). Senior, student, and children's discounts available Mon–Thurs evening and Sat matinee.

Andrews Lane Theatre   This relatively new venue has an ascending reputation for fine theater. It consists of a 220-seat main theater where contemporary work from home and abroad is presented, and a 76-seat studio geared for experimental productions. 9–17 St. Andrews Lane, Dublin 2. © 01/679-5720. Box office Mon–Sat 10:30am–7pm; shows Mon–Sat 8pm in theater, 8:15pm in studio. Tickets €13–€20 ($12–$18).

The City Arts Centre   The City Arts Centre is an affiliate of Trans Europe Halles, the European network of independent arts centers. It presents a varied program, from dramatic productions, theatrical discussions, and readings by local writers to shows by touring companies from abroad. In May 2000, it was home to the World Stories Festival. 23–25 Moss St., at City Quay. © 01/677-0643. Tickets €8.50–€12 ($7.55–$11).

The Gate   Just north of O'Connell Street off Parnell Square, this recently restored 370-seat theater was founded in 1928 by Hilton Edwards and Michael MacLiammoir to provide a venue for a broad range of plays. That policy prevails today, with a program that includes a blend of modern works and the classics. Although less known by visitors, The Gate is easily as distinguished as the Abbey. 1 Cavendish Row, Dublin 1. © 01/874-4368. Box office Mon–Sat 10am–7pm; shows Mon–Sat 8pm. Tickets €21–€25 ($19–$22) or €15 ($13) for previews. AE, DC, MC, V.

The Peacock   In the same building as the Abbey, this 150-seat theater features contemporary plays and experimental works. It books poetry readings and one-person shows, as well as plays in the Irish language. Lower Abbey St., Dublin 1. © 01/878-7222. www.abbeytheatre.ie. Box office Mon–Sat 10:30am–7pm; shows Mon–Sat 8:15pm, Sat 2:45pm. Tickets €8.50–€20 ($7.55–$18).

CONCERTS

Dublin is a great town for live music. On a given night, you can find almost anything—rock, pop, jazz, blues, traditional Irish, country, or folk—so check listings magazines to find out what's on and where. Music and dance concerts take place in a range of Dublin venues—theaters, churches, clubs, museums, sports stadiums, castles, parks, and universities. Again, the online booking site, Ticketmaster (**www.ticketmaster.ie**) is an excellent place to get a quick look at who's playing where and buy your tickets. While you're probably more likely to choose your entertainment based on the performer rather than the venue, these institutions stand out as venues where most international performers play.

National Concert Hall   This magnificent 1,200-seat hall is home to the National Symphony Orchestra and Concert Orchestra, and host to an array of international orchestras and performing artists. In addition to classical music, there are evenings of Gilbert and Sullivan, opera, jazz, and recitals. The box office is open Monday to Friday from 10am to 3pm and from 6pm to close of concert. Open weekends 1 hour before concerts. Parking is available on the street. Earlsfort Terrace, Dublin 2. ℂ 01/475-1572. www.nch.ie. Box office Mon–Sat 11am–7pm, Sun (on perform-ance days) from 7pm. Tickets €10–€32 ($8.90–$28). Lunchtime concerts €5 ($4.45). DC, MC, V.

The Point Depot   With a seating capacity of 3,000, The Point is one of Dublin's larger indoor theater/concert venues, attracting top Broadway-caliber shows and international stars such as Neil Young and Sarah Brightman. The box office is open Monday to Saturday 10am to 6pm. Parking is €4 ($3.55) per car. East Link Bridge, North Wall Quay. ℂ 01/836-3633. Tickets €13–€65 ($12–$58). AE, DC, MC, V.

Royal Dublin Society (RDS)   Although best known as the venue for the Dublin Horse Show, this huge indoor arena also hosts major concerts (Andrea Bocelli, Bon Jovi, and The Eagles were recent performers), with seating and standing room for more than 6,000 people. Merrion Rd., Ballsbridge, Dublin 2. ℂ 01/668-0645. www.rds.ie. Box office hours vary according to events; shows 8pm. Most tickets €13–€40 ($12–$36).

SMALLER CONCERT VENUES

If you prefer smaller, more intimate settings, check out the listings magazines for who's performing at these favorite venues:

Temple Bar Music Centre, Temple Bar, Dublin 2 (ℂ **01/670-9202**)

Vicar Street, 99 Vicar St., Dublin 8 (ℂ **01/609-7788;** www.vicarstreet. com)

Whelans, 25 Wexford St., Dublin 2 (ℂ **01/478-0766**)

Eamonn Doran's, 3A Crown Alley, Temple Bar, Dublin 2 (ℂ **01/679-9114**)

Club Mono, 26 Wexford St., Dublin 2 (ℂ **01/475-8555**)

Midnight at the Olympia, 74 Dame St., Dublin 2 (ℂ **01/677-7744**)

10 Side Trips from Dublin

Fanning out a little over 19km (12 miles) in each direction, Dublin's southern and northern suburbs offer a variety of interesting sights and experiences. All are easy to reach by public transportation or rental car.

DUBLIN'S SOUTHERN SUBURBS

Stretching southward along Dublin Bay from Ballsbridge is the harbor town of Dun Laoghaire, followed by Dublin's poshest suburbs, the seaside towns of **Dalkey** 🏵🏵 and **Killiney**—nicknamed "Bel Eire" for their beauty and density of celebrity residents. All three towns offer lovely seaside views and walks. Dun Laoghaire has a long promenade and a bucolic park, Killiney has a stunning, cliff-backed expanse of beach. The prettiest is Dalkey, a heritage town with a lovely medieval streetscape and something for just about everyone.

Thanks to DART service, these towns are easily accessible from downtown Dublin. They offer a good selection of restaurants and fine places to stay. A hill-side overlooking Dublin Bay outside the village of Killiney is the setting for the Dublin area's only authentic deluxe castle hotel, Fitzpatrick Castle (see "Where to Stay," below).

If you're traveling to Ireland by ferry from Holyhead, Wales, your first glimpse of Ireland will be the port of Dun Laoghaire. Many people decide to base themselves here and commute into downtown Dublin each day. As a base, it is less expensive than Dalkey, but less attractive too.

ATTRACTIONS

Dalkey Castle and Heritage Centre   Housed in a 16th-century tower house, the center and its fascinating exhibitions unfold this venerable town's remarkable history. After taking in the exhibit, you can visit the battlements to put it all in place and enjoy vistas of the Dublin area coastline. Adjoining the center is a medieval graveyard and the Church of St. Begnet, Dalkey's patron saint, whose foundations may be traced to Ireland's Early Christian period. Booklets sketching the history of the town, the church, and the graveyard are available at the Heritage Centre. You'll see and appreciate more of this landmark town if you purchase these and take them next door to the Queens Bar for a pint and quick scan. "Those who are patient," wrote the playwright Hugh Leonard, "and will sit, wait and listen or will linger along the tree-shaded roads running down to the sea, can hear the centuries pass."

Castle St., Dalkey, county Dublin. (© 01/285-8366. Admission €3 ($2.65) adults, €2.50 ($2.25) seniors and students, €2 ($1.80) children, €10 ($8.90) family. Apr–Oct Mon–Fri 9:30am–5pm, Sat–Sun 11am–5pm; Nov–Mar Sat–Sun 11am–5pm DART: Dalkey. Bus: 8.

The Ferryman 🏯 *Kids*   Young Aidan Fennel heads the third generation of Fennels to ferry visitors to nearby Dalkey Island, whose only current inhabitants are a small herd of wild goats and the occasional seal. Aidan is a boat builder, and his brightly-painted fleet comes mostly from his hand. The island, settled about 6000 B.C., offers three modest ruins: a church that's over 1,000 years old, ramparts dating from the 15th century, and a martello tower constructed in 1804 to make Napoleon think twice. Now the island is little more than a lovely picnic spot. If you want to build up an appetite and delight your children or sweetheart, row out in one of Aidan's handmade boats.

Coliemore Rd. (at stone wharf, adjacent to a seaside apartment complex). (© 01/283-4298. Island ferry round-trip €6.50 ($5.80) adults, €4 ($3.55) children; rowboat rental €10 ($8.90)/hr. June–Aug, weather permitting.

James Joyce Museum 🏯🏯   Sitting on the edge of Dublin Bay about 9.7km (6 miles) south of the city center, this 12m (40-ft.) granite monument is one of a series of martello towers built in 1804 to withstand an invasion threatened by Napoleon. The tower's great claim to fame is that James Joyce lived here in 1904. He was the guest of Oliver Gogarty, who rented the tower from the Army for an annual fee of IR£8 (€10, $8.90). Joyce, in turn, made the tower the setting for the first chapter of *Ulysses*, and it has been known as Joyce's Tower ever since. Its collection of Joycean memorabilia includes letters, documents, first and rare editions, personal possessions, and photographs.

Sandycove, county Dublin. (© 01/280-9265. Admission €3.50 ($3.10) adults, €3 ($2.65) seniors and students, €2 ($1.80) children, €10 ($8.90) family. Apr–Oct Mon–Sat 10am–1pm and 2–5pm; Sun 2–6pm. Closed Nov–Mar. DART: Sandycove. Bus: 8.

WHERE TO STAY
Expensive

The Gresham Royal Marine   A landmark since 1870, this five-story hotel sits on a hill overlooking the harbor, 11km (7 miles) south of Dublin City. It's a good place to stay for ready access to the ferry across the Irish Sea to and from

Side Trips from Dublin

Balbriggan
Bernagearagh Bay

0 — 2 1/2 mi
0 — 2.5 km

R127
St. Patrick's Island
Skerries 9
10
Shenick's Island

N1

R127

R128

Area of Detail
Dublin ★
REPUBLIC OF IRELAND

R108

R126
11 **Donabate**

Lambay Island

Swords 12
R106 **Malahide**
13 14

Irish Sea

R122
N1
R106

Dublin Airport ✈
6
M1

Portmarnock

Ireland's Eye

R107
R104
Sutton **Howth** 16 17
N2 3 4
2 R103 5
15 ▲ *Ben of Howth*
R105

N3
1 **Clontarf** *North Bull Island*

N4 ★ **DUBLIN** *Dublin Bay*
Liffey
N7
R119
Royal Canal

N11
R117
18 19
R112 20 21 22 23
Dun Laoghaire
24
Sandycove 25 *Dalkey Island*
Dalkey 26 27
R113 *Dalkey Hill* ▲ 29 28
Killiney Hill ▲ 30
To Shankill ↓ **Killiney**
31

ATTRACTIONS ●
Ardgillan Castle **7**
Casino Marino **5**
Dalkey Castle Heritage Centre **29**
The Ferryman **25**
The Fry Model Railway **13**
Howth Castle Rhododendron Gardens **15**
James Joyce Museum **21**
Malahide Castle **14**
National Botanic Gardens **2**
Newbridge House and Park **11**
Skerries Mills **8**

ACCOMMODATIONS ■
Clontraf Castle Hotel **1**
The Court Hotel **31**
Egan's House **3**
Fitzpatrick Castle Hotel **30**
Forte Travelodge **12**
The Gresham Royal Marine **18**
Iona House **4**
Posthouse **6**
Red Bank Lodge & Guesthouse **9**
Tudor House **23**

DINING ◆
Abbey Tavern **16**
Brasserie na Mara **19**
Caviston's **20**
Dee Gee's Wine and Steak Bar **17**
Guinea Pig **26**
Morels Bistro **24**
Munkberrys **28**
P.D.'s Woodhouse **22**
The Red Bank **10**
The Queens Bar & Restaurant **27**

Wales. Basically a Georgian building with a wing of modern rooms, the Royal Marine has public areas that have been beautifully restored and recently refurbished, with original molded ceilings and elaborate cornices, crystal chandeliers, marble-mantled fireplaces, and antique furnishings. The older rooms, many of which offer wide-windowed views of the bay, carry through the Georgian theme, with dark woods, traditional floral fabrics, and four-poster or canopy beds. Newer rooms are less atmospheric, with more contemporary light woods and pastel tones.

Marine Rd., Dun Laoghaire, county Dublin. (C) **800/44-UTELL** in the U.S., or 01/280-1911. Fax 01/280-1089. www.ryan-hotels.com. 103 units. €216 ($192) double. Rates include full breakfast and service charge. AE, DC, MC, V. DART: Dun Laoghaire. Bus: 7, 7A, or 8. **Amenities:** Restaurant (international); bar; concierge; room service; laundry service; nonsmoking rooms. *In room:* TV, radio, tea/coffeemaker, hair dryer, garment press, voice mail.

Moderate

The Court Hotel   Situated on 1.6 hectares (4 acres) of gardens and lawns, this three-story Victorian hotel enjoys a splendid location overlooking Killiney Bay and convenient access to Dublin with the nearby DART. The hotel's multiple lounges and popular restaurants show off their Victorian origins with corniced ceilings and old wood, and are bright and welcoming. The guest rooms are comfortably, though unremarkably, furnished, so it pays to request a room with a view of the bay. The real draw of this hotel is its lovely setting, which is convenient for excursions to Dublin as well as evening strolls on one of the most beautiful beaches on Ireland's east coast.

Killiney Bay Rd., Killiney, county Dublin. (C) **800/221-2222** in the U.S., or 01/285-1622. Fax 01/285-2085. www.killineycourt.ie. 86 units. €140–€200 ($125–$178) double. Rates include full Irish breakfast and service charge. AE, DC, MC, V. DART: Killiney. Bus: 59. **Amenities:** 2 restaurants (Continental, grill); bar; lounge; concierge; room service; laundry service. *In room:* TV, radio, hair dryer.

Fitzpatrick Castle Hotel ✦   With a fanciful Victorian facade of turrets, towers, and battlements, this restored 1741 gem is an ideal choice for those who want to live it up a bit. A 15-minute drive from the center of the city, it is between the villages of Dalkey and Killiney, on 3.6 hectares (9 acres) of gardens and hilltop grounds with romantic vistas of Dublin Bay. Two generations of the Fitzpatrick family pamper guests with 21st-century comforts in a regal setting of medieval suits of armor, Louis XIV–style furnishings, Irish antiques, original oil paintings, and specially woven shamrock-pattern green carpets. Most of the guest rooms have four-poster or canopy not-so-firm beds, and many have balconies with sweeping views of Dublin and the surrounding countryside. In spite of its size and exacting standards, the castle never fails to exude a friendly, family-run atmosphere.

Killiney Hill Rd., Killiney, county Dublin. (C) **01/230-5400.** Fax 01/230-5430. www.fitzpatrickhotels.com. 113 units. €145 ($129) double. No service charge. Breakfast €14 ($12). AE, DC, MC, V. DART: Dalkey. Bus: 59. **Amenities:** 2 restaurants (Continental, grill); 2 bars; nightclub; indoor swimming pool; guest privileges at nearby 18-hole golf course; squash and tennis courts; gym; saunas; children's playroom; concierge; courtesy minibus service to downtown and airport; salon; room service; laundry service; nonsmoking rooms. *In room:* TV, tea/coffeemaker, hair dryer, garment press.

Tudor House ✦   This handsome Gothic Revival Victorian manor house, built in 1848, has been lovingly restored to its original elegance by Katie and Peter Haydon. It has an enviable location back from the town center but still near many good pubs and restaurants. Set on a hill in its own manicured grounds, Tudor House gives all the guest rooms a pleasing view of Dublin Bay over the rooftops of Dalkey. Rooms are individually decorated with antiques and quality upholstery, and brightened with fresh flowers. The blue Wedgwood Room is particularly spacious and offers a firm double bed beneath a glittering chandelier; down the hall, the cozy corner room is bright and comfortable, with twin beds. The nearby DART commuter rail cannot be seen but may be heard by a light sleeper; the Dun Laoghaire ferry port is 2.8km (1¾ miles) away. What sets this place apart is the Haydon's attention to detail and the splendid breakfast.

Dalkey (off Castle St. between the church and Archbolds Castle), county Dublin. ✆ **01/285-1528.** Fax 01/284-8133. 6 units (all with shower only). €114–€149 ($101–$133) double. Rates include full breakfast and service charge. MC, V. Free private parking. DART: Dalkey, then 7-min. walk. **Amenities:** Babysitting, laundry service. *In room:* TV, hair dryer.

WHERE TO DINE
Expensive

Brasserie na Mara ✿ SEAFOOD   Award-winning chef Adrian Spelman keeps this fine seafood restaurant high on the charts, despite ever-steepening competition. Set squarely in the bustle of Dun Laoghaire's busy seafront, this restaurant, elegantly converted from the old Kingstown terminal building, has been a benchmark for South Dublin cuisine since 1971. In addition to a wide selection of fish and shellfish, you can count on an array of poultry and meat dishes, from guinea fowl to Irish beef, as well as vegetarian options. Flaming desserts—another specialty—provide both high drama and suitable closure to a memorable meal.

1 Harbour Rd., Dun Laoghaire, county Dublin. ✆ **01/280-6767.** Reservations required. 4-course table d'hôte lunch €17 ($15); 4-course fixed-price dinner €29 ($26); main courses €13–€20 ($12–$18). Mon–Sat 12:30–2:30pm and 6:30–10pm. DART: Dun Laoghaire. Bus: 7, 7A, 8, or 46A.

Guinea Pig INTERNATIONAL   This eatery is small and easily overlooked, but to do so would be a shame—it's a fine restaurant with a well-deserved following. The menu emphasizes whatever is freshest and in season. It often includes a signature dish called *symphony de la mer* (a potpourri of fish and crustaceans), wild salmon with coriander sauce, filets of lemon sole with cockle and mussel sauce, and rack of lamb. In addition to a worthy wine list, the Guinea Pig also offers good house wines in white and red. The culinary domain of chef-owner Mervyn Stewart, a former mayor of Dalkey, the restaurant is decorated in Irish country style with Victorian touches.

17 Railway Rd., Dalkey, county Dublin. ✆ **01/285-9055.** Reservations recommended. 5-course table d'hôte €38 ($34) special-value menu Sun–Fri 6–8pm, Sat 6–7pm €19 ($17). AE, DC, MC, V. Sun 5–9:30pm; Mon–Sat 5:30–11:30pm. DART: Dalkey. Bus: 8.

Morels Bistro ✿✿✿ *Value* INTERNATIONAL   This is one of the Dublin area's most popular and best-value restaurants, particularly for Sunday lunch (it's also sister restaurant to the Morels in Stephen's Hall, p. 104). The vividly colorful room is a perfect backdrop for chef John Dunne's imaginatively prepared, yet approachable food. He's just as talented when making old stalwarts like his excellent Caesar salad or roast duckling in a red-onion marmalade as he is when he plays with fusion—try the soy-marinated salmon with sesame and lime dressing. The atmosphere is buzzing, the wines sparkling, the crowd duly appreciative.

18 Glasthule Rd. (above the Eagle House pub), Sandycove, county Dublin. ✆ **01/230-0210.** Avg. lunch €19 ($17); avg. dinner €35 ($31). AE, DC, MC, V. Mon–Fri 5:30–9:45pm; Sat 6:30–10:30pm; Sun 12:30–3pm and 6–9pm.

Moderate

Caviston's ✿✿ SEAFOOD   Fresh, fresh fish is the hallmark of this tiny lunch spot in Sandycove, run by the Caviston family, whose neighboring delicatessen and fish shop is legendary. There's no doubt that having the inside track on fresh produce transfers to the preparation of fish in the restaurant itself; chef

Noel Cusack checks out the daily catch before creating the menu of simply pre-pared dishes, relying on just one or two well-chosen ingredients to bring out the seafood's delicate flavors. The daily menu might include roast monkfish with pasta in a saffron-and-basil sauce, chargrilled salmon with béarnaise, or mari-nated red mullet with roasted red peppers. Unfortunately, the three lunchtime sittings can make for frantic service, so your best bet is to arrive at noon sharp before things get too hectic, or else aim for the last sitting and enjoy your meal without feeling like your table has been earmarked for somebody else.

59 Glasthule Rd., Sandycove, county Dublin. ✆ 01/280-9120. Reservations recommended. Main courses €10–€19 ($8.90–$17). DC, MC, V. Tues–Fri 3 sittings: noon, 1:30pm, 3pm; Sat: noon, 1:45pm, and 3:15pm.

Munkberrys ✿ MODERN CONTINENTAL   Crisp linens, candlelight, and tasteful contemporary art lend an immediate calm to this intimate restaurant on Dalkey's most animated street. The excitement here lies in the food, which pro-vokes both the eye and the palate. The crostini of goat's cheese with fresh figs and spicy tomato chutney arrives on a swirl of delicious and mysterious sauces. The spinach ricotta tortellini with a stilton, pistachio, and cognac sauce is per-fectly prepared and elegant to behold. It's a struggle to decide between desserts: The lemon crème brûlée with hazelnut biscuit? Or perhaps the steamed date pudding with butterscotch? Or—sigh—the Italian ice cream. While the service is especially attentive, there is no true separation of smokers and nonsmokers, who are potentially at arm's length from each other.

Castle St., Dalkey, county Dublin. ✆ 01/284-7185. Reservations recommended. 4-course fixed-price dinner €28 ($25); main courses €11–€23 ($10–$20); early-bird fixed-price dinner (Mon–Sat 5:30–7pm) €19 ($17). AE, DC, MC, V. Mon–Fri noon–2:30pm; and 5:30–10pm; Sat 5:30–10:30pm; Sun noon–6pm. DART: Dalkey.

P. D.'s Woodhouse IRISH/MEDITERRANEAN   The first and only oak-wood barbecue bistro in Ireland, P. D.'s Woodhouse cooks everything over chips from oaks ripped up by Hurricane Charlie, the worst tropical storm to hit Ireland in recent memory. The wild Irish salmon in caper and herb butter is fabulous, as is the white sole. And whatever you do, don't miss the Halumi cheese kebabs—conversation-stopping grilled Greek goat cheese. On the other hand, the nut kebabs, one of several vegetarian entrees, are unnecessarily austere.

1 Coliemore Rd., Dalkey center, county Dublin. ✆ 01/284-9399. Reservations recommended. Main courses €10–€23 ($8.90–$20). AE, DC, MC, V. Mon–Sat 6–11pm; Sun 4–9:30pm. DART: Dalkey.

Moderate/Inexpensive

The Queens Bar and Restaurant ✿ INTERNATIONAL   One of Ireland's oldest inns, this historic establishment has won a pocketful of awards, including county Dublin's best pub in 1992. It has great atmosphere and food to match. In the center of town, the informal trattoria has an open-grill kitchen, a departure from the usual pub grub. The low end of the menu leans toward pastas and pizzas, while the high end includes spicy Jamaican jerk chicken, T-bone steak, roast half crispy duck, and the catch of the day. In addition, there are daily specials and an interesting selection of antipasti. Upstairs, the Vico Restaurant and Piano Bar adds new flavors and style to this revered and flourishing establishment.

12 Castle St., Dalkey, county Dublin. ✆ 01/285-4569. Reservations not accepted. Dinner main courses €10–€18 ($8.90–$16); bar menu €2.50–€10 ($2.25–$8.90). AE, DC, MC, V. Bar daily noon–midnight; bar food Mon–Sat noon–5pm, Sun 12:30–5pm. Restaurant Mon–Sat 6–11pm; Sun 6–10pm. DART: Dalkey. Bus: 8.

PUBS

P. McCormack and Sons   This popular pub offers three distinctive atmos-pheres. The main bar has an old-world feel, with globe lamps, stained-glass windows, books and jugs on the shelves, and lots of nooks and crannies for a quiet drink. In the skylit, plant-filled conservatory area, classical music fills the air, and outdoors you'll find a festive courtyard beer garden. The pub grub here is top-notch, with a varied buffet table of lunchtime salads and meats. 67 Lower Mounttown Rd. (off York Rd.), Dun Laoghaire, county Dublin. ℭ 01/284-2634.

The Purty Kitchen   Housed in a building that dates from 1728, this old pub has a homey atmosphere, with an open brick fireplace, cozy alcoves, a large fish mural, and pub poster art on the walls. There's always something going on—be it a session of Irish traditional music in the main bar area, blues upstairs in the Loft, or a DJ spinning dance music. Call ahead for entertainment details. Old Dunleary Rd., Dun Laoghaire, county Dublin. ℭ **01/284-3576.** No cover for traditional music; cover €6–€8 ($5.35–$7.10) for blues in the Loft.

DUBLIN'S NORTHERN SUBURBS

Dublin's northern suburbs make a convenient base to **Dublin International Airport,** and they're also home to a delightful assortment of castles, historic buildings, gardens, and other attractions. In addition, the residential suburbs of **Drumcondra** and **Glasnevin** offer many good lodgings.

Just north of Dublin, the picturesque suburbs of **Howth** and **Malahide** offer panoramic views of Dublin Bay, beautiful hillside gardens, and many fine seafood restaurants. Best of all, they are easily reached on the DART. Farther north along the coast, but only 20 minutes from Dublin Airport, lies the bustling and attractive harbor town of **Skerries** 𝕘. Skerries is a convenient and appealing spot to spend your first or last night in Ireland; or stay longer and explore all this area has to offer, including a resident colony of gray seals and the lowest annual rainfall in Ireland.

ATTRACTIONS

Ardgillan Castle and Park 𝕘   Between Balbriggan and Skerries, this exquisitely restored 18th-century castellated country house sits right on the coastline on sumptuously manicured lawns. The house was built in 1738 and contains some fine period furnishings and antiques. But the real draw is the setting, right on the edge of the Irish Sea, with miles of walking paths and coastal views as well as a rose garden and an herb garden. Behind the lavish rose garden, there's also a nice cafe for grabbing a quick bite or some ice cream. Balbriggan, county Dublin. ℭ 01/849-2212. Admission to house €4 ($3.55) adults, €2.50 ($2.25) seniors and students, €8.50 ($7.55) family. Castle open Oct–Dec and Feb–Mar Tues–Sun 11am–4:30pm; Apr–June Tues–Sun 11am–6pm; July–Aug daily 11am–6pm; Sept Tues–Sun 11am–6pm. Park open daily dawn to dusk. Closed Jan. Free parking year-round. Signposted off N1. Bus: 33.

Casino Marino   Standing on a gentle rise 4.8km (3 miles) north of the city center, this 18th-century building is considered one of the finest garden temples in Europe. Designed in the Franco-Roman neoclassical style by Scottish architect Sir William Chambers, it was constructed in the garden of Lord Charlemont's house by the English sculptor Simon Vierpyl. Work commenced in 1762 and was completed 15 years later. It is particularly noteworthy for its elaborate stone carvings and compact structure, which make it appear to be a single story (it is actually two stories tall). Malahide Rd., Marino, Dublin 3. ℭ 01/833-1618. Admission €2.50 ($2.25) adults, €2 ($1.80) seniors and group members, €1.25 ($1.10) students and children, €6.50 ($5.80) family. Feb–Apr and Nov Sun and Thurs noon–4pm; May and Oct daily 10am–5pm; June–Sept daily 9:30am–6:30pm. Closed Dec–Jan. Bus: 20A, 20B, 27, 27A, 27B, 42, 42B, or 42C.

The Fry Model Railway *Kids*   On the grounds of Malahide Castle (see listing below), this is an exhibit of rare handmade models of more than 300 Irish trains, from the introduction of rail to the present. The trains were built in the 1920s and 1930s by Cyril Fry, a railway engineer and draftsman. The complex includes items of Irish railway history dating from 1834, and models of stations, bridges, trams, buses, barges, boats, the River Liffey, and the Hill of Howth.

Malahide, county Dublin. (℃ **01/846-3779.** Admission €3.70 ($3.30) adults, €2.80 ($2.50) seniors and students, €2 ($1.80) children, €10 ($8.90) family. Apr–Oct Mon–Sat 10am–5pm, Sun 2–6pm; Nov–Mar Sun 2–5pm. Closed for tours 1–2pm year-round. Suburban Rail to Malahide. Bus: 42.

Howth Castle Rhododendron Gardens   On a steep slope about 13km (8 miles) north of downtown, this 12 hectare (30-acre) garden was first planted in 1875 and is best known for its 2,000 varieties of rhododendrons. Peak bloom time is in May and June. *Note:* The castle and its private gardens are not open to the public.

Howth, county Dublin. (℃ **01/832-2624.** Free admission. Apr–June daily 8am–sunset. DART: Howth. Bus: 31.

Malahide Castle *⋆⋆* *Kids*   About 13km (8 miles) north of Dublin, Malahide is one of Ireland's most historic castles. Founded in the 12th century by Richard Talbot, it was occupied by his descendants until 1973. The fully restored interior is the setting for a comprehensive collection of Irish furniture, dating from the 17th to the 19th centuries. One-of-a-kind Irish historical portraits and tableaux on loan from the National Gallery line the walls. The furnishings and art reflect life in and near the house over the past 8 centuries. After touring the house, you can explore the 100-hectare (250-acre) estate, which includes 8 hectares (20 acres) of prized **gardens** with more than 5,000 species of plants and flowers, and a children's playground. The Malahide grounds also contain the **Fry Model Railway** museum (see above) and **Tara's Palace,** an antique dollhouse and toy collection.

Malahide, county Dublin. (℃ **01/846-2184.** malahidecastle@dublintourism.ie. Admission €4 ($3.55) adults, €3.40 ($3) students and seniors, €2 ($1.80) children under 12, €11 ($10) family; gardens free. AE, MC, V. Combination tickets with Fry Model Railway and Newbridge House available. Apr–Oct Mon–Sat 10am–5pm, Sun 11am–6pm; Nov–Mar Mon–Fri 10am–5pm, Sat–Sun 2–5pm; gardens May–Sept daily 2–5pm. Closed for tours 12:45–2pm (restaurant remains open). Suburban Rail to Malahide. Bus: 42.

National Botanic Gardens *⋆⋆*   Established by the Royal Dublin Society in 1795 on a rolling 20-hectare (50-acre) expanse of land north of the city center, this is Dublin's horticultural showcase. The attractions include more than 20,000 different plants and cultivars, a Great Yew Walk, a bog garden, a water garden, a rose garden, and an herb garden. A variety of Victorian-style glass houses are filled with tropical plants and exotic species. Remember this spot when you suddenly crave refuge from the bustle of the city. It's a quiet, lovely haven, within a short walk of Glasnevin Cemetery. All but the rose garden is wheelchair accessible. There's free roadside parking outside the garden gates.

Botanic Rd., Glasnevin, Dublin 9. (℃ **01/837-7596.** Free admission. Guided tour €2 ($1.80). Apr–Oct Mon–Sat 9am–6pm and Sun 11am–6pm; Nov–Mar Mon–Sat 10am–4:30pm and Sun 11am–4:30pm. Bus: 13, 19, or 134.

Newbridge House and Park *⋆* *Kids*   This country mansion 19km (12 miles) north of Dublin dates from 1740 and was once the home of Dr. Charles Cobbe, an archbishop of Dublin. Occupied by the Cobbe family until 1984, the house is a showcase of family memorabilia such as hand-carved furniture, portraits, daybooks, and dolls, as well as a museum of objects collected on world travels. The

Great Drawing Room, in its original state, is one of the finest Georgian interiors in Ireland. The house sits on 140 hectares (350 acres), laid out with picnic areas and walking trails. The grounds also include an 8-hectare (20-acre) working Victorian farm stocked with animals, as well as a craft shop and a coffee shop. There's also a terrific, up-to-the-minute playground for children to let off some energy. The coffee shop remains open during the lunch hour (1–2pm).

Donabate, county Dublin. ℂ **01/843-6534.** Admission €4 ($3.55) adults, €3.30 ($2.95) seniors and students, €2 ($1.80) children, €10 ($8.90) family. Apr–Sept Tues–Sat 10am–1pm and 2–5pm, Sun 2–6pm; Oct–Mar Sat–Sun 2–5pm. Suburban rail to Donabate. Bus: 33B.

Skerries Mills This fascinating new 18-hectare (45-acre) historical complex has been open for only a few years and is already a major attraction. Why? Well, bread, for one thing. This site has provided it on and off since the 12th century. Originally part of an Augustinian Priory, the mill has had many lives (and deaths). Last known as the Old Mill Bakery, providing loaves to the local north coast, it suffered a devastating fire in 1986 and lay in ruins until it was reborn as Skerries Mills in 1999. An ambitious restoration project brought two restored windmills and a water mill—complete with grinding, winnowing, and threshing wheels—back into operation. And there's even an adjoining field of grains— barley, oats, and wheat, all that's needed for the traditional brown loaf—sown, harvested, and threshed using traditional implements and machinery. The result is not only the sweet smell of fresh bread but an intriguing glimpse into the past, brought to life not only by guided tours but also by the opportunity to put your own hand to the stone and to grind your own flour on rotary or saddle querns. Then, if you've worked up an appetite, there's a lovely tearoom, often hosting live music, Irish dancing, and other events. Besides all this, there are rotating special exhibits and a fine gift shop of Irish crafts.

Skerries, county Dublin. ℂ **01/849-5208.** Admission €4 ($3.55) adults, €3 ($2.65) seniors, students, and children, €10 ($8.90) family. Apr–Sept daily 10:30am–6pm; Oct–Mar daily 10:30am–4:30pm. Closed Dec 20–Jan 1. Suburban Rail. Bus: 33. Skerries town and the Mills signposted North of Dublin off the N1.

WHERE TO STAY
Very Expensive
Clontarf Castle Hotel ⚐ If you want to be within striking distance of Dublin airport (8km/5 miles away), you can't beat this luxurious castle hotel in Clontarf, a pretty seaside suburb served by both the DART and several bus routes. But if you'll be spending most of your time in the city center, this hotel will probably feel too remote. The castle was built in 1172 by Normans and retains its impressive castellated exterior. Much later, in the 1600s, it was given to one of Oliver Cromwell's loyal servants, whose family retained ownership for the next 300 years. There's a regal quality about the magnificent entrance hall and the guest rooms, some of which boast four-poster beds. The place was completely refurbished in 1998, blending the medieval elements of the castle with bang-up-to-date facilities. Clontarf Castle is also a leading entertainment venue, welcoming a variety of musical and comedic guests throughout the year.

Castle Ave., Clontarf, Dublin 3. ℂ **01/833-2321.** Fax 01/833-0418. www.clontarfcastle.ie. 111 units. €292 ($260) double. Rates include service charge and full breakfast. AE, DC, MC, V. Free parking. Bus: 130. **Amenities:** Restaurant (international); 2 bars; gym; room service; babysitting; laundry service; nonsmoking rooms. *In room:* A/C, TV, dataport, radio, tea/coffeemaker, hair dryer, garment press, voice mail.

Moderate
Posthouse This is the only hotel on the airport grounds, 11km (7 miles) north of the city center. Behind a modern three-story brick facade, it has a

sunken skylit lobby with a central courtyard surrounded by the guest rooms. The rooms are comfortable and functional, with windows looking out into the courtyard or toward distant mountain vistas.

Dublin Airport, county Dublin. ℂ 800/225-5843 in the U.S., or 01/808-0500. Fax 01/844-6002. 249 units. €115–€230 ($102–$205) double. Rates include service charge and full breakfast. AE, DC, MC, V. Bus: 41 or 41C. **Amenities:** 2 restaurants (Continental, Chinese); bar; concierge; courtesy airport coach; room service; laundry service; nonsmoking rooms. In room: TV, tea/coffeemaker, hair dryer, garment press.

Inexpensive

Egan's House   This two-story red-brick Victorian guesthouse is in the center of a pleasant residential neighborhood that's within easy access of the city center. It's within walking distance of the Botanic Gardens and a variety of sports facilities, including tennis, swimming, and a gym. Operated by John and Betty Egan, it offers newly redecorated rooms in a variety of sizes and styles, including ground-floor rooms. The comfortable public rooms feature traditional dark woods, brass fixtures, and antiques.

7/9 Iona Park (between Botanic and Lower Drumcondra rds.), Glasnevin, Dublin 9. ℂ 800/937-9767 in the U.S., or 01/830-3611. Fax 01/830-3312. 23 units. €75 ($67) double. Continental breakfast €6 ($5.35); full Irish breakfast €8 ($7.10). MC, V. Limited free parking available. Bus: 3, 11, 13, 13A, 16, 19, 19A, 41, 41A, or 41B. **Amenities:** Dining room; lounge; nonsmoking rooms. In room: TV, tea/coffeemaker, hair dryer.

Forte Travelodge   About 13km (8 miles) north of downtown and 2.4km (1½ miles) north of Dublin airport, this recently expanded two-story motel offers adequate, no-frills accommodations at reasonable prices. Each of the basic rooms, with a double bed and sofa bed, can sleep up to four people. The hotel is located alongside the N1 motorway, and the interior is clean and modern. Public areas are limited to a modest reception area, public pay phone, and adjacent budget-priced Little Chef Irish chain restaurant and lounge.

N1 Dublin-Belfast road, Swords, county Dublin. ℂ 800/CALL-THF in the U.S., or 1800/709-709 in Ireland. Fax 01/840-9235. 100 units. €76 ($68) double. No service charge. AE, DC, MC, V. Bus: 41 or 43. In room: TV, hair dryer.

Iona House   A sitting room with a glowing open fireplace, chiming clocks, brass fixtures, and dark wood furnishings sets a welcoming tone for guests at this two-story red-brick Victorian home. Built around the turn of the 20th century, it has been operated as a guesthouse by John and Karen Shouldice since 1963. Iona House is in a residential neighborhood 15 minutes from the city center, within walking distance of the Botanic Gardens. Guest rooms offer modern hotel-style appointments, orthopedic beds, and contemporary Irish-made furnishings.

5 Iona Park, Glasnevin, Dublin 9. ℂ 01/830-6217. Fax 01/830-6732. 10 units. €86 ($77) double. No service charge. Rates include full breakfast. MC, V. Closed Dec–Jan. Parking available on street. Bus: 19 or 19A. **Amenities:** Lounge; patio; nonsmoking rooms. In room: TV, hair dryer.

Red Bank Lodge & Guesthouse ⋆ (Value   Within a leap of each other, these two comfortable nooks in the heart of Skerries town are only 20 to 30 minutes by car from Dublin Airport, so they can provide a convenient first or last night's lodging for your Ireland holiday. Better yet, they virtually abut the award-winning Red Bank restaurant (see "Where to Dine," below), so you are guaranteed a memorable introductory or farewell meal in the country. The seven rooms in the guesthouse are a bit more spacious than the five in the lodge. There's an invitingly simply country style to the guest rooms—cream walls, dark woods, crisp white bedspreads, and floral drapes. The powerful showers are just the ticket after or before a long journey.

7 Church St. and Convent Lane, Skerries, county Dublin. ☎ **01/849-1005** or 01/849-0439. Fax 01/849-1598. www.redbank.ie. 12 units (several with shower only). Guesthouse €90 ($80) double. Lodge €65 ($58) double. Rates include service and full Irish breakfast. Guesthouse B&B and dinner for 2 €152 ($135). Lodge B&B and dinner for 2 €140 ($125). AE, DC, MC, V. Parking on street and lane. Suburban rail. Bus: 33. **Amenities:** Restaurant (seafood). *In room:* TV, dataport, tea/coffeemaker, hair dryer.

WHERE TO DINE
Expensive
The Red Bank ★★ SEAFOOD   The hugely popular Red Bank has been winning friends, influencing people, and garnering awards for nearly 20 years. A bank in a former life, the restaurant uses the old vault as its wine cellar. The mood here is charmingly old-fashioned and classy. Your waiter takes your order in the cozy lounge, where you wait with a drink until your meal is ready and you're brought to your table. Owner-chef Terry McCoy is an exuberant and inspired chef, who gets his exceptional fresh seafood from local waters. His *Paddy Attley* is a platter of three fish of the day landed in the Skerries Harbor, each served in a uniquely enhancing sauce. McCoy is at his best with timeless icons such as scallops in a sauce of butter, cream, and white wine, or a truly divine lobster thermidor. A dinner here is a both a spectacle and a feast. Service is correct and respectfully old school, highlighted when the dessert trolley is wheeled in, laden with a mouthwatering selection of confections.

7 Church St., Skerries, county Dublin. ☎ **01/849-1005.** www.redbank.ie. Reservations required. Dinner main courses €14–€24 ($12–$21); fixed-price dinners €36–€39 ($32–$35). AE, DC, MC, V. Mon–Sat 7–9:30pm; Sun 12:30–4pm. Suburban rail. Bus: 33.

Moderate
Abbey Tavern SEAFOOD/INTERNATIONAL   Well known for its nightly traditional music ballad sessions, this 16th-century tavern also has a full-service restaurant upstairs. Although the menu changes by season, entrees often include scallops *Ty Ar Mor* (with mushrooms, prawns, and cream sauce), *crêpes fruits de mer* (seafood crepes), poached salmon, duck with orange and Curaçao sauce, and veal à la crème. After a meal, you might want to join the audience downstairs for some lively Irish traditional music.

Abbey St., Howth, county Dublin. ☎ **01/839-0307.** Reservations recommended. Main courses €14–€28 ($13–$25). MC, V. Mon–Sat 7–11pm. DART: Howth. Bus: 31.

Dee Gee's Wine and Steak Bar INTERNATIONAL   Facing Howth Harbour and Dublin Bay, this informal seaside spot opposite the DART station is ideal for a cup of coffee, a snack, or a full meal. A self-service snackery by day and a more formal, table-service restaurant at night, it offers indoor and outdoor seating. Dinner entrees range from steaks and burgers to shrimp scampi and vegetable lasagna. At lunchtime, soups, salads, and sandwiches are featured. Sit, relax, and watch all the activities of Howth from a front-row seat.

Harbour Rd., Howth, county Dublin. ☎ **01/839-2641.** Dinner main courses €9–€18 ($8–$16). MC, V. Oct–Apr daily 7am–7pm; May–Sept daily 7am–9pm. DART: Howth. Bus: 31.

5

Out from Dublin

If your time in Ireland is limited to 10 days or less, there are good reasons for focusing your itinerary on what the distinguished Trinity geographer, J. H. Andrews, labeled "the eastern triangle"—a wedge of Ireland's east coast, extending north to south from county Wicklow to county Louth, and west to county Westmeath. Like a stage, compact and prominent, this relatively small space has witnessed and preserved more of the Irish drama than perhaps any other comparable part of the country. So, while the region doesn't deliver the West's spellbinding landscapes, you won't get a bigger bang of Irish history and culture for your buck.

The stretch of level coast from Dundalk to the Wicklow Mountains marks the greatest breach in Ireland's natural defenses, made worse by the inviting estuaries of the Liffey and the Boyne. These "opportunities" were not lost on explorers, settlers, and invaders across the millennia. Once taken, whether by Celts, Danes, Normans, or English, this area's strategic importance was soon recognized as the most likely command and control center for the whole of Ireland. Here lay Tara, the hill of kings; Dublin, the greatest of the Viking city-states; and the Pale, the English colonial fist, holding the rest of Ireland in its grip. Here, too, are Newgrange and Knowth, marking one of the most profound prehistoric sites in the world; Kells, where Ireland's greatest treasure was fished from a bog; Mellifont, where the Irish Cistercian movement made its beginning; and the Valley of the Boyne, where the Irish finally lost their country to the English.

Rimmed by the Irish Sea, this eastern triangle—every point of which is an easy distance from Dublin City—has less rain, less bog, and more history than any other region of comparable concentration on the island. To the south, county Wicklow presents a panorama of gardens, lakes, mountains, and seascapes. To the east sit the flat plains of county Kildare, Ireland's prime horse country. In the north are the counties of Meath and Louth, packed with historic sites. In a nutshell, this is an area that is both a great hub from which to explore and a historical and geographic microcosm for those who don't have time to hit the four corners of the land.

1 County Wicklow & County Carlow

County Wicklow extends from Bray, 19km (12 miles) S of Dublin, to Arklow, 64km (40 miles) S of Dublin

The borders of county Wicklow, nicknamed the "Garden of Ireland," start just a dozen or so miles south of downtown Dublin. Within this county, you'll find some of Ireland's best rural scenery. If you're based in Dublin, you can easily spend a day or afternoon in Wicklow and return to the city for dinner and the theater, but you'll probably want to linger overnight at one of the many fine country inns.

One accessible, charming gateway to county Wicklow is the small harbor town of **Greystones** ★★, which you may not want to tell your friends back home about for fear of spoiling the secret. It is hands-down one of the most unspoiled and attractive harbor towns on Ireland's east coast. It has no special attractions except itself, and that's enough.

In general, though, Wicklow's most stunning scenery and most interesting towns and attractions are inland, between Enniskerry and Glendalough. A raised granite ridge runs through the county, containing two of the highest mountain passes in the country—the **Sally Gap** and the **Wicklow Gap.** The best way to see the **Wicklow Mountains** is on foot, following the **Wicklow Way** past mountain tarns and secluded glens. In this region, don't miss the picturesque villages of **Roundwood, Laragh,** and **Aughrim.**

In the southernmost corner of Wicklow, the mountains become hills and share with the villages they shelter an unassuming beauty, a sleepy tranquility that can be a welcome respite from the bustle of Wicklow's main tourist attractions. Near **Shillelagh** village are lovely forests and the curious edifice of **Huntington Castle.**

Just over the border of county Wicklow lies less-frequented county Carlow, home to many a delightful surprise. Carlow, one of Ireland's smallest counties, is bordered by the scenic **Blackstairs Mountains** to the east. The fertile limestone land of the Barrow Valley and the Killeshin Hills lie in the west of Carlow. The county's most prominent feature is the 5,000-year-old granite formation known as **Browne's Hill Dolmen.** It's believed to have the largest capstone in Europe, weighing a colossal 100 tons.

ESSENTIALS
GETTING THERE   **Irish Rail** (✆ 01/836-6222; www.irishrail.ie) provides daily train service between Dublin and Bray and Wicklow.

Bus Eireann (✆ 01/836-6111) operates daily express bus service to Arklow, Bray, and Wicklow towns. Both Bus Eireann and **Gray Line Tours** (✆ 01/605-7705) offer seasonal sightseeing tours to Glendalough, Wicklow, and Powerscourt Gardens.

But the best way to see Wicklow is by car, so that you can stop where you like and let serendipity guide your way. Take the N11 south from Dublin City and follow turnoff signs for major attractions. Or, as noted in Chapter 2, "Planning Your Trip to Ireland," you can try out the "Route Planning" facility offered by Ireland's **AA Roadwatch** (**www.aaroadwatch.ie**). Simply plug in your starting point and destination, with as many places in between that you'd like to visit. It lets you avoid the rush or save money with nifty options like "avoid motorways" and "avoid toll roads."

VISITOR INFORMATION   The **Wicklow Tourist Office,** Fitzwilliam Square, Wicklow Town, county Wicklow (✆ 0404/69117; www.wicklow.ie) is open Monday to Friday year-round, Saturday during peak season. The **Carlow Tourist Office,** Presentation Buildings, Tullow Street, Carlow Town, county Carlow (✆ 0503/31554; www.countycarlow.com), is open Monday to Friday year-round, 9:30am to 1pm and 2 to 5:30pm; and Saturday during peak season, 10am to 5pm.

SEEING THE SIGHTS
Altamount Gardens   The lush, colorful extravagance of Altamount is the result of 55 years of nurturing by the late Corona North. A shadowy avenue of venerable beech trees leads to bright lawns and the splash of flowers growing

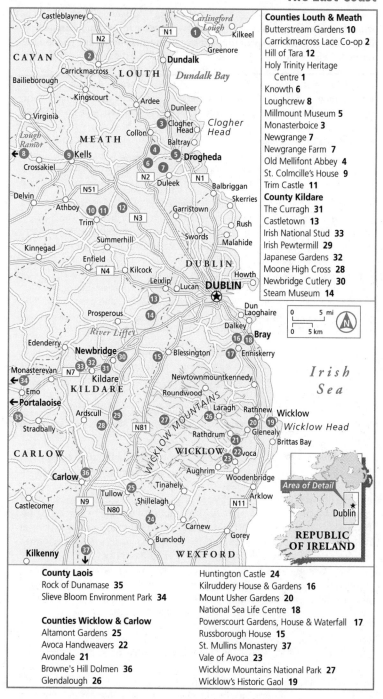

Counties Louth & Meath
Butterstream Gardens **10**
Carrickmacross Lace Co-op **2**
Hill of Tara **12**
Holy Trinity Heritage
  Centre **1**
Knowth **6**
Loughcrew **8**
Millmount Museum **5**
Monasterboice **3**
Newgrange **7**
Newgrange Farm **7**
Old Mellifont Abbey **4**
St. Colmcille's House **9**
Trim Castle **11**
County Kildare
The Curragh **31**
Castletown **13**
Irish National Stud **33**
Irish Pewtermill **29**
Japanese Gardens **32**
Moone High Cross **28**
Newbridge Cutlery **30**
Steam Museum **14**

County Laois
Rock of Dunamase **35**
Slieve Bloom Environment Park **34**

Counties Wicklow & Carlow
Altamont Gardens **25**
Avoca Handweavers **22**
Avondale **21**
Browne's Hill Dolmen **36**
Glendalough **26**

Huntington Castle **24**
Kilruddery House & Gardens **16**
Mount Usher Gardens **20**
National Sea Life Centre **18**
Powerscourt Gardens, House & Waterfall **17**
Russborough House **15**
St. Mullins Monastery **37**
Vale of Avoca **23**
Wicklow Mountains National Park **27**
Wicklow's Historic Gaol **19**

beneath ancient yew trees. Graveled walks weave around a large lake, constructed as a famine relief project, and the delights of this garden lie not only in its aesthetic and botanical diversity but also in the many birds that find sanctuary here. In early June, spectacular drifts of bluebells fill the forest floor on slopes overlooking the River Slaney. The moss-green depths of the Ice Age Glen, a rock-strewn cleft leading to the river, are currently closed to the public, but the walk through the Glen can sometimes be made with a guide, by request—and it's a beautiful walk, concluding with an ascent up 100 hand-cut granite steps through the bluebell wood, and past a small temple with fine views of the southern Wicklow Mountains.

Tullow, county Carlow. ✆ **0503/59444.** Admission €2.50 ($2.25) adults, €2 ($1.80) seniors and students, €1.30 ($1.15) children under 16, €6.35 ($5.65) family. Easter–Sept Thurs–Sun 10:30am–6:30pm.

Avondale House & Forest Park ✪   In a fertile valley between Glendalough and the Vale of Avoca, this is the former home of Charles Stewart Parnell (1846–91), one of Ireland's great political leaders. Built in 1779, the house is now a museum dedicated to his memory. Set in the surrounding 209-hectare (523-acre) estate and boasting signposted nature trails alongside the Avondale River, Avondale Forest Park is considered the cradle of modern Irish forestry. A new exhibition area commemorates the American side of the Parnell family, most notably Admiral Charles Stewart of U.S.S. *Constitution.* The coffee shop serves teas and light lunches, featuring homemade breads and pastries.

Off R752, Rathdrum, county Wicklow. ✆ **0404/46111.** Admission €4.50 ($4) adults, €4 ($3.55) seniors and children under 16, €11 ($10) family. Daily mid-Mar to Oct 31 11am–5pm. Parking €4 ($3.55).

Browne's Hill Dolmen   A field monument of huge proportions, the 5,000-year-old capstone, also known as the Druid's Altar, is believed to be the largest in Europe. The purpose of this Megalithic structure has been the subject of conjecture for centuries. Most likely it marks the burial place of a local king of long ago, but it has been invested with a rich overlay of myth and legend.

Off Rathvilly Rd., Carlow, county Carlow. Admission free. Daily, year-round. Access via car park and enclosed pedestrian pathway.

Glendalough ✪✪✪   This is Wicklow's top sight. In the 6th century, St. Kevin chose this idyllically secluded setting—whose name derived from the Irish phrase *Gleann Da Locha,* meaning "The Glen of the Two Lakes"—for a monastery. Over the centuries, it became a leading center of learning, with thousands of students from Ireland, Britain, and all over Europe, including St. Lawrence O'Toole, who visited in the 12th century. But like so many early Irish religious sites, Glendalough fell into the hands of plundering Anglo-Norman invaders, and its glories came to an end by the 15th century.

Today, visitors can stroll from the upper lake to the lower lake and walk through the remains of the monastery complex, long since converted to a burial place. Although much of the monastic city is in ruins, the remains do include a nearly perfect round tower, 31m (103 ft.) high and 16m (52 ft.) around the base, as well as hundreds of timeworn Celtic crosses and a variety of churches. One of these is St. Kevin's chapel, often called St. Kevin's Kitchen, a fine specimen of an early Irish barrel-vaulted oratory with a miniature round belfry rising from a stone roof. A striking new visitor center at the entrance to the site provides helpful orientation, with exhibits on the archaeology, history, folklore, and wildlife of the area. Unfortunately, the main entrance to the monastic complex has been spoiled by a sprawling hotel and hawkers of various sorts, so you may want to cross the river at the visitor center and walk along the banks. You can

---

Tips   Getting to Glendalough

If you plan on driving a car from Dublin to Glendalough, consider taking R155. The trip may take a little longer, and the signage may not be the best, but the spectacular vistas and awe-inspiring scenery are well worth seeing. If you don't have a car, Gray Line offers a bus tour from Dublin to Glendalough. For information, contact Gray Line Desk, Dublin Tourism Centre, Suffolk Street, Dublin 2 (✆ **01/605-7705**; grayline@tlp.ie).

---

cross back again at the monastic site, bypassing the trappings of commerce that St. Kevin once fled.

County Wicklow (11km/7 miles east of Wicklow on T7 via Rathdrum). ✆ **0404/45325** or 0404/45352. Free admission; exhibits and audiovisual presentation €2.50 ($2.25) adults, €2 ($1.80) seniors, €1.30 ($1.15) children and students under 16, €6.35 ($5.65) family. Daily mid-Oct to mid-Mar 9:30am–5pm; mid-Mar to May and Sept to mid-Oct 9:30am–6pm; June–Aug 9am–6:30pm.

Huntington Castle ✯   Movie buffs might recall that Stanley Kubrick used this castle, with its famed lime-tree avenue, for the setting of his film *Barry Lyndon.* Another interesting bit of trivia: The castle is said to be the most haunted building in Ireland, with at least 10 resident ghosts. You might find it unsurprising, then, that it has a lived-in feel, despite a magnificent decrepitude derived in part from the sometimes-overwhelming assortment of debris left by previous generations. The house has many stories to tell, and young Alexander Durdin-Robertson, whose ancestors built the place, gives an anecdote-rich tour. At the confluence of the rivers Derry and Slaney, this castle was of great strategic importance from the time it was built, in the early 17th century. It was at the center of conflicts in the area until the early 20th century, when the IRA briefly used it as a headquarters. Nowadays the castle's basement is home to a temple of the Fellowship of Isis, a religion founded here in 1976.

Clonegal, county Carlow (off N80, 6.5km/4 miles from Bunclody). ✆ **054/77552.** Guided tour €4.50 ($4) adults, €2 ($1.80) children. Jun–Aug daily 2–6pm; May and Sept Sun 2–6pm; other times by appointment.

Kilruddery House & Gardens ✯✯   This estate has been the seat of the earl of Meath since 1618. The original part of its mansion, dating from 1820, features a Victorian conservatory modeled on the Crystal Palace in London. The gardens are a highlight, with a lime avenue, a sylvan theater, foreign trees, exotic shrubs, twin canals, and a fountain-filled, round pond edged with beech hedges. They are the only surviving 17th-century French-style gardens in Ireland.

Kilruddery, Bray, county Wicklow (off the N11) ✆ **01/286-2777.** House and garden tour €5.75 ($5.10) adults, €4 ($3.55) seniors and students over 12, €1.30 ($1.15) children; gardens only €4 ($3.55) adults, €2.50 ($2.25) seniors and students, €.65 (60¢) children. House May–June and Sept daily 1–5pm; gardens Apr–Sept daily 1–5pm.

Mount Usher Gardens ✯   Encompassing 8 hectares (20 acres) along the River Vartry, this sylvan site was once home to an ancient lake and more recently laid out in the informal, free-range, "Robinsonian" style. It contains more than 5,000 tree and plant species from all parts of the world, including spindle trees from China, North American swamp cypresses, and Burmese juniper trees. Fiery rhododendrons, fragrant eucalyptus trees, giant Tibetan lilies, and snowy camellias also compete for your attention. Informal and responsive to their natural setting, these gardens have an almost untended feel—a floral woodland, without pretense yet with considerable charm. A spacious tearoom overlooks the river and gardens. The courtyard at the entrance to the gardens contains an interesting assortment of shops, which are open year-round.

Ashford, county Wicklow (off the N11). ℂ 0404/40116. http://homepage.eircom.net/~gardens. Admission €5 ($4.45) adults, €4 ($3.55) seniors, students, and children 5–12. Guided tours €30 ($26.70); call for reservation. Mar 17–Oct 31 daily 10:30am–6pm.

National Sea Life Centre ⭐ *Kids*   The national aquarium and sea park offers good family fun, even if it's overpriced considering its size (which is quite small). Situated at water's edge, the center provides a child-focused introduction to the denizens of the deep. The labyrinthine path through the aquarium begins with a rock tunnel carved by a winding freshwater stream; from there, you follow the water's course toward the open sea, from freshwater river to tidal estuary to storm-pounded harbor and finally to the briny deep. Along the way, kids are quizzed on what they're learning, as they use "magic" glasses to read coded questions and find the answers on special scratchpads they've been given. One remarkable feature here is the close access visitors have to the sea life. When you bend over and eyeball the fish, they as often as not return the favor, surfacing and staring back only inches from your face. Once you reach "the Deep," the emphasis is on scary critters, like sharks (of course) and the blue-ringed octopus. Count on spending an hour or so here.

Strand Rd., Bray, county Wicklow. ℂ 01/286-6939. www.sealife.ie. Admission €7 ($6.25) adults, €5.75 ($5.10) seniors, €5 ($4.45) students and children, €22 ($20) family. Open year-round daily 10am–5pm.

Powerscourt Gardens, House Exhibition, and Waterfall ⭐⭐⭐   If you only have time to visit one of Wicklow's fabulous gardens, then let this be the one. On a 400-hectare (1,000-acre) estate less than 19km (12 miles) south of Dublin city, Powerscourt is one of the finest gardens in Europe, designed and laid out by Daniel Robertson between 1745 and 1767. This property is filled with splendid Greek- and Italian-inspired statuary, decorative ironwork, a petrified-moss grotto, lovely herbaceous borders, a Japanese garden, a circular pond and fountain with statues of winged horses, and the occasional herd of deer. Stories have it that Robertson, afflicted with gout, was pushed around the grounds in a wheelbarrow to oversee the work. An 18th-century manor house designed by Richard Cassels, the architect of Russborough House (see below) and the man credited with the design of Dublin's Parliament house, stood proudly on the site until it was gutted by fire in 1974. The real reason to come is for the gardens. Don't opt for the additional entrance fee to "the house," as the exhibition consists primarily of a mediocre video on the history of Powerscourt. The cafeteria serves up delicious, reasonably priced lunches and a view that's not to be believed. The adjacent garden center is staffed with highly knowledgeable green thumbs who can answer all your horticultural questions. If you've brought the kids, they can occupy themselves at a nearby playground. The waterfall is the highest in Ireland, at 121m (398 ft.), and is a favorite picnic spot.

Enniskerry, county Wicklow (off the N11). ℂ 01/204-6000. Gardens and house exhibition €6.35 ($5.65) adults, €5.75 ($5.10) seniors and students, €4 ($3.55) children 5–16, free for children under 5; gardens only €5 ($4.45) adults, €4.50 ($4) seniors and students, €2.50 ($2.25) children 5–16, free for children under 5; waterfall €2.50 ($2.25) adults, €2 ($1.80) seniors and students, €1.30 ($1.15) children 5–16, free for children under 5. AE, MC, V. Gardens and house exhibition daily Mar–Oct 9:30am–5:30pm, Nov–Feb 9:30am–dusk; waterfall daily Mar–Oct 9:30am–7pm, Nov–Feb 10:30am–dusk.

Russborough House ⭐⭐   Ensconced in this 18th-century Palladian house is the world-famous Beit Art Collection, with paintings by Vernet, Guardi, Bellotto, Gainsborough, Rubens, and Reynolds. Since 1974, Russborough has suffered three art burglaries. The most recent was a 3-minute heist in June 2001, when thieves made away with a Gainsborough and a Bellotto, together worth €3.88 million ($3.45 million). Most of the artworks were eventually recovered. The house is furnished with European pieces and decorated with bronzes, tapestries, and some fine Francini plasterwork. On the premises are a restaurant, shop, and playground.

Blessington, county Wicklow (off N81). (© **045/865239.** Admission to main rooms €5 ($4.45) adults, €4 ($3.55) seniors and students, €2.50 ($2.25) children under 12. May–Sept daily 10:30am–5:30pm; Oct Sun 10:30am–5:30pm. Closed Nov–Apr.

St. Mullin's Monastery *Finds*   This little gem is a well-kept secret. On a sunny day its idyllic setting—in a sleepy hamlet beside the River Barrow, ringed by soft carpeted hills—is reason enough for a visit. Besides that, this is a fascinating spot, an outdoor minimuseum of sorts, spanning Irish history from the early Christian period to the present, all in no more than several acres. There are the ruins of a monastery founded here by St. Moling (Mullin) in roughly A.D. 614. Plundered again and again by the Vikings in the 9th and 10 centuries, it was annexed in the 12th century by a nearby Augustinian abbey. Here, too, is a steep grassy motte (grove) and the outline of a bailey (the outer wall or court of a castle) constructed by the Normans in the 12th century. In the Middle Ages, the monastery ruins were a popular destination, especially during the height of the Black Death in 1348, when pilgrims would cross the river barefoot, circle the burial spot of St. Mullin nine times in prayer, adding small stones to the cairn marking the spot, and drink from the healing waters of the saint's well. These ruins and waters are still the site of an annual pilgrimage near or on July 25.

Adjoining the monastery buildings is an ancient cemetery still in use, where, contrary to common practice, Protestants and Catholics have long lain side by side. You'll also find the graves of 20 heroes from the 1798 Rebellion, including that of General Thomas Cloney. Even if the Heritage Centre is closed (it opens at the discretion of the caretaker, Seamus Fitzgerald), there's a helpful site map and history mounted at the entrance to the cemetery. Remarkably, the ferry across the River Barrow, instituted by St. Mullin in the 7th century, remained in use until the 20th century, and the bell in the founder's chapel still rings for burials in the abbey cemetery.

On the scenic Barrow Dr., 12km (7½ miles) north of New Ross, St. Mullins, county Carlow. Admission free at any time to site.

Vale of Avoca *✦*   Basically a peaceful riverbank, the Vale of Avoca was immortalized in the writings of 19th-century poet Thomas Moore. It's here at the "Meeting of the Waters" that the Avonmore and Avonbeg rivers join to form the Avoca River. It's said that the poet sat under "Tom Moore's Tree" looking for inspiration and penned the lines, "There is not in the wide world a valley so sweet / as the vale in whose bosom the bright waters meet . . ." The tree itself is a sorry sight—it's been picked almost bare by souvenir hunters—but the place is still worth a visit.

Rte. 755, Avoca, county Wicklow.

Wicklow Mountains National Park *✦✦✦*   Nearly 20,000 hectares (50,000 acres) of county Wicklow make up this new national park. The core area surrounds Glendalough, including the Glendalough Valley and Glendalough Wood Nature Reserves. Hikers note: The most mountainous stretch of the Wicklow Way cuts through this park (see **www.irishwaymarkedways.ie**). You'll

find an information station at the Upper Lake at Glendalough. Information is available here on hiking in the Glendalough Valley and surrounding hills, including maps and descriptions of routes. (See "Sports & Outdoor Pursuits," below, for suggestions.) Free guided nature walks—mainly through rolling woodland—begin from the center on Tuesdays (departing 11am and returning 1:30pm) and Thursdays (departing 3pm and returning 4pm). The closest parking is at Upper Lake, where you'll pay €2 ($1.80) per car; instead, just walk up from the Glendalough Visitor Centre, where the parking's free.

Glendalough, county Wicklow. ⓒ **0404/45425**. Visitor center admission €4 ($3.55). May–Aug daily 10am–6pm; Apr and Sept Sat–Sun 10am–6pm; closed other months.

Wicklow's Historic Gaol ⭐ It's hard to believe that Wicklow Gaol closed its doors only as recently as 1924, after more than 2 centuries of terror. After passing under the hanging beam, visitors are lined up against the wall of the "day room" and confronted with some dark facts of prison life in 1799, when more than 400 prisoners, most of them rebels, occupied the jail's 42 cells. After being fed once every 4 days and allowed to walk in the prison yard for just 15 minutes a month, prisoners must have warmed to the idea of facing the hangman's noose. Within the main cellblock, you can roam the jail's individual cells and visit a series of exhibitions and audiovisual presentations. The impact of these stories is immediate and powerful for children as well as for adults, because this jail held both. Because many prisoners were sent off to penal colonies in Australia and Tasmania, that story, too, is told here, with the help of a stage-set wharf and prison ship. There's an in-house cafe, but your appetite might have been killed off by the time you've finished your tour. Overall, it's very informative and moving.

Kilmantin Hill, Wicklow Town, county Wicklow. ⓒ **0404/61599**. www.wicklow.ie/gaol. Tour €5.75 ($5.10) adults; €4.50 ($4) seniors and students, €3 ($2.65) children, €15 ($14) family with up to 3 children. Apr 17–Sept daily 10am–6pm (last admission at 4:50pm).

SHOPPING
Wicklow and Carlow offer a wide array of wonderful craft centers and workshops. Here is a small sampling.

Avoca Handweavers Dating from 1723, this cluster of whitewashed stone buildings and a mill houses the oldest surviving hand-weaving company in Ireland. It produces a wide range of tweed clothing, knitwear, and accessories. The dominant tones of mauve, aqua, teal, and heather reflect the local landscape. You're welcome to watch as craftspeople weave strands of yarn spun from the wool of local sheep. The weaving shed is open daily May to October from 9:30am to 5:30pm. The complex has a retail outlet and a tea shop (see "Where to Dine," later in this chapter). A second outlet shop, on the main N11 road at Kilmacanogue, Bray, county Wicklow (ⓒ **01/286-7466**), is open daily 9:30am to 5:30pm. Avoca, county Wicklow. ⓒ 0402/35105. www.avoca.ie.

Bergin Clarke Studio In this little workshop, Brian Clarke hand-fashions silver jewelry and giftware, and Yvonne Bergin knits stylish, colorful apparel using yarns from county Wicklow. Open May to September daily 10am to 8pm; October to April Monday to Saturday 10am to 5:30pm. The Old Schoolhouse, Ballinaclash, Rathdrum, county Wicklow. ⓒ **0404/46385**.

Fisher's of Newtownmountkennedy This shop, in a converted schoolhouse, stocks a wide array of men's and women's sporting clothes—quilted jackets, raincoats, footwear, blazers, and accessories. There's also a new tearoom.

Open Monday to Saturday 9:30am to 5:30pm, Sunday 2 to 6pm. The Old Schoolhouse, Newtownmountkennedy, county Wicklow. © **01/281-9404.**

The Woolen Mills Glendalough   This long-established crafts shop in a converted farmhouse offers handcrafts from all over Ireland, such as Bantry Pottery and Penrose Glass from Waterford. Books, jewelry, and a large selection of handknits from the area are also sold. Open daily 10am to 6:30pm. Laragh, county Wicklow. © **0404/45156.**

SPORTS & OUTDOOR PURSUITS

CYCLING   The Lorum Old Rectory (see below, under "Where to Stay") is also the base for **Celtic Cycling** (www.celticcycling.com; see chapter 3, "Ireland Outdoors"), which offers an array of 1- or 2-week cycling tours, or simply the gear you need to go it alone, with or without accommodation. The "sunny south" (not always, but offering better odds than most), with its rolling hills and gentle breezes, is great cycling country, and Don Smith will help you make the most of it. In addition, **Cycling Safaris** (© **01/260-0749;** fax 01/706-1168; www.cyclingsafaris.com) offers a 7-day self-led tour of Wicklow for €540 ($481), including accommodation and luggage transfers.

FISHING   During brown trout season (Mar 15–Sept 30), you'll find lots of angling opportunities on the Aughrim River (contact Dudley Byrne in Woodenbridge; © **0402/36161**) and on the Avonmore River (contact Peter Driver in Rathdrum; © **0404/46304**). The Dargle River flows from Enniskerry to the sea at Bray and offers great sea trout fishing in season from February 1 to October 12 (contact Hugh Duff in Enniskerry; © **01/286-8652**). Unfortunately, the Avoca River south of the Meeting of the Waters is polluted due to old copper mines and is unsuitable for fishing. Shore angling is hugely popular from beaches along the coast; contact the **Irish Federation of Sea Anglers** (© **01/ 280-6873**) for information on how to obtain permits.

GOLF   County Wicklow's verdant hills and dales offer ample opportunity for golfing. If you're looking for cachet, head to the championship **Druids Glen Golf Club,** Newtonmountkennedy (© **01/287-3600;** www.druidsglengolf. com), an inland beauty of a course that bears more than a fleeting resemblance to Augusta. Green fees are €95 ($85) weekdays and weekends. Nearby, the seaside **European Club,** Brittas Bay (© **0404/47415**), is a championship links with greens fees of €52 ($46) year-round. For a more affordable day out, try the parkland **Glenmalure Golf Club,** Greenane, Rathdrum (© **0404/46679**), where greens fees start at €20 ($18) weekdays and €25 ($22) weekends. The **Arklow Golf Club** (© **0402/32492**), a seaside par-68 course, charges greens fees of €23 ($20).

HORSEBACK RIDING   With its valleys, glens, secluded paths, and nature trails, county Wicklow is a dream for horseback riding. More than a dozen stables and equestrian centers offer horses for hire and instructional programs. Rates for horse hire average €13 to €25 ($12–$22) per hour. Among the leading venues are **Broomfield Riding School,** Broomfield, Tinahely (© **0402/ 38117**), and **Brennanstown Riding School,** Hollybrook, Kilmacanogue (© **01/286-3778**). At the **Paulbeg Riding School,** Shillelagh (© **055/29100**), experienced riders can explore the beautiful surrounding hills, and beginners can receive expert instruction from Sally Duffy, a friendly woman who gives an enthusiastic introduction to the sport.

Devil's Glen Holiday and Equestrian Village, Ashford, county Wicklow (© **0404/40637;** www.devilsglen.ie), splendidly situated at the edge of Devil's Glen, offers a full range of equestrian opportunities, from lessons to jumping to trekking to cross-country. Accommodation is offered in spotless, spacious, fully-equipped, self-catering two-bedroom apartments, two-bedroom bungalows, and three-bedroom cottages. This makes a great base from which to explore the Wicklow Mountains and coastline, whether or not you ever climb into a saddle. Weekly rates run from €180 to €395 ($160–$352), depending on season and size of unit. Weekend (Fri–Sun) and midweek (Mon–Thurs) rates are also available. Most lessons and rides cost €20 ($18) per hour for adults and €15 ($14) per hour for children under 12. Both the equestrian center and the self-catering village are open year-round.

HUNTING The **Broomfield Riding School,** Broomfield, Tinahely (© **0402/38117**), offers access to the hunt for those who can demonstrate adequate equestrian skills, including jumping. The riding school is open year-round for lessons and trail rides.

WALKING The **Wicklow Way** is a 132km (82-mile) signposted walking path that follows forest trails, sheep paths, and country roads from the suburbs south of Dublin, up into the Wicklow Mountains, and down through country farmland to the trail's terminus in Clonegal. It takes about 5 to 7 days to walk its entirety, with overnight stops at B&Bs and hostels along the route. Most people choose to walk sections as day trips.

You can pick up information and maps at the Wicklow National Park center in Glendalough, at any local tourist office, or on the website **www.irishway markedways.ie/TheWicklowWayE8.htm.** Information on less strenuous walks can be found in the *Wicklow Trail Sheets,* which provides a map and route description for several short walks and is available at tourist offices.

The most spectacular walks in Wicklow are in the north and central parts of the county, an area traversed by the Wicklow Way and numerous short trails. One lovely walk on the Way begins at the **Deerpark parking lot** near the Dargle River and continues to Luggala, passing Djouce Mountain; the next section, between Luggala and Laragh, traverses some wild country around Lough Dan.

St Kevin's Way, one of the oldest pilgrim routes in Ireland, for a period stretching back more than 1,000 years, has been recently restored. The path runs for 30km (18 miles) through scenic countryside from Hollywood to Glendalough, following the route taken by pilgrims visiting the ancient monastic city of Glendalough, and winds its way through a combination of roads, forest paths and open mountainside. It takes in many of the historical sites associated with St Kevin, who travelled the route in search of a mountain hermitage, as well as areas of geological interest and scenic beauty.

For folks who prefer less strenuous walking, a wonderful option is the **southern section of the Wicklow Way,** through Tinahely, Shillelagh, and Clonegal. Although not as rugged as the terrain in central Wicklow, the hills here are voluptuously round, with delightful woods and glens hidden in their folds. Through much of this section the path follows country roads that have been chosen for their lack of vehicular traffic. Consider treating yourself to a night at **Park Lodge B&B,** Clonegal, Shillelagh (© **055/29140**), near the trail's terminus; double rooms run €95 to €105 ($85–$93). If you're on foot, the hospitable Osborne family (who run the B&B) can arrange to pick you up at one of several points along the trail between Shillelagh and Clonegal.

WATERSPORTS & ADVENTURE SPORTS   Serenely set in the foothills of the Wicklow Mountains, the Blessington Lakes, created by a dam completed in 1940 for the Electricity Supply Board, are a 2,000-hectare (5,000-acre) playground of tranquil, clean, speedboat-free water. Less than an hour's drive from Dublin center, and signposted on N81, the **Blessington Adventure Centre,** Blessington, county Wicklow (© **045/865092**), offers water-based activities such as canoeing, kayaking, sailing, and windsurfing. On land, there's archery, orienteering, tennis, pony trekking, and riding lessons for all levels. Some representative prices per hour for adults are €7 ($6.25) for canoeing and kayaking, €14 ($12) for sailing and windsurfing, and €15 ($13) for pony trekking. Full- and half-day multiactivity prices are also available.

For the more adventurous, the **National Mountain and Whitewater Centre,** The Devil's Glen Forest, Ashford, county Wicklow (© **0404/40169;** www. tiglin.com), is an innovative state-funded facility that offers weekend courses in white-water kayaking, mountaineering, and rock climbing in locations around Ireland. Basic equipment is provided; fees for 1- to 5-day courses range from €50 to €450 ($46–$401). The center attracts a young clientele, and lodging is in hostels unless you arrange otherwise.

WHERE TO STAY
EXPENSIVE

Brook Lodge Hotel ⋆⋆   Brook Lodge is a revolutionary idea in Ireland—not so much a hotel as a planned village built from scratch to include accommodations, fine dining, good pubs (nearby Acton's is a microbrewery), a chapel, a bakery, landscaped gardens, and a half-dozen or so shops selling homemade wines, jams, crafts, and the like. The hotel itself is modern and comfortable, done up in warm, energized colors. Rooms have firm king-size four-poster beds, wood-paneled window seats, deep tubs, quality linens, and contemporary furnishings of natural elements. Service is excellent and the personal touch extends to a decidedly Irish nightly turn down: chocolates on your pillow and a hot water bottle between the sheets. The hotel's flagship is the Strawberry Tree restaurant—a fine, all-organic restaurant transplanted from Killarney, county Kerry. It's just as popular at its new Brook Lodge home, still delivering exceptional meals created from all free-range, wild, and additive-free produce. It's quite difficult to find, so call for directions.

Macreddin Village (between Aughrim and Aghavannagh), county Wicklow. © **0402/36444.** Fax 0402/ 36580. www.brooklodge.com. 40 units. €175–€235 ($156–$209) double. Rates include full Irish breakfast and service charge. AE, DC, MC, V. **Amenities:** Restaurant (organic); 2 pubs; laundry service. *In room:* TV, hair dryer.

Rathsallagh House Hotel & Golf Club ⋆⋆   It's only an hour's drive from Dublin, but any trace of city tension or travel fatigue evaporates as soon as you cross the threshold of Rathsallagh House. A recent recipient of the American Express Best-Loved Hotels of the World award, this country house hotel has a particularly warm, welcoming, unpretentious feel to it; it's a splendid place to relax and recharge. Converted from Queen Anne stables in 1798, the rambling, ivy-covered country house sits amid 212 hectares (530 acres) of parkland with its own walled garden and is surrounded by Rathsallagh Golf Course. The general mood here is cheerful and easygoing, with log or turf fires roaring in the public lounge areas. Return guests request their favorite rooms by name—the Buttercup, the Romantic, the Over Arch, or the Yellow Room, whose bathtub is set in an alcove. Rooms are priced according to size, starting with standard

Service Charges

A reminder: Unless otherwise noted, room rates don't include service charges (usually 10%–15% of your bill).

rooms, which are rather cramped. A superior room costs €40 ($36) more but offers considerably more space. Most rooms have a sitting area, a huge walk-in closet, and window seats, and some have Jacuzzis. There are good reading lamps over the beds and antique furnishings throughout the hotel.

Dunlavin, county Wicklow. (C) **800/323-5463** in the U.S., or 045/403112. Fax 045/403343. www.rathsallagh househotel.com. 17 units. €230–€270 ($205–$240) double. No service charge. Rates include full breakfast. Greens fees: €40–€70 ($36–$62). AE, DC, MC, V. Closed Dec 23–31. No children under 12 accepted. **Amenities:** Restaurant (modern Continental); lounge/bar; small indoor pool; 18-hole championship golf course; tennis court; archery; croquet; billiards; sauna. *In room:* TV, tea/coffeemaker, hair dryer.

Tinakilly Country House & Restaurant ★★★   Tinakilly is one of Ireland's most relaxing, sought-after small hotels—the kind of place the Irish come to celebrate an anniversary or special event, and the kind of place that remains in your memory long after you've departed. Everything conspires to spoil you: luxurious accommodations, attentive service, and an award-winning restaurant. Dating from the 1870s, this was the home of Capt. Robert Charles Halpin, commander of the *Great Eastern,* who laid the first successful cable connecting Europe with America. With a sweeping central staircase said to be the twin of the one on the ship, Tinakilly is full of seafaring memorabilia, paintings, and Victorian antiques. Every room is unique and in keeping with the Victorian style; most have either four-poster or half-tester canopy beds. The best have views of the Irish Sea. Don't be daunted by the wide selection of rooms here, from doubles to junior suites to Captain's Suites, because you really can't go wrong. The Captain's Suites are quite grand (with enormous bathrooms), but even the standard doubles are cozy and charming in the true sense of the word. The restaurant, Brunel (p. 188), is duly famous for ennobling the "Irish country house" style of cooking—think modern, French-influenced dishes that use the freshest Irish produce available. In the 17 years since opening, Tinakilly House has garnered a wall of prestigious awards, including being ranked no. 75 in the "Top 100 Hotels of the World" by the London *Times* several years ago.

On R750, off the Dublin-Wexford rd. (N11), Rathnew, county Wicklow. (C) **800/525-4800** in the U.S., or 0404/ 69274. Fax 0404/67806. www.tinakilly.ie. 51 units. €190–€210 ($169–$187) double; €235–€265 ($209–$236) junior suite; €315–€360 ($280–$320) captain's suite with sea view. No service charge. Rates include full breakfast and VAT. AE, DC, MC, V. **Amenities:** Restaurant (modern country house); lounge. *In room:* TV, radio, hair dryer.

MODERATE

Glendalough Hotel   Without spending the night in a round tower, you can't get any closer to St. Kevin's digs than this seasoned, veteran inn situated in a wooded glen at the very entrance to Glendalough, beside the Glendasan River and within the Wicklow Mountains National Park. Dating from the 1800s, it was refurbished and updated in the mid-1990s with traditional Irish furnishings and standard modern comforts. This was once a sleepy and idyllic spot, but it is now rather overrun with tourists, their buses, and all that caters to them.

Glendalough, county Wicklow. (C) **800/365-3346** in the U.S., or 0404/45135. Fax 0404/45142. 44 units. €80–€105 ($71–$93) double. Rates include full breakfast. AE, DC, MC, V. Closed Jan. **Amenities:** Restaurant (Irish/Continental); pub. *In room:* TV, hair dryer.

Kilgraney Country House ★★ Pass through the Georgian front door, and the eclectic tastes of the proprietors, Martin Marley and Bryan Leech, take over. High ceilings and ochre walls complement the bold lines of 20th-century drawings and hammered metal furniture of Asian influence. Rooms are soothing and simple and demonstrate a careful consideration of the tactile as well as the visual, but even here the unexpected slips in: Perhaps the light pull is a horn-headed cane, or a Thai puppet waves from a bedside table. Such attention to detail invites a slow, lingering sojourn. Dinner, served communal style on a long table of Kilkenny black marble, is also a fusion of old and new, of the exotic and the traditionally Irish—wild salmon is wrapped with a band of Japanese seaweed, and a creamy potato soup is laced with curry. The ritual of dinner and the conversation it inspires means that the meal can last well into the night. Breakfasts are equally satisfying—perhaps raisin and orange pancakes as a first course, a truly superlative soda bread, and more standard second-course offerings of scrambled eggs with salmon or bacon and sausage.

Just off the R705 (L18), 5.6km (3½ miles) from Bagenalstown on the Borris rd., Bagenalstown, county Carlow. ✆ **0503/75283.** Fax 0503/75595. www.kilgraneyhouse.com. 6 units, all with private bathroom (4 with shower only). €90–€140 ($80–$125) double. Rates include full breakfast. Dinner €38 ($34). AE, MC, V. Closed Nov–Feb. **Amenities:** Lounge; nonsmoking rooms. *In room:* TV, hair dryer.

Lorum Old Rectory ★ Set well back from the road and surrounded by cultivated fields, rolling pastures, and casual gardens in the serene Barrow Valley, the Old Rectory stands weathered and welcoming. Its hallmarks are hospitality and cuisine, both unforgettable. There is something contagious about the congeniality of this house. Don and Bobbie Smiths are consummate hosts, perhaps because they love doing what they do. Bobbie is a standout chef and the meals here are memorable. The individual bedrooms, like siblings, are all of a piece, even as each holds its own. All are spacious, clean, comfortable, and peaceful, with half- or full-canopy beds, and are gifted with lovely views of the sensuous Carlow countryside. Smoking is not permitted in bedrooms or in the dining room, but smokers have their own cozy snug, complete with fireplace. There's a small gift shop just for guests, displaying the work of local artisans, including Bobbie. This is a place to which you will find yourself returning, either in happy memory or in fact.

Just off the R705 (L18), 7km (4⅓ miles) from Bagenalstown on the Borris rd., Bagenalstown, county Carlow. ✆ **0503/75282.** Fax 0503/75455. www.lorum.com. 5 units, all with private bathroom (with shower only). €95–€105 ($85–$93) double. Rates include full breakfast. Dinner €36 ($32). AE, MC, V. Closed Dec 22–Jan 2. **Amenities:** Drawing room. *In room:* TV, tea/coffeemaker, hair dryer.

INEXPENSIVE

Derrybawn Mountain Lodge This elegant, comfortable fieldstone manor house in an idyllic parkland setting looks out over the surrounding hills. The rooms are spacious, bright, tastefully furnished, and outfitted with orthopedic beds. Located just outside Laragh village, the place is convenient to fishing streams and hiking trails (including the Wicklow Way), and a great place from which to explore Wicklow's natural wonders.

Laragh, county Wicklow. ✆ **0404/45644.** Fax 0404/45645. derrybawnlodge@eircom.net. 8 units. €65–€76 ($58–$68) double. No service charge. Rates include full breakfast. MC, V. **Amenities:** Sitting room; recreation/billiards room; nonsmoking rooms. *In room:* TV.

The Lord Bagenal Inn ★★ This storybook country inn has heaps of real charm—an old stone entrance archway, a lovely location alongside the Barrow River, and prices that won't break the bank. It's difficult to imagine two more courteous and hospitable innkeepers than James and Mary Kehoe, who offer a dozen adorably prim rooms featuring half-tester beds and chic country fabrics. The multi-award-winning restaurant delivers exceptionally good, modern country fare—French-influenced classics created with fresh local produce—and is of particularly good value. Overall, this is a great address to know about when you want to unwind and be comforted. And, if you've got the kids along, the outdoor playground is a perfect antidote for the sick-of-the-car blues.

Main St., Leighlinbridge, Co. Carlow. ℂ 0503/21668. Fax 0503/22629. www.lordbagenal.com. 12 units. €76–€90 ($68–$80) double. No service charge. Rates include full breakfast. MC, V. **Amenities:** Restaurant (modern country); pub; boat hire. In room: TV, tea/coffeemaker, hair dryer.

Sherwood Park House   An 18th-century Georgian country house and working farm, Sherwood Park is a place of green fields, distant mountains, the promise of hot tea, and real sheep to count from the warmth of a canopy bed piled high with pillows. There are only four guest rooms. All are comfortably large, and the two on the second floor have smaller, adjoining rooms with twin beds that are perfect for children. Guests are invited to use the sitting room, where peat fills the fireplace and an old piano sits in the corner, ready to command center stage when played by guests. Patrick and Maureen Owens are the genial hosts, and they help create a festive occasion of even the rainiest evening. Maureen prepares the dinner, served in a high-ceilinged dining room. Conversation is encouraged as everyone is seated together at a long polished table, although it's difficult to get beyond contented murmurs over soup made from vegetables grown on the estate or delighted exclamations about the flavor of homemade strawberry ice cream.

Kilbride, Ballon, county Carlow. (off the N80, 3km/1.8 miles south of Ballon). ℂ 0503/59117. Fax 0503/59355. info@sherwoodparkhouse.ie. 4 units. €65–€76 ($58–$68) double. 25% reduction for children. Dinner €25 ($22). AE, MC, V. **Amenities:** Sitting room. In room: TV.

Slievemore   This mid-19th-century harbor house offers white-glove cleanliness, spacious comfort, and (if you book early and request a seafront room) a commanding view of Greystones Harbor, Bray Head, and the Irish Sea. Proprietor Pippins Parkinson says that "people stumble on Greystones, find it by accident." But forget relying on serendipity. Reserve a room in advance, as well as a table for dinner at nearby Coopers (see "Where to Dine," below).

The Harbour, Greystones (signposted on N11), county Wicklow. ℂ 01/287-4724. 8 units (all with shower only). €62 ($55) double. No service charge. Rates include full Irish breakfast. No credit cards. Bus: 84. **Amenities:** Sitting room. In room: TV.

Tudor Lodge   The whitewashed walls of Tudor Lodge are fresh and inviting, recalling the rusticity of a country cottage. Bedrooms are spacious, and each has a small desk as well as both a double and a single bed. The dining room and living room are equally hospitable, with large windows opening onto views of green meadows and the slopes of the Wicklow Mountains. A brick fireplace and beamed ceilings make the living room a cozy retreat. A generous stone terrace lies just outside, and a riverside patio overlooks the Avonmore River at the end of the garden. Hosts Des and Liz Kennedy offer guests an appetizing array of breakfast choices, and will also prepare dinner for larger groups. Otherwise, the restaurants and pubs of Laragh are a short and scenic walk away.

Laragh, county Wicklow. ℂ and fax 0404/45554. 6 units, all with private bathroom (shower only). June–Sept €66 ($58) double; Sept–May €58 ($52) double. MC, V. **Amenities:** Living room; sunroom; nonsmoking rooms. In room: TV, tea/coffeemaker, hair dryer.

SELF-CATERING

Fortgranite   Fortgranite is—and has been for centuries—a working farm in the rolling foothills of the Wicklow Mountains. Its meadows and stately trees create a sublime retreat. Its unique stone cottages, formerly occupied by the estate's workers, are being restored and refurbished with appreciable care and charm by M. P. Dennis. Three are available to rent for a week or longer. The gate lodges—Doyle's and Lennon's—each have one double bedroom fully equipped with all essentials. The third, Stewards's Cottage, sleeps four and is furnished with lovely antiques. All have open fireplaces, and each has its own grounds and garden. Tranquility, charm, and warmth are the operative concepts at Fortgranite, so those in search of something grand and luxurious will be disappointed. Think "cottage" and "character," and you will be delighted. Also, it's best to plan ahead because word is out, and availability is at a premium. Golf, fishing, hiking, horse racing and riding, and clay-pigeon shooting can all be found nearby. Smoking is discouraged.

Baltinglass, county Wicklow. (4.8km/3 miles southeast of Baltinglass on R747). ✆ **0508/81396.** Fax 0508/73510. 3 cottages. €250–€550 ($223–$490) per week. No credit cards. *In room:* TV, kitchen, no telephone.

Manor Kilbride   Gracefully situated amid 16 hectares (40 acres) of mature gardens and wooded walks in the Wicklow Mountain foothills, just 29 km (18 miles) from Dublin, Charles and Margaret Cully's Manor is a haven of charm and cordiality. The grounds include two small lakes and a stretch of the River Brittas. Four lovely stone self-catering cottages are available. The two courtyard cottages and the river lodge each sleeps four; the gate lodge is better suited to a couple. These are chic cottages, with original beams, exposed stone walls, and every amenity. The Cullys are rather lavish in their welcome baskets, so there's no need for an immediate trip to the market.

N. Blessington, county Wicklow (on N81 6.5km/4 miles north of Blessington, take Kilbride/Sally Gap turn, then left at sign for Sally Gap). ✆ **01/458-2105.** Fax 01/458-2607. 4 cottages. Cottages €360–€635 ($320–$565) per week year-round. AE, MC, V. *In room:* TV, kitchen, microwave, washing machine.

Tynte House ✦ *Kids*   Dunlavin is a sleepy three-pub town in western Wicklow, 48km (30 miles) southwest of Dublin. It's as convenient as it is peaceful. Tynte House, a lovingly preserved 19th-century family farm complex with new apartment units and holiday cottages, offers an attractive array of options for overnight and longer-term guests. The driving force is Mrs. Caroline Lawler, "brought up in the business" of divining visitors' needs and surpassing their expectations. In 2000 she was named one of the top 20 "landladies" in the United Kingdom and Ireland.

The self-catering mews (renovated stables) houses have one to three bedrooms; the apartments hold one or two bedrooms; and the four new cottages range from two to four bedrooms and have working fireplaces. All are brilliantly designed and furnished with one eye on casual efficiency and the other on good taste. They have bold, bright color schemes, light pine furniture, and spacious tiled bathrooms. The no. 3 mews house and the open-plan apartment are favorites, but none will disappoint. This makes a great home base for families, with a grassy play area and treehouse, an outdoor barbecue and picnic tables, a tennis court, and a game room with Ping-Pong and pool. Exact prices depend on the season and the size of the unit. Shorter stays and weekend discounts may be negotiated in the off-season.

Dunlavin center, county Wicklow. ✆ **045/401561.** Fax 045/401586. www.iol.ie/~jclawler. 7 units, 4 homes, 4 apts, 4 cottages. Self-catering units €190–€400 ($169–$356) per week. Dinner €19 ($17). AE, MC, V. *In room:* TV, kitchens, microwave, dishwasher, washer/dryer.

Wicklow Head Lighthouse *(Finds* This 18th-century octagonal lighthouse, situated on Wicklow Head just 3.2km (2 miles) from Wicklow Town, makes for a very unique getaway. The lighthouse was established in 1781, then struck by lightning and subsequently gutted by fire in 1836. It remained a neglected shell until the Irish Landmark Trust (ILT), whose mission is to rescue neglected historic buildings, transformed it into a wonderful place to get away from it all. The interior is chic rustic, with whitewashed walls, pine furnishings, brass beds, and nautical memorabilia. There are five floors, each of which is an octagonal room: two double bedrooms, one bathroom, one sitting room, and the kitchen. The ground floor also has a sitting area and a small bathroom. Every window has a view to make even the most cynical jaw drop, and the sitting room is equipped with a telescope (great for watching seals frolicking below, or fishing trawlers returning home in the evening). Like all ILT properties, there is no TV. One caveat: The spiral staircase that corkscrews up the tower is not suitable for folks with hampered mobility or children under age 5.

Wicklow, county Wicklow. Contact the Irish Landmark Trust ✆ **01/670-4733**. Fax 01/670-4887. landmark@ iol.ie. €380 ($338) for 4 nights in low season, sliding up to €1,020 ($908) per week in high season. **Amenities:** Kitchen.

WHERE TO DINE
EXPENSIVE

Brunel Restaurant ✿✿✿ MODERN COUNTRY This extraordinary restaurant, which *Bon Appétit* magazine once called "a beacon to restore hope to the traveller's heart," has won as many accolades as the Tinakilly Country House hotel, to which it belongs (see above). The table d'hôte menu changes daily and is confidently balanced—sophisticated without being fussy; elegant without acrobatics. The service, too, is precise and intuitive, letting the ritual follow its own course. All this makes for a meal you remember, like the chargrilled tiger prawns and lemongrass with fennel oil, the cream of roast chestnut and celery soup, the caramelized scallops on saffron potato mash, and the loin of Wicklow lamb. The wine list is vast and, while international, focuses on France.

In Tinakilly Country House. Rathnew, county Wicklow (on R750, off the N11). ✆ **0404/69274**. Fixed-price dinner €48 ($43). AE, DC, MC, V. Year-round 12:30–2pm and 7:30–9pm.

MODERATE

Coopers ✿✿ INTERNATIONAL/SEAFOOD Coopers is the perfect reward after making the cliff walk from Bray to Greystones. To start with, the dining room is breathtaking—vaulted beamed ceilings, exposed brick and stone walls, stained glass, three fireplaces, wrought-iron fixtures, and linen table settings. It's a warm, relaxed, comfortable place for couples and families of any age. The menu is a rarity in that it understates its offerings, with ordinary descriptions like "smoked lamb" for extraordinary fare. Roast duckling and steamed sea trout are specialties, and there's a fine wine list. There are spectacular views of the open sea on two sides, and a piano player on Friday and Saturday nights. Alas, Coopers is no secret, so book well ahead.

Above the Beach House, The Harbour, Greystones, county Wicklow. ✆ **01/287-3914**. Reservations recommended. Fixed-price early-bird 2-course dinner (Mon–Fri 5:30–7:30pm) €13 ($12). Main courses €12–€24 ($11–$21); no service charge. AE, MC, V. Mon–Sat 5:30–11pm; Sun 12:30–4pm and 5:30–10pm.

Danette's Feast ✿ MEDITERRANEAN Should your itinerary put you in Carlow between Wednesday and Sunday, make an effort to get to this superb little restaurant. Be sure, however, to book ahead—it seats only 30, and is very popular with locals as well as visitors. The restaurant is in the main Georgian section of the very large house, and an 18th-century two-story cottage is now the kitchen. Bright, strong colors are used throughout; drinks and "nibbles" are served in a room the color of Rioja wine. From there, you proceed to one of the two dining rooms. Partners Danette O'Connell and David Milne are both musicians, and if things are quiet enough you may find David at the piano.

In the kitchen, Danette makes the most of Mediterranean flavors—try her chiles rellenos with goat cheese, Parma ham, and a puree of sun-dried tomatoes, or Mediterranean minced lamb with a red pepper sauce. The menu selection is quite varied and always includes a vegetarian dish, as well as organically grown vegetables whenever possible. Two things not to be missed: Danette's tomato and fennel bread and, to finish off the meal, her caramelized lemon tart made from the eggs of their free-range hens. There is a separate nonsmoking dining room. Musical evenings are held once a month between September and May.

5.2km/3¼ miles from Carlow town, immediately off the Hacketstown Rd., Urglin Glebe, Bennekerry, Carlow, county Carlow. ☎ **0503/40817**. Reservations required. Fixed-price dinner €38 ($34); Sun lunch €27 ($24). MC, V. Wed–Sat 7–9:30pm, Sun 1–2:30pm.

Roundwood Inn ⊛ IRISH/CONTINENTAL   Dating from 1750, this old coaching inn is the one of the best reasons to head to Roundwood, a place of unspoiled mountain beauty. It has an old-world atmosphere, with open log fireplaces and antique furnishings. Nearly everything is home baked or locally grown or raised—from steaks and sandwiches to traditional Irish stew, fresh lobster and salmon from Greystones, and seafood pancakes. In good weather, there's a lovely, secluded garden to sit in, and in the bar between meal times, there's outstanding pub grub.

Main St. (R755), Roundwood, county Wicklow. ☎ **01/281-8107**. Reservations recommended for dinner. Main courses €15–€23 ($13–$20). MC, V. Wed–Sat 1–2:30pm and 7:30–9:30pm.

INEXPENSIVE

Avoca Handweavers Tea Shop ⊛⊛ BISTRO/VEGETARIAN   Forget for a moment that this is an informal cafeteria—at a tourist magnet, no less. It is a great place to eat, virtually guaranteed to deliver one of the better meals on your trip. The menu changes frequently, but starters might include a delicate pea-and-mint soup or the terrific Caesar salad. Main courses might offer sesame-glazed chicken, honey roasted ham, Mediterranean sweet frittata, or smoked Wicklow trout. The tea shop attracts a loyal local clientele, in addition to the busloads of visitors who come to shop. Go for lunch, even if you're not interested in woolens.

Avoca, county Wicklow. ☎ **0402/35105**. Lunch €4–€9 ($3.55–$8). Daily 9:30am–5pm. AE, DC, MC, V.

The Opera House ITALIAN   This Irish trattoria is a good budget standby in this lovely, traditional harbor town. The faux Mediterranean decor is warm and tasteful; in fine weather, picnic tables provide street-side dining for nonsmokers. The smoked salmon and tagliatelle flamed in a cream-and-vodka sauce is a delicious bargain, and the house French table wine (€15/$13) suits both wallet and palate. The service is enthusiastic, if stretched a bit thin on weekends. For a delightful conclusion, treat yourself to the lemon brûlée.

Market Sq., Wicklow Town, county Wicklow. ☎ **0404/66422**. Reservations recommended Fri–Sun. Main courses €8–€20 ($7.10–$18). No service charge. MC, V. Daily June–Aug 11am–11pm, Sept–May 6–11pm. Occasionally closes on Tues in the winter.

Poppies Country Cooking IRISH HOME-STYLE   This 10-table self-service eatery opposite the main square is justifiably popular for light meals and snacks all day. The menu ranges from homemade soups and salads to hominy pie, nut roast, baked salmon, vegetarian quiche, and lasagna.

Enniskerry, county Wicklow. ✆ **01/282-8869.** All items €1–€8 (90¢–$7.10). No credit cards. Daily 9am–7pm.

Poppies Country Cooking IRISH HOME-STYLE   A second branch of Poppies, this time in Greystones, is just a short walk from the bus or train. With the warm, familiar feel of a neighbor's kitchen—that is, a neighbor who can really cook—this is a local hangout. From fist-sized whole-grain scones to vegetarian nut roast, the portions are generous. Seating overflows the 10 tables into a lovely flowered tea garden out back when the sun appears (Apr–Oct). *A warning:* The desserts are diet-breakers, so try not to even look unless you are prepared to fall. Homemade jams, preserves, salad dressing, and even local artwork are on sale.

Trafalgar Rd., Greystones, county Wicklow. ✆ **01/287-4228.** All items €1–€8 (90¢–$7.10). No credit cards. Mon–Sat 10am–6pm; Sun 11:30am–7pm.

PUBS

Cartoon Inn   With walls displaying the work of many famous cartoonists, this cottagelike pub claims to be the country's only cartoon-themed pub. It's the headquarters for Ireland's Cartoon Festival, held in late May or early June each year. Pub grub is available at lunchtime. Main St., Rathdrum, county Wicklow. ✆ **0404/46774.**

The Coach House   Adorned with lots of colorful hanging flowerpots, this Tudor-style inn sits in the mountains, in the heart of Ireland's highest village. Dating from 1790, it is full of local memorabilia, from old photos and agricultural posters to antique jugs and plates. It's well worth a visit, whether to learn about the area or to get some light refreshment. Main St., Roundwood, county Wicklow. ✆ **01/281-8157.**

The Meetings   This Tudor-style country-cottage pub stands idyllically at the "Meeting of the Waters" associated with poet Thomas Moore. An 1889 edition of Moore's book of poems is on display. Good pub grub is served daily, with traditional Irish music April to October every Sunday afternoon (from 4–6pm), and weekend nights all year. Avoca, county Wicklow. ✆ **0402/35226.**

2 County Kildare: Ireland's Horse Country

County Kildare is 24 to 48km (15–30 miles) W of Dublin

A TV quiz show host once asked a Kildare man if he knew who wrote *Gone With the Wind.* "No, but I can tell you who trained him," came the reply. Old jokes aside, Kildare is synonymous with horse racing. It's home of the Curragh (pronounced *ker*-ah), the racetrack where the Irish Derby is held in late June, and smaller tracks at Naas and Punchestown. County Kildare is also the heartland of Ireland's flourishing bloodstock industry and the National Stud. In this panorama of open grasslands and limestone-enriched soil, you'll find many of Ireland's 300 stud farms.

Once the stronghold of the Fitzgerald Clan, Kildare got its name from Cill Dara, which means Church of the Oak Tree, a reference to St. Brigid's monastery, which sat beneath an oak tree. Brigid was a bit ahead of her time as an early exponent for women's equality—she founded her coed monastery in the 5th or 6th century.

Kildare's rolling countryside is very pretty but also less diverse than nearby Wicklow.

ESSENTIALS

GETTING THERE   **Irish Rail** (© 01/836-6222; www.irishrail.ie) provides daily train service to Kildare.

Bus Eireann (© 01/836-6111; www.buseireann.ie) operates daily express bus service to Kildare.

By car, take the main Dublin-Limerick road (N7) west of Dublin from Kildare, or the main Dublin-Galway road (N4) to Celbridge, turning off on local road R403.

VISITOR INFORMATION   Contact the **Wicklow Tourist Office,** Wicklow Town (© 0404/69117). It's open year-round Monday to Friday, and Saturday during peak season. There is also a seasonal (mid-May to Sept) information office on The Square, Kildare Town, county Kildare (© 045/522696).

SEEING THE SIGHTS

Castletown 🏛️   Castletown—designed by Italian architect Alessandro Galilei for William Connolly (1662–1729), then Speaker of the Irish House of Commons—is the grandest Palladian-style mansion in Ireland. In a 1722 letter to Bishop Berkeley, this architectural gem was touted as a "magnificent pile of a building . . . [destined to be] the finest Ireland ever saw." For all too long, "pile" came sadly close to the truth, as the once and future gem underwent extensive renovation in the hands of the Office of Public Works, its current overseer. Work continues, but Castletown was reopened to the public in 1999.

R403, off main Dublin-Galway road (N4), Celbridge, county Kildare. © 01/628-8252. Admission €4 ($3.55) adults, €2.50 ($2.25) seniors, €1.30 ($1.15) children and students, €10 ($8.90) family. Easter day–Sept Mon–Fri 10am–6pm, Sat–Sun 1–6pm; Oct Mon–Fri 10am–5pm, Sun 1–5pm; Nov Sun 1–5pm. Closed Dec–Easter.

The Curragh ⭐⭐⭐   Sometimes called the Churchill Downs of Ireland, this is the country's best-known racetrack, just 48km (30 miles) west of Dublin. Majestically placed at the edge of Ireland's central plain, it's home to the **Irish Derby,** held in late June. Horses race at least one Saturday a month from March to October. A couple of years ago, the main stand was extensively renovated, a new betting hall added, and dining facilities (bars, restaurants, and food court) greatly expanded.

The track has rail links with all major towns. Irish Rail offers a round-trip "Racing by Rail" package from Dublin (Heuston Station) for €15 ($13), including courtesy coach to the main entrance. There's also a "Racing Bus" leaving Dublin (Busaras) each race day. Call Bus Eireann for details (© 01/836-6111; www.buseireann.ie).

Dublin-Limerick rd. (N7), Curragh, county Kildare. © 045/441205. www.curragh.ie. Admission €10–€15 ($8.90–$13) for most days of racing; €20–€45 ($18–$40) on Derby day. AE, DC, MC, V. Hours vary; first race usually 2pm but check newspaper sports pages.

Impressions

Pat: He was an Anglo-Irishman.

Meg: In the name of God what's that?

Pat: A Protestant with a horse.

—Brendan Behan (1923–64), *The Hostage*

Irish National Stud with Japanese Gardens & St. Fiachra's Garden ★★
Some of Ireland's most famous horses have been bred on the grounds of this government-sponsored stud farm. A prototype for other Irish horse farms, it has 288 stalls to accommodate mares, stallions, and foals. Visitors are welcome to walk around the 383-hectare (958-acre) grounds and see the noble steeds being exercised and groomed. A converted groom's house has exhibits on racing, steeplechasing, hunting, and show jumping, plus the skeleton of Arkle, one of Ireland's most famous horses.

The **Japanese garden** ★ is among the finest Asian gardens in Europe. Laid out between 1906 and 1910, it's designed to symbolize the journey of the soul from oblivion to eternity. The Japanese-style visitor center has a restaurant and craft shop. The Commemorative Garden of St. Fiachra, in a natural setting of woods, wetlands, lakes, and islands, opened in 1999. The reconstructed hermitage houses a Waterford crystal garden of rocks, ferns, and delicate glass orchids.

Off the Dublin-Limerick rd. (N7), Tully, Kildare, county Kildare. ✆ **045/521617.** www.irish-national-stud.ie. Admission €8 ($7.10) adults, €6.50 ($5.80) seniors, students, and children over 12, €4 ($3.55) children under 12, €18 ($16) family. MC, V. Feb 12–Nov 12 daily 9:30am–6pm. Bus: From Busaras, Dublin, each morning, returning each evening.

The Irish Pewtermill Ensconced in an 11th-century mill constructed for the nunnery of St. Moling—after whom the village of Timolin ("House of Moling") is named—Ireland's oldest pewter mill makes for a nice diversion. Six skilled craftsmen cast traditional Irish, silver-bright pewter in antique molds, some 300 years old. Casting takes place just about every day, usually in the morning. The showroom displays and sells a wide selection of high-quality hand-cast pewter gifts, from bowls to brooches. Prices are very reasonable. Custom-made gifts, such as tankards engraved with family crests, may be commissioned. An additional attraction here is a set of excellent reproductions of the principal panels from Moone High Cross (see the listing below), with explanatory plaques. They're helpful in further understanding and appreciating the nearby treasure. If he is about, be sure to meet Sean Cleary, a veritable font of information on pewter casting, local history, and all things Irish, and a formidable storyteller to boot.

Timolin-Moone (signposted off N9 in Moone), county Kildare. ✆ **0507/24164.** http://kildare.ie/molinpewter. Free admission. Year-round Mon–Fri 9:30am–4:30pm.

Larchill Arcadian Garden ★ (Kids) One of Ireland's most important rediscovered gardens, Larchill is the only surviving "ornamental farm" of its type in Europe. During the 18th century's Romantic Movement, ornamental farms were popular throughout Europe. Designed around a working farm, the natural landscape was embellished with ornamental buildings, statuary, water features, and picturesque walls. Larchill has a lake dotted with Gothic castle follies; miles of wooded nature trails; meadows stocked with rare breeds of animals, including emus and llamas; a walled garden filled with pigs, goats, geese, and peacocks; and even a resident ghost haunting a medieval tower covered in cockle shells. Especially for kids, there is a wooden adventure trail with traditional games, a playground, a sand pit, and a pet's corner with guinea pigs and rabbits. A tea room serves snacks and ice cream. Larchill was saved from dereliction in 1994, restored, then opened to the public in 1999.

Kilcock, county Kildare. Signposted off N4 near Maynooth. Admission €6 ($5.35), free for children under 4. May and Sept, Sat–Sun noon–6pm; June–Aug daily noon–6pm.

Moone High Cross ★ This renowned high cross, recently restored on-site, stands in the ruins of Moone Abbey, the southernmost monastic settlement established by St. Columba in the 6th century. The ruins and grounds are given a curious formula of neglect and care; for instance, the path to the site is overgrown, but lined with bright annuals. The high cross, nearly 1,200 years old, is quite magnificent. A splendid example of Celtic stone carving, it contains finely crafted Celtic designs as well as numerous biblical scenes, such as the temptation of Adam and Eve, the sacrifice of Isaac, and Daniel in the lions' den. The cross also holds several surprises, such as representations of a dolphin and a species of Near Eastern fish that reproduces when the male feeds the female her own eggs, which eventually hatch from her mouth. If you're in the vicinity, it's well worth a look.

Moone, county Kildare. Signposted off N9 on southern edge of Moone village.

Newbridge Cutlery   Look closely at the silverware when you sit down to eat at one of Ireland's fine hotels or restaurants—there's a good chance it was made by Newbridge, which for some 60 years has been Ireland's leading manufacturer of fine silverware. In the visitor center, you can see a display of place settings, bowls, candelabras, trays, frames, and one-of-a-kind items. A video on silver making is also shown. Silver pieces are sold here, including "sale" items.

Off Dublin-Limerick rd. (N7), Newbridge, county Kildare. ✆ **045/431301.** Free admission. Mon–Fri 9am–5pm; Sat 11am–5pm; Sun 2–5pm.

Steam Museum   Housed in a converted church, this museum is a must for train-spotters and steam-engine buffs. It contains two collections. The Richard Guinness Hall has more than 20 prototypical locomotive engines dating from the 18th century, and the Power Hall has rare industrial stationary engines. The shop stocks a variety of recent books and videos on the Irish Railway, and serves as the sole outlet for National Trust Enterprises gifts, which can be excellent values. The 18th-century walled garden is comprised of several verdant "rooms," extending to a delightful rose garden. Call ahead for information on when the engines will be in operation.

Straffan, county Kildare. Signposted off N7 at Kill Village. ✆ **01/627-3155.** Admission €4 ($3.55) adults, €2.50 ($2.25) seniors, children, and students, €13 ($12) family. Garden €2.50 ($2.25). Museum Apr–May and Sept Sun 2:30–5:30pm; June–Aug Tues–Sun 2–6pm. Walled garden June–July Tues–Fri and Sun 2–6pm; Aug Tues–Fri 2:30–5:30pm.

SPORTS & OUTDOOR PURSUITS

CYCLING   Kildare's mainly flat-to-rolling landscape makes it perfect for cyclists who aren't looking for anything strenuous. Unfortunately, most organized tours bypass Kildare for regions with more scenic diversity, but you can always plan your own route if you don't mind traveling light.

GOLF   The flat plains of Kildare offer some lovely settings for parkland layouts, including two 18-hole championship courses. The Arnold Palmer-designed, par-72 **Kildare Hotel & Country Club,** Straffan (✆ **01/601-7300**), charges greens fees of €110 to €245 ($98–$218) for nonresidents. For a less costly game, the par-70 **Kilkea Castle Golf Club,** Castledermot (✆ **0503/45555**), charges €34 ($30) all week. Or try the par-72 championship course at the **Curragh Golf Club,** Curragh (✆ **045/441238**), with greens fees of €25 ($22) weekdays, €28 ($25) weekends.

HORSEBACK RIDING   Visitors can expect to pay an average of €13 to €19 ($12–$17) per hour for trekking or trail riding in the Kildare countryside. To arrange a ride, contact the **Kill International Equestrian Centre,** Kill (✆ **045/877208**), or the **Abbeylands Equestrian Centre,** Clane (✆ **045/868188**).

Beyond the Pale in County Laois

A couple hours southwest of Dublin in the midlands of county Laois (pronounced "Leash"), **Portlaoise** makes a convenient stopover between the capital and Cork or Kerry. Book a room in the award-winning **Ivyleigh House** ⭐⭐, Bank Place, Portlaoise, county Laois (© **0502/ 22081;** fax 0502/63343; www.ivyleigh.com). This historic Georgian home, a stone's throw from the heart of the town, has been lavishly restored and furnished with opulent antiques. The breakfast here is a gourmet feast and the €105 ($93) for a double room is a terrific value. Have dinner at **Jim's Country Kitchen,** 27 Church St., Portlaoise, county Laois (© **0502/62061**), a disciple of Ireland's "slow food" movement, where the best of Irish produce and ingredients are properly prepared, nothing rushed and nothing lost.

If you want some outdoor recreation, the nearby **Slieve Bloom Environmental Park** ⭐ is a magnificently unspoiled mecca for walkers and cyclists. Before setting out, pack a picnic provisioned at **Jim's Food Hall** (same Jim and same location as above). Archaeology buffs can head to the ancient **Rock of Dunamase** (6.4km/4 miles outside of Portlaoise, signposted SE off N80) to explore an open site under excavation, of a captivatingly ruined 12th-century castle. After some modest climbing, you'll be rewarded with stunning, panoramic views of the sensuously molded Laois landscape, all soft hillocks and quilted fields.

WALKING One of Ireland's marked long-distance trails, the **Grand Canal Way** cuts through part of Kildare and is ideal for beginners because it is flat. The canal passes through many towns, such as Sallins, Robertstown and Edenderry, where you can find accommodation and stock up on provisions. For more information, contact the tourist office or see the **Irish Waymarked Ways** website at **www.irishwaymarkedways.ie/TheGrandCanalWay.htm**.

WHERE TO STAY
VERY EXPENSIVE
Kildare Hotel & Country Club ⭐   The K Club, as it is better known, is one of Ireland's most expensive and exclusive hotels. The darling of the affluent, sporty set, it's perhaps most famous for its 18-hole Arnold Palmer–designed golf course, which will host the Ryder Cup in 2006. Located a 45-minute drive from Dublin, this 132-hectare (330-acre), no-expense-spared resort makes a luxurious base from which to visit both Dublin and the sights of Kildare. The surroundings are gorgeous and the service excellent, but the atmosphere here is less personal and relaxed than at many of Ireland's other manor hotels.

Straffan House, a Georgian mansion, serves as the core of the hotel, with two wings that replicate the original building. Throughout the hotel, hand-painted wall coverings and murals enhance the Georgian high ceilings, bow windows, wide staircases, antiques, and period pieces. The guest rooms are spread out among the main hotel, courtyard suites, and a private lodge. Each room is sumptuously appointed with period antiques and upholsteries, the best Egyptian cotton linens, and marble bathrooms with thick bathrobes and heated towel racks. Prices reflect only room size, but the level of luxury is consistent through-out the hotel. The house overlooks a 1.6km (1-mile) stretch of the River Liffey. The main restaurant, the Byerley Turk, is formal (and a tad snooty) and features French food. Do adjourn for drinks to the library, one of the most wonderful rooms in the house and the showcase for a sumptuous collection of Jack B. Yeats paintings.

Straffan, county Kildare. ℂ **800/221-1074** in the U.S., or 01/601-7200. Fax 01/601-7299. www.kclub.ie. 95 units. €270–€445 ($240–$396) double; €460–€575 ($409–$512) 1-bedroom suite; €485–€700 ($432–$623) 2-bedroom suite; €3,100–3,800 ($2,759–$3,382) Viceroy Suite or Penthouse Suite. Greens fees for residents €65–€105 ($58–$93). No service charge. AE, DC, DISC, MC, V. **Amenities:** 2 restaurants (French, bistro); pub; indoor swimming pool; 18-hole golf course; private access to salmon and trout fishing; 2 indoor and 2 outdoor tennis courts; squash courts; gym; sauna; concierge; room service; babysitting; beauty treatments; library; massage; solarium; laundry. *In room:* A/C, TV/VCR, minibar, hair dryer.

Kilkea Castle Hotel & Golf Club ⭐⭐ Nestled beside the River Greese and surrounded by lovely formal gardens, this striking multiturreted hotel is the old-est inhabited castle in Ireland, built around 1180 for Walter de Riddlesford, a great warrior. It is supposedly haunted by the 11th earl of Kildare, who is said to gallop around the castle walls every 7 years. The hotel really delivers a medieval feel, thanks to displayed suits of armor and medieval banners, as well as a mix of Irish antiques and Asian tables, chests, and urns. About a third of the guest rooms are in the original castle building, with the rest in a newer court-yard addition. The decor in the guest rooms continues the Middle Ages theme, with plenty of dark woods, half-tester beds, armoires, chandeliers, brass fixtures, gilt-framed paintings and mirrors, and floral designer fabrics. The Geraldine Bar owes its 12th-century atmosphere to original stone walls, stained-glass windows, and a huge fireplace crowned by a copper flue. Local outdoor pursuits include fishing for brown trout, tennis, clay-pigeon shooting, and archery.

Castledermot, county Kildare. ℂ **0503/45156.** Fax 0503/45187. www.kilkeacastlehotelgolf.com. 40 units. €200–€310 ($178–$276) double. Rates include full Irish breakfast and service charge. AE, DC, MC, V. **Amenities:** Restaurant (Continental); bar; indoor swimming pool; 18-hole golf course; exercise room; spa pool; sauna; concierge; room service; babysitting; laundry; tanning bed. *In room:* TV, hair dryer.

EXPENSIVE

Barberstown Castle ⭐ Within easy reach of Dublin, this is a perfect coun-try getaway with more than a touch of class. This exquisite hotel spans 750 years of Irish history within its walls. Its four segments—constructed in the 13th, 16th, 18th, and 20th centuries—somehow form a coherent and pleasing whole. Each luxurious guest room is named after one of the castle's former lords or pro-prietors. They begin with Nicholas Barby, who constructed the battlemented rectangular keep in the late 13th century, and include Eric Clapton, who sold it to the present owners, Kenneth and Catherine Healy. The Barberstown story—from fortress to guesthouse—is a long one, with a happy ending for anyone deciding to stay here. The rooms are warm and elegant, with sitting areas, four-poster beds, antique desks, chandeliers, and spacious bathrooms. Two-bedroom family accommodations are available, as is a room designed for guests with dis-abilities. Smoking is limited to the lounge.

Straffan, county Kildare. ℂ **800/323-5463** in the U.S., or 01/628-8157. Fax 01/627-7027. www.barberstown castle.com. 22 units. €175–€195 ($156–$174) double; €260 ($231) suite. Service charge 10%. Rates include full Irish breakfast. AE, DC, MC, V. Closed Jan–Feb. From Dublin, drive south on N7, take turn for Straffan at Kill; from west on N4, then turn for Straffan at Maynooth. **Amenities:** Restaurant (Continental); lounge; non-smoking rooms. *In room:* TV, hair dryer.

MODERATE

Tonlegee House ★★ Marjorie Molloy's wonderful B&B has a cult following of in-the-know Dubliners who come down for a few days of the three Rs (in Kildare, that's rest, relaxation, and racing). What sets it apart from other moderately-priced places to stay is the wonderful home-style meals served here—in fact, the restaurant is a destination of its own in the county. The house is an elegant 18th-century manor that exudes warmth and hospitality with roaring fires and antique furnishings. Guest rooms are nicely appointed in an inviting country style, with very large bathrooms (some furnished with old-style claw-foot tubs). Athy is an attractive town on the Grand Canal, which is used today for recreation and pleasure boating, and makes for lovely walks.

Athy, county Kildare (leave Athy by Barrow Bridge and Canal Bridge, then pass Tergal and take next left). ℂ and fax **0507/31473**. www.tonlegeehouse.com. 12 units. €110–€130 ($98–$116) double. Dinner Mon–Sat €28 ($25). Rates include full Irish breakfast. AE, DC, MC, V. **Amenities:** Restaurant (country style); drawing room. *In room:* TV, hair dryer.

WHERE TO DINE
EXPENSIVE

Moyglare Manor ★★ FRENCH A half-hour's drive on the Dublin-Galway road (N4) delivers you to this grand Georgian mansion and inn, whose restaurant is surprisingly intimate. Elegance is the operative word here. Roast quail, baked plaice stuffed with shrimp, grilled sea trout, and steaks, all with fresh vegetables from the manor's own garden, are all memorable. Service is excellent, and the desserts are worth saving room for.

Maynooth, county Kildare. ℂ **01/628-6351**. Reservations required. Fixed-price dinner €36 ($32). AE, DC, MC, V. Sun–Fri 12:30–2pm; daily 7–9:30pm. Closed Good Friday and Dec 25–27.

MODERATE

Ballymore Inn ★★ INTERNATIONAL It may look like a modest country pub, but Georgina O'Sullivan's inspired cooking belies such simplicity. Her menu is like a hit list of all-time favorite casual foods, each made with the freshest ingredients and plenty of flair—chic pizzas topped with oven-dried tomatoes and loads of cheese, linguini with mussels, garlicky stir-fried veggies and black beans, sautéed beef with mushrooms and paprika-laced sour cream. An excellent address to know about if you're heading to or from Dublin on the N81.

Ballymore Eustace, county Kildare (off the N81, southeast of Blessington). ℂ **045/864747**. Reservations required. Main courses €27 ($24). MC, V. Mon 12:30–3pm; Tues–Thurs 12:30–3pm and 6–9pm; Sat–Sun 12:30–9:30pm.

MODERATE/INEXPENSIVE

Silken Thomas ★ GRILL Formerly known as Leinster Lodge, this historic inn offers an old-world pub and restaurant with an open fire. The menu offers a good selection of soups, sandwiches, burgers, and salads, as well as steaks, roasts, mixed grills, and fresh seafood platters. The inn is named after a famous member of the Norman Fitzgerald family, whose stronghold was in Kildare and who led an unsuccessful rebellion against Henry VIII.

The Square, Kildare, county Kildare. ℂ **045/521264**. Reservations recommended for dinner. Main courses €9–€18 ($8–$16). AE, MC, V. Mon–Sat 12:30–3pm and 6–10pm; Sun 12:30–3pm and 6–9pm.

PUBS

The Moone High Cross Inn Run by a granny named Bridget Clynch who "won't see 80 again," this rambling 18th-century pub is ideal for a road stop.

There's genuine hospitality and excellent pub grub—toasted sandwiches, Shepherd's pie, all the classics—not to mention an open fire, finely pulled pints, and convivial conversation. Moone, county Kildare. No phone.

The George Inn   The back room of this pub is what makes it special. It was more than likely the kitchen of the original cottage, which has seen more than a few additions. The focal point is a lovely, large fireplace with warm inglenooks and a brass-and-leather horse harness hanging over the mantel. The walls have wainscoting and there's a random hodgepodge of cozy pine tables and chairs, kettles and pots, and a kitchen cupboard filled with crockery. Prosperous, county Kildare. © 045/861041.

3 Counties Meath & Louth/The Boyne River Valley

48km to 80km (30–50 miles) N and W of Dublin

Less than 48km (30 miles) north of Dublin along Ireland's east coast runs the River Boyne, surrounded by the rich, fertile countryside of counties Meath and Louth. More than any other river in the country, this meandering body of water has been at the center of Irish history.

The banks of the Boyne hold reminders of almost every phase of Ireland's past, from the prehistoric passage tombs of Newgrange to the storied Hill of Tara, seat of the High Kings, to early Christian sites. This land was also the setting for the infamous Battle of the Boyne, when on July 1, 1690 (July 12 on modern calendars), King William III defeated the exiled King James II for the crown of England.

ESSENTIALS
GETTING THERE   Irish Rail (© 01/836-6222; www.irishrail.ie) provides daily train service between Dublin and Drogheda.

Bus Eireann (© 01/836-6111; www.buseireann.ie) operates daily express bus service to Slane and Navan in county Meath, and Collon and Drogheda in county Louth. Bus Eireann and **Gray Line Tours** (© 01/605-7705; www.guide friday.com) offer seasonal sightseeing tours to Newgrange and the Boyne Valley.

By car, take N1 north from Dublin City to Drogheda, then N51 west to Boyne Valley; N2 northwest to Slane and east on N51 to Boyne Valley; or N3 northwest via Hill of Tara to Navan, and then east on N51 to Boyne Valley.

VISITOR INFORMATION   Contact the **Dundalk Tourist Office,** Jocelyn Street, county Louth (© 042/35484); the **Drogheda Tourist Office,** Headfort Place (behind the town hall), Drogheda, county Meath (© 041/983-7070); or the **Bru na Boinne Center,** Newgrange, Donore, county Meath (© 041/80305).

COUNTY MEATH: THE ROYAL COUNTY
The best reason to come to Meath is to learn about Ireland's pagan and early Christian history. Meath is known as Ireland's spiritual capital and is the richest treasure trove of Ireland's past, from the Megalithic passage tomb at **Newgrange** to the **Hill of Tara,** seat of the High Kings, to early Christian sites. Meath consists almost entirely of a rich limestone plain, with verdant pasturelands and occasional low hills. Once a separate province that included neighboring county Westmeath, Meath was usually referred to as the "Royal County Meath," because it was ruled by the kings of Ireland, from the Hill of Tara near Navan. Centuries later, however, Ireland fell under Anglo-Norman clout, and **Trim**

Castle was constructed in the 12th and 13th centuries to make certain that the fact of British rule was not lost on anyone.

The chief town of county Meath is **Navan,** but nearby **Kells** is better known to the traveler because of its association with the famous Book of Kells, the hand-illustrated gospel manuscript on display at Trinity College in Dublin (see chapter 4). The town of Kells, known in Gaelic as *Ceanannus Mor* ("Great Residence"), was originally the site of an important 6th-century monastic settlement founded by St. Columcille. Monks driven from Iona in the 9th century by the Vikings occupied it for a time. The monks may have brought with them at least an incomplete Book of Kells. The book was stolen in 1007, and recovered months later from a bog. The monastery was dissolved in 1551, and today only ruins and a number of crosses survive.

Less than 40km (25 miles) southeast of Kells, beside the River Boyne, stand the alluring ruins of **Bective Abbey,** a Cistercian monastery founded in 1147 and fortified in the 15th century. Today, the fortress aspect of the abbey prevails, and it feels more like a castle than a monastery. It is a great climbing ruin, with myriad staircases, passageways, and chambers—a favorite hide-and-seek venue for local children, and perfect for a family picnic.

A focal point of county Meath is **Slane,** a small crossroads village and gateway to prehistoric Newgrange. Nearby is the Hill of Slane, a lofty 150m (500-ft.) mound overlooking one of the loveliest parts of the Boyne Valley. On this hill, tradition has it, Patrick lit the Christian paschal fire in direct defiance of the Irish King Laoghaire, throwing down the gauntlet for a confrontation between Ireland's old and new religious orders.

Even though Meath is primarily an inland county, it is also blessed with a 9.7km (6-mile) stretch of coastline and two fine sandy beaches, **Bettystown** and **Laytown.** History pops up everywhere in county Meath, even on the beach: the Tara Brooch was found at Bettystown in 1850. Often copied in modern jewelry designs, the brooch is one of Ireland's finest pieces of early Christian gold-filigree work, embellished with amber and glass. It's on view at the National Museum in Dublin.

SEEING THE SIGHTS

Butterstream Gardens   Butterstream is an idyllic orchestration of garden rooms, each holding the delights of spring and summer. Garden designer Jim Reynolds and his sole assistant meld the brilliant reds and yellows of a garden of hot colors with the gentle green foliage flanking a pond and the pale scepter of a white garden. Architectural notes resound throughout the garden, with vegetation marked by a Doric folly or reshaped into topiary pyramids.

Trim, county Meath. ✆ 046/36017. Admission €5 ($4.45). May–Sept daily 11am–6pm.

Hill of Tara ✹✹   This glorious hill is best remembered as the royal seat of the high kings in the early centuries of the millennium before Christianity came to Ireland. Every 3 years a *feis* (a banquet reaching the proportions of a great national assembly) was held. It's said that more than 1,000 people—princes, poets, athletes, priests, druids, musicians, and jesters—celebrated for a week in a single immense hall. The poet Thomas Moore wrote, "The harp that once through Tara's halls / the soul of music shed. . . ." A feis wasn't all fun and games, though: laws were passed, tribal disputes settled, and matters of peace and defense decided. The last feis was held in A.D. 560, and thereafter, Tara went into a decline associated with the rise of Christianity. Admittedly, the remains are not as impressive today as they were centuries ago. All that remains of Tara's former glories are grassy mounds, some ancient pillar stones, and depressions where the Iron Age ring forts stood. There's no access to the interior. All the wooden halls rotted long ago, so you'll have to rely on your imagination. But it's still a magnificent spot, with the hill rising 90m (300 ft.) above the surrounding countryside, and the views surely as awesome as they were 1,500 years ago. A visitor center, with exhibits and a stirring audiovisual presentation, is in the old church beside the entrance to the archaeological area. There's no picnicking, but there is a coffee shop/tearoom.

Off the main Dublin rd. (N3), Navan, county Meath. ✆ **046/25903**. Admission €2 ($1.80) adults, €1.30 ($1.15) seniors, €.75 (65¢) children and students, €5 ($4.45) family. Early May to mid-June and mid-Sept to Oct daily 10am–5pm; mid-June to mid-Sept daily 9:30am–6:30pm. Closed Nov–Apr.

Knowth ★★   Dating from the Stone Age and under seemingly perpetual excavation, this great mound is believed to have been a burial site for the high kings of Ireland. In historical importance, it's second only to Newgrange (see below). Archaeological evidence points to occupation from 3000 B.C. to A.D. 1200. Knowth is more complex than Newgrange, with two passage tombs surrounded by 17 smaller satellite tombs. The site has the greatest collection of passage tomb art ever uncovered in western Europe. There is no access to the interior of the tombs at this time. All tickets are issued at the new visitor center. Combined tickets with Newgrange are available.

Drogheda, county Meath (1.6km/1 mile northwest of Newgrange, between Drogheda and Slane). ✆ **041/ 988-0300**. www.knowth.com. Admission to Knowth and Bru na Boinne Centre €3.80 ($3.40) adults, €2.50 ($2.25) seniors, €1.50 ($1.35) students and children over 6, €9.50 ($8.45) family. MC, V. Daily Nov–Feb 9:30am–5pm; Mar–Apr and Oct 9:30am–5:30pm; May 9am–6:30pm; June to mid-Sept 9am–7pm; mid- to late Sept 9am–6:30pm.

Loughcrew ★   The 30 passage tombs of Loughcrew, also known as *Slieve na Calliaghe* or "the hill of the witch," crown three hilltops in western Meath. From their summits, the views of the plains of Meath and of the lakelands of Cavan are spectacular on a clear day. Two of the cairns—ornamented with Neolithic carvings—can be entered with a key. Guided tours of the eastern cairn are offered from mid-June to mid-September, and a key is available at the office for the western tomb (in many ways the more interesting of the two). A €25 ($23) deposit is required for the key. From October to May the keys to both cairns are available from Mrs. Basil Balfe (✆ **049/41256**), whose home is the first house on your right after turning into the Loughcrew drive.

Outside Oldcastle, county Meath. Admission €1.30 ($1.15) adults, €1 (90¢) seniors, €.50 (45¢) children and students, €4 ($3.55) family. Mid-June to mid-Sept daily 10am–6pm. Other times: key is available (see above). From N3, take R195 through Oldcastle toward Mullingar. 2.4km/1½ miles out of Oldcastle, look for a signposted left turn. The next left turn into Loughcrew is also signposted.

Newgrange ★★★   Ireland's best-known prehistoric monument is one of the archaeological wonders of western Europe. It's classified as a World Heritage Site by UNESCO. Built as a burial mound more than 5,000 years ago—long before the Great Pyramids and Stonehenge—it sits atop a hill near the Boyne, massive and impressive. The huge mound—11m (36 ft.) tall and approximately 78m (260 ft.) in diameter—consists of 200,000 tons of stone, a 6-ton capstone, and other stones weighing up to 16 tons each, many of which were hauled from as far away as county Wicklow and the Mountains of Mourne. Each stone fits perfectly in the overall pattern, and the result is a watertight structure, an amazing feat of engineering. Carved into the stones are myriad spirals, diamonds, and concentric circles. Inside, a passage 18m (60 ft.) long leads to a central burial chamber with a 5.7m (19-ft.) ceiling.

Fascination with Newgrange reaches a peak at the winter solstice, when sunlight pierces the inner chamber with an orange-toned glow for about 17 minutes at dawn from December 19 to 23. This occurrence is so remarkable that, as of this writing, the waiting list for viewing extends through the year 2005. Admission to Newgrange is by guided tour only. It's 3.2km (2 miles) east of Slane.

Logistical tips: All tickets are issued at the visitor center, Bru na Boinne. Combined tickets with Knowth, another nearby megalithic passage tomb, are available. Because of the great numbers of visitors, especially in the summer, expect delays; access is not guaranteed.

Off N51, Slane, county Meath. ℂ **041/988-0300.** Fax 041/982-3071. www.knowth.com/newgrange.htm. Guided tour and admission to Bru na Boinne Centre €5 ($4.45) adults, €3.80 ($3.40) seniors, €2.50 ($2.25) students and children over 6, €12.60, ($11.20) family. MC, V. Daily Nov–Feb 9:30am–5pm; Mar–Apr and Oct 9:30am–5:30pm; May 9am–6:30pm; June to mid-Sept 9am–7pm; mid- to late Sept 9am–6:30pm.

Newgrange Farm *(Kids)*   In contrast to all the surrounding antiquity in the Boyne Valley, this busy 133-hectare (333-acre) farm is very much a 21st-century attraction. Farmer Willie Redhouse and his family invite visitors on a 1½-hour tour of their farm, which grows wheat, oats, barley, rapeseed oil, corn, and linseed (flax). You can throw feed to the ducks, groom a calf, or bottle-feed the baby lambs or kid goats. Children can hold a newborn chick, pet a pony, or play with the pigs. In the aviaries are pheasants and rare birds. Horses, donkeys, and rare Jacob sheep romp in the fields. The high point of the week occurs at roughly 3pm every Sunday, when the sheep take to the track with Teddy Bear jockeys for the weekly Derby. This is especially engaging for children, who are given "part-owner" badges for the sheep of their choice so that they can shout their own ball of wool to victory. There is also a go-carting and toy tractor play area for children.

Demonstrations of sheepdog working, threshing, and horseshoeing are given. The Redhouses spin and dye their own wool and have put together an exhibit of the fibers produced and the natural dyes used to color them. At the herb garden, visitors receive a lesson on picking edible plants and herbs. Many of the farm buildings are from the 17th century. There is a coffee shop and indoor and outdoor picnic areas.

Off N51, 3.2km (2 miles) east of Slane (signposted off N51 and directly west of Newgrange monument), county Meath. ℂ **041/982-4119.** Admission €4.50 ($4) per person, €15 ($14) family. Daily 10am–5pm. Closed Sept–Easter.

St. Colmcille's House   St. Colmcille's Oratory, whose oldest parts date from the 9th century, sits in ancient glory amidst a row of modern terraced housing. Once an ancient church holding relics of St. Colmcille, the first-floor room still contains the traces of an ancient fireplace and entryway. But this isn't all: A narrow metal staircase ascends 4.5m (15 ft.) to a dark vault just under the roof. The small two-chambered space has both a structural and a mythical dimension. It is thought to help reinforce the stone arch of the oratory roof and—though this is more conjectural—is also said to be the place where the Book of Kells was completed.

About 180m (200 yd.) NW of St. Columba's Church, Church Lane, Kells, county Meath. Free admission. Ask for key from caretaker Mrs. B. Carpenter, next door to the oratory on Church Lane.

Trim Castle *(⚜⚜)*   This is the most massive and important Anglo-Norman castle in Ireland, and a magnificent sight for anyone still rapt by knights in armor and all things medieval. After years of being closed due to restoration, Trim Castle (aka King John's Castle, and best known today as a central set for the film *Braveheart*) reopened to the public in 2000. Norman lord Hugh de Lacy occupied the site in 1172 and completed the enclosed cruciform keep or great tower before the end of the century. In the 13th century, his son Walter enlarged the keep, circled it with a many-towered curtain wall, and added a Great Hall as an upgraded venue for courts, parliaments, and feasts.

The decision of the Heritage Service to restore it as a "preserved ruin" is a wise and effective one. What stands revealed now is the grand skeleton of the once-grand symbol of Anglo-Norman clout, just enough for visitors to reconstruct the flourishing whole in their imaginations.

Take the guided tour of the keep, but get there early. It's usually a sellout and can't be booked in advance. Note that this tour is unsuitable for small unruly children and anyone unable to tolerate steep climbs and formidable heights. It's perfectly safe but it involves narrow, steep steps in places and calls for obedience to the guide's restrictions.

Trim, county Meath. © 041/988-0300. Admission to grounds and tour of keep €3 ($2.65) adults, €2.50 ($2.25) seniors, €1.30 ($1.15) children and students, €8 ($7.10) family. Admission to grounds €1.30 ($1.15) adults, €1 (90¢) seniors, €.50 (45¢) children and students, €4 ($3.55) family. June–Sept daily 10am–6pm (last admission at 5:15pm). Tours every 30 min: 1st tour at 10:15am and last tour at 5:15pm. Closed Oct–May.

SPORTS & OUTDOOR PURSUITS
GOLF   The rolling hills of Meath set the stage for some lovely parkland lay-outs. The par-73 **County Meath Golf Club,** Trim (© **046/31463**), charges greens fees of €26 ($23) on weekdays and €33 ($29) on weekends. Even more reasonably-priced is **Headfort Golf Club,** Kells (© **046/40146**), with greens fees of €23 ($20) weekdays, €26 ($23) weekends. If you prefer links courses, the **Laytown and Bettystown Golf Club,** Bettystown (© **041/982-7534**), charges greens fees of €24 ($21) weekdays, €27 ($24) weekends.

HORSEBACK RIDING   Visitors can expect to pay an average of €13 to €19 ($12–$17) per hour for trekking or trail riding in the Meath countryside. To arrange a ride, contact the **Kells Equestrian Centre,** Kells (© **046/46638**).

SHOPPING
Mary McDonnell Craft Studio   Textile artist Mary McDonnell welcomes vis-itors to watch as she creates beautiful leather items, ceramics, jewelry, quilts, cush-ions, and wall hangings. Her shop also stocks the work of other local artisans, with a wide selection of crafts inspired by ancient Celtic designs uncovered in the Boyne Valley. The studio also incorporates Slane Antiques, operated by Mark McKeever. It's worth a detour. Open Tuesday to Saturday from 10:30am to 6pm, Sunday from 3 to 6pm. Newgrange Mall Studio, Slane, county Meath. © 041/982-4722.

WHERE TO STAY
MODERATE
Conyngham Arms Hotel ✦   On the main drag of one of the Boyne Valley's loveliest villages, this three-story stone-faced inn dates from 1850 and has been run by the same family for more than 60 years. The current proprietors, Kevin and Vonnie Macken, work hard to blend old-world charm and personal atten-tion with 21st-century efficiency and innovative innkeeping. The guest rooms offer traditional dark wood furnishings, some with four poster beds, rich pri-mary-color fabrics, and good reading lights. Other features include writing desks and towel warmers—but, in keeping with the building's character, there's no ele-vator. Exceptionally good bar food is available all day in the lounge. Dinner is served in the adjacent Flemings restaurant.

Main St., Slane, county Meath. ℂ **800/44-UTELL** in the U.S., or 041/988-4444. Fax 041/982-4205. www. conynghamarms.com. 14 units. €100–€110 ($89–$98) double. No service charge. Rates include full breakfast. DC, MC, V. Free parking. **Amenities:** Bar/lounge; babysitting. *In room:* TV, hair dryer.

INEXPENSIVE

Lennoxbrook Country House ⭐ A dense arch of ancient rhododendrons marks the entry to Lennoxbrook, the Mullan family home for five generations. Pauline Mullan and her three daughters offer a quartet of beautifully furnished guest rooms—antique chairs are positioned beside bay windows, and high, old-fashioned beds have firm, new mattresses. Two guest rooms have private bathrooms that are bright, pine-paneled, and quite large. For those who prefer character to convenience, the two rooms without their own bathrooms are particularly charming, and one of the two common bathrooms holds an enormous, old claw-foot tub. The Mullans provide for guests' needs in a way that is not done in more generic B&Bs. For example, laundry can be done for a reasonable fee, and Pauline and her daughters will spend extra time at breakfast in helping guests plan the day's itinerary. For those who want a longer stay, one of the upstairs rooms can be used as a self-catering apartment, with its own kitchen and sitting room on the ground floor.

Kells, county Meath. ℂ and fax 046/45902. 4 units, 2 with private bathroom (shower only). €50 ($46) double without bathroom, €54 ($48) double with bathroom. 20% reduction for children. V.

The Old Workhouse ⭐⭐ Niamh Colgan's lovely B&B used to be—as its name suggests—a workhouse, but today it feels like you're the special guest of a lovable granny. The atmosphere is anything but hard and foreboding; if anything, the interior design veers toward the feminine, a conglomeration of pastels, floral fabrics, fringed lampshades, and crystal chandeliers. The entrance hall and downstairs drawing room are both grand and majestic, the guest rooms are ultracomfy (just like at Granny's). Niamh's fruitcake—served with the obligatory cup of tea when you arrive—is excellent, and her breakfasts are legendary; especially her ham simmered in cider.

Ballinlough, Dunshaughlin, county Meath (on the N3, a mile south of Dunshaughlin). ℂ and fax **01/ 825-9251.** 5 units. €80–€90 ($71–$80) double. No service charge. Rates include full breakfast. MC, V. **Amenities:** Drawing room.

WHERE TO DINE
MODERATE

Hudson's Bistro ⭐ INTERNATIONAL This snappy little bistro, decked out with sunny colors and bright pottery, is a treat for travelers passing through the Navan area, especially couples or small groups of friends who enjoy quiet talk, wine, and terrific food. Try the tender Greek lamb kebabs with saffron rice, ratatouille chutney, and crisp salad, or authentic, delicious spicy Thai curry with vegetables, or saffron fettuccine with prawns. The desserts are worth waiting for. The staff is friendly and the chefs gladly accommodate vegetarian requests.

Railway St., Navan, county Meath. ℂ **046/29231.** Reservations required Fri–Sat. Main courses €11–€22 ($10–$20). Early-bird (before 6pm) dinner €13 ($12). Service charge 10%. AE, MC, V. Mon–Sat 5:30–11pm; Sun 5:30–10pm.

COUNTY LOUTH/CUCHULAINN COUNTRY

To the north and east of Meath is Louth, the smallest of Ireland's counties at only 824 sq. km (318 sq. miles). The two largest towns are Drogheda and Dundalk (the hometown of the Corrs), but both pale in comparison with **Carlingford** ⭐⭐, one of Ireland's heritage towns and easily the prettiest town in Louth.

It is wonderfully situated on a spur of the Cooley Mountains, overlooking Carlingford Lough and the Irish Sea at the northernmost point of Ireland's east coast, south of Northern Ireland. Established by the Vikings, it is very much a medieval town dominated by a massive 13th-century castle. Legend has it that long before the Vikings came, Carlingford was part of the warriors' hunting grounds. On the heights above the town, folk hero Cuchulainn is said to have single-handedly defeated the armies of Ulster in an epic battle.

Louth is not a place of outstanding scenic beauty, and most visitors move on after exploring a few sites of historic interest.

SEEING THE SIGHTS

Holy Trinity Heritage Centre   In a beautifully restored medieval church, this center has exhibits that detail the town's history from its Norman origins. If you book ahead, a visit can include a free guided walking tour of the town and a look at King John's Castle, the Mint, the Tholsel (the sole surviving, though altered, gate to the old medieval town), and a Dominican friary. The center overlooks the south shore of Carlington Lough, at the foot of Sliabh Foy, the highest peak of the Cooley Mountains.

Carlingford, county Louth. Ⓒ 042/9373454. Admission €1.30 ($1.15) adults, €.65 (60¢) children under 16. Sept–May Sat–Sun noon–5pm; June–Aug daily 10am–7pm.

Millmount Museum and Martello Tower ⚜   In the courtyard of 18th-century Millmount Fort, this museum offers exhibits on the history of Drogheda and the Boyne Valley area. A Bronze Age oracle, medieval tiles, and a collection of 18th-century guild banners are on display. Also on display are domestic items, such as spinning, weaving, and brewing equipment; antique gramophones; mousetraps; and hot-water jars. A geological exhibit contains specimens of stone from every county in Ireland, every country in Europe, and beyond. The tower was opened to the public in summer 2000 and houses an exhibition on the military history of Drogheda.

Duleek St., off the main Dublin rd. (N1), Drogheda, county Louth. Ⓒ 041/983-3097. Admission €4.50 ($4) adults, €3 ($2.65) students, €2.50 ($2.25) children under 12, €11 ($10) family. Mon–Sat 10am–5:30pm; Sun 2:30–5pm.

Monasterboice ⚜   Once a great monastery and now little more than a peaceful cemetery, this site is dominated by Muiredeach's High Cross. At 5m (17 ft.) tall, it's one of the most perfect crosses in Ireland. Dating from the year 922, the cross is ornamented with sculptured panels of scenes from the Old and New Testaments. On the monastery grounds are the remains of a round tower, two churches, two early grave slabs, and a sundial.

Off the main Dublin rd. (N1), 9.7km (6 miles) northwest of Drogheda, near Collon, county Louth. Free admission. Daily dawn–dusk.

Old Mellifont Abbey   "Old Mellifont" (distinct from "New Mellifont," a Cistercian monastery several miles away) was established in 1142 by St. Malachy of Armagh. Although little more than foundations survive, this tranquil spot is worth a visit for a few moments of quiet. Remnants of a 14th-century chapter house, an octagonal lavabo dating from around 1200, and several Romanesque arches remain. A visitor center contains sculpted stones from the excavations.

On the banks of the Mattock River, 9.7km (6 miles) west of Drogheda, off T25, Collon, county Louth. Ⓒ 041/ 982-6459. Admission €2 ($1.80) adults, €1.30 ($1.15) seniors, €.75 (65¢) students and children under 12, €5 ($4.45) family. Daily May to mid-June and mid-Sept to Oct 10am–5pm; mid-June to mid-Sept 9:30am–6:30pm.

WHERE TO STAY & DINE

Ballymascanlon House Hotel   A stone-faced Victorian mansion dating from the early 1800s, Ballymascanlon was formerly the home of Baron Plunkett. The house has been enlarged several times, including a new wing completed just last summer. The hotel stands on 52 hectares (130 acres) of award-winning gardens and grounds, a peaceful oasis just 4.8km (3 miles) south of the Northern Ireland border. Rooms vary in size but are decorated in traditional style with antiques and rich fabrics. The Cellar Bar offers traditional Irish music on weekends.

Off the Dublin-Belfast rd. (N1), Dundalk, county Louth. © **800/528-1234** in the U.S., or 042/93-71124. Fax 042/93-71598. 74 units. €136–€150 ($121–$134) double. No service charge. Rates include full breakfast. AE, DC, MC, V. **Amenities:** Restaurant (Continental); pub; swimming pool; golf course; tennis courts; squash courts; gym; sauna; solarium. *In room:* TV, hair dryer.

Jordan's Townhouse & Restaurant *★★*   Here is a place of many incarnations: In the 16th century, it was a row of small fishermen's cottages; later it was a coal store, then a shop selling mineral water. Today it's a gem of a townhouse hotel in the heart of a lovely medieval village, with a bistro that's a culinary destination in itself. Harry and Marian Jordan don't follow fads—they just do things right. Their five guest rooms are very popular with Dubliners traveling north and northerners traveling south, who take a couple of nights in Carlingford as a break from the road. Both the decor and the food are comfortably timeless and elegant, and the service is terrific.

Newry St., Carlingford, county Louth. © **042/9373223.** Fax 042/9373827. 5 units. €118–€140 ($105–$125) double. No service charge. Rates include full breakfast. AE, MC, V. **Amenities:** Restaurant (bistro/seafood). *In room:* TV, hair dryer.

McKevitts Village Inn   This is a great hotel for unwinding and taking long walks along the shores of Carlingford Lough. It's a vintage two-story property that has been updated and refurbished in recent years. Guest rooms vary in size and shape, but all have standard Irish furnishings and are very comfortable, with nice views of the town.

Market Sq., Carlingford, county Louth. © **800/447-7462** in the U.S., or 042/9373116. Fax 042/9373144. 15 units. €66–€104 ($59–$93) double. No service charge. Rates include full breakfast. AE, DC, MC, V. **Amenities:** Restaurant (seafood); bar. *In room:* TV.

SHOPPING

Celtic Clays   This little pottery shop sells the exquisite wares of Ciaran O'Conboirne, whose work has developed an international following since he opened his shop in 1995. O'Conboirne's uses Celtic motifs and rich, earthy tones to create pieces that look and feel sturdy and decidedly Irish. Every item is handmade and truly individual, making a superb souvenir. Open Monday to Friday 9am to 5:30pm; Sunday noon to 6pm. 2 Riverlane, Carlingford, county Louth. © **042/938-3996.** celticclays@eircom.net.

AN EASY EXCURSION FROM COUNTY LOUTH

Eight kilometers (5 miles) from county Louth's northwest border, the town of **Carrickmacross** in county Monaghan has been famous for its tradition of lace-making for more than 150 years.

Seeing the Sights

Carrickmacross Lace Co-op *★*   Since the 1820s, lace has been made in the surrounding countryside, with the tradition being passed through many hands to the present accomplished lace makers, who now display their works in this gallery. On view are the beautiful, intricate handmade laces produced locally; some are for sale. Demonstrations are given every once in a while; call to inquire.

Market Square, Carrickmacross. © **042/966-2506.** Apr–Oct Wed and Sat 9:30am–12:30pm, and Mon, Tues, Thurs, and Fri 9:30am–12:30pm and 1:30–5:30pm.

Where to Stay & Dine

Nuremore Hotel   In a town famous for its lace, this modern three-story hotel is equally well known for its hospitality and high standards. Set amid 40 hectares (100 acres) of parkland and woods (including three lakes), it has been totally refurbished and expanded in recent years. The decor is traditional, with dark woods, marble fireplaces, and antique framed prints of the area. Most of the guest rooms feature bright colors, reproduction furniture, and half-tester beds; some have light woods and more contemporary styling. All afford lake or garden views. Guests have access to a nearby leisure center with a squash court, two tennis courts, sauna, steam room, gym, and whirlpool, and to trout fishing on the privately stocked lake.

Ashbourne-Slane-Ardee rd. (N2), Carrickmacross, county Monaghan. © **042/966-1438.** Fax 042/966-1853. www.nuremore-hotel.ie. 69 units. €165–€250 ($147–$223) double. No service charge. Rates include breakfast. AE, DC, MC, V. **Amenities:** Restaurant (international); bar; indoor swimming pool; 18-hole championship golf course. *In room:* TV, minibar, hair dryer.

6

The Southeast

Wexford, Waterford, South Tipperary, and Kilkenny are often referred to as Ireland's "sunny southeast" because these counties usually enjoy more hours of sunshine than the rest of the country. No matter what the weather, they also provide a varied touring experience, from the world-famous Waterford Crystal Factory to the Viking streets of Wexford, and from the majestic Rock of Cashel to Kilkenny's medieval splendor.

The website for all Southeast Tourism is **www.southeastireland. travel.ie**.

1 County Wexford

Wexford Town is 142km (88 miles) S of Dublin, 63km (39 miles) E of Waterford, 90km (56 miles) S of Wicklow, 187km (116 miles) E of Cork, 214km (133 miles) SE of Shannon Airport

County Wexford is most remarkable for the long stretches of pristine beach that line its coast, and for the evocative historic monuments in Wexford Town and on the Hook Peninsula. The Blackstairs Mountains dominate the western border of the county, and provide excellent hill walking. Bird-watchers can find an abundance of great sites, including Wexford Wildfowl Reserve and Great Saltee Island.

The modern English name of Wexford evolved from *Waesfjord,* which is what the Viking sea-rovers called it when they settled here in the 9th century. It means "the harbor of the mud-flats." Like the rest of Ireland, Wexford was under Norman control by the 12th century, and some stone reminders of their dominance in this region survive.

With a population of about 10,000, Wexford is a hard-working Irish harbor town with a surprisingly sophisticated social calendar, highlighted by the opera festival in late October.

WEXFORD TOWN ESSENTIALS
GETTING THERE   Irish Rail provides daily train service to Wexford and Rosslare Pier. It serves **O'Hanrahan Station,** Redmond Place, Wexford (© 053/22522; www.irishrail.ie).

Bus Eireann operates daily bus service to Wexford and Rosslare, into O'Hanrahan Station and Bus Depot, Redmond Place, Wexford (© 053/22522; www.buseireann.ie).

If you're driving from Dublin and points north, take the N11 or N80 to Wexford; if you're coming from the west, take the N25 or N8. Two bridges lead into Wexford from the north—the Ferrycarrig Bridge from the main Dublin road (N11) and the Wexford Bridge from R741. The Ferrycarrig Bridge takes you into town from the west. The Wexford Bridge leads right to the heart of town along the quays.

Ferries from Britain run to Rosslare Harbour, 19km (12 miles) south of Wexford Town. **Stena Line** (© 053/33115; www.stenaline.co.uk) handles service from Fishguard, Wales. **Irish Ferries** (© **053/33158;** www.irishferries.ie) has a route between Rosslare and Pembroke, Wales. (Irish Ferries also provides service from Le Havre and Cherbourg, France.)

If you're traveling between county Wexford and county Waterford, there's a waterborne shortcut. The **Passage East Ferry County Ltd.,** Barrack Street, Passage East, county Waterford (© **051/382488**), operates a car-ferry service across Waterford Harbour. It links Passage East, about 16km (10 miles) east of Waterford, with Ballyhack, about 32km (20 miles) southwest of Wexford. The shortcut saves about an hour's driving time between the cities. Crossing time averages 10 minutes. It's continuous drive-on, drive-off service, with no reservations required. Fares are €6 ($5.35) one way and €8.50 ($7.55) round-trip for car and passengers; €2 ($1.80) round-trip and €1.30 ($1.15) single trip for foot passengers; €2.50 ($2.25) one way and €3 ($2.65) round-trip for cyclists. It operates April to September, Monday to Saturday 7am to 10pm, Sunday 9:30am to 10pm; October to March, Monday to Saturday 7am to 8pm, Sunday 9:30am to 8pm.

VISITOR INFORMATION   Contact the **Wexford Tourist Office,** Crescent Quay, Wexford (© **053/23111**); the **Gorey Tourist Office,** Town Centre, Gorey (© **055/21248**); and the **Rosslare Harbour Tourist Office,** Ferry Terminal, Rosslare Harbour (© **053/33622**), or visit the website at **www.wexford tourism.com**. The Wexford and Gorey Town offices are open year-round Monday to Saturday 9am to 6pm. The Rosslare Harbour office opens daily to coincide with ferry arrivals. **Seasonal offices,** open June to August, are at Enniscorthy, Town Centre (© **054/34699**), and at New Ross, Town Centre (© **051/21857**).

TOWN LAYOUT   Rimmed by the River Slaney, Wexford is a compact and congested town with many narrow streets—successors of the 9th-century market trails—lined with 18th-century houses and shop fronts. You'll want to explore it on foot, not behind the wheel. Four quays (Custom House, Commercial, Paul, and the semicircular Crescent) run beside the water. Crescent Quay marks the center of town. One block inland is Main Street, a long, narrow thoroughfare that you can easily walk. Wexford's shops and businesses are on North and South Main Street and the many smaller streets that fan out from it.

GETTING AROUND   Wexford is small and compact, with narrow streets. There is no town bus transport, but **Bus Eireann** (© **051/22522;** www.bus eireann.ie) operates daily service between Wexford and Rosslare. Other local services operate on certain days only to Kilmore Quay, Carne, and Gorey.

The best way to see Wexford Town is to walk it. Park your car along the quays; parking operates according to the disc system, at €.40 (35¢) per hour. Discs are on sale at the tourist office and many shops. There is free parking off Redmond Square, beside the train and bus station. You'll need a car to reach county Wexford attractions outside of town.

If you need to rent a car, contact **Budget** at the Quay, New Ross (© **051/ 421670**); **Murrays Europcar,** Wellington Place, Wexford (© **053/33634**), or Rosslare Ferryport, Rosslare (© **053/33634**); or **Hertz,** Ferrybank, Wexford (© **053/23511**), or Rosslare Harbour, Wexford (© **053/33238**).

If you want a cab, call **Abbey Cabs** (© **053/41741**) or **Wexford Taxi** (© **053/46666**).

FAST FACTS   If you need a drugstore, try **John Fehily/The Pharmacy,** 28 S. Main St., Wexford (© **053/23163**); **Sherwood Chemist,** 2 N. Main St.,

The Southeast

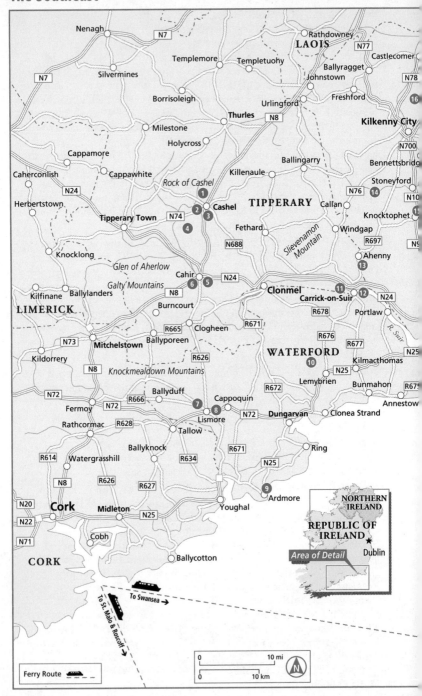

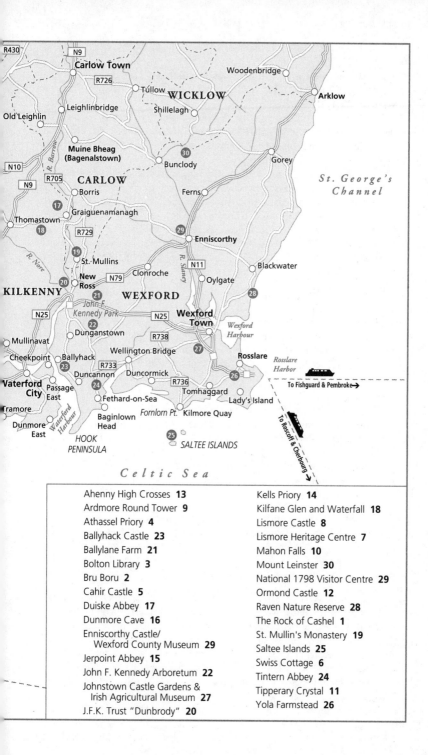

R430
N9
Carlow Town
R726
Woodenbridge○
○Tullow **WICKLOW**
Arklow
○Leighlinbridge
Shillelagh○
Old Leighlin○
**Muine Bheag
(Bagenalstown)**
N10
30
Gorey
N9 R705 ○Bunclody
CARLOW
*St. George's
Channel*
○Borris
Ferns○
17
○Graiguenamanagh
Thomastown○
29
18 R729 ●Enniscorthy
R. Nore
19
○St. Mullins
Blackwater○
N11
Clonroche
20 ●New N79
Ross
Oylgate○
KILKENNY **21** **WEXFORD**
28
*John F.
Kennedy Park*
N25 **Wexford
Town**
N25 *Wexford
Harbour*
22 ○Dunganstown
R738
Mullinavat○ **27**
Cheekpoint○ Wellington Bridge
Rosslare *Rosslare
Harbour*
○Ballyhack R733
23 Duncannon Duncormick
26
**Waterford
City** Passage
East R736
To Fishguard & Pembroke→
○Fethard-on-Sea Tomhaggard
Tramore○ Lady's Island
Dunmore
East *Waterford
Harbour* Baginlown
Head *Fornlorn Pt.* Kilmore Quay
**HOOK
PENINSULA** **25** ○
○ *SALTEE ISLANDS*

C e l t i c   S e a

To Roscoff & Cherbourg ↓

Wexford (© **053/22875**); or **Fortune's Pharmacy,** 82 N. Main St., Wexford (© **053/42354**).

In an emergency, dial © **999.** The **Garda Station** (police) is on Roches Road, Wexford (© **053/22333**). **Wexford General Hospital** is on Richmond Terrace, Wexford (© **053/42233**).

Like most towns in Ireland today, Wexford offers free Internet access in its **Public Library** (© **053/21637**), which is in Selskar House, off Redmond Square just in from Commercial Quay. Its hours are Tuesday 1 to 5:30pm, Wednesday 10am to 4:30pm and 6 to 8pm, Thursday and Friday 10am to 5:30pm, and Saturday 10am to 1pm. The demand is so great, however, that it's usually necessary to call in advance to reserve time on a PC. Otherwise, every day but Sunday between 9am and 5pm you can go to the **Westgate Computer Centre,** Westgate (© **053/46291**), next to the Heritage Tower. The center offers Internet access for €2.50 ($2.25) per each 30 minutes online.

The weekly *Wexford People* covers town and county events and entertainment.

The **General Post Office** on Anne Street, Wexford (© **053/22587**), is open Monday to Saturday 9am to 5:30pm.

EXPLORING WEXFORD TOWN

The best way to see the town is by walking the entire length of North and South Main Street, taking time to detour up and down the alleys and lanes that cross the street. The tourist office can supply you with a free map. You may want to start out by visiting the Westgate Heritage Tower (see below), which will provide you with valuable context and background information before you explore the rest of the city.

The Bull Ring 🐦 In 1798, the first declaration of an Irish Republic was made here, and a statue memorializes the Irish pikemen who fought for the cause. Earlier, in the 17th century, the town square was a venue for bull baiting, a sport introduced by the butcher's guild. Tradition has it that, after a match, the hide of the ill-fated bull was presented to the mayor and the meat used to feed the poor. Today, activity at the ring is much tamer: a weekly outdoor market, open Friday and Saturday from 10am to 4:30pm.

Off N. Main St., Wexford, county Wexford. Free admission.

Cornmarket Until a century ago, this central marketplace buzzed with the activity of cobblers, publicans, and more than 20 other businesses. Today it's just a wide street. The Wexford Arts Centre, in a structure dating from 1775, dominates the street.

Off Upper George's St., Wexford, county Wexford.

Irish National Heritage Park 🐦🐦 This 14-hectare (36-acre) living history park on the banks of the River Slaney provides an ideal introduction for visitors of all ages to life in ancient Ireland, from the Stone Age to the Norman invasion. Each reconstructed glimpse into Irish history is beautifully crafted and has its own natural setting and wildlife. The 20-minute orientation video is engaging and informative, but can't hold a candle to a guided tour by head guide Jimmy O'Rourke. He is a master in bringing each site to life, captivating children and intriguing adults. There's also a nature trail and interpretive center, complete with gift shop and cafe. Plan to spend several hours in the park.

Off Dublin-Wexford rd. (N11), Ferrycarrig, county Wexford. © 053/20733. www.inhp.com. Admission €7 ($6.25) adults, €5.50 ($4.90) seniors and students, €4 ($3.55) youths 13–16, €3.50 ($3.10) children 4–12, €17.50 ($15.60) family. Mar–Oct daily 9:30am–6:30pm. Last admission 5pm.

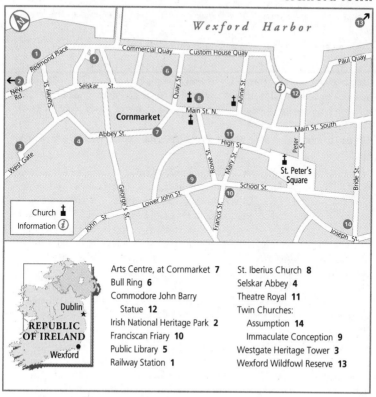

Wexford Harbor

Paul Quay

Commercial Quay — Custom House Quay

Redmond Place

New Rd.

Slaney St.

Selskar St.

Cornmarket

Main St. N.

Abbey St.

West Gate

Main St. South

High St.

Rowe St.

Mary St.

St. Peter's Square

Peter St.

Bride St.

School St.

George's St.

Lower John St.

Francis St.

John St.

Joseph St.

Church ✝

Information ⓘ

REPUBLIC OF IRELAND

Dublin ★

Wexford ●

Arts Centre, at Cornmarket **7**
Bull Ring **6**
Commodore John Barry
   Statue **12**
Irish National Heritage Park **2**
Franciscan Friary **10**
Public Library **5**
Railway Station **1**

St. Iberius Church **8**
Selskar Abbey **4**
Theatre Royal **11**
Twin Churches:
   Assumption **14**
   Immaculate Conception **9**
Westgate Heritage Tower **3**
Wexford Wildfowl Reserve **13**

John Barry Monument   This bronze statue, a gift from the American people in 1956, faces out to the sea as a tribute to John Barry, a favorite son who became the father of the American Navy. Born at Ballysampson, Tacumshane, 16km (10 miles) southeast of Wexford Town, Barry emigrated to the colonies while in his teens and volunteered to fight in the American Revolution. One of the U.S. Navy's first commissioned officers, he became captain of the *Lexington*. In 1797, George Washington appointed him commander-in-chief of the U.S. Navy.
Crescent Quay, Wexford, county Wexford.

St. Iberius Church   Erected in 1660, St. Iberius was built on hallowed ground—the land has been used for houses of worship since Norse times. The church has a lovely Georgian facade and an interior known for its superb acoustics. Free guided tours are given according to demand.
N. Main St., Wexford, county Wexford. ℂ **053/43013.** Free admission; donations welcome. May–Sept daily 10am–5pm; Oct–Apr Tues–Sat 10am–3pm.

Selskar Abbey   Said to be one of the oldest sites of religious worship in Wexford, this abbey dates from at least the 12th century. It was often the scene of synods and parliaments. The first Anglo-Irish treaty was signed here in 1169, and it's said that Henry II spent the Lent of 1172 at the abbey doing penance for having Thomas à Becket beheaded. Although the abbey is mostly in ruins, its choir is part of a Church of Ireland edifice, and a portion of the original tower is a vesting room. The adjoining graveyard has suffered a disturbing amount of vandalism over the years. The entrance most likely to be open is to the left of Westgate.

Off Temperance Row at Westgate St., Wexford, county Wexford. Open site (except when it's locked).

The Twin Churches: Church of the Assumption and Church of the Immaculate Conception ⊛   These twin Gothic structures (1851–58) were designed by architect Robert Pierce, a pupil of Augustus Pugin. Their 69m (230-ft.) spires dominate Wexford's skyline. Mosaics on the main door of both churches list relevant names and dates.

Bride and Rowe sts., Wexford, county Wexford. ℂ 053/22055. Free admission; donations welcome. Daily 8am–6pm.

Westgate Heritage Tower   Westgate once guarded the western entrance of Wexford Town. Sir Stephen Devereux built it in the 13th century, on instructions from King Henry. Like other town gates, it consisted of a toll-taking area, cells for offenders, and accommodations for guards. Fully restored and reopened in 1992 as a heritage center, it presents artifacts, displays, and a 27-minute audiovisual display, titled *In Selskar's Shadow,* which provides an informative introduction to Wexford's complex and turbulent history. If you see this presentation prior to exploring the city, your ambles will likely be a good deal more meaningful to you.

Westgate St., Wexford, county Wexford. ℂ 053/46506. Admission €2 ($1.80) adults, €.70 (60¢) children and students, €5 ($4.45) family. May–Aug Mon–Fri 9am–4:30pm, Sat–Sun noon–5pm; Sept–Apr Mon–Fri 9:30am–4:30pm.

Wexford Wildfowl Reserve ⊛   This national nature reserve is part of the unfortunately-named North Slob, adjacent to Wexford Harbour, 4.8km (3 miles) east of Wexford Town. About 10,000 Greenland white-fronted geese—more than one-third of the world's population—spend the winter here, as do brent geese, Bewick's swans, and wigeons. The area is immensely attractive to other wildfowl and birds as well; more than 240 species have been seen here. The reserve has a visitor center, an audiovisual program, a new exhibition hall, and an observation tower and blinds.

North Slob, Wexford, county Wexford. ℂ 053/23129. cjwilson@esatclear.ie. Free admission. Apr 16–Sept daily 9am–6pm; Oct–Apr 15 daily 10am–5pm.

SIGHTSEEING TOURS

Walking Tours of Wexford   Proud of their town's ancient streets and vintage buildings, the people of Wexford spontaneously started to give tours to visitors more than 30 years ago. Eventually organized as the Old Wexford Society, the local folk have developed a real expertise over the years, and continue to give tours on a regular basis. All tours depart from Westgate Heritage Tower.

c/o Seamus Molloy, "Carmeleen," William St., Wexford, county Wexford. ℂ 053/22663. €5 ($4.45) adults, €1.50 ($1.34) children. Individual tours arranged when you call.

SHOPPING

Shops in Wexford are open Monday to Thursday 9am to 5:30pm, Friday and Saturday 9am to 6pm; some shops stay open until 8pm on Friday.

Barkers   Established in 1848, this shop has long been a mainstay in Wexford. It stocks a large selection of Waterford crystal, Belleek china, and Royal Irish Tara china, as well as Irish linens and bronze and international products such as Aynsley, Wedgwood, and Lladró. 36–40 S. Main St., Wexford, county Wexford. ℂ 053/23159.

Faller Sweater Shop   As its name implies, this shop specializes in Aran hand-knit sweaters (of which it carries a large selection) and mohair, cotton, and linen knits. To warm and accessorize other parts of your body, you'll also find ties, scarves, wool socks, and tweed caps. 39 N. Main St., Wexford, county Wexford. © 053/24659.

The Wexford Bookshop   This extensive and bustling emporium, spread out on three levels, offers much more than books. There's a long wall-full of magazines and newspapers, a selection of stationery, arts and crafts and supplies, and a slew of toys. 31 N. Main St., Wexford, county Wexford. © 053/22223.

Wexford Silver   Pat Dolan, one of Ireland's leading silversmiths, plies his craft at this shop. He and his sons create gold, silver, and bronze pieces by hand using traditional tools and techniques. They are members of a long line of Dolans who trace their silversmithing connections back to 1647. Open 10am to 5:30pm. A second workshop is in Kinsale (see "Kinsale Silver" listing in chapter 8). 115 N. Main St., Wexford, county Wexford. © 053/21933.

The Wool Shop   In the heart of the town's main thoroughfare, this is Wexford's long-established best source for hand-knit items. The selection runs from caps and tams to sweaters and jackets, as well as tweeds, linens, mohairs, and knitting yarns. 39 S. Main St., Wexford, county Wexford. © 053/22247.

ATTRACTIONS FARTHER AFIELD IN COUNTY WEXFORD

The rounded granite form of **Mount Leinster,** the highest in Wexford, is a landmark throughout the region. One of the most popular hang-gliding spots in Ireland, the summit is always windy, and often shrouded in clouds. If you can get to the top on a clear day, however, it will be an experience you won't soon forget. To get there, follow signs for the Mount Leinster Scenic Drive from the sleepy town of **Kiltealy** on the eastern slopes of the mountain. Soon you will begin climbing the exposed slopes; don't get too distracted by the dazzling views, because the road is twisting and quite narrow in places. There's a parking area at the highest point of the auto road, and a paved access road (closed to cars) continues approximately 2.4km (1½ miles) to the summit. From the top you can scramble along the ridge to the east, known as Black Rock Mountain. To return, continue along the Scenic Drive, which ends a few miles outside the town of Bunclody.

Ballyhack Castle   On a steep slope overlooking the Waterford estuary, about 32km (20 miles) west of Wexford, this large tower house is considered a Crusader castle. It's thought to have been built around 1450 by the Knights Hospitallers of St. John, one of the two great military orders founded at the beginning of the 12th century during the Crusades. The castle has been recently restored and turned into a heritage information center, with displays on the Crusader knights, medieval monks, and Norman nobles.

Off R733, Ballyhack, county Wexford. © 051/389468. Admission €1.30 ($1.15) adults, €1 (90¢) seniors, €.50 (45¢) students and children, €4 ($3.55) family. June–Sept daily 9:30am–6:30pm. Closed Oct–May.

Ballylane Visitor Farm   In the heart of county Wexford's verdant countryside, this 80-hectare (200-acre) farm is owned by the Hickey family. They invite visitors to get a firsthand look at their farm life, which includes such activities as tillage, sheep raising, and deer and pheasant husbandry. Guided tours, lasting about an hour, follow a set route covering fields of crops, woodlands, bog lands, ponds, and farm buildings. A tearoom, shop, and picnic area have been added in addition to a fully equipped caravan/RV park.

Signposted off New Ross–Wexford rd. (N25), 44km (27 miles) west of Wexford Town and 4.8km (3 miles) east of New Ross, county Wexford. ℭ **051/425666**. Admission €5 ($4.45) adults, €3 ($2.65) seniors, students, and children, €15 ($13) family. April noon–6pm Sun; May–Sept daily 10am–6pm; Oct–Mar Sun and holidays noon–6pm (but call first to confirm).

Enniscorthy Castle/Wexford County Museum ✦

Overlooking the River Slaney at Enniscorthy, 24km (15 miles) north of Wexford Town, this castle was built by the Prendergast family in the 13th century. It's said that the poet Edmund Spenser once owned it briefly. Remarkably well preserved and restored, it's now home to the Wexford County Museum, which focuses on the area's ecclesiastical, maritime, folk, agricultural, industrial, and military traditions. Displays include an old Irish farm kitchen, early modes of travel, nautical memorabilia, and items connected with Wexford's role in Ireland's struggle for independence, especially the 1798 and 1916 risings.

Castle Hill, Enniscorthy, county Wexford. ℭ **054/35926**. Admission €4 ($3.55) adults, €2.50 ($2.25) seniors and students, €.70 (60¢) children. June–Sept daily 10am–6pm; Oct–Nov and Feb–May daily 2–5:30pm; Dec–Jan Sun 2–5pm.

Irish Agricultural Museum and Famine Exhibition ✦

The importance of farming in Wexford's history is the focus of this museum, on the Johnstown Castle Demesne 6.5km (4 miles) southwest of Wexford Town. In historic farm buildings, the museum contains exhibits on rural transport, planting, and the diverse activities of the farm household. There are also extensive displays on dairying, crafts, and Irish country furniture. Large-scale replicas illustrate the workshops of the blacksmith, cooper, wheelwright, harness maker, and basket maker. The 19th-century Gothic Revival castle on the grounds is not open to the public except for its entrance hall, where tourist information is available. Visitors can enjoy the 20 hectares (50 acres) of ornamental gardens, which contain more than 200 kinds of trees and shrubs, three lakes, a tower house, hothouses, a statue walk, and a picnic area.

Johnstown Castle. Bridgetown Rd., off Wexford-Rosslare rd. (N25), Wexford, county Wexford. ℭ **053/42888**. Admission to museum €3 ($2.65) adults, €2 ($1.80) students and children, €10 ($8.90) family; gardens €2 ($1.80) adults, €.70 (60¢) children and students, or €4 ($3.55) by the car. No credit cards. Museum June–Aug Mon–Fri 9am–5pm, Sat–Sun 11am–5pm; Apr–May and Sept–Nov Mon–Fri 9am–12:30pm and 1:30–5pm, Sat–Sun 2–5pm; Dec–Mar Mon–Fri 9am–12:30pm and 1:30–5pm. Gardens year-round daily 9am–5:30pm.

John F. Kennedy Arboretum ✦✦

Dedicated to the memory of the 35th U.S. president, this 240-hectare (600-acre) arboretum is near a hill known as Slieve Coilte, about 32km (20 miles) west of Wexford. The arboretum overlooks the simple thatched cottage where JFK's great-grandfather was born. Opened in 1968, the arboretum was initiated with financial help from a group of Irish Americans; the Irish government funds its development and maintenance. More than 4,500 species of plants and trees from five continents grow here. There are an information center, play and picnic areas, and a small miniature railway. A hilltop observation point (at 266m/888 ft.) presents a sweeping view of county Wexford and five neighboring counties, the Saltee Islands, the Comeragh Mountains, and parts of the rivers Suir, Nore, and Barrow.

Off Duncannon rd. (R733), New Ross, county Wexford. ℭ **051/388171**. Admission €2.50 ($2.25) adults, €2 ($1.80) seniors, €1.30 ($1.15) students and children, €7 ($6.25) family. Apr and Sept daily 10am–6:30pm; May–Aug daily 10am–8pm; Oct–Mar daily 10am–5pm.

J.F.K. Trust Dunbrody

Housed in twin 18th-century grain mills, the center tells the story of the Irish Diaspora: their lives and achievements abroad, beginning with the monks who went to Europe in the 6th century and continuing to the present day. A computerized data bank for tracing county Wexford roots is being developed with the Ellis Island Immigration Museum in New York and other immigration centers as far away as Australia and Argentina, and will contain more than four million names. A section of the center is devoted to John F. Kennedy, who was descended from a county Wexford family.

The **Dunbrody,** the largest tall ship ever built in the Republic of Ireland— 458 tons and 53m (176 ft.) long—was opened to visitors in May 2001. It is moored on the New Ross quays as a floating exhibition center.

The Quay, New Ross, county Wexford. (*C* 051/425239. Fax 051/425240. www.dunbrody.com. Admission €4 ($3.55) adults, €2 ($1.80) seniors, students, and children, €10 ($8.90) family. Sept–June Mon–Fri 10am–5pm, Sat–Sun noon–5pm; July–Aug daily 10am–7pm.

The National 1798 Visitor Centre   Just south of Enniscorthy Castle, this visitor center, dedicated to the 1798 Rebellion and its aftermath, gives visitors insight into the birth of modern democracy in Ireland. Interactive computers, an audiovisual presentation, and an array of artifacts are on display to help dramatize the events in an interesting and exciting way. The center also incorporates a pleasant tearoom and gift shop.

Millpark Rd., Enniscorthy, county Wexford. (*C* **054/37596.** Admission €5 ($4.45) adults, €4 ($3.55) seniors and students, €16 ($14) family. Mon–Sat 9:30am–6pm; Sun 11am–6pm.

Tintern Abbey ★★   In a lovely rural setting overlooking Bannow bay, Tintern Abbey was founded under the patronage of William, the Earl of Marshall, by the Cistercian monks of Tintern in South Wales. The parts that remain— nave, chancel, tower, chapel, and cloister—date from the early 13th century, though they have been much altered since then. The grounds are quite beautiful, and include a restored stone bridge spanning a narrow sea inlet.

Saltmills, New Ross, county Wexford. (*C* **051/562650.** Admission €2 ($1.80) adults, €1.30 ($1.15) seniors, €.80 (70¢) students and children, €5 ($4.45) family. Mid-June to Sept daily 9:30am–6:30pm. Signposted 19km (12 miles) south of New Ross off of R733.

Yola Farmstead   A voluntary community project, this theme park depicts a Wexford farming community as it would have been 200 or more years ago. Thatched-roof buildings have been constructed, including barns housing farm animals. Bread and butter making are demonstrated, and craftspeople can be seen at work blowing and hand-cutting crystal at Wexford Heritage Crystal, a glass-production enterprise. It's touristy, but not hokey. The **Genealogy Center** (*C* **053/31177;** fax 053/32612; wexgen@iol.ie) is open May to October daily 9:30am to 5pm; January to April and November Monday to Friday 9:30am to 4:30pm. Closed in December. Consultation or one name search costs IR£20 (25€/$23). The website is www.irishroots.net/Wexford.htm.

16km (10 miles) south of Wexford Town, 2.4km (1½ miles) from Rosslare Ferry-port, Wexford-Rosslare rd. (N25), Tagoat, county Wexford. (*C* **053/32610.** yolafst@iol.ie. Admission €5 ($4.45) adults, €3.50 ($3.10) seniors and students, €1.30 ($1.15) children, €10 ($8.90) family. June–Sept daily 9:30am–5pm; Mar–Apr and Nov Mon–Fri 9:30am–4:30pm. Closed other months.

SPORTS & OUTDOOR PURSUITS
BEACHES   County Wexford's beaches at **Courtown, Curracloe, Duncannon,** and **Rosslare** are ideal for walking, jogging, or swimming.

BICYCLING   You can rent mountain bikes at two Raleigh Rent-a-Bike locations in Wexford Town: **Hayes Cycle Shop,** 108 S. Main St. (*C* **053/22462**); and the **Bike Shop,** 9 Selskar St. (*C* **053/22514**), which allows one-way rentals. From Wexford, the road north up the coast through Curracloe to Blackwater is

A Trip Through History: Exploring the Ring of Hook

The **Hook Peninsula** in southwest county Wexford is a place of rocky headlands and secluded beaches. It sits between Bannow Bay and Waterford Harbor, two of the most significant inlets in medieval times for travelers from Britain to Ireland, and the abundance of archaeological remains reflects the area's strategic importance. The end of the peninsula is popular with birders as a site for watching the spring and fall passerine migration, and holds a lighthouse reputed to be one of the oldest in Europe. The route described below will guide you through a driving or biking tour, and hikers can see most of the places listed from the Wexford Coastal Pathway.

Start your exploration of the peninsula at the town of **Wellington Bridge**. Just west of town on R733 is a roadside stop on the left by a cemetery; from here you can look across Bannow Bay to the ruins of **Clonmines**, a Norman village established in the 13th century. This is one of the finest examples of a walled medieval settlement in Ireland, with remains of two churches, three tower houses, and an Augustinian priory. You can drive to the ruins—just follow R733 another mile west to a left turn posted for the Wicklow Coastal Pathway, and continue straight on this road where the Coastal Pathway turns right. The ruins are on private land, so you should ask permission at the farmhouse at the end of the road.

Continuing west on R733, turn left on R734 at the sign for the Ring of Hook, and turn right at the sign for **Tintern Abbey** (see above). The abbey was founded by the monks of Tintern in South Wales in the 13th century, and it has been much altered. The grounds are beautiful and contain a restored stone bridge that spans a narrow sea inlet.

a scenic day trip. For complete 1- or 2-week cycling holidays in the Southeast, contact Don Smith at **Celtic Cycling,** Lorum Old Rectory, Bagenalstown (© **0503/75282**).

BIRD-WATCHING   A good starting place for bird-watching in the region is the **Wexford Wildfowl Reserve** (see above); warden Chris Wilson can direct you to other places of interest.

The **Great Saltee Island** is one of the best places in Ireland to watch seabirds, especially during May, June, and July, when the place is mobbed with nesting parents and their young. Like something out of a Hitchcock feature, the cliffs on the island's southernmost point are packed to overflowing with raucous avian residents, and the combined sound of their screeching, squawking, and chortling is nearly deafening at times. This is a place to get up close and personal with puffins, which nest in underground burrows, or graceful guillemots. Other species include cormorants, kittiwakes, gannets, and Manx shearwaters. The island is privately owned, but visitors are welcome on the condition that they do nothing to disturb the bird habitat and the island's natural beauty. From April to September, weather permitting, **Declan Bates** (© **053/29684**) provides boat rides to the island and back from the town of Kilmore Quay (about 16km/10

At **Baginbun Head** is a fine beach nestled against the cliffs, from which you can see the outline of the Norman earthwork fortifications on the head. Here the Norman presence in Ireland was first established with the victory of Norman forces over the Irish at the Battle of Baginbun.

The **tip of the peninsula,** with its line of low cliffs, eroded in places to form blowholes, has been famous for shipwrecks since Norman times. There has long been a **lighthouse** on this site; the present structure consists of a massive base, built in the early 13th century, and a narrower top dating from the 19th century.

The Ring of Hook road returns along the western side of the peninsula, passing the beaches at **Booley Bay** and **Dollar Bay.** On a promontory overlooking the town of Duncannon is a **fort** built in 1588 to protect Waterford Harbour from the threat of attack by the Spanish Armada. Just north of Duncannon, along the coast, is the village of **Ballyhack,** where a ferry operates to Passage East in county Waterford, and a Knights Hospitallers castle (see "Ballyhack Castle," above) stands on a hill over the harbor.

A visit to the Hook Peninsula wouldn't be complete without a stop at **Dunbrody Abbey,** in a field beside the road about 6.5km (4 miles) north of Duncannon. The abbey, founded in 1170, is a magnificent ruin and one of the largest Cistercian abbeys in Ireland. Despite its grand size, it bears remarkably little ornamentation. Tours are sometimes available; inquire at the visitor's center across the road.

At the eastern end of Enniscorthy is Vinegar Hill (117m/390 ft.), where the Wexford men of 1798 made their last stand. Now a scenic viewing point, it offers panoramas of Wexford from its summit.

miles south of Wexford Town). He charges €80 ($71) minimum for the boat, or €16 ($14) per person for groups of at least five people.

Hook Head is a good spot for watching the spring and autumn passerine migration—the lack of sizable cliffs means that it isn't popular with summer nesting seabirds. In addition to swallows, swifts, and warblers, look out for the less common cuckoos, turtle doves, redstarts, and blackcaps.

While driving south from Gorey toward Ballycanew on R741, keep an eye out for a reddish **cliff** on the left, about 2.4km (1½ miles) out of Gorey; this is a well-known peregrine aerie, with birds nesting until the early summer. The land is private, but it is possible to watch the birds from the roadside.

Other places of interest are **Lady's Island Lake** near Carnsore Point, an important tern colony, and neighboring **Tacumshin Lake.**

DIVING   The Kilmore Quay area, south of Wexford Town, offers some of the most spectacular diving in Ireland. For answers to all your questions and needs, consult **Wexford Diving Centre and Dive Charters,** Riverstown Farm, Murrintown, county Wexford (© **053/39373**).

FISHING   One center for sea angling in Wexford is the town of **Kilmore Quay,** south of Wexford Town on R739. Several people offer boats for hire, with all the necessary equipment; Dick Hayes runs **Kilmore Quay Boat Charters** (*(C) 053/29704*) and is skipper of the *Cottage Lady.* The most popular rivers for fishing are the Barrow and the Slaney, where the sea trout travel upstream from mid-June to the end of August.

GOLF   In recent years, Wexford has blossomed as a golfing venue. One of the newest developments is an 18-hole championship seaside par-72 course at **St. Helens Bay Golf Club,** Kilrane (*(C) 053/33669*). Greens fees are €30 ($27) on weekdays and €35 ($31) on weekends. Tennis courts, sauna, and luxury cottages are available. The **Enniscorthy Golf Club,** Knockmarshall, Enniscorthy (*(C) 054/33191*), an inland par-70 course with greens fees of €25 ($23) on weekdays, €28 ($25) on weekends, also welcomes visitors.

HORSEBACK RIDING   **Horetown House** ✦, Foulksmills (*(C) 051/ 565771*), offers riding lessons by the hour or in a variety of packages that include meals and lodging. One of the better residential equestrian centers in Ireland, it caters particularly to families and children. For more experienced riders, lessons in jumping and dressage are available, as is a game called polocross, which combines polo and lacrosse. Training in hunting and admission to the hunt can also be arranged. Riding is €18 ($16) per hour; bed-and-breakfast costs €60 to €72 ($53–$64) for a double.

WALKING   Along the entire coastline, you'll see brown signs with a picture of a hiker on them. The signs mark the **Wexford Coastal Path,** which theoretically allows you to walk the whole coast on beaches and country roads. In reality, the roads are often too full of traffic to make it a good idea to walk the whole route—especially on the bypass around Wexford Town. The markers are handy, however, for shorter walks along and between Wexford's beaches.

In the northern part of the county, the section of beach from Clogga Head (county Wicklow) to Tara Hill is especially lovely, as is the walk to the top of Tara Hill, which offers many viewpoints over sloping pastures to the sea. A good base for both these walks is **Carrigeen B&B,** Tara Hill, Gorey, county Wexford (*(C) 055/21732*). It offers basic accommodations, a spectacular view of the sea, and a welcoming family (the Leonards) who are quite familiar with the local walks. Double rooms with private bathroom are €60 ($53). Farther south, the path veers off the roads and sticks to the beach from Cahore Point south to Raven Point and from Rosslare Harbour to Kilmore Quay.

There's a lovely coastal walk near the town of Wexford in the **Raven Nature Reserve,** an area of forested dunes and uncrowded beaches. To get there, take R741 north out of Wexford, turn right on R742 to Curracloe just out of town, and in the village of Curracloe, turn right and continue 1.6km (1 mile) to the beach parking lot. The nature reserve is to your right. You can get there by car, driving another half mile south, or walk the distance along the beach. The beach extends another 4.8km (3 miles) to Raven Point, where at low tide you can see the remains of a shipwreck, half-buried in the sand. The point is also a great place to watch migratory birds in winter and spring—the flight of the white-fronted geese at dusk is an experience you shouldn't miss.

On the border between counties Wexford and Carlow is a long, rounded ridge of peaks known as the **Blackstairs Mountains,** which offer a number of beautiful walks in an area remarkably unspoiled by tourism. A good guide is *Walking the Blackstairs,* by Joss Lynam, which includes trail descriptions and information on local plants and wildlife. It's available at Wexford tourist offices.

WHERE TO STAY
EXPENSIVE/VERY EXPENSIVE

Marlfield House ★★ Formerly the principal residence of the earl of Courtown, this splendid Regency manor home, 65km (40 miles) north of Wexford Town in the northernmost part of the county, was built around 1850. Thanks to the current owners, Ray and Mary Bowe, it has been masterfully transformed into a top-notch country house and restaurant with award-winning gardens. Although the individually-decorated rooms have every modern convenience and comfort, they haven't sacrificed their old-world charm. Most have four-poster or canopied beds, hand-carved armoires, sumptuous fabrics, and one-of-a-kind, period antiques. Bathrooms tend to be quite large, stocked with thick towels and bathrobes and plenty of upscale toiletries. The public rooms and lounge are also quite posh, with gilt-edge mirrors, crystal chandeliers, and marble fireplaces. Marlfield is rightly celebrated for its cuisine, which incorporates organically grown fruits and vegetables from the garden. It's served in the main dining area or in a fanciful skylit Victorian-style conservatory room.

Courtown Rd., Gorey, county Wexford. ☎ **800/323-5463** in the U.S., or 055/21124. Fax 055/21572. www. marlfieldhouse.ie. 20 units. €222–€240 ($198–$214) double; state rooms from €400 ($356). Dinner from €50 ($45). Rates include full breakfast and service charge. AE, DC, MC, V. Closed Dec 15–Jan. **Amenities:** Restaurant (local/French/Mediterranean); lounge; tennis court; croquet lawn; nonsmoking rooms. *In room:* TV, CD player, hair dryer, garment press, iron.

MODERATE/EXPENSIVE

Kelly's Resort Hotel ★ *(Value* *(Kids* Four generations of the Kelly family have turned this hotel into one of Ireland's best-loved family resorts. Over the years it's proved an honest-to-goodness pioneer in the country's hotel industry, being the first Irish hotel to introduce an indoor swimming pool, sauna baths, squash courts, and indoor tennis courts. It's also unique in being a true resort hotel; prices are all-inclusive for multiple-night stays, so you don't have to worry about paying extra for meals and access to leisure facilities. And in the best resort tradition, there's excellent dining and nighttime entertainment. Rooms aren't luxurious, but they are bright, well kept, and very comfortable. Before you balk at the price (don't forget to divide by the number of nights), consider what it might cost you to feed your family three meals a day at another hotel.

Wexford–Rosslare Harbour rd. (N25), about 16km (10 miles) south of Wexford Town, Rosslare, county Wexford. ☎ **053/32114.** Fax 053/32222. www.kellys.ie. 100 units. €520 ($463) double for 2 nights to €1,580 ($1,406) double for 7 nights. Children's discounts available. AE, MC, V. **Amenities:** 2 restaurants (Continental, bistro); bar; 2 indoor swimming pools; indoor tennis; squash; miniature golf; billiard room; gym; Jacuzzi; outdoor hot tub; sauna; steam room; beauty/spa treatments; children's playground. *In room:* TV, radio, tea/coffeemaker, hair dryer.

Rosslare Great Southern ★ *(Kids* If you're taking the ferry to or from Britain or France, or if you've brought the kids, this modern three-story hotel is an appealing overnight stop in Rosslare. The Great Southern is a branch of a popular, good-value chain that specializes in family-friendly accommodation. The Rosslare version is on a cliff top overlooking the harbor, and less than a mile from the ferry terminals. The decor is bright and airy, with lots of wide floor-to-ceiling

Service Charges
A reminder: Unless otherwise noted, room rates don't include service charges (usually 10%–15% of your bill).

windows and colorful contemporary furnishings in the guest rooms and public areas. Families are well taken care of, with special kids' meals, recreation areas, and even swimming lessons in the summertime.

Wexford–Rosslare Harbour rd. (N25), about 19km (12 miles) south of Wexford Town, Rosslare Harbour, county Wexford. 𝒞 **800/44-UTELL** in the U.S., or 053/33233. Fax 053/33543. www.gsh.ie. 100 units. €160–€210 ($142–$187) double. AE, DC, MC, V. **Amenities:** Restaurant (international); bar; lounge; leisure center with indoor pool, tennis; gym, sauna, children's playground and indoor supervised playroom; salon; room service; babysitting; nonsmoking rooms; conservatory. *In room:* TV, radio, tea/coffeemaker, hair dryer, garment press.

MODERATE

Ballinkeele House 🏠🏠 This grand Irish manor B&B, built in 1840 and in the Maher family for four generations now, is a wonderful place to appreciate Irish country house living. As soon as you enter into the majestic entrance hall with its Corinthian columns and fireplace, John and Margaret Maher see to it that you feel immediately at home. And you will: With only five guest rooms, there's the impression that you're a guest of the family. Rooms are old-fashioned in the grandest sort of way, with four-poster or half-tester beds and period touches everywhere. Dinner (book before noon) is served by candlelight in a chandeliered dining room. The food is excellent: starters might include avocado paté or carrot and parsnip soup, while main courses range from trout with fennel to steak with whiskey sauce to pheasant in cream-and-brandy sauce; vegetarian options are also available. Some 140 hectares (350 acres) of fields and woodlands surround the house, with gardens created around a pond. Strolling the grounds, you may well encounter pheasants, foxes, black rabbits, all manner of birds, and, if you're lucky, the resident hedgehog.

Signposted off the N11 north of Wexford at Oylgate, Ballymurn, Enniscorthy, county Wexford. 𝒞 **053/38105.** Fax 053/38468. www.ballinkeele.com. 5 units. €126–€164 ($112–$146) double. Dinner Tues–Sun, €35 ($31). MC, V. Rates include full breakfast. Closed mid-Nov to Feb. **Amenities:** Dining room; lounge. *In room:* TV, hair dryer.

Riverside Park Hotel 🏠 Set on the green banks of the River Suir, the Riverside Park Hotel is a striking new (1998) addition to the bustling market town of Enniscorthy. The contemporary design of the hotel attracts the eye with a rich terra-cotta and blue facade, lots of glass, and a bold stone tower centerpiece, which houses a circular atrium lobby. A flower-fringed terrace allows for dining and relaxing with a view of the River Slaney and its promenade. Guest rooms have a warm, bright feel to them, with bold print fabrics. They are thoughtfully designed, providing all the cubbies and counter space travelers need. Front-facing rooms enjoy a fine view of the river from their own small balconies. The Riverside Park Hotel makes a great base from which to explore the Blackstair Mountains, Wexford Town, the Wexford coast, and local attractions; and it's only a short walk from the town center of Enniscorthy.

At the junction of N11 and N30 on the south edge of town, The Promenade, Enniscorthy, county Wexford. 𝒞 **054/37800.** Fax 054/37900. www.riversideparkhotel.com. 60 units. €154 ($137) double; €155–€180 ($138–$160) suite. Rates include full Irish breakfast. AE, DC, MC, V. **Amenities:** 2 restaurants (international, Mexican); 2 bars; discounts at nearby leisure center and golf course; babysitting. *In room:* TV, tea/coffeemaker, hair dryer.

White's Dating from 1779, this vintage hotel is right in the middle of town, with its older section facing North Main Street. White's—now part of Best Western Hotels Worldwide—has been expanded and updated over the years, resulting in lots of connecting corridors and guest rooms of varying size and standards. Some have four-poster or canopy beds, others a more contemporary feel with blond-wood furnishings. The public rooms reflect the aura of an old coaching inn, complete with two lively bars: the Shelmalier, where jazz and folk music often plays on weekends, and Speakers, a popular lounge-style watering hole.

George and Main sts., Wexford, county Wexford. (© **800/528-1234** in the U.S., or 053/22311. Fax 053/ 45000. www.bestwestern.com. 82 units. €100–€130 ($89–$116) double. No service charge. Rates include full breakfast. AE, MC, V. **Amenities:** 2 restaurants (international, brasserie); 2 bars; minigym; sauna; solarium; concierge; room service; babysitting; laundry service. *In room:* TV, tea/coffeemaker, hair dryer.

INEXPENSIVE

Clone House   You're sure to receive a gracious welcome at this 120-hectare (300-acre) working farm, the home of Tom and Betty Breen. The five guest rooms are furnished with handsome antiques, as is the rest of the 250-year-old farmhouse. A courtyard opens onto a garden in back, and you can walk through the fields to the bank of the River Bann. Tom prides himself on his knowledge of the area (both the local region and Ireland as a whole), and will be glad to assist you in making plans for touring or outdoor activities. Only three rooms are designated nonsmoking; if this is important to you, book well in advance.

Ferns, Enniscorthy, county Wexford. (© **054/66113.** Fax 054/66225. 5 units, 4 with bathroom. €58–€70 ($52–$62) double. No service charge. Rates include full breakfast. No credit cards. Closed Nov–Feb. **Amenities:** Nonsmoking rooms. *In room:* TV in 3 rooms.

McMenamin's Townhouse   This feel-good B&B has a well-deserved reputation for taking good care of its guests, and subsequently does a huge amount of repeat business. At the western end of town, opposite the railroad station, this lovely Victorian-style townhouse offers warm, hospitable accommodations at an affordable price. Guest rooms are individually furnished with local antiques, including brass beds and caned chairs. All the guest rooms are nonsmoking and have orthopedic beds. Not all of them have televisions, so if this is important to you, ask. McMenamin's is run by Seamus and Kay McMenamin, who formerly ran the Bohemian Girl pub and restaurant, so your stomach is in luck: Kay puts her culinary skills to work by providing copious, gourmet breakfasts (homemade breads and cereals, juice, eggs any which way, and plenty of coffee or tea) for guests in the nonsmoking dining room.

3 Auburn Terrace, Redmond Rd., Wexford, county Wexford. (© **053/46442.** Fax 053/46442. mcmem@indigo.ie. 6 units. €66 ($59) double. No service charge. Rates include full breakfast. MC, V. **Amenities:** Babysitting; nonsmoking rooms. *In room:* TV in some rooms, tea/coffeemaker.

WHERE TO DINE
MODERATE

Mange2   FRENCH FUSION   This is French cooking with global flair—inventive without any wild antics, and quite eclectic, while retaining the subtlety and attention to detail that seem to be part of the French genetic code. The roast red pepper and fennel samosa with baby beets and yogurt dressing is delicately crisp, as is the pine-nut fritter that accompanies the filets of sole. The roast breast of chicken comes with thin strips of pan-fried chorizo and savory cabbage. Veggie side dishes begin with ingredients at the peak of freshness and arrive crisp and steaming, wrapped in parchment packets. The wine list is modest and judicious, with a quite decent house wine for roughly €14 ($12). The dessert menu features a devastating baked passion-fruit ricotta cake with orange ice cream. Portions are generous, so you may want to pace yourself, sharing starters and desserts. If you're sensitive to smoke, this isn't the place for you; there's no designated nonsmoking section.

100 S. Main St., Wexford, county Wexford. (C) **053/44033**. Reservations recommended. Main courses €12–€18 ($11–$16). AE, MC, V. Daily 6–10:30pm.

The Neptune ⋆ SEAFOOD   On the western edge of county Wexford, about 32km (20 miles) from Wexford Town, this little gem is in an old house on the waterfront of a sheltered harbor town. The interior has an airy modern motif, with paintings and pottery by Irish artisans; tables are also set up outside on sunny days. Dinner options might include scallops in orange and ginger sauce, filet of hake in citrus sauce, hot buttered lobster, Ballyhack wild salmon baked in cream, or the signature dish, hot crab Brehat (sautéed in port and baked with mushrooms, béchamel sauce, and cheese). The restaurant is easily accessible from Waterford (on the Ballyhack–Passage East car ferry) or Wexford, and worth the trip from any direction.

The Neptune is also home to the **Ballyhack Cookery Centre** (C) **051/ 389284**), which offers classes by prior arrangement in the summer months.

Ballyhack Harbor, Ballyhack, county Wexford. (C) **051/389284**. Reservations required. Main courses €14–€20 ($12–$18); lobster averages €25 ($23). AE, DC, MC, V. High season Mon–Sat 7–9pm; low season Thurs–Sat 7–9pm. Closed Dec–Jan.

INEXPENSIVE
Bohemian Girl PUB GRUB   Named for an opera written by one-time Wexford resident William Balfe, this is a Tudor-style pub, with lantern lights, barrel-shaped tables, and matchbook covers on the ceiling. Its excellent pub lunches include fresh oysters, patés, sandwiches, and homemade soups.

2 Selskar St., Wexford, county Wexford. (C) **053/24419**. All items €2.50–€10 ($2.25–$8.90). MC, V. June–Aug 10:30am–11:30pm; Sept–May 10:30am–11pm; pub lunches year-round 12:30–3pm.

Cellar Bistro VEGETARIAN/HEALTH   Housed in the Wexford Arts Centre, this charming eatery has a country-kitchen atmosphere, with stone walls, pine furnishings, and home cooking prepared by Chef Caroline. Selections include salads, soups, quiches, pizzas, and chili, with an emphasis on vegetarian items.

Cornmarket, at Abbey St., Wexford, county Wexford. (C) **053/23764**. Reservations not accepted. All items €2.50–€10 ($2.25–$8.90). No credit cards. Daily 10am–6pm.

WEXFORD AFTER DARK
THE PERFORMING ARTS
Famed for the **Wexford Festival Opera** each October, Wexford is a town with a fine tradition of music and the arts. Year-round performances are given at the **Theatre Royal,** High Street, Wexford ((C) **053/22144**), a beautiful theater dating from 1832. Booking for the opera festival (www.wexfordopera.com) opens in June for the following October. Tickets range from €10 to €75 ($8.90–$67).

There's always something interesting going on at the **Wexford Arts Centre,** Cornmarket, Wexford ((C) **053/23764**). Built as the market house in 1775, this building has served as a dance venue, concert hall, and municipal office. It has provided a focal point for all the arts in Wexford since 1974, and now houses three exhibition rooms and showcases a range of theatrical and artistic events. Open year-round from 10am to 6pm daily.

To see traditional Irish music and dancing, head 16km (10 miles) south of Wexford to the **Yola Farmstead,** Wexford-Rosslare road (N25), Tagoat, county Wexford ((C) **053/32610**). For groups, by prior arrangement, the Farmstead stages traditional Irish banquets and ceili evenings of Irish music, song, dance, and recitations. If you're not traveling with a group and a banquet is planned, you might be able to join in. The average cost is €32 ($28) per person.

PUBS

Antique Tavern   It's worth a 24km (15-mile) trip from Wexford City to Enniscorthy to see this unique Tudor-style pub, located off the main Dublin-Wexford road (N11). True to the name, the walls are lined with memorabilia from the Wexford area—old daggers, pikes, farming implements, lanterns, pictures, and prints. You'll also see mounted elk heads, an antique wooden birdcage, and a glass case full of paper money from around the world. 14 Slaney St., Enniscorthy, county Wexford. ✆ **054/33428.**

Con Macken's, The Cape of Good Hope   Long a favorite with photographers, this pub is unique for the trio of services it offers, aptly described by the sign outside the door: BAR-UNDERTAKER-GROCERIES. Hardly any visitor passes by without a second look at the windows; one displays beer and spirit bottles, the other plastic funeral wreaths. An alehouse for centuries, the Cape has always been at the center of Wexford political events, and rebel souvenirs, old weapons, and plaques line the bar walls. The Bull Ring, off N. Main St., Wexford, county Wexford. ✆ **053/22949.**

The Crown Bar   Once a stagecoach inn, this tiny pub in the center of town has been in the Kelly family since 1841. Besides its historical overtones, it is well known for its museumlike collection of antique weapons. You'll see 18th-century dueling pistols, pikes from the 1798 Rebellion, powder horns, and blunderbusses, as well as vintage prints, military artifacts, and swords. Unlike most pubs, it's not always open during the day, so it's best to visit in the evening. Monck St., Wexford, county Wexford. ✆ **053/21133.**

Oak Tavern   Dating back over 150 years, this pub—originally a tollhouse—is 3.2km (2 miles) north of town, overlooking the River Slaney near the Ferrycarrig Bridge. Bar lunch choices are of the beef and vegetable hot pot and shepherd's pie variety. There is a riverside patio for outside seating on fine days, and traditional music sessions are held most evenings in the front bar. Wexford-Enniscorthy rd. (N11), Ferrycarrig, county Wexford. ✆ **053/20945.**

The Wren's Nest   Near the John Barry Memorial on the harbor, 5 minutes from the bus and train station, this pub has redesigned its front bar to include an old-style wood floor and ceiling, and attractive pine tables and chairs. The varied pub grub includes Wexford mussel platters, house patés, soups, salads, and vegetarian entrees. There is free traditional Irish music on Tuesday and Thursday nights. Custom House Quay, Wexford, county Wexford. ✆ **053/22359.**

2 County Waterford

Waterford City is 65km (40 miles) W of Wexford, 53km (33 miles) W of Rosslare Harbour, 158km (98 miles) SW of Dublin, 126km (78 miles) E of Cork, and 153km (95 miles) SE of Shannon Airport

Waterford City (pop. 42,500) is the main seaport of the southeast. Only 11km (7 miles) from the Atlantic, it is one of Ireland's windiest cities, boasting gale-force winds an average of 180 days every year. More significantly, this is Ireland's oldest city, founded by Viking invaders in the 9th century. In fact, Waterford is older than any of the major Nordic capitals of modern Europe, including Oslo, Stockholm, and Copenhagen. In recent years, a major archaeological endeavor has excavated nearly a fourth of the ancient Viking city, and some of the more striking finds from these excavations can be seen in the new **Waterford Treasures at the Granary Museum.**

Although the historic district around Reginald's Tower is quite intriguing, the city is primarily a commercial center, dominated by its busy port. Because the rest of county Waterford is so beautiful, many travelers don't linger long in the capital city, though it is currently enjoying a fresh wave of renewal and development, some of which is aimed directly at visitors. Truth is, there's a good deal to see and to do here.

Coastal highlights south of Waterford include **Dunmore East,** a picturesque fishing village; **Dungarvan,** a major town with a fine harbor; **Ardmore,** an idyllic beach resort; and **Passage East,** a tiny seaport from which you can catch a ferry across the harbor and cut your driving time from Waterford to Wexford in half. Of all the coastal towns in county Waterford, Ardmore stands out as the perfect getaway. It has a beautiful and important early Christian site, a pristine Blue Flag beach, a stunning cliff walk, a fine craft shop, an excellent restaurant, comfortable seaside accommodations, and a quaint town recently named Ireland's tidiest. **Portally Cove,** near Dunmore East, is the home of Ireland's only Amish-Mennonite community.

In northwest county Waterford, the **Comeragh Mountains** provide many opportunities for beautiful walks, including the short trek to Mahon Falls. These mountains also have highly scenic roads for biking. Farther west, there's great fishing and bird-watching on the **Blackwater estuary.**

WATERFORD CITY ESSENTIALS

GETTING THERE   Air service from Britain operates into **Waterford Airport,** off R675, Waterford (© 051/75589). Carriers include **Suckling Airlines** from Luton, and **British Airways** (operated by British Regional) from London (Stansted) and Manchester.

Irish Rail offers daily service from Dublin and other points into Plunkett Station, at Ignatius Rice Bridge, Waterford (© **051/873401;** www.irishrail.ie).

Bus Eireann operates daily service into Plunkett Station Depot, Waterford (© **051/879000;** www.buseireann.ie), from Dublin, Limerick, and other major cities throughout Ireland.

Four major roads lead into Waterford: N25 from Cork and the south, N24 from the west, N19 from Kilkenny and points north, and N25 from Wexford.

The Passage East Ferry County Ltd., Barrack Street, Passage East, county Waterford (© **051/382480** or 051/382488), operates car ferry service across Waterford Harbour. It links Passage East, about 16km (10 miles) east of Waterford, with Ballyhack, about 32km (20 miles) southwest of Wexford. This shortcut saves about an hour's driving time. The crossing time averages 10 minutes. It's continuous drive-on, drive-off service, with no reservations required. See p. 206, "Wexford Town Essentials," for fare and schedule information.

VISITOR INFORMATION   The **Waterford Tourist Office** is at 41 The Quay, Waterford (© 051/875788). It's open April to June and September, Monday to Saturday 9am to 6pm; July and August, Monday to Saturday 9am to 6pm, Sunday 11am to 5pm; October, Monday to Saturday 9am to 5pm; November to March, Monday to Friday 9am to 5pm. The year-round office on the Square in Dungarvan (© **058/41741**) keeps comparable hours. The seasonal tourist office on the Square at Tramore (© 051/381572) is open from mid-June to August, Monday to Saturday 10am to 6pm. Additionally, here is a website that will keep you up on Waterford goings-on: **www.waterford-today.ie.**

CITY LAYOUT   Rimmed by the River Suir, Waterford is a commercial city focused from the start on its quays. The city center sits on the south bank of the Suir. Traffic from the north, west, and east enters from the north bank over the

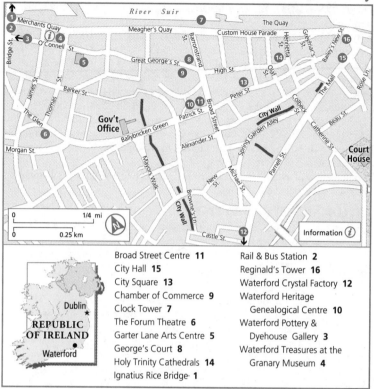

Broad Street Centre **11**
City Hall **15**
City Square **13**
Chamber of Commerce **9**
Clock Tower **7**
The Forum Theatre **6**
Garter Lane Arts Centre **5**
George's Court **8**
Holy Trinity Cathedrals **14**
Ignatius Rice Bridge **1**

Rail & Bus Station **2**
Reginald's Tower **16**
Waterford Crystal Factory **12**
Waterford Heritage
Genealogical Centre **10**
Waterford Pottery &
Dyehouse Gallery **3**
Waterford Treasures at the
Granary Museum **4**

Ignatius Rice Bridge and onto a series of four quays (Grattan, Merchants, Meagher, and Parade), but most addresses simply say "The Quay." Most shops and attractions are concentrated near the quay area or on two thoroughfares that intersect the quays: The Mall and Barronstrand Street (changing their names to Broad, Michael, and John sts.). Both of these streets were once rivers flowing into the Suir; and, in fact, the original waterways continue to flow roughly 15m (50 ft.) beneath today's pavement.

GETTING AROUND   Bus Eireann operates daily **bus service** within Waterford and its environs. The flat fare is €.90 (80¢). **Taxi** ranks are outside Plunkett Rail Station and along the Quay opposite the Granville Hotel. If you need to call a taxi, try **Rapid Cabs** (© 051/844440), **Metro Cabs** (© 051/857157), or **Waterford Taxi Co-op** (© 051/877778).

To see most of Waterford's sights (except the Waterford Crystal factory), it's best to walk. Park along the quays; parking is operated by machines or by the disc system. Discs are on sale at the tourist office and in many shops. It will cost you €1.30 ($1.15) for 3 hours, or €2.50 ($2.25) for a full day. You'll need a car to reach the Waterford Crystal and county Waterford attractions outside of town.

To rent a car, contact **Hertz,** Dublin Road, Waterford (© 051/878737), or **Budget Rent A Car,** Waterford Airport (© 051/421670).

FAST FACTS   If you need a drugstore, try **Gallagher's Pharmacy,** 29 Barronstrand St. (© 051/878103); or **Mulligan's Chemists,** 40–41 Barronstrand

St. (© **051/875211**), and City Square Shopping Centre, Unit 12A (© **051/ 853247**).

In an emergency, dial © **999. Garda Headquarters** (© **051/874888**) is the local police station. **Holy Ghost Hospital** is on Cork Road (© **051/374397**), and **Waterford Regional Hospital** is on Dunmore Road (© **051/873321**).

Among the resources for gay travelers is the **Gay and Lesbian Line Southeast** (© **051/879907**). The **Waterford Gay and Lesbian Resource Centre** is at the Youth Resources Centre, St. John's Park (© **087/638-7931**).

The **Voyager Internet Cafe,** Parnell Court, off Parnell Street (© **051/ 843843**), isn't actually a cafe, but it does provide high-speed access with all the peripherals for €2 ($1.80) per 15 minutes. Open Monday to Saturday 11am to 11pm, Sunday 3 to 11pm.

The **General Post Office** on Parade Quay (© **051/874444**) is open Monday to Friday 9am to 5:30pm, Saturday 9am to 1pm.

EXPLORING WATERFORD CITY

The best way to see the city is by walking along the quays and taking a right at Reginald's Tower on the Mall (which becomes Parnell St.). Turn right onto John Street (which becomes Michael, Broad, and Barronstrand St.), which brings you back to the quays. The tourist office can supply you with a free map.

City Hall   Headquarters of the local city government, this late-18th-century building houses local memorabilia, including information on the city's charter, which was granted in 1205. In addition, a display is dedicated to Thomas Francis Meagher, a leader in an 1848 Irish insurrection. Meagher was sentenced to death but eventually escaped to America, where he fought in the Civil War, earned the rank of brigadier general, and was appointed acting governor of Montana. City Hall's other treasures include an 18th-century Waterford glass chandelier, a complete dinner service of priceless antique Waterford glasses, and a painting of Waterford City in 1736 by the Flemish master William Van der Hagen.

The Mall, Waterford, county Waterford. © 051/73501. Free admission. Mon–Fri 9am–1pm and 2–5pm.

Garter Lane Arts Centre   One of Ireland's largest arts centers, the Garter Lane occupies two buildings on O'Connell Street. No. 5, the site of the former Waterford Library, holds exhibition rooms and artists' studios, and No. 22a, the former Friends Meeting House, is home of the Garter Lane Theatre, with an art gallery and outdoor courtyard. The gallery showcases works by contemporary and local artists.

5 and 22a O'Connell St., Waterford, county Waterford. © 051/855038. Free admission to exhibitions. Gallery Mon–Sat 10am–6pm.

Holy Trinity Cathedrals 🐀🐀   Waterford has two impressive cathedrals, one Catholic and the other Protestant, both built by the same architect, John Roberts. Roberts lived 82 years (1714–96), fathered 22 children with the same beloved partner (in business and in bed), and built nearly every significant 18th-century building in and around Waterford. Holy Trinity on Barronstrand is the oldest Catholic and the only baroque Cathedral in Ireland and boasts 10 unique Waterford Crystal chandeliers. It's open daily 7:30am to 7pm. The Anglican or Church of Ireland Holy Trinity Cathedral (conveniently nicknamed Christ Church) on Henrietta Street has a most peculiar spire and only clear glass, because its first bishop and rector disliked stained glass.

Barronstrand and Henrietta sts., Waterford, county Waterford.

Reginald's Tower Circular, topped with a conical roof, and with walls 3m (10 ft.) thick, this mighty tower stands at the eastern end of the Quay beside the river. It's said to have been built in 1003 by a Viking governor named Reginald and has never fallen into ruin, which makes it Ireland's oldest standing building in continuous use. Still dominating the Waterford skyline, it's particularly striking at night when fully floodlit. Over the centuries, it's been a fortress, a prison, a military depot, a mint, an air-raid shelter, and now a museum.

The Quay, Waterford, county Waterford. ✆ 051/73501. Admission €2 ($1.80) adults, €1.30 ($1.15) seniors, €.80 (70¢) children. Combined ticket with Waterford Treasures available. June–Aug daily 9:30am–9pm; May and Sept daily 9:30am–6pm; Oct–Apr daily 10am–5pm.

Waterford Crystal Factory and Gallery ✵✵✵ This is Waterford's number-one attraction. Since the glasswork's founding in 1783, Waterford has been a byword for the crystal of connoisseurs. The devastating effects of the Irish famine forced the factory to close in 1851. Happily, it was revived in 1947, and Waterford has since regained its prominence among prized glassware. With more than 2,000 employees, Waterford is the largest crystal factory in the world and the major industry in Waterford.

The bi-level Waterford Crystal Gallery contains the most comprehensive display of Waterford Crystal in the world, from all the glassware patterns to elaborate pieces like trophies, globes, and chandeliers. Crystal is on sale in the gallery. (But don't look for any discounts at the factory; there are no seconds to be had. The main advantage in shopping here is simply the wide selection.)

There is a free 17-minute audiovisual presentation on the glass-making process and an excellent, 35-minute tour of the factory to see it firsthand, from mouth-blowing and shaping of molten glass to delicate hand-cutting. *Note:* Children under 10 are not permitted on the factory tour. Reservations are not required.

Cork Rd., Waterford, county Waterford. ✆ 051/373311. Tour €5 ($4.45) adults, €2.50 ($2.25) students, free for children under 12. Free admission to audiovisual presentation and gallery. Tours Apr–Oct daily 8:30am–4pm; Nov–Mar Mon–Fri 9am–3:15pm. Showrooms Apr–Oct daily 8:30am–6pm; Nov–Mar Mon–Fri 9am–5pm.

Waterford Heritage Genealogical Centre Did your ancestors come from Waterford? If so, follow the small lane between George's and Patrick streets to this historic building adjoining St. Patrick's, one of Ireland's oldest churches. The center specializes in tracing county Waterford ancestry. Church registers dating from 1655 and other surveys, rolls, and census lists are used as resources. An audiovisual presentation examines the heritage of the local people.

St. Patrick's Church, Jenkins Lane, Waterford, county Waterford. ✆ 051/876123. Fax 051/850645. www.waterford-heritage.ie. Free admission; basic search fee €40 ($36). Mon–Thurs 9am–5pm; Fri 9am–2pm.

Waterford Pottery and The Dyehouse Gallery ✵ Liz McCay is both the resident potter and the gallery director of this combined venue, where you'll find not only her own unique "Waterford Ware," inspired by a black ceramic style discovered in local Viking excavations, but also contemporary paintings and prints by many of Ireland's leading visual artists. The gallery hosts seven or eight exhibitions per year.

Dyehouse Lane, Waterford, county Waterford. Pottery ✆ 051/878166, www.waterfordpottery.com; Gallery ✆ 051/850399, www.dyehouse-gallery.com. Free admission to exhibitions. Shop and gallery open Mon–Sat 10:30am–5:30pm, or phone for appointment.

Waterford Treasures at the Granary Museum ✵✵ This impressive heritage center and museum, housed in a converted granary, unfolds Waterford's

---

Tips **Walking Your Way Through Waterford**

The very best way to begin you explorations of Waterford is to take a **Waterford City Walking Tour** . Jack Burtchaell, well-versed in the history, folklore, and witty anecdotes of the city, conducts an engaging hour-long tour of the old city, leaving daily from the reception area of the Granville Hotel on the Quay. Tours are offered daily at noon and 2pm from March through October and cost €6 ($5.35) for adults, free for accompanied small children. For more information, call Waterford Tourist Services at ② **051/873711.**

---

history from its earliest Viking origins to the present. An exceptional collection of Viking and medieval artifacts recovered from Waterford's lower levels is on display. The Granary, however, is no ordinary museum of artifacts under glass and walls of small print. It's also an ambitious state-of-the-art multimedia experience aimed at all ages, and launched with a three-dimensional audiovisual sea voyage viewed from the hull of a Viking boat actually rolling with the waves you're watching. But despite its ambitions, the museum's myriad exhibitions can seem like a circus with too many rings, more chaotic than enticing. (Still, the Granary was named the Irish Museum of the Year in 1999–2000.) If you move along at your own pace, however, there's a lot to see and to learn here; and the building and conversion itself is truly beautiful. There's also a gift shop and cafe.

Merchant's Quay, Waterford, county Waterford. ② **051/304500.** www.waterfordtreasures.com. Admission €5 ($4.45) adults, €4 ($3.55) seniors and students, €2.50 ($2.25) children, €16 ($14) family. Combined ticket with Reginald's Tower available. June–Aug daily 9:30am–9pm; May and Sept daily 9:30am–6pm; Oct–Apr daily 10am–5pm.

SHOPPING

Most people come to Waterford for the crystal, but there are many other fine products in the shops and in the three multilevel enclosed shopping centers: **George's Court,** off Barronstrand Street, **Broad Street Centre** on Broad Street, and **City Square** off Broad Street. Hours are usually Monday to Saturday from 9 or 9:30am to 6 or 6:30pm. Some shops are open until 9pm on Thursday and Friday.

Aisling   Beside the Granville Hotel, this interesting shop (pronounced "Ashling," the name means "dream" or "vision" in Gaelic) offers an assortment of handmade crafts, from quilts, tartans, and kilts to floral art, miniature paintings, and watercolors of Irish scenes and subjects. 61 The Quay, Waterford, county Waterford. ② **051/873262.**

The Book Centre   This huge, four-level bookstore sells all types of books, newspapers, and magazines, as well as posters, maps, and music tapes and CDs. You can also make a photocopy or zap off a fax. Barronstrand St., Waterford, county Waterford. ② **051/873823.**

Joseph Knox   For visitors, this store has long been a magnet for its large selection of Waterford crystal, particularly specialty items like chandeliers. 3 Barronstrand St., Waterford, county Waterford. ② **051/875307.**

Kelly's   Dating from 1847, this store offers a wide selection of Waterford crystal, Aran knitwear, Belleek and Royal Tara china, Irish linens, and other souvenirs. 75/76 The Quay, Waterford, county Waterford. ② **051/873557.**

Penrose Crystal   Established in 1786 and revived in 1978, this is Waterford's other glass company, which turns out delicate hand-cut and engraved glassware. The craftspeople practice the stipple engraving process, the highest art form in glass. A retail sales outlet is at Unit 8 of the City Square Shopping Centre. Both are open the usual hours, but the factory is also open Sunday from June to August, 2 to 5:30pm. 32A Johns St., Waterford, county Waterford. ℂ 051/876537.

Woolcraft   For more than 100 years, the Fitzpatrick family has operated this reliable source for quality Irish knitwear. The focus here is on a huge selection of hand-loomed and hand-knit Aran sweaters at exceptionally low prices. 11 Michael St., Waterford, county Waterford. ℂ 051/874082.

ATTRACTIONS FARTHER AFIELD IN COUNTY WATERFORD

Ardmore High Cross ⚛   Ardmore (Irish for "the great height") may well be the oldest Christian settlement in Ireland. St. Declan, its founder, is said to have been a bishop in Munster as early as the mid–4th century, well before Patrick came to Ireland. Tradition has it that the small stone Oratory, situated in a cemetery high above the town, marks his burial site. St. Declan's Oratory is one of several stone structures here composing the ancient monastic settlement, which you can explore freely on your own. The most striking is the perfectly intact 30m (97-ft.) high round tower, arguably the finest of all round towers in Ireland. There are also the ruins of a medieval cathedral and, nearby, St. Declan's well and church. For more in-depth explorations, pick up a copy of *The Pilgrim's Round of Ardmore, County Waterford,* at the local newsdealer for €2.55 ($2.30), or join the local walking tour of ancient Ardmore led by Mary Murray, which leaves twice daily (11am and 3pm), Monday to Saturday, from the Tourist Information Office in the harbor. Ardmore, county Waterford. Open site.

Lismore Castle ⚛   Perched high on a cliff above the River Blackwater, this turreted castle dates to 1185, when Prince John of England built a similar fortress on this site. Local lore says that Lismore Castle was once granted to Sir Walter Raleigh for IR£12 (€15/$14) a year, although he never occupied it. One man who did live here was Richard Boyle, the first earl of Cork. He rebuilt the castle, including the thick defensive walls that still surround the garden, in 1626. Richard's son Robert, who was born at the castle in 1627, was the celebrated chemist whose name lives on in Boyle's Law. Most of the present castle was added in the mid–19th century. Today the 3,200-hectare (8,000-acre) estate of gardens, forests, and farmland is the Irish seat of the duke and duchess of Devonshire, whose primary home is in England. Although the castle itself is not open for tours, the public is welcome in the splendid walled and woodland gardens.

The castle can be rented, complete with the duke's personal staff, to private groups for a minimum of €1550 ($1,396) per day, which includes dinner, afternoon tea, breakfast, and staff. Contact Elegant Ireland (ℂ 01/475-1632; www.elegant.ie).

Lismore, county Waterford. ℂ 058/54424. Admission to gardens €4 ($3.55) adults, €2 ($1.80) children under 16. Mid-Apr to mid-Oct daily 1:45–4:45pm. From Cappoquin, take N72 6.5km (4 miles) west.

Lismore Heritage Centre   This interpretative center, in the town's Old Courthouse, tells the history of Lismore, a charming town founded by St. Carthage in the year 636. "The Lismore Experience" is an exceptional award-winning multimedia presentation on the town's unique treasures, including the Book of Lismore, which dates back 1,000 years, and the Lismore Crozier

---

Finds A Walk to Mahon Falls

Mahon Falls is located in the Comeragh Mountains, on R676 between Carrick-on-Suir and Dungarvan. At the tiny village of Mahon Bridge, 26km (16 miles) south of Carrick-on-Suir, turn west on the road marked for Mahon Falls, then continue to follow signs for the falls and the "Comeragh Drive." In about 4.8km (3 miles), you reach a parking lot along the Mahon River (in fact, just a tiny stream). The trail, indicated by two boulders, begins across the road from the parking lot. Follow the stream along the floor of the valley to the base of the falls. From here you can see the fields of Waterford spread out below you, and the sea a glittering mirror beyond. Walking time is about 30 minutes, round-trip.

(1116). Both were discovered hidden in the walls of Lismore Castle in 1814. The presentation also provides an excellent introduction to the surrounding area and its attractions. In addition, the center offers tours of the Lismore town and cathedral. There's a souvenir/gift shop adjacent to the heritage center.

Lismore, county Waterford. ℭ 058/54975. www.lismore-ireland.com/heritage/index.htm. Admission €4 ($3.55) adults, €3 ($2.65) seniors, €2.50 ($2.25) children, €8 ($7.10) family. Apr–Oct daily 9:30am–5:30pm; Nov–Mar Mon–Fri 9:30am–5:30pm.

SPORTS & OUTDOOR PURSUITS

BEACHES   For walking, jogging, or swimming, visit one of county Waterford's wide sandy beaches at **Tramore, Ardmore, Clonea,** or **Dunmore East.**

BICYCLING   Wright's Cycle Depot Ltd., Henrietta Street, Waterford (ℭ **051/874411**), offers bikes only. At **Altitude Cycle and Outdoor,** 22 Ballybricken, Waterford (ℭ **051/870356**), prices start at €13 ($12) daily, €75 ($67) weekly. Altitude Cycle offers helmets and emergency repair service for travelers, and can complete just about any repair on the same day you bring the bike in.

From Waterford City, you can ride 13km (8 miles) to Passage East and take the ferry (€3/$2.65 with a bicycle) to Wexford and the beautiful Hook Peninsula. Or continue on from Passage East to Dunmore East, a picturesque seaside village with a small beach hemmed in by cliffs. The road from there to Tramore and Dungarvan is quite scenic. For a complete 1- or 2-week biking vacation in the Southeast, contact Don Smith at **Celtic Cycling,** Lorum Old Rectory, Bagenalstown, county Carlow (ℭ and fax **0503/75282;** www.celticcycling.com).

FISHING   The Colligan River is excellent for both sea trout and salmon. For permit information, contact Baumann's Jewellers, 6 St. Mary St., Dungarvan (ℭ **058/41395**). For sea angling, there are a number of licensed charter-boat companies operating out of Kilmore Quay, roughly 24km (15 miles) southwest of Wexford. One such operation is **Kilmore Quay Boat Charters;** contact Dick Hayes (ℭ **053/29704**). For landlubbers, the River Slaney, brimming with salmon and sea trout, can be fished from the old bridge in Enniscorthy.

GOLF   County Waterford's golf venues include three 18-hole championship courses. **Waterford Castle Golf and Country Club,** The Island, Ballinakill, Waterford (ℭ **051/871633**), is a par-72 parkland course; greens fees are €36 ($32) on weekdays, €38 ($35) on weekends. **Faithlegg Golf Club,** Faithlegg House (ℭ **051/382241**), a par-72 parkland course beside the River Suir, charges greens fees of €28 ($25) Monday to Thursday, €35 ($31) Friday to Sunday. **Dungarvan Golf Club,** Knocknagranagh, Dungarvan (ℭ **058/43310**), a par-72 parkland course, has greens fees of €25 ($23) on weekdays, €33 ($29) on weekends. In addition, the 18-hole par-71 inland course at **Waterford Golf Club,** Newrath, Waterford (*C* 051/876748), is a mile from the center of the city. Its greens fees are €28 ($25) on weekdays, €32 ($29) on weekends.

HORSEBACK RIDING County Waterford is filled with trails. You can arrange to ride at **Killotteran Equitation Centre,** Killotteran, Waterford (*C* 051/384158); or **Nire Valley Equestrian Trail-Riding and Trekking,** Ballmacarberry (*C* 052/36147). Fees average €16 ($14) per hour.

SAILING, WINDSURFING & SEA KAYAKING From May to September, the **Dunmore East Adventure Centre,** Dunmore East (*C* 051/383783), offers courses of 1 to 4 days that cost €24 to €39 ($21–$35) per day, including equipment rental. Summer programs for children are also available. This is a great spot for an introductory experience, but there isn't much wave action for thrill-seeking windsurfers.

WHERE TO STAY
VERY EXPENSIVE
Waterford Castle ☆☆☆ There's something simply magical about taking a boat back to your room for the night. Islands are natural oases, and Waterford Castle is no exception. Dating back 800 years, this is the most secluded of Ireland's castles, on a private 124-hectare (310-acre) island in the River Suir, surrounded by woodland and an 18-hole championship golf course. It's only 3.2km (2 miles) south of Waterford and yet accessible only by the castle's private car ferry. Comprising an original Norman keep and two Elizabethan-style wings, it is built entirely of stone, with leaded roofs, mullioned windows, granite archways, ancient gargoyles, and fairy-tale turrets, towers, and battlements. The castle's interior is full of oak-paneled walls, ornate plaster ceilings, colorful tapestries, spacious sitting areas with huge stone fireplaces, original paintings, and elegant antiques. Four of the five suites are furnished with four-poster or canopied beds, and all have hand-carved armoires, designer fabrics, and other regal accessories. All of the castle's 19 rooms have big, firm beds, huge claw-foot bathtubs, and splendid views. The atmosphere is warm and graciously informal; the staff is excellent and members work together as a congenial team. They can help make arrangements for horseback riding, fishing, watersports, and other local activities.

The Island, Ballinakill, Waterford, county Waterford. *C* **051/878203.** Fax 051/879316. www.waterfordcastle. com. 19 units. €180–€420 ($160–$374) double; €355–€600 ($316–$534) suite. AE, MC, V. **Amenities:** Restaurant (international); bar; indoor heated pool; 18-hole championship golf course; tennis courts; concierge; room service; laundry and valet service. *In room:* TV, CD player, radio, hair dryer.

MODERATE
The Bridge Taking its name from its location on the waterfront at the foot of the Ignatius Rice Bridge, this attractive, red, vintage hotel is one of the city's oldest. The public rooms have retained their warm, old-world character, but the guest rooms have been renovated, trading old character for contemporary convenience. The rooms have blonde-wood furnishings, firm beds, and bright floral fabrics; they are surprisingly quiet, despite the hotel's harried location.

1 The Quay, Waterford, county Waterford. *C* **800/221-2222** in the U.S., or 051/877222. Fax 051/877229. www.minotel.com. 100 units. €120–€160 ($107–$142) double. Rates include full Irish breakfast and service charge. MC, V. **Amenities:** 2 restaurants (Continental, cafe); 2 bars; room service; babysitting. *In room:* TV, tea/coffeemaker, hair dryer.

Granville   Along the quay-side strip of Waterford's main business district, this historic hotel looks out onto the south side of the River Suir. The Granville was originally a coaching inn, and an adjacent section was the home of Irish patriot Thomas Francis Meagher and a meeting place for Irish freedom fighters. The Cusack family bought it in 1980, and totally restored and enlarged it. Today the Granville is a member of Best Western International. The chain's 1998 refurbishment of the hotel preserved its architectural blend while providing handsome individually styled rooms with orthopedic beds, as well as a new floor of penthouse suites. Many of the front rooms look out onto the river.

Meagher Quay, Waterford, county Waterford. *C* **800/538-1234** in the U.S., or 051/305555. Fax 051/305566. www.bestwestern.com or www.granville-hotel.ie. 100 units. €150–€198 ($134–$176) double. No service charge. Rates include full breakfast. AE, MC, V. Closed Dec 24–27. **Amenities:** Restaurant (international); bar; concierge; room service; laundry; valet. *In room:* TV, radio, dataport, hair dryer, ironing board, garment press.

Jurys Waterford Hotel ★★   Set amid 15 hectares (38 acres) of gardens and lawns, this modern six-story hotel with a fantastic leisure center is perched on a hill along the River Suir's northern bank. Every room enjoys a sweeping view of Waterford City. Recently refurbished, the guest rooms offer a Victorian-style decor of frilly floral fabrics, dark woods, and brass trim. The restaurant and bar are quite pleasant, but the bang for your buck comes with the terrific leisure center and all its amenities.

Ferrybank, Waterford, county Waterford. *C* **800/843-3311** in the U.S., or 051/832111. Fax 051/832863. www.jurys.com. 98 units. €126 ($112) double. AE, DC, MC, V. Closed Dec 24–26. **Amenities:** Restaurant (international); bar; leisure center with swimming pool, tennis courts, gym, Jacuzzi, two saunas, and steam room; concierge; salon; room service; babysitting; dry cleaning and laundry. *In room:* TV, tea/coffeemaker, hair dryer.

INEXPENSIVE

Aglish House   This corner of the Waterford countryside possesses a mix of sleepy pastoral charm and wild beauty, and Aglish House is an ideal base from which to explore the area. The B&B is set in a 17th-century manor home, alongside a working dairy farm. Tom and Teresa Moore are generous hosts, and breakfast is especially good; dinner is served with advance reservation. All the guest rooms are comfortably furnished, and the orthopedic beds ensure a good night's sleep. As numerous photos and trophies attest, this is a family of avid cyclists, and they are well versed in the local bicycling routes. A short walk from the house are the Kiltera Ogham stones, inscribed pillars dating from pre-Christian times; also nearby is the lovely Blackwater estuary. A short drive brings you to the coast or the Knockmealdown Mountains.

Aglish, Cappoquin, county Waterford. *C* **024/96191.** Fax 024/96482. www.aglishhouse.com. 4 units, 3 with private bathroom. €68 ($61) double. No service charge. Rates include full breakfast. MC, V. **Amenities:** Non-smoking rooms. *In room:* TV.

Buggy's Glencairn Inn ★★ *(Finds*   Ken and Cathleen Buggy are semicelebrities among Ireland's B&B aficionados, having run the beloved Old Presbytery in Kinsale, county Cork, for years before moving to Waterford. Their latest venture, a lovely honey-yellow farmhouse with an extraordinary restaurant and bar, is another testimony to their incredible talent for getting the details right. The guest rooms are chock-full of covetable auction finds: Victorian desks, steamer trunks above beefy, country armoires, and darling iron-and-brass beds. A bed at Buggy's is like something out of a fairy tale—a decadent effect created with a firm mattress, a small mountain of pillows, and miles of crisp, billowy sheets of Irish linen. The restaurant (see below) is a foodie's destination in itself, with the red-and-white checked bistro tablecloths and country pine furniture the perfect backdrop to Ken's traditional, mouthwatering cooking. The adjoining bar was described by one Irish newspaper as "a dream of a local pub." Waking up in one of those fabulous beds, with the sunlight softly tickling your face and Ken's delectable breakfast (his homemade soda bread is legendary) awaiting downstairs, is as good as it gets.

Glencairn, county Waterford (4.8km/3 miles from Lismore). © **058/56232**. www.lismore.com. 5 units. €100 ($89) double. No service charge. Rates include full breakfast. MC, V. Closed Christmas. **Amenities:** Restaurant (Irish); bar. *In room:* TV.

Foxmount Farm ⭐ This elegant, secluded, 17th-century country home is the perfect place to relax and collect yourself after a busy day of sightseeing. Margaret and David Kent are superlative hosts and do all they can to ensure that your stay will be a memorable one. Two adjacent guest rooms share a separate alcove, perfect for a family, and four double rooms have private bathrooms. All have views of the fields around the house. Margaret's breakfasts are bountiful affairs and have won national awards. A guide to walks in the area is available. The terrific Jack Meades pub (see listing below) is within walking distance.

Passage East Rd., Waterford, county Waterford. © **051/874308**. Fax 051/854906. foxmount@iol.ie. 5 units. €90 ($80) double. 25% discount for children under 12. No service charge. Rates include full breakfast. Dinner €25 ($23). No credit cards. Closed Nov–Feb. *In room:* TV, hair dryer.

WHERE TO DINE
EXPENSIVE

The Tannery ⭐⭐ *Value* ECLECTIC EUROPEAN Until 1995 this impressive stone monument of a building on the quays was an operating tannery; then it reappeared as a stylish contemporary restaurant that took off like a rocket. The reason for its success is Paul Flynn, one of the most innovative and iconoclastic chefs working in Ireland today. He takes every dish—be it an Irish stalwart such as bacon and colcannon (mashed potatoes and onions) or a Provençal specialty such as bouillabaisse—and puts his stamp on it to make it his own. His forte is blending unlikely ingredients to create interesting, creative dishes that seem impossible on paper but really work—a perfect plum tomato soup; sea bream with pepperoni and saffron-laced potatoes; French toast with baked apples and Chantilly cream. There is great discipline and artistry here, and the value for the money is exceptional.

Quay St., Dungarvan, county Waterford (beside the library). © **058/545420**. Reservations recommended. Main courses €15–€20 ($14–$18). AE, DC, MC, V. Tues–Sat 12:30–2:30pm and 6:30–10pm.

MODERATE

Buggy's Glencairn Inn ⭐⭐ COUNTRY IRISH Ken Buggy is the best sort of chef to run across: Utterly talented but without a pretentious bone in his body. He writes out his menu on a chalkboard, focusing on simple food that people like to eat. Then he cooks everything to perfection. His grilled steak is wonderfully grilled, his smoked salmon expertly smoked. He's particularly gifted with seafood, sourcing the best local catch and dressing it with just what's needed to let the natural flavors shine through. Prices are more than reasonable for this quality of cooking. The Inn itself is reviewed in the previous section.

Glencairn, county Waterford (4.8km/3 miles from Lismore). © **058/56232**. www.lismore.com. Reservations recommended. Main courses €13–€19 ($12–$17). MC, V. Wed–Mon 7:30–9pm.

O'Grady's CONTINENTAL Midway between downtown and the Waterford Crystal Factory, this restaurant is in a 19th-century Gothic-style stone gate lodge.

Modern Irish art enhances the light, airy interior, and the menu blends mainly European cuisine and fresh local ingredients, with an emphasis on seafood. It offers dishes such as seafood ravioli with brunoise of black olives, peppers, and saffron cream; and rack of lamb with red currants and Madeira. The O'Gradys also offer B&B in nine sweetly decorated, good-sized rooms for €70 ($62) double.

Cork Rd., Waterford, county Waterford. ✆ 051/378851. Reservations recommended. Fixed-price lunch €15 ($13) for 2 courses, €19 ($17) for 3 courses; dinner main courses €13–€19 ($12–$17). AE, DC, MC, V. Mon–Sun 12:30–2:15pm and 6:30–9:30pm. Closed holidays.

The Reginald MODERN EUROPEAN   One of the city's original walls (ca. A.D. 850) is part of the decor at this pub and restaurant next to Reginald's Tower. In keeping with its Viking-inspired foundations, the Reginald is laid out in a pattern of caverns, alcoves, and arches. The restaurant offers innovative choices using local ingredients, such as filet steak Aoife topped with avocado, chives, tomatoes, and green peppercorn sauce; and filet of pink trout with vermouth sauce. There's live music midweek to Sunday. After hours from Thursday to Saturday, the Reginald becomes the Excalibur "Knight Club" (named after the film and housing a number of its props), with live music and dancing. There's no cover charge before 10pm.

2/3 The Mall, Waterford, county Waterford. ✆ 051/855087. Reservations recommended for dinner. Bar food €2.50–€10 ($2.25–$8.90); early-bird (before 7pm) 3-course dinner €15 ($13); dinner main courses €13–€22 ($12–$20). MC, V. Daily 9:30am–10:30pm.

The Strand Seafood Restaurant ⚜ SEAFOOD   This intimate restaurant, attached to two pubs, has an independent reputation for outstanding cuisine. If you manage to look up from your plate, the views of Waterford Harbour and the Celtic Sea are stunning. Four or five daily seafood specials augment the excellent menu. Grilled wild salmon with green gooseberry sauce sounds risky but generously rewards all takers, and fresh lemon sole stuffed with seafood mousse is gorgeous. A vegetarian choice is provided each evening; and plates of crisp sautéed vegetables are liable to appear all by themselves, so be forewarned. An alluring dessert cart lies in wait at the end of your meal.

In the Strand Inn, Dunmore East, county Waterford. ✆ 051/383174. Reservations recommended. Main courses €16–€18 ($14–$16). No service charge. AE, MC, V. Mar–Oct daily 6:30–10pm; Nov–Dec and Feb Wed–Sun 6:30–10pm. Closed Jan.

The Wine Vault ⚜⚜ WINE BISTRO   Waterford's famed wine merchants have been popping corks for 800 years, and David Dennison is the city's current wine master. The food here is great, the wines are great, but the real magic of this place is that the room is so welcoming and clubby—red bricks and wood paneling, just like in your favorite trattoria. Chef Paul Brady features several daily specials, often focused on the most alluring catch of the day. His herb-crusted salmon with peppered cucumber and cabernet sauvignon dressing is disarmingly simple and perfect, the marinated squid with garlic and ginger a memorable delicacy. Dennison thinks about how to best match foods to wines and wines to foods, and he never misses. Desserts, such as the Chocolate Nemesis and homemade lemon curd ice cream, provide the perfect finish to a wonderful meal. The service here is exceptional—attentiveness without fuss, sophistication with warmth and humor. Smoking is permitted on the main floor; nonsmokers have the romantic wine vault to themselves.

High St., Waterford, county Waterford. ✆ 051/853444. www.waterfordwinevault.com. Reservations recommended. Main courses €10–€24 ($8.90–$21). No service charge. AE, DC, MC, V. Mon–Sat 12:30–2:30pm and 5:30–10:30pm.

INEXPENSIVE

Bewley's CAFE/TEAROOM   On the second level of the Broad Street Shopping Centre, this self-service spot is a branch of the famous Dublin coffeehouse of the same name. It serves breakfast, lunch, and coffee and tea all day. Homemade scones, fresh pastries, and soups are specialties.

Broad St., Waterford, county Waterford. ℭ 051/870506. All items €1–€11 (90¢–$10). Mon–Sat 8am–6pm.

WATERFORD AFTER DARK

Waterford has two main entertainment centers. Housed in one of Ireland's largest arts centers, the **Garter Lane Theatre,** 22a O'Connell St. (ℭ **051/ 855038**), presents the work of local production companies such as the Red Kettle and Waterford Youth Drama. Visiting troupes from all over Ireland also perform contemporary and traditional works at the 170-seat theater. Performances are usually Tuesday to Saturday, and tickets average €8 to €14 ($7.10–$12) for most events. The box office is open Monday to Saturday 10am to 6pm, and accepts MasterCard and Visa.

When big-name Irish or international talents come to Waterford, they usually perform at the **Forum Theatre** at the Glen (ℭ **051/871111**), a 1,000-seat house off Bridge Street. Tickets average €13 to €20 ($12–$18), depending on the event. The box office is open Monday to Friday, 11am to 1pm and 2 to 4pm. The Forum opens a late-night bar, Deja Vu, every Friday and Saturday. There's no cover, and the patrons are mostly in their mid- to late 30s.

From May to September, on Tuesday, Thursday, and Saturday (and Wed in July and Aug) at 8:45pm, the historic Waterford City Hall is home to the **Waterford Show,** a festive evening of music, storytelling, song, and dance. In high season, be sure to reserve a place in advance. Credit-card bookings (ℭ **051/ 875823,** or 051/381020 after 5pm) are accepted. Admission is €10 ($8.90), which includes a preshow drink and a glass of wine during the show.

There's also a new **Waterford Viking Show,** a 90-minute celebration of Waterford's Viking Heritage through music, dance, storytelling, and humor at the Granary, Merchants Quay. It happens in July and August at 8pm on Monday, Wednesday, and Friday. The cost is €13 ($12) per person. Call the Granary (ℭ **051/304500**) to reserve in advance.

Otherwise, Waterford's nightlife is centered in the hotel lounges and in the city's interesting assortment of pubs.

PUBS

Egans   In the heart of the city center, this friendly pub is a showcase of Tudor style and decor, from its neat black-and-white facade to its cozy interior. 36/37 Barronstrand St., Waterford, county Waterford. ℭ 051/875619.

Jack Meade   Waterford's most unusual pub is not in the city, but nestled beneath an old stone bridge in an area known as Halfway House, 6.5km (4 miles) south of town. Dating from 1705, the pub is widely known by the locals as Meades Under the Bridge, or "Ireland's only fly-over pub." As a public house with a forge, it was a stopping-off point for travelers between Waterford and Passage East in the old days. The facade and interior—wooden beams, historical paintings, antiques, and open, crackling fireplaces—haven't changed much in the intervening years. In July and August, there's music with singalong sessions on Wednesday night, and all year, impromptu evening sessions can occur. The grounds include an icehouse, a corn mill, lime kilns, a viaduct, and a beer garden and barbecue area. On Sundays in summer, barbecues with outdoor music start at 2pm and run until roughly 7:30pm. From May to September, bar food is served daily. Cheekpoint Rd., Halfway House, county Waterford. ℂ 051/873187.

The Kings This pub just off the Mall dates from 1776, when it was called the Packet Hotel because of its proximity to the Waterford docks and the packet ships sailing to England. It was often a send-off point for emigrants from Ireland. Today it retains its original Georgian-style facade, and the interior reflects old-world charm, particularly in the cozy 20-seat front bar. Check out the mid-19th-century bar counter—it has panels that used to hold sandpaper for customers to strike a match. 8 Lombard St., Waterford, county Waterford. ℂ 051/874495.

The Munster The flavor of old Waterford prevails in this 300-year-old building, which also can be entered from the Mall. Often referred to as Fitzgerald's (the name of the family that owns it), this pub is rich in etched mirrors, antique Waterford glass sconces, and dark wood walls, some of which are fashioned out of timber from the old Waterford Toll Bridge. Among the many rooms are an original "Men's Bar" and a lively modern lounge, which often features traditional Irish music on weekends. Bailey's New St., Waterford, county Waterford. ℂ 051/874656.

T. & H. Doolan Once a stagecoach stop, this 170-year-old pub in the center of town claims to be Waterford's oldest public house. It is a favorite venue for evening sessions of ballad, folk, and traditional music. Lanterns light the whitewashed stone walls and a collection of old farm implements, crocks, mugs, and jugs. 32 George's St., Waterford, county Waterford. ℂ 051/841504.

3 South Tipperary

South Tipperary is one of Ireland's best-kept secrets. Here, far from the tour buses and the clicking of camera shutters, you may just find the Ireland everyone is looking for: lush, welcoming, unspoiled, and splendidly beautiful.

VISITOR INFORMATION The **Clonmel Tourist Office** is on Sarsfield Street, Clonmel (ℂ 052/22960). It's open year-round Monday to Saturday, 9:30am to 5:30pm. **Seasonal offices,** open June to August, Monday to Saturday, 9:30am to 6pm, are at Castle Street, Cahir (ℂ 052/41453), and at the Town Hall, Cashel (ℂ 062/61333). The website for all Southeast Tourism is **www.southeastireland.travel.ie.** To get the latest on news, listings, and events in Clonmel and the surrounding area, buy a copy of the local **Nationalist,** which hits the stands every Saturday. Among other things, it will tell you what's on at the Regal Theatre or the White Memorial Theatre, Clonmel's principal venues for the arts.

EXPLORING THE AREA

Clonmel, the capital of Tipperary and the largest inland town in Ireland, is the unassuming gateway to the region. A working town, as yet undistorted or distracted by massive tourism, Clonmel has everything you need to establish a strategic, pleasant base of operations in the southeast. Poised on the banks of the Suir, Clonmel once had the distinction of withstanding a Cromwellian siege for 3 months. More recently, the town has successfully resisted the lure of rapid, unplanned tourism, preserving its own landscape and character and so making itself all the more attractive to visitors. Its 8km (5-mile) riverfront walkway, bustling vitality, and prime location all make it a perfect base for exploring one of the most pristine and stunningly beautiful regions of Ireland.

Whether you're staying in Clonmel or just passing through, several marvelously scenic drives converge here: the **Comeragh or Nire Valley Drive** deep into the Comeragh Mountains, which rise from the south banks of the Suir; the **Knockmealdown Drive,** through the historic village of Ardfinnan and the Vee (see below); and the **Suir Scenic Drive.** All are signposted from Clonmel.

North of Clonmel and deep in the Tipperary countryside, **Cashel** is not to be missed. Because it's on the main N8 road, most people pass through en route from Dublin to Cork. If your travels don't take you to Cashel, a side trip from Waterford is worth the drive. In particular, two scenic routes are well worth a detour:

At Cahir, head north through the **Galtee Mountains** ⍟, Ireland's highest inland mountain range, to the Glen of Aherlow. Often called "Ireland's Greenest Valley," the 11km (7-mile) Glen of Aherlow is a secluded and scenic area that was an important pass between the plains of counties Tipperary and Limerick.

If you're driving south into Waterford, head for the **"Vee."** This 18km (11-mile) long road winds through the Knockmealdown Mountains from Clogheen to Lismore and Cappoquin in county Waterford. It's one of the most dramatic drives in the southeast or, for that matter, anywhere in Ireland. The high point of the Vee is at the Tipperary-Waterford border, where the two slopes of the pass converge to frame the patchwork fields of the Galtee Valley far below. At this point, numerous walking trails lead to the nearby peaks and down to the mountain lake of Petticoat Loose—named after a, shall we say, less-than-exemplary lady. A more edifying local character was Samuel Grubb, of Castle Grace, who so loved these slopes that he left instructions that he should be buried upright overlooking them. And so he is. The rounded stone cairn you might notice off the road between Clogheen and the Vee is where he stands in place, entombed, facing the Golden Vale of Tipperary.

Ahenny High Crosses   You're likely to have this little-known and rarely visited site to yourself, except for the cows whose pasture you will cross to reach it. The setting is idyllic and, on a bright day, gorgeous. The remarkably well-preserved Ahenny high crosses are among the oldest in Ireland, dating from the 8th or 9th century. Tradition associates them with seven saintly bishops, all brothers, who are said to have been waylaid and murdered. Their unusual stone "caps," thought by some to be bishops' miters, more likely suggest the transition from wood crosses, which would have had small roofs to shelter them from the rain. Note too their intricate spiral and cable ornamentation in remarkably high relief, which may well have been inspired by earlier Celtic metalwork. Irish high crosses compose some of the most striking monuments of early Christianity in Ireland, and these are among the finest and most important examples of the form.

Kil Crispeen Churchyard, Ahenny, county Tipperary. 8km (5 miles) north of Carrick-on-Suir, signposted off R697. Open site. Box for donations.

Athassel Priory   This is the largest medieval priory in Ireland, spread out over 1.6 hectares (4 acres), and although it is in ruins, many delightful details from the original structure remain. This was an Augustinian priory, founded in the late 12th century; the remaining structures date from that time until the mid–15th century. The main approach is over a low stone bridge and through a gatehouse that was the focal point of the outer fortifications. The church entrance is a beautifully carved doorway at its west end. To the south of the church is the cloister, whose graceful arches have been largely eroded by time. Don't miss the carved face protruding from the southwest corner of the chapel tower, about 9m (30 ft.) above ground level.

3.2km (2 miles) south of Golden, county Tipperary. Take signposted road from Golden, on the N74; the priory is in a field just east of the road. Open site.

The Bolton Library   In this library, you'll see the smallest book in the world, as well as other rare, antiquarian, and unusual books dating from the 12th century. Ensconced here are works by Dante, Swift, Calvin, Newton, Erasmus, and Machiavelli. Also on display are some silver altar pieces from the original cathedral on the Rock of Cashel.

On the grounds of St. John the Baptist Church, John St., Cashel, county Tipperary. (C) **062/61944**. Admission €2 ($1.80) adults, €1.30 ($1.15) seniors and students, €.70 (60¢) children. Mon–Fri 9:30am–5:30pm; Sun 2:30–5:30pm. Closed Mon Mar–Sept.

Brú Ború Heritage Centre (*)   At the foot of the Rock of Cashel, this modern complex adds a musical element to the historic Cashel area. Operated by Comhaltas Ceoltoiri Eireann, Ireland's foremost traditional music organization, Brú Ború presents daily performances of authentic Irish traditional music at an indoor theater. Many summer evenings feature concerts in the open-air amphitheater. A gift shop, restaurant, and self-service snack bar are also on hand.

Rock Lane, Cashel, county Tipperary. (C) **062/61122**. Free admission to center; show €10 ($8.90); show and dinner €32 ($29). Daily Oct–Apr 9am–5:30pm; May–Sept 9am–6pm. Shows mid-June to mid-Sept Tues–Sat 9pm.

Cahir Castle (*)(*)   On a rock in the middle of the River Suir, this is one of Ireland's largest medieval fortresses. Its origins can be traced from the 3rd century, when a fort was built on the rock—hence the town's original name, City of the Fishing Fort. The present structure, which belonged to the Butler family from 1375 to 1961, is Norman and dates to the 13th and 15th centuries. It has a massive keep, high walls, spacious courtyards, and a great hall, all fully restored. The interpretive center offers an engaging 20-minute video introduction to the region's major historic sites, as well as guided tours of the castle grounds. Be sure to walk through the castle buildings, which are not included in the tour.

Cahir, county Tipperary. (C) **052/41011**. Admission €2.50 ($2.25) adults, €2 ($1.80) seniors, €1.30 ($1.15) students and children, €6.50 ($5.80) family. Daily mid-Mar to mid-June and mid-Sept to mid-Oct 9:30am–5:30pm; daily mid-June to mid-Sept 9am–7:30pm; daily mid-Oct to mid-Mar 9:30am–4:30pm.

Ormond Castle   The mid-15th-century castle built by Sir Edward MacRichard Butler on this strategic bend of the River Suir has lain in ruins for centuries. What still stands, attached to the ancient battlements, is the last surviving Tudor manor house in Ireland. Trusting that "if he built it, she would come," Thomas Butler constructed an extensive manor in honor of his most successful relation, Queen Elizabeth I—whose mother, Anne Boleyn, is rumored to have been born in Ormond Castle. She never came, but many others have, especially since the Heritage Service partially restored this impressive piece of Irish history. Current plans include an elaborate furnishing of the Earl's Room in period style. The manor's plasterwork, carvings, period furniture, and startling collection of original 17th- and 18th-century royal charters will make you glad you bothered to visit and wonder why Queen Elizabeth didn't.

Signposted from the center of Carrick-on-Suir, Carrick-on-Suir, county Tipperary. (C) **051/640787**. Admission €2.50 ($2.25) adults, €2 ($1.80) seniors, €1.30 ($1.15) students and children, €6.50 ($5.80) family. June–Sept daily 9:30am–6:30pm. Closed Oct–May.

The Rock of Cashel (*)(*)   When you reach the town of Cashel, look for signs to the Rock of Cashel, which dominates the Tipperary countryside for miles. An outcrop of limestone reaching 60m (200 ft.) into the sky, "the Rock" tells the tales of 16 centuries. It was the castled seat of the kings of Munster at least as far back as A.D. 360, and it remained a royal fortress until 1101, when King Murtagh O'Brien granted it to the church. Among Cashel's many great moments was the legendary baptism of King Aengus by St. Patrick in 448. Remaining on the rock are the ruins of a two-towered chapel, a cruciform cathedral, a 28m (92-ft.) round tower, and a cluster of other medieval monuments. The views of and from the Rock are spectacular. Forty-five-minute guided tours are available on request.

Cashel, county Tipperary. ☎ 062/61437. Admission €5 ($4.45) adults, €3 ($2.65) seniors, €2 ($1.80) students and children, €10 ($8.90) family. Daily mid-June to mid-Sept 9am–7:30pm; daily mid-Sept to mid-Mar 9am–4:30pm; mid-Mar to mid-June daily 9am–5:30pm. Last admission 45 min. before closing.

Swiss Cottage   The earls of Glengall used the Swiss Cottage as a hunting and fishing lodge as far back as 1812. It's a superb example of "cottage orné": a rustic house embodying the ideal of simplicity that so appealed to the Romantics of the early 19th century. The thatched-roof cottage has extensive timberwork, usually not seen in Ireland, and is believed to have been designed by John Nash, a royal architect. The interior has some of the first wallpaper commercially produced in Paris. The guided tour (the only way to see the building) lasts approximately 40 minutes.

Off Dublin-Cork rd. (N8), Cahir, county Tipperary. ☎ 052/41144. Guided tour €2.50 ($2.25) adults, €2 ($1.80) seniors, €1.30 ($1.15) students and children, €6.50 ($5.80) family. Late Mar and mid-Oct to Nov Tues–Sun 10am–1pm and 2–4:30pm; Apr Tues–Sun 10am–1pm and 2–6pm; May to mid-Oct daily 10am–6pm.

Tipperary Crystal 👁👁   This crystal factory, one of Ireland's top producers, is laid out in the style of traditional Irish cottages, complete with a thatched roof. Visitors are welcome to watch master craftspeople as they mouth-blow and hand-cut crystal. Unlike other crystal factories, Tipperary imposes no restriction on photographs and video recorders. The facility includes a showroom and restaurant.

Waterford-Limerick rd. (N24), Ballynoran, Carrick-on-Suir, county Tipperary. ☎ 051/641188. Free admission. Tours Mon–Fri 10am–3:30pm; shop and restaurant Mon–Fri 9am–5:30pm, Sun 11am–5pm.

SPORTS & OUTDOOR PURSUITS

BIRD-WATCHING   As many as 15 species of Irish waterbirds—including mute swans, coots, wigeons, gadwalls, teals, grey herons, and moorhens—can be seen at the **Marlfield Lake Wildfowl Refuge,** several miles west of Clonmel in Marlfield. This is a little lake with an astonishing number of birds. On your way, you will likely pass signposts for **St. Patrick's Well,** less than a mile away, a tranquil spot with an effervescent pool of reputedly healing crystalline water. In the middle of the pool rises a seriously ancient Celtic cross. The legend that Patrick visited here seems more solidly rooted than most such claims. Even saints get thirsty.

BICYCLING   For complete 1- or 2-week cycling holidays in the Southeast, contact Don Smith at **Celtic Cycling,** Lorum Old Rectory, Bagenalstown, county Carlow (☎ and fax **0503/75282**).

FISHING   The **River Suir,** from Carrick-on-Suir to Thurles, was once one of the finest salmon rivers in Europe, but recent excessive trawling at its mouth has threatened its stock. It's still a decent salmon river, especially in the February run and from June to September. Trout (brown and rainbow) are in abundance here in the summer. Here you'll find some of the least expensive game fishing in

Ireland; single weekday permits cost €19 to €32 ($17–$29) for salmon, €6.50 ($5.80) for trout. They are available from **Kavanagh Sports,** Westgate, Clonmel, county Tipperary (© and fax **052/21279**), as is everything else you'll need. Manager Declan Byrne can outfit you with the all essentials and more. To orient yourself and to consider your options, pick up a copy of *Angling on the Suir,* a quite helpful pamphlet available at the Tourist Office. The **River Nore** and the nearby **River Barrow** are also known for good salmon and trout fishing.

For sea fishing, picturesque Dunmore East, 13km (8 miles) south of Waterford, is a good bet. Contact **John O'Connor** (© **051/383397**) to charter a boat for reef, wreck, and shark fishing. Boat charter rates are €200 to €290 ($178–$258) per day; rod and reel can also be rented. The species you're likely to encounter in this area during the summer include blue shark, cod, bass, whiting, conger, and ling.

HORSEBACK RIDING   Hillcrest Riding Centre, Glenbally, Tipperary (© **062/37915**), is a registered riding stable based in the Galtee Mountains offering trail rides, a cross-country course, and instruction in show jumping. Trail rides range from €13 ($12) an hour to €50 ($46) for a full day's ride. Hillcrest is a keen hunting stable, and for those anxious for the chase, horses and participation in local and neighboring hunts can be arranged. Hillcrest also offers longer trekking holidays, up to a week in duration. For trekking and trail riding on the slopes of the Comeragh Mountains, you can't do better than **Melodys Nire Valley Equestrian Centre,** Nire View, Ballycarbry, Clonmel (© **052/36147**).

SWIMMING   If you're staying in the area, you're welcome to swim at the **Clonmel Civic Swimming Pool** (© **052/21972**), near the Market Place. It's open Monday to Friday 10am to 10pm, Saturday and Sunday 10am to 8pm. Call for specific public swimming hours.

TENNIS   The courts of the **Hillview Sports Club,** Mountain Road, Clonmel (© **052/21805**), may be used by visitors.

WALKING   R668 between Clogheen and Lismore is one of the most scenic stretches of road in the southeast, and some great walks begin at the **Vee Gap,** a dramatic notch in the Knockmealdown Mountains. About 2.4km (1½ miles) north of R669 and R668, you reach the highest point in the gap; there is a parking lot, as well as a dirt road continuing down to a lake nestled into the slope below. This is Bay Lough, and the dirt road used to be the main thoroughfare over the gap; it now offers a fine walk to the shores of the lake, with outstanding views of the valley to the north. For a panoramic perspective of the region, start walking due east from the gap parking lot to the summit of Sugarloaf Hill; the hike is extremely steep, but well worth the effort—the views from the ridge are superb.

In the Clonmel area, there are a number of excellent river and hill walks, some more challenging than others. The most spectacular is the ascent of famed **Slievenamon,** a mountain rich in myth and lore. Inexpensive, detailed trail maps for at least a half a dozen walks are available at the Clonmel Tourist Office on Sarsfield Street, Clonmel. Also available is a free leaflet guide to the birds, butterflies, and flora of nearby **Wilderness Gorge.**

The **Galtee Mountains,** northwest of the Knockmealdowns, offer some great long and short walks. One beautiful route on a well-defined trail is the circuit of **Lake Muskry,** on the north side of the range. To get there, take R663 west out of Bansha, and follow signs for the town of Rossadrehid. To get to the trail, ask for directions in Rossadrehid; there are several turns, and the landmarks change frequently because of logging in the region. The trail leads you up a glaciated valley to the base of a ring of cliffs, where the crystalline waters of Lake Muskry lie; from here you can walk around the lake, take in the tremendous views of the valley, and return the way you came. Walking time to the lake and back is 3 hours.

Another option on this walk is to continue up past the lake to the top of the ridge, and from there along the ridge top to Galtymore, a prominent dome-shaped peak about 4.8km (3 miles) west of Lake Muskry. It is a beautiful but extremely demanding walk, about 6 hours to Galtymore and back. This is only one of many extraordinary walks in the Glen of Aherlow. Trail maps and all the information and assistance you could think of asking for are available at the **Glen of Aherlow Failte Centre,** Coach Road, Newtown (© **062/56331**), ably directed by Helen Morrissey. It's open year-round, Monday to Friday 10am to 4pm, and daily June to October from 9am to 6pm. Guided 2-hour walks are best booked in advance. Or drop in, and one might be leaving shortly.

WHERE TO STAY
EXPENSIVE
Cashel Palace Hotel ⚐   Originally built in 1730 as a residence for Church of Ireland archbishops, this mammoth red-brick Palladian mansion has been a hotel for over 30 years. It has an ideal location, right in the middle of Cashel town yet within its own walled grounds, and recent owners have thoroughly updated the property and filled it with antiques and designer-coordinated fabrics. The house itself is a proud display of lofty, corniced ceilings, Corinthian pillars, mantelpieces of Kilkenny marble, and a paneled early Georgian staircase of red pine. Guest rooms in the main house are beautifully appointed to reflect the taste of the 18th-century upper crust, and have big four-poster or mahogany beds and spacious bathrooms. The 10 rooms in the charming Mews House give visitors a cozy nook next to the hotel. The Bishop's Buttery restaurant offers splendid views of the revered Rock, especially at night when it is floodlit. The well-tended back garden holds mulberry bushes planted in 1702 to commemorate the coronation of Queen Anne, and a private pathway known as the Bishop's Walk that runs up a hill to the Rock of Cashel.

Main St., Cashel, county Tipperary. © **800/221-1074,** 800/223-6510 in the U.S., or 062/62707. Fax 062/61521. www.cashel-palace.ie. 23 units. €170–€270 ($151–$240) double. Rates include full Irish breakfast and service charge. AE, DC, MC, V. **Amenities:** 2 restaurants (international, cafe); bar; babysitting; drawing room. *In room:* TV, hair dryer.

MODERATE/EXPENSIVE
Hotel Minella ⚐⚐   The attractive centerpiece of this sprawling hotel complex along the River Suir was built in 1863. Its many additions have made it not only a haven for tourists but also a haunt for locals, whether they're celebrating a wedding or merely a Friday night out. Its riverbank location and attractive landscaping give it an appeal beyond its somewhat-incongruous mix of architectural styles. Once you're inside, its warm, welcoming, and utterly comfortable atmosphere take over. The standard guest rooms are furnished traditionally in dark woods and paisley prints. The Jacuzzi suites have Jacuzzi tubs, while the steam room suites are especially spacious and luxuriant, with rich colors, four-poster canopy beds, and private steam rooms with showers. All the rooms have views either of the river or of the nearby mountains. Perhaps the chief appeal of this hotel is its new, fully-equipped, state-of-the-art health and fitness club to which guests have unlimited free access. You could easily spend several days making use of the facilities.

1.6km (1 mile) east of Clonmel center on the south bank of the River Suir, Coleville Rd., Clonmel, county Tipperary. © **052/22388.** Fax 052/24381. www.hotelminella.ie. 70 units. €140 ($125) double; €180–€200 ($160–$178) suite. Rates include full breakfast and service charge. AE, DC, MC, V. **Amenities:** Restaurant (international); bar; 2 lounges; indoor swimming pool; outdoor hot tub; all-season tennis court; gym; indoor Jacuzzi; sauna; aquacruisers; aromatherapy steam room; therapy rooms; room service; massage; babysitting; laundry/dry cleaning; nonsmoking rooms; currency exchange. *In room:* TV, tea/coffeemaker, garment press, iron.

MODERATE

Dundrum House Hotel   Located 9.7km (6 miles) northwest of Cashel, this impressive Georgian country manor is nestled in the fertile Tipperary countryside, surrounded by 40 hectares (100 acres) of grounds and gardens. The River Multeen runs through the property. Originally built as a residence in 1730 by the earl of Montalt, it was used as a convent school, then transformed into a hotel in 1978 by local residents Austin and Mary Crowe. It is furnished with assorted heirlooms, vintage curios, Victorian pieces, and reproductions. Each room is individually decorated in a traditional and slightly dated, feminine feel, some with four-poster beds or hand-carved headboards, armoires, vanities, and other traditional furnishings. There are exceptional weekend specials on offer all year, such as €130 ($116) double for 2 nights B&B plus one dinner from May to September. The hotel's bar is especially appealing, set in a former chapel with stained-glass windows.

Dundrum, county Tipperary. © **800/447-7462** in the U.S., or 062/71116. Fax 062/71366. www.dundrum househotel.com. 60 units. €140–€154 ($127–$139) double. Rates include full Irish breakfast. Weekend discounts available. AE, DC, MC, V. **Amenities:** Restaurant (Irish/Continental); bar; indoor pool; 18-hole championship golf course; 2 tennis courts; gym; sauna; horseback riding; trout fishing privileges. *In room:* TV, radio, hair dryer.

Kilcoran Lodge Hotel   A former hunting lodge nestled on 8 hectares (20 acres) of wooded grounds, this old Victorian treasure is on a hillside set back from the main road a few miles west of Cahir. It was totally renovated and refurbished in 1998. The public areas retain their old-world charm, with open fireplaces, grandfather clocks, antique tables and chairs, brass fixtures, and tall windows that frame expansive views of the Suir Valley and Knockmealdown Mountains. Guest rooms are basically but comfortably appointed and have modern bathrooms. The bar is noted for its excellent daytime pub grub, which includes Irish stew, traditional boiled bacon and cabbage, homemade soups, and hot scones.

Dublin-Cork rd. (N8), Cahir, county Tipperary. © **800/447-7462** in the U.S., or 052/41288. Fax 052/41994. 25 units. €90–€110 ($80–$98) double. Rates include full breakfast and service charge. AE, MC, V. **Amenities:** Restaurant (international); bar; lounge; indoor swimming pool; gym; Jacuzzi; sauna; solarium. *In room:* TV, radio, tea/coffeemaker, hair dryer, garment press.

Mobarnane House ✸   This elegant, splendidly restored 18th-century farmhouse was opened in 2000 as a B&B and immediately became popular with discerning travelers in search of a period setting, tranquil surroundings, and warm hospitality. Richard Craik-White is a terrific chef, and his wife, Sandra, is a warm hostess. Dinner is served at 8pm at a communal table for all the guests. Guest rooms are pretty in cream or blue, furnished with mahogany pieces and antiques. The best two rooms have mountain views and their own sitting rooms; the other two face the lake and are equally pretty but not as large. The 24-hectare (60-acre) estate of woodlands, meadows, and gardens—complete with a 1.2-hectare (3-acre) lake—makes this a particularly wonderful base for walkers.

Fethard, county Tipperary. © and fax **052/31962.** www.mobarnanehouse.com. 4 units. €140–€166 ($125–$148) double. Rates include full breakfast and service charge. MC, V. **Amenities:** Drawing room. *In room:* TV.

INEXPENSIVE

Bansha House   Mary and Jone Marnane have won many well-deserved awards during 25 years of offering accommodations in their elegant, comfortable Georgian manor farmhouse. The guest rooms are nicely appointed with sturdy country furniture and have a feminine feel, but unfortunately the largest rooms lack private bathrooms. The self-catering Primrose Cottage, which sleeps five, is perfect for families and folks who want to do their own cooking. The town of Bansha sits at the base of the magnificent Galtee Mountains, which dominate the skyline on a clear day and make this house a great base for walking and bicycling or just taking in the scenery. A main activity here is **horseback riding** ✪ at the adjacent Bansha House Stables, one of the area's top professional breeding stables.

Bansha, county Tipperary. Ⓒ **062/54194**. Fax 062/54215. www.tipp.ie/banshahs.htm. 8 units, 5 with private bathroom. €60–€70 ($53–$62) double. No service charge. Rates include full breakfast. Cottage €330–€450 ($294–$401) per week. MC, V. Closed Dec 20–Jan 1. **Amenities:** Sitting room.

Kilmaneen Farmhouse *(Value)*   This small gem of a B&B has recently been winning both national and regional accommodation and landscaping awards. The guest rooms are spotless and beautifully appointed. Better yet, the mountain location is breathtaking and there is great fishing available on the farm. You can cast for trout here, into either the Suir or the Tar, without any permit required, and you will be provided with a fisherman's hut for tying flies, storing equipment, and drying waders. If the mountains hold more allure for you, your host, Ken O'Donnell, is trained in mountaineering and leads trekking and walking tours into the nearby Knockmealdowns, Comeraghs, or Galtee mountains.

If you decide you want to stay a week and not a night, you may want to consider the O'Donnells' fully equipped guest cottage, cozy enough for two and spacious enough for five. It rents for anywhere from €130 to €390 ($116–$347), depending on the season and the number of occupants. Finding your way here can be tricky, so call ahead and ask for detailed directions.

Newcastle, county Tipperary. Ⓒ and fax **052/36231**. 3 units (2 with shower only). €52 ($46) double. No service charge. Rates include full breakfast. Dinner €19 ($17). MC, V. Open year-round. **Amenities:** Non-smoking rooms.

Legends Guesthouse & The Kiln ✪✪ *(Finds)*   What sets this new guesthouse apart from the pack is its fabulous Kiln restaurant and the fact that, after dinner, you can climb upstairs and into bed and enjoy an unobstructed view of the floodlit Rock of Cashel. Downstairs in The Kiln's kitchen, Michael O'Neill is celebrated for his simple but wonderful cooking. As a starter, try the twice-baked cheese soufflé roasted in cream with spring onion and tomato, before moving on to a fish dish, perhaps pan-fried brill with chive butter and tomato fondue. Desserts, like the star anise crème brûlée with poached pear, are models of understated elegance. The dining room has a terrific placement, looking onto the Rock of Cashel. Guest rooms are modest but homey, with pine furniture and modern bathrooms. Breakfasts are wonderful.

The Kiln, Cashel, county Tipperary. Ⓒ **062/61292**. Fax 062/62876. 7 units. €58–€80 ($52–$71) double. No service charge. Rates include full breakfast. MC, V. **Amenities:** Restaurant (Continental). *In room:* TV.

Mr. Bumbles *(Value)*   Located above Declan Gavigan's Mr. Bumbles restaurant (see "Where to Dine," below), with their own exterior staircase, these four rooms are basic but bright and simple. They are meticulously clean and have firm beds. The family room sleeps three. If you crave a night off from the social rituals of the standard B&B and want an excellent breakfast, this is the place. Better yet, it's possible to negotiate a B&B-and-dinner combination, which all but guarantees sweet dreams.

Richmond House, Kickham St., Clonmel, county Tipperary. (top of Clonmel Market Place.) ℂ **052/29380.** Fax 052/29007. 4 units, all with shower only. €52 ($46) double; €58 ($52) family room. No service charge. Rates include full breakfast. MC, V. **Amenities:** Restaurant (international). *In room:* TV.

SELF-CATERING

Ballyknockane Estate Once the hunting lodge and grounds of the Marquess of Ormonde, this 2,000-hectare (5,000-acre) estate is the ultimate retreat and wooded wonderland. Composing a large part of Slievenamon ("the Mountain of Women"), a hauntingly beautiful peak steeped in Irish legend, the estate has 81km (50 miles) of private roads and paths, a paradise for hikers, climbers, and birders. The cottages (each with three bedrooms, sleeping six) and the coach house (which has four bedrooms and sleeps eight) are situated within a beautifully maintained 21 hectare (52-acre) arboretum, boasting many rare and exotic species of trees and shrubs. The fully equipped (TV, washing machine, microwave) and cozy cottages are meticulously maintained and tastefully landscaped. The coach house, with its own walled enclosure, is far grander though a bit fraying here and there. Whichever you choose, you will be warmly welcomed and well attended during your stay here.

2.4km (1½ miles) west of Ballypatrick off N76, Ballypatrick, Clonmel, county Tipperary. ℂ **052/33234.** Fax 052/33255. robinmc@gofree.indigo.ie. 3 cottages, 1 coach house. Cottages €802 ($714) per week; coach house €1,162 ($1,034) per week. No credit cards. *In room:* TV, kitchen, washing machine.

Coopers Cottage ⟨★⟩ This adorable Victorian cottage is perfect for a family wanting to explore the southeastern counties of Tipperary, Waterford, and Kilkenny. Stella and Eamonn Long have lovingly restored and renovated this 19th-century cooper's cottage, once Eamonn's family home, into an extraordinarily comfortable and tasteful country hideaway. While retaining the original cozy proportions and traditional lines, the Longs have created a house full of light, with generous skylights and windows opening to spectacular views of the Galtee Mountains. The furnishings have a bright, contemporary feel. The house, which has three bedrooms and sleeps six, comes with absolutely everything, and there's even a barbecue and a lovely modest fenced-in garden, with a patio area for sunny days.

1.6km (1 mile) off N24 at Bansha, Raheen, Bansha, county Tipperary. ℂ **062/54027.** Fax 062/54027. www. dirl.com/tipperary/coopers.htm. 1 cottage. €380–€500 ($338–$445) per week. No credit cards. **Amenities:** Patio. *In room:* TV, kitchen, microwave, dishwasher, washing machine, dryer.

Knocklofty Country House & Leisure Centre ⟨★★⟩ Knocklofty House is a grand, sprawling country house hotel and self-catering complex whose torso dates from the 17th century, with various extremities added in the 18th and 19th centuries. Restoration and redecoration of the units was completed in April 2000. The setting—42 hectares (105 acres) of rolling park and pastureland along the River Suir—is exquisite. The river views are serene. Each guest room and apartment has its own character, but all share high ceilings, great wide windows, and orthopedic beds (many are king-size). The elegant oak-paneled dining room (see "Where to Dine," below) serves extraordinary cuisine, which guests can enjoy after a drink in the grand two-story Georgian library.

The well-appointed self-catering units offer an appealing array of options. There are hotel apartments, mews town houses, and cottages, some freestanding and some in a row. Cottages came from varied incarnations—for example, a stable, a barn, or a shed. Favorites include the garden lodge, a cozy one-bedroom stone cottage; "Mrs. Phelan's House," a stone three-bedroom cottage that once belonged to the long-standing (literally) housekeeper of Lady Dunoughmore; and the mews houses with one, two, three, or four bedrooms, circling a court-yard adjoining the great house. There are many memorable walks and drives nearby. Fishing is free (no permits required) for guests on this stretch of the Suir, known for brown and rainbow trout.

4.8km (3 miles) west of Clonmel (signposted from R665), Clonmel, county Tipperary. Hotel ✆ 052/38222. Fax 052/38300. Self-catering ✆ 052/25444. Fax 052/26444. www.tipp.ie/knocklof.htm. 17 hotel units, 4 with shower only. €100–€130 ($89–$116) double. Rates include full Irish breakfast and service charge. 17 self-catering units. €230–€530 ($205–$472) per week. AE, MC, V. **Amenities:** Restaurant (Continental); bar/library; indoor pool; gym; Jacuzzi; massage and beauty treatments; tanning bed. *In room:* TV.

WHERE TO DINE
EXPENSIVE
Chez Hans ✸✸✸ CONTINENTAL/SEAFOOD   It's not surprising that the Rock of Cashel, a landmark in Irish royal and ecclesiastical history, would inspire a great restaurant. The dining room is one of the prettiest places to eat in Ireland—a former Gothic chapel in the shadow of the mighty rock. The cathedral-style ceiling, original stone walls, lyrical background music, and can-dlelight atmosphere create the perfect setting for the cooking of Jason Matthaie, son of owner Peter Hans Matthaie, who started his restaurant in 1968. His repertoire includes such dishes as Dublin Bay prawn bisque, cassoulet of seafood, roast sea scallops, succulent herb-crusted roast Tipperary lamb, and free-range duckling with honey and thyme. The flavors are luxurious, the por-tions generous, the crowd appreciative.

Rockside, Cashel, county Tipperary. ✆ 062/61177. Reservations required. Main courses €18–€29 ($16–$26). MC, V. Tues–Sat 6:30–10pm. Closed Jan and Sept 5–12.

MODERATE/EXPENSIVE
Knocklofty House Restaurant CONTINENTAL   A special spot fre-quented by locals as well as visitors, this restaurant boasts excellent cuisine served in a warm oak-paneled dining room overlooking the Suir River. It's a ritual to peruse the menu over drinks in the library; you are called when your meal is ready. The fixed-price lunch menu offers a range of international dishes, from chicken with mozzarella and sweet jalapeño chile to roast beef with Yorkshire pudding. At dinner, we found the tender rack of lamb with sun-dried tomato and basil-scented *jus* and the whole pan-fried back sole meunière truly delicious. Fresh ingredients, inventive sauces, and generous portions are the hallmarks of this most pleasant restaurant. The menu changes weekly to take advantage of what's available at local markets.

In Knocklofty Country House, 4.8km (3 miles) west of Clonmel (signposted from R665), Clonmel, county Tip-perary. Hotel ✆ 052/38222. Reservations recommended. Fixed-price lunch €18 ($16); fixed-price dinner €34 ($30); dinner main courses €15–€23 ($13–$20). AE, MC, V. Daily 7:30–10:30am and 12:30–2:30pm; Mon–Sat 7–9:30pm; Sun 6:30–8pm.

MODERATE
Mr. Bumbles ✸ INTERNATIONAL   With its natural woods, bright colors, and bistro feel, this split-level restaurant is very inviting and the food simply first-rate. Many dishes are grilled or pan-seared with a Mediterranean slant to the spic-ing, and all are brilliantly fresh. Wild sea trout, Tipperary sirloin, and Mediterranean vegetables are representative entrees. The presentation is gorgeous,

and portions are generous. The French house wines are quite fine and reasonable at roughly €14 ($12), and the French and Australian entries on the international wine list are particularly strong.

Richmond House, Kickham St., Clonmel, county Tipperary. ℂ 052/29188. www.tipp.ie/mrbumbles.htm. Reservations recommended. Fixed-price 4-course dinner €29 ($26); main courses €13–€19 ($12–$17). No service charge. MC, V. Daily noon–3pm and 6–10pm.

INEXPENSIVE

Angela's Wholefood Restaurant ⟨★⟩ ⟨Value⟩ CAFETERIA Angela's offers scrumptious, substantial fare at remarkable value. The blackboard menu might include custom-made breakfast omelets, spicy Moroccan lamb stew, savory tomato-and-spinach flan Provençal, homemade soups, sandwiches made to order, and an array of delicious salads. The food is vibrant, fresh, and appreciated by the bustling patrons who line up with trays in hand, from barristers (in garb) to babysitters.

14 Abbey St., Clonmel, county Tipperary. ℂ 052/26899. Breakfast menu €2.50–€5 ($2.23–$4.45); lunch menu €2.50–€9 ($2.25–$8). No service charge. No credit cards. Mon–Fri 9am–5:30pm; Sat noon–5pm.

PUBS

Gerry Chawkes Chawkes is a Clonmel landmark, a shrine not so much to stout as to sport. A fanatic fan of hurling and racing (dogs and horses), Gerry Chawke has made his pub a cult place, lined with fascinating sports memorabilia. Athletic clubs from throughout Ireland make a point of stopping here, as do local politicians in recovery from council meetings. You too will be quickly at home— Gerry will see to that. 3 Gladstone St. Upper, Clonmel, county Tipperary. ℂ 052/21149.

Railway Bar ⟨Finds⟩ You'll need on-the-ground directions to find Kitty's, which is what locals call this pub. Roughly, it's in a cul-de-sac behind the train station. Any effort you make to find your way will not be wasted, especially on weekends, when a traditional music session is likely to break out at any time. This is the mother of all Irish music pubs in Clonmel. No one is paid or even invited to play here; they just do. Often, there are so many musicians and so many wanting to hear them that the music spills outside, down the lane. No frills here—just the best Irish music around, and a pub out of the who-knows-when past. Sadly, Kitty has now passed away, but her two daughters and son are carrying on admirably in her name and tradition. Clonmel, county Tipperary. No phone.

The Ronald Reagan Yes, there really is a pub named after the former U.S. president, right in the middle of the town that was home to his great-grandfather, Michael Reagan. Filled with pictures and mementos of the president's June 3, 1984, visit to Ballyporeen, with a mural of the original Reagan homestead cottage on the back wall, the bar is part of the pub and gift-shop complex of local entrepreneur John O'Farrell. Partisan politics aside, it's worth a stop for a toast or at least a picture. Main St., Ballyporeen, county Tipperary. ℂ 052/67133.

Tierney's This is truly a show pub, with all of the ribbons to prove it. In 8 of the past 12 years, it was named Tipperary Pub of the Year and twice the Munster Pub of the Year. First of all, it's remarkably classy, with lots of dark carved wood, shiny brass railings and fitments, and stained glass. It goes on and on from one level to another, with all manner of separate lounges, dining rooms, nooks, and snugs. Upstairs, there are a full-service restaurant with several distinct dining rooms, each with its own character, and a walled floral beer garden for outside drinks and meals when the weather is gracious. 13 O'Connell St., Clonmel, county Tipperary. ℂ 052/24467.

4 County Kilkenny

Kilkenny City is 48km (30 miles) N of Waterford, 81km (50 miles) NW of Wexford, 121km (75 miles) SW of Dublin, 137km (85 miles) SE of Shannon Airport, 148km (92 miles) NE of Cork, and 61km (38 miles) NE of Cashel

Kilkenny City ✦, the centerpiece of county Kilkenny and the southeast's prime inland city, is considered the medieval capital of Ireland because of its remarkable collection of well-preserved castles, churches, public buildings, streets, and lanes. But, perhaps more interestingly for shoppers, it's also the national center for crafts and design, with perhaps the country's best selection of pottery, woodwork, jewelry, and other handmade items. Its lively pub and entertainment circuit (including several comedy festivals throughout the year) also make Kilkenny a top weekend getaway destination for Dubliners and Corkonians.

Situated along the banks of the River Nore, Kilkenny (pop. 11,000) takes its name from a church founded in the 6th century by St. Canice. In the Irish language, *Cill Choinnigh* means "Canice's Church."

Like most Irish cities, Kilkenny had fallen into Norman hands by the 12th century. Thanks to its central location, it became a prosperous walled city and served as the venue for many parliaments during the 14th century. Fortunately, much of Kilkenny's great medieval architecture has been preserved and restored, and the basic town plan has not changed much with the passing of the centuries. It's still a very walkable community of narrow streets and arched lanes.

The oldest house in town is purported to be **Kyteler's Inn** on St. Kieran Street. It was once the home of Dame Alice Kyteler, a lady of great wealth who was accused of witchcraft in 1324. She escaped and forever disappeared, but her maid, Petronilla, was burned at the stake. Now restored, the inn is currently used as a pub and restaurant, but it retains an eerie air, with appropriately placed effigies of witches and other memorabilia and decorations.

One building that stands out on the streetscape is the **Tholsel,** on High Street, with its curious clock tower and front arcade. Otherwise known as the town hall or city hall, it was erected in 1761 and served originally as the tollhouse or exchange. Milk and sugar candy were sold at the Tholsel, and dances, bazaars, and political meetings were held here. Today, completely restored after a fire in 1987, it houses the city's municipal archives.

Kilkenny is often referred to as the Marble City. Fine black marble used to be quarried on the outskirts of town. Until 1929, some of the city streets also had marble pavements.

Primarily a farming area, the surrounding county Kilkenny countryside is dotted with rich river valleys, rolling pasturelands, gentle mountains, and picture-postcard towns. Don't miss **Jerpoint Abbey,** on the River Nore just southwest of Thomaston on N9, one of the finest of Ireland's Cistercian ruins. Also on the Nore is the village of **Inistioge** ✦, about 24km (15 miles) southeast of Kilkenny City. Inistioge has an attractive tree-lined square and a much-photographed 18th-century bridge of nine arches spanning the river.

The town of Graiguenamanagh—its name means "village of the monks"—is home to **Duiske Abbey.** Surrounded by vistas of Brandon Hill and the Blackstairs Mountains, Graiguenamanagh is at a bend of the River Barrow, about 32km (20 miles) southeast of Kilkenny City.

Kells, about 9.7km (6 miles) south of Kilkenny City (not to be confused with Kells in county Meath), is the only completely walled medieval town in Ireland. The extensive curtain walls, seven towers, and some of the monastic buildings have been well preserved.

KILKENNY CITY ESSENTIALS

GETTING THERE **Irish Rail** provides daily service from Dublin into the Irish Rail McDonagh Station, Dublin Road, Kilkenny (© **056/22024;** www.irishrail.ie).

Bus Eireann, McDonagh Station, Dublin Road, Kilkenny (© **056/64933;** www.buseireann.ie), operates daily service from Dublin and all parts of Ireland.

Many roads pass through Kilkenny, including the N9/N10 from Waterford and Wexford, the N8 and N76 from Cork and the southwest, the N7 and N77 from Limerick and the west, and the N9 and N78 from Dublin and points north and east.

VISITOR INFORMATION For information, maps, and brochures about Kilkenny and the surrounding area, contact the **Kilkenny Tourist Office,** Shee Alms House, Rose Inn Street, Kilkenny (© **056/51500;** www.southeastireland.travel.ie). It's open May to September, Monday to Saturday 9am to 6pm, Sunday 11am to 1pm and 2 to 6pm; April and October, Monday to Saturday 9am to 6pm; November to March, Monday to Saturday 9am to 1pm and 2 to 5pm.

CITY LAYOUT The main business district sits on the west bank of the River Nore. A mile-long north-south thoroughfare, High Street, runs the length of the city, changing its name to Parliament Street at midpoint. It starts at the Parade, on the south end near Kilkenny Castle, and continues through the city to St. Canice's Cathedral at the northern end. Most of the city's attractions are along this route or on offshoot streets such as Patrick, Rose Inn, Kieran, and John. The tourist office can supply you with a good street map.

GETTING AROUND There is no downtown bus service in Kilkenny. Local buses run to nearby towns on a limited basis, departing from the Parade. Check with **Bus Eireann** (© **056/64933;** www.buseireann.ie) for details.

If you need a taxi, call **Nicky Power Taxi** (© 056/63000), **Billy Delaney Cabs** (© 056/22457), **David Nagle Taxi** (© 056/63300), or **Phonecab** (© 056/63017).

Don't even try to drive in town—Kilkenny's narrow medieval streets make for extremely slow-moving traffic, and you'll almost certainly get stuck. If you have a car, park it at one of the designated parking areas at the Parade, the rail station, or one of the shopping centers. Some parking is free, and other spaces have coin-operated machines, usually for €.30 (25¢) per hour. There's also a central multistory car park on Ormonde Street, which costs €.70 (60¢) per hour until you reach €6.50 ($5.80), which will last you for 24 hours. If you need to rent a car to see the surrounding countryside, call Barry Pender, Dublin Road, Kilkenny (© **056/65777** or 056/63839).

The best way to see Kilkenny City is on foot. Plot your own route or join a guided walking tour (see below).

FAST FACTS If you need a drugstore, try **John Street Pharmacy,** 47 John St. (© **056/65971**); **John O'Connell,** 4 Rose Inn St. (© **056/21033**); or **White's Chemist,** 5 High St. (© **056/21328**).

In an emergency, dial © **999.** The local **Garda Station** is on Dominic Street (© **056/22222**).

If you need to access the Internet, try the **Kilkenny Library** at 6 John's Quay (© **056/22021**), open Tuesday to Saturday 10:30am to 1pm; Tuesday to Friday 2 to 5pm; Tuesday and Wednesday 7 to 9pm. **Web-Talk,** Rose Inn Street (no phone), is an Internet cafe with ISDN Internet access; open Monday to Saturday

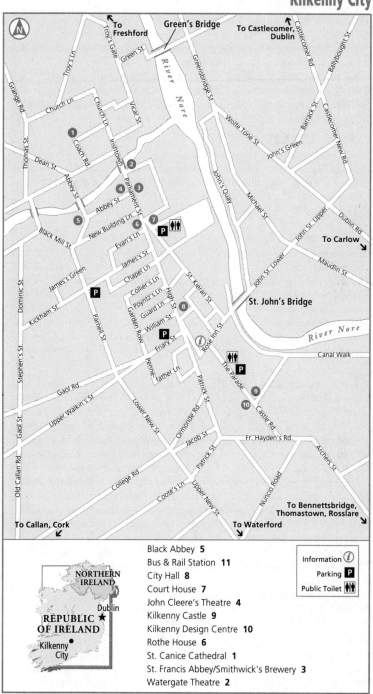

Black Abbey **5**
Bus & Rail Station **11**
City Hall **8**
Court House **7**
John Cleere's Theatre **4**
Kilkenny Castle **9**
Kilkenny Design Centre **10**
Rothe House **6**
St. Canice Cathedral **1**
St. Francis Abbey/Smithwick's Brewery **3**
Watergate Theatre **2**

Information 🛈
Parking P
Public Toilet 🚻

10am to 10pm and Sunday 2 to 8pm, for €1.50 ($1.35) every 10 minutes and €6.50 ($5.80) an hour.

For information on upcoming events and festivals, visit **www.kilkenny.ie**, **www.countykilkenny.com**, or **www.kilkennycraic.com**. When you're in town, check out the weekly *Kilkenny People* (**www.kilkennypeople.ie**), which also covers local happenings. The **Kilkenny District Post Office,** 73 High St. (✆ **056/21813**), is open Monday to Friday 9:30am to 5:30pm, Saturday 9:30am to 1pm.

EXPLORING KILKENNY CITY

Black Abbey   Nobody is sure why this Dominican church, founded in 1225, is named Black Abbey. It may be because the Dominicans wore black capes over their white habits, or perhaps because the Black Plague claimed the lives of eight priests in 1348. The Black Abbey's darkest days came in 1650, when Oliver Cromwell used it as a courthouse; by the time he left, all that remained were the walls. The abbey reopened in 1816 for public worship, a new nave was completed in 1866, and the entire building was fully restored in 1979. Among the elements remaining from the original abbey are an alabaster sculpture of the Holy Trinity that was carved about 1400, and a pre-Reformation statue of St. Dominic carved in Irish oak, which is believed to be the oldest such piece in the world. The huge Rosary Window, a stained-glass work of nearly 45 sq. m (500 sq. ft.) that represents the 15 mysteries of the rosary, was created in 1892 by Mayers of Munich.

Abbey St. (off Parliament St.), Kilkenny, county Kilkenny. ✆ 056/21279. Free admission; donations welcome. Apr–Sept Mon–Sat 7:30am–7pm, Sun 9am–7pm; Oct–Mar Mon–Sat 7:30am–5:30pm. No visits during worship.

Kilkenny Castle ⊛⊛⊛   Majestically standing beside the River Nore on the south side of the city, this landmark medieval castle—built in the 12th century and remodeled in Victorian times—was the principal seat of the Butler family, who were the earls, marquesses, and dukes of Ormonde. In 1967, the castle was given to the Irish government to be restored to period splendor as an enduring national monument. From its sturdy corner towers to its battlements, Kilkenny Castle retains the imposing lines of an authentic fortress and sets the tone for the entire city. The exquisitely restored interior includes a fine collection of Butler family portraits, some from as far back as the 14th century. The old castle kitchen operates as a tearoom in the summer. The 20-hectare (50-acre) grounds include a riverside walk, extensive gardens and parkland, and a well-equipped children's playground. Access to the main body of the castle is by guided tour only, prefaced by an informative video introduction to the rise, demise, and restoration of the splendid structure. This is a very busy site, so get there early to avoid waiting.

The Parade, Kilkenny, county Kilkenny. ✆ 056/21450. Admission €5 ($4.45) adults, €3.50 ($3.10) seniors, €2 ($1.80) children and students, €10 ($8.90) family. Daily Apr–May 10:30am–5pm; daily June–Sept 10am–7pm; Oct–Mar Tues–Sat 10:30am–12:45pm and 2–5pm, Sun 11am–12:45pm and 2–5pm.

Rothe House ⊛   This is a typical middle-class house from the Tudor period. Originally a merchant's home, built in 1594, it consists of three stone buildings divided by three cobbled courtyards. It has an arcaded shop front and a remarkable timber ceiling. Purchased in 1961 by the Kilkenny Archeological Society, it was restored and opened to the public in 1966. Inside are a museum of Kilkenny artifacts and a collection of period costumes. A family history research service for Kilkenny city and county has its offices here.

Parliament St., Kilkenny, county Kilkenny. © **056/22893.** Admission €2.50 ($2.25) adults, €2 ($1.80) seniors and students, €1.30 ($1.15) children. Jan–Mar and Nov–Dec Mon–Sat 1–5pm, Sun 3–5pm; Apr–June and Sept–Oct Mon–Sat 10:30am–5pm, Sun 3–5pm; July–Aug Mon–Sat 10am–6pm, Sun 3–5pm.

St. Canice Cathedral 🕭   At the northern end of the city, this is the church that gave Kilkenny its name. The St. Canice's Cathedral that stands today is a relative newcomer, built in the 13th century on the site of the 6th-century church of St. Canice. The cathedral has benefited from much restoration work in recent years. It is noteworthy for its rich interior timber and stone carvings, its colorful glasswork, and the structure itself. Its roof dates from 1863; its marble floor is composed of the four marbles of Ireland; and its massive round tower, 30m (100 ft.) high and 14m (46 ft.) in circumference, is believed to be a relic of the ancient church (although its original conical top has been replaced by a slightly domed roof). If you want to climb to the tip of the tower, it will cost you €1.30 ($1.15) and more calories than you can count. The steps that lead to the cathedral were constructed in 1614. The library contains 3,000 volumes from the 16th and 17th centuries.

Coach Rd., Irishtown, Kilkenny, county Kilkenny. © **056/64971.** Free admission; suggested donation €1.30 ($1.15) adults, €1 (90¢) students. Easter–Sept Mon–Sat 9am–1pm, daily 2–6pm; Oct–Easter Mon–Sat 10am–1pm, daily 2–4pm.

St. Francis Abbey Brewery 🕭   Established in 1710 by John Smithwick, the brewery occupies a site that originally belonged to the 12th-century Abbey of St. Francis. A popular local beer called Smithwick's (pronounced *Smit*-icks) is produced here, as are Budweiser and Land Kilkenny Irish beer. A video presentation and free samples are offered in the summer.

Parliament St., Kilkenny, county Kilkenny. © **056/21014.** Free admission. June–Aug Mon–Fri at 3pm.

ORGANIZED TOURS

Kilkenny Panoramic   This open-top, double-decker bus tour hits the highlights of medieval Kilkenny. It runs all day in a loop; so when you see something you want to explore, you just hop off. Or you can just stay on to get a feel for how the city is laid out. Further details are available from the Kilkenny Tourist Office.

Grayline Irish City Tours, Kilkenny, county Kilkenny. © **01/670-8822.** €8 ($7.10) adults, €4 ($3.55) children. Apr–Oct daily (hours change seasonally according to demand).

Tynan's Walking Tours   Local historian Pat Tynan leads you through the streets and lanes of medieval Kilkenny, providing historical facts and anecdotes along the way. Tours depart from the tourist office, Rose Inn Street.

10 Maple Dr., Kilkenny, county Kilkenny. © **056/65929.** Tickets €4 ($3.55) adults, €2.50 ($2.25) seniors and students, €1.30 ($1.15) children. Mar–Oct Mon–Sat 9:15 and 10:30am, 12:15, 1:30, 3, and 4:30pm; Sun 11am, 12:15, 2, and 3pm; Nov–Feb Tues–Sat 10:30am, 12:15, and 3pm.

SHOPPING

If you're an enthusiast of Irish crafts, Kilkenny City is perhaps the best shopping destination in Ireland. To assist visitors in discovering smaller workshops, the local tourist office provides a free **Craft Trail map** and information on local artisans.

Kilkenny shopping hours are normally Monday to Saturday 9am to 6pm; many shops stay open until 9pm on Thursday and Friday.

The newest major addition to the shopping scene is **Market Cross,** a new shopping center off High/Parliament Street (© **056/65534**), with its own multistory parking lot.

The Book Centre   This shop offers a fine selection of books about Kilkenny and the area, as well as books of Irish interest. Current bestsellers, maps, stationery, cards, and posters are sold. You can grab a quick daytime snack at the Pennefeather Cafe, upstairs. 10 High St., Kilkenny, county Kilkenny. © 056/62117.

Kilkenny Crystal   Established in 1969, this is the retail shop for Kilkenny's hand-cut crystal enterprise. It specializes in footed vases, rose bowls, bells, ring holders, wineglasses, carafes, and decanters. The factory is on Callan Road (© **056/25132**), 16km (10 miles) outside of town, and also welcomes visitors. 19 Rose Inn St., Kilkenny, county Kilkenny. © 056/21090.

Kilkenny Design Centre   This classy emporium is the shopper's reason for visiting Kilkenny. The 18th-century coach house and stables of Kilkenny Castle, with its arched gateway and a copper-domed clock tower, have been wonderfully converted into an assembly of shops and workshops for craftspeople from all over Ireland. The center and the smaller shops collected nearby provide a showcase for many of the country's top handcrafted products—jewelry, glassware, pottery, clothing, candles, linens, books, leather work, and furniture. An excellent coffee shop and restaurant is on the upstairs level of the Design Centre. Open Monday to Saturday from 9am to 6pm, Sunday from 10am to 6pm. Castle Yard, The Parade, Kilkenny, county Kilkenny. © 056/22118.

Liam Costigan   This alumnus of the Kilkenny Design Centre produces fine hand-crafted jewelry in this tiny studio-cum-shop. You can watch him work as you browse. Colliers Lane, off High St., Kilkenny, county Kilkenny. © 056/62408.

P. T. Murphy   The sign above the entrance says it all: watchmaker, jeweler, optician, and silversmith. This is Kilkenny's master jeweler. The shop is a very good source for Irish Claddagh and heraldic jewelry. 85 High St., Kilkenny, county Kilkenny. © 056/21127.

ATTRACTIONS FARTHER AFIELD IN COUNTY KILKENNY

Duiske Abbey 🅰   Duiske Abbey (1204) is a fine example of an early Cistercian abbey. It was suppressed in 1536, but its monks continued to occupy the site for many years. In 1774, the tower of the ruined abbey church collapsed. In 1813, the roof was replaced and religious services returned to the church, but the abbey didn't approach its former glory until the 1970s, when a group of local people mounted a major reconstruction effort. Now, with its fine lancet windows and a large effigy of a Norman Knight, the abbey is the pride of Graiguenamanagh. The adjacent visitor center has an exhibit of Christian art and artifacts. Graiguenamanagh, county Kilkenny. © **0503/24238**. Free admission; donations welcome. Daily 8am–7:30pm.

Dunmore Cave   Known as one of the darkest places in Ireland, this series of chambers, formed over millions of years, contains some of the finest calcite formations found in any Irish cave. Known to humans for many centuries, the cave may have been the site of a Viking massacre in A.D. 928. Exhibits at the visitor center tell the story of the cave. It's about 11km (7 miles) from Kilkenny City. Off Castlecomer rd. (N78), Ballyfoyle, county Kilkenny. © **056/67726**. Admission €2.50 ($2.25) adults, €2 ($1.80) seniors, €1.30 ($1.15) students and children, €6.50 ($5.80) family. Mid-Mar to mid-June and mid-Sept to Oct daily 10am–5pm; mid-June to mid-Sept daily 10am–7pm; winter Sat–Sun and holidays 10am–5pm.

Jerpoint Abbey 🅰🅰   About 18km (11 miles) southeast of Kilkenny, this is an outstanding Cistercian monastery, founded in the latter half of the 12th century. Preserved in a peaceful country setting, one of the abbey's highlights is a sculptured cloister arcade. There is also a splendid array of artifacts from medieval times—from unique stone carvings on 16th-century tombs and Romanesque architecture in the north nave of the abbey church. A tasteful interpretive center with an adjoining picnic garden makes this a perfect midday stop. Ms. Sheila Walsh is quite knowledgeable and articulate about the abbey, its art, and its history.

On the N9, 2.4km (1½ miles) south of Thomastown, Thomastown, county Kilkenny. ℂ 056/24623. Admission €2.50 ($2.25) adults, €2 ($1.80) seniors, €1.30 ($1.15) students and children, €6.50 ($5.80) family. Mar–May and mid-Sept to mid-Nov daily 10am–5pm; June to mid-Sept daily 9:30am–6:30pm; late Nov Wed–Mon 10am–4pm.

Kells Priory ★★★   With its encompassing fortification walls and towers, as well as complex monastic ruins, enfolded into the sloping south bank of the King's River in unspoiled countryside, Kells is the largest and one of the most spectacular monastic ruins complexes in Ireland. It's a wonderful oxymoron, an intact ruin, a feast for the eyes and the imagination. In 1193, Baron Geoffrey FitzRobert founded the priory and established a Norman-style town beside it. The current ruins date from the 13th to 15th centuries, while the burgess, where the livestock was kept, dates from the 15th to 16th centuries.

The priory is less than a half mile from the village of Kells. Be sure to find the new footbridge behind the priory, which takes you across the river and intersects a riverside walk leading to an old mill.

Kells, county Kilkenny. Off N76 or N10. From N76 south of Kilkenny, follow signs for R699/Callan and stay on R699 until you see signs for Kells.

Kilfane Glen and Waterfall   The main place of interest in this small garden is the glen, created in true picturesque style, with an artificial waterfall and a rustic cottage. The paths have been strategically placed to enhance one's sense of the place's grandeur. Views of cottage and waterfall have been carefully composed, and the sound of water creates a counterpoint to the visual delights of the garden. An installation by the American artist James Turrell, *Air Mass,* is open to visitors, although the time of day when it was intended to be seen—dusk—unfortunately doesn't correspond with the garden's hours in summer.

Thomastown, county Kilkenny. ℂ 056/24558. Admission €4 ($3.55) adults, €3 ($2.65) seniors, €2.50 ($2.25) students and children. Apr–June and Sept Sun 2–6pm; July–Aug daily 11am–6pm. Closed Oct–Mar. Other times by appointment.

SHOPPING
The Bridge Pottery   The studio of Mary O'Gorman and Mark Campden is perhaps the brightest and most cheerful pottery workshop in Ireland. The place is a dazzling kaleidoscope of Mediterranean colors and warm, earthen tones. Jugs, mugs, bowls, tiles, plates, even drawer handles—there's something here for every taste and budget, with prices from €4 to €400 ($3.55–$355). Open year-round Monday to Saturday from 10am to 5pm. Chapel St., Bennettsbridge, county Kilkenny. ℂ 056/27077. www.bridgepottery.com.

Jerpoint Glass Studio   Last stop on the "Craft Trail" from Kilkenny to Stoneyford, here you can witness the creation of Jerpoint Glass, which you've probably been admiring in shops all across Ireland. The lines of their goblets, candlesticks, pitchers, vases, and much more are simple and fluid, often highlighted or infused with swirls of color. You can watch the glass being blown and then gladly blow your own budget next door at the factory shop, which includes an entire room of discounted seconds. Open Monday to Friday from 9am to

---

⌢ *Fun Fact* **The City of Marble**

The Irish often refer to Kilkenny as Marble City. Fine black marble used to be quarried on the outskirts of town and up until 1929, some of the town's streets were paved in marble.

6pm and Saturday from 11am to 6pm. Signposted from the N9 just south of Jerpoint Abbey, Stoneyford, county Kilkenny. ℭ 056/24350.

Nicholas Mosse Pottery In a former flour mill on the banks of the River Nore, this is the studio of Nicholas Mosse, a potter since age 7. Using hydropower from the river to fire the kilns, he produces colorful country-style earthenware from Irish clay, including jugs, mugs, bowls, vases, and plates. All are hand-slipped and hand-turned, then decorated by hand with cut sponges and brushes. An on-site museum displays antique Irish earthenware made with this process. Pottery firsts and seconds are available. The shop expanded greatly in 1999 to included tasteful housewares. Open year-round Monday to Saturday from 9am to 6pm, July and August also Sunday from 1:30pm to 5pm. The Mill, Bennettsbridge, county Kilkenny. ℭ 056/27105. www.nicholasmosse.com.

Stoneware Jackson Here's yet another fine pottery studio located in Bennettsbridge, fast becoming a one-stop village for some of Ireland's most beautiful earthenware. All the pieces are handthrown and unique, featuring lovely two-color glazing and Celtic motifs. Open Monday to Saturday from 10am to 6pm. Bennettsbridge, county Kilkenny. ℭ 056/27175. www.stonewarejackson.com.

SPORTS & OUTDOOR PURSUITS

BICYCLING Rent a bike to ride around the outskirts of Kilkenny, especially along the shores of the River Nore. Consult the Kilkenny Tourist Office, or contact **J. J. Wall,** 88 Maudlin St. (ℭ 056/21236), or **Kilkenny Cycles,** Lower Michael St. (ℭ 056/64374). Rates average €10 ($8.90) per day. For complete 1- or 2-week cycling holidays in the Southeast, contact Don Smith at **Celtic Cycling,** Lorum Old Rectory, Bagenalstown, county Carlow (ℭ and fax **0503/ 75282;** www.celticcycling.com).

FISHING The **River Nore,** southeast of Kilkenny, is known for salmon and trout. For advice, permits, and supplies, visit the **Sports Shop,** 82 High St., Kilkenny (ℭ 056/21517), or the **Noreside Adventure Centre,** Thomastown, county Kilkenny (ℭ 056/27273).

GOLF The most prestigious course in the county is the **Mount Juliet Golf and Country Club,** Thomastown, county Kilkenny (ℭ 056/73000), 16km (10 miles) south of Kilkenny City. The 18-hole, par-72 championship course, designed by Jack Nicklaus, charges greens fees from €60 ($53) on weekdays, and from €70 ($62) on weekends. The price drops for Mount Juliet guests, and reduced early-bird and "sunsetter" rates are also available. Alternatively, try the 18-hole championship course at the **Kilkenny Golf Club,** Glendine, county Kilkenny (ℭ 056/65400), an inland par-71 layout 1.6km (1 mile) from the city. Greens fees are €54 ($48) on weekdays, €66 ($59) on weekends.

WHERE TO STAY
VERY EXPENSIVE

Mount Juliet Estate ✦✦✦ A private 3.2-km (2-mile) lane wends its way beside the pastures of the Ballylinch Stud Farm to this exclusive hotel, an

18th-century manor house set on a hillside overlooking the River Nore and surrounded by 600 walled hectares (1,500 acres) of formal gardens, lawns, woodlands, and parkland. Built in the 1760s, the house was named after the wife of the eighth Viscount Ikerrin, the first earl of Carrick. The McCalmont family, leaders in the Irish horse-breeding industry, later owned it. Mount Juliet is most famous for its Jack Nicklaus–designed golf course, and is also the home of Ireland's oldest cricket club. Unsurprisingly, Mount Juliet is hugely popular with the affluent sporting set, who appreciate the combination of luxurious accommodation and extensive leisure possibilities. Guests can choose between the manor house, the Hunters Yard, and the Rose Garden lodges. Rooms are individually and sumptuously decorated with mahogany antiques and designer fabrics, and public areas are full of period pieces and original art.

The Paddocks, a cluster of 12 self-catering luxury lodges lying between the 10th and 16th fairways, are also available. Each has a fully equipped kitchen, an elegantly furnished lounge/dining room, and en suite bedrooms. Weekly rentals start at 2,311€ ($2,093) for a two-bedroom lodge.

Thomastown, county Kilkenny. ⓒ 800/525-4800 in the U.S., or 056/73000. Fax 056/73019. www.mount juliet.ie. 56 units. €220–€400 ($196–$356) double; €400–€500 ($356–$445) suite; €420–€540 ($374–$481) 2-bedroom garden lodge. No service charge. AE, DC, MC, V. Amenities: 3 restaurants (international, bistro, Alpine); bar; indoor swimming pool; 18-hole golf course; tennis courts; badminton; squash; gym; sauna; Jacuzzi; riding stables; salmon and trout fishing on exclusive 2.4-km (1½-mile) stretch of River Nore; pheasant shooting; fox hunting; concierge; room service; valet and laundry service; nonsmoking rooms. *In room:* A/C, TV, minibar, hair dryer, garment press.

EXPENSIVE

Kilkenny Ormonde Hotel 𝘒𝘪𝘥𝘴 ★★★   When this chic new hotel opened in the heart of Kilkenny town a couple of years ago, it immediately became the city's premier guest address. Its dead-center location leaves it without scenic views, but its exceptional design and decor provide some striking scenery of their own. The emphasis is on bright open spaces with insightful use of natural materials—woods, stone, glass, metals, and quality textiles—to create tones and textures. The halls are wide and full of light, from windows and light shafts. Kilkenny is a particularly hectic town, and the soft, restful color palate of the guest rooms provides a welcome antidote to the day. More stress relief lies next door at the state-of-the-art leisure club, connected by an underground walkway to the hotel. Deluxe rooms are smartly done up in a warm, contemporary decor and are quite spacious, with a queen-sized bed and a single bed as well as every expected comfort and amenity, including plush bathrobes. The ascending order of executive rooms, superior rooms, and suites extends the size of the beds and of the guest quarters, culminating in the five-room presidential suite. Of all the options, the superior rooms offer the best value for money.

Ormonde St., Kilkenny, county Kilkenny. ⓒ 056/23900. Fax 056/23977. www.kilkennyormonde.com. 118 units. €170–€230 ($151–$205) double; €290–€380 ($258–$338) suite. Rates include full breakfast and VAT. Service charge at the discretion of guests. AE, DC, MC, V. Amenities: 3 restaurants (international, cafe, bistro); 2 bars; gym; indoor pool; kiddie pool; gym; Jacuzzi; sauna/steam room; tanning bed; children's playroom; condierge; room service; massage; laundry service; nonsmoking rooms; currency exchange. *In room:* TV, minibar, hair dryer, garment press.

MODERATE

Abbey House   This attractive period B&B alongside the Little Argile River was once part of the Jerpoint Abbey's estate. The front garden with sitting area is a perfect spot to relax, and the house's spacious sitting room, complete with piano and stacks of books, suits both quiet reading and a round of songs. Mrs.

Helen Blanchfield has done a fine job of maintaining the period character of her Georgian (ca. 1750) home. She serves guests complimentary tea and scones on arrival. The comfortable, pleasant rooms vary in size; all have firm, orthopedic beds. The nearby town of Thomastown and the grand abbey across the way are well worth a good look, and the area is known for its crafts.

Thomastown, county Kilkenny. On the N9, directly across from Jerpoint Abbey. ⓒ **056/24166.** Fax 056/ 24192. 6 units. €90–€130 ($80–$116) double. Rates include full Irish breakfast and service charge. AE, MC, V. Closed Dec 21–30. **Amenities:** Sitting room. *In room:* TV on request, tea/coffeemaker.

Berryhill ⭐⭐ The ivy-clad gables of this whimsical country house overlook the River Nore, just outside the plucked-from-a-storybook village of Inistioge. George and Belinda Dyer have created a uniquely pleasant retreat of this rambling house, built by the Dyer family in 1780. The three spacious, immensely comfortable bedrooms are attached to a private sitting room, and each is decorated with a particular, unmistakable animal theme. The resulting feeling is good-natured fun rather than schlock. The Elephant Room's distinctive feature is its bathroom, where a red bathtub and small sofa sit before a fireplace, so you can bathe by firelight; the sole drawback here is the ground-floor location, adjacent to the car park. In the Frog Room (on the second floor), an abundance of ivy makes a private nook of the veranda (there's a great view of the river). Lastly, there's the Pig Suite, on the western side of the house, with views toward the river. There are walks on the hill behind the house, and a path provides a short walking route to Inistioge village. Breakfast here is a memorable occasion, and options include fresh trout from the river.

Inistioge, county Kilkenny. ⓒ and fax **056/58434.** www.berrryhillhouse.com. 3 units. €120 ($107) double. Rates include full breakfast. MC, V. Closed Nov–Apr. **Amenities:** Nonsmoking rooms. *In room:* TV.

Butler House ⭐ Built in 1770 by the 16th earl of Ormonde as an integral part of Kilkenny Castle, this elegant building with a series of conical rooftops has a front door facing busy Patrick Street and a backyard overlooking lovely, secluded 17th-century–style gardens, the Kilkenny Castle stables, and the Kilkenny Design Centre. Converted into a guesthouse in the late 1980s, it has a sweeping staircase, marble fireplaces, and guest rooms of various sizes with an eclectic mix of contemporary and period furnishings.

16 Patrick St., Kilkenny, county Kilkenny. ⓒ **056/65707.** Fax 056/65626. www.butler.ie. 13 units. €114–€240 ($101–$214) double; €250 ($223) suite. No service charge. Rates include full breakfast. AE, DC, MC, V. **Amenities:** Restaurant (international); bar; babysitting. *In room:* TV/VCR, tea/coffeemaker, hair dryer.

Hotel Kilkenny ⭐ *Value* In a residential neighborhood on the southwest edge of the city, this contemporary hotel is one of the best-value finds in the city. The whole place has been recently refurbished, and even the standard double rooms are huge. Guest rooms are decked out in a smart chocolate-and-cream palette and are close to the excellent leisure center.

College Rd., Kilkenny, county Kilkenny. ⓒ **056/62000.** Fax 056/65984. www.griffingroup.ie. 103 units. €114–€160 ($101–$142) double. No service charge. Rates include full breakfast. AE, MC, V. **Amenities:** Restaurant (international); bar; indoor swimming pool; 2 tennis courts; gym; sauna; hot tub; babysitting; solarium. *In room:* TV, hair dryer.

Lacken House Restaurant and Guesthouse ⭐⭐ A husband and wife duo, Trevor Toner and Jackie Kennedy, has made this handsome yellow Victorian home into one of the area's best places to stay and eat. The real pull here is the award-winning restaurant (see listing below), and the chance to just flop upstairs to bed after a great meal and, perhaps, an after-dinner drink in the bar.

The guest rooms are small but comfortable and brightly furnished—some are nonsmoking and all have orthopedic beds. In the morning, breakfasts are copious and delicious. Lacken is on its own grounds with gardens, in the northeast corner of the city, about 10 minutes' walking distance from High Street and within a long block of the rail and bus station.

Dublin Rd., Kilkenny, county Kilkenny. ℂ 056/61085. Fax 056/62435. www.lackenhouse.ie. 9 units. €100 ($89) double. No service charge. Rates include full breakfast. MC, V. **Amenities:** Restaurant (international); bar; limited room service; nonsmoking rooms. *In room:* TV, tea/coffeemaker.

The Newpark Hotel 🐦   This lovely hotel about a mile north of the city center is part of the Best Western chain. Set amid 20 hectares (50 acres) of gardens and parkland, it was opened as a small Victorian-style country hotel more than 35 years ago, and it has grown in size and gained in reputation ever since. The rooms are done up in light woods with colorful Irish textiles, and the recently refurbished public areas have a stylish, contemporary flair.

Castlecomer Rd., Kilkenny, county Kilkenny. ℂ 800/528-1234 in the U.S., or 056/22122. Fax 056/61111. www.newparkhotel.com. 111 units. €114–€160 ($101–$142) double. No service charge. DC, MC, V. **Amenities:** Indoor swimming pool; 2 tennis courts; gym; Jacuzzi; sauna/steam room; solarium. *In room:* TV, hair dryer.

INEXPENSIVE

Cullintra House   A slightly bohemian atmosphere is tangible at this quaint country farmhouse, presided over by Patricia Cantlon, an accomplished artist and cook, and her several cats. The 92-hectare (230-acre) farm is a sanctuary for birds and all sorts of animals. As you would expect in a 200-year-old, ivy-clad farmhouse, each rustic guest room is charming and unique. Patricia's lovely art studio and conservatory has tea-making facilities and a piano. Morning brings a relaxed breakfast schedule (served 9am–noon), and perhaps a walk to Mount Brandon or the nearby *cairn* (prehistoric burial mound); a trail departs from the back gate. Dinner—costing €24 ($21)—begins around 9pm, announced by the sound of a gong, and guests sometimes don't depart from the candlelit dining room until the wee hours. Mrs. Cantlon is an enthusiastic hostess, and clearly enjoys entertaining her guests and making them feel at home. This is a good bet if you like good food, candlelight, and cats.

The Rower, Inistioge, county Kilkenny. On R700, 9.7km (6 miles) from New Ross. ℂ 051/423614. 6 units, 3 with bathroom. €60–€78 ($53–$69) double. No service charge. Rates include full breakfast. No credit cards. **Amenities:** Conservatory.

SELF-CATERING

Clomantagh Castle *Finds* 🐦🐦   Yet another one-of-a-kind rental property from the nonprofit Irish Landmark Trust, this huge, rambling farmhouse sleeps 10 and is ideal for a large family or group. The complex of buildings at Clomantagh includes the ruins of a 12th-century church and an early-15th-century crenellated tower house, which is attached to an 18th-century farmhouse. There are four large double bedrooms in the farmhouse, with a connecting staircase leading to a fifth wonderfully medieval double bedroom in the tower itself. The decor throughout the house is pleasingly old-fashioned and rustic, with many fine period pieces and brass beds. There are several reception rooms, but the house's beating heart is the enormous, old-fashioned country kitchen with a flagstone floor, timbered ceiling, and Stanley range. Like all Irish Landmark Trust properties, Clomantagh Castle has no TV, but there is a well-equipped kitchen with a dishwasher and laundry facilities. Although the setting is rural, Kilkenny City is only about 20 minutes away by car.

Freshford, county Kilkenny. Contact the Irish Landmark Trust: ℂ **01/670-4733.** Fax 01/670-4887. landmark@ iol.ie. €500 ($445) for 4 nights in low season, sliding up to €1,500 ($1,335) per week in high season. *In room:* Kitchen, dishwasher, washing machine.

WHERE TO DINE
EXPENSIVE

Lacken House ★★ INTERNATIONAL   A stately Victorian house is the setting for this restaurant, on the northeast edge of the city. Chef Nicola O'Brien runs the show, creating wonderful meals with local produce. The menu changes daily but starters might include spring onion-and-red cheddar soup or a delicious ballotine of salmon on a bed of cucumber ribbons with homemade chive dressing. For your main course, consider the roast leg of lamb in tangy jus; breast of chicken with blue cheese and bacon wrapped in phyllo pastry; or the Oriental pan-fried salmon in tomato vinaigrette. Roast crispy duckling in orange-and-star anise sauce is a house specialty.

Dublin Rd., Kilkenny, county Kilkenny. ℂ **056/61085.** Reservations required. Fixed-price dinner €33 ($30). MC, V. Tues–Sat 7–10:30pm.

MODERATE

Café Sol ★★ SOUTHERN AMERICAN/MEDITERRANEAN   The Café Sol is just what the name implies: A friendly cafe of bright colors with light streaming in through its floor-to-ceiling windows, with dishes that evoke the feeling of warm sunshine. Its diminutive size and unassuming informality are, however, largely a ruse—chef Gail Johnson runs one of the most appealing eateries in Ireland. It's open all day, starting with homemade scones and biscuits at breakfast time. A few hours later, the lunch menu consists of staple comfort foods for busy Kilkenny shoppers and business folk—mainly homemade soups, salads, sandwiches, and hot plates. But the place really comes into its own at dinnertime, when the menu comes alive with zingier, zestier options, like Louisiana crab cakes with tomato salsa; chicken and mozzarella wrapped in phyllo; salade Savoyarde; fresh pasta with sun-dried tomatoes, chile peppers, and olives; and steamed mussels with wine and garlic.

6 William St. (opposite the Town Hall), Kilkenny, county Kilkenny. ℂ **056/64987.** Reservations recommended for dinner. Lunch main courses €8–€13 ($7.10–$12); dinner main courses €10–€19 ($8.90–$17). MC, V. Mon–Sat 10am–5:30pm; Wed–Sat 7–10pm.

The Maltings CONTINENTAL   Overlooking the River Nore about 16km (10 miles) southeast of Kilkenny City, this much-loved restaurant offers simple, well-prepared food in an idyllic, romantic county-house setting. The menu includes chicken Kiev, roast half duck, filet steak, and grilled salmon. No provisions are made for nonsmokers other than prohibiting pipes and cigars.

Bridge House, Inistioge, county Kilkenny. ℂ **056/58484.** Reservations required. Early-bird (6–8:30pm) fixed-price menu €10–€16 ($8.90–$14). Main courses €13–€20 ($12–$19). MC, V. Tues–Sun noon–3pm and 7–9:30pm.

The Motte ★ MODERN CONTINENTAL   In both cuisine and ambience, The Motte is fresh and exuberant. The intimate dining room simmers with gilt and candlelight, with each table crowned by a bouquet of Irish field flowers. Clearly, the chef loves experimenting with the cornucopia of local ingredients like fresh trout and farmhouse cheeses. Some of the most unlikely combinations of flavors really worked beautifully. Though it looks like a stretch on paper, the profiteroles filled with Cashel Blue cheese and laced with chile chocolate sauce are airy pastry pockets that melt away into a sharp bite of cheese chased by a smooth thread of slightly bitter chocolate—simply delicious.

Main courses range from sirloin in burgundy butter sauce to a selection of fish. Filets of plaice arrive with a delicately flavored lemon butter, cooked to tongue-tantalizing perfection. Sorbet precedes an excellent choice of diet-busting desserts, like the velvety-rich chocolate cardamom truffle cake, which is served with custard and a drizzle of raspberry sauce. Final orders are taken at 9:30pm, although diners often remain until late in the evening; just book a table well in advance and surrender your evening to conversation and good food.

Plas Newydd Lodge, Inistioge, county Kilkenny. (Ⓒ **056/58655**. Reservations recommended. 3-course set menu €32 ($28). MC, V. Tues–Sat 7–9:30pm.

Parliament House Restaurant CONTINENTAL Overlooking busy Parliament Street, this upstairs restaurant has a plush, old-style, Edwardian decor, with high ceilings, chandeliers, and floral wallpaper. The menu offers a fine selection of local beef, veal, and lamb, as well as tasty combination dishes, such as prawns and mussels with hazelnuts; Nore salmon in pastry with lobster sauce; duckling in wine and garlic butter; and chicken Parliament (stuffed with seafood mousse and lobster sauce).

Parliament St., Kilkenny, county Kilkenny. (Ⓒ **056/63666**. Reservations recommended. Main courses €15–€23 ($13–$20). AE, MC, V. Daily noon–3pm and 6–10:30pm.

INEXPENSIVE

Kilkenny Design Restaurant CAFETERIA Above the Kilkenny Design shop, this spacious self-service restaurant is a classy place to eat, with white-washed walls, circular windows, beamed ceilings, framed art prints, and fresh, delicious food. The ever-changing menu often includes local salmon, chicken and ham platters, salads, and homemade soups. The pastries and breads offer some unique choices, such as cheese and garlic scones.

The Parade, Kilkenny, county Kilkenny. (Ⓒ **056/22118**. Reservations not accepted. All items €3–11 ($2.65–$10). AE, DC, MC, V. Year-round Mon–Sat 9am–5pm; Sun 10am–5pm.

The Water Garden TEAROOM Just outside Thomastown on the road to Kilkenny, you'll find this tearoom and small garden, operated by a local Camphill community for mentally and physically disabled children and adults. The cafe serves lunch, tea, and baked goods; meals are prepared with organic vegetables and meats raised on the community farm. Lunches include sandwiches made with home-baked bread, soups, and a vegetable or meat paté. The garden (admission €1.30/$1.15 adults, €.65/60¢ children) takes the form of a stroll along a small stream, with numerous aquatic plants on display; there's also a garden shop.

Thomastown, county Kilkenny. (Ⓒ **056/24690**. Lunch €5–€8 ($4.45–$7.10). No credit cards. Tues–Fri 10am–5pm; Sun 12:30–5pm. Closed Sun from Christmas to Easter.

KILKENNY AFTER DARK

To find out what's going on around town, visit **www.kilkennycraic.com** or pick up a copy of the local weekly paper *Kilkenny People*. Kilkenny is home to one of Ireland's newest theaters (opened in 1993), the **Watergate Theatre,** Parliament Street (Ⓒ **056/61674**). The 328-seat showplace presents both local talent and visiting professional troupes performing a variety of classic and contemporary plays, concerts, opera, ballet, one-person shows, and choral evenings. Ticket prices average €5 to €14 ($4.45–$13). Most evening shows start at 8 or 8:30pm, matinees at 2 or 3pm.

Across the street is **John Cleere's,** 28 Parliament St. (Ⓒ **056/62573**), a small pub theater that presents a variety of local productions, including the *Cat Laughs* comedy fest. It is also a venue for the Kilkenny Arts Week. Tickets average €4 to €8 ($3.55–$7.10), and most shows start at 8:15 or 9:30pm.

PUBS

Caislean Ui Cuain (The Castle Inn) A striking facade with a mural of old Kilkenny welcomes guests to this pub, founded in 1734 as a stagecoach inn. The interior is a pub-lover's dream, with dark wood furnishings, globe-style lights, a paneled ceiling, and local memorabilia. Traditional music sessions—both scheduled and spontaneous—often start up, and many patrons and staff speak Irish. The Parade, Kilkenny, county Kilkenny. © 056/65406.

Kyteler's Inn This inn has served up spirits for over 650 years. The ground floor restaurant and bar is done up in cozy, contemporary pine. But if you are in a medieval mood, head downstairs to the cellar, where a deep-set window overlooks Kieran's Well, which predates the inn itself, and the original stone pillars still reach from floor to ceiling. This was once the home of Dame Alice Kyteler, a colorful character who made the tavern into a den of merrymaking. Between all the joviality, however, she laid four husbands to rest in the Kilkenny graveyard. She was tried for being a witch, and condemned to burn at the stake. Alice escaped and was never heard from again, but her maid wasn't so lucky and was burned. You may feel Alice's presence in the cellar, thanks to a life-size doll of her overseeing the proceedings. St. Kieran St., Kilkenny, county Kilkenny. © 056/21064.

Eamon Langton's No self-respecting Irishman—or anyone, for that matter— would pass through Kilkenny without stopping for a pint in this frequent "Pub of the Year" winner. In fact, rival publicans joke that Eamon (pronounced *Ay-mun*) Langton has won so many awards that he should close shop just to give someone else a chance. The place has everything you look for in a pub: Low ceilings so you don't feel like you're conversing in a warehouse, a lovely fireplace with a carved wooden mantelpiece, the smell of polished wood everywhere, etched mirrors, stained-glass windows, brass globe lamps, and burgundy leather banquettes. On summer days, everyone heads to "the back room"—actually a lush, plant-filled conservatory with Gothic-style windows and a garden area backed by the old city walls. Langton's has won plaudits for its pub grub, too, so bring your appetite. 69 John St., Kilkenny, county Kilkenny. © 056/65133.

Marble City Bar One of the best shop-front facades in Ireland belongs to this pub in the middle of the city. Its exterior is a showcase of carved wood, wrought iron, polished brass, and globe lamps, with flower boxes overhead—and the interior is equally inviting. Even if you don't stop for a drink here, you'll certainly want to take a picture. 66 High St., Kilkenny, county Kilkenny. © 056/62091.

Tynan's Bridge House *(Finds* Ask anyone who knows Kilkenny to tell you about his all-time favorite pub, and you're guaranteed to hear a lot of votes for this one. It stands along the River Nore next to St. John's Bridge. Before a man named Tynan turned it into a pub in 1919, this 225-year-old building was used to house a pharmacy and a grocery shop. Behind the horseshoe-shaped marble-top bar, side drawers marked "cloves," "almonds," "mace," "citron," and "sago" are vestiges from these earlier incarnations, as is the 200-year-old scale with its little set of cup weights. The place is lit by nostalgic globe gas lamps, and adorned everywhere with shiny brass fixtures, silver tankards, shelves holding shaving mugs, old teapots, and even a tattered copy of Chaucer's *Canterbury Tales* for rainy days. An intricate old clock chimes the hour. 2 Horseleap Slip, St. John's Bridge, Kilkenny, county Kilkenny. © 056/21291.

7

Cork: The Rebel City

Cork City (pop. 240,000, including environs) may be far smaller than Dublin, but to a Corkman there isn't even the remotest possibility for comparison; Cork is simply superior. Any native will tell you that his beloved Cork provides all the conveniences of a city but retains its small town, leisurely pace of life. And don't let the size mislead you. There's a thriving arts culture in Cork, where you'll find the **Crawford Art Gallery,** the most important gallery outside the capital, and the refurbished **Cork Opera House,** packing sell-out seasons.

But Cork's real draw is its fabulous dining scene. It is a foodie's paradise, with more good restaurants per capita than anywhere else in Ireland. (Now that we mention it, that's true for the entire county of Cork. Nearby Kinsale has its own gourmet food festival; in West Cork, seemingly every little hamlet possesses a wonderful little place to dine; and East Cork boasts the internationally-acclaimed Ballymaloe House cooking school.)

In the Rebel City, check out the covered **Old English Market** and sample the fare, but leave room for a superb meal in one of the city's many top-flight restaurants. Though you can find Guinness drinkers everywhere in Ireland, many would argue that a true Corkonian will only drink Murphy's or Beamish, the two locally brewed stouts. (Walk into any pub and order a "home and away" and you'll be presented with a pint of Murphy's and one of Guinness.)

The city was founded by St. Finbarr in the 6th century on a swampy estuary of the River Lee. He called it Corcaigh, which means "marsh" in Irish. The Lee is near and dear to every Corkonian's heart. If you're in a pub at closing time, you might hear someone's rendition of the Cork anthem, "The Banks of My Own Lovely Lee," also known as "Da Banks." (For the full lyrics, search Celtic Lyrics at **http://celtic-lyrics.com**).

The city is often called "Rebel Cork" because it was a center of the 19th-century Fenian movement and played an active part in the Irish struggle for independence. But today, Cork is a busy commercial hub for the south of Ireland. Be warned that the traffic moves fast, and the locals talk even faster in their lovely singsong accent. They are also known for their particularly dry sense of humor. Cork slang is so rich, and so particular to Cork, that it makes even other Irish feel out of the loop. If you want to keep up with the locals, pick up *A Dictionary of Cork Slang* by Sean Beecher, available in all Cork bookshops. While it's said that kissing the Blarney Stone (at nearby **Blarney Castle**) gives Corkonians their gift of the gab, in truth, most Corkonians have never kissed it. So, yes, it's touristy. But sometimes you just gotta do those touristy things.

1 Orientation

Cork is 258km (160 miles) SW of Dublin, 206km (128 miles) SE of Galway, 101km (63 miles) S of Limerick, 122km (76 miles) S of Shannon Airport, 126km (78 miles) W of Waterford, and 87km (54 miles) E of Killarney

ARRIVING

GETTING THERE **Aer Lingus** (© 021/432-7155; www.aerlingus.ie) flights from Dublin regularly serve Cork Airport, Kinsale Road (© 021/ 313131; www.cork-airport.com), 13km (8 miles) south of the city. In addition, there are direct flights from Amsterdam, Bristol, Exeter, Glasgow, Guernsey, Isle of Mann, London, Manchester, Paris, Plymouth, and Rennes. Cork Airport is in the process of dramatically expanding its services, and it may eventually handle transatlantic flights.

Bus Eireann (© 021/450-8188; www.buseireann.ie) provides bus service from the airport to Parnell Place Bus Station in the city center; the fare is €3.20 ($2.85) one way, €4.50 ($4) round-trip. The trip takes between 18 and 24 minutes, depending on time of day. Buses from all parts of Ireland arrive at **Bus Eireann's Passenger Depot,** Parnell Place, in the downtown area, 3 blocks from Patrick Street.

Iarnrod Eireann/Irish Rail (toll-free © 1850/366222 or 01/836-6222; www.irishrail.ie) operates the train services in Ireland. Trains from Dublin, Limerick, and other parts of Ireland arrive at **Kent Station,** Lower Glanmire Road, Cork (© 021/450-4777), on the city's eastern edge

Car ferry routes into Cork from Britain include service from Swansea on **Swansea/Cork Ferries** (© 021/427-1166; www.swansea-cork.ie), and from Roscoff on **Brittany Ferries** (© 021/427-7801; www.brittany-ferries.com). All ferries arrive at Cork's Ringaskiddy Ferryport.

If you're approaching Cork from the east, take the Carrigaloe-Glenbrook ferry from Cobh across Cork Harbour. This ferry can save you an hour's driving time on the rim of Cork Harbour, and you'll bypass Cork City traffic. The ferry runs from 7:15am to 12:30am. Cars cost €2.50 ($2.25) one way, €4 ($3.55) round-trip, plus €.65 (60¢) for each additional passenger. For cyclists and pedestrians, the fare is €.75 (65¢) one way, €1.30 ($1.15) round-trip. The trip lasts less than 5 minutes. For more information, contact Cross River Ferries Ltd., Westland House, Rushbrooke, Cobh (© 021/481-1485).

Many main national roads lead into Cork, including N8 from Dublin, N25 from Waterford, N20 from Limerick, N22 from Killarney, and N71 from West Cork.

VISITOR INFORMATION

For brochures, maps, and other information, visit the **Cork Tourist Office,** Tourist House, 42 Grand Parade, Cork (© 021/427-3251). Its hours are October to May, Monday to Saturday 9:15am to 1pm and 2:15 to 5:30pm; June and September, Monday to Saturday 9am to 6pm; July and August, Monday to Saturday 9am to 7pm and Sunday 10am to 5pm. For online information, consult **Local Cork** (http://cork.local.ie) or the **Cork Guide** (www.cork-guide.ie). For accommodation in Cork, consult our recommendations (below), then try www.book-a-hotel-in-cork.com.

CITY LAYOUT

There are lots of bridges in Cork, which can be quite confusing. Before you start thinking you're going around in circles, realize that central Cork is actually on

Cork City

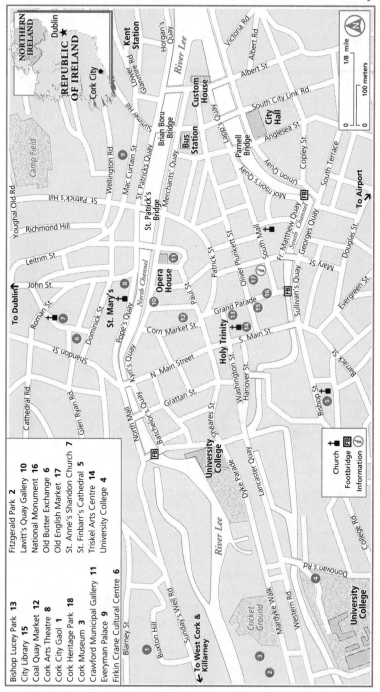

Bishop Lucey Park **13**
City Library **15**
Coal Quay Market **12**
Cork Arts Theatre **8**
Cork City Gaol **1**
Cork Heritage Park **18**
Cork Museum **3**
Crawford Municipal Gallery **11**
Everyman Palace **9**
Firkin Crane Cultural Centre **6**

Fitzgerald Park **2**
Lavitt's Quay Gallery **10**
National Monument **16**
Old Butter Exchange **6**
Old English Market **17**
St. Anne's Shandon Church **7**
St. Finbarr's Cathedral **5**
Triskel Arts Centre **14**
University College **4**

an island which lies between two limbs of the River Lee. The city is divided into three sections:

SOUTH BANK   South of the River Lee, South Bank encompasses the grounds of St. Finbarr's Cathedral, the site of St. Finbarr's 6th-century monastery, and also includes 17th-century city walls, the remains of Elizabeth Fort, City Hall, built in 1936, and Cork's chief administrative center.

FLAT OF THE CITY   This is the downtown core, surrounded on the north and south by channels of the River Lee. This area includes the **South Mall,** a wide tree-lined street with mostly Georgian architecture and a row of banks, insurance companies, and legal offices; the **Grand Parade,** a spacious thoroughfare that blends 18th-century bow-fronted houses and the remains of the old city walls with modern offices and shops; and a welcome patch of greenery, the **Bishop Lucey Park,** a fairly new (1986) addition to the cityscape.

Extending from the northern tip of the Grand Parade is the city's main thoroughfare, **St. Patrick Street.** Referred to simply as Patrick Street by Corkonians, this broad avenue was formed in 1789 by filling in an open channel in the river. It is primarily a street for shopping, but it is also a place for folks to stroll, be seen, and greet friends. (In Cork slang, hanging out on Patrick Street is "doing a Pana"). Patrick Street is also the site of one of the city's best-known meeting places: the statue of 19th-century priest Fr. Theobald Matthew, a crusader against drink who is fondly called the "apostle of temperance." The statue stands at the point where Patrick Street reaches St. Patrick's Bridge and is the city's central point of reference.

NORTH BANK   St. Patrick's Bridge (or Patrick's Bridge), opened in 1859, leads over the river to the north side of the city, a hilly, terraced section where Patrick Street becomes **St. Patrick's Hill.** And is it ever a hill, with an incline so steep that it is nearly San Franciscan. If you climb the stepped sidewalks of St. Patrick's Hill, you will be rewarded with a sweeping view of the Cork skyline.

East of St. Patrick's Hill is **MacCurtain Street,** a commercial thoroughfare that runs east, leading to Summerhill Road and up into the Cork hills to the residential districts of St. Luke's and Montenotte. West of St. Patrick's Hill is one of the city's oldest neighborhoods, **St. Ann's Shandon Church,** and the city's original Butter Market building.

2 Getting Around

BY PUBLIC TRANSPORTATION   **Bus Eireann** operates bus service from Parnell Place Bus Station (✆ 021/450-8188; www.buseireann.ie) to all parts of the city and its suburbs, including Blarney and Kinsale. The flat fare is €.90 (80¢). Buses run frequently from 7am to 11pm Monday to Saturday, with slightly shorter hours on Sunday.

BY TAXI   Taxis are readily available throughout Cork. The main taxi ranks are along St. Patrick's Street, along the South Mall, and outside major hotels. To call for a taxi, try **ABC Cabs** (✆ 021/496-1961), **Cork Taxi Co-Op** (✆ 021/427-2222) or **Shandon Cabs** (✆ 021/450-2255).

BY CAR   It's best to park and explore the city on foot or by public transport. Unless your hotel has a parking lot, it can be a hassle finding street parking. If you have to park in public areas, it costs €.65 (60¢) per hour, whether you park in one of the city's two multistory parking lots, at Lavitt's Quay and Merchant's Quay, or on the street, where the disc system is in use. Parking discs, sold singly or in books of 10 for €6.50 ($5.80), are available at many shops and newsstands. There are also at least a dozen ground-level parking lots throughout the city.

Many international car-rental firms maintain rental desks at Cork Airport, including **Alamo** (© 021/431-8636), **Budget** (© 021/431-4000), **Hertz** (© 021/496-5849), **National** (© 021/431-8623), and **Murray's Europcar** (© 021/491-7300). **Avis** also has a large depot in Cork City at Emmet Place (© 021/428-1111).

ON FOOT Because of the problem finding street parking, the best way to see Cork is on foot, but don't try to do it all in a single day. The South Bank and the central part, or flat, of the city can easily take a day to explore; save the Cork Hills and the North Bank for another day. You might want to follow the sign-posted Tourist Trail to guide you to all the major sights.

FAST FACTS: Cork City

Drugstores Try **Duffy's Dispensing Chemists,** 96 Patrick St. (© 021/427-2566); **Hayes Conyngham and Robinson,** Wilton Shopping Centre (© 021/454-6500); or **Murphy's Pharmacy,** 48 N. Main St. (© 021/427-4121).

Emergencies For emergencies, dial © 999.

Gay & Lesbian Resources For information and aid, call the **Lesbian and Gay Resource Group and Community Centre,** 8 S. Main St. (© 021/427-8470). The **Gay Information** line (© 021/427-1087) is open Wednesday 7 to 9pm and Saturday 3 to 5pm. The **Lesbian Line** (also © 021/427-1087) is open Thursday 8 to 10pm.

Hospitals Try **Cork University Hospital,** Wilton Road (© 021/454-6400); **Bon Secours Hospital,** College Road (© 021/454-2807); or **City General Hospital,** Infirmary Road (© 021/431-1656).

Information See "Visitor Information," under "Orientation," above.

Internet Access **Cork Central Library,** 57 Grand Parade (© 021/427-7110), has a bank of public Internet workstations available. You can also log on at the **Cyber Café, Internet Center,** Thompson House, MacCurtain Street (© 021/450-3511).

Library **Cork Central Library,** 57 Grand Parade (© 021/427-7110), is the best stocked public library in Cork.

Police The local Garda Headquarters is on Barrack Street (© 021/431-6020).

Post Office The **General Post Office,** on Oliver Plunkett Street (© 021/427-2000), is open Monday to Saturday 9am to 5:30pm.

3 Where to Stay

VERY EXPENSIVE

Hayfield Manor Hotel ★★ This is Cork's only true luxury hotel, with sky-high tariffs to prove it. Spend just 1 night and you'll note how its designers thought of everything. Despite its period appearance and feel, Hayfield Manor was built in 1996 and expanded in 1999. The entire hotel is done with a warm palette of apricots and ochres, including the magnificent foyer with marble columns and grand mahogany staircase. Guest rooms are especially spacious and evoke an elegant private manor home, with large windows, exquisite furnishings, and bright marble bathrooms. This place provides the level of comfort and attention to detail you expect from one of Ireland's great manor home hotels.

Although less than a mile from the city center and beside Cork's University College, Hayfield Manor is genuinely secluded. Its modest 1.2 hectares (3 acres) of mature trees, orchard, and formal garden give the feeling of a grand estate, providing lovely views from virtually every window. The fully equipped conservatory/leisure center—reserved exclusively for hotel guests—is singularly inviting.

Perrott Ave., College Rd., Cork, county Cork. ✆ 021/431-5600. Fax 021/431-6839. www.hayfieldmanor.ie. U.S. reservations through Small Luxury Hotels of the World, ✆ 800/525-4800. 87 units. €343 ($305) double; €380 ($338) junior suite; €535 ($476) executive suite; €890 ($792) master suite. Rates include full Irish breakfast and service charge. AE, DC, MC, V. Free parking. **Amenities:** Restaurant (Continental); bar; drawing room; indoor swimming pool; health club; Jacuzzi; sauna; concierge; health and beauty treatments; room service; babysitting; laundry service. *In room:* A/C, TV, hair dryer, garment press.

EXPENSIVE

The Imperial Hotel 🌟🌟   This vintage four-story hotel is a local landmark and the sentimental favorite in Cork. Since opening in 1845, the hotel has played host to a number of renowned figures including Sir Walter Scott, William Makepeace Thackeray, Charles Dickens, and the composer Franz Liszt. Michael Collins, who negotiated the Free State Treaty in 1921, spent his last night in the hotel. With Waterford crystal chandeliers, marble floors, and brass fittings, the reception area and public rooms exude an aura of 19th-century grandeur. The guest rooms recently received an injection of much-needed attention, and are extremely attractive with a warm, golden backdrop to complement dark woods, antique fixtures, and half-tester beds. The executive bedrooms have DVD players, dataports, minibars, and fax machines. Of the three hotels in this price range, the Imperial has the best location, right in the city center of Cork.

South Mall, Cork, county Cork. ✆ 800/44-UTELL in the U.S., or 021/427-4040. Fax 021/427-5375. www.flynn hotels.com/imperial. 88 units. €190 ($169) double. Rates include full breakfast and service charge. AE, MC, V. Street parking only. **Amenities:** 2 restaurants (international, brasserie); 2 bars; concierge; room service; laundry service. *In room:* TV, radio, tea/coffeemaker, iron, garment press, voice mail.

Jurys Cork Hotel 🌟   On the western edge of town, Jurys is well positioned, next to University College of Cork and along the banks of the River Lee, yet just a 5-minute walk from the city center. The modern two-story multiwinged structure was refurbished just a few years ago. The light-filled public areas include a skylit atrium, and there's a wall-length mural of Cork characters in the lobby. Guest rooms are furnished in traditional dark woods with designer fabrics and have views of either the central courtyard gardens or the river and city. Like most Jurys hotels, this one has the look and feel of a business person's hotel.

Western rd. (N22), Cork, county Cork. ✆ 800/44-UTELL in the U.S., or 021/427-6622. Fax 021/427-4477. www.jurys.com. 188 units. €197–€242 ($175–$215) double. Rates include full breakfast and service charge. AE, DC, MC, V. Free parking. **Amenities:** Restaurant (international); 2 bars; indoor-outdoor swimming pool; squash court; exercise room; sauna; concierge; room service, laundry and dry cleaning; nonsmoking rooms. *In room:* TV, radio, hair dryer, garment press.

EXPENSIVE/MODERATE

Clarion Hotel & Suites, Morrisons Island 🌟🌟 *(Kids)*   Overlooking the River Lee, just off the South Mall, this six-story downtown property is centrally located and is ideal for business travelers or families, as most of the units are suites. The rooms, decorated with contemporary furniture and modern art, have views of the river, cityscape, and nearby bridges. Each suite contains a sitting room, a dining area, a kitchen, a bathroom, and one or two bedrooms. Connecting rooms easily accommodate large parties.

Morrison's Quay, Cork, county Cork. ℂ **800/44-UTELL** in the U.S., or 021/427-5858. Fax 021/427-5833. 40 units. €160 ($142) double; from €205 ($182) suite. No service charge. AE, DC, MC, V. Free parking. **Amenities:** Restaurant (bistro); bar; concierge; room service; laundry/valet service; laundromat; nonsmoking rooms. *In room:* TV, dataport, hair dryer, iron.

MODERATE

Arbutus Lodge Hotel ⭐ *(Value)*   Arbutus Lodge is a Cork institution and very much a part of the fabric of the city. Perched in the fashionable, hilly Montenotte neighborhood, the former residence of the city's Lord Mayor affords extraordinary views of Cork from the dining room (and quite possibly from your room), yet the city center is an easy walk away. Though better known for its award-winning restaurant (see "Where to Dine," below), the hotel offers superb value for this price range. Each room is beautifully decorated and very individual, and several feature hand-carved, four-poster beds. The Oriental Room and the Tivoli Room are especially elegant and spacious, and have city views. The first guest in the presidential suite was Andrew Lloyd Webber, and the second was Mary Robinson, the former president of Ireland. Suites have queen sofa beds in the living rooms, kitchenettes, VCRs, and fax/modems.

St. Luke's Hill, Montenotte, Cork, county Cork. ℂ **021/450-1237.** Fax 021/450-2893. www.arbutuslodge.net. 20 units, 16 with private bathroom. €125 ($111) standard double; €170 ($151) superior double. No service charge. Rates include full breakfast. AE, DC, MC, V. Free parking. **Amenities:** Restaurant (Continental); bar; room service; laundry service. *In room:* TV, hair dryer, garment press.

Maranatha Country House ⭐ *(Finds)*   Olwen Venn is the energetic hostess at this 19th-century manor house, situated on 11 hectares (27 acres) of fine woodland. Each room is astonishing, offering a unique and sumptuous experience. One room is fit for a princess, with a regal-style canopy of velvet and florals; another evokes a cool forest; yet another uses over 365m (400 yd.) of material in its draperies. Traditional rules of decorating have been discarded in favor of thoughtful (and often whimsical) effusiveness. The most luxurious quarters are in the ground-floor suite, which contains a canopy bed and a large Jacuzzi within its ample floor plan. The breakfast conservatory houses an abundance of fresh blossoms, and the breakfast itself is plentiful and delicious.

Tower, Blarney, county Cork. ℂ and fax **021/438-5102.** www.maranathacountryhouse.com. 6 units, all with private bathroom (5 with shower only, 1 with Jacuzzi). €53–€90 ($47–$80) double. 50% reduction for children under 12. Rates include full breakfast. MC, V. Closed mid-Nov to Mar. Free parking. **Amenities:** TV lounge; babysitting; nonsmoking rooms. *In room:* Hair dryer.

Seven North Mall Guesthouse ⭐⭐   This lovely waterside town house guesthouse has attained cult status among travelers who know Ireland well. It dates from 1750 and looks out on the River Lee from the north bank. Angela Hegarty is obviously a detail-oriented person; every furnishing is carefully chosen, every accoutrement perfectly timbered, right down to the eating utensils. The result is an atmosphere of relaxation and elegant understatement. Up the narrow stairs, the rooms with river views are very appealing, but those in the back of the house are more spacious. The one ground-floor room is popular with travelers who have trouble with stairs.

7 North Mall, Cork, county Cork. ℂ **021/439-7191.** Fax 021/430-0811. 7 units. €90–€120 ($80–$107) double. No service charge. MC, V. Closed Christmas. Free parking. *In room:* TV, hair dryer.

Silver Springs Hotel ⭐   On a hillside overlooking the River Lee from 3.2km (2 miles) out of the city, this modern seven-story hotel is a popular choice for the wedding receptions of Corkonians. Surrounded by 17 hectares (42 acres) of gardens and grounds, the Silver Springs features an exterior glass elevator that offers great views of the surrounding countryside. Each room, outfitted with handcrafted Irish furniture and designer fabrics, has lovely views of the river, city, or gardens.

Dublin Rd., Tivoli, Cork, county Cork. ℂ 021/450-7533. Fax 021/450-7641. 109 units. €108–€229 ($96–$204) double. Rates include full breakfast and service charge. AE, DC, MC, V. Free parking. **Amenities:** 2 restaurants (international, bistro); 2 bars; indoor swimming pool; 9-hole golf course; tennis courts; squash court; health club; Jacuzzi; sauna; steam room; concierge; room service; laundry service. *In room:* TV, tea/coffeemaker, garment press, hair dryer.

INEXPENSIVE

Garnish House *(Finds)*   This is the very best B&B on the Western Road and, since B&Bs are absolutely chockablock along the entire thoroughfare, that's saying a helluva lot. Hansi Lucey is a simply wonderful innkeeper, the kind who makes a fuss for you as if you were a much-cherished friend or relative instead of a paying customer. Her breakfasts are legendary and her rooms exceedingly comfortable. Never content to rest on her laurels, a few years ago she added family suites and champagne breakfasts.

Western Rd., Cork, county Cork. ℂ 021/427-5111. Fax 021/427-3872. www.garnish.ie. 14 units. €60–€100 ($53–$89) double. No service charge. AE, DC, MC, V. Free parking. **Amenities:** Lounge; nonsmoking rooms. *In room:* TV, hair dryer.

Jurys Cork Inn *(Kids)*   This comfortable but functional hotel overlooking the River Lee is an excellent choice for families traveling on a budget. The flat-rate room price covers up to three adults or two adults and two children—exceptional value for a city-center location. The brick facade and mansard-style roof blend in with Cork's older architecture, yet the interior is bright and modern, with contemporary light-wood furnishings.

Anderson's Quay, Cork, county Cork. ℂ 800/44-UTELL in the U.S., or 021/427-6444. Fax 021/427-6144. www.jurys.com. 133 units. €69–€75 ($61–$67) per room. No service charge. AE, DC, MC, V. Free parking. **Amenities:** Restaurant (international); bar; laundry service; nonsmoking rooms. *In room:* TV, tea/coffeemaker, hair dryer.

Lotamore House *(Value)*   Overlooking the River Lee on 1.6 hectares (4 acres) of wooded grounds and gardens, 3.2km (2 miles) east of Cork City, this Georgian manor is one of the county's best guesthouses. It is exceedingly well run and public rooms are elegantly furnished with antiques, a sweeping staircase, ornate plasterwork, crystal chandeliers, and a fireplace dating from 1791. Guest rooms are old-fashioned and primly comfy, as if decorated by your granny or dearest old aunt. Breakfast is exceptional, with freshly squeezed juices, fresh fruit, and homemade scones, along with the traditional Irish fry.

Dublin-Waterford rd. (N8/N25), Tivoli, county Cork. ℂ 021/482-2344. Fax 021/482-2219. http://lotamore.iewebs.com. 20 units. €75–€85 ($67–$76) double. No service charge. Rates include full breakfast. AE, MC, V. Closed Dec 20–Jan 7. Free parking. **Amenities:** Lounge; laundry service; nonsmoking rooms. *In room:* TV, tea/coffeemaker, hair dryer, garment press.

4 Where to Dine

EXPENSIVE

Arbutus Lodge CONTINENTAL   Overlooking the city skyline from a hilltop, this lovely Georgian town-house restaurant has long been synonymous with gourmet cuisine in Cork—and, for that matter, in Ireland. It has long ranked among a handful of restaurants setting the standard toward which everyone else strives; and now, with a new chef, it too must strive to maintain its place. To even a jaded palate, a meal here can be startling. On many evenings, the chef prepares an eight-course tasting menu, which is an excellent way to discover the full scope of his talent. The wine list has won more decorations than Patton and offers a more delicate finish. It provides marvelous reading, even before a cork is lifted. The skilled, gracious service staff adds to the rare pleasure of a dinner at Arbutus Lodge.

St. Luke's Hill, Montenotte, Cork, county Cork. © **021/450-1237.** Reservations required. Fixed-price lunch €23 ($20); fixed-price dinner €46 ($41); dinner main courses €16–€26 ($14–$23). AE, DC, MC, V. Daily 1–2:30pm and 7–10pm.

The Ivory Tower MODERN CONTINENTAL   Seamus O'Connell has made a name as one of the most innovative chefs in the British Isles, and once told *Bon Appétit* magazine that he likes to "challenge the customer with complexity in flavors and textures." And so he does. He sources the freshest ingredients from local markets, and concentrates on adding layers of ingredients, much like a composer does with music. His style is intense and iconoclastic, and his menu reads like a roster of unlikely flavors. Who else would try swordfish on banana ketchup with mango salsa? Hot smoked salmon with lemon geranium sauce? Kumquats in Rioja wine? Not for the faint of heart, but this is food you experience with every sense of your being.

The Exchange Buildings, 35 Princes St., Cork, county Cork. © **021/427-4665.** Main courses €17–€23 ($15–$20). MC, V. Wed–Sun 6–11pm.

MODERATE

Café Paradiso VEGETARIAN   This is not only the best vegetarian restaurant in Ireland, but one of the best restaurants of any kind. Devotees include vegans and carnivores alike, because the fact that meat doesn't appear on the menu simply isn't an issue when the food is this good. Denis Cotter elevates vegetables to a higher plain, always pushing the envelope. The menu features organic local produce whenever possible, complemented by the finest Irish farmhouse cheeses. At lunchtime, there's light fare such as understated-but-tasty sandwiches and cleverly combined soups. For dinner, you might begin your meal with balsamic-roasted beets with organic salad leaves and sugar snaps, pesto dressing, and Knoackalara sheep's cheese. Then move on to mange-tout, rocket and red-onion risotto with Parmesan shavings and balsamic-roasted cherry tomatoes. Dark chocolate tart or strawberry baked Alaska make an ideal finish for a fine meal. The well-selected wine list offers a number of choices by the glass or half-bottle. Cotter and his partner, Bridget Healy, have spilled their secrets in their very popular *Café Paradiso Cookbook,* on sale here and in bookstores for €25 ($23).

16 Lancaster Quay, Western Rd., Cork, county Cork. (across from Jurys hotel). © **021/427-7939.** Reservations recommended. Dinner main courses €15–€19 ($13–$17). AE, MC, V. Tues–Sat 12:30–3pm and 6–10pm. Closed Christmas week.

Isaacs INTERNATIONAL   Isaacs is so integral to the fabric of Cork's dining scene that we can hardly imagine the city without it. The dining room itself is quite beautiful and contemporary, with soaring warehouse-style ceilings, exposed brick walls, and that intangible feel-good factor that comes from eating in a place where everyone is having a grand old time. Chef Canice Sharkey's signature is modern, understated cuisine, with absolutely no showing off. Think simple, fresh pasta dishes, hearty stews, mouthwatering grilled meats, and interesting salads. Every dish is perfectly prepared, be it a classic

Caesar salad, a chargrilled burger, or the prawn tempura with soy and ginger dip. Daily blackboard specials add to the variety. Isaacs was the winner of the Year 2000 Bord Bia New Irish Cuisine Award. The best-value deal is at lunchtime, when you can easily get out of here for €11 ($10) a head.

48 MacCurtain St., Cork, county Cork. ℭ 021/450-3805. Reservations recommended. Dinner main courses €9–€14 ($8–$12). AE, DC, MC, V. Mon–Sat 10am–10pm; Sun 6:30–9pm.

Jacob's On the Mall ⚜⚜ INTERNATIONAL   Housed in what was once the city's old Turkish bathhouse, this eatery, showcasing Mercy Fenton's confident, harmonious cooking, is the talk of the town. She doesn't so much cook as compose meals using fresh ingredients and side dishes to heighten the taste of her main dishes. Her grilled mackerel comes with buttery new potatoes and the licoricey hint of fennel, her crispy salmon is served with Chinese greens and noodles, and her breast of chicken with a dollop of lemon aioli. The place is truly lovely, with tall windows flooding the dining room with light.

30A South Mall, Cork, county Cork. ℭ 021/425-1530. Main courses €11–€24 ($10–$20). AE, MC, V. Wed–Sun 6–11pm.

Jacques ⚜⚜ INTERNATIONAL   Amazingly, after nearly 20 years in business, this stylish bistro still generates the buzz of a hot new kid on the block. All of Cork adores the creations of sisters Eithne and Jacqueline Barry, which seem to effortlessly stay contemporary and give people what they want. Lately, the menu is highly influenced by Mediterranean and Asian ingredients, as seen in main dishes like roast swordfish with couscous and lemon; roast brace of quail served on Oriental thread noodles; Tuscan chicken with polenta and Parmesan cheese with roast vegetables; and tagliatelle with wild mushroom in a garlic cream sauce. There are also perennial classics like beef Bordelaise and their deservedly famous roast duck with potato and apricot stuffing. The small dining room, whose cheery lemon, tangerine, and green walls are lined with modern artwork, is the perfect backdrop for the buzzy, fresh, and dynamic experience of eating here.

9 Phoenix St., Cork, county Cork. ℭ 021/427-7387. Reservations recommended. Fixed-price lunch €15 ($13); early-bird dinner (6–7pm) €15 ($13); fixed-price dinner €29 ($26); dinner main courses €15–€23 ($13–$20). AE, MC, V. Mon–Fri noon–3pm; Mon–Sat 6–10:30pm.

Number 5 Fenn's Quay ⚜⚜ INTERNATIONAL   Eilish and Pat O'Leary's superbly restored 18th-century terrace house attracts a well-heeled clientele and looks set to be a long-distance runner among Cork's many excellent restaurants. The secret to Brenda Harrington's cooking is an utter lack of pretension and a talent for making the most of potent ingredients. Flavors are paired to complement and contrast, and the palate is never, ever bored. A spinach-and-cream cheese strudel might be served with a sauce of roasted red pepper and black olives. Lamb kebabs come with Mediterranean couscous, while Spicy Toulouse sausages get paired with sauerkraut, mashed spuds, and herb jus. The place gets jammed at the good-value lunchtime, so be prepared to wait for a table or, better yet, go for a more leisurely dinner.

5 Fenn's Quay, Cork, county Cork. ℭ 021/427-9527. Reservations recommended. Lunch avg. €14 ($12); dinner main courses €10–€15 ($8.90–$13). AE, MC, V. Mon–Sat noon–3pm and 6–10pm.

INEXPENSIVE

Crawford Gallery Cafe ⚜ COUNTRY HOUSE   In a ground-floor room at the Crawford Art Gallery, this restaurant, decorated with oil paintings and statuary, is run by the Allen family of Ballymaloe House fame (see "East Cork" in chapter 8). It serves breakfast, lunch, and afternoon tea. The menu includes such traditional dishes as lamb braised with vegetables and rosemary and served with champ (a traditional dish of buttery mashed potatoes with chopped green onions, made here with parsley, chives, and young nettle tops), and more contemporary open-faced sandwiches such as a wonderful smoked salmon, cheese, and pickle combination. All fish are brought in fresh daily from Ballycotton Bay, and breads and baked goods are from Ballymaloe kitchens.

Emmet Place, Cork, county Cork. ✆ **021/427-4415.** Reservations recommended for parties of 6 or more. All items €4–€14 ($3.55–$12). MC, V. Mon–Sat 10am–5pm.

Quay Co-op ⭐ VEGETARIAN/CAFETERIA   The ground floor of this insider establishment is a whole-foods store that also sells delicious breads and cakes. The main attraction, however, is on the second floor. Reached by a narrow, steep, winding staircase, the self-service restaurant far surpasses its rather inauspicious first impression. An array of delicious hot and cold dishes spread out before you, including spinach and sun-dried tomato roulade, spanakopita, and lentil and coconut soup. Homemade breads and cakes are especially good here. Although some vegan offerings may seem bland if you're not used to this diet, don't let that deter you; they make up a small portion of the menu. The clientele includes much of Cork's countercultural community, both young and old.

24 Sullivan's Quay, Cork, county Cork. ✆ **021/431-7026.** Dinner main courses €5–€9 ($4.45–$8). MC, V. Daily 9:30am–10:30pm.

5 Attractions

IN TOWN

Coal Quay Market *Overrated*   This is Cork's open-air flea market, a trove of secondhand clothes, old china, used books, memorabilia, and—well, to be truthful—plenty of junk. It all happens on a street, now a little ragged, that was once Cork's original outdoor market.

Cornmarket St., Cork, county Cork. Free admission. Mon–Sat 9am–5pm.

Cork City Gaol ⭐   About a mile west of the city center, this restored prison was infamous in the 19th century, when it housed many of Ireland's great patriots. Sound effects and lifelike characters inhabiting the cells re-create the social history of Cork. The "Radio Museum Experience," an exhibition drawn from the RTE Museum Collection, depicts a restored 6CK Radio Studio and an array of antique radio equipment and memorabilia.

Convent Ave., Sunday's Well, Cork, county Cork. ✆ **021/430-5022.** Admission to gaol or exhibition €5 ($4.45) adults, €4 ($3.55) seniors, students, and children, €14 ($12) family. Mar–Oct daily 9:30am–6pm; Nov–Feb Sat–Sun 10am–5pm. Last admission 1 hr. before closing.

Cork Heritage Park ⭐   About 3.2 km (2 miles) south of the city center, this newish park is in a 19th-century courtyard on lovely grounds beside an estuary of Cork Harbour. The site was originally part of the estate of the Pike family, Quakers who were prominent in banking and shipping in Cork in the 1800s. The exhibits trace the maritime and shipping routes of Cork as well as the history of the Pike family, in a series of colorful tableaux. There is also an environmental center, an archaeology room, a small museum dedicated to the history of Cork fire fighting from 1450 to 1945, and stables that house models of a saddler and blacksmith.

Bessboro Rd., Blackrock, Cork, county Cork. ✆ **021/435-8854**. Admission €5 ($4.45) adults, €3 ($2.25) seniors and students, €2 ($1.80) children, €10 ($8.90) family. Apr Sun noon–5:30pm; May–Sept Mon–Fri 10:30am–5:30pm, weekends noon–5:30pm. Closed Oct–Mar.

Cork Public Museum ✿ This museum occupies a magnificent Georgian building in a park on the western edge of the city. Exhibits include models depicting early medieval times; artifacts recovered from excavations in the city, some dating as far back as 4,000 years; and a working model of an early flour mill with an unusual horizontal water wheel. There's an archive of photographs and documents relating to Cork-born Irish patriots Terence McSwiney, Thomas MacCurtain, and Michael Collins. Antique Cork silver, glass, and lace are on display. An extension to the museum has recently been completed.

Fitzgerald Park, Cork, county Cork. ✆ **021/427-0679**. Admission Sun €1.30 ($1.15), €2.50 ($2.25) family; Mon–Fri free. Mon–Fri 11am–1pm and 2:15–5pm; Sun 3–5pm (until 6pm July–Aug). Bus: 8.

Crawford Municipal Art Gallery ✿✿✿ Works by such well-known Irish painters as Jack B. Yeats, Nathaniel Grogan, William Orpen, Sir John Lavery, James Barry, and Daniel Maclise are the focal point of this excellent gallery in Cork's 18th-century former customs house. Also on display are sculptures and handcrafted silver and glass pieces. A fine restaurant and bookstore are on the premises. In 2000, the Gallery received a dramatic face-lift, with a major futuristic extension.

Emmet Place, Cork, county Cork. ✆ **021/4273377**. www.synergy.ie/crawford. Free admission. Mon–Sat 10am–5pm.

Lavitts Quay Gallery Operated by the Cork Arts Society, this gallery promotes the area's contemporary visual arts. It's in an early 18th-century Georgian house that overlooks the River Lee. The ground floor presents a variety of works by established artists, and the upper floor showcases up-and-coming talent.

5 Father Matthew St., Cork, county Cork. ✆ **021/427-7749**. Free admission. Mon–Sat 10am–6pm.

Old Butter Exchange ✿ Started in 1770, Cork's butter exchange became the largest exporter of salted butter in the world, exporting around 500,000 casks of butter a year by 1892. Although the exchange closed in 1924, it's become a popular museum in this city of good food. Situated opposite the famous Shandon Bells, the exchange now houses the Shandon Craft Centre and the Firkin Crane Centre, a hot venue for contemporary dance performances.

John Redmond St., Cork, county Cork. Free admission to Centres. ✆ **021/430-0600**. Mon–Sat 10am–5pm.

Old English Market ✿✿ Ireland's best food market dates from a Charter of James 1 in 1610. The present building, finished in 1786, was damaged by fire in 1980 and was refurbished by Cork Corporation to an award-winning design by T. F. MacNamara, the city architect. Foodstuffs peculiar to Cork may be purchased here. Stands brim with meats, fish, vegetables, and fruit, and you'll also see such traditional Cork foods as hot buttered eggs, *tripe* (animal stomach), *crubeens* (pig's feet), and *drisheens* (local blood sausage). The market's name is a holdover from the days of English rule.

Grand Parade; enter from Patrick St., Grand Parade, Oliver Plunkett St., or Princes St., Cork, county Cork. Free admission. Mon–Sat 9am–6pm.

St. Anne's Church ✿✿ Cork's prime landmark, also known as Shandon Church, is famous for its giant pepper pot steeple and its eight melodious bells. Virtually no matter where you stand in the downtown area, you can see the stone tower, crowned with a gilt ball and a unique fish weather vane. Seen on

TV as the background to a Murphy's Stout ad, up to recently it was known as "the four faced liar" because each of its four clock faces used to show a different time, except on the hour, when they all managed to synchronize. Somewhat sadly, that charming quirk was fixed a few years ago. Built in 1722, the steeple has red sandstone (south) and limestone (west) walls, from which the colors of the Cork hurling and football teams are taken. A climb to the belfry rewards with the chance to play a tune on the famous Shandon Bells, immortalized in the poem by Francis Mahony called "The Bells of Shandon." Consequently, you might hear the bells of Shandon ringing at all times of the day. Continue on a sometimes-precarious climb up past the bells, and you'll be further rewarded with a spectacular view of Cork city and the Lee Valley.

Church St., Cork, county Cork. ℭ 021/450-1672. Admission €5 ($4.45) adults, €4 ($3.55) seniors and students, €9 ($8) family. Mon–Sat 8:30am–6pm.

St. Finbarr's Cathedral ☆ This Church of Ireland cathedral sits on the spot St. Finbarr chose in A.D. 600 for his church and school. The current building dates from 1880 and is a fine example of early French Gothic style; its three giant spires dominate the skyline. The interior is highly ornamented with unique mosaic work. The bells were inherited from the 1735 church that previously stood on this site.

Bishop St., Cork, county Cork. ℭ 021/496-3387. Free admission; donations welcome. Apr–Sept Mon–Sat 10am–5:30pm and Oct–Mar Mon–Sat 2–5:30pm.

University College, Cork (U.C.C.) A component of Ireland's National University, with about 7,000 students, this center of learning is housed in a pretty quadrangle of Gothic Revival–style buildings. Lovely gardens and wooded grounds grace the campus. Tours include the Crawford Observatory, the lovely Harry Clarke stained-glass windows in the Honan Chapel, and the Stone Corridor, a collection of stones inscribed with the ancient Irish Ogham style of writing.

Western Rd., Cork, county Cork. ℭ 021/490-2371. Tours by arrangement.

BUS TOURS

In July and August, **Bus Eireann,** Parnell Place Bus Station (ℭ **021/450-8188**), offers narrated tours to all of Cork's major landmarks and buildings, including nearby Blarney. Fares start at €8 ($7.10).

Cork Panoramic These open-top buses let you hop on and hop off to explore the sights of Ireland's second city. They run all day in a loop, so when you see something you want to explore, just get off and rejoin the tour later. Or you can stay on the bus and use the tour to get oriented. Tour highlights include the Cork City Gaol, St. Ann's Church, and UCC (University College, Cork). Further details are available from the Cork Tourist Office.

Grayline Tours, Cork, county Cork. ℭ 01/670-8822. Apr–Oct daily, with hours and number of tours reflecting seasonal demand. Admission €11 ($10) adults, €9 ($8) students, €3.50 ($3.10) children.

NEARBY: BLARNEY CASTLE & MORE

Ballincollig Gunpowder Mills This industrial complex beside the River Lee was a hub for the manufacture of gunpowder from 1794 to 1903, a time of wars between Britain and France. In its heyday as Cork's prime industry, it employed about 500 men as coopers, millwrights, and carpenters. You can tour the restored buildings, and there are exhibits and an audiovisual presentation that tell the story of gunpowder production in the Cork area.

About 8km (5 miles) west of Cork City on the main Cork-Killarney rd. (N22), Ballincollig, county Cork. © 021/487-4430. Admission €4 ($3.55) adults, €3 ($2.65) seniors and students, €2.50 ($2.25) children, €10 ($8.90) family. Apr–Sept daily 10am–6pm.

Blarney Castle and Stone ✦✦✦   While aspects of Blarney Castle are very touristy, it is still one of the most haunting and striking castles in Ireland. What remains of this impressive castle is a massive square tower, with a parapet rising 25m (83 ft.). The infamous Blarney Stone is wedged far enough underneath the battlements to make it uncomfortable to reach, but not far enough that count-less tourists don't literally bend over backwards, hang upside down in a parapet, and kiss it. It's customary to tip the attendant who holds your legs (you might want to do it before he hangs you over the edge).

After bypassing the stone, take a stroll through the gardens and a nearby dell beside Blarney Lake. The Badger Cave and adjacent dungeons, penetrating the rock at the base of the castle, can be explored by all but the claustrophobic with the aid of a flashlight.

R617, 8km (5 miles) northwest of Cork City, Blarney, county Cork. © 021/438-5252. Admission €5 ($4.45) adults, €3 ($2.65) seniors and students, €1.30 ($1.15) children, €10 ($8.90) family (2 adults and 2 children 8–14). May and Sept Mon–Sat 9am–6:30pm, Sun 9:30am–5:30pm; June–Aug Mon–Sat 9am–7pm, Sun 9:30am–5:30pm; Oct–Apr Mon–Sat 9am–sundown, Sun 9:30am–5:30pm. Bus: 154 from bus station on Par-nell Place, Cork City.

6 Spectator Sports & Outdoor Pursuits

SPECTATOR SPORTS

GAELIC GAMES   Hurling and Gaelic football are both played on summer Sunday afternoons at Cork's **Pairc Ui Chaoimh Stadium,** Marina Walk (© 021/496-3311). Check the local newspapers for details or log on to the Gaelic Athletics Association's site at www.gaa.ie.

GREYHOUND RACING   Go to the dogs, as they say in Cork, at **Cork Greyhound Track,** Western Road, Cork (© 021/454-3013), on Wednesday, Thursday, and Saturday at 8pm. Admission is €6.50 ($5.80).

HORSE RACING   The nearest racetrack is **Mallow Race Track,** Killarney Road, Mallow (© 022/50207), approximately 32km (20 miles) north of Cork. Races are scheduled in mid-May, early August, and early October.

OUTDOOR PURSUITS

The **Tent Shop & Outside World,** 7 Parnell Place (© 021/278833), is a one-stop source for outdoor needs, from canoe and tent rentals to surfing and moun-taineering gear. Express repairs are offered for tourists in distress.

BICYCLING   Although walking is probably the ideal way to get around Cork, you can rent a bike at **Cyclescene,** 396 Blarney St. (© 021/430-1183). It costs €14 ($12) per day or €50 ($46) per week. Open Monday to Saturday, 8:30am to 6pm.

FISHING   The **River Lee,** which runs through Cork, the nearby **Blackwater River,** and the many area lakes present fine opportunities. Salmon licenses, lake fishing permits, tackle, and equipment can be obtained from **T. W. Murray,** 87 Patrick St. (© 021/427-1089), and the **Tackle Shop,** Lavitt's Quay (© 021/ 427-2842).

GOLF   Local clubs that welcome visitors are the **Cork Golf Club,** Little Island (© 021/435-3451), 8km (5 miles) east of Cork, with greens fees of €58 ($52) weekdays, €64 ($57) weekends; **Douglas Golf Club,** Maryboro Hill, Douglas

(© **021/489-5297**), 4.8km (3 miles) south of Cork, with greens fees of €46 ($41) weekdays, €54 ($48) weekends; and **Harbour Point,** Little Island (© **021/435-3094**), 6.5km (4 miles) east of Cork, with greens fees of €30 ($27) weekdays, €34 ($30) weekends.

WALKING The **Old Railway Line** is a dismantled train route running from Cork to the old maritime town of Passage West. It is from here that Captain Roberts set out and crossed the Atlantic in the first passenger steamship, *The Sirius*. Following along the rails, a scenic walk affords the visitor excellent views of the inner harbor.

7 Shopping

Patrick Street is the main shopping thoroughfare, and many stores are scattered throughout the city on side streets and in lanes. In general, shops are open Monday to Saturday 9:30am to 6pm, unless indicated otherwise. In the summer, many shops remain open until 9:30pm on Thursday and Friday, and some are open on Sunday.

The city's antiques row is **Paul's Lane,** an offshoot of Paul Street, between Patrick Street and the Quays in the Huguenot Quarter. There are three shops along this lane, each brimming with old Cork memorabilia and furnishings: **Anne McCarthy,** 2 Paul's Lane (© **021/427-3755**); **Mills,** 3 Paul's Lane (© **021/427-3528**); and **O'Regan's,** 4 Paul's Lane (© **021/427-2902**). All are open Monday to Saturday 10am to 6pm.

The main mall is **Merchant's Quay Shopping Centre,** Merchant's Quay and Patrick Street. This enclosed complex houses large department stores, such as **Marks and Spencer** (© **021/427-5555**), as well as small specialty shops, such as **Laura Ashley** (© **021/427-4070**).

Cork's best department store is **Cash's,** 18 St. Patrick St. (© **021/427-6771**). Dating from 1830, it offers three floors of wares and gift items, including Waterford crystal, Irish linen, and all types of knitwear and tweeds.

BOOKS & MUSIC

The Living Tradition This small shop on the North Bank specializes in Irish folk and traditional music—CDs, cassettes, books, videos, sheet music, and songbooks—as well as instruments such as *bodhrans* (Irish frame drums) and tin whistles. Here's where to buy the real thing, the kind of music you actually hear in Ireland at a pub session or a Fleadh Ceoil (Irish music festival). In addition, it stocks a good selection of recordings of musicians from around the world, along with handcrafted goods. 40 MacCurtain St., Cork, county Cork. © **021/450-2040.** www.ossian.ie.

Mainly Murder Tucked between French Church and Academy streets, this tiny bookshop is a huge treasure trove of whodunits for amateur sleuths or anyone looking for a good read. It stocks volumes on murder, mystery, and mayhem from Ireland, England, and many other English-speaking lands. It's well worth a visit to stock up for a rainy day. 2A Paul St., Cork, county Cork. © **021/427-2413.**

Mercier Press and Bookshop Long a part of Cork's literary tradition, this shop stocks a variety of books, including those published by Cork-based Mercier Press, founded in 1944 and now Ireland's oldest independent publishing house. It has an extensive Irish-interest section, including volumes on history, literature, folklore, music, art, humor, drama, politics, current affairs, law, and religion. 5 French Church St., Cork, county Cork. © **021/427-5040.**

Waterstone's Booksellers   With entrances on two streets, this large branch of the British-owned chain is always busy. It has a good selection of books about Cork and of Irish interest, as well as sections on art, antiques, biography, religion, and travel. 69 Patrick St. and 12 Paul St., Cork, county Cork. ℂ **021/427-6522.**

CRAFTS

Crafts of Ireland   Just a block off Patrick Street, this well-stocked shop presents an array of local crafts, including weavings, wrought iron, batik hangings, candles, glass, graphics, leather work, pottery, toys, Irish wildlife mobiles, and Irish floral stationery. Open Monday to Saturday 9:30am to 5:30pm. 11 Winthrop St., Cork, county Cork. ℂ **021/427-5864.**

Meadows & Byrne   This shop, with branches in many of Ireland's larger towns, claims the finest Irish home store, and unquestionably offers a wide and attractive array of contemporary furniture, furnishings, and household items. In this multilevel center, you'll find some of the best contemporary Irish design and crafts, including Jerpoint glass, Shanagarry and Jack O'Patsy pottery, and wrought-iron works by John Forkin. Academy St., Cork, county Cork. ℂ **021/427-2324.**

Shandon Craft Centre   Inside the Old Butter Exchange (see "Attractions," above), this enclosed emporium showcases the workshops of artisans, who practice a range of traditional trades and display their wares for sale. The crafts include porcelain dolls, jewelry, clothing, crystal, pottery, and handmade violins, cellos, and violas. From June to August, folk, traditional, jazz, and classical musicians offer free concerts from 1 to 2pm. Cork Butter Exchange, John Redmond St., Cork, county Cork. ℂ **021/450-8881.**

TWEEDS & WOOLENS

Blarney Woollen Mills   About 9.7km (6 miles) northwest of Cork City, on the same grounds as the famous castle of the same name, this huge store is housed in an 1824 mill. It's a one-stop source for Irish products, from cashmeres to crystal glassware, hats to heraldry, and tweeds to T-shirts, as well as the distinctive Kelly green Blarney Castle–design wool sweaters, made on the premises. Best of all, it's open until 10pm every night in summer. Blarney, county Cork. ℂ **021/438-5280.**

House of Donegal   "Tailoring to please" is the theme of this showroom and workshop. You can buy ready-made or specially tailored raincoats, classic trench coats, jackets, suits, and sportswear for men and women. The handsome rainwear, with Donegal tweed linings, is a special souvenir to bring home from Ireland. 6 Paul St. (off the Grand Parade), Cork, county Cork. ℂ **021/427-2447.**

Quills   For tweeds, woolens, and knits at the best prices, don't miss this family-run enterprise on Cork's busy main thoroughfare. It's a branch of a shop that started small more than 20 years ago at Ballingeary, in the heart of the West Cork Gaeltacht. It now has similar shops in Killarney, Kenmare, and Sneem. 107 Patrick St., Cork, county Cork. ℂ **021/427-1717.**

8 Cork After Dark

PUBS

An Bodhran   There's Irish traditional music at this friendly pub Monday to Thursday, starting at 9pm. The old-world decor includes stone walls, dark woods, and a huge stained-glass window with Book of Kells–inspired designs depicting Irish monks playing traditional Irish instruments. 42 Oliver Plunkett St., Cork, county Cork. ℂ **021/427-4544.**

Impressions

An Irishman is just a machine for turning Guinness into urine, which as any Murphy's drinker will tell you is a superfluous exercise.
                                    —Niall Tóibín, Irish comedian (b. 1929)

An Spailpin Fanac (The Migrant Worker)   Located opposite the Beamish Brewery, this is another of the city's choice spots for traditional Irish music, Sunday to Friday starting at 9:30pm. It dates from 1779, making it one of Cork's oldest pubs. It is a lovely, soothing place—as all the best pubs are—with low ceilings, exposed brick walls, flagstone floors, open fireplaces, a simple wooden bar, and woven rush seats. Oh, and there's a darling, authentic snug. 28–29 S. Main St., Cork, county Cork. ✆ 021/427-7949.

The Hibernian   This is a real insider's place, which everyone calls by its nickname, "the Hi-B." Located up a linoleum-covered flight of stairs (the entrance is beside the Minahan Chemist shop), this is as quintessential an old-style lounge pub as you're likely to find. It looks like a living room gone astray, with a mishmash of slightly threadbare upholstered armchairs and sofas strewn about at odd angles. The one-room bar is always crammed with a wonderful cross-section of Cork—blue-collar types, students, artists, writers, eccentrics, and the beautiful, well-heeled set. 108 Oliver Plunkett St. (corner of Winthrop St.), Cork, county Cork. ✆ 021/427-2758.

John Henchy & Sons   It's worth a walk up steep Summerhill Road, a northeast continuation of busy MacCurtain Street, to reach this classic pub near the Arbutus Lodge hotel. Established by John Henchy in 1884, it looks much the same as it did then, with lots of polished brass fittings, leaded-glass windows, silver tankards, thick red curtains, and a small snug. The original Henchy family grocery store still operates adjacent to the pub. 40 St. Luke's, Cork, county Cork. ✆ 021/450-7833.

The Long Valley *(Finds*   This is one of those exceptional, family-run, old-fashioned bars that you fall in love with as soon as you enter—or, rather, even before you enter. To the left of the entrance hallway is a snug with etched glass doors and chased silver doorknobs. Those doors came from the *Celtic*, a White Star ocean liner (of *Titanic* fame) which ran aground in Cork Harbor—just one example of the craftsmanship of a pub that's been seducing Cork folk since 1842. And this is before you even step into the bar itself. For anyone who knows and loves Cork, this is a place of pilgrimage. It could be called The Long Bar: one endless, low-slung room with the bar running its full length. Along the opposite wall are small wooden tables, chairs, and benches, with historic photos on the wall above. The barmen wear white butchers coats, Victorian-style, and provide a constant supply of pints to the laid-back, predominantly 30-something crowd. If you're hungry, order one of the excellent sandwiches at the bar, served deli-style on home-baked bread. Winthrop St., Cork, county Cork. ✆ 021/427-2144.

Maguire's Warehouse Bar   Just off Patrick Street in the heart of town, this Edwardian-style pub has a conversation-piece interior, with vintage bicycles, unicycles, and lots of old brass fixtures. Daunt Sq., Grand Parade, Cork, county Cork. ✆ 021/427-7825.

Mutton Lane Inn   Old Cork is alive and well at this tiny pub down an alley that was first trod as a pathway for sheep going to market. It was opened in 1787 as a public house by the Ring family, who used to make their own moonshine whiskey. It's now the domain of Maeve and Vincent McLoughlin, who have preserved the old-world aura, which incorporates lantern lights, dark wood-paneled walls, exposed-beam ceilings, and an antique cash register. 3 Mutton Lane, off Patrick St., Cork, county Cork. © 021/427-3471.

CLUBS: COMEDY, DANCE & MUSIC
You're likely to have the last laugh at the **City Limits,** every Friday and Saturday night at The Comedy Club, 2 Coburg St. (© **021/450-1206**).

Half Moon After the main stage empties, the Cork Opera House Bar, the Half Moon, swings into action. It schedules an ever-changing program of contemporary music, from blues and ragtime to pop and rock, with comedy gigs on occasion. Open Thursday to Sunday from 11:30pm to 3am. Cork Opera House, Emmet Place, Cork, county Cork. © 021/427-0022. Cover €7–€15 ($6.25–$13).

The Lobby Bar This bar opposite City Hall presents a variety of musical entertainment, from folk, traditional, bluegrass, and blues to jazz, gypsy, rock, classical, and New Age. Most performances start at 9pm. 1 Union Quay, Cork, county Cork. © 021/431-1113. www.lobby.ie. Cover €5–€10 ($4.45–$8.90).

The Red Room The DJs in this popular nightclub spin everything from hip-hop to techno. 17 Liberty St., Cork, county Cork. © 021/425-1855. Free admission before 10.30pm, then €4–€7 ($3.55–$6.25).

Sir Henry's Cork's biggest (three floors) and best-known nightclub has been on the front line of Irish club culture since it opened. It used to be a place for live acts in the '80s and '90s (Sonic Youth, Pavement, and Wedding Present all played here), but in recent years, the scene has moved to DJs spinning bleeding edge dance music, from acid house to techno to disco. It gets packed on weekends with 20-something beautiful things. S. Main St., Cork, county Cork. © 021/427-4391. Cover €6–€10 ($5.35–$8.90).

THE PERFORMING ARTS
Cork Opera House Just off Lavitt's Quay along the River Lee, this is southwest Ireland's major venue for opera, drama, musicals, comedies, dance, concerts, and variety nights. The original century-old opera house was completely gutted by a fire in 1955; this 1,000-seat replacement opened a decade later, in 1965. Emmet Place, Cork, county Cork. © 021/427-0022. www.corkoperahouse.ie. Tickets €8–€40 ($7.10–$36); avg. €20 ($18). Box office 9am–7pm; curtain usually 8pm; matinees 1:30 or 3pm.

Firkin Crane Cultural Centre Dating from the 1840s, this unique rotunda was part of Cork's original Butter Exchange, and the building's name derives from Danish words pertaining to measures of butter. Although destroyed by fire in 1980, the site was completely rebuilt and opened as a cultural center in 1992. Today, Firkin Crane is singularly dedicated to the understanding and development of contemporary dance throughout Ireland. It serves as both a producing venue for new dance works and a presenting venue for touring national and international dance companies. John Redmond St., Shandon, Cork, county Cork. © 021/450-7487. Tickets €10–€14 ($8.90–$12). Curtain usually 8pm.

Triskel Arts Centre This ever-growing arts center just goes from strength to strength. Its program presents a variety of entertainment, including drama, poetry readings, musical recitals, opera, and popular Irish and traditional music concerts. There is also a full curriculum of daytime art workshops and gallery talks. The restaurant with bar is open for day and evening events, and is a stylish place to have a light meal or a cappuccino. Tobin St., off S. Main St., Cork, county Cork. ℭ 021/427-2022. Tickets €2–€10 ($1.80–$8.90). Box office Mon–Sat 10am–5:30pm; curtain usually 8pm; some Sat–Sun matinees at 1:15 or 1:30pm.

THEATERS

Cork Arts Theatre   Across the river from the Opera House, this busy theater presents a wide variety of contemporary dramas, comedies, and musical comedies, almost always to full houses. A multistory parking garage and the city center main street are a 10-minute walk away. Knapp's Sq., Cork, county Cork. ℭ 021/450-8398. Tickets €11 ($10) adults, €6.50 ($5.80) seniors and students. Shows Tues–Sat 8pm.

Everyman Palace   This lovely, refurbished historic theater 2 minutes from the bus and train station is well known as a showcase for new plays, both Irish and international. The Irish National Ballet also performs here regularly. 17 MacCurtain St., Cork, county Cork. ℭ 021/450-1673. Tickets €7–€11 ($6.25–$10). Box office Mon–Fri 10am–7pm; curtain 8pm.

8

Out from Cork

Once the haunt of outlaws, Cork long had a reputation as an inaccessible and unruly corner of the country. Cork is often called "The Rebel County" for the independent spirit of those that reside here, both past and present.

It is the largest of the 32 Irish counties, and one of the most diverse. The landscape has hardly been tamed, either, and West Cork holds some of Ireland's most beautifully remote and wild coastal regions, with long sandy beaches (called "strands" in Ireland), high rugged cliffs, and a scattering of off-shore islands. The rivers Blackwater, Lee, and Bandon flow west to east along the fertile valleys between these limestone ridges, each turning sharply southwards to empty into the sea. There are rocky, heather-clad mountains, subtropical gardens (thanks to the congenial Gulf Stream), and still, dark corrie lakes. You can find dark forests, old walled villages, deserted mining towns, colorful spinnakers of racing yachts, and plenty of seafaring folklore about shipwrecks. After all, it was in the harbor town of Cobh (pronounced *Cove*), once known as Queenstown in honor of a visit by Queen Victoria, that the *Titanic* made her last port of call.

Little bays and harbors are indented all along the county's 1,095km-long (680-mile) coastline (one-fifth of the national coastline), making Cork an ideal location for sailing. The oldest yacht club in the world is based at Crosshaven and dates from 1720, and Ireland's only cable car service links Dursey Island with the mainland at Beara peninsula.

There's no better place to start a tour of county Cork than in Kinsale, a small harbor town directly south of Cork City.

1 Kinsale ⚘

Kinsale is 29km (18 miles) S of Cork, 87km (54 miles) SE of Killarney, 156km (97 miles) SE of Shannon Airport, 285km (177 miles) SW of Dublin, and 32km (20 miles) E of Clonakilty

Only 29km (18 miles) south of Cork City, **Kinsale** is a small fishing village with a sheltered semicircular harbor rimmed by hilly terrain. It is one of the most darling harbor towns in Europe. Considered the gateway to the western Cork seacoast, this compact town of 2,000 residents has also made a big name for itself as the "gourmet capital of Ireland." Home to more than a dozen award-winning restaurants and pubs, Kinsale draws food lovers year-round, particularly in October during the 4-day **Gourmet Festival,** when the atmosphere in town is especially convivial.

Kinsale fits the picture-postcard image of what a charming Irish seaport should look like—narrow, winding streets; well-kept 18th-century houses; imaginatively painted shop fronts; window boxes and street stanchions brimming with colorful flowers; and a harbor full of sailboats. The downside of all this is that the secret is out: Kinsale is a tourist mecca, so add parking problems and tour buses to the list of the city's sights.

County Cork

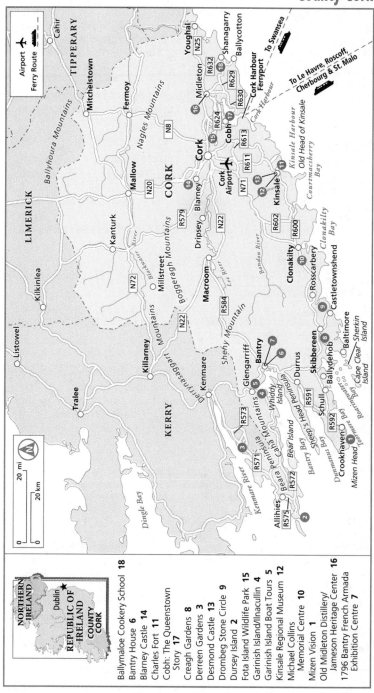

In 1601, the town was the scene of the Battle of Kinsale, a turning point in Irish history. The defeat of the Irish helped to establish English domination. After the battle, a new governor representing the British crown was appointed. His name was William Penn. Ring any bells? For a time, Penn's son William served in Kinsale as clerk of the admiralty court, but Penn Jr. did not stay long; he was soon off to the New World to found the state of Pennsylvania.

Just off the coast of the Old Head of Kinsale—about 8km (5 miles) west of the town—a German submarine sank the *Lusitania* in 1915. More than 1,500 people were killed, and many are buried in a local cemetery.

ESSENTIALS

GETTING THERE   **Bus Eireann** (© **021/450-8188;** www.buseireann.ie) operates regular daily service from Cork City to Kinsale. The arrival and departure point is the Esso gas station on Pier Road, opposite the tourist office.

Kinsale is 29km (18 miles) south of Cork City on the Airport Road; if you're coming by car from the west, use N71. From East Cork, Cross River Ferries Ltd. provides regular service across Cork Harbour (see "East Cork" later in this chapter).

VISITOR INFORMATION   The **Kinsale Tourist Office,** Pier Road, Kinsale (© **021/477-2234;** www.kinsale.ie), is open March through November.

GETTING AROUND   Kinsale's streets are so narrow that walking is the best way to get around. There is no local transport; if you need a taxi to outlying areas, call **Kinsale Cabs** (© **021/477-2642**), **O'Dea & Sons** (© **021/477-4900**), or **Allied Cabs** (© **021/477-3600**).

EXPLORING THE TOWN

Charles Fort ⭐   Southeast of Kinsale, at the head of the harbor, this coastal landmark dates from the late 17th century. A classic star-shaped fort, it was constructed to prevent foreign naval forces from entering the harbor of Kinsale, then an important trading town. Additions and improvements were made throughout the 18th and 19th centuries, and the fort remained garrisoned until 1921. Across the river is James Fort (1602). The complex includes an exhibition center and cafe.

Off the Scilly Rd., Summer Cove, county Cork. © 021/477-2263. Admission €3 ($2.65) adults, €2.50 ($2.25) seniors, €1.30 ($1.15) students, €8 ($7.10) family. Tours available on request. Mid-Apr to mid-Oct daily 10am–6pm; mid-Oct to mid-Mar weekends 10am–5pm; last admission 45 min. before closing.

Desmond Castle ⭐   The castle is now the home of the **International Museum of Wine,** celebrating the "wine geese"—the Irish emigrants who colonized the wine trade throughout the world after being forced to leave their own shores. Built around 1500 as a customhouse by the earl of Desmond, this tower house has a colorful history. The Spanish occupied it in 1601, and the British used it as a prison for captured American sailors during the War of Independence. Locally, it's known as "French Prison" because 54 French prisoners died here in a 1747 fire. During the Great Famine, the castle became a workhouse for the starving populace.

Cork St., Kinsale, county Cork. © 021/477-4855. Admission €3 ($2.65) adults, €2 ($1.80) seniors and students, €1.30 ($1.15) children, €6.50 ($5.80) family. Mid-Apr to mid-June Tues–Sun 10am–6pm; mid-June to early Oct daily 10am–6pm. Last admission 45 min. before closing. Closed mid-Oct to mid-Apr.

Kinsale Regional Museum ⭐   This museum tells the town's story from its earliest days, with exhibits, photos, and memorabilia highlighting such events as the Battle of Kinsale in 1601 and the sinking of the *Lusitania* in 1915, and featuring extensive traditional craft exhibits. It's in the Market House (1600), which gained an arched facade in 1706. An extensive renovation and extension, doubling its exhibition space, was completed in July 2000.

Market Sq., Kinsale, county Cork. ℭ 021/477-2044. Admission €2.50 ($2.25) adults, €1.30 ($1.15) students, €.70 (60¢) children. Apr–Sept daily 10am–6pm; Oct–Mar Mon–Fri 11am–1pm and 3–5pm. Closed Jan.

SHOPPING

Boland's Irish Craft Shop   This is a good spot to buy exclusively Irish-made crafts—such as traditional Kinsale smocks, Aran sweaters, pottery, Ogham plaques, woolly and ceramic sheep, quilts, Irish leather belts, and miniature paintings by Irish artists. Pearse St., Kinsale, county Cork. ℭ 021/477-2161. www.boland kinsale.com.

Granny's Bottom Drawer   Traditional Irish linens and lace are the ticket here. It's well stocked with tablecloths, pillowcases, Victorian table runners, and hand-crocheted place mats. 53 Main St., Kinsale, county Cork. ℭ 021/477-4839.

The Irish Print Shop   The *London Times* named this spacious shop one of the two standout galleries in Kinsale's flourishing fine-arts scene. Oliver Sears, the proprietor, first came to Ireland from London as a chef. Since switching careers, he has assembled the largest selection of original Irish prints in the country. If you can't find something you love here, you might as well stop looking. The shop is closed from mid-January to mid-February. 20/21 Main St., Kinsale, county Cork. ℭ 021/477-2565 or 087/261-9154.

Jagoes Mill Pottery   Just over 3.2km (2 miles) from Kinsale, Irene Gahan Ryle runs a small pottery workshop in an old mill dating from the 17th century. She makes individual pieces that appeal to lovers of studio pottery because of the work's distinctive, practical and beautiful forms. Included in many private collections around the world, the work is only sold from the studio workshop and selected galleries. Jagoes Mill, Kinsale, county Cork. ℭ 021/477-2771.

Kinsale Crystal   Started in 1991 by a former Waterford Crystal master craftsman, this small workshop produces traditional full-lead, mouth-blown, and hand-cut crystal, with personalized engraving. Visitors are welcome to watch the entire fascinating process and admire the sparkling results, which are only sold in this shop; you'll find it nowhere else in Ireland. Market St., Kinsale, county Cork. ℭ 021/477-4493. www.kinsalecrystal.ie.

Kinsale Silver   Kinsale silver traces its origins back more than 300 years. The Dolan family runs this silversmith workshop (see the section on Wexford shopping in chapter 6, "The Southeast"). You can watch as each piece is wrought and forged by hand, using tools of yesteryear. Pearse St., Kinsale, county Cork. ℭ 021/477-4359. www.iol.ie/~dolan.

SPORTS & OUTDOOR PURSUITS

BICYCLING   Biking along Kinsale Harbor is an exhilarating experience. To rent a bike, contact **The Hire Shop,** 18 Main St. (ℭ 021/477-4884). Rentals average €11 ($10) a day, €55 ($49) per week, depending on equipment. The shop is open Monday through Friday from 8:30am to 6pm and weekends during summer from 9:30am to 6pm.

FISHING   Kinsale is one of the southern Irish coast's sea-angling centers. There are numerous shipwrecks in the area for wreck fishing, including the *Lusitania,* near the Old Head of Kinsale. As many as 22 species of fish have been caught off Kinsale in a single day. If you like shark and wreck fishing, the

Castlepark Marina Centre (✆ 021/477-4959; www.activeireland.com) has three 13m (43-ft.) sea-angling boats that can be chartered by groups of up to 12 people for €285 to €350 ($254–$316) per day. A full day's fishing with rod hire is €45 ($40) per person. Operating out of the White Lady Hotel in Kinsale, **John O'Mahony** (pronounced "O Manny" in Ireland) is the skipper of a 9m (30-ft.) boat that can be chartered for €285 to €305 ($254–$271) per day, plus €40 ($36) for rod hire. **Sporting Tours Ireland,** 71 Main St. (✆ and fax 021/477-4727), arranges sea fishing from Kinsale Harbor or game fishing for salmon and trout in nearby rivers. The fee for sea fishing averages €25 ($22) per day with a three-person minimum; river fishing is €50 ($45) per day. It's open year-round Monday to Friday 9am to 5:30pm.

For fishing tackle or to rent a rod and other equipment, try **The Hire Shop** (see above). They offer a bicycle/fishing-tackle rental package of €20 ($18) for the day.

GOLF Embraced by the sea on three sides, the nothing-short-of-spectacular **Old Head Golf Links** (✆ 021/477-4722; www.oldheadgolflinks.com) is Tiger Woods's favorite Irish course. Named one of *Golf Magazine's* "Top 100 Courses in the World," it is hauntingly beautiful, rain or shine. Old Head has long been home to many species of wildlife, including rare migratory birds. The course retains a resident environmentalist to ensure that crucial habitats are not disturbed. But golfing here costs big money: Greens fees are currently a whopping €250 ($223) for one 18-hole round. Caddy fees run €25 ($23) for a junior caddy, €32 ($29) for a senior caddy.

There is a fine par-72 championship course at the **Fota Island Golf Club,** Carrigtwohill (✆ 021/488-3700), with greens fees of €50 ($46). Less expensive still is the **Kinsale Golf Club,** Kinsale (✆ 021/477-4722), which has an 18-hole, par-71 course at Farrangalway, 4.8km (3 miles) north of town. Greens fees are €35 ($31) on weekends, €30 ($27) weekdays.

SAILING Yacht charters are available from **Sail Ireland Charters,** Trident Hotel, county Cork (✆ 021/477-2927; www.sailireland.com). From Kinsale it is possible to sail to Bantry Bay and back on a 1-week charter, or to the Dingle Peninsula on a 2-week charter. Prices for a six-berth, 11m (35-ft.) yacht run €1,250 to €1,895 ($1,113–$1,687) per week, not including outboard or skipper. A 10-berth, 15m (51-ft.) yacht runs €2,115 to €2,850 ($1,882–$2,537) per week.

TENNIS Court time can be had at the **Oysterhaven Activity Centre** (✆ 021/477-0738), 8km (5 miles) from Kinsale, for €7 ($6.25) per hour. Racket rental is an additional €1.50 ($1.35). It's open Monday to Thursday 4:30 to 9pm, Friday to Sunday 10am to 6pm.

WALKING The **Scilly Walk** is a signposted pedestrian path along the sea that runs from Scilly, the community across the harbor from Kinsale, all the way to Charles Fort. If you continue to walk south along the sea from Charles Fort, you'll find another path that follows the headland to the tip of **Frower Point,** which offers great views across the harbor to the Old Head of Kinsale. The complete walk from Kinsale to Frower Point is 8km (5 miles) each way, and every part of it is quite rewarding.

WATERSPORTS At **Sporting Tours Ireland,** 71 Main St. (✆ and fax 021/477-4727), prices for scuba diving start at €40 ($36) per dive, minimum three persons. Canoeing, windsurfing, and dinghy sailing cost at least €15 ($13) per hour. Pleasure yacht hire prices are at a minimum of €130 ($116) per half day.

Hours are daily 9am to 5:30pm. The **Oysterhaven Activity Centre** (© 021/ 477-0738), 8km (5 miles) from Kinsale, rents Windsurfers, dinghies, and kayaks. It's open Monday to Thursday 10am to 9pm, Friday to Sunday 10am to 7pm.

WHERE TO STAY
EXPENSIVE

The Old Bank House ☆☆ This is a vital address in Kinsale: A splendidly restored, waterside Georgian town house-turned-B&B that is a soothing oasis in this bustling, vibrant town. The place breathes unobtrusive luxury, from the period furnishings to the plush Egyptian cotton towels and bathrobes. *A tip when booking:* Rooms at the front of the house overlook the sailboat-dotted harbor, and the views get significantly better the higher you go. The largest (and priciest) room is the Postmaster's Suite, with a lovely sitting room and a fireplace. The owner, Michael Riese, is a terrific chef and breakfasts are exceptional.

11 Pearse St. (next to Post Office), Kinsale, county Cork. © 021/477-4075. Fax 021/477-4296. www.old bankhousekinsale.com. 17 units. €170–€195 ($151–$174) double. No service charge. Rates include full breakfast. AE, MC, V. **Amenities:** Concierge. *In room:* TV.

MODERATE

Blindgate House ☆☆ (Value) Here's a fabulous new entry to this year's guide: the immensely stylish, inarguably luxurious, and decidedly low-stress Blindgate House. Owner Maeve Coakley and designer Beatrice Blake have combined contemporary dark-wood furnishings, natural fabrics, wood flooring, and serene lighting to achieve an effect that feels wonderfully indulgent and calming. Guest rooms are spacious and elegantly simple, while providing modern conveniences such as satellite TV and modem connections. All in all, you don't normally expect to find this level of designer savvy at this price level. It's a Zen haven amid the bustle of Kinsale town.

Blindgate, Kinsale, county Cork. © 021/477-7858. Fax 021/477-78868. www.blindgatehouse.com. 11 units. €115–€150 ($102–$134) double. No service charge. Rates include full breakfast. AE, MC, V. Closed Nov–Feb. Free parking. **Amenities:** Residents' lounge; babysitting; nonsmoking rooms. *In room:* TV, radio, dataport, tea/coffeemaker, hair dryer.

The Blue Haven ☆ In the heart of town on the old Fish Market, the Blue Haven is everything a small, old-world inn should be: inviting, convivial, and possessing both an excellent restaurant (see "Where to Dine," below) and a fine pub. All the rooms are individually furnished in bright, contemporary style, with local crafts and artwork, and views of either the town or the back gardens. Request one of the rooms in the new wing, which are named for the so-called "wine geese"—Irish exiles who established wineries in France with names like Château McCarthy and Château Dillon. These newer rooms have traditional decor, with canopy beds, window seats, armoires, and brass fixtures.

3 Pearse St., Kinsale, county Cork. © 021/477-2209. Fax 021/477-4268. 17 units. €96–€195 ($85–$174) double. No service charge. Rates include full breakfast. AE, MC, V. **Amenities:** Restaurant (seafood); bar. *In room:* TV.

The Moorings ☆ Beautifully situated overlooking the harbor and marina, Pat and Irene Jones's wonderfully-appointed guesthouse has a bright, contemporary decor with lots of wide-windowed views of the water. All the rooms are nonsmoking, and are individually furnished with brass beds, pastel-colored quilts, and modern art. The best five rooms have balconies facing the harbor— you could nearly swan dive right into the water—while the rest overlook the garden. Guests enjoy use of a cozy, traditional parlor and a large sunlit conservatory with panoramic maritime views. Scilly, this part of Kinsale, is a 10-minute walk along the harbor from the bustling town center. Consequently, it's a much quieter alternative than the Blue Haven, but also further from the action.

Scilly, Kinsale, county Cork. ☎ 021/477-2376. Fax 021/477-2675. 8 units. €130–€140 ($116–$125) double. No service charge. Rates include full breakfast. AE, DC, MC, V. Closed early Nov to Dec 27. Free parking. **Amenities:** Nonsmoking rooms; conservatory; sitting room. *In room:* TV, tea/coffeemaker, hair dryer.

O'Connor's *(Value)* Des O'Connor's popular B&B offers a fabulous standard of comfort and attention to detail for the price. Perched in Scilly above Kinsale Harbor, with uncompromised views of the town and seascape below, this spacious Georgian brick house offers a quartet of lovely guest rooms. Each is decorated in a peaceful shade of fern green or rose, each has terrific views of the harbor, and each is priced exactly the same. The best rooms are the two suites, which have semicircular sunrooms (where breakfast is served) and spa bathtubs. The other two rooms are large doubles with huge picture windows and smaller bathrooms with shower stalls. The several-course breakfast can be served in your room, a copious affair that includes fresh fruit salad, fresh squeezed juices in chilled goblets, smoked salmon, bacon, eggs, sausages, fried tomatoes, toast, and so on. Like The Moorings, this place is in the quieter Scilly district of Kinsale.

Scilly, Kinsale, county Cork. ☎ **021/477-3222**. Fax 021/477-3224. www.kinsale.ie/oconnor.htm. 4 units, 2 with shower only. €120–€170 ($107–$151) double. Rates include full Irish breakfast and service charge. AE, MC, V. Free parking. *In room:* TV, hair dryer.

INEXPENSIVE

Castlepark Marina Centre *(Value)* This is an ideal hostel if you're budget-minded and crazy about fishing (or simply like waterside accommodations). Poised on the southern shore of Kinsale Harbor (opposite the town) and housed in a striking 200-year-old stone-and-slate boatyard, Castlepark Marina is a complex of facilities. It contains a B&B, restaurant, pub, marina, and sea-fishing outfitter. It's ideal for those wanting modest, clean, comfortable lodging and excellent no-frills dining at the water's edge. Hostel rooms are available for 2, 4, 6, 8, or 10 persons, all with bunk beds; some doubles and quadruples have private showers. The flat rate includes linens, duvets, showers, and use of the open kitchen. In cleanliness and taste, this place is streaks ahead of the average hostel; Eddie and Ann McCarthy have created a place that other hostels should emulate. The dining room serves excellent meals, including the day's catch from the marina's own boats. The center is wheelchair accessible. Ferry service is available from the marina to the center of Kinsale every hour for €1.50 ($1.35).

Castlepark, Kinsale, county Cork. ☎ 021/477-4959. Fax 021/477-4958. www.activeireland.com. €30 ($27) double with private shower; from €10 ($8.90) per person for bed and shared showers. MC, V. Closed Nov–Feb. **Amenities:** Restaurant (seafood); bar; self-catering kitchen; laundromat.

WHERE TO DINE
EXPENSIVE

The Blue Haven SEAFOOD Of all the restaurants in Kinsale, this has the hugest following because there's something to suit every budget and appetite. There are really two places to eat: the atmospheric bar for first-rate pub grub or the lovely, skylit restaurant for a full a la carte menu. The bar menu tends toward smoked seafood quiches, seafood pancakes, oak-smoked salmon, steaks, pastas, and a lamb stew that's to die for. The restaurant offers a wide array of fresh seafood, including a house special of salmon slowly cooked over oak chips. Other specialties include brill and scallop bake, farmyard duck with sage-and-onion stuffing, and local venison (in season). The wines have Irish connections;

they come from many of the French wineries that were started by Irish exiles— the Châteaux Dillon, McCarthy, Barton, Kirwan, Lynch, and Phelan. The wines are also on sale in the Blue Haven's wine and cheese shop.

3 Pearse St., Kinsale, county Cork. (✆ 021/477-2209. Reservations recommended. Main courses at the bar €7–€18 ($6.25–$16); fixed 3-course dinner €40 ($36); dinner main courses €23–€30 ($20–$27), €45 ($40) for lobster. AE, MC, V. Bar daily 12:15–3pm and 5:30–9:30pm; restaurant daily 7–10pm.

The Vintage 🌟🌟 SEAFOOD/CONTINENTAL   In an elegant 200-year-old house in the heart of Kinsale, this landmark restaurant offers truly wonderful food in a charming setting. House specialties include Irish salmon baked in a pastry crust, whole black sole meunière, oven-roasted Barbary duck, and grilled whole lobster. The gourmet daily specials menu is enhanced by the expanded new wine list of more than 160 vintages.

50/51 Main St., Kinsale, county Cork. (✆ **021/477-2502.** www.vintagerestaurant.ie. Reservations recommended. Main courses €20–€30 ($18–$27). AE, MC, V. Mar–Apr and mid-Oct to Dec Tues–Sat 6:30–10pm; May to mid-Oct daily 6:30–10:30pm.

MODERATE

Cottage Loft 🌟 CONTINTENTAL   This pleasing shop-front restaurant has a cottage-style decor, with pink linens, antiques, caned chairs, leafy hanging plants, and wooden ceiling beams. The eclectic menu includes such items as farmyard duck in apple brandy sauce, filet of lemon sole rolled in smoked salmon, prawns with lobster sauce, and a delicious rack of lamb. A house specialty is seafood Danielle—salmon stuffed with crab, prawns, and peppers with prawn or nettle sauce.

6 Main St., Kinsale, county Cork. (✆ **021/477-2803.** Reservations recommended. Main courses €8–€20 ($7.10–$18); fixed-price dinner €24 ($21). AE, MC, V. May–Oct daily 5:30–10:30pm; Nov–Apr Tues–Sun 6:30–10:30pm.

Jim Edwards 🌟 CONTINENTAL   This classy, nautical-inspired pub is known for its exceptionally refined pub grub. Dishes include boneless duck with cassis and red-currant sauce, rack of lamb, king prawns in light basil cream sauce, medallions of monkfish with fresh herbs, a variety of steaks, and a range of vegetarian dishes.

Market Quay, off Emmet Place, Kinsale, county Cork. (✆ 021/477-2541. Reservations recommended for dinner. Dinner main courses €10–€22 ($8.90–$20). AE, MC, V. Daily 10:30am–11pm for bar food; lunch 12:30–3pm; dinner 6–10:30pm.

Kinsale Gourmet Store & Fishy Fishy Café 🌟🌟 SEAFOOD DELI/ BISTRO   This is the "It" lunch spot in Kinsale—exactly the sort of hip, relaxed place you wish you had in your hometown. The food is outstanding, prices are fair, and the only apparent drawback is that it's not open for dinner. There's nothing complicated about the reasons behind its success: fresh seafood from the very best local sources (the owner and chef, Martin Shanahan, is up at 5am to handpick the best fish off the boats), perfectly-prepared fresh vegetables, yummy farmhouse cheeses, imaginative salads, and homemade breads. The cold dishes at the counter are wonderful, but Shanahan's culinary talents really shine through with his hot dishes. Start with a bowl of his exceptional seafood chowder, then move on to grilled John Dory with a tomato-and-coriander salsa, or tiger prawns with chick peas and bacon. The dozen or so tables are very much in demand, so go for an early or late lunch to avoid the rush.

Guardwell (next to St. Multoge Church in center of town), Kinsale, county Cork. (✆ **021/477-4453.** Lunch avg. €16–€20 ($14–$18). MC, V. Sept–May, Mon–Sat 11:30am–4:30pm (shop open 9am–6pm); June–Aug, daily 11:30am–4:30pm.

Max's Wine Bar Restaurant INTERNATIONAL   For more than 20 years, this old-world town house with an outdoor patio has been a local favorite for a light snack or a full meal. Although Max is long gone and the place is now in the hands of Anne Marie Galvin, the place now turns out even better fare. Grilled mussels remain a specialty. Other dishes include goat-cheese pastas, fresh soups, and roast lamb with lavender sauce. Nonsmoking conservatory seating is available.

Main St., Kinsale, county Cork. ℂ 021/477-2443. Reservations recommended. Fixed-price early-bird 3-course dinner €18 ($16); dinner main courses €13–€20 ($12–$18). MC, V. Daily 12:30–3pm and 6:30–10:30pm. Closed Nov–Feb.

PUBS

The Bulman   About a mile along the quay in the direction of Fort Charles, the Bulman draws a sweater-and-Wellington boot contingent made up of both fishermen and the yachtsmen. There's also a smattering of artists, students, and foreign expatriates, all of whom come for the good pints and lovely location. Twilight is a special time, when you can take your pint outside, listen to the waves lap up against the wharf, and watch the gulls turn a shimmery orange as the sun sets. Summercove, Kinsale, county Cork. ℂ 021/477-2131.

The Greyhound   Photographers are enchanted with the exterior of this pub, with its neat flower boxes, rows of stout barrels, and handmade signs depicting its namesake, the swift Irish racing dog. The interior rooms are cozy and known for hearty pub grub, such as farmhouse soups, seafood pancakes, shepherd's pie, and Irish stew. Market Sq., Kinsale, county Cork. ℂ 021/477-2889.

Lord Kingsale   A touch of elegance prevails at this handsome pub, decorated with lots of polished horse brass and black-and-white Tudor-style trappings. It takes its name (and ancient spelling) from the first Anglo-Norman baron who took charge of this Irish port in 1223. You'll often find evening singalongs here, and the soup-and-sandwich pub grub is very good. There is nightly live entertainment in the summer. Main St. and Market Quay, Kinsale, county Cork. ℂ 021/477-2371.

The Shanakee   With an Anglicized name (derived from the Irish word *seanachie,* meaning "storyteller"), this vintage pub is known for its music—traditional tunes and ballads nightly—and recently added a full restaurant. 6 Market St., Kinsale, county Cork. ℂ 021/477-7077.

1601   Named after the year of the Battle of Kinsale, this vintage pub is popular with locals and visitors alike. There are three sections: pub, restaurant, and coffeehouse. If you've come to have a pint, head into the intimate back room, where there's a fireplace and seating for only about 50 people. Pearse St., Kinsale, county Cork. ℂ 021/477-2529.

The Spaniard (Finds   Set high on Compass Hill overlooking the harbor, this is perhaps Kinsale's most atmospheric pub. Its exterior, with its whitewashed walls and thatched roof is much photographed, and you can have your pint outside at a table while watching the sun set. Inside, low ceilings and seafaring memorabilia create an intimate feel, and there's a fireplace in the main room. Named for Don Juan de Aguila, who rallied his fleet with the Irish in a historic but unsuccessful attempt to defeat the British in 1601, this old pub draws large crowds for live music nightly in the summer, and on weekends at other times of the year. On Sunday year-round, there is a jazz-blues session at 5pm. Scilly, Kinsale, county Cork. ℂ 021/477-2436.

The White House With its Georgian facade and distinctive name over the front entrance, this is yet another pub that tempts many a visitor to take a photograph. Inside, you will find a popular new bistro, the Antibes Room, with bright decor and a comfortable bar. End of Pearse St., Kinsale, county Cork. (© 021/477-2125.

2 East Cork

County Cork east of Cork City is notably more tame than West Cork. What the region lacks in rugged splendor, it makes up in sophisticated amenities: **Ballymaloe House,** run by Darina Allen, Ireland's answer to Julia Child, is famed for its cooking school and gourmet cuisine, while **Crosshaven** holds the world's most venerable yacht club.

Lying 24km (15 miles) east of Cork City is the harbor town of **Cobh** (pronounced *Cove,* meaning "haven" in Irish). In the days before airline travel, Cobh was Ireland's chief port of entry and exit, with three or four transatlantic liners calling each week. For thousands of Irish emigrants, particularly during the famine years and in the early part of the 20th century, Cobh was the last sight of Ireland they ever saw. Tragically, it was also the last port of call for the RMS *Titanic* before it sank in April 1912. Cobh is still an important, heavily industrialized port. The new visitor attraction, Cobh: The Queenstown Story (see below), tells the city's history, which includes the construction of a magnificent Gothic Revival cathedral, completed in 1915.

The county's major coastal town is **Youghal** (pronounced *Yawl*), 48km (30 miles) east of Cork City, near the Waterford border. A leading beach resort and fishing port, Youghal is loosely associated with Sir Walter Raleigh, who was once the mayor and is said to have planted Ireland's first potatoes here. From a tourist's-eye view, present-day Youghal is a moderately attractive, congested town with a grand stretch of beach just beyond the center.

ESSENTIALS

GETTING THERE If you're driving from Cork City, take the main Waterford road (N25) east. Exit at R624 for Fota and Cobh, or R632 for Shanagarry and Ballycotton. Midleton and Youghal have their own signposted exits. If you're coming from West Cork and want to bypass Cork City (a good idea during rush hour), take the car ferry operated by **Cross River Ferries Ltd.,** Atlantic Quay, Cobh (© 021/481-1485). It links Carrigaloe, near Cobh, with Glenbrook, south of Cork City. Ferries run daily from 7:15am to 12:45am; average crossing time is 5 minutes. No reservations are necessary. Fares are payable on the ferry. Cars cost €3 ($2.65) one way, €4.50 ($4) round-trip, plus €.70 (60¢) for each additional passenger.

Irish Rail (© 021/450-64777; www.irishrail.ie) operates daily train service between Cork City and Cobh via Fota Island. **Bus Eireann** (© 021/450-8188; www.buseireann.ie) also provides daily service from Cork City to Cobh and other points in East Cork.

VISITOR INFORMATION The **tourist office** is open daily 9:30am to 5:30pm at the Old Yacht Club in the lower harbor at Cobh (© 021/481-3301). **Seasonal tourist offices** operate at 4 Main St., Midleton (© 021/461-3702), and Market Square, Youghal (© 024/92390), from May or June through September.

SEEING THE SIGHTS

Ballymaloe Cookery School ⭐ Professional and amateur cooks from all over the world flock here to learn from Darina Allen, the Irish answer to Julia Child. It all started with Darina's mother, Myrtle, whose evangelization of Ireland's bounty of fresh produce at Ballymaloe House restaurant (see "Where to Stay & Dine," below) elevated Irish "country house" cooking to gourmet status. The Allen family's success then led to various other ventures, including the founding of this cooking school and a line of epicurean foods (look for Darina Allen ice cream in Irish supermarkets). The cooking school offers more than 35 different courses a year, which range in length from 1 day to 12 weeks. Topics include bread making, weekend entertaining, hors d'oeuvres, seafood, vegetarian cuisine, family food, barbecue, mushrooms, and Christmas cooking. There are also courses for absolute beginners, on new trends in cooking, and for chef certificates. The beautiful, extensive **gardens** ⭐ on the grounds are open to visitors from April to October, and half-day gardening courses are available. Admission to the gardens is €5 ($4.45) adults, family discounts available. The Garden Café, open Wednesday to Sunday 11am to 6pm, serves memorable morning coffee, light lunches, and afternoon tea.

Kinoith, Shanagarry, county Cork. © 021/464-6785. Fax 021/464-6909. www.ballymaloe-cookery-school.ie. 1- to 5-day courses €175–€665 ($156–$592). Accommodations for students €23 ($20) per night extra. Open year-round; schedule varies.

Cobh: The Queenstown Story ⭐⭐ If there's one thing you learn here, it's that you really don't want to sail from Cobh. Because more than 2.5 million people from all over Ireland departed from Cobh in the mid-1800s (it was then known as Queenstown) for new lives in the United States, Canada, and Australia, the city became synonymous with farewells. This heritage center commemorates Cobh's identity as the last port of call for emigrants: convict ships to Australia, coffin ships to America, and finally transatlantic liners like the *Titanic* and *Lusitania*, both of which sank after leaving Cobh. In a beautifully restored Victorian railway station, the center tells the story of the city, its harbor, and the Irish exodus in a series of displays, with an audiovisual presentation and exhibits that re-create the sinkings of the *Titanic* and the *Lusitania*. The center also has a restaurant, a shop, and a new genealogical referral service.

Cobh Railway Station, Cobh, county Cork. © **021/481-3591.** Admission €5 ($4.45) adults, €4 ($3.55) seniors and students, €2.50 ($2.25) children, €14 ($12) family. Feb–Dec daily 10am–6pm. Last admission 5pm. Closed Jan.

Fota Island Wildlife Park & Arboretum ⭐⭐⭐ Fota Wildlife Park is no ordinary zoo. Wherever possible the animals roam free with no obvious barriers, while mixed with other species and with us human visitors. It's home to rare and endangered types of giraffes, zebras, ostriches, antelopes, cheetahs, flamingos, penguins, and peafowl. Monkeys swing through the trees, and kangaroos, macaws, and lemurs have the run of 16 hectares (40 acres) of grassland. Only the cheetahs are behind conventional fencing. Admission includes entrance to the adjacent **Fota Arboretum.** First planted in the 1820s, it contains trees and shrubs from the world's temperate and subtropical regions, from China to South America and the Himalayas. A coffee shop, a small amusement park for young children, a tour train, picnic tables, and a gift shop are on the grounds.

Fota Island, Carrigtwohill (16km/10 miles east of Cork on Cobh Rd.), county Cork. © **021/481-2678.** www. fotawildlife.ie. Admission €7 ($6.25) adults, €4.20 ($3.75) students, seniors, and children, €27.90 ($25) family. Mid-Mar to Sept daily 10am–5pm; Oct–early Mar weekends 11am–5pm. Rail: Cork-Cobh line from Cork City to Fota station.

The Old Midleton Distillery/Jameson Heritage Centre ☆ If you've always wanted to know what makes Irish whiskey different from Scotch, you've come to the right place. At the production center for Jameson Whiskey and other leading Irish brands, you find the largest pot still in the world (with a capacity of more than 30,000 gallons) and many of the original 1825 structures, which have been meticulously preserved. They include the mill building, maltings, corn stores, still houses, warehouses, kilns, water wheel, and last copper stills manufactured in Ireland. The modern distillery uses high-tech methods, but the production areas are closed to visitors. The center offers an audiovisual presentation, photographs, working models, and a demonstration, followed by a tasting after the tour. The restaurant at the center serves country Irish fare for lunch only.

Distillery Rd., off Main St., Midleton, county Cork. ☎ 021/461-3594. Admission €5 ($4.45) adults, €2 ($1.80) children. Daily 10am–6pm. Tours on request; last tour at 4:45pm.

SHOPPING

Stephen Pearce Pottery One of Ireland's most successful potters, Stephen Pearce creates his popular terra-cotta-and-white earthenware pieces in this huge, skylit studio showroom. Downstairs is the workshop and upstairs is the shop that stocks a selection of Simon Pearce glass, jewelry, linens, and the entire range of Stephen Pearce pottery. You are welcome to watch the team of potters perform this ancient craft and, whenever possible, children get a piece of clay to make their own masterpieces. The workshop is open Monday to Thursday from 8am to 5pm, Friday from 8am to 4:15pm, Saturday from 10am to 6pm, and Sunday from noon to 6pm. Shanagarry, county Cork. ☎ 021/464-6807.

Youghal Pottery This workshop offers a very good selection of pottery and ceramics in stoneware, earthenware, porcelain, and smoke-fired raku, all handmade on the premises. The shop also offers a selection of crafts, woolens and textiles. On N25 to Waterford, 1km (½ mile) from Youghal. ☎ 024/91222.

WHERE TO STAY & DINE
EXPENSIVE

Ballymaloe House ☆ Combining a Georgian farmhouse facade with the tower of a 14th-century castle, this ivy-covered enclave of hospitality run by the Allen family is on a 160-hectare (400-acre) farm, complete with grazing sheep and cows. Ballymaloe is about 23km (20 miles) southeast of Cork City, less than 3.2km (2 miles) from Ballycotton Bay. The only road sign you'll see is one that alerts you to the importance of four-legged traffic: DRIVE SLOW—LAMBS CROSSING. The guest rooms are furnished in informal, comfortable, rather rustic style. Make no mistake—the high cost of a room here reflects the celebrity of Ballymaloe House, to which you may want to assign your own value. The biggest reason for coming is the dining room, a pioneer of Ireland's "country house" culinary school. It is French-inspired and relies on local seafood and produce, accompanied by fresh vegetables from the garden. The kitchen's success has spawned an acclaimed cooking school (see "Seeing the Sights," above) and a shelf of Allen family cookbooks. If you're interested in Ballymaloe only for the food, consider staying at the more stylish Barnabrow Country House, nearby, and popping over here for dinner.

Shanagarry, Midleton, county Cork. ☎ **800/323-5463** in the U.S., or 021/465-2531. Fax 021/465-2021. www.ballymaloe.ie. 33 units. €180–€240 ($160–$214) double. Dinner avg. €46 ($41). No service charge. Accommodation rates include full breakfast. AE, DC, MC, V. **Amenities:** Restaurant (Country House); outdoor swimming pool; 9-hole golf course; tennis courts; sitting room. *In room:* Hair dryer.

MODERATE

Aherne's Seafood Restaurant & Luxury Hotel ⋆⋆   In the heart of a busy seaside resort, this cozy restaurant with rooms has been inked into many travelers' journals because of its first-rate seafood. The Fitzgibbon family has made Aherne's into an icon in Irish hospitality, and after three generations they continue to get the details right. Along with being very comfortably and stylishly furnished, the guest rooms are all quite large by Irish standards. The best five are more like hotel suites than rooms—each with an enormous, king-plus bed and a sea of antiques and designer fabrics. There are two bars and a library-style sitting room, but the main reason to stay here is to be near the superb, classic seafood restaurant. David Fitzgibbon's French-influenced cooking makes the most of the local catch—any fresher and it would still be swimming—including Blackwater salmon, giant prawn tails, rock oysters, and lobsters from the tank. Even the bar food is worth a detour—seafood pies, chowders, crab sandwiches, and crisp salads. Breakfasts here are a real indulgence, served in front of the fire.

163 N. Main St., Youghal, county Cork. ℂ **800/223-6510** in the U.S., or 024/92424. Fax 024/93633. www. ahernes.com. 12 units. €140–€210 ($125–$187) double. Bar lunch from €9 ($8); dinner main courses €16–€21 ($14–$19). No service charge. Accommodation rates include full breakfast. AE, DC, MC, V. **Amenities:** Restaurant (seafood); 2 bars; nonsmoking rooms; library. *In room:* TV, hair dryer, garment press.

Barnabrow Country House ⋆⋆ *(Kids)*   Who in his right mind would open a country house hotel and restaurant within spitting distance of the celebrated Ballymaloe House? But it's not fair to compare this handsome, historic house to Ballymaloe, since they are like apples and oranges. Barnabrow is a terrific place to stay in its own right. Geraldine O'Brien eschews clichés and has created a completely original, highly romantic, and incredibly stylish place to stay in the rolling hills of East Cork. Guest rooms, which are located both in the main house and in stone buildings off the courtyard, are bathed in warm hues of terracottas, apricots, and ochers, and decorated with polished hardwood floors, brass beds, and a wonderful collection of African furniture and crafts. Some of the bathrooms boast old-fashioned, claw-foot tubs. For families, this is that elusive (no, make that near-impossible) find: the truly family-friendly-style hotel. There are cots, cribs, babysitters, and special children's menus. Kids are safe to roam freely, and there are plenty of tame animals to meet and pet—donkeys, ducks, hens, geese, sheep, goats—plus a playground for letting off steam.

Cloyne, Midleton, county Cork. ℂ **021/465-2534.** www.barnabrowhouse.com. 19 units. €100–€150 ($89–$134) double. No service charge. Rates include full breakfast. AE, MC, V. **Amenities:** Restaurant (Continental); lounge; babysitting. *In room:* TV, hair dryer.

Rathcoursey House ⋆   This is exactly the kind of place you imagine when you go looking for that perfect Irish country house. Less than a half hour's drive from Cork airport, this gracious Georgian country manor house is set on 14 hectares (35 acres) of peaceful meadowlands and woods. Beth Hallinan, the owner, has hit the perfect note of casual elegance here, from the infinitely welcoming common rooms to her delicious dinners (served in the dining room, communal style). The guest rooms are all spacious and beautifully decorated with sumptuous colors, quality fabrics, lovely antiques, and open fires.

Ballinacurra, county Cork. ℂ **021/461-3418.** www.rathcoursey.com. 5 units. €170 ($151) double. No service charge. Rates include full breakfast. MC, V. **Amenities:** Drawing room; library. *In room:* Hair dryer.

SELF-CATERING

Myrtleville Oceanside Retreat   This timbered ocean-side retreat—a curiosity in Ireland, where most cottages are built of stone—offers a touch of Cape Cod and a lot more. It's right on the sea, with stunning views from the wraparound deck and living room. Convenient to Cork City, Kinsale, golfing, yachting, deep-sea fishing, and a sandy beach, it's on a small country road, facing the Atlantic at precisely the spot where Victor Hugo worked on *Les Misérables*. Although the house is 80 years old, its kitchen appliances are new, its decor graciously inviting. It sleeps six people comfortably.

Contact Elegant Ireland *C* **01/475-1632.** Fax 01/475-1012. www.elegant.ie. 3 double bedrooms (1 with king-size bed, 2 with queens). €1,325–€1,600 ($1,179–$1,424) per week, including utilities. MC, V. **Amenities:** Babysitting (by prior arrangement). *In room:* Full kitchen, washer/dryer.

3 West Cork

For many, West Cork is Ireland's ultimate destination—not as tourist-heavy as Kerry, yet every bit as alluring. It shares with Kerry the craggy topography and jagged coastline that create many hidden corners and seldom-explored byways. It's impossible to make good time on the roads here, as they tend to be narrower and more sinuous than in other parts of the country, twisting along rivers, through valleys, around mountains, and passing through small town after small town. But those willing to slow down and go with the flow are amply rewarded. You'll probably come across at least one country intersection that's completely unsignposted, and have to slow for a herd of sheep slowly making its way down a country lane. In places, the public route that hugs the coast narrows to just one lane and delivers some of the most heart-stopping views you'll ever experience. You may even come to think of the roads here as one of West Cork's great pleasures.

West Cork's most and least favorite son was Michael Collins, who was immortalized in an eponymous film starring Liam Neeson, Aidan Quinn, and Julia Roberts. Collins was both born and murdered in West Cork and everyone here has an opinion on him. A hero to some, a traitor to others, the "Big Fella" was unquestionably a larger-than-life, utterly charismatic man. The memory of Collins, often referred to as "the man who made Ireland," is preserved, in particular, at the Michael Collins Memorial Center and the ambush site near Macroom.

Some of the most beautiful coastal scenery (and severe weather) is on the islands. **Cape Clear** *€*, home to a bird-watching observatory, is also a well-known *gaeltacht:* Many schoolchildren and adults come to work on their Irish language skills each summer. **Dursey Island,** off the tip of the Beara Peninsula, is accessible by a rickety cable car. **Garinish Island** in Glengarriff is the site of Ilnacullen, an elaborate Italianate garden.

West Cork is known for its enticing and colorful towns. A cluster of artists gives **Ballydehob** a creative flair. At the local butcher, colorful drawings of cattle, pigs, and chickens indicate what's available, and a mural on the outside wall of a pub depicts a traditional music session. Other notable enclaves include the buzzy, seaside town of **Skibbereen** (meaning "little boat harbor"), where live, impromptu traditional music sessions are commonplace in its 22 pubs; the immaculate, flower-box-on-every-sill town of **Clonakilty;** the yachting town **Schull;** and **Barleycove,** a remote, windswept resort that's the last stop before Mizen Head and the sheer cliffs at the island's southernmost tip.

ESSENTIALS

GETTING THERE   N71 is the main road into West Cork from north and south; from Cork and points east, N22 also leads to West Cork.

Bus Eireann (*C* **021/450-8188;** www.buseireann.ie) provides daily bus service to the principal towns in West Cork.

VISITOR INFORMATION Contact the **Skibbereen Tourist Office,** North Street, Skibbereen, county Cork (℃ **028/21766**). It is open year-round Monday to Friday 9:15am to 5:30pm, with weekend and extended hours May through September. There are **seasonal tourist offices** in the Square, Bantry (℃ **027/50229**); Rossa Street, Clonakilty (℃ **023/33226**); and Main Street, Glengarriff (℃ **027/63084**), operating from May or June through August or September.

EXPLORING THE REGION

A number of local historians offer **personalized and group tours** of archaeological and historical sites in West Cork. Each tour has its own specific focus. A range of tours is offered **by Don Healy,** Ardagh, Rosscarbery, West Cork (℃ **023/48726;** mobile 086/818-2580); and **Dolores and Tim Crowley** (℃ **023/46107**). Call for details and bookings. The cost begins around €14 ($12) and diminishes as the group increases in size. Currently, on Saturday mornings at 11am in summer, there's a **Michael Collins Tour** at the ambush site (Béal na mBláth, near Macroom), focused on the assassination of Michael Collins. This tour costs €6 ($5.35) and is conducted and booked by **Fachtna O'Callaghan,** Barley Hill, Rosscarbery (℃ **023/33223;** mobile 086/235-7343).

There is a magnificent **Sheep's Head Loop** drive that begins outside Bantry along the Goat's Path to Kilcrohane, then back through Ahakista, and on to Durrus. The north side is all sheer cliffs and stark beauty (the sunsets are incredible) while the more lush south side road runs right alongside the wondrous Dunmanus Bay.

You may also want to explore **Dursey Island,** a barren promontory extending into the sea at the tip of the Beara Peninsula. It offers no amenities for tourists, but the adventuresome will find great seaside walks and a memorable passage from the mainland on Ireland's only operating cable car. To get there, take R571 past Cahermore to its terminus. As you sway wildly in the rickety wooden cable car, reading the text of Psalm 91 (which has kindly been posted to comfort the nervous), you might wonder whether a ferry might not have been a wiser option. It wouldn't. Apparently the channel between island and mainland is often too treacherous to permit regular crossing by boat. There is no lodging on the island, so be sure you know when the last cable car departs for the mainland; for schedule information, call ℃ **027/73017.**

SEEING THE SIGHTS

Bantry House ⟨★★ On the edge of the town of Bantry, this house was built around 1750 for the earls of Bantry. It has a mostly Georgian facade with Victorian additions. Its interior contains many items of furniture and objets d'art from all over Europe, including four Aubusson and Gobelin tapestries said to have been made for Marie Antoinette. Bantry House has been in the White family, descendants of the third earl of Bantry, since 1739. The gardens, with original

---

Impressions

Oh, well do I remember the black December day
The landlord and the sheriff came to drive us all away;
They set my roof on fire with their cursed English spleen,
And that's another reason why I left old Skibbereen.
—Anonymous (19th c.)

statuary, are beautifully kept and well worth a stroll. Climb the steps behind the building for a panoramic view of the house, gardens, and Bantry Bay.

In both the east and west wings of Bantry House, **bed-and-breakfast rooms** are available, tastefully furnished with reproductions in keeping with the period and style of the house. Prices for bed-and-breakfast, including a tour of the house and gardens, run €220 to €240 ($196–$214) for a double room with private bathroom.

Bantry, county Cork. ℭ 027/50047. www.bantryhouse.ie. Admission €9.50 ($8.45) adults, €8 ($7.10) students and seniors, free for children under 14. Mar 17–Oct daily 9am–6pm. Closed Nov–Feb.

Creagh Gardens ★   This is one of the most beautiful lesser-known gardens in Ireland, hemmed in by colorful meadows and the waters of an exquisitely picturesque estuary. Serpentine paths wind among magnificent old oaks, maples, and beeches, with occasional prospects through meadow and wood to the weathered facade of Creagh House. In the early summer, the garden is loud with the drone of bees and the blazing colors of the massive rhododendrons, fuchsia, and hydrangeas. A walled garden encloses a greenhouse, vegetable garden, and collection of domestic fowl. Despite its modest size (8-plus hectares/20 acres), Creagh contains many surprises and hidden corners, and really shouldn't be missed by garden lovers. A tearoom offers light lunches that feature produce from the walled organic garden.

On R595, 5.6km (3½ miles) S of Skibbereen, Creagh, Skibbereen, county Cork. ℭ 028/22121. Admission €4 ($3.55) adults, €2.50 ($2.25) children. Daily 10am–6pm.

Derreen Gardens ★   The benign climate of West Cork and Kerry has made this subtropical informal garden a site of great natural beauty, blessedly situated on a hilly promontory on the breathtaking north coast of the Beara Peninsula. In the late 19th century, the garden was planted with American species of conifer, many of which have become venerable giants. One path follows the sweep of the shoreline through tunnels of rhododendron, while others wind through the dense foliage of the promontory, opening occasionally to a view of the mountains or an entrancing rocky glen. The garden is home to several rarities, most notably the New Zealand tree ferns that flourish in a small glade, among giant blue gum and bamboo.

Signposted 1.6km (1 mile) off R571 in Lauragh, county Kerry. ℭ 064/83588. Admission €4 ($3.55). Apr–Oct daily 10am–6pm.

Drombeg Stone Circle ★★   This ring of 17 standing stones is the finest example of a megalithic stone circle in county Cork. Hills slope gently toward the sea nearby, and the builders could hardly have chosen a more picturesque spot. The circle dates from sometime between 153 B.C. and A.D. 127, but little is known about its ritual purpose. Just west of the circle are the remains of two huts and a cooking place; it is thought that heated stones were placed in a water trough (which can be seen adjacent to the huts), and the hot water was used for cooking. The cooking place dates from between A.D. 368 and 608.

Off R597 between Rosscarbery and Glandore, county Cork.

Ilnacullin (Garinish Island) ★★   Officially known as Ilnacullin, but usually referred to as Garinish, this balmy island was once barren. In 1919, it was transformed into an elaborately planned Italianate garden, with classical pavilions and myriad unusual plants and flowers from many continents. It's said that George Bernard Shaw wrote parts of *St. Joan* under the shade of its palm trees. The island can be reached on a covered ferry operated by **Blue Pool Ferry,** the

Moments Southern Exposure: An Excursion to Cape Clear Island

Cape Clear Island, 13km (8 miles) off the mainland, is the southernmost inhabited point in Ireland. It is a *Gaeltacht,* or Irish-speaking area, which welcomes nearly 200 students every year who come to perfect their Irish. The country's islands are part of its last frontier, the last bits of rugged untamed splendor. Even Cape Clear is struggling to preserve the balance of beauty and livelihood that allows remote settlements to remain both remote and settled. This place can be bleak, with a craggy coastline and no trees to break the rush of sea wind, but that very barrenness appeals to many for its stark beauty, rough and irregular, but not without solace and grace. In early summer, wildflowers brighten the landscape, and in October, passerine migrants, some on their way from North America and Siberia, fill the air. Seabirds are present in abundance during the nesting season, especially from July to September. At any time, Cape Clear is unforgettable.

The first step to enjoying the island is reaching it. The *Naomh Ciarán II* offers passenger-only ferry service year-round, seas permitting. In the highest season (July–Aug), the *Naomh Ciarán II* leaves Baltimore Monday to Saturday at 11am, 2:15, and 7pm, and Sunday at noon, 2:15, 5, and 7pm; return service from Cape Clear departs Monday to Saturday at 9am and 6pm, and Sunday at 11am, 1, 4, and 6pm. Service is always subject to the seas and is more limited off-season. The passage takes 45 minutes, and a round-trip ticket costs €11 ($10). For inquiries, contact Captain Conchúr O'Driscoll (© **028/39135**).

Summer service is also available aboard *Karycraft,* departing Schull daily in July and August at 10am, 2:30, and 4:30pm; and departing Cape Clear at 11am, 3:30, and 5:30pm. In June and September, service is limited to one crossing daily, departing Schull at 2:30pm and Cape Clear at 5:30pm. The passage takes 45 minutes. For inquiries, contact Captain Kieran Molloy (© **028/28138**).

Blue Pool, Glengarriff (© **027/63333**). Boats operate every 30 minutes during the island's visiting hours.

Glengarriff, county Cork. © **027/63040**. Admission €3.50 ($3.15) adults, €2.50 ($2.25) seniors, €1.50 ($1.35) students and children, €8 ($7.10) family. Boat trips €6.50 ($5.80) per person. Mar and Oct Mon–Sat 10am–4:30pm, Sun 1–5pm; Apr–June and Sept Mon–Sat 10am–6:30pm, Sun 1–7pm; July–Aug Mon–Sat 9:30am–6:30pm, Sun 11am–7pm. Closed Nov–Feb. Last landing 1 hr. before closing.

Michael Collins Memorial Centre The truth is, there is very little to see here. More a shrine than an "attraction," this is a place for those who revere Collins rather than those who want to learn more about him. The stone farmhouse in which Collins and all his siblings were born was later turned into outbuildings, which survive. The new, larger farmhouse into which his family moved when Michael was 10 was burned to the ground in 1921 by the Black and Tans. Only the foundation remains. Equally shrinelike is the ambush site at Béal na mBláth, near Macroom, where he was assassinated. For better insight

Once you're on Cape Clear, there are a number of things to see, including birds galore, seals, dolphins, the occasional whale, ancient "marriage stones," and a goat farm offering courses on everything you ever wanted to know (about goats). Don't miss the hauntingly spectacular castle ruins on the island's western shore.

There's also a lot to do apart from hiking and sightseeing. **Cléire Lasmuigh,** Cape Clear Island Adventure Centre (☏ **028/39198**), offers an array of outdoor programs, from snorkeling and sea kayaking to hill walking and orienteering. Instruction or accompanied sessions are available by the hour, day, or week. For example, prices for a 5-day sea-kayaking package (including meals, housing, instruction, and equipment rental) start at €250 ($223). Coastal cruises—for sea angling, scuba diving, or bird-watching—are the specialty of **Ciarán O'Driscoll** (☏ and fax **028/39153**). There are no plans for a shopping mall, but you will enjoy the local art and crafts and books in Harpercraft and the Back Room in Cotter's Yard, North Harbour, as well as the nearby pottery shop. While you're at it, pick up a copy of Chuck Kruger's *Cape Clear Island Magic.* There's no better introduction to the wonder of this place.

Modest hostel, B&B, and self-catering accommodations are available by the day, week, or month. The island's **An Óige Youth Hostel** (☏ **028/39198**) is open March through October. Most B&Bs are open year-round. They include **Fáilte** (contact Eleanór Uí Drisceoil, ☏ **028/ 39135**); and **Ard na Gaoith** (contact Eileen Leonard, ☏ **028/39160**). For self-catering cottages by the day or week, contact **Ciarán O'Driscoll** (☏ **028/39135**). To drop anchor, the **Southernmost House** (see "Self-Catering," later in this section) is without parallel. You can't miss the town's three pubs and two restaurants, which will keep you well fortified. (Also, the fruit scones baked and served at Cistin Chléire on North Harbour are the among the best in Ireland.)

Cape Clear has a helpful website at **www.oilean-chleire.ie**.

into Michael Collins and his childhood, read the excellent biographies by Frank O'Connor and Tim Pat Coogan, available at all good Irish bookshops.

Signposted off N71, 5.6km (3½ miles) west of Clonakilty, Woodfield, county Cork.

Mizen Vision ★★★   At the southernmost part of Ireland, the land falls precipitously into the Atlantic breakers in a procession of spectacular sea cliffs. A suspension bridge permits access to the Irish Lights signal station, now a visitor center, on a small rock promontory, the southernmost point on the Irish mainland. It affords pinch-yourself-it-can't-be-real views of the surrounding cliffs, open sea, and nearby Three Castle Head. Whales, seals, dolphins, porpoises, and daredevil seabirds contribute to the spectacle. Even on a foggy day, the excellent guided tour and exhibitions make the fascinating history of the Mizen come alive for visitors. On a clear day, this is an absolute must.

On the way out to Mizen Head, you'll pass Barleycove Beach, one of the most beautiful beaches in southwest Ireland, and a great place to explore.

Mizen Head, county Cork. © **028/35591**, or 028/35115 (Mar–Nov). Fax 028/35603. www.mizenvision.com. Admission €4.50 ($4) adults, €3.50 ($3.15) seniors and students, €2.50 ($2.25) children, free for children under 5, €14 ($12) family. Apr, May, and Oct daily 11am–5pm; June–Sept daily 10am–5:30pm; Nov to Mar Sat–Sun 12pm–6pm. Closed weekdays Nov–Mar. Take R591 to Goleen, and follow signs for Mizen Head.

1796 Bantry French Armada Exhibition Centre   This center commemo-rates Bantry Bay's role in the battle of 1796, when a formidable French armada—inspired by Theobold Wolfe Tone and the United Irishmen—sailed from France to expel the British. Almost 50 warships carried nearly 15,000 soldiers to this cor-ner of southwest Ireland. Thwarted by storms and a breakdown in communica-tions, the invasion never came to pass. Ten ships were lost. Too storm-damaged to return to France, the frigate *Surveillante* was scuttled off Whiddy Island, and lay undisturbed for almost 200 years. The centerpiece of this exhibition is a giant scale (1:6) model of the ship in cross section, illustrating life in the French Navy 200 years ago and various activities as they happened on board.

East Stables, Bantry House, Bantry, county Cork. © **027/51796**. Admission €4 ($3.55) adults, €2.50 ($2.25) seniors and students. Daily mid-Apr to mid-Oct, 10am–4pm.

SHOPPING

Bandon Pottery Shop   Right in the town center, this attractive shop pro-duces a colorful line of hand-thrown tableware, vases, bowls, and other acces-sories. Paintings, sculpture, and other works of art are on display and for sale. St. Finbarr's Place, Bandon, county Cork. © **023/43525**.

Courtmacsherry Ceramics   Overlooking the sea, this studio and shop offers an array of porcelain animals, birds, butterflies, and tableware, all inspired by the flora and fauna of West Cork. Visitors are welcome to watch potter Peter Wolstenholme at work on new creations. Main St., Courtmacsherry, county Cork. © **023/ 46239**.

Prince August Ltd   Prince August is Ireland's only toy-soldier factory. The shop produces and displays a huge collection of metal miniatures based on J. R. R. Tolkien's classic books *The Hobbit* and *The Lord of the Rings*. Factory tours are available. Kilnamartyra, Macroom, county Cork. © **026/40222**. Off the N22, north-west of Kinsale.

Quills Woollen Market   This family-run enterprise is headquartered in a small village deep in the heart of West Cork's Gaelic-speaking region. You'll find wonderful handmade sweaters, knitwear, and garments made from wool and goatskins. Main St., Ballingeary, county Cork. © **026-47008**.

Rossmore Country Pottery   This family-run studio produces a lovely range of practical domestic stoneware and a colorful collection of earthenware deco-rated flower pots. Rossmore, county Cork (11km/7 miles from Clonakilty on Bandon-Bantry Rd.) © **023/38875**.

SPORTS & OUTDOOR PURSUITS

BEACHES   **Barleycove Beach** is a vast expanse of pristine sand and a fine view out toward the Mizen Head cliffs; despite the trailer park and holiday homes on the far side of the dunes, large parts of the beach never seem to get crowded. Take R591 to Goleen, and follow signs for Mizen Head. There is a public parking lot at the Barleycove Hotel.

Inchydoney Beach, on Clonakilty Bay, is famous for both its gorgeous, extrawide beach and the salubrious **Inchydoney Lodge & Spa** (© **023/33143**), which specializes in thalasso (seawater) treatments. For more information, visit **www.inchydoneyisland.com**.

BICYCLING   The **Mizen Head, Sheep's Head, and Beara peninsulas** offer fine roads for cycling, with great scenery and few cars. The Beara Peninsula is the most spectacular; the other two are less likely to be crowded with tourists during peak season. The loop around Mizen Head, starting in Skibbereen, is a good 2- to 3-day trip, and a loop around the Beara Peninsula from Bantry, Glengarriff, or Kenmare is at least 3 days at a casual pace.

In Skibbereen, 18- and 21-speed bicycles can be rented from **Roycroft's Stores** (✆ **028/21235;** roycroft@iol.ie); prices start at €45 ($40) per week. If you call ahead, you can reserve a lightweight mountain bike with toe clips at no extra cost—an enormous advantage over the leaden, battleship-like bicycles rented at most stores. One-way riding from Skibbereen to Killarney or Kenmare can be arranged for an additional €20 ($18).

BIRD-WATCHING   Cape Clear Island is the prime birding spot in West Cork, and one of the best places in Europe to watch seabirds and passerine migrants (see the box above). The best time for seabirds is July to September, and October is the busiest month for passerines (and for bird-watchers, who flock to the island). There is a bird observatory at the **North Harbour,** with a warden in residence from March to November, and accommodations for bird-watchers; to arrange a stay, write to **Kieran Grace,** 84 Dorney Court, Shankhill, county Dublin. **Ciarán O'Driscoll** (✆ **028/39153**), who operates a B&B on the island, also runs boat trips for bird-watchers and has a keen eye for vagrants and rarities.

DIVING   The **Baltimore Diving & Watersports Centre,** Baltimore, county Cork (✆ **028/20300**), provides equipment and boats to certified divers for exploring the many shipwrecks, reefs, and caves in this region. The cost is €40 ($36) per dive with equipment. Various 2-hour to 15-day certified PADI courses are available for all levels of experience. For example, beginners can take a 2- to 3-hour snorkeling course for €16 to €20 ($14–$18), or a scuba-diving course for €25 to €40 ($22–$36); experienced divers can take the 2-week PADI instructor course.

FISHING   The West Cork Coast is known for its many shipwrecks, which are quickly taken over by all manner of marine life after they hit the ocean floor. Wreck fishing is popular all along the Irish coast, and this is one of the best places for it. **Mark and Patricia Gannon** of Woodpoint House, Courtmacsherry (✆ **023/46427**), offer packages that include bed-and-breakfast in their idyllic stone farmhouse and a day's sea angling aboard one of their two new Aquastar purpose-built fishing boats. A day's fishing costs €40 ($36) per person. Boats holding up to 12 people can be chartered for €300 to €330 ($267–$294) per day, including a qualified skipper. For sea angling in Baltimore, contact **Michael Walsh** (✆ **028/20352**) or **Kieran Walsh** at the Algiers Inn (✆ **028/20145**).

KAYAKING   With hundreds of islands, numerous inviting inlets, and a plethora of sea caves, the coast of West Cork is a sea kayaker's paradise. **Lough Ine** offers warm, still waters for beginners, a tidal rapid for the intrepid, and access to a nearby headland riddled with caves that demand exploration. In Castletownbere on the dramatic and rugged Beara Peninsula, **Beara Outdoor Pursuits** (✆ **027/70692;** www.bearaoutdoors.com), specializes in accompanied trips out and around Bere Island and as far as Glengariff. Frank Conroy is a terrific guide and can lead you to waters that are as protected or as rough as you want them.

SAILING   The **Glenans Irish Sailing Club** (www.glenans-ireland.com) was founded in France and has two centers in Ireland, one of which is in Baltimore Harbor. The centers provide weeklong courses at all levels, using dinghies, cruisers, catamarans, or windsurfers; prices are €349 to €549 ($303–$481). The living facilities are spartan, with dorm-style accommodations and you cook for yourself. The clientele is mostly middle-aged and younger, from Ireland and the Continent. Weekend sailing courses are available in Baltimore in May, June, September, and October for €165 ($147) per person; call ✆ **028/20154** or fax 028/20312 for advance booking.

WALKING   One of the most beautiful coastal walks in West Cork begins along the banks of **Lough Ine,** the largest saltwater lake in Europe. Connected to the sea by a narrow isthmus, the lake is in a lush valley of exceptional beauty. To get there, follow signs for Lough Ine along R595 between Skibbereen and Baltimore; there is a parking lot at the northwest corner of the lake. The wide trail proceeds gradually upward from the parking lot through the woods on the west slope of the valley, with several viewpoints toward the lake and the sea beyond. Once you reach the hilltop, there is a sweeping view of the coast from Mizen Head to Galley Head. Walking time to the top and back is about 1½ hours.

At the vertigo-inducing high cliffs of **Mizen Head,** it was once possible, for the sure of foot and steady of spirit, to explore the surrounding heights. No more. Access to the cliffs is limited to the suspension bridge leading to the "Mizen Vision" lighthouse. No ticket or admission is required for access to the bridge.

Near Lauragh on the Beara Peninsula is the abandoned town of **Cummingeera,** at the base of a cliff in a wild, remote valley. The walk to the village gives you a taste for the rough beauty of the Caha Mountains, and a sense for the lengths to which people in pre-famine Ireland would go to find a patch of arable land. To get to the start of the walk, take the road posted for Glanmore Lake south from R571; the road is 1.3km (⁸⁄₁₀ mile) west of the turnoff for Healy Pass. Follow the Glanmore Lake road 1km (⁶⁄₁₀ mile), then turn right at the road posted for "stone circle"; continue 2.1km (1⅓ miles) to the point at which the road becomes dirt, and park on the roadside. From here, there is no trail—simply walk up the valley to its terminus, about 2km (1¼ miles) away, where the ruins of a village hug the cliff's base. Where the valley is blocked by a headland, take the route around to the left, which is less steep. Return the way you came; the whole walk—4km (2½ miles)—is moderately difficult, and takes about 2 hours.

An easy seaside walk on the **Beara Peninsula** begins at Dunboy Castle, just over a mile west of Castletownbere on R572; this stretch of trail is part of the O'Sullivan Beara trail, which may eventually extend from Castletownbere to Leitrim. You can park your car along the road, by the castellated gatehouse, or drive up to the castle; the entry fee is €.70 (60¢) for pedestrians, €2.50 ($2.25) for a car. The castle is a ruined 19th-century manor house overlooking the bay, with some graceful marble arches spanning the grand central hall. Just down the road are the sparse ruins of a medieval fortress. Beyond, the trail continues to the tip of Fair Head through overarching rhododendrons, with fine views across to Bere Island. A walk from the gatehouse parking lot to the tip of Fair Head and back takes about 2 hours.

The **Sheep's Head Way,** voted "Best Walk in Ireland," by *Country Walking* magazine, makes a 89km (55-mile) loop, and incorporates numerous smaller day loops. The *Guide to the Sheep's Head Way,* available in most local stores and tourist offices, combines history, poetry, and topography in a fantastic introduction to the region. In the 17th century, the Sheep's Head Peninsula was described as "being all rocky and frequented only by eagles and birds—never to be inhabited by reason of the rough incommodities." It still is a rough place, and you won't find many tourists in its more remote reaches. There are treasures to be found, but you might have to work a little harder to unearth them here than in regions long since "discovered."

One of Ireland's most beautiful spots, **Gougane Barra** (which means "St. Finbar's Cleft") is a still, dark, romantic lake a little northeast of the Pass of Keimaneigh, 24km (15 miles) northeast of Bantry off T64 (also well signposted on the Macroom-Glengarriff rd.). This is the source of the River Lee, where St. Finbar founded a monastery in these deeply wooded mountains, supposedly on the small island connected by a causeway to the mainland. Though nothing remains of the saint's 6th-century community, the setting is idyllic, with rhododendrons spilling into the still waters where swans glide by. The island now holds an elfin chapel and eight small circular cells, dating from the early 1700s, as well as a modern chapel. Today Gougane Barra is a national forest park, and there are signposted walks and drives through the wooded hills. There's a small admission charge per car to enter the park.

WINDSURFING   Weeklong courses and equipment rental are available at the **Glenans Sailing Club** (see "Sailing," above), in Baltimore. If you'd rather spend just a day, try the **Courtmacsherry Leisure Center** (© 023/46177), where rates are €11 ($10) per hour. There is a sheltered beach in Courtmacsherry where beginners can get started and another beach that's good for wave jumping nearby.

WHERE TO STAY
EXPENSIVE

Ballylickey Manor House 🏵🏵   Could any setting be more romantic? Ballylickey Manor is hidden in rugged inlets with a stunning view of Bantry Bay, nestled on 4 hectares (10 acres) of award-winning lawns and gardens, with a backdrop of mountains and moorlands. The 300-year-old manor house, built as a shooting lodge for Lord Kenmare, has five large suites, and there are an additional seven more rustic, modern wood cottages clustered around the swimming pool. Every room is decorated with country-style furnishings. This inn has an international ambience, thanks to the influence of its owners, the Franco-Irish Graves family, and a largely European clientele.

Bantry-Glengarriff Rd. (N71), Ballylickey, county Cork. © **800/323-5463** in the U.S., or 027/50071. Fax 027/50124. www.ballylickeymanorhouse.com. 12 units. €204–€340 ($182–$303) double. Rates include full breakfast. AE, DC, MC, V. Closed Nov to mid-Apr. **Amenities:** Restaurant (Continental); outdoor swimming pool; drawing room. *In room:* TV, hair dryer, garment press.

Longueville House Hotel 🏵🏵🏵   This is one of those rare places that is refined enough to please the most sophisticated traveler and yet one that remains charmingly rural, without a hint of pretense. The house itself is a white palatial affair built about 1720 and situated on a 200-hectare (500-acre) farmland estate with its own winery. All this grandness is saved from pomposity by

---

Service Charges
A reminder: Unless otherwise noted, room rates don't include service charges (usually 10%–15% of your bill).

the down-to-earth, laid-back manner of the O'Callaghan family. Guest rooms are sumptuous without going overboard, furnished in old-world style, with family heirlooms and period pieces, and most have bucolic views of the gardens, grazing pastures, or vineyards. The beacon of Longueville is the Presidents' Room, an award-winning restaurant where William O'Callaghan continues to demonstrate why he is one of Ireland's most gifted chefs. He sources produce and vegetables from the hotel's farm and gardens and from local markets, and transforms them into something memorable. In the summer, meals are also served in a gorgeous, skylit Victorian conservatory.

Killarney road (N72), Mallow, county Cork. © 800/323-5463 in the U.S., or 022/47156. Fax 022/47459. www.longuevillehouse.ie. 22 units. €168–€336 ($150–$299) double. Rates include full breakfast. Dinner €48 ($43). AE, DC, MC, V. Closed mid-Dec to early Mar. **Amenities:** Restaurant (modern Continental); nonsmoking rooms; drawing rooms. *In room:* TV, hair dryer, garment press.

MODERATE

Baltimore Harbour Hotel 🗷🗷 (Kids)   Nearly every room in this strategically placed harbor hotel has a lovely view. The public rooms—bar, garden room, and Clipper Restaurant—are fresh, bright, and inviting, with a contemporary nautical feel. The guest rooms are quite comfortable, with extraordinary views of the harbor and mountainous coastline. Rooms 216 and 217 are especially spacious, at no extra cost. A host of weekend, multiple-night, and B&B-and-dinner packages offer special rates. The hotel also features 18 self-catering apartments, which are ideal for families, as is the kids' club (for ages 4 and older) that offers activity programs in the summer and on bank holiday weekends.

Signposted off R595 in Baltimore, county Cork. © 028/20361. Fax 028/20466. www.bhrhotel.ie. 64 units. €110–€160 ($98–$142) double. Rates include full Irish breakfast and service charge. Packages available. AE, DC, MC, V. **Amenities:** Restaurant (international); bar; indoor swimming pool; gym; Jacuzzi; steam room; nonsmoking rooms. *In room:* TV, tea/coffeemaker, hair dryer.

Kilbrittain Castle 🗷   Built by the grandson of Brian Boru, high king of Ireland, in 1035, this is the oldest habitable castle in Ireland. In fact, it is very much lived in by the Cahill-O'Briens, who followed a long line of Irish chieftains, Norman invaders, Cromwellian troops, and English planters and made this their family home. Kilbrittain looks and feels like an authentic castle because that's exactly what it is. Climb the steep, winding tower staircase to the great Medieval hallway, and then up another staircase to your room, and you'll appreciate why it's best to leave your expectations below. The history in these walls is the history of Ireland, and Tim's stories make the stones speak. Spending the night here—in surprising comfort and absolute peace—is a unique experience. The public rooms are full of historical gems, while the guest rooms are spacious, the views enchanting, and the breakfasts generous.

9.7km (6 miles) from Bandon, 56km (35 miles) from Cork airport, Kilbrittain, county Cork. © 023/49601. Fax 023/49702. 5 units. €125 ($113) double. Rates include full Irish breakfast but not VAT. Family discounts available. No credit cards. **Amenities:** Nonsmoking rooms; reading room.

Sea View House 🗷🗷   This handsome, seaside hotel is homey and full of interesting heirlooms, fine antiques, and an utter disregard for fads and trends. Instead, Kathleen O'Sullivan and her staff just stick to the old-fashioned principles of good service and make sure that every guest is taken care of. The cheerily decorated rooms are individually furnished in a manner Grandma would like, with dark woods, busy fabrics, and mattresses firm enough to bounce a penny off of. Request a room in the front of the house for peekaboo views of Bantry Bay through the leafy trees. The establishment is best known for Kathleen's award-winning cuisine, the sort of hearty comfort food that's reassuringly still devoted to using politically incorrect dollops of fresh cream, real butter, a slug of booze, and salt.

Bantry-Glengarriff road (N71), Ballylickey, county Cork. (📞) **800/447-7462** in the U.S., or 027/50073. Fax 027/ 51555. 17 units. €135–€175 ($120–$156) double. Rates include full breakfast. AE, MC, V. Closed mid-Nov to mid-Mar. **Amenities:** Restaurant (Continental); bar; outdoor patio. *In room:* TV, hair dryer.

West Cork Hotel ★★ *(Finds)*   The name to know here is John Murphy, one of the most congenial, hospitable, and hardworking innkeepers in Ireland. His is the sort of comfy, old-style hotel that is stylish in spite of itself. Everything is designed to induce contentment and familiarity, and it's a testimony to its success that the public areas—particularly the buzzy pub—always draw a big local crowd. Murphy is the kind of host who can work the crowd, juggle a dozen tasks at once, and still make you feel like you're his one and only personal guest. Guest rooms are very relaxing in the old-fashioned Irish way, with lots of traditional dark woods and mismatched patterns. The handsome, yellow building at the Kennedy bridge is the first thing you see if you enter Skibbereen from the west on N71, or the last as you leave town if you're heading in the opposite direction.

Ilen St., Skibbereen, county Cork. (📞) **028/21277**. Fax 028/22333. 36 units. €95–€135 ($85–$120) double. Rates include full breakfast. AE, MC, V. Closed Dec 22–28. **Amenities:** Restaurant (Continental), bar. *In room:* TV.

Westlodge Hotel ★ *(Kids)*   Though more than a tad generic-looking from the outside, this modern three-story hotel is ideal for budget-conscious families. What separates it from the ho-hum pack is its spanking new leisure center and wide array of child-friendly amenities. The public areas and guest rooms are bright and airy, enhanced by wide windows, blonde-wood furnishings, and bright Irish fabrics. Westlodge specializes in family holidays and offers organized activities for children June through August. For even better value, ask about the multiple-day packages.

Off Bantry-Glengarriff rd. (N71), Bantry, county Cork. (📞) **027/50360**. Fax 027/50438. www.westlodgehotel. ie. 95 units. €114 ($101) double. Rates include full breakfast and service charge. AE, DC, MC, V. **Amenities:** Restaurant (international); bar; indoor swimming pool; tennis; squash; gym; Jacuzzi; steam room; kids' playroom; babysitting; nonsmoking rooms. *In room:* TV, tea/coffeemaker.

INEXPENSIVE

Ballinatona Farm ★ *(Finds)*   Like the region that surrounds it, this working dairy farm is a little-known treasure, just far enough off the beaten track to be spared the crowds that congest much of the southwest during the summer. While the landscape isn't wild and rugged like that of the West Cork coast, its gentler beauty is still magnificent. The energetic hosts, Jytte Storm and Tim Lane, know the region well and their excitement over its hidden delights is truly infectious. Just a 15-minute walk brings you to the stunning valley that holds Coomeenatrush waterfall at its head, while longer walks take you along the ridgeline of the surrounding hills. The house is tucked high onto the hillside at 240m (800 ft.) above sea level and commands magnificent views. A modern addition has been designed to take full advantage of the site, and all but one room command striking vistas. The second-floor front room, reached by a spiral staircase, offers a breathtaking view, with glass walls on three sides.

4.8km (3 miles) out of Millstreet on the Macroom rd., Millstreet, county Cork. (📞) **029/70213**. Fax 029/ 70940. 6 units. €55 ($49) double. Rates include full breakfast. 25% discount for children under 12 sharing B&B with parents. MC, V. Closed Dec 15–Jan 1. *In room:* TV, tea/coffeemaker.

Fortview House ✹✹   This former winner of the Irish Agritourism Award for "best B&B in the South" boasts pristine country-style rooms, with antique pine furniture, wood floors, iron and brass beds, and crisp Irish linens. Beamed ceilings and a warm color palette add to the comfortable feeling, and the spacious, inviting sitting room, equipped with tea and coffee facilities and an honor-system bar, completes the welcome. Violet Connell's copious breakfasts are legendary, with seven varieties of fresh-squeezed juices jostling for space on a menu that includes hot potato cakes, pancakes, kippers, smoked salmon, and eggs prepared however you'd like.

If you prefer self-catering, there is also a three-bedroom cottage (sleeps six) on the Fortview grounds that rents for €330 ($294) per week in low season and €600 ($534) per week in the summer.

On R591 from Durrus toward Goleen, Gurtyowen, Toormore, Goleen, county Cork. ✆ **028/35324.** 5 units. €70 ($62) double. Rates include full breakfast. No credit cards. Closed Nov–Feb. **Amenities:** Sitting room. *In room:* TV.

Glebe Country House ✹   Built in 1690 as a rectory, Glebe House is now the gracious home of Jill Bracken. The charming guest rooms, each comfortable and individually decorated, enjoy views of the rose and herb gardens that wreath the house. A fireplace and piano accent the peaceful living room. The enticing breakfast menu includes waffles, scrambled eggs with rosemary shortbread, "cheesy French toast" (a Glebe House invention), and homemade brown and soda breads. The spacious dining room provides a lovely setting for candlelit five-course dinners partly drawn from the house's garden. Dinners cost €25 ($23); book before noon and bring your own wine.

The Coach House apartments behind the main house offer comfortable self-catering accommodations. The ground-floor, two-bedroom garden apartment sleeps five, with a double and single bed in one room and twin beds in the other. Equipped with all the essentials, it has an open living-dining-kitchen area decorated in simple country-cottage style. The ideal choice for families is the one-bedroom loft apartment that sleeps five, with a double and single bed in one room and a pullout sofa in the living room. A compact kitchen is equipped with all you need to prepare substantial meals. Both apartments have linens, and each has a private patio-garden. A chalet in the garden, Beech Lodge, is available for up to six guests.

Balinadee (off Balinadee center), Bandon, county Cork. ✆ **021/4778294.** Fax 021/4778456. http://indigo.ie/ ~glebehse. 6 units. €64–€90 ($57–$80) double. Rates include full Irish breakfast and service charge. 3 self-catering units. €285–€508 ($254–$452) per week. MC, V. **Amenities:** Living room. *In room:* Tea/coffeemaker.

Heron's Cove ✹✹   Locals on the Mizen Head peninsula know the Heron's Cove as a terrific seafood restaurant (see below), but it's really what the Irish call a restaurant with rooms and a very inviting place to stay. Its three sea-view rooms, with balconies overlooking a beautiful, sheltered cove, are tremendously appealing. The rooms are comfortably furnished, and the atmosphere of the entire B&B is so friendly, it's almost familial. Enjoying a wonderful dinner with wine over sunset and then scampering upstairs to your room for a moonlit view of the harbor is paradise found.

Signposted in the center of Goleen, county Cork. ✆ **028/35225.** Fax 028/35422. www.westcorkweb.ie/ heron. 5 units. €70 ($62) double; €84 ($75) triple. Rates include full breakfast. AE, MC, V. Children under 12 (except infants) not accepted. *In room:* TV, tea/coffeemaker, hair dryer.

Rock Cottage ✹   This new B&B offers a wonderfully secluded, relaxing retreat in what was once Lord Bandon's hunting lodge. The spacious guest rooms, in the tastefully restored Georgian building, combine ample shares of elegance and comfort. Here's the best news: Your hostess, Barbara Klötzer, used to be the head chef at Blair's Cove and is now able to focus her culinary wizardry on a handful of lucky guests.

Barnatonicane (11km/7 miles from Durrus on R591), Schull, county Cork. ℂ 028/35538. www.mizen.net/ rockcottage. 3 units. €68 ($61) double. Rates include full breakfast. 3-course dinner from €32 ($28). MC, V. Free parking. *In room:* TV, hair dryer.

Rolf's Holiday Hostel ✿ Rolf's is a long-established, award-winning, family-run hostel beautifully situated on Baltimore Hill overlooking the harbor and the Mizen peninsula. This appealing cut-stone complex of buildings—somehow alpine, with steep lofts and wide beams—offers an array of lodging and dining options. All guests have access to the open self-catering kitchen, which is unlikely to compete with Rolf's Cafe Art and Restaurant. The art here refers to the rotating exhibits of contemporary Irish painting and sculpture selected by Frederika Haffner, Rolf's daughter, a fine sculptor. Both cafe and restaurant are open daily from 8am to 9:30pm, providing excellent value across their impressive menus and wine lists. Johannes Haffner, Rolf's son, grew up here and takes great pride in offering the finest in hostel hospitality.

0.5km (⅓ mile) off R595, signposted just outside Baltimore center, Baltimore, county Cork. ℂ and fax 028/ **20289**. €18 ($18) per person double room; €12–€14 ($11–$12) per person in 4-bed dorm; €5 ($4.45) per person for camping. MC, V. **Amenities:** Restaurant (international); bicycle hire. *In room:* Full kitchen, washing machine.

SELF-CATERING

Ahakista ✿ Simplicity, charm, and an alluring location on the Sheep's Head Peninsula (the least touristy of Cork's three peninsulas) make this recently restored stone cottage a magnificent getaway. It's a short walk to the two-pub farming and fishing village of Ahakista. The old-fashioned cottage, whose low-slung ceilings and traditional, narrow staircase lend intimacy, enjoys fine views of Dunmanus Bay and is surrounded by 97km (60 miles) of marked walking paths along the wild coastline, which the Nobel-winning poet Seamus Heaney has described as "water and ground in their extremity." The two-bedroom cottage has one double and one twin.

Contact Elegant Ireland. ℂ 01/475-1632. Fax 01/475-1012. www.elegant.ie. 1 cottage. From €770 ($654) per week. MC, V. *In room:* TV, full kitchen, dishwasher, washing machine, dryer.

Anne's Grove Medieval Miniature Castle ✿✿ *Finds* What could be more romantic than a tiny, Gothic castle just big enough for two? Designed by the distinguished architect Benjamin Woodward in 1853, this gate lodge of Anne's Grove Gardens was conceived as a medieval castle in miniature. It had been vacant and neglected from the 1940s to the 1990s, when the Irish Landmark Trust turned it into something immensely cozy and enchanting. There is a living room with a fireplace, a well-equipped kitchen, one double bedroom, and a bathroom. There are hardwood floors throughout the lodge and the furnishings are rustic and inviting. The architectural lines of the rooms—leaded windows, doorways, and ceilings—all echo the classic Gothic arch. There is perhaps no more dreamy base from which to explore northwest Cork, and the price is downright unbeatable.

Castleownroach, county Cork. Contact the Irish Landmark Trust ℂ 01/670-4733. Fax 01/670-4887. www. irishlandmark.com. €194 ($173) for 4 nights in low season, sliding up to €441 ($392) per week in high season. *In room:* Kitchen, microwave.

Baltimore Holiday Homes ✿ *Kids* These well-established holiday cottages form an attractive cluster safely set back from the road and overlooking a lovely inlet near Baltimore, a charming harbor town. They are best suited to families wanting to settle in for a week's self-contained seaside and island-hopping holiday. Tennis courts and pitch-and-putt (miniature golf) are offered, and the new leisure center of the nearby Baltimore Harbour Hotel is accessible for a fee. The cottages are bright and inviting, with white walls and pine furniture, and each has an open fireplace and three bedrooms. They are fully equipped, including washer, dryer, and microwave. Baltimore's two small food shops are minutes away on foot, and there is regular bus service to Skibbereen.

Off R595 just before Baltimore center, Baltimore, county Cork. Contact Home From Home Holidays, 26/27 Rossa St., Clonakilty, county Cork. ℂ 023/33110. Fax 023/333131. 32 cottages. €254–€635 ($226–$565) per week. 2-day rates available in low and midseason. MC, V. *In room:* TV, kitchen, microwave, washing machine, dryer.

Galley Head Lightkeeper's House ★★ *(Finds* A recent addition to the wonderful stable of Irish Landmark Trust properties, this lightkeeper's house stands next to the lighthouse on the tip of breathtaking Galley Head, just south of Clonakilty. It's actually two connecting houses, which can be rented separately or together. In the first house, downstairs comprises a fully-equipped kitchen, sitting room, and lounge/bedroom with bathroom. Upstairs, there are two bedrooms (one double, one twin) and a bathroom. The second house has the same basic floor plan, minus the downstairs lounge and bathroom. Both houses are chockablock with old-world charms—sturdy mahogany furnishings, oversized sofas and armchairs, quality Irish linens, a fireplace in every room, wide plank floors, and deep windowsills with wooden interior shutters. It's location is idyllic: As remote as you'd hope for from a lighthouse, and still only a 20-minute drive to bustling Clonakilty, a little jewel in West Cork. As with all ILT properties, there is no TV. One of the property's best assets is its caretaker, Gerald Butler, a third-generation lightkeeper (on both sides of his family!) who actually grew up in this house. He's a marvelous storyteller and history buff and can give you a private tour of the lighthouse.

Galley Head, county Cork. Contact the Irish Landmark Trust ℂ **01/670-4733.** Fax 01/670-4887. www.irish landmark.com. €294 ($262) for 4 nights in low season, sliding up to €782 ($696) per week in high season. *In room:* Kitchen, dishwasher, washing machine.

The Southernmost House ★ This exquisitely situated cottage is the southernmost dwelling on the southernmost inhabited Irish island, Cape Clear. Quite simply, it redefines the word *getaway*. Five years were devoted to the restoration of this centuries-old traditional island cottage, and everything was done to perfection. The exposed stone walls, pine ceilings and floors, multiple skylights, and simple, tasteful furnishings make it a most pleasing and comfortable nook, and the views from virtually every window are stunning. It's cozy enough for a love nest, and spacious enough for a family of six (it has three bedrooms). If it rains—and this has been known to happen on the "Cape"—the massive stone fireplace is the perfect antidote. The one down side: This place is so popular that you'll need to book up to 9 months in advance.

Glen West, Cape Clear, county Cork. ℂ and fax **028/39157.** http://indigo.ie/~ckstory. 1 cottage. €250–€550 ($223–$490) per week. No credit cards. Discounts for longer-term rentals. *In room:* TV, kitchen, washing machine.

WHERE TO DINE
EXPENSIVE
Blair's Cove ★★★ INTERNATIONAL This restaurant boasts one of the most romantic, captivating dining rooms in Ireland: a stone-walled, high-ceilinged

affair with open fireplaces overlooking majestic Dunmanus Bay. Owners Philip and Sabine de Mey have converted a stone barn with a 250-year-old Georgian courtyard and terrace into one of the best dining experiences in southwest Ireland. You begin with the hors d'oeuvre buffet of cold starters (perhaps salmon fumé, prawns, oysters, or mousse), a display large enough to satisfy some dinner appetites. Moving on to your main course, the menu is particularly strong on grilled meats—rack of lamb, grilled rib of beef—and fresh fish, such as monkfish filet flambéed in Pernod. For dessert, step up to the grand piano that doubles as a sweets trolley. Naturally, the cheese course includes plenty of Irish farmhouse varieties, including the local specialty, Durrus. Don't look for cutting-edge, break-the-mold fusion; this place is all about classic dishes done in a familiar way, only better than you've likely had them elsewhere. There are also a small number of rooms available for nightly B&B, costing €100 ($89) for a double room. For longer stays, there are also four duplex apartments and two cottages available for rent, for €250 to €1,050 ($223–$935) per week.

Barley Cove Rd., Durrus, county Cork. ✆ 027/61127. Fax 027/61487. Reservations required. Dinner with starter buffet €40 ($35); buffet and dessert €29 ($26). MC, V. Apr–June and Sept–Oct Tues–Sat 7:30–9:30pm; July–Aug Mon–Sat 7:30pm–9:30pm. Closed Nov–Mar.

Chez Youen ✮✮ SEAFOOD   Overlooking the marina of this picturesque harbor town, Frenchman Youen Jacob's restaurant has been wooing West Cork since 1978. The decor evokes Jacob's native Brittany and is tremendously relaxing, with beamed ceilings, candlelight, colorful pottery, and an open copper fireplace. Lobster is the specialty, fresh from local waters, but the steaks, poached wild salmon in fennel, and leg of lamb are also very good. The chef's signature dish—the one that commands the €40 ($35) price tag—is a mountainous gourmet shellfish platter, which includes Galley Head prawns, Baltimore shrimp, and velvet crab, as well as local lobster and oysters, all served in the shell. The owners also run the neighboring Baltimore Bay Guesthouse and the lower-priced bistro, La Jolie Brise.

The Pier, Baltimore, county Cork. ✆ 028/20136. Reservations required. Fixed-price dinner €29 ($26); dinner main courses €14–€40 ($12–$35). AE, DC, MC, V. Mar–Oct daily 6pm–midnight, Sun noon–4pm.

MODERATE

Casino House ✮✮ INTERNATIONAL   Kerrin and Michael Relja's enchanting little restaurant is yet another West Cork eatery with a fabulous setting and terrific ambience. The views of Courtmacsherry Bay will make you gasp, and the interior is Nantucket meets Provence. Michael's cooking is invariably inventive and eclectic, yet thankfully focused on bringing out the flavors of the main ingredient. His menu changes according to what's fresh at the market, but starters might include cream of carrot soup served with caramelized walnuts, or terrine of quail with pistachio nuts and shiitake mushrooms. Main dishes might include roast duck with Madeira, or Michael's melt-in-your-mouth sole with spring onions and wild rice. The globe-trotting wine list includes many good-value options from Germany and Italy.

16km (10 miles) from Kinsale on coast rd. (R600), Coulmain Bay, Kilbrittain, county Cork. ✆ 023/49944. Reservations recommended. Main courses €13–€20 ($12–$18). MC, V. Tues–Sat 12:30–3pm, 6:30–10:30pm. Closed Christmas, Easter, last 2 weeks Aug.

The Customs House ✮✮ *Finds* SEAFOOD   This just may be the best fish restaurant in Ireland, and is certainly in the top three. Susan Holland is a truly talented chef (not to mention artist—check out her paintings on the walls) who finds inspiration in Mediterranean ingredients but is restrained enough to heighten the fish's flavors without overpowering them. The blackboard menu lists mouthwatering choices such as red mullet with tapenade, grilled squid with hot salsa, and John Dory with spinach, soy, and ginger. Duck also appears on the menu (both as confit and roast), though it would be a pity to dine here on anything other than fish. The dress code is smart casual, with the emphasis on smart. Children under 12 would most likely feel like a fish out of . . . well, you know.

50m (164 ft.) from the Pier (beside the Garda Station), Baltimore, county Cork. ℂ 028/20200. Reservations recommended. Dinner main courses €12–€18 ($11–$16). No credit cards. Wed–Sat 7–10pm. Closed Oct to mid-Mar.

The Heron's Cove ⟨★⟩ SEAFOOD   This is a regular port of call for locals, who know they can count on the Heron's Cove for excellent dining free of formality and risk. The casual, modest dining room enjoys a splendid view of a secluded cove. The menu, while focused on local seafood, has selections for vegetarians and carnivores alike. The fisherman's broth is exceptional, as are monkfish in red pepper cream sauce and Dunmanus Bay scallops pan-fried with leek and smoked bacon cream sauce. For dessert, indulge in the Russian cheesecake. Do visit the open-for-browsing cellar of 50 to 60 international wines. Study the labels, discuss them with other diners, and make your selection. Sue Hill, your host, is a knowledgeable oenophile and will help out if you find yourself deadlocked in indecision.

Signposted in the center of Goleen, county Cork. ℂ **028/35225.** Reservations recommended. Main courses €15–€28 ($13–$25). AE, DC, MC, V. May–Oct daily noon–10pm.

Lettercollum House ⟨★★⟩ IRISH COUNTRY HOUSE   In this county overflowing with excellent places to eat, Lettercollum is one of the standard bearers. Owner and chef, Con McLoughlin, creates simple, original dishes based on organic produce from the adjacent walled garden, pigs raised on the premises, and locally-caught fish. His menu changes daily, and there are always several vegetarian choices. Choices might include grilled wild salmon with sorrel sauce, a perfectly grilled steak, cannelloni of sea spinach and brie with tomato butter sauce, or organic lamb tahini. The dining room was once a convent's chapel and a lovely stained-glass window remains. The service is informal in the best way possible, the desserts worth saving room for, the crowd duly appreciative.

Timoleague, county Cork. ℂ **023/46251.** www.lettercollum.ie. Reservations required. Fixed-price 5-course dinner €32 ($28). AE, MC, V. Mid-Mar to Nov daily 7:30–9:30pm, Sun 1–3pm. Open same hours on weekends Dec to mid-Mar.

Mary Ann's ⟨★★⟩ PUB GRUB   Here is one of those darling little places for which you'll thank yourself for making the effort to stop by. Dating from 1844, this rustic pub perched halfway up a hill is decorated with ships' wheels, lanterns, and bells—but you don't go to Mary Ann's for the cute decor. You go for the superlative-inspiring pub grub. The menu offers seafood salads and West Cork cheese plates, as well as more ambitious dishes, such as scallops meunière, sirloin steak with garlic butter, chicken Kiev, and deep-fried prawns. Weather permitting, you can sit outside in the attractive courtyard.

Castletownshend, Skibbereen, county Cork. ℂ **028/36146.** Reservations recommended for dinner. Bar food €4–€20 ($3.55–$18); restaurant 5-course fixed-price dinner €30 ($27). MC, V. Daily 12:30–2pm and 6–9pm. Closed holidays.

Wine Vaults INTERNATIONAL   Established in 1854, this is Skibbereen's oldest pub and one of its most popular. The look is classic Irish rural pub, with plenty of nooks and crannies, soft lighting, brick, woodwork, and open fires. It is a handy place for lunch or a light meal in transit. The menu includes soups, sandwiches on pita bread, and pizzas (the house special is topped with mushrooms, peppers, onions, ham, and salami). There is live traditional music or jazz and blues nightly.

73 Bridge St., Skibbereen, county Cork. ✆ **028/23112.** All items €4–€18 ($3.55–$16). No credit cards. Food served daily noon–9pm; music and drinks until 12:30am.

INEXPENSIVE

Adele's ⭐⭐ *Value* SEAFOOD/PASTA   By day, this tiny establishment is a hip tearoom, serving up delicious baked goods, teas, and excellent sandwiches (the ciabatta with tomato and slabs of local Gubbeen cheese is a real treat). But the place really takes off in the evening, when the upstairs dining room opens and Simon Connor prepares meals with his creative use of basic, local ingredients. The menu changes daily and each dish is so enticing that it's always a challenge to choose: perhaps fresh mussels with angel-hair pasta and leeks, or tagliatelle with rosemary and parsley pesto. Panzanella, a marinated salad with red peppers, capers, and soaked bread crumbs, is a delicious summer appetizer. The atmosphere is casual, and families are welcome. There's a separate nonsmoking dining room. This place is one of the few good restaurants in Cork that won't take a big bite out of your budget. B&B is also available, at budget rates.

Main St., Schull, county Cork. ✆ **028/28459.** Reservations recommended. Lunch and baked goods €7–€14 ($6.25–$12); dinner main courses €11–€20 ($10–$18). MC, V. Apr–June and Sept–Nov Wed–Sun 9:30am–10pm; July–Aug daily 9:30am–10pm. Closed Dec–Mar.

9

County Kerry: "The Kingdom"

For many first-time travelers to this island, Kerry is the Ireland they've imagined in their mind's eye. To start with, it's picture-postcard gorgeous, with three jagged peninsulas chock-ablock with spectacular coastal vistas and vibrant towns. Spend a bit of time here, and you'll also see that Kerry is a place of disorienting contrasts, where the crassest tourist attractions coexist with some of Ireland's most spectacular scenic wonders. It's a rugged place for the most part, some of it so rugged that it's seldom visited and remains quite pristine; Ireland's two highest mountains, Carrantuohill and Mount Brandon, are examples of such places. You could be driving along—say, on the famous and much-trafficked Ring of Kerry, which traces the shores of the Iveragh Peninsula—make one little detour from the main road, and be in true wilderness. The transition can be startling.

Like many of Ireland's western counties, county Kerry has always been an outpost of Gaelic culture. Poetry and music are intrinsic to the lifestyle, as is a love of the outdoors and sports. Gaelic football is an obsession in this county, and "The Kingdom" wins more than their share of national championships. You'll also find some of Ireland's best golf courses, and the fishing for salmon and trout is equally hard to resist.

1 The Iveragh Peninsula

For the majority of the literally millions of annual tourists to county Kerry, whose explorations follow the turn of a bus driver's wheel, the Iveragh Peninsula is synonymous with the Ring of Kerry. It's important to realize, however, that the Ring is a two-lane strip of road measuring roughly 178km (110 miles), tracing the peninsula's shores and missing its tip altogether, while the Iveragh Peninsula itself is nearly 1,813 sq. km (700 sq. miles) of wild splendor, which you'll notice once you get off the tourist strip. Admittedly, almost everyone who gets this far feels compelled to "do" the Ring of Kerry; so, once it's done, why not take an unplanned turn, get truly lost and let serendipity lead you to the unexpected and the unspoiled?

ESSENTIALS

GETTING THERE   **Bus Eireann** (*C* **064/34777**; www.buseireann.ie) provides limited daily service from Killarney to Caherciveen, Waterville, Kenmare, and other towns on the Ring of Kerry. The best way to get to the Ring is by car, on N70 and N71. Some Killarney-based companies offer daily sightseeing tours of the Ring (see section 2, "Killarney," later in this chapter).

VISITOR INFORMATION   Stop in at the **Killarney Tourist Office,** Aras Fáilte, at the Town Centre Car Park, Beech Road, Killarney (*C* **064/31633**), before you explore the area. For hours, see section 2, later in this chapter. The **Kenmare Tourist Office,** Market Square, Kenmare (*C* **064/41233**), is open

County Kerry

Blennerville Windmill **2**
Ceardlann Craft Village **7**
Crag Cave **8**
Derrynane House National Historic Park **12**
Dingle Oceanworld **7**
Eask Tower **6**
Gallarus Oratory **4**
Gap of Dunloe **15**

Ionad An Bhlascaoid Mhoir (The Blasket Centre) **5**
Kenmare Druid Circle **14**
Kenmare Heritage Centre **13**
Kerry Bog Village Museum **9**
Kerry the Kingdom **1**
Skellig Experience **10**
Staigue Fort **11**
Tralee Steam Railway **3**

daily Easter through September, 9:15am to 5:30pm, with extended hours in July and August. The rest of the year (from Oct–Easter), it's open Monday to Saturday.

THE RING OF KERRY ✸✸✸

Undoubtedly Ireland's most popular scenic drive, the Ring of Kerry is a 178-km (110-mile) route around the Iveragh Peninsula, a panorama of seacoast, mountain, and lake-land vistas. Bicyclists usually avoid this route, because the scores of tour buses that thunder through every day in the summer aren't always generous about sharing the road. For the most part, the Ring follows N70 and circles the Iveragh Peninsula; most people start and finish at the largest hub, Killarney, but Kenmare makes for a more charming, more classy, and more peaceful base. The drive runs in either direction, but we strongly recommend a counterclockwise route for the most spectacular views.

Although it's possible to circle the peninsula in as little as 4 hours, the only way to get a feel for the area and the people is to leave the main road, get out of your car, and explore some of the inland and coastal towns. **Portmagee** is a lovely seaside town, connected by a bridge to **Valentia Island,** which houses the informative Skellig Heritage Centre. **Caherdaniel** has a museum devoted to Daniel O'Connell, one of Ireland's great historical figures.

The most memorable and magical site to visit on the Iveragh Peninsula is **Skellig Michael,** a rocky pinnacle towering over the sea, where medieval monks built their monastery in ascetic isolation. The crossing to the island can be rough, so you'll want to visit on as clear and calm a day as possible. Seabirds nest here in abundance, and more than 20,000 pairs of gannets inhabit neighboring Little Skellig during the summer nesting season.

Kenmare is by far the most enchanting town on the Ring of Kerry route. Originally called Neidin (pronounced Nay-*deen,* meaning "little nest" in Irish), Kenmare is indeed a little nest of verdant foliage nestled between the River Roughty and Kenmare Bay. It's an ideal base for Kerry sightseeing because it is well laid out and immaculately maintained—flower boxes in the windows, litter-free sidewalks—and full of excellent restaurants and places to stay.

From Kenmare to **Killarney,** the Ring road takes you through a scenic mountain stretch known as **Moll's Gap.** Killarney is best known for the scenic beauty surrounding the town, and in particular for the spectacular, 10,000-hectare (25,000-acre) **Killarney National Park,** which includes the famous **Killarney Lakes** and the scenic **Gap of Dunloe.** The town itself, while colorful and bustling, has become a victim of its own success in recent years. Tourism is more in-your-face here than perhaps anywhere else in Ireland, with generic souvenir shops and overpriced restaurants chockablock.

Departing Killarney, follow the signs for **Killorglin.** When you reach this little town, you're on N70. You might want to stop and walk around Killorglin, a spot that's widely known for its annual mid-August horse, sheep, and cattle fair. It's officially called the **Puck Fair,** because local residents capture a wild goat (symbolizing the *puka* or *puki,* a mischievous sprite) from the mountains and enthrone it in the center of town as a sign of unrestricted merrymaking.

Continue on N70, and vistas of Dingle Bay will soon appear on your right. **Carrantuohill,** at 1,041m (3,414 ft.) Ireland's tallest mountain, is to your left. The open bogland constantly comes into view. From it, the local residents dig pieces of peat, or turf, to burn in their fireplaces. Formed thousands of years ago, the boglands are mainly composed of decayed trees. They tend to be bumpy if you attempt to drive over them too speedily, so do be cautious.

Impressions of Kenmare

As I leave behind Neidin it's like purple splashed on green
My soul is strangely fed through the winding hills ahead
She plays a melody on wind and streams for me
Won't you remember, won't you remember, won't you remember me?
And we wind and climb and fall like the greatest waltz of all
Float across the floor, her sweet breath outside the door
And it's time that I was gone across the silver tear
Won't you remember, won't you remember, won't you remember me?
—Jimmy MacCarthy, Irish songwriter

The Ring winds around cliffs and the edges of mountains, with nothing but the sea below—another reason you will probably average only 48kmph (30 mph), at best. As you go along, you'll notice the remains of many abandoned cottages. They date from the famine years, in the mid-1840s, when the Irish potato crop failed and millions of people starved to death or were forced to emigrate. This peninsula alone lost three-fourths of its population.

The next town on the Ring is **Glenbeigh,** a palm-tree-lined fishing resort with a lovely duned beach called Rossbeigh Strand. You might want to stop here or continue the sweep through the mountains and along the sea's edge to **Cahirciveen.** From Cahirciveen, you can make a slight detour to see **Valentia** (which you may also see spelled "Valencia"). The offshore island is 11km (7 miles) long and one of Europe's westernmost points. Connected to the mainland by a bridge at Portmagee, this was the site from which the first telegraph cable was laid across the Atlantic in 1866. In the 18th century, the Valentia harbor was famous as a refuge for smugglers and privateers; it's said that John Paul Jones, the Scottish-born American naval officer in the War of Independence, also anchored here quite often.

Head next for **Waterville,** an idyllic spot wedged between Lough Currane and Ballinskelligs Bay off the Atlantic. For years, it was known as the favorite retreat of Charlie Chaplin; today it's the home of the only Irish branch of Club Med.

If you follow the sea road north of town out to the Irish-speaking village of **Ballinskelligs,** at the mouth of the bay, you can also catch a glimpse of the two Skellig Rocks. Continuing on N70, the next point of interest is **Derrynane,** at **Caherdaniel,** the home of Daniel O'Connell, remembered as "the Liberator" who freed Irish Catholics from the last of the English Penal Laws in 1829. Derrynane is now a national monument and park and a major center of Gaelic culture.

Watch for signs to **Staigue Fort,** about 3.2km (2 miles) off the main road. One of the best preserved of all ancient Irish structures, this circular fort is constructed of rough stones without mortar of any kind. The walls are 4m (13 ft.) thick at the base, and the diameter is about 27m (90 ft.). Not much is known of its history, but experts think it probably dates from around 1000 B.C.

Sneem, the next village on the circuit, is a colorful little hamlet with twin parklets. Its houses are painted in vibrant shades of blue, pink, yellow, purple, and orange, like a little touch of the Mediterranean plunked down in Ireland.

As you continue on the Ring, the foliage becomes lusher, thanks to the warming waters and winds of the Gulf Stream. When you begin to see lots of palm trees and other subtropical vegetation, you'll know you are in **Parknasilla,** once a favorite haunt of George Bernard Shaw.

SEEING THE SIGHTS

Derrynane House National Historic Park ⚑ On a 128-hectare (320-acre) site along the Ring of Kerry coast between Waterville and Caherdaniel, this is where Ireland's Great Liberator, Daniel O'Connell, lived for most of his life. The Irish government maintains the house as a museum. It's filled with documents, illustrations, and memorabilia related to O'Connell's life, including a 25-minute audiovisual display about him titled *Be You Perfectly Peaceable.*

Caherdaniel, county Kerry. ✆ **066/947-5113.** Admission €2.50 ($2.25) adults, €2 ($1.80) seniors, €1.30 ($1.15) students and children, €6.50 ($5.80) family. Nov–Mar Sat–Sun 1–5pm; Apr and Oct Tues–Sun 1–5pm; May–Sept Mon–Sat 9am–6pm, Sun 11am–7pm.

Kenmare Druid Circle ⚑ On a small hill near the center of town, this large Bronze Age Druid stone circle is magnificently intact, with 15 standing stones surrounding a dolmen tomb.

Kenmare, county Kerry.

Kenmare Heritage Centre ⚑ To learn more about the delightful town of Kenmare, the Ring of Kerry's "little nest," step inside this visitor center. Exhibits recount Kenmare's history as a planned estate town that grew up around the mine works founded in 1670 by Sir William Petty, ancestor of the Lansdownes, the local landlords. The center also displays locally made lace, and tells the story of the woman who originated the craft. A scripted walking trail around the town is also under development.

The Square, Kenmare, county Kerry. ✆ **064/41491.** Admission €3 ($2.65) adults, €2 ($1.80) seniors, €1.30 ($1.15) students and children, €6.50 ($5.80) family. Mon–Sat 9:15am–5:30pm, with extended summer hours.

Kerry Bog Village Museum This little cluster of thatched-roof cottages shows what life was like in Kerry in the early 1800s. The museum village has a blacksmith's forge and house, turf-cutter's house, laborer's cottage, thatcher's dwelling, tradesman's house, and stable and dairy house. Stacks of newly cut turf sit piled high beside the road. There are also a football pitch and other recreational facilities. The interiors are furnished with authentic pieces gathered from all parts of Kerry.

Ring of Kerry rd. (N71), Ballycleave, Glenbeigh, county Kerry. ✆ **066/976-9184.** Admission €4.50 ($4) adults, €4 ($3.55) students, €10 ($8.90) family. AE, DC, MC, V. Mar–Nov daily 9am–6pm; Dec–Feb by appointment.

Seafari Eco-nature Cruises and Seal-Watching Trips ⚑⚑ This is the very best way to see the sights and splendors of Kenmare Bay: On board a 15m (50-ft.) covered boat. The 2-hour cruises cover 16km (10 miles) and are narrated by well-versed guides who provide information on local history, geography, and geology. The guides frequently point out sea otters, gray seals, herons, oyster catchers, and kingfishers. Boats depart from the pier next to the Kenmare suspension bridge. Reservations are recommended.

Kenmare Pier, Kenmare, county Kerry. ✆ **064/83171.** www.seafariireland.com. Tickets €13 ($12) adults, €10 ($8.90) students, €6.50 ($5.80) children under 12, €32 ($28) family. May–Oct 4 cruises daily.

The Skellig Experience ⚑⚑ Eleven kilometers (7 miles) off the mainland Ring of Kerry route (R765) on Valentia Island, this relatively new attraction blends right into the terrain, with a stark stone facade framed by grassy mounds. Inside, through a series of displays and audiovisual presentations, the center offers a detailed look at the area's birds and plant life. In particular, it tells the story of the Skellig Rocks, Skellig Michael, and Little Skellig. The experience isn't complete without the sea cruise, which circuits the islands.

Skellig Heritage Centre, Valentia Island, county Kerry. ℂ **066/947-6306.** Exhibition and audiovisual €4.50 ($4) adults, €4 ($3.55) seniors and students, €2 ($1.80) children under 12, €9 ($8) family of 2 adults and up to 4 children; exhibition, audiovisual, and sea cruise €20 ($18) adults, €18 ($16) seniors and students, €10 ($8.90) children under 12, €52 ($46) family. AE, MC, V. Apr–Oct 10am–6pm. Closed Nov–Mar.

THE SKELLIG ISLANDS ✦✦✦

A visit to these two crags rising precipitously from the sea, about 14km (8 miles) off the coast of the Iveragh Peninsula, is sure to be one of your more memorable experiences in Ireland. Seen from the mainland, the islands have a fantastic aspect, seeming impossibly steep and sharp-angled. Yet it was on the highest pinnacle of the larger island, **Skellig Michael,** that a community of monks chose to build a monastery in the 6th or 7th century. They carved steps out of the rock to provide access from the stormy waters below. Rough seas make it inaccessible for much of the year, but records surviving from this remote community include the kidnap of one of the monks by the Vikings and the death of the abbot in A.D. 823. The island later became a marriage destination for 16th-century couples after the change to the Gregorian calendar meant that they were forbidden to get married during lent on the mainland.

You'll start off by taking a 45-minute boat passage from the mainland. Upon disembarking, you'll begin a long ascent of the island using the same steps trodden by the monks for 6 centuries, until the monastery was abandoned in the 12th or 13th century. The monastic enclosure consists of six beehive-shaped huts of mortarless stone construction, two oratories, and a church; there is also a collection of carved stones that have been found on the island. The smaller of the Skellig Islands has no space for human habitation, but is home during nesting season to more than 20,000 pairs of gannets.

Ferries leave daily from Ballinskelligs, usually between 9am and noon; call **Joe Roddy** (ℂ **066/947-4268**) or **Sean Feehan** (ℂ **066/947-9182**). Ferries from Valentia Island are run by **Des Lavelle** (ℂ **066/947-6124,** while those from Portmagee are run by **O'Keefe's** (ℂ **066/947-7103**). The cost is €34 ($30) per person.

SHOPPING

Many good craft and souvenir shops lie along the Ring of Kerry, but those in **Kenmare** offer the most in terms of variety and quality. Kenmare shops are open year-round, usually Monday to Saturday 9am to 6pm. From May to September, many shops remain open till 9 or 10pm, and some open on Sunday from noon to 5 or 6pm.

Avoca Handweavers at Moll's Gap   In one of the most scenic settings, this shop is on a high mountain pass (288m/960 ft. above sea level) between Killarney and Kenmare. It's a branch of the famous tweed makers of Avoca, county Wicklow, dating from 1723. The wares range from colorful hand-woven capes, jackets, throws, and knitwear to pottery and jewelry. Chefs trained at the Ballymaloe Cookery School staff the excellent coffee shop. Closed from November to mid-March. Ring of Kerry rd. (N71), Moll's Gap, county Kerry. ℂ **064/34720.**

Cleo   A branch of the long-established Dublin store of the same name, this newly expanded trendy women's-wear shop is known for its beautiful, vibrantly colorful tweed and linen fashions, as well as specialty items such as Kinsale cloaks. 2 Shelbourne Rd., Kenmare, county Kerry. ℂ **064/41410.**

Kenmare Bookshop This shop specializes in books on Ireland, particularly biographies and books by Irish writers, as well as maps and guides to the surrounding area. Offerings include ordinance survey maps, walking and specialist guides, and marine charts. There are also art cards and craft items relating to the Book of Kells. An upstairs room holds a display and audiovisual presentation on the Book of Kells, for those who can't get to Dublin to see the real thing. Admission to the upstairs exhibit is €2.50 ($2.25) adults, €1.30 ($1.15) children. Closed January through March. Shelbourne St., Kenmare, county Kerry. ⓒ **064/41578.**

Nostalgia In a town known for its lace, it's a natural to stop into this shop. It carries new and antique lace, table and bed linens, traditional teddy bears, and accessories. Closed from January to mid-March. 27 Henry St., Kenmare, county Kerry. ⓒ **064/41389.**

Quills Woolen Market These are branches of the store of the same name in Killarney. They're known for Aran hand knits, Donegal tweed jackets, Irish linen, Celtic jewelry, and hand-loomed knitwear. Market Sq. and Main St., Kenmare, county Kerry. ⓒ **064/32277.** North Sq., Sneem, county Kerry. ⓒ **064/45277.**

SPORTS & OUTDOOR PURSUITS

GOLF Home to a myriad of seascapes and sand dunes, the Ring of Kerry is known for its great golf courses, particularly **Waterville Golf Links,** Waterville (ⓒ **066/947-4102;** www.kerrygems.ie/golf/watervillegolfclub), on the edge of the Atlantic. On huge sand dunes, bounded on three sides by the sea, the 18-hole championship course is one of the longest in Ireland (7,184 yd.). Visitors are welcome. Greens fees are €95 ($85) daily.

Other challenging 18-hole courses on the Ring include **Dooks Golf Club,** Glenbeigh (ⓒ **066/976-8205;** www.dooks.com), a links par-70 course on the Ring of Kerry road, with greens fees of €34 ($30). The expanded **Kenmare Golf Club,** Kenmare (ⓒ **064/41291;** www.kenmaregolfclub.com), is a parkland par-71 course; greens fees run €25 ($22) weekdays and Saturdays, and €38 ($34) on Sundays.

WALKING Ireland's longest low-level, long-distance path, the **Kerry Way,** traverses the Ring of Kerry. The first stage, from Killarney National Park to Glenbeigh, is inland, through wide and scenic countryside. The second stage is a circuit of the Iveragh Peninsula, linking Cahirciveen, Waterville, Caherdaniel, Sneem, and Kenmare, with a farther inland walk along the old Kenmare Road back to Killarney, for a total of 202km (125 miles). The route consists primarily of paths and "green" (unsurfaced) roads, such as old driving paths, butter roads, and routes between early Christian settlements. A leaflet outlining the route is available from the Killarney and Kenmare tourist offices.

WHERE TO STAY
VERY EXPENSIVE

The Park Hotel Kenmare ⭐⭐⭐ Ensconced in palm tree–lined gardens beside Kenmare Bay, this imposing limestone building was built at the end of the 19th century by the Great Southern Railway as a hotel for train travelers. It was totally restored and refurbished about 20 years ago under the masterful ownership and management of Francis Brennan. The interior is rich in high-ceilinged sitting rooms and lounges, crackling open fireplaces, original oil paintings, tapestries, plush furnishings, and museum-worthy antiques (including an eye-catching cistern decorated with mythological figures and supported by gilded sea horses and dolphins).

The individually decorated guest rooms are decked out in a mix of Georgian and Victorian furnishings and rich upholsteries. Many have four-poster or canopy beds, hand-carved armoires, china lamps, curios, and little extra touches like telephones in the bathroom and heated towel rails. Most rooms offer river and mountain vistas. Amid all the elegance, this hotel exudes an intrinsically welcoming atmosphere and service is top-notch without being stuffy. The elegant dining room, with romantic views of the water and gardens, is one of the most acclaimed hotel restaurants in Ireland, meriting a Michelin star.

Kenmare, county Kerry. ⓒ 800/323-5463 in the U.S., or 064/41200. Fax 064/41402. www.parkkenmare.com. 49 units. €362–€498 ($322–$443) double. No service charge. Rates include full breakfast. AE, DC, MC, V. Closed Nov–Dec 22 and Jan 3–Mar. **Amenities:** Restaurant (Continental); bar; 18-hole golf course; joggers' trail; tennis court; croquet lawn; salmon fishing; concierge; room service; babysitting; laundry service; non-smoking rooms; drawing room. *In room:* TV, CD player, minibar, hair dryer, garment press.

Sheen Falls Lodge ★★★ Everything at Sheen Falls conspires to make you feel stress-free and pampered—the fabulous service, the faultless attention to detail—whether you stay a night or a week. No wonder it's a favorite getaway for Irish and Hollywood celebrities, and no wonder *Condé Nast Traveler* magazine voted it the number-three hotel in Europe. Originally the 18th-century home of the Earl of Kerry, this salubrious resort sits beside a natural waterfall on 120 hectares (300 acres) of lawns and semitropical gardens where the River Sheen meets the Kenmare Bay estuary. The public areas are graceful, with pillars and columns, polished woodwork, open fireplaces, traditional furnishings, and original oil paintings. The staff make an effort to address guests by name, the bar feels like a drawing room, and the 1,000-volume library, with its green leather sofas and floor-to-ceiling bookshelves, feels like a fine gentlemen's club. The guest rooms are spacious, decorated in elegant contemporary style; each overlooks the falls (stunning when floodlit at night) or the bay. The hotel also maintains a vintage 1922 Buick to provide local excursions for guests. It comes at a price, but this is the perfect Irish country house atmosphere: elegant and yet relaxed.

Kenmare, county Kerry. ⓒ 800/537-8483 in the U.S., or 064/41600. Fax 064/41386. www.sheenfallslodge.ie. 61 units. €240–€393 ($214–$350) double; €413–€600 ($368–$534) suite. No service charge. AE, DC, MC, V. Closed Dec 24–Feb 1. **Amenities:** 2 restaurants (French, bistro); bar; indoor swimming pool; private salmon fishing; horseback riding; tennis; croquet; billiard room; gym; Jacuzzi; sauna/steam room; health and beauty treatments; concierge; room service; laundry/dry cleaning; library; helicopter pad. *In room:* A/C, TV/VCR, radio, minibar, hair dryer, garment press.

MODERATE

Derrynane Hotel ★ Perched on a precipice between the mountainous coast and the open waters of the Atlantic, this contemporary hotel boasts one of the Ring's most dramatic and remote locations, next to the Derrynane National Park and midway between Waterville and Sneem. The guest rooms are standard, but greatly enhanced by superb views from every huge window. A local guide is available to take guests on weekend walking trips.

Off Ring of Kerry rd. (N71), Caherdaniel, county Kerry. ⓒ 800/528-1234 or 066/947-5136. Fax 066/947-5160. www.derrynane.com. 75 units. €107–€133 ($95–$118) double. Rates include full Irish breakfast and service charge. AE, DC, MC, V. Closed early Oct to mid-Apr. **Amenities:** Restaurant (international); lounge; outdoor swimming pool; tennis court; gym; sauna/steam room. *In room:* TV.

Dromquinna Manor Hotel ★ A bit over 3.2km (2 miles) west of Kenmare, this Victorian-style hotel was originally a private home dating from 1850. It lies on 17 hectares (42 acres) of woodland, with almost a mile of land facing the Kenmare River. Refurbished and expanded in recent years, it retains an old-world ambience, with log fireplaces, original oak paneling, ornate ceilings, and authentic bric-a-brac. Guest rooms are individually furnished, some with four-poster or Victorian-style beds, and some in a more modern style, with light woods and frilly floral fabrics; some face the water. Lastly, there's an immensely popular, 4.5m-high (15-ft.) treehouse suite—said to be the only one in the British Isles—with two bedrooms and a large balcony affording great views.

Blackwater Bridge P.O., off Ring of Kerry rd. (N71), Kenmare, county Kerry. © 064/41657. Fax 064/41791. www.dromquinna.com. 46 units. €114–€202 ($101–$180) double; €254 ($226) treehouse suite. No service charge. Rates include full Irish breakfast. AE, MC, V. **Amenities:** Restaurant (international); tennis; croquet; rowboats. *In room:* TV, hair dryer.

Sallyport House ★★ This wonderful country house B&B won the Irish Automobile Association's "Guest Accommodation of the Year" award in 2000. It's got a great location, just 2 minutes on foot into Kenmare, yet set on extensive, well-kept grounds that run down to the Kenmare River. After spending years refurbishing her brother's B&B in California, Janey Arthur returned to Kenmare and did up her own handsome manor splendidly with a sophisticated, uncluttered, and luxurious feel. The spacious, individually decorated guest rooms are furnished with well-chosen antiques, including very large beds and exceptionally grand bathrooms. Each room has a striking feature—extradeep window seats that beg you to take in mountain views, an enormous king-size four-poster bed, or perhaps a lovely river view.

Glengarriff Rd., Kenmare, county Kerry. © 064/42066. Fax 0646/42067. www.sallyporthouse.com. 5 units. €127 ($113) double. Rates include full breakfast and service charge. No credit cards. Closed Nov through mid-Apr. **Amenities:** Lounge; nonsmoking rooms. *In room:* TV, hair dryer.

Shelburne Lodge ★★ Yet another fabulous, reasonably priced place to ink into your travel journal. This time, it's a Georgian farmhouse that the owners Maura and Tom Foley have transformed into one of the most original, stylish, and comfortable B&Bs on the island. Every room in the house has polished wood parquet floors, truly beautiful (and beautifully arranged) antique furnishings, contemporary artwork, and boldly colored walls that go pow. The guest rooms are all large and gorgeously appointed, with particularly sumptuous bathrooms (heated towel rails and handmade mirrors). The breakfasts are nothing short of decadent, and Maura and Tom really take care of you throughout your stay.

Killowen, Cork Rd., Kenmare, county Kerry. © 064/41013. Fax 0646/42135. 9 units. €98–€122 ($87–$109) double. Rates include full breakfast and service charge. MC, V. Closed Nov–Mar. **Amenities:** Tennis court; drawing room. *In room:* TV.

MODERATE/INEXPENSIVE

Kenmare Bay ★ Here's a place that offers good value for money, so long as you prioritize a good view over outstanding decor. On a hillside at the edge of town, just off the main road that winds around the Ring of Kerry, this modern hotel was recently expanded and upgraded. The guest rooms are furnished comfortably, if generically, with blonde-wood furnishings and tweedy or quilted upholsteries, and nearly all of their large windows afford good views of the mountainous landscape.

Sneem Rd., Kenmare, county Kerry. © 064/41300. Fax 064/41541. kenmare@leehotels.ie. 136 units. €70–€110 ($62–$98) double. Rates include full breakfast and service charge. AE, DC, MC, V. Closed Nov–Mar. **Amenities:** Restaurant (international); bar. *In room:* TV.

INEXPENSIVE

Hawthorn House ★★ ⓥ*alue* On a quiet side street in Kenmare, this excellent-value town house B&B has attracted a huge following over the years. Mary

O'Brien is a congenial, gifted hostess, and her hospitality sets the tone for your stay. Her guest rooms all have a pretty, feminine feel, with floral bedspreads and pastel walls. Rooms here may be slightly smaller than you'd find at rural B&Bs that were built for this purpose, but they are certainly comfortable. Breakfasts are bountiful and delicious.

Shelbourne St., Kenmare, county Kerry. ✆ **064/41035.** Fax 064/41932. 8 units. €60 ($53) double. Rates include full breakfast and service charge. MC, V. Closed Christmas. **Amenities:** Sitting room. *In room:* TV, hair dryer.

Hillcrest   The guest rooms of this Georgian-style bungalow are spacious and cheerful, with pastel walls offset by bright contemporary floral fabrics, painted white furniture, and dark-stained window frames. Ask for one of the front rooms, which enjoy views of the nearby hills. This is a pleasant bargain on the Ring.

Killarney Rd., 0.5km (⅓ mile) outside of Killorglin town, county Kerry. ✆ **066/976-1552.** Fax 066/976-1996. 5 units. €50 ($45) double. Rates include full breakfast and service charge. MC, V. Closed Jan–Mar. *In room:* TV, tea/coffeemaker, hair dryer.

WHERE TO DINE
EXPENSIVE
Café Indigo 🕮🕮 MODERN CONTINENTAL/SEAFOOD   This ultrahip, ultrastylish restaurant has recently expanded the bar and added a grill, but the focus continues to be the talents of Vanessa Falvey, one of Ireland's hottest young chefs. Her cooking is a model of sophistication and simplicity, using a combination of fresh, local ingredients to bring one strong flavor to the fore. She's especially good with fish and seafood, with dishes like oven-baked salmon complimented by sun-dried-tomato tapenade, or celeriac purée with perfectly grilled sea scallops. The dining room is understated, the food is classy and memorable, the crowd happy.

The Square (above Square Pint pub), Kenmare, county Kerry. ✆ **064/42356.** Reservations recommended. Main courses €18–€23 ($16–$20); main courses, grill menu €10–€15 ($8.90–$13). AE, DC, MC, V. Wed–Mon, 7–11pm. Closed mid-Jan to mid-Mar.

MODERATE
The Blue Bull 🕮 TRADITIONAL IRISH   Sneem is so small that if you blink as you pass through it, you'd miss it completely. Yet it has five good pubs, and this one, in particular, serves excellent food. With a blue straw bull's head resting over the doorway, this old place has long been a favorite on the Ring of Kerry route. Sir Andrew Lloyd Webber even called it the best bar restaurant in the world. There are three small rooms, each with an open fireplace and walls lined with old prints of county Kerry scenes and people, plus a skylit conservatory room in the back. Traditional Irish fare, like smoked salmon and Irish stew, shares the menu with such dishes as salmon stuffed with spinach, Valencia scallops in brandy, and chicken Kiev. There's traditional Irish entertainment most evenings.

South Sq., Ring of Kerry rd. (N70), Sneem, county Kerry. ✆ **064/45382.** Reservations recommended. Main courses €13–€20 ($12–$18). AE, MC, V. Bar food daily year-round 11am–8pm. Restaurant daily Mar–Oct 6–10pm.

d'Arcy's 🕮🕮 CONTINENTAL   In a two-story stone house at the top end of Kenmare, this restaurant has a homey atmosphere with a big open fireplace. The owner, Pat Gath, and head chef, James Mulchrone, make a great team, and this place is a standout even in this restaurant-rich town. Using fresh local ingredients, the menu includes classics such as peppered filet of beef with crispy onions and baked salmon with rosemary butter. Mulchrone's penchant for Mediterranean flavors is evident in dishes like the goat's cheese starter that comes with olive-and-tomato sauce or the rack of lamb main course that comes stuffed with garlic and sun-dried tomatoes. The homemade breads and desserts are also excellent.

Main St., Kenmare, county Kerry. (C) 064/41589. Reservations recommended. Main courses €16–€23 ($14–$20). MC, V. Wed–Mon, 7–10pm (open daily in summer). Closed Jan to mid-Mar.

The Huntsman SEAFOOD   It's worth a trip to Waterville just to dine at this contemporary restaurant on the shores of Ballinskelligs Bay. Owner-chef Raymond Hunt takes the time to circulate and chat with diners, offering suggestions on the extensive menu, which uses only the freshest local catch and produce. Skellig lobster fresh from the tank and Kenmare Bay scampi are among the seafood specialties; meat dishes include rack of lamb, seasonal pheasant, rabbit, duck, and Irish stew.

The Strand, Waterville, county Kerry. (C) 066/947-4124. Reservations recommended. Lunch and bar food items from €4 ($3.55); dinner main courses €14–€25 ($12–$22). AE, DC, MC, V. Mar–Oct daily 10am–10pm; Nov–Feb Thurs–Sun 6–10pm. Closed Dec 23–27.

Lime Tree ☆ MODERN CONTINENTAL   Innovative cuisine is the focus at this restaurant, in an 1821 landmark renovated schoolhouse next to the Park Hotel. Paintings by local artists line the stone walls, and the menu offers such dishes as goat's-cheese potato cake with balsamic glaze, oak-planked wild salmon, filet of Irish beef with colcannon (mashed potatoes with spring onions), and oven-roasted Kerry lamb.

Shelbourne Rd., Kenmare, county Kerry. (C) 064/41225. Reservations recommended. Main courses €15–€23 ($13–$20). MC, V. Apr–Nov daily 6:30–10pm.

MODERATE/INEXPENSIVE

Packie's ☆☆ BISTRO   If you're looking for a stylish place to have a great meal that won't break the bank, this little place is it. There's always a buzz here, and the smart crowd fits in perfectly with the bistro look—colorful window boxes, slate floor, stone walls filled with contemporary art, and dark oak tables and chairs. Everyone comes for the food, and chef-owner Maura Foley is known for never serving a bad meal. Her menu includes tried-and-true favorites such as Irish stew, delicious potato pancakes, mint-infused rack of lamb, and crab claws in garlic butter. But there are also more creative combinations, such as gratin of crab and prawns, beef braised in Guinness with mushrooms, and curry sabayon with Castletownberre prawns. Desserts are terrific, too.

Henry St., Kenmare, county Kerry. (C) 064/41508. Reservations recommended. Main courses €14–€25 ($12–$22). MC, V. Easter to mid-Nov, Tues–Sat 5:30–10pm.

The Vestry ☆ MODERN IRISH   As its name implies, this building is an 18th-century Church of Ireland that's been wonderfully restored. In 1993, it was tastefully converted into a restaurant, retaining much of its original decor, including many fixtures. Recently, the modern Irish menu, highlighting fresh local seafood and vegetables, was expanded—"ecumenically," as it were—to include more exotic items such as kangaroo, ostrich, and wild boar. All dishes are expertly prepared by award-winning chef Garrett O'Mahony.

Ring of Kerry rd. (N71), on Kenmare Bay about 6.5km (4 miles) west of Kenmare, Templenoe, Kenmare, county Kerry. (C) 064/41958. Reservations recommended. Main courses €14–€24 ($12–$21). MC, V. Mar–Sept daily 6–9:30pm.

INEXPENSIVE

Purple Heather ☆☆ *Finds* IRISH   This lovely little eatery is *the* place to lunch in Kenmare. The food is all about tearoom classics with a gourmet twist—wild smoked salmon or prawn salad, smoked trout paté, vegetarian omelets, and Irish cheese platters, as well as homemade soups.

Henry St., Kenmare, county Kerry. © **064/41016.** All items €3–€20 ($2.65–$18). No credit cards. Mon–Sat 11am–7pm. Closed Christmas week.

2 Killarney

Killarney is 135km (84 miles) SW of Shannon, 309km (192 miles) SW of Dublin, 87km (54 miles) W of Cork, 111km (69 miles) SW of Limerick, and 193km (120 miles) SW of Galway

Killarney is the busiest beehive of tourism in Ireland—the Grand Central Station of the southwest, with all the positive and negative connotations that this implies. The town becomes one giant traffic jam of battling tour buses every summer, and a Mecca for pushy jaunting-car (horse-and-buggy) drivers. The locals are well practiced at dispensing a professional brand of Irish charm, and accommodation and restaurant prices are hiked up to capitalize on the hordes descending from the motorcoaches. If that's not your scene, it's easy enough to resist Killarney's gravitational pull and instead explore the incredibly picturesque hinterlands that border the town on all sides. You might sneak into town at some point to sample the best of what this tourist megalopolis has to offer.

It's important to remember that the reason Killarney draws millions of visitors a year has nothing to do with the town. It's all about the valley in which the town is nestled, a landscape of lakes and mountains that's so truly spectacular that Brendan Behan once said, "even an ad man would be ashamed to eulogize it." And entering these wonders is ever so easy. Walk from the town car park toward the cathedral, and turn left into the National Park. In a matter of minutes, you'll see the reason for all the fuss. During the summer, the evenings are long, the twilight is often indescribable, and you needn't share the lanes. Apart from deer and locals, the park is all yours until dark.

The park's three lakes are Killarney's main attraction. The first, the Lower Lake, is sometimes called "Lough Leane" or "Lough Lein," which means "the lake of learning." It's the largest, more than 6.5km (4 miles) long, and is dotted with 30 small islands. The second lake is aptly called the "Middle Lake" or "Muckross Lake," and the third simply "Upper Lake." Upper Lake, the smallest, is full of storybook islands covered with a variety of trees—evergreens, cedars of Lebanon, juniper, holly, and mountain ash.

The lakes and the surrounding woodlands are part of the 65-sq.-km (25-sq.-mile) **Killarney National Park.** The ground is a soft carpet of moss and the air fragrant with wildflowers. Cars are banned from most of the ferny trails, so take a hike or hire a "jarvey," an old-fashioned horse-and-buggy that's a holdover from the days when the Victorians waxed poetically about Killarney and brought it to the attention of the world. Found within the park's limits are two major estates, **Muckross** and **Knockreer,** and the remains of major medieval abbeys and castles. A profusion of foliage, such as rhododendrons, azaleas, magnolias, camellias, hydrangeas, and tropical ferns, blossoms in season. At almost every turn, you'll see Killarney's own botanical wonder, the arbutus, or strawberry tree, plus eucalyptus, redwoods, and native oak.

The most noteworthy of Killarney's islands is **Innisfallen,** or "Fallen's Island," which seems to float peacefully in the Lower Lake. You can reach it by rowboat, available for rental at Ross Castle. St. Fallen founded a monastery here in the 7th century, and it flourished for 1,000 years. It's said that Brian Boru, the great Irish chieftain, and St. Brendan the Navigator were educated here. From 950 to 1320, the "Annals of Innisfallen," a chronicle of early Irish history, was written at the monastery; it's now in the Bodlein Library at Oxford University. Traces of an 11th-century church and a 12th-century priory can still be seen today.

ESSENTIALS

GETTING THERE **Aer Lingus** offers flights from Dublin into Kerry County Airport, Farranfore, county Kerry (© 066/976-4644; www.kerryairport.ie), about 16km (10 miles) north of Killarney. **Ryanair** flies direct from London (Stansted) to Kerry, and Manx Airlines flies to Kerry from Luton and Manchester.

Irish Rail trains from Dublin, Limerick, Cork, and Galway arrive daily at the **Killarney Railway Station** (© 064/31067; www.irishrail.ie), Railway Road, off East Avenue Road.

Bus Eireann operates regularly scheduled service into Killarney from all parts of Ireland. The bus depot (© 064/34777; www.buseireann.ie) is adjacent to the train station at Railway Road, off East Avenue Road.

Kerry folk like to say that all roads lead to Killarney, and at least a half dozen major national roads do. They include N21 and N23 from Limerick, N22 from Tralee, N22 from Cork, N72 from Mallow, and N70 from the Ring of Kerry and West Cork.

VISITOR INFORMATION The **Killarney Tourist Office,** Aras Fáilte, is at the Town Centre Car Park, Beech Road (© 064/31633). It's open October to April, Monday to Saturday 9:15am to 1pm and 2:15 to 5:30pm; May, Monday to Saturday 9:15am to 5:30pm; June, Monday to Saturday 9am to 6pm, Sunday 10am to 1pm and 2 to 6pm; July to August, Monday to Saturday 9am to 8pm, Sunday 10am to 1pm and 2 to 6pm; September, Monday to Saturday 9am to 6pm, Sunday 10am to 1pm and 2:15 to 6pm. It offers many helpful booklets, including the *Tourist Trail* walking-tour guide and the *Killarney Area Guide,* with maps.

Useful local publications include *Where: Killarney,* a quarterly magazine distributed free at hotels and guesthouses. It is packed with current information on tours, activities, events, and entertainment.

TOWN LAYOUT Killarney is small, with a full-time population of approximately 7,000. The town is built around one central thoroughfare, Main Street, which changes its name to High Street at midpoint. The principal offshoots of Main Street are Plunkett Street, which becomes College Street, and New Street, which, as its name implies, is still growing. The Deenagh River edges the western side of town, and East Avenue Road rims the eastern side. It's all very walkable in an hour or two.

The busiest section of town is at the southern tip of Main Street, where it meets East Avenue Road. Here the road curves and heads southward out to the Muckross road and the entrance to the Killarney National Park.

GETTING AROUND Killarney Town is so small and compact that there is no local bus service; the best way to get around is on foot. To see the best of Killarney Town, follow the signposted "Tourist Trail," encompassing the highlights of the main streets and attractions. It takes about 2 hours to complete the walk. A booklet outlining the trail is available at the tourist office.

Taxi cabs line up at the rank on **College Square** (© 064/31331). You can also phone for a taxi from **John Burke** (© 064/32448), **Dero's Taxi Service** (© 064/31251), or **O'Connell Taxi** (© 064/31654).

Killarney

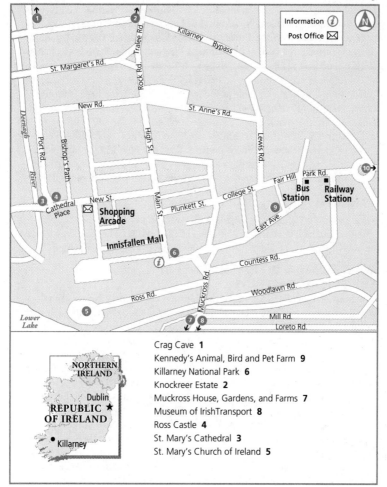

Information (i)
Post Office ✉

Crag Cave **1**
Kennedy's Animal, Bird and Pet Farm **9**
Killarney National Park **6**
Knockreer Estate **2**
Muckross House, Gardens, and Farms **7**
Museum of Irish Transport **8**
Ross Castle **4**
St. Mary's Cathedral **3**
St. Mary's Church of Ireland **5**

In Killarney Town, it's best to park your car and walk. Most hotels and guest-houses offer free guest parking. If you must park on the street, buy a parking disc and display it on your car; parking costs €.50 (45¢) per hour, and hotels and shops sell discs. You'll need a car to drive from town to Killarney National Park on the Muckross and Kenmare road (N71).

If you need to rent a car in Killarney, contact **Avis,** the Glebe Arcade (© **064/ 36655**); **Budget,** c/o International Hotel, Kenmare Place (© **064/34341**); **Hertz,** 28 Plunkett St. (© **064/34126**); or **Randles Bros.,** Muckross Road (© **064/31237**).

Horse-drawn **jaunting cars** (light, two-wheeled vehicles), also known as "jar-veys," line up at Kenmare Place in Killarney Town. They offer rides to Killarney National Park sites and other scenic areas. Depending on the time and distance, prices range from €16 to €40 ($14–$36) per jaunting car (up to four persons). (For details, see "Organized Tours," below.)

FAST FACTS If you need a drugstore, try **O'Sullivans Pharmacy,** 81 New St. (© **064/35866**), or **Donal Sheahan,** 34 Main St. (© **064/31113**).

In an **emergency,** dial © **999.** The **Killarney District Hospital** is on St. Margaret's Road (© **064/31076**). The **Killarney Garda Station** is on New Road (© **064/31222**).

Full Internet access (over superfast ISDN lines), plus secretarial services, tea, coffee, and pastries, are available Monday through Saturday at **Café Internet,** 49 Lower New St. (© **064/36741;** www.cafe-internet.net). Facilities include scanners, color printers, and quick-cams. Internet fees run €1 (90¢) for up to 10 minutes or €5 ($4.45) per hour. Open 9:30am to 7pm (10pm June–Sept).

The **Killarney Public Library,** on Rock Road (© **064/32972**), also provides Internet access from its bank of computers.

If you need to do your laundry, head for the **Gleeson Launderette,** Brewery Lane, off College Square (© **064/33877**).

Where: Killarney, a quarterly magazine, is chock-full of helpful, up-to-date information for visitors; it is distributed free at top hotels and guesthouses.

The **Killarney Post Office,** New Street (© **064/31051**), is open Monday and Wednesday to Saturday 9am to 5:30pm, Tuesday 9:30am to 5:30pm.

WHAT TO SEE & DO IN KILLARNEY
THE TOP ATTRACTIONS

The town of Killarney sits right on the doorstep of **Killarney National Park** ⚘, out Kenmare road (N71), 10,000 hectares (25,000 acres) of natural beauty. You'll find three storied lakes—the **Lower Lake** (or Lough Leane), the **Middle Lake** (or Muckross Lake), and the **Upper Lake**—myriad waterfalls, rivers, islands, valleys, mountains, bogs, woodlands, and lush foliage and trees, including oak, arbutus, holly, and mountain ash. Large areas of the park are infested with rhododendron bushes, which have grown rampantly to the delight of visitors but the dismay of park rangers, because these runaway rhododendrons thwart the growth of indigenous plant life. There's also a large variety of wildlife, including a rare herd of red deer. You can't explore the park by car, so plan on hiking, biking, or hiring a horse-drawn jaunting car. The park offers four nature trails along the lakeshore.

There's access from several points along the Kenmare road (N71). The main entrance is at Muckross House, where a visitor center features a restaurant and background exhibits on the park and a film titled *Mountain, Wood, Water.* Call © **064/31440** for more information on the park. Admission is free, and it's open in all daylight hours year-round.

Amid mountains and lakelands, the winding, rocky, incredibly scenic **Gap of Dunloe** ⚘⚘ is about 9.7km (6 miles) west of Killarney. The route through the gap passes a kaleidoscope of craggy rocks, massive cliffs, meandering streams, and deep gullies. The road ends at Upper Lake. One of the best ways to explore the gap is by bicycle (see "Bicycling," under "Sports & Outdoor Pursuits," below). Horse fanciers may want to take one of the excursions offered by **Castlelough Tours,** 7 High St. (© **064/31115**); **Corcoran's Tours,** Kilcummin (© **064/36666**); **Dero's Tours,** 22 Main St. (© **064/31251** or 064/31567); or **Tangney Tours,** Kinvara House, Muckross Road (© **064/33358**). Combination coach/horse/boat tours cost €37 ($33). If you'd rather have someone else handle the horse, you can take an 11km (7-mile) jaunting-car tour. Excursions go from Kate Kearney's Cottage through the Gap of Dunloe to Lord Brandon's Cottage and back.

Knockreer Estate ⚘ The house isn't open to the public, but the gardens offer lovely views of the Lower Lake. Once the home of Lord Kenmare, the estate has a turn-of-the-20th-century house, a pathway along the River Deenagh, and gardens that mix 200-year-old trees with flowering cherries, magnolias, and azaleas. Main access to Knockreer is through Deenagh Lodge Gate, opposite the cathedral, in town.

Cathedral Place, off New St., Killarney, county Kerry. ⓒ **064/31440**. Free admission to gardens. Daily during daylight hours.

Muckross House & Gardens ⚘⚘⚘ The focal point of the Middle Lake and, in many ways, of the entire national park, is the Muckross Estate, often called "the jewel of Killarney." It consists of a gracious ivy-covered Victorian mansion, **Muckross House,** and its elegant surrounding gardens. Dating from 1843, the 20-room Muckross House has been converted into a museum of county Kerry folk life, showcasing locally carved furniture, prints, maps, paintings, and needlework. Imported treasures like Oriental screens, Venetian mirrors, Chippendale chairs, Turkish carpets, and curtains woven in Brussels are on display. Also on site are a restaurant and craft workshops, where local artisans demonstrate traditional trades such as bookbinding, weaving, and pottery. The adjacent mature gardens, known for their fine collection of rhododendrons and azaleas, are also worth exploring.

The ruin of the 15th century **Muckross Abbey,** founded about 1448 and burned by Cromwell's troops in 1652, is also near the house. The abbey's central feature is a vaulted cloister around a courtyard that contains a huge yew tree, said to be as old as the abbey itself.

Kenmare rd. (N71), Killarney, county Kerry. ⓒ **061/31440**. www.muckross-house.ie. Admission €5 ($4.45) adults, €3.80 ($3.40) seniors, €2 ($1.80) students and children, €12.70 ($11) family. July–Aug daily 9am–7pm; mid-Mar to June and Sept–Oct daily 9am–6pm; Nov to mid-Mar daily 9am–5:30pm.

Muckross Traditional Farms ⚘⚘ *Kids* Located near the Muckross House estate, this 28 hectare (70-acre) park is home to displays of traditional farm life and artisans' shops. The farmhouses and buildings are so authentically detailed that visitors feel they are dropping in on working farms and lived-in houses. The animals and household environments are equally fascinating for children and adults, making for a great family outing.

You'll be able to watch sowing and harvesting or potato picking and hay making, depending on the season. Farmhands work in the fields and tend the animals, while the blacksmith, carpenter, and wheelwright ply their trades in the old manner. Women draw water from the wells and cook meals in traditional kitchens with authentic utensils, crockery, and household items. *Note:* The combination ticket allows you to visit Muckross House for €2.50 ($2.25) extra per person.

Kenmare rd. (N71), Killarney, county Kerry. ⓒ **064/31440**. www.muckross-house.ie. Admission €5 ($4.45) adults, €3.80 ($3.40) seniors, €2 ($1.80) students and children, €12.70 ($11) family. Combination ticket with Muckross House €7.50 ($6.70) adults, €5.50 ($4.90) seniors, €3 ($2.65) students and children, €19 ($17) family. Mid-Mar to Apr and Oct Sat–Sun 1–6pm; May daily 1–6pm; June–Sept daily 10am–7pm. Closed Nov to mid-Mar.

Ross Castle ⚘ Newly restored, this 15th-century fortress sits on the edge of the Lower Lake, 3.2km (2 miles) outside Killarney Town. Built by the O'Donoghue chieftains, the castle distinguished itself in 1652 as the last stronghold in Munster to surrender to Cromwell's forces. All that remains today is a tower house, surrounded by a fortified *bawn* (walled garden) with rounded turrets. The tower has been furnished in the style of the late 16th and early 17th centuries, and offers a magnificent view of the lakes and islands from its top. Access is by guided tour only. A lovely lakeshore walk stretches for 3.2km (2 miles) between Killarney and the castle. Lake cruises are run from the castle (see "Boat Tours," below), including boats to **Inisfallen Island** 🏰🏰, home to the ruins of a 7th-century monastery and a 12th-century oratory.

Ross Rd., off Kenmare rd. (N71), Killarney, county Kerry. ✆ 064/35851. Admission €3.80 ($3.40) adults, €2.50 ($2.25) seniors, €1.50 ($1.35) students and children, €10 ($8.90) family. Apr daily 10am–5pm; May and Sept daily 10am–6pm; June–Aug daily 9am–6:30pm; Oct Tues–Sun 10am–5pm. Last admission 45 min. before closing. Closed Nov–Mar.

St. Mary's Cathedral Officially known as the Catholic Church of St. Mary of the Assumption, this limestone cathedral is the town's most impressive building. Designed in the Gothic Revival style by Augustus Pugin, it's cruciform in shape. Construction began in 1842, was interrupted by the famine years, and concluded in 1855. The magnificent central spire was added in 1912. The entire edifice was extensively renovated from 1972 to 1973. It's at the edge of town, on the far end of New Street.

Cathedral Place, off Port Rd., Killarney, county Kerry. ✆ **064/31014.** Free admission; donations welcome. Daily 10:30am–6pm.

MORE ATTRACTIONS

Crag Cave 🏰 Believed to be more than a million years old, these limestone caves were discovered and first explored in 1983. Guides accompany you 3,753m (12,510 ft.) into the passage on a well-lit tour revealing some of the largest stalactites in Europe. Exhibits, a craft shop, and a restaurant are on the premises, 24km (15 miles) north of Killarney.

Off Limerick rd. (N21), Castleisland, county Kerry. ✆ 066/41244. www.cragcave.com. Admission €5 ($4.45) adults, €3.80 ($3.40) seniors and students, €2.50 ($2.25) children over 6, €15 ($13) family (up to 4 children). Mid-Mar to June and Sept–Oct daily 10am–6pm; July–Aug 10am–7pm.

Kennedy's Animal, Bird and Pet Farm *Kids* At this 30-hectare (75-acre) dairy and sheep farm surrounded by mountain vistas, you'll see cows being milked, piglets being fed, and peacocks strutting their stuff. Horse-drawn machinery is on display.

9.7km (6 miles) east of Killarney, off the main Cork rd. (N22), Glenflesk, Killarney, county Kerry. ✆ **064/54054.** Admission €3.80 ($3.40) adults, €2.50 ($2.25) children. May–Oct daily 10am–6pm. Closed Nov–Apr.

Museum of Irish Transport This museum presents a unique collection of vintage and classic cars, motorcycles, bicycles, carriages, and fire engines. It includes an 1825 hobby-horse bicycle; a 1907 Silver Stream, the only model ever built; a 1904 Germain, one of four remaining in the world; a 1910 Wolseley Siddeley once driven by William Butler Yeats; and an ill-fated De Lorean, a futuristic, stainless-steel car manufactured during its short life at a plant in Ireland. Lining the walls are early motoring and cycling periodicals, and license plates from all over the world.

E. Avenue Rd., Killarney, county Kerry. ✆ 064/34677. Admission €3.80 ($3.40) adults; €2.50 ($2.25) seniors, students, and children; €8 ($7.10) family. Apr–Oct daily 10am–6pm. Closed Nov–Mar.

St. Mary's Church It's commonly believed that St. Mary's, an 1870 neo-Gothic church, stands on the site of the original "Church of the Sloe Woods" (in Irish, *Cill Airne*—the Anglicization of which is *Killarney*). It's in the heart of town, across from the tourist office.

Church Place, Killarney, county Kerry. ℭ 064/31832. Free admission; donations welcome. Daily 9:30am–5pm.

ORGANIZED TOURS
Bus Tours

To get your bearings of the Killarney environs, consider one of these sightseeing tours:

Dero's Tours   Besides showing off Killarney's lakes from the best vantage points, this 3-hour tour takes you to Aghadoe, the Gap of Dunloe, Ross Castle, Muckross House and Gardens, and Torc Waterfall.

7 Main St., Killarney, county Kerry. ℭ **064/31251** or 064/31567. Tour €10 ($8.90). May–Sept daily at 10:30am; schedules vary.

Gap of Dunloe   This tour takes you through the spectacularly scenic Gap of Dunloe and includes a boat tour of the Killarney lakes.

Castlelough Tours, 7 High St., Killarney, county Kerry. ℭ **064/31115**. Tour €18 ($16). May–Sept; call for hours and reservations.

In addition to Killarney's main sights, some bus tours also venture into the two prime scenic areas nearby: the Ring of Kerry and Dingle Peninsula. From May to September, tours are offered daily; prices range from €18 to €23 ($16–$20) per person. The following companies offer tours outside Killarney: **Bus Eireann,** Bus Depot, Railway Road, off East Avenue Road (ℭ **064/34777;** www.buseireann.ie); **Castlelough Tours,** 7 High St. (ℭ **064/31115**); **Corcoran's Chauffeur Tours,** 10 College St. (ℭ **064/36666;** www.corcorantours. com); and **Dero's Tours,** 22 Main St. (ℭ **064/31251** or 064/31567; www. derostours.com).

Jaunting-Car Tours

If you enjoy walking or bicycling, just say no to the numerous drivers who will inevitably offer their services as you make your way around the Killarney lakes. The quaint horse-driven buggies are one of the main features of the landscape. If you decide to give them a try, keep in mind that jaunting-car rates are set and carefully monitored by the Killarney Urban District Council. Current rates, all based on four persons to a jaunting car, run roughly from €16 to €40 ($14–$36) per jaunting car, for up to four persons. The price depends on the destinations, which include Ross Castle, Muckross House and Gardens, Torc Waterfall, Muckross Abbey, Dinis Island, and Kate Kearney's Cottage, gateway to the Gap of Dunloe. To arrange a tour in advance, contact **Tangney Tours,** Kinvara House, Muckross Road, Killarney (ℭ **064/33358**).

Boat Tours

There is nothing quite like seeing the sights from a boat on the lakes of Killarney. Two companies operate regular boating excursions, with full commentary.

M.V. *Lily of Killarney* Tours   Departing from the pier at Ross Castle, this enclosed water bus cruises the lakes for just over an hour. Make reservations.

Old Weir Lodge, Muckross Rd., Killarney, county Kerry. ℭ **064/31068**. Tour €8 ($7.10) adults, €3.80 ($3.40) children, €20 ($18) family. Apr–Oct 10:30am, noon, 1:45, 3:15, and 4:30pm.

M.V. *Pride of the Lakes* Tours   This enclosed boat offers daily sailings from the pier at Ross Castle. The trip lasts just over an hour, and reservations are suggested.

Scotts Gardens, Killarney, county Kerry. ℭ **064/32638**. Tour €6.50 ($5.80) adults, €3 ($2.65) children, €18 ($16) family. Apr–Oct 11am, 12:30, 2:30, 4, and 5:15pm.

SHOPPING

Shopping hours are usually Monday to Saturday 9am to 6pm, but from May through September or October, most stores are open every day until 9 or 10pm. Almost all stores carry Kerry Glass products, a unique Killarney-made souvenir.

Although there are more souvenir and craft shops in Killarney than you can shake a shillelagh at, here are a few of the best.

Anu Design   This little shop specializes in jewelry, stationery, and clothing with Celtic design imprints and engravings inspired by the original art of Newgrange, the Book of Kells, and other historic symbols. The items range from T-shirts and art cards to stone, brass, ceramics, bronze, and silver jewelry. 8 Main St., Killarney, county Kerry. ℂ 064/34799.

Blarney Woollen Mills   A branch of the highly successful county Cork–based enterprise, this large store occupies a beautiful shop front on the corner of Plunkett Street in the center of town. The wares range from hand-knit or hand-loomed sweaters to tweeds, crystal, china, pottery, and souvenirs of all sizes, shapes, and prices. 10 Main St., Killarney, county Kerry. ℂ 064/33222.

Frank Lewis Gallery   This gallery shows and sells a variety of contemporary and traditional paintings, sculptures, and photographic work—much of it with a Kerry theme—by some of Ireland's most acclaimed emerging artists. It's on one of Killarney's enchanting lanes, in a restored artisan's dwelling near the post office. 6 Bridewell Lane, Killarney, county Kerry. ℂ 064/31108.

Killarney Art Gallery   This shop-front gallery features original paintings by leading Irish artists, from the Killarney area and elsewhere, as well as art supplies, Irish prints, and engravings. 3 Plunkett St., Killarney, county Kerry. ℂ 064/34628.

Killarney Bookshop   Stop at this shop for books and maps on the history, legends, and lore of Killarney and Kerry. It also stocks good maps of the area and other books of Irish and international interest. The mail-order catalog is available on request. 32 Main St., Killarney, county Kerry. ℂ 064/34108.

Mucros Craft Centre   Located on the grounds of the famous Muckross House, this studio-cum-shop carries on many county Kerry craft traditions and features an on-premises weaver's workshop as well as a working pottery. There is also a wide selection of quality crafts from all over Ireland and a skylit cafeteria overlooking the walled garden area. Muckross House, Muckross Road, Killarney ℂ 064-31440.

Quill's Woollen Market   This is one of the best spots in town for hand-knit sweaters of all colors, sizes, and types, plus tweeds, mohair, and sheepskins. There are also branches in Sneem and Kenmare on the Ring of Kerry, in Cork City, and at Ballingeary, county Cork (the original shop). 1 High St., Killarney, county Kerry. ℂ 064/32277.

Serendipity   The shelves of this tidy shop feature a wide range of unusual crafts from local artisans, such as hand-thrown pottery from the likes of Nicholas Mosse and Stephen Pearce, Jerpoint glass, and hand-crafted jewelry. 15 College St., Killarney, county Kerry. ℂ 064/31056.

SPORTS & OUTDOOR PURSUITS

BICYCLING   Killarney National Park, with its many lakeside and forest pathways, trails, and byways, is a paradise for bikers. Various vehicles are available for rent, from 21-speed touring bikes and mountain bikes to tandems. Rental charges average €10 ($8.90) per day, €45 ($40) per week. Bicycles can be rented from **O'Neills Cycle Shop,** 6 Plunkett St. (© **064/35357**), and **David O'Sullivan's Cycles,** Bishop Lane, New Street (© **064/31282**). Most shops are open year-round daily 9am to 6pm, until 8 or 9pm in the summer.

One great ride beginning in Killarney takes you through the Gap of Dunloe along a dirt forest road, where you'll see some of the best mountain scenery in the area. It can be made into a 56km (35-mile) loop if you return on N71.

FISHING Fishing for salmon and brown trout in Killarney's unpolluted lakes and rivers is a big attraction. Brown trout fishing is free on the lakes, but a permit is necessary for the rivers Flesk and Laune. A trout permit costs €4 to €14 ($3.55–$12) per day.

Salmon fishing anywhere in Ireland requires a license; the cost is €4 ($3.55) per day, €14 ($12) for 21 days. In addition, some rivers also require a salmon permit, which costs €10 to €14 ($8.90–$12) per day. Permits and licenses can be obtained at the Fishery Office at the **Knockreer Estate Office,** New Street (© **064/31246**).

For fishing tackle, bait, rod rental, and other fishing gear, as well as permits and licenses, try **O'Neill's,** 6 Plunkett St. (© **064/31970**). The shop also arranges the hire of boats and *ghillies* (fishing guides) for €80 ($71) per day on the Killarney Lakes, leaving from Ross Castle. Gear and tackle can also be purchased from Michael Collins at **Angler's Paradise,** Loreto Road (© **064/33818**).

GOLF Visitors are always welcome at the twin 18-hole championship courses of the **Killarney Golf & Fishing Club,** Killorglin Road, Fossa (© **064/31034;** www.killarney-golf.com), 4.8km (3 miles) west of the town center. Widely praised as one of the most scenic golf settings in the world, these courses, known as "Killeen" and "Mahony's Point," are surrounded by lake and mountain vistas. Greens fees are €70 ($62).

HORSEBACK RIDING Many trails in the Killarney area are suitable for horseback riding. Hiring a horse costs about €20 ($18) per hour at **Killarney Riding Stables,** N72, Ballydowney (© **064/31686**), and **Rocklands Stables,** Rockfield, Tralee Road (© **064/32592**). Lessons and weeklong trail rides can also be arranged.

WALKING Killarney is ideal for hiking. On the outskirts of town, the **Killarney National Park** offers four signposted nature trails. The **Mossy Woods Nature Trail** starts near Muckross House, by Muckross Lake, and rambles 2.4km (1½ miles) through yew woods along low cliffs. **Old Boat House Nature Trail** begins at the 19th-century boathouse below Muckross Gardens and leads half a mile around a small peninsula by Muckross Lake. **Arthur Young's Walk** (4.8km/3 miles) starts on the road to Dinis, traverses natural yew woods, and then follows a 200-year-old road on the Muckross Peninsula. The **Blue Pool Nature Trail** (2.4km/1½ miles) goes from Muckross village through woodlands and past a small lake known as the Blue Pool. Leaflets with maps of the four trails are available at the park visitor center.

Rising steeply from the south shore of Muckross Lake, **Torc Mountain** provides spectacular views of the Killarney Lakes and nearby **MacGillycuddy's Reeks,** a moody mountain range. Start at the **Torc Waterfall** parking lot, about 6.5km (4 miles) south of Killarney, and follow the trail to the top of the falls. At a T intersection, turn left toward the top parking lot, and almost immediately turn right on the Old Kenmare Road, which follows a small stream along the south slopes of Torc Mountain. After leaving the woods, you will see Torc Mountain on your right. Look for a crescent-shaped gouge in the side of the road, about 9m (30 ft.) across, with a small cairn at its far edge. This is the beginning of the path to the ridge top, marked somewhat erratically by cairns along the way. Return the way you came; the whole trip is 9.7km (6 miles), takes about 4 hours, and is moderate in difficulty.

In addition to walking independently, visitors to the Killarney area can use a range of guided walks varying in grade and duration (from 1 day to a weekend to a full week). These walks and full guided walking holidays are offered by **SouthWest Walks Ireland Ltd.,** 40 Ashe St., Tralee, county Kerry (© **066/712-8733;** swwi@iol.ie). Or you can arrange in advance to meet up with the **Wayfarers,** an international organization of passionate pedestrians, who schedule 5-week-long footloose circuits of the Ring of Kerry each spring, summer, and fall. To receive a schedule and reserve your place, contact the **Wayfarers,** 172 Bellevue Ave., Newport, RI 02840 (© **800/249-4620;** www.thewayfarers.com).

For long-distance walkers, the 202km (125-mile) **"Kerry Way"** is a signposted walking route that extends from Killarney around the Ring of Kerry (see "Sports & Outdoor Pursuits," in section 1, above).

SPECTATOR SPORTS

GAELIC GAMES The people of Killarney are passionately devoted to the national sports of hurling and Gaelic football. Games are played almost every Sunday afternoon during the summer at **Fitzgerald Stadium,** Lewis Road (© **064/31700;** www.gaa.ie). For complete details, consult the local *Kerryman* newspaper or the Killarney Tourist Office.

HORSE RACING Killarney has two annual horse-racing meets, in early May and mid-July. Each event lasts for 3 or 4 days and draws large crowds. For more information, contact the **Killarney Racecourse,** Ross Road (© **064/31125**), or the tourist office.

WHERE TO STAY
VERY EXPENSIVE/EXPENSIVE

Killarney Park Hotel ⭐⭐ With a handsome yellow neo-Georgian facade, this elegant four-story property is on the eastern edge of town, between the railway station and the tourist office. Public rooms are posh and spacious and evoke a distinguished Victorian country house, with brass fixtures, oil paintings, wainscot paneling, deep-cushioned seating, open fireplaces, and a sunlit conservatory-style lounge overlooking the gardens. The guest rooms have a traditional, conservative style, with quality provincial furnishings, quilted designer fabrics, and marble-finished bathrooms.

Kenmare Place, Killarney, county Kerry. © 064/35555. Fax 064/35266. www.killarneyparkhotel.ie. 75 units. €220–€335 ($196–$298) double; €320–€650 ($285–$579) suite. No service charge. Rates include full breakfast. AE, DC, MC, V. **Amenities:** Restaurant; bar; indoor swimming pool; gym; Jacuzzi; sauna/steam room; concierge; room service; massage; babysitting; laundry service; library. *In room:* TV, minibar, hair dryer, garment press.

EXPENSIVE

Hotel Europe ⭐⭐ Part of the same group as the Dunloe Castle, this modern, five-story hotel has the edge because it enjoys one of the most picturesque settings in Killarney. It sits right on the shores of the Lower Lake, 4.8km (3 miles) west of town, adjacent to Killarney's two 18-hole championship golf courses, and surrounded by dozens of mountain peaks. The hotel's public areas are spacious, open, and filled with antiques, while guest rooms offer contemporary furnishings. You pay about €70 ($62) more for a lakeside view, but it's spectacular and well worth it. Most rooms have private balconies.

Service Charges

A reminder: Unless otherwise noted, room rates don't include service charges (usually 10%–15% of your bill).

Off Killorglin Rd., Fossa, Killarney, county Kerry. (© **800/221-1074** in the U.S., or 064/31900. Fax 064/32118. www.iol.ie/khl. 205 units. €180–€251 ($160–$223) double. No service charge. Rates include full breakfast. V. Closed Nov to mid-Mar. Free parking. **Amenities:** 2 restaurants (international, cafe); 2 lounges; bar; indoor pool; tennis; boating; fishing; bicycling; horseback riding; gym; saunas; salon; babysitting. *In room:* TV, hair dryer.

Killarney Great Southern ★★ Set amid 14 hectares (36 acres) of gardens and lush foliage on the eastern edge of town, this four-story, ivy-covered land-mark is the grande dame of Killarney hotels. Dating from 1854, it was built around the time of Queen Victoria's visit to Killarney and has since hosted pres-idents, princes, and personalities from all over the world, as well as many a modern-day tour group. The public areas retain the charm of yesteryear, with high ceilings rimmed by ornate plasterwork, tall windows looking onto nearby mountain vistas, glowing fireplaces, and Waterford crystal chandeliers. The guest rooms also have a traditional decor, and are quite spacious and comfort-able. Train and bus terminals are opposite the hotel.

Railway Rd., off E. Avenue Rd., Killarney, county Kerry. (© **800/44-UTELL** in the U.S., or 064/31262. Fax 064/ 31642. www.gsh.ie. 180 units. €200–€240 ($178–$214) double. Rates include full breakfast. AE, DC, MC, V. Street parking only. **Amenities:** 2 restaurants (international, bistro); bar; lounge; indoor heated swimming pool; 2 tennis courts; gym; Jacuzzi; sauna/steam room; concierge; salon; room service; laundry; dry cleaning. *In room:* TV, hair dryer, garment press.

MODERATE/EXPENSIVE

Randles Court ★★ A former rectory dating from the turn of the 20th cen-tury, this attractive yellow gabled four-story house sits on a raised site off the main road outside Killarney Town on the road to Muckross House. Totally restored, enlarged, and refurbished, it opened as a hotel in 1992. Since then, the Randle family has worked together to enhance their new hotel venture with much suc-cess. The public areas of Randles Court harken back to earlier days, with marble floors, fireplaces, chandeliers, gilt mirrors, tapestries, and old prints. Three of the guest rooms are in the original building and the rest are in a new wing. All have distinctive furnishings, including armoires, antique desks, or vanities.

Muckross rd. (N71), Killarney, county Kerry. (© **800/4-CHOICE** in the U.S., or 064/35333. Fax 064/35206. www.randleshotels.com. 37 units. €110–€200 ($98–$178) double. Rates include full breakfast and service charge. AE, DC, MC, V. Free parking. **Amenities:** Restaurant (international); bar; fitness center; limited room service; babysitting; laundry service. *In room:* TV, hair dryer.

MODERATE

Castlerosse Hotel and Leisure Centre ★ Set on its own parklands between the Lower Lake and surrounding mountains, this modern, rambling, ranch-style inn is 3.2km (2 miles) from the heart of town and next to Killarney's two golf courses. The recently refurbished rooms offer bright, contemporary fur-nishings and views of the lake. If you're interested in longer term rentals, there are also 27 well-equipped two-bedroom, two-bathroom apartments available for €264 to €850 ($235–$757) per week, depending on the season. Special rates are often exclusively available on the hotel's website.

Killorglin Rd., Killarney, county Kerry. (© **800/528-1234** in the U.S., or 064/31114. Fax 064/31031. www. towerhotelgroup.ie. 110 units. €130 ($116) double. Rates include full Irish breakfast and service charge. AE,

DC, MC, V. Closed Nov to early Mar. Street parking only. **Amenities:** Restaurant (international); bar; lounge; indoor pool; 9-hole golf course; tennis courts; gym; Jacuzzi; sauna/steam room; babysitting; laundry service; nonsmoking rooms. *In room:* TV.

Earl's Court House ⚐

Award-winning Earl's Court, a 5-minute walk from the town center, is among Killarney's most attractive quality guesthouses. On arrival, guests are greeted with tea and scones in a lovely, old-fashioned lounge. The rooms are spacious and furnished with good taste and a range of Irish antiques. They are immaculately clean and immediately peaceful and pleasing, with a distinct Victorian flair. Some have half-tester beds, others have sitting areas, and nearly all have balconies. The second-floor rooms, in particular, have clear views of the mountains. The breakfast menu offers a range of selections, from apple crepes to kippers and tomatoes; you can eat in the gracious, formal dining room or, by request, in your room.

Signposted off N71, Woodlawn Junction, Muckross rd., Killarney, county Kerry. © 064/34009. Fax 064/34366. www.killarney-earlscourt.ie. 11 units, 1 single with shower only. €80–€128 ($71–$114) double. Rates include full Irish breakfast and service charge. MC, V. Closed Nov 6–Feb. Free parking. **Amenities:** Room service; nonsmoking rooms. *In room:* TV, radio, dataport, hair dryer.

Kathleen's Country House ⚐⚐

Of the many guesthouses in the area, this one stands out. About 1.6km (1 mile) north of town on 1.2 hectares (3 acres) of gardens next to a dairy farm, it's a two-story contemporary stone house with a modern mansard-style roof and many picture windows. Enthusiastic, efficient hostess Kathleen O'Regan-Sheppard offers totally refurbished guest rooms with antique pine furniture and light floral paisley fabrics, complemented by Kathleen's collection of contemporary pastels and paintings. Smoking is permitted only in the enclosed front foyer.

Madam's Height, Tralee rd. (N22), Killarney, county Kerry. © 064/32810. Fax 064/32340. www.kathleens. net. 17 units. €90–€126 ($80–$112) double. No service charge. Rates include full breakfast. AE, MC, V. Closed mid-Nov to early Mar. Free parking. **Amenities:** Nonsmoking rooms; drawing room; sunroom. *In room:* TV, tea/coffeemaker, hair dryer, garment press.

Killeen House Hotel ⚐

Dating from 1838 and set on high ground overlooking Killarney's lakes and golf courses, this rambling Edwardian country manor house is surrounded by mature gardens in a quiet residential area about 3.2km (2 miles) northwest of town. It has a relaxed, homey feel, with many of the comforts of a hotel. The guest rooms, which vary in size and decor, feature orthopedic beds and standard furniture. The golf-themed bar is probably the only pub in the world that accepts golf balls as legal tender.

Aghadoe, Killarney, county Kerry. © 064/31711. Fax 064/31811. www.killeenhousehotel.com. 23 units. €102–€204 ($91–$182) double. Rates include full breakfast. AE, DC, MC, V. Free parking. **Amenities:** Restaurant (Continental); bar; lounge. *In room:* TV, radio.

Muckross Park Hotel ⚐

This charming hotel sits across the road from Muckross House in the heart of Killarney National Park. Although it was built recently, it incorporates parts of the oldest hotel in Killarney, dating from 1795. It's furnished in country-house style, with paneled walls, open fireplaces, and equestrian-theme oil paintings. The rooms, which vary in size and decor, have period furniture, including some half-tester beds, quilted fabrics, frilly draperies, and Victorian-style ceiling fixtures. Molly Darcy's, the house watering hole, is a traditional thatched-roof pub (see "Pubs," below).

Muckross rd. (N71), Killarney, county Kerry. © 064/31938. Fax 064/31965. www.muckrosspark.com. 27 units. €150–€206 ($134–$182) double. No service charge. Rates include full breakfast. AE, DC, MC, V. Closed Nov–Feb. Free parking. **Amenities:** Restaurant (Continental); bar; lounge. *In room:* TV, hair dryer, garment press.

INEXPENSIVE

Gleann Fia Country House ⚘ Although it's just a mile from town, this modern guesthouse feels pleasantly secluded, tucked away in 10 hectares (26 acres) of lawns and woodlands. Jerry and Nora Galvin are thoughtful hosts whose presence makes it a highly personable place. The house has an airy conservatory with tea-making facilities, a guest lounge, and an unusually extensive breakfast menu. Although the entire house is modern, it has been thoughtfully and tastefully constructed, and definitely isn't your average purpose-built guesthouse. There is a nature walk along the stream by one side of the house.

Deerpark, Killarney, county Kerry. ✆ 064/35035. Fax 064/35000. www.gleannfia.com. 17 units. €80–€116 ($71–$103) double. Rates include full breakfast. AE, MC, V. Closed Dec–Feb. Free parking. **Amenities:** Lounge; nonsmoking rooms; conservatory. *In room:* TV.

Killarney Town House This appealing three-story guesthouse is on one of the busiest streets in the heart of town. It's ideal for those who want a good, clean room and don't need a bar or restaurant on the premises. The guest rooms, identified by Killarney flowers rather than by numbers, offer all the basic comforts. Breakfast is served in a bright, airy ground-floor dining room. It's a 10-minute walk from the bus and train station.

31 New St., Killarney, county Kerry. ✆ 064/35388. Fax 064/35259. 11 units. €64–€70 ($57–$62) double. No service charge. Rates include full breakfast. MC, V. Free parking. **Amenities:** Nonsmoking rooms. *In room:* TV.

WHERE TO DINE
EXPENSIVE

Gaby's Seafood Restaurant ⚘⚘ SEAFOOD   One of Killarney's longest established restaurants, this nautically themed place is a mecca for seafood lovers. Its walls are adorned with commendations and awards, which could be a tacky turnoff if the food weren't so good. Gaby's is known for its succulent lobster, served grilled or in a house sauce of cognac, wine, cream, and spices. Other choices include haddock in wine, a delectable tempura of prawns, and a giant Kerry shellfish platter—a veritable feast of prawns, scallops, mussels, lobster, and oysters.

27 High St., Killarney, county Kerry. ✆ 064/32519. Reservations recommended. Main courses €16–€40 ($13–$36) AE, DC, MC, V. Mon–Sat 6–10pm. Closed late Feb to mid-Mar and Christmas week.

MODERATE

Bricín ⚘⚘ TRADITIONAL IRISH   Old-time Kerry boxty dishes (potato pancakes with various fillings, such as chicken, seafood, curried lamb, or vegetables) are the trademark of this restaurant above a very good craft and bookshop. The menu also offers a variety of fresh seafood, pastas, and Irish stew. Specials might include filet of pork with sage and apricot stuffing, and chicken Bricín (breast of chicken in red-currant and raspberry sauce). Bricín is in one of Killarney's oldest buildings, dating from the 1830s. It sports original stone walls, pine furniture, turf fireplaces, and—very rare in Ireland—a completely nonsmoking room that seats 40. Snacks and light fare are served during the day. In addition to the shop downstairs, the building houses the Bricín Art Gallery, which displays oils and watercolors by local artists.

26 High St., Killarney, county Kerry. ✆ 064/34902. Reservations recommended for dinner. Snacks €3–€8 ($2.65–$7.10); dinner main courses €11–€20 ($10–$18). AE, DC, MC, V. Year-round Tues–Sat 10am–4:30pm; Easter–Oct Mon–Sat 6–9:30pm.

Coopers Café and Restaurant ⚘⚘ MODERN CONTINENTAL   Open just a couple of years, this creation of "Martin and Mo," two of Ireland's most touted restaurateurs, has created quite a buzz among both locals and tourists. Coopers has clearly broken the mold here in Killarney, with its chic, urban, nightclub decor, making the most of glass, stone, aluminum, and sharp black-and-white contrasts. Overhead, the many-tendrilled wire-sculpture chandeliers with flower-cup lights cast a magical fairylike illumination. The total effect is as captivating as the inventive and varied menu, which focuses on local Irish seafood and wild game. Menu options include wild pheasant cooked in Irish cream liqueur, escalop of venison, filet of wild pigeon, grilled swordfish and salmon, wild filet of sea trout, and baked cod Provençal. For vegetarians, the warm goat-cheese salad with two pestos is but one tasty selection. The alluring array of desserts includes crumbles, tarts, homemade ice creams, meringues, and crème brûlées, although it requires rare strength of character to get past the duo of dark chocolate and pistachio mousse.

Old Market Lane, off High St. (at New St.), Killarney, county Kerry. ☎ 064/37716. Reservations recommended. Main courses €11–€20 ($10–$18). MC, V. Mon–Sat 12:30–3pm; Mon–Thurs 6:30–9:30pm; Fri–Sat 6:30–10pm; Sun 4–9:30pm.

Green's ✪ VEGETARIAN   It may be a cliché to say that big surprises come in small parcels, but it's true in the case of this uncommonly good, fanciful nook of a restaurant tucked away in one of Killarney's many back lanes. The cooking has a light touch and is creative enough to pull in carnivores and vegetarians alike. The menu changes with the season and with what's best in the markets, but you can expect the likes of carrot and coriander loaf with crème fraîche; whole-wheat spinach crepe filled with organic avocado, Brazil nuts, and three cheeses; or baked aubergine (eggplant) gâteau. The modest selection of house wines, by bottle or glass, suits the cuisine well and is reasonably priced. An assortment of puddings, tarts, and other sweet whims awaits you at the finish line.

4 Bridewell Lane, off New St. across from Dunnes Stores, Killarney, county Kerry. ☎ 064/33083. Reservations recommended. Dinner main courses €11–€18 ($10–$16). MC, V. Tues–Sun 12:30–3pm and 6:30–9:30pm.

KILLARNEY AFTER DARK

At the **Killarney Manor Banquet,** Loreto Road (☎ 064/31551), you can have a five-course dinner in 19th-century style with a complete program of songs, ballads, and dance. It's held in a stately 1840s stone-faced mansion that was built as a hotel and later served as a convent and school. Of course, it's in the nature of these shows to be touristy, which doesn't mean the Irish don't enjoy them every now and then. The performers are talented and really get into it, and people have a good time. The mansion is on a hillside 3.2km (2 miles) south of town overlooking the Killarney panorama. From April through October, the banquet is staged 6 nights a week (usually closed on Sun) starting at 7:45pm. The price is €38 ($34) per person for complete banquet and dinner. If you don't want to eat there, the entertainment-only segment costs €15 ($13) and runs from 9 to 10:30pm. Reservations are required; most credit cards accepted.

Dero's Tours, 22 Main St. (☎ 064/31251), offers a special bus and theater ticket to **Siamsa Tire,** the National Folk Theatre of Ireland, at Town Park, Tralee, 32km (20 miles) northwest of Killarney. (See "Tralee After Dark," in section 4, later in this chapter.)

PUBS

Dunloe Lodge   This simple pub in the heart of town has a friendly, comfortable atmosphere. Don't be surprised if a local patron spontaneously pulls out a harmonica, an accordion, a banjo, or a fiddle and starts to play. Most nights you'll hear anything from Irish ballads to folk or rock music. It can be touristy, but it's fun. Plunkett St., Killarney, county Kerry. ✆ **064/33503.**

Kate Kearney's Cottage   This is a place of pilgrimage in Killarney, and it's worth a stop if only for tradition's sake. Almost everyone who ventures through the famous Gap visits this former coaching inn, and it's been that way for more than a century. Elegantly attired Victorians were served illegal poteen (potato moonshine) by Kate herself, who was believed by some to be a witch. From this point on, all cars are left behind and it's into the Gap on foot, horseback, bike, or horse-and-buggy. Today this outpost 15km (9 miles) west of town is more than a little touristy—a glorified refreshment stop with souvenirs for sale. But from May through September, very good traditional music is performed on Sunday, Tuesday, and Wednesday from 9 to 11:30pm. Gap of Dunloe, Killarney, county Kerry. ✆ **064/44146.**

The Laurels   One of the more popular "singsong" pubs in town, this place rings to the rafters with the lilt of Irish ditties. Ballad singers are booked nightly from April through October, starting at 9pm. Main St., Killarney, county Kerry. ✆ **064/ 31149.**

Molly Darcy's   Across from Muckross House, this is one of Killarney's best traditional pubs, with a thatched roof, stone walls, an oak-beamed ceiling, open fireplaces, alcoves, snugs, public phones in what were confession boxes salvaged from a monastery, and lots of Killarney memorabilia. There's dancing on Sunday evenings. Muckross Village, Muckross Rd., Killarney, county Kerry. ✆ **064/34973.**

Tatler Jack   This traditional pub is a favorite gathering place for followers of Gaelic football and hurling. Traditional music or ballads are scheduled from June through September, nightly from 9:30pm. Plunkett St., Killarney, county Kerry. ✆ **064/32361.**

3 The Dingle Peninsula

Dingle Town is 48km (30 miles) W of Tralee and 80km (50 miles) NW of Killarney

Like the Iveragh Peninsula, Dingle has a spectacularly scenic peripheral road, and a tourist trade has blossomed along it. But as soon as you veer off the main roads, or penetrate to such hinterlands of the peninsula as the Blasket Islands or Brandon Head, you'll discover extraordinary desolate beauty, seemingly worlds away from the tour buses and shamrock-filled shops. Dingle Town itself is definitely touristy, but it's smaller and less congested than Killarney and retains more traces of being a real, year-round town with an identity beyond the tourist trade.

ESSENTIALS
GETTING THERE   **Bus Eireann** (✆ **066/712-3566;** www.buseireann.ie) provides daily coach service to Dingle from all parts of Ireland. The boarding and drop-off point is on Upper Main Street.

If you're driving from Tralee to Dingle, follow R559, or take R561 from Castlemaine.

VISITOR INFORMATION   **The Dingle Tourist Office** is on Main Street, Dingle (✆ **066/915-1188**). It is open seasonally, usually mid-April through October. Regular hours are Monday to Saturday 10am to 1pm and 2:15 to 6pm. (extended and Sun hours in peak summer season).

For extensive, detailed tourist information on the Dingle Peninsula, see **www. dingle-peninsula.ie** or **www.kerrygems.ie.**

Impressions

I walked up this morning along the slope from the east to the top of Sybil Head, where one comes out suddenly on the brow of a cliff with a straight fall of many hundreds of feet into the sea. It is a place of indescribable grandeur, where one can see Carrantuohill and the Skelligs and Loop Head and the full sweep of the Atlantic, and over all, the wonderfully tender and searching light that is seen only in Kerry. One wonders in these places why there is anyone left in Dublin, or London, or Paris, when it would be better, one would think, to live in a tent or hut with this magnificent sea and sky, and to breathe this wonderful air, which is like wine in one's teeth.

—John Millington Synge (1871–1909), Irish playwright

GETTING AROUND   Dingle Town has no local bus service. **Bus Eireann** (📞 **066/712-3566**) provides service from Dingle to other towns on the peninsula. For local taxi or minibus service, contact **John Sheehy** (📞 **066/915-1301**). The best way to get around Dingle Town, with its narrow, winding, hilly streets, is to walk. The town is small, compact, and easy to get to know.

To see the sights beyond the town, drive west along R559 or take one of the sightseeing tours suggested below.

FAST FACTS   In an emergency, dial 📞 **999**. The **Dingle Hospital** is on Upper Main Street (📞 **066/915-1455** or 066/915-1172). The local **Garda Station** is at Holy Ground, Dingle (📞 **066/915-1522**).

The **Niallann and Daingean** (Dingle Laundry) is on Green Street (📞 **066/915-1837**).

The **Dingle District Library** is on Green Street, Dingle (📞 **066/915-1499**).

In & About Dingle Peninsula is a newspaper-style publication distributed free at hotels, restaurants, shops, and the tourist office. It lists events, attractions, activities, and more.

WHAT TO SEE & DO

Don't miss **Slea Head,** at the southwestern extremity of the peninsula. It's a place of pristine beaches, great walks, and fascinating archaeological remains. The village of **Dunquin,** stunningly situated between Slea Head and Clogher Head, is home to the Blasket Centre. **Dunbeg Fort** sits on a rocky promontory just south of Slea Head, its walls rising from the cliff edge. Although much of the fort has fallen into the sea, the place is well worth a visit at the bargain-basement rate of €1.50 ($1.35) per person. From Slea Head, the Dingle Way continues east to Dingle Town (24km/15 miles) or north along the coast toward Ballyferriter.

Just offshore from Dunquin are the seven **Blasket Islands;** a ferry (📞 **066/915-6455**) connects Great Blasket with the mainland when the weather permits. Alternatively, you can take a 3-hour cruise around the islands with Blasket Island Tours (📞 **066/915-6422**), leaving from Dunquin Pier. The islands were abandoned by the last permanent residents in 1953 and now are inhabited only by a few summer visitors who share the place with the seals and seabirds. A magnificent 13km (8-mile) walk goes to the west end of Great Blasket and back, passing sea cliffs and ivory beaches; you can stop along the way at the only cafe on the island, which serves lunch and dinner.

East of Ballyferriter is **Gallarus Oratory,** one of the best-preserved early Christian church buildings in Ireland. With a shape much like an overturned boat, it's constructed of unmortared stone, yet is still completely watertight after more than 1,000 years.

Dingle's Oceanworld Aquarium *(Kids)*

Despite the big-sounding name, this is a relatively small aquarium with little to see to justify the ticket price. There are various sea critters behind glass in the aquarium's 29 tanks, and members of the young staff carry around live lobsters, crabs, starfish, and other "inner space" creatures, and introduce them up-close to visitors. During feeding times, children are allowed to hand out the grub. In addition, there are exhibits on Brendan the Navigator and the Spanish Armada, a cafe, and a gift shop. This is a compact, hands-on, interactive place that gets bonus points for effort, but in the end doesn't provide the wow factor of many other aquariums.

Dingle Harbour, Dingle, county Kerry. (C) **066/915-2111.** www.dingle-oceanworld.ie. Admission €7.50 ($6.70) adults, €6 ($5.35) seniors and students, €4.50 ($4) children, €20 ($18) family. MC, V. Daily Sept and June 9:30am–7pm; July–Aug 9:30am–8:30pm; Oct–May 9:30am–6pm.

Eask Tower *(★)*

Built in 1847 as a signal for Dingle Harbour, Eask Tower was a famine relief project. It is a remarkable edifice, a 12m (40-ft.) tower built of solid stone some 4.5m (15 ft.) thick, with a wooden arrow pointing to the mouth of the harbor. The main reason for making the 1.6km (1-mile) climb to the summit of Carhoo Hill is not the tower, but the incredible panoramic views of Dingle Harbour, Connor Pass, Slea Head, and, on the far side of Dingle Bay, the high peaks of the Iveragh Peninsula. This is a great place to get your bearings in the region—you can see most of the southern part of the Dingle Peninsula. Save this for a clear day.

Carhoo Hill, Dingle, county Kerry. (C) **066/915-1850.** Admission €1.30 ($1.15). Daily 8am–10pm. From Dingle, follow Slea Head Rd. 3.2km (2 miles), turn left at road signposted for Colâiste Ide, and continue another 3.2km (2 miles).

Ionad An Bhlascaoid Mhoir/The Blasket Centre *(★★)*

This relatively new heritage center is perched on the westerly tip of the Dingle Peninsula, overlooking the Atlantic and the distant vistas of the remote Blasket Islands. The Great Blasket was once an outpost of Irish civilization and a nurturing ground for a small group of great Irish-language writers, but its inhabitants abandoned the island in 1953. Through a series of displays, exhibits, and a video presentation, this center celebrates the cultural and literary traditions of the Blaskets and the history of Corca Dhuibhne, the Gaeltacht area. The center also has a research room, a bookshop specializing in local literature, and a wide-windowed restaurant with views of the Blaskets.

Dunquin, county Kerry. (C) **066/915-6371.** Admission €3.50 ($3.10) adults, €2.50 ($1.95) seniors, €1.30 ($1.15) children and students, €8 ($7.10) family. Apr–June and Sept–Oct daily 10am–6pm; July–Aug daily 10am–7pm. Closed Nov–Mar.

SIGHTSEEING TOURS

Fungie the Dolphin Tours *(★★) (Kids)*

Forget Flipper. In Dingle, the name to know is Fungie the Dolphin. Every day, fishing boats ferry visitors out into the nearby waters to see the famous village mascot. Trips last about 1 hour and depart regularly, roughly every 2 hours off-season and as frequently as every half-hour in high season. Fungie really does swim up to the boat, and the boatmen stay out long enough for ample sightings—and long, wonderful eyefuls of the gorgeous bay. If you want to get up close and personal with Fungie, you can also arrange an early-morning dolphin swim (see "Swimming with a Dolphin," below).

The Pier, Dingle, county Kerry. ✆ **066/915-1967** or 066/915-2626. Tour €10 ($8.90) adults, €5 ($4.45) children under 12. Year-round daily 10am–6pm.

Sciuird Archaeological Adventures A local expert leads these archaeological tours, which last 2½ hours and involve a short bus journey and some easy walking. Four or five monuments, from the Stone Age to medieval times, are on the route. All tours, limited to 8 to 10 people, start from the top of the pier. Reservations are required.

Holy Ground, Dingle, county Kerry. ✆ **066/915-1937**. Tour €10 ($8.90) per person. May–Sept daily 10:30am and 2pm.

SHOPPING

Annascaul Pottery This shop sells colorful, locally-made pottery and ceramics with wildflower designs. The wares come in all sizes and shapes, including jewelry. The factory at nearby Annascaul is open year-round. The shop is open from Easter to October, from 10am to 6pm. Green St. Courtyard, off Green St., Dingle, county Kerry. ✆ **066/915-7186**.

Brian De Staic Considered by many to be Ireland's leading gold- and silversmith, Brian de Staic plies his trade in his workshop, located just west of the Dingle Pier. He specializes in Celtic jewelry, handcrafted and engraved with ancient Celtic symbols or the letters of the Ogham alphabet, an ancient Irish form of writing dating from the 3rd century. His collection includes pendants, bracelets, earrings, cuff links, brooches, and tie clips. From June to October, the shop is open daily from 9am to 9pm; from November to May, hours are Monday to Saturday, from 9am to 6pm. There are two other retail shops: Green Street, Dingle (✆ **066/915-1298**), and 18 High St., Killarney (✆ **064/33822**). The Wood, Dingle, county Kerry. ✆ **066/915-1298**. www.brian-de-staic.ie.

Ceardlann Craft Village Just west of the Dingle Marina, this cluster of traditional cottages is a circular craft village, set on a hillside above the town and harbor. A local craft worker who produces and sells his or her craft staffs each workshop. Handmade felts, fun jewelry and mosaics, and traditional Irish musical instruments are offered, as well as silver jewelry and ceramic pictures. A cafe on the premises serves excellent homemade soups, salads, and hot dishes. Open daily from 10am to 6pm. The Wood, Dingle, county Kerry. ✆ **066/915-1778**.

Greenlane Gallery This gallery and shop offers a wide selection of contemporary Irish paintings, watercolors, sculpture, and ceramics. Works by leading Irish artists are always available, and private viewings can be arranged. Images are also available by e-mail upon request. In summer, the shop is open from 10am to 9pm; in winter, hours are 11am to 5pm. Green St., Dingle, county Kerry. ✆ **066/915-2018**. www.greenlanegallery.com.

Holden Leathergoods Conor Holden is one of Ireland's most talented leather craftsmen. Here, in his schoolhouse-turned-studio, he offers beautiful handcrafted suede and silk-lined leather handbags, suede and leather pouches, and duffel and travel bags, as well as briefcases, belts, wallets, and key cases. Open Monday to Saturday from 8:30am to 6:30pm and Sunday 10:30am to 5pm (in low season, open Mon–Fri 9am–5pm). The Old School House, signposted 4.8km (3 miles) west of town on the Ventry rd. (R559), off the Slea Head Dr., Burnham, Dingle, county Kerry. ✆ **066/915-1796**.

Louis Mulcahy Pottery 🌟🌟 Located north of Dunquin, this is the studio of master craftsman Louis Mulcahy. He produces a stunning, sophisticated range of pottery made from local clay and glazes devised at the shop. The finished products include everything from tableware to giant vases, teapots, platters, and huge lamps. Complementary furniture and hand-decorated silk and cotton lampshades are available, as is a selection of Lisbeth Mulcahy's tapestries and weavings. The Mulcahys have opened a new shop and cafe in Ballyferriter Village, just down the road. The shop specializes in distinctive painted lampshades and housewares. Open daily from 10am to 6pm. Clogher, Ballyferriter, county Kerry. C 066/915-6229. www.louismulcahy.com.

The Weavers' Shop   One of Ireland's leading weavers, Lisbeth Mulcahy creates fabrics and tapestries inspired by seasonal changes in the landscape and seascape. She uses pure wool, Irish linen, cotton, and alpaca in weaving scarves, shawls, knee rugs, wall hangings, tapestries, table mats, and napkins. Everything is gorgeous, but expensive. From October to May, open Monday to Saturday from 9am to 6pm; June to September, open Monday to Saturday from 9am to 9pm, Sunday from 10am to 6pm. Green St., Dingle, county Kerry. C 066/915-1688.

SPORTS & OUTDOOR PURSUITS

BEACHES   The Dingle Peninsula has some of the most dramatic beaches in Ireland. The most famous is **Inch Strand,** which plays a cameo in county Kerry Tourism's TV ad with the tag line, "Where an inch is a mile." Actually, it's a 4.8km-long (3-mile) dune-covered sandy spit—one of the largest dune fields in Ireland. To walk eastward from the crashing waves of the Atlantic surf of Dingle Bay through the large, active dunes to the quiet lagoons and mud flats behind in Cromane Bay is to witness nature caught in a dynamic dance of wind, sea, and sand. It is also steeped in history, archaeology and wildlife. Part of *Ryan's Daughter,* the 1969 David Lean production with Robert Mitchum and Sarah Miles, was filmed here.

If you've never seen a boulder beach, then **Kilmurray Bay at Minard** 🎉🎉 is a Lilliputian dream come to life. Here in the shadow of Minard Castle, giant sausage-shaped sandstone boulders form a beach unlike anything you have ever seen. Definitely not a place for swimming, but a wonderful place for a surrealistic picnic lunch.

Like Minard, **Trabeg Beach** confronts the southwest storms of the Atlantic head on. Here, on an ebbing tide, you will find exquisite wave-sculptured maroon sandstone forms marching seaward from sheer rock cliffs and small sea caves lined with veins of crystalline quartz. The beauty of the rock sculptures combined with the roar of the surf is magical.

Some of the calmest beaches in this area for swimming are east of Castlegregory, on the west side of Tralee Bay. The beach at **Maherabeg** has a coveted European Blue Flag (a symbol of high environmental and safety standards), and the beaches of **Brandon Bay** are exceptionally scenic, and good for walking and swimming.

BICYCLING   Mountain bikes can be rented at the **Mountain Man,** Strand Street, Dingle (C **066/915-1868**), for €10 ($8.90) per day or €44 ($39) per week. Mike Shea knows the area well, and can suggest a number of 1-day or overnight touring options on the Dingle Peninsula. A great day trip is the road out to the tip of the peninsula past Slea Head and Clogher Head, which is outrageously beautiful and not too hilly. Touring and mountain bikes are also available year-round from **Foxy John Moriarty,** Main Street, Dingle (C **066/915-1316**). High-season prices start at €9 ($8) per day, €35 ($31) per week.

BIRD-WATCHING   **Great Blasket Island** is of some interest for the fall passerine migration. In summer, the small, uninhabited islands surrounding

Great Blasket attract an abundance of nesting seabirds, including more than 20,000 pairs of storm petrels. From Clogher Head north of Dunquin at the western extremity of the Dingle Peninsula, rare autumn migrants can sometimes be seen. Inch Peninsula, extending into Castlemaine Harbour south of Inch town, is a wintering ground for brent geese, which arrive in late August and move on in April; there is also a large wigeon population during the fall.

DIVING   The **Dingle Marina Centre,** on the marina, Dingle (© **066/915-2422;** www.divedingle.com), offers a full range of PADI lessons and certification courses for beginners and experienced divers, as well as day-trip dives. A 1-hour lesson followed by an ocean dive is €60 ($53). A day trip to the Blasket Islands, including two dives, gear hire, and tanks, also runs €60 ($53). On the North Dingle Peninsula, **Harbour House,** The Maharees, Castlegregory, county Kerry (© **066/713-9292;** www.waterworld.ie/harbour.html), is a diving center that offers packages including diving, room, and board at remarkable rates. The house is yards from the Scraggane Pier, and a 5- to 15-minute boat ride from most of the diving sites. All members of the Fitzgibbon family are active divers, and they offer a great vacation for people who share their passion. Classes for beginners are also available.

GOLF   Sixteen kilometers (10 miles) west of Dingle Town, on the western edge of the Dingle Peninsula, overlooking the Atlantic, the **Dingle Golf Club (Ceann Sibéal),** Ballyferriter (© **066/915-6255;** www.iol.ie/~dinglegc), welcomes visitors to play its 18-hole, par-72 course. Greens fees are €25 to €50 ($22–$45) on weekdays and €32 to €57 ($28–$51) on weekends, depending on the season.

HORSEBACK RIDING   At **Dingle Horse Riding,** Ballinaboula House, Dingle (© **066/915-2018**), rides are available along nearby beaches or through the mountains. A 1½-hour mountain ride costs €24 ($21). Half-day, full-day, and 3- to 5-day packages including accommodations, meals, and riding can be arranged.

SAILING   The **Dingle Sailing Club,** c/o The Wood, Dingle (© **066/915-1984**), offers an array of courses taught by experienced, certified instructors. Summer courses run €120 to €145 ($107–$129). To charter a yacht, contact **Dingle Sea Ventures,** Dingle (© **066/915-2244;** www.charterireland.com). Yachts that sleep 6 to 10 are available; prices run €1,200 to €2,700 ($1,068–$2,403) per week. Skippers' fees are €65 ($58) per day.

SEA ANGLING   For packages and day trips, contact Nicholas O'Connor at **Angler's Rest,** Ventry (© **066/915-9947**); or Seán O'Conchúir (© **066/915-429**), representing the **Kerry Angling Association.**

WALKING   The **Dingle Way** begins in Tralee and circles the peninsula, covering 153km (95 miles) of gorgeous mountain and coastal landscape. The most rugged section is along Brandon Head, where the trail passes between Mount Brandon and the ocean. The views are tremendous, but the walk is long (about 24km/15 miles, averaging 9 hr.) and strenuous, and should be attempted only when the sky is clear. The section between Dunquin and Ballyferriter (also 24km/15 miles) follows an especially lovely stretch of coast. For more information, see *The Dingle Way Map Guide,* available in local tourist offices and shops.

The best walk in the region, and one of the best in Ireland, is the ascent to **Brandon's summit** ✮✮. The approach from the west is a more gradual climb, but the walk from the eastern, Cloghane side is far more interesting and includes the beautiful Paternoster Lakes. The road to the trailhead is signposted just past

Moments Swimming with a Dolphin

A unique watersport in Dingle Bay is swimming with the resident dolphin, Fungie. Although Fungie can swim about 40kmph (25 mph), he enjoys human company and is usually willing to slow down and swim with his new acquaintances, often playfully jumping clear over their heads. He's free and lives in the wild, but regularly comes by to interact with people. To arrange a dolphin encounter, contact Bridgit Flannery (© 066/915-1967), almost any day from 8am to 8pm. You book a swim the day before, when you rent your gear (semi-dry suit, mask, snorkel, boots, and fins, all in one duffel). The full overnight outfitting cost is €20 ($18) per person. Then you show up in your gear early the next morning to be brought out by boat to your aquatic rendezvous. The 2-hour escorted swim costs an additional €15 ($13). If you prefer, you can use your rented outfit and swim out on your own; Fungie also welcomes drop-ins. This outing is for teenagers on up, although smaller children will certainly enjoy watching.

Cloghane on the road to Brandon town; drive about 4.8km (3 miles) on this road to a small parking lot and the Lopsided Tea House. Be sure to bring plenty of water and food, gear for wind and rain, and a good map. The trail climbs through fields, past an elaborate grotto, and along the slope of an open hillside where flashy red and white poles mark the way. As you round the corner of the high open hillside, the Paternoster Lakes and Brandon come into view. The walk through this glacial valley toward the base of the mountain is the most beautiful part of the trail; when the weather's bad, you won't have wasted your time if you turn around before reaching the summit. The only seriously strenuous leg of the journey is the climb out of this valley to the ridge, a short but intense scramble over boulders and around ledges. Once you reach the ridge top, turn left and follow the trail another quarter mile or so to the summit. You can return the way you came or continue south along the ridge, returning to Cloghane on the Pilgrim's Route, an old track that circumnavigates the Dingle Peninsula. Although this is a day hike (about 4 hr. to the summit and back), and very well marked, it shouldn't be taken too lightly—bring all necessary supplies, and let someone know when you expect to return. Information on climbing routes and weather conditions is available at the Cloghane visitor's center.

Hidden Ireland Tours, Dingle (© **888-246-9026** in the U.S., or 087/221-4002; www.hiddenirelandtours.com), offers a week of easy to moderate guided hiking through some of Ireland's most beautiful scenery. It takes in parts of the Kerry Way, Killarney National Park, the Beara Peninsula in County Cork, Skellig Michael, and the Dingle Peninsula. Costs, including luggage transfers and accommodations, run €2,475 ($2,203) per person. Available April to September.

WINDSURFING   The beaches around Castlegregory offer a variety of conditions for windsurfing. Those on the eastern side of the peninsula are generally calmer than those to the west. Equipment can be hired from **Jamie Knox Watersports,** Maharees, Castlegregory, county Kerry (© **066/713-9411;** www.jamieknox.com), on the road between Castlegregory and Fahamore. Kayaks can also be rented for €16 ($14) per hour.

WHERE TO STAY

MODERATE/EXPENSIVE

Dingle Skellig Hotel ⭐ Named for the fabled Sceilig (or Skellig) Rocks off the coast, this three-story hotel enjoys an idyllic location next to Dingle Bay on the eastern edge of town. Expanded and upgraded in recent years by the Cluskey family, the public areas are decorated with Irish pine and brass touches. The guest rooms can feel dated, with busy fabrics and nondescript furnishings, but they have fabulous views of the sea.

Throughout the summer season, the Dingle Bay Cabaret puts on a 3-hour spectacle, including audience participation in the Irish dancing. A range of children's entertainment is also available.

Annascaul Rd., Dingle, county Kerry. © 066/9151144. Fax 066/9151501. www.dingleskellig.com. 116 units. €140–€230 ($125–$205) double. Rates include full breakfast. AE, MC, V. Closed Jan–Feb. Free parking. **Amenities:** Restaurant (seafood); bar; lounge; indoor pool; gym; Jacuzzi; steam room; children's playroom; health treatments; room service. In room: TV, radio, hair dryer.

MODERATE

Benners Hotel ⭐⭐ (Value) One of the few hotels out here that stay open year-round, Benners is a good-value choice with character that's right in the heart of town. The lovely Georgian doorway with a fanlight at the front entrance sets the tone. Dating from more than 250 years ago, the hotel blends old-world charm and modern comforts, thanks to a recent refurbishment and expansion. It's furnished with Irish antique pine furniture, including four-poster beds and armoires in the guest rooms. Special 2- and 3-night rates are available on the hotel's website.

Main St., Dingle, county Kerry. © 066/915-1638. Fax 066/915-1412. www.bennershotel.com. 52 units. €133–€222 ($118–$198) double. Rates include full Irish breakfast and service charge. AE, DC, MC, V. **Amenities:** Restaurant (Continental); 2 bars. In room: TV, tea/coffeemaker, hair dryer.

Doyle's Townhouse ⭐⭐ Sister to the successful Doyle's Seafood Restaurant next door, this three-story guesthouse is a favorite Dingle hideaway. It has a lovely Victorian fireplace in the drawing room area, and many of the antique fixtures date from 250 years ago or more. Period pieces and country pine predominate in the guest rooms, although they're totally up-to-date with firm beds and good-size Italian marble bathrooms with towel warmers. Most are so spacious that they have a pullout couch that can accommodate a third person. Front rooms look out onto the town, and back rooms have a balcony or patio and face a garden, with mountain vistas in the background. Two ground-floor rooms are perfect for folks who have difficulty with stairs. In addition, just down the road, off a little courtyard, there are four little town houses—each with its own entrance and a sitting room downstairs, with a bedroom and bathroom on the upper level.

5 John St., Dingle, county Kerry. © 800/223-6510 in the U.S., or 066/915-1174. Fax 066/915-1816. www. doylesofdingle.com. 12 units. €105–€112 ($93–$100) double. Rates include full breakfast. DC, MC, V. Closed Christmas and mid-Jan to mid-Feb. **Amenities:** Drawing room. In room: TV, hair dryer.

INEXPENSIVE/MODERATE

Milltown House ⭐⭐ You couldn't wish for a more picturesque setting than this bay-side haven. Tucked away on the bank of a tidal inlet, Milltown House enjoys a privileged location just minutes from Dingle Town, providing both easy access and serene remove. The simple white-and-black 19th-century exterior conceals the exceptional class and comfort of a fine family-run guesthouse. It incorporates the amenities of a hotel with the informal warmth of a B&B. The spacious guest rooms—each uniquely designed—have sitting areas and firm, orthopedic beds. Half have sea views and nearly all have patios. Two are wheelchair accessible. The nonsmoking sitting room—all easy chairs and open fires— is elegant and comfortable, while the conservatory breakfast room (where you'll enjoy a lavish breakfast menu) looks out on Dingle Bay. Film buffs might want to request room 2, where Robert Mitchum stayed while filming *Ryan's Daughter.*

Milltown (off Ventry Rd), Dingle, county Kerry. © **066/915-1372.** Fax 066/915-1095. http://indigo.ie/ ~milltown. 10 units. €84–€138 ($75–$123). Rates include full breakfast. MC, V. **Amenities:** Conservatory; sitting room. *In room:* TV, tea/coffeemaker, hair dryer.

INEXPENSIVE

The Captain's House ★★ Jim and Mary Milhench own and run this friendly, dapper little B&B right smack in the middle of Dingle. The name is inspired more by the location (the house is landlocked, except for a river that runs through the well-manicured yard) than by Jim's former life as a sea captain. Everything here is done with an eye for orderly, shipshape detail. When you arrive, you're offered tea with scones or a slice of rich porter cake (don't decline—it's wonderful) and made to feel genuinely welcome. As in many town houses, rooms were built to a smallish scale, but the whole place is done up so delightfully that the overall effect is cozy rather than cramped. Returning guests often ask specifically to stay in room 10, which is tucked under the gables and has a sloping ceiling. Mary's breakfasts are excellent—homemade muesli, baked ham, local cheeses, homemade honey and marmalade, along with the usual eggs any which way with sausages and bacon.

The Mall, Dingle, county Kerry. © **066/915-1531.** Fax 066/915-1079. 9 units. €80–€90 ($71–$80) double. No service charge. Rates include full breakfast. AE, MC, V. Closed Dec–Jan. **Amenities:** Sitting room. *In room:* TV.

Greenmount House ★★ Perched on a hill overlooking Dingle Bay and the town, this modern bungalow-style bed-and-breakfast home is a standout in its category. It was named RAC (Royal Automobile Club—the British equivalent of AAA) 1997 "Small Hotel of the Year" for Ireland. It has all the comforts of a hotel at bargain prices, including spacious guest rooms, each with its own sitting area and large bathroom. Breakfasts, ranging from smoked salmon omelets to ham-and-pineapple toasties, have won awards for proprietors Mary and John Curran.

John St., Dingle, county Kerry. © **066/915-1414.** Fax 066/915-1974. www.greenmounthouse.com. 12 units. €68–€108 ($61–$96) double. No service charge. Rates include full breakfast. MC, V. Closed Dec 20–26. **Amenities:** Nonsmoking rooms; conservatory; sitting room. *In room:* TV, tea/coffeemaker.

WHERE TO DINE
EXPENSIVE

Beginish ★★★ SEAFOOD If you're looking for the best seafood in Dingle, you've come to the right place. Mrs. Pat Moore runs this delightful small restaurant, and she's managed to achieve an atmosphere of quiet elegance, unassuming and comfortable. There's a lovely conservatory overlooking the garden in back, with room for outdoor tables in summer. Although there are lamb and beef dishes and a vegetarian special each night, the emphasis is on fish—the cooking is simple, traditional, and always delightful. Among the starters, the smoked salmon with shallots, capers, and horseradish cream is exquisite— nothing fancy, just excellent ingredients combined in the perfect proportions. Also delicious is the tomato and goat's-cheese mousse with fennel. You can't go wrong with any of the fish courses, such as the old-fashioned fish chowder as a starter, or main courses like Monkfish with Provençal sauce or Cod on thyme-scented potatoes and sweet red peppers. For dessert, chef Pat Moore's hot rhubarb soufflé tart is legendary in these parts.

Green St., Dingle, county Kerry. ✆ **066/915-1321.** Reservations recommended. Dinner main courses €16–€30 ($14–$27). MC, V. Tues–Sun noon–2pm and 6–10pm. Closed Jan.

Doyle's Seafood Bar 🌟🌟 SEAFOOD   It's been almost 25 years since John and Stella Doyle left Dublin to open the town's first seafood bar. John meets the fishing boats each morning and brings in the best of the day's catch, and Stella perfects her culinary skills—a combination that has achieved international acclaim. The atmosphere is homey, with stone walls and floors, sugan (a kind of straw) chairs, tweedy place mats, and old Dingle sketches. All the ingredients come from the sea, the Doyles' gardens, or nearby farms—and the Doyles even smoke their own salmon. Specialties include baked filet of lemon sole with prawn sauce, salmon filet in puff pastry with sorrel sauce, rack of lamb, and a signature platter of seafood (sole, salmon, lobster, oysters, and crab claws).

4 John St., Dingle, county Kerry. ✆ **066/915-1174.** Reservations required. Main courses €15–€28 ($13–$25). MC, V. Mon–Sat 6–10pm. Closed mid-Dec to mid-Feb.

MODERATE

The Chart House 🌟🌟 MODERN COUNTRY   This is the hottest table in Dingle—in fact, it's quickly become a destination restaurant that draws folks from outside Kerry—so book ahead and prepare to enjoy. As the *Sunday Tribune* food critic gushed, "The food, the service, and the buzz all conspire to set this place apart." There's the ubiquitously inviting bistrolike atmosphere—cue the country half-door and chunky pine furniture—but everyone comes for Laura Boyce's confident, simple cooking. Think wonderful comfort food with a flair—filet of beef with garlicky mashed spuds, herb-marinated John Dory on a bed of citrus-infused couscous, roast monkfish with zucchini (called courgette in Ireland) and mustard sauce, home-smoked pork with apple frittatas. It's the kind of food you never tire of. And the service is, as the Irish would say, "spot on."

The Mall, Dingle, county Kerry. ✆ **066/915-2255.** Reservations required. Dinner main courses €15–€29 ($13–$26). MC, V. Daily 6:30 –10pm. Closed Jan 8–Feb 12.

Lord Bakers 🌟 SEAFOOD/PUB GRUB   Named after a 19th-century Dingle poet, politician, and publican, this restaurant is part of a building that is reputedly the oldest pub in Dingle. The decor blends an old-world stone fireplace and cozy alcoves with a sunlit conservatory and art deco touches. The menu offers standard bar food, as well as crab claws or prawns in garlic butter, fried scampi, Kerry oysters, seafood Mornay, and steaks. Dinner specialties include sole stuffed with smoked salmon and spinach in cheese sauce, lobster thermidor, and rack of lamb.

Main St., Dingle, county Kerry. ✆ **066/915-1277.** Reservations recommended for dinner. Bar food €3–€15 ($2.65–$13); dinner main courses €15–€28 ($13–$25). AE, MC, V. Fri–Wed 12:30–2pm and 6–10pm.

INEXPENSIVE

An Cafe Liteartha 🌟 CAFE/TEAROOM   "The Literary Cafe" is a self-service tearoom and a fabulous bookstore with books and maps of Irish interest, and a focus on life in this corner of county Kerry. The cafe section features soups, salads, seafood, and freshly baked scones and cakes, as well as traditional dishes such as Irish stew. It's an ideal spot to browse and to enjoy a quick lunch or snack in the middle of town.

Dykegate St., Dingle, county Kerry. © **066/915-2204**. All items €3–€16 ($2.65–$14). No credit cards. Mon–Sat 9am–6pm, later in summer.

PUBS

An Driochead Beag/The Small Bridge   Built on a bridge, with a stone floor and a rustic interior and a friendly atmosphere, this pub in the heart of town draws crowds throughout the year for sessions of traditional Irish music, usually starting at 9:30pm. Be sure to arrive early if you want even standing room! Lower Main St., Dingle, county Kerry. © **066/915-1723**.

Dick Mack's   Although one of Dingle's most famous old characters, Richard "Dick" Mack, died a few years ago, his family carries on his traditions. In his day, Dick ran the place as a pub and shoeshine shop all in one. The small leather shop is still on the left, opposite a tiny bar. Old pictures, books, and mugs, all part of the Dick Mack legend, line the walls. It's a favorite among locals, as it has been for celebrities such as Robert Mitchum, Timothy Dalton, and Paul Simon, whose names are commemorated with stars on the sidewalk just outside. Green St., Dingle, county Kerry. © **066/915-1070**.

O'Flaherty's   This big, barnlike, rustic pub reflects the true flavor of the Dingle Peninsula. Old posters, prints, clippings, and photos of Irish literary figures line the walls. You'll also see poems on the Dingle area by local authors, and favorite Gaelic phrases. In the evenings, you'll usually find excellent traditional music sessions. Bridge St., Dingle, county Kerry. © **066/915-1983**.

4 Tralee

Tralee is 32km (20 miles) NW of Killarney

Tralee is the commercial center of county Kerry; with a population of 22,000, it's three times the size of Killarney. This is more a functioning town than a tourist center, and locals outnumber visitors, except during the ever-popular **Rose of Tralee festival** in August. The town is the permanent home of the National Folk Theatre of Ireland, Siamsa Tire, which operates year-round but is most active during July and August.

The harbor of Tralee is 6.5km (4 miles) northwest of the town, at Fenit. A major sailing center, Fenit is where St. Brendan the Navigator was born in 484, or so it's said. Brendan is credited with sailing the Atlantic in a small leather boat known as a *coracle* and arriving in America long before Columbus.

ESSENTIALS

GETTING THERE   **Aer Lingus** operates daily nonstop flights from Dublin into **Kerry County Airport,** Farranfore, county Kerry (© **066/976-4644;** www.kerryairport.ie), about 24km (15 miles) south of Tralee.

Buses from all parts of Ireland arrive daily at the **Bus Eireann Depot,** John Joe Sheehy Road (© **066/712-3566;** www.buseireann.ie).

Trains from major cities arrive at the **Irish Rail Station,** John Joe Sheehy Road (© **066/712-3522;** www.irishrail.ie).

Four major national roads converge on Tralee: N69 and N21 from Limerick and the north, N70 from the Ring of Kerry and points south, and N22 from Killarney, Cork, and the east.

VISITOR INFORMATION   The **Tralee Tourist Office,** Ashe Memorial Hall, Denny Street (© **066/712-1288**), offers information on Tralee and the Dingle Peninsula. It is open weekdays 9am to 1pm and 2 to 5pm, with weekend and extended hours in the spring and summer. There is also a first-rate cafe on the premises. For Tralee tourist information on the Web, explore **www. tralee-insight.com**.

GETTING AROUND   The best way to get around Tralee's downtown area is to walk. If you prefer to take a taxi, call the **Taxi Rank** (8am–midnight), The Mall (✆ **066/718-1888**); **Kingdom Cabs,** Boherbee (✆ **066/712-7828**); or **Tralee Radio Cabs,** Monavelley (✆ **066/712-5451**).

FAST FACTS   If you need a drugstore, try **Kelly's Pharmacy,** 9 The Mall (✆ **066/712-1302**), or **Cahill Sharon Chemist,** 37 Upper Castle St. (✆ **066/712-1205**).

In an emergency, dial ✆ **999. Bon Secours Hospital** is on Strand Street (✆ **066/712-1966**). **Tralee General Hospital** is on Killarney road (N22; ✆ **066/712-6222**). The local **Garda Station** is off High Street (✆ **066/712-2022**).

SEEING THE SIGHTS

During July and August, **Tralee Tourism,** Ostendia, Oakpark (✆ **066/712-5364**), sponsors guided walks that take in the local churches, the Square, Market Lane, Ashe Hall, Siamsa Tire, the Town Park, and principal streets. Departures are at 10am and 4 and 9pm. After the 9pm walks, participants are taken to the local pubs to enjoy folk and traditional music. Prices start at €3 ($2.65).

Blennerville Windmill   Just 4.8km (3 miles) west of Tralee and reaching 20m (65 ft.) into the sky, this landmark is the largest working windmill in Ireland or Britain. Built in 1800 by Sir Rowland Blennerhasset, it flourished until 1850. After decades of neglect, it was restored in the early 1990s and is now fully operational, producing 5 tons of ground whole-meal flour per week. The visitor complex has an emigration exhibition center, an audiovisual theater, craft workshops, and a cafe.

R559, Blennerville, county Kerry. ✆ 066/712-1064. Admission €4 ($3.55) adults, €3 ($2.65) seniors and students, €2 ($1.80) children over 5, €10 ($8.90) family. Apr–Oct daily 10am–6pm. Closed Nov–Mar.

Kerry the Kingdom 🔍   One of Ireland's largest indoor heritage centers, the Kingdom offers three attractions that give an in-depth look at 7,000 years of life in county Kerry. A 10-minute video, *Kerry in Colour,* presents seascapes and landscapes; the Kerry County Museum chronologically examines the county's music, history, legends, and archaeology through interactive and hands-on exhibits; and a unique exhibit explores Gaelic football. Many items of local origin that were previously on view at the National Museum in Dublin are now here. Complete with lighting effects and aromas, a theme park–style ride, "Geraldine Tralee," takes you through a re-creation of Tralee's streets and houses during the Middle Ages. The gift shop was recently expanded to include many unique items.

Ashe Memorial Hall, Denny St., Tralee, county Kerry. ✆ 066/712-7777. Admission €7 ($6.25) adults, €6.50 ($5.80) students, €4 ($3.55) children, €22 ($20) family. Mar–Oct daily 10am–6pm; Nov–Dec 2–5pm. Closed Jan–Feb.

Tralee Steam Railway 🔍🔍   Europe's westernmost railway, this restored steam train offers narrated, scenic 3.2km (2-mile) trips from Tralee's Ballyard Station to Blennerville. It uses equipment that was once part of the Tralee and Dingle Light Railway (1891–1953), one of the world's most famous narrow-gauge railways.

Ballyard, Tralee, county Kerry. ✆ 066/712-1064. Round-trip fare €4 ($3.55) adults, €3 ($2.65) students and seniors, €2 ($1.80) children, €9 ($8) family. Daily May–Oct. Trains depart Blennerville on the ½ hour (1st departure 10:30am) and depart Tralee on the hour (last departure 5pm). **Note:** Near the end of every month, the trains are off-track and serviced for a day or two; call before you visit.

SPECTATOR SPORTS

DOG RACING Greyhounds race year-round on Tuesday and Friday starting at 8pm at the **Kingdom Greyhound Racing Track,** Oakview, Brewery Road (✆ **066/712-4033**). Admission is €6 ($5.35) per person, including program.

HORSE RACING Horse racing takes place twice a year (in early June and late Aug) at **Tralee Racecourse,** Ballybeggan Park (✆ **066/713-6148,** or on race days 066/712-6188). Post time is usually 2:30pm. Admission starts at €11 ($10) adults, €6 ($5.35) seniors and students, and is free for children under 14.

SPORTS & OUTDOOR PURSUITS

GOLF Like its neighbor Killarney, Tralee is great golfing turf. The **Tralee Golf Club,** Fenit/Churchill Road, West Barrow, Ardfert (✆ **066/713-6379;** www. traleegolfclub.com), overlooking the Atlantic 13km (8 miles) northwest of town, was the first Arnold Palmer–designed course in Europe. One of Ireland's newer courses, it's expected in time to rank among the best in the world. Greens fees are €95 ($85).

About 40km (25 miles) north of Tralee in the northwest corner of county Kerry is Bill Clinton's favorite Irish course, the fabulous **Ballybunion Golf Club** ✿, Ballybunion, county Kerry (✆ **068/27146;** www.ballybuniongolf-club.ie). This facility offers visitors a relatively new clubhouse and the chance to play on two challenging 18-hole seaside links, both on the cliffs overlooking the Shannon River estuary and the Atlantic. Tom Watson has rated the Old Course one of the finest in the world; the Cashen Course was designed by Robert Trent Jones. Greens fees are €110 ($98) for the Old Course, €75 ($67) for the Cashen Course, and €135 ($120) for golf both courses in the same day.

HORSEBACK RIDING If you'd like to see the Tralee sights from horseback, you can't do better than to hire a horse from **El Rancho Farmhouse and Riding Stables,** Ballyard (✆ **066/712-1840;** elrancho@iol.ie). Prices start at €18 ($16) per hour for 1- or 2-hour rides on the Slieve Mish Mountains and Queen Scotia's Glen. El Rancho also offers 3- or 6-day trail rides along the Dingle Peninsula.

WHERE TO STAY
EXPENSIVE

Ballyseede Castle Hotel ✿✿ Ballyseede Castle, a 15th-century castle complete with live-in ghost, was once the chief garrison of the legendary Fitzgeralds, the earls of Desmond. The Blennerhassett family occupied it until 1966 and, in 1985, turned it into a hotel. The lobby has Doric columns and a hand-carved oak staircase. Two drawing rooms are decorated with cornices of ornamental plasterwork and warmed by marble fireplaces. Guest rooms are spacious and elegantly appointed with period furnishings. The castle is 3.2km (2 miles) east of Tralee, on 30 acres of parkland.

Tralee-Killarney rd., Tralee, county Kerry. ✆ **066/712-5799.** Fax 066/712-5287. 12 units. €180–€250 ($160–$223) double. MC, V. **Amenities:** Restaurant (international); piano lounge; library. *In room:* TV, hair dryer, garment press.

MODERATE/EXPENSIVE

Brandon Hotel ✿ Named for nearby Mount Brandon, this is a modern, dependable five-story hotel at the west edge of town, with vistas of the Dingle Peninsula in the distance. The rooms are functional and well maintained, but it's the amenities and leisure center that make this hotel a very good value. The convenient location is another plus—just a block from the National Folk Theatre and tourist office, and within easy strolling distance of shops and downtown restaurants.

Princes St., Tralee, county Kerry. ℂ **800/44-UTELL** in the U.S., or 066/712-3333. Fax 066/712-5019. www. whites-hotelsireland.com. 182 units. €90–€205 ($80–$182) double. No service charge. Rates include full breakfast. AE, DC, MC, V. Closed Dec 24–28. **Amenities:** 2 restaurants (international, cafe); 2 bars; indoor pool; gym; sauna/steam room. *In room:* TV, tea/coffeemaker, hair dryer.

MODERATE

Abbey Gate Hotel ✯   This new three-story hotel brings much-needed quality lodging and a broader dimension of social activity to the center of Tralee town. The hotel is ideally located within walking distance of Tralee's prime attractions, shops, and pubs. Guest rooms, like the public areas, are furnished with new reproductions, and fabrics, art, and accessories convey an air of Georgian and Victorian Tralee.

Maine St., Tralee, county Kerry. ℂ **066/712-9888.** Fax 066/712-9821. www.abbeygatehotel.com. 100 units. €110–€140 ($98–$125) double. No service charge. AE, DC, MC, V. Limited parking. **Amenities:** 2 restaurants (international, bistro); bar; room service; nonsmoking rooms. *In room:* TV, tea/coffeemaker, hair dryer.

Ballygarry House Hotel   About 1.6km (1 mile) south of town, this country inn is on the edge of a residential neighborhood, surrounded by well-tended gardens and sheltering trees. The guest rooms vary in size; each is individually decorated and named after different aspects of county Kerry, such as Arbutus, Muckross, Valentia, and Slea Head. The public areas have a horsey theme, with pictures of prize-winning thoroughbreds, brass accessories, and other equestrian touches. The Monarchs restaurant and lounge bar are in the hotel.

Tralee-Killarney rd., Leebrook, Tralee, county Kerry. ℂ **066/712-1233.** Fax 066/712-7630. 30 units. €90–€140 ($80–$125) double. Rates include full Irish breakfast and service charge. AE, MC, V. Closed Dec 20–28. **Amenities:** Restaurant (international); bar. *In room:* TV.

INEXPENSIVE

Barnagh Bridge Country Guesthouse ✯   Perched on a hillside overlooking Tralee Bay, this stunning two-story contemporary house was built as a guesthouse by the Williams family. It is located on the quieter, north side of the peninsula, and makes an ideal touring base for those who prefer a country setting to a town. Each guest room takes its theme from a flower in the surrounding gardens, such as Fuchsia, Bluebell, and Rose. The rooms have light pine furnishings and orthopedic beds, and most have views of the mountains and sea. Smoking is limited to the guest lounge.

Cappalough, Camp, county Kerry. ℂ **066/713-0145.** Fax 066/713-0299. 5 units. €55–€70 ($49–$62) double. No service charge. Rates include full breakfast. AE, MC, V. Closed Nov–Mar 15. **Amenities:** Lounge; nonsmoking rooms. *In room:* TV, tea/coffeemaker, hair dryer.

The Shores ✯✯ *Value*   This is a modern house, tastefully extended in 1999, on the south side of Brandon Bay. It commands wonderful views of Tralee Bay and Mount Brandon. Annette O'Mahoney is an avid interior decorator and has extended a Victorian theme and a feeling of luxury throughout the house. Furnishings are lavish, with a canopy bed in one room and writing desks in three rooms. A downstairs room has a private entrance and a fireplace. All rooms have orthopedic beds, with crisp white cotton and cream lace linen. There's a sun deck and a beach for when the heavens are kind, and a guest library and video rentals for when they are not. Breakfast options are particularly extensive, with smoked salmon and waffles as alternatives to the standard fry. The latest addition is a new self-catering cottage.

.8km (½ mile) west of Stradbally on the Conor Pass Rd., Cappatigue, Castlegregory, county Kerry. ℂ **066/ 713-9196.** 6 units. €56–€68 ($50–$61) double. Rates include full breakfast. MC, V. Closed Dec–Jan. **Amenities:** Nonsmoking rooms. *In room:* TV, tea/coffeemaker.

SELF-CATERING

Illauntannig Island Cottage   For those who really want to get away from it all, in a stunningly beautiful place, this cottage presents a unique opportunity. Illauntannig is one of the seven Maharees Islands, about 1.6km (1 mile) offshore from Scraggane Bay, on the north shore of the Dingle Peninsula. The island covers an area of about 14 hectares (36 acres), and has been inhabited at least since the 6th century, when St. Seanach founded a monastery here. The remains of this monastic site, now a national monument, are a short walk from the house; perched on the water's edge are several beehive huts, an oratory, some beautiful stone crosses, and an enclosing wall. There is only one cottage on the island. The small stone structure has four bedrooms (sleeps eight), one bathroom, a sitting room with fireplace, and a sunny kitchen with dining alcove.

Make no mistake—you're roughing it, with oil lamps substituting for electric, and precious drinking water brought over from the mainland. Still, the basic necessities are provided, with gas-powered refrigeration, a hot-water heater, and a toilet with shower. Your only companions for the week will be seabirds (many species nest on the island) and cows, the island's only year-round residents. Bob Goodwin, a venerable seaman with a wealth of knowledge on local birds and history, will check in on you every day by two-way radio, and can take you to the mainland as often as necessary for supplies. Although some might balk at the isolation or the austerity, for the right person, this place is a getaway dream come true.

Contact Bob Goodwin, Maharees, Castlegregory, county Kerry. ℂ and fax **066/713-9443.** 1 cottage. Apr–May and Sept–Oct €355 ($315) per week; June–Aug €420 ($374) per week. Rates include transport to and from the island, bedding, and all utilities. No credit cards. Closed Nov–Mar. *In room:* Kitchen.

Kerry Cottages 🎯🎯 *Kids*   If you want to be on the coveted Dingle Peninsula but away from the crowds, look no further. These 10 cottages are off a quiet back road, just a few minutes on foot to the beach and another 20 minutes or so to Castlegregory village on the north side of the peninsula. All the cottages are furnished in a charming country Irish style, with pine furnishings, terra-cotta floors (carpeting upstairs), and whitewashed walls. The smallest cottage is a cozy two-bedroom retreat with a small private garden; six cottages have three bedrooms and semiprivate backyards. "The Sands" is the largest house, with five bedrooms, each with a private bathroom. In another five-bedroom house, three bedrooms have private bathrooms. Second-story bedrooms in the larger cottages have great sea views. Each place is equipped with a washer-dryer and dishwasher, and the kitchens are well equipped with everything you need to prepare most meals. A small playground area for kids, with swing set and slide, is part of the complex. Rates vary seasonally; the cottages are an especially good value outside the summer season.

Castlegregory, Dingle Peninsula, county Kerry (1.6km/1 mile from Castlegregory). ℂ **01/284-4000.** Fax 01/ 284-4333. www.kerrycottages.com. Book through Kerry Cottages, 3 Royal Terrace West, Dun Laoghaire, county Dublin. 10 cottages. €261–€1,015 ($232–$903) per week for a 2- or 3-bedroom cottage; €785–€1,915 ($708–$1,704) per week for a 5-bedroom cottage. MC, V. *In room:* TV, kitchen, microwave, dishwasher, washing machine, dryer, no phone.

WHERE TO DINE
MODERATE

The Tankard SEAFOOD   This is one of the few restaurants in the area that capitalizes on sweeping views of Tralee Bay. Situated on the water's edge, it has wide picture windows and a sleek, contemporary decor. The straightforward menu primarily features local shellfish and seafood, such as lobster, scallops, prawns, and black sole. It also includes rack of lamb, duck, quail, and a variety of steaks. Bar food is available all day, but this restaurant is at its best in the early evening, especially at sunset.

9.7km (6 miles) northwest of Tralee, Kilfenora, Fenit, county Kerry. ✆ **066/713-6164**. Reservations recommended. Main courses €11–€20 ($10–$18). AE, DC, MC, V. Daily bar food 12:30–10pm; restaurant 6–10pm.

TRALEE AFTER DARK

Siamsa Tire, the National Folk Theatre of Ireland, is at Town Park (✆ **066/ 712-3055;** www.siamsatire.com). Founded in 1974, Siamsa (pronounced *Sheem*-sha) offers a mixture of music, dance, and mime. Its programs focus on three themes: Fado Fado/The Long Ago; Sean Agus Nua/Myth and Motion; and Ding Dong Dedero/Forging the Dance. The scenes depict old folk tales and farmyard activities, such as thatching a cottage roof, flailing sheaves of corn, and twisting a *sugan* (straw) rope.

In addition to folk theater entertainment, Siamsa presents a full program of drama and musical concerts (from traditional to classical) performed by visiting amateur and professional companies. Admission is €16 ($14) for adults, €14 ($12) for seniors, students, and children. Performances take place Monday, Tuesday, Thursday, and Saturday in May and from September to mid-October; Monday to Thursday and Saturday in June; and Monday to Saturday in July and August. Curtain time is 8:30pm. Call ahead for reservations.

PUBS

An Blascaod (The Blasket Inn)   Named for the Blasket Islands, this pub has a lovely modern facade and interior, and a stark red-and-black color scheme. Inside, there's a two-story atrium with an open fireplace, plus shelves lined with old books and plates. Castle St., Tralee, county Kerry. ✆ **066/712-3313.**

Harty's Lounge Bar   This pub is celebrated as the original meeting house where the Rose of Tralee festival was born. It is also known for its traditional pub grub, such as steak and kidney pie, shepherd's pie, and Irish stew. 30 Lower Castle St., Tralee, county Kerry. ✆ **066/712-5385.**

Kirby's Olde Brogue Inn   This pub has a barnlike layout, with an interior that incorporates agricultural instruments, farming memorabilia, and rush-work tables and chairs. There's excellent pub grub, specializing in steaks, as well as traditional music and folk ballads when the right people show up. Rock St., Tralee, county Kerry. ✆ **066/712-3357.**

Oyster Tavern   The nicest location of any pub in the Tralee area belongs to this tavern, just 4.8km (3 miles) west of downtown, overlooking Tralee Bay. The pub grub available includes seafood soups and platters. Fenit Rd., The Spa, Tralee, county Kerry. ✆ **066/713-6102.**

10

The Mouth of the Shannon: Limerick & Clare

If you're one of the millions of visitors arriving at Shannon Airport, you'll be at the doorstep of three counties: Limerick, Clare, and Galway. Unlike Galway (the county and the town), Limerick and Clare, for all that they have to offer, are not principal tourist destinations—but neither are they well-kept secrets. For instance, the Cliffs of Moher in county Clare is one of the natural wonders of Europe with a constant stream of tourists to prove it, while the Burren, also in county Clare, is a unique spectacle, with seldom a tour bus in sight.

We'll leave Galway aside for now (we'll get to it in chapters 11, "Galway City," and 12, "Out from Galway"). This chapter focuses on its surprising western neighbors in the hope of encouraging you to explore beyond the bus-beaten track.

1 Limerick City & Environs

Limerick is 24km (15 miles) E of Shannon Airport, 198km (123 miles) SW of Dublin, 105km (65 miles) N of Cork, 111km (69 miles) NE of Killarney, and 105km (65 miles) S of Galway

Situated along the midwest coast of Ireland, Limerick is the third-largest city in the Republic, with a population approaching 80,000. As a port on the River Shannon, Limerick has been a city of strategic and commercial importance since its beginnings as a Viking settlement in the 10th century.

If you read Frank McCourt's best-selling novel, *Angela's Ashes,* you may envision Limerick as a sprawling, struggling, hard-working city with limited resources. But that's only part of the picture. In recent years, it's been shaking off its reputation for high unemployment and general neglect and is reemerging as a city revitalized by new industries and impressive renovation projects. In particular, Limerick's recently developed riverside cultural and historic area, the Medieval Heritage Precinct on King's Island, has considerable appeal both by day and by night, when the 13th century **King John's Castle** is floodlit. Don't miss the excellent **Hunt Museum,** which houses the best collection of Bronze Age, Celtic, and medieval treasures outside Dublin. The **Limerick City Gallery of Art** is well worth a visit for its excellent permanent collection, which includes works by Jack B. Yeats. Limerick has also seen a resurgence in the number of stylish cafes and fine restaurants serving a range of different cuisines. After dark, you can head for one of the city's lively pubs or take in a play at the well-known **Belltable Arts Centre.** This is a time of renaissance for this proud city, which has known such a turbulent past.

The countryside around Limerick has a number of interesting sights. Southwest of Limerick, the village of Adare is worth a visit, as are Glin Castle, Lough Gur, and Rathkeale. See "Side Trips from Limerick City," at the end of this section, for suggestions.

ESSENTIALS

GETTING THERE   From the United States, Aer Lingus, Continental, and Delta Airlines operate regularly scheduled flights into **Shannon Airport,** off the Limerick-Ennis road (N18), county Clare (© **061/471444;** www.shannonair port.com), 24km (15 miles) west of Limerick. Domestic flights from Dublin and overseas flights from Britain and the Continent are available from a range of carriers. (See "Getting There" in chapter 2 for all the airlines' toll-free numbers and websites.) A taxi from the airport to the city center costs about €20 ($18).

Bus Eireann (© **061/313333;** www.buseireann.ie) provides bus service from Shannon Airport to Limerick's Railway Station. The fare is €5 ($4.45). Bus services from all parts of Ireland come into Limerick's Colbert Station, Parnell Street.

Irish Rail operates direct trains from Dublin, Cork, and Killarney, with connections from other parts of Ireland. They arrive at Limerick's Colbert Station, Parnell Street (© **061/315555;** www.irishrail.ie).

Limerick City can be reached on N7 from the east and north; N20, N21, N24, and N69 from the south; and N18 from the west and north.

VISITOR INFORMATION   The **Limerick Tourism Centre** is on Arthur's Quay, Limerick (© **061/317522**). It is open Monday to Friday 9:30am to 5:30pm, Saturday 9:30am to 1pm, with expanded and weekend hours in summer. Ask for a free copy of the *Shannon Region Visitors Guide,* which is packed with helpful information about activities and events in Limerick and the surrounding areas.

A seasonal tourist office is open March to November in the **Adare Heritage Centre,** Main Street, Adare (© **061/396255**).

For good all-around visitor information on the Web, see **www.visitlimerick. com** or **www.limerick.com.**

GETTING AROUND   Bus Eireann (© **061/313333**) operates local bus service around Limerick and its environs; the flat fare is €1 (90¢). Buses depart from Colbert Station, Parnell Street.

Taxis line up outside Colbert Station, at hotels, and along Thomas and Cecil streets, off O'Connell Street. To reserve a taxi, call **Economy Taxis** (© **061/ 411422**), **Express Taxis** (© **061/417777**), or **Top Cabs** (© **061/417417**).

Driving around Limerick can be a little confusing because of the profusion of one-way streets—it's best to park your car and walk to see the sights. You might want to drive to King's Island for the Medieval Heritage Project, which includes King John's Castle and the other historic sights (there's a free parking lot opposite the castle). If you must park downtown, head for the lot at Arthur's Quay, which is convenient to sightseeing and shopping, and well signposted. Parking is €1.30 ($1.15) per hour.

If you need to rent a car in Limerick, contact **Alamo/Treaty Rent-A-Car** (© **061/363663**) or **Payless Car Rental** (© **061/328328**). Most major international car-rental firms maintain desks at Shannon Airport (see the "County Clare" section, later in this chapter).

The best way to get around Limerick is to walk. Follow the signposted "Tourist Trail" to see most of the city's main attractions; a booklet outlining the trail is available at the tourist office and in bookshops.

FAST FACTS   If you need a drugstore, try **Hogan's Pharmacy,** 45 Upper William St. (© **061/415195**). After-hours service is available by calling © **088/ 526800.**

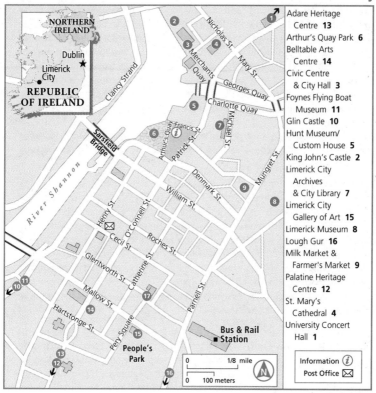

Adare Heritage
  Centre **13**
Arthur's Quay Park **6**
Belltable Arts
  Centre **14**
Civic Centre
  & City Hall **3**
Foynes Flying Boat
  Museum **11**
Glin Castle **10**
Hunt Museum/
  Custom House **5**
King John's Castle **2**
Limerick City
  Archives
  & City Library **7**
Limerick City
  Gallery of Art **15**
Limerick Museum **8**
Lough Gur **16**
Milk Market &
  Farmer's Market **9**
Palatine Heritage
  Centre **12**
St. Mary's
  Cathedral **4**
University Concert
  Hall **1**

Information ⓘ
Post Office ✉

In an emergency, dial ✆ **999. St. John's Hospital** is on St. John's Square (✆ **061/415822**). The local **Garda Headquarters** is on Henry Street (✆ **061/414222**).

The **General Post Office** is on Post Office Lane, off Lower Cecil Street (✆ **061/314636**). There is a branch of the post office at Arthur's Quay Centre, Patrick Street (✆ **061/415261**).

SEEING THE SIGHTS

Hunt Museum ⭐⭐ The Hunt Museum is housed in the tastefully restored Old Custom House, the finest 18th-century building in Limerick. The facade is a reduced copy of the Petit Trianon at Versailles. The museum's 2,000-work collection of ancient, medieval, and modern treasures—the finest in Ireland outside of Dublin's National Museum—includes antiquities and art objects from Europe and Ireland, ancient Irish metalwork, and medieval bronzes, ivories, and enamels. The late John and Gertrude Hunt, antiquarians and art historians, presented the collection to the Irish nation. The museum has a shop and an attractive restaurant that serves snacks and full meals.

The Custom House, Rutland St., Limerick, county Limerick. ✆ 061/312833. www.ul.ie/~hunt. Admission €5 ($4.45) adults, €3.50 ($3.10) students, seniors, and children, €12 ($11) family. Tues–Sat 10am–5pm; Sun 2–5pm.

King John's Castle ⭐⭐⭐ Strategically built on the banks of the Shannon River, this royal fortress is the centerpiece of Limerick's historic area. It is said to date from 1210, when King John of England visited and was so taken with the site that he ordered a "strong castle" to be built here. It survives today as one of the oldest examples of medieval architecture in Ireland, with rounded gate towers and curtain walls. Thanks to a recent $7 million restoration, the interior includes an authentic archaeological excavation dating from Hiberno-Norse times, as well as gallery displays and an audiovisual presentation portraying Limerick's 800 years of history. On the outside, the impressive facade has battlement walkways along the castle's walls and towers, offering sweeping views of the city. It is floodlit at night.

Nicholas St., Limerick, county Limerick. ✆ 061/411201. Admission €6 ($5.35) adults, €4.50 ($4) seniors and students, €3.20 ($2.85) children, €16 ($14) family. Apr–Oct daily 9:30am–5:30pm (last admission 4:30pm). Closed Nov–Mar.

Limerick City Gallery of Art 🏵🏵   Expanded and renovated in 1998 to occupy the whole neo-Romanesque Carnegie Building (1903), this gallery is in the People's Park, on the corner of Mallow Street. It houses a permanent collection of 18th-, 19th-, and 20th-century art, including some fine paintings by Ireland's most celebrated artist, Jack B. Yeats. It also plays host to a wide range of traveling contemporary art exhibitions, including touring exhibitions from the Irish Museum of Modern Art. On some evenings, the gallery holds literary readings or traditional or classical music concerts at 8pm.

Pery Sq., Limerick, county Limerick. ✆ 061/310633. www.iol.ie/eva. Free admission. Mon–Fri 10am–6pm; Thurs 10am–7pm; Sat 10am–1pm; Sun 2–5pm.

Limerick Museum 🏵   This museum provides an insight into the history of Limerick. It contains displays on Limerick's archaeology, natural history, civic treasures, and traditional crafts of lace, silver, furniture, and printing. Also on view are historical paintings, maps, prints, and photographs. Of particular interest are the city's original charters from Oliver Cromwell and King Charles II and the civic sword presented by Queen Elizabeth I.

Castle Lane, at Nicholas St., Limerick, county Limerick. ✆ 061/417826. Free admission. Tues–Sat 10am–1pm and 2:15–5pm.

St. Mary's Cathedral 🏵   Founded in the 12th century on a hill on King's Island, this site was originally home to a palace belonging to one of the kings of Munster, Donal Mor O'Brien. In 1172, he donated it for use as a church. The building contains many fine antiquities, including a Romanesque doorway, a pre-Reformation stone altar, and a huge stone coffin lid said to be that of Donal Mor O'Brien himself. Features added in later years include 15th-century *misericords* (supports for standing worshippers) with carvings in black oak, and a *reredos* (ornamental partition) on the high altar carved by the father of Irish patriot Patrick Pearse. St. Mary's is now a Church of Ireland property.

Bridge St., Limerick, county Limerick. ✆ 061/416238. Donation €1.30 ($1.15). June–Sept Mon–Sat 9am–5pm; Oct–May Mon–Sat 9am–1pm.

SHOPPING

Shopping hours in Limerick are Monday to Saturday 9:30am to 5:30pm. Many stores also stay open until 9pm on Thursday and Friday.

At the corner of Ellen Street and Wickham Street, in the heart of Limerick's old Irishtown, you'll find the **Milk Market,** a venue that hosts a memorable **Farmer's Market** every Saturday morning from 8am to noon or 1pm. On Fridays, from roughly 11am to 4pm, this becomes an **Arts and Crafts Market.**

Monday to Saturday in the Milk Market you'll find an informal bazaar of booths and stands selling everything from pottery to potato chips.

Arthur's Quay Centre   With a striking four-story brick facade, this shopping complex overlooks Arthur's Quay Park and the Shannon River. It houses more than three dozen shops and services, ranging from Irish handcrafts to fashions, casual wear, shoes, music recordings, and books. Open Monday to Wednesday 9am to 7pm, Thursday and Friday 9am to 9pm, Saturday 9am to 6pm. Arthur's Quay, Limerick, county Limerick. ℂ **061/419888.**

Cruises Street Shopping Centre   This is the centerpiece of Limerick's downtown shopping district. Taking an original city street, the developers spent €22.9 million ($20.7 million) and turned it into an old-world village-style mall, with a total of 55 retail outlets and 20 residential apartments and offices. Cruises St. (off Patrick St.), Limerick, county Limerick. No central phone.

Heirlooms   Long established in downtown Limerick, this shop moved to a larger space in the new Cruises Street Shopping Centre. Come here for a vast stock of local collectibles, including old books and maps, dolls, puppets, and biscuit tins, as well as frames, wood carvings, pottery, clocks, sculptures, jewelry, and candles. 32A Cruises St., Limerick, county Limerick. ℂ **061/419111.**

Irish Handcrafts   Dating back more than 100 years, this family-run business specializes in products made by people from the Limerick area. The particular emphasis is on women's hand-knit and -loomed sweaters of all types, colors, and styles. There are also linen and lace garments. 26 Patrick St., Limerick, county Limerick. ℂ **061/415504.**

Todd William & Co   For more than 100 years, this has been Limerick's leading department store. It sells an array of Waterford crystal, Aran knitwear, Donegal tweeds, and ready-to-wear clothing. O'Connell St., Limerick, county Limerick. ℂ **061/417222.**

White and Gold   Irish Dresden figurines, the delicate porcelain pieces made at nearby Drumcollogher, are the special attraction of this chic gift shop. Other wares include fanciful European Christmas ornaments, intricate wind chimes, and Hummels. 34 O'Connell St. (at Roches St.), Limerick, county Limerick. ℂ **061/419977.**

SPECTATOR SPORTS & OUTDOOR PURSUITS

FISHING   Visitors are welcome to cast a line in the River Shannon for trout and other freshwater fish. For information, licenses, permits, and equipment, contact **Steve's Fishing and Shooting Store,** 7 Denmark St. (ℂ **061/413484**). **Celtic Angling,** in nearby Ballingarry, Adare (ℂ **069/68202;** www.celtican-gling.com), can provide day-long salmon fishing excursions on the Shannon, including pick-up from Limerick City, equipment, licenses, and everything else you need. A day tour costs €130 ($116) per day for one person or €150 ($134) for groups of two to four people, plus €65 ($58) per person for tackle, licenses, permits, and lunch.

GOLF   The Limerick area has three 18-hole golf courses, including a championship par-72 parkland layout at the **Limerick County Golf & Country Club,** Ballyneety (ℂ **061/351881;** www.limerickcounty.com), 8km (5 miles) east of Limerick. It charges greens fees of €45 ($40) weekends, €33 ($29) weekdays. The par-70 inland course at the **Limerick Golf Club,** Ballyclough (ℂ **061/415146;** www.limerickgolfclub.com), 4.8km (3 miles) south of Limerick, has greens fees of €42 ($37) weekends, €22 ($20) weekdays. The par-71 inland course at **Castletroy Golf Club,** Castletroy, county Limerick (ℂ **061/335753**),

4.8km (3 miles) east of Limerick, charges greens fees of €32 ($28) weekdays, €40 ($36) weekends.

HORSEBACK RIDING   County Limerick's fertile fields provide good turf for horseback riding and pony trekking. Rates start at about €32 ($28) per hour. The **Clonshire Equestrian Centre,** Adare, county Limerick (€ 061/ 396770; www.clonshire.com), offers riding for all levels of ability, horsemanship classes, and instruction for cross-country riding, dressage, and jumping. Clonshire is also home to the Limerick Foxhounds; in the winter it's a center for hunting in the area. Per-hour rates average €28 ($25) adults, €17 ($15) students and children. Riding and board packages are available.

WHERE TO STAY
EXPENSIVE

Jurys Limerick Hotel ★★   On the leafy banks of the Shannon across the Sarsfield Bridge in a residential section, this contemporary-style, business traveler's hotel is just a 3-minute walk from O'Connell Street. Recently renovated, it's laid out in a bright and airy style, with a skylit, atrium-style foyer. The up-to-date guest rooms are spacious and practical, with conservative, mahogany-like furniture and brass fixtures, and wide-windowed views of the gardens and river. Like other Jurys properties (and so many business hotels), this one does everything right but lacks a certain individuality. *Money-saving tip:* Promotions available through the Jurys website can be outstanding. In July and August, it's been possible to land a double for as little as €85 ($76).

Ennis Rd. (N18), Limerick, county Limerick. € 800/44-UTELL in the U.S., or 061/327777. Fax 061/326400. www.jurys.com. 95 units. €184 ($164) double. Rates include full Irish breakfast and service charge. AE, DC, MC, V. **Amenities:** 2 restaurants (international, bistro); bar; indoor pool; tennis court; gym; Jacuzzi; sauna/steam room; concierge; room service; laundry service; nonsmoking rooms. *In room:* TV, radio, hair dryer, garment press.

MODERATE

Castle Oaks House ★★   Set on 10 hectares (26 acres) of mature oak woodlands along the Shannon River, this two-story Georgian manor house is more than 150 years old. In former lives, it has been a private residence and a convent. Among the original fittings are classic bay windows, a decorative staircase, and a skylit central dome. Vestiges from its convent days include stained-glass windows and a chapel (now used as a banquet room). The comfortable guest rooms are furnished with crown-canopy beds, soft pastel fabrics, and choice antiques from the area. The suites are grand, with king-size beds and Jacuzzi tubs.

> **Service Charges**
> *A reminder:* Unless otherwise noted, room rates don't include service charges (usually 10%– 15% of your bill).

9.7km (6 miles) east of Limerick City, off Dublin Rd. (N7), Castleconnell, county Limerick. € 800/223-6510 in the U.S., or 061/377666. Fax 061/377717. www.castle-oaks.com. 20 units. €111–€132 ($99–$117) double, €145–€154 ($129–$137) suite. Rates include full breakfast. AE, DC, MC, V. **Amenities:** Restaurant (Continental); bar; indoor pool; tennis court; gym. *In room:* TV, tea/coffeemaker.

Limerick Gresham Ardhu ★★ *Value*   Formerly the Limerick Ryan, this hotel on the main road 1.6km (1 mile) west of the city center was recently renamed to reflect its absorption into the Gresham Hotel group. The smart decor and amenities combine to make this place a particularly good value for the money. The hotel combines one of Limerick's oldest buildings, the 1780 Ardhu House, with a modern wing of guest rooms. The public areas, part of the original house, are decorated in classic Georgian style. Guest rooms are conservatively decorated, but very comfortable and well appointed.

Ardhu House, Ennis Rd. (N18), Limerick, county Limerick. ⓒ 800/44-UTELL in the U.S., or 061/453922. Fax 061/326333. www.gresham-hotels.com. 181 units. €115 ($102) double. No service charge. Rates include full breakfast. AE, DC, MC, V. **Amenities:** Restaurant (international); 2 bars; room service; laundry service; nonsmoking rooms. *In room:* TV, radio, tea/coffeemaker, hair dryer, garment press.

INEXPENSIVE

Jurys Inn Limerick 🎇🎇   The budget arm of the Jurys chain has a knack for providing centrally situated, attractive, affordable accommodation in Ireland's major cities. This property's riverfront location is particularly appealing. The river-facing rooms, especially on the upper floors, have splendid views of the Shannon and the city's historic area. If you can get a corner room, you'll feel positively spoiled. Rooms are tastefully contemporary and eminently functional, with firm beds, large bathtubs, desks, and ample shelf and wardrobe space—everything you need and very little you don't. All rooms accommodate up to three adults or two adults and two children.

Lower Mallow St., Limerick, county Limerick. ⓒ 800/843-3311 in the U.S., or 061/207000. Fax 061/400966. www.jurys.com. 151 units. €75 ($67) room. No service charge. AE, DC, MC, V. Discounted parking available at adjoining car park **Amenities:** Restaurant (international); bar; laundry service; nonsmoking rooms. *In room:* TV, dataport, tea/coffeemaker, hair dryer.

Shannon Grove   In a quiet residential area a mile north of the city center, this modern two-story guesthouse, surrounded by lovely gardens, is just a quarter-mile walk from a curve of the Shannon River. The guest rooms have contemporary furnishings and firm beds. There are two cheery breakfast rooms and outdoor seating in fine weather. Proprietor Noreen Marsh provides a particularly warm welcome and can help you plan an insider's tour of Limerick. If you don't have a car, you can take the local bus service that stops nearby.

Athlunkard, Killaloe Rd. (R463), Limerick, county Limerick. ⓒ 061/345756. Fax 061/343838. 9 units. €66–€80 ($59–$71) double. Rates include full Irish breakfast. MC, V. Closed Dec 15–Jan 6. **Amenities:** TV lounge. *In room:* Tea/coffeemaker.

WHERE TO DINE
MODERATE

Green Onion Caffé 🎇🎇 MODERN CONTINENTAL   There are two don't-miss stops on any foodie's visit to the Limerick area: The first is The Wild Geese (see "Where to Dine around County Limerick," later), and this is the second. This is one of the most happening restaurants of the moment in Limerick City, and a shining light in the still-working-on-it renaissance of this culinary landscape. Jeff Gloux is an extremely talented chef and his down-to-earth cooking is all about letting the wonderful flavors of natural ingredients shine through. His wild mushroom-and-garlic soup packs a tremendous punch of flavor—but then, nothing is bland here. For a main course, go for comfort food—perhaps beef-and-Guinness stew (again with loads of mushrooms) or a perfect pasta with pesto. Add a great wine list, a terrific staff, fun background music, and you'll see why Limerick folks just can't get enough of the Green Onion. Come for lunch before or after visiting the Hunt Museum, just across the street. Or better yet, book for dinner, when the place is buzzing.

Old Town Hall Building, Rutland St., Limerick, county Limerick. ⓒ 061/229588. Reservations recommended for dinner. Main courses €11–€20 ($10–$18). AE, MC, V. Mon–Sat noon–10pm.

Patrick Punch's 🎇 INTERNATIONAL   This popular pub-restaurant is on the main road on the southern edge of town, surrounded by gardens, ancient trees, and lots of parking. It has a three-tier lounge area, a glass-enclosed conservatory overlooking the gardens, and a clubby main room decorated with Tiffany-style lamps, dark woods, an open turf fireplace, and old photos of movie stars. The menu is equally varied, with dishes such as filet of beef Wellington, chicken Cleopatra (with lemon and prawn sauce), and vegetable lasagna.

O'Connell Ave. (N20), Punchs Cross, Limerick, county Limerick. ✆ **061/229588**. Reservations recommended for dinner. Main courses €12–€20 ($11–$18). MC, V. Daily 10:30am–11:30pm.

INEXPENSIVE

Piccola Italia 👤 ITALIAN   Its name means "Little Italy," and this basement ristorante brings a touch of the Mediterranean to the heart of Limerick. The tables have traditional trattoria red-and-white-checked tablecloths, and Chianti baskets hang from the ceiling. The menu reads like the "best of Italy," from mushroom soup, cannelloni, lasagna, and fettuccine to scampi, salmon alla griglia, and steak pizzaiola.

55 O'Connell St., Limerick, county Limerick. ✆ **061/315844**. Reservations recommended. Main courses €7–€16 ($6.25–$14). Daily 6–11pm.

LIMERICK CITY AFTER DARK

PUBS

The Locke   Established in 1724, this is one of Limerick's oldest and most popular pubs, situated beside the east bank of the Shannon, just off Bridge Street. It's what's known in Ireland as a "black-and-white" pub—meaning a white facade with black trim. It's a lovely, rambling sort of place, with lots open fires roaring, and nooks and crannies for quiet conversations over a pint. Although it started as a haven for sea captains visiting the port, today it's known for its traditional Irish music—played on Sunday and Tuesday year-round. It's a particularly good place to come on a summer's evening, when there is outdoor riverside seating and little Japanese lanterns strung along a cobbled walkway lend a romantic, festive air. The pub has recently added a comfortable restaurant that offers seafood specialties. 2A/3 Georges Quay, Limerick, county Limerick. ✆ **061/413733**.

Nancy Blake's   Nancy's hasn't changed for years—flock wallpaper and little to hide that the room was once someone's drawing room. Nancy is still there, reigning over the place with a gentle hand, as it's been since anyone can remember. It's a cozy, old-world pub known for its free traditional music sessions, year-round Sunday to Wednesday at 9pm. An added attraction, weather permitting, is the outdoor beer garden. 19 Upper Denmark St., just off Patrick St., Limerick, county Limerick. ✆ 061/416443.

South's   This timeless old pub has a black-and-white checkerboard floor, a high, white marble bar, and a succession of Victorian mahogany arches behind the bar that frames bottles, mirrors, and curios. The snug, off to the side, is lined with milk glass, and there's a skylit back room with hunting tapestries on the wall. Oh, and one other little thing: It also has a reputation for pouring the best Guinness in town. Top of O'Connell St., Limerick, county Limerick. ✆ **061/318850**.

Vintage Club   In one of Limerick's older sections near the quays, this pub used to be a wine cellar, and the decor reflects it: barrel seats and tables, oak casks, and dark-paneled walls. A new attractive feature is the indoor/outdoor beer garden. 9 Ellen St., Limerick, county Limerick. ✆ **061/410694**.

THE PERFORMING ARTS

Belltable Arts Centre   A fine program of dramas, musicals, and concerts are staged year-round at this midcity theater and entertainment center. The summer program includes weeks of professional Irish theater. By day, the building is open for gallery exhibits, showing the works of modern Irish artists as well as local crafts. There is a bar and a coffee shop. It's a 5-minute walk from the bus and train station. Most shows run Monday to Saturday at 8pm, but call ahead to confirm showtimes. 69 O'Connell St., Limerick, county Limerick. © 061/319709. Tickets €8–€16 ($7.10–$14).

University Concert Hall   On the grounds of the University of Limerick, just northeast of the city, this 1,000-seat hall offers a broad program of national and international solo stars, variety shows, and ballet. It also books the Irish Chamber Orchestra, RTE Concert Orchestra, University of Limerick Chamber Orchestra, Limerick Singers, and European Community Orchestra. The monthly list of events is available from the tourist office. Most performances start at 8pm, but call ahead for details. University of Limerick, Plassey, county Limerick. © 061/331549. www.uch.ie. Tickets €14–€20 ($12–$18).

SIDE TRIPS FROM LIMERICK CITY

Dotted about the county Limerick countryside, within a 40km (25-mile) radius of Limerick City, are many historic and cultural attractions. A particularly nice excursion is to the lovely village of **Adare** 🏛🏛, one of Ireland's most beautiful places. It's full of thatched-roof and Tudor-style houses, beautiful gardens, and ivy-covered medieval churches that occupy wooded surroundings on both sides of the street beside the River Maigue. Here are a few suggestions of things to do and see around the county:

Adare Heritage Centre 🏛   Those who want to linger and learn more about Adare can drop in on this heritage center. Housed in a stone building with a traditional courtyard, it offers a walk-through display on Adare's colorful history, along with a model of the town as it looked in medieval times. There is also a 20-minute audiovisual presentation illustrating the many facets of Adare today. The center also houses a cafe, craft shop, knitwear shop, and library.

Main St., Adare, county Limerick. © 061/396666. Admission €4 ($3.55) adults, €2.50 ($2.25) children, €8 ($7.10) family. Daily 9am–6pm.

Foynes Flying Boat Museum 🏛   For aviation buffs, this museum is a must. This is the "first" Shannon Airport, the predecessor to the modern runways of Shannon Airport in county Clare, restored and reopened as an attraction. It commemorates an era begun on July 9, 1939, when Pan Am's luxury flying boat *Yankee Clipper* landed at Foynes, marking the first commercial passenger flight on the direct route between the United States and Europe. On June 22, 1942, Foynes was the departure point for the first nonstop commercial flight from Europe to New York. This is also where bartender Joe Sheridan invented Irish coffee in 1942. (At a festival each Aug, there's a contest to select the world Irish-coffee-making champion.) The complex includes a 1940s-style cinema and cafe, the original terminal building, and the radio and weather rooms with original transmitters, receivers, and Morse code equipment.

Foynes, county Limerick. © 069/65416. Admission €4.50 ($4) adults, €4 ($3.55) seniors and students, €2.50 ($2.25) children, €11 ($10) family. MC, V. Apr–Oct daily 10am–6pm. Closed Nov–Mar. 37km (23 miles) east of Limerick on N69.

Glin Castle 🏛🏛   Lilies of the valley and ivy-covered ash, oak, and beech trees line the driveway leading to this gleaming-white castle, home to the knights of Glin for the past 700 years. On the south bank of the Shannon Estuary, the sprawling estate contains 160 hectares (400 acres) of gardens, farmlands, and forests. Although there were earlier residences on the site, the present home was built in 1785. It is more of a Georgian house than a castle, with added crenellations and gothic details. The current (29th) knight of Glin, Desmond Fitz Gerald, a noted historian and preservationist, maintains a fine collection of 18th-century Irish furniture and memorabilia. The house features elaborate plaster-work, Corinthian columns, and a unique double-ramp flying staircase. It's protected by three sets of toy fort lodges, one of which houses a craft shop and cafe. In addition, quite royal accommodations can be arranged for €220 to €350 ($196–$312) double, with an additional €40 ($36) per person for dinner.

Limerick-Tarbert Rd. (N69), county Limerick. ℂ 068/34173. www.glincastle.com. Admission (for nonguests) to house and gardens €4 ($3.55) adults, €1.30 ($1.15) students. May–June daily 10am–noon, 2–4pm, and by appointment. Approximately 40km (25 miles) east of Limerick City.

Irish Palatine Heritage Centre Ireland's unique links with Germany are the focus of this museum, 29km (18 miles) south of Limerick off the main road. Reflecting on the history of the several hundred Palatine families who emigrated from Germany and settled in this part of Ireland in 1709, it includes an extensive display of artifacts, photographs, and graphics. In addition, the museum seeks to illustrate the Palatines' innovative contributions to Irish farming life and their formative role in the development of world Methodism.

Limerick-Killarney Rd. (N21), Rathkeale, county Limerick. ℂ 069/63511. Admission €2.50 ($2.25) adults, €2 ($1.80) seniors, €1.30 ($1.15) students, €6.50 ($5.80) family. June–Aug Mon–Sat 10am–noon, daily 2–5pm, and by appointment.

Lough Gur Visitor Centre ✰✰ Lough Gur is one of Ireland's principal archaeological sites. The area was occupied continuously from the Neolithic period to late medieval times, and the site includes the foundations of a small farmstead built about A.D. 900, a lake island dwelling built between A.D. 500 and 1000, a wedge-shaped tomb that was a communal grave around 2500 B.C., and the Grange Stone Circle, the largest and finest of its kind in Ireland. There's free access to its lake and shores, which make a great place to explore and have a picnic.

The museum and audiovisual program, however, are worth neither the time nor the fee. It's better to explore on your own and use your imagination.

11km (7 miles) SE of Limerick City on R512, Lough Gur, county Limerick. ℂ 061/361511. Museum and audiovisual presentation €3.50 ($3.10) adults, €2 ($1.80) seniors, students and children, €8 ($7.10) family. Visitor Centre mid-May to Sept daily 10am–6pm (last admission 5:30pm); site open year-round.

WHERE TO STAY AROUND COUNTY LIMERICK
Very Expensive
Adare Manor ✰✰✰ Most people wouldn't expect to find a five-star hotel in a village as tiny and secluded as Adare, 16km (10 miles) south of Limerick, but Ireland is surprising, with little gems tucked in all corners. This one is a 19th-century Tudor Gothic mansion, nestled on the banks of the River Maigue on an 336-hectare (840-acre) estate. It recently added a full-service spa to its already impressive list of amenities. The former home of the earls of Dunraven, it has been masterfully restored and refurbished as a deluxe resort, with original barrel-vaulted ceilings, 15th-century carved doors, Waterford crystal chandeliers, ornate fireplaces, and antique-filled guest rooms (all nonsmoking). New two- to four-bedroom garden town houses for families and larger groups are also available.

Adare, county Limerick. ℂ 800/462-3273 in the U.S., or 061/396566. Fax 061/396124, or 201/425-0332 in the U.S. www.adaremanor.com. 63 units.€210–€260 ($187–$231) double. AE, DC, MC, V. **Amenities:** Restaurant (Continental); bar; indoor swimming pool; 18-hole Robert Trent Jones golf course; riding stables;

salmon and trout fishing; fox hunting; clay-pigeon shooting; nature trails; gym; sauna; spa treatments; concierge; room service; babysitting; laundry service. *In room:* TV, minibar, hair dryer, garment press.

Expensive

Dunraven Arms ★★★ Lolling on the banks of the River Maigue, this 18th-century inn is a charming country retreat just 16km (10 miles) south of Limerick City. The public areas have an old-world ambience, with open fireplaces and antiques. Half of the rooms are in the original house, half in a new wing, and all are furnished in traditional style, with Victorian accents and period pieces such as four-poster and half-tester beds, and big, beefy armoires. Gwyneth Paltrow stayed here a couple of years ago while in Ireland for a friend's wedding. *Warning:* The pub here—all woody and sink-into-your-chair comfortable—is habit-forming.

Main St. (N21), Adare, county Limerick. ⓒ **800/447-7462** in the U.S., or 061/396633. Fax 061/396541. www.dunravenhotel.com. 74 units. €146–€184 ($130–$164) double, €254 ($226) suite. Breakfast €12–€15 ($11–$13). AE, DC, MC, V. **Amenities:** Restaurant (international); bar; indoor pool; gym; steam room; massage and beauty treatments; room service. *In room:* TV, radio, hair dryer.

Moderate/Expensive

The Mustard Seed at Echo Lodge ★★★ *Finds* Built in 1884 as a parochial house, then later turned into a convent, this is now one of the best places to stay and eat in Ireland. Every element of Daniel Mullane's stylish restaurant-with-rooms hits a delightfully whimsical aesthetic note, be it the color schemes and carefully chosen artworks for each guest room or the perfect pieces of fruit hand-picked and placed on a small silver plate. Mullane is a world traveler, and it shows in the furnishings, colors, and fabrics, which all manage to come together in harmony here, making the Mustard Seed a very relaxing place to stay. The restaurant is a destination in itself, with a menu that presents a creative mix of dishes, such as roulade of spinach encasing a pepper and tomato filling on warm salad of tomato and spinach, or maybe chicken coated in honey, garlic, and green peppercorns with scallion cream sauce. Organic produce and cheeses are included in the food preparation, and the atmosphere is peaceful and lovely.

13km (8 miles) from Adare, off the Newcastle West rd. from the center of Ballingarry, county Limerick. ⓒ **069/68508.** 18 units. €165–€254 ($147–$226) double. Fixed-price 4-course dinner €54 ($48). AE, MC, V. Daily 7–9:30pm. Closed mid-Feb to mid-Mar. **Amenities:** Restaurant (modern Continental). *In room:* TV, hair dryer.

Inexpensive

Abbey Villa ★ *Value* Mrs. May Haskett's home is a modern bungalow in a scenic setting, and she greets each guest warmly. Like the best of hosts, she will invite you to sit and chat while working out the best travel routes, yet she also recognizes the need to retire to your own room. The comfortable rooms are tastefully decorated, and all have satellite TV and electric blankets.

Kildimo Rd., Adare, county Limerick. ⓒ **061/396113.** Fax 061/396969. 6 units. €54–€68 ($48–$61) double. 33% discount for children. Rates include full breakfast. MC, V. **Amenities:** Laundry machines; sitting room. *In room:* TV, hair dryer.

WHERE TO DINE AROUND COUNTY LIMERICK
Expensive

The Wild Geese ★★★ MODERN INTERNATIONAL This is Limerick's most exciting restaurant. After spending years making other people's restaurants absolutely fabulous, owner-chef David Foley struck out on his own and created a gem in what many believe to be the prettiest town in Ireland. His trick? He starts with superb local ingredients and puts his indelible stamp on them. His cooking is complex, flavorful, and refined, yet always controlled and deliberate. His duck confit, which comes served on wontons with sesame dressing, is absolutely superb, as is his Clare crabmeat soufflé. In season, he does a fabulous wild pheasant stuffed with rosemary and currants. Desserts are to die for, service is impeccable, and the atmosphere is always alive with the clink of glasses and the buzz of conversation. What else could anyone want?

Rose Cottage, Adare, county Limerick. © 061/396451. Reservations required. Main courses €14–€25 ($12–$22). AE, MC, V. Tues–Sat 6:30 –9:30pm.

Moderate

Inn Between 🐾 INTERNATIONAL   Tucked in a row of houses and shops, this thatched-roof brasserie-style restaurant has a surprisingly airy skylit interior dominated by warm red and yellow tones, and a back courtyard for outdoor seating. Choices range from homemade soups and traditional dishes to more innovative concoctions, such as medallions of beef filet with green peppercorn sauce, wild salmon on leek fondue with tomato-and-chive butter sauce, and the classic Inn Between Burger, with homemade relish and french fries.

Main St., Adare, county Limerick. © 061/396633. Reservations recommended. Main courses €12–€20 ($11–$18). AE, DC, MC, V. Thurs–Mon 6:45–9:30pm, summer also 12:30–2:30pm.

PUBS AROUND COUNTY LIMERICK

Matt the Thrasher   About 24km (15 miles) northeast of Limerick—and well worth the drive—this roadside tavern is a replica of a 19th-century farmers' pub. A rustic, cottagelike atmosphere prevails, with antique furnishings, agricultural memorabilia, traditional snugs (private rooms), and lots of cozy alcoves. A new patio and small restaurant have been added recently, and there's music on many evenings. Dublin Rd. (N7), Birdhill, county Tipperary. © 061/379227.

M. J. Finnegan's   Dating from 1776, this wonderfully restored and newly renovated alehouse takes its name from James Joyce's *Finnegan's Wake,* and the decor reflects a Joycean theme, albeit with appropriate Limerick overtones. Special features include Irish ceili music on weekends, picnic tables for sitting by the rose garden on warm summer days, and excellent fare. A recent winner of many prestigious awards—including Black and White Pub of the Year, the International Dining Club Gold Award, and 1998 Pub of Distinction—Finnegans has expanded into a full-service inn and restaurant. Dublin Rd. (N7), about 8km (5 miles) east of Limerick City, Annacotty, county Limerick. © 061/337338.

2 County Clare

Clares's chief town (Ennis) is 67km (42 miles) S of Galway, 27km (17miles) NW of Shannon Airport, 37km (23 miles) NW of Limerick, 235km (147 miles) SW of Dublin, and 133km (83 miles) NW of Cork.

After stepping off the plane at Shannon, your first sight of Ireland will be the vistas of county Clare: rich green fields and rolling hills joined by the meandering Shannon River. If you turn left off the main road, the barren, rocky Atlantic coast awaits you; if you continue north, you'll be heading into the historic market town of **Ennis** and then to **the Burren** 🐾🐾🐾—rocky plains of Karst limestone.

Among the counties of Ireland, Clare is not a major celebrity on the tourist trail. This isn't just a pity, it's a mystery. (The Irish, for their part, have always been smitten.) Though less dramatic and less touristy than its neighbors, Kerry and Galway, Clare boasts a dazzling coast, including the take-your-breath-away **Cliffs of Moher** and the darling seaside summer resorts of **Lahinch** and **Kilkee.** The county is a hotbed for traditional music, especially in the charming villages of **Doolin,** Miltown Malby, Fanore, and Ennistymon. It's the proud heir to a number of impressive ancient sites and monuments, from the **Poulnabrone**

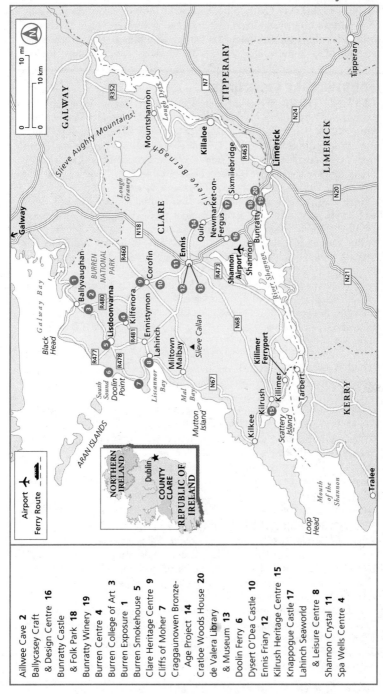

County Clare

Airport ✈
Ferry Route ⎯ ⎯

GALWAY

Galway

Galway Bay

Black Head

ARAN ISLANDS

South Sound

Doolin Point

Liscannor Bay

Mal Bay

Mutton Island

Slieve Aughty Mountains

BURREN NATIONAL PARK

Ballyvaughan

Lisdoonvarna

Kilfenora

Corofin

Ennistymon

Lahinch

Miltown Malbay

Slieve Callan

CLARE

Ennis

Quin

Newmarket-on-Fergus

Sixmilebridge

Shannon Airport

Shannon

River Shannon

Killimer Ferryport

Kilrush

Kilkee

Killimer

Scattery Island

Tarbert

Loop Head

Mouth of the Shannon

KERRY

Slieve Bernagh

Lough Derg

Mountshannon

Killaloe

TIPPERARY

Tipperary

LIMERICK

Limerick

Lough Graney

10 mi
10 km

R352 R460 R480 R481 R478 R477 N18 N67 N68 N473 N7 N24 N463 N20 N21

NORTHERN IRELAND
Dublin ★
COUNTY CLARE
REPUBLIC OF IRELAND

383

Dolmen to **Bunratty Castle,** with its better-than-you-would-think folk park. The Burren's magnificent lunar-like landscape, with its turloughs (limestone-bedded lakes that take on water after rainfall, then dry up again), wildflowers, and butterflies, and the birds of the cliffs from Hag's Head to **Loop Head** all contribute to Clare's appeal.

COUNTY CLARE ESSENTIALS

GETTING THERE From the United States, Aer Lingus, Aeroflot, Continental, and Delta Airlines operate regularly scheduled flights into **Shannon Airport,** off the Limerick-Ennis road (N18), county Clare (© 061/471444; www.shannonairport.com), 24km (15 miles) west of Limerick. Domestic flights from Dublin and overseas flights from Britain and the Continent are available from a range of carriers. See "Getting There" in chapter 2, "Planning Your Trip to Ireland," for the airlines' phone numbers and websites.

Irish Rail provides service to **Ennis Rail Station,** Station Road (© 065/684-0444; www.irishrail.ie), and Limerick's **Colbert Station,** Parnell Street (© 061/315555), 24km (15 miles) from Shannon.

Bus Eireann provides bus services from all parts of Ireland into **Ennis Bus Station,** Station Road (© 065/682-4177; www.buseireann.ie), and other towns in county Clare.

By car, county Clare can be reached on N18. Shannon Airport has offices of the following international firms: **Alamo** (© 061/472342), **Avis** (© 061/471094), **Budget** (© 061/471361), and **Hertz** (© 061/471739). Several local firms also maintain desks at the airport; among the most reliable is **Dan Dooley Rent-A-Car** (© 061/471098).

From points south, county Clare can be reached directly, bypassing Limerick, on the **Tarbert-Killimer Car Ferry.** It crosses the Shannon River from Tarbert, county Kerry, to Killimer, county Clare. Trip time for the drive-on/drive-off service is 20 minutes; no reservations are needed. Crossings from Tarbert are on the half hour; from Killimer, on the hour. Ferries operate April to September, Monday to Saturday 7 or 7:30am to 9 or 9:30pm, Sunday 9 or 9:30am to 9 or 9:30pm; October to March, Monday to Saturday 7 or 7:30am to 7 or 7:30pm, Sunday 10 or 10:30am to 7 or 7:30pm. Summer fares for cars with passengers are €13 ($12) one way, €20 ($18) round-trip. For more information, contact **Shannon Ferry Ltd.,** Killimer/Kilrush, county Clare (© 065/905-3124; www.shannonferries.com). The Killimer Ferry terminal has a gift shop and restaurant. Open daily 9am to 9pm.

VISITOR INFORMATION A **tourist office** is in the Arrivals Hall of Shannon Airport (© 061/471644). Hours coincide with flight arrivals and departures.

The **Ennis Tourist Office,** Clare Road, Ennis, county Clare (© 065/682-8366), is about 1.6km (1 mile) south of town on the main N18 road. Open year-round Monday to Friday 9:30am to 5:15pm, with weekend and extended hours April to October.

Seasonal tourist offices in county Clare are at the Cliffs of Moher (© 065/708-1171); O'Connell Street, Kilkee (© 065/905-6112); and Town Hall, Kilrush (© 065/905-1577). These offices are usually open May or June to early September.

You can also find visitor information at **www.county-clare.com**.

FROM SHANNON AIRPORT TO ENNIS

The 24km (15-mile) road from Shannon Airport to Ennis, a well-signposted section of the main Limerick-Galway road (N18), is one of the most traveled routes in Ireland. It has the feel of a superhighway—a feel you won't often encounter in Ireland, and a misleading introduction to the land of *boreens* (country, single-lane roads). The whole point in Ireland, unless you know exactly where you must arrive in a hurry, is to turn off the straight-and-wide and get lost.

Now that you're on N18, turn right and proceed for 8km (5 miles). The village of **Bunratty** is before you, with its 15th-century medieval castle and theme park. Turn left, heading toward Ennis, and you pass through the charming river town of **Newmarket-on-Fergus,** home of **Dromoland Castle.**

The main town of county Clare, **Ennis** (pop. 18,000) is a compact enclave of winding, narrow streets on the banks of the River Fergus. The original site was an island on the river—hence the name *Ennis,* an Anglicized form of the Gaelic word *inis,* meaning "island." Easily explored on foot, Ennis offers a walking trail developed by the Ennis Urban District Council. A leaflet outlining the route is available free throughout the town.

ATTRACTIONS

Ballycasey Craft & Design Centre 🕊   Signposted within the airport complex, 4.8km (3 miles) from the main terminal, en route to the main road, this craft center is located in the courtyard of a restored Georgian manor house. The workshops feature handcrafted items ranging from pottery, jewelry, and metalwork to knitwear and fashions. You can watch the artisans as they work and learn more about their trades.

Airport Rd. (N19), Shannon Airport, county Clare. ℭ **061/362105.** Free admission. Mon–Sat 9:30am–6pm.

Bunratty Castle and Folk Park 🕊🕊   Long before you reach the village of Bunratty, vistas of this striking 15th-century fortress will stand out along the main road from the airport. Nestled beside the O'Garney River, Bunratty Castle (1425) is Ireland's most complete medieval castle. The ancient stronghold has been carefully restored, with authentic furniture, armorial stained glass, tapestries, and works of art. By day, the building's inner chambers and grounds are open for public tours; at night, the castle's Great Hall serves as a candlelit setting for medieval banquets and entertainment (see "Where to Dine," later in this chapter).

Bunratty Castle is the focal point of an 8-hectare (20-acre) theme park, Bunratty Folk Park. Don't just write it off as a giant cliché; it's actually done very well. The re-creation of a typical 19th-century Irish village includes thatched cottages, farmhouses, and an entire village street, with school, post office, pub, grocery store, print shop, and hotel—all open for browsing and shopping. Fresh scones are baked in the cottages, and craftspeople ply such trades as knitting, weaving, candle making, pottery, and photography.

Limerick-Ennis Rd. (N18), Bunratty, county Clare. ℭ **061/360788.** Admission €8 ($7.10) adults, €5 ($4.45) students and seniors, €4 ($3.55) children, €17 ($15) family. Daily 9:30am–5:30pm.

Bunratty Winery   Housed in a coach house dating from 1816, this winery produces mead, a medieval drink made from honey, fermented grape juice, water, matured spirits, and a selection of herbs. Long ago, it was served by the jugful at regal gatherings and weddings. In fact, custom required that a bride and groom continue to drink mead for one full moon to increase the probability of a happy marriage. (Some speculate that this is where the term *honeymoon* came from.) Today, the Bunratty Winery produces mead primarily for consumption at Bunratty Castle's medieval-style banquets. Visitors are welcome to

Knowing Your Castles

Ireland, as even the most casual visitor will notice, has no shortage of stones. When the first Irish farmers began to turn over the soil, the stones merely got in their way. Eventually, they put the stones to use, to build walls.

The earliest stone fortifications in Ireland—round forts, often on hilltops—date from the Iron Age, sometime after 500 B.C. **Dún Aengus** on the Aran Islands, **Staigue Fort** in county Kerry, and the newly restored **Lisnagun Ring Fort** are among the survivors of as many as 30,000 stone forts that once protected the Irish from each other.

Later, in the early Christian period, the centers of Irish civilization— the monastic communities—came under attack from Vikings. Round towers that climbed up to 30m (100 ft.) were constructed to lift life, limb, and everything else precious out of harm's reach. The flaw with this strategy was that it depended on the enemy's going away, like a dog that tires of waiting for a treed cat to come down. Vikings, how- ever, had patience. They tended to stay and burn or starve the monks down from their towers.

Next came the Normans, who constructed their castles with massive rectangular keeps. **Trim Castle** in county Meath and **Carrickfergus Castle** in county Antrim are impressive reminders of Norman clout. **Cahir Castle** in county Tipperary—with eight towers in its encircling battlements— has no equal in Ireland for sheer scale. Then came the tower house, a fortified residence. **Bunratty Castle** in county Clare and **Dunguaire Castle** in county Galway are splendidly restored examples of this kind of "safe house," which remained in vogue for several centuries. Wealthy merchants and others with less to protect built semifortified mansions, of which a well-preserved example is **Rothe House** in Kilkenny.

Nearly all of the above might loosely be called "castles." Even today, we say that a man's home is his castle—a point now made with dead- bolts, motion detectors, and alarm systems.

---

stop by the working winery, watch the production in progress, and taste the brew. Also available is traditional Irish *poteen,* the first of this heady potato moonshine to be legally made and bottled in Ireland since it was banned in 1661.

Bunratty, county Clare. ℂ **061/362222.** Free admission. Daily 9:30am–5:30pm.

Craggaunowen Bronze-Age Project *(Overrated* Making use of an actual cas- tle, *crannóg* (fortified island), and ring fort, the Craggaunowen Project has attempted to reconstruct and present glimpses of Ireland's ancient past, from the Neolithic period to the Christian Middle Ages. A special glass house has been created to exhibit Tim Severin's sea-proven replica of the curragh in which Bren- dan and his brother monks may have sailed to America in the 5th century. This project must have been launched with great vision and enthusiasm, but much of the original wind seems to have left its sails. As a "living history" project, it is currently on life support. The possibilities here are exciting, but the reality is disappointing.

About 16km (10 miles) from Ennis, signposted off R469, Quin, county Clare. ℭ **061/367178**. Admission €5 ($4.45) adults, €4.50 ($4) seniors, €3.20 ($2.85) children. AE, DC, MC, V. Sat–Sun mid-Mar to end Oct 10am–6pm. Last admission 5pm.

Cratloe Woods House   This 17th-century house is a fine example of a long-house, a type of Irish architecture that's almost obsolete. Steeped in history and long associated with the O'Brien clan, who trace their ancestry back to Brian Boru, the house is still lived in. It's filled with family portraits, works of art, and curios, and the grounds feature a collection of horse-drawn farming machinery. The primeval Garranon Oak Wood, which provided timbers for the Westminster Hall in London, is also part of the estate.

Cratloe, county Clare. ℭ **061/327028**. Admission €3.20 ($2.85) adults, €2 ($1.80) seniors and students, €1.30 ($1.15) children. Mon–Sat 2–6pm. Closed mid-Sept to May.

de Valera Library & Museum 👁   This museum and library, housed in a renovated 19th-century Presbyterian church, pays tribute to Ireland's American-born freedom fighter and president, Eamon de Valera (1882–1975). It contains many of de Valera's personal possessions, including his car. There is also an art collection, and interesting area relics, such as a door from a Spanish Armada galleon that sank off the Clare coast in 1588 at a place now known as Spanish Point. A bronze statue of de Valera stands several blocks away at the Ennis Courthouse.

Harmony Row, off Abbey St., Ennis, county Clare. ℭ **065/684-6353**. Free admission. Mon, Wed, and Thurs 10am–5pm; Tues and Fri 10am–8pm; Sat 10am–2pm.

Ennis Friary 👁   Founded in 1241, this Franciscan abbey, a famous seat of learning in medieval times, made Ennis a focal point of western Europe for many years. Records show that in 1375 it buzzed with the activity of no fewer than 350 friars and 600 students. Although it was finally forced to close in 1692, and thereafter fell into ruin, the abbey still contains many interesting sculpted tombs, decorative fragments, and carvings, including the famous McMahon tomb. The nave and chancel are the oldest parts of the friary, but other structures, such as the 15th-century tower, transept, and sacristy, are also rich in architectural detail.

Abbey St., Ennis, county Clare. ℭ **065/682-9100**. Admission €1.30 ($1.15) adults, €1 (90¢) seniors, €.50 (45¢) children and students, €4 ($3.55) family. Daily 9:30am–6:30pm. Closed Oct to mid-May.

Knappogue Castle 👁👁   Midway between Bunratty and Ennis, this castle was built in 1467 and was the home of the McNamara clan, who dominated the area for more than 1,000 years. The original Norman structure includes elaborate late-Georgian and Regency wings that were added in the mid–19th century. Now fully restored, it is furnished with authentic 15th-century pieces. Like Bunratty Castle, it serves as a venue for nightly medieval banquets in the summer (see "Where to Dine," below).

Quin, county Clare. ℭ **061/360788**. Admission €4 ($3.55) adults, €2.50 ($2.25) seniors and students, €2 ($1.80) children, €10 ($8.90) family. Daily 9:30am–5:30pm. Last admission 4:30pm. Closed Nov–Mar.

Shannon Crystal   In the north end of town (on the way to Galway rd.), this is the Shannon area's own crystal-making enterprise, producing original hand-cut glassware on the premises. The showroom is open to visitors, who can watch demonstrations by the master cutter.

Sandfield Rd., Ennis, county Clare. ℭ **065/682-1250**. Free admission. Daily 9am–6pm.

SHOPPING

Avoca This pink, thatched-roof cottage shop is a branch of the legendary county Wicklow–based Avoca Handweavers, the oldest company of its kind in Ireland, dating from 1723. Like its sister shops, this one carries the colorful tweeds and mohairs that have made the Avoca line famous, plus linen-cotton fashions, stylish sweaters, tweed totes, and a wide array of hats. A coffee shop, serving lunch and snacks, is on the premises. Limerick-Ennis rd. (N18), Bunratty, county Clare. ℂ 061/364029.

Belleek Shop In the heart of Ennis, overlooking the 16th-century Franciscan Abbey, this newly expanded shop is more than 90 years old. It was the first Belleek china outlet in southern Ireland. The shop is renowned for its extensive range of Waterford, Galway, and Tipperary crystals, fine china, tableware, and figurines. In recent years, it has expanded to include other Irish products, such as handmade character dolls, turf crafts, pewter, jewelry, and fashionable tweeds. 36 Abbey St., Ennis, county Clare. ℂ 065/682-9607. www.belleekshop.com.

Bunratty Village Mills On the grounds of the Bunratty Castle Hotel, there's a dozen fine shops laid out like a 19th-century village. This includes a branch of Tipperary Crystal; the wonderful housewares shop, Meadows & Byrne; Linen Shop; Aran Shop, for knitwear; Celtic Sounds Music & Book Shop; Patio & Garden Shop; Bargain Loft; and Bunratty Cottage, for clothing, gifts, and jewelry. Main St., Bunratty, Co. Clare. ℂ 061/364321.

Custy's Traditional Music Shop If you'd like to bring back the melodious sounds of county Clare, this is the place to shop. The selection includes a full range of traditional and folk music tapes and CDs, as well as books, photos, paintings, and crafts pertaining to traditional music. You can also buy a fiddle, a tin whistle, a banjo, a concertina, an accordion, or a flute. 2 Francis St., Ennis, county Clare. ℂ 065/682-1727.

Shannon Duty Free Shops Founded in 1947, this airport complex offers one of the world's best duty-free shops. It offers tax-free bargains to shoppers passing through the airport. Most of the products are Irish, such as Waterford crystal, Belleek china, Donegal tweeds, Aran knitwear, Connemara marble, ceramic leprechauns, shillelaghs, and smoked salmon. You'll also find such names as Wedgwood, Bing and Grondahl, Lladró, Anri, Limoges, Orrefors, and Pringle. Shannon Airport, county Clare. ℂ 061/475047 or 061/471777.

HITTING THE LINKS

Where else but in Ireland can you step off a plane and right up to the first tee? The 18-hole, par-72 championship course at the **Shannon Golf Club,** Shannon Airport (ℂ **061/471020;** www.shannongolf.com), welcomes visitors. Greens fees are €35 to €45 ($31–$40). Within a half mile of the main terminal, it is surrounded by scenic vistas of county Clare, the Shannon River, and the busy runways.

Other choices in the area include the par-71 **Dromoland Golf Club,** Newmarket-on-Fergus, county Clare (ℂ **061/368444**), with greens fees of €50 to €60 ($45–$53), or €27 ($24) for guests at the castle hotel. The par-71 parkland course at the **Ennis Golf Club,** Drumbiggle, Ennis, county Clare (ℂ **065/682-4074;** http://golfclub.ennis.ie), charges greens fees of €25 to €35 ($22–$31).

WHERE TO STAY
VERY EXPENSIVE

Dromoland Castle ★★ Just 13km (8 miles) from Shannon Airport, this impressive castle hotel of turrets and towers (and every 20th-century luxury) makes for a fairy-tale first or last night in Ireland. The castle was built in 1686 by the O'Brien clan, the high kings of Ireland, and was restored and refurbished 30 years ago as a hotel. It's nestled beside the River Rine, amid 160 hectares (400 acres) of parklands and gardens that are home to various species of wildlife, including a deer herd. As befits its royal exterior, the castle's drawing rooms and stately halls are full of splendid wood and stone carvings, medieval suits of armor, rich oak paneling, and original oil paintings. The guest rooms are individually and lavishly decorated with designer fabrics and reproduction furniture; many look out onto the water or the romantic walled gardens. Service is excellent, if a bit stiff and self-conscious.

Limerick-Ennis rd. (N18), Newmarket-on-Fergus, county Clare. ✆ **800/346-7007** in the U.S., or 061/368144. Fax 061/363355. www.dromoland.ie. 100 units. €194–€469 ($173–$417) double; €372–€1,130 ($331–$1,006) suite. Full Irish breakfast €20 ($18). No service charge. AE, DC, MC, V. **Amenities:** 2 restaurants (French, country club); bar; 18-hole golf course; tennis courts; walking/jogging trails; concierge; fishing and boating equipment; room service; babysitting; laundry service. *In room:* TV, hair dryer, garment press.

MODERATE

Bunratty Castle Hotel *✿✿*   The newly refurbished, greatly expanded Bunratty Castle Hotel, which adjoins Bunratty Castle, opened in 1998. The hotel itself isn't a castle, nor does it pretend to be one, with its sunny yellow facade. But it is heir to a long tradition of hospitality, beginning with a wooden fortress 700 years back, later an inn and nightclub housed in an 18th-century stone structure. Add a tasteful extension, and you have a gracious hotel offering every comfort and convenience with a touch of elegance. The public rooms are both interesting and appealing, with an antique marble altar as a reception desk and a number of other fine antiques. The spacious guest rooms are furnished in the traditional style of dark woods, floral fabrics, and brass fixtures. Double rooms have orthopedic king-size beds.

Bunratty, county Clare. ✆ **061/364116.** Fax 061/364891. www.bunrattycastlehotel.com. 60 units. €130–€165 ($116–$147) double. Executive suites also available. Rates include full breakfast. AE, DC, MC, V. **Amenities:** Restaurant (Irish); bar; babysitting. *In room:* A/C, TV, tea/coffeemaker, hair dryer.

Clare Inn Resort Hotel *✿✿* *(Kids)*   Panoramic views of the River Shannon and the Clare hills are part of the scene at this contemporary Tudor-style hotel. Situated 13km (8 miles) from Shannon Airport, it's surrounded by the Dromoland Castle golf course and thousands of acres of woodland. The public areas are bright and airy, with large picture windows. The guest rooms are well appointed and very comfortable, and the roster of leisure facilities is excellent for this price bracket.

Limerick-Ennis rd. (N18), Newmarket-on-Fergus, county Clare. ✆ **800/473-8954** in the U.S., or 065/682-3000. Fax 065/682-3759. www.lynchotels.com. 183 units. €80–€140 ($71–$125) double. No service charge. Rates include full breakfast. AE, DC, MC, V. **Amenities:** 2 restaurants (international, cafe); bar; indoor swimming pool; 18-hole golf course; 2 tennis courts; jogging track; miniature golf; gym; Jacuzzi; sauna; solarium; supervised children's facilities. *In room:* TV, radio, hair dryer.

Old Ground Hotel *✿✿*   Long a focal point in the busy market town of Ennis, this ivy-covered hotel dates from 1749. According to a citation at the front entrance, it has been known variously as the Great Inn of Jayl Street and the Kings Arms; part of the hotel was once used as the Town Hall and the Town Jail. Many of the furnishings are antiques—you'll find vintage tea chests in the halls, and there's even a 1553 fireplace that once warmed the interior of nearby Lemaneagh Castle. The guest rooms are done up in rich, restful tones and are truly beautiful. They are furnished with antiques and some have lovely canopied beds. On many summer evenings, cabaret-style entertainment is offered in the pub.

O'Connell St., Ennis, county Clare. ✆ **065/682-8127.** Fax 065/682-8112. http://flynnhotels.com/oldground. 83 units. €95–€160 ($85–$142) double. No service charge. Rates include full breakfast. AE, DC, MC, V. **Amenities:** 2 restaurants (international, grill); bar; lounge. *In room:* TV, hair dryer, garment press.

INEXPENSIVE

Bunratty Woods ★★ *Value*   A 10-minute walk from Bunratty Folk Park and only 9.7km (6 miles) from Shannon Airport, Bunratty Woods is an ideal spot to spend your first or last night in Ireland, or both. Just beyond the tourist thicket, you'll enjoy both convenience and tranquility in this especially tasteful guesthouse, furnished in antique pine, with bare wood floors and handmade patchwork quilts. Most rooms have lovely views of the rolling Clare countryside. Smoking is permitted in the guest rooms, but not in the lounge or breakfast room. Be sure to ask the delightful hostess, Maureen O'Donovan, about local lore—she has some startling stories ready for the sharing.

Low Rd., Bunratty, county Clare. ✆ 061/369689. Fax 061/369454. www.iol.ie/~bunratty. 15 units. €64 ($57) double. No service charge. Rates include full breakfast. DC, MC, V. Closed mid-Nov to Feb. **Amenities:** Lounge. *In room:* TV, tea/coffeemaker, hair dryer.

Cill Eoin House ★   Just off the main N18 road at the Killadysert Cross, .8km (½ mile) south of Ennis, this two-story yellow guesthouse is a real find. It offers bright, comfortable rooms with hotel-quality furnishings and firm beds at a very affordable price, capped by attentive service from the McGann family. Although it's within walking distance of Ennis, the rooms offer lovely views of the countryside. The house is named after the nearby medieval Killone Abbey ("Killone" is the Anglicization of *Cill Eoin*).

Killadysert Cross, Clare Rd., Ennis, county Clare. ✆ **065/6841668.** Fax 065/6841669. www.euroka.com/cilleoin. 14 units. €60–€70 ($53–$62) double. No service charge. Rates include full breakfast. AE, MC, V. Closed Dec 24–Jan 8. **Amenities:** TV lounge; sunroom. *In room:* TV.

WHERE TO DINE
MEDIEVAL BANQUETS & TRADITIONAL MEALS WITH MUSIC

The medieval banquets at Bunratty and Knappogue castles and the traditional evening at Bunratty Folk Park can be booked in the United States through a travel agent or by calling ✆ **800/CIE-TOUR.** They're all very touristy, but fun nevertheless, and even the locals have been known to attend once in a while.

Bunratty Castle ★★   Built in 1425, this splendid structure is the most complete and authentic example of a medieval castle in Ireland. Every evening, a full medieval banquet is re-created with music, song, and merriment. Seated at long tables in the castle's magnificent baronial hall, you'll feast on ancient recipes using modern Irish ingredients, all served in strictly medieval use-your-fingers style. For refreshment, there's mulled wine, claret, and mugs of mead (the traditional honey-based drink). To add to the fun, at each banquet a "lord and lady" are chosen from the participants to reign over the 3-hour proceedings, and someone else is thrown into the dungeon.

Castle Limerick-Ennis rd. (N18), Bunratty, county Clare. ✆ **061/360788.** Reservations required. Dinner and entertainment €45 ($40). AE, DC, MC, V. Daily year-round at 5:30 and 8:45pm.

Knappogue Castle ★   Once the stronghold of the McNamara clan, this castle was built in 1467. Now fully restored, it's the setting for authentic medieval banquets. This castle is smaller and more intimate than Bunratty, but you'll still feast on a medieval meal, followed by a colorful pageant of Irish history celebrating the influential role of women in Celtic Ireland. The program includes rhyme and mime, song, and dance.

Quin, county Clare. ✆ **061/360788.** Reservations required. Dinner and entertainment €45 ($40). AE, DC, MC, V. May–Oct daily 5:30 and 8:45pm.

Traditional Irish Night ✿ Irish country life of yesteryear is the focus of this "at home" evening in a thatched farmhouse cottage. You'll have a traditional meal of Irish stew, homemade bread, and apple pie and fresh cream. Then the music begins: the flute and fiddle, accordion, bodhran, and spoons—all at a spirited, foot-tapping pace.

Bunratty Folk Park, off the Limerick-Ennis rd. (N18), Bunratty, county Clare. ✆ **061/360788.** Reservations required. Dinner and entertainment €35 ($31). AE, DC, MC, V. May–Sept daily 5:30 and 8:45pm.

Kathleen's Irish Nights ✿ The highlight of the entertainment program at the Bunratty Castle Hotel starts at 7pm every summer evening. More like a family party than a stage show, this 2½-hour gala dinner with traditional music is a great way to celebrate your arrival or to console yourself before departure.

Kathleen's Irish Pub, Bunratty Castle Hotel, Bunratty, county Clare. ✆ **061/364116.** Fax 061/364891. Reservations recommended. €35 ($31) adults, €17 ($15) children.

MODERATE

The Cloister ✿✿ MODERN CONTINENTAL Built right into the remains of a 13th-century Franciscan friary, with windows overlooking what was the friary garden, this old-world pub offers innovative cuisine. The decor is warmly elegant, with open turf fireplaces and stoves, beamed ceilings, and reproductions from the Book of Kells adorning the walls. The menu includes poached monkfish with red-pepper sauce, wild venison with juniper-and-Armagnac sauce, and supreme of chicken layered with Carrigline cheese and Irish Mist. A house specialty starter is Inagh goat cheese laced with port-wine sauce. Pub-style lunches are served in the skylit Friary Bar, adjacent to the old abbey walls.

Club Bridge, Abbey St., Ennis, county Clare. ✆ **065/682-9521.** Reservations recommended. Bar food €4–€14 ($3.55–$12); dinner main courses €14–€23 ($12–$20). AE, DC, MC, V. Restaurant daily 12:30–3pm and 6–9:30pm; bar daily 12:30pm–midnight.

Cruise's Pub Restaurant GRILL Housed in a 1658 building, this restaurant has low beamed ceilings, timber fixtures and fittings, crackling fires in open hearths, lantern lighting, a rough flagstone floor strewn with sawdust, memorabilia from crockery to books, and a snug appropriately dubbed "The Safe Haven." On warm days, seating extends into an outdoor courtyard overlooking the friary. The menu offers a good selection of pub grub, including Irish stew, along with seafood, steaks, and vegetarian stir-fry. There are often impromptu music sessions.

Abbey St., Ennis, county Clare. ✆ **065/684-1800.** Reservations recommended. Main courses €10–€24 ($8.90–$21). MC, V. Daily 12.30–10pm.

AFTER-DARK FUN

In addition to the medieval banquets and traditional ceili evenings synonymous with this area, county Clare offers much to delight the visitor. A number of hotels present music or shows, particularly in the high season.

Cois na hAbhna For pure traditional entertainment, try Cois na hAbhna (pronounced *Cush*-na *How*-na). This center stages sessions of music, song, and dance, followed by ceili dancing with audience participation. Tea and brown bread are served. Traditional dance sessions are run year-round by Dick

O'Connell, Wednesdays from 8:30 to 11:30pm. Call for the most current schedule of ceilis and other events. Gort Rd., Ennis, county Clare. © **065/682-0996.** Admission €3–€7 ($2.65–$6.25), depending on the event.

Durty Nellie's   Established in 1620 next door to Bunratty Castle, this ramshackle, thatched-roof cottage was originally a watering hole for the castle guards. Now, with a mustard-colored facade and palm trees at its entrance, it's a favorite before-and-after haunt of locals and of tourists who join the nightly medieval banquets at the castle. That the place is now commercialized is no matter—it's still sheer fun. The decor—mounted elk heads and old lanterns on the walls, sawdust on the floors, and open turf fireplaces—hasn't changed much over the centuries. It's a warren of little nooks, crannies, snugs, and "courtin' corners." The walls are covered in old photos, manifestos, and historical documents, and make a good primer in Irish history. This is also a good spot for a substantial pub lunch or a full dinner in one of the two restaurants. Spontaneous Irish music sessions erupt here on most evenings. Limerick-Ennis rd. (N18), Bunratty, county Clare. © **061/364861.**

THE BURREN ✸✸✸

Moving west from Ennis into the heart of county Clare, you'll come to an amazing district of 259 sq. km (100 sq. miles) called the Burren. The word *burren* derives from the Irish word *boirreann,* which means "a rocky place."

It is a strange, lunarlike region of bare carboniferous limestone, bordered by the towns of **Corofin, Ennistymon, Lahinch, Lisdoonvarna,** and **Ballyvaughan.** Massive sheets of rock, jagged boulders, caves, and potholes are visible for miles in a moonscape pattern, yet this is also a setting of little lakes and streams, and an amazing assemblage of flora. There is always something in bloom, even in winter, from fern and moss to orchids, rock roses, milkwort, wild thyme, geraniums, violets, and fuchsia. The Burren is also famous for its butterflies, which thrive on the rare flora. The pine marten, stoat, and badger, rare in the rest of Ireland, are common here.

The story of the Burren began more than 300 million years ago, when layers of shells and sediment were deposited under a tropical sea. Many millions of years later they were thrust above the surface and left open to the erosive power of Irish rain and weather, producing the limestone landscape that appears today. As early as 7,000 years ago, humans began to leave their mark on this landscape in the form of Stone Age burial monuments, such as the famed Poulnabrone Dolmen and Gleninsheen wedge tomb.

In addition to rock, the area has other unique attractions. Lisdoonvarna, on the western edge, is a town known for its spa of natural mineral springs. Each summer it draws thousands of people to bathe in its therapeutic waters of sulfur, chalybeate (iron), and iodine. Lisdoon, as the natives call it, is also known worldwide for playing host to an annual matchmaking festival (see "Ireland Calendar of Events" in chapter 2, "Planning Your Trip to Ireland," for details).

One of the most scenic Burren drives is along R480. The corkscrew-shaped road leads from Corofin to Ballyvaughan, a delightful little village overlooking Galway Bay.

EXPLORING THE REGION

Burren National Park ✸✸ presently encompasses 1,653 hectares (4,133 acres), but will acquire more land as it becomes available. It's a remarkable limestone plateau dotted with ruined castles, cliffs, rivers, lakes, valleys, green road walks, barren rock mountains, and plant life that defies all of nature's conventional rules. The area is particularly rich in archaeological remains from the Neolithic through the medieval periods—dolmens and wedge tombs (approximately 120), ring forts (500), round towers, ancient churches, high crosses, monasteries, and holy wells. The park is centered at Mullaghmore Mountain but there is as of yet no official entrance point, and no admission charges or restrictions to access.

With its unique terrain and pathways, the Burren lends itself to **walking.** Visitors who want to amble through the hills, turloughs, limestone pavements and terraces, shale uplands, and inland lakes should follow the **Burren Way.** The 42km (26-mile) signposted route stretches from Ballyvaughan to Liscannor. An information sheet outlining the route is available from any tourist office. **Burren Walking Holidays,** in conjunction with the Carrigann Hotel (see "Where to Stay," below), Lisdoonvarna (© **065/707-4036**), offers a wide selection of guided and self-guided walks, from one day to a week or more.

Aillwee Cave ⚐ One of Ireland's oldest underground sites, Aillwee was formed millions of years ago but remained hidden until a local farmer discovered it less than 50 years ago. The cave has more than 1,020m (3,400 ft.) of passages and hollows running straight into the heart of a mountain. Its highlights are bridged chasms, deep caverns, a frozen waterfall, and the Bear Pits—hollows scraped out by the brown bear, one of the cave's original inhabitants. Guided tours, which last approximately half an hour, are conducted continuously. The site has a cafe and a craft-rock shop; a unique farmhouse cheese-making enterprise called Burren Gold Cheese, near the cave's entrance; and an apiary where honey is produced.

Ballyvaughan, county Clare. © **065/707-7036.** www.aillweecave.ie. Admission €7.50 ($6.70) adults, €6 ($5.35) seniors, €4.50 ($4) children, €21 ($19) family. V. Daily 10am–5:30pm. Closed mid-Nov to Feb.

The Burren Centre Established in 1975 in the heart of the Burren as a community development cooperative, this is a fine place to acquaint yourself with all facets of the area. The facility includes a new 25-minute audiovisual presentation, plus landscape models and interpretive displays that highlight the unique features of the region's geology, geography, flora, and fauna. Also here are tearooms, a shop stocked with locally made crafts and products, and picnic tables.

R476 to Kilfenora, county Clare. © **065/708-8030.** Admission €3.50 ($3.10) adults, €2.50 ($2.25) students and children over age 8. MC, V. Oct and Mar–May daily 10am–5pm; June–Sept daily 9:30am–6pm. Closed Nov–Feb.

Burren College of Art If ever there were a great place for an artist to paint or a photographer to snap a picture, it's the Burren. Bearing that in mind, this new center of artistic learning has sprung up in the midst of the dramatic landscapes. On the grounds of a 16th-century castle, the newly constructed college opened in 1993. Although geared to 15-week semester programs and to granting full 4-year bachelor of fine arts degrees, it also offers a range of weekend and 1-week courses that are ideal for visitors. Fees vary according to the specifics of the course. The facilities include bright studios for sculpture, painting, photography, and drawing, plus a lecture theater, an exhibition area, a library, a cafeteria, and a shop. The restored castle and grounds are open to the public.

N67 to Ballyvaughan, Newtown Castle, Ballyvaughan, county Clare. © **065/707-7200.** www.iol.ie/~burren. Admission to castle or nature trail €3 ($2.65) adults, €2 ($1.80) children, €8 ($7.10) family; to both €4 ($3.55) adults, €2.50 ($2.25) children, €16 ($14) family.

Burren Exposure ⚐⚐ This compact multimedia exhibition center provides an exciting and essential introduction to the extraordinary natural wonders and the rich historical legacy of the Burren. If you intend to explore the area at all, the 35 minutes you spend here will be worthwhile—the center's beautifully crafted visuals and narratives bring out the salient points quickly and intelligently. Side by side with Burren Exposure is the Whitethorn Restaurant, one of the most tasteful, tastiest cafes in county Clare. It offers excellent seaside snacks and full lunches, as well as dazzling seascapes through slanted, floor-to-ceiling glass panels. Last but not least, the third component is a fine gift shop, containing a discerning selection of Irish clothing, crafts, jewelry, and books.

Galway Rd. (N67), .4km (¼ mile) north of Ballyvaughan, county Clare. ℂ 065/707-7277. Admission €5 ($4.45) adults, €3.20 ($2.85) seniors and students, €14 ($12) family. 1 week before Easter to Oct daily 10am–6pm (last admission 5:20pm).

The Burren Smokehouse Ltd ⭐ Aficionados of smoked salmon flock here to see the fish-smoking process firsthand and to buy right from the source. Visitors are welcome to watch as fresh Atlantic salmon is sorted, hand-treated, salted, and then slowly smoked over Irish oak chips in the traditional way. Each side of salmon is then vacuum-sealed and chilled. Tours are given throughout the day. Smoked mackerel, eels, and trout are also produced here. The smokehouse provides a worldwide mail-order service. Yum.

Kincora Rd., Lisdoonvarna, county Clare. ℂ 065/707-4432. www.burrensmokehouse.ie. Free admission. Daily 9am–7pm. Closed Dec–Feb.

Clare Heritage Centre If you have Clare family roots, you'll be especially fascinated by this heritage museum and genealogical research center. Even if you don't, this center is worth a visit to learn about Irish history and emigration. Housed in a former Church of Ireland edifice built by a first cousin of Queen Anne in 1718, it has exhibits on Clare farming, industry, commerce, education, forestry, language, and music. All are designed to reflect life in county Clare during the past 300 years. There is also a tearoom and gift shop. The genealogical research facility is open year-round.

R476 to Corofin, county Clare. ℂ 065/683-7955. Admission €3 ($2.65) adults, €2 ($1.80) seniors, students, and children. Apr–Sept Mon–Fri 9am–6pm, Sat–Sun 10am–5pm; Oct–Mar Mon–Fri 9am–5:30pm.

Dysert O'Dea Castle and Archaeology Centre ⭐⭐ Built in 1480 by Diarmaid O'Dea on a rocky outcrop of land, this castle was badly damaged during the Cromwellian years. It was restored and opened to the public in 1986 as an archaeology center and museum. Today, the castle offers exhibitions and an audiovisual show on the history of the area. It is also the starting point for a signposted trail that leads to 25 sites of historical and archaeological interest within a 3.2km (2-mile) radius. They include a church founded by St. Tola in the 8th century that contains a unique Romanesque doorway surrounded by a border of 12 heads carved in stone. The O'Deas, who were chieftains of the area, are buried under the church. Also at the center are a round tower from the 10th or 12th century, a 12th-century high cross, a holy well, a 14th-century battlefield, and a stone fort believed to date to the Iron Age. The castle bakery is currently under excavation.

R476 to Corofin, county Clare. ℂ 065/683-7401. Admission €4 ($3.55) adults, €3 ($2.65) seniors and students, €2 ($1.80) children, €9 ($8) family. Daily 10am–6pm. Closed mid-Oct to Apr.

Spa Wells Centre ⭐ Nestled in a shady park on the edge of town, this is Lisdoonvarna's famous Victorian-style spa complex, dating from the 18th century. The stinky-but-healthy sulfur-laced mineral waters are served hot or cold in the pump room, drawn from an illuminated well. Sulfur baths can also be arranged. Videos of the Burren and the Shannon area are shown continuously in the visitor center.

Kincora Rd., Lisdoonvarna, county Clare. ℂ **065/707-4023**. Free admission. Daily 10am–6pm. Closed Nov–May.

WHERE TO STAY
Expensive/Very Expensive

Gregans Castle Hotel ⭐⭐ If you want to spoil yourself utterly on your first night in Ireland as you recover from jet lag in tranquility, this elegant haven is the place. Only an hour's drive from Shannon, just over 4.8km (3 miles) outside Ballyvaughan, it's nestled in the exotic floral moonscape of the Burren. The mid-19th-century, ivy-clad, stone country house is full of light and color, and offers lovely views of the Burren or Galway Bay from every window. Although not strictly a castle, it is on the site of the ancient family estates of the Martyn family and the O'Loughlens, princes of the Burren. Owned and managed by the Hayden family, Gregans embodies decades of attention to detail and gracious hospitality. The public areas contain heirlooms and period pieces, antique books, and Raymond Piper's mural paintings of Burren flora. Each guest room is individually decorated with designer fabrics, dark woods, and brass accents; some have four-poster or canopied beds. The suites and superior rooms are especially spacious and luxuriant, but none of the rooms will disappoint.

Ballyvaughan-Lisdoonvarna Rd. (N67), Ballyvaughan, county Clare. ℂ **800/323-5463** in the U.S., or 065/707-7005. Fax 065/707-7111. www.gregans.ie. 22 units. €155–€270 ($138–$240) double. Suites available. No service charge. Rates include full breakfast. AE, MC, V. Closed Nov–Mar. **Amenities:** Restaurant (seafood); bar; drawing room; library. In room: TV, hair dryer.

Moderate

Clifden House ⭐⭐ This handsome, romantic Georgian mansion has a splendid location at the southern tip of the Burren, at the foot of a wooded hill on the shores of Lough Inchiquin, with the River Fergus flowing through the stable yard. The house was abandoned for many years, but Jim and Bernadette Robson are coaxing it back into use with some modern updates. Some parts of the house are as elegant as a luxury hotel but work is ongoing, so there's a real opportunity to witness a thoughtful restoration of a historic home in progress. The resulting effect is epicurean comfort meets gentle ruin, which somehow sidesteps time. The guest rooms are finished—each one elegant and beautiful in its own right. Bernadette is a passionate cook and breakfasts are wonderful. Just 32km (20 miles) from Shannon Airport, this makes for a wonderfully idiosyncratic entrance into Ireland.

Corofin, county Clare. ℂ **065/683-7692**. 4 units. €120 ($107) double. Rates include full breakfast. MC, V. Closed mid-Dec to Feb. **Amenities:** Sitting room. In room: TV, hair dryer.

Inexpensive

Carrigann Hotel ⭐ Rose bushes and flower-filled gardens surround this country-house hotel, on a hillside on the outskirts of town. Most of the guest rooms, which are cheerfully decorated with standard furnishings and firm beds, enjoy garden views. The Carrigann offers guided and self-guided walks in the Burren (see "Exploring the Region," above). Horse riding, cycling, and fishing can also be arranged on request.

Lisdoonvarna, county Clare. ℂ **065/707-4036**. Fax 065/707-4567. www.gateway-to-the-burren.com. 20 units. €80 ($71) double. Rates include full breakfast. Dinner €29 ($26). MC, V. Closed Nov–Feb. **Amenities:** Restaurant (Continental); bar; lounge. In room: TV, radio, tea/coffeemaker, hair dryer.

Rusheen Lodge ⭐ On the main road just south of Ballyvaughan village, this award-winning, bungalow-style guesthouse is completely surrounded by flowers. The innkeepers are Rita and John McGann, whose father, Jacko McGann, discovered the nearby Aillwee Caves, one of the area's most remarkable natural attractions. Rooms are decorated in blonde woods and have firm, half-tester beds and floral fabrics. Breakfast, served in a cheery pastel-toned room overlooking the gardens, includes freshly caught local fish as an option. Burren flowers enhance the decor throughout the house.

Knocknagrough, Ballyvaughan, county Clare. ✆ 065/707-7092. Fax 065/707-7152. €70–€80 ($62–$71) double. No service charge. Rates include full breakfast. AE, MC, V. Closed Dec–Feb. **Amenities:** Nonsmoking rooms. *In room:* TV, tea/coffeemaker, hair dryer.

WHERE TO DINE

Bofey Quinn's SEAFOOD/GRILL   An informal atmosphere prevails at this pub-restaurant in the center of Corofin. Dinner specialties include lobster, fresh wild salmon, and cod, as well as a variety of steaks, chops, mixed grills, and also pizza. Pub-grub lunches are available throughout the day. From May to mid-September, Mondays to Thursdays from 7:30 to 9:30pm, there's a harpist to serenade you.

Main St., Corofin, county Clare. ✆ 065/683-7321. Main courses €7–€20 ($6.25–$18); lobster €33 ($29). MC, V. Jan–Mar and Oct–Dec daily noon–9pm; Apr–Sept daily 10:30am–10pm.

Tri na Cheile CONTINENTAL   This homey, intimate restaurant in the middle of Ballyvaughan village is now the common venture of Adele Laffan and Barry Richards, committed to offering meals made with the freshest Irish ingredients at reasonable prices. The menu includes sirloin; mussels and linguini; whole crab; beef curry; filet of salmon; roast lamb with anchovies, garlic, and rosemary; and roast chicken. Vegetarian options are also available.

Main St., Ballyvaughan, county Clare. ✆ 065/707-7029. Reservations recommended. Main courses €13–€18 ($11–$16). MC, V. May–Sept Mon–Sat 6–10:45pm; Sun 12:30–3:30pm.

THE CLARE COAST

One of Ireland's most photographed scenes, the **Cliffs of Moher** ✰✰✰, draw busloads and carloads of visitors to Clare's remote reaches every day of the year. Rising to vertigo-inducing heights over 210m (700 ft.) above the Atlantic and extending about 8km (5 miles) along the coast, the cliffs are county Clare's foremost natural wonder.

The Cliffs are only the beginning, however. Another highlight of the Clare Coast includes **Lahinch,** the old-fashioned seaside resort, with its wide beach and long promenade along the horseshoe bay. Lahinch is also world-renowned for its golf course. Dubbed by golfers the "St. Andrews of Ireland," it is the paradigm of Irish links golf and is ranked among the 50 best courses in the world by *Golf* magazine.

Farther up the coast is the secluded fishing village of **Doolin,** which is also the unofficial capital of Irish traditional music. Doolin, like Galway to the north, is also a departure point for the short boat trip to the Aran Islands.

The Clare Coast is dotted with a variety of **seaside resorts,** such as Kilrush, Kilkee, Miltown Malbay, and Ennistymon, that are particularly popular with Irish families. As you drive around this craggy coastline, you'll find many off-the-beaten-path delights with intriguing names, like Pink Cave, Puffing Hole, Intrinsic Bay, Chimney Hill, Elephant's Teeth, Mutton Island, Loop Head, and Lover's Leap.

ATTRACTIONS

Cliffs of Moher ✰✰✰   One of Ireland's natural wonders, these 228m (760-ft.) cliffs stretch for over 8km (5 miles) along Clare's Atlantic coast. They offer spirit-raising, panoramic views, especially from the 19th-century O'Brien's

Tower at the northern end. It's a very dramatic place, with the roar of the waves crashing below and the call of circling seagulls. On a clear day you can see the Aran Islands in Galway Bay. It's also a very touristy place, with a constant throng of coaches and cars clogging the parking lot below, and tacky souvenir stalls set up along the footpath to the cliffs. No bother. Just walk on past and enjoy the view. The visitor center houses a tearoom, an information desk, and a craft and souvenir shop.

R478, 11km (7 miles) north of Lahinch, county Clare. ✆ 065/708-1171. Free admission to cliffs; to O'Brien's Tower €2 ($1.80) adults, €.80 (70¢) children. Cliffs visitor center daily 9:30am–5:30pm; O'Brien's Tower May–Sept daily 9:30am–5:30pm (weather permitting).

Kilrush Heritage Centre   Housed in the town's historic Market House, this center provides historic and cultural background on Kilrush—the "capital of West Clare"—and the south Clare coast. An audiovisual presentation, *Kilrush in Landlord Times,* tells of the struggles of the area's tenant farmers during the 18th and 19th centuries, particularly during the Great Famine. The museum is also the focal point of a signposted heritage walk around the town. The building, erected in 1808 by the Vandeleur family, the area's chief landlords, was burned to the ground in 1892 and rebuilt in its original style in 1931.

Town Hall, Martyrs Sq., off Henry St., Kilrush, county Clare. ✆ 065/9051047. Admission €3 ($2.65) adults, €1.30 ($1.15) children, €6.50 ($5.80) family. May–Sept Mon–Sat 10am–5pm.

Lahinch Seaworld and Leisure Centre ⭐   After stretching your legs along the vast strand and exploring its countless tide pools, you can get a closer look at the aquatic denizens of the Clare Coast by visiting this compact, well-designed local aquarium. Among the sea creatures in residence are conger eels, sharks, and rays. In the "touch pool," you can tickle a starfish or surprise an anemone. If you are then inspired to take to the water yourself, the leisure center next door charges very reasonable rates. For extra savings, combination tickets are available.

The Promenade, Lahinch, county Clare. ✆ 065/708-1900. www.lahinchseaworld.com. Admission to aquarium €5.90 ($5.25) adults, €4.90 ($4.35) seniors and students, €3.90 ($3.45) children, €18.90 ($17) family. Daily 10am–9pm.

Scattery Island ⭐   Scattery, a small, unspoiled island in the Shannon Estuary near Kilrush, is the site of a group of monastic ruins dating from the 6th century. A high round tower and several churches are all that remain of what was once an extensive settlement, founded by St. Senan. Legends tell of a massive sea monster defeated by the saint on the island, from which the place derives its name in Gaelic. To visit the island, contact one of the boatmen who arrange the 20-minute ferry rides—frequency depends on demand, and even in summer there may be only one trip per day. Or ask at the Information Center on the mainland—in the village of Kilrush, just past the pier—when the next ferry departs. The Information Center also houses exhibits on the history and folklore of the island.

Information Center, Merchants Quay, Kilrush, county Clare. ✆ 065/905-2144. Free admission. Ferry: €12 ($11) round-trip. Mid-June to mid-Sept daily 10:30am–6:30pm.

TRIPS TO THE ARAN ISLANDS

Doolin Ferry Co   Although most people come to Doolin to enjoy the music, many also come to board this ferry to the Aran Islands. The three fabled islands—Inishmore, Inishmaan, and Inisheer—sitting out in the Atlantic, are closer to Doolin than they are to Galway (roughly 8km/5 miles, or 30 min.). Ferries operate at least daily during the season, with expanded service in the summer. (For more information about excursions to the Aran Islands, see "Side Trips from Galway City" in chapter 11.)

The Pier, Doolin, county Clare. © **065/707-4455.** www.doolinferries.com. Inisheer €20 ($18) round-trip, Inishmaan €25 ($22) round-trip, Inishmore €27 ($24) round-trip. Student, child, and family discounts available. Mid-Apr to Sept. Call for current schedule.

SHOPPING

Doolin Crafts Gallery   Since 1982, this has been an oasis of fine craftsmanship in the heart of the Clare coast. Surrounded by gardens and next to the churchyard, this shop is the brainchild of two artisans: Matthew O'Connell, who creates batik work with Celtic designs on wall hangings, cushion covers, ties, and scarves; and Mary Gray, who hand-fashions contemporary gold and silver jewelry, inspired by the Burren's rocks, flora, and wildflowers. There are also products by other Irish craftspeople. There is a good coffee shop on the premises. Ballyvoe, Doolin, county Clare. © **065/707-4309.**

Traditional Music Shop   In this town known for its traditional music, this small shop is a center of attention. It offers all types of Irish traditional music on cassette tape and compact disc, as well as books and instruments, including tin whistles and bodhrans. Ballyreen, Doolin, county Clare. © **065/707-4407.**

SPORTS & OUTDOOR PURSUITS

BIRD-WATCHING   The **Bridges of Ross,** on the north side of **Loop Head,** is one of the prime autumn bird-watching sites in Ireland, especially during northwest gales, when several rare species have been seen with some consistency. The **lighthouse** at the tip of the Head is also a popular spot for watching seabirds.

BOATING & FISHING   The waters of the lower Shannon estuary and the Atlantic coastline are known as a good place to fish for shark, skate, turbot, ray, conger eel, tope, pollock, and more. The new Kilrush Creek Marina, an attraction in itself, is the base for **Michael McLaughlin** (© and fax **065/905-5105;** m_mc_ laughlin@hotmail.com), who offers boat charters for deep-sea angling. Prices are €40 ($36) per person for a day's fishing, €400 ($356) for an 8-hour boat charter for up to 12 persons. Rods and reels can be hired for €7 ($6.25) per day. Anne and Michael McLaughlin also provide comfortable accommodations, year-round, in their guesthouse, **San Esteban.** It is quite splendidly situated at the water's edge, just outside Doonbeg. The price of a double room with breakfast is €48 ($43).

Sea Angling is also available from **Kilrush Deep Sea Angling,** Cappa Road, Kilrush (© **065/905-1327;** shannondolphins@eircom.net). Fees run €40 ($36) per angler daily, €320 ($285) daily charter, €1,500 ($1,335) weekly charter.

DOLPHIN WATCHING   The Shannon Estuary is home to about 70 bottlenose dolphins, one of four such resident groups of dolphins in Europe. Cruises run by **Dolphinwatch** leave daily May to September from Carrigaholt. Advance booking is essential. During July and August, call © **065/9058156;** or visit www.dolphinwatch.ie. Fees are €17 ($15) for adults, €9 ($8) for children under 14.

GOLF   "I tell everybody about this course. I tell them that I have got the best site in the world and it's in Doonbeg in Ireland," gushes Greg Norman about **Doonbeg Golf Club,** Doonbeg (©**065/905-5246;** www.doonbeggolfclub. com), whose opening in 2002 was a highlight in the Irish golf calendar. The Norman-designed links course has a breathtaking setting and a magnificent 15th hole, which ends in a funnel-shaped green surrounded by sky-high dunes.

With a nearby helipad and a complex that includes a country club, hotel, and deluxe cottages in the works, Doonbeg has quickly become a haunt for the moneyed set. Greens fees are a hefty €185 ($165) daily.

Also famous, but far less pricey, is **Lahinch Golf Club,** Lahinch (℗ 065/708-1003; www.lahinchgolf.com). Lahinch is a treat for any golfer. There are two 18-hole links courses, but the longer championship links course is the one that has given Lahinch its far-reaching reputation. This course's elevations, such as those at the 9th and 13th holes, reveal open vistas of sky, land, and sea; they also make the winds an integral part of the scoring. Watch out for the goats, Lahinch's legendary weather forecasters. If they huddle by the clubhouse, it means a storm is approaching. Visitors are welcome to play, especially on weekdays; greens fees range from €42 ($37) on weekdays to €64 ($57) on weekends.

WHERE TO STAY
Moderate

Aberdeen Arms ✿ In the heart of town, within view of the golf course that has made Lahinch famous, this hotel is over 140 years old. It's said to be the oldest golf links hotel in Ireland and is convenient for budget-minded golfers touring the Clare coast. The guest rooms are pretty in an old-fashioned, pastel-and-chintz sort of way, and the public rooms have a country-inn atmosphere.

Main St., Lahinch, county Clare. ℗ 065/708-1100. Fax 065/708-1228. 55 units. €80–€140 ($71–$125) double. Rates include full Irish breakfast and service charge. AE, DC, MC, V. **Amenities:** 2 restaurants (international, grill); bar; tennis court; squash court; gym; Jacuzzi; sauna. *In room:* TV.

Aran View House ✿✿ Dating from 1736, this three-story, yellow Georgian-style stone house stands on a hill on the main road and sits on 40 hectares (100 acres) of farmland just north of town. It offers panoramic views of the Clare coastline and, on a clear day, of the Aran Islands. The house is furnished in traditional Irish style, and the guest rooms are surprisingly luxurious for this price bracket. They are spacious and appointed with mahogany furnishings, some with four-poster beds and armoires. The ambience here is convivial, the staff is efficient and friendly, and there is traditional music in the pub three times a week.

Doolin, county Clare. ℗ 065/707-4061. Fax 065/707-4540. 19 units. €92–€130 ($82–$116) double. Rates include full breakfast. AE, DC, MC, V. Closed Nov–Mar. **Amenities:** Restaurant (international); bar. *In room:* TV, hair dryer.

Ballinalacken Castle Country House ✿✿ The first delight of Ballinalacken is its location: Situated just below the crest of a hill overlooking the Aran Islands, all rooms but three command fine sea views. The hotel itself, run by the O'Callaghan family for over 40 years, was built in the 1840s. Most of the guest rooms are in a new wing, but it's worthwhile to request a room in the old house, where you'll find high ceilings, marble fireplaces, and, in room 16, a sweeping panorama of hill and sea. All rooms are traditionally furnished and are quite spacious. Bathrooms are compact, white tiled, and modern, with strong showers (two of the rooms have showers only, no tubs). An added bonus: The exceptional ruined 15th-century castle tower of the O'Brien clan just behind the hotel is open only to guests. Before you leave, be sure to climb its worn stairs to its dizzy top to scan the sea from crumbling battlements.

Doolin, county Clare. ℗ and fax 065/74025. www.ballinalackencastle.com. 12 units. €102 ($91) double. AE, DC, MC, V. Closed Oct–Mar. **Amenities:** Restaurant (Continental). *In room:* TV, hair dryer.

Inexpensive

Doonmacfelim Guest House ✿ *Value* On the main street a few hundred feet from the famous Gus O'Connor's Pub (see below), this modern two-story guesthouse is a great value in the heart of Doolin. Although it's close to the center of everything, the house is also surrounded by a dairy farm. Guest rooms have standard furnishings and nice views of the neighboring countryside and town.

Doolin, county Clare. ✆ **065/707-4503.** Fax 065/707-4129. www.kingsway.ie/doonmacfelim. 8 units. €51–€65 ($45–$58) double. No service charge. Rates include full breakfast. MC, V. **Amenities:** Tennis court; sitting room. *In room:* Tea/coffeemaker, hair dryer.

Knockerra House ★ *Kids* The Troy family house is set in the shelter of a beautiful grove of old trees, which is rare on Ireland's windswept west coast. The place defines serenity, with gardens tucked into a hillside and views of the neighboring fields. The house (built ca. 1875) has aged well, and bears the marks of time on its ivy-covered facade and the antiques that populate the spacious rooms. This is a good place for families—each room has a double and a twin bed, and the extensive grounds offer many places to explore. Fishing is free at Knockerra Lake, a 10-minute walk from the house.

Ennis Rd, 6.5km (4 miles) north of Kilrush, county Clare. ✆ **065/905-1054.** 3 units, 2 with private bathroom. €64 ($57) double with bathroom. Rates include full breakfast. 50% discount for children under 12. No credit cards.

Self-Catering

Loop Head Lightkeeper's House ★★ *Finds* Here is yet another of the splendid new properties run by the Irish Landmark Trust (ILT), an organization that has gone from strength to strength. This lightkeeper's house stands next to the lighthouse on the tip of remote Loop Head, just southwest of Kilkee. The downstairs contains a fully equipped kitchen, sitting room, two bathrooms, and a double bedroom. Upstairs, there are two bedrooms (one double, one twin) and a small sitting room. The house is brimming with old-world charms—sturdy mahogany furnishings, brass beds, oversized sofas and armchairs, quality Irish linens, a fireplace in every room, wide plank floors, and deep windowsills with wooden interior shutters. Its location is perfect for a get-away-from-it-all vacation: as remote as you'd hope for from a lighthouse, and still only a 20-minute drive to bustling Kilkee, a little seaside resort with old-fashioned appeal. As with all ILT properties, there is no TV, but there is a radio.

Loop Head, county Clare. Contact the Irish Landmark Trust ✆ **01/670-4733.** Fax 01/670-4887. www.irishlandmark.com. €247 ($220) for 4 nights in low season, sliding up to €651 ($579) per week in high season. *In room:* Kitchen.

WHERE TO DINE

Barrtrá Seafood Restaurant ★★ SEAFOOD On the ground floor of a country house overlooking Liscannor Bay, this intimately-scaled, wide-windowed restaurant is a great place to tuck into fabulous fish and take in some smashing views of the Atlantic. It's a simple, family-run place where the menu changes daily but always pairs tried-and-true fish with interesting flavors: baked hake with orange and ginger, turbot with parsley pesto, shark steak with sun-dried tomatoes, haddock with lime and ginger sauce, salmon with Dijon mustard sauce, or John Dory with Thai spices. The menu also features such local Clare cheeses as Kilshanny (in five flavors: garlic, pepper, herb, cumin, and plain), Poolcoin (Burren goat cheese), and Cratloe Hills Gold (sheep's cheese). There's a fun, interesting wine list and good desserts, too.

Barrtrá, Lahinch, county Clare. ✆ **065/708-1280.** Reservations recommended. Fixed-price dinner €33 ($29); early-bird 5–6:30pm €20 ($18); main courses €18–€24 ($16–$21). AE, MC, V. Feb–Apr and Oct Thurs–Sun 5–10pm; May–June and Sept Tues–Sat 5–10pm; July–Aug daily 5–10pm.

The Mermaid ✸✸ SEAFOOD   The wonder of rural Ireland is that it's capable of producing culinary gems like The Mermaid in unlikely settings. Just up the coast from Lahinch, here is a place that, despite its modest atmosphere, does everything right and wins you over with its exceptional food and service. Word of mouth has turned this into a hot destination on this laid-back Clare coastline, and nobody ever seems to leave disappointed. You may never again have crab Florentine as good as the one Neville Fitzpatrick makes here. And his swordfish with lime and pepper butter is a dish worthy of the best seafood restaurants anywhere. The dessert list is fabulous, the wines terrific.

Liscannor, county Clare. ✆ **065/708-1076.** Reservations recommended in summer. Main courses €16–€23 ($14–$20). MC, V. Apr–Oct daily 6–11pm.

Mr. Eamon's Restaurant ✸ SEAFOOD/CONTINENTAL   This mom-and-pop place is an institution in Lahinch and one of those places you wish would move to your hometown. Eamon and Rita Vaughan's secret of success is knowing what they do best and running with it. In the kitchen, Eamon knows how to choose accent ingredients to make the most of simple fish: pan-fried turbot with a rosti crust, scallops in vermouth sauce, or perhaps fried monkfish fingers with tartar sauce. Starters, such as the warm St. Tola goat cheese with sesame seeds, are some of the most appetizing items on the menu, and desserts are mouthwatering, too. The atmosphere is bubbly, the service is great, and the crowd is content.

Kettle St., Lahinch, county Clare. ✆ **065/708-1050.** Reservations recommended. Main courses €12–€24 ($11–$21). AE, DC, MC, V. Apr–Oct daily 7–9:30pm.

DOOLIN'S TRADITIONAL MUSIC PUBS

Gus O'Connor's Pub   No discussion of Doolin is complete without mention of Gus O'Connor's. Situated in a row of thatched fishermen's cottages less than a mile from the roaring waters of the Atlantic, this simple pub beckons people from many miles around each evening. Besides its historic charm (it dates from 1832), its big draw is music, with an international reputation for Irish traditional music sessions. If your hunger extends beyond music, the pub serves meals, specializing in seafood. Doolin, county Clare. ✆ **065/707-4168.**

McGann's *Finds*   Sure, Gus O'Connor's has the farthest-reaching reputation, but it pays the price by being jammed with tourists. On many nights, you couldn't find a local inside there if your life depended on it. That's because the Irish are all just up the road, downing pints of Guinness and listening to just-as-wonderful traditional music at McGann's. Join them. Doolin, County Clare. ✆ **065/ 707-4133.**

11

Galway City

Ask an Irishman to recommend his favorite Irish city, and you're likely to hear, "Without a doubt, Galway." As one of Europe's fastest-growing cities, with a population of 61,000, Galway is a major city by Irish standards, yet it still manages to retain much of the accessibility and congeniality of a small town. Galway is perhaps the most prosperous city in Ireland and arguably the most immediately appealing.

As the home to many artists, writers, and artisans, and because it has a proliferation of art galleries and is the home to a lively arts scene, Galway has earned the reputation of the unofficial arts capital of Ireland. The excellent Galway Arts Festival, held every summer, is perhaps the most accessible and friendly culture fest in Europe. But while Galway attracts droves of outsiders, it does so without alienating its long-standing population. The result is a city that feels lived-in—a real place that, at the same time, accommodates (and charms) masses of visitors.

Galway City is billed as the "Gateway to the west," and that's exactly what it is—a welcoming, colorful doorway through which you pass on your way to the gigantic, melancholy solitude of Connemara and the western Gaeltacht. The city has a blessed location, tucked between the Atlantic and the grand expanse of Lough Corrib, which spreads out over 176 sq. km (68 sq. miles) and holds some of the world's best fishing. With 365 islands, the lake is said to have an island for every day of the year.

Like most ancient cities, Galway was founded because of its strategic access to water. It began as a fishing village, but after an invasion by the Anglo-Norman forces of Richard de Burgo in the early 13th century, Galway developed into a walled town. Elevation to city status followed with the granting of a royal charter by Richard III in 1484. Around this time, 14 wealthy merchant families ruled the city, giving Galway the nickname it still bears today—"City of Tribes." These families, mostly of Welsh and Norman origin, ruled the town as an oligarchy, and you still see storefronts and businesses bearing these names today: Athy, Blake, Bodkin, Browne, Darcy, Deane, Font, Ffrench, Joyce, Kirwan, Lynch, Martin, Morris, and Skerret. By far the most important name in medieval times was Lynch, whose clan gave the city not only its first mayor, in 1484, but 83 other mayors during the next 169 years.

In the center of town, on Shop Street, is **Lynch's Castle,** dating from 1490 and renovated in the 19th century. It's the oldest Irish medieval town house used daily for commercial purposes (it's now a branch of the Allied Irish Bank). The exterior is full of carved gargoyles, impressive coats of arms, and other decorative stonework. Walk northwest 1 block to Market Street, and you'll see the **Lynch Memorial Window** embedded in a wall above a built-up Gothic doorway. It commemorates the 16th-century Mayor James Lynch FitzStephen, who condemned his son to death for the murder of a Spanish merchant. After finding no one to carry out the deed, he acted as executioner. He later retreated into seclusion, broken-hearted. During the 170-year heyday of the tribes, Galway grew wealthy and cosmopolitan, with particularly strong trade links to Spain. Close to the city docks, you can still see the area where Spanish merchants unloaded cargo from their galleons. The **Spanish Arch** was one of four arches built in 1594, and the Spanish Parade is a small open square where visitors strolled in the evening. Local legend has it that Christopher Columbus attended mass at Galway's **St. Nicholas Collegiate Church** before setting sail for the New World in 1477. Originally built in 1320, the church has been enlarged, rebuilt, and embellished over the years. It has also changed denominations at least four times.

The hub of the city is a pedestrian park at Eyre Square (pronounced Air Square), officially called the John F. Kennedy Park in commemoration of his visit here in June 1963, just months before his assassination. A bust of JFK shares space in the park with a statue of a man sitting on a limestone wall—a depiction of Galway-born local hero Padraig O'Conaire, a pioneer in the Irish literary revival of the early 20th century and the epitome of a Galway Renaissance man.

From Eyre Square, it's a minute's walk to the medieval quarter and its festive, Left Bank atmosphere. What makes Galway particularly engaging is that this bohemian facet coexists so infectiously with the city's history. Despite Galway's population boom, the city core remains astonishingly similar to how it was in the Middle Ages. In fact, a street map from the 1700s would still get you around today!

All in all, Galway is a city bursting with life. Music is everywhere—wafting from pub entryways, lilting from the street musicians on seemingly every corner, and humming from milkmen on their rounds (yes, bottled milk is still delivered door-to-door here). Chances are that your only regret in visiting Galway will be not being able to stay longer.

Fun Fact **Souvenir Stories: The Claddagh Ring**

One of the most popular souvenirs to take home from Ireland is a Claddagh ring. It's story began in Galway, or more precisely, just over the Father Griffin Bridge, on the west bank of the River Corrib, in Claddagh. Claddagh is now a residential satellite to Galway, but in ancient times, it was a kingdom with its own royalty, laws, fleet, and customs. The people of Claddagh were descendants of early Gaelic families and spoke only Irish. The earliest known Claddagh ring was made in the 17th century.

The ring depicts two hands holding a heart topped by a crown. The hands represented friendship, the crown stood for loyalty, and the heart for love—the three ingredients, it was said, of a perfect marriage. Originally, the ring was a wedding band worn facing out for engagement and facing in for marriage. Though no longer widely worn as a wedding band, it is still frequently worn in Ireland by men and women as a friendship ring and makes a lovely memento of your trip to Ireland.

1 Orientation

Galway is 92km (57 miles) north of Shannon Airport, 219km (136 miles) west of Dublin, 105km (65 miles) northwest of Limerick, 209km (130 miles) northwest of Cork, and 193km (120 miles) north of Killarney

ARRIVING   Aer Lingus operates twice-daily service from Dublin into Galway Airport, Carnmore (© **091/755569;** http://fly.to/galway), about 16km (10 miles) east of the city. A taxi to the city center costs about €16 ($14); the occasional bus, if it coincides with your arrival, costs €4 ($3.55) and drops you off at Galway Rail Station.

Irish Rail trains from Dublin and other points arrive daily at **Ceannt Station** (© **091/564222;** www.irishrail.ie), off Eyre Square, Galway.

Buses from all parts of Ireland arrive daily at **Bus Eireann Travel Centre,** Ceannt Station, Galway (© **091/562000;** www.buseireann.ie).

As the gateway to West Ireland, Galway is the terminus for many national roads. They lead in from all parts of Ireland, including N84 and N17 from the north points, N63 and N6 from the east, and N67 and N18 from the south.

VISITOR INFORMATION   For information about Galway and the surrounding areas, contact or visit **Ireland West Tourism (Aras Fáilte),** Victoria Place, off Eyre Square (© **091/563081;** www.westireland.travel.ie). Hours are May, June, and September daily 9am to 5:45pm; July and August daily 9am to 7:45pm; October to April Monday to Friday 9am to 5:45pm, Saturday 9am to 12:45pm. For further detailed information on events in Galway, consult **www.galway.net**.

CITY LAYOUT   The core of downtown Galway lies between Eyre Square on the east and the River Corrib on the west. The main thoroughfare begins west of Eyre Square. Its name changes—from William to Shop, Main Guard, and Bridge—before it crosses the River Corrib and changes again. If that sounds confusing, don't worry. The streets are all short, well marked, and, with a map in hand, easy to follow.

GETTING AROUND   Galway has excellent local bus service. Buses run from the **Bus Eireann Travel Centre** (© **091/562000**) or Eyre Square to various suburbs, including Salthill and the Galway Bay coastline. The flat fare is €.90 (80¢).

There are taxi ranks at Eyre Square and all the major hotels in the city. If you need to call a cab, try **Abbey Cabs** (© **091/569369**), **Cara Cabs** (© **091/ 563939**), or **Galway Taxis** (© **091/561112**).

A town of medieval arches, alleyways, and cobblestone lanes, Galway is best explored on foot (wear comfortable shoes). Once you check in at your hotel or guesthouse, it's best to leave your car and tour by walking. (To see the highlights, follow the signposts on the Tourist Trail of Old Galway. A handy 32-page booklet, available at the tourist office and at most bookshops, explains the tour.) If you must bring your car into the center of town, park it and then walk. There is free parking in front of Galway Cathedral, but most street parking uses the disc system. It costs €.60 (55¢) for 1 hour; a book of 10 discs costs €5 ($4.45). Multistory parking garages average €1.50 ($1.35) per hour or €11 ($10) per day.

To rent a car, contact one of the following firms: **Avis Rent-A-Car,** Higgins Garage, Headford Road (© **091/568886**); **Budget Rent-A-Car,** Galway Airport (© **091/556376**); or **Murrays Rent-A-Car,** Headford Road (© **091/562222**).

FAST FACTS   If you need a drugstore, try **Flanagan's Pharmacy,** 32 Shop St. (© **091/562924**); **Matt O'Flaherty Chemist,** 16 William St. (© **091/561442;**

Galway City

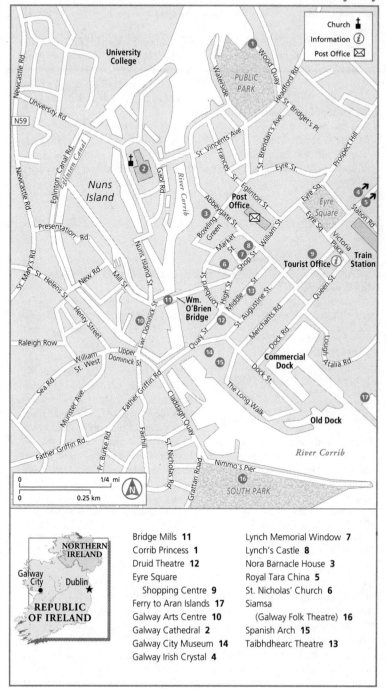

Church ✝
Information ⓘ
Post Office ✉

University College

PUBLIC PARK

Nuns Island

Post Office ✉

Eyre Square

Tourist Office ⓘ

Train Station

Wm. O'Brien Bridge

Commercial Dock

Old Dock

River Corrib

Nimmo's Pier

SOUTH PARK

0 — 1/4 mi
0 — 0.25 km

NORTHERN IRELAND

Galway City ● ★ Dublin

REPUBLIC OF IRELAND

Bridge Mills **11**
Corrib Princess **1**
Druid Theatre **12**
Eyre Square
  Shopping Centre **9**
Ferry to Aran Islands **17**
Galway Arts Centre **10**
Galway Cathedral **2**
Galway City Museum **14**
Galway Irish Crystal **4**

Lynch Memorial Window **7**
Lynch's Castle **8**
Nora Barnacle House **3**
Royal Tara China **5**
St. Nicholas' Church **6**
Siamsa
  (Galway Folk Theatre) **16**
Spanish Arch **15**
Taibhdhearc Theatre **13**

after hours 091/525426); or **Whelan's Chemist,** Williamsgate Street (© **091/ 562291**).

In an emergency, dial © **999. University College Hospital** is on Newcastle Road (© **091/580580**). There's also **Merlin Park Regional Hospital** (© **091/ 757631**). The local **Garda Station** is on Mill Street (© **091/563161**).

For information, gay and lesbian travelers might contact the **Galway Gay Help Line** (© **091/566134**), Tuesday and Thursday 8 to 10pm; **Galway Lesbian Line** (© **091/564611**), Wednesday 8 to 10pm.

For Internet access in Galway, try **Net Access,** in the heart of the city in The Olde Malte Arcade, High Street (© **091/569772;** www.netaccess.ie). **Hotlines**, 4 High St. (© **091/562838**), offers net access and low-cost international phone calls and is open 7 days a week. The **Galway Library/An Leabhar,** in the Hynes Building, Augustine Street (© **091/561666**), is open Monday 2 to 5pm, Tuesday to Thursday 11am to 8pm, Friday 11am to 5pm, Saturday 11am to 1pm and 2 to 5pm.

The **Post Office,** Eglinton Street (© **091/562051**), is open Monday to Saturday 9am to 5:30pm.

2 Where to Stay

VERY EXPENSIVE

Glenlo Abbey Hotel ★★★ About 3.2km (2 miles) outside of Galway on the main Clifden road, this secluded, sprawling stone hotel overlooks Lough Corrib in a tranquil, sylvan setting, surrounded by a 9-hole golf course. Dating from 1740, it was originally the ancestral home of the Ffrench and Blake families, two of the 14 tribes that ruled the city for centuries. It's been totally restored and has retained its grandeur in the public areas, which feature hand-carved wood furnishings, hand-loomed carpets, ornate plasterwork, and an extensive collection of Irish art and antiques. The guest rooms, which have lovely views of Lough Corrib and the countryside, are luxuriously decorated with traditional furnishings as well as marbled bathrooms.

> **Service Charges**
>
> *A reminder:* Unless otherwise noted, room rates don't include service charges (usually 10%– 15% of your bill).

Bushy Park, Galway, county Galway. © 091/526666. Fax 091/527800. www.glenlo.com. 46 units. €195–€310 ($174–$276) double. Suites also available. No service charge. Rates include full breakfast. AE, DC, MC, V. Free parking. **Amenities:** 2 restaurants (international, Continental); 2 bars; 9-hole golf course; fishing in Lough Corrib; concierge; room service; laundry service; drawing room. *In room:* TV, hair dryer, garment press, safe.

EXPENSIVE

Galway Great Southern Hotel ★★★ Dating from 1845, and built as a resting place for train travelers, this handsome five-story hotel is the grande dame of the Galway area. In the heart of the city, overlooking Eyre Square, its location couldn't be more central—next to the bus and rail station and within walking distance of all the major sights. The spacious public areas have high ceilings, elaborate plasterwork, crystal chandeliers, and original Connemara marble fireplaces. The guest rooms are elegant, with mahogany furnishings, half-tester beds, designer fabrics, and brass touches. Request a room overlooking Eyre Square for views of the whole city. The public areas are a favorite meeting place for Galwegians, and the hotel is always buzzing.

15 Eyre Sq., Galway, county Galway. © 800/44-UTELL in the U.S., or 091/564041. Fax 091/566704. www.gsh.ie. 106 units. €198–€240 ($176–$214) double. Rates include full Irish breakfast and service charge. AE, DC, MC, V. Street parking only. **Amenities:** Restaurant (seafood, Continental); bar; rooftop indoor swimming pool; sauna/steam room; concierge; room service; babysitting; laundry service. *In room:* TV, radio, tea/coffeemaker, hair dryer, garment press.

MODERATE/EXPENSIVE

Ardilaun House Hotel ✦   This Georgian-style country-house hotel takes its name from the Irish *Ard Oilean*, meaning "high island" and referring to a picturesque island nearby in Lough Corrib. Built in 1840 as a town house for a prominent Galway family, it has extensive gardens with ancient trees, set within a hilly residential section about 1.6km (1 mile) west of the downtown area. It has been expanded and updated in recent years, and most of the rooms are now housed in a modern three-story addition. They are very comfortably appointed with traditional furnishings and floral fabrics.

Taylor's Hill, Galway, county Galway. © 800/44-UTELL in the U.S., or 091/521433. Fax 091/521546. www.ardilaunhousehotel.ie. 90 units. €150–€200 ($134–$178) double. Rates include full Irish breakfast and service charge. AE, DC, MC, V. Closed Dec 22–28. Free parking. **Amenities:** Restaurant (Continental); bar; indoor swimming pool; gym; massage and beauty treatments; solarium. *In room:* TV.

Corrib Great Southern Hotel ✦   Set on high ground 3.2km (2 miles) east of the city, this contemporary five-story hotel offers panoramic views of Galway Bay, from its skylit atrium-style lobby to the wraparound windows in the public areas. Guest rooms are equally bright and airy, with lovely bay views, and are decked out in traditional furnishings and warm colors. This property is newer and more functional than its elegant sister hotel, the Galway Great Southern (see above), and attracts largely a business crowd.

Dublin rd. (N6), Galway, county Galway. © 800/44-UTELL in the U.S., or 091/755281. Fax 091/751390. www.gsh.ie. 180 units. €170–€230 ($151–$205) double. Rates include full Irish breakfast and service charge. AE, DC, MC, V. Free parking. **Amenities:** Restaurant (international); bar; indoor swimming pool; Jacuzzi; sauna/steam room; children's program (school holidays); concierge; room service; babysitting; laundry service; table tennis. *In room:* TV, dataport, tea/coffeemaker, hair dryer, garment press.

MODERATE

Brennans Yard Hotel ✦✦ *(Finds)*   One of the most clever restorations in Galway's historic area, right next to the Spanish Arch, this four-story stone building was formerly a warehouse. It has compact, skylit public areas enhanced by modern Irish art. Guest rooms overlook the city's Spanish Arch area and are decorated in a hip, contemporary style, with Irish pine furnishings, designer fabrics, and locally-made pottery. For a hotel that puts you in the center of Galway's vibrant nightlife and shopping, you can't beat this.

Lower Merchant's Rd., Galway, county Galway. © 800/44-UTELL in the U.S., or 091/568166. Fax 091/568262. www.brennansyardhotel.com. 45 units. €89–€133 ($79–$118) double. No service charge. Rates include full breakfast. AE, DC, MC, V. Free parking at nearby car park. **Amenities:** Restaurant (modern Continental), bar. *In room:* TV, tea/coffeemaker, hair dryer.

Killeen House ✦✦ *(Value)*   Catherine Doyle has always loved antiques, and in her handsome circa-1840 manor she has themed her guest rooms according to period: Art Deco, Victorian, Georgian, Edwardian, and Regency. Everything harmonizes very well, and there are no false notes—just a lot of design fun and a sense of quiet luxury. The decor in the rest of the house is equally aesthetic, with lots of grand, look-at-me pieces of furniture and high-backed chairs in the sitting room. Overall, this lovely house offers better value than you'd normally find at this price.

On N59, 6km (4 miles) from Galway, Bushy Park, Galway, county Galway. ☎ **091/524179.** Fax 091/528065. www.killeenhousegalway.com. 5 units. €120–€140 ($107–$125) double. No service charge. Rates include full breakfast. AE, MC, V. Closed Christmas. Free parking. **Amenities:** Sitting room. *In room:* TV.

INEXPENSIVE

Devondell 🎴🎴 *Value* You'd be hard-pressed to find a better budget B&B in Galway than Berna Kelly's much-lauded house in the Lower Salthill residential area, about 2.4km (1½ miles) from Galway's city center. It's a modern house, but guest rooms are spacious and done up with period furnishings and brass beds covered in superb, crisp Irish linens. The award-winning breakfasts are truly exceptional, offering everything from cereals and fresh fruit to yogurt and cheese to hash browns and kippers to eggs and French toast. Devondell is within walking distance of the seafront.

47 Devon Park, Lower Salthill, county Galway. ☎ **091/528306.** www.iol.ie/~devondel. 4 units. €62–€76 ($55–$68) double. No service charge. Rates include full breakfast. MC, V. Closed Dec–Feb. Free parking. **Amenities:** Sitting room. *In room:* TV.

Eyre Square Hotel 🎴 Just a block from the swish Galway Great Southern Hotel on Eyre Square (see above) is this great little find: a gently-priced hotel with a convenient address, spacious rooms, an accommodating staff, and a terrific traditional Irish breakfast. The decor is traditional Irish, with lots of dark wood and patterned carpet, but the place is kept in good condition with frequent refurbishments and feels well tended. This hotel and Jurys Inn (see below) have the most central locations of the recommended budget hotels.

Forster St., Galway, county Galway. ☎ **091/5696333.** www.byrne-hotels-ireland.com/eyresquare-hotel. htm. 4 units. €100 ($89) double. No service charge. Rates include full breakfast. MC, V. Street parking only. **Amenities:** Restaurant (Irish); bar. *In room:* TV, tea/coffeemaker.

Jurys Inn Galway 🎴 *Value* This relatively new four-story hotel opposite the Spanish Arch was designed in keeping with the area's historic character. Geared to the cost-conscious traveler, it was the first of its kind in downtown Galway, providing quality hotel lodgings at guesthouse prices. The real draw is the central location, right in the heart of things yet bounded on one side by an almost-lulling canal. The guest rooms, with expansive views of the river or nearby Galway Bay, are rather functionally decorated in contemporary "motel" style, with light-wood furniture and prints of Old Galway and Connemara.

Quay St., Galway, county Galway. ☎ **800/44-UTELL** in the U.S., or 091/566444. Fax 091/568415. www.jurys.com. 128 units. €68–€94 ($61–$84) double. No service charge. Prices may be higher at New Year's and in mid-July during the Arts Festival and Galway Races. DC, MC, V. Discounted parking at nearby car park. **Amenities:** Restaurant (international); bar; laundry service; nonsmoking rooms. *In room:* TV, tea/coffeemaker, hair dryer.

Knockrea Guest House 🎴 In operation since the 1960s, Knockrea is situated on a commercial street in Salthill, a 15-minute walk from Galway's city center and 5 minutes from the waters of Galway Bay. Eileen and Padraic Storan purchased the place in 1995, and since then, they've completely transformed the interior, bringing this cozy guesthouse up-to-date. The guest rooms are furnished in simple pine furniture with pine floors. There are two family rooms, which offer more space and two twin beds in addition to the double bed found in most rooms. Bathrooms are about the size of your average closet. Eileen Storan is an able and sympathetic host—she knows the area well, and helps her guests make the most of their time in Galway.

55 Lower Salthill, Galway, county Galway. ☎ **091/520145.** Fax 091/529985. www.galway.net/pages/ knockrea. 9 units (3 with shower only). €50–€90 ($45–$80) double. 25% reduction for children. Rates

include full breakfast. MC, V. Free parking. **Amenities:** 3 sitting rooms; use of kitchen; nonsmoking rooms. *In room:* TV.

Roncalli House ✱   The O'Halloran home is an exceptionally comfortable base for your explorations in Galway. Carmel and her husband, Tim, have been welcoming guests to their home for many years, and they're great hosts. A glowing fireplace takes the chill off cool evenings, and in good weather, guests can relax on the outdoor patio or in an enclosed sun porch at the front of the house. There are two ground-floor bedrooms and four others upstairs, all exceptionally clean and moderate to small in size, while bathrooms are quite compact. The breakfast is admirably diverse—oatmeal, French toast, and pancakes are among the plentiful options. Galway city is a 12-minute walk from the house.

24 Whitestrand Ave., Lower Salthill, Galway, county Galway. ✆ and fax **091/584159.** 6 units, all with shower only. €60 ($53) double. 20% reduction for children. Rates include full breakfast. MC, V. Free parking. **Amenities:** Conservatory; sitting room. *In room:* TV, tea/coffeemaker, hair dryer.

3 Where to Dine
EXPENSIVE

The Archway ✱✱ *Value* FRENCH   With a great location right across from the tourist office, just a stone's throw from Eyre Square, this excellent little restaurant is a temple of French country cooking. It's more formal than nearly every eatery in Galway's sea of casual bohemia, so it's perfect for a special night out. The menu reads like it was plucked straight from the Dordogne—lovely rack of lamb with *gratin dauphinois,* duck's liver fried in balsamic vinaigrette, steak with peppercorn sauce, a mouthwatering pan-fried fois gras with potato *galette,* magret of duck with Madeira sauce, and to finish things off, a delectable crème brûlée. The service is very good—if a tad stiff—and so is the value for your money.

Victoria Place, Galway, county Galway. ✆ **091/563693.** www.galway.net/pages/archway. Reservations recommended. Main courses €15–€25 ($13–$22). MC, V. Tues–Sat 12:30–2:30pm and 7–10pm.

deBurgos ✱ INTERNATIONAL   Named after one of Galway's most important Norman tribes, deBurgos is housed in what was originally the wine vault of a 16th-century merchant's house. Because of this, it has an impressive, cavelike interior—whitewashed walls, caverns, arches, turreted dividers, Oriental carpets, and medieval-style wall hangings—enhanced by flickering candles, fresh flowers, pink linens, and Irish music playing in the background. The imaginative menu offers dishes such as deBurgos three filets (pork, veal, and beef) on a confit of shallots and stuffed with farci of chicken, shrimp, and chervil cream sauce. There's an array of seafood as well as vegetarian offerings.

15/17 Augustine St., Galway, county Galway. ✆ **091/562188.** Reservations recommended. Main courses €15–€25 ($13–$22). AE, MC, V. Mon–Sat 6pm–midnight.

Kirwan's Lane ✱✱ CONTINENTAL   Chef-owner Michael O'Grady's stylish, inviting restaurant is one of the most-acclaimed in Galway. The dining room is rustic chic, with pine furnishings, a terra-cotta floor, and walls painted alternatively warm ocher and vivid red. It's a particularly good value at lunchtime, when the menu includes a nice starter of Irish brie crostini and marinated salmon roulade. The dinner menu features *mille-feuille* of fresh crab, stuffed breast of guinea fowl, and sautéed fresh monkfish.

Kirwan's Lane, Galway, county Galway. ✆ **091/568266.** Reservations recommended. Main courses €20–€25 ($18–$22). AE, MC, V. Daily 12:30–2:30pm and 6–10:30pm. Closed Sun Sept–June.

Finds **Picnic Fare Beyond Compare**

Sheridans Cheesemongers, 1 Kirwan's Lane (© **091/564829;** www.irish cheese.com), is *the* headquarters for putting together a gourmet movable feast. Myriad vats of gorgeous olives, mounds of fine Irish cheeses, baskets of crisp fresh loaves, savory arrays of sausages and sliced meats, and shelves of gourmet mustards, quince paste, eggplant caviar, and other delicacies all conspire to endanger the high chefs of Ireland. Open Monday to Saturday 9:30am to 6pm. If you're in town on Saturday morning, look for a Sheridans stand at the Galway Street Market, which forms around the walls of Saint Nicholas' Collegiate Church, a short walk away.

Park Room Restaurant ✿ SEAFOOD/CONTINENTAL   Just half a block east of Eyre Square, at the back of the Park House Hotel, this fine restaurant—sporting many awards, including the Galway Oyster Festival Best Seafood Award—has an old-world decor of stained glass, dark woods, oil paintings, and plants. Entrees include sirloin steak au poivre, roast duckling with peach and brandy sauce, fresh Carna scallops Mornay, and Dublin Bay prawns thermidor. As the awards testify, the seafood is particularly good here.

Forster St., Eyre Sq., Galway, county Galway. © **091/564924.** Reservations recommended. Main courses €18–€32 ($16–$28). AE, DC, MC, V. Daily 12:30–3pm and 6–10pm.

MODERATE

Nimmo's ✿✿ WINE BAR/CONTINENTAL   This is one of Galway's coolest, smartest tables—a place to see and be seen that manages to serve up fantastic food and still be fun. It's ideal for a festive, buzzy meal out. Pass the stone facade, climb a winding stairway, and you'll find yourself in one of the most romantic dining rooms in Galway, particularly on a starry night when you can see through the skylights. The menu changes according to season and tends to feature seafood in the summer and game during the winter. Start with the zesty fish soup or the smoked salmon salad, then move on to the delicious Parmesan chicken or beef bourguignon with a pile of fluffy mashed spuds. Save room for dessert, which is brought in by Goya's, the best bakery in Galway (see below). The wines are terrific, too.

Long Walk, Spanish Arch, Galway, county Galway. © **091/561114.** Reservations recommended. Main courses €12–€20 ($11–$18). MC, V. Tues–Sun 12:30–3pm and 7–10pm.

INEXPENSIVE/MODERATE

The Cobblestone ✿ VEGETARIAN   This is one of Galway's brightest fixtures on the cuisine scene, located on Galway's oldest medieval lane. Proprietor Kate Wright serves up excellent fresh salads, vegetarian soups, quiches, pastas, and innovations on classic dishes such as "beanie shepherd pie" and vegetable-and-walnut bake. Seafood and meats are also available as is a wide array of freshly baked croissants, breads, muffins, cakes, and cookies. This is a good place to know about when you're in the mood for a light meal or snack.

Kirwan's Lane, Galway, county Galway. © **091/567227.** Main courses €5–€14 ($4.45–$12). MC, V. Daily 10am–7pm.

Conlon ✿ SEAFOOD   If you love seafood, this is a good address to know. Conlon boasts approximately 20 varieties of fresh fish and shellfish at any given time. The house specialties are wild salmon and oysters. Entrees include grilled wild salmon, steamed Galway Bay mussels, and fishermen's platters (smoked salmon, mussels, prawns, smoked mackerel, oysters, and crab claws).

Eglinton Court, Galway, county Galway. © 091/562268. Seafood bar items €4–€8 ($3.55–$7.10); main courses €7–€20 ($6.25–$18); lobster thermidor €25 ($22). DC, MC, V. Mon–Sat 11am–midnight; Sun 5pm–midnight.

G.B.C. (Galway Bakery Company) ⋆ BISTRO   With a distinctive Old Galway shop-front facade, this building is two eateries in one: a ground-level self-service coffee shop and a full-service bistro upstairs. The restaurant menu lists a variety of dishes, priced to suit every budget, from steaks and seafood dishes to chicken Kiev or cordon bleu, as well as quiches, omelets, salads, and stir-fried vegetable platters. Baked goods, particularly the homemade brown bread, are an added attraction.

7 Williamsgate St., Galway, county Galway. © 091/563087. Coffee-shop items under €7 ($6.25); dinner main courses €8–€20 ($7.10–$18). AE, DC, MC, V. Coffee shop daily 8am–10pm; restaurant daily noon–10pm.

McDonagh's ⋆⋆ FISH AND CHIPS/SEAFOOD   For seafood straight off the boats, served up in an authentic maritime atmosphere, this is Galway's best choice. The place is divided into three parts: a traditional "chipper" for fish and chips, a smart restaurant in the back, and a fish market where you can buy raw fish. The McDonaghs, fishmongers for more than four generations, buy direct from local fishermen every day—and it shows; crowds line up every night to get in. The menu includes salmon, trout, lemon or black sole (or both), turbot, and silver hake, all cooked to order. In the back restaurant, you can crack your own prawns' tails and crab claws in the shell, or tackle a whole lobster.

22 Quay St., Galway, county Galway. © 091/565001. Reservations not accepted June–Aug. Main courses €8–€34 ($7.10–$30). AE, MC, V. Daily noon–10pm.

The River God Cafe ⋆ 𝘝𝘢𝘭𝘶𝘦 IRISH/CONTINENTAL   This is a rewarding destination for those with hearty appetites and modest budgets. The byword here is rib-sticking comfort food in a rustic setting. The casserole of cod and potatoes Connemara style, served in a wide, deep tureen, will put the color back into any hungry face. An equally lavish portion of wild mushroom tart with paprika potatoes will restore the vegetarian visitor. Other offerings include sheep-cheese Gouda with pesto and loin of pork with Guinness mustard sauce. A full lunch special at roughly €6.50 ($5.80) is an especially savory bargain here.

Quay St. (at Cross St.), Galway, county Galway. © 091/565811. Reservations not accepted. Dinner main courses €9–€16 ($8–$14). AE, DC, MC, V. Mon–Sat noon–10pm; Sun 4–10pm.

INEXPENSIVE

Da Tang Noodle House ⋆ CHINESE   The noodles at Da Tang are superlative. Bowls of homemade soup noodles are large and result in more than a few appreciative slurps. The broth, seasoned with fresh coriander and chiles, has a pleasant bite. Vegetables abound: carrot, mushroom, bamboo shoots, and shreds of Chinese cabbage are all cooked to crunchy perfection. Go for a midafternoon meal, when the service is admirably fast, making this a great place to nourish your noodle along with a steady stream of Galwegians looking for a quick, healthy lunch.

Middle St., Galway, county Galway. © 091/561443. Main courses €10–€14 ($8.90–$12). MC, V. Daily noon–10pm. Closed Sun off-season.

Goya's ⋆⋆ TEAROOM/BAKED GOODS   Goya's recently moved from its tiny spot on Quay Street to this bright, much more spacious venue. Its reputation for seductive pastries has followed, and the new cafe is every bit as crowded as the old, with Galwegians lining up for Emer Murray's pastries and desserts. The emphasis is on simplicity. You probably won't find anything unexpected, but everything is delightful. Stop in for tea and a scone, or buy a loaf of exceptional soda bread for lunch.

Kirwan's Lane, Galway, county Galway. ℂ **091/567010.** All items under €8 ($7.10). No credit cards. Mon–Sat 10am–6pm.

4 Attractions

Some of Galway's top attractions are outdoors and free of charge. Leading the list is Galway Bay. Additionally, no one should miss a stroll around the Spanish Arch and Spanish Parade, through Eyre Square and the John F. Kennedy Park, or along the banks of the River Corrib. Here are some of the top indoor attractions:

Galway Arts Centre ⭐⭐   Originally the town house of W. B. Yeats's patron, Lady Augusta Gregory, this building was for many years the offices of the Galway Corporation (Galway City's government offices). Now it's an arts center, offering an excellent program of concerts, readings, and exhibitions by Irish and international artists.

47 Dominick St. and 23 Nuns Island, Galway, county Galway. ℂ **091/565886.** Free admission to exhibits; concerts €3–€8 ($2.65–$7.10). Mon–Fri 10am–9:30pm; Sat 10am–5:30pm.

Galway Cathedral ⭐   Dominating the city's skyline, Galway Cathedral is officially known by the more unwieldy name of Cathedral of Our Lady Assumed into Heaven and St. Nicholas. Mainly in the Renaissance style, it's constructed of fine-cut limestone from local quarries, with Connemara marble floors. It was completed in 1965, after 8 years of building. Contemporary Irish artisans designed the statues, stained-glass windows, and mosaics. It's beside the Salmon Weir Bridge on the west bank of the River Corrib.

University and Gaol rds., Galway, county Galway. ℂ **091/563577.** Free admission; donations welcome. Daily 8am–6pm.

Galway City Museum ⭐   This little museum offers a fine collection of local documents, photographs, city memorabilia, examples of medieval stonework, and revolving exhibits.

Off Spanish Arch, Galway, county Galway. ℂ **091/567641.** Admission €1.30 ($1.15) adults, €.70 (60¢) students and children. Apr–Sept daily 10am–1pm and 2–5pm; Oct–Mar Tues–Thurs 10am–1pm and 2–5pm.

Galway Irish Crystal Heritage Centre ⭐⭐   Visitors to this distinctive crystal manufacturer are welcome to watch the craftsmen at work—blowing, shaping, and hand-cutting the glassware—as part of a great tour through the heritage center. Demonstrations are continuous on weekdays. The shop and restaurant are open daily.

East of the city on the main Dublin rd. (N6), Merlin Park, Galway, county Galway. ℂ **091/757311.** www. galwaycrystal.ie. Free admission. Guided tour €2.50 ($2.25) adults, €2 ($1.80) seniors and students, €1.30 ($1.15) children, €6.50 ($5.80) family. June–Aug Mon–Fri 9am–7pm, Sat 9am–6pm, Sun 10am–6pm; Sept–May Mon–Sat 9am–5:30pm, Sun 10am–5:30pm.

Nora Barnacle House ⭐   Opposite the St. Nicholas church clock tower, this restored 19th-century terrace house was once the home of Nora Barnacle, wife of James Joyce. It contains letters, photographs, and other exhibits on the lives of the Joyces and their connections with Galway.

Bowling Green, Galway, county Galway. ℂ **091/564743.** Admission €1.50 ($1.35). Mid-May to mid-Sept Mon–Sat 10am–5pm (closed for lunch), and by appointment.

Royal Tara China Visitor Centre ★★   One of Galway's oldest enterprises, this company manufactures fine bone china gift and tableware, distinguished by delicate shamrock patterns and designs inspired by the Book of Kells, the Tara brooch, and the Claddagh ring. The showrooms are quite beautiful, and the tearooms are a congenial place to rest. Look for the sign 1.6km (1 mile) east of Galway City, off the main Dublin road.

Tara Hall, Mervue, Galway, county Galway. ☎ 091/751301. www.royal-tara.com. Free admission and tours. Jan–June and Oct–Dec daily 9am–6pm; July–Sept daily 9am–9pm.

St. Nicholas' Collegiate Church ★★   It's said that Christopher Columbus prayed here in 1477 before setting out for the New World. Established about 1320, it has changed from Roman Catholic to Church of Ireland (Episcopal) and back again at least four times and is currently under the aegis of the latter denomination. Highlights include an authentic crusader's tomb dating from the 12th or 13th century, with a rare Norman inscription on the grave slab. In addition, there is a freestanding *benitier* (a holy-water bowl) that's unique in Ireland, as well as a carved font from the 16th or 17th century and a stone lectern with barley-sugar twist columns from the 15th or 16th centuries. The belfry contains 10 bells, some of which date from 1590. Guided tours, conducted by Declan O Mordha, a knowledgeable and enthusiastic church representative, depart from the south porch according to demand, except on Sunday morning.

Lombard St., Galway, county Galway. ☎ 091/564648. Free admission to church; donations of €2 ($1.80) adults, €1.30 ($1.15) seniors and students requested. Tours €3 ($2.70); reservations required. Mid-Apr to Sept Mon–Sat 9am–5:45pm, Sun 1–5:45pm; Oct to mid-Apr Mon–Sat 10am–4pm, Sun 1–5pm.

CRUISES & TOURS

Corrib Princess ★★   This 157-passenger, two-deck boat cruises along the River Corrib, with commentary on all points of interest. The trip lasts 90 minutes, passing castles, sites of historical interest, and assorted wildlife. There is full bar and snack service. You can buy tickets at the dock or at the *Corrib Princess* desk at the tourist office.

Woodquay, Galway, county Galway. ☎ 091/592447. Cruise €9 ($8) adults, €6.50 ($5.80) seniors and students, €3 ($2.70) children, €20 ($18) family. May, June, and Sept daily 2:30 and 4:30pm; July–Aug daily 12:30, 2:30, and 4:30pm.

Galway Panoramic ★★   These open-top buses are a great way to explore the highlights of Galway and its spectacular environs. They run all day in a loop, and when you see something you want to explore, you just hop off and hop back on when you want to. Or just stay on all day and get a feel for the way the city is laid out. The tour includes vistas of the western coast of Ireland, Galway Bay, and distant views of the Aran Islands (p. 399). Further details are available from the Galway Tourist Office.

Grayline/Guide Friday Irish City Tours, Galway, county Galway. ☎ 01/670-8822. Apr–Oct daily, with schedule varying according to demand. €9 ($8) adults, €6.50 ($5.80) students, €2.50 ($2.25) children.

5 Spectator Sports & Outdoor Pursuits

SPECTATOR SPORTS

GREYHOUND RACING   The hounds race year-round every Tuesday and Friday at 8:15pm at the **Galway Greyhound Track,** College Road, off Eyre Square (☎ **091/562273**). Admission is €4 ($3.55) and includes a racing card.

HORSE RACING   For 6 days at the end of July, thoroughbreds ply the track at the **Galway Racecourse,** Ballybrit (☎ **091/753870**), less than 3.2km (2 miles) east of town. Two-day race meetings are scheduled in early September and late October. Admission is €10 to €15 ($8.90–$13), depending on the event and the day of the week.

OUTDOOR PURSUITS

BICYCLING To rent a bike, contact **Celtic Cycles,** Queen Street (© **091/56 6606**), or **Richard Walsh Cycles,** Headford Road, Woodquay (© **091/565 710**).

FISHING Dotted beside the River Corrib, Galway City and nearby Connemara are popular fishing centers for salmon and sea trout. For the latest information on requirements for licenses and local permits, check with the **Western Regional Fisheries Board (WRFB),** Weir Lodge, Earl's Island, Galway (© **091/563118;** www.wrfb.ie). The extraordinarily accessible WRFB also provides free consultation for overseas anglers on where to go at different times of the season for salmon or trout, where to find the best *ghillies* (guides), and which flies and gear to use. Maps and brochures are available on request. For gear and equipment, try **Duffys Fishing,** 5 Main Guard St. (© **091/562367**); **Freeney Sport Shop,** 19 High St. (© **091/568794**); or **Great Outdoors Sports Centre,** Eglinton Street (© **091/562869**).

GOLF Less than 8km (5 miles) east of Galway is the 18-hole, par-72 championship **Galway Bay Golf & Country Club,** Renville, Oranmore, county Galway (© **091/790503;** www.gbaygolf.com). It charges greens fees of €55 ($49) weekdays, €60 ($53) weekends. Less than 3.2km (2 miles) west of the city is the 18-hole, par-69 seaside course at **Galway Golf Club,** Blackrock, Galway (© **091/522033**), with greens fees of €28 ($25) weekdays, €30 ($27) weekends.

HORSEBACK RIDING Riding enthusiasts head to **Aille Cross Equestrian Centre,** Aille Cross, Loughrea, county Galway (© **091/841216;** www.aille-cross.com), about 32km (20 miles) east of Galway. Run by personable Willy Leahy (who has appeared often on American television), this facility is one of the largest in Ireland, with 50 horses and 20 Connemara ponies. For about €16 ($14) an hour, you can ride through nearby farmlands, woodlands, forest trails, and mountain lands. Weeklong trail rides in the scenic Connemara region are another specialty, as is hunting with the Galway Blazers in the winter. For information on trail tours, in the United States call © **800/757-1667,** or check out **www.connemaratrail.com.**

6 Shopping

Galway offers malls of small shops clustered in some of the city's well-preserved and restored historic buildings. They include the **Cornstore** on Middle Street, the **Grainstore** on Lower Abbeygate Street, and the **Bridge Mills,** a 430-year-old mill building beside the River Corrib. **Eyre Square Centre,** the downtown area's largest shopping mall with 50 shops, has incorporated a major section of Galway's medieval town wall into its complex.

Most shops are open Monday to Saturday 9 or 10am to 5:30 or 6pm. In July and August, many shops stay open late, usually until 9pm on weekdays, and some also open on Sunday from noon to 5pm.

Here's a sampling of some of Galway's best shops.

ANTIQUES & CURIOS

Cobwebs   Established almost 25 years ago, this little shop is across from the Spanish Arch. It offers unique jewelry, antique toys, curios, and rarities from all parts of Ireland and beyond. 7 Quay Lane, Galway, county Galway. ℂ 091/564388.

The Winding Stair   Three floors crammed with antiques—just the place to pick up an Art Nouveau lamp, painted wooden chest, or church pew. 4 Mainguard St., Galway, county Galway. ℂ 091/561682.

BOOKS

Charlie Byrne's Bookshop   Prices are good in this mostly secondhand bookshop, specializing in paperback fiction and Irish-interest books. There are also some surprising finds to be had, with a fair selection of titles in archaeology, art history, the cinema, and music. The Cornstore, Middle St., Galway, county Galway. ℂ 091/561766. www.charliebyrne.com.

Hawkins House Bookshop   This shop stocks new books concentrating on Irish poetry, drama, fiction, history, art, archaeology, genealogy, mythology, and music. It also has a great selection of children's. It's beside St. Nicholas' Collegiate Church. 14 Churchyard St. (off Shop St.), Galway, county Galway. ℂ 091/567507.

Kenny's Book Shop and Galleries Ltd.   A Galway fixture for more than 50 years, this shop is an attraction unto itself. You'll find old maps, prints, engravings, and books on all topics—many on local history, as well as whole sections on Yeats and Joyce—are wedged on shelves and window ledges and piled in crates and turf baskets. Lining the walls are signed photos of more than 200 writers who have visited the shop over the years. In addition, Kenny's is famous for its antiquarian department, its bookbinding workshop, and an ever-changing gallery of local watercolors, oils, and sculptures. Enough goes on here to keep eight members of the Kenny family busy. Middle and High sts., Galway, county Galway. ℂ 091/562739. www.kennys.ie.

CRYSTAL, CHINA & SOUVENIRS

Moons   This is Galway's long-established midcity department store, with crystal, china, linens, and gifts, as well as clothing and household items. William St. (at Eglinton St.), Galway, county Galway. ℂ 091/565254.

Treasure Chest   For more than 25 years, this attractive shop with a Wedgwood-style exterior has been a treasure trove of top-quality crafts, fashions, and gifts. You'll find everything from Waterford crystal chandeliers to Royal Tara and Royal Doulton china, Irish Dresden figurines, Lladró figures, and Belleek china. It also carries Irish designer clothing, Aran knitwear, lingerie, and swimwear, not to mention touristy souvenirs such as hand-carved wooden leprechauns and Irish whiskey marmalade. 31–33 William St. and Castle St., Galway, county Galway. ℂ 091/563862.

HANDCRAFTS

Design Concourse Ireland   Don't miss potter Judy Green's exhibition shop for hand-thrown pottery painted by hand with Irish floral designs. Her wares include goblets, vases, candleholders, dinner and tea services, garden pots, cutwork lamps, miniatures, and jewelry. There is also craftware from other artisans here, and everything is in fabulous taste. Kirwan's Lane, Galway, county Galway. ℂ 091/566016.

Design Ireland Plus   Ceramics, pottery, linen, lace, jewelry, leather bags, rainwear, blankets, stationery, candlesticks, multicolored sweaters and capes, and handcrafted batik ties and scarves—all designed and made in Ireland—are sold here and at a second location on Lower Abbeygate Street. The Cornstore, Middle St., Galway, county Galway. (© 091/567716.

Kevin McGuire & Son   Housed in a whitewashed cottage and a gray stone building 1 block from Eyre Square, this specialty leather shop offers Celtic and modern handbags, briefcases, music cases, wallets, watch straps, belts, pendants, and sheepskin rugs. 3 Lyndon Court, Rosemary Ave., Galway, county Galway. (© 091/568733.

Meadows & Byrne   The Galway branch of this excellent housewares shop (with other branches in Dublin and Cork) features crafts from the most popular artisans in the country. You'll find earthenware pottery, hand-blown glass, woodenware, kitchen utensils and gadgets, textiles, tableware, scented beeswax candles, and Irish preserves and honey. Castle St., Galway, county Galway. (© 091/567776.

Twice As Nice   This charming, small shop is filled with fine white linens and cottons for the bedroom and dining room, as well as antique linens, Victorian nighties, and sumptuous christening gowns. Owner Deirdre Grundy started up this shop 19 years ago and has earned a cult following since. 5 Quay St., Galway, county Galway. (© 091/566332.

JEWELRY

Fallers of Galway   Dating from 1879, Fallers has long been a prime source of Claddagh rings, many of which are made on the premises. It also sells Celtic crosses, some inlaid with Connemara marble, as well as gold and silver jewelry and crystal. Williamsgate St., Galway, county Galway. (© 800/229-3892 in the U.S. (for catalogs), or 091/561226. www.fallers.com.

Hartmann & Son Lt.   The Hartmann family, which began in the jewelry business in the late 1800s in Germany, brought their skills and wares to Ireland in 1895, and opened this shop in 1942. They enjoy a far-reaching reputation as watchmakers, goldsmiths, and makers of Claddagh rings. The store also stocks Celtic crosses, writing instruments, crystal, silverware, and unusual clocks. It's in the heart of town, just off Eyre Square. 29 William St., Galway, county Galway. (© 091/562063. www.hartmanns.ie.

MUSIC & MUSICAL INSTRUMENTS

Mulligan   Mulligan's boasts that it has the largest stock of Irish and Scottish traditional records, CDs, and cassettes in Ireland. There is also a good selection of folk music from all over the world, including Cajun, Latin American, and African, as well as country music, blues, and jazz. 5 Middle St. Court, Middle St., Galway, county Galway. (© 091/564961.

P. Powell & Sons/The Music Shop   Opposite Lynch's Castle, where William Street meets Abbeygate Street, this shop is known for Irish traditional music. In addition to cassettes and CDs, it sells tin whistles, flutes, bodhrans, accordions, and violins, as well as sheet music and a full range of music books. The Four Corners, William St., Galway, county Galway. (© 091/562295.

TWEEDS, WOOLENS & CLOTHING

Mac Eocagain/Galway Woollen Market   This shop brims with traditional Aran hand-knits and colorful hand-loomed sweaters and capes, as well as linens, lace, sheepskins, jewelry, and woolen accessories. Each item has two prices, one including value-added tax (VAT) and one tax-free for non–European Union (EU) residents. 21 High St., Galway, county Galway. (© 091/562491.

O'Máille (O'Malley)   Established in 1938, this shop became famous in the 1950s for outfitting the entire cast of *The Quiet Man,* starring John Wayne and Maureen O'Hara, and has done a fabulous business ever since. It's synonymous with quality Irish tweeds, Irish-designed knitwear, and traditional Aran knits. There is always a good selection of sweaters, jackets, coats, suits, capes, kilts, caps, and ties. 16 High St., Galway, county Galway. © 091/562696. www.omaille.com.

7 Galway City After Dark

PUBS

An Pucan   A block east of Eyre Square, this old-fashioned nautical-theme pub is a great place to find some of the best Irish traditional music in Galway (daily from 9pm). It's also an Irish-language pub, where most of the patrons are native Irish speakers. 11 Forster St., Galway, county Galway. © 091/561528.

Busker Browne's   This relatively new pub and bistro has an Old Galway ambience, with alcoves and nooks and crannies, and offers a choice of bars. This is one of Galway's most mobbed spots, so secure your space early. Traditional music is performed throughout the week, and the place swings to Dixieland jazz on Sunday afternoons. Cross St., Galway, county Galway. © 091/563377.

Crane Bar   In the southwestern part of Galway, at the corner of an open market area called "the Small Crane," this rustic pub is known for its nightly musical entertainment. It gives special rates to fiddlers, pipers, singers, and banjo and accordion players who pass the "efficiency" test. From 9pm every night, there is country and western downstairs and traditional Irish tunes upstairs. 2 Sea Rd., Galway, county Galway. © 091/567419.

Hole in the Wall   Topped with a thatched roof, this sports pub stands out on a busy shopping street one block from Eyre Square. It has a low-beamed ceiling, open fireplaces, old sporting prints, and an old-fashioned jukebox. Cable TV screens show major sports events in this regular gathering spot for fans of Gaelic football and horse racing. Between the sports talk, traditional Irish music starts nightly in the summer at 9:30pm. 9 Eyre St., Galway, county Galway. © 091/565593.

O'Malley's   Claiming to be Galway's oldest music pub, this informal watering hole has traditional Irish and folk music sessions with special guests on Fridays from October to March, and music with dancing in the summer. 30 Prospect Hill, Galway, county Galway. © 091/564595.

The Quays   With an interior imported from a French medieval church, the Quays (pronounced "Keys") is a little treasure in the heart of the city, a half block from the Druid Theatre. It's full of tinted glass, carved wood, Gothic arches, and even pews. Evening music ranges from traditional Irish to '70s retro to Dixieland and usually starts at 9pm. Quay St. and Chapel Lane, Galway, county Galway. © 091/568347.

Rabbitt's   Dating from 1872, this pub is much the way it was a century ago. Old lanterns hang in the corners, skylights brighten the bar area, and pictures of Galway in horse-and-carriage days line the walls. Run by the fourth generation of the Rabbitt family, it's a block east of Eyre Square. 23–25 Forster St., Galway, county Galway. © 091/566490.

Tigh Neachtain (Naughton's) *(Finds)*   Voted one of the top-six pubs in Ireland by *Himself* magazine, this pub is what the Irish call "the genuine article." It is housed in one of the last buildings in Galway that date from the Middle Ages and is the only one with an intact oriel window. Inside, the place positively breathes atmosphere. The labyrinth of tiny snugs are over a century old, and the interior has scarcely been changed since 1894. A piece of local trivia: This was once the home of Richard Martin, a Galway politician and animal-rights activist known as "Humanity Dick." Today it's known for its theatrical and literary clientele and for its superb sessions of traditional Irish music. 17 Cross St., Galway, county Galway. ✆ 091/568820.

CLUBS

Like a late relay, the clubs take up at 11:30pm when the pubs leave off. The places to see and be seen are **Central Park,** 36 Upper Abbeygate St. (✆ **091/ 565976**); **Cuba,** Eyre Square (✆ **091/566135**), for seriously cool Latin jazz funk Saturday nights; and the **GPO,** Eglinton Street (✆ **091/563073**). In nearby Salthill, new dance clubs with hot guest DJs are popping up all the time. Two of the best are **Bogarts** (✆ **091/582357**), with its big dance floor and giant video screen, and the smaller, award-winning **Liquid** (✆ **091/522715**).

Zulu's Bar, Raven's Terrace (near Jury's Inn; ✆ **091/58124**), is Galway's first exclusively gay bar. Fridays and Saturdays are gay nights at **The Attic @ Liquid,** Liquid, Salthill (✆ **091/522715**).

A MEDIEVAL BANQUET

On the shores of Galway Bay, **Dunguaire** is a splendid 16th-century castle that features a medieval banquet with a literary-themed show. In south county Galway on Ballyvaughan Road (N67), Kinvara, the castle is a nightlife option for people staying in Galway City, just a half-hour's drive away (see "Side Trips from Galway City," below). The show features the work of Synge, Yeats, Gogarty, and other Irish writers who knew and loved this area. Banquets are staged in the summer months in keeping with demand and cost €40 ($36) per person. Reservations can be made at ✆ **061/361511.**

THEATERS

Druid Theatre Irish folk dramas, modern international dramas, and Anglo-Irish classics are the focus at this professional theater in the heart of Galway. Founded in 1975, the theater is located in a converted grain warehouse and configured with 65 to 115 seats, depending on the production. Lunchtime performances are often staged during the summer. The Druid Theatre Company, of international repute, is much in demand and frequently on tour, so make your plans well in advance. Box office hours are Monday to Saturday from noon to 8pm; evening shows start at 8pm. Chapel Lane, Galway, county Galway. ✆ 091/ 568617. www.druidtheatre.com. Evening tickets €11–€20 ($10–$18).

Siamsa, The Galway Folk Theatre This delightful blend of traditional Irish music, dance, and folk drama will definitely put you in the Celtic mood. If you wished that *Riverdance* would never end, here you'll discover that it hasn't. It's just over the Wolfe Tone Bridge in Claddagh, a 10-minute walk at most from Jurys. Box office hours are June through August, weekdays 10am to 5pm. Shows take place June through August, Monday to Friday at 8:45pm. Additional weekend shows are added depending on demand. Claddagh Hall, Nimmos Pier, Galway, county Galway. ✆ 091/755479. http://homepage.tinet.ie/~siamsa. Tickets €13–€16 ($12–$14).

Taibhdhearc Theatre Pronounced *Thive*-yark and officially known as *An Taibhdhearc na Gaillimhe* (the Theater of Galway), this is Ireland's national stage of the Irish language. Founded in 1928, it is a 108-seat, year-round venue for Irish plays and visiting troupes (such as ballet). In the summer, the theater presents *Spraci,* a program of traditional music, song, dance, and folk drama. The box office is open Monday to Saturday from 1 to 6pm (until 8pm on show nights); most shows start at 8pm. The Spraci program is performed July to August Monday to Friday at 8:45pm. Middle St., Galway, county Galway. © 091/ 563600. taibh@iol.ie. Tickets €14 ($12).

8 Side Trips from Galway City

THE ARAN ISLANDS

West from the mouth of Galway Bay, 48km (30 miles) out at sea, the storied **Aran Islands** ✿—**Inis Mór (Inishmore), Inis Meain (Inishmaan),** and **Inis Oirr (Inisheer)**—are outposts of Gaelic culture and language. Here the rugged islanders, immortalized in John Millington Synge's play *Riders to the Sea* and Robert Flaherty's film *Man of Aran,* maintain their hardscrabble traditional life, clinging like moss to the islands' harsh rocks and fishing from *currachs,* small craft made of tarred canvas stretched over a timber frame.

The island's 1,500 inhabitants live in stone cottages, often rely on pony-drawn transport, and speak Irish among themselves, breaking into English when necessary to converse with nonislanders. Inevitably, booming tourism has altered things somewhat, and many distinctively Aran traditions hang on more as curios than as everyday elements of life. Among them are *crios*—finger-braided belts made of colored wool that traditionally held up the islanders' heavy wool trousers, but are now more commonly made for the tourist trade. The classic hand-knit *bainin* sweaters that originated here are still worn, as there's nothing better for keeping out the chill. You'll see plenty of them, both on people's backs and in the islands' many woolen and craft shops.

Most visitors debark from the ferries at Kilronan, Inishmore's main town and possibly the easiest place in the world in which to arrange or rent transportation. The mode is up to you: Jaunting cars can be hailed like taxis as you step off the boat, minivans stand at the ready, and bicycle rentals are within sight.

The chief attraction on the Arans is **Dún Aengus** ✿✿, a stone cliff fortress on Inishmore that extends over more than 4.4 hectares (11 acres). Dating back 2,000 years, the fort is believed to have been of great significance. Less certain is what that significance was. Some think it was not a military structure at all, but rather a vast ceremonial theater. It's on the edge of a cliff that drops 90m (300 ft.) to the sea, and offers a spectacular view of Galway Bay, the Burren, Connemara, and (with sharp eyes and clear skies) the Blasket Islands. A Dún Aengus Interpretive Centre opened in 1999.

The new heritage center, **Ionad Arann,** Kilronan, Inishmore (© 099/ 61355), explores the history and culture of the islands. Exhibits examine the harsh yet beautiful landscape, the Iron Age forts, and the churches of the first Christians. In addition, the 1932 film *Man of Aran,* directed by Robert Flaherty, is shown six times daily. The center is open March to October daily 11am to 5pm. Admission to the center is €4 ($3.55) adults, €2.50 ($2.25) students, €2

Impressions

Some time ago, before the introduction of police, all the people of the islands were as innocent as the people here remain to this day. I have heard that at that time the ruling proprietor and magistrate of the north island used to give any man who had done wrong a letter to a jailer in Galway, and send him off by himself to serve a term of imprisonment.

—J. M. Synge (1871–1909), *The Aran Islands*

($1.80) seniors and children, €8 ($7.10) family. Discounted combination tickets to the center and film are available. The cafe serves soups, sandwiches, and pastries throughout the day.

Here are the best ways to arrange an excursion to the Aran Islands:

Aer Arann   The fastest way to get from the mainland to the Aran Islands is on this local airline, which departs from Connemara Airport, approximately 29km (18 miles) west of Galway City. Flight time is 10 minutes, and bus service between Galway City and the airport is available. You can book your flight at the Galway Tourist Office or at Aer Arann Reservations. A range of specials is usually on offer, combining flights with bus/ferry/accommodation, and so forth.

Connemara Airport, Inverin, county Galway. ✆ 091/593034. Fax 091/593238. www.aerarann.ie. Fare €44 ($39) adult round-trip, €25 ($22) child round-trip. MC, V. Daily Apr–Sept 9am, 10:30am, 4, and 5pm; Oct–Mar 9am, 10:30am, and 3pm.

Aran Island Ferries   This company, with a number of offices in Galway center, offers extensive year-round daily service to all three Aran Islands. Most boats leave from Rossaveal in Connemara, 37km (23 miles) west of the city for the 40-minute trip. Island Ferries provides coach connection service from its Victoria Place office 90 minutes before sailing time. During peak summer season, there are daily excursions from Galway Dock, which cost up to €6.50 ($5.80) more than tickets from Rossaveal. Inquire about times for the newest fast ferry in the fleet.

Victoria Place, off Eyre Sq., Galway, county Galway. ✆ 091/568903. Fax 091/568538. www.aranisland ferries.com. Round-trip fare €19 ($17) adults, €15 ($13) seniors and students, €10 ($8.90) children; family and group rates on request. From Rossaveal Nov–Mar daily 10:30am and 5:30pm; Apr–Oct 10:30am, 1:30, and 6:30pm. Additional sailings July–Aug according to demand.

O'Brien Shipping   The M.V. *Oileain Arann,* a 240-passenger, air-conditioned, three-deck ship launched in 1993, is the newest on the Galway–Aran Islands route. It has a full bar, snack bar, TV, and public telephone on board. Sailing time is 90 minutes. The booking office is at the Galway Tourist Office. Ask about discounts for seniors and children.

Galway Docks, Galway, county Galway. ✆ 091/567676. Fare €20 ($18) per person round-trip, €15 ($13) students, €10 ($8.90) one way interisland. From Galway Dock, June–Sept daily 10:30am; from Aran, June–Sept daily 5pm. Oct–May schedule varies.

WHERE TO STAY ON THE ARAN ISLANDS

Kilmurvey House ★★   This has been the place to stay on Inishmore since Dún Aengus fell into ruin. The 18th-century stone family home of the "Ferocious O'Flahertys" forms the core of this most hospitable and pleasant guesthouse, expanded to offer 12 diverse rooms, all quite comfortable and impeccably clean. Despite its origins, the spirit of the house could not be more gracious, thanks to Teresa Joyce's hospitality. An array of delights awaits you at breakfast, and an optional four-course dinner is served at 7pm with advance reservation. Kilmurvey House lies just below Dún Aengus, Inishmore's prime attraction. A handful of shops, cafes, and restaurants, as well as a "blue flag" (that is, pristine) white-sand beach, are within a short stroll.

8km (5 miles) from the ferry on the coast rd., Kilmurvey, Kilronan, Inis Mór, Aran Islands, county Galway. ✆ 099/61218. Fax 099/61397. 12 units. €70 ($62) double. Rates include full breakfast. MC, V. Closed Nov–Easter. **Amenities:** Sitting room.

Radharc An Chlair ★ *Finds*   Leaving the ferry and trodding onto tiny Inisheer, you're met by Peadar Poil and given a lift up to the house—wait for it—on his tractor. Peadar's wife, Brigid, runs a spit-and-polish B&B operation and the guest rooms are all very comfortable and cozy. She is also a superb cook and a terrific baker, so even a scone and a cup of tea is a real pleasure. For those who find Inishmore a bit too busy and touristy (as it can be in the summer), think about hopping over here for the ideal of Aran.

Inis Oirr, Aran Islands, county Galway. (**099/61218.** Fax 099/61397. 6 units. €50 ($45) double. Rates include full breakfast. MC, V. Closed Nov–Easter. **Amenities:** Sitting room.

WHERE TO DINE ON THE ARAN ISLANDS

Man of Aran CONTINENTAL ★★ If the Man of Aran restaurant looks familiar, it may be because you just saw it in the film at the Heritage Centre. It is the traditional thatched seaside cottage constructed in 1934 for the filming of *Man of Aran.* The resemblance stops there, however—the Man himself never for one day ate as well as you will here. After years of culinary training and experience in London, Maura Wolfe returned to Aran with her husband, Joe, and created one of the island's great surprises. It's a first-class restaurant drawing upon the organic vegetables and herbs grown with great toil in their garden. Maura conjures each day's menu on the spot, inspired by what is fresh and available from the sea and from the soil just beyond her front door. The result is exquisite home cooking, perfect, simple, and without pretense. Tables are limited, especially in the separate nonsmoking room. If you can't stay for dinner, at least stop by for lunch. B&B accommodations are also available for €68 ($60) double. Though the cottage remains rustic and true to the film, the three guest-rooms are quite comfortable and homey, with whitewashed walls, simple pine furnishings, and character galore.

Kilmurvey, Kilronan, Aran Islands, county Galway. (**099/61301.** Reservations required for dinner. Fixed-price dinner €25 ($22). No credit cards. Mon–Sat 12:30–3pm and 7:30–10pm.

OYSTER COUNTRY

On the main road south (N18) of Galway are two small fishing villages, **Claren-bridge** and **Kilcolgan.** Each year at the end of September, the villages host the annual **Galway Oyster Festival.** Launched in 1954, the 5-day festival is packed with traditional music, song, dancing, sports, art exhibits, and, above all, oyster-tasting events and oyster-opening competitions. A Galway beauty is crowned "Oyster Pearl," and she reigns over the festival. Even if you can't be there for the festival, you can enjoy some of Ireland's best oysters during any month with an "r" in it—that is, September through April.

If you continue south on N18 for another 16km (10 miles), you'll see signs to **Coole Park** ((**091/631804**). Irish red deer, pine martens, red squirrels, and badgers inhabit this national forest. **Coole House** was once the home of Lady Augusta Gregory, dramatist and folklorist. With W. B. Yeats and Edward Martyn, she founded the Abbey Theatre. Her house no longer stands, but an "autograph tree" bears initials carved by George Bernard Shaw, Sean O'Casey, John Masefield, Oliver St. John Gogarty, W. B. Yeats, and Douglas Hyde, the first president of Ireland. The restored courtyard has a visitor center, tearooms, picnic tables, and a garden with nature trails that run to the lake. Admission is €2.50 ($2.25) adults, €2 ($1.80) seniors, €1.30 ($1.15) students and children, and €6.50 ($5.80) family. It's open mid-April to mid-June, Tuesday to Sunday 10am to 5pm; mid-June to August, daily 9:30am to 6:30pm; September, daily 10am to 5pm. Last admission 1 hour before closing.

In Gort, also on the N18, is **Thoor Ballylee** ((**091/631436**). This restored 16th-century Norman tower house was the summer home of the Nobel Prize–winning poet William Butler Yeats. Yeats described the house as "a tower set by a stream's edge"; it served as the inspiration for his poems "The Winding Stair" and "The Tower." In the interpretive center, an audiovisual presentation examines the poet's life. Also on the grounds are the original Ballylee Mill, partially restored, and a bookshop specializing in Anglo-Irish literature. Admission is €5 ($4.45) adults, €4 ($3.55) seniors and students, €1.30 ($1.15) children. It's open from Easter to September daily 10am to 6pm. There's a seasonal **Tourist Information Office** (© **091/631436**) located here, open May to September daily 10am to 6pm.

West off the main road, between Gort and Kilcolgan, is **Dunguaire Castle**, Kinvara (© **061/360788**). On N67 just east of Kinvara, this tower house and *bawn* (fortified enclosure) sits on the south shore of Galway Bay. It was erected in the 16th century by the O'Heynes family at the royal seat of the 7th-century King Guaire of Connaught. The castle was later the country retreat of Oliver St. John Gogarty, Irish surgeon, author, poet, and wit. The castle's greatest appeal is the view from its battlements of the nearby Burren and Galway Bay. Admission is €4 ($3.55) adults, €2.50 ($2.25) seniors and students, €2 ($1.80) children, and €10 ($8.90) family. It's open daily from mid-April through September 9:30am to 5:30pm. Medieval banquets also take place here on summer evenings (p. 398).

WHERE TO EAT OYSTERS

Moran's Oyster Cottage ★★ SEAFOOD Presidents, prime ministers, movie stars, and locals who know their fish make a point of finding their way here. The food is simply legendary. For six generations, the Morans have been catching salmon and shucking oysters and preparing them to perfection here on the weir. In 1960, Willie Moran caught 105 wild salmon in a single day on the Dun Killen River in front of the family pub, and went on to win the world title in oyster opening. Two of his staff members, Vincent Graham and Gerry Grealish, are also world champions. The wild smoked salmon is exquisite—sheer velvet. Willie Moran believes in a small menu, fresh and wild and with nothing in the way. Ambience? It's a thatched cottage with 36 swans and a blue heron outside the front door. It's rustic, but a helluva nice place to eat oysters.

The Weir, Kilcolgan, county Galway. © **091/796113**. Main courses €5–€20 ($4.45–$18). AE, MC, V. Mon–Sat 10:30am–11:30pm, Sun noon–11:30pm.

Paddy Burke's ★ SEAFOOD Platters of local oysters and mussels are served throughout the day at this homey tavern, with its lemon color and thatched roof. You can pick your favorite spot to relax in the half-dozen rooms and alcoves with original stone walls, open fireplaces, pot-bellied stoves, fishing nets on the walls, and traditional *sugan* chairs (wood chairs with twisted straw rope seats). In good weather, there is seating in a back garden. Lunch and snack items range from seafood soups and chowders to sandwiches, salads, and omelets. In the evening, you can also order full meals, with choices such as Atlantic plaice and crab with prawn sauce, honey roast duck with mead sauce, and medallions of beef with whiskey and mustard. The tavern is on the main road, 16km (10 miles) south of Galway City.

Ennis-Galway rd. (N18), Clarenbridge, county Galway. © **091/796226**. Reservations recommended for dinner. Main courses €10–€20 ($8.90–$18). AE, DC, MC, V. Mon–Sat 10:30am–10:30pm, Sun noon–9:30pm.

SHOPPING

Clarenbridge Crystal and Fashion Shop This shop features all types and styles of Clarenbridge crystal, a local glass product hand-cut, engraved, and decorated at a factory 1.6km (1 mile) away. You'll also find a beautiful range of classic quality ladies' fashions and men's country clothing, framed prints, watercolors, and jewelry. Open Monday to Saturday from 9:30am to 6pm, Sunday from noon to 6pm. N18, Clarenbridge, county Galway. © **091/796178**. 16km (10 miles) south of Galway City. Mon–Sat 9:30am–6pm, Sun noon–6pm.

12

Out from Galway

Along the rocky western coast of Ireland, Galway is the country's second-largest county, forming (with Mayo, see chapter 13) the heart of the province of Connaught. The area northwest of Galway City is one of Ireland's most spellbinding landscapes—a combination of bogland, heather-clad moors, rocky hillocks, and everywhere the most fantastic light you may ever witness in your travels. In the heyday of the "Island of Saints and Scholars," the remote and rugged Connemara region was favored by early Christian monks for their awe-inspiring beauty and isolation. Important monasteries were founded on islands like Inishboffin, Inishshark, High Island, and Omey Island. Today, no fewer than 17 islands off the Connemara coast have monastic remains.

Yet, ironically, for a landscape that inspires so much serenity, medieval history was particularly unkind to this part of Ireland. In the 17th century, after the merciless Oliver Cromwell and his armies ravaged everything in their path, he famously told the native Irish to go "to hell or to Connaught." It was effectively a condemnation to destitution, and for many it was a

death sentence. While English landlords divvied up Ireland's most fertile lands, Connaught was so barren, so uncultivable, so desolate, that nobody could hope for better than to eke out a impoverished existence on minute, rock-infested farms. It was also here, where it seemed people had little left to lose, that the Great Famine of 1845–49 took its largest toll. Masses of people either starved or took off on ships sailing west, never to return. Haunting reminders can still be found in the many deserted farms and villages that are scattered throughout Connemara.

History aside, this moody, melancholy, magical outpost is stunningly beautiful—a fact you can appreciate if you don't have to eat the scenery to survive. It is indeed a feast of eye candy, and, as it happens, the feast provides for everyone, because tourism is bringing prosperity to the west that the potato never did. If you're concerned that there might be too much tourism here, well, you shouldn't be. It's a destination that seems to swallow people; no matter how many visitors come, the solitude is always vast and healing.

1 The Galway Bay Coast

It's certainly a pleasure to drive up the majestic, spectacular Galway Bay coast, with the Aran Islands sitting 48km (30 miles) out at sea to your left like three giant whales at rest, and the heather-clad stony foothills of Connemara to your right. Departing Galway, and certainly once you pass Spiddal, you have the sense of passing through a gateway into Ireland's wild west, a land strikingly remote, melancholy, and moody in contrast to the exuberance of Galway. Count on it taking about 40 minutes from Galway to Rossaveel, and another 40 minutes to Carna.

GALWAY BAY COAST ESSENTIALS

GETTING THERE & GETTING AROUND   The best way to see the sights along the Galway Bay coast is to drive. From Galway City, follow the coast road (R336). From Galway City to Inverin, it's about 32km (20 miles).

VISITOR INFORMATION   Contact or visit **Ireland West Tourism,** Aras Fáilte, Victoria Place, Galway, county Galway (✆ **091/563081;** www.west ireland.travel.ie). It's open year-round; see p. 384 for hours. Seasonal offices, open from late May to mid-September, are at Clifden (✆ **095/21163**) and Salthill (✆ **091/563081**).

EXPLORING THE COAST

Head west from Galway, following signs for the coast road (R336). Within 3.2km (2 miles), you'll be in **Salthill,** a modern beach resort that is a summer mecca for Irish families and that is somewhat reminiscent of the New Jersey shore in the United States. It has a boardwalk and a fine beach, plus lots of bars, fast food, amusement rides, and game arcades. You will likely prefer to continue on this scenic road to little towns like **Barna** and **Spiddal,** both of which are Irish-language towns. Spiddal, 19km (12 miles) west of Galway City, is also an ideal spot to shop for locally made Aran knit sweaters and other handcrafts produced by the people in the surrounding cottages.

The road continues as far as **Inverin,** then turns northward, with signposts for **Rossaveal.** From Rossaveal, you can make the shortest sea crossing from the Galway mainland to the Aran Islands (see "Side Trips from Galway City" in chapter 11). You might want to combine this coastal drive with a trip to the islands.

If you continue on R336, you'll leave the Galway Bay coast and travel past the rocky and remote scenery approaching the center of Connemara. **Casla (Costelloe)** is the home of Raidio na Gaeltachta, the Irish-language radio station, and **Rosmuc** is the site of the **Padraic Pearse Cottage.** This simple thatched-roof structure served as a retreat for Dublin-based Pearse (1879–1916), who was one of the leaders of Ireland's 1916 Rising. He used his time here to improve his knowledge of the Irish language. Now a national monument, the cottage contains documents, photographs, and other memorabilia. Admission is €1.30 ($1.15) for adults, €.90 ($80¢) for seniors, €.50 (45¢) for students and children, and €4 ($3.55) for families. It's open from mid-June to mid-September, daily 9:30am to 6:30pm (last admission 45 min. before closing).

At this point, you can continue north into the heartland of Connemara or retrace your route back to Galway, setting out afresh the next day for Connemara.

SHOPPING

Ceardlann an Spideil/Spiddal Craft Village   Overlooking Galway Bay, this is a cluster of cottage shops where craftspeople ply their trades. You're welcome to browse around and watch crafts being made. The selection includes pottery, weaving, knitwear, silk-screen printing and design, jewelry, and wood turning. The art galleries feature original hand-carved stone crafts, sculpture, paintings, prints, posters, and cards, and there's a very good coffee shop on the premises. For a snack, lunch, or light meal, **Jackie's Bistro,** in a rustic cottage at the Craft Village, offers highly-recommended fare. The shops are open Monday to Saturday from 9:30am to 6:30pm and Sunday from 2 to 5:30pm in July and August; and Monday to Saturday from 9:30am to 5:30pm September through June. Coast Rd., Spiddal, county Galway. ✆ 091/553041.

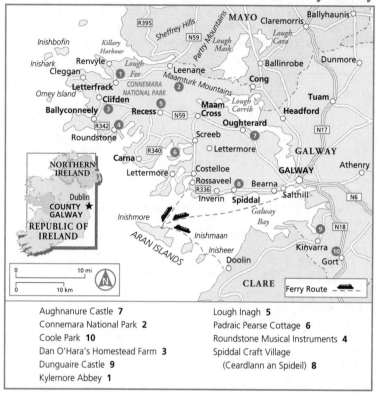

Aughnanure Castle **7**
Connemara National Park **2**
Coole Park **10**
Dan O'Hara's Homestead Farm **3**
Dunguaire Castle **9**
Kylemore Abbey **1**

Lough Inagh **5**
Padraic Pearse Cottage **6**
Roundstone Musical Instruments **4**
Spiddal Craft Village
  (Ceardlann an Spideil) **8**

Standun   A fixture on the Connemara coast since 1946, this shop has long been known as a good source for authentic bainin sweaters, handcrafted by local women from the nearby Aran Islands and the surrounding Connemara countryside. Recently enlarged, it also offers colorful knits, tweeds, sheepskins, linens, glassware, china, pottery, jewelry, books, and maps. In addition, there's a wide-windowed cafe that faces Galway Bay and the Aran Islands. Open from March to December, Monday to Saturday from 9:30am to 6:30pm. Coast Rd., Spiddal, county Galway. ⓒ 091/553108.

SPORTS & OUTDOOR PURSUITS
FISHING   Rimmed by the waters of Galway Bay and the Atlantic, this area is prime territory for sea fishing, especially for mackerel, pollock, cod, turbot, and shark. To locate a boat-hire service in the area where you plan to stay, contact the **Western Regional Fisheries Board,** the Weir Lodge, Earl's Island, Galway (ⓒ **091/563118;** fax 091/566335; www.wrfb.ie), for recommendations. The cost per person per day, including permit, rods, reels, and bait, is likely to average €52 to €65 ($46–$59).

For those who prefer trout fishing, there's **Crumlin Fisheries,** Inverin, county Galway (ⓒ **091/593105**). This fishery has a lake stocked with sea-reared rainbow trout and allows two fish per person to be taken per day. Prices range from €14 ($12) for fishing from the bank to €34 ($30) for fishing with a boat;

ghillies (guides) are available for €35 ($31) extra. Fishing starts at 9am daily; reservations must be made at least a day in advance.

SWIMMING The Silver Strand at Barna and the beach at Spiddal are clean, sandy, and ideal for swimming.

WHERE TO STAY
MODERATE/EXPENSIVE
Connemara Coast Hotel 🏰🏰 Only 9.7km (6 miles) west of Galway City and with Galway Bay at it's back door, this place has a lot going for it. Recently refurbished and expanded, the guest rooms are decorated in bold, tweedy plaids—that look smart, not frumpy—and each has a picture-window view of the water. Most have views of the Aran Islands or Clare hills, and some have turf-burning fireplaces and private verandas. The pub, Sin Sceal Eile (meaning "That's Another Story"), was named the 1998 Irish hotel bar of the year and offers traditional entertainment nightly in summer and on weekends the rest of the year.

Coast Rd., Furbo, county Galway. ✆ **091/592108.** Fax 091/592065. www.sinnotthotels.com/connemara. 112 units. €140–€200 ($125–$178) double. Suites also available. No service charge. Rates include full breakfast. AE, DC, MC, V. **Amenities:** Restaurant (Continental); bar; indoor swimming pool; 2 tennis courts; gym; Jacuzzi; steam bath; nonsmoking rooms. *In room:* TV, tea/coffeemaker.

INEXPENSIVE
Cloch na Scíth, Kellough Thatched Cottage 🏰 If you want more than a touch of charm and authenticity on the shores of Galway Bay, this place is right up your alley. The trio of guest rooms in Nancy Hopkins Naughton's centuries-old thatched farmhouse are warm and welcoming, with antique pine furniture, polished wood floors, and patterned quilts. The whole house is open to guests and is full of antiques and keepsakes from many generations of Naughtons. Tomas Naughton, Nancy's husband, is both a talented painter and an all-Ireland *sean-nos* (traditional a cappela Gaelic) singer; guests are often treated to traditional Irish sessions around the fire in the evening. As an afternoon snack, Nancy bakes a fresh corn cake in the open hearth each day and leaves it out for her guests, who have included an appreciative Julie Christie. A small sandy beach is minutes away by foot.

> ### Service Charges
> *A reminder:* Unless otherwise noted, room rates don't include service charges (usually 10%–15% of your bill).

In addition, there is an inviting **self-catering thatched stone cottage,** built by Tomas's great-grandfather. It rents for €200 to €420 ($178–$374) per week, depending on the season. It has two bedrooms, a kitchen-dining-living room with a wood stove, a spacious sunroom, and 1½ bathrooms.

15km (9 miles) from Galway center, just east of Spiddal, Coast Rd., Kellough, Spiddal, county Galway. ✆ **091/553364.** 3 units. €54 ($48) double. Rates include full breakfast. No credit cards. **Amenities:** Non-smoking rooms. *In room:* No phone.

WHERE TO DINE
Boluisce 🏰🏰 SEAFOOD The name of this restaurant comes from an old Irish phrase meaning "patch of grazing by the water." The draw here is delicious and fresh seafood—scallops, prawns, lobster, smoked salmon, and crab plate. The West Coast platter includes prawns, crab, lobster, mussels, and salmon. The house chowder is a meal in itself, brimming with salmon, prawns, monkfish, mussels, and more. Home-baked brown bread, made with whole meal, bran,

---

Impressions

I have a total irreverence for anything connected with society except that which makes the roads safer, the beer stronger, the food cheaper, the old men and old women warmer in the winter and happier in the summer.
—Brendan Behan (1923–64)

---

and buttermilk, accompanies every meal; it's rich and nutty, and genial proprietor John Glanville will gladly share the recipe with you.

Coast Rd., Spiddal, county Galway. © **091/553286.** Reservations recommended. Dinner main courses €10–€25 ($8.90–$22). AE, DC, MC, V. Daily 12:30–10pm.

Twelve Pins SEAFOOD   Named for the famous mountain range of Connemara, this old-world roadside inn is a good place to come for fresh oysters or a seafood platter (oysters, mussels, smoked salmon, and prawns). Other creatively prepared seafood choices include scallops en croûte and trout *Oisin* (stuffed with almonds and seafood). For non-fish-eaters, the menu offers a traditional roast of the day, plus steaks, rack of lamb, duckling, vegetarian stir-fry, and lasagna.

Coast Rd., Barna, county Galway. © **091/592368.** Reservations recommended. Dinner main courses €9–€20 ($7.10–$18). AE, MC, V. Daily 12:30–3pm and 6:30–10pm.

2 Connemara

If you look at an average map or road sign, you won't see a marking or directions for Connemara, because it's not a city or town or county, but rather an area or region, like the Burren in county Clare. In general, Connemara constitutes the section west of Galway City, starting at Oughterard and continuing toward the Atlantic. It is an area of astounding barrenness and beauty.

Connemara is the Anglicization of *Conmaicne mara,* the "descendants of Conmac by the sea." One could say that there are two Connemaras. South of the Galway-Clifden road, you'll find a vast bog-mantled, granite moorland sown with innumerable lakes, and with a low indented coastline that is a labyrinth of land and sea. North of the Galway-Clifden road, the tall quartzite domes and cones of the Maum Turks and the Twelve Bens rise steeply, while other mountains, formed of schist and gneiss, continue the highlands northward to the beautiful Killary fjord—the only fjord in the British Isles—where Mayo replaces Galway. "Connemara is a savage beauty," Oscar Wilde once remarked. And he was right.

CONNEMARA AREA ESSENTIALS

GETTING THERE & GETTING AROUND   From Galway City, **Bus Eireann** (© **091/562000;** www.buseireann.ie) provides daily service to Clifden and other small towns en route. The best way to get around Connemara is to drive, following N59 from Moycullen and Oughterard. Or you can take a guided tour (see "Sightseeing Tours," below). Clifden is 65km (40 miles) west of Galway City.

VISITOR INFORMATION   Contact or visit **Ireland West Tourism,** Aras Fáilte, Victoria Place, Galway, county Galway (© **091/563081;** www.west ireland.travel.ie). Open May, June, and September daily 9am to 5:45pm; July and August daily 9am to 7:45pm; October to April Monday to Friday 9am to 5:45pm, Saturday 9am to 12:45pm. The **Oughterard Tourist Office,** Main Street, Oughterard (© **091/552808**), is open year-round, Monday to Friday from 9am to 5pm, with extended hours in the summer season. In addition, a

---

Impressions

Constantly the heart releases
Wild geese to the past
Look, how they circle poignant places.
                              —Thomas Kinsella (b. 1928): "A Lady of Quality"

---

seasonal office, open Monday to Saturday 9am to 5pm between March and October, is maintained at Clifden (℃ **095/21163**).

EXPLORING THE AREA

The "capital," or largest town in Connemara, is **Clifden.** The road marked N59 takes you around the heart of Connemara and then to county Mayo. You can also follow many of the smaller roads and wander around Connemara for days. Many people stay in this region for a week or so, usually basing themselves in one or more of the fine resorts and inns that dot the countryside, especially in places like **Cashel, Ballynahinch, Renvyle,** and Clifden.

In recent years, Clifden has exploded into a major tourist center, and it shows. B&Bs, pubs, and shops arm wrestle for space in the town center, which for the first time in its history is experiencing gridlock. Even so, it remains an attractive town, whose past and present can be seen on the two sides of its buildings— their backs gray and worn, their fronts bright and alluring.

Better yet, for a slower, more intact taste of Connemara town life, give the small, active fishing port of **Roundstone** ⭐ a try. Roundstone is definitely on the move and already has all of the essentials: glorious, pristine beaches; comfortable guesthouses; good restaurants; quality galleries and shops; and more than its share of natural charm. It's not exactly a secret, but for the time being it is blessedly just off the well-beaten track.

Another untrammeled Connemara treasure lies 11km (7 miles) offshore. A day spent on the island of **Inishbofin**—provided the weather is on your side— is one you'll not soon forget. (See "An Excursion to Inishbofin," below.)

Little bays and inlets, small harbors, and beaches dot the coastline. At almost every turn are lakes, waterfalls, rivers, and creeks, while a dozen glorious mountains, known as the **Twelve Bens** (sometimes called the Twelve Pins), rise at the center. All of this is interspersed with rock-strewn land and flat fields of open bog, rimmed with gorse and heather, rhododendrons, and wildflowers. The tableau presents a dramatic panorama of sea and sky, land and bog.

Connemara's **boglands** began forming 2,500 years ago. During the Iron Age, the Celts preserved their butter in the bog. Today, with one-third of Connemara classified as bog, the turf (or peat) that's cut from the bog remains an important source of fuel. Cutting and drying turf is an integral part of the rhythm of the seasons in Connemara. Cutting requires a special tool, a spade called a *slane,* which slices the turf into bricks about 18 inches long. The bricks are spread out to dry and stiffen so that they can be stacked in pyramids to permit air circulation for further drying. Finally, they're piled up along the roadside for transport. You can always tell when a family is burning turf in a fireplace—the smoke coming out of the chimney is blue and sweet-scented.

As you drive around Connemara, you're sure to notice the absence of trees, felled and dragged off long ago for building English ships, houses, and furniture. (More of Cromwell's handiwork.) In recent years, however, the Irish government has undertaken an aggressive reforestation program, and vast areas of land have been set aside for planting trees, mostly pines, as a crop.

A trademark of this region is the **donkey,** still a worker on the farms. In some places, you'll see a sturdy little horse known as the **Connemara pony,** the only horse breed native to Ireland (although it's had an infusion of Spanish blood over the centuries). Often raised in tiny fields with limestone pastures, these animals have great stamina and are invaluable for farming and pulling equipment. The Connemara pony is also noted for its gentle temperament, which makes it ideal for children's riding.

A major part of Connemara is designated as a *Gaeltacht,* or Irish-speaking area, so you may hear many of the people conversing in their native tongue. Traditional music thrives in this part of the countryside, as do handcrafts and cottage industries.

The much-imitated **Aran knit sweaters** are synonymous with this region. Made of oatmeal-colored wool from the native sheep, these semi-waterproof sweaters were first knit by the women of the nearby Aran Islands for their fishermen husbands and sons, and each family had a different stitch or pattern. Years ago, the patterns were not only a matter of aesthetics; they served as the chief way to identify men who had drowned in the treacherous waters off the coast. Today these sweaters are hand-knit in the homes of Connemara and the nearby Aran Islands, then sold in the many craft shops throughout the region.

THE TOP ATTRACTIONS

Aughnanure Castle ⭐ Standing on a rocky island close to the shores of Lough Corrib, this castle is a well-preserved example of a six-story Irish tower house, with an unusual double bawn (a fortified enclosure) and a watchtower. It was built around A.D. 1500 as a stronghold of the O'Flaherty clan.

32km (20 miles) west of Galway City, signposted off N59, Clifden Rd., Oughterard, county Galway. ℂ 091/ 552214. Admission €2.50 ($2.25) adults, €2 ($1.80) seniors, €1.30 ($1.15) students and children, €6.50 ($5.80) family. Mid-June to mid-Sept daily 9:30am–6:30pm.

Connemara National Park ⭐⭐⭐ *(Kids* This stunning national park incorporates nearly 2,000 hectares (5,000 acres) of Connemara's mountains, bogs, heaths, and grasslands. The grounds are home to herds of Connemara ponies and Irish red deer, as well as a variety of birds and smaller mammals. To orient and acquaint visitors with all the aspects of the park, the handsome exhibition center offers a series of displays and an informative 20-minute audiovisual presentation. Tea, coffee, soup, sandwiches, and freshly baked goods are on hand in the tearoom. If you're up to it, test your willpower against the cheesecake. During July and August, Tuesday and Thursday are "nature days" for children; on Monday, Wednesday, and Friday there are guided walks for the whole family. Call the center for information on these and other special programs.

Clifden-Westport rd. (N59), Letterfrack, county Galway. ℂ 095/41054. http://homepage.tinet.ie/~knp/ connemara. Admission €3 ($2.70) adults, €2 ($1.80) groups and seniors, €1.30 ($1.15) children and students, €6.50 ($5.80) family. Park open year-round. Visitor center open daily Apr–May and Sept to mid-Oct 10am–5:30pm; June 10am–6:30pm; July–Aug 9:30am–6:30pm. Visitor center closed late Oct–Mar.

Dan O'Hara's Homestead Farm ⭐ For insight into how Connemara farmers find soil to till on this rocky land, head to this small farm. It was once owned by Dan O'Hara, but the harsh conditions and high taxes of the time forced him to emigrate to the United States. Today, the expanded center incorporates a 3.2-hectare (8-acre) prefamine farm and reflects daily life in the 1840s, with local people using traditional tilling and farming methods. The land also contains a reconstructed *crannóg* (fortified lake dwelling), an authentic megalithic tomb, and a dolmen. Attached to the farm and heritage center, farmhouse accommodations and some self-catering cottages are available.

About 6.5km (4 miles) east of Clifden off the main N59 rd., Lettershea, Clifden, county Galway. ℂ 095/21246. Admission €4.50 ($4) adults, €4 ($3.55) seniors and students, €2.50 ($2.25) children, €14 ($12) family. Daily 10am–6pm. Closed Nov–Mar.

Kylemore Abbey ✦✦ Originally a private residence (ca. 1868), this castellated house overlooking Kylemore Lake is a splendid example of neo-Gothic architecture. In 1920 it was turned over to the Benedictine nuns, who have since opened the grounds and part of the house to the public. The highlight is the recently restored Gothic chapel, considered a miniature cathedral. The complex also includes a cafe, which serves produce grown on the nuns' farm; a shop with a working pottery studio; and a visitor center where a video presentation gives you an overview of life at Kylemore, both past and present. The abbey is most atmospheric when the bells are rung for midday office or for vespers at 6pm. Admission to the Abbey is through two gates, each providing access to different attractions and facilities, and each requiring a separate fee. (It might help to think of it as a double collection.) The Abbey Gate offers access to the Abbey receptions rooms, the exhibition, the church, the lake walk, and the video; the Garden Gate opens to the walled garden, the exhibition, the tea house, the shop, and the wilderness walk. Though increasingly commercialized in recent years, it is still a lovely site.

Kylemore, county Galway. ℂ 095/41146. www.kylemoreabbey.com. Admission to Abbey Gate €4.50 ($4) adults, €3.20 ($2.85) seniors and students, €9 ($8) family; Garden Gate €4.50 ($4) adults, €3.20 ($2.85) seniors and students, €9 ($8) family; Abbey year-round daily 9am–5:30pm. Garden Easter–Sept daily 10:30am–4:30pm.

SIGHTSEEING TOURS

Several companies offer sightseeing tours of Connemara from Galway or Clifden.

Bus Eireann Departing from the bus station in Galway, this 8-hour tour of Connemara takes in Maam Cross, Recess, Roundstone, and Clifden, as well as Kylemore Abbey, Leenane, and Oughterard.

Ceannt Station, Galway, county Galway. ℂ 091/562000. www.buseireann.ie. Tour €15 ($13) adults, €14 ($12) seniors and students, €10 ($8.90) children, €45 ($40) family, with up to 3 children. Sun–Fri 10am.

Connemara Walking Centre This company's expert local guides lead walking tours of Connemara, with an emphasis on history and archaeology as well as scenery. The walks cover different sections—from the Renvyle Peninsula and Roundstone Bog to the Kylemore Valley, the Maumturk Mountains, and Sky Road. The tour to Inishbofin Island includes a 45-minute boat trip. Weeklong walking trips are based at Dun Gibbons, a center dedicated to exploring Connemara's countryside. All walks assemble at Island House in Clifden and include bus transportation to the walking site. Advance reservations are required.

The Island House, Market St., Clifden, county Galway. ℂ 095/21379. www.walkingireland.com. Tours €20 ($18) Tours offered Mar–Oct; call for times and a detailed price list.

Corrib Cruises Departing from the pier at Oughterard, this company's sightseeing boat cruises across Lough Corrib, Ireland's largest lake, measuring 176 sq. km (68 sq. miles) with 365 islands. The cruise stops at Inchagoill Island, home of a 12th-century monastery that was inhabited until the 1940s. One trip visits the island only, and the other goes to the island and to Cong in county Mayo, site of Ashford Castle (p. 428) and the area where the movie *The Quiet Man* was filmed. The Cong-Oughterard round-trip cruise can start at either place. In fact,

(Moments **An Excursion to Inishbofin**

It has been said that Ireland's last unspoiled frontiers are its islands, and Inishbofin, on its own, makes a strong contribution to that claim. This small emerald-green gem lies 11km (7 miles) off the northwest coast of Connemara and offers not only seclusion, but spectacular beauty, provided the skies are clear enough to deliver the not-to-be-believed views of and from its shores. Once the domain of monks, then the lair of pirate queen Grace O'Malley, later Cromwell's infamous priest-prison, and currently home to a mere 180 year-round residents, Inishbofin is both steeped in history and oozing with charm. It's well worth a day's expedition or a 1- or 2-day stay.

Numerous ferries to the island leave from and return to the sleepy port of Cleggan (13km/8 miles northwest of Clifden off N59) daily April through October. **Inishbofin Island Tours,** Kings of Cleggan, Cleggan, county Galway (© **095/44642**), operates the largest, newest, and fastest boat, the *Island Discovery.* Tickets cost €16 ($14) per adult and €8 ($7.10) per child, round-trip, and are available at the company office in Cleggan. *Note:* It's important, even necessary, to book in advance. The other option, which we prefer, is to ride with **Paddy O'Halloran** (© **095/45806**) on the *Dun Aengus,* the island's worn and worthy mail boat. The *Dun Aengus* remains the vessel of choice for most locals. It has both more charm and more roll than its newer rival, and skipper O'Halloran, after a half century at the wheel, definitely knows the way. Tickets (€15/$13 per person, round-trip) for the *Dun Aengus* are available at the **Spar Foodstore** in Cleggan (© **095/44750**).

there are currently four different day cruises on offer, as well as an evening Irish Hour (happy-hour) cruise.

Oughterard, county Galway. © **092/46029** or 091/552808. www.corribcruises.com. 90-min. round-trip cruise to island €12 ($11) adults, €6 ($5.35) children, €25 ($22) family; Cong-Oughterard round-trip day cruise €16 ($14) adults, €7 ($6.25) children, €32 ($28) family. May–Sept daily. Be sure to book ahead and to confirm times.

SHOPPING

Avoca Handweavers   This is the Connemara branch of the famous Wicklow weavers. About 9.7km (6 miles) north of Clifden on an inlet of the bay, surrounded by colorful flower gardens, this shop has one of the loveliest and most photographed locations in Ireland. It features colorful tweeds, as well as all sorts of Connemara-made marble souvenirs, candles, jewelry, books, music, wood carvings, pottery, and knits. A snack shop is on the premises. Open April through October daily from 9:30am until at least 6pm. Clifden-Leenane Rd. (N59), Dooneen Haven, Letterfrack, county Galway. © **095/41058.**

Celtic Shop   This shop offers a wide array of arts and crafts, including gold and silver Celtic jewelry, hand-woven Irish rugs, knitwear, hats, ceramics, and crystal. You'll also find a good selection of Irish and Celtic books. Open daily 9am to 6pm from September through June; daily from 9am to 9pm in July and August. Main St., Clifden, county Galway. © **095/21064.**

Malachy Kearns, the Bodhrán Maker

I remember the first time I saw a bodhrán. I remember the first time I heard one. I was about 8 years old. I can remember the hair standing up on the back of my neck!

My father brought me to a family funeral in Donegal. It was away up in the north of Donegal somewhere near Crolly, and this would have been in the late Fifties.

We buried the man. I remember it was a cold afternoon too and afterwards the men adjourned to a pub in the village and, like a million boys of my age before and since, I was stuffed to the tonsils with orange squash and lemonade while the grown-ups drank fiery glasses of whiskey and big black pints of porter. There was a fireplace with an open fire and I remember sitting beside it, late in the evening, bored and stupefied with fizzy drinks and adult talking.

Then there was a bit of excitement at the door of the bar and who came in but the legendary fiddle player called Johnny Doherty, a man whose name is still spoken with near reverence by Irish musicians everywhere. He was thin and hardy and he had his fiddle, I think, in a green velvet sack instead of a timber case. He had small quick hands and a very quiet way about him. There was another man with him and he had a sack with him, too, a jute one this time, and when he left it down on the floor beside me, carefully, I heard it make a boomy kind of noise.

Johnny Doherty, still regarded as the prince of Donegal fiddlers, was a master musician who was also a semi-traveller. He moved all around Donegal at different times of the year staying and playing in selected

Connemara Marble Visitor Centre   Connemara's unique green marble—diverse in color, marking, and veining—is quarried, cut, shaped, and polished here. Estimated by geologists to be about 500 million years old, the marble shows twists and interlocking bands of serpentine in various shades, ranging from light lime green to dark emerald. On weekdays, you'll see craftspeople at work hand-fashioning marble jewelry, paperweights, ashtrays, Celtic crosses, and other giftware. Open daily from 9am to 5:30pm. 13km (8 miles) west of Galway City on Galway-Clifden Rd. (N59), Moycullen, county Galway. © 091/555102.

Fuchsia Craft   Wedged in the center of Oughterard's main thoroughfare, this small shop is a treasure trove of unusual, hard-to-find crafts, produced by more than 100 craftspeople throughout Ireland. The items include handmade fishing flies, products made from pressed Irish peat, bronze sculptures, recycled art cards of Connemara scenes, decorative metal figurines fashioned from nails, and lithographs of early Ireland—as well as pottery, crystal, jewelry, knitwear, and much more. Open daily 9am to 10pm from June through September; daily 9am to 7pm in April, May, and October; and Mon to Sat 9am to 6pm from November through March. The Square, Oughterard, county Galway. © 091/552644.

Millars Connemara Tweed Ltd   This is the home of the colorful Connemara tweeds, an industry started in 1900 by Robert Millar as a small mill to process wool from local mountain sheep. Although most people travel to Clifden just to buy Millar's skeins of wool or hand-woven materials—plus houses for weeks and months at a time. It was a great honour to have him stay in your house and make his music under your roof. People came from everywhere just to hear him play.

Even as a child I knew there was something special about him when he began to play in that pub. He was sitting in the chair opposite me, swaying a bit in the gale of his own jigs and reels, his eyes empty and full in his face at the same time, as if they were seeing the music, in some strange way, and nothing else. The men that were standing listening, and sitting listening, were silent, except to say, "Good man, Johnny" now and again, and they even forgot that they had drinks in their hands. It was beautiful stuff.

But after a while it was even better because the other man that was with Johnny Doherty . . . and somebody told me he was a real traveller . . . he eventually took the first bodhrán I ever saw out of the jute bag. He warmed it to the fire, rubbing it now and again so that it muttered and grumbled almost, and then, without any beater, just like I am now this minute, he began to play.

And it was absolutely mighty.

I'm telling ye that the hair stood up on the back of my neck. I was mesmerized. That was certainly the occasion that determined, later in life, that I would become a bodhrán maker.

—From *Wallup!* by Malachy Kearns. Printed with permission of the author. Available at bookstores and from Roundstone Musical Instruments (www.bodhran.com).

ready-made ties, hats, caps, scarves, blankets, and bedspreads—today's shop is more than just an outlet for wool. You'll also find Irish patchwork, rush baskets, Aran crios belts, embroidery work, handmade miniature currachs, tin whistles, and blackthorn pipes, plus an art gallery of regional paintings. Open Monday to Saturday from 9am to 6pm, with extended summer hours. Main St., Clifden, county Galway. ✆ **095/21038**.

Roundstone Musical Instruments   A master craftsman, Malachy Kearn is one of the only full-time *bodhrán* (an ancient one-sided frame drum) makers in the world, and one of Ireland's most beloved celebrities. His contributions to Irish music recently earned him a place on a postage stamp. For the most resonant results on a bodhran, it is vital to have one of the quality goatskins Malachy seeks out from his various far-flung suppliers. Many of Ireland's most renowned musicians, including those who created the sounds of *Riverdance,* play Malachy Kearns's instruments. While you wait, his artist wife, Anne, can decorate the skin with Celtic designs, initials, family crests, or any design you request in old Gaelic script. Malachy's workshop also makes wooden flutes (ebony), tin whistles, and Irish harps, and he has an excellent mail-order service. Open daily 9am to 6pm from May through October; Monday to Saturday from 9:30am to 6pm November through April. The Monastery, Michael Killeen Park, Roundstone, county Galway. ✆ **095/35875**. www.bodhran.com.

Sheepchandler Gallery   Ensconced in an attractive location in the center of Roundstone, Katherine Parisot's fine gallery is a true delight. Her thoughtful selection of works by many of the finest contemporary artists in Ireland provides a focused glimpse into the country's art scene as well as many temptations to bring home more than a sweater or a cap. Open Monday to Friday from 9:30am to 5pm; Saturday from 10am to 2pm. Roundstone Harbor, county Galway. ℂ 095/35040.

Síla Mag Aoide Designs (Shelagh Magee)   Shelagh Magee is one of Ireland's most noteworthy artisans. Although inspired by ancient Celtic images and designs, her work is original and contemporary. In addition to a wide selection of her handmade silver jewelry, the shop offers a range of works, including watercolor prints and art cards of Connemara scenes, baskets, handmade wooden pencils, and miniature frames. Open daily from 9am to 9pm May to September, with shorter off-season hours. The Monastery, Michael Killeen Park, Roundstone, county Galway. ℂ 095/35912.

SPORTS & OUTDOOR PURSUITS

For location, facilities, and quality of instruction, **Delphi Adventure Center** *⋆*, Leenane, county Galway (ℂ **095/42307;** www.delphiadventureholidays.ie), is one of the best of the many adventure centers in Ireland. Courses are available in a wide range of water sports, as well as in mountaineering, pony trekking, tennis, and archery. Accommodation is in bright, simply furnished single or dorm-style rooms. The food in the dining room is good and plentiful, and vegetarian meals can be arranged. Residential adventure holidays for children are offered. Weekend prices for room, full board, and activities begin at €165 ($147) for an adult. The nonresidential activities fee for 1 full day is €32 ($28). Water-skiing and horseback riding are available at additional cost. This place caters primarily to people in their 20s and 30s.

BICYCLING   Bicycles can be hired year-round from **John Mannion & Son,** Bridge Street, Clifden, county Galway (ℂ **095/21160**). The rate for a regular touring bike in high season is €9 ($8) per day. Mountain bikes can be hired from May through October at the **Little Killary Adventure Company,** Leenane, county Galway (ℂ **095/43411;** www.killary.com). They go for €20 ($18) per day, and road bikes for €14 ($12) per day.

DIVING   You can rent equipment and receive instruction at **Scubadive West,** Renvyle, county Galway (ℂ **095/43922;** fax 095/43923; www.scubadivewest.com).

FISHING   Lough Corrib is renowned for brown-trout and salmon fishing. Brown-trout fishing is usually good from the middle of February, and salmon best from the end of May. The mayfly fishing begins around the middle of May and continues for up to 3 weeks.

Angling on Lough Corrib is free, but a state license is required for salmon. For expert advice and rental equipment, contact the **Cloonnabinnia Angling Centre,** Moycullen, county Galway (ℂ **091/555555**).

For salmon and sea trout, the **Ballynahinch Castle Fishery** at Ballynahinch, Recess (ℂ **095/31006**), is an angler's paradise. State fishing licenses, tackle hire and sales, maps, and great advice are available at the hotel.

At **Portarra Lodge,** Tullykyne, Moycullen, county Galway (ℂ **091/555-051;** fax 091/555-052; www.irishfarmholidays.com/portarra-lodge.html), packages are available, including B&B accommodation in a modern guesthouse on the shores of Lough Corrib, dinners, and boats and tackle. Michael Canney is an

Lough Inagh & the Walk to Maum Ean Oratory

Lough Inagh, nestled between the Maumturk and The Twelve Ben Mountains in the heart of Connemara, is situated in one of the most spectacularly beautiful valleys in Ireland. The mountain slopes rise precipitously from the valley floor, and many small streams cascade into the lake in a series of sparkling waterfalls. The R344 cuts through the valley, linking Recess to the south and Kylemore Lake to the north.

The **Western Way,** a walking route that traverses the high country of Galway and Mayo, follows a quiet country road above the R344 through the Lough Inagh Valley. To reach the beginning of the walk, drive north on the R344, turning right on a side road—sign for Maum Ean—about 200m (656 ft.) before the Lough Inagh Lodge Hotel. Continue on this side road for 6.5km (4 miles) to a large gravel parking lot on the left. Park here, and follow the well-worn trail 2km (1¼ miles) to the top of the pass, through glorious mountain scenery.

This short (4km/2½-mile) walk follows the Western Way to the top of a mountain pass which has long been associated with St. Patrick, and which is now the site of a small oratory, a hollow in the rock known as **Patrick's Bed,** a life-size statue of the saint, and a series of cairns marking the Stations of the Cross. Together, these monuments make a striking ensemble, strangely eerie when the mists descend and conceal the far slopes in their shifting haze. On a clear day there are great views from here, with the Atlantic Ocean and Bertraghboy Bay to the southwest and another range of mountains to the northeast. The round-trip walking time is about 1 hour.

---

avid angler and a great guide to this part of Galway. A double room with full breakfast is €60 ($53) per night. Weekly packages that include half-board, boat, and *ghillie* (guide) are also available.

GOLF   Visitors are welcome at the 18-hole, par-72 championship seaside course of the **Connemara Golf Club,** Ballyconneely, Clifden (© **095/23502**), nestled in the heart of Connemara and overlooking the Atlantic. Greens fees from May to September are €48 ($43); October to April, €30 ($27).

The **Oughterard Golf Club,** Oughterard, county Galway (© **091/552131**), is an 18-hole, par-70 inland course. Greens fees are €27 ($24).

HORSEBACK RIDING   Explore the stunningly beautiful Connemara Coast from May to September with **Connemara and Coast Trails,** Loughrea, county Galway (© **091/841216;** www.connemara-trails.com). Rides are for experienced and beginning riders alike. **Glen Valley Stables,** Glencroff, Leenane, county Galway (© **095/42269**), has one of the best equestrian programs in Connemara. Treks of 1 to 3 hours take you into the hills surrounding beautiful Glen Valley, or along the shores of Killary Harbour. The program is run by Niall O'Neill, whose mother, Josephine O'Neill, has offered B&B accommodations at Glen Valley House and Stables for over a decade (see "Where to Stay," below). Riding is €20 ($18) per person, per hour.

WALKING   **Killary Harbour,** Ireland's only fjord, rimmed by mountains on both sides, is remote and wild at its western, seaward end. The green road, now a sheep track for much of its length, was once the primary route from the Rinvyle Peninsula to Leenane. The famine devastated this area; you'll pass an abandoned prefamine village on the far side of the harbor, the fields rising at a devilishly steep slope from the ruined cottages, clustered at the water's edge. This is a walk into Ireland's recent past, when many lived by subsistence farming and fishing, always perilously close to disaster.

WATERSPORTS Hobie Cat sailing and sail-boarding can be arranged at the **Little Killary Adventure Company,** Leenane, county Galway (© **095/43411;** www.killary.com). Daily rates are €50 ($46) per day (two sessions), which entitles you to use the watersports equipment and participate in all the center's supervised sporting activities, including kayaking, water-skiing, hill and coastal walking, rock climbing, archery, and more.

WHERE TO STAY
MODERATE/EXPENSIVE
Ballynahinch Castle 🏵🏵🏵 Set on an enchanting 140-hectare (350-acre) estate at the base of Ben Lettery, one of the Twelve Ben mountains, this turreted, gabled manor house overlooks the Owenmore River. Dating from the 16th century, it has served over the years as a base for the O'Flaherty chieftains and the sea pirate Grace O'Malley. It was also the sporting residence of the Maharajah Jans Sahib Newanagar, better known as Ranjitsinhgi, the famous cricketer. The ambience can be best described as country house casual; the place feels luxurious and your every need will be satisfied by the efficient staff, yet there's absolutely no stuffiness or pretentiousness here. The guest rooms are individually decorated, and many have fireplaces and four-poster or canopy beds (all are orthopedic). Most of all, however, this is a sportsman's lodge, one that is particularly renowned for top-notch sea trout and salmon fishing. Each evening, the day's catch is weighed in and recorded at the Fishermen's Bar, usually creating a cause for celebration.

Recess, county Galway. © **095/31006.** Fax 095/31085. www.ballynahinch-castle.com. 40 units. €143–€216 ($127–$192) double. Suites also available. Rates include full breakfast. AE, DC, MC, V. Closed Feb. **Amenities:** Restaurant (Continental); bar; tennis courts; private fishing; limited room service; babysitting; library. *In room:* TV, hair dryer.

Cashel House Hotel 🏵 Set on 20 hectares (50 acres) of exotic gardens and woodlands, this 150-year-old country house is nestled deep in the mountains and lakelands of Connemara. Run since 1968 by Dermot and Kay McEvilly, it has attracted a range of discerning guests over the years, including President and Madame de Gaulle, who spent 2 weeks here in 1969 and put Cashel House on the map. Guest rooms, which have wide-windowed views of the bay or the gardens, are decorated with Irish floral fabrics, European antiques, sheepskin rugs, rattan pieces, vintage paintings, and local heirlooms. The hotel has a private beach on the bay, a tennis court, fishing, boating, and signposted walking paths. The private stables offer riding lessons, dressage, and mountain trekking.

Cashel Bay, Cashel, county Galway. © **800/323-5463** or 800/735-2478 in the U.S., or 095/31001. Fax 095/31077. www.cashel-house-hotel.com. 32 units. €150–€180 ($134–$160) double; €210 ($187) garden suite. Rates include full breakfast. AE, DC, MC, V. Closed Jan 12–Feb 10. **Amenities:** Restaurant (Continental); bar; tennis court; horseback riding; nonsmoking rooms; library; private beach. *In room:* TV, hair dryer.

Lough Inagh Lodge 🏵🏵 This handsome fishing-and-sporting lodge has one of the most enviable locations in Connemara, standing alone on the shore of the tranquil Lough Inagh. Without another building in sight, you truly feel like you're swallowed up in the region's stunning solitude, with only the splashing of fish in Lough Inagh to disturb the silence. It is an infinitely relaxing place. Inside, the public rooms strike a note of warm hospitality, with open log fires in the library and the oak-paneled bar. Guest rooms are beautifully appointed with period furnishings and are quite spacious for this price range; most include a separate dressing room. Request a room in the front of the house, overlooking the lake and the Twelve Bens.

Recess, county Galway. © **800/323-5463** or 800/735-2478 in the U.S., or 095/31001. Fax 095/31077. www.commerce.ie/inagh. 32 units. €144–€298 ($128–$265) double. Rates include full breakfast. AE, MC, V. Closed Jan–Feb. **Amenities:** Restaurant (Continental); bar; library. *In room:* TV, hair dryer.

Renvyle House 🏵🏵   Originally the residence of the Blake family, this grand old house sits on a 80-hectare (200-acre) estate along the Atlantic shoreline in the wilds of Connemara. It was purchased in 1917 by Oliver St. John Gogarty, a leading Irish poet, wit, surgeon, and politician, who fondly called this secluded seascape and mountain setting "the world's end." That's putting it mildly: It really is off the beaten track, not ideal for a quick overnight, but perfect for a stay of a few days or longer. In his day, Gogarty invited his many friends to visit; W. B. Yeats honeymooned here, and Churchill was a frequent guest. Updated and refurbished in recent years by current owner Hugh Coyle, it retains a turn-of-the-20th-century ambience, particularly in its public areas. Guest rooms vary in size and decor, from grand rooms with balconies to cozy attic rooms with dormer windows. Along with a long list of sporting amenities, the hotel also hosts a range of events, such as murder-mystery weekends, fly-fishing clinics, and painting weekends.

Renvyle, county Galway. © **095/43511.** Fax 095/43515. www.renvyle.com. 65 units. €102–€203 ($91–$180) double. Rates include full Irish breakfast and service charge. AE, DC, MC, V. Closed Jan–Feb. **Amenities:** Restaurant (Continental); bar; outdoor swimming pool; 9-hole golf course; 2 tennis courts; boating; horseback riding. *In room:* TV.

Zetland Country House Hotel 🏵   Here's yet another fine fishing lodge in Connemara, and the staff is extraordinarily accommodating to anglers. Built in 1850 as a sporting lodge, this three-story manor house was named for the earl of Zetland, a frequent visitor during the 19th century. Surrounded by lush gardens and ancient trees, Zetland is run by John Prendergast, a Paris-trained hotelier. The guest rooms, many of which look out onto the bay, have antique or reproduction furnishings. The dining room is known for its local seafood and lamb dishes, and its vegetables and fruit come from the inn's kitchen garden. The Zetland owns the Gowla Fishery, one of the best private sea-trout fisheries in Ireland, encompassing 14 lakes and 6.5km (4 miles) of river.

Cashel Bay, Cashel, county Galway. © **800/448-8355** in the U.S., or 095/31111. Fax 095/31117. www. zetland.com. 19 units. €150–€210 ($134–$187) double. Rates include full breakfast and service charge. AE, MC, V. Closed Nov–Mar. **Amenities:** Tennis court; croquet; billiards room. *In room:* TV, hair dryer.

MODERATE

Abbeyglen Castle 🏵🏵   On a hilltop overlooking Clifden and the bay, this property dates from the 1820s, although it gained its castlelike facade only within the past 20 years. Happily, the turrets and battlements blend in well with the Connemara countryside. Abbeyglen is a splendidly informal Irish hotel—the kind of place where a parrot in reception confuses staff by mimicking the telephone, and the piano bar brings guests together in a house party atmosphere. The recently refurbished public areas have brass candelabra chandeliers, arched windows, and vintage settees. Guest rooms are large and comfortable and have crown canopies. Personable proprietor Brian Hughes can arrange fishing trips, packed lunches, and a host of other local activities.

Sky Rd., Clifden, county Galway. © 800/447-7462 in the U.S., or 095/21201. Fax 095/21797. www.abbey glen.ie. 29 units. €150–€175 ($134–$156) double. Rates include full breakfast. AE, MC, V. Closed early Jan–Feb. **Amenities:** Restaurant (Continental); bar; outdoor swimming pool; tennis court; sauna; solarium. *In room:* TV.

Connemara Gateway   Less than 1.6km (1 mile) from the village of Oughterard and 26km (16 miles) west of Galway City, this contemporary two-story inn is well positioned. It sits on its own grounds, near the upper shores of Lough Corrib and across the road from an 18-hole golf course. Although it has a rambling modern exterior, a hearth-side ambience permeates the interior, with leafy plants and homey bric-a-brac in the corridors. Guest rooms have a smart look, with local tweed fabrics and hangings, oak dressers and headboards, and scenes of Connemara. A fine collection of original paintings by landscape artists John MacLeod and Kenneth Webb enhances the restaurant.

Galway-Clifden Rd. (N59), Oughterard, county Galway. © 091/552328. Fax 091/552332. www.connemara gatewayhotel.com. 62 units. €140–€180 ($125–$160) double. No service charge. Rates include full break-fast. AE, DC, MC, V. Closed Jan. **Amenities:** Restaurant (international); bar; indoor swimming pool; tennis court; gym; sauna; solarium; croquet; nonsmoking rooms; walking trails. *In room:* TV, tea/coffeemaker.

Delphi Lodge ★★ *Finds*   Ranked among the top-20 fishing lodges in Ireland, Delphi Lodge is a gorgeous private country house in a breathtaking, wild, unde-filed setting. Built in the early 19th century as a sportsman's hideaway for the marquis of Sligo, it occupies a landscape of crystalline lakes and rivers, hard-wood forests, unspoiled ocean beaches, and luminous mountain slopes. All that, plus salmon and sea trout outside the front door, just waiting to be caught. The rooms are spacious and fashionably simple, furnished in antiques with an infor-mally elegant touch. Owner and fly fisherman Peter Mantle can supply you with everything you need to go fishing—permits, licenses, and equipment rental. The kitchen staff can prepare your own catch of the day, or send it to you at home, smoked, after you return. Special 3-day weekend packages, including courses in fly tying, watercolors, wine appreciation, and other diversions, are also available in the off-season.

The Delphi Estate and Fishery, Leenane, county Galway. © 095/42222. Fax 095/42296. www.delphilodge.ie. 12 units, 5 cottages. €120–€180 ($107–$160) standard double; €150–€210 ($134–$187) lakeside double. No service charge. Rates include full Irish breakfast. 2- and 3-bedroom self-catering cottages €400–€1,000 ($356–$890) per week. AE, MC, V. Closed Christmas and New Year's holidays. **Amenities:** Sitting room. *In room:* TV.

Dolphin Beach House ★★   Originally a homestead in the early 19th cen-tury, Dolphin Beach House is a stylish, restful place to base yourself in Con-nemara. The main house has been restored, and bedrooms have been added—spacious bedrooms with soaring ceilings, underfloor heating, antique furnishings, pristine bed linens, spellbinding views, and the beach just a stone's throw away. It all combines for a feeling of homespun luxury. Meals are fash-ioned mainly from ingredients produced on the 5.6-hectare (14-acre) estate; you can even collect your own eggs for breakfast if you wish. This is a truly special destination in itself.

Lower Sky Rd., Clifden, county Galway. © 095/21204. Fax 095/22935. www.connemara.net/dolphinbeach house. 8 units. €100–€130 ($89–$116) double. Rates include full breakfast and service charge. MC, V. Closed mid-Nov to mid-Mar. **Amenities:** Restaurant (Continental). *In room:* TV.

Rock Glen Manor House ★   Originally an 18th-century hunting lodge, this rambling country house sits amid lovely gardens about 2.4km (1½ miles) south of Clifden. Expanded over the years and now in the hands of John and

Evangeline Roche, Rock Glen is set back from the road, with views of Ardbear Bay and the Atlantic Ocean. It's a restful spot, with tastefully furnished rooms and public areas. Most rooms, including the restaurant, face the sea, and half the guest rooms are on the ground floor.

Ballyconneely Rd., Clifden, county Galway. ⓒ **095/21035.** Fax 095/21737. www.connemara.net/rockglen-hotel. 27 units. €140–€164 ($125–$146) double. Rates include full breakfast and service charge. AE, DC, MC, V. Closed Nov to mid-Mar. **Amenities:** Restaurant (Continental); tennis court; putting green; fishing privileges. *In room:* TV, radio, hair dryer, garment press.

Sweeney's Oughterard House ⭐   A favorite with anglers, this ivy-covered, 200-year-old Georgian house has been run by the Sweeney-Higgins family since 1913. Across the road from the rushing, salmon-filled waters of the Owenriff River, the inn is surrounded by flowering gardens and ancient trees on the quiet western end of the village. The public rooms have an old-world charm, thanks to multipaned bow windows, a fine selection of Victorian, Edwardian, and Georgian furnishings, and original artworks by 20th-century Irish artists. The guest rooms vary in size and decor, from antique-filled to modern light-wood styles, some with four-poster or king-size beds. It's a great spot for fishing, taking long country walks, or catching up on your reading. There's a good dining room (book ahead) with an extensive wine cellar (more than 300 wines).

Galway-Clifden Rd. (N59), Oughterard, county Galway. ⓒ **091/552207.** Fax 091/552161. www.sweeneys-hotel.com. 20 units. €100–€180 ($89–$160) double. No service charge. Rates include full breakfast. AE, MC, V. Closed late Dec to mid-Jan. **Amenities:** Sitting room. *In room:* TV, tea/coffeemaker, hair dryer.

INEXPENSIVE/MODERATE

Doonmore Hotel ⭐ *(Kids)*   This seasoned waterfront hotel enjoys a prime location on Inishbofin, with stunning views of the open sea and of nearby Inishshark and High Island. Small boats dot the bay and there is even a seal colony just beyond the hotel's front doors. A range of room options is available, including spacious family units with children's bunk beds. The appealing, unpretentious rooms in the newish expansion are clean, full of light, and tastefully furnished with simple pine furniture. The older rooms in the original hotel building are somewhat worn but comfortable; some enjoy the hotel's finest sea views. All rooms have firm beds. The hotel offers facilities for sea angling and scuba diving. Inishbofin is well known for both. The Doonmore is a short walk from the ferry and provides van service to and from the main harbor on request.

Inishbofin Island, county Galway. ⓒ and fax **095/45804.** www.doonmorehotel.com. 25 units. €72–€110 ($64–$98) double. No service charge. Rates include full breakfast. AE, MC, V. Closed Nov–Mar. **Amenities:** Restaurant (Continental); bar; sitting room. *In room:* TV, tea/coffeemaker.

INEXPENSIVE

Errisbeg Lodge ⭐   Conveniently proximate to Roundstone yet blessedly ensconced between mountainside and sea, Errisbeg Lodge is a place where you may plan to spend a night and wind up lingering for days. Jackie and Shirley King's family land, reaching high onto the slopes of Errisbeg Mountain and sloping down to the sea, is a sublime haven for innumerable rare species of wildflowers and birds, and Jackie loves nothing more than sharing these wonders with his guests. The Atlantic is spread out before you, with two glorious white-sand beaches a few hundred yards away on foot. Guest rooms are rustic and serenely spare, with stucco walls, light pine furniture, and pastel floral comforters, with either mountain or ocean views. It's all about tranquility here and warm, gracious hospitality.

Just over 1.6km (1 mile) outside of Roundstone on Clifden Rd., Roundstone, county Galway. ℰ and fax 095/35807. www.connemara.net/errisbeg-lodge. 5 units. €58 ($52) double. No service charge. Rates include full breakfast. No credit cards. Closed Dec–Feb. **Amenities:** Nonsmoking rooms.

Glen Valley House and Stables   At the base of a remote glaciated valley, this award-winning B&B redefines "secluded." The entrance drive follows the base of the valley for over a mile before you arrive at the house, which has great views across to the far line of hills. The O'Neills are helpful yet unobtrusive hosts, and their home attracts people looking for a serene, restful setting. Don't miss the spectacular section of the Western Way walking trail that passes near the house and follows the hills rimming Killary Harbour, Ireland's only fjord, with unforgettable views of the harbor mouth—this is a great place to watch the sun set. Glen Valley is a specialist in horseback riding holidays (see "Sports & Outdoor Pursuits" on p. 414).

Signposted 5.6km (3½ miles) west of Leenane on the Clifden rd., Glencroff, Leenane, county Galway. ℰ 095/ 42269. Fax 095/42365. www.irishfarmholidays.com/glen-valley.html. 4 units, 2 with private bathroom. €50–€60 ($46–$53) double. No service charge. Closed Nov–Feb. **Amenities:** Sitting room. *In room:* Tea/ coffeemaker.

WHERE TO DINE
EXPENSIVE

Erriseask Country House ★★★ MODERN CONTINENTAL   An international stream of foodies flock to this little country inn for the imaginative cooking of Stefan Matz. There seems to be no dish he can't pull off successfully, no matter how unlikely. Vanilla-cured duck on warm vegetable salad, sautéed monkfish in ginger sauce, sorbet of beet and buttermilk are artful, light-spirited, complex dishes that, at their best, represent some of the best food in the British Isles. Erriseask House also offers extremely stylish B&B accommodations from €140 ($125).

Ballyconeely, Connemara, county Galway. ℰ 095/23553. Reservations recommended. Main courses €16–€24 ($14–$21). AE, DC, MC, V. Mon–Sun 6:30–9pm (Wed for hotel guests only). Closed Oct–Easter.

MODERATE

Beola ℱ SEAFOOD   This attractive restaurant serves perhaps the best seafood in Roundstone at near-budget prices. Beola, which belongs to the adjacent Eldon's Hotel, has an exceptionally welcoming staff to go with its fine cuisine. Smoked salmon parcels in phyllo pastry or hot avocado and prawns make a splendid first course. To follow, try the roast filet of monkfish with lemon soy sauce or grilled cod with nut dressing. For a memorable finish, it's got to be the Baileys and ginger cheesecake. The wine list offers a fine international selection at surprisingly affordable prices, and the South African house wine (Armiston Bay) is a high-quality surprise at €16 ($14) a bottle. The only drawback here is that no significant provision is made for nonsmokers—the restaurant is a single unpartitioned space.

Roundstone Harbor, Connemara, county Galway. ℰ 095/35933. Reservations recommended. Main courses €13–€20 ($11–$18). AE, DC, MC, V. Easter to mid-Oct daily 6:30–9:30pm.

Burke's ℱ FOOD   The first thing you'll notice here is that everyone, from the barman to the waiters, is very friendly. The bright dining room is hidden beyond a long, dark barroom, where traditional music often starts at around 10pm. The meal begins well, with delicious home-baked breads. Vegetables that accompany the meal are locally grown and mostly organic. Main courses include honey roast duck breast with orange port sauce and grilled lamb cutlets with red currant sauce. The vegetarian special changes daily and is a fine example of how to eat well without meat. The food here is consistently simple in its conception and presentation, and it is consistently satisfying.

Mount Gable House, Clonbur, county Galway. ⊙ **092/46175.** Reservations recommended. Main courses €11–€20 ($10–$18). MC, V. Apr–Oct Mon–Sat 6–9pm.

High Moors ✹✹ *(Finds* MODERN CONTINENTAL   Less than 1.6km (1 mile) from Clifden, a narrow country road leads to this modern bungalow-style restaurant, set high on a hill with panoramic views of the Atlantic and the wild countryside. A homey ambience prevails—and well it should, because this is the home of Hugh and Eileen Griffin, host and chef, respectively. The food and menu appear quite simple, based on what is fresh at the markets and what vegetables and herbs are in season in Hugh's organic gardens. Eileen's specialties include such classics as breast of chicken with basil and tomato; filet of pork with three spices; wild salmon with sorrel butter sauce; and roast leg of Connemara lamb with red currant and rosemary. Just when things seem a bit too routine, the menu throws you some innovative zingers: monkfish with Thai green curry or perhaps prawn-and-dill tartlet with saffron. Try to book a table for sunset—if you can tear your attention away from the food, the views are incredible. The views, the wonderful service, the attention that goes into each dish—everything conspires to give a truly intimate experience.

Off the Ballyconeely rd., Dooneen, Clifden, county Galway. ⊙ **095/21342.** Reservations recommended. Main courses €14–€20 ($12–$18). AE, MC, V. Wed–Sun 6:30–10pm. Closed Nov–Easter.

O'Grady's ✹ SEAFOOD   Since the mid-1960s, this restaurant has been drawing seekers of great seafood to Clifden. The menu features all that is freshest from the sea, with choices such as Clifden lobster with lemon or garlic butter and filet of Cleggan brill. For non-fish-eaters, there's filet of beef with radish sauce, pork with peach stuffing in peppercorn cream sauce, and lamb with rosemary sauce.

Market St., Clifden, county Galway. ⊙ **095/21450.** Reservations recommended for dinner. Dinner main courses €14–€25 ($12–$22). AE, MC, V. Apr–Oct Mon–Sat 12:30–2:30pm and 6:30–10pm.

INEXPENSIVE

Two Dog Café ✹✹ MEDITERRANEAN   This bright, smoke-free cafe is a great place to relax and enjoy an array of homemade soups, Mediterranean sandwiches (constructed on baguettes, tortillas, and ciabatta), salads, fresh pastries, tea, and Italian coffee. The baguette with goat's cheese and grilled red peppers was particularly enticing. Wine is served by the glass or bottle.

There is also an Internet cafe on the second floor, where Dell PCs and Apple iMacs, loaded with the latest browsing software, are at the ready. You pay €2 ($1.80) for the first 15 minutes, €.65 (60¢) for each additional 5 minutes, or €8 ($7.10) per hour, with discounts for students.

Church St., Clifden, Connemara, county Galway. ⊙ **095/22186.** www.twodogcafe.ie. All items €2–€8 ($1.80–$7.10). MC, V. June–Sept daily 9:30am–10pm; Oct–May Tues–Sun 10:30am–6:30pm.

13

The Northwest: Mayo, Sligo & Donegal

North of county Galway on the Atlantic coast are counties Mayo, Sligo, Leitrim, and Donegal.

Southern Mayo is a continuation of stunning Connemara (see chapter 12), with Westport being one of the most popular resort towns in Ireland.

Traveling northward, the next county is Sligo. The main appeal here is not in its towns, which tend to be functional rather than colorful and vibrant, but out in the countryside. This is Yeats Country, the landscape that soothed W. B. Yeats's soul and inspired his poetry. A century later, Sligo's unspoiled marvels are still a healing tonic for the workaday lifestyle. The county possesses a wealth of historic sites, and fans of Yeats can plot a course of pilgrimages to the plethora of places associated with the poet and his writings.

For most visitors (and, if truth be told, for most Irish, too), Leitrim is simply somewhere you pass through on your way to and from Donegal. There are a few sites in Leitrim— Glencar Waterfall, Dromahair, and Parke's Castle—that can most easily be visited from Sligo town, and for this reason, we've included them in this chapter. You'll find more details on Leitrim in chapter 14, "The Midlands: Along the River Shannon."

If you're looking for the least-inhabited, least-touristed, and most liberating landscape of majestic wilderness and splendor, Donegal is definitely the place to go. While it's true that Donegal's austere beauty can be rather bleak when the weather turns gray and rainy, there's nothing like warming yourself by a peat fire while Mother Nature wreaks havoc outside. Donegal is particularly loved by the outdoorsy, sporty crowd. Several of Ireland's greatest natural wonders are here, such as the Slieve League cliffs and Horn Head. And the most remote, pristine, and beautiful beaches in the country are tucked into the bays and inlets of Donegal's sharply indented coast.

The towns of Donegal are less developed for tourism than pretty much everywhere else on the island. While buildings in many Irish towns tend to be prettified with vibrant shades of paint and adorned with flower boxes, Donegal's towns tend to remain the gray color of the natural stone. Make no mistake: This is what all of Ireland looked like before tourism took over, so there's a real feeling of authenticity here. Sure, fewer tourists mean fewer amenities. It might be harder to ferret out a gourmet restaurant or upscale guesthouse in a tiny seaside hamlet. In addition, you'll have to contend with the road signs, which are cryptic or nonexistent on all but the national roads. But for those willing to venture to Ireland's last outpost, the thrill of discovery is its own reward.

1 County Mayo

Mayo's chief town (Ballina) is 101km (63 miles) N of Galway, 193km (120 miles) N of Shannon Airport, 246km (153 miles) NW of Dublin, and 311km (193 miles) NW of Cork

Rimmed by Clew Bay and the Atlantic Ocean, county Mayo boasts many diverse attractions, although it has been widely identified as *The Quiet Man* country since the classic John Wayne movie was filmed here in 1951. The setting for the film was **Cong,** a no-longer-so-quiet village wedged between Lough Mask and Lough Corrib and backed up against the county Galway border. Most of Mayo, however, has resisted the pull of Hollywood, and still has remote bogs, beaches, cliffs, and crags where quiet splendor prevails.

Among Mayo's other attractions are the 5,000-year-old farmstead settlement at Ceide Fields, the Marian shrine at Knock, and some of Europe's best fishing waters at Lough Conn, Lough Mask, and the River Moy. **Ballina,** Mayo's largest town, calls itself the home of the Irish salmon. And **Westport** is a little resort town guaranteed to steal your heart.

COUNTY MAYO ESSENTIALS

GETTING THERE   Aer Lingus provides daily service from Dublin into **Knock International Airport,** Charlestown, county Mayo (© 094/67222; www.knockinternationalairport.ie). Charter flights from the United States operate in the summer. From Britain, there's service to Knock on **Aer Lingus** from Birmingham, **British Regional Airlines** from Manchester, and **Ryan Air** from London's Stansted. See "Getting There," in chapter 2, "Planning Your Trip to Ireland," for the airlines' phone numbers and websites.

Irish Rail and Bus Eireann (© 096/21011; www.buseireann.ie) provide daily service from Dublin and other cities into Ballina, Westport, and Castlebar, with bus connections into smaller towns. There is also express service from Galway into most Mayo towns.

From Dublin and points east, the main N5 road leads to many points in county Mayo; from Galway, take N84 or N17. From Sligo and points north, take N17 or N59. To get around county Mayo, it's best to rent a car. Two firms with outlets at Knock International Airport are **Casey Auto Rentals, Ltd.** (© 094/24618) and **National Car Rental** (© 094/67252).

VISITOR INFORMATION   For year-round information, visit or contact the **Westport Tourist Office,** The Mall, Westport (© 098/25711; http://westport. mayo-ireland.ie). It's open September through May, Monday to Saturday, from 9am to 5:45pm and June through August, Monday to Friday, 9am to 7pm.

The **Knock Airport Tourist Office** (© 094/67247) is open June to September at times coinciding with flight arrivals.

Seasonal tourist offices, open from May or June to September or October, are the **Ballina Tourist Office,** Cathedral Road, Ballina, county Mayo (© 096/ 70848); **Castlebar Tourist Office,** Linenhall Street, Castlebar, county Mayo (© 094/21207); **Knock Village Tourist Office,** Knock (© 094/88193); **Cong Village Tourist Office** (© 092/46542); **Achill Tourist Office,** Achill Sound (© 098/45384); and **Newport Tourist Office** (© 098/41895).

EXPLORING THE COUNTY

Unlike many other counties, county Mayo does not have one central city (although Westport is rapidly approaching that stature). It's a county of many towns, from large market and commercial centers, such as Castlebar, Claremorris, and Ballinrobe in the southern part of the county, to Ballina in the northern reaches. Most of the attractions of interest to visitors lie in the hinterlands, in smaller communities like Knock, Foxford, Ballycastle, Louisburgh, and Newport.

County Mayo's loveliest town, **Westport** 𝔸𝔸, is nestled on the shores of Clew Bay. Once a major port, it is one of the country's few planned towns, designed by Richard Castle with a tree-lined mall, rows of Georgian buildings, and an octagonal central mall.

Southeast of Westport is **Croagh Patrick,** a 750m (2,500-ft.) mountain dominating the vistas of western Mayo for many miles. St. Patrick is said to have prayed and spent the 40 days of Lent here in A.D. 441. To commemorate this belief, each year on the last Sunday of July, thousands of Irish people make a pilgrimage to the site, which has become known as St. Patrick's Holy Mountain.

The rugged, bog-filled, thinly populated coast of Mayo provides little industry for the locals, but offers scenic drives and secluded outposts to intrigue visitors. Leading the list is **Achill Island,** a heather-filled bogland with sandy beaches and cliffs dropping into the Atlantic. A bridge links it to the mainland. **Clare Island,** once the home of Mayo's amazing pirate queen, Grace O'Malley, sits south of Achill in Clew Bay.

The drive from Ballina along the edge of the northern coast to Downpatrick Head is particularly scenic. It includes a visit to **Killala,** a small, secluded harbor village that came close to changing the course of Ireland's history. In August 1798, France's General Humbert landed at Killala in an abortive attempt to lead the Irish in a full-scale rebellion against the British. For this reason, the phrase "The Year of the French" is part of the folk memory of Mayo. Novelist Thomas Flanagan used the incident as the basis for his best-selling novel of the same name.

You'll find two extraordinary, ruined, 15th-century Franciscan friaries signposted off the R314 between Killala and Ballina. Moyne and Rosserk are located about 3.2km (2 miles) apart, and both are dramatically situated on the shores of Killala Bay. The last friar at **Moyne Abbey** probably died in the 1800s, but processions of brown robed monks are easily imagined in the beautiful stone cloister. **Rosserk Abbey** is particularly fascinating: not only are its chapel windows well preserved but visitors can climb a winding stone stair to see the domestic rooms of the friary and look out across the bay. The *piscina* of the church (a place for washing altar vessels) is carved with angels, and on its lower-left-hand column is a delightful detail: a tiny, elegant carving of a Round tower that recalls its 23m-tall (75-ft.) counterpart in nearby Killala.

Ballintubber Abbey 𝔸   This is known as the abbey that refused to die, because it is one of the few Irish churches that's been in continuous use for almost 800 years. Founded in 1216 by Cathal O'Connor, king of Connaught, it has survived fires and other tragedies. Although the forces of Oliver Cromwell took off the church's roof in 1653 and attempted to suppress services, clerics persisted in discreetly conducting religious rites. Completely restored in 1966, the interior includes a video display and an interpretive center, and the grounds are landscaped to portray spiritual themes.

Off the main Galway-Castlebar rd. (N84), about 32km (20 miles) west of Knock, Ballintubber, county Mayo. (𝒸) 094/30934. Free admission; €2.50 ($2.25) donation requested. Daily 9am–midnight.

Ceide Fields 𝔸   Here, in a dramatic sea-edge setting, lies the oldest enclosed landscape in Europe, revealing a pattern of once-tilled fields as they were laid out and lived in 50 centuries ago. Preserved for millennia beneath the bog to which it had been lost, this Neolithic farming settlement, home to the builders of the

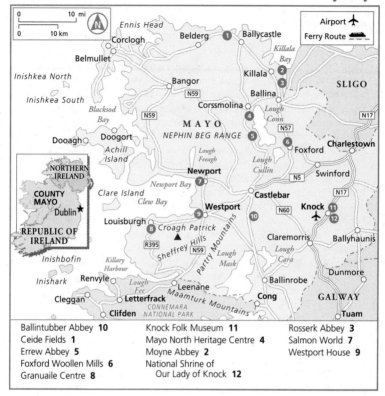

Ballintubber Abbey **10**	Knock Folk Museum **11**	Rosserk Abbey **3**
Ceide Fields **1**	Mayo North Heritage Centre **4**	Salmon World **7**
Errew Abbey **5**	Moyne Abbey **2**	Westport House **9**
Foxford Woollen Mills **6**	National Shrine of	
Granuaile Centre **8**	Our Lady of Knock **12**	

nearby megalithic tombs, now shows its face again. Admittedly, it's a nearly inscrutable face, requiring all the resources of the interpretive center to make a visit meaningful. The visitor center offers a 20-minute video presentation and tours of the site.

On R314, the coastal road north of Ballina, between Ballycastle and Belderrig, Ballycastle, county Mayo. © 096/43325. Admission €3.50 ($3.10) adults, €2.50 ($2.25) seniors, €1.30 ($1.15) students and children, €8 ($7.10) family. Mid-Mar to May and Oct daily 10am–5pm; June–Sept daily 9:30am–6:30pm; Nov daily 10am–4:30pm.

Errew Abbey ✪ This ruined 13th-century Augustinian church sits on a tiny peninsula in Lough Conn and has great views of the lake. The cloister is well preserved, as is the chancel with altar and *piscina*. An oratory with massive stone walls is in the field adjacent to the abbey—on the site of a church founded in the 6th century, and known locally as Templenagalliaghdoo, or "Church of the Black Nun." The site of the abbey is a remarkably tranquil place, and great for a picnic.

Signposted about 3.2km (2 miles) south of Crossmolina on the Castlebar road, then 5km (3 miles) down a side road, county Mayo. No phone. Free admission.

Foxford Woollen Mills Visitor Centre ✪✪ Founded in 1892 by a local nun to provide work for a community ravaged by the effects of the Irish famine, Foxford Woollen Mills brought prosperity to the area through the worldwide sales of beautiful tweeds, rugs, and blankets. Using a multimedia presentation, the center

Moments **A Trip to Clare Island**

Floating a mere 5.6km (3½ miles) off the Mayo coast, just beyond Clew Bay, Clare Island is roughly 104 sq. km (40 sq. miles) of unspoiled splendor. Inhabited for 5,000 years and once quite populous—with 1,700 prefamine residents—Clare is now home to 150 year-round islanders, plus perhaps as many sheep. But the island is best known as the haunt of Grace O'Malley, the pirate queen, who controlled the coastal waters 400 years ago. O'Malley's modest castle, and the partially restored Cistercian Abbey where she is buried, are among the island's few attractions. The rest is a matter of remote natural beauty, in which Clare abounds. The sea cliffs on the north side of the island are truly spectacular. Two ferry services, operating out of Roonagh Harbour, 29km (18 miles) south of Westport, charge €16 ($14) one way or €30 ($27) round-trip, for the 15-minute journey: O'Malley's Ferry Service, aboard the *Island Princess* (℗ **098/25045**); and Clare Island Ferries, aboard the *Pirate Queen* (℗ **098/26307**).

Once you arrive on Clare, if you want the grand tour, look for Ludwig Timmerman's 1974 Land Rover. Ludwig offers cordial, informative tours from June to August. Otherwise, your transport options are mountain bikes or your own legs.

tells the story of this local industry, then offers an on-site tour of the working mills, which produce the famous Foxford woolen products. Tours run every 20 minutes and last approximately 45 minutes. A restaurant, a shop, an exhibition center, an art gallery, a heritage room, and other craft units (including a doll-making and -restoration workshop and a jewelry designer) are also part of the visit.

Off the Foxford-Ballina rd. (N57), 16km (10 miles) south of Ballina, St. Joseph's Place, Foxford, county Mayo. ℗ **094/56488**. Admission €5 ($4.45) adults, €4 ($3.55) seniors, students, and children; €16 ($14) family. May–Oct Mon–Sat 10am–6pm and Sun noon–6pm; Nov–April Mon–Sat 10am–6pm and Sun 2pm–6pm. Last tour at 5:30pm.

Granuaile Centre 𝕣 Using an audiovisual display and graphic exhibits, this center tells the story of one of Ireland's great female heroes, Granuaile (Grace) O'Malley (1530–1600). Known as the "pirate queen," Grace led battles against the English and ruled the baronies of Burrishoole and Murrisk, around Clew Bay. Her extraordinary exploits are recounted in Elizabethan state papers. The center also includes a craft shop and coffee shop.

Louisburgh, county Mayo. ℗ **098/66341**. Admission €3.50 ($3.10) adults, €2 ($1.80) seniors and students, €1.60 ($1.40) children. June to mid-Sept Mon–Sat 10am–6pm.

Mayo North Heritage Centre If your ancestors came from Mayo, this center will help you trace your family tree. The data bank includes indexes to church registers of all denominations, plus school roll books, leases, and wills. Even if you have no connections in Mayo, you'll enjoy the adjacent museum, with its displays of rural household items, farm machinery, and farm implements, including the *gowl-gob*, a spadelike implement exclusive to this locality. The center also offers a new 5- to 10-day blacksmithing course. The lovely Enniscoe Gardens adjoin the center; combined tickets to the center and gardens are available. There is also a tearoom on the premises.

Note: If your ancestors were from the southern part of Ireland, try the **South Mayo Family Research Centre,** Town Hall, Neale Road, Ballinrobe, county Mayo (© **092/41214**). It's open Monday to Friday 9:30am to noon and 1:30 to 4pm.

On Lough Conn, about 3.2km (2 miles) south of Crossmolina, off R315, Enniscoe, Castlehill, Ballina, county Mayo. © **096/31809**. Fax 096/31885. www.mayoroots.com. Admission to museum €5 ($4.45) adults, €2 ($1.80) children. Oct–May Mon–Fri 9am–4pm; June–Sept Mon–Fri 9am–6pm and Sat–Sun 2–6pm.

National Shrine of Our Lady of Knock ⭐ It's said that here, in 1879, local townspeople witnessed an appearance of Mary, the mother of Jesus. Considered the Lourdes or Fatima of Ireland, Knock came to the world's attention in 1979, when Pope John Paul II visited the shrine. Knock's centerpiece is a huge circular basilica seating 7,000 people and containing artifacts or furnishings from every county in Ireland. The grounds also hold a folk museum and a religious bookshop.

On the N17 Galway rd., Knock, county Mayo. © **094/88100**. Free admission to shrine; museum €2.50 ($2.25) adults, €1.30 ($1.15) seniors and children over age 5; free for children under 5. Shrine and grounds year-round daily 8am–6pm or later; museum May–Oct daily 10am–6pm.

Westport House ⭐ *Kids* At the edge of town you can visit Westport House, a late 18th-century residence that's the home of Lord Altamont, the marquis of Sligo, who is in residence with his family. The work of Richard Cassels and James Wyatt, the house is graced with a staircase of ornate white Sicilian marble, unusual art nouveau glass and carvings, family heirlooms, and silver. The grandeur of the residence is admittedly compromised by the commercial enterprises on its grounds, including a small children's zoo and amusement park.

Westport, county Mayo. © **098/25430**. www.westporthouse.ie. Admission to house and children's animal and bird park €16 ($14) adults, €11 ($10) students, €9 ($8) seniors, €6.50 ($5.80) children; to house only €8 ($7.10) adults, €5 ($4.45) seniors and students, €4.50 ($4) children. Westport House only: Apr–May Sun 2–5pm and Sept daily 2–5pm. Westport House and children's animal and bird park: June daily 1:30–5:30pm; July–Aug Mon–Fri 11:30am–5:30pm and Sat–Sun 1:30–5:30pm.

SPORTS & OUTDOOR PURSUITS

FISHING The waters of the River Moy and loughs Carrowmore and Conn offer some of the best fishing in Europe, and are some of Ireland's premier sources for salmon and trout. For general information about fishing in county Mayo, contact the **North Western Regional Fisheries Board,** Ardnaree House, Abbey Street, Ballina (© **096/22788;** www.cfb.ie).

To arrange a day's fishing, contact **Cloonamoyne Fishery** ⭐, Castlehill, near Crossmolina, Ballina (© **096/31851**). Managed by an Irish-born former New Yorker, Barry Segrave, this professional angling service will advise and equip you to fish the local waters—for brown trout on loughs Conn and Cullin; for salmon on loughs Beltra, Furnace, and Feeagh; and for salmon and sea trout on the rivers Moy and Deel. The fishery rents fully equipped boats and tackle, teaches fly-casting, and provides transport to and from all fishing. Daily rates average €18 ($16) for a boat, €40 ($36) for a boat with engine, and €65 ($58) for a boat with engine and *ghillie* (guide).

County Mayo is also home to the **Pontoon Bridge Fly Fishing School,** Pontoon, county Mayo (© **094/56120;** http://pontoon.mayo-ireland.ie/FlySchl/FlySchl.htm). Daily rates average €32 ($28) for a boat, €45 ($40) for a boat with engine, and €77 ($69) for a boat with engine and *ghillie*. This school offers 1- to 4-day courses in the art of fly-casting, as well as fly tying, tackle design, and other information necessary for successful game fishing. Fees range from €45 to

€134 ($40–$119), depending on the duration of the course. Courses run daily from April to late September. The newly expanded Pontoon Bridge Hotel also runs painting and cooking classes.

Permits and state fishing licenses can be obtained at the **North Mayo Angling Advice Centre** (Tiernan Bros.), Upper Main Street, Foxford, county Mayo (© **094/56731**). It also offers a wide range of services, including boat hire and *ghillies.*

For fishing tackle, try **Jones Ltd., General Merchants,** Main Street, Foxford, county Mayo (© **094/56121**), or **Walkins Fishing Tackle,** Tone Street, Ballina, county Mayo (© **096/22442**).

GOLF   County Mayo's 18-hole golf courses include a par-72 links course at **Belmullet Golf Course,** Carne, Belmullet, county Mayo (© **097/82292; www.belmulletgolfclub.ie**), with greens fees of €35 ($31); and a par-71 inland course at **Castlebar Golf Club,** Rocklands, Castlebar, county Mayo (© **094/ 21649**), with greens fees of €28 ($25) weekdays and €32 ($28) weekends. The par-73 championship course at **Westport Golf Club,** county Mayo (© **098/ 28262; www.golfwestport.com**), charges greens fees of €35 ($31) weekdays, €41 ($36) weekends. Set on the shores of Clew Bay, the course winds around the precipitous slopes of Croagh Patrick Mountain. It's one of western Ireland's most challenging and scenic courses.

KAYAKING   Courses for adults and children are offered at the **Killala Bay Adventure and Education Centre,** operated with the Killala Youth Hostel, Killala, county Mayo (© **096/37172**). The kayaking is mostly in Killala Bay, a beautiful inlet north of Ballina, and very reasonable rates are available for packages including room, full board, and activities.

WALKING   The region to the east of the Mullet peninsula offers a spectacular array of sheer sea cliffs and craggy islands. The small, secluded beach at **Portacloy,** 14km (8½ miles) north of Glenamoy on the R314 is a good starting point for a dramatic walk. On a sunny day, its aquamarine waters and fine-grained white sand recall the Mediterranean more than the North Atlantic. At its western edge, there is a concrete quay. From here, head north up the steep green slopes of the nearest hill. Don't be too distracted by the fantastic view or adorable little sheep: The unassuming boggy slopes on which you are walking end precipitously at an unmarked cliff edge—the walk is not recommended for children. Exercise caution and resist the urge to try to get a better view of mysterious sea caves or to reach the outermost extents of the coast's promontories. Instead, use a farmer's fence as a guide and head west toward the striking profile of **Benwee Head,** about 2.4km (1½ miles) away. Return the same way to have a swim in the chilly, tranquil waters of Portocloy.

WHERE TO STAY
VERY EXPENSIVE

Ashford Castle ★★★   From turrets and towers to drawbridge and battlements, this sprawling castle is indeed a fairy-tale resort. It dates from the 13th century, when it was first the home of the De Burgo (Burke) family and later the country residence of the Guinnesses. A hotel since 1939, it has been enlarged and updated over the years. It drew worldwide media attention in 1984 when President Ronald Reagan stayed here during his visit to Ireland, and in 2001 when 007 himself, Pierce Brosnan, held his wedding here. On the shores of Lough Corrib amid 140 forested, flowering hectares (350 acres), it sits in the heart of the scenic territory that was the setting for the film classic *The Quiet Man.*

The interior is rich in baronial furniture, medieval armor, carved oak paneling and stairways, objets d'art, and masterpiece oil paintings. Guest rooms are decorated with designer fabrics and traditional furnishings, some with canopied or four-poster beds. Jacket and tie are required for men in the restaurant after 7pm.

Cong, county Mayo. ℂ **800/346-7007** in the U.S., or 092/46003. Fax 092/46260. www.ashford.ie. 83 units. €194–€466 ($173–$415) double. Suites also available. Rates include tax and service charge. AE, DC, MC, V. **Amenities:** Restaurant (Continental, French); bar; 9-hole golf course; tennis court; gym; Jacuzzi; sauna; salmon and trout fishing; boating; concierge; room service; babysitting; laundry service. *In room:* TV, minibar, hair dryer, garment press.

EXPENSIVE

Newport House Hotel ★★★ *(Finds* Everybody gushes in superlatives about Newport House, perhaps the most magnificent—and magnificently unselfconscious country house hotel in Ireland. Close to the Clew Bay coast, this ivy-covered Georgian mansion sits at the edge of town along the Newport River, making it a favorite base for salmon anglers. It was originally part of the estate of the O'Donnell family, ancient Irish chieftains. There's fine, ornate plasterwork on the soaring ceilings, and a dramatic, skylit dome crowns the cascading central staircase. The public areas make you feel like

> ### Service Charges
> *A reminder:* Unless otherwise noted, room rates don't include service charges (usually 10%– 15% of your bill).

you have a bit part in lavish period film—all antique furnishings, oil paintings, and cases of fishing trophies. The guest rooms are spread among the main house and two smaller courtyard buildings. They're quite spacious and elegant, with Georgian sash windows, high ceilings, antique furnishings, and original paintings and prints. Then there's the restaurant, a destination in itself and a place of pilgrimage for any food lover. If you want to experience the Irish country house at its best, you really won't find anything better than the Newport House.

Newport, county Mayo. ℂ **800/223-6510** in the U.S., or 098/41222. Fax 098/41613. www.newporthouse.ie. 18 units. €202–€252 ($180–$224) double. No service charge. Rates include full breakfast. AE, DC, MC, V. Closed Oct to mid-Mar. **Amenities:** Restaurant (Continental); bar; drawing room; private salmon and sea-trout fishing. *In room:* TV, hair dryer.

MODERATE

Breaffy House ★ If you've always wanted to stay in one of those trumpets-blaring, grand castle hotels but didn't think you could afford it, here's your chance. A long paved driveway leads to this sprawling baronial mansion, picturesquely ensconced amid 40 hectares (100 acres) of gardens and woodlands. The public areas are furnished with traditional and period pieces. Guest rooms aren't as luxurious as those in many other (more expensive) castle hotels, and they vary in size and shape. Yet each is attractive and comfortable, if a bit functional. Breaffy House is part of the Best Western chain.

Claremorris Rd., Castlebar, county Mayo. ℂ **800/528-1234** in the U.S., or 094/22033. Fax 094/22276. www. breaffyhouse.ie. 62 units. €110–€130 ($98–$116) double. No service charge. AE, DC, MC, V. Free parking. **Amenities:** Restaurant (Continental); bar; minigym; babysitting; drawing room. *In room:* TV, tea/coffeemaker, hair dryer, garment press.

Enniscoe House ★★ This is a terrific place for unwinding and escaping the real world. Overlooking Lough Conn and surrounded by a wooded estate with more than 4.8km (3 miles) of nature walks, this two-story Georgian country inn has been described as "the last great house of North Mayo." It is owned and run by Susan Kellett, a descendant of the original family that settled on the lands in the 1660s. Enniscoe's interior is truly magnificent, with delicate plasterwork, lovely fireplaces, and a fabulous staircase. The place abounds with family portraits, antique furniture, early drawings, and pictures of the house and surrounding area. Guest rooms are individually furnished; those at the front of the house are particularly impressive, with huge hand-carved armoires and canopied or four-poster beds with firm mattresses. All rooms have views of parkland or the lake. Meals here feature fish from local rivers, produce from the house's farm, and vegetables and herbs from the adjacent garden. Enniscoe also has its own fishery (see Cloonamoyne Fishery under "Fishing" in "Sports & Outdoor Pursuits," above). Self-catering apartments are also available.

3.2km (2 miles) south of Crossmollina, off R315, next to the North Mayo Heritage Centre, Castlehill, near Crossmolina, Ballina, county Mayo. ✆ 800/223-6510 in the U.S., or 096/31112. Fax 096/31773. www.ennis coe.com. 6 units. €144–€172 ($128–$153) double. Dinner from €36 ($32). No service charge. Rates include full breakfast. AE, MC, V. Closed mid-Oct to Mar. **Amenities:** Nonsmoking rooms; drawing room. *In room:* TV.

Mount Falcon Castle 🏰🏰 If you love fishing, this award-winning, ivy-clad country house is nirvana—complete with dogs, Wellington boots, and many a tale about the one that got away. A stay here entitles you to salmon and trout fishing on Lough Conn and to fishing in a salmon preserve on the River Moy. Built in 1876 by the same man who did much of the exterior work at Ashford Castle in Cong (see above), this handsome, gabled, Victorian-style manor is set in a 40-hectare (100-acre) wooded estate 6.5km (4 miles) south of Ballina. The decor in both the public areas and the guest rooms is an eclectic blend of comfort pieces—fluffy throw pillows, carved chests, and gilded mirrors. The Aldridge family enthusiastically caters to anglers' needs and will prepare and serve you your day's catch for dinner.

Foxford Rd. (N57), Ballina, county Mayo. ✆ 800/223-6510 in the U.S., or 096/70811. Fax 096/71517. 9 units. €90–€154 ($80–$137) double. Rates include full breakfast. Dinner €32 ($28). AE, DC, MC, V. Closed Feb–Mar and Christmas week. **Amenities:** Tennis court; private salmon and trout fishing; drawing room.

The Olde Railway Hotel 🏰 William Thackeray's description of this hotel in 1834—"one of the prettiest, comfortablest inns in Ireland"—remains true. The Olde Railway Hotel, built in 1780 by Lord Sligo to accommodate his "overflow" houseguests, has been tastefully restored by the Rosenkranz family. Its bright yellow facade is warm and welcoming; inside, it exudes charm and a touch of elegance. No two rooms are alike; each has been given a distinctive character. Twenty-two rooms face the tree-lined Carrowbeg River. The superior rooms are more spacious and include a sitting area with sofa. Bicycles are also available for guests who wish to take a pedal through town.

The Mall, Westport, county Mayo. ✆ **098/25166.** Fax 098/25090. www.anu.ie/railwayhotel. 27 units. €100–€180 ($89–$160) double. No service charge. Rates include full breakfast. AE, DC, MC, V. **Amenities:** Bar. *In room:* TV.

INEXPENSIVE

Drom Caoin 🏰 *(Kids* The view of Blacksod Bay is terrific from Mairin Maguire-Murphy's comfortable home, a short walk from the center of Belmullet. Two of the guest rooms have recently been renovated into self-catering apartments that can be rented by the night or by the week, with or without breakfast. It's a great concept—you can actually settle in, cook some of your own meals, and enjoy the extra space of a suite for a little more money than an average B&B room. The ground-floor apartment faces a parking lot at the back of the house—not a great view, but there's plenty of room for a family with a pullout couch in the sitting room, a bedroom with a double bed, and a loft-nook, which is just the right size for a small child. The other apartment is on the upper floor of the house, and is very comfortable for a couple—the kitchen adjoins a small dining room/sitting room with a sloping ceiling and a skylight view of the bay. It's not spacious, but it is very comfortable. The other two bedrooms are small, with compact bathrooms. Breakfast is something to look forward to here— omelets, fresh fish, and toasted cheese are offered periodically as alternatives to the standard fry, and the fresh scones are delicious.

Belmullet, county Mayo. ✆ and fax **097/81195**. 4 units (2 with shower only, no tub). €54 ($48) double; €250 ($223) apts by the week (without breakfast). 33% reduction for children. MC, V. *In room:* TV.

Dun Maeve ★★ *Value*   This beautifully restored and expanded 19th-century Georgian townhouse provides elegance, comfort, and extraordinary convenience—it is in the heart of Westport town, just around the corner from the tourist office. It is clearly a cut above almost any B&B you'll come across. Each room is unique and eminently tasteful and the range of accommodations meets the needs of couples, families, and single travelers. The beds are firm, the bathrooms are spacious, and the breakfast-room conservatory is a real treat.

If you want to stay in the Westport area for a week or more, hostess Maria Hughes also offers two self-catering, four-bedroom holiday homes. Each sleeps seven. They're less than a mile from the town, near the harbor, and come fully furnished. Rates range roughly from €380 to €640 ($338–$570) per week.

Newport Rd., Westport, county Mayo. ✆ **098/26529**. Fax 098/25055. 6 units. €80 ($71) double. Rates include full breakfast. MC, V. **Amenities:** Sitting room. *In room:* TV.

WHERE TO DINE
MODERATE
Echoes ★★ *Finds* CONTINENTAL   Look out for the lilac-colored, two-story building in the middle of Main Street in Cong, for it's one of the most likable eateries in western Ireland. Tom Ryan Jr. gets his meats from his dad's butcher shop, right next door, and the quality of the produce is exceptional. He does all the classics—lamb with rosemary sauce, steak with peppercorns—only better than almost everybody else, and always with very punchy, distinct flavors. Tom's fish dishes are likewise fresh and flavorful, be it dreamy scallops with bacon in garlic butter or his prawn scampi with tomato-and-basil sauce. Starters and desserts are also impressive (the homemade ice creams have attained near-legend status in these parts), and it's hard to find a downside to this happy, fun place.

Main St., Cong, county Mayo. ✆ **092/46059**. Reservations recommended. Dinner main courses €11–€18 ($10–$16). AE, MC, V. Mon–Sun 6:30–10pm.

The Quay Cottage ★ SEAFOOD   Overlooking Westport Harbour, Quay Cottage is done up from top-to-bottom with nautical bric-a-brac. The menu presents fresh, beautifully prepared seafood, such as lemon sole beurre blanc or wild local salmon, with an array of daily specials; a request for a plain steak can also be fulfilled. A separate nonsmoking room is available. You can take a waterside stroll after your meal.

The Quay, Westport, county Mayo. ✆ **098/26412**. Reservations recommended. Main courses €16–€22 ($14–$20). AE, MC, V. Daily 6–10pm. Closed Christmas.

INEXPENSIVE
The Continental Cafe ★ VEGETARIAN   Comforting, hearty food is the hallmark of the Continental Cafe. The salad of the day, made with fresh, crisp greens and crunchy vegetables, accompanies hearty pita sandwiches, pasta casseroles, or quiche heavy with sharp cheddar. The menu is as eclectic: gado-gado

from Thailand is served alongside the more prosaic stuffed baked potatoes and toasted sandwiches. Service is conscientious and friendly, and a whole floor is set aside for nonsmoking diners.

High St., Westport, county Mayo. ✆ **098/26679.** Main courses €3–€10 ($2.67–$8.90). No credit cards. Thurs–Tues noon–7pm.

The Old Mill CAFE/TEAROOM   On the grounds of the historic Foxford Woollen Mills (see the "Exploring the County," section earlier in this chapter), this is a nice place to grab a bite in a setting that's bright and airy. On the menu: soups, salads, sandwiches, and cold meat plates, as well as quiche, lasagna, sausage rolls, scones, muffins, and desserts. There are also daily hot meal specials.

Foxford Woollen Mills, Foxford, county Mayo. ✆ **094/56756.** All items €3–€10 ($2.65–$8.90). MC, V. Mon–Sat 10am–5:30pm; Sun noon–5:30pm.

2 Sligo & Yeats Country

Sligo Town is 219km (136 miles) NE of Shannon Airport, 217km (135 miles) NW of Dublin, 76km (47 miles) NE of Knock, 60km (37 miles) NE of Ballina, 140km (87 miles) NE of Galway, 118km (73 miles) N of Athlone, and 337km (209 miles) N of Cork

Sligo Town (pop. 18,000) is northwest Ireland's most important town, a thriving merchant's hub that sits mostly on the south side of the River Garavogue and is surrounded on three sides by mountains, the most famous of which are Ben Bulben to the north and Knocknarea to the south. More importantly, it's at the epicenter of Yeats Country. Though born in Dublin, W. B. Yeats spent so much time in county Sligo that it became a part of him, and he a part of it.

Sligo Town is in the midst of a major renaissance. Roughly half to two-thirds of the town center has been refurbished in the past 9 years. From a visitor's perspective, the focus of this radical rejuvenation has been Sligo's new "Left Bank," where cafes and restaurants spill onto the waterfront promenade whenever weather permits.

When you plan your itinerary, give yourself plenty of time to explore the surrounding countryside. As you'll quickly discover in Yeats Country, every hill, rill, cottage, vale, and lake seems to bear a plaque indicating its relation to the poet or his works.

SLIGO TOWN ESSENTIALS

GETTING THERE   Aer Aeran operates daily flights into **Sligo Airport,** Strandhill, county Sligo (✆ **071/68280;** www.sligoairport.com), 8km (5 miles) southwest of Sligo Town. The bus to Sligo town from the airport will cost you under €3 ($2.65), while you can expect a taxi to cost around €12 ($11).

Irish Rail, with its station on Lord Edward Street (✆ **071/69888;** www. irishrail.ie), operates daily service into Sligo from Dublin and other points.

Bus Eireann, also pulling into Lord Edward Street (✆ **071/60066;** www. buseireann.ie), operates daily bus service to Sligo from Dublin, Galway, and other points, including Derry in Northern Ireland.

Four major roads lead to Sligo: N4 from Dublin and the east, N17 from Galway and the south, N15 from Donegal to the north, and N16 from county Fermanagh in Northern Ireland.

VISITOR INFORMATION   For information about Sligo and the surrounding area, contact the **North West Regional Tourism Office,** Aras Reddan, Temple Street, Sligo (✆ **071/61201;** www.northwestireland.travel.ie). It's open year-round, weekdays 9am to 5pm, with weekend and extended hours April to

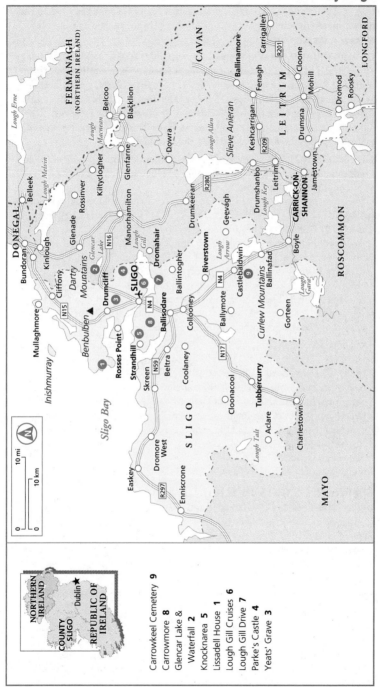

County Sligo

Carrowkeel Cemetery **9**
Carrowmore **8**
Glencar Lake &
  Waterfall **2**
Knocknarea **5**
Lissadell House **1**
Lough Gill Cruises **6**
Lough Gill Drive **7**
Parke's Castle **4**
Yeats' Grave **3**

August. The most comprehensive local Internet source for Sligo can be found at **www.sligotourism.ie**.

TOWN LAYOUT   Edged by Sligo Bay to the west, Sligo Town sits beside the Garavogue River. Most of the city's commercial district lies on the south bank of the river. **O'Connell Street** is the main north-south artery of the downtown district. The main east-west thoroughfare is **Stephen Street,** which becomes Wine Street and then Lord Edward Street. The **Tourist Office** is in the south-west corner of the town on Temple Street, 2 blocks south of O'Connell Street. Three bridges span the river; the **Douglas Hyde Bridge,** named for Ireland's first president, is the main link between the two sides.

GETTING AROUND   There is no public transport in the town of Sligo. During July and August, **Bus Eireann** (© 071/60066) runs from Sligo Town to Strandhill and Rosses Point.

Taxis line up at the taxi rank on Quay Street. If you prefer to call for a taxi, try **A Cabs** (© 071/45777), **ACE Cabs** (© 071/44444), **Greenline Hackney Cabs** (© 071/69000), or **Sligo Cabs** (© 071/71888).

You'll need a car to see the sights outside Sligo Town. If you need to hire a vehicle locally, contact **Budget Rent-A-Car,** Sligo Airport, Strandhill (© 0903/ 24614); or **Murrays Europcar,** Sligo Airport (© 071/68400).

The best way to see Sligo Town itself is on foot. Follow the signposted route of the Tourist Trail. The walk takes approximately 90 minutes. From mid-June to September, the **Tourist Office,** Temple Street, Sligo (© 071/61201), offers guided tours; contact the office for details and reservations.

FAST FACTS   In an emergency, dial © **999. St. John's Hospital** is at Ballytivan, Sligo (© 071/42606), or you can try **Sligo county Hospital,** The Mall (© 071/ 42620). The local **Garda Station** is on Pearse Road (© 071/42031).

Need to check your e-mail? Three minutes' walk from the center of Sligo Town, you'll find the **Galaxy Cyber Cafe,** Millbrook Riverside (© 071/40441; www.cisl.ie). There are also Internet-accessible PCs at the **county Sligo Library,** on Stephen Street (© 071/42212), which is open Tuesday to Friday 10am to 5pm, Saturday 10am to 1pm and 2 to 5pm.

The **Sligo General Post Office,** Wine Street (© 071/42646), is open Monday through Saturday 9am to 5:30pm.

SEEING THE SIGHTS IN SLIGO TOWN

Model Arts Centre ⪑   Although this is a relatively new development in Sligo (it opened in 1991), it carries on the Yeatsean literary and artistic traditions. Housed in an 1850 Romanesque-style stone building that was originally a school, it offers nine rooms for touring shows and local exhibits by artists, sculptors, writers, and musicians. In the summer, there are often poetry readings and arts lectures.

The Mall, Sligo, county Sligo. © 071/41405. Free admission. Readings and lectures €4–€7 ($3.55–$6.25). No credit cards. Mon–Sat 11am–6pm; evening events 8pm.

Sligo Abbey ⪑⪑   Founded as a Dominican house in 1252 by Maurice Fitzgerald, earl of Kildare, Sligo Abbey was destroyed by fire in 1414 and rebuilt 2 years later. It flourished in medieval times and was the burial place of the kings and princes of Sligo. After many raids and sackings, the abbey was closed in 1641. Much restoration work has been done in recent years, and the cloisters are considered outstanding examples of stone carving; the 15th-century altar is one of the few intact medieval altars in Ireland.

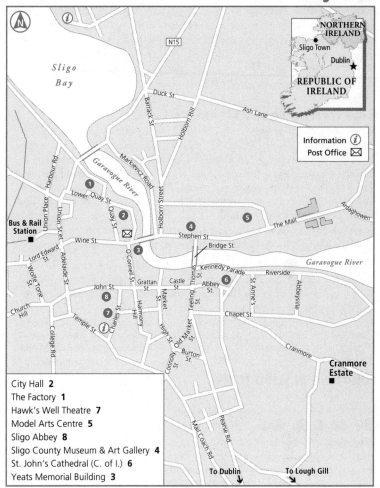

NORTHERN IRELAND

Sligo Town

Dublin ★

REPUBLIC OF IRELAND

Information *i*
Post Office ✉

Sligo Bay

N15

Duck St.

Barrack St.

Holborn Hill

Ash Lane

Harbour Rd.

Markievicz Road

Garavogue River

Lower Quay St.

❶

Union Place

Union St.

Quay St.

❷

Holborn Street

Ardaghowen

❺

The Mall

Bus & Rail Station

✉

Wine St.

Stephen St.

❹

Bridge St.

Lord Edward St.

Adelaide St.

O'Connell St.

❸

Kennedy Parade

Riverside

Garavogue River

Wolfe Tone St.

John St.

Grattan St.

Castle St.

Thomas St.

Abbey St.

❻

St Anne's

Abbeyville

Church Hill

College Rd.

Temple St.

❽

Charles St.

Harmony Hill

Market St.

Teeling St.

Chapel St.

Cranmore

Burton St.

❼

i

High St.

Old Market St.

Connolly St.

Cranmore Estate

Mall Coach Rd.

Pearse Rd.

To Dublin ↓

To Lough Gill ↘

City Hall **2**
The Factory **1**
Hawk's Well Theatre **7**
Model Arts Centre **5**
Sligo Abbey **8**
Sligo County Museum & Art Gallery **4**
St. John's Cathedral (C. of I.) **6**
Yeats Memorial Building **3**

Abbey St., Sligo, county Sligo. ✆ **071/46406.** Admission €2 ($1.75) adults, €1.30 ($1.15) seniors, €.80 (70¢) students and children, €5 ($4.45) family. No credit cards. Daily 9:30am–6:30pm. Closed Oct–May.

Sligo County Museum & Niland Gallery ⋆⋆   Housed in a church manse of the mid–19th century, this museum exhibits material of national and local interest dating to pre-Christian times. One section, devoted to the Yeats family, includes a display of William Butler Yeats's complete works in first editions, poems on broadsheets, letters, and his Nobel Prize for literature (1923). This same section contains the Niland Gallery, a collection of oils, watercolors, and drawings by Jack B. Yeats (W. B. Yeats's brother) and John B. Yeats (William and Jack's father). There is also a permanent collection of 20th-century Irish art, including works by Paul Henry and Evie Hone.

Stephen St., Sligo, county Sligo. ✆ **071/42212.** sligolib@iol.ie. Free admission. Tues–Sat 10am–noon and 2–4:50pm. Closed Oct–May.

Yeats Memorial Building ✦   In a 19th-century red-brick Victorian building, this memorial contains an extensive library with items of special interest to Yeats scholars. The building is also headquarters of the Yeats International Summer School and the Sligo Art Gallery, which exhibits works by local, national, and international artists. The latest addition to the memorial is a full cafe.

Douglas Hyde Bridge, Sligo, county Sligo. ℂ **071/42693**. www.yeats-sligo.com. Free admission. Year-round Mon–Fri 9:30am–5pm.

SIGHTSEEING TOURS & CRUISES

JH Transport   This fine family-operated company offers narrated minibus tours of the Sligo area, departing daily from the Sligo Tourist Office. The morning tour follows the Lough Gill Drive, and the afternoon tour visits Yeats's grave, Lissadell House, Glencar Lake and Waterfall, and—if time permits and the popular will is there—Carrowmore (see below). Phone ahead to confirm schedules and booking. With the morning tour, you have the option of returning to Sligo on a water bus via Innisfree Island.

57 Mountain Close, Carton View, Sligo, county Sligo. ℂ **071/42747** or 086/833-9084 (mobile). Bus tours €14 ($12) adults, €6.50 ($5.80) children 6–16. Water bus return option €4.50 ($4) extra.

Lough Gill Cruises   On this tour, you cruise on Lough Gill and the Garavogue River aboard the 72-passenger *Wild Rose* water bus while listening to the poetry of Yeats. Trips to the Lake Isle of Innisfree are also scheduled. An onboard bar serves refreshments.

Blue Lagoon, Riverside, Sligo, county Sligo. ℂ **071/64266**. Lough Gill cruise €8 ($7.10) adults, €4 ($3.55) children over 10; Innisfree cruise €6.50 ($5.80) adults, €3.20 ($2.85) children over 10. June–Sept Lough Gill cruise daily 2:30 and 4:30pm; Innisfree tour daily 12:30, 3:30, and 6:30pm. Apr–May and Oct (Sun only) cruise and tour schedule subject to demand; call ahead.

SHOPPING IN SLIGO TOWN

Most Sligo shops are open Monday to Saturday 9am to 6pm, and some may have extended hours during July and August.

The Cat & the Moon   This shop offers uniquely-designed crafts from throughout Ireland, ranging from beeswax candles and baskets to modern art, metal and ceramic work, wood turning, hand weaving, Celtic jewelry, and furniture. An expanded gallery displays a large variety of paintings, limited-edition prints, and occasionally sculpture. 4 Castle St., Sligo, county Sligo. ℂ **071/43686**.

Kates Kitchen/Hopper & Pettit   Kates has an outstanding delicatessen section, with gourmet meats, cheeses, salads, patés, and breads baked on the premises, all ideal makings for a picnic by Lough Gill. Don't miss the handmade Irish chocolates and preserves. Hopper & Pettit stocks potpourri, soaps, and natural oils as well as Crabtree & Evelyn products. 24 Market St., Sligo, county Sligo. ℂ **071/ 43022**.

M. Quirke   Michael Quirke started out as a butcher, but a few years ago he traded his cleaver for woodcarving tools and transformed his butcher shop into a craft studio. Step inside and watch as he transforms chunks of native timbers into Ireland's heroes of mythology, from Sligo's Queen Maeve to Cu Chulainn, Oisin, and other folklore characters. He also carves chess sets and other Irish-themed wood items. The price of an individual carving averages €85 ($76). Wine St., Sligo, county Sligo. ℂ **071/42624**.

Music Room   Just off O'Connell Street, this small cottagelike store draws you to it with the sounds of Irish music. This is a great spot to purchase Irish musical instruments and accessories. A sister shop, the Record Room, a half a block away on Grattan Street (ℭ **071/43748**), offers cassettes, CDs, videos, and records. Harmony Hill, Sligo, county Sligo. ℭ **071/44765**.

Sligo Craft Pottery   This shop features the work of one of Ireland's foremost ceramic artists, Michael Kennedy, who produces pottery and porcelain with layers of textured markings and drawings that form a maze of intricate patterns. He then applies glazes that reflect the strong tones and shades of the Irish countryside. The result is one-of-a-kind vases, jars, dishes, figurines, buttons, jewelry, and other pieces. Market Yard, Sligo, county Sligo. ℭ **071/62586**.

Sligo Crystal & Giftware Ltd   This workshop, in new premises in Sligo Town, is noted for its personalized engraving of such items as family crests on mirrors or glassware. The craftspeople also produce hand-cut crystal candlesticks, glasses, and curio items like crystal bells and scent bottles. Crystal pieces can be cut to a pattern of your creation or choice. Weekdays, you'll see the craftspeople at work. 2 Hyde Bridge House, Hyde Bridge, Sligo, county Sligo. ℭ **071/43440**.

Wehrly Bros. Ltd   Established in 1875, this is one of Sligo's oldest shops, noted for a fine selection of jewelry and watches, as well as cold-cast bronze sculptures of Irish figures, silverware, Claddagh rings, Waterford crystal, Belleek china, and Galway crystal. 3 O'Connell St., Sligo, county Sligo. ℭ **071/42252**.

EXPLORING THE SURROUNDING COUNTRYSIDE

Sligo's great antiquity can be counted in the seemingly numberless grave mounds, standing stones, ring circles, and dolmens still marking its starkly stunning landscape. The county contains the greatest concentration of megalithic sites in all of Ireland.

A fitting place to begin exploring ancient Sligo is at **Carrowmore** (see listing below), a vast Neolithic cemetery that once contained perhaps as many as 200 passage tombs, some of which predate Newgrange by 500 years. From Carrowmore, the Neolithic mountaintop cemetery of **Carrowkeel** is visible in the distant south. Less than an hour's drive away (ask for detailed directions at the Carrowmore Visitors Centre), it offers an experience beyond any account: After a breathtaking ascent on foot, you'll find yourself alone with the past. The tombs, facing Carrowmore below and aligned with the summer solstice, are rarely visited.

To the west is **Knocknarea** (323m/1,078 ft.), on whose summit sits a gigantic unexcavated *cairn* (grave mound). It's known as ***Miscaun Meadhbh* (Maeve's Mound),** even though it predates Maeve—an early Celtic warrior queen who plays a central role in the *Táin Bó Cuilnge*, the Celtic epic—by millennia. Legend has it that she's buried standing, in full battle gear, spear in hand, facing her Ulster enemies even in death. This extraordinary tomb is 189m (630 ft.) around at its base, 24m (80 ft.) high, 30m (100 ft.) in diameter, and visible for miles.

At the foot of Knocknarea is **Strandhill,** 8km (5 miles) from Sligo Town. This delightful resort area stretches into Sligo Bay, with a sand-duned beach and a patch of land nearby called Coney Island, which is usually credited with lending its name to the New York beach amusement area. Across the bay, about 6.5km (4 miles) north of Sligo Town, is another beach resort, Rosses Point.

Northwest of Sligo Bay, 6.5km (4 miles) offshore, lies the uninhabited island of **Inishmurray** ⟡, which contains the haunting ruins of one of Ireland's earliest monastic settlements. Founded in the 6th century and destroyed by the Vikings in 807, the monastery of St. Molaise contains in its circular walls the remains of several churches, beehive cells, altars, and an assemblage of "cursing stones" once used to bring ruin on those who presumably deserved it. For transportation to the island, call **Joe McGowan** (✆ **071/66267**) or **Brendan Merrifield** (✆ **071/41874**).

Most of Sligo's attractions are associated in some way with the poet William Butler Yeats, as you'll note below.

Carrowmore Megalithic Cemetery ★★★ Here, at the dead center of the Coolera Peninsula, sits the giant's tomb, a massive passage grave that once had a stone circle of its own. Circling it, and in nearly every instance facing it, were as many as 100 to 200 passage graves, each circled in stone. Tomb 52A, excavated in August 1998, is estimated to be 7,400 years old, making it the earliest known piece of freestanding stone architecture in the world. Circles within circles within circles describe a stone-and-spirit world of the dead whose power touches every visitor who stops to see and consider it—it's one of the great sacred landscapes of the ancient world. The cemetery's interpretive center offers informative exhibits and tours.

Carrowmore Visitors Centre (signposted on N4 and N15), county Sligo. ✆ **071/61534.** Admission €2 ($1.80) adults, €1.30 ($1.15) seniors, €.80 (70¢) students and children, €5 ($4.45) family. No credit cards. Daily 9:30am–6:30pm. Both visitor center and site closed Oct–Apr.

Glencar Lake ★★ This Yeats Country attraction is just over the border in county Leitrim. Lovely Glencar Lake stretches east for 3.2km (2 miles) along a verdant valley, highlighted by two waterfalls, one of which rushes downward for 15m (50 ft.). Yeats's "The Stolen Child" speaks wondrously of this lake.

Off N16, Glencar, county Leitrim.

Lissadell House ★★ On the shores of Sligo Bay, this large neoclassical building was another of Yeats's favorite haunts. Dating from 1830, it has long been the home of the Gore-Booth family, including Yeats's friends Eva Gore-Booth, a fellow poet, and her sister Constance, who became the Countess Markievicz after marrying a Polish count. She took part in the 1916 Irish Rising and was the first woman elected to the British House of Commons and the first woman cabinet member in the Irish Dáil. The house is full of such family memorabilia as the travel diaries of Sir Robert Gore-Booth, who mortgaged the estate to help the poor during the famine. At the core of the house is a dramatic two-story hallway lined with Doric columns leading to a double staircase of Kilkenny marble.

Off N15, 13km (8 miles) north of Sligo, Drumcliffe, county Sligo. ✆ **074/63150.** Admission €4 ($3.55) adults, €1.30 ($1.15) children. June to mid-Sept Mon–Sat 10:30am–12:30pm and 2–4:30pm.

The Lough Gill Drive ★★★ This 42km (26-mile) drive-yourself tour around Lough Gill is well signposted. Head 1.6km (1 mile) south of town and follow the signs for **Lough Gill,** the beautiful lake that figured so prominently in Yeats's writings. Within 3.2km (2 miles) you'll be on the lower edge of the shoreline. Among the sites are **Dooney Rock,** with its own nature trail and lakeside walk (inspiration for the poem "Fiddler of Dooney"); the **Lake Isle of Innisfree,** made famous in Yeats's poetry and in song; and the **Hazelwood Sculpture Trail,** a unique forest walk along the shores of Lough Gill, with 13 wood sculptures.

The storied Innisfree is only one of 22 islands in Lough Gill. You can drive the whole lakeside circuit in less than an hour, or you can stop at the east end and visit **Dromahair** ★, a delightful village on the River Bonet, in county Leitrim. The road along Lough Gill's upper shore brings you back to the northern end of Sligo

Town. Continue north on the main road (N15), and you'll see the graceful profile of **Ben Bulben** (519m/1,730 ft.), one of the Dartry Mountains, rising to the right. County Sligo and county Leitrim.

Parke's Castle ✿✿   On the north side of the Lough Gill Drive, on the county Leitrim side of the border, Parke's Castle stands out as a lone outpost amid the natural tableau of lake view and woodland scenery. Named after an English family that gained possession of it during the 1620 plantation of Leitrim (when land was confiscated from the Irish and given to favored English families), this castle was originally the stronghold of the O'Rourke clan, rulers of the kingdom of Breffni. Beautifully restored using Irish oak and traditional craftsmanship, it exemplifies the 17th-century, fortified manor house. In the visitor center, informative exhibits and a splendid audiovisual show illustrate the history of the castle and introduce visitors to the rich, diverse sites of interest in the surrounding area. This is an ideal place from which to launch your own local explorations. The tearoom offers fresh and exceptionally enticing pastries.
Lough Gill Dr., county Leitrim. ✆ 071/64149. Admission €2.50 ($2.25) adults, €2 ($1.80) seniors, €1.30 ($1.15) students and children, €6.50 ($5.80) family. St. Patrick's weekend 10am–5pm; Apr–May Tues–Sun 10am–5pm; June–Sept daily 9:30am–6:30pm; Oct daily 10am–5pm.

Yeats's Grave ✿   Eight kilometers (5 miles) north of Sligo Town is Drumcliffe, site of the Church of Ireland cemetery where W. B. Yeats is buried. It's well signposted, so you can easily find the poet's grave with the simple headstone bearing the dramatic epitaph he composed: "Cast a cold eye on life, on death; Horseman, pass by." This cemetery also contains the ruins of an early Christian monastery founded by St. Columba in A.D. 745.
Drumcliffe Churchyard, Drumcliffe (off N15), county Sligo.

SPORTS & OUTDOOR PURSUITS
BEACHES   For walking, jogging, or swimming, there are safe sandy beaches with promenades at **Strandhill, Rosses Point,** and **Enniscrone** on the Sligo Bay coast.

BICYCLING   With its lakes and woodlands, Yeats Country is particularly good biking territory. To rent a bike, contact **Gary's Cycles Shop,** Quay Street, Sligo (✆ **071/45418**), or **Conways Shop,** 6 Hugh St., Sligo (✆ **071/61370**).

FISHING   Boats, with or without guides, are available at the **Blue Lagoon,** Riverside, Sligo (see "Pubs," later in this chapter). Contact Peter Henry (✆ **071/ 45407** or 071/44040).

GOLF   With its seascapes, mountain valleys, and lakesides, county Sligo is known for challenging golf courses. Leading the list is **County Sligo Golf Club** ✿, Rosses Point Road, Rosses Point (✆ **071/77134;** www.countysligogolf club.ie), overlooking Sligo Bay under the shadow of Ben Bulben mountain. It's an 18-hole, par-71 championship seaside links famed for its wild, natural terrain and constant winds. Greens fees are €55 ($49) weekdays, €70 ($62) weekends.

Eight kilometers (5 miles) west of Sligo Town is **Strandhill Golf Club,** Strandhill (✆ **071/68188;** www.strandhillgc.com), a seaside par-69 course with greens fees of €35 ($31) weekdays, €45 ($40) weekends.

In the southwestern corner of the county, about 40km (25 miles) from Sligo Town and overlooking Sligo Bay, the **Enniscrone Golf Club,** Enniscrone (✆ **096/36297;** http://homepage.tinet.ie/~enniscronegolf), is a seaside par-72 course. Greens fees are €45 ($40) weekdays, €60 ($53) weekends.

Impressions

Every St. Patrick's Day every Irishman goes out to find another Irishman to make a speech to.

—Shane Leslie, *American Wonderland,* 1936

HORSEBACK RIDING An hour's or a day's riding on the beach, in the countryside, or over mountain trails can be arranged at **Sligo Riding Centre,** Carrowmore (© **071/61353**), or at **Woodlands Equestrian Centre,** Loughill, Lavagh, Tubbercurry, county Sligo (© **071/84207**). Rates average €14 to €17 ($12–$15) per hour.

WHERE TO STAY
EXPENSIVE/VERY EXPENSIVE

Cromleach Lodge 🌟🌟 Thirty-two kilometers (20 miles) south of Sligo Town, this lovely, modern sprawling hotel, nestled in the quiet hills above Lough Arrow, is run by Moira and Christy Tighe. Though not a period house, it's decorated to feel like one. Views from the restaurant, lounges, and most guest rooms deliver a stunning panorama of lakeland and mountain scenery. Guest rooms are extralarge by Irish standards and feature sitting areas, oversized orthopedic beds, designer fabrics, and original oil paintings. Each room is named after a different part of the Sligo countryside (from Ben Bulben and Knocknarea to Moytura and Carrowkeel) and is decorated with colors reflecting its namesake. Half the rooms are nonsmoking, and there are separate smoking and nonsmoking lounges. The place is beautiful, the setting divine, but the best reason of all to come is for the award-winning restaurant and Moira's fabulous cooking (see "Where to Dine," below).

Ballindoon, Castlebaldwin, county Sligo. © 071/65155. Fax 071/65455. www.cromleach.com. 10 units. €210–€300 ($187–$267) double. No service charge. Rates include full breakfast. AE, DC, MC, V. Closed Nov–Jan. **Amenities:** Restaurant (modern Continental); 2 lounges; nonsmoking rooms. *In room:* TV, tea/coffeemaker, minibar, safe.

MODERATE

Ballincar House Hotel 🌟 Nestled on 2.4 tree-shaded pastoral hectares (6 acres) overlooking Sligo Bay, and just a stone's throw from Rosses Point, this handsome country house was built as a private residence in 1848 and was extended and opened as a lodging in 1969. The public rooms preserve the house's charm, with open fireplaces, period furnishings, and original oil paintings of the area. Guest rooms are decorated in contemporary country style, and most look out onto the gardens or vistas of Sligo Bay.

3.2km (2 miles) northwest of the Sligo Town, Rosses Point Rd., Sligo, county Sligo. © **800/447-7462** in the U.S., or 071/45361. Fax 071/44198. www.infowing.ie/ballincarhousehotel. 25 units. €110–€140 ($98–$125) double. Rates include full breakfast and service charge. AE, MC, V. **Amenities:** Restaurant (international); bar; tennis court; sauna; snooker table. *In room:* TV.

Markree Castle 🌟🌟 *Finds* If you are hoping to spend at least a night in an Irish castle, this one—four stories high, with a forbidding entrance, a monumental stone staircase, and a sea of turrets—packs all the drama you could wish for. This is one of the county's oldest inhabited castles, and the current owner, Charles Cooper, is the 10th generation of his family to live at Markree. Even the approach to the castle is impressive—a mile-long driveway, along pasturelands grazed by sheep and horses and past lovely gardens that stretch down to the

Unsin River. The interior is equally regal, with a hand-carved oak staircase, ornate plasterwork, and a stained-glass window that traces the Cooper family tree back to the time of King John of England. The guest rooms, restored and equipped with modern facilities, have lovely views of the gardens, and the restaurant, known as Knockmuldowney (see "Where to Dine," below), draws customers from far and wide. If you like horseback riding, there's an excellent stable attached to the castle that can organize rides through county Sligo (from an afternoon to a week).

Collooney (13km/8 miles south of Sligo Town), county Sligo. ✆ **800/223-6510** or 800/44-UTELL in the U.S., or 071/67800. Fax 071/67840. www.markreecastle.ie. 30 units. €170–€190 ($151–$169) double. No service charge. Rates include full breakfast. AE, MC, V. Closed several days at Christmas. **Amenities:** Restaurant (Continental); horseback riding; salmon fishing. *In room:* TV, tea/coffeemaker, hair dryer.

Sligo Park Hotel ✪ *Value* With a glass-fronted facade and skylit atrium lobby, this is Sligo's most contemporary hotel. It's set back from the road on 2.8 hectares (7 acres) of parkland, and surrounded by lovely gardens, with distant views of Ben Bulben to the north. The interior is like that of a zillion other hotels—modern and attractive, but completely lacking in distinction. The decor in the guest rooms is also generic but inoffensive, with light woods, pastel-toned floral fabrics, quilted headboards, orthopedic beds, and framed scenes of the Sligo area. Still, it's hard to beat this price if you're looking for a place with a leisure center.

Pearse Rd. (just over 1.6km/1 mile south of Sligo on the Dublin rd./N4), Sligo, county Sligo. ✆ **071/60291.** Fax 071/69556. www.leehotels.ie. 110 units. €126–€156 ($112–$139) double. Rates include full breakfast and service charge. DC, MC, V. **Amenities:** 2 restaurants (international, cafe); bar; indoor swimming pool; tennis court; gym; Jacuzzi; sauna/steam room; nonsmoking rooms. *In room:* TV, radio, tea/coffeemaker, hair dryer.

Temple House ✪✪ This vast Georgian mansion is beautifully situated in 400 hectares (1,000 acres) of woods and parkland, overlooking a lake and the ruins of a Knights Templar castle, for which the place is named. The house has seen better days and is a bit frayed at the edges, but impresses with the sheer magnitude of its spaces and the antiquity of its eclectic furnishings. The grand, sweeping staircase in the foyer is magnificent. The Percevals have lived here since 1665, and Sandy and Deb Perceval run the place with a sense of casual elegance and affable unpretentiousness. The two double rooms in the front of the house are particularly stately and have canopied beds; book them well in advance. The walled garden is a short walk from the house and supplies vegetables for the excellent evening meals.

Two caveats: The atmosphere is more intimate than you might want, much like a house party; guests meet for drinks in the drawing room and dine together at a communal table. Also, Sandy has an acute chemical sensitivity and asks guests to avoid the use of cosmetic products in the house, such as perfume, after-shave, scented lotions, or hair spray.

Ballymote, county Sligo. ✆ **071/83329.** Fax 071/83808. www.templehouse.ie. 5 units. €120–€130 ($107–$116) double. Rates include full breakfast. Dinner €30 ($27). AE, MC, V. Closed Dec–Easter. Free parking. **Amenities:** Nonsmoking rooms.

Yeats Country Hotel Golf and Leisure Club ✪ Located between an 18-hole golf course and Rosses Point, this hilltop property has great views of Ben Bulben and the sandy beaches of Sligo Bay. Slightly reminiscent of the Edwardian period, the public rooms are elegant while guest rooms are blandly traditional in dark woods and floral bedspreads. The Sligo Park Hotel (see above) offers better value for a similar standard of accommodation, but this place has a more spectacular location.

Rosses Point Rd. (8km/5 miles northwest of Sligo Town), Rosses Point, county Sligo. ✆ **800/44-UTELL** in the U.S., or 071/77211. Fax 071/77203. 79 units. €130–€205 ($116–$182) double. Rates include full Irish breakfast and service charge. AE, DC, MC, V. Closed Jan. **Amenities:** Restaurant (international); bar; indoor swimming pool; gym; Jacuzzi; sauna/steam room; babysitting. *In room:* TV, tea/coffeemaker, hair dryer.

INEXPENSIVE

Dunfore Farmhouse ⭐ Ita Leyden, winner of two recent tourism awards, is an outgoing and energetic host who has done a great job of making this recently renovated farmhouse a pleasant base for exploring Sligo. Guest rooms have firm beds and fine views of the surrounding countryside (some across the bay to Rosses Point, others to Ben Bulben or the nearby Lissadell Wood). Breakfast is often enlivened by Ita's ardent recitation of her favorite Irish poetry, and you'll find literary touches throughout the house, from portraits of Irish writers to a painting by Yeats's brother Jack. When the weather is good, visitors can arrange a tour of the local coast in the Leydens' small motorboat, docked at nearby Raghly Harbor. If you'd like to rent the entire house by the week or month, inquire well in advance.

Ballinful (turn off N15 at Drumcliffe), county Sligo. ✆ 071/63137. Fax 071/63574. www.irishfarmholidays.com/dunfore-farmhouse.html. 4 units. €60 ($53) double. Rates include full breakfast. 50% discount for children under 12. MC, V. Closed Nov–Feb. *In room:* TV, tea/coffeemaker.

SELF-CATERING

Beech Cottage ⭐⭐ Beech Cottage, just outside beautiful Dromahair, focuses on its riding school and offers an array of packages that include horse riding, lessons, accommodations, and meals. They range from 1-day trekking trips to 7-day all-inclusive instructional holidays at all levels. Guests who love horses but prefer to watch are also warmly welcomed. If your interests include horses, Yeats, and ancient Irish Neolithic sites, you will never want to leave. The tasteful, quiet 19th-century manor house sleeps seven in excellent beds. The four self-catering apartments, attractively converted from old stone stables, have open-plan kitchen/dining and living rooms with fireplaces, and are equipped with all the essentials including cable TV and washing machines. The stoves have hobs (burners), but no ovens. The deluxe three-person apartment is the gem of the four, with exposed stone walls, skylights, and a massive open stone fireplace.

Lough Gill Dr., Dromahair, county Leitrim. ✆ 071/64110. 1 house, 4 apts. House €670–€1,060 ($593–$943) per week; apt €188–€465 ($167–$414) per week. MC, V. Free parking. **Amenities:** TV, kitchen, washing machine, no phone.

WHERE TO DINE
EXPENSIVE

Cromleach Lodge ⭐⭐⭐ MODERN CONTINENTAL It's worth the drive 32km (20 miles) south of Sligo Town to dine at this lovely country house overlooking Lough Arrow. The panoramic views are secondary, however, to chef Moira Tighe's culinary creations, which have won a fistful of prestigious awards. The menu changes nightly, depending on what is freshest and best from the sea and garden. It may include such dishes as boned stuffed roast quail with a vintage port sauce, halibut with Parmesan crust, and loin of lamb scented with garlic and Irish Mist. For dessert, the white chocolate mousse can be counted on for perfect closure. The nonsmoking dining room is a delight, with decorated plaster moldings and chair rails, curio cabinets with figurines and crystal, ruffled valances, potted palms, and place settings of Rosenthal china and fine Irish linens and silver.

Ballindoon, Castlebaldwin, county Sligo. ✆ **071/65155.** Reservations required. Fixed-price 7-course tasting menu €52 ($46); main courses €16–€26 ($14–$23). AE, MC, V. Daily 6:30–9pm. Closed Nov–Jan.

Markree Castle Hotel and Restaurant ✿✿ INTERNATIONAL Long before Charles and Mary Cooper took over Markree Castle (see "Where to Stay," above), they were winning culinary plaudits for Knockmuldowney restaurant, then in a small house at the base of Knocknarea Mountain on the shores of Ballisodare Bay. When they inherited the castle, they brought the restaurant's name with them and have now changed it to match the castle. Even though it's now in a more regal and spacious 60-seat setting, under 19th-century Louis Philippe–style plasterwork, the spotlight is still on the food. It includes such entrees as supreme of chicken with Cashel blue cheese, escallops of pork with Morvandelle cream sauce, and roast farmyard duckling with black-cherry-and-port sauce.

Collooney, county Sligo. ✆ **071/67800.** Reservations required. Fixed-price dinners €32–€37 ($28–$33). AE, DC, MC, V. Daily 7–9:30pm; Sun 1–2:30pm. Closed several days at Christmas.

MODERATE

Austie's/The Elsinore ✿ SEAFOOD Set on a hill with lovely views of Sligo Bay, this pub-restaurant boasts nautical knickknacks and fishnets, periscopes and corks, and paintings of sailing ships. Substantial pub grub is available during the day—open-faced "sandbank" sandwiches of crab, salmon, or smoked mackerel; crab claw or mixed seafood salads; and hearty soups and chowders. The dinner menu offers such fresh seafood choices as pan-fried Dover sole and crab au gratin, as well as steaks and chicken curry. Lobster is also available, at market prices. Outdoor seating on picnic tables is available in good weather.

Rosses Point Rd. (6.5km/4 miles northwest of Sligo), Rosses Point, county Sligo. ✆ **071/77111.** Reservations recommended. Main courses €9–€20 ($8–$18). MC, V. Daily 6–10pm.

INEXPENSIVE

The Cottage ✿ VEGETARIAN For a light meal or snack, try this cottage-style vegetarian place in the heart of town. The emphasis is on fresh local ingredients, organic whenever possible. It's known for quiche, chili, pizza, baked potatoes with varied fillings, crab claws, seafood chowders, and hot open sandwiches on French bread topped with melted cheese. There is self-service and table service. The evening menu is eclectic, ranging from ethnic dishes to superb local seafood. All pastries and desserts are homemade, and you can tell.

4 Castle St., Sligo, county Sligo. ✆ **071/45319.** All items €3–€15 ($2.70–$13). No credit cards. Daily 9am–5:30pm; Fri–Sun 7:30–10:30pm.

The Winding Stair ✿ IRISH The sister shop of the Winding Stair in Dublin offers both food and food for thought. There's a wide selection of new, secondhand, and antiquarian books, along with self-service food that is simple and healthy—sandwiches made with additive-free meats or fruits (such as banana and honey), organic salads, homemade soups, confections, and natural juices.

Hyde Bridge House, Sligo, county Sligo. ✆ **071/41244.** All items €3–€8 ($2.70–$7.10). MC, V. Mon–Sat 10am–6pm.

SLIGO AFTER DARK
PUBS

The Crossbar In the heart of Sligo's rich traditional music scene, this bright yellow pub stands at the center of the little village of Gurteen. There's always a lively buzz from the local crowd, who are drawn by the congeniality of owners Adrian Tansey and Pauline Walsh and the warmth of the open fireplace. This is the preferred hangout of the Sligo Gaelic Football team, with the requisite big screen television to air major sporting events. Gurteen, county Sligo. ℂ 071/82203.

Hargadon Brothers   This pub is legendary. More than a century old, this is the most atmospheric bar in the center of the downtown area. Although it is strictly a pub now, it also used to be a grocery shop, as you'll see when you enter if you glance at the shelves on the right. The decor is a mélange of dark-wood walls, mahogany counters, stone floors, colored glass, old barrels and bottles, a pot-bellied stove, and alcoves lined with early prints of Sligo. There are four snugs, each with its own special features. Strung together, they are reminiscent of an old-fashioned railway carriage—a bit cramped but extremely conducive to conversation. 4 O'Connell St., Sligo, county Sligo. ℂ 071/70933.

Stanford's Village Inn   Five generations of the McGowan family have run this old tavern, and thankfully not much about its appearance has changed over the years. There are several comfortable bars with open fires, and there's a delightful blend of old stone walls, vintage pictures and posters, oil lamps, and tweed-covered furnishings. If you're driving around Lough Gill from Sligo, this 160-year-old pub is a great midway stop for a drink or a snack. Main St., Dromahair, county Leitrim. ℂ 071/64140.

The Thatch   Established in 1638 as a coaching inn, this pub is about 8km (5 miles) south of Sligo on the main road. Before you enter, stand outside for a moment and admire its thatched roof and whitewashed exterior, a look that has withstood modernization without loosing a smidgen of charm. Inside, there's a country-cottage motif with plenty of photos showing Irish life from the turn of the 19th century. Irish traditional music usually starts at 9pm on Thursdays and Sundays year-round and Tuesday through Sunday in August. Dublin-Sligo Rd. (N4), Ballisodare, county Sligo. ℂ 071/67288.

Yeats Tavern   Some 6.5km (4 miles) north of Sligo, across the road from the famous churchyard where William Butler Yeats is buried, this pub honors the poet's memory with quotations from his works, photos, prints, and murals. A modern tavern and restaurant with a copper-and-wood decor, it is a convenient place to stop for a snack or a full meal when touring Yeats Country. Donegal Rd. (N15), Drumcliffe, county Sligo. ℂ 071/63117.

THE PERFORMING ARTS

The Factory   This is home to Sligo's award-winning Blue Raincoat Theatre Company. It is one of only three professional Irish acting companies (the Abbey in Dublin and the Druid in Galway are the others) that own their own theaters. During July and August, the Blue Raincoat Theatre Company often presents lunchtime performances of Yeats's plays as well as other Sligo-related productions. Evening shows usually start at 8pm. Lower Quay St., Sligo, county Sligo. ℂ 071/70431. Tickets cost €7–€10 ($6.25–$8.90).

Hawk's Well Theatre   The premier stage of Ireland's northwest region, this modern 350-seat theater presents a varied program of drama, comedy, ballet, opera, and concerts of modern and traditional music. It derives its name from *At the Hawk's Well,* a one-act play by Yeats. The theater occasionally produces shows, but mostly books visiting professional and local companies. Temple St., Sligo, county Sligo. ℂ 071/61518. Tickets average €10 ($8.90). Mon–Sat box office 10am–6pm; most shows at 8pm.

3 Donegal Town

Donegal Town is 222km (138 miles) NW of Dublin, 283km (176 miles) NE of Shannon Airport, 66km (41 miles) NE of Sligo, 69km (43 miles) SW of Derry, 180km (112 miles) W of Belfast, 205km (127 miles) NE of Galway, 403km (250 miles) N of Cork, and 407km (253 miles) NE of Killarney

Situated on the estuary of the River Eske on Donegal Bay, Donegal Town (pop. 3,000) is a small, pedestrian-friendly metropolis that's a pivotal gateway to touring the county. As recently as the 1940s, the town's central mall (called "the Diamond") was used as a market for trading livestock and goods. Today the marketing is more in the form of tweeds and tourist goods.

ESSENTIALS

GETTING THERE   **Aer Arann** (© 01/814-5240; www.aerarann.ie) and **Aer Lingus** (© 01/886-8888; www.aerlingus.ie) operate regularly scheduled flights from Dublin to **Donegal Airport,** Carrickfinn, Kincasslagh, county Donegal (© 075/48284; www.donegalairport.ie), about 65km (40 miles) northwest of Donegal Town on the Atlantic coast.

Bus Eireann (© 074/21309; www.buseireann.ie) operates daily bus service to Donegal Town to and from Dublin, Derry, Sligo, Galway, and other points. All tickets are issued on the bus. The pickup and boarding point is in front of the Abbey Hotel on The Diamond.

There are also a small number of private bus companies serving the northwest region. For example, **McGeehan's Coaches** (© 075/46150; www.mgbus.com) operates multiple daily buses between Donegal and Dublin. They leave from the Garda Station opposite the Donegal Tourist Office. Between Galway and Donegal (via Ballyshannon, Bundoran, and Sligo), **Feda O'Donnell** (© 075/48114 in Donegal or 091/761656 in Galway) operates at least one daily private coach. Other routes are also available.

If you're driving from the south, Donegal is reached on N15 from Sligo or A46 or A47 from Northern Ireland; from the east and north, it's N15 and N56; from the west, N56 leads to Donegal Town.

VISITOR INFORMATION   The **Donegal Tourist Office,** Quay Street (© 073/21148), is open Easter through September, Monday to Friday 9am to 5pm, Saturday 10am to 2pm, with extended hours in July and August. For a wealth of online tourist information, the best websites are **www.goireland.com/donegal** and **www.donegaltown.ie**.

TOWN LAYOUT   Donegal Town which sits to the east of the River Eske, is laid out around a triangular central mall or market area called "The Diamond," where the roads from Killybegs, Ballyshannon, and Ballybofey converge. **Main Street** and **Upper Main Street,** which form the prime commercial strip, extend northeast from The Diamond.

GETTING AROUND   Easily walked, Donegal has no local bus service within the town. If you need a taxi, call **McGroary Cabs** (© 073/35240) or **Marley Taxis** (© 074/33013).

There is free parking along the Quay beside the tourist office and off of Main Street.

A booklet outlining the signposted walking tour of Donegal Town is available at the tourist office and most bookshops.

FAST FACTS   In an emergency, dial © **999.** Donegal **District Hospital** is on Upper Main Street (© **073/21019**). The local Garda Station is on Quay Street (© 073/21021).

Donegal County Library, Mountcharles Road (© **073/21105**), is open Monday, Wednesday, and Friday 3 to 6pm, Saturday 11am to 1pm and 2 to 6pm. Internet access is free (for the time being), but there is a limit of 1 hour per session. Book ahead.

The **Donegal Post Office** on Tirconnail Street (© **073/21001**) is open Monday, Tuesday, and Thursday to Saturday 9am to 5:30pm, Wednesday 9:30am to 5:30pm.

EXPLORING DONEGAL TOWN

The greatest attraction of Donegal Town is the town's layout itself, a happy mix of medieval and modern buildings. Most of the structures of interest are there for you to enjoy at will, with no admission charges, no audiovisuals, no interpretive exhibits, and no crowds.

The Diamond is the triangular market area of town. It's dominated by a 7.5m-high (25-ft.) obelisk erected as a memorial to four early-7th-century Irish clerics from the local abbey who wrote *The Annals of Ireland,* the first recorded history of Gaelic Ireland.

Lough Derg, filled with many islands, lies about 16km (10 miles) east of Donegal. Legend has it that St. Patrick spent 40 days and 40 nights fasting in a cavern at this secluded spot, and since then it has been revered as a place of penance and pilgrimage. From June 1 to August 15, thousands of Irish people take turns coming to Lough Derg to do penance for 3 days at a time, remaining awake and eating nothing but tea and toast. It's considered one of the most rigorous pilgrimages in all of Christendom. To reach the lake, take R232 to Pettigo, then R233 for 8km (5 miles).

Donegal Castle 👣👣 Built in the 15th century beside the River Eske, this magnificent castle was once the chief stronghold for the O'Donnells, a powerful Donegal clan. In the 17th century, during the Plantation period, it came into the possession of Sir Basil Brook, who added an extension with 10 gables, a large bay window, and smaller mullioned windows in Jacobean style. Much of the building has survived the centuries, and both the interior and exterior of the castle were beautifully restored in 1996. Free 25-minute guided tours are available.
Castle St., Donegal, county Donegal. © **073/22405**. Admission €4 ($3.55) adults, €2 ($2.65) seniors, €1.30 ($1.15) students and children, €6.50 ($5.80) family. Daily 9:30am–6:30pm. Closed Nov to mid-Mar.

Old Abbey 👣 This old Franciscan monastery was founded in 1474 by the first Red Hugh O'Donnell and his wife, Nuala O'Brien of Munster. Sitting in a peaceful spot where the River Eske meets Donegal Bay, it was generously endowed by the O'Donnell family and became an important center of religion and learning. Great gatherings of clergy and lay leaders assembled here in 1539. It was from this friary that some of the scholars undertook to salvage old Gaelic manuscripts and compile *The Annals of the Four Masters* (1632–36). Enough remains of its glory days—some impressive ruins of a church and a cloister—for you to imagine what once was.
The Quay, Donegal, county Donegal. Free admission.

SIGHTSEEING TOURS & CRUISES

Donegal Bay Waterbus 👣👣 The 60-seat, enclosed Waterbus makes daily tours into Donegal Bay, allowing you to see the bay and the surrounding scenery. The tour lasts about 90 minutes and passes many local points of interest, including the Old Abbey and Seal Island (where a colony of about 200 seals lives). Sailing times are usually morning and afternoon or evening, but are dependant upon weather and the tides. Tickets can be obtained from the ticket office on the pier. There is a detailed commentary on the sights during the trip.

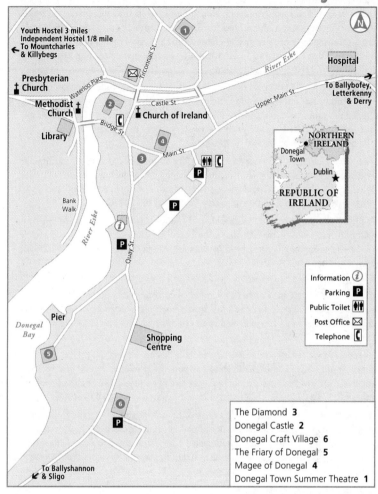

Donegal Town

Youth Hostel 3 miles
Independent Hostel 1/8 mile
← To Mountcharles
& Killybegs

Presbyterian
† Church

Methodist †
Church

Library

Ticonnail St.

Waterloo Place

Bridge St.

Castle St.

† Church of Ireland

Main St.

River Eske

Upper Main St.

To Ballybofey,
Letterkenny
& Derry

NORTHERN
IRELAND
●
Donegal
Town
Dublin ★

REPUBLIC OF
IRELAND

Hospital

Bank
Walk

River Eske

Quay St.

*Donegal
Bay*

Pier

Shopping
Centre

Information ⓘ
Parking P
Public Toilet ♿
Post Office ✉
Telephone ☎

To Ballyshannon
↙ & Sligo

The Diamond **3**
Donegal Castle **2**
Donegal Craft Village **6**
The Friary of Donegal **5**
Magee of Donegal **4**
Donegal Town Summer Theatre **1**

The Pier, Donegal Town, Donegal. ☎ **073/22312** or 073/23666. €8 ($7.10) adults, €4.50 ($4) seniors and children under 12. Closed Oct–Apr.

Donegal Town Walks ⭐   This 1-hour guided walking tour hits all of Donegal's historic sites and is a good way to get oriented the day of your arrival.

Donegal Tourist Office, Quay St. ☎ **073/21148**. €4 ($3.55) per person. June–Aug Mon–Sat 5:30pm.

SHOPPING

Most Donegal shops are open Monday to Saturday from 9am to 6pm, with extended hours in summer and slightly shorter hours in winter.

Donegal Craft Village   This cluster of artisans' shops lies in a rural setting about a mile south of town. This project provides a creative environment for an ever-changing group of craftspeople who practice a range of ancient and modern trades: porcelain, ceramics, hand weaving, batik, jewelry, metalwork, visual art, and Irish musical instrument making. You can buy some one-of-a-kind treasures or just browse from shop to shop and watch the craftspeople at work. The coffee shop serves snacks and lunch in the summer only, and the grounds are a great place for a picnic. The craft studios are open year-round Monday to Saturday 10am to 6pm and Sunday noon to 6pm. Ballyshannon Rd., Donegal, county Donegal. ℂ 073/22015. celticforest@eircom.net.

Forget-Me-Not/The Craft Shop This shop features a wide selection of gifts both usual and unusual. Items include handmade jewelry, Celtic art cards, Donegal county banners and hangings, woolly sheep mobiles, Irish traditional music figures, tweed paintings, bog oak sculptures, and beaten-copper art. The Diamond, Donegal, county Donegal. ℂ 073/21168.

The Four Master Bookshop Facing the monument commemorating the Four Masters, this shop specializes in books of Irish and Donegal interest, plus Waterford crystal, Celtic-design watches, Masons ironstone figures, and souvenir jewelry. The Diamond, Donegal, county Donegal. ℂ 073/21526.

Magee of Donegal Ltd Established in 1866, this shop is *the* name for fine Donegal hand-woven tweeds, including beautiful suits, jackets, overcoats, hats, ties, and even material on the bolt. The Diamond, Donegal, county Donegal. ℂ 073/22660. www.mageeshop.com.

Melody Maker Music Shop If you're enchanted by the traditional and folk music of Donegal, stop in here for tapes, recordings, and posters. This is also the main ticket agency for the southwestern section of county Donegal, handling tickets for most concerts and sports nationwide. The Diamond, Donegal, county Donegal. ℂ 073/22326.

Wards Music Shop If you'd like to take home a harp, bodhran, bagpipe, flute, or tin whistle, this is the shop for you. It specializes in the sale of Irish musical instruments and instructional books. The stock also includes violins, mandolins, and accordions. Castle St., Donegal, county Donegal. ℂ 073/21313.

William Britton & Sons Established in 1874, this shop stocks antique jewelry, silver, crystal, clocks, sports-related sculptures, pens, and watches. W. J. Britton is a registered appraiser and a fellow of the National Association of Goldsmiths of Great Britain and Ireland. Main St., Donegal, county Donegal. ℂ 071/21131.

SPORTS & OUTDOOR PURSUITS

WALKING Crossing Boyce's Bridge on the Killybegs road will bring you to the beginning of the **Bank Walk** to your left. This 2.5km (1½-mile) walk is delightful, following the west bank of the River Eske as it empties into Donegal Bay. It offers a stunning view of the Old Abbey, Green Island, and Donegal Bay.

BICYCLING The north side of Donegal Bay offers great cycling roads—tremendously scenic and very hilly. One good but arduous route from Donegal Town follows the coast roads west to Glencolumbkille (day 1), continues north to Ardara and Dawros Head (day 2), and then returns to Donegal (day 3). It takes in some of the most spectacular coastal scenery in Ireland along the way. Rental bikes are available from **Pat Boyle** (ℂ 073/22515). The cost is roughly €10 ($8.90) a day, €62 ($55) a week.

FISHING For advice and equipment for fishing in Lough Eske and other local waters, contact **Doherty's Fishing Tackle,** Main Street (ℂ 073/21119). The shop stocks a wide selection of flies, reels, bait, and fishing poles. It's open Monday to Saturday 9am to 6pm.

WHERE TO STAY
VERY EXPENSIVE

St. Ernan's House Hotel ★★   This is one of the area's most unusual lodgings—an 1826 country house that is the only structure on a small island in Donegal Bay that is connected to the mainland by its own causeway. The island, named for a 7th-century Irish monk, is planted with hawthorn and holly bushes that have been blooming for almost 3 centuries. The public areas and the Georgian-theme dining room, which is acclaimed for its cuisine, have all been magnificently restored. They hold delicate plasterwork, high ceilings, crystal chandeliers, gilt-framed oil paintings, heirloom silver, antiques, and open log fireplaces. The guest rooms, all individually decorated by proprietors Brian and Carmel O'Dowd, have traditional furnishings, with dark woods, designer fabrics, floral art, and period pieces; most have views of the water. It's a delightful spot, almost like a kingdom unto itself, yet less than 3.2km (2 miles) south of Donegal Town.

St. Ernan's Island, Donegal, county Donegal. ℂ **800/323-5463** in the U.S., or 073/21065. Fax 073/22098. www.sainternans.com. 12 units. €115–€140 ($102–$125) double. Suites also available. No service charge. Rates include full breakfast. MC, V. Closed Nov–Mar. **Amenities:** Drawing room. *In room:* TV.

MODERATE

The Abbey ★   In the heart of town, with The Diamond at its front door and the River Eske at its back, this vintage three-story hotel has been updated and refurbished in recent years. The guest rooms, about half of which are in a newish wing overlooking the river, have standard furnishings and bright floral fabrics. The pub has views of the River Eske, and an outdoor beer garden and patio also offer great waterside views.

The Diamond, Donegal, county Donegal. ℂ **073/21014.** Fax 073/23660. www.whites-hotelsireland.com. 49 units. €120–€148 ($107–$132) double. Rates include full breakfast and service charge. AE, MC, V. **Amenities:** Restaurant (international); bar; lounge; patio. *In room:* TV, hair dryer, garment press.

Ardnamona House ★★ *Finds*   Ardnamona, on Lough Eske under the Blue Stack mountains, was described in the *Topographical Dictionary of Ireland 1837* as "one of the most picturesque domains in rural Ireland." The writer Violet French was equally captivated: "I first saw Ardnamona from the lake on a fine August evening, romantic and picturesque with an appealing beauty which clings around the heart as if it belonged to a dream world."

A few miles west of town on the shores of the lake, this gorgeous, idiosyncratic house on 16 hectares (40 acres) of lovely grounds is like a breath of fresh air when compared to Donegal Town's mainly run-of-the-mill accommodations. Run by Amabel and Kieran Clarke, it's that perfect cross between a grand manor and an intimate country house. Guest rooms are beautifully done with just the right combination of color, flair and restraint. The gardens are a highlight here; the ideal time to visit is April and May, when the rhododendrons and azaleas are in full fury. The house is also musically inclined, with a Steinway upon which Paderewski once played and a small musical theater where concerts are held. Try to book here first, and use the more conventional Harvey's Point (see below) as your backup.

Lough Eske, Donegal, county Donegal. ℂ **073/22650.** Fax 073/22819. www.ardnamona.com. 6 units. €114–€140 ($101–$125) double. Rates include full breakfast. Dinner €33 ($29). AE, MC, V. Closed Dec 20–Jan 2. **Amenities:** Sitting room. *In room:* TV.

Harvey's Point Country Hotel ★★   About 6.5km (4 miles) northwest of town, this modern, rambling, Swiss-style lodge occupies a 5.2-hectare (13-acre) woodland setting on the shores of Lough Eske at the foot of the Blue Stack Mountains. The guest rooms, most of which feature views of Lough Eske and the hills of Donegal, have traditional mahogany furnishings—some with four-poster beds. The excellent restaurant was recently expanded down to the edge of the Lough, so ask for a table by the window and enjoy the sunset on the water.

Lough Eske, Donegal, county Donegal. © **073/22208.** Fax 073/22352. www.harveyspoint.com. 20 units. €138–€158 ($123–$141) double. Rates include full breakfast. AE, DC, MC, V. Closed weekdays Nov–Mar. **Amenities:** Restaurant (French); bar; lounge; 2 tennis courts; bicycle hire; boat hire. *In room:* TV, minibar, tea/coffeemaker, hair dryer.

Hyland Central ★ *(Value)*   Owned and operated by the Hyland family since 1941, this four-story hotel faces Donegal's main thoroughfare; in back, a modern extension overlooks Lough Eske—so request a view of the water. Guest rooms are outfitted with traditional furnishings of dark woods, light florals, and quilted fabrics. The leisure center pushes this place into the value-for-the-money category.

The Diamond, Donegal, county Donegal. © **800/528-1234** in the U.S., or 073/21027. Fax 073/22295. www.whites-hotelsireland.com. 91 units. €90–€130 ($80–$116) double. Service charge 10%. Rates include full breakfast. AE, DC, MC, V. Closed Dec 24–27. **Amenities:** Restaurant (bistro); pub; indoor swimming pool; gym; Jacuzzi; steam room; solarium. *In room:* TV, tea/coffeemaker, garment press.

INEXPENSIVE

Rhu-Gorse ★★ *(Value)*   This has to be one of the most simply satisfying B&Bs in Ireland. It's a little out of the way (8km/5 miles outside Donegal), but winding your way here is an effort well rewarded. A modern home of stature and character, Rhu-Gorse has a North Woods feel, with an ample stone fireplace, open beams, duvets, and lots of custom-fitted pine. Best of all are the panoramic views of Lough Eske and the encircling Blue Stack Mountains. Beds are firm, and smoking is not permitted in the rooms.

Lough Eske Dr. (8km/5 miles outside of Donegal), Lough Eske, Donegal, county Donegal. © and fax **073/21685.** 3 units. €68–€74 ($61–$66) double. Rates include full breakfast. MC, V. Closed Nov–Mar. Free parking. **Amenities:** Nonsmoking rooms. *In room:* TV.

WHERE TO DINE

Like many towns in northwest Ireland, the best restaurants are the dining rooms in the hotels. Nevertheless, the below is a good place for a snack or light meal:

The Weaver's Loft CAFETERIA   Upstairs from Magee's tweed shop, this 60-seat self-service restaurant with its huge mural of Donegal on the wall conveys an aura of times past. The menu changes daily, but usually includes prawn, cheese, and fruit salads as well as tasty sandwiches, soups, cakes, and tarts.

Magee Shop, The Diamond, Donegal, county Donegal. © **073/22660.** Main courses €5–€8 ($4.45–$7.10). AE, MC, V. Mon–Sat 9:45am–5pm.

DONEGAL AFTER DARK

If you're in Donegal during July and August, try to take in a performance of the Donegal Drama Circle at the **Donegal Town Summer Theatre,** O'Cleary Hall, Tirconnaill Street (no phone). Performances are held on Tuesdays, Wednesdays, and Thursdays at 9pm and feature works by Donegal-based playwrights. No reservations are necessary; admission prices start at €5 ($4.45) for adults, €2.50 ($2.25) for students.

PUBS

Biddy O'Barnes *(Finds)*   It's worth a detour into the Blue Stack Mountains and the scenic Barnesmore Gap, 11km (7 miles) northeast of Donegal Town, to visit this pub, which has been in the same family for four generations. Passing through the front door—with its etched glass window and iron latch—is like entering a country cottage, with blazing turf fires, stone floors, wooden stools and benches, and old hutches full of plates and bric-a-brac. A commanding portrait of Biddy, who once owned the house, hangs over the main fireplace. On most evenings there's a spontaneous music session. Donegal-Ballybofey Rd. (N15), Barnesmore, county Donegal. © 073/21402.

The Olde Castle Bar   There is an old-Donegal aura at this little pub, which has a welcoming open fireplace, etched glass, whitewashed walls, and old jars and crocks. Castle St., Donegal, county Donegal. © 073/21062.

The Schooner Inn   Model ships and seafaring memorabilia decorate this pub. There is music on most summer evenings, with traditional Irish music on Monday and Saturday, folk on Wednesday, and singing acts on Thursday, Friday, and Sunday. Upper Main St., Donegal, county Donegal. © 073/21671.

4 The Donegal Bay Coast

The Donegal Bay coast extends for 80km (50 miles): from Bundoran, 32km (20 miles) S of Donegal Town, to Glencolumbkille, 48km (30 miles) W of Donegal Town

The Donegal Bay coast is composed of two almost equal parts: the area from Ballyshannon north to Donegal Town (Southern Donegal Bay) and the area west of Donegal Town, stretching to Glencolumbkille (Northern Donegal Bay). On a map, the coast looks like a lobster claw reaching out from Donegal Town to grasp the bay's beautiful waters. Beaches, watersports, and coastal scenery are definitely the main drawing cards, but the Donegal Bay coast holds many other attractions, from bustling seaport towns to folk museums and craft centers.

For scenic beauty, the two sides of the coast are far from equal. The southern side tends more toward the tourist (read tacky) seaside resort, with Bundoran as the litmus; Rossnowlagh is somewhat more appealing, however, and does have one of the finest beaches in the region. The northern Donegal Bay coast, on the other hand, is nothing short of spectacular. Once you travel west of Killybegs, the mountains reach right to the sea, creating the beautifully indented coastline around Kilcar and the incomparable Slieve League cliffs.

AREA ESSENTIALS

GETTING THERE & GETTING AROUND   **Ireland Airways** operates regularly scheduled flights from Dublin to Donegal Airport, Carrickfinn, Kincasslagh, county Donegal (© 075/48284), about 65km (40 miles) north of Killybegs.

Bus Eireann (© 074/21309; www.buseireann.ie) operates daily bus service to Killybegs and Glencolumbkille, on the northern half of the bay, and to Ballyshannon and Bundoran, on the southern half of the bay.

The best way to get to and around Donegal Bay is by car. Follow the N15 route on the southern half of the bay, the N56 route on the northern half of the bay.

VISITOR INFORMATION   Contact the **North West Tourism Office,** Aras Reddan, Temple Street, Sligo (© 071/61201; www.northwestireland.travel.ie); the **Letterkenny Tourist Office,** Derry Road, Letterkenny (© 074/21160); or **Bundoran Tourist Office,** Main Street, Bundoran, county Donegal (© 072/41350). The first two are open year-round; the third is open from June through August.

SOUTHERN DONEGAL BAY

To reach the southern section of Donegal Bay from Sligo, take the N15 road up the Atlantic coast, and at about 32km (20 miles) north, you'll come to **Bundoran,** the southern tip of county Donegal and a major beach resort.

Continuing up the coast, you'll pass **Ballyshannon,** dating from the 15th century and one of the oldest inhabited towns in Ireland; it's another favorite with beachgoers, and it boasts some 21 lively pubs, many offering traditional music in the evenings. In late July or early August, there's the **Ballyshannon Folk Festival,** when music rings through the streets day and night.

Two kilometers (just over a mile) northwest of town, the once-famous Cistercian **Assaroe Abbey,** founded in 1184, now lies in ruins, although its mill wheel has been restored and is driven by water from the Abbey River just as in ancient days. Some 50m (164 ft.) away, at the edge of the Abbey River, **Catsby Cave** is a grottolike setting where a rough-hewn altar reminds you that mass was celebrated here during the penal years, when the ritual was prohibited by law.

At this point, leave the main road and head for the coastal resort of **Rossnowlagh,** one of the loveliest beaches in this part of Ireland. At over 3.2km (2 miles) long and as wide as the tides allow, it's a flat sandy stretch shielded by flower-filled hills and ideal for walking. You'll see horses racing on it occasionally. This spot is a splendid vantage point for watching sunsets over the churning foam-rimmed waters of the Atlantic.

Overlooking the beach from a hilltop is the **Franciscan Friary,** Rossnowlagh (© **072/51342**), which houses a small museum of local Donegal history. The complex also contains beautiful gardens and walks overlooking the sea, a tearoom with outdoor seating, and a shop with religious objects. It's open daily from 10am to 8pm. There's no admission charge, but donations are welcome.

From Rossnowlagh, return to the main road via the **Donegal Golf Club** (see "Sports & Outdoor Pursuits," below) at Murvagh, a spectacular setting nestled on a rugged sandy peninsula of primeval duneland, surrounded by a wall of dense woodlands. From here, the road curves inland and it's less than 16km (10 miles) to Donegal Town.

SHOPPING

Britton and Daughters   In a cottage opposite the Sand House Hotel, this workshop is a source of unusual artistic crafts. Its wares include mirrors or glass hand-etched with local scenes and Celtic, nautical, floral, and wildlife designs; prints of traditional musicians; carved rocks (heads, Celtic designs, dolphins, and so on); posters; and pottery with surfing and Irish music themes. Off the Ballyshannon-Donegal rd., Rossnowlagh, county Donegal. © **072/52220.**

Donegal Parian China   Established in 1985, this pottery works produces wafer-thin Parian china gift items and tableware in patterns of the shamrock, rose, hawthorn, and other Irish flora. Free guided tours (every 20 min.) enable visitors to watch as vases, bells, spoons, thimbles, wall plaques, lamps, and eggshell coffee and tea sets are shaped, decorated, fired, and polished. There is also an audiovisual room, an art gallery, a tearoom, and a showroom and shop here. Bundoran Rd. (N15), Ballyshannon, county Donegal. © **072/51826.**

SPORTS & OUTDOOR PURSUITS

BEACHES   Donegal Bay's beaches are wide, sandy, clean, and flat—ideal for walking. The best are **Rossnowlagh** and **Bundoran.**

County Donegal

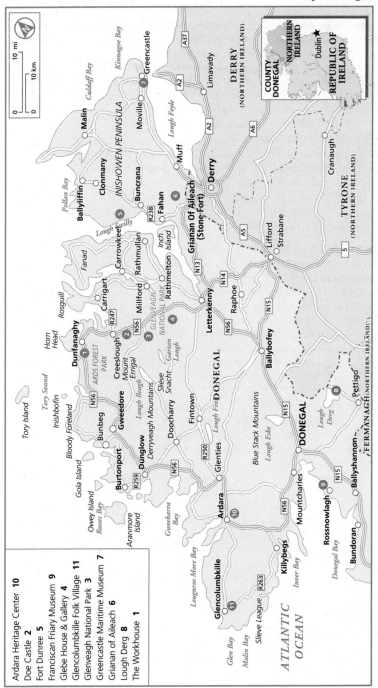

Legend:
- Ardara Heritage Center **10**
- Doe Castle **2**
- Fort Dunree **5**
- Franciscan Friary Museum **9**
- Glebe House & Gallery **4**
- Glencolumbkille Folk Village **11**
- Glenveagh National Park **3**
- Greencastle Maritime Museum **7**
- Grianan of Aileach **6**
- Lough Derg **8**
- The Workhouse **1**

GOLF   The Donegal Bay coast is home to two outstanding 18-hole championship seaside golf courses. **Donegal Golf Club,** Murvagh, Ballintra, county Donegal (© **073/34054;** www.donegalgolfclub.ie), is 4.8km (3 miles) north of Rossnowlagh and 11km (7 miles) south of Donegal Town. It's a par-73 course with greens fees of €35 ($31) weekdays, €42 ($37) weekends.

The **Bundoran Golf Club,** off the Sligo-Ballyshannon road (N15), Bundoran, county Donegal (© **072/41302;** www.bundorangolfclub.com), is a par-69 course designed by the great Harry Vardon. The greens fees are €27 ($24) weekdays, €32 ($28) weekends.

HORSEBACK RIDING   Stracomer Riding School Ltd., off the Sligo-Ballyshannon road (N15), Bundoran, county Donegal (© **072/41787**), specializes in trail riding on the surrounding farmlands, beaches, dunes, and mountain trails. An hour's ride averages €15 ($13).

SURFING   Bundoran has hosted the European Surfing Championships. Rossnowlagh is also a surfer's mecca. When the surf is up, you can rent boards and wet suits locally for roughly €4 ($3.55) per hour per item.

WHERE TO STAY

Great Northern Hotel   Set on 52 hectares (130 acres) of grounds that include parkland, sand dunes, and an 18-hole golf course, this sprawling multi-winged hotel is right on Donegal Bay. The hotel's interior was recently refurbished with a bright modern Irish motif, and the rooms were spruced up with a new, contemporary look; most rooms have views of the sea or the golf course. A favorite with Irish families, it's on the northern edge of Bundoran.

Sligo-Donegal rd. (N15), Bundoran, county Donegal. © **072/41204.** Fax 072/41114. www.greatnorthern hotel.com. 112 units. €156 ($139) double. Rates include full Irish breakfast and service charge. AE, MC, V. Closed Jan. **Amenities:** 2 restaurants (international, grill); bar; indoor swimming pool; tennis court; gym; children's playroom; room service. *In room:* TV, tea/coffeemaker, hair dryer.

Sand House Hotel   On a crescent of beach overlooking the Atlantic coast, this award-winning three-story hotel is a standout in county Donegal. It is reminiscent of those old-fashioned beach resort hotels where people strolled on the beach in crisp linen trousers and then returned to the hotel for martinis before dinner. The Sand House began as a fishing lodge in 1886. In 1949, Vincent and Mary Britton moved in and began their quest to create a top-notch hotel. With open log and turf fireplaces, the public rooms are decorated with antiques and local artwork, and a sunlit, plant-filled conservatory offers great views of the sea. Guest rooms vary in size but all are decorated with designer fabrics, antiques, and such period pieces as hand-carved armoires and vanities; a few have canopied or four-poster beds. The best rooms have wide picture windows with vistas of the Atlantic. The dining room—which, surprisingly, does not overlook the sea—is presided over by a creative chef who specializes in locally harvested Donegal Bay lobster, oysters, scallops, mussels, and other seafood. In keeping with the vintage resort aura, there's a midweek cabaret as well as weekend entertainment.

Off the Ballyshannon-Donegal rd. (N15), Rossnowlagh, county Donegal. © **800/44-UTELL** in the U.S., or 072/51777. Fax 072/52100. www.sandhouse-hotel.ie. 45 units. €140–€220 ($125–$196) double. Rates include full Irish breakfast. AE, MC, V. Closed late Oct to early Apr. **Amenities:** Restaurant (seafood); bar; lounge; private 3.2km/2-mile beach; tennis court; croquet; conservatory. *In room:* TV, hair dryer.

WHERE TO DINE

Smuggler's Creek   SEAFOOD   For great food and grand sunset views, head to this little gem perched on a cliff overlooking Donegal Bay. It's in an

1845 stone building that has been restored and enlarged to include a conservatory-style dining area with open fireplaces, beamed ceilings, stone walls, wooden stools, porthole windows, crab traps, and lobster pots. Seafood is the star attraction, and proprietor Conor Britton pulls his own oysters and mussels from local beds. The bar menu ranges from soups, salads, and sandwiches to buttered garlic mussels or fresh paté. Dinner entrees include Smugglers sea casserole (scallops, salmon, and prawns with Mornay sauce), deep-fried squid with Provençal sauce, tiger prawns in garlic butter, wild Irish salmon hollandaise, steaks with whiskey sauce, and vegetarian pasta or stir-fry dishes. The restaurant is nonsmoking; the bar is not. More than a dozen B&B rooms with private bathroom are available for €74 ($66) double.

Rossnowlagh, county Donegal. (✆ 072/52366. Reservations required for dinner. Dinner main courses €12–€24 ($11–$21); lobster €26 ($23). DC, MC, V. Daily 12:30–3pm and 6–9:30pm; evening sittings 6:30 and 8:30pm. Closed Mon–Tues Oct–Easter.

SOUTHERN DONEGAL BAY AFTER DARK

In summer, **Rossnowlagh** is a hub of social activity. People flock to the **Sand House Hotel,** on Rossnowlagh beach, Rossnowlagh, county Donegal (✆ **072/ 51777;** www.sandhouse-hotel.ie), for the nautical atmosphere of the Surfers Bar and the Slice of Ireland Cabaret. It's a 1-hour show of Donegal-theme music, song, dance, poetry, comedy, and drama, presented July and August on Wednesdays at 9pm. Admission is roughly €7 ($6.25).

Farther south, **Dorrian's Thatch Bar,** Main Street, Ballyshannon, county Donegal (✆ **072/51147**), holds nightly sessions of Irish traditional music in summer.

NORTHERN DONEGAL BAY

From Donegal Town, follow the main road (N56) for a slow, spectacularly scenic drive along the northern coast of Donegal Bay. You'll encounter narrow, winding roads, sheer cliffs, craggy rocks, boglands, panoramic mountain and sea views, and more than a few sheep. You'll also see the distinctive thatched-roof cottages that are typical of this area—with rounded roofs, because a network of ropes (*sugans*) ties down the thatch and fastens it to pins beneath the eaves, to protect it from the prevailing winds off the sea. It's only 48km (30 miles) to Glencolumbkille, but plan on it taking over an hour.

Your first stop could be at **Killybegs**—where, if you arrive around sundown, you can watch the fishing boats unloading the day's catch—or at Studio Donegal in Kilcar, if you're casting for tweed (see "Shopping," below). A must-stop is **Slieve League** ✮✮, the highest sea cliffs in Europe. The turnoff for the Bunglas viewing point is at Carrick. Once at the cliffs, you must decide whether you want to merely gaze at their 300m (1,000-ft.) splendor or to experience them in-your-face close and personal on the wind-buffeted walk along the ridge. This walk should only be for the fearless and fit. Including the climb up and then back down, the hike is about 10km (6 miles) and takes 4 or 5 hours.

Just before you come to Killybegs, the N56 road swings inland and northward. Continue on the coastal road west to **Glencolumbkille** ✮✮, an Atlantic outpost dating back 5,000 years. It's what the Irish would call "the back of beyond." The rest of us would call it a dead end; the road literally stops here right before the sea. It is said that St. Columba established a monastery here in the 6th century and gave his name to the glen. In the 1950s, this area was endangered by a 75% emigration rate, until the parish priest, James McDyer, focused the energies of the town not only on ensuring the community's future, but also on preserving its past. He helped accomplish both by founding the **Glencolumbkille Folk Park** (© 073/30017). Built by the people of Glencolumbkille in the form of a tiny village, or *clachan,* this modest theme park of thatched cottages—each outfitted with period furniture and artifacts—reflects life in this remote corner of Ireland over the past several centuries. Two miniature playhouses are on hand for children. The tearoom serves a simple menu of traditional Irish dishes, such as stews and *brútin,* composed mainly of hot milk and potatoes. Don't miss the Guinness cake, a house specialty. In the *sheebeen,* a shop of traditional products, don't dismiss the admittedly bizarre-flavored local wines—fuchsia, heather, seaweed, and tea and raisin—until you've tried them all. They're surprisingly good. Recent additions to the folk park include a visitors' reception hall and an interpretive center, housing a range of engaging exhibits. Admission and tour are €3 ($2.65) for adults, €2 ($1.80) for seniors and children, €10 ($8.90) for family. It's open from Easter through September, Monday to Saturday 10am to 6pm, Sunday noon to 6pm.

To continue touring from Glencolumbkille, follow the signs for Ardara over a mountainous inland road. Soon you'll come to one of the most breathtaking drives in Ireland, through **Glengesh Pass,** a narrow, sinuous, scenic roadway that rises to a height of 270m (900 ft.) before plunging, in a zigzag pattern into the valley below. The road leads eventually to **Ardara,** known for its tweed and woolen craft centers (see section 5, "The Atlantic Highlands," later in this chapter).

SHOPPING

Folk Village Shop   Part of Glencolumbkille's folk park mentioned above, this is well worth a visit in its own right for smart shopping. The well-stocked shelves of this whitewashed cottage feature the arts and crafts of members of the local community—hand-knit sweaters and other woolen items, turf-craft art, books, jewelry, and assorted cottage industry souvenirs. Since the Folk Village operates as a charitable trust, purchases are not subject to VAT (sales tax), so you save some money and help a good cause by shopping here. Glencolumbkille, county Donegal © 073-30017.

Studio Donegal   Started in 1979, this hand-weaving enterprise is distinguished by its knobby tweed, subtly colored in tones of beige, oat, and ash. You can walk around both the craft shop and the mill and see the chunky-weave stoles, caps, jackets, and cloaks in the making. Other products fashioned of this unique tweed include tote bags, cushion covers, table mats, tapestries, and wall hangings. Kilcar is on the R263 between Killybegs and Glencolumbkille, about 32km (20 miles) west of Donegal Town. Glebe Mill, Kilcar. © 073/38194. www. studiodonegal.ie.

Taipeis Gael   The name says it all. "Gaelic Tapestry" refers to a group of artists who create fabulously unique, quintessentially Irish tapestries. They have learned the traditional skills of natural dyeing, carding, spinning, and weaving from others in Donegal, handed down from generation to generation. Their tapestries are strongly influenced by Gaelic culture, music, archaeology, folklore, and social history. The group hosts weeklong courses during the summer months. Considering the work and skill involved, these works of art are a bargain. Malin Beg, Glencolumbkille, county Donegal. © 073/30325.

SPORTS & OUTDOOR PURSUITS

BEACHES   Glencolumbkille has two fine beaches: One is the flat, broad, sandy beach at the end of Glencolumbkille village, where the R263 swings left; the lesser-known gem is a tiny beach surrounded by a horseshoe of cliffs, accessible from the small road signposted to Malin More (off the R263) about a mile southwest of town.

BICYCLING   If you're very fit, the north side of Donegal Bay offers great cycling roads—tremendously scenic though very hilly. One good but arduous route from Donegal Town follows the coast roads west to Glencolumbkille (day 1), continues north to Ardara and Dawros Head via Glengesh Pass (day 2), and then returns to Donegal (day 3). It takes in some of the most spectacular coastal scenery in Ireland along the way. Rental bikes are available in Donegal from Pat Boyle (© **073/22515**) at The Bike Shop, Waterloo Place, Donegal, for roughly €10 ($8.90) per day and €62 ($55) per week.

FISHING   Surrounded by waters that hold shark, skate, pollock, conger, cod, and mackerel, **Killybegs** is one of the most active centers on the northwest coast for commercial and sport sea-fishing. **Brian McGilloway** (© **073/32444**) operates full-day fishing expeditions on the 12m (40-ft.) *Aquarius,* from Blackrock Pier. Prices average €35 ($31) per person per day, plus €7 ($6.25) for rods and tackle, or €265 ($236) for a party of 8 to 10 (eight is preferable for comfort). The daily schedule and departure times vary according to demand; reservations are required.

At **Mountcharles,** a coastal town midway between Donegal Town and Killybegs, **Michael O'Boyle,** Old Road (© **073/35257**), organizes deep-sea fishing trips. Outings are slated daily from 11am to 5pm and cost €20 ($18) per person. This company also offers guided boat trips and wildlife cruises on demand; prices start at €20 ($18) per person, with a 2-hour minimum booking.

WALKING   The peninsula that extends westward from Killybegs boasts some of the most spectacular coastal scenery in Ireland, and much of it is accessible only from the sea or on foot. The grandeur of the **Slieve League** cliffs is not to be missed, but only if you have good hiking boots and basic provisions. The best way to visit this natural monument is to hike from the Bunglass lookout point to Trabane Strand in Malin Beg, a few miles southwest of Glencolumbkille. This walk involves crossing the renowned "One Man's Pass," a vertigo-inducing narrow ridge with steep drops on both sides. The distance from Bunglass to Trabane Strand is 15km (9 miles), and you will have to arrange a pickup at the end. The summits of the Slieve League, rising almost 600m (2,000 ft.) above the sea, are often capped in clouds, and you should think twice about undertaking the walk if there is danger of losing visibility along the way.

Another lesser-known walk that is just as spectacular is the coastal walk between Glencolumbkille and the town of **Maghera** (not so much a town as a small cluster of houses). Glen Head, topped by a Martello tower, overlooks Glencolumbkille to the north. This walk begins with a climb to the tower and continues along the cliff face for 24km (15 miles), passing only one remote outpost of human habitation along the way, the tiny town of Port. For isolated sea splendor, this is one of the finest walks in Ireland, but only experienced walkers with adequate provisions should undertake the walk, and only in fine weather.

WHERE TO STAY

Bay View Hotel ⚘   Right on the harbor in the middle of Killybegs, this four-story hotel is as close to the water as you can get without getting wet. Guest rooms are decorated in contemporary style with light pine furnishings, bright quilted fabrics, and brass accessories, all enhanced by wide-windowed views of the marina and fishing boats. Ask about special deals for multinight stays.

1–2 Main St., Killybegs, county Donegal. ☎ **073/31950**. Fax 073/31856. www.bayviewhotel.ie. 40 units. €120–€152 ($107–$135) double. No service charge. Rates include full breakfast. AE, MC, V. **Amenities:** 2 restaurants (international, brasserie); 2 bars; indoor swimming pool; gym; Jacuzzi; sauna/steam room. *In room:* TV.

Bruckless House ✦   Clive and Joan Evans have restored their mid-18th-century farmhouse with such care and taste that every room is a pleasure to enter and enjoy. Furniture and art they brought back from their years in Hong Kong add a special elegance. All the guest rooms are smoke-free, spacious, and bright. Joan's gardens have taken first prize in county Donegal's country garden competition at least twice in recent years. Inside and out, Bruckless House is a gem. Be sure to ask Clive to introduce you to his fine Connemara ponies, which he raises and treasures.

Signposted on N56, 19km (12 miles) west of Donegal, Bruckless, county Donegal. ☎ **073/37071**. Fax 073/ 37070. 4 units, 1 with private bathroom. €92 ($82) double with bathroom; €80 ($71) double with shared bathroom. No service charge. Rates include full Irish breakfast. AE, MC, V. Closed Oct–Mar. **Amenities:** Sitting room; nonsmoking rooms. *In room:* No phone.

Dún Ulún House ✦ *Value*   Dún Ulún House, one of the best bargains in this part of the world, caters to a remarkably diverse clientele. First there's the B&B, in a modern, purpose-built guesthouse. The building is unremarkable, but remains in the memory long after you've left, thanks to the graciousness of the Lyons family and the extraordinary beauty of the seaside scene it overlooks. The rooms (with orthopedic beds) are pleasant and comfortable. Then there's the cottage, also overlooking the sea, with an open fire in the kitchen and basic, functional furnishings in the bedrooms; rates are €14 to €24 ($12–$21) per person per night. There's also a separate self-catering cottage across the street, which rents by the week for €260 ($231) plus electricity. Finally, there's an in-house, eponymous band made up of five teenage girls—the Lyonses' daughter, two nieces, and two friends—who play some of the best traditional music you'll hear anywhere. They play locally in the Piper's Rest (see below) and also for guests at the B&B. Denis Lyons is a great source of information on the archaeology of the Kilcar region and can direct you to many fascinating and little-known sites.

R263 (1.6km/1 mile west of Kilcar), Kilcar, county Donegal. ☎ **073/38137**. 10 units, 9 with private bathroom. €48–€54 ($43–$48) double. Rates include full breakfast. MC, V. Free parking. **Amenities:** Sitting room. *In room:* TV.

The Glencolumbkille Hotel ✦   If you want to get away from it all, this hotel is the westernmost outpost in Donegal. Edged by Malin Bay and the Atlantic Ocean, encircled by craggy mountains that are populated mostly by meandering woolly sheep, it's a lovely spot, with turf fireplaces to warm you and a cottage atmosphere to cheer you. There's also a good dining room, with panoramic views of the countryside. A renovation of the entire hotel was completed in 2000. Most rooms have views of the sea or the valley.

Glencolumbkille, county Donegal. ☎ **073/30003**. Fax 073/30222. 38 units. €90–€104 ($80–$93) double. No service charge. Rates include full breakfast. MC, V. **Amenities:** Restaurant (international); bar. *In room:* TV.

WHERE TO DINE

The Blue Haven ✦ CONTINENTAL   On a broad, open sweep of Donegal Bay between Killybegs and Kilcar, this modern skylit restaurant offers 180° views of the bay from a semicircular bank of windows. It's an ideal stop for a meal or light refreshment while touring. The bar-food menu, available throughout the day, offers soups, sandwiches, and omelets with unusual fillings. The dinner menu includes filet of rainbow trout, T-bone and sirloin steaks, and savory mushroom pancakes. A new addition with 15 bedrooms opened in 2000, offering views of Donegal Bay and bed and breakfast for €68 ($61).

Largymore, Kilcar, county Donegal. ✆ 073/38090. Reservations recommended for dinner. Dinner main courses €7–€16 ($6.25–$14). MC, V. Open Apr–Sept only, daily 11am–11pm.

Fleet Inn ★★ *Value* SEAFOOD/CONTINENTAL   This little pub-and-restaurant-with-rooms is a great example of how it's the simple things that work best. The pub is on the ground floor, with the restaurant one flight up. Finally, on the top floor, there are a few cozy rooms under the eaves, done up in bright colors. Marguerite Howley is a classically trained chef and her dishes hit the right notes—blackened mackerel with scallion-infused mashed potatoes, wild salmon with spinach, and loin of lamb with rosemary jus. Her excellent desserts are French-inspired, like the prune-and-armagnac parfait, the tarte tatin (here made with pineapples) and a scrumptious crème brûlée.

Killybegs, county Donegal. ✆ 073/38090. Reservations recommended for dinner. Dinner main courses €10–€16 ($8.90–$14). MC, V. Open Sept–mid-Feb and mid-Mar–June, Tues–Sat, 7–10pm; July–Aug daily 7–10pm. Closed mid-Feb to mid-Mar.

PUBS

Harbour Bar   This popular meeting place holds an Irish music night on Tuesdays during July and August. Main St., Killybegs, county Donegal. ✆ 073/31049.

Piper's Rest   This thatched-roof pub has a country half-door, original stone walls, arches, flagged floors, an open turf fire, and a unique stained-glass window depicting a piper. Music may erupt at any time, and usually does on summer nights; the pub also features a fine collection of pipes, many of which are likely to be in use. Watch out for a local band called Dún Ulún, five teenage girls whose traditional music brings down the house. Kilcar, county Donegal. ✆ 073/38205.

5 The Atlantic Highlands

The Atlantic Highlands start at Ardara, 40km (25 miles) NW of Donegal Town, 16km (10 miles) N of Killybegs

Scenery is the keynote to the Atlantic Highlands of Donegal—vast stretches of coastal and mountain scenery, beaches and bays, rocks and ruins. It's sometimes lonely, but always breathtaking. Set far off the beaten track and deep amid the coastal scenery is Mount Errigal, the highest mountain in Donegal (740m/2,466 ft.). It gently slopes down to one of Ireland's greatest visitor attractions, the **Glenveagh National Park.**

The best place to start a tour of Donegal's Atlantic Highlands is at **Ardara** ★,, an adorable small town on the coast about 40km (25 miles) northwest of Donegal Town. From here, it's easy to weave your way up the coast. This drive can take 4 hours or 4 days, depending on your schedule and interests.

The deeper you get into this countryside, the more you'll be immersed in a section known as the *Gaeltacht,* or Irish-speaking area. This should present no problems, except that most of the road signs are only in Irish. If you keep to the main road (N56), you should have no difficulties. If you follow little roads off to the seashore or down country paths, you might have a problem figuring out where you're going (unless you can read Irish). In many cases, the Irish word for a place bears no resemblance to the English equivalent (*An Clochan Liath* in Irish is *Dungloe* in English), so our best advice is to buy a map with place names in both languages or stick to the main road.

ATLANTIC HIGHLANDS ESSENTIALS

GETTING THERE & GETTING AROUND Ireland Airways operates regularly scheduled flights from Dublin to **Donegal Airport,** Carrickfinn, Kincasslagh, county Donegal (© 075/48284), in the heart of the Atlantic coast.

Bus Eireann (© 074/21309; www.buseireann.ie) operates daily bus service to Ardara and Glenties.

The best way to get to and around Donegal's Atlantic Highlands is by car, following the main N56 route.

VISITOR INFORMATION Contact the **North West Tourism Office,** Aras Reddan, Temple Street, Sligo (© 071/61201; www.northwestireland.travel.ie); the **Letterkenny Tourist Office,** Derry Road, Letterkenny (© 074/21160); or the **Donegal Tourist Office,** Quay Street, Donegal (© 073/21148). The first two are open year-round; the third is open from May through September.

EXPLORING THE REGION

Ardara, known for its local tweed and sweater industries, is one of the northwest's most charming little towns. It's particularly worth a stop for shoppers (see the listings below, under "Shopping"). North of Ardara, the route travels inland near Gweebarra Bay and passes through Dungloe to an area known as the **Rosses,** extending from Gweebarra Bridge as far north as Crolly. This stretch presents a wealth of rock-strewn land, with many mountains, rivers, lakes, and beaches. Here you can visit **Burtonport** (otherwise known as *Ailt an Chorrain*), one of the country's premier fishing ports; it's said that more salmon and lobster are landed here than at any other port in Ireland or Britain.

North of the Rosses, between Derrybeg and Gortahork, is an area known as the **Bloody Foreland,** a stretch of land that derives its name from the fact that its rocks take on a warm ruddy color when lit by the setting sun. This is a sight that should not be missed.

Next you'll approach the top rim of Donegal, which is dominated by a series of small peninsulas or fingers of land jutting out into the sea. Chief among these scenic areas are **Horn Head** and **Ards.** The latter contains a forested park with a wide diversity of terrain: woodlands, a salt marsh, sand dunes, seashore, freshwater lakes, and fenland.

In Tory Sound, 15km (9 miles) north of the mainland, the treeless **Tory Island** lies, desolate and seemingly uninhabitable. The truth is that Tory Island, all of 4km (2½ miles) long and less than 1.6km (1 mile) wide, has been settled for thousands of years and currently boasts nearly 200 year-round inhabitants. Known for its painters and pirates, ruins and bird cliffs, Tory makes for a great adventure. The crossing can be made daily, weather permitting, from Bunbeg or Magheraroarty with **Donegal Coastal Cruises,** Strand Road, Middletown, Derrybeg, county Donegal (© 075/31320 or 075/31340). There are four daily sailings June through September, five sailings per week the rest of the year. Round-trip fares are €22 ($20) adults, €16 ($14) seniors and students, €10 ($8.90) children under 15, free for children under 5.

After Horn Head, the next spit of land to the east is **Rosguill.** The 16km (10-mile) route around this peninsula is called the Atlantic Drive. This leads you to yet another peninsula, the **Fanad,** with a 73km (45-mile) circuit between Mulroy Bay and Lough Swilly. The resort of **Rathmullan** is a favorite stopping point here.

After you drive to all these scenic peninsulas, it might come as a surprise that many of the greatest visitor attractions of the Atlantic Highlands are not along the coast, but inland, a few miles off the main N56 road near Kilmacrennan.

Ardara Heritage Centre ★ Ardara has long been a center for weaving, and varied displays represent the history of tweed production in the region. The weaver in residence is sometimes present to demonstrate techniques. A video provides an outline of nearby places of interest. The center opened in 1995 and is building its collections and exhibits. A cafe serves inexpensive teas, soups, and simple meals.

On N56 in the center of Ardara, county Donegal. © 075/41704. Admission €2.50 ($2.25) adults, €1.30 ($1.15) seniors and students, €.65 (60¢) children under 14. Open Easter–Sept Mon–Sat 10am–6pm; Sun 2–6pm.

Doe Castle ★★ This tower house is surrounded on three sides by the waters of Sheep Haven Bay and on the fourth by a moat carved into the bedrock that forms its foundation. A battlement wall with round towers at the corners encloses the central tower; the view from the battlements across the bay is superb. Built in the early 16th century, the castle was extensively restored in the 18th century and inhabited until 1843. If the entrance is locked, you can get the key from the caretaker in the house nearest the castle. With its remote seaside location and sweeping views of the nearby hills, this is one of the most beautifully situated castles in Ireland.

5.6km (3½ miles) off N56; turnoff signposted just south of Creeslough, county Donegal. Free admission.

Glebe House and Gallery ★★ *Finds* Sitting in woodland gardens on the shores of Lough Gartan, about 6.5km (4 miles) southwest of Glenveagh, this Regency-style house was built as a rectory in the 1820s. It was owned until recently by English artist Derek Hill, who donated the house and his art collection to the Irish government for public use and as an enhancement to the area he loves. The house is decorated with Donegal folk art, Japanese and Islamic art, Victoriana, and William Morris papers and textiles. The adjacent stables have been converted into an art gallery housing the 300-item Hill Collection of works by Picasso, Bonnard, Kokoschka, Yeats, Annigoni, Pasmore, and Hill. It's more than surprising to find this first-rate 20th-century art collection in a remote part of Donegal, but then, this is a surprising place.

18km (11 miles) northwest of Letterkenny on the Churchill rd. (R251), Church Hill, county Donegal. © **074/ 37071.** Admission €2.50 ($2.25) adults, €2 ($1.80) seniors, €1.30 ($1.15) students and children, €6.50 ($5.80) family. Mid-May to Sept Sat–Thurs 11am–6:30pm, last tour at 5:30pm.

Glenveagh National Park ★★★ Deep in the heart of county Donegal, far off the coastal path, this 14,000-hectare (35,000-acre) estate is considered by many to be Ireland's finest national park. The core of the park is the Glenveagh Estate, originally the home of the notorious landlord John George Adair, much despised for his eviction of Irish tenant farmers in 1861. He built the castle in the 1870s. From 1937 to 1983, the estate prospered under the stewardship of Henry McIlhenny, a distinguished Philadelphia art historian who restored the baronial castle and planted gardens full of exotic species of flowers and shrubs. McIlhenny subsequently gave Glenveagh to the Irish nation for use as a public park, and today the fairy-tale setting includes woodlands, herds of red deer, alpine gardens, a sylvan lake, and the highest mountain in Donegal, Mount Errigal. Visitors can tour the castle and gardens and explore the park on foot. The complex includes a visitor center with a continuous audiovisual show; displays on the history, flora, and fauna of the area; and nature trails. There is a restaurant in the visitor center, and a tearoom in the castle.

Main entrance on R251, Church Hill, county Donegal. © **074/37090.** Park admission and castle tour €2.50 ($2.25) adults, €2 ($1.80) seniors, €1.30 ($1.15) students and children, €6.50 ($5.80) family. No credit cards. Mid-Mar to 1st Sun in Nov daily 10am–6:30pm; closed Fri in Oct.

The Workhouse ⭐ This imposing stone structure was constructed in 1844, just before the height of the famine, and it provided meals and a roof for more than 300 local people. Life in a workhouse was miserable, and they were places of last resort: families were separated, inmates were subjected to harsh physical labor on a minimal food allowance, and once you entered, you were forbidden to leave. Still, by 1846 most of the 100,000 places in workhouses throughout Ireland were filled. The exhibits portray the life of workhouse inmates and relate local famine history. There is also an exhibit on the history of Dunfanaghy and an audiovisual presentation on the natural history of the region. Occasionally, evening music, poetry, or drama events are offered. A cozy tea and gift shop with an open fire serves baked goods.

Just west of Dunfanaghy on N56, county Donegal. ✆ **074/36540.** Admission €3.50 ($3.10) adults, €2.50 ($2.25) seniors and students, €2 ($1.80) children. Mid-Mar to mid-Oct Mon–Fri 10am–5pm; Sat–Sun noon–5pm.

SHOPPING

Ardara is a hub of tweed and woolen production. Most shops are open Monday to Saturday 9am to 5:30pm, with extended hours in summer. Unless otherwise noted, shops are on the main street of the town (N56).

C. Bonner & Son With 500 hand-knitters throughout county Donegal and 50 weavers in its factory, C. Bonner & Son produces a wide selection of hand-knit and hand-loomed knitwear, including linen-cotton and colorful sheep-patterned lamb's-wool sweaters, all for sale here in its factory outlet. Also for sale is a broad selection of crafts and gifts, including sheepskins, pottery, wildlife watercolors, wool hangings, linens, crystal, and china. Closed January and February. Front St., Ardara, county Donegal. ✆ **075/41303.**

C. Kennedy & Sons Ltd Established in 1904, this family-owned knitwear company employs about 500 home workers who hand-knit or hand-loom bainin sweaters, hats, scarves, and jackets in native Donegal patterns and colors. The shop also sells turf crafts, pottery, and dolls. Ardara, county Donegal. ✆ **075/41106.**

Eddie Doherty A hand-weaver with over 40 years experience, Eddie produces hand-woven material throws, scarves, caps, and shawls in a variety of colors and designs, some of which reflect the colors of the Donegal landscape. The loom is on display and the weaving is demonstrated to visitors. Ardara, county Donegal. ✆ **075/41304.**

John Molloy In the heart of wool and weaving country, this factory shop is well stocked with hand-knits, homespun fashions, sports jackets, tweed scarves and rugs, and all types of caps, from kingfisher to ghillie styles. There's even a bargain bin. Factory tours and a shop weaving demonstration are available. Ardara, county Donegal. ✆ **075/41133.**

SPORTS & OUTDOOR PURSUITS

BEACHES Some of the most pristine and secluded beaches in Ireland are along the northern and western coasts of Donegal. There are few such places anywhere else where you can be so alone on such magnificent expanses of sand. The only problem is hitting the good weather. There are several popular beaches on Dawros Head, including **Traighmore Strand** in Rossbeg, and extensive beaches in Portnoo and Navan. **Magheroarty,** near Falcarragh on the northern coast, has a breathtaking beach, unspoiled by crowds or commercial development. The same goes for **Tramore** beach on the western side of Horn Head near

Dunfanaghy; you have to hike a short distance, but the rewards are miles of white sand and seclusion. Other secluded and sandy beaches ideal for walking and jogging include Carrigart, Downings, Marble Hill, and Port na Blagh.

BICYCLING Raleigh mountain bikes can be rented with panniers and accessories from **Church Street Cycles,** Letterkenny, county Donegal (✆ 074/ 26204). They cost €15 ($13) per day, €60 ($53) per week, with a €65 ($58) deposit. Letterkenny is a good starting point for exploring the coast of northern Donegal—Horn Head, Inishowen Peninsula, Tory Island, and Bloody Foreland Head are all within an easy day's ride. Cycles rented here can be returned in Sligo Town, Donegal Town, or Galway City for an additional fee of €20 ($18).

BIRD-WATCHING **Horn Head,** a nesting site for many species of seabirds, has the largest nesting population of razorbills in Ireland. **Malin Head,** at the end of the Inishowen Peninsula, is the northernmost point on the Irish mainland, and once was the site of a bird observatory; it's a good site for watching migrants in late autumn.

FISHING The rivers and lakes in this area produce good catches of salmon, sea trout, and brown trout, and the coastal waters yield flounder, pollock, and cod. Fishing expeditions are offered by charter boats, fishing boats, and trawlers. For details, contact the **North Western Regional Fisheries Board,** Abbey Street, Ballina, county Mayo (✆ 096/22788; fax 096/70543; NWRFB@iol.ie).

GOLF One of Ireland's most challenging golf courses is the **Rosapenna Golf Club,** Atlantic Drive, Downings, county Donegal (✆ 074/55301), an 18-hole championship seaside par-70 links course that was laid out in 1983 by Tom Morris of St. Andrews. Greens fees are €30 ($27) weekdays, €37 ($33) weekends.

Other 18-hole courses in this part of Donegal are **Dunfanaghy Golf Club,** Dunfanaghy, county Donegal (✆ 074/36335), a seaside par-68 course with greens fees of €19 ($17) weekdays, €24 ($21) weekends; **Narin & Portnoo Golf Club,** Narin-Portnoo, county Donegal (✆ 075/45107), a par-69 seaside course with greens fees of €20 ($18) weekdays, €24 ($21) weekends; and **Portsalon Golf Club,** Portsalon, county Donegal (✆ 074/59459), a seaside par-69 course with greens fees of €24 ($21) weekdays, €28 ($25) weekends.

HORSEBACK RIDING **Dunfanaghy Stables,** Arnolds Hotel, Dunfanaghy, county Donegal (✆ 074/36208), specializes in trail riding on the surrounding beaches, dunes, and mountain trails. An hour's ride averages €15 ($13).

WALKING A section of the **Ulster Way** passes through Donegal between the towns of Falcarragh to the north and Pettigo to the south, on the border with Fermanagh. This trail traverses some remote and wild terrain, passing Errigal Mountain and Glenveagh Park before heading south into the Blue Stack Mountains.

There are some incredible walks on **Hook Head,** signposted off N56 just west of Dunfanaghy. Follow Hook Head Drive to the concrete lookout point. From here you can walk out to a ruined castle on the headland and continue south along a line of impressive quartzite sea cliffs that glitter in the sun as though covered with a sheet of ice. This is a moderately difficult walk.

The **Ards Forest Park** is on a peninsula jutting out into Sheep Haven Bay, about 5.6km (3½ miles) south of Dunfanaghy on N56. The park is mostly forested and includes an area of dunes along the water. There are signposted nature trails, and you can buy a guidebook as you enter the park.

WHERE TO STAY

MODERATE/EXPENSIVE

Rathmullan House 🏵🏵🏵 This is one of the most pleasurable places to stay in northern Donegal. On the western shores of Lough Swilly, Donegal's great sea lake, about .8km (½ mile) north of town, this secluded, sprawling, white country mansion is surrounded by colorful rose gardens and mature trees. The mostly Georgian (ca. 1760) interior features intricate plastered ceilings, crystal chandeliers, oil paintings, white marble log-burning fireplaces, and an assortment of antiques and heirlooms collected over the years by owners Bob and Robin Wheeler. Rooms vary in size, but all are comfortably and attractively furnished. The most expensive are luxurious, with sitting areas and views of the lake, while the least expensive are more compact with a garden view. All have orthopedic beds, and two are wheelchair accessible. The award-winning breakfast buffet is copious and imaginative. Rathmullan House is more luxurious overall than its neighbor, the Fort Royal (see below), so try here first.

Lough Swilly, Rathmullan, county Donegal. ℂ **800/223-6510** in the U.S., or 074/58188. Fax 074/58200. www.rathmullanhouse.com. 23 units. €160–€200 ($142–$178) double. Rates include full Irish breakfast and service charge. AE, DC, MC, V. Closed Jan to mid-Feb. **Amenities:** Restaurant (modern country); bar; drawing room; library; indoor swimming pool; private beach; 2 tennis courts; steam room; massage treatments. *In room:* TV, hair dryer.

MODERATE

Arnold's Hotel 🏵 Right on Sheephaven Bay, this family-run place offers warm hospitality and great views of the Atlantic and Horn Head. In the Arnold family for three generations, brothers Derek and William act as desk clerks, porters, waiters, and whatever else needs doing. Rooms are comfortable and attractive, if slightly bland. Arnold's is an ideal base for touring northwest Donegal and for exploring Glenveagh National Park. Golf, fishing, and pony trekking can be arranged at the front desk.

Dunfanaghy, county Donegal. ℂ **800/44-UTELL** in the U.S., or 074/36208. Fax 074/36352. www.arnolds hotel.com. 30 units. €110–€140 ($98–$125) double. No service charge. Rates include full breakfast. AE, MC, V. Closed Nov–Mar 15. **Amenities:** Restaurant (international). *In room:* TV.

Fort Royal Hotel 🏵🏵 Built in 1819, this rambling, three-story country house owned by the Fletcher family has been a hotel since 1948. It's set on 7.2 hectares (18 acres) of gardens and woodlands, with a small sandy beach overlooking the water on the western shore of Lough Swilly, 1.6km (1 mile) north of the village. Both the public areas and the recently refurbished guest rooms are decorated in an upscale country style, with traditional furnishings, period pieces, and oil paintings showing scenes of Donegal. Though not as luxurious as Rathmullan House (see above), Fort Royal delivers an extremely comfortable country house experience. All but three guest rooms have lake views.

Rathmullan, county Donegal. ℂ **800/447-7462** in the U.S., or 074/58100. Fax 074/58103. www.fortroyal hotel.com. 15 units. €134–€160 ($119–$142) double. No service charge. Rates include full breakfast. AE, V. Closed Nov–Easter. **Amenities:** Restaurant (Continental); bar; lounge; golf course; tennis court; squash court. *In room:* TV.

Ostán Na Rosann/Hotel of the Rosses 🏵 *Value* On a hill overlooking the Atlantic, this modern ranch-style hotel sits in a scenic Gaelic-speaking area in the heart of the Rosses overlooking Dungloe Bay. The guest rooms have wide-windowed sea views and comfortable, standard furnishings. Quite frankly, the public rooms and guest rooms are nothing special, but the leisure center and sea views make it very good value. A popular hotel with Irish families, it has a very lively bar and a nightclub/disco.

Dungloe, county Donegal. ✆ 075/22444. Fax 075/22400. www.ostannarosann.com. 48 units. €114–€126 ($101–$112) double. Rates include full breakfast. AE, MC, V. **Amenities:** Restaurant (Continental); lounge; nightclub/disco; indoor swimming pool; gym; Jacuzzi; sauna; nonsmoking rooms. *In room:* TV, tea/coffeemaker, hair dryer.

Rosapenna Golf Hotel ⚜ Surrounded by Sheephaven Bay and the hills of Donegal, this contemporary two-story hotel is a favorite with golfers, who flock here to enjoy the hotel's 18-hole links course. Nongolfers come for the scenery, the seclusion (280 hectares'/700 acres' worth), and the hotel's proximity to northern Donegal attractions. The guest rooms, dining area, and lounges enjoy panoramic views of land and sea.

Atlantic Dr., Downings, county Donegal. ✆ 074/55301. Fax 074/55128. www.rosapenna.ie. 53 units. €140–€160 ($125–$142) double. Rates include service charge and full breakfast. AE, MC, V. Closed late Oct to mid-Mar. **Amenities:** Restaurant (international); bar; indoor swimming pool; 18-hole golf course; 2 tennis courts. *In room:* TV.

INEXPENSIVE

Croaghross ⚜⚜ This terrific house, set on a hill overlooking Lough Swilly, has been penned into many a budget traveler's journal. It's the kind of modest place that strikes an endearing, nostalgic chord, for everything is done here with the attention and care of a doting grandmother. Guest rooms are very comfortable, the setting divine, and breakfasts legendary. Kay Deane's sophisticated dinnertime meals are a fabulous, soulful, perfect end to a windblown Donegal day.

Portsalon, Letterkenny, county Donegal. ✆ and fax 074/59548. www.croaghross.com. 5 units. €60–€90 ($53–$80) double. No service charge. Rates include full breakfast. AE, MC, V. Closed Oct–Mar 18. **Amenities:** Nonsmoking rooms; sitting room. *In room:* No phone.

SELF-CATERING

Donegal Thatched Cottages ⚜⚜ This cluster of cottages has a spectacular situation on Cruit Island, an enchanting landscape of rock and sand just off the Donegal coast near Dungloe. Accessible by a small bridge, Cruit is a narrow spit of land reaching into the Atlantic, dwarfed by its nearby neighbors Aranmore and Owey islands. The cottages are on the Atlantic side, which alternates rocky headlands with unspoiled beaches; on the lee side is a lovely quiet beach that extends for miles. The view west toward Owey Island is captivating, and sunsets are notoriously glorious. There's a great seaside walk along the western side of the island, which takes in a series of lovely half-moon beaches.

Each cottage is built according to a traditional plan, resembling many of the rural homes you're sure to have seen while exploring the region. The interiors are simple and appealing, with wooden and tiled floors, high ceilings in the living/dining rooms, and a great loft bedroom on the second floor. The kitchen comes equipped with a dishwasher and a washer and dryer for your laundry, and there's a master bedroom with its own private bathroom. Each cottage has three bedrooms, and can sleep up to seven guests. Although the location is somewhat remote, there are a number of pubs and restaurants within a short driving distance.

Cruit Island, c/o Conor and Mary Ward, Rosses Point, county Sligo. Signposted opposite Viking House Hotel on Kincasslagh Rd., 9.5km (6 miles) north of Dungloe, Cruit Island. ✆ 071/77197. Fax 071/77500. www.donegalthatchedcottages.com. 10 cottages. €225–€795 ($200–$708) per cottage per week, plus €7 ($6.25) per person per week. Weekend discounts available. MC, V. **Amenities:** TV, kitchen, dishwasher, washer/dryer, no phone.

WHERE TO DINE

The Mill Restaurant 🏵🏵 INTERNATIONAL This buzzy place is deservedly one of the hottest destination restaurants in this part of Donegal. The draw is Derek Alcorn's cooking, which confidently manages to simultaneously be both adventurous and restrained. It's all about pairing ingredients to achieve disarming results. The Doe Castle mussels with Smithwick ale and sage is surprising and terrific, as is the lime-and-coriander couscous paired with mushroom-and-eggplant moussaka. Desserts are simple and elegant, and the wine list is well chosen.

Figart (.8km/½ mile past village of Dunfanaghy, beside lake), county Donegal. 🕐 **074/36985.** Reservations recommended for dinner. Dinner main courses €18–€26 ($16–$23). MC, V. Tues–Sun 7–9pm; Sun also 12:30–2pm.

Water's Edge 🏵 INTERNATIONAL   As its name implies, this restaurant is on the edge of picturesque Lough Swilly, on the south end of town. Although a glassy facade on three sides gives the 70-seat dining area a modern look, the interior is quite traditional, with beamed ceilings, an open fireplace, nautical bric-a-brac, and watercolors of Donegal landscapes. The menu blends Irish dishes with such international favorites as wild salmon in brandy-bisque sauce, chicken Kiev, prawns Provençal, and steaks. Bar food, served all day, ranges from soups and sandwiches to patés, scampi, and fish and chips. Rooms with a view and breakfast are available, for €56 ($50) double.

The Ballyboe, Rathmullan, county Donegal. 🕐 **074/58182.** Reservations recommended for dinner. Dinner main courses €14–€20 ($12–$18). MC, V. Easter–Sept daily noon–10pm; Oct–Easter daily 6:30–10pm.

PUBS

Almost all the pubs in this Irish-speaking area provide spontaneous sessions of Irish traditional music in summer. Two places especially renowned for music are the **Lakeside Centre,** Dunlewey (🕐 **075/31699**), and **Leo's Tavern** 🏵, Meenaleck, Crolly (🕐 **075/48143**). The highly successful Irish group Clannad and the vocalist Enya (all part of the talented Brennan family) got their starts at Leo's.

The don't-miss pub in Ardara is **Nancy's** 🏵🏵 (🕐 **075/41187**) on Front Street, which has to be one of the smallest pubs in Ireland. It's an old Victorian house with the pub in the sitting room. As the crowd pours in, other rooms open up in hospitality.

6 The Inishowen Peninsula

Buncrana, the peninsula's chief town, is 113km (70 miles) NE of Donegal Airport, 84km (52 miles) NE of Donegal Town, 19km (12 miles) NW of Derry, 145km (90 miles) NE of Sligo, 359km (223 miles) NE of Shannon, and 259km (161 miles) NW of Dublin

This long, broad finger of land stretching north to the Atlantic between Lough Swilly to the west and Lough Foyle to the east is Ireland's northernmost point. It is arguably the most beautiful area in all of Ireland. Along the shores of both loughs and the Atlantic Ocean, long stretches of sandy beaches are backed by sheer cliffs. Inland are some of Ireland's most impressive mountains, with the 615m (2,019-ft.) Slieve Snacht dominating the center of the peninsula. Its heritage reaches back beyond recorded history, with relics of those distant days scattered across its face.

The Inishowen gets its name from Eoghain, a son of King Niall of the Nine Hostages, who lived at the time of St. Patrick in the 5th century. The king named this amazing finger of land for his son—Inis Eoghain means "the island of Owen."

To drive around the Inishowen is to traverse a ring of seascapes, mountains, valleys, and woodlands. It's been said that Donegal is a miniature Ireland; Donegal folk claim that Inishowen is a miniature Donegal.

Relatively undiscovered by most visitors to Ireland, Inishowen is a world apart, where present-day residents revere their ancient heritage, treasure the legends and antiquities of this remote region, and still observe many traditions of their ancestors. Traditional music and dance thrive here, and it's unlikely you'll face an evening when there's not a music session in a nearby pub. No place this spectacularly beautiful and unspoiled goes unappreciated for its splendors forever; just go before everyone else discovers it.

INISHOWEN PENINSULA ESSENTIALS

GETTING THERE & GETTING AROUND   **North West Busways** (© 074/ 82619) offers service between Letterkenny and Moville, via Cardonagh and Buncrana, and there's daily Dublin-Inishowen service on offer by John McGinley (© 074/35201).

The best way to get to and around the Inishowen Peninsula is by car, following the signposted 161km (100-mile) Inishowen route.

VISITOR INFORMATION   Contact the **North West Tourism Office,** Aras Reddan, Temple Street, Sligo (© 071/61201; www.northwestireland.travel.ie); the **Letterkenny Tourist Office,** Derry Road, Letterkenny (© 074/21173); or the **Inishowen Tourism Society,** Chapel Street, Cardonagh, county Donegal (© 077/74933; www.visitinishowen.com). All three are open year-round, Monday to Friday 9:30am to 5:30pm, with extended summer hours.

SEEING THE SIGHTS

In spite of its remote location, the Inishowen Peninsula circuit is one of the best-marked roads in Ireland, with all directions clearly printed in English and Irish, miles and kilometers. Among the many features of this 161km (100-mile) route (which runs from Letterkenny to Moville) is a string of beach resorts like Ballyliffin, Buncrana, Greencastle, and Moville. Natural wonders include the **Gap of Mamore,** 8km (5 miles) north of Buncrana, a pass rising to 240m (800 ft.) and then slowly descending on a corkscrew path to sea level, and **Slieve Snacht,** a 606m (2,019-ft.) mountain.

The peninsula's most impressive historic monument is the hilltop fort known as **Grianan of Aileach,** 16km (10 miles) south of Buncrana. One of the best examples of a ring fort in Ireland, it was built as a temple of the sun around 1700 B.C. From the mid–5th century to the early 12th, it was the royal residence of the O'Neills, the kings of this area.

After you've toured the Inishowen, or perhaps stayed a few days, head south through **Letterkenny** (pop. 5,000). The largest town in the county, it's on a hillside overlooking the River Swilly. There you can pick up N56, the main road, and drive to the twin towns of Ballybofey and Stranorlar. Change here to N15, which takes you to yet another scenic Donegal drive, the **Barnesmore Gap,** a vast open stretch through the Blue Stack Mountains, which leads you into Donegal Town and points south.

Fort Dunree Military Museum ✭   Perched on a cliff overlooking Lough Swilly, Fort Dunree is a military and naval museum incorporating a Napoleonic Martello tower at the site of World War I defenses on the north Irish coast. It features a wide range of exhibitions, an audiovisual center, and a cafeteria housed in a restored forge. Even if you have no interest in military history, it's worth a trip for the view. Dunree has one of Donegal's best vantage points for observing unencumbered seascapes and broad mountain vistas.

Signposted on the coast rd. north of Buncrana, county Donegal. © 077/61817 or 077/21173. Admission €2.50 ($2.25) per car. June–Sept Tues–Sat 10:30am–6pm; Sun 12:30–8pm.

Greencastle Maritime Museum ✯   This compact maritime museum, in the harbor home of one of the busiest fishing fleets in Ireland, is housed in the old 1857 coast-guard station. Before you go in, be sure to take in the grand views of Lough Foyle, as well as the monument to those lost in nearby waters. The museum's modest, intriguing exhibits focus on the everyday struggles as well as the historic events beyond Greencastle Harbour, from Armada wrecks to famine-period emigration to the heroism of the Irish lifeboat rescue teams. In addition, there's a Mesolithic exhibit with local 8,000-year-old finds. A small coffee, craft, and souvenir shop is also at hand. Best of all, Maire McCann's stories bring the museum's exhibits to life. A planetarium, built in 2000, has three shows daily: Call ahead to confirm times.

Harbour, Greencastle, county Donegal. © 077/81363. Admission €2.50 ($2.25) adults, €1.30 ($1.15) seniors and students, €6.50 ($5.80) family. June–Sept daily 10am–6pm; other times by appointment.

SPORTS & OUTDOOR PURSUITS
BEACHES   **Ballyliffin, Buncrana, Greencastle,** and **Moville** have safe, sandy beaches that are ideal for swimming or walking.

GOLF   Donegal's northern coast is believed to be one of the first places where golf was played in Ireland, and it's been played on the Inishowen Peninsula for more than 100 years.

The Inishowen has three 18-hole golf courses. The **Ballyliffin Golf Club,** Ballyliffin, county Donegal (© 077/76119; www.ballyliffingolfclub.com), the northernmost golf course in Ireland, is a par-71 links course with greens fees of €38 ($34) weekdays, €42 ($38) weekends. The **North West Golf Club,** Fahan, Buncrana, county Donegal (© 077/61027), founded in 1890, is a par-69 seaside course with greens fees of €23 ($20) weekdays, €28 ($25) weekends. **Greencastle Golf Course,** Greencastle, county Donegal (© 077/781013), is a par-69 parkland course with greens fees of €23 ($20) weekdays, €24 ($21) weekends.

WATERSPORTS   The Inishowen's long coastline, sandy beaches, and combination of open ocean and sheltered coves offer great opportunities for watersports. The northwest coast presents some of the most challenging surfing conditions in the world. For advice and specific information, contact the **Irish Surfing Association,** Tirchonaill Street, Donegal (© 073/21053; www.isas-urf.ie).

WHERE TO STAY
MODERATE
Mount Errigal ✯   South of Lough Swilly and less than .8km (1 mile) east of Letterkenny, this contemporary two-story hotel is a handy place to stay. It's midway between the Inishowen Peninsula and Donegal Town, within 32km (20 miles) of Glenveagh National Park. Although it has a rather ordinary gray facade, the inside is bright and airy, with skylights, light woods, hanging plants, colored and etched glass, and brass fixtures. The guest rooms are outfitted in contemporary style, with cheerful colors and modern art, and good reading lights over the beds.

Derry Rd., Ballyraine, Letterkenny, county Donegal. © 074/22700. Fax 074/25085. www.mounterrigal.com. 82 units. €108–€145 ($96–$129) double. No service charge. Rates include full breakfast. AE, DC, MC, V. **Amenities:** 2 restaurants (international, cafe); bar; indoor swimming pool; gym; sauna/steam room; massage treatments. *In room:* TV, tea/coffeemaker, hair dryer, garment press.

Redcastle Hotel ★★ *Value*   Right on the shores of Lough Foyle on the Inishowen's eastern coast, this country inn-style hotel offers a combination of old-world charms and modern comforts. The guest rooms are done up in designer fabrics, and each has a view of the lake or the adjacent golf course. When you consider the lakeside location, the leisure center, and the golf course, it's hard to beat this place for the price. If you're interested in using the Redcastle as a base, ask about their multiple-night deals.

Redcastle, Moville, county Donegal. © 077/82073. Fax 077/82214. www.redcastlehotel.com. 31 units. €94–€147 ($84–$131) double. No service charge. Rates include full breakfast. AE, MC, V. **Amenities:** 2 restaurants (international, cafe); bar; indoor swimming pool; 9-hole golf course; tennis court; gym; sauna/steam room. *In room:* TV, tea/coffeemaker, hair dryer.

INEXPENSIVE

Brooklyn Cottage ★★ *Value*   You're not going to find a nicer lakeside B&B for this price. Only tall panes of glass separate the living room of Brooklyn Cottage from the lapping waves. This modern bungalow is right on the brink of the Inishowen peninsula, and guests eat breakfast in a conservatory that takes advantage of a spectacular sea view (as do the living room and two of the guest rooms). A small coastal path skirts the rocky shore in front of the house, and it's possible to follow it to the neighboring town of Moville, about 3.2km (2 miles) away. The guest rooms are small, but each is meticulously kept. Peter Smith, who serves as host along with his wife, Gladys, is involved with the nearby Maritime museum and shares his knowledge of the area with guests. Brooklyn Cottage is within walking distance of the center of Greencastle, yet occupies a seemingly remote site just beyond the port.

Greencastle, Inishowen, county Donegal. © 077/81087. 3 units (2 with shower only, no tub). €54 ($48) double. Rates include breakfast. No credit cards. Closed Jan–Feb. **Amenities:** Living room. *In room:* Tea/coffeemaker, no phone.

The Strand ★   On a hillside overlooking Pollen Strand, with views of nearby Malin Head, this small family-run hotel is on the edge of town, set apart in its own palm tree–lined rose gardens. The decor throughout the hotel is contemporary Irish, with wide windows and traditional touches. Guest rooms are attractively, though not imaginatively, appointed with beech furnishings, patterned carpeting, and neutral fabrics. Bathrooms are modern but smallish. Still, if you're looking for a slightly old-style family hotel, it's hard to beat the price. The bar is known for its local entertainment.

Ballyliffin, Clonmany, county Donegal. © 077/76107. Fax 077/76486. www.ballyliffin.com/strand/location. htm. 21 units. €60–€80 ($53–$71) double. No service charge. Rates include full breakfast. MC, V. **Amenities:** Restaurant (international); bar. *In room:* TV, tea/coffeemaker, hair dryer.

SELF-CATERING

Ballyliffin Self Catering ★★   Ballyliffin is a tiny seaside village on the west coast of Inishowen, with two golf courses in close proximity. This group of cottages is situated along the main road through town, a 10-minute walk from the fine sand and clear waters of Pollan Bay. The six connected cottages are all built in stone and pine, with lofty vaulted ceilings in the living rooms and massive central fireplaces, which the stairs circle on their way to the second floor. Each cottage has three bedrooms and two bathrooms—two of the bedrooms have a double bed and an attached bathroom, while the third bedroom has three single beds. In some cottages, second-floor bedrooms overlook the living room, where a foldout couch provides yet more sleeping space. The well-equipped kitchen includes a microwave, an electric stove, a dishwasher, and a washing machine and dryer.

Rossaor House, Ballyliffin, county Donegal. ℂ and fax 077/76498. 6 cottages. €475–€630 ($423–$561) per week. Rates include oil-fired heat. MC, V. **Amenities:** TV, kitchen, microwave, dishwasher, washer/dryer, no phone.

WHERE TO DINE

The Corncrake ✰✰ MODERN CONTINENTAL A restaurant like the Corncrake is as rare as the endangered bird from which it takes its name. The setup is "dead simple," as the Irish like to say—just one room and two talented women at the helm. The freshest of ingredients are sought out by Brid McCartney and Noreen Lynch and then transformed using a selection of herbs grown in their own gardens in a way that is nothing short of sublime. Starters include a prawn chowder where lemon and fresh coriander bring out the flavor of locally caught fish and a cheese soufflé whose golden crown topples to reveal a velvet textured filling of egg, cream, and sharp cheddar. Meat and fish dishes are coupled with sauces and seasonings so masterful that they seem to give lamb a new tenderness and monkfish an unanticipated delicacy. Vegetarians need to book a day in advance but will be rewarded by something downright delectable, such as goat cheese wrapped in red peppers. Desserts range from a wholesome gooseberry fool to a blissful orange and Grand Marnier *panna cotta* (an Italian dessert made with cream and eggs).

Malin St., Carndonagh, county Donegal. ℂ 077/74534. Reservations recommended. Dinner main courses €12–€18 ($11–$16). No credit cards. Easter–Sept daily 6–9pm; Oct–Dec weekends only. Closed Jan–Easter.

Kealy's Seafood Bar ✰✰ SEAFOOD Right across the road from the pier in Greencastle, Tricia Kealy's always-buzzing little fish house is a terrific place to know about. Tricia knows what to pair with just-off-the-boat fish—poached hake in saffron sauce, plaice in anchovy butter, cod with Stilton—which makes dining here a surprisingly refined experience. If you prefer, sidle up to the bar for an afternoon bite, and you can have a simple bowl of chowder or smoked salmon on brown bread. Locals claim the fish is so fresh, it's reeled onto your plate. This is food, of the people, by the people, and for the people, and you can taste the difference.

Greencastle, county Donegal. ℂ 077/81010. Reservations recommended for dinner. Dinner main courses €14–€21 ($12–$19). MC, V. Daily 12:30–3pm and 7–9:30pm; bar snacks 3–5pm. Closed Mon–Wed in off-season (usually Oct–Easter).

St. John's Country House and Restaurant ✰ CONTINENTAL On its own grounds overlooking Lough Swilly, this lovely Georgian house has two cozily elegant dining rooms. Open turf fireplaces, Waterford crystal, embroidered linens, and richly textured wallpaper add to the ambience. Importantly, the food is dependably good—baked Swilly salmon with lemon sauce, roast duck with port-and-orange sauce, spiced lamb en croûte with gooseberry-and-mint sauce, and John Dory with fennel. B&B is available for €94 to €200 ($84–$178) double.

Fahan, county Donegal. ℂ 077/60289. Fax 077/60612. Reservations required. Fixed-price 6-course dinner €40 ($36). AE, DC, MC, V. Tues–Sat 6–10pm.

14

The Midlands: Along the River Shannon

No matter where in the midlands you find yourself, you're never far from the River Shannon. It is Ireland's fluid, winding spine, dividing east from west, flowing through lowland fields and bogs, and communing with countless lakes and lesser rivers. The Shannon is the constant by which you should take your bearings in Ireland's heartland.

At 371km (230 miles), the Shannon is the longest river in Ireland or Great Britain. It influences and defines more of the Irish landscape than any other body of water. Rising in county Cavan, it flows south through the heartland of Ireland, touching nine other counties— Leitrim, Roscommon, Longford, Westmeath, Offaly, Galway, Tipperary, Clare, and Limerick—before reaching its mouth and separating counties Kerry and Clare as the Shannon estuary waters meet the Atlantic.

The Shannon takes many shapes and forms as it flows. At some points, it's almost 16km (10 miles) across; at others, it narrows to a few hundred yards. For centuries, the river was primarily a means of transportation and commerce, Ireland's most ancient highway; more recently, it's chiefly been a source of enjoyment and recreation.

The river can be divided into three segments: the **Lower Shannon and Lough Derg,** stretching from Killaloe, county Clare, to Portumna, county Galway; the **Middle Shannon,** a narrow passage from the Birr/Banagher area in county Offaly to Athlone, Westmeath; and the **Upper Shannon,** from Westmeath's Lough Ree to Leitrim's Lough Allen and on to the river's source in county Cavan. In this chapter, we'll explore the river from south to north. This is not to imply that the river flows in that direction; rather, it's to help you start touring in the area that has the most to do and see.

While it's unlikely that you will follow the Shannon for all of its 345 navigable kilometers (214 miles), you'll encounter it in almost every cross-country route you take. So, whether you trace or cross its path, it makes sense here to point out some of the many delights to be found along and near the Shannon's shores.

1 Lower Shannon: The Lough Derg Drive

Killaloe is 26km (16 miles) NE of Limerick and 40km (25 miles) E of Ennis; Portumna is 65km (40 miles) SE of Galway and 44km (27 miles) E of Gort

The Lower Shannon, stretching from Killaloe, county Clare, north to Portumna, county Galway, encompasses one huge lake, Lough Derg. Often called an inland sea, **Lough Derg** was the main inland waterway trading route between Dublin and Limerick when canal and river commercial traffic was at its height in Ireland in the 18th and 19th centuries. It is the Shannon River's largest lake and widest point: 40km (25 miles) long and almost 16km (10 miles) wide, with more than 10,000 hectares (25,000 acres) of water. Today, Lough Derg can be described as Ireland's pleasure lake, because of all the recreational and sporting opportunities it provides.

AREA ESSENTIALS

GETTING THERE & GETTING AROUND   The best way to get to the Lough Derg area is by car or boat. Although there is limited public transportation in the area, you will need a car to get around the lake. Major roads that lead to Lough Derg are the main Limerick-Dublin road (N7) from points east and south, N6 and N65 from Galway and the west, and N52 from the north. The Lough Derg Drive, which is well signposted, is a combination of R352 on the west bank of the lake and R493, R494, and R495 on the east bank.

VISITOR INFORMATION   Because Lough Derg unites three counties (Clare, Galway, and Tipperary), there are several sources of information about the area. They include the **Shannon Development Tourism Group,** Shannon, county Clare (© 061/361555; www.shannon-dev.ie); **Ireland West Tourism,** Victoria Place, Eyre Square, Galway (© 091/563081; www.westireland.travel.ie); and **Tipperary Lake Side & Development,** The Old Church, Borrisokane, county Tipperary (© 067/27155). Seasonal information offices include the **Nenagh Tourist Office,** Connolly Street, Nenagh, county Tipperary (© 067/31610), open early May to early September; and the **Killaloe Tourist Office,** The Bridge, county Clare (© 061/376866), open May to September.

EXPLORING THE AREA

The road that rims the lake for 153km (95 miles), the **Lough Derg Drive,** is one of the most scenic routes in Ireland. It's a continuous natural setting where panoramas of hilly farmlands, gentle mountains, bucolic forests, and glistening waters are unspoiled by commercialization. Most of all, the drive is a collage of colorful shoreline towns, starting with **Killaloe** 𝕬, county Clare, and Ballina, county Tipperary, on the south banks of the lake. They're called "twin towns" because they're usually treated as one community—only a splendid 13-arch bridge over the Shannon separates them.

Killaloe is a darling little village and home to Ireland's largest inland marina and a host of watersports centers. Of historical note is a 9th-century oratory, said to have been founded by St. Lua—hence the name Killaloe, which comes from the Irish *Cill* ("church") of Lua.

Nearby is another oratory and cathedral, built in the 12th century and named for 6th-century St. Flannan; it boasts an exquisite Romanesque doorway. **Kincora,** on the highest ground at Killaloe, was the royal settlement of Brian Boru and the other O'Brien kings, but no trace of any building remains. Killaloe is a lovely town with lakeside views at almost every turn and many fine restaurants and pubs offering outdoor seating on the shore.

Eight kilometers (5 miles) inland from Lough Derg's lower southeast shores is **Nenagh,** the chief town of north Tipperary. It lies in a fertile valley between the Silvermine and Arra Mountains.

On the north shore of the lake is **Portumna,** which means "the landing place of the oak tree." A major point of traffic across the Shannon, Portumna has a lovely forest park and a remarkable castle that's currently being restored.

Memorable little towns and harborside villages like **Mountshannon** and **Dromineer** dot the rest of the Lough Derg Drive. Some towns, like **Terryglass** and **Woodford,** are known for atmospheric old pubs where spontaneous

The River Shannon's Shores

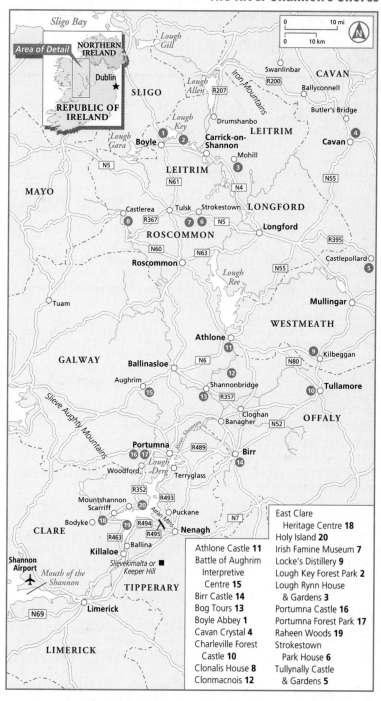

0   10 mi
0   10 km

Sligo Bay

Area of Detail

NORTHERN
IRELAND

Dublin ★

REPUBLIC OF
IRELAND

Lough Gill

Lough Allen R207

Lough Key

SLIGO

Iron Mountains

Swanlinbar R200 CAVAN

Ballyconnell

Butler's Bridge

Drumshanbo

LEITRIM

Cavan ④

Lough Gara

Boyle ❶ ❷

Carrick-on-Shannon

Mohill

N5

LEITRIM

N61

N4

❸

MAYO

Castlerea Tulsk Strokestown LONGFORD

❽ R367 ❼ ❻ N5

Longford ○

ROSCOMMON

R395

N55

Castlepollard ○
⑤

N60

N63

Roscommon ○

Lough Ree

N55

Tuam ○

Mullingar ○

WESTMEATH

Athlone ○
⑪

GALWAY

Ballinasloe ○

N6

Kilbeggan
⑨

N80

Aughrim

⑮

Shannonbridge

⑫

Tullamore ○
⑩

⑬ R357

Cloghan

Banagher N52

OFFALY

River Shannon

Portumna ○
⑯ ⑰ R489

Birr ○
⑭

Woodford ○ *Lough Derg* Terryglass ○

R352

Mountshannon
Scarriff ⑳ R493

Bodyke ○ ⑱ ⑲ R494 Puckane ○ N7

CLARE

R463 R495

Killaloe ○ Ballina

Shannon
Airport *Slievekimalta or Keeper Hill* ■

Mouth of the Shannon

TIPPERARY

N69

Limerick ○

LIMERICK

Arran Mtns.

Nenagh ○

East Clare
  Heritage Centre **18**
Holy Island **20**
Irish Famine Museum **7**
Locke's Distillery **9**
Lough Key Forest Park **2**
Lough Rynn House
  & Gardens **3**
Portumna Castle **16**
Portumna Forest Park **17**
Raheen Woods **19**
Strokestown
  Park House **6**
Tullynally Castle
  & Gardens **5**

Athlone Castle **11**
Battle of Aughrim
  Interpretive
  Centre **15**
Birr Castle **14**
Bog Tours **13**
Boyle Abbey **1**
Cavan Crystal **4**
Charleville Forest
  Castle **10**
Clonalis House **8**
Clonmacnois **12**

sessions of traditional Irish music are likely to occur. Others, like **Puckane** and **Ballinderry,** offer unique crafts or locally made products.

The Lough Derg Drive is the Shannon River at its best.

East Clare Heritage Centre/Holy Island Tours ⭑⭑ Housed in the restored 10th-century church of St. Cronan (Ireland's oldest church in continuous use), this center explains the heritage and history of the East Clare area through a series of exhibits and an audiovisual presentation. A pier across the road is the starting point for a 15-minute boating excursion on Lough Derg to nearby Inishcealtra (Holy Island), one of the most famous monastic sites in Ireland. Like all monasteries, it was a target of Viking attacks, the first occurring in A.D. 836. Brian Boru rebuilt the monastery and his brother Marcan was abbot there. The trip includes a 45-minute guided tour of the island.

Off the Portumna-Ennis rd. (R352), Tuamgraney, county Clare. ✆ 061/921351. Admission to the center €2.50 ($2.25) adults, €1.30 ($1.15) children, €6.50 ($5.80) family; Holy Island Tours €6.50 ($5.80) adults, €2.50 ($2.25) children. Centre May–Sept daily 10am–6pm; Holy Island Tours Apr–Sept 11am–6pm, weather permitting.

Portumna Castle ⭑ Built in 1609 by Earl Richard Burke, this castle on the northern shores of Lough Derg is said to have been one of the finest 17th-century manor houses in Ireland. A fire gutted the castle in 1826, but spared its Dutch-style decorative gables and rows of stone mullioned windows. The castle is in the process of being restored, with limited access to the public. The gardens are open, and worth a visit as well.

Off N65, Portumna, county Galway. No phone. Admission to castle: €2.25 ($2.00) adults, €1 (89¢) for seniors and children under 12. Free admission to gardens. Daily 8am–4pm.

Portumna Forest Park ⭑⭑ On the shores of Lough Derg, this 560-hectare (1,400-acre) park is east of the town, off the main road. It offers trails and signposted walks, plus viewing points and picnic areas.

Off N65, Portumna, county Galway. ✆ 0905/42365. Admission €2 ($1.80) adults, €1.30 ($1.15) students and seniors, €.80 (70¢) children over 5, €5 ($4.45) family. Daily dawn–9pm.

SIGHTSEEING CRUISES

R&B Marine Services Ltd Enjoy a cruise of Lough Derg on board the 48-seat *Derg Princess,* a covered river bus. Departing from Killaloe Marina, the one-hour cruise travels past the fort of Brian Boru and into Lough Derg.

Killaloe Marina, Killaloe, county Clare. ✆ 061/375011. Cruise €7 ($6.25) adults, €4 ($3.55) children, €18 ($16) family. May–Sept Sunday 3:15pm or by arrangement.

Shannon Sailing Ltd. This company operates a covered 53-seat water bus, the *Ku-ee-tu.* It sails from the southeastern shore of Lough Derg at Dromineer on a 1½-hour cruise with full commentary on local sights.

New Harbor, Dromineer, Nenagh, county Tipperary. ✆ 067/24499. Cruise €7 ($6.25) adults, €3.50 ($2.85) children, €18 ($16) family. May–Sept daily; schedule varies.

SHOPPING

Eugene & Anke McKernan A husband-and-wife team, Eugene and Anke offer a colorful array of distinctive tweed scarves, jackets, vests, and blankets. The couple hand-weaves all items on the premises, which were formerly police barracks. Visitors are welcome to visit the workshop and observe the weaving process. Open daily 10am to 7pm from May through September; hours vary October to April. Handweavers, Main St., Tuamgraney, county Clare. ✆ 061/921527.

Old Church Craft Shop & Gallery Built on the site of the original abbey of St. Columba (A.D. 549), this stone-faced building dates from 1838. Transformed into a craft shop in 1984, it is a treasure trove of locally produced crafts and products. You might see Terryglass pottery, Rathbone traditional beeswax candles, Irish bonsai plants, bog oak pendants, wildlife mobiles, boxwood products from Birr Castle, Jerpoint glass, decorated horseshoes, miniature watercolors of Shannon River scenes, and books about the Shannon. The gallery has watercolors by artist-owner Jenny Boelens on permanent display. Open Easter to October daily from 9am to 6pm. The Old Church, R493, Terryglass, county Tipperary. © 067/22209.

Walsh Crafts A rustic thatched-roof cottage, complete with a traditional half-door (the top and bottom open and close separately), serves as the workshop for Paddy Walsh, a craftsman who carves and paints on natural wood. His works depict Ireland past and present, with Celtic and rural scenes and pieces with heraldic and religious themes. The items range from pendant-size figurines and symbols—such as St. Patrick, the harp, or a dove—to portrait-size scenes of Irish music sessions, pub facades and interiors, farmyards, cottages, castles, sporting events, and Christmas tableaux. The craft is ingenious and truly Irish, a great souvenir. Visitors are welcome to watch Paddy and his staff as they carve the wood and paint the colorful motifs. Open weekdays from 9am to 5pm. R493, Puckane, Nenagh, county Tipperary. © 067/24229.

BOATING & OTHER WATERSPORTS

Watersports are the pièce de résistance of a visit to Lough Derg. If you enjoy boating, tubing, water-skiing, windsurfing, canoeing, or other watersports, this is the place for you.

Below we've listed a few of the businesses that specialize in these activities. In addition, the following companies also rent cabin cruisers along this section of the Shannon: **R&B Marine Services Ltd.,** Derg Marina, Killaloe, county Clare (© 061/375011); **Emerald Star Line,** The Marina, Portumna, county Galway (© 0509/41120; www.emeraldstar.ie); **Shannon Castle Line,** The Marina, Williamstown, county Clare (© 061/927042; www.shannoncruisers.com); and **Shannon Sailing,** New Harbor, county Tipperary (© 067/24499; www. shannonsailing.com). The crafts range from two to eight berths; rates average €140 to €270 ($125–$240) per person per week.

Lough Derg Sailing With its still waters and numerous bays, islands, and harbors, Lough Derg is ideal for sailing. This company offers daily sailing trips on the 8.7m (29-ft.) yacht *Sangazure,* with instruction and training on board. The activities are especially geared toward beginners who want to learn the basics of sailing. Mountshannon Harbour, Mountshannon, county Clare. © 061/927131. Cruise €48 ($43) per day; hourly rates available. May–Sept daily by appointment.

Watersports Lough Derg This outdoor center offers water-skiing, speed-boat rides, tubing, and jet-skiing. Two Mile Gate, Killaloe, county Clare. © 088/588430 (mobile). Water-skiing from €16 ($14); speedboat rides from €4 ($3.55) per person; tubing from €8 ($7.10); jet skis from €16 ($14). May–Oct daily 11am–dusk.

Whelan's Boat Hire Whelan's rents 5.7m (19-ft.) lake boats with outboard engines for sightseeing or fishing in the waters of Lough Derg. Prices include fuel, fishing gear, life jackets, and rainwear. In the summer, Whelan's offers an hourly river tour that provides lots of local history and lore.

At the bridge, Killaloe, county Clare. © **061/376159.** Boat rental €14 ($12) 1st hour, €6.50 ($5.80) each additional hour; €40 ($36) per day; €140 ($125) per week. Daily 9am–9pm.

OTHER SPORTS & OUTDOOR PURSUITS

FISHING　An angler's paradise, Lough Derg has good stocks of brown trout, pike, bream, and perch. Fish weighing 36 to 90 pounds have been caught here. Brown trout average 1 to 6 pounds. For tackle and guidance on local fishing, visit **Eddie Fahey,** Ballyminogue, Scariff, county Clare (© **061/921019**); or **Whelan's,** Summerhill, Nenagh, county Tipperary (© **067/31301**).

GOLF　Lovely parkland and woodland golfing in the Lough Derg area is offered at 18-hole clubs such as **Portumna Golf Club,** Portumna, county Galway (© **0509/41059**), with greens fees of €22 ($20) weekdays, €25 ($22) weekends; and **Nenagh Golf Club,** Beechwood, Nenagh (© **067/31476**), with greens fees of €18 ($16) weekdays, €22 ($20) weekends. The **East Clare Golf Club,** Scariff/Killaloe Road, Bodyke, county Clare (© **061/921322**), is an 18-hole championship course. Greens fees are €19 ($17) weekdays, €22 ($20) weekends.

SWIMMING　Lough Derg is known for clear, unpolluted water that's ideal for swimming, particularly at **Castle Lough, Dromineer,** and **Portumna Bay.** Portumna Bay has changing rooms and showers.

WALKING　There are some excellent walks in **Portumna Forest Park,** in **Raheen Woods,** and along the shoreline of **Lough Derg.** For a touch of scenic wilderness, walk a portion of the **Slieve Bloom Way,** a circular 34km (21-mile) signposted trail that begins and ends in Glenbarrow, county Laois.

WHERE TO STAY
MODERATE

Dromineer Bay Hotel ⭐　Tucked along the shores of Lough Derg beside the Dromineer Yacht Club, this recently expanded two-story hotel, long a favorite with anglers, now also appeals to anyone looking for an informal riverside retreat. More than 100 years old, it was originally a coast-guard inn. The rooms are small and simply furnished, although some have four-poster beds and antiques. For a little local color and history, look at the bar walls; they're decorated with photographs of the hotel and the village.

Dromineer Bay, Nenagh, county Tipperary. © **067/24114.** Fax 067/24444. 24 units. €96–€170 ($80–$147) double. No service charge. Rates include full breakfast. AE, MC, V. **Amenities:** 2 restaurants (international, cafe); bar. *In room:* TV, hair dryer.

Lakeside Hotel ⭐　Perched on the southern banks of Lough Derg and shaded by ancient trees, this two-story country-house-style hotel has one of the loveliest settings of any property in the area. The guest rooms have standard furnishings but are greatly enhanced by wide-windowed views of the lake or gardens. The hotel is on the Ballina side of the bridge, on the edge of town next to the marina.

Killaloe, county Clare. © **800/447-7462** in the U.S., or 061/376122. Fax 061/376431. 46 units. €88–€120 ($78–$107) double. No service charge. Rates include full breakfast. AE, MC, V. **Amenities:** Restaurant (Continental); bar; indoor swimming pool; tennis court; gym; Jacuzzi; steam room; nonsmoking rooms. *In room:* TV.

Roundwood House ⭐⭐ *(Finds)*　Roundwood House offers a put-up-your-feet casual elegance equaled by few other guesthouses. The Kennan family's warmth and taste pervade the splendid, perfectly-proportioned 18th-century Palladian country villa, set in 7.2 hectares (18 acres) of secluded woods, pasture, and gardens. Roundwood breathes relaxation and leisure, although more active pursuits are close at hand—particularly the Slieve Bloom Way, a 50km (31-mile) hill walk through Ireland's most untrammeled range. The six double guest rooms in the main house are spacious and deco-rated with a gifted eye for charm and simplicity. The two on the second floor share a large central play area that's ideal for families with children. The "Yellow House," across the herb garden and courtyard from the main building, dates from the 17th century

Service Charges
A reminder: Unless otherwise noted, room rates don't include service charges (usually 10%–15% of your bill).

and has been tastefully restored to offer four delightful double rooms. Round-wood's soft couches, firm beds, lovely views, myriad good books, large bathtubs, and exquisite meals may not inspire an active holiday, but they go a long way toward calming the soul. FYI: The nearest TV is a good walk away.

4.8km (3 miles) northwest of Mountrath, on R440 toward the Slieve Bloom Mountains, Mountrath, county Laois. ℭ 0502/32120. Fax 0502/32711. 10 units. €120 ($107) double. No service charge. Rates include full Irish breakfast. Dinner (book by 2pm) €34 ($30). AE, DC, MC, V. **Amenities:** Croquet; drawing room.

INEXPENSIVE

Lantern House ℱ   This pleasant, unpretentious guesthouse enjoys wide vistas of Lough Derg. Palm trees grow on the well-tended hilltop grounds. All the pub-lic rooms overlook the Shannon, as do some of the guest rooms. Furnishings are homey and comfortable. The cozy lounge has a fireplace, and residents can enjoy a drink at a small bar. The restaurant (see "Where to Dine," below) is quite pop-ular among locals. One caveat: Some of the beds are soft enough to prove chal-lenging for the dorsally afflicted.

9.7km (6 miles) north of Killaloe on the main rd., Ogonnelloe, Tuamgraney, county Clare. ℭ 061/923034. Fax 061/923139. 9 units. €68 ($61) double. Rates include full breakfast. AE, DC, MC, V. Closed Dec to mid-Feb. **Amenities:** Restaurant (Continental); lounge; bar; nonsmoking rooms. *In room:* TV.

SELF-CATERING: RENT-A-COTTAGE

For an area of such amazing beauty and wide-open spaces, the Lough Derg region has surprisingly few hotels. In many ways, that's part of its allure—natural lakelands and forests unspoiled by condos, hotels, motels, and fast-food joints.

When the "Rent an Irish Cottage" program was pioneered here almost 30 years ago, the idea was simple: Build small rental cottages designed in traditional style, with exteriors of white stucco, thatched roofs, and half doors. But aside from the turf fireplaces, all of the interior's furnishings, plumbing, heating, and kitchen appliances inside are totally up-to-date. The cottages, built in groups of 8 to 12, are on picturesque sites in remote villages such as Puckane, Terryglass, and Whitegate, overlooking or close to Lough Derg's shores. As there are no restaurants or bars on-site, you shop in local grocery stores, cook your own meals, and mix with locals in the area's pubs at night. In other words, it's a chance to become part of the community. Rates range from €165 to €1,145 ($147–$1,019) per cottage per week, depending on the size (one to six bed-rooms) and time of year. Rental rates include bed linen and color TV; towels and metered electricity are extra.

In recent years, individual owners have built modern cottages with slate or tile roofs. One of the loveliest cottage settings belongs to **Mountshannon,** county Clare, a cluster of 12 pastel-toned one- and two-story cottages on the shores of Lough Derg at Mountshannon Harbour. Grouped like a private village around a garden courtyard, the three-bedroom cottages cost €215 to €585 ($191–$521) per week, depending on the time of year. Also on the shores of Lough Derg, there are 12 cottages in a country village setting in **Puckane,** county Tipperary. Rates for two- and three-bedroom cottages cost €178 to €585 ($159–$521) per week, depending on season and number of bedrooms.

For more information, contact **Rent an Irish Cottage,** 85 O'Connell St., Limerick, county Limerick (✆ **061/411109;** fax 061/314821; www.rentacottage.ie).

WHERE TO DINE
EXPENSIVE
Brocka-on-the-Water ★★★ *Finds* INTERNATIONAL A small country lane, signposted off the Lough Derg Drive, leads to this country-house restaurant in a garden setting near the shores of Lough Derg. Rather than seeking waterside views, people flock here for the Byrne family's innovative cuisine and warm hospitality. The atmosphere is one of an intimate family house, and the food is akin to the best home cooking you've ever had. Each table is set with Waterford crystal lamps, Newbridge silver, hand-embroidered linens, and fresh flowers. The menu changes nightly, but specialties often include breaded pork with gooseberry herb sauce, baked stuffed sole with a sauce of dill and lemon cream, panfried sirloin steak Gaelic-style (flamed in whiskey), and ribbons of chicken breast with gingerroot and honey. Many of the dishes are decorated with or incorporate fresh edible flowers from the garden. To finish, don't miss the carragin mousse or farmhouse cheeses from local farms. Service is attentive but unobtrusive.

Kilgarvan Quay, Nenagh, county Tipperary. ✆ **067/22038.** Reservations required. Fixed-price dinner €38 ($34); main courses €16–€24 ($14–$21). No credit cards. May–Oct Mon–Sat 7–9:30pm.

MODERATE
Galloping Hogan's Restaurant ★ CONTINENTAL In a restored old railway station, this restaurant sits beside Lough Derg, overlooking the water on the Ballina side of the Killaloe bridge. The plant-filled conservatory-style room has a patio-terrace for fair-weather dining. The menu here includes rack of lamb and a variety of steaks. Seafood choices might be fresh lobster; grilled or poached scallop of salmon with chive butter sauce; panfried black sole on the bone with nut brown butter and chopped parsley; or baked cod with roasted peppers, tomatoes, fresh spinach, and chile oil. Bar food is also available from noon to 10pm.

Ballina, county Clare. ✆ **061/376162.** Reservations recommended. Main courses €15–€24 ($13–$21); lobster €27 ($24). AE, MC, V. Daily 6:30–10pm.

Goosers ★★ SEAFOOD With a thatched roof and bright mustard-colored exterior, this very popular pub and restaurant sits on the Ballina side of the Shannon, looking out at the river and the broad vista of Killaloe. Its two informal rooms have open fireplaces, stone walls and floors, and beamed ceilings, and its pub area contains window seats, *sugan* chairs (traditional wood chairs with twisted straw rope seats), and lots of nautical and fishing memorabilia. The restaurant has booth seating and windows that overlook an adjacent garden, and there's picnic-table seating outside in good weather. The bar-food menu lists the usual standards, including such traditional dishes as bacon and cabbage and Irish stew. The restaurant menu focuses on seafood—lobster, salmon, sole, and monkfish.

Ballina, county Clare. ✆ **061/376791.** Reservations recommended for dinner. Bar food €3–€15 ($2.70–$13); dinner main courses €16–€32 ($14–$28). AE, MC, V. Daily 11am–11pm.

Lantern House ⭐ CONTINENTAL   Perched high on a hillside amid palm tree-lined gardens just north of Killaloe, this country-house restaurant enjoys panoramic views of Lough Derg and the verdant hills of the surrounding countryside. Host Phil Hogan extends a warm welcome, and the candlelit dining room exudes old-world charm, with a beamed ceiling, wall lanterns, and lace tablecloths. Menu choices might include poached fresh local salmon, pan-fried sole, scallops Mornay, or sirloin steak.

Ogonnelloe, county Clare. ℂ 061/923034. Reservations recommended. Main courses €14–€22 ($12–$20). AE, MC, V. Mid-Feb to Oct daily 6–9pm. Closed Mon off-season.

INEXPENSIVE

Country Choice ⭐ CAFE   Country Choice is just that: Its shelves are brimming with the finest of Irish foodstuffs from an acclaimed local marmalade to farmhouse cheeses. Floury loaves of bread are heaped on the counter, and on the floor, baskets glisten with the clear, green orbs of local gooseberries. This is the best place to fill up on picnic fixings before heading out to the shores of Lough Derg. A cafe at the back of the shop is the place to sit with a cup of good coffee and find out what's happening locally—it's a popular gathering place for locals and visitors. There's an inexpensive lunch menu, and freshly baked goods are served in the morning.

25 Kenyon St., Nenagh, county Tipperary. ℂ 067/32596. Lunch main courses €4–€8 ($3.55–$7.10). Mon–Sat 9am–6pm; lunch served noon–6pm.

Molly's Bar and Restaurant ⭐⭐ CONTINENTAL   Next to the Killaloe bridge, this brightly colored pub and restaurant offers views of Killaloe Harbour from most of its windows. The informal interior is like that of a comfortable cottage, with beamed ceilings, wall shelves lined with old plates, vintage clocks, pine and mahogany furnishings, period pictures and prints of the Shannon area, and a stove fireplace. The menu offers both light fare and full dinner selections, such as baked Limerick ham with Madeira sauce, Atlantic salmon Hibernian, and chargrilled steaks. The open-faced fresh crab sandwich on brown bread is especially delicious. Outdoor seating is available on picnic-style tables. There's live music, traditional and modern, Thursday to Sunday evenings, as well as a disco and sports bar in the basement.

Killaloe/Ballina, county Clare. ℂ 061/376632. Reservations recommended for dinner. All items €3–€18 ($2.65–$16). AE, MC, V. Daily 12:30–11:30pm.

PUBS

There are public houses in every town around the Lough Derg route. The pubs of Terryglass, county Tipperary, on the east shore, and of Woodford, county Galway, on the west shore, are particularly well known for their lively sessions of Irish traditional music.

The Derg Inn   With three cozy rooms and a beer garden in the courtyard, this is one of the lake's best watering holes. It's worth a visit just to see this pub's decor of Tipperary horse pictures, old plates, books, beer posters, vintage bottles, hanging tankards, and lanterns. However, most people come for the free traditional music on Wednesday and Sunday evenings. Terryglass, county Tipperary. ℂ 067/22037.

J. Walsh's Forest Bar   If you're lucky enough to be here when there's a traditional music session, then sit back and enjoy. One hometown favorite is fiddler and tin-whistle player Anthony Coen, who is often accompanied by his talented daughters, Dearbhla, on the flute and tin whistle, and Eimer, on the concertina and bodhran. Sessions are totally informal and usually unscheduled; if you want to catch one, you can try asking the barmen or calling the pub in advance. Woodford, county Galway. ℂ 0509/49012.

Moran's Overlooking the Woodford River, this place (correct pronunciation is *mor*-ins) is a curiosity—it's probably the only pub in Ireland where you'll find two clerics serving drinks at the bar during the summer. Both Carmelite Order priests, they are the owner's sons and spend their vacation time helping out in the family business—only in Ireland! Woodford, county Galway. ℂ 0509/49063.

Paddy's Pub From the harbor, it's a short walk up a winding lane to this small, dark pub. A fine display of antiques and nightly traditional music in summer make it a jewel among Lake Derg's pubs. Terryglass, county Tipperary. ℂ 067/22147.

2 Middle Shannon: From Birr to Athlone

Birr is 24km (15 miles) E of Portumna; Athlone is 97km (60 miles) E of Galway

The middle section of the Shannon River is where you'll find one of Ireland's greatest historic sites: the early Christian settlement of **Clonmacnois,** a spot that has been drawing visitors since the 6th century. This region also includes vast stretches of boglands; the inland town of Birr, known for its magnificent and historic gardens; and **Banagher,** a river town with a picturesque harbor. In addition, this stretch of the river curves into **Athlone,** the largest town on the Shannon and a leading inland marina for mooring and hiring boats. Athlone's other claim to fame is that it produced Ireland's most famous operatic tenor, the great John McCormack.

AREA ESSENTIALS

GETTING THERE & GETTING AROUND The best way to get to the Middle Shannon area is by car or boat. Although there's public transportation, you'll need a car to get around the riverbanks. Major roads that lead to this area are the main Galway-Dublin road (N6) from points east and west, N62 from the south, and N55 and N61 from the north.

VISITOR INFORMATION Information on this area can be obtained from the **Ireland West Tourism Office,** Victoria Place, Eyre Square, Galway (ℂ 091/63081; www.westireland.travel.ie), and the **Midlands Tourism Office,** Clonard House, Dublin Road, Mullingar, county Westmeath (ℂ 044/48650). Both are open Monday to Friday 9am to 6pm, plus Saturdays during peak season.

Seasonal tourist information points are open from May or June to September at signposted sites in **Athlone** (ℂ 0902/94630), **Ballinasloe** (ℂ 0905/42131), **Birr** (ℂ 0509/20110), and **Clonmacnois** (ℂ 0905/74134).

EXPLORING THE AREA

Athlone Castle ⭐ Built in 1210 for King John of England, this mighty stone fortress sits on the edge of the Shannon. It played an important part in Athlone's history, first as the seat of the presidents of Connaught and later as the headquarters of the governor of Athlone during the first Siege of Athlone in 1690 and the second in 1691. Declared a national monument in 1970, it was recently restored and adapted for use as a visitor center, museum, gallery, and tearoom. The exhibition area offers an audiovisual presentation on the Siege of Athlone. It also contains displays on the castle, the town, the flora and fauna of the Shannon region, and the great Irish tenor John McCormack, Athlone's most honored son. The castle's original medieval walls have been preserved, as have two large cannons dating from the reign of George II and a pair of 10-inch mortars that were cast in 1856.

Athlone, county Westmeath. ℭ **0902/92912**. Admission €5 ($4.45) adults, €3 ($2.70) seniors and students, €1.30 ($1.15) children under 13, €10 ($8.90) family. May to mid-Oct daily 10am–5pm. On the riverbank, signposted from all directions.

Battle of Aughrim Interpretative Centre ⋒   Using a high-tech three-dimensional audiovisual presentation, this center invites visitors to relive the Battle of Aughrim, on July 12, 1691. On that day, the army of James II of England confronted the forces of his son-in-law, William of Orange, and staged the bloodiest battle in Irish history. The confrontation involved 45,000 soldiers from eight European countries and cost 9,000 lives, changing the course of Irish and European history. (For more on the conflict between William and James, see "Irish History" in the appendix.) The center, which also houses a bookshop, craft shop, and cafe, is in Aughrim village, adjacent to the actual Aughrim battlefield, which is signposted for visitors. Aughrim is on the main Dublin-Galway road, about 19km (12 miles) west of the Shannonbridge/Clonmacnois area.

Galway-Dublin rd. (N6), Aughrim, near Ballinasloe, county Galway. ℭ **0905/73939**. Admission €3.50 ($3.10) adults, €2.50 ($2.25) seniors and students, €6.50 ($5.80) family. June–Aug Tues–Sat 10am–6pm; Sun 2–6pm.

Birr Castle Demesne ⋒⋒   The main attraction of this inland estate 19km (12 miles) east of the river is its 40-hectare (100-acre) **garden.** The demesne (or estate) of the Parsons family, now the earls of Rosse, it's laid out around a lake and along the banks of the two adjacent rivers. It contains more than 1,000 species of trees and shrubs, including magnolias, cherry trees, chestnut, and weeping beech. The box hedges are featured in the *Guinness Book of Records* as the tallest in the world, and the hornbeam cloisters are a unique feature. Farther along the path you may combine a bit of stargazing with the garden stroll—the grounds also contain an astronomical exhibit, including an 1845 1.8m (6-ft.) reflecting telescope, then the largest in the world, built by the third earl of Rosse and recently restored to form as part of the Historic Science Centre. The telescope operates twice daily, at noon and 3pm. During the summer, you can usually find additional rotating exhibits dealing with the history of Birr Castle and its residents. The 17th-century castle and residence is not open to the public.

Birr, county Offaly. ℭ **0509/20336**. www.birrcastle.com. Admission €6.50 ($5.80) adults, €4.50 ($4) students and seniors, €3.20 ($2.85) children over 5, free for children under 5, €16 ($14) family. V. Year-round daily 9am–6pm. Take N52 37km (23 miles) southwest of Tullamore.

Bog Train Tours ⋒   Bogland discoveries are the focus of this tour in the heart of the Irish midlands, on the east bank of the Shannon. Visitors board the narrow-gauge Clonmacnois and West Offaly Railway for an 8km (5-mile) circular ride around the Blackwater bog. The commentary explains how the bogland was formed and became a vital source of fuel. The route includes a firsthand look at turf cutting, stacking, drying, and close-up views of bog plants and wildlife. Participants can even take a turn at digging the turf or picking some bog cotton. The ride lasts approximately 45 minutes. The visitor center also offers an audiovisual story about the bog. For groups who make advance arrangements, a 2- to 4-hour nature trail and field-study tour is available.

Bord na Mona/The Irish Peat Board, Blackwater Works, Shannonbridge, county Offaly. ℭ **0905/74114**. Tours €5 ($4.45) adults, €4.50 ($4) seniors and students, €3.20 ($2.85) children, €14 ($12) family. Apr–Oct daily 10am–5pm; tours on the hour. Signposted from Shannonbridge.

Charleville Forest Castle 🐦🐦 Designed in 1798 by Francis Johnston, one of Ireland's foremost architects, this castle took 12 years to build and was the first of the great Gothic houses. Today it's considered one of the best of the early-19th-century castles still standing in Ireland. The castle has a fine limestone exterior, with fanciful towers, turrets, and battlements. The rooms have spectacular ceilings and plasterwork and great hand-carved stairways, as well as secret passageways and dungeons. Admission includes a guided tour.

Off N52/Birr rd., Tullamore, county Offaly. 🕐 **0506/21279.** Guided tour €4.50 ($4) adults, €2.50 ($2.25) children. Apr–May Sat–Sun 2–5pm; June–Sept Tues–Sun 11am–5pm.

Clonmacnois 🐦🐦🐦 Resting silently on the east bank of the Shannon, this is one of Ireland's most profound ancient sites. St. Ciaran founded the monastic community of Clonmacnois in 548 at the crucial intersection of the Shannon and the Dublin-Galway land route, and it soon became one of Europe's great centers of learning and culture. For nearly 1,000 years, Clonmacnois flourished under the patronage of numerous Irish kings. The last high king, Rory O'Conor, was buried here in 1198. In the course of time, Clonmacnois was raided repeatedly by native chiefs, Danes, and Anglo-Normans, until it was finally abandoned in 1552. Today you can see the remains of a cathedral, a castle, eight churches, two round towers, three sculpted high crosses, and more than 200 monumental slabs. The site includes an exemplary visitor center with a beautifully designed exhibition, a first-rate audiovisual program, and pleasant tearooms.

On R357, 6.5km (4 miles) north of Shannonbridge, county Offaly. 🕐 **0905/74195.** Admission €5 ($4.45) adults, €3.20 ($2.85) seniors, €2 ($1.80) students and children, €11 ($10) family. Nov to mid-Mar daily 10am–5:30pm; mid-Mar to mid-May and mid-Sept to Oct daily 10am–6pm; mid-May to early Sept daily 9am–7pm.

Locke's Distillery Museum 🐦 Established in 1757, this 18th- and 19th-century enterprise was one of the oldest licensed pot-still whiskey distilleries in the world. After producing whiskey for almost 200 years, it closed in 1953; over the past 15 years, a local group has restored it as a museum. In 1998, a major exhibition space opened in the restored front grain loft to display a host of distilling artifacts. A 35-minute tour will not only tell you how whiskey was distilled using old techniques and machinery, but also inform you about the area's social history. It's almost midway between Dublin and Galway, making it a good stop-off point while you're on a cross-country journey or touring in the area. On the premises, you'll find a restaurant, coffee shop, and craft shop.

On N6, east of Athlone, Kilbeggan, county Westmeath. 🕐 **0506/32134.** Admission €5 ($4.45) adults, €3.20 ($2.85) seniors and students, €11 ($10) family. Apr–Oct daily 9am–6pm; Nov–Mar daily 10am–4pm.

SIGHTSEEING CRUISES

Athlone Cruisers Ltd 🐦 This company operates cruises around Lough Ree on board the 60-passenger M.V. *Ross.* The average cruise time is 90 minutes, and the boat has a sun deck and a covered deck with a bar and coffee shop.

Jolly Mariner Marina, Athlone, county Westmeath. 🕐 **0902/72892.** www.iol.ie/wmeathtc/acl. Cruise €8 ($7.10) adults, €5 ($4.45) children. May–Sept, times vary.

Rosanna Cruises 🐦🐦 This is the cruise to take if you only have time for one, since it offers live commentary and more enthusiasm than the other somewhat canned deliveries. This company offers cruises of the inner lakes of Lough Ree or to Clonmacnois on board the 71-passenger *Viking I.* Patrons hear live commentary on the 300-year Viking history on the Shannon and Lough Ree and refreshments. The Lough Ree trip takes 1½ hours; the 4-hour Clonmacnois trip includes a 1-hour stopover at the monastic site. The company furnishes children with Viking helmets, costumes, and plastic swords for the duration of the trip to add a touch of berserk authenticity. Buy tickets at the Strand Fishing Tackle Shop (✆ **0902/79277**), from where you'll also depart.

15 Church St., Athlone, county Westmeath (office address). ✆ **0902/73383**. Lough Ree trip €8 ($7.10) adults, €5 ($4.45) children; Clonmacnois trip €14 ($12) adults, €8 ($7.10) seniors, students, and children. May–Sept Lough Ree trip daily 2:30 and 4:30pm; Clonmacnois trip daily 9am.

Silverline Cruisers Ltd ✿   This company operates 90-minute cruises on the *River Queen,* a 54-seat enclosed river bus. The trip starts out by passing under the seven-arched Banagher Stone Bridge, then passes Martello towers and fortresses on its way downstream to Victoria Lock, the largest lock on the Shannon system. The taped commentary covers all the historical aspects of the route, but it lacks the spontaneity of the live commentary you get on the Rosanna Cruises. There's a bar on board.

The Marina, Banagher, county Offaly. ✆ **0509/51112**. Cruise €5 ($4.45) adults, €3.20 ($2.85) children. June–Sept, times vary.

OUTDOOR PURSUITS & SPECTATOR SPORTS

BICYCLING   Bikes can be rented from **Shannon Holidays,** Jolly Mariner Marina, Athlone, county Westmeath (✆ **0902/72892**), for €9 ($8) per day or €40 ($36) per week.

BOATING   The following companies rent cabin cruisers, usually for a minimum of 1 week, along this section of the Shannon: **Athlone Cruisers,** Jolly Mariner Marina, Athlone, county Westmeath (✆ **0902/72892;** www.iol. ie/wmeathtc/acl); **Silverline Cruisers,** The Marina, Banagher, county Offaly (✆ **0509/51112**); and **Tara Cruiser Ltd.,** Kilfaughna, Knockvicar, county Roscommon (✆ **079/67777**). Crafts range from three to eight berths; rates average €435 to €2,390 ($387–$2,127) per week in high season.

GOLF   **Birr Golf Club,** Birr, county Offaly (✆ **0509/20082**), is an 18-hole course on 112 acres of parkland countryside; the greens fees are €16 ($14) weekdays, €18 ($16) weekends.

In the Athlone area are the 18-hole **Athlone Golf Club,** Hodson Bay, Athlone, county Roscommon (✆ **0902/92073**), with greens fees of €26 ($23) weekdays, €28 ($25) weekends; and the 18-hole championship **Mount Temple Golf Club,** Moate, county Westmeath (✆ **0902/81841**), 8km (5 miles) east of Athlone, with greens fees of €22 ($20) weekdays, €24 ($21) weekends.

HORSE RACING   Horse racing takes place in July, August, and September at the **Kilbeggan Racecourse,** Loughnagore, Kilbeggan, county Westmeath (✆ **0506/32176**), off the main Mullingar road (N52), 1.6km (1 mile) from town. Admission is €7 ($6.25) for adults, €3.50 ($3.10) for students.

WHERE TO STAY & DINE
VERY EXPENSIVE

Temple Country House & Spa ✿✿✿   This is something of a cult address in Ireland. Temple Country House is a 250-year-old manor that operates as a B&B–cum–health spa—a wonderful place to truly chill out for a couple of days, at a price that's reasonable when you consider the rates include spa treatments and all meals. If you're willing to "lose" a day or two of vacation time, you can indulge in some pampering treatments and in Bernadette Fagan's low-fat cooking—nothing chaste and depriving here, just rich, tasty food without the animal fat. The health and spa facilities are all spanking modern, but otherwise there's a real old-world feel to the place that's incredibly restorative for the body and soul. Rooms are comfortably and attractively appointed, if not overtly luxurious. The spa is closed Sunday afternoons and all day Monday. Weekends at Temple Country House tend to be booked solid about 8 weeks in advance; figure on booking 3 weeks ahead for a midweek stay.

Horseleap, Moate, county Westmeath. © 0506/35118. Fax 0506/35008. www.templespa.ie/. 8 units. Spa stays from €370 ($329) double for 24-hr. stay, including all meals. €680–€1,030 ($605–$917) double for 2–3-day spa stays, including all meals. AE, MC, V. Free parking. **Amenities:** Sauna/steam room; salon; aromatherapy; bicycle rental; hydrotherapy bath; massage and reflexology treatments; sitting room. *In room:* TV.

MODERATE

Crookedwood House ★★ This excellent country restaurant with rooms makes a terrific base for touring around this part of the midlands. Originally the house was an old parish rectory, but it's now known for its basement restaurant. Noel Kenny is one of those terrifically talented chefs who delights in giving earthy flavors a bit of a kick. Think baked crabmeat with chardonnay over tagliatelle, rib of beef with horseradish, and venison and wild duck with juniper berries. The guest rooms are spacious and nicely furnished, and best of all, they allow you to just fall into bed after one of Noel's fabulous meals.

Crookedwood, Mullingar, county Westmeath. © 044/72165. Fax 044/72166. www.crookedwoodhouse.com. 8 units. €150 ($134) double. No service charge. Rates include full breakfast. Dinner €33 ($29). MC, V. Free parking. **Amenities:** Restaurant (country house). *In room:* TV.

INEXPENSIVE

Brosna Lodge Hotel ★ *Value* Although it sits on the main thoroughfare in Banagher, a busy river town near Clonmacnois, this two-story hotel has a warm country atmosphere, thanks to a beautiful flower-filled front garden and enthusiastic innkeeper-owners Geraldine and Aidan Hoare. The public areas are furnished with traditional period pieces and local antiques. The rooms are bright and airy, and overlook the gardens or the town. Best of all, it's just a short walk to the riverfront.

Main St., Banagher, county Offaly. © 0509/51350. Fax 0509/51521. 14 units. €74 ($66) double. No service charge. Rates include full breakfast. MC, V. Free parking. **Amenities:** Restaurant (international); bar; lounge. *In room:* TV.

Dooly's Hotel ★ Dating from 1747, this three-story Georgian hotel is in the center of Birr. Although one of Ireland's oldest former coaching inns, it's been thoroughly restored and refurbished in recent years. The public areas retain their Georgian charm, while the guest rooms are comfortably modern with views of the town or back garden.

Emmet Sq., Birr, county Offaly. © 0509/20032. Fax 0509/21332. www.doolyshotel.com. 18 units. €95 ($85) double. No service charge. Rates include full breakfast. AE, DC, MC, V. Free public parking. **Amenities:** 2 restaurants (international, cafe); bar. *In room:* TV, tea/coffeemaker.

PUBS

Of all the river towns in this section of the Shannon, Banagher, in county Offaly, is particularly well known for lively Irish traditional music sessions at two of its pubs. At **J. J. Hough's,** Main Street (no phone), there's music every night during the summer, and Friday to Sunday the rest of the year. The **Vine House,** West End (© 0902/51463), offers music every night during the summer. Here are two more pubs with considerable character:

Killeen's   Just 6.4km (4 miles) south of Clonmacnoise, tucked into the little village of Shannonbridge—so named for the graceful bridge of 16 arches that spans the river—here's yet another great watering hole that outgrew its pub-cum-grocery origins with tremendous style and grace. There are turf fires, excellent pints of Guinness, and faultless Irish Coffees. Shannonbridge, county Offaly. ⑦ **0905/ 74112.**

Sean's *Finds*   This is a classic old-time pub—long and narrow with small, scarred wooden tables, low ceilings, and a fireplace to warm your hands by. There's live music (mainly traditional) here practically all the time, which only adds to the appeal. 13 Main St., Athlone, county Westmeath. ⑦ **0902/92358.**

3 Upper Shannon: From Lough Ree to Lough Allen

Roscommon is 82km (51 miles) NE of Galway, 147km (91 miles) NW of Dublin; Longford is 129km (80 miles) NW of Dublin, 44km (27 miles) NE of Athlone; Carrick-on-Shannon is 56km (35 miles) SE of Sligo; Cavan is 105km (65 miles) NW of Dublin

The Upper Shannon River region is home to a remarkable assortment of castles, great houses, and museums. One of Ireland's newest and most significant collections, the **Irish Famine Museum,** Strokestown, county Roscommon, is of special importance as Ireland commemorates the 150th anniversary of the Great Hunger. This museum chronicles the great tragedy that changed the course of history in Ireland and the world, sending forth the Irish diaspora to England, the United States, Canada, and Australia.

In addition, the shores of the Upper Shannon encompass **Lough Ree,** the second largest of Shannon's lakes. Considered almost an inland sea, it's distinguished by long, flat vistas across the farming countryside of counties Roscommon, Westmeath, and Longford.

County Longford gives the river its literary associations. This eastern bank of the Shannon is often referred to as "Goldsmith country," because 18th-century dramatist, novelist, and poet Oliver Goldsmith was born at Pallas, near Ballymahon. Although Goldsmith did much of his writing in London, it's said that he drew on many of his Irish experiences for his works, including *She Stoops to Conquer.*

Above Lough Ree, the river is relatively narrow until it reaches the town of **Carrick-on-Shannon,** county Leitrim. It's situated on one of the great ancient crossing places of the Shannon. The town is particularly known as a center for boating, with a vast marina in the middle of the town where many companies rent cabin cruisers.

The whole county of **Leitrim** is uniquely affected by the Shannon's waters. It's divided into two parts, almost wholly separated by Lough Allen. A storage reservoir for a nearby hydroelectric plant, Lough Allen is the Shannon's third-largest lake, 11km (7 miles) long and 4.8km (3 miles) wide. North of Lough Allen, in county Cavan, is the source of the river: the **Shannon Pot,** on the southern slopes of the Cuilcagh Mountain.

The scope of the Shannon has been broadened in recent years, so it's now possible to travel from the Shannon River to Lough Erne, using a stretch of water known as the Ballinamore-Ballyconnell Canal. Following a painstaking restoration, it was reopened in spring 1994, after a lapse of 125 years. Because it provides a clear path from the Shannon in the Republic of Ireland to Lough Erne in Northern Ireland, the new passage is officially designated the Shannon-Erne Waterway. It's a symbol of cross-border cooperation and a touchstone in a new golden age of Irish waterway travel.

AREA ESSENTIALS

GETTING THERE & GETTING AROUND   The best way to get to the Upper Shannon area is by car or boat. Although there is public transportation, you will need a car to get around the riverbanks and to the various attractions. Among major roads that lead to this area are the main Dublin-Sligo road (N4), the main Dublin-Cavan road (N3), N5 and N63 from Castlebar and the west, and N61 and N55 from the south.

VISITOR INFORMATION   Information on **county Roscommon** is available from the **Ireland West Tourism Office,** Victoria Place, Eyre Square, Galway (℃ 091/63081; www.westireland.travel.ie). Hours are May, June, and September daily 9am to 5:45pm; July and August daily 9am to 7:45pm; October to April, Monday to Friday, 9am to 5:45pm and Saturday 9am to 12:45pm. Information on **county Longford** is available from the **Midlands East Tourism Office,** Clonard House, Dublin Road, Mullingar, County Westmeath (℃ 044/48761), open Easter through September, Monday to Friday 9am to 5pm, Saturday 10am to 2pm, with extended hours in July and August; on **county Cavan** from the **Cavan Tourist Office,** Farnham Street, Cavan, County Cavan (℃ 049/4331942), open May through September, Monday to Friday 10am to 5pm, Saturday 10am to 2pm; on **county Leitrim** from the **North-West Tourism Office,** Aras Reddan, Temple Street, Sligo (℃ 071/61201), open Easter through September, Monday to Friday 9am to 5pm, Saturday 10am to 2pm, with extended hours in July and August; and from the tourist office at **Carrick-on-Shannon** (℃ 078/20170), open May through September, Monday to Friday 10am to 5pm, Saturday 10am to 2pm.

   Seasonal information points, operating from June to August, are signposted in **Boyle** (℃ 079/62145), **Longford** (℃ 043/46566), and **Roscommon** (℃ 0903/26342).

EXPLORING THE AREA

Boyle Abbey ⚘   Boyle Abbey was founded in 1161 as a daughter house of the Cistercian Abbey at Mellifont. Today, it is the most impressive survivor of the early Irish Cistercian settlements of the late 12th and early 13th centuries. The Cistercian Order was founded in 11th-century France as a return to the uncompromising simplicity and tranquil austerity of the monastic calling. The abbey was to be a haven of otherworldliness, and yet the world's savagery descended on Boyle Abbey more than once. Its walls were torn down in the mid-1600s, when the English murdered the resident monks and used the monastery as a military garrison. What remains is a complex fossil clearly imprinted with both the serene and violent aspects of the abbey's history. The ruins of Boyle Abbey evoke in visitors a sense of what this place has seen, suffered, and enjoyed. The interpretive center, housed in the restored gatehouse, is informative and thoughtfully designed.

N4, Boyle, county Roscommon. ℃ **079/62604.** Admission €1.30 ($1.15) adults, €.90 (80¢) seniors, €.50 (45¢) children and students, €4 ($3.55) family. Early Apr–Oct daily 9:30am–6:30pm.

Cavan Crystal Craft & Design Centre ⚘⚘   One of the country's top three crystal companies, this establishment is known for its delicate glassware, mouth-blown and hand-cut by skilled craftspeople. Visitors are invited to watch as skilled master blowers fashion the molten crystal into intricate shapes and designs, followed by the precision work of the master cutters. The glassware is sold in the extended craft and factory shop. The center also includes a restaurant.

Dublin rd. (N3), Cavan, county Cavan. ℃ **049/433-1800.** www.cavancrystaldesign.com. Free admission. Mon–Fri 9:30am–6pm; Sat 10am–5pm; Sun noon–5pm.

Clonalis House ★★ Standing on land that has belonged to the O'Conors for more than 1,500 years, this is one of Ireland's great houses. It's the ancestral home of the O'Conors, kings of Connaught, and the home of the O'Conor Don, the direct descendant of the last high king of Ireland. The house, built in 1880, is a combination of Victorian, Italianate, and Queen Anne architecture, with mostly Louis XV–style furnishings, plus antique lace, horse-drawn farm machinery, and other memorabilia. It's primarily a museum of the O'Conor (O'Connor) family, with portraits, documents, and genealogical tracts dating back 2,000 years. Displays also include a rare ancient harp that's said to have belonged to Turlough O'Carolan (1670–1738), the blind Irish bard who composed tunes that are still played today. The grounds, with terraced and woodland gardens, also hold the O'Conor inauguration stone, similar to the Stone of Scone at Westminster Abbey.

On the N60 west of Castlerea, county Roscommon. ✆ 0907/20014. Admission €4.50 ($4) adults, €3.20 ($2.85) seniors and students, €2 ($1.80) children over 7, free for children under 8. June–Sept 15 Mon–Sat 11am–5pm.

Lough Key Forest Park ★★ *Kids* If you're driving cross-country and want to stop for a picnic and a walk, or if you're traveling with children and are in search of a perfect place to let them loose, look no further. Spanning 336 hectares (840 acres) along the shores of Lough Key and made up of mixed woodlands, a lake, and more than a dozen islands, this is one of Ireland's foremost lakeside parks. The grounds include nature walks, ancient monuments, ring forts, a central viewing tower, picnic grounds, a cafe, and a shop. In addition to cypress groves and other diverse foliage, you'll find a unique display of bog gardens, where a wide selection of peat-loving plants and shrubs flourishes. Deer, otters, hedgehogs, birds, pheasants, and many other forms of wildlife roam the park. The lake is navigable from the Shannon on the Boyle River. Powerboats and rowboats are available to rent, and there are pony and cart rides through the park.

Enter from the main Dublin-Sligo rd. (N4), 3.2km (2 miles) east of Boyle, county Roscommon. ✆ 079/62363. Admission to park €4 ($3.55) per car (charged Apr–Sept only). Year-round daily dawn–dusk.

Lough Rynn House & Gardens ★ Seat of the Clements, the earls of Leitrim, this estate comprises 40 hectares (100 acres) of woodland, ornamental gardens, open pastures, and lakes. Of particular interest is the 1.2-hectare (3-acre) terraced walled garden dating from 1859. It's one of the largest of its kind in the country, laid out in the manner of a Victorian pleasure garden. The arboretum contains specimens of the tulip tree, California redwood, and other exotic species, including the oldest monkey puzzle tree in Ireland. Four thousand years of history can be seen at the rear of the house in one 180° sweep of the eye. The Neolithic burial tomb atop Druids Hill was constructed about 2000 B.C.; Reynolds Castle, a lonely sentinel by the lakeshore, dates from the 16th century; and Lough Rynn House (which you can see the inside of as well) was built in 1832.

South of Carrick-on-Shannon, on the outskirts of Mohill, 5.2km (3¼ miles) from the main Dublin-Sligo rd. (N4), county Leitrim. ✆ 078/31427. Admission €4.50 ($4) per car. Guided tour €1.30 ($1.15) adults, €.65 (60¢) children. May–Aug daily 10am–7pm.

Strokestown Park House, Gardens & Famine Museum ★★ One of the defining events of Ireland's history, the Great Potato Famine of the 1840s is the focus of this museum. Housed in the stable yards of Strokestown Park House, this museum illustrates how and why the famine started, how English colonial officials failed to prevent its spread, and how it reduced the Irish population of

8.1 million by nearly 3 million through death and mass emigration. This museum is particularly interesting for Irish Americans, tens of millions of whom trace their ancestry to those who left the country during and after the famine. The museum also seeks to relate the events of the Irish famine to contemporary world hunger and poverty.

Strokestown Park House was the seat of the Pakenham-Mahon family from 1600 to 1979. The 45-room Palladian house, designed for Thomas Mahon by German architect Richard Castle in the 1730s, incorporates parts of an earlier tower house. The north wing houses Ireland's last existing galleried kitchen (where the lady of the house could observe the culinary activity without being part of it). The south wing is an elaborate vaulted stable, often described as an equine cathedral.

On the main Dublin-Castlebar rd. (N5), Strokestown Park, Strokestown, county Roscommon. © 078/33013. www.strokestownpark.ie. Admission to gardens €4.50 ($4) adults, €.65 (60¢) children, €10 ($8.90) family. Admission to house and museum €4.50 ($4) adults, €3.20 ($2.85) seniors and students, €2 ($1.80) children, €10 ($8.90) family. Apr–Oct daily 11am–5:30pm.

Tullynally Castle and Gardens ⭐ A turreted and towered Gothic Revival manor, this house has been the home of the Pakenham family, the earls of Longford, since 1655. The highlights include a great hall that rises two stories, with a ceiling of plaster Gothic vaulting, and a collection of family portraits, china, and furniture. There's also a collection of 19th-century gadgets. The 12-hectare (30-acre) grounds are an attraction in themselves, with woodland walks, a linear water garden, a Victorian grotto, and an avenue of 200-year-old Irish yew trees. Tullynally is near Lough Derravaragh, an idyllic spot featured in the legendary Irish tale *The Children of Lir*. The tearoom is open daily May to August.

About 32km (20 miles) east of Longford and 21km (13 miles) north of Mullingar, off the main Dublin-Sligo rd. (N4), Castlepollard, county Westmeath. © 044/61159. Admission to gardens €4 ($3.55) adults, €1.30 ($1.15) children; admission to both castle and gardens €6.50 ($5.80) adults, €3.20 ($2.85) children. Castle mid-June to July daily 2:30–6pm; gardens May–Aug daily 2–6pm. Closed Sept–Apr.

SPORTS & OUTDOOR PURSUITS

BOATING The following companies rent cabin cruisers along this part of the Shannon: **Athlone Cruisers,** Jolly Mariner Marina, Athlone, county Westmeath (© **0902/72892**); **Carrick Craft,** The Marina, Carrick-on-Shannon, county Leitrim (© **078/21248**); **Crown Blue Line,** The Marina, Carrick-on-Shannon, county Leitrim (© **44-1603-630513** headquartered in Britain; www.crown-blueline.com); and **Emerald Star Line,** The Marina, Carrick-on-Shannon, county Leitrim (© **078/20234**).

GOLF There are two 18-hole championship golf courses in the area that should not be missed. The **Glasson Golf Hotel and Country Club,** Glasson, county Westmeath (© **0902/85120;** www.glassongolf.ie), is on the shores of Lough Ree, 9.7km (6 miles) north of Athlone. Green fees are €45 to €50 ($40–$45) weekdays, €50 to €60 ($45–$53) weekends. The **Slieve Russell Hotel Golf Club,** Cranaghan, Ballyconnell, county Cavan (© **049/26444;** www.quinn-hotels.com), charges greens fees of €50 ($45) weekdays, €65 ($58) weekends, for nonguests of the hotel. Guests (see review, below) pay €34 ($30) weekdays, €42 ($37) weekends.

Two other 18-hole courses in the area are **County Cavan Golf Club,** Arnmore House, Drumellis, county Cavan (© **049/433-1283;** www.cavangolf. ie), with greens fees of €23 ($20) weekdays, €25 ($22) weekends; and **County Longford Golf Club,** Dublin Road, Longford (© **043/46310**), with greens fees of €18 ($16) weekdays, €24 ($21) weekends.

HORSEBACK RIDING Moorlands Equestrian & Leisure Center, Drumshanbo, county Leitrim (✆ **078/41095**), offers lessons, as well as trail rides along Lough Allen and the nearby hills. Children are welcome. During the off-season, courses in equestrian science are offered. Book lessons or trail rides at least a day in advance. Mountain walking, watersports, and accommodations are also offered.

WHERE TO STAY & DINE
EXPENSIVE
Slieve Russell Hotel ★★★ *(Kids)* Set on 160 hectares (400 acres) of parklands and gardens, including 20 hectares (50 acres) of lakes and ponds, this impressive resort hotel is a popular destination among the Irish looking for quality down time. (The easy, 2-hour drive from the capital makes it particularly big with Dubliners.) Although barely a decade old, the hotel captures the opulence and charm of a bygone era, with public areas that boast marbled colonnades, huge open fireplaces, plush carpets, marble staircases, and wrought-iron trim. The conservatory-style Fountain Room exudes an Italianate garden atmosphere, with its skylit glass dome, Corinthian columns, stone fountain, and array of leafy plants. Guest rooms are modern and large, with traditional furnishings, quality period fabrics, and brass accessories. For families, there is an excellent, supervised playroom, children's menus at meal times, and a general child-friendly atmosphere. Situated near the Shannon-Erne Waterway, this hotel is a good base for touring not only the upper Shannon area, but also the attractions of Enniskillen and Northern Ireland. Excellent 2- and 3-day packages are available year-round.

Ballyconnell, county Cavan. ✆ **049/952-6444.** Fax 049/952-6474. www.quinn-hotels.com. 151 units. €216 ($192) double. No service charge. Rates include full breakfast. DC, MC, V. Free parking. **Amenities:** 2 restaurants (international, brasserie); 2 bars; indoor swimming pool; 18-hole championship golf course; 4 tennis courts; 2 squash courts; exercise room; Jacuzzi; sauna/steam room; children's playroom; concierge; salon; room service; babysitting; laundry and dry cleaning; walking trails. *In room:* TV, tea/coffeemaker, minibar, hair dryer, garment press.

MODERATE
Hotel Kilmore ★ Located 3.2km (2 miles) south of Cavan Town, this modern hotel (built in the 1980s) was totally refurbished and redecorated a few years ago to provide a new level of comfort. The public areas are airy and bright, done up in warm rusts and golds, and overlook the garden with its trio of fountains. Guest rooms are comfortable and well appointed.

Dublin rd. (N3), Cavan, county Cavan. ✆ **049/433-2288.** Fax 049/4332458. www.quinn-hotels.com. 39 units. €110 ($98) double. No service charge. Rates include full breakfast. AE, DC, MC, V. **Amenities:** Restaurant (seafood, game); bar/nightclub; babysitting; nonsmoking rooms. *In room:* TV, tea/coffeemaker, hair dryer, garment press.

The Park Hotel ★ Set on 40 hectares (100 acres) of woodlands and gardens beside Lough Ramor, this old-style hotel dates from 1751. Originally known as Deer Park Lodge, a sporting and summer residence of the Marquis of Headfort, it became a hotel in the 1930s. It has since undergone a number of renovations and extensions, making for lots of connecting corridors and varying standards of guest rooms. The public areas retain a definite 18th-century charm, with high ceilings, elaborate chandeliers, period furnishings, and original oil paintings. The hotel and its kitchen are used as the Irish campus for the Baltimore International (Culinary) College in the off-season.

Deer Park Lodge, Cavan-Dublin rd. (N3), Virginia, county Cavan. ✆ **049/854-7235.** Fax 049/854-7203. www.bichotels.com. 19 units, 16 with bathroom. €96–€140 ($85–$125) double. No service charge. Rates include full breakfast. AE, MC, V. **Amenities:** Restaurant (Continental); bar; 9-hole golf course; tennis court; fishing privileges; walking trails. *In room:* TV.

INEXPENSIVE

Glencarne House ★★ *Value*   Situated on a 40-hectare (100-acre) working farm, Glencarne is a beautifully restored and recently redecorated late Georgian house with great charm and warmth. The two front rooms (nos. 1 and 2) enjoy a sweeping view of the valley below, and an especially spacious double with an adjoining twin combine to make an elegant family suite. Rooms feature brass poster beds, antique furnishings, and fresh flowers in abundance. Dinner is the high point of life at Glencarne; the Harringtons draw from their own produce and meats and present a fresh, sumptuous feast. Then, when there's nothing left to do but collapse, firm beds are there to catch you.

Signposted on N4, between Carrick-on-Shannon and Boyle, Ardcarne, Carrick-on-Shannon, county Leitrim. ℂ 079/67013. 6 units. €65 ($58) double. No service charge. Rates include full Irish breakfast. Fixed-price dinner €24 ($21). No credit cards. Closed mid-Oct to Feb. **Amenities:** Drawing room. *In room:* TV.

Ross Castle and House ★★ *Value*   This 160-hectare (400-acre), family-run horse, cattle, and sheep farm on Lough Sheelin offers appealing options for accommodations and activities. It's a unique place, and one of the nicest hide-aways in this very affordable corner of Ireland. Ross Castle is a 16th-century fortified tower that's said to be haunted by a lovesick bride-to-be named Sabrina, whose lover, Orwin, drowned in Lough Sheelin en route to their elopement. They're buried together in a nearby field. Today, the place is restored, with central heating throughout (even in the tower rooms). It contains four guest rooms, including one family room. Rooms aren't quite as luxurious as at pricier castles, but they're comfortable and quite atmospheric. Nearby Ross House is a spacious, comfortable manor house with seven guest rooms. The oldest portions of the building date from the mid–17th century. Fishing is a particularly popular pastime here—the place is noted for its brown trout and is stocked with pike and perch. On request, three-course dinners are served, with an excellent small selection of wines, modestly priced. Whether you fish or not, for trout or ghosts, this is a most congenial spot.

Mount Nugent, county Cavan. Ross Castle. ℂ 049/854-0237. Ross House ℂ and fax 049/854-0218. www.ross-castle.com. 10 units. €80–€100 ($71–$89) double. No service charge. MC, V. Closed Dec–Feb. **Amenities:** Tennis court; Jacuzzi; sauna; massage treatments; babysitting; drawing room; horseback riding. *In room:* TV (house only).

A PUB

Although there are many good pubs in the area, don't miss the **Derragarra Inn,** Butlersbridge, county Cavan (ℂ **049/433-1003**), for a drink or a meal. More than 200 years old, it's full of local farm implements and crafts, as well as exotic souvenirs collected by former owner John Clancy during his travels around the world. Relax by the old turf fireplace or on the garden patio. It's 6.5km (4 miles) north of Cavan Town.

15

Northern Ireland

Technically, the province of Ulster comprises the six counties of Northern Ireland and Donegal. But the terms Ulster, Northern Ireland, "the Six Counties," and "the North" are used interchangeably by everyone in Ireland. And each is a byword for a historically troubled land. John Hume, one of Northern Ireland's most distinguished statesmen and a Nobel-winning peacemaker, once said, "Anyone who isn't confused in Northern Ireland doesn't really understand what is going on." These are sobering words for anyone about to sketch, in a few paragraphs, this unique place, its remarkable people, and fraught history. But here it is in a nutshell.

The strife in Northern Ireland can be traced back to a point over 800 years ago when Britain decided to take control of its neighboring island. Over the past 8 centuries there have been various unsuccessful attempts by the Irish to eject the British. And in that same time period, the British have made concerted efforts to make Ireland, and the Irish, more British. Tactics have included outlawing the Gaelic language, banning the practice of Catholicism, barring Catholics from land ownership, and relocating Britons to Ireland—often enticing them with land. The descendants of these British settlers, generally speaking, make up the modern-day Protestant population of Ireland.

Ireland finally won its independence from Britain in 1921, in the aftermath of the 1916 rebellion. During negotiations, in which the Irish government was represented by Michael Collins, it was decided that the border would be drawn to divide the island in two. Twenty-six Irish counties would form an independent, free state (later the Republic of Ireland), while six counties in the Ulster province would become Northern Ireland and remain a part of the United Kingdom. Why these six counties? Because their populations were mainly Protestant—and as such were presumably more loyal to Britain—while the vast majority of the island's other 26 counties was, and still is, Catholic. A provision in the agreement stated that Northern Ireland could later join the other 26 counties if it was the will of the people—that is, if the Northern Irish people voted for reunification in a referendum.

When the Six Counties were detached from the rest of the island, two conflicting ideological bodies emerged in the North: Unionists, associated with the Protestant majority, who want to remain a part of the United Kingdom, and Nationalists, associated with the Catholic minority, who want the whole of Ireland united as one independent nation. It's important to realize that being a Unionist or a Nationalist doesn't by itself imply the approval of violence as a means to an end. In fact, the overwhelming majority of Northern Irish people, regardless of whether they want British rule or Irish rule, don't belong to any paramilitary group.

By all accounts, there was considerable unfairness in how Catholics were treated by the police and British government in Northern Ireland. Things

Northern Ireland

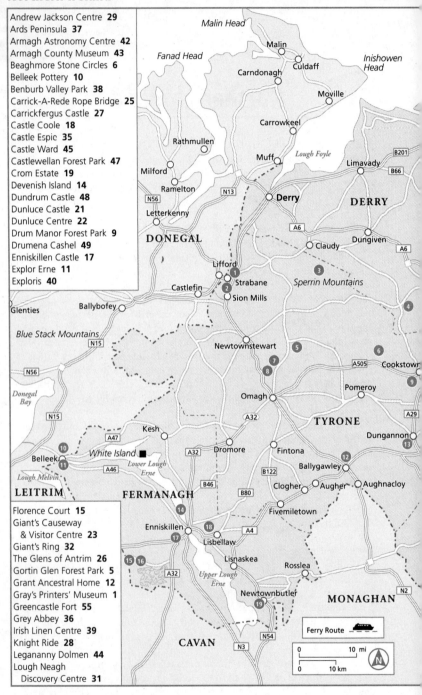

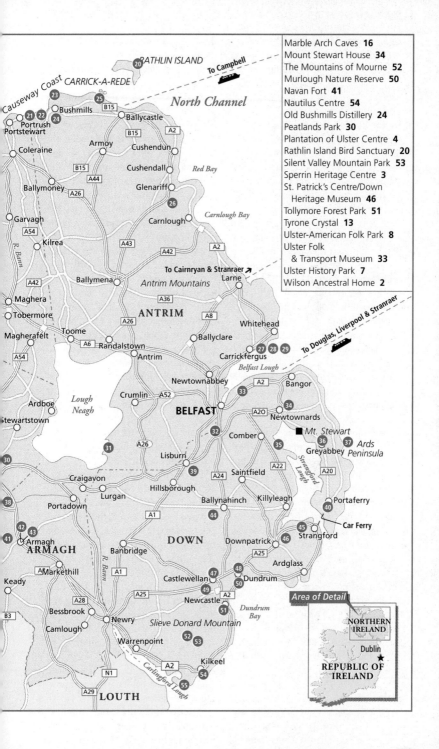

Marble Arch Caves **16**
Mount Stewart House **34**
The Mountains of Mourne **52**
Murlough Nature Reserve **50**
Navan Fort **41**
Nautilus Centre **54**
Old Bushmills Distillery **24**
Peatlands Park **30**
Plantation of Ulster Centre **4**
Rathlin Island Bird Sanctuary **20**
Silent Valley Mountain Park **53**
Sperrin Heritage Centre **3**
St. Patrick's Centre/Down
   Heritage Museum **46**
Tollymore Forest Park **51**
Tyrone Crystal **13**
Ulster-American Folk Park **8**
Ulster Folk
   & Transport Museum **33**
Ulster History Park **7**
Wilson Ancestral Home **2**

RATHLIN ISLAND

To Campbell

Causeway Coast CARRICK-A-REDE

North Channel

Bushmills
Portrush
Portstewart
Coleraine
Ballycastle
B15

B15   A2

Armoy
Cushendun

B15
A44
Ballymoney
A26
Cushendall   Red Bay

Glenariff

Garvagh
A54
Kilrea
Carnlough   Carnlough Bay

R. Bann

A43
A42   A2

Maghera
Tobermore
Magherafelt
A54

Toome
A6
Randalstown
Antrim

Ballymena
Antrim Mountains
To Cairnryan & Stranraer
Larne

A36
ANTRIM
A8

Whitehead

Ballyclare
To Douglas, Liverpool & Stranraer

Ardboe
Stewartstown

Lough
Neagh

Crumlin   A52
Newtownabbey
Carrickfergus
Belfast Lough
Bangor

A2

BELFAST
A2O
Newtownards

A26
Comber
Mt. Stewart   Ards
Peninsula
Greyabbey

Lisburn
Strangford
Lough
A20

Craigavon
Hillsborough
Saintfield
A22
Portaferry

Portadown
Lurgan
Ballynahinch
Killyleagh
Car Ferry

A1
DOWN
Downpatrick
Strangford

Armagh
ARMAGH
Banbridge
A25
Ardglass

Markethill
A1
Castlewellan
Dundrum

Keady
A28
Newcastle
A2
Dundrum
Bay

Bessbrook
A25
Slieve Donard Mountain

B3
Camlough
Newry
Warrenpoint
Kilkeel

N1
Carlingford Lough
A2

A29 LOUTH

came to a head in the late 1960s, when the minority Catholic population began a civil rights campaign to protest their treatment as second-class citizens. When their demonstrations and marches were squelched forcefully by the police force, the stage was set for the Irish Republican Army, a violent paramilitary Nationalist group, to emerge. The break-out of the so-called "Troubles" in 1969 was the beginning of violence as an everyday fact of life for the people of Northern Ireland. This isn't to say that every Northern Irishman has encountered violence in his lifetime, but it certainly has been a pervasively stressful environment in which to live. Since 1969, the North has seen the emergence of a half-dozen other paramilitary groups on both sides of the fence.

To many outsiders, the "Troubles" are as incomprehensible and distant as the Middle East conflict. Other people's prejudices and quarrels usually are. Yet from a visitor's perspective, the violence has been remarkably contained. Like diplomats, foreigners have enjoyed a certain immunity. Derry and Belfast at their worst have been as safe for visitors as almost any comparable American city, and the Ulster countryside has been as idyllic and serene as Vermont. For the outsider, driving through Northern Ireland was and is no more cause for fear than driving to work. Not so for the people of Northern Ireland, whose wounds and grief run deep.

Fortunately, their resilience and resolve for peace run even deeper. On May 22, 1998, Northerners and their fellow islanders in the Republic voted for a fresh future, one that would not be rutted or wrecked by the past. The Belfast Agreement, aka the "Good Friday Agreement," dismantled the claims of both Ireland and Britain to the North and acknowledged the sovereign right of the people of Northern Ireland to take charge of their political

destiny. As a consequence, the government was devolved from London to Belfast. Yes, there have been teething pains. But the people of Northern Ireland, it is to be hoped, will unite to nurture their fascinatingly diverse island, unique in its history, which they all have made and shared. Even the Troubles have been shared, and held painfully in common, and will make their own contribution to the future.

As this book goes to press, the mood is cautiously optimistic. For the past 4 years (1998–2002) since the Good Friday Agreement was signed, the new government of the North has had a turbulent time. After finally appointing its legislative body, the new Northern Ireland Assembly encountered obstacle after hurdle after stumbling block as all sides began finger pointing and failed to reach an agreement on how and when the peace process should proceed. A most crucial breakthrough came, in August 2001, when the Irish Republic Army finally put forward a plan to decommission its weapons. Decommissioning had been a prickly point since negotiations began.

For many visitors to Ireland, the North offers a new, uncharted, and exciting destination. While tourism to the Republic has soared, the North has been relatively unvisited. Even the majority of the Irish people in the Republic have never set foot in the North. All of this is bound to change, and none too soon. The truth is that Northern Ireland is as welcoming and gracious as the Republic, and surely as beautiful. Furthermore, because tourism has taken much shorter and more careful steps in the North, the countryside is all the more unspoiled. Much of Northern Ireland is just waiting to be discovered.

The first thing that strikes you once you cross the border and take your bearings is how small Northern Ireland is. The next thing is how much there is to see and do. As the Tourist Board puts it, Northern Ireland is a nation that only pretends to be small. This said, there are really only two cities in the North likely to serve as major destinations in themselves and bases for exploration: **Belfast** and **Derry City,** and their environs. After these, the major destinations in the North lie in its magnificent countryside, in regions officially designated as areas of outstanding natural beauty: the **Causeway Coast** and the **Glens of Antrim,** the **Mourne Mountains,** the **Sperrin Mountains,** and the **Fermanagh Lakelands.**

1 Northern Ireland Essentials

VISITOR INFORMATION

The **Northern Ireland Tourist Board** headquarters is at 59 North St., Belfast BT1 1NB (© **028/9024-6609;** fax 028/9031-2424; www.discovernorthernireland. com). In addition, there are more than 30 tourist information centers (TICs) scattered around the province, most of which are open year-round. The obliging, friendly personnel are eager to help with any problem and to make sure you see the highlights of their area. Local accommodations may be booked in any TIC, and most are hooked up to online reservations systems that can secure reservations throughout all of Ireland and the United Kingdom. To make your own reservations anywhere in Ireland using a credit card, you can call the Central Accommodations free-phone number (© **0800/6686-6866**).

GETTING TO THE NORTH

BY AIR   Aer Lingus (© **800/474-7424;** www.aerlingus.ie) offers scheduled flights from Boston and New York via Shannon to **Belfast International Airport** (© **028/94-422888;** www.belfastairport.com). Other major carriers offer connecting flights from the United States and Canada via London/Heathrow, Glasgow, or Manchester. Charter service to Shannon, Dublin, and Belfast is offered by a range of operators, such as **Sceptre Charters** (© **800/221-0924**) and **Irish Charters** (© **888/431-6688**) in the United States, and **World of Vacations** (© **800/263-8776;** www.worldofvacations.com) in Canada.

Direct flights into **Belfast International Airport** include service by **British Airways** (© **0345/222111;** www.british-airways.com) from Birmingham, Edinburgh, and London/Heathrow; and by **Virgin Express** (© **800/891199;** www.virgin-atlantic.com) from London/Heathrow. In addition, there is service into **Belfast City Airport** (© **028/9045-7745;** www.belfastcityairport.com) by a range of carriers, including **British Airways** flights from Edinburgh, Glasgow, Leeds, Liverpool, and Manchester, and by **Jersey European** (© **0990/676676**)

Tips **Keeping Your Irish Up**

If you want to brush up on your knowledge of Northern Ireland, **Newshound** (www.nuzhound.com) is an indispensable resource. Run by American expat John Fay, this is an extremely well-organized catalog of news articles culled from international newspapers, covering everything from a history of "the Troubles" to stories on dining and shopping in Belfast. The vast array of articles about the Republic (click "News of the Irish") includes culture, travel, and even dining reviews from Dublin to Donegal. The site is intelligent, user-friendly, and searchable.

---

from Birmingham, Bristol, Exeter, London Stansted, and London Gatwick. Service to **City of Derry Airport** (© 028/7181-0784; www.derrynet.net/airport) is provided by **British Airways** from Glasgow and Manchester, and by **Ryanair** (© 0541/569569 in Britain; www.ryanair.com) from London Stansted.

Most international flights into Ireland land in Dublin, with connecting flights to Belfast.

BY FERRY   The quickest sea crossing from Britain to Northern Ireland is the 90-minute **SeaCat** (© 08705/523523; www.seacat.co.uk), a catamaran service from Stranraer, Scotland, to Belfast. Other ferry services into Belfast include **Norse Merchant Ferries** (© 0870/6004321 in Britain or 01/819-2999 in Ireland; www.norsemerchant.com), which takes 8 hours from Liverpool, and the **Isle of Man Steam Packet Co.** (© 08705/523523) which takes 2 hours and 45 minutes from Douglas, on the Isle of Man. In addition, **Stena Sealink** (© 08705/707070; www.stenaline.com) operates both fast craft (105 min.) and ferry service (3 hr., 15 min.) from Stranraer, Scotland, to Belfast; **P&O European Ferries** (© 0870/242-4777; www.poferries.com) from Cairnryan, Scotland, to Larne; and, in July and August, **SeaCat** from Campbell, Scotland, to Ballycastle, county Antrim. The shortest of the routes is from Cairnryan, aboard a fast craft (60 min.) or a superferry (105 min.).

BY CRUISE SHIP   Derry City is rapidly becoming a premier international cruise destination, with a reputation for friendliness and charm. Every year more cruise ships, including six-star luxury liners, call at the deep-water facilities at Lisahally or at the city center's refurbished Queen's Quay. For the latest information on cruises to Derry Port, contact the **Cruise Development Officer,** Derry City Council, 98 Strand Rd., Derry BT48 7NN (© 028/7136-5151; fax 028/7126-4858).

BY TRAIN   Trains on the **Irish Rail** (© 1850/366222; www.irishrail.ie) and **Northern Ireland Railways** (© 888/BRITRAIL or 028/9089-9411) systems travel into Northern Ireland from Dublin's **Connolly Station** daily. They arrive at Belfast's Central Station, East Bridge Street (© 028/9089-9411). Monday to Saturday, eight trains a day connect Dublin and Belfast; on Sunday, five. The trip takes about 2 hours.

BY BUS   Ulsterbus (© 028/9033-3000; www.translink.co.uk) runs buses from the Republic to Belfast and virtually all bus service in and between 21 localities in Northern Ireland. To purchase or reserve a ticket, call © 028/9032-0011. The express bus from Dublin to Belfast takes 3 hours and runs seven times daily Monday to Saturday, three times on Sunday.

BY CAR   Northern Ireland is directly accessible from the Republic of Ireland on many main roads and secondary roads. It is possible, but unlikely, that you will encounter checkpoints when crossing the border. Main roads leading to Northern Ireland from the Republic include N1 from Dublin, N2 from Monaghan, N3 from Cavan, N14 and 15 from Donegal, and N16 from Sligo. *Important note:* If you are renting a car and taking it across the border, make certain that all your insurance coverage is equally valid in the North and in the Republic. Don't forget to check any coverage provided by your credit card as well.

GETTING AROUND IN THE NORTH

Northern Ireland has recently launched a major initiative called **Translink** (www.translink.co.uk) to coordinate rail, bus, and auto travel in the North, which will expand and enhance transportation services.

BY TRAIN   The hub of **Northern Ireland Railways** (© 028/9089-9411) is Belfast, with two principal rail stations: **Great Victoria St. Station,** across from the Europa Bus Centre; and **Belfast Central Station,** East Bridge Street. Trains from Larne arrive at Yorkgate Station; otherwise, trains to and from all destinations depart from and arrive at Belfast Central. The three main routes in the North's rail system are north and west from Belfast to Derry via Ballymena; east to Bangor, tracing the shores of Belfast Lough; and south to Dublin via Newry. Be sure to refer to the box called "Money-Saving Rail & Bus Passes" in the "Getting Around" section of chapter 2. For example, the **Irish Rover** pass is for use both in the Republic of Ireland and in the North.

BY BUS   Ulsterbus (© 028/9033-3000; www.translink.co.uk) runs daily scheduled service from Belfast to major cities and towns throughout Northern Ireland. From the **Laganside Bus Centre,** Oxford Street, Belfast (© 028/9023-2356), buses leave for destinations in counties Antrim, Down (eastern), Derry (eastern), and Cookstown. Buses to most every other destination in the North, including Belfast International Airport and the Larne ferries, as well as the Republic, depart from the **Europa Bus Centre,** Glengall Street, Belfast (© 028/9032-0011). Bus service in the North is remarkably thorough and will get you to the most unlikely and remote destinations. For extra savings, be sure to investigate the bus and rail passes outlined in the above-mentioned box in the "Getting Around" section of chapter 2.

BY SIGHTSEEING TOUR   From June to August, **Ulsterbus** operates a wide variety of full- and half-day coach tours from the Europa Bus Centre, Glengall Street, Belfast. They run to places such as the Glens of Antrim, Causeway Coast, Fermanagh Lakelands, Sperrin Mountains, the Mountains of Mourne, and Armagh. There are also tours designed to take you to specific attractions, such as the Giant's Causeway, Old Bushmills Distillery in Bushmills, Navan Centre in Armagh, Ulster-American Folk Park in Omagh, and Tyrone Crystal Factory in Dungannon. For full information on the day tours and holiday packages, visit or phone the Ulsterbus tourism office at the Europa Bus Centre, Glengall Street (© 028/9033-3000). To consider in advance the range of tours available, take a look at **www.tourulster.com** and click the "Guided Tours" link.

BY CAR   The best way to travel around the Northern Ireland countryside is by car. The roads are in extremely good condition and are well signposted. Distances between major cities and towns are short. If you want to rent a car, **Avis** (© 028/9024-0404), **Budget** (© 028/9023-0700), **Europcar** (© 028/9031-3500), **Hertz** (© 028/9073-2451), and **McCausland** (© 028/9073-2451) have offices in Belfast city, in at least one of the Belfast airports, or both. If you rent a car in the Republic, you can drive it in the North as long as you arrange the proper insurance.

FAST FACTS: Northern Ireland

Area Code   The area code for all of Northern Ireland is **028.** Drop the "0" when dialing from within Northern Ireland.

Business Hours   Banks are generally open Monday to Friday 10am to 12:30pm and 1:30 to 3 or 4pm; they're closed on bank holidays. In Belfast and Derry City, banks tend not to close for lunch. Most shops are open

Monday to Saturday 9 or 9:30am to 5 or 5:30pm, with one early-closing day a week, usually Wednesday or Thursday. Shops in tourist areas are likely to be open Sunday and to have extended hours, especially in the summer months.

Currency Since Northern Ireland is a part of the United Kingdom, it uses the pound sterling and not the Euro.

Electricity The electrical current (220 volts/AC) and outlets (requiring three-pin flat, fused plugs) are the same in the North as in the Republic. Note that they are not the two-pin round plugs standard throughout Europe.

Embassies & Consulates The **U.S. Consulate General** is at Queen's House, 14 Queen's St., Belfast BT1 6EQ (*ⓒ* **028/9032-8239**). Other foreign offices include the **Australian High Commission,** Australia House, Strand, London WC2 B4L (*ⓒ* 020/7379-4344); **Canadian High Commission,** Macdonald House, Grosvenor Square, London W1X 0AB (*ⓒ* **020/7499-9000**); **New Zealand High Commission,** New Zealand House, 80 Haymarket Sq., London SW1Y 4TQ (*ⓒ* **020/7930-8422**).

Emergencies Dial *ⓒ* **999** for fire, police, and ambulance.

Mail United Kingdom postal rates apply, and mailboxes are painted red. Most post offices are open weekdays 9am to 5pm, Saturday 9am to 1pm.

Newspapers & Magazines For listings of upcoming cultural events throughout Northern Ireland, check the free bimonthly *Arts Link* brochure, published by the Arts Council of Northern Ireland and available at any Northern Ireland Tourist Board office.

Parking Because of long-standing security concerns, parking regulations are more restrictive and more relentlessly enforced in the North than in the Republic.

Petrol (Gas) Filling up the tank is far cheaper in the Republic, so do it before you cross the border. In the North, the approximate price of 1 liter of unleaded gas is 73p sterling ($1.05). There are 4 liters to the U.S. gallon, which makes the price of a gallon of unleaded gas a whopping £2.92 ($4.15).

Police The Northern Ireland police are now known as the **Northern Ireland Police Service.** Following the Good Friday Agreement, the name was changed from the Royal Ulster Constabulary (RUC) to reflect the British devolvement. Dial *ⓒ* **999** in an emergency.

Safety Contrary to the media image, the North has one of the lowest levels of crime in western Europe. Historically, the high rate of serious crime, such as homicide and robbery, have been almost exclusively associated with terrorism and the "Troubles." Yet common sense dictates using care to avoid pickpockets in crowded areas and to follow other basic rules of safety.

Taxes You pay a **VAT (value-added tax)** of 17.5% on almost everything, except B&B accommodations. The percentages vary with the category of the services and purchases. It is usually already included in the prices you're quoted by hotels and the prices you see marked on merchandise tags. VAT is already included in the hotel prices we've quoted in this guide. Many shops offer tax-free shopping schemes, such as "Cashback," and are pleased to explain the details. The refund procedure is essentially the same as for the Republic, outlined in "VAT Refunds" in chapter 2. Vouchers from the North can be presented at the Dublin or Shannon airports before departure from Ireland. For further information, contact HM Customs and Excise, Belfast International Airport (© **028/9441-3439** or 028/9442-3439; www.hmce.gov.uk).

Telephone To reach Northern Ireland from anywhere but the Republic of Ireland or Great Britain, dial the country code (44) and then 28 (the area code minus the initial 0) and finally the local eight-digit number. From the Republic of Ireland, omit the country code; dial 048 and then the local eight-digit number. From Great Britain, dial 028 and the eight-digit number. For local calls within Northern Ireland, simply dial the eight-digit local number.

2 Belfast

Belfast is 166km (103 miles) N of Dublin, 340km (211 miles) NE of Shannon, 201km (125 miles) E of Sligo, and 422km (262 miles) NE of Cork

Now is a great time to visit Belfast because it's a vibrant place that's on the way up. You only have to look at how the city's dining scene is exploding, with exciting restaurants opening up all the time, to feel the buzz that is Belfast today. As Bono of U2 put it, "Belfast is really happening at the minute. I'm looking around and the people are looking good, and the place is looking good. It's the perfect time for it to be happening with the European Capital of Culture 2008 bid."

Nestled beside the River Lagan and Belfast Lough and ringed by gentle hills, Belfast occupies a lovely setting, often called "the Hibernian Rio." First-time visitors are in for a number of pleasant surprises. To begin with, Belfast is a vibrant, fast-moving place with great sightseeing and shopping, as well as wonderful places to eat, drink and stay. Secondly, it is an arts hub with an outstanding program of all-year-round events. And finally, Belfast is a pleasingly walkable city laid out on a human scale. You could cross the city in an hour on foot or, as the locals say, "just take a wee dander" to admire exquisite examples of Georgian, Victorian and Edwardian architecture, dominated by the magnificently domed City Hall.

The core of downtown Belfast sits beside the west bank of the River Lagan. The city revolves around a central point, **Donegall Square,** which holds the city hall; all roads radiate out from there. Donegall Place, which extends north from the square, leads to Royal Avenue, a prime shopping district. Bedford Street, which extends south from the square, becomes Dublin Road, which, in turn, leads to the Queen's University area. Nearly half a million people, a third of Northern Ireland's population, reside within Belfast city limits.

With its large port, Belfast is an industrialized city, often referred to as the engine room that drove the whirring wheels of the industrial revolution in Ulster. Major industries range from linen production to shipbuilding to aircraft manufacturing. The *Titanic* was built in Belfast port, and today the world's largest dry dock is here.

The city's architecture is particularly rich in Victorian and Edwardian buildings with elaborate sculptures over the doors and windows. Busts of gods, poets, scientists, kings, and queens peer down from the high ledges of banks and old linen warehouses. Some of Belfast's grandest buildings are on the banks of Waring Street. The Ulster Bank, dating from 1860, has an interior like a Venetian palace, and the Northern Bank, dating from 1769, was originally a market house.

The **Queen's University,** with its Tudor cloister, dominates the southern sector of the city. The original edifice was built in 1849 by Charles Lanyon, who designed more of Belfast's buildings than anyone else. The university was named for Queen Victoria, who visited Belfast in that year and had just about everything named in her honor for the occasion—dozens of streets, a hospital, a park, a man-made island, and the harbor's deepwater channel are all named after her. Today, the university enrolls 12,000 students and is the setting for the Belfast Festival at Queen's, one of Europe's major annual arts events.

ESSENTIALS

GETTING THERE For details, see "Getting to the North," in section 1, earlier in this chapter. Belfast has two airports—Belfast International and Belfast City—and gets considerable sea traffic at Belfast Harbour and at Larne (30 min. from Belfast by train, bus, or car).

From Belfast International Airport, nearly 31km (19 miles) north of the city, your best option is the **Airbus** coach into the city center. It operates daily, leaves every half hour, and costs £5 ($7.10) per person for a one-way ticket and £8 ($11) for a round-trip. A taxi will run closer to £22 ($28).

From Belfast City Airport, less than 6.4km (4 miles) from the city center, there are several options. The most convenient is a taxi, which costs roughly £6 ($8.50) to get into the city. You can also take Citybus no. 21 from the airport terminal or the Sydenham Halt train from the station directly across from the airport, both for 80p ($1.15).

In Northern Ireland, all roads really do lead to Belfast. It's the point of origin for the country's principal motorways and also the rail hub of the North.

VISITOR INFORMATION Brochures, maps, and other data about Belfast and the North are available from the **Belfast Welcome Centre,** at 47 Donegall Place (© 028/9024-6609; www.gotobelfast.com). It's open June through September, Monday to Saturday, 9am to 7pm, and Sunday noon to 5pm; October through May, Monday to Saturday 9am to 5:30pm. The tourist information desk at **Belfast City Airport** (© 028/9045-7745) is open year-round Monday to Friday 5:30am to 10pm, Saturday 5:30am to 9pm, Sunday 5:30am to 10pm. The desk at **Belfast International Airport** (© 028/9442-2888) is open March to September daily 24 hours, October to February daily 6:30am to 11pm. If you're wired, **www.belfast.net** is a comprehensive guide to the city, featuring tourism, news, accommodation, events, and nightlife rubrics.

GETTING AROUND **Citybus,** Donegall Square West, Belfast (© 028/9024-6485; www.citybus.co.uk), provides local bus service within the city. Departures are from Donegall Square East, West, and North, plus Upper Queen Street, Wellington Place, Chichester Street, and Castle Street. There is an information kiosk on Donegall Square West. Fares are determined by the number of zones traversed. The maximum fare for city-center travel is £1.10 ($1.55). Multiple-trip tickets, day tickets, and 7-day passes offer significant savings.

If you've brought a **car** into Belfast, it's best to leave it parked at your hotel and take public transportation or walk around the city. If you must drive and want to park your car downtown, look for a blue P sign that shows a parking lot or a parking area. Belfast has a number of "control zones," indicated by a pink-and-yellow sign, where no parking is permitted. In general, on-street parking is

Belfast

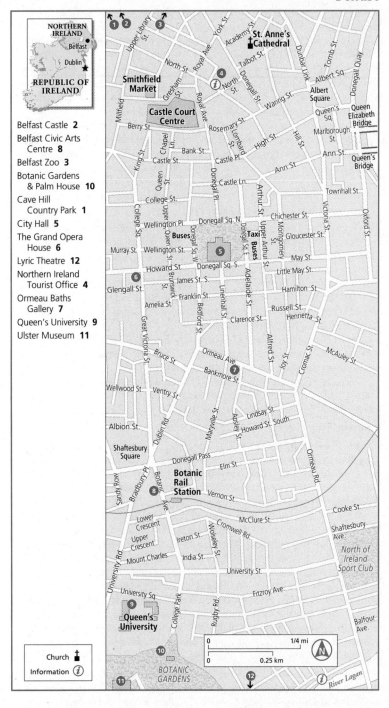

Belfast Castle **2**

Belfast Civic Arts
  Centre **8**

Belfast Zoo **3**

Botanic Gardens
  & Palm House **10**

Cave Hill
  Country Park **1**

City Hall **5**

The Grand Opera
  House **6**

Lyric Theatre **12**

Northern Ireland
  Tourist Office **4**

Ormeau Baths
  Gallery **7**

Queen's University **9**

Ulster Museum **11**

Church †

Information ⓘ

NORTHERN IRELAND

Belfast

Dublin ★

REPUBLIC OF IRELAND

St. Anne's Cathedral

Smithfield Market

Castle Court Centre

Albert Square

Queen's Sq.

Queen Elizabeth Bridge

Queen's Bridge

Buses

Taxi Buses

Botanic Rail Station

Shaftesbury Square

Shaftesbury Ave.

North of Ireland Sport Club

Queen's University

BOTANIC GARDENS

River Lagan

0   1/4 mi

0   0.25 km

limited to an area behind City Hall (south side), St. Anne's Cathedral (north side), and around Queen's University and Ulster Museum.

Taxis are available at all main rail stations, ports, and airports, and in front of City Hall. Most metered taxis are London-type black cabs with a yellow disc on the window. Other taxis may not have meters, so you should ask the fare to your destination in advance. Except for reasonably inexpensive service down the Shankill Road and the Falls Road, Belfast taxi fares are on the high side, with a £2 ($2.85) minimum and an additional £1 ($1.40) per mile.

Belfast is a good city for **walking.** To guide visitors on the best and safest areas for a stroll, the Belfast City Council has produced five self-guided walking-tour leaflets. They are city center south to Shaftesbury Square, city center north to the Irish News office, Shaftesbury Square south to the university area, city center northeast to the port area, and Donegall Square south to Donegall Pass. Each walk is about a mile and lasts an hour. Ask for a leaflet for the walk or walks that interest you at the Belfast Welcome Centre.

FAST FACTS The **U.S. consulate general** is at Queen's House, 14 Queen's St., Belfast BT1 (© **028/9032-8239**). For other embassies and consulates, see "Fast Facts: Northern Ireland," above.

In an **emergency,** dial © **999** for fire, police, and ambulance. The most central hospital is Shaftesbury Square Hospital, 16–20 Great Victoria St. (© **028/9032-9808**). Farther south, on Lisburn Road, is Belfast City Hospital (© **028/9032-9241**). West of the city center on Grosvenor Road is the Royal Victoria Hospital (© **028/9024-0503**).

At the **Revelations Café,** 27 Shaftesbury Sq. (© **028/9032-0337**; www.revelations.co.uk), you can surf the Internet for £1 ($1.40) per 15 minutes. It's on Bradbury Place just south of Donegall Road.

The main post office, the **Belfast GPO (General Post Office)** is at Castle Place, at the intersection of Royal Avenue and Donegall Place. It's open Monday to Friday 9am to 5:30pm, Saturday 9am to 7pm.

SEEING THE SIGHTS

Citybus Tours (© **028/9045-8484**; www.citybus.co.uk) offers a 1½-hour **Belfast City Tour** that gives you a good overview of the city. It departs at 11am Monday to Saturday from Castle Place, beside the GPO (post office), late June to September. It costs £9 ($13) for adults, £8 ($11) seniors and children, £23 ($33) family. The 2-hour **Black Taxi Tour** is also very popular, and disturbing—it encompasses local sites and stories of the barely historical Troubles. The fare is £20 ($28) for the first two passengers, or £7.50 ($11) per head for three or more passengers. If you're interested in this tour, call Michael at © **0800/052-3914** (toll-free) or 07860/127207 (mobile), or find all the details at **www.belfasttours.com**.

Themed walking tours are commonly offered during the summer, but they tend to be organized on a year-by-year basis. Up-to-date information on current specialty tours is available from the Belfast Welcome Centre at 47 Donegall Place (© **028/9024-6609**; www.gotobelfast.com). Typically, the selection includes **Historical Pub Tours of Belfast** (© **028/9268-3665**), departing twice a week to pay visits to six pubs. Tours take 2 hours and cost £6 ($8.50), not including drinks.

Belfast Botanic Gardens & Palm House ★★ Dating from 1828, these gardens were established by the Belfast Botanic and Horticultural Society. Ten years later they gained a glass house, or conservatory, designed by noted Belfast architect Charles Lanyon. Now known as the Palm House, this unique building is one of the earliest examples of curvilinear cast-iron glass-house construction. It

---

Tips **Tracing Your Roots**

Contact the **Ulster Historical Foundation,** Balmoral Buildings, 12 College Sq. E., Belfast BTI 6DD (© **028/9033-2288;** fax 028/9023-9885; www.uhf. org.uk), for help in tracking down Irish ancestors, particularly in Belfast, county Antrim, and county Down. The staff will furnish a list of helpful publications and help you find the appropriate genealogical source. A brand-new, excellent genealogy resource covering all 32 counties on the island is the **Irish Family History Foundation**'s new Internet site at www.irishroots.net. Much of the archived information is free for your perusal, and you can also avail of researchers to do the work for you. Initial searches cost €75 ($67) and comprehensive family searches cost €250 ($223). See also "Tracing Your Irish Roots" in chapter 2.

Two private organizations that can also help are **Irish Genealogical Services,** 2 Lower Crescent, Belfast B17 1NR (© **028/9024-1412;** fax 028/9023-9972); and **Historical Research Associates,** Glen Cottage, Glenmachan Road, Belfast BT4 2NP (© **028/9076-1490**). For a list of members and details of services for the **Association of Ulster Genealogists and Record Agents,** write **AUGRA,** Glen Cottage, Glenmachan Road, Belfast BT4 2NP.

---

contains many rare plant specimens, including such tropical plants as sugar cane, coffee, cinnamon, banana, aloe, ivory nut, rubber, bamboo, guava, and the striking bird of paradise flower. The Tropical Ravine, also known as the fernery, provides a setting for plants to grow in a sunken glen. Take time to stroll in the surrounding outdoor gardens of roses and herbaceous borders, established in 1927.

Signposted from M1/M2 (Balmoral exit), Stranmillis Rd., county Antrim. © 028/9032-4902. Free admission. Palm House and Tropical Ravine Apr–Sept Mon–Fri 10am–noon, daily 1–5pm; Oct–Mar Mon–Fri 10am–noon, daily 1–4pm. Gardens daily 8am–sunset. Bus: 61, 71, 84, or 85.

Belfast Castle ★★★   Northwest of downtown and 120m (400 ft.) above sea level stands Belfast Castle, whose 80-hectare (200-acre) estate spreads down the slopes of Cave Hill. The castle, which affords panoramic views of Belfast Lough and the city, was completed in 1870. It was the family residence of the third marquis of Donegall, and was presented to the city of Belfast in 1934 and used for private functions. After extensive restoration, the castle reopened to the public in 1988; 2 years later, its cellars were transformed into a Victorian arcade, including an antiques and craft shop, a bar, and a bistro restaurant. The extensive grounds include a public park, which is ideal for walking, jogging, picnicking, and enjoying extraordinary views of the city.

Signposted off the Antrim Rd., 4km (2½ miles) north of the city center, county Antrim. © 028/9077-6925. Free admission and parking. Castle daily 9am–6pm.

Belfast Zoo ★ *Kids*   In a picturesque mountain park on the slopes of Cave Hill overlooking the city, this zoo was founded in 1920 as Bellevue Gardens. A completely new, modern zoo was built in recent years. It emphasizes conservation, education, and breeding rare species, including Hawaiian geese, Indian lions, red lechwe, and golden lion tamarinds.

8km (5 miles) north of the city on A6, Antrim Rd., county Antrim. © 028/9077-6277. www.belfastzoo.co.uk. Admission £6 ($7.80) adults, £3 ($4.25) children 4–16, free for seniors and children under 4. Apr–Sept daily 10am–5pm; Oct–Mar daily 10am–3:30pm (to 2:30pm on Fri). Bus: 9, 45, 46, 47, 48, 49, 50, or 51.

Cave Hill Country Park 🎨 *Kids*   This lovely park atop a 360m (1,200-ft.) basalt cliff, said to resemble the profile of Napoleon (a Gallic Mount Rushmore in Ireland?), offers panoramic views, walking trails, and a number of interesting archaeological and historical sights. There are the Neolithic caves that gave the hill its name, and MacArt's Fort, an ancient earthwork built against the Vikings. In this fort, in 1795, Wolfe Tone and fellow United Irishmen planned the 1798 rebellion. On a lighter note, there's an adventure playground for the kids.

Off the Antrim Rd., 6.5km (4 miles) north of city center, county Antrim. Parking at Belfast Castle or Belfast Zoo (above).

City Hall 🎨🎨   Completed in 1906, this magnificent public building is the core of Belfast, the axis around which the city radiates. It was built of Portland stone after Queen Victoria granted Belfast the status of a city in 1888. Similar to an American State capitol building (except for the big statue of Queen Victoria at the front), it dominates the main shopping area.

Donegall Sq., Belfast, county Antrim. ℂ **028/9027-0456.** Free admission. Guided tours June–Sept Mon–Fri 10:30am, 11:30am, and 2:30pm, Sat 2:30pm; Oct–May Mon–Sat 2:30pm. Otherwise by arrangement. Reservations required.

Ormeau Baths Gallery 🎨🎨   Occupying the site of, and partly incorporating, the old Victorian swimming baths designed by Robert Watt, Ormeau Baths Gallery opened in 1995 as the city's principal exhibition space for contemporary visual art. This striking and versatile facility can program multiple simultaneous exhibitions in a variety of media, and has become the premier showcase for the best of Northern Irish contemporary art.

18A Ormeau Ave., Belfast, county Antrim. ℂ **028/9032-1402.** Free admission. Tues–Sat 10am–6pm.

Ulster Museum 🎨🎨🎨   Built in the grand Classical Renaissance style, with an Italian marble interior, this museum summarizes 9,000 years of Irish history with exhibits on art, furniture, ceramics, costume, industrial heritage, and a permanent display of products "Made in Belfast." One of the best-known exhibits is the collection of gold and silver jewelry recovered by divers in 1968 off the Antrim coast from the 1588 wreckage of the Armada treasure ship *Girona*. Other permanent collections focus on water wheels and steam engines, linen making, the post office, coins and medals, early Ireland, flora and fauna, and the living sea.

Signposted from M1/M2 (Balmoral exit); next to the Botanic Gardens, Stranmillis Rd., county Antrim. ℂ **028/9038-3000.** Free admission, except to major special exhibitions. Mon–Fri 10am–5pm; Sat 1–5pm; Sun 2–5pm. Bus: 61, 71, 84, or 85.

SHOPPING

Shops in Belfast city center are generally open Monday to Saturday 9am to 5:30pm, with many shops remaining open until 8 or 9pm on Thursday.

A great place to start your spree is **Craftworks Gallery,** Bedford House, Bedford Street (ℂ **028/9024-4465**), a one-stop showcase and shop for the work of individual craftspeople from all over Northern Ireland. The gallery can supply a free copy of the brochure "Crafts in Northern Ireland," detailing local crafts and where to find them. It is just behind Belfast City Hall.

The main shopping street is **Royal Avenue,** home of well-known names such as Waterstone's, Jaeger, and Virgin Megastore. The **Castlecourt Shopping Centre** on Royal Avenue is Belfast's main downtown multistory shopping mall and the largest in Northern Ireland, with more than 70 boutiques and shops.

Belfast's leading department stores are **Anderson & McAuley** and **Marks & Spencer,** both on Donegall Place, and **Debenham's** in the Castlecourt Shopping Centre on Royal Avenue. Other shops to look for include the following:

St. George's Market   This is Belfast's original "Variety Market," dating from the 19th century and now standing across from the new Waterfront Hall. The market was completely restored in 1999, and is a colorful outlet for fresh fruit, flowers, fish, vegetables, clothing, crafts, and lots more. Open Tuesday and Friday starting at 8am. May St. at Oxford St., Belfast ⓒ 028/9032-0202.

Smyth's Irish Linens   If you want to stock up on fine Irish linen damask tablecloths, napkins, and handkerchiefs, head for this shop in the heart of the city's prime shopping thoroughfare. It also stocks other traditional gift items and souvenirs, and offers VAT-free export. 65 Royal Ave., Belfast, county Antrim. ⓒ 028/9024-2232.

The Steensons   This is the main showroom of Bill and Christina Steenson, two of the most celebrated goldsmiths in Ireland. On display and for sale is the widest collection anywhere of the Steensons' unique gold and silver jewelry, as well as work by a select number of top designers from afar. Bedford St. (behind Belfast City Hall), Belfast, county Antrim. ⓒ 028/9024-8269.

Tom Caldwell Gallery   Come here for a selection of paintings, sculptures, and ceramics by living artists, as well as handcrafted furnishings, rugs, and cast-iron candelabras. Open Monday to Friday from 9:30am to 5pm, Saturday from 10am to 1pm. 40 Bradbury Place, Belfast, county Antrim. ⓒ 028/9032-3226.

SPORTS & OUTDOOR PURSUITS

FISHING   The 8.9km (5½-mile) stretch of the Lagan River from Stranmillis weir to Shaw's Bridge offers decent coarse fishing, especially on summer evenings. From May to July, Lough Neagh has good shore and boat fishing. Contact Paddy Prunty at the **Kinnego Marina,** Oxford Island, Craigavon (ⓒ 028/3832-7573). For info, tackle, and bait, try the **Village Tackle Shop,** 55a Newtownbreda Rd., Belfast (ⓒ 028/9049-1916), or **Shankill Fishing Tackle,** 366 Shankill Rd., Belfast (ⓒ 028/9033-0949).

GOLF   The Belfast area offers four 18-hole courses within 6.5km (4 miles) of the city center. Some 4.8km (3 miles) southwest of the city, there's the **Balmoral Golf Club,** 518 Lisburn Rd., Belfast (ⓒ 028/9038-1514), with greens fees of £22 ($31) weekdays (except Wed), £33 ($47) weekends and Wednesday. About 6.5km (4 miles) southwest of the city center is the **Dunmurry Golf Club,** 91 Dunmurry Lane, Dunmurry, Belfast (ⓒ 028/9061-0834; www.dunmurrygolf club.co.uk), £19 ($27) weekdays, £30 ($43) weekends. About 4.8km (3 miles) south of the city center is the **Belvoir Park Golf Club,** 73 Church Rd., Newtownbreda, Belfast (ⓒ 028/9049-1693), £35 ($50) weekdays, £40 ($57) weekends; and 4.8km (3 miles) north, the **Fortwilliam Golf Club,** Downview Avenue, Belfast (ⓒ 028/9037-0770; www.fortwilliam.co.uk), £24 ($34) weekdays, £30 ($43) weekends. Weekdays are usually better for visitors, and each club has preferred weekdays. Phone ahead. Club pros offer lessons, usually for about £25 ($36) per hour; book at least 2 days ahead.

HORSEBACK RIDING   Saddle up at the **Drumgooland House Equestrian Centre,** 29 Dunnanew Rd., Seaforde, Downpatrick, county Down (ⓒ 028/4481-1956; www.activityholidaysireland.com). It offers 1- to 4-hour treks, beach rides, and lessons. Full equestrian holidays are available.

WHERE TO STAY
VERY EXPENSIVE

Culloden Hotel ★★★   The Belfast area's finest hotel is not in the city itself, but 8km (5 miles) east on the shore of Belfast Lough, in county Down. Set on 4.8 hectares (12 acres) of secluded gardens and woodlands, this hotel was originally built as a palace for the bishops of Down. Later, it was sold and remained a private home until it opened as a hotel in 1963. The place is overflowing with luxurious—no, make that palatial—style, complete with many fine antiques and paintings, plasterwork ceilings, Louis XV chandeliers, and exceptional service. Guest rooms offer contemporary furnishings with lovely designer upholsteries, and many enjoy views of Belfast Lough.

142 Bangor Rd., county Down. ℂ **028/9042-5223.** Fax 028/9042-6777. www.hastingshotels.com. 75 units. £180–£210 ($256–$298) double. Rates include full breakfast. AE, DC, MC, V. Free valet parking. **Amenities:** Restaurant (Continental); bar; indoor swimming pool; tennis court; squash court; putting green; croquet; gym; Jacuzzi; steam room; bicycle rental; concierge; beauty treatments; room service; babysitting; laundry service. *In room:* TV, hair dryer, garment press.

Europa Hotel ★★   In the heart of the city beside the Grand Opera House and the start of Belfast's "Golden Mile," this is the city's largest and most modern hotel. Total renovation of this landmark hotel was completed in 1995, after it was damaged in a 1993 bombing. The Europa was host to Bill Clinton, the first U.S. president to visit Northern Ireland, during his stay in Belfast. The guest rooms, though modern, are luxuriously appointed in a traditional style with mahogany furnishings, opulent fabrics, and marble bathrooms. A recent extension added 56 new guest rooms, bringing the total to 240. The Europa is also home to the Ulster Cabaret, a traditional evening of harp, fiddle, fife, Lambeg drum, dance, and Ulster humor, every weekend in July and August. Dinner (at 7pm) and cabaret (at 8:15pm) costs £34 ($48) per person.

> ### Service Charges
> *A reminder:* Unless otherwise noted, room rates don't include service charges (usually 10%–15% of your bill).

Great Victoria St., Belfast, county Antrim. ℂ **028/9032-7000.** Fax 028/9032-7800. www.hastings hotels.com. 240 units. £135–£153 ($192–$217) double. Luxury suites available. AE, DC, MC, V. Free valet parking. **Amenities:** 2 restaurant (Continental, brasserie); bar; access to nearby health club; concierge; room service; babysitting; laundry service. *In room:* TV, tea/coffeemaker, hair dryer.

The McCausland Hotel ★★★   Whereas the Europa is huge and modern, the McCausland is the more intimate, boutique option in a historic setting. Both hotels are luxurious, but the McCausland feels more personal and exclusive (there's even butler service). This sister hotel of the Hibernian in Dublin was magnificently created from two classically ornate Italianate warehouses designed by William Hastings in the mid-1850s, and many stunning architectural details remain. Already listed among the "Small Luxury Hotels of the World," the McCausland offers sophistication and comfort. The guest rooms are spacious and beautifully decorated in warm, Mediterranean tones, with oak furnishings and quality fabrics.

34–38 Victoria St., Belfast, county Antrim. ℂ **800/525-4800** in the U.S., or 028/9022-0200. Fax 028/9022-0220. www.slh.com. 69 units. £150–£170 ($213–$241) double; £190 ($270) junior suite. Rates include full Irish breakfast. AE, DC, MC, V. Free valet parking. **Amenities:** 2 restaurants (Continental, cafe); access to health club; concierge; 24-hr. room service; nonsmoking rooms; foreign currency exchange; twice-daily maid service. *In room:* TV, dataport, tea/coffeemaker, minibar, hair dryer, garment press.

EXPENSIVE

TENsq 🐾🐾   This funky boutique hotel is Belfast's first Pudong-style hotel, but let's hope it's not the last. The Pudong district, in Shanghai, is renowned for its five-star hotels, and TENsq (pronounced "ten square") aims to emulate this Asian luxury. Low-level beds with white comforters and dark headboards lie on cream coir carpet. Armoires, shutters, and double doors are all inlaid with white opal glass. The overall feel is one of luxurious, elegant minimalism. Downstairs, there's a quartet of restaurants and bars that have become buzzy meeting places for hip Belfasters: A cutting-edge, excellent Asian fusion restaurant called Porcelain; a gourmet sandwich bar; a sleek city bar called Red; and the China Club, an exclusive member's bar (open to guests).

10 Donegall Square, Belfast, county Antrim. ✆ **028/9024-1001.** Fax 028/9024-3210. www.ten-sq.com. 23 units. £130–£185 ($185–$277) double. AE, MC, V. Street parking only. **Amenities:** 2 restaurants (fusion, deli); 2 bars; concierge. *In room:* TV, hair dryer.

MODERATE

Ash Rowan 🐾🐾   On a quiet, tree-lined street in a residential neighborhood, this four-story Victorian house sits near Queen's University. Proprietors Evelyn and Hazlett have outfitted it with country-style furnishings, family heirlooms, and antiques, along with bouquets of fresh flowers from the garden. The mood here is relaxed and old-style, with morning papers and late breakfasts. The rates include a choice of 12 traditional breakfasts, including the Ulster fry or scrambled eggs with kippers or smoked salmon. The location is ideal, just a short stroll into the city center.

12 Windsor Ave. (between Lisburn and Malone rds.), Belfast, county Antrim. ✆ **028/9066-1758.** Fax 028/9066-3227. 5 units. £88 ($125) double. Rates include full breakfast. AE, MC, V. Private parking. *In room:* TV.

Dukes Hotel 🐾   In a tree-lined residential area near the university, this hotel is in a former Victorian residence. The interior is bright and modern, with Art Deco furnishings, waterfalls, and plants. Guest rooms are contemporary, with double-glazed windows, light-wood furnishings, floral fabrics, and modern art. The hotel is within a half-mile walk of the center of the city.

65–67 University St. (off Botanic Ave.), Belfast, county Antrim. ✆ **028/9023-6666.** Fax 028/9023-7177. www.dukeshotelbelfast.co.uk. 21 units. £110 ($156). Rates include full breakfast. AE, DC, MC, V. Street parking only. **Amenities:** Restaurant (Continental); bar; gym; sauna; room service; nonsmoking rooms. *In room:* TV, tea/coffeemaker, hair dryer, garment press.

INEXPENSIVE

Ashberry Cottage 🐾 *Value*   "Cozy" is the word for Hilary and Sam Mitchell's modern bungalow, and you'll be completely spoiled from the moment they greet you with a welcome tray of tea and goodies. Not only do they both know the Belfast area well, but Hilary works for the Northern Ireland Tourist Board and is well qualified to help you plan your travels throughout the province. Guest rooms are attractive and very comfortable. Sam is the morning cook, and his breakfasts are legendary. Evening meals also draw raves from guests. Sam will meet you at the airport or railway station with advance notice.

19 Rosepark Central, Belfast, county Antrim. ✆ **028/9028-6300.** 3 units, 1 with bathroom. £42 ($60) double. Rates include full breakfast. No credit cards. Free parking. Take A20 to Rosepark, the 2nd turn on the right past the Stormont Hotel. **Amenities:** Nonsmoking rooms. *In room:* TV, tea/coffeemaker.

WHERE TO DINE
EXPENSIVE

Cayenne 🐾🐾🐾 FUSION   Prepare for culinary liftoff. Chef-owner Paul Rankin is one of this island's cleverest, most imaginative chefs and is famous for pairing the best of Ulster produce with exotic combinations of ingredients. His book, *Hot Food*, is full of fun, wildly enticing fusion recipes and the resulting dishes appear on the extremely extensive menu here—starters, soups, pastas, risottos, main courses, and desserts. Stellar main courses include chargrilled calamari with chorizo and arugula; duck confit with cucumber-and-lemongrass salad; and miso-glazed salmon with spinach and soy-lime vinaigrette. If possible, save room for the lovingly prepared vanilla panna cotta or the honeycomb ice cream.

7 Lesley House, Shaftesbury Sq., Belfast, county Antrim. © 028/9033-1532. www.cayennerestaurant.com. Reservations required. Main courses £10–£18 ($14–$26). AE, DC, MC, V. Mon–Fri noon–2:30pm; Mon–Sat 6–11:15pm.

Restaurant Michael Deane ★★★ FUSION   There are actually two separate establishments at Michael Deane's: the brasserie, where the cooking has been inconsistent in recent times, and the baroque restaurant where the Michelin-star-winning chef himself, Michael Deane, presides over the stove for Friday lunchtimes and dinner from Wednesday to Saturday. This place is more formal than most Irish establishments; to some this is a welcome change, to others, it's off-putting. But come for the food, for there's no arguing that Deane's cooking is modern and sublime, a hip pairing of Asian ingredients with classic French methods. Deane's signature dishes include a carpaccio of salmon with grilled scallops, sticky rice, and cucumber; confit of eggplant with goat's cheese that's melt-in-your-mouth delectable; roasted scallops with a velouté of Jerusalem artichokes; and a filet of beef with lemongrass-infused mashed spuds and (gulp) haggis.

38–40 Howard Place, Belfast, county Antrim. © 028/9033-1134. Reservations required. www.deanes belfast.com. 2-course dinner menu: £29 ($41). Dinner main courses £14–£20 ($20–$28). AE, DC, MC, V. Fri noon–2pm; Wed–Sat 7–9:30pm.

MODERATE

Alden's ★★ FUSION   Alden's is one of the most consistently good, exciting places to eat out in Ireland. Chef Cathy Gradwell's cooking is full of punch and yet thoughtfully restrained, not half-cocked as so many fusion pretenders can be. Start with something suitably complex to put you in the right frame of mind— perhaps the terrific grilled squid with black bean dressing and bok choy. Then follow with something slightly more subtle, such as the pan-fried scallops with noodle salad and chile dressing—one of those dishes you keep returning to each time you visit. Desserts are wonderful, the wine list intelligent, the staff eager to please.

229 Upper Newtownards Rd., Belfast, county Antrim. © 028/9065-0079. Reservations recommended. Dinner main courses £8–£16 ($11–$23). AE, DC, MC, V. Mon–Fri noon–2:30pm; Mon–Sat 6–10pm.

Ginger ★★ MODERN EUROPEAN   There's no denying that this hip, fast-rising restaurant is all about the food: pared-down decor with no menus, no tablecloths, and no hype. There's just a cool soul soundtrack (James Brown and the like) and the wonderful, earthy cooking of Simon McCance. He offers homespun stalwarts like filet of beef with french fries, but he's got a real talent with seafood, so don't miss his wonderful crabmeat salad with mango and just a little mayo, or his hake with roast eggplant and garlicky potatoes. Alas, this establishment has no liquor license, so bring your own bottle of wine.

217 Ormeau Rd., Belfast, county Antrim. © 028/9049-3143. Reservations recommended. Dinner main courses £8–£13 ($11–$18). MC, V. Sat noon–3pm; Tues–Sat 5–9:30pm.

Le Tavole ★★ MEDITERRANEAN   This is a fabulous neighborhood restaurant, the kind you wish was located in your hometown. Johnnie Ritchie delivers a menu of tasty, rustic dishes with the flair that comes with understanding that delicious food starts with the best ingredients. Start with the warm salad of poached salt cod with potatoes and Greek walnut pesto. The seared roast beef is delicious, with manchego cheese, pickled onions, and olives. The lamb is cooked with garlic and comes with mashed potatoes, roasted red pepper, and tomato sauce.

479–481 Lisburn Rd., Belfast, county Antrim. ✆ 028/9066-3211. Reservations recommended. Dinner main courses £7–£13 ($9.95–$18). MC, V. Tues–Sat noon–3:30pm and 6–10pm.

Nick's Warehouse ★★ INTERNATIONAL   In an old warehouse between St. Anne's Cathedral and the tourist office, this extremely popular place offers a worldview of rib-sticking, soulful, hearty food. Nick Price gets his influence from everywhere—you might see Scandinavian dishes on the menu alongside Mediterranean ones—but he is clear-headed enough to be true to each individual dish. There's a wine bar setting downstairs and a classy dining room upstairs, with brick walls and an open kitchen. Appetizers run from gazpacho to curly kale soup to a platter of Italian salami or gravlax (cured Norwegian salmon). Main courses include sirloin steaks, lamb chops with honey and ginger sauce, and filet of salmon with fennel hollandaise.

35 Hill St., Belfast, county Antrim. ✆ **028/9043-9690.** www.nickswarehouse.co.uk. Reservations recommended. Main courses £7–£14 ($9.95–$20). AE, DC, MC, V. Mon–Fri noon–3pm; Tues–Sat 6–9:30pm (drinks until midnight).

INEXPENSIVE

Planet Harveys *Kids* INTERNATIONAL   This is a good, easy place to bring the kids for dinner. An American atmosphere prevails here, with U.S. flag decor and a menu that offers choices such as steaks, burgers, salads, pizza, tacos, pasta, and a signature Frisco Bay platter (prawns, crab claws, scampi, mussels, and crawfish). Other options include beef stroganoff, chicken Kiev, and pork filet stuffed with cheese and smoked bacon.

95 Great Victoria St., Belfast, county Antrim. ✆ **028/9023-3433.** Main courses £5–£8 ($7.10–$11). MC, V. Tues–Thurs and Sun 5–11:30pm; Fri–Sat 5pm–midnight.

BELFAST AFTER DARK
PUBS

Pub hours are generally Monday to Saturday from 11:30am to 11pm, and Sunday from 12:30 to 2:30pm and from 7 to 10pm. Children are not permitted on licensed premises.

Crown Liquor Saloon *Finds*   This is the jewel in Northern Ireland's crown of pubs. Dating from 1826 and situated opposite the Europa Hotel and the Grand Opera House, this gaslit pub has what many architecture buffs believe to be the finest example of Victorian Gothic decor found anywhere. Owned by the National Trust and run by Bass Ireland, the pub boasts stained glass windows, which lend a marvelous baroque-cathedral feel when the sun is out. There's a tin ceiling, a tile floor, etched and smoked glass, a beveled mirror with floral and wildlife decorations, scalloped lamps, and a long bar with inlaid colored glass and marble trim. Of special note is the array of 10 snugs on the right, each guarded by a mythological beast with an armor shield. Inside each room are all the accoutrements any good Victorian could hope for: gunmetal plates for striking matches, little windows to peep discreetly out of, and even an antique system of bells to summon service. Great Victoria St., Belfast, county Antrim. ✆ **028/9024-9476.**

Kelly's Cellars   Belfast's oldest tavern in continuous use, this pub dates from 1720 and has a storied history, including being a headquarters for leaders in the

1798 Insurrection. It's also been a favorite haunt for actors and novelists over the years. The interior certainly shows its age—vaulted ceilings, barred windows covered in cobwebs, little snugs, whitewashed stone archways, and heaps of memorabilia such as old ledgers, coins, china, prints, maps, and international soccer caps. There is often traditional music in the evenings. 32 Bank St. (just off Royal Ave.), Belfast, county Antrim. ℭ **028/9032-4835.**

Pat's Bar   For a taste of Belfast's harbor atmosphere, join the sailors, dockers, and local businesspeople at this pub at the gates of Prince's Dock. You'll see an antique hand-carved beech bar, pinewood furnishings, a red-tile floor, and black-and-white photos of the pub's earliest days. There's an interesting collection of memorabilia given to the bar's owner by sailors passing through the port—clogs, swords, tom-toms and maracas, a telescope, and a bayonet. There's traditional Irish music on Friday and Saturday night at 9pm. 19 Prince's Dock St., Belfast, county Antrim. ℭ **028/9074-4524.**

White's Tavern   Tucked into a historic cobblestone trading lane, this old tavern was established in 1630 as a wine and spirit shop. It's full of old barrels and hoists, ornate snugs, brick arches, large copper measures, framed newspaper clippings of 200-year-old vintage, quill pens, and other memorabilia. It's a good pub for conversation and browsing, and features jazz and traditional music, as well as quiz nights, darts, and theme nights. 2–4 Winecellar Entry (between High and Rosemary sts.), Belfast, county Antrim. ℭ **028/9024-3080.**

THE PERFORMING ARTS

For up-to-date listings of shows and concerts, there are several sources. *That's Entertainment* is free and widely available at tourist offices and pubs, as are *The Big List* and *Artslink*. And there's always the *Belfast Daily Telegraph* and *The Irish News*. Also, both the **www.gotobelfast.com** and the **www.belfast.net** sites have very useful "events" and "nightlife" pages.

The latest, largest venue to appear on the arts scene is the **Belfast Waterfront Hall,** Oxford Street, Laganside (ℭ **028/9033-4455** for credit card reservations, or 028/9033-4400 for program information; www.waterfront.co.uk). The other leading concert and performance halls in Belfast are the **Grand Opera House,** Great Victoria Street (ℭ **028/9024-1919;** www.goh.co.uk), which presents a wide variety of entertainment; **Ulster Hall,** Bedford Street (ℭ **028/9032-3900;** www.ulsterhall.co.uk), which stages major concerts from rock to large-scale choral and symphonic works by the Ulster Orchestra and Northern Ireland Symphony Orchestra; and **Kings Hall Exhibition and Conference Centre,** Balmoral (ℭ **028/9066-5225;** www.kingshall.co.uk), for superstar concerts and other musical events, as well as everything from sheep sales to bridal fairs.

Theaters include the **Belfast Civic Arts Theatre,** 41 Botanic Ave. (ℭ **028/9031-6900**), for popular shows, musicals, and comedies; the **Lyric Theatre,** Ridgeway Street (ℭ **028/9038-1081;** www.lyrictheatre.co.uk), for new plays by Irish and international playwrights; and the **Group Theatre,** part of Ulster Hall on Bedford Street (ℭ **028/9032-9685;** www.ulsterhall.co.uk), for performances by local drama societies.

For stand-up comedy, the Belfast epicenter is in the basement of the **Empire Music Hall,** 42 Botanic (ℭ **028/9032-8110**). It's home every Tuesday at 9pm to *The Empire Laughs Back.* If you'd rather sit down than stand up, get there at least an hour early. Other occasional comedy venues include the **Factory,** 52 Hill St. (ℭ **028/9024-4000**), and the **Old Museum Arts Centre,** College Square North (ℭ **028/9023-5053;** www.oldmuseumartscentre.org).

Tickets, which cost £7 to £30 ($9.95–$43) for most events, can be purchased in advance from the **Virgin Ticket Shop,** Castle Court, Belfast (② **028/ 9032-3744**) or online at **www.ticketmaster.ie.** (You can always arrange to have tickets purchased online delivered to your hotel.)

3 Side Trips from Belfast

CARRICKFERGUS

Carrickfergus is 19km (12 miles) NE of Belfast

It's said that Carrickfergus, county Antrim, was a thriving town when Belfast was a sandbank. In 1180, John de Courcy, a Norman, built a massive keep at Carrickfergus, the first real Irish castle, to guard the approach to Belfast Lough.

Stop into the **Carrickfergus Tourist Information Office,** Heritage Plaza, Antrim Street, Carrickfergus, county Antrim (② **028/9336-6455**). It's open June to September Monday to Friday 9am to 6pm, Saturday 10am to 6pm, Sunday noon to 6pm; October to May weekdays 9am to 5pm.

Andrew Jackson Centre   This simple one-story cottage with earthen floor and open fireplace was the ancestral home of Andrew Jackson, seventh president of the United States. His parents emigrated to the United States in 1765. The house now contains a display on the life and career of Andrew Jackson and Ulster's connections with America. On weekends in July and August, there are craft demonstrations reflecting rural folk life, such as sampler making, basket weaving, griddle making, quilting, and lace making.

Boneybefore, Carrickfergus, county Antrim. ② 028/9336-6455. Admission £1.50 ($2.15) adults, 60p (85¢) seniors and children, £3 ($4.25) family. June–Sept Mon–Fri 10am–1pm, daily 2–6pm; reduced hours in Apr–May and Oct. Closed Nov–Mar.

Carrickfergus Castle ⭐⭐   This remarkably well-preserved and formidable castle, with Ireland's oldest Norman keep, strikes a menacing pose at the strategic entrance to Belfast Lough. The site's guides, audiovisual presentation, and exhibits help visitors imagine and consider the castle's turbulent past. In the summer, medieval banquets, a medieval fair, and a crafts market are held, adding a touch of play and pageantry. Gifts and refreshments are also available.

Marine Highway, Antrim St., Carrickfergus, county Antrim. ② 028/9335-1273. Admission £3 ($4.25) adults, £1.50 ($2.15) seniors and children, £7.50 ($11) family. Combination ticket with Knight Ride £5 ($7.10) adults, £2.50 ($3.55) seniors and children, £13 ($18) family. Apr–Sept Mon–Sat 10am–6pm, Sun 2–6pm; Oct–Mar Mon–Sat 10am–4pm, Sun 2–4pm.

Knight Ride *(Kids*   The Knight Ride is an action-packed monorail theme ride spanning 8 centuries of Carrickfergus history, from sailing ships to haunted houses to historic invasions. This is one way to fill the imaginations of the whole family with pictures of the past before you explore Carrickfergus Castle.

The Heritage Plaza, Antrim St., Carrickfergus, county Antrim. ② 028/9336-6455. Admission £3 ($4.25) adults, £1.50 ($2.15) seniors and children, £7.50 ($11) family. Combination ticket with Carrickfergus Castle £5 ($7.10) adults, £2.50 ($3.55) seniors and children, £13 ($18) family. Apr–Sept Mon–Sat 10am–6pm, Sun noon–6pm; Oct–Mar Mon–Sat 10am–5pm, Sun noon–5pm.

CULTRA

11km (7 miles) E of Belfast

Ulster Folk & Transport Museum ⭐⭐⭐ *(Kids*   This 70-hectare (176-acre) site, which brings together many parts of Ulster's past, is deservedly one of the North's most popular attractions. Twenty-four hectares (60 acres) are devoted to a unique outdoor folk museum featuring a collection of 19th-century buildings, all saved from the bulldozer's path and moved intact from their original sites in various parts of Northern Ireland. You can walk among centuries-old farmhouses, mills, and churches; climb to the terraces of houses; and peruse rural schools, a forge, a bank, a print shop, and more. Actors in period dress reenact tasks of daily life—cooking over an open hearth, plowing the fields with horses, thatching roofs, and practicing traditional Ulster crafts such as textile making, spinning, quilting, lace making, printing, spade making, and shoemaking. The transport museum's collection ranges from donkey carts to De Loreans, and includes an exhibit on the Belfast-built *Titanic*. The exhibit on Irish railways is considered one of the top 10 of its kind in Europe.

153 Bangor Rd. (11km/7 miles northeast of Belfast on the A2), Cultra, Holywood, county Down. © 028/9042-8428, or 028/9042-1444 for 24-hr. information. www.nidex.com/uftm. Day ticket to both museums £4 ($5.70) adults, £2.50 ($3.55) seniors, students, and children, £11 ($16) family. Apr–June and Sept, Mon–Fri 9:30am–5pm, Sat 10:30am–6pm, Sun noon–6pm; July–Aug Mon–Sat 10:30am–6pm, Sun noon–6pm; Oct–Mar Mon–Fri 9:30am–4pm, Sat–Sun 12:30–4:30pm.

THE ARDS PENINSULA

The Ards Peninsula, beginning about 16km (10 miles) east of Belfast, curls around the western shore of **Strangford Lough** ✿, and at 29km (18 miles) long is one of the largest sea inlets in the British Isles. A place of great natural beauty, the peninsula boasts a wonderful bird sanctuary and wildlife reserve, and its shores are home to many species of marine life. Two roads traverse the peninsula: A20 (the Lough road) and A2 (the coast road). The Lough road is the more scenic.

At the southern tip of the Lough, continuous car ferry service connects Portaferry with the Strangford Ferry Terminal (© **028/4488-1637**), in Strangford, on the mainland side. It runs every half hour, weekdays 7:30am to 10:30pm, Saturday 8am to 11pm, Sunday 9:30am to 10:30pm. No reservations are needed. A one-way trip takes 5 minutes and costs £4.80 ($6.80) for a car and driver, £1 ($1.40) for each additional passenger.

The **Portaferry Tourist Information Office,** Shore Street, near the Strangford ferry departure point (© **028/4272-9882**), is open Monday to Saturday 9am to 5pm, Sunday 2 to 6pm. There are two National Trust properties in this area, one on the Ards Peninsula and the other just across the lough at Portaferry. For a wealth of excellent information about where to stay, eat, and play on the peninsula, visit the region's website at **www.kingdomsofdown.com**.

Castle Espie ✿ *Kids*   This marvelous center, owned and managed by the Wildlife and Wetlands Trust, is home to a virtual U.N. of geese, ducks, and swans, many of which are extraordinarily rare. Many are so accustomed to visitors that they will eat grain from your hand. Children can have the disarming experience of meeting Hooper swans eye-to-eye. Guided trails are specially designed for children and families, and the center sponsors a host of activities and events throughout the year. The reserve is also, in the words of center manager James Orr, a "honey pot" for serious bird-watchers in search of waterfowl. Up to 3,000 pale-bellied brent can be seen in early winter. The center's book and gift shop is enticing for naturalists of all ages, and the restaurant serves deliciously diverting lunches and home-baked sweets.

78 Ballydrain Rd., Comber, county Down. © 028/9187-4146. Admission £3.50 ($4.95) adults, £2.50 ($3.55) seniors and students, £2 ($2.85) children, £8.50 ($12.05) family. Mar–Oct Mon–Sat 10:30am–5pm, Sun 11:30am–6pm; Nov–Feb Mon–Sat 11:30am–4pm, Sun 11:30am–5pm. 21km (13 miles) SE of Belfast, sign-posted from the A22 Comber-Killyleagh-Downpatrick rd.

Castle Ward ✿   Situated 2.4km (1½ miles) west of Strangford village, this National Trust house dates from 1760 and is half classical and half Gothic in architectural style. It sits on a 280-hectare (700-acre) country estate of formal gardens, woodlands, lakelands, and seashore. A restored 1830s corn mill and a Victorian-style laundry are on the grounds, and the theater in the stable yard is a venue for operatic performances in summer.

Strangford, county Down. © **028/4488-1204.** www.nationaltrust.org.uk. House admission £4.50 ($6.40) adults, £1.75 ($2.50) children, £9.50 ($13) family; estate admission £3 ($4.25) per car. House Apr–May and Sept–Oct Sat–Sun 1–6pm; June–Aug Fri–Wed 1–6pm. Castle tour at 5pm; estate open year-round dawn–dusk.

Exploris *Kids*   Northern Ireland's aquarium concentrates on the rich diversity of life found in Strangford Lough and the nearby Irish Sea. Displays include models of the saltwater environment found beneath the surface of Strangford Lough, as well as examples of thousands of species of local and regional sea life. The newest addition is the seal sanctuary, a guaranteed crowd pleaser. The aquarium complex contains a cafe and gift shop, a park, a picnic area, a children's playground, a bowling green, tennis courts, and woodlands.

Castle St., Portaferry, county Down. © **028/4272-8062.** Admission £5.40 ($7.65) adults, £3.20 ($4.55) children, £15 ($21) family. Apr–Aug Mon–Fri 10am–6pm, Sat 11am–6pm, Sun 1–6pm; Sept–Mar Mon–Fri 10am–5pm, Sat 11am–5pm, Sun 1–5pm.

Giant's Ring   This massive prehistoric earthwork, 180m (600 ft.) in diameter, has more or less at its center a megalithic chamber with a single capstone. It was doubtlessly a significant focus of local cults as long as 5,000 years ago. Today this 2.8-hectare (7-acre) ritual enclosure is a place of wonder for the few who visit; the site is largely neglected by tourists.

Ballynahatty, county Down. 8km (5 miles) SW of Belfast center, west off A24; or 1.6km (1 mile) S of Shaw's Bridge, off B23.

Grey Abbey *★★*   The impressive ruins of Grey Abbey enjoy a beautifully landscaped setting, perfect for a picnic or just some quiet reflection. It was founded in 1193 for the Cistercians and contained one of the earliest Gothic churches in Ireland. True to Cistercian simplicity, there was and is very little embellishment here, but the Cistercians, like the Shakers, knew well that restraint is no impediment to beauty. All the same, amid the bare ruined choirs, there is a fragmented stone effigy of a knight in armor, possibly a likeness of John de Courcy, husband of the abbey's founder, Affrica of Cumbria. There's also a small visitor center.

Greyabbey, county Down. Admission £1 ($1.40) adults, 50p (70¢) children. Apr–Sept Tues–Sat 10am–7pm, Sun 2–7pm. Closed Oct–Mar. On the east side of Greyabbey, 3.2km (2 miles) southeast of Mt. Stewart.

Legananny Dolmen *★★*   This renowned, impressive granite dolmen (Neolithic tomb) on the southern slope of Slieve Croob looks, in the words of archaeologist Peter Harbison, like "a coffin on stilts." This is one of the most photographed dolmens in Ireland, but you have to see it up close to admire it fully. The massive capstone seems almost weightlessly poised on its three supporting uprights.

Slieve Croob, county Down. Take A24 from Belfast to Ballynahinch, B7 to Dromara, then ask directions.

Mount Stewart House *★★★*   Once the home of Lord Castlereagh, this 18th-century house sits on the eastern shore of Strangford Lough. It has one of the greatest gardens in the care of the National Trust, with an unrivaled collection of rare and unusual plants. The house is noteworthy for its artwork, including *Hambletonian* by George Stubbs, one of the finest paintings in Ireland, and family portraits by Batoni, Mengs, and Lazlo. The Temple of the Winds, a banqueting house built in 1785, is also on the estate. In 1999, the gardens of Mount Stewart was one of 32 sites in the United Kingdom nominated as a potential World Heritage Site. Final selection (which can take years) would place it in the company of such sites as the Taj Mahal and the Great Wall of China.

On the east shore of Strangford Lough, southeast of Newtownards, 24km (15 miles) southeast of Belfast, on A20, Newtownards, county Down. (© 028/4278-8387. www.nationaltrust.org.uk. House, garden, and temple admission £4.75 ($6.75) adults, £2.25 ($3.20) children, £9.75 ($13.85) family. House Apr and Oct Sat–Sun 1–6pm; May–Sept Mon and Wed–Sun 1–6pm. Garden mid-Mar Sun 11am–6pm; Apr–Sept daily 11am–6pm; Oct Sat–Sun 11am–6pm. Temple Apr–Oct Sat–Sun 2–5pm. Bus: 9, 9A, or 10 from Laganside Bus Centre (Mon–Sat).

SPORTS & OUTDOOR PURSUITS

BICYCLING   If you want to explore the area on your own two wheels, you can rent bicycles at the **Strangford Arms Hotel,** 92 Church St., Newtownards (© **028/9181-4141**), for roughly £10 ($14) a day. Cycle rental by the day or week, and delivery in the North Down/Ards area, are available from **Gary Harkness Cycle Hire,** 53 Frances St., Newtownards (© **028/9181-1311**). If you want some guidance and companionship, contact Tony Boyd at **The Emerald Trail Bicycle Tours,** 15 Ballyknocken Rd., Saintfield (© **028/9081-3200;** www.emeraldtrail.com).

DIVING   The nearby loughs and offshore waters are a diver's dream—remarkably clear and littered with wrecks. To charter a diving expedition in Strangford Lough, contact **Des Rogers** (© **028/4272-8297**). **Norsemaid Sea Enterprises,** 152 Portaferry Rd., Newtownards, county Down (© **028/9181-2081**), caters 4- to 10-day diving parties along the Northern Irish coast, in Belfast Lough and Strangford Lough, amid the St. Kilda Isles and along the coast of Scotland. One of Europe's finest training centers, **DV Diving,** 138 Mountstewart Rd., Newtownards, county Down (© **028/9146-4671;** www.dvdiving.co.uk), offers a wide range of diving courses.

FISHING   For info, tackle, and bait, try the **Village Tackle Shop,** 55a Newtownbreda Rd., Belfast (© **028/9049-1916**), or **H.W. Kelly,** 54 Market St., Downpatrick, county Down (© **028/4461-2193**). Sea-fishing trips from Portaferry into the waters of Strangford Lough and along the county Down coast are organized by Peter Wright, **Norsemaid Sea Enterprises,** 152 Portaferry Rd., Newtownards, county Down (© **028/9181-2081**). Reservations are required. This company also offers diving charters, day cruises, hill walking, and wildlife cruises. To outfit yourself and fish for rainbow trout year-round, visit **Ballygrangee Fly Fishery,** Mountstewart Road, Carrowdore, county Down (© **028/ 4278-8883**).

GOLF   There are several well-established courses a short drive from Belfast in north county Down. They include the **Bangor Golf Club,** Broadway, Bangor (© **028/9127-0922**), with greens fees of £20 ($28) weekdays, £25 ($36) weekends; **Downpatrick Golf Club,** 43 Saul Rd., Downpatrick (© **028/4461-5947;** www.downpatrickgolfclub.com), with greens fees of £18 ($26) weekdays, £23 ($33) weekends; and the 71-par **Scrabo Golf Club,** 233 Scrabo Rd., Newtownards (© **028/9181-2355;** www.scrabo-golf-club.org), with greens fees of £18 ($26) weekdays, £23 ($33) weekends.

WHERE TO STAY IN THE AREA
Moderate

Portaferry Hotel 🌟🌟   Set in a designated conservation area and incorporating a terrace dating from the mid–18th century, the Portaferry Hotel retains the charm of a seasoned waterside inn while offering all the amenities of a modern hotel. Guest rooms are in keeping with the hotel's traditional character, with dark woods and floral fabrics, which lend a slightly feminine feel. Many have excellent views of the lough.

The Strand, Portaferry (47km/29 miles from Belfast), county Down. ☎ **028/4272-8231.** Fax 028/4272-8999. www.portaferryhotel.com. 14 units. £95 ($135) double. Rates include full breakfast. AE, DC, MC, V. **Amenities:** Restaurant (seafood); bar; nonsmoking rooms. In room: TV, radio, hair dryer.

Inexpensive

Ballycastle House 🌟   Mrs. Margaret Deering's home is a beautiful 300-year-old farmhouse that has been elegantly refurbished. The guest rooms are nicely appointed with pretty floral bedspreads and dark woods, and offer restful rural views. A two-bedroom self-catering cottage is also available for £300 ($426) per week.

20 Mountstewart Rd. (8km5 miles southeast of town on A20), Newtownards, county Down. ☎ and fax **028/4278-8357.** 3 units. £45 ($64) double. Children's and senior discounts available. Rates include full breakfast. No credit cards. **Amenities:** Laundry facilities; nonsmoking rooms; sitting room. In room: Tea/coffeemaker, hair dryer.

The Cottage 🌟 *Value*   Your enchantment with The Cottage is likely to begin as you pull up in the driveway and get a full view of a lovely lawn and colorful flower beds. Mrs. Elizabeth Muldoon has realized every cottage lover's dream—she has lovingly retained the original charm of the house and installed modern conveniences. The living room is picture-pretty, as is the rustic dining area. Guest rooms are beautifully furnished, with many antiques scattered about. The Cottage is one of the most inviting budget accommodations in the area.

377 Comber Rd. (4.8km/3 miles east of Belfast on A20), Dundonald, county Down. ☎ **028/9187-8189.** 2 units. £45 ($64) double. Children's discount available. Rates include full breakfast. No credit cards. **Amenities:** Conservatory; sitting area.

Greenlea Farm   Greenlea, a comfortable old farmhouse, looks out from its hilltop to the Ards Peninsula and across to the coast of Scotland and the Isle of Man. The warm, friendly hostess, Mrs. Evelyn McIvor, teaches crafts and enjoys sharing her considerable knowledge of the area with guests. The lounge and dining room have picture windows that frame the spectacular view, and the dining room holds lovely antique pieces, with lots of silver and crystal. Mrs. McIvor has one large family room with bunk beds for two children and a double for parents, as well as accommodations for singles and doubles. Greenlea Farm is about 37km (23 miles) southeast of Belfast on A2, at the top of the Ards Peninsula. The biggest drawback here is that none of the guest rooms has a private bathroom.

48 Dunover Rd. (off A2), .8km/½ mile north of Ballywalter, county Down. ☎ and fax **028/4275-8218.** 5 units, none with bathroom. £40 ($57) double. 50% discount for children under 12 (under 5 free). 10% senior discount. Rates include full breakfast. No credit cards. **Amenities:** Sitting room. In room: TV.

WHERE TO DINE IN THE AREA
Moderate/Expensive

The Narrows 🌟🌟🌟 *Finds* MEDITERRANEAN   If you'd travel anywhere to discover a good restaurant, then set your compass for the sleepy little waterside hamlet of Portaferry. Here, Danny Millar demonstrates why he's one of the most gifted, exciting, passionate young chefs on this island, enough to inspire *Food & Wine* magazine to have once gushed, "If your dream meal lies somewhere between the little quayside bistro you frequented last summer in Brittany and the exalted heights of Michelin-starred precision cooking then look no further than the Narrows in the picturesque village of Portaferry." Here is a chef who adores all the keynote Mediterranean flavors and peppers his menu with items like tapenade (a black olive paste), aioli (garlicky mayonnaise), red peppers, pesto, sun-dried tomatoes, and goat's cheese. This is complex cooking, but with tastes that are nevertheless grounded, earthy, and sensuous—think roast pheasant served with truffle aioli with wild mushroom and fennel risotto; seared fois gras with peach chutney and hazelnut brioche; monkfish saltimbocca with red pepper, creamed penne, and Parma ham. After dinner here, it's heavenly to amble upstairs to one of the chic, white-on-beige guest rooms, priced at £90 ($128) for a double.

8 Shore Rd., Portaferry, county Down. ⓒ **028/4272-8148.** www.narrows.co.uk. Dinner main courses £10–£17 ($14–$24). AE, MC. V. Daily 11am–11:30pm.

Moderate

Primrose Bar and Restaurant PUB GRUB   The Primrose—an erstwhile blacksmith shop—is known locally for its steak casseroles, open-faced prawn sandwiches, and fresh-baked bread. Other offerings include chicken dishes, pizza, and a variety of salads. There's always a nice fire blazing, and local opinion concurs that "the craic is always good" (meaning there's always a good time to be had). The adjacent Primrose Pop-In tearoom serves up good quiches and pies Monday to Saturday 9am to 4:30pm.

30 Main St., Ballynahinch, county Down. ⓒ **028/9756-3177**. Dinner main courses £6–£12 ($8.50–$17). AE, MC. V. Daily 11am–11:30pm.

DOWNPATRICK

37km (23 miles) SE of Belfast

Downpatrick, one of the North's oldest cities, is closely identified with St. Patrick. Legend tells us that when Patrick came to Ireland in 432 to begin his missionary work, strong winds blew his boat into this area. He had meant to sail up the coast to county Antrim, where as a young slave he had tended flocks on Slemish Mountain. Instead, he settled here and converted the local chieftain Dichu and his followers to Christianity. Over the next 30 years, Patrick roamed to many other places in Ireland, carrying out his work, but this is where he died. He is said to be buried in the graveyard of Downpatrick Cathedral. A large stone claims to mark the spot.

For information in the Down District, stop into the **Downpatrick Tourist Information Centre,** 74 Market St., Downpatrick, county Down (ⓒ **028/ 4461-2233**). It's open October to mid-June Monday to Friday 9am to 5pm, Saturday 9am to 1pm and 2 to 5pm; mid-June to September Monday to Saturday 9am to 6pm and Sunday 2 to 6pm. A "St. Patrick's Country" coach tour is offered according to demand and can be booked through this office.

Down Cathedral 👉   As its name suggests, Downpatrick was once a *dún* (fort), perhaps as early as the Bronze Age. Eventually, here on the Hill of Down, ancient fortifications gave way to a line of churches, which have superseded each other for 1,800 years, like a stack of Russian nesting dolls. Today's cathedral represents an 18th- and 19th-century reconstruction of its 13th- and 16th-century predecessors. Just south of the cathedral stands a relatively recent monolith inscribed with the name *Patric.* By some accounts, it roughly marks the grave of the saint, who is said to have died at Saul, 3.2km (2 miles) northeast. The tradition identifying this site as Patrick's grave seems to go back no further than the 12th century, when John de Courcy reputedly transferred the bones of saints Bridgit and Columbanus here to lie beside those of St. Patrick.

The Mall, Downpatrick, county Down. ℂ 028/4461-4922. Mon–Fri 9:30am–5pm; Sat–Sun 2–5pm.

St. Patrick Heritage Centre/Down County Museum ⚑ Next to the cathedral and sharing an extensive 18th-century jail complex, the St. Patrick Centre and the County Museum provide some intriguing glimpses into the rich history of this area. You'll also be introduced to some of the county's more notorious figures, from St. Patrick to a handful of prisoners sent off to Australia in the 19th century.

The Mall, Downpatrick, county Down. ℂ 028/4461-5218. Free admission, except for some special events. June–Aug Mon–Fri 10am–5pm, Sat–Sun 2–5pm; Sept–May Tues–Fri 10am–5pm, Sat 2–5pm.

WHERE TO DINE
Down Arts Centre Café CAFETERIA   You won't have any difficulty finding this place. Look for the clock tower atop a Victorian red-brick building in the very center of Downpatrick, and enter below. Its soups, salads, sandwiches, and pastries provide a satisfying snack or lunch break on your day's outing from Belfast.

Irish St., Downpatrick, county Down. ℂ 028/4461-5283. All items £2–£9 ($2.85–$13) Mon–Wed and Fri–Sat 9am–5pm; Thurs 9am–9pm.

LISBURN
16km (10 miles) SE of Belfast

Irish Linen Centre and Lisburn Museum   The focus of this center and museum is the linen industry, long synonymous with Northern Ireland. Through the re-creation of factory scenes and multimedia presentations, visitors can trace the history of Irish linen production, from its earliest days in the 17th century to the high-tech industry of today. There are opportunities to see linen in all stages of production, and to watch skilled weavers at work on restored 19th-century looms in the workshop. There are also a cafe and a research library. If you're a big fan of linen and want to give over a whole day to its consideration, you can book a place in an **Irish Linen Tour** by calling the Banbridge Gateway Tourist Information Centre (ℂ **028/4062-3322**). From May to September, there are tours every Wednesday and Saturday.

Market Sq., Lisburn, county Antrim. ℂ 028/9266-3377. Free admission. Mon–Sat 9:30am–5pm.

LOUGH NEAGH
16km (10 miles) W of Belfast

Lough Neagh, at 396 sq. km (153 sq. miles), is the largest lake in the British Isles. Often called an inland sea, the lough is 32km (20 miles) long and 16km (10 miles) wide, with a 105km (65-mile) shore. It's said that Lough Neagh was created by the mighty, Fionn MacCumhail (anglicized to Finn McCool) when he flung a sod into the sea to create the Isle of Man. But before you think about taking a dip, consider this: The lake's claim to fame is its eels. Yep, the waters are positively infested with the slimy things. Hundreds of tons of eels are taken from Lough Neagh and exported each year, mainly to Germany and Holland. This extraction has been going on since the Bronze Age, and shows no sign of letting up. The age-old method involves the use of a "long line," baited with up to 100 hooks. There are often as many as 200 boats trailing a few of these lines each on the lake each night (the best time to go fishing for eels), with a nightly catch of up to 10 tons of eels.

If you're not entirely creeped out by that, you can take a **boat trip** on Lough Neagh, departing regularly from the nearby **Kinnego Marina** (© **0374/ 811248** mobile), signposted from the main road. They last about 45 minutes and cost £5 ($7.10) for adults, £3 ($4.25) for children.

Lough Neagh Discovery Centre ⊛ Midway between Belfast and Armagh city, this center is on the southern shore of Lough Neagh at Oxford Island, a 108-hectare (270-acre) nature reserve with a range of habitats such as reed beds, woodlands, and wildflower meadows. The center provides an excellent introduction to all that the lough has to offer. It contains historical and geographic exhibits, an interactive lab explaining the ecosystems of the lough, walking trails, bird-watching observation points, and picnic areas. For a closer look at everything in sight, the center has binoculars for hire.

Oxford Island, Craigavon, county Armagh. © **028/3832-2205.** Admission £3 ($4.95) adults, £2.30 ($3.80) seniors, £1.80 ($2.95) children, £6.70 ($11.05) family. Apr–Sept daily 10am–7pm; Oct–Mar Wed–Sun 10am–5pm.

ARMAGH
65km (40 miles) SW of Belfast

One of Ireland's most historic cities, Armagh takes its name from the Irish *Ard Macha,* or Macha's Height. The legendary pagan queen Macha is said to have built a fortress here in the middle of the first millennium B.C. Most of Armagh's history, however, focuses on the 5th century, when St. Patrick chose this place as a base from which to spread Christianity; he called it "my sweet hill" and built a stone church here. Ever since, Armagh has been considered the ecclesiastical capital of Ireland. Today there are two St. Patrick's cathedrals, one Catholic and one Anglican. Each is the seat of the primate of its denomination.

Many of the public buildings and the Georgian town houses along the Mall are the work of Francis Johnston, a native of Armagh, who also left his mark on Georgian Dublin. Buildings, doorsteps, and pavements are made of warm-colored pink, yellow, and red local limestone that make the city glow even on a dull day. In addition to being Ireland's spiritual capital, this area is known for its apple trees, earning Armagh the title "the Orchard of Ireland."

Stop into the **Armagh Tourist Information Office,** the Old Bank Building, 40 English St., Armagh (© **028/3752-1800**). It's open April to September, Monday to Saturday 9am to 5pm, Sunday 1 to 5:30pm; October to March, Monday to Saturday 9am to 5pm, Sunday 2 to 5pm. For a host of tourist information on county Armagh, take a look at **www.armagh-visit.com**.

Armagh Astronomy Centre and Planetarium ⊛ (Kids) On your way up College Hill from the Mall, you'll pass the 200-year-old Armagh Observatory, still in service but closed to the public. Farther up the hill stands the Astronomy Centre and Planetarium complex, whose Astropark, Lindsay Hall of Astronomy, Eartharium Gallery, and Star Theatre planetarium offer an engaging array of exhibits and shows, with lots of hands-on learning for the whole family. *Note:* The Star Theatre is currently closed for renovations, but shows and demonstrations will take place in the Lindsay Hall of Astronomy in the meantime.

College Hill, Armagh, county Armagh. © **028/3752-3689.** www.armagh-planetarium.co.uk. Admission to show and exhibition area £3 ($4.25) adults, £2 ($2.85) seniors and children, £9 ($13) family. Mon–Fri 10am–4:45pm; Sat 1:15–4:45pm.

Armagh County Museum ⊛ Housed in what appears to be a miniature Greek temple, this is the oldest county museum in Ireland. Its rather extensive collection, documenting local life across the millennia, ranges from prehistoric ax heads to wedding dresses. In addition to natural history specimens and folklore items, the museum has an extensive art collection, which includes works by George Russell and John Luke. There is also a rotating exhibition. The museum's maps, photographs, and research library can also be consulted.

The Mall East, Armagh, county Armagh. ✆ **028/3752-3070.** Free admission. Mon–Fri 10am–5pm; Sat 10am–1pm and 2–5pm.

Benburb Valley Park, Castle, and Heritage Centre ⟨★★⟩

Begin in the town and explore the dramatic banks of the River Blackwater, a favorite for canoeists and anglers. The park follows the river and brings you to a tree-lined gorge with a partially restored 17th-century castle perched on a cliff high overhead. Another half mile brings you to the Benburb Valley Heritage Centre, a restored linen mill, and the Benburb Castle site, within the grounds of a Servite monastery.

89 Milltown Rd., Benburb, county Armagh. ✆ **01861/548170** or 028/3754-8170. Park: Free admission. Daily until dusk. Castle and heritage center: Admission £2 ($2.85). Apr–Sept Mon–Sat 10am–5pm. 11km (7 miles) northwest of Armagh; take B128 off A29.

Navan Fort ⟨★★⟩

Navan Fort (in Irish, *Emain Macha*) was, in pre-Christian Ireland, a seat of power and a site of ritual. It was the royal and religious capital of Ulster. As at Tara, very little remains—only mounds, mute and unimpressive until their remarkable stories are told. Thankfully, the adjacent interpretive center does just this, quite strikingly. The Navan Centre is an artificial mound, barely visible until you're upon it. Inside, the magic begins. Through a series of exhibits and two multimedia presentations, the history and prehistory of Emain Macha, its mysteries and legends, unfold. A book and gift shop and cafe are also on hand. The center is also the focus of educational and artistic programs and events year-round.

The Navan Centre, 81 Killylea Rd., Armagh, county Armagh. ✆ **028/3752-5550.** Fax 028/3752-2323. Admission £4.50 ($6.40) adults, £3 ($4.25) students and seniors, £2.50 ($3.55) children, £7–£10 ($9.95–$14) family. Year-round Mon–Sat 10am–5pm; Sun 11am–5pm. 3.2km (2 miles) from Armagh on A28, signposted from Armagh center.

Peatlands Park ⟨★⟩

Once a part of the Churchill Estate, Peatlands Park consists of more than 240 hectares (600 acres) of peat faces and small lakes in the southwest corner of the Lough Neagh basin, designated as a Natural Nature Reserve. To preserve the park's protected fauna and flora, you're asked to stay on the system of marked walking paths or to take a ride on a narrow-gauge railway. Nature walks and events are offered through the year.

33 Derryhubbert Rd. (11km/7 miles southeast of Dungannon, at exit 13 off M1), The Birches, county Armagh. ✆ **028/3885-1102.** Free admission to park. Rail ride £1 ($1.40) adults, 50p (70¢) children. Vehicle access to park daily 9am–dusk. Railway June–Aug 2–6pm.

St. Patrick's Trian Visitor Complex ⟨★⟩

Housed in the old Second Presbyterian Church in the heart of Armagh, this modern visitor complex provides an informative and engaging introduction to Armagh, the "motherhouse" of Irish Christianity. Its dramatic presentations, including the *Armagh Story* and *The Land of Lilliput* (complete with a giant Gulliver beset by Lilliputians), are entertaining for the whole family. This is a good first stop to get your bearings in local history and culture. There are a craft courtyard and a cafe, as well as a visitor genealogical service, if you have local roots.

40 English St. (off Friary Rd, a 10-min. walk from town), Armagh, county Armagh. ✆ **028/3752-1801.** Admission (includes 3 multimedia exhibitions) £4 ($5.70) adults, £3 ($4.25) seniors and students, £2 ($2.85) children, £10 ($14) family. July–Aug Mon–Sat 10am–5:30pm, Sun 1–6pm; Sept–June Mon–Sat 10am–5pm, Sun 2–5pm.

4 The Causeway Coast & the Glens of Antrim

106km (66 miles) from Larne to Portstewart on the coastal A2; Larne is 40km (25 miles) from Belfast

Over 9,000 years ago, the first visitors to Ireland made landfall on the Causeway Coast. It was accessible, attractive, and there—all that was needed then, or now, to invite the curious to these spectacular shores. Steeped in myth and legend, pounded by its own history, and graced with true grandeur, the North Antrim Coast is one of the most dramatic coastlines in Ireland.

Heralded in story and song, the Glens of Antrim consist of nine green valleys, sitting north of Belfast and stretching from south to north. The glens have individual names, each based on a local tale or legend. Although the meanings are not known for certain, the popular translations are as follows: Glenarm (glen of the army), Glencloy (glen of the hedges), Glenariff (ploughman's glen), Glenballyeamon (Edwardstown glen), Glenaan (glen of the rush lights), Glencorp (glen of the slaughter), Glendun (brown glen), Glenshesk (sedgy glen), and Glentaisie (Taisie's glen).

Many residents of the Glens of Antrim are descendants of the ancient Irish and the Hebridean Scots, so this area is one of the last strongholds in Northern Ireland of the Gaelic tongue. To this day, the glen people are known to be great storytellers.

Two of Ireland's foremost attractions are also here: the **Giant's Causeway** and **Old Bushmills Distillery.** For bird-watchers, the coastal moors and cliffs and the offshore nature reserve on **Rathlin Island** are prime destinations. There are plenty of opportunities for exploring and outdoor adventuring. Each August, the seaside town of **Ballycastle** plays host to one of Ireland's oldest traditional gatherings, the Oul' Lammas Fair.

VISITOR INFORMATION The principal **tourist information centers** in North Antrim are at Narrow Guarge Road, **Larne** (© 028/2826-0088); Sheskburn House, 7 Mary St., **Ballycastle** (© 028/2076-2024); 44 Causeway Rd., **Bushmills** (© 028/2073-1855); and Dunluce Centre, Sandhill Drive, **Portrush** (© 028/7082-3333). All but the Dunluce Centre are open year-round; hours vary seasonally. Summer hours, at the minimum, are Monday to Friday 10am to 5pm, Saturday 10am to 4pm, Sunday 2 to 6pm.

EXPLORING THE COAST

The area identified as the Antrim coast is 97km (60 miles) long, stretching north of **Larne** and west past Bushmills and the Giant's Causeway to **Portrush.** The route takes in marine seascapes and white, chalky cliffs. It includes the National Trust village of **Cushendun** 𝕬𝕬, rife with pretty Cornish-style cottages, as well as a string of old-style beach resorts, such as **Portrush, Portstewart,** and **Portballintrae.** This coastal drive also meanders under bridges and arches, passing bays, sandy beaches, harbors, and huge rock formations.

Carrick-A-Rede Rope Bridge 𝕬𝕬𝕬 *(Moments* Eight kilometers (5 miles) west of Ballycastle off the A2 road, this open rope bridge spans a chasm 18m (60 ft.) wide and 24m (80 ft.) above the sea between the mainland and a small island. Local fishermen put up the bridge each spring to allow access to the island's salmon fishery, but visitors can use it for a thrilling walk and the chance to call out to each other, "Don't look down!" (This is excellent advice.) If you are acrophobic, stay clear; if you don't know whether you are, this is not the place to find out. *Note:* The 19km (12-mile) coastal cliff path from the Giant's Causeway to the rope bridge is always open and is well worth the exhaustion.

Larrybane, county Antrim. ✆ **028/2073-1159.** Free admission. Bridge, center, and tearoom Apr–June and early Sept daily 10am–6pm; July–Aug 10am–8pm. Parking £2 ($2.85).

Dunluce Castle ★★   This site was once the main fort of the Irish MacDonnells, chiefs of Antrim. It's the largest and most sophisticated castle in the North, consisting of a series of fortifications built on rocky outcrops extending into the sea, and was the power base of the north coast for 400 years. In 1639, part of the castle fell into the sea, taking some of the servants with it. The castle ruins incorporate two of the original Norman towers dating from 1305. The visitor center shows an audiovisual presentation with background on the site.

87 Dunluce Rd. (5.6km/3½ miles east of Portrush off A2), Bushmills, county Antrim. ✆ **028/2073-1938.** www.northantrim.com/dunlucecastle.htm. Admission £1.50 ($2.15) adults, 75p ($1.05) seniors and children under 16. Apr–May and Sept Tues–Sat 10am–6pm, Sun 2–6pm; June–Aug Mon–Sat 10am–7pm, Sun noon–6pm; Oct–Mar Tues–Sat 10am–4pm, Sun 2–6pm. Last admission 30 min. before closing.

Dunluce Centre ★ *Kids*   This family-oriented entertainment complex provides a variety of indoor activities. It offers a multimedia show, *Myths & Legends,* that illustrates the folklore of the Antrim coast, as well as "Turbo Tours," a thrill ride that simulates a space ride, and "Earthquest," an interactive display on the wonders of nature. There's also a viewing tower with panoramic views of the coast and a Victorian-style arcade of shops, and a restaurant with a children's play area.

Dunluce Rd., Bushmills, Country Antrim. ✆ **028/7082-3333.**

Giant's Causeway ★★★   A World Heritage Site, this natural rock formation is often called the eighth wonder of the world. It consists of roughly 40,000 tightly packed basalt columns that extend for 4.8km (3 miles) along the coast. The tops of the columns form stepping stones that lead from the cliff foot and disappear under the sea. They're mostly hexagonal, and some are as tall as 12m (40 ft.). Scientists estimate that they were formed 60 or 70 million years ago by volcanic eruptions and cooling lava. The ancients, on the other hand, believed the rock formation to be the work of giants. Another legend has it that Finn MacCool, the Ulster warrior and commander of the king of Ulster's armies, built the causeway as a highway over the sea to bring his girlfriend from the Isle of Hebrides. To reach the causeway, follow the walk from the parking area past amphitheaters of stone columns and formations with fanciful names like Honeycomb, Wishing Well, Giant's Granny, King and his Nobles, and Lover's Leap, and up a wooden staircase to Benbane Head and back along the cliff top. ***Note:*** In spring 2000, the new Giant's Causeway Visitors Centre tragically burned to the ground. There is currently a well-outfitted temporary center in place, and a new, permanent center is expected to open in spring 2003.

Causeway Rd., Bushmills, county Antrim. ✆ **028/2073-1159.** www.giantscausewayofficialguide.com. Mon–Sat 9:30am–6pm; Sun 10am–5pm.

Old Bushmills Distillery ★★   Licensed to distill spirits in 1608, but with historical references dating from as far back as 1276, this is the oldest distillery in the world. Visitors are welcome to tour the facility and watch the whiskey-making process, starting with fresh water from the adjacent River Bush and continuing through distilling, fermenting, and bottling. At the end of the tour, you can sample the wares in the Poststill Bar, where there are fascinating exhibits on the long history of the distillery. Tours last about 25 minutes. The Bushmills coffee shop serves tea, coffee, homemade snacks, and lunches.

Main St., Bushmills, county Antrim. ✆ **028/2073-1521.** www.bushmills.com. Admission £3.50 ($4.95) adults, £3 ($4.25) seniors and students, £1.50 ($2.15) children, £9 ($13) family. Apr–Oct tours offered fre-

Moments　Going to the Birds: A Trip to Rathlin Island

Looking for peace and solitude? Plan a trip to **Rathlin Island** ✶✶, 9.7km (6 miles) off the coast north of Ballycastle and 23km (14 miles) south of Scotland. It is almost 6.5km (4 miles) long, but less than 1.6km (1 mile) wide at any point. Rathlin Island is almost completely treeless, with a rugged coast of 60m-high (200-ft.) cliffs, a small beach, and a native population of 100. Don't worry—there is also a pub, a restaurant, and a guesthouse, in case you get stranded. This is a mecca for bird-watchers, especially in spring and early to midsummer. Free admission to the **Rathlin Island RSPB Seabird Viewpoint** is available by appointment April through August.

Boat trips operate daily from Ballycastle pier; crossing time is 50 minutes. The one-way fare is £4.20 ($5.95) for adults, and £3.20 ($4.55) for seniors, students, and children. The number and schedule of crossings vary from season to season and from year to year, and are always subject to weather, but there are usually several crossings a day. It's best to confirm departures by phoning the **Caledonian MacBrayne** ticket office (© 028/2076-9299; www.calmac.co.uk) well in advance.

On the island, a minibus (summer only) will take you from Church Bay to the West Light Platform and the Kebble Nature Reserve for roughly £3 ($4.25) adults, £2 ($2.85) children, round-trip. There are also minibus tours offered by **McCurdy's Minibus Tours** (© 028/2076-3909) or **Irene's Minibus Tours** (© 028/2076-3949). Bicycles can be rented from **Soerneog View Hostel** (© 028/2076-3954).

For more information on the island and its offerings, call © 028/2076-3948 or surf over to **www.island-trail.com**.

quently throughout the day Mon–Sat 9am–5pm, Sun noon–5pm (last tour leaves 4pm); Nov–Mar tours offered Mon–Sat at 10:30am, 11:30am, noon, 1:30, 2:30, and 3:30pm, Sun at 1:30, 2:30, and 3:30pm.

A SHOPPING STOP

The Steensons　This is the workshop-showroom of Bill and Christina Steenson, two of the most celebrated goldsmiths in Ireland. On display and for sale is a small, impressive selection of their pieces, as well as a sampling of the work of other distinguished Irish goldsmiths and silversmiths with a similar contemporary eye. Toberwine St., Glenarm, county Antrim. © and fax **028/2884-1445**.

SPORTS & OUTDOOR PURSUITS

ADVENTURE SPORTS　The **Ardclinis Activity Centre,** High Street, Cushendall, county Antrim (© and fax **028/2177-1340**), offers a range of year-round outdoor programs and courses. They include everything from rock climbing and mountain biking to windsurfing and rafting. Half-day, full-day, and weeklong activities for ages 8 and older are offered, as well as 5- and 6-night scenic walking and cycling tours. It's best to book at least several weeks ahead. The center will arrange local B&B or hostel accommodations.

FISHING　The best time to fish in the North Antrim Glens is July to October, both for salmon and for sea trout. The rivers of choice are the Margy, Glenshesk, Carey, and Dun. The **Marine Hotel** (see "Where to Stay," below) in Ballycastle offers an array of services to the game angler. For locally arranged game fishing, contact **Gillaroo Angles,** 7 Cooleen Park, Jordanstown, Newtownabbey, county Antrim (© **028/9086-2419**). For info, tackle, and bait, try **Red Bay Boats,** Coast Road, Cushendall (© **028/2177-1331**).

GOING SKY HIGH   You can book a spectacular helicopter ride over the North Antrim Coast by calling **The Helicopter Centre,** Newtownards Airfield (© **028/9182-0028**). While you're at it, keep your eyes peeled for a familiar sight—a monk from Dublin who hang-glides off the Causeway cliffs every month or so. He's known by locals only as "Flyer Tuck."

GOLF   North Antrim boasts several notable courses, including the **Royal Portrush Golf Club,** Dunluce Road, Portrush (© **028/7082-2311;** www. royalportrushgolfclub.com). Royal Portrush has three links courses, including the celebrated Dunluce Course, ranked number three in the United Kingdom. Greens fees are £85 ($121) weekdays and £95 ($135) weekends. Just over the border in county Londonderry is the **Portstewart Golf Club,** 117 Strand Rd., Portstewart (© **028/7083-2015;** www.portstewartgc.co.uk). Of its three links courses, the 72-par Strand Course is the celebrated one here. Some days and times are more accessible than others for visitors, so it's advisable to call ahead for times and fees, which range from £10 to £80 ($14–$114) for 18 holes, depending on the course and the day of the week.

PONY TREKKING   **Watertop Farm Family Activity Centre,** 188 Cushendall Rd., Ballycastle (© **028/2076-2576**), offers pony trekking and other outdoor family activities, daily in July and August and weekends in late June and early September. In the Portrush area, contact **Maddybenny Riding Centre** (© **028/7082-3394;** www.maddybenny.freeserve.co.uk), also offering accommodation which won "Farmhouse of the Year" award for all of Ireland in 1999. B&B accommodation runs £50 to €55 ($71–$78) for a double. Also, in Castlerock, there's **Hillfarm Riding and Trekking Centre** (© **028/7084-8629**). Fees are typically around £10 ($14) per hour.

WALKING   The **Ulster Way,** 904km (560 miles) of marked trail, follows the North Antrim Coast from Glenarm to Portstewart. The **Moyle Way** offers a spectacular detour from Ballycastle south to Glenariff. Maps and accommodations listings for both ways are in the free NITB booklet *The Ulster Way: Accommodation for Walkers.* Or pick up a copy of *Walking the Ulster Way,* by Alan Warner (Appletree Press, 1989). The NITB also offers *An Information Guide to Walking,* full of useful information for avid pedestrians.

Last but far from least is the **Causeway Coast Path.** It stretches from Bushfoot Strand, near Bushmills, in the west to Ballintoy Harbour in the east. Short of sprouting wings, this is surely the way to take in the full splendor of the North Antrim coast.

WHERE TO STAY
MODERATE
Bushmills Inn 🏚🏚   In the center of the famous whiskey-making village of the same name, this inn dates from the 17th century. Some of the guest rooms are in the original coaching inn and the others are in the newer mill house. The interior of the coaching inn has old-world charm, with open turf fireplaces, gas lamps, and antique furnishings. Guest rooms here are comfortable, with country pine and caned furniture, floral wallpaper, brass fixtures, and vintage prints.

The mill house rooms have less character but they are considerably more spacious and modernized.

9 Dunluce Rd., Bushmills, county Antrim. ℂ 028/2073-2339. Fax 028/2073-2048. www.bushmills-inn.com. 33 units, 26 with private bathroom. £110–£150 ($156–$213) double. Family rooms available. Rates include full breakfast. MC, V. **Amenities:** Restaurant (Continental); bar; babysitting; nonsmoking rooms; drawing room. *In room:* TV, dataport, hair dryer, garment press, iron.

Londonderry Arms Hotel ✦✦ At the foot of Glencloy, one of the nine Antrim glens, this ivy-covered former coaching inn dates back to 1848; at one point Sir Winston Churchill owned it through a family inheritance. (He once slept in room 114.) It has been a hotel in the hands of the O'Neill family since 1947. It sits in the heart of a delightful coastal town with views of the harbor across the street. The hotel recently expanded, and a surprising degree of tasteful continuity was achieved between the original Georgian structure and the newer wing. Each room has its own character, yet is furnished with the same fine eye and excellent taste. This is a family-run hotel, and it shows in the warmth of hospitality and careful attention to detail.

20 Harbour Rd., Carnlough, county Antrim. ℂ 800/44-PRIMA in the U.S., or 028/2888-5255. Fax 028/2888-5263. www.glensofantrim.com. 35 units. £90 ($128) double. Rates include full breakfast. High tea £14 ($20); dinner £20 ($28). AE, DC, MC, V. **Amenities:** Restaurant (seafood); bar. *In room:* TV, radio, tea/coffeemaker.

Magherabuoy House Hotel ✦✦ Nestled amid gardens at the edge of Portrush, this country manor-style hotel enjoys panoramic views of the town and seacoast, yet is away from the resort hubbub. The traditional ambience—dark woods, gilded mirrors, and open fireplaces—contrasts with the guest rooms, which are contemporary and smart, with frilly fabrics, brass fittings, and floral wallpapers.

41 Magheraboy Rd., Portrush, county Antrim. ℂ 028/7082-3507. Fax 028/7082-4687. www.magherabuoy. co.uk. 38 units. £110 ($156) double. Rates include full breakfast. AE, DC, MC, V. **Amenities:** 2 restaurants (Continental, cafe); bar/nightclub; gym; Jacuzzi. *In room:* TV.

Marine Hotel ✦ *Value* Sitting right on the harbor at Ballycastle, just a 10-minute drive from the Giant's Causeway, this refurbished three-story contemporary-style hotel is a favorite with Irish vacationers. The guest rooms offer lovely views of the sea and bright modern furnishings.

The Marine Hotel and Country Club complex includes 27 **self-catering apartments** (ℂ 028/9066-7110) that sleep up to eight people. They are rented only by the week in high season. During the rest of the year, they're available by the night or for a weekend. Weekly rates range from £230 to £400 ($327–$568).

1 North St., Ballycastle, county Antrim. ℂ 028/2076-2222. Fax 028/7076-9507. www.marinehotel.net. 32 units. £80 ($114) double. Rates include full breakfast. Dinner £14 ($20). AE, DC, MC, V. **Amenities:** Restaurant (Continental); bar; nightclub; indoor swimming pool; gym; sauna; nonsmoking rooms. *In room:* TV, tea/coffeemaker.

INEXPENSIVE

Cushendall Youth Hostel ✦ Renovated only a few years ago, this superior hostel has been in service for 30 years; clearly, practice makes perfect. It is quite attractive and close to immaculate. The dining and guest rooms are all nonsmoking. A comfortable TV and reading lounge, complete with open fireplace, is also available. The commodious kitchen offers far more than most hostels, both in facilities (including ovens and microwave) and in spotlessness. On an old farm half a mile outside the village center, the hostel is accessible by bus and is near the Ulster Way. There's a locked bike shed.

42 Layde Rd., Cushendall, county Antrim. ℂ **028/2177-1344.** Fax 028/2177-2042. Dorm and family rooms £9 ($13) per person over 17, £7–£8 ($9.95–$11) per person 17 and under. MC, V. Daily 7:30–10:30am and 5–11:30pm. Closed Dec 23–Feb. Signposted from Cushendall center. **Amenities:** Nonsmoking rooms; kitchen facilities; TV lounge.

The Meadows 🛈   This newly built guesthouse provides spacious, well-designed accommodations in a lovely coastal setting. The front-room views of the sea and, on a clear day, of Scotland are quite splendid. There's one family room, and one unit is fully adapted for travelers with disabilities. A 10-minute walk from the center of Cushendall, the Meadows offers exceptional convenience, comfort, and good value. Anne Carey, your host, will gladly arrange for you to eat at the private boat club across the road.

81 Coast Rd., Cushendall, county Antrim. ℂ **028/2177-2020.** 6 units, all with shower only. £40 ($57) double. Family rates negotiable. Rates include full Irish breakfast and service charge. V. **Amenities:** Non-smoking rooms; sitting room. *In room:* TV, tea/coffeemaker.

Sanda   Perched high at the mouth of Glenariff, the Queen of the Glens, Sanda affords truly spectacular views. The two guest rooms are modest and immaculate. The beds are very firm, and a pleasant lounge, complete with TV and a stack of intriguing books about the area, is available to guests. Host Donnell O'Loan is quite knowledgeable and articulate about the area—its ancient sites, as well as its current attractions.

29 Kilmore Rd., Glenariff, county Antrim. ℂ **028/2177-1785.** sanda@antrim.net. 2 units, both with shower only. £34–£40 ($48–$57) double. Family rates negotiable. Rates include full Irish breakfast and service charge. No credit cards. Closed Dec–Feb. **Amenities:** Nonsmoking rooms; TV lounge.

SELF-CATERING

Bellair Cottage 🛈 *Value*   This century-old whitewashed farmhouse and attached barn have been beautifully converted into a gracious, inviting traditional home away from home for one or two families. It has three bedrooms, and sleeps six. The house occupies a lovely secluded setting high on Glenarm Glen, with an enclosed stone-walled garden that's a safe play area for children. The kitchen has its original open fireplace and the exquisite master bedroom could win a design award. For an extended working holiday or summer—or sabbatical year, for that matter—Bellair is a good size for two people, giving each a private workplace. The nearby North Antrim Coast is all the inspiration any writer, painter, photographer, or gazer could ask for. You can book any desired activities through RCH—horseback riding, day boats, trekking, rock climbing, or bicycling.

Glenarm, county Antrim. Contact RCH, ℂ **028/9024-1100.** Fax 028/9024-1198. www.cottagesinireland.com. 1 cottage. £300–£430 ($426–$611) per week. Also available for 2- or 3-day stays. MC, V. **Amenities:** Full kitchen; fridge; oven/stove; microwave; washing machine. *In room:* TV, no phone.

Tully Cottage 🛈   This is one of the loveliest self-catering cottages available for the money. Although it has two bedrooms and is just large enough to accommodate four people quite comfortably, Tully is the perfect love nest or honeymoon nook. It is both elevated and secluded, affording spectacular views of Glenarm Glen and the North Channel down to the Mull of Galloway, plus total privacy. The old farm cottage has been lovingly restored and tastefully appointed to offer equal charm and comfort. The beds are firm, the tub is extralong, the traditional fireplace is up to the task, and the kitchen is well equipped. This is a perfect base for exploring the stunning North Antrim coast. Horse riding, day boats, trekking, and rock climbing can be arranged in advance; bicycles can be waiting for you at the cottage, all through RCH.

Glenarm, county Antrim. Contact RCH, ℂ **028/9024-1100.** Fax 028/9024-1198. www.cottagesinireland. com. 1 cottage. £280–£400 ($398–$568) per week. Also available for 2- to 3-day stays. MC, V. **Amenities:** Kitchen; fridge; oven/stove; microwave; washing machine. *In room:* TV.

WHERE TO DINE
EXPENSIVE

Ramore ★★ MODERN CONTINENTAL On your first look-see of Portrush, you'd never believe this small, slightly frayed resort town would possess such a wonderful beacon of good cooking. But there it is. On the east end of the harbor overlooking boats and the sea, this stylish, hip, buzzy restaurant is home to George McAlpin's highly original, very modern cooking. On any given day, the menu might include chicken breast with fresh asparagus and vinaigrette of pine nuts, sun-dried tomatoes, Parmesan, and truffle oil; a fabulous black bean ratatouille with filet of steak; or smoked squid with bacon fries. For dessert, choose something with wow appeal, like a chocolate soufflé. And cap off your night with a drink downstairs at The Harbour Bar, also owned by McAlpin.

Ramore St., The Harbour, Portrush, county Antrim. ℂ **028/7082-4313.** Reservations required. Main courses £12–£16 ($17–$23). MC, V. Wine bar Mon–Sat noon–2pm and 5:30–9pm; restaurant Tues–Sat 6:30–10:30pm.

MODERATE

Hillcrest Country House ★ IRISH Surrounded by lovely gardens and situated opposite the entrance to the Giant's Causeway, this restaurant offers lovely wide-windowed views of the coast, which are particularly beautiful at sunset. The menu emphasizes local ingredients and creative sauces: salmon baked with cucumbers, mushrooms, and fennel sauce; grilled venison with game mousse laced with Black Bush Irish whiskey; and roast North Antrim duck with sage and onion stuffing and peach brandy. Bed-and-breakfast is also available for £80 ($114) for a double, or less with special off-season weekend packages.

306 Whitepark Rd., Giant's Causeway, county Antrim. ℂ **028/2073-1577.** Reservations required. Main courses £9–£12 ($13–$17). MC, V. Mon–Sat noon–9:30pm; Sun noon–9pm.

INEXPENSIVE

Sweeney's Wine Bar ★ PUB GRUB This is a popular, informal spot on the coast, with a conservatory-style extension and outdoor seating in good weather. The menu offers good pub grub—burgers, pasta, seafood plates (prawns, scampi, cod, and whitefish); steak-and-kidney pie, and stir-fry vegetables.

6b Seaport Ave., Portballintrae, county Antrim. ℂ **028/2073-2405.** Reservations recommended for dinner. Main courses £5–£8 ($7.10–$11). No credit cards. Mon–Sat 12:30–8pm; Sun 12:30–2:30pm and 7–9pm.

Victoriana Restaurant CAFETERIA In the Dunluce Center, this Victorian-theme bilevel restaurant is a handy place to stop for refreshment when touring the Antrim coast. The menu includes sandwiches, omelets, salads, pastas, and steaks, as well as sausage, beans, and "Ulster fry" (a cheese-and-onion pie).

Dunluce Ave., Portrush, county Antrim. ℂ **028/7082-4444.** Main courses £2–£5 ($2.85–$7.10). No credit cards. Apr–June and Sept daily noon–5pm; July–Aug daily 10am–8pm; Oct Sat–Sun noon–5pm.

PUBS

Harbour Bar George McAlpin's place is reputed to serve the best Guinness in the North. It's a particularly good place for a before- or after-dinner libation, with a location just under the terrific Ramore restaurant (see "Where to Dine," above) on the wharf overlooking the harbor. You'll find mostly locals in the plain, old-style bar. It's all so very Irish. The Wharf, Portrush, county Antrim. ☎ **028/ 7082-5047.**

J. McCollam   Known to locals as Johnny Joe's, J. McCollam has been the hottest scene in Cushendall for traditional music and Antrim atmosphere for nearly a century. You have to be willing to wedge yourself in, but you're not likely to have any regrets. Mill St., Cushendall, county Antrim. ☎ **028/2177-1992.**

M. McBride's   Opened in 1840, Mary McBride's was the smallest pub or bar in Europe until, quite recently, it expanded to include a bistro and restaurant. The old Guinness record–holding pub is still intact, so squeeze in and partake of the legend for yourself. Live, traditional music tends to break out in the pub's conservatory on weekend evenings. The Riverside Bistro serves light lunches and dinners (noon–9pm). The Waterside Restaurant, specializing in seafood, has a dinner menu (6–9pm) that features Torr Head lobster and Cushendum salmon; main courses run £7 to £16 ($9.95–$23). 2 Main St., Cushendun Village, county Antrim. ☎ **028/2176-1511.**

O'Malley's *Finds*   This is a favored fisherman's haunt and a great place to have a drink and kick back without being up to your elbows in tourists. The bar is off the wood-paneled lobby of the Edgewater Hotel, facing the magnificent beach at Portstewart. The Edgewater Hotel, 88 Strand Rd., Portstewart, county Derry. ☎ **028/7083- 3314.**

5 The Mourne Mountains

48km (30 miles) SW of Belfast

South and west from Downpatrick lie the rolling foothills of the Mournes, the highest mountains in Northern Ireland. A dozen of their nearly 50 summits rise above 600m (2,000 ft.), all of which are dominated by the barren peak of **Slieve Donard** (839m/2,796 ft.). Its breathtaking vista includes the full length of Strangford Lough, Lough Neagh, the Isle of Man, and, on a crystalline day, the west coasts of Wales and Scotland. (The recommended ascent of Slieve Donard is from Donard Park on the south side of Newcastle.)

Described by C. S. Lewis as "earth-covered potatoes," all but two of the Mournes's purple peaks are soft and rounded. Remote and veined by very few roads, the mountains are a hiker's dream—barren windswept moors galore. The ancestral home of the Brontës is here, in ruin. But all is not desolate. There are forest parks, sandy beaches, lush gardens, and, of course, pubs.

Besides walking and climbing and sighing at the wuthering splendor of it all, there's **Newcastle,** a popular, lively seaside resort, complete with beach and one of the finest golf courses in Ireland. Several other coastal towns strung along A2—**Kilkeel, Rostrevor,** and **Warrenpoint**—have their own charms. But here the mountains are the thing, and naturally you can't have cliffs and the sea without birds and castles and the odd dolmen. Finally, if at the end of the day your idea of nightlife has mostly to do with the stars, the Mourne Mountains provide a luminous getaway.

ESSENTIALS

GETTING THERE   If you're driving up from Dublin, turn east off the Dublin-Belfast road at Newry and take A2, tracing the north shore of Carlingford Lough, between the mountains and the sea. It's a drive you won't soon forget.

VISITOR INFORMATION For information in the Down District, stop into the **Downpatrick Tourist Information Centre,** 74 Market St., Downpatrick, county Down (© **028/4461-2233**), open October to mid-June Monday to Friday 9am to 5pm, Saturday 9am to 1pm and 2 to 5pm; mid-June to September Monday to Saturday 9am to 6pm and Sunday 2 to 6pm. (Downpatrick, covered in section 3 of this chapter, "Side Trips from Belfast," is a good gateway stop as you head into the Mourne Mountains from Belfast.)

There's also the **Newcastle Tourist Information Centre,** 10–14 Central Promenade, Newcastle, county Down (© **028/4372-2222;** fax 028/4372-2400). It's open Monday to Saturday 9am to 5pm and Sunday 2 to 6pm, with extended hours in the summer. A coach tour of the Mournes, offered according to demand, can be booked here. Or try the **Mourne Countryside Centre,** 91 Central Promenade, Newcastle, county Down (© **028/4372-4059**), open June to September Monday to Friday 9am to 7pm, weekends noon to 6pm. The center dispenses plenty of information and maps and sponsors guided mountain walks every Monday and Saturday.

SEEING THE SIGHTS

Castlewellan Forest Park *★★* Surrounding a fine trout lake and watched over by a magnificent private castle, this splendid forest park just begs for picnics and outdoor activities. Woodland walks, a lakeside sculpture trail, formal walled gardens, and even excellent trout fishing (brown and rainbow) await. The real draw is the National Arboretum, begun in 1740 and now grown to 10 times its original size. The largest of its three greenhouses features aquatic plants and a collection of free-flying tropical birds. The town of Castlewellan, elegantly laid out around two squares, is also worth a stroll.

6.5km (4 miles) northwest of Newcastle on A50, The Grange, Castlewellan Forest Park, Castlewellan, county Down. © 028/4377-8664. Free admission. Parking £4 ($5.70). Daily 10am–dusk; coffeehouse open summer, 10am–5pm.

Drumena Cashel (Stone Fort) *★* The walls of this irregularly shaped ancient stone-ring fort—a farmstead, dating from the early Christian period—were partially rebuilt in 1925–26 and measure 2.7m (9 ft.) to 3.6m (12 ft.) thick. The *souterrain* (underground stone tunnel) is T-shaped and was likely used in ancient times for cold storage. In the extreme, it hopefully provided some protection from Viking raiders. There were once, it seems, tens of thousands of such fortifications in Ireland, and this is one of the better-preserved examples in this region.

3km (2 miles) southwest of Castlewellan, off A25, county Down.

Dundrum Castle *★* This was the site of an early Irish fortification, of which nothing is visible now. The oldest portions of the castle's striking and quite extensive ruins date from the late 12th century, and the most recent are from the 17th century. The hilltop setting is quite lovely, and the views from the keep's parapet are especially grand. This was once the mightiest of the Norman castles along the Down coast. It still commands the imagination, if nothing else.

6.5km (4 miles) east of Newcastle, off A2, Dundrum, county Down. No phone. Admission £1 ($1.40) adults, 50p (70¢) children. Apr–Sept Tues–Sat 10am–1pm and 1:30–7pm, Sun 2–7pm; Oct–Mar Tues–Sat 10am–1pm and 1:30–4pm, Sun 2–4pm.

Greencastle Fort *★* The first castle on this site, built in 1261, faced its companion, Carlingford Castle, across the lough. It was a two-story rectangular tower surrounded by a curtain wall with corner towers. Very little survives. Most of what you see is from the 14th century, a fortress that fell to Cromwell in 1652, never to rise again.

6.5km (4 miles) southwest of Kilkeel, Greencastle, Cranfield Point, Mouth of Carlingford Lough, county Down. No phone. Admission £1 ($1.40) adults, 50p (70¢) children. Apr–Sept Tues–Sat 10am–1pm and 1:30–7pm, Sun 2–7pm; Oct–Mar Tues–Sat 10am–1pm and 1:30–4pm, Sun 2–4pm.

Murlough Nature Reserve ⚐ Sand dunes, heathland, and forest, surrounded by estuary and sea, make for a lovely outing on a clear bright day, but you'll want to bring a windbreaker, and some binoculars; this is a prime habitat for a host of waders and sea birds. Take a picnic, and you may find your dessert on the dunes, which are strewn with wild strawberries in the summertime.

On the main Dundrum-Newcastle rd. (A2), southeast of Dundrum, county Down. ✆ 028/4375-1467. Free admission. Parking £2 ($2.85).

Nautilus Centre ⚐ Opened in spring 1998, this multipurpose center is an ideal place to begin your exploration of Kilkeel, Northern Ireland's premier fishing port. For a start, you can have a fisherman's breakfast in the center's Sea Breeze Diner (see "Where to Dine," below). The Nautilus Heritage Centre features a compact exhibition with an interactive multimedia display, introducing visitors to the mission and development of Northern Ireland's modern fishing fleet. You'll also find, in the center's Harbour Store, fresh fish on ice, fishing gear and tackle, and a selection of gifts and souvenirs.

Rooney Rd., Kilkeel Harbour, Kilkeel, county Down. ✆ 028/4176-5555. Free admission. Year-round Mon–Sat 10am–6pm; Sun noon–6pm.

Silent Valley Mountain Park (Kids) More than 90 years ago, the 36km (22-mile) dry-stone Mourne Wall was built to enclose Silent Valley, which was dammed to create the Silent Valley Reservoir, to this day the major source of water for county Down. The 36km (22-mile) **Mourne Wall trek** threads together 15 of the range's main peaks—more than most hikers want to take on. A fine alternative is the more modest walk from the fishing port of Kilkeel to the Silent Valley and Lough Shannagh. An even less strenuous alternative is to drive to the Silent Valley Information Centre and take the shuttle bus to the top of nearby Ben Crom. The bus runs daily in July and August, weekends only in May, June, and September, and costs £2 ($2.85) round-trip, 75p ($1.05) for children. There is also a restaurant, gift shop, children's playscape, and picnic area.

6.5km (4 miles) north of Kilkeel on Head Rd., Silent Valley, county Down. ✆ 028/9074-6580. Admission £3 ($4.25) per car. Information Centre Easter–Sept daily 10am–6:30pm; Oct–Easter 10am–4:30pm.

Tollymore Forest Park ⚐ Tollymore House is no more. What remains is a delightful 480-hectare (1,200-acre) wildlife and forest park. The park offers a number of walks along the Shimna River, noted for its salmon, or up into the north slopes of the Mournes. The forest is a nature preserve inhabited by a host of local wildlife, including badgers, foxes, otters, and pine martens. Don't miss the trees for the forest—there are some exotic species here, including magnificent Himalayan cedars and a 30m-tall (100-ft.) sequoia in the arboretum.

Off B180, 3.2km (2 miles) northwest of Newcastle, Tullybrannigan Rd., Newcastle, county Down. ✆ 028/4372-2428. Free admission. Parking £3 ($4.25). Daily 10am–dusk.

SHOPPING

The Celtic Crafts Gallery You'll find an impressive array of Celtic-design crafts here, as well as original gold and silver jewelry by Mary Doran. In addition, there are a pleasant cafe and panoramic views of the Mourne Mountains. 45 Dromara Rd., Dundrum, county Down. ℭ 028/4375-1327.

The Mourne Grange Craft Shop and Tea Room This gift shop is a browser's paradise, full to the brim with unique quality handcrafted goods, from pottery and silk scarves to toys for young and old. There's also a fine selection of books of local interest and beyond. The cheerful, nonsmoking tearoom serves an array of freshly baked pastries to complement a cup of coffee or pot of tea. The proceeds of this shop help support the Rudolf Steiner–inspired Kilkeel Camphill Community for children and adults with special needs. Camphill Village Community, 169 Newry Rd., Kilkeel, county Down. ℭ 028/4176-0103.

SPORTS & OUTDOOR PURSUITS

AIRPLANE TOURS You and two friends can book a guaranteed-to-render-you-speechless ride in a 4-seater airplane over the Mountains of Mourne by calling **WEAC Flight Training,** Belfast International Airport (ℭ **028/9442-2789**). Flights cost approximately £140 ($199).

BICYCLING The Mourne roads are narrow and often bordered by 1.7m-high (5½-ft.) dry-stone walls. There is also precious little traffic, and the vistas are spectacular. The decision's yours; if you decide to pedal across the Mournes, you can rent touring and mountain bikes for £8 ($11) per day from **J. P. Quinn,** 4–6 Bridge St., Kilkeel (ℭ **028/4176-2654**). Weekly rates are available.

The foothills of the Mournes around Castlewellan are ideal for cycling, with panoramic vistas and very little traffic. In these parts, the perfect year-round outfitter is **Ross Cycles,** 44 Clarkhill Rd., signposted from the Clough-Castlewellan road, one-half mile out of Castlewellan (ℭ **028/4377-8029**), which has light-frame, highly geared mountain bikes for the whole family, with helmets and children's seats. All cycles are fully insured, as are their riders. You can park and ride, or request local delivery. Daily rates are £7 to £10 ($9.95–$14). Family and weekly rates are available.

FISHING The best time to fish for trout and salmon is August to October. Some sizable sea trout can be seen on the Whitewater River in the Mournes, and not all of them get away. The **Burrendale Hotel** in Newcastle (ℭ **028/ 4372-2599**) and the **Kilmorey Arms Hotel** in Kilkeel (ℭ **028/4176-2220**) offer special holiday breaks for game anglers. For further information, as well as tackle, bait, and outfitting needs, try **Four Seasons,** 47 Main St., Newcastle (ℭ **028/4372-5078**).

GOLF ⛳ **Royal County Down,** Newcastle, county Down (ℭ **028/4372-3314;** www.royalcountydown.org), is nestled in huge sand dunes with the Mountains of Mourne in the background. This 18-hole, par-71 championship course was created in 1889 and is considered one of the best in the British Isles. Greens fees are £90 ($128) weekdays, £100 ($142) weekends. For a fraction of the cost, try the **Kilkeel Golf Club,** Mourne Park, Ballyardle, Kilkeel (ℭ **028/ 4176-5095**), a beautiful parkland course on the historic Kilmorey Estate. The best days for visitors are weekdays except Tuesday, and greens fees are £19 ($27) weekdays, £24 ($34) weekends.

HORSEBACK RIDING The **Mount Pleasant Trekking and Horse Riding Centre** (ℭ **028/4377-8651**) offers group trekking tours into Castlewellan Forest Park for £8 ($11) an hour. For riding in the Tollymore Forest Park or on local trails, contact the **Mourne Trail Riding Centre,** 96 Castlewellan Rd., Newcastle (*C* **028/4372-4315**). They have quality horses and offer beach rides for highly skilled riders. The **Drumgooland House Equestrian Centre,** 29 Dunnanew Rd., Seaforde, Downpatrick, county Down (*C* **028/4481-1956**), also offers trail riding in the Mournes, including 1½-hour trekking around Tollymore and Castlewellan Forest Parks from £20 ($28). Full equestrian holidays are also available.

SAILING   For leisure sailing cruises—from sightseeing to a meal afloat—contact Pamela or Aidan Reilly at **Leisure Sailing Cruises,** 5 Coastguard Villas, Newcastle (*C* **028/4372-2882**).

WHERE TO STAY
EXPENSIVE
Glasdrumman Lodge Country House and Restaurant 𝑅𝑅   "Simple elegance" is the mark Graeme and Joan Hall set in establishing this extraordinary place, and they have achieved just that. Poised between sea and mountains, with splendid views of each, Glasdrumman Lodge is encrusted with awards for fine dining and gracious accommodation, including the Irish "Most Romantic Hotel" award in 1997. Here is a place that knows what really good service is all about: Shoes are shined and cars cleaned overnight. Some of the light-filled rooms have working fireplaces, and no. 4, "Knockree," has an especially grand view of the sea. Note that the lodge is only 3.2km (2 miles) from the Silent Valley. The restaurant specializes in organic, natural produce and ingredients.

85 Mill Rd., Annalong, county Down. *C* 028/4376-8451. Fax 028/43767041. 10 units. £140 ($199) double. Rates include full breakfast. MC, V. **Amenities:** Restaurant (organic); bar; room service; nonsmoking rooms; valet service. *In room:* TV, hair dryer.

The Slieve Donard Hotel 𝑅𝑅𝑅   From this turreted, red-brick Victorian hotel on the seafront, you look across Dundrum Bay to where the Mountains of Mourne sweep down to the sea. Outside, you can walk along the 6.5km (4-mile) curving sandy strand to their very feet. When the hotel was built in 1897, there were coal fires in every bathroom. These days, the public areas and well-appointed guest rooms incorporate every modern convenience. Front rooms overlooking the sea are especially appealing. Other rooms look out onto the mountains or Royal County Down Golf Course.

Downs Rd., Newcastle, county Down. *C* 028/4372-3681. Fax 028/4372-4830. www.hastingshotels.com. 130 units. £140 ($199) double. Children's discount available. Rates include full breakfast. AE, DC, MC, V. **Amenities:** Restaurant (Continental); bar; indoor swimming pool; miniature golf; tennis court; gym; Jacuzzi; steam room; salon. *In room:* TV, hair dryer.

MODERATE
Burrendale Hotel and Country Club 𝑅𝑅 𝐾𝑖𝑑𝑠   This meticulously maintained modern hotel enjoys a fine location between the Mournes and the shore, and is a 15-minute walk from Newcastle Centre and the Royal County Down Golf Course. The gracious, contemporary rooms are spotless and spacious. In addition, so much attention has been paid to the needs of guests with disabilities that the Burrendale is a past recipient of the British Airways award for disabled access and amenities, both in the hotel and in the country club. If you're traveling with kids, the spacious family rooms are the way to go.

51 Castlewellan Rd., Newcastle, county Down. *C* 028/4372-2599. Fax 028/4372-2328. www. burrendale.com. 69 units. £110–£130 ($156–$185) double. Rates include full buffet breakfast. AE, DC, MC, V. **Amenities:** Restaurant (seafood, vegetarian); bar; indoor swimming pool; gym; beauty treatments; room service; massage; babysitting; laundry service; nonsmoking rooms. *In room:* TV, tea/coffeemaker, hair dryer.

Kilmorey Arms Hotel ⭐ In this pleasant seaside resort, the Kilmorey Arms is a delightful small inn that dates back 200 years. It's the kind of place Irish and Northern Irish families return to year after year, and there's a slightly threadbare, comforting atmosphere that permeates the entire hotel. Local townspeople use the attractive public rooms as meeting places, and consequently it's one of the busiest places in town. One caveat: The nightclub can get quite loud on weekend nights, so ask for a room up and away from the fray.

41 Greencastle St., Kilkeel, county Down. ✆ 028/4176-2220. Fax 028/4176-5399. www.kilmoreyarms hotel.co.uk. 26 units. £80 ($114) double. Children's and senior discounts available. Rates include full breakfast. MC, V. **Amenities:** Restaurant (international); bar; nightclub; nonsmoking rooms. *In room:* TV.

INEXPENSIVE

Briers Country House ⭐⭐ ⓥ*alue* Mary and David Bowater have lovingly converted their 200-year-old house into an award-winning B&B, keeping its old-world charm. There are some .8 hectares (2 acres) of gardens, with a trout pond, and the Bowaters grow most of their own fruit and vegetables and make their own breads and preserves. The full-service restaurant overlooks the pond and gardens, and the home-style guest rooms have good views. The house is in the foothills of the Mountains of Mourne, beside the Tollymore Forest Park.

39 Middle Tollymore Rd. (2.5km/1½ miles from the beach at Newcastle, off B180), Newcastle, county Down. ✆ 028/4372-4347. Fax 028/4372-6633. www.thebriers.co.uk. 9 units. £50 ($71) double. Rates include full breakfast. 3-day and weekly rates available. MC, V. **Amenities:** Restaurant (seafood); nonsmoking rooms; sitting room. *In room:* TV.

Grasmere Mrs. McCormick presides over this pleasant, well-kept modern bungalow in a residential area on the edge of Newcastle, off the Bryansford-Newcastle road (B180), with views of the Mournes. Grasmere is only a 10-minute walk from the beach, and there are a golf course and some forest walks nearby. With only three rooms, this B&B definitely feels more intimate than some travelers might want. But for those on a budget, it offers a comfortable, clean, relaxed place to stay.

16 Marguerite Park, Bryansford Rd., Newcastle, county Down. ✆ 028/4372-6801. 3 units, 2 with private bathroom. £38 ($54) double. Rates include full breakfast. No credit cards. Closed Dec 25. *In room:* TV, tea/coffeemaker.

Slieve Croob Inn ⭐⭐ ⓥ*alue* This small, family resort offers what is perhaps the best value for money in the Mournes. The setting—a patchwork of drumlin pastureland just shy of the Mournes's peaks—is exceptional. The panoramic views of Slieve Croob, Newcastle Bay, and the Isle of Man are breathtaking. This is a rambler's fantasy, with 8km (5 miles) of trails on Slieve Croob and a plethora of lazy mountain lanes to explore. The spotless inn is tastefully designed and outfitted in a homey, mountain-lodge style. There's simple pine furniture throughout. In addition to standard doubles, there's a fabulous three-bedroom family apartment with its own outer door. The Branny Bar features traditional music Tuesday to Sunday. There are also 10 one- to three-bedroom self-catering cottages—appealingly rustic in decor, yet fitted with the conveniences of modern life.

Seeconnell Centre, 119 Clanvaraghan Rd. (signposted 1.6km/1 mile out of Castlewellan on the A25), Castlewellan-Clough Rd., Castlewellan, county Down. ✆ 028/4377-1412. Fax 028/4377-1162. www.slieve croob.mcmail.com. 7 units in the inn; 10 1- to 3-bedroom self-catering cottages. Inn £75 ($107) double. Cottages £200–£360 ($284–$511) per week. AE, MC, V. **Amenities:** Restaurant (international); bar; 18-hole golf course; horseback riding; laundry facilities. *In room:* TV, tea/coffeemaker, garment press.

SELF-CATERING

Hannas Close ★★ *Kids*   Hannas Close is a meticulously restored *clachan,* or medieval-style extended-family settlement, founded in 1640 and restored/refurbished in 1997. On a low bluff over a lovely shallow stream, facing the spectacular Mountains of Mourne, this born-again *clachan* is so quiet that there's little to wake you other than birdsong. In the refurbishment of the cottages, every effort was made to re-create the past while attending to contemporary codes and standards of comfort. The cottages, which sleep from two to seven, have everything you'll need, including central heating. Additionally, all have an open fireplace or a wood stove. They are ideal for families with kids over 4 years old, though the steep steps and rustic character of the cottages won't suit everyone. A small museum in the Close can help you imagine the former life of the rural mountainside world you'll enter here.

Aughnahoory Rd., Kilkeel, county Down. Contact RCH at ℂ 028/9024-1100. Fax 028/9024-1198. www. cottagesinireland.com. 7 cottages. £185–£400 ($263–$568) per week. Also available for 2- to 3-day stays. Additional charge for heat and electricity. V. **Amenities:** Kitchen; fridge; oven/stove; microwave; washing machine.

WHERE TO DINE

Most of the dining in the Mournes, with or without frills, gourmet or generic, happens in hotels, guesthouses, and pubs. When your stomach growls, be sure to also consider the accommodations listed above and the pubs listed below.

The Fisherman ★ SEAFOOD   Locals consider this seafood joint to be the best in town. Luscious seasonal lobster stuffed with prawns competes for attention with mixed seafood Creole, and grilled haddock with bacon and fine herbs. Diners preferring fare from terra firma will do well to try the lamb cooked in red wine sauce with a julienne of carrots and mange tout, or tarragon chicken. The Fisherman is on the main street, opposite the BP station.

68 Greencastle St., Kilkeel, county Down. ℂ 028/4176-2130. Dinner main courses £7–£16 ($9.95–$23). MC, V. Wed–Sat noon–2:30pm; Thurs–Fri 6–9:30pm; Sat 6–10:30pm; Sun 5–10:30pm.

Pavilion Bistro and Restaurant ★★ INTERNATIONAL   On the north end of Newcastle's waterfront, facing the sea, you will find this gracious restaurant. Royal County Down golfers especially appreciate its mission of serving tasty fresh fare in generous portions, all day, every day. Gilded mirrors and tile fireplaces accent the tasteful Victorian dining rooms (smoking and nonsmoking). The bistro-style menu changes daily and includes such entrees as savory pork loin and fresh plaice with lemon herb sauce. On any given day, the dinner menu might include filet of sole served with fresh salmon and dill mousse or roast chestnut and apple duck. The tempting finales include shortbread with fruit coulis and brandy cream.

36 Downs Rd., Newcastle, county Down. ℂ 028/4372-6239. Reservations recommended. Dinner main courses £5–£12 ($7.10–$17); fixed-price dinner £22 ($31). MC, V. Daily noon–10pm.

Sea Breeze Diner ★ SEAFOOD   This informal harborside spot in the new Kilkeel Nautilus Centre offers fresh home cooking with an emphasis on the catch of the day. From this vantage point, you can see the catch coming in. Start with a salad of fresh prawns, then move on to something modest, such as fresh fish cakes, or go full sail with sole and prawns or the "land and sea" steak and prawns special. No spirits are served, but you can bring your own wine or beer (from the Kilkeel Wine Market, across from the Kilmorey Arms Hotel on Greencastle Street in Kilkeel center).

Nautilus Centre, Rooney Rd., Kilkeel Harbour, Kilkeel, county Down. ✆ 028/4176-4888. No reservations. Dinner main courses £6–£12 ($8.50–$17). No credit cards. Mon–Sat 10am–7pm; also open Sun in summer.

PUBS

Harbour Inn   You won't find a quainter "wee" harbor on the Down Coast than Annalong, and the Harbour Inn, as its name suggests, is poised right on the dock. The black guillemots tend to outnumber anyone else here, but they too welcome visitors. Awaiting a warm day, picnic tables sit out front for the perfect dockside happy hour. Otherwise, there's an inviting lounge and full restaurant serving lunch, high tea, dinner, and bar snacks. A live band, often of the Irish country-western persuasion, shows up every Saturday, and there's an unpredictable disco now and then. 6 Harbour Dr., Annalong Harbour, Annalong, county Down. ✆ 028/4376-8678.

Jacob Halls   If there's a chill in the air, you'll leave it behind in Jacob Halls, with its three massive fires blazing at the least pretense. This well-worn pub is a hub of hospitality for all ages—all over 18, that is. Vintage local photographs line the walls. There's live music Wednesday to Sunday, and pub grub from lunch on. Greencastle St., Kilkeel, county Down. ✆ 028/4176-4751.

The Percy French   The Percy French has stood watch over the gates of the Slieve Donard Hotel for a century. It's named after the famed Irish composer who died in 1920, leaving behind these words as an epitaph:

> *Remember me is all I ask—and yet*
> *If remembrance proves a task—forget.*

Forgetting is not a real option, however, as long as this fine old faux-Tudor pub pours the perfect pint and serves delicious fare. The same beamed roof encloses both the lounge and a full-service restaurant, with a traditional Irish menu. There's live traditional music on Saturday, and disco every Friday. Downs Rd., Newcastle, county Down. ✆ 028/4372-3175.

6 Derry City

Derry City is 118km (73 miles) NW of Belfast, 63km (39 miles) SW of Portrush, 113km (70 miles) NW of Armagh, 98km (61 miles) NE of Enniskillen, 232km (144 miles) NW of Dublin, and 354km (220 miles) NE of Shannon

Is it Derry or Londonderry? What's in a name? Traditionally in Northern Ireland, what you called the second-largest city of Northern Ireland (pop. 75,000) was politically loaded. During "the Troubles," the name issue became a sore point, with Unionists calling it Londonderry and Catholics calling it Derry. Visitors were left scratching their heads and walking a tightrope of political correctness. Things are still confusing, though less fraught: Though Londonderry remains the official name of the city, the official title of the city council is Derry. More important these days is that Derry is the more commonly used name. The people of the city have become accustomed to (and amused by) the fine line over this issue walked by many newspaper and broadcasting organizations. The local BBC radio station, for example, now routinely refers to the city as "Derry-stroke-Londonderry." And tourist authorities now speak of "the Maiden City," a coy reference to the fact that the city has never fallen to siege.

Derry is the unofficial capital of the northwestern region of the province. The city derives its name from the Irish words *Doire Calgach,* meaning "the oak grove of Calgach." Calgach was a warrior who set up a camp here in pre-Christian times. The name survived until the 10th century, when it became *Doire Colmcille* in honor of St. Columba, who founded his first monastery in Derry in A.D.

Derry City

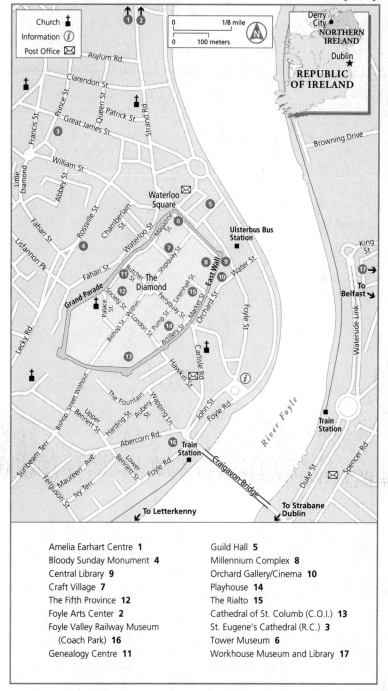

Church ✝
Information ⓘ
Post Office ✉

0 ___ 1/8 mile
0 ___ 100 meters

Derry City •
NORTHERN IRELAND
Dublin ★
REPUBLIC OF IRELAND

Asylum Rd.
Clarendon St.
Prince St.
Queen St.
Patrick St.
Strand Rd.
Great James St.
Francis St.
William St.
Abbey St.
Little Diamond
Fahan St.
Rossville St.
Chamberlain St.
Waterloo St.
Lisfannon Pk.
Fahan St.
Butcher St.
The Diamond
Grand Parade
Society St.
Palace St.
Bishop St. Within
London St.
Bishop St. Pump St.
Artillery St.
Lecky Rd.
Hawkin St.
The Fountain
Bishop Street Without
Upper Bennett St.
Harding St.
Aubery St.
Wapping Ln.
Sunbeam Terr.
Ferguson St.
Maureen Ave.
Lower Bennett St.
Ivy Terr.
Abercorn Rd.
Foyle Rd.
John St.
Carlisle Rd.
Browning Drive
Waterloo Square
Magazine St.
Shipquay St.
Linenhall St.
Ferryquay St.
Market St.
Orchard St.
East Wall
Water St.
Foyle St.
Ulsterbus Bus Station
King St.
To Belfast
Waterside Link
River Foyle
Train Station
Duke St.
Spencer Rd.
Craigavon Bridge
To Strabane Dublin
To Letterkenny
Train Station

Legend

Amelia Earhart Centre **1**
Bloody Sunday Monument **4**
Central Library **9**
Craft Village **7**
The Fifth Province **12**
Foyle Arts Center **2**
Foyle Valley Railway Museum (Coach Park) **16**
Genealogy Centre **11**

Guild Hall **5**
Millennium Complex **8**
Orchard Gallery/Cinema **10**
Playhouse **14**
The Rialto **15**
Cathedral of St. Columb (C.O.I.) **13**
St. Eugene's Cathedral (R.C.) **3**
Tower Museum **6**
Workhouse Museum and Library **17**

546. He is supposed to have written, "The angels of God sang in the glades of Derry and every leaf held its angel." Over the years, the name was anglicized to Derrie, or simply Derry.

Set on a hill on the banks of the Foyle estuary, strategically close to the open sea, Derry has often been threatened by invaders. At the time of the Plantation of Ulster in the 17th century, the City of London sent master builders and money to reconstruct the ruined medieval town, and the name became, for some of its inhabitants, Londonderry. The city's great 17th-century walls, about a mile in circumference and 5.4m (18 ft.) thick, are a legacy from that era. Although they were the focus of attacks (including sieges in 1641, 1649, and 1689), the walls withstood many tests of time and remain unbroken. They make Derry one of the finest examples of a walled city in Europe. The rest of the city's architecture is largely Georgian, with brick-fronted town houses and imposing public buildings. Basement-level pubs and shops are common.

About 19km (12 miles) east of the city is another Georgian enclave, the town of **Limavady** 🔊 in the Roe Valley. It was here that Jane Ross wrote down the tune of a lovely air she heard, played by a fiddler passing through town. It became the famous "Londonderry Air," otherwise known as "Danny Boy."

For longer than anyone wants to remember, Derry was immersed in, and all but identified with, the Troubles. In the 1960s and 1970s, the North's civil rights movement was born here and baptized in blood. The victims of Bloody Sunday are the symbols of the struggle for equality in the North, an effort for which this city and its people paid dearly. By 1980, nearly a third of the inner city was in ruins. But that was then, and this is now. In the years since, Derry has rebuilt some walls and dismantled others, and has become increasingly engaged in the struggle to build a new North. Today, Derry is emerging as one of the most vibrant, happening, and appealing centers of culture and commerce in Northern Ireland, and it's destined to become a major tourist mecca, once word gets out.

Another secret about Derry is how close it is to many of the major sights of Ireland's northwest corner. To cite a few highlights, the Inishowen Peninsula, the Giant's Causeway and the North Antrim Coast, the Northwest Passage and the Sperrins, and Glenveagh National Park in Donegal are all within an hour's drive. Derry is an ideal base of operations from which to explore one of Ireland's most unspoiled and dazzling regions.

ESSENTIALS

GETTING THERE   By Plane   Service to **City of Derry Airport** (📞 028/7181-0784; www.cityofderryairport.com) is provided by **British Airways** (📞 0345/222111; www.british-airways.com) from Glasgow and Manchester, and by **Ryanair** (📞 0541/569569 in Britain; www.ryanair.com) from London Stansted. The no. 43 Limavady **bus** stops at the airport. A **taxi** for the 13km (8-mile) journey to the city center costs about £11 ($16). If you're landing in either of the Belfast airports, without a connection to Derry, the **Airporter** coach can take you straight to Derry. Call 📞 **028/7126-9996** for information and reservations.

By Cruise Ship   Derry City is an important port of call for an increasing number of cruise ships, including six-star luxury liners, which call at the deep-water facilities at Lisahally or at the city center's Queen's Quay. For the latest information on cruises to Derry Port, contact the **Cruise Development Officer,** Derry City Council, 98 Strand Rd., Derry BT48 7NN (📞 **028/7136-5151**).

By Train Northern Ireland Railways (© 888/BRITRAIL or 028/9089-9411) operate frequent trains from Belfast and Portrush, which arrive at the **Northern Ireland Railways Station** (© **028/7134-2228**), on the east side of the Foyle River. A free Linkline bus brings passengers from the train station to the city center.

By Bus The fastest bus between Belfast and Derry, the no. 212 Maiden City Flyer, operated by **Ulsterbus** (© **028/9033-3000** in Belfast or 028/7126-2261 in Derry; www.translink.co.uk), is about twice as fast as the train; it takes a little over 90 minutes. **Ulsterbus** also has service from Portrush and Portstewart. From the Republic, **Bus Eireann** offers three buses a day from Galway's **Bus Eireann Travel Centre,** Ceannt Station, Galway (© **091/562000**; www.buseireann.ie), via Sligo and Donegal; and there's one bus daily to and from Cork. **Lough Swilly Bus Service** (© **028/7126-2017**) serves Derry from a number of towns in county Donegal, including Dunfanaghy and Letterkenny.

VISITOR INFORMATION The **Derry Visitor and Convention Bureau and Tourist Information Centre** is at 44 Foyle St., Derry (© **028/7126-7284;** fax 028/7137-7992). It's open October to Easter, Monday to Thursday 9am to 5:15pm, Friday 9am to 5pm; Easter to May, Monday to Thursday 9am to 5:15pm, Friday 9am to 5pm, Saturday 10am to 5pm; June to September, Monday to Friday 9am to 7pm, Saturday 10am to 6pm, Sunday 10am to 5pm. For all you ever wanted to know about Derry, consult **www.derryvisitor.com** and **www.derry.net**.

GETTING AROUND Ulsterbus, Foyle Street Depot, Derry (© **028/7126-2261;** www.translink.co.uk), operates local bus service to the suburbs. There is no bus service within the walls of the small, easily walkable city. The black London-style taxis you'll see are known in Derry and Belfast as "people's taxis." These taxis primarily serve nationalist areas outside the walls and will not go to most areas of interest to tourists. Use any of the other taxis available throughout the city, which are plentiful and reasonably priced.

There are taxi stands at the **Ulsterbus Depot,** Foyle Street (© **028/7126-2262**), and at the **Northern Ireland Railways Station,** Duke Street, Waterside (© **028/7134-2228**). To call a cab, contact **Co-Op Taxis** (© **028/7137-1666**), **Derry Taxi Association** (© **028/7126-0247**), or **Foyle Taxis** (© **028/7126-3905**).

Local car-rental offices include **Europcar** (© **028/7130-1312**) at the City of Derry Airport, and **Desmond Motors** (© **028/7136-0420**), 173 Strand Rd.

The focal point of Derry is **the Diamond,** a square in the center of the city, just west of the banks of the Foyle River. Four streets radiate out from the Diamond: Bishop, Ferryquay, Shipquay, and Butcher. Each extends for several blocks and ends at a walled gateway of the same name (Bishop's Gate, Ferryquay Gate, Shipquay Gate, and Butcher's Gate). A massive wall that rings the inner city connects the gates.

Two bridges connect the east and west banks of the River Foyle. The Craigavon Bridge, built in 1933, is one of the few examples of a double-decker bridge in the British Isles. The Foyle Bridge, Ireland's longest bridge, opened in 1984 and provides a dual-lane highway about 3.2km (2 miles) north of the Craigavon Bridge. West of the river are two major areas: the walled inner city and, farther west, an area known as the Bogside. East of the Foyle is the area usually referred to as Waterside, where most of the fine hotels and many of the city's restaurants are located. Also in Waterside is a small grassy viewing point called the **"Top of the**

> **Fun Fact** **A Poetic Persona**
>
> Born and educated in Derry, the celebrated contemporary poet Seamus
> Heaney (b. 1939) has been called Ireland's Robert Frost and, perhaps more
> appropriately, a latter-day Yeats. Heaney's poems about his homeland in
> the North of Ireland appear in his collections *North* (1975), *Field Work*
> (1979), *Station Island* (1984), and *Seeing Things* (1991). In 1995 he was
> awarded the Nobel Prize for Literature, the fourth Irishman to be so
> honored.

Hill," where you can enjoy spectacular eagle's-eye views of the city and its splendid environs. You'll never find your own way there, so take a taxi and bring your
map. Short of a helicopter tour, this is the best way to get your initial bearings.

FAST FACTS   In the city center, the **Bank of Ireland** (© 028/7126-4992) is
on Shipquay Street, and the **Ulster Bank** (© 028/7126-1882) is at Waterloo
Place. Both are open weekdays 9:30am (10am on Wed) to 4:30pm. The **Northern Bank** (© 028/7126-5333) at Shipquay Place is open Saturday 9:30am to
12:30pm, in addition to the typical weekday hours.

In an emergency, dial © **999** for fire, police, and ambulance. **Altnagevin
Hospital** is on Glenshane Road (© 028/7134-5171). The main **RUC or police
station** is on Strand Road (© 028/7136-7337).

Internet access is available at the **Central Library,** 35 Foyle St. in the city
center (© 028/7127-2300), for £3 ($4.25) per hour.

The main **Post Office,** 3 Custom House St. (© 028/7136-2563), is open
Monday 8:30am to 5:30pm, Tuesday to Friday 9am to 5:30pm, Saturday 9am
to 12:30pm.

SEEING THE SIGHTS

In July and August, **Ulsterbus** operates **Civic Bus Tours** of the Derry sights.
Tours are Tuesday at 2pm and cost £3.50 ($4.95) adults, £2.50 ($3.55) seniors
and children. Tours leave from the Ulsterbus Depot, Foyle Street. For further
information, call the **Tourist Information Centre** (© 028/7126-7284).

The Derry Visitor and Convention Bureau sponsors **Inner City Walking
Tours,** June to September Monday to Friday. They depart at 10:30am and
2:30pm from the Tourist Information Centre, 44 Foyle St. The price is £4
($5.70) adults, £3 ($4.25) seniors and children. **McNamara Walking Tours**
(© 028/7134-5335) offers an informative, entertaining walking tour of the city
June to September, daily at 10am, noon, 2, and 4pm. The cost is £4 ($5.70)
adults, £2 ($2.85) seniors and children.

Another fine option is the "Essential Walking Tour of Historic Derry," offered
by **Northern Tours** (© 028/7128-9051). It leaves from the Tourist Information Centre, May to September, daily at 10:30am and 2:30pm. The cost is £3
($4.25) adults, free for children.

Finally, if you're tired of walking and want to be conducted in regal fashion,
Martin McGowan will take you by horse-drawn carriage through the old city
and unravel its history as you go. Excursions cost around £34 ($48) for 90 min-
utes. Call **Charabanc Tours** (© 028/7127-1886) for details and reservations
from May to October.

Amelia Earhart Centre   Located 4.8km (3 miles) north of Derry off the A2
road, this cottage commemorates Amelia Earhart's landing here in 1932, as the

first woman to fly the Atlantic solo. The grounds encompass the Ballyarnett Community Farm and Wildlife Centre, with a range of farmyard animals and wildlife.

Ballyarnett, county Derry. ✆ 028/7135-4040. Free admission. Cottage Mon–Fri 10am–4pm; farm and sanctuary daily 10am–dusk.

Cathedral of St. Columb ✯
Within the city walls, near the Bishop's Gate, this cathedral, built as a Church of Ireland edifice between 1628 and 1633, is a fine example of the Planters Gothic style of architecture. It was the first cathedral built in Europe after the Reformation. Several sections were added afterward, including the impressive spire and stained-glass windows that depict scenes from the great siege of 1688–89. The chapter house contains a display of city relics, including the four original keys to the city gates, and an audiovisual presentation that provides background on the history of the building and the city.

London St., Derry, county Derry. ✆ 028/7126-7313. £1 ($1.40) donation requested. Mar–Oct Mon–Sat 9am–5pm; Nov–Feb Mon–Sat 9am–1pm and 2–4pm.

The Fifth Province ✯✯
This ambitious multimedia experience was many years in the making. Drawing from remote legends of a fifth Irish province at the navel of ancient Ireland, the idea here is to imagine and experience a once and future Ireland untroubled and unified. This multistage high-tech tour through time—past, present, and future—is designed to be absorbing for adults and children alike.

Calgach Centre, 4–22 Butcher St., Derry, county Derry. ✆ 028/7137-3177. Admission £3 ($4.25) adults, £1 ($1.40) seniors and children, £7 ($9.95) family. Mon–Fri 9:30am–4pm. Extended summer hours.

Foyle Valley Railway Centre ✯ *Kids*
Just outside the city walls near the Craigavon Bridge, where four railway lines once crossed paths, this center focuses on the local history of letting off steam. Besides viewing exhibits and retired trains, you can take a 20-minute narrow-gauge trip through the Foyle Riverside Park.

Foyle Rd., Derry, county Derry. ✆ 028/7137-3177. Free admission. Train rides £3 ($4.25) adults, £1.50 ($2.15) seniors and children, £7 ($9.95) family. Centre Tues–Sat 10am–4:30pm; trains Mon–Fri 10am–4:30pm, Sat 11:30am–4:30pm.

Genealogy Centre
Did your ancestors come from Derry or nearby? If you're of Irish ancestry, it's possible, and maybe even likely. Derry served as the principal port for thousands of emigrants who left Ulster for the New World in the 18th and 19th centuries; records show that Ulster men and women became the second-most-numerous group in the colonial population, and played an important role in the American Revolution and the settlement of the West. This heritage library and Genealogy Centre, in the heart of the old walled city, can help you research your Derry roots.

Calgach Centre, 4–22 Butcher St., Derry, county Derry. ✆ 028/7137-3177. Fax 028/7137-4818. www.irishroots.net/derry. £24 ($34) initial search fee. Mon–Fri 9am–5pm.

Guild Hall ✯✯
Just outside the city walls, between Shipquay Gate and the River Foyle, this Tudor Gothic–style building looks much like its counterpart in London. The site's original structure was built in 1890, but it was rebuilt after a fire in 1908 and after a series of bombings in 1972. The hall is distinguished by its huge four-faced clock and by its stained-glass windows, made by Ulster craftsmen, that illustrate almost every episode of note in the city's history. The hall is used as a civic and cultural center for concerts, plays, and exhibitions.

Shipquay Place, Derry, county Derry. ✆ 028/7137-7335. Free admission. Mon–Fri 9am–5pm; Sat–Sun by appointment. Free guided tours July–Aug.

Orchard Gallery ★★★   The Orchard Gallery, founded in 1978, is Derry's prime venue for contemporary visual art. Mounting 20 or more exhibitions and events each year, the gallery fosters and displays the work of a wide range of contemporary local, Irish, and international artists. Central to the gallery's mission, as well, is its innovative, multifaceted Education and Community Outreach Scheme. The art that originates here is meant to provoke a generously creative and collaborative response from the wider community, especially Derry's youth. Sharing the same building with the Orchard Gallery is the Orchard Cinema, where you're likely to find the latest international films.

Orchard St., Derry, county Derry. ✆ **028/7126-9675.** Free admission. Tues–Sat 10am–6pm.

St. Eugene's Cathedral ★★   Designed in the Gothic Revival style, this is Derry's Catholic cathedral, nestled in the heart of the Bogside district just beyond the city walls. The foundation stone was laid in 1851, but work continued until 1873. The spire was added in 1902. It's built of local sandstone and is known for its stained-glass windows depicting the Crucifixion, by Meyer of Munich.

Fransic St., Derry, county Derry. Free admission. Mon–Sat 7am–9pm; Sun 7am–6:30pm.

Tower Museum ★★   Housed in O'Doherty Tower, a medieval-style fort, this award-winning museum presents the history of the city, from its geological formation to the present day. Visitors are invited to walk through time, and a series of exhibits and audiovisual presentations provoke their imaginations along the way. The Tower's collection of historical artifacts includes items salvaged from the Spanish Armada, ravaged by storms off the Irish coast in 1588. The Tower Museum, a must for all visitors to Derry, is just inside the city walls next to Shipquay Gate, and was recently expanded to include a new Spanish Armada museum.

Union Hall Place, Derry, county Derry. ✆ **028/7137-2411.** Admission £4 ($5.70) adults, £1.50 ($2.15) children, £8 ($11) family. July–Aug Mon–Sat 10am–5pm, Sun 2–5pm; Sept–June Tues–Sat 10am–5pm.

The Workhouse Museum and Library ★★   This splendid, compact museum on the Waterside, only minutes from Derry Centre, opened in May 1998 and is still being developed. It occupies the central building—the inmates' dorms and the master's quarters—of a 19th-century workhouse complex. The story told here is both grim and moving. Built to employ and maintain the poor, the workhouse was little more than a concentration camp. A visit ensures that you will leave feeling deliriously fortunate. This museum also presents intriguing multimedia exhibitions focused on two moments in Derry's history: the Great Famine, when between 1845 and 1849 roughly 12,000 people a year left Ireland forever from the port of Derry; and the Battle of the Atlantic, when Derry played a major role in the defeat of the Kriegsmarine. The German U-boat fleet surrendered at Derry in May 1945.

23 Glendermott Rd., Waterside, Derry, county Derry. ✆ **028/7131-8328.** Free admission. Sept–June Mon–Thurs and Sat 10am–4:30pm; July–Aug Mon–Sat 10am–4:30pm, Sun 2–4pm.

SHOPPING

The city center offers some fine shopping, including two modern multistory malls: the **Richmond Centre,** facing the Diamond at the corner of Shipquay and Ferryquay Streets; and the new **Foyleside Shopping Centre,** just outside the walls. **London Street,** beside St. Columb's Cathedral, is Derry's antique row, where most of the city's antique and curio shops cluster.

In general, shops are open Monday to Saturday 9am to 5:30pm. Shops in the two large shopping centers are open Monday to Wednesday and Saturday 9am to 5:30pm, Thursday and Friday 9am to 9pm. In the summer, some shops are open on Sunday.

Austin & Co., Ltd   This is the city's landmark three-story Victorian-style department store, specializing in fashions, perfumes, china, crystal, and linens. It's the island of Ireland's oldest department store, established in 1839. The coffee shop on the third floor looks out on a panorama of the city. The Diamond, Derry, county Derry. ✆ **028/7126-1817.**

Derry Craft Village   In the heart of the inner city near the Tower, this unique shopping complex reflects Old Derry, with architecture of the 16th to 19th centuries. It houses retail shops, workshops, residential units, and a thatched-cottage pub offering an Irish Night (ceili and supper) almost every Thursday in July and August. Shipquay St. (enter on Shipquay or Magazine St.), Derry, county Derry. ✆ **028/7126-0329.**

MTM   Whether you've left home without your favorite tapes or are looking for something more local on the Irish traditional scene, you're likely to find it here. You can book tickets for major concerts and plays throughout the island. Richmond Centre, Derry, county Derry. ✆ **028/7137-1970.**

SPORTS & OUTDOOR PURSUITS

BICYCLING   Whether you want to rent a bike and do your own exploring, or sign up for a cycling tour of county Derry and county Donegal, **An Mointean Rent-a-Bike and Cycle Tours,** 245 Lone Moor Rd., Derry (✆ **028/7128-7128**), offers excellent service. Rental of mountain or touring bikes costs £10 ($14) a day, £45 ($64) a week. Package tours with bed-and-breakfast included are also available.

FISHING   The Foyle System of rivers makes this a promising area for snagging brown and sea trout (Apr to early July and Sept) and a variety of salmon (Mar–Sept). In addition, there is a stocked lake at Glenowen. Call **Glenowen Fisheries Co-operative** (✆ **028/7137-1544**) for bookings. You can outfit yourself and get useful information at **Rod and Line,** 1 Clarendon St., Derry (✆ **028/7126-2877**). If you're looking for an experienced local *ghillie* (guide) or boatman, contact **Mark Stewart,** Salmon Anglers Northwest, c/o Glenowen Fisheries Co-operative (✆ **028/7137-1544**), or **Lance Thompson,** Faughan Angler's Association, 26a Carlisle Rd., Derry (✆ **028/7126-7781**). For a game-fishing rod license, contact the **Foyle and Carlingford Locks Agency,** 8 Victoria Rd., Derry (✆ **028/7134-2100**).

GOLF   Derry has two 18-hole parkland courses: the **City of Derry Golf Club,** 49 Victoria Rd. (✆ **028/7134-6369**), with greens fees of £24 ($34) weekdays, £28 ($40) weekends; and the very inexpensive **Foyle International Golf Centre,** 12 Alder Rd., Derry (✆ **028/7135-2222;** www.foylegolfcentre.co.uk), which charges greens fees of £12 ($17) weekdays, £15 ($21) weekends. It is always best to phone ahead. Weekdays are best for visitors at the City of Derry Golf Club; any day of the week should be fine at the Foyle Golf Centre.

HORSEBACK RIDING   **Ardmore Stables,** 8 Rushall Rd., Ardmore (✆ **028/7134-5187**), offers lessons, trail rides, and pony trekking. Across the border, only 6.5km (4 miles) from Derry in county Donegal, **Lenamore Stables,** Muff, Inishowen (✆ **077/84022;** lenamorestable@eircom.net), also offers lessons and trekking, and has guest accommodations.

WALKING   In Derry, walking the **city walls** is a must. Just outside the city, off the main Derry-Belfast road, you'll come across **Ness Woods,** where there are scenic walks and nature trails, as well as the North's highest waterfall.

Value **A Note on Prices**

Derry prices for both accommodations and dining are exceptionally reasonable. The fact that Derry has barely any expensive hotels or restaurants does not mean that it lacks first-class lodging or dining. The city offers more for less and is, for the foreseeable future, a real bargain.

WHERE TO STAY
MODERATE

Beech Hill Country House Hotel ★★   In a residential area southeast of the city, this lovely country-house hotel dates from 1729. Antiques and marble fireplaces decorate the public areas, and some of the pleasant guest rooms have four-poster beds with frilly floral covers. The hotel's elegant Ardmore restaurant is, amazingly, all nonsmoking. The wooded grounds are lovely, and there's an arbor of beech trees for which the hotel is named.

32 Ardmore Rd., Derry, county Derry. ℂ **800/44-PRIMA** in the U.S., or 028/7134-9279. Fax 028/7134-5366. www.beech-hill.com. 27 units. £92 ($131) double. Rates include full breakfast. AE, MC, V. Free parking. **Amenities:** Restaurant (Continental); bar; lounge; mini gym; Jacuzzi; sauna/steam room. *In room:* TV, tea/coffeemaker, hair dryer, garment press.

Broomhill Hotel ★   Lovely views of Lough Foyle are a feature of this modern hotel, on its own grounds in a residential area 2.4km (1½ miles) east of the city, on the main road near the Foyle Bridge. Rooms are modern, with standard furnishings, welcome trays, and garment presses. The Garden Restaurant offers views of the river and the city.

Limavady Rd., Derry, county Derry. ℂ **028/7134-7995.** Fax 028/7134-9304. 42 units. £70 ($99) double. Rates include full breakfast. MC, V. Free parking. **Amenities:** Restaurant (international); bar. *In room:* TV, tea/coffeemaker, garment press.

Everglades Hotel ★★ *Value*   This is Derry's best hotel. On a hill overlooking the east bank of Lough Foyle in the prosperous Waterside district, this three-story contemporary hotel takes its name from Florida's Everglades. Like much of Florida, the hotel is built on reclaimed waterfront land. Guest rooms are luxuriously decorated in quality contemporary furnishings and smart designer fabrics. The tasteful Library Bar features live jazz on weekends.

Prehen Rd., Derry, county Derry. ℂ **028/7134-6722.** Fax 028/7134-9200. 64 units. www.hastingshotels.com. £80–£110 ($114–$156) double. Rates include full breakfast. High tea £10 ($14); dinner £17 ($24). AE, DC, V. Free parking. **Amenities:** Restaurant (international); bar; room service; laundry service; nonsmoking rooms. *In room:* TV, tea/coffeemaker, hair dryer, garment press.

Trinity Hotel ★★   One of the city's newest hotels, the Trinity merges clean modern lines with more traditional design elements. Large windows overlooking the street echo the surrounding Georgian neighborhood. The spacious rooms are tastefully decorated in warm, restful tones, accented by modern furniture in attractive maple veneer. The overall effect is chic and fanciful without compromising comfort. The brilliant bathrooms with towel warmers softly whisper "bubble bath." Fans of *Who Wants to Be a Millionaire* should note that Nolan's Bistro is a convivial late-night spot with a Wednesday quiz night.

22–24 Strand Rd., Derry, county Derry. ℂ **028/7127-1271.** Fax 028/7127-1277. 40 units. £90 ($128) double. Luxury suites available. Rates include Irish/continental breakfast and service charge. AE, DC, MC, V.

Free parking. **Amenities:** 2 restaurants (international, bistro); bar; complimentary access to nearby fitness center; currency exchange. *In room:* TV, tea/coffeemaker, hair dryer, garment press.

White Horse Hotel ⚘ ✓Value   This hotel, once an old inn and now part of the Best Western chain, is a favorite of tour operators and one of the more appealing moderately-priced hotels in the North. Its countryside setting 6.5km (4 miles) northeast of the city, on the Limavady road, is restful, and there's good, frequent bus service into Derry. Guest rooms are spacious and well appointed in a homey, traditional style.

68 Clooney Rd., Campsie, county Derry. ✆ **028/7186-0606.** Fax 028/7186-0371. 43 units. £54–£75 ($77–$107) double. Rates include full breakfast. Weekly and weekend discounts available. AE, DC, MC, V. Free parking. **Amenities:** Restaurant (international); bar; laundry facilities. *In room:* TV, tea/coffeemaker.

INEXPENSIVE

Clarence House ⚘   Mrs. Eleonora Slevin offers singles, doubles, twin rooms, and family rooms in this well-kept brick guesthouse. Rooms are quite comfortable, and the house and its hostess have become favorites of BBC and RTE television crews, who return again and again. The washing and ironing facilities are a bonus. Dinner and babysitting can be arranged for an extra charge, and there are restaurants within easy walking distance.

15 Northland Rd., Derry, county Derry. ✆ and fax **028/7126-5342.** 9 units, 7 with private bathroom. £54 ($77) double with bathroom. Children's discount available. Rates include full breakfast. MC, V. Limited free parking available. **Amenities:** Babysitting; laundry facilities; sitting room. *In room:* TV.

The Saddlers House and the Merchant's House ⚘⚘ ✓Value   Peter and Joan Pyne have beautifully restored these two 19th-century town houses. The Saddlers House is cozy Victorian. The more elegant Merchant's House is late Georgian and has been revived with such care that it won a Civic Trusts Ireland conservation award. It is among the last Georgian-style houses still in service as residences in Derry. These two noteworthy houses are several blocks from each other and are only minutes away by foot from Derry center. At the risk of runaway alliteration, they offer considerable comfort, convenience, character, and charm at budget rates.

Saddlers House, 36 Great James St., Derry, county Derry. ✆ **028/7126-9691.** Fax 028/7126-6913. 7 units, 3 with private bathroom. £52 ($74) double. Merchant's House, 16 Queen St., Derry. ✆ **028/7126-4223.** Fax 028/7126-6913. 5 units, 1 with private bathroom. £52 ($74) double. Children's and senior discounts available. Rates include full breakfast. No credit cards. **Amenities:** Sitting room. *In room:* TV, tea/coffeemaker.

WHERE TO DINE
EXPENSIVE

Ardmore Room Restaurant ⚘⚘ CONTINENTAL   Lunch in this pretty dining room draws many business types, who can relax in what was once a billiard room overlooking gardens while enjoying a superb meal. In the evening, there's a soft, romantic ambience. Among the outstanding specialties are monkfish accompanied by vegetables with ginger and balsamic vinaigrette, and brill poached in champagne with dill butter sauce. There's an extensive international wine list, as well as an extraordinary selection of home-baked specialty breads.

Beech Hill Country House Hotel, 32 Ardmore Rd., Derry, county Derry. ✆ **028/7134-9279.** Reservations recommended. Fixed-price 4-course dinner £29 ($41). MC, V. Daily 12:30–2:30pm and 6:30–9:30pm.

MODERATE

Brown's Bar and Brasserie ⚘⚘ MODERN INTERNATIONAL   Behind the unassuming exterior of this Waterside area row house, you will find some of the finest food in Derry. This lively spot has won a dedicated local clientele and attracted the attention of distant connoisseurs. The decor is warm, streamlined, and minimalist, with sculptural dried-flower arrangements—conducive to quiet conversation or a gathering of friends. The innovative menu blends the best of modern Irish, Italian, and Thai influences with an emphasis on fresh and, when possible, organic ingredients. Dishes include seared loin of lamb with porcini cream and reduced pan juices atop a bacon and pea potato cake; supreme of chicken with parsnip puree and tiger prawn–coconut sauce; and fresh monkfish on tagliatelle with tarragon and paprika cream. For a dramatic climax, go for the architecturally ambitious pineapple and toffee sponge with citrus fruit salad.

1–2 Bond's Hill, Waterside, Derry, county Derry. ℂ **028/7134-5180**. Reservations recommended. Main courses £7–£15 ($9.95–$21). MC, V. Tues–Fri noon–2:30pm; Tues–Sat 5–11pm.

Da Vinci's Bar and Restaurant ✿ INTERNATIONAL   The glow of candlelight and rich Renaissance reds and blues romantically warm the rough stone walls, arched doorways, and dramatic wrought-iron fittings. But it's the food that will coax the informed diner to venture a short distance (5 min.) from Derry center. You can choose from delights such as grilled sea bass with tikka crust and lime-cherry relish, or pesto cream over tender chicken breast stuffed with sun-dried tomatoes. Stop in to see the magnificent mahogany central bar and its towering three-faced clock, which just might have sprung from Leonardo's imagination after a few pints.

15 Culmore Rd., Derry, county Derry. ℂ **028/7137-2074**. Reservations recommended. Dinner main courses £9–£16 ($13–$23). AE, MC, V. Mon 5:30–9:30pm; Tues–Fri 5:30–10pm; Sat 5:30–10:30pm; Sun 5:30–9pm.

Oysters ✿ INTERNATIONAL   It bodes well that Oysters is always crowded with locals, even on weeknights. The nautical theme pervades every room to the point that you can almost convince yourself that you're below deck. The bistro-like menu is vast, featuring Thai, Portuguese, Caribbean, Indian, and traditional Irish entrees. Choices include coconut-crusted chicken with coriander and tiger prawns, or seared salmon with mango and chile sauce with fresh linguine. The modest wine list is well selected and affordable.

Spencer Rd., Waterside, Derry, county Derry. ℂ **028/7134-4875**. Reservations recommended. Dinner main courses £6–£11 ($8.50–$16). MC, V. Mon–Sat 5:30–10pm; Sun 12:30–2:30pm and 5:30–9pm.

Reggie's Seafood Restaurant ✿ SEAFOOD   The freshest fish go into tasty seafood dishes in this bright, cheerful eatery that offers very good value. Recommendable dishes include seafood in a pasta nest with creamy white-wine sauce and filet of turbot with hazelnut mousseline sauce. There is a good cheese board, a selection of teas, and freshly ground Bewley's coffee.

165 Strand Rd., Derry, county Derry. ℂ **028/7126-2050**. Dinner main courses £7–£13 ($9.95–$18). No credit cards. Mon–Fri noon–2:30pm and 5:30–10pm; Sat 5–10:30pm.

INEXPENSIVE

Badger's ✿ PUB GRUB   This comfortable corner pub restaurant is just the place to enjoy a simple, satisfying dinner before the theater, or to settle into after your day's adventures for a drink and a chat. Tastefully decorated and graced with stained glass and wood paneling, the two levels have a Victorian feel but were designed with a more modern appreciation of light and openness. It's a popular meeting spot for locals who come for the friendly service and such well-prepared favorites as savory steak, vegetable and Guinness casserole with a crisp puff-pastry lid, or the flavorful hot sandwiches known as "damper melts."

16–18 Orchard St., Derry, county Derry. ℂ **028/7136-0763**. Reservations not accepted. Dinner main courses £5–£8 ($7.10–$11). MC, V. Mon noon–3pm; Tues–Thurs noon–7pm; Fri–Sat noon–9:30pm.

Ramsey's Cafe ☆ CAFETERIA   At this great budget-minded drop-in eatery in the heart of the city, Anne Ramsey dishes up heaping plates of hot meals, fresh salads, fish and chips, and a variety of bakery items. It's self-service and very busy at almost any hour.

10 William St., Derry, county Derry. ℂ 028/7126-9236. Main courses under £6 ($8.50). No credit cards. Mon–Sat 8am–midnight; Sun 6pm–midnight.

DERRY AFTER DARK

One thing to keep in mind as you're sketching out your after-dark plans is that Derry is one of Ireland's most youthful cities—roughly 40% of its population is under 30. This fact, coupled with an 18-year-old drinking age, means that the night scene is mostly driven by the young—few, if any, gray hairs appear in the hottest spots. On weekends, after 1 or 2am when the clubs empty, the city center can become a rather loud and volatile area.

THE PERFORMING ARTS

Derry has long been associated with the arts, especially theater, poetry, and music. While its financial resources have been modest, its commitment remains inventive and tenacious. Last year's completion of the new **Millennium Forum,** Newmarket Street (box office ℂ 028/7126-4455), inside the city walls, brought a grand cultural meeting place and superb theater into Derry's art scene. Other principal venues for concerts, plays, and poetry readings are the **Guild Hall,** Shipquay Place (ℂ 028/7136-5151); the **Foyle Arts Centre,** Lawrence Hill (ℂ 028/7126-6657); the **Playhouse,** 5–7 Artillery St. (ℂ 028/7126-8027); and the **Rialto,** 5 Market St. (ℂ 028/7126-0516). Ticket prices for most performances range from £12 to £15 ($17–$21).

PUBS

Derry City pubs rarely resemble the small, cozy nooks you often find in the Republic. They tend to be rather grand by comparison and a bit theatrical, more like stage sets than parlors. In addition, Derry pubs are known for their music and communal quiz evenings, when teams compete in a free-range Irish form of Trivial Pursuit. There are even pub debating contests, in the midst of which you'll hear Irish eloquence at its well-lubricated best. Here's a small sampling of Derry's more-than-ample pub options.

Along **Waterloo Street,** just outside the city walls, are a handful of Derry's most traditional and popular pubs, known for their live music and simply as the place to be. The **Dungloe,** the **Gweedore,** and **Peador O'Donnells** are three well-established hot spots. Walk from one end of Waterloo to the other, which will take you all of 2 minutes, and you'll likely find the bar for you.

In addition to visiting Sandinos (see below), gay and lesbian travelers might want to check out **Ascension,** at 64 Strand Rd. It's open until 1am most days and has free disco on Tuesdays and Thursdays and karaoke on Sundays.

The Clarendon   This inviting bar offers more quiet and calm than most of Derry's bars. It's a congenial pub for those who have broken 30 and are somewhere beyond the sonic boom. You can have a conversation here as well as a drink. Sundays and Tuesdays are quiz nights, when you can display whatever wisdom might have come with your years. 48 Strand Rd., Derry, county Derry. ℂ 028/7126-3705.

River Inn/Glue Pot   These two adjoining bars make up the oldest pub in Derry. The downstairs River Inn inhabits cellars opened to the thirsty public in 1684. The upstairs Glue Pot is a more modern cocktail bar, not as appealing as the cellars, but a good deal more appealing than its name. Shipquay St., Derry, county Derry. 🕐 028/7137-1965.

Sandino's Cafe Bar In 1999, the *Irish Times* named this tiny place one of the 100 top pubs in Ireland. It's certainly one of Derry's trendiest bars, where many of the city's gays and lesbians and literary folks prefer to settle in for the evening. Its "South of the Border" theme refers to the States' Mexican border, not to the North's border on the Republic. There are blues on Friday, jazz on Saturday, and an open mike for local poets every Sunday. This intriguing shoe box of a bar can only fit 30 people comfortably, so come early to secure a place for the evening. Water St., Derry, county Derry. 🕐 028/7130-9297.

THE CLUB SCENE

Provided you're under 25 and have no plans to be a piano tuner, there are several places where you'll want to be seen if not heard. Two multientertainment complexes stand out. First, there's **Squires Night Club,** 33 Shipquay St. (🕐 028/ 7126-6017), behind the Townsman bar. Once you pay the cover charge, usually £4 to £7 ($5.70–$9.95), you can make your way up to the VIP or farther back to the 1,200-capacity voxbox. Second, there's **Earth** (possibly recognizable as such), 122–124 Strand Rd. (🕐 028/7130-9372), where your club choices are Café Roc and Coles Bar. The **Strand,** 35–38 Strand Rd. (🕐 028/7126-0494), features a classy bar serving mostly pub grub, and downstairs, an open venue for live bands. On weekend nights, in the bar, the tables are moved aside and the Strand morphs into a nightclub for the 20-plus crowd.

The night scene in Derry, like anywhere else, is a movable feast, so be sure to check the current *What's On?* listings.

7 The Sperrin Mountains

65km (40 miles) E to W along the Derry-Tyrone border

Southeast of Derry, the Sperrin Mountains slowly rise up out of county Tyrone. They reach their highest point at Sawel, from which you can see as far as the Foyle Estuary and across the Northern Ireland countryside to Lough Neagh and the Mournes. This is splendid wide-open walking country that golden plover, red grouse, and thousands upon thousands of sheep call home.

In the Sperrins, you won't be likely to find the tallest, oldest, deepest, or most famous of anything in Ireland. Even the highest peak in the range—Sawel, at 661m (2,204 ft.)—is an easy climb. This is Ireland in a minor key. It is a corner of Ireland largely unsung and unspoiled. You'll see mostly wildflowers here, rather than formal gardens, and cottages rather than castles. All the same, gold has been found in these mountains. Poetry, too. The Nobel-winning poet Seamus Heaney grew up on the edge of the Sperrins and found words to suit their subtle splendor.

Unless you come to farm, chances are you'll spend your time exploring the dark russet blanket bogs and purple heathland, the gorse-covered hillsides, and the lovely forest parks, whether on foot, cycle, or horseback. For the more acquisitive, there are salmon and trout on the Foyle System from Strabane to Omagh, as well as game on the moors. There are also a few first-rate historical museums and sights for the whole family. As for minor destinations for a morning walk or an afternoon drive, there's no shortage of standing stones (about 1,000 have been counted), high crosses, dolmens, and hill forts—more reminders that every last bit of bog on this island has its own slew of stories, if only we could hear them told.

VISITOR INFORMATION   There are four nationally networked tourist information centers in county Tyrone. The **Cookstown Centre,** 48 Molesworth St., Cookstown (✆ **028/8676-6727**), is open weekdays 9am to 5pm, with weekend and extended hours Easter to September. The **Kilmaddy Centre,** Ballgawley Road (off A4), Dungannon (✆ **028/8776-7259**), is open Monday to Thursday 9am to 5pm, with Friday and weekend hours in the spring and summer. The **Omagh Centre,** 1 Market St., Omagh (✆ **028/8224-7831**), is open Easter to September Monday to Saturday 9am to 5pm; October to Easter Monday to Friday 9am to 5pm. The **Strabane Centre,** Abercorn Square, Strabane (✆ **028/ 7188-3735**), is open April to October Monday to Saturday 9:30am to 5pm.

SEEING THE SIGHTS

An Creagán Visitors' Centre   This is a helpful place to get your bearings in the Sperrins. Besides viewing interpretive exhibitions on the region, you can find the best cycling and trekking routes, rent bicycles, and have a meal in the restaurant.

A505 (20km/12½ miles east of Omagh), Creggan, county Tyrone. ✆ **028/8076-1112.** Admission £2 ($2.85) adults, £1 ($1.40) children. Apr–Sept daily 11am–6:30pm; Oct–Mar Mon–Fri 11am–4:30pm.

Beaghmore Stone Circles ✦   In 1945, six stone circles and a complex assembly of cairns and alignments were uncovered here, in remote moorland north of Evishbrack Mountain and near Davagh Forest Park on the southern edge of the Sperrins. The precise function of this intriguing concentration of Bronze Age stonework is unknown, but it may have involved astronomical observation and calculation.

17km (10½ miles) northwest of Cookstown, signposted from A505 to Omagh, county Tyrone.

Drum Manor Forest Park ✦   Once a private estate, this extensive park and woodland has numerous trails and three old walled gardens, one of which has been designed as a butterfly garden. There is also a pond that attracts a variety of wildfowl, a heronry, and a visitor center with exhibits on butterflies and other local wildlife.

4km (2½ miles) west of Cookstown on A505, county Tyrone. ✆ **028/8676-2774.** Admission £3 ($4.25) per car; pedestrians £1 ($1.40) adults, 50p (70¢) children. Daily 10am–dusk.

Gortin Glen Forest Park ✦✦   Nearly 400 hectares (1,000 acres) of planted conifers make up this beautiful nature park, established in 1967. The woodlands are a habitat to a variety of wildlife, including a herd of Japanese silka deer. The park's 7.3km (4½-mile) forest drive offers some splendid vistas of the Sperrins. There is also a nature center, wildlife enclosures, trails, and a cafe. For those planning to arrive and leave on foot, the Ulster Way passes through the park.

B48 (11km/7 miles north of Omagh), Cullion, county Tyrone. ✆ **028/8164-8217.** Free admission. Parking £3 ($4.25). Daily 9am to 1 hr. before sunset.

Grant Ancestral Home   This farm cottage was the home of the ancestors of Ulysses S. Grant, 18th president of the United States. Grant's maternal great-grandfather, John Simpson, was born here and emigrated to Pennsylvania in 1738 at the age of 22. The cottage has two rooms with mud floors and has been restored and furnished with period pieces, including a settle bed and dresser. The site includes a visitor center with an audiovisual presentation, a tearoom, and various exhibits, including a collection of typical 18th-century agricultural implements.

32km (20 miles) southeast of Omagh off A4, Dergina, Ballygawley, county Tyrone. ✆ **028/7188-3735.** Admission £1 ($1.40) adults, 50p (70¢) seniors and children. Apr–Sept Mon–Sat noon–5pm; Sun 2–6pm.

Gray's Printers' Museum   The museum and print shop housed together here are unrelated (apart from being "flatmates"). The print shop, maintained by the National Trust, dates from 1760. It has an attractive bow-front window and an exhibit of 19th-century hand-operated printing presses. John Dunlop, founder of the first daily newspaper in the United States and printer of the American Declaration of Independence, learned his trade here. An audiovisual show provides insight into how the original presses operated and the part Dunlop played in America's early printing days. The museum, operated by the local district council, is a venue for changing exhibits germane to the history and culture of the region. Access to the printing press is through the museum.

49 Main St., Strabane, county Tyrone. ℭ **028/7188-4094**. Admission £2 ($2.85) adults, £1 ($1.40) children, £5 ($7.10) family. Museum Tues–Fri 11am–5pm; Sat 11:30am–5pm. Guided tours of printing press Apr–Sept Tues–Sat 2–5pm.

Plantation of Ulster Visitor Centre ⚑   This newish interpretive center tells the story of the Ulster Plantation of 1610, which marked the completion of the Elizabethan Conquest of Ireland. To do so, it uses an array of graphic images, audiovisual presentations, and interactive displays. Anyone wanting to understand the divisions that to this day define Irish geography and disrupt Irish life would do well to consider the center's informative and moving exhibits. The restaurant serves homemade meals, and the gift shop stocks a selection of local crafts.

50 High St., Draperstown, county Derry. ℭ **028/7922-7800**. Admission £3 ($4.25) adults, £2.50 ($3.55) seniors and students, £1.50 ($2.15) children, £8 ($11) family. Apr–Sept daily 10am–5pm; Oct–Mar daily 10am–4pm.

Sperrin Heritage Centre ⚑⚑   Here, in the heart of the Sperrins, is *the* place to get the local bearings and background. A range of computerized presentations and other exhibits introduce the history, culture, geology, and wildlife of the region. This is a gold-mining area, and for a small additional fee (65p/90¢ adults, 35p/50¢ children) you'll get a chance to try your hand at panning for gold. A cafeteria, craft shop, and nature trail share the grounds.

274 Glenelly Rd. (east of Plumbridge off B47), Cranagh, county Tyrone. ℭ **028/8164-8142**. Admission £2 ($2.85) adults, £1 ($1.40) seniors and children. Apr–Sept Mon–Fri 11am–6pm; Sat 11:30am–6pm; Sun 2–7pm.

Tyrone Crystal ⚑⚑   With a 200-year-old tradition, this crystal factory is one of Ireland's oldest and best known. Visitors are welcome to tour the operation and see glass being blown and crafted, carved, and engraved by hand. A 25-minute audiovisual presentation tells the story of the development of Tyrone Crystal, a showroom displays the finished products, and a very good cafe adds sustenance.

Oaks Rd. (3.2km/2 miles east of town), Killybrackey, Dungannon, county Tyrone. ℭ **028/8772-5335**. Admission £2 ($2.85) adults, free for seniors and children. Craft shop Mon–Sat 9am–5pm. Tours every 30 min. Apr–Oct Mon–Thurs and Sat 9:30am–3:30pm, Fri 9:30am–noon; Nov–Mar Mon–Thurs 9:30am–3:30pm, Fri 9:30am–noon.

Ulster-American Folk Park ⚑⚑   This outdoor museum presents the story of emigration from this part of rural Ireland to America in the 18th and 19th centuries. There are reconstructions of the thatched cottages the emigrants left behind, and replicas of the log cabins that became their homes on the American frontiers. The park developed around the homestead where Thomas Mellon was born in 1813. He went to Pittsburgh and prospered to the point where his son Andrew became one of the world's richest men. The Mellon family donated part of the funding to build this excellent park. Walk-through exhibits include a forge, weaver's cottage, smokehouse, schoolhouse, post office, Sperrin Mountain famine cabin, and full-scale replica of an emigrant ship in a dockside area that features original buildings from the ports of Derry, Belfast, and Newry. A self-guided tour of all the exhibits, which are staffed by interpreters in period costume, takes about 2 hours. Musical events that tie in with the Ulster-American theme, such as a bluegrass music festival in September, take place each year.

Mellon Rd. (4.8km/3 miles north of Omagh on A5), Castletown, Camphill, Omagh, county Tyrone. ℂ 028/ 8224-3292. www.folkpark.com. Admission £4 ($5.70) adults, £2.50 ($3.55) seniors and children 5–16, £10 ($14) family. Oct–Easter Mon–Fri 10:30am–5pm; Easter–Sept Mon–Sat 10:30am–6pm, Sun 11am–6:30pm. Last admission 1 hour before closing.

Ulster History Park ★   Ireland's history from the Stone Age to the 17th-century plantation period is the focus of this outdoor theme park. There are full-scale models of homes, castles, and monuments through the ages, including a Mesolithic encampment, Neolithic dwelling, crannóg lake dwelling, church settlement with round tower, and motte-and-bailery type of castle common. The park also contains an audiovisual theater, a gift shop, and a cafeteria.

Cullion (on B48, 11km/7 miles north of Omagh), Omagh, county Tyrone. ℂ 028/8164-8188. Admission £4 ($5.70) adults, £2.50 ($3.55) seniors, students, and children, £10 ($14) family. Apr–Sept Mon–Sat 10:30am–6:30pm, Sun 11:30am–7pm; Oct–Mar Mon–Fri 10:30am–5pm. Last admission 90 min. before closing. Bus: From Omagh.

Wilson Ancestral Home   This small thatched, whitewashed cottage on the slopes of the Sperrin Mountains was the home of Judge James Wilson, grandfather of Woodrow Wilson, 28th president of the United States. James Wilson left the house in 1807 at the age of 20. It contains some of the family's original furniture, including a tiny out-shot bed (sleeping nook) in the kitchen close to the fire, larger curtained beds, and a portrait of the president's grandfather over the fireplace. Wilsons still occupy the modern farmhouse next door. *Note:* Opening hours are subject to change; phone in advance.

Off Plumbridge Rd., Dergalt, Strabane, county Tyrone. ℂ 028/8224-3292. Admission £1 ($1.40) adults, 50p (70¢) children. Apr–Sept daily 2–6pm.

SPORTS & OUTDOOR PURSUITS

BICYCLING   The Sperrin countryside is ideal for cycling. Bicycles can be rented by the day or week from the **An Creagán Visitors' Centre** (see "Seeing the Sights," above), or from **Conway Cycles,** 1 Old Market Place, Omagh (ℂ 028/ 8224-6195). Bike rentals run roughly £8 ($11) a day or £34 ($48) a week.

BIRD-WATCHING   The Sperrins are home to golden plovers, peregrines, ravens, grouse, and hen harriers. **Sawel Mountain,** the highest of the Sperrins, is a great place to take out your binoculars and field guide.

FISHING   The **Foyle System** of rivers, from Derry to Omagh and Limavady to Dungiven, makes this a promising area for snagging brown and sea trout (Apr to early July and Sept) and a variety of salmon (Mar–Sept). There's also some good coarse fishing available north and west of Omagh, on the Baronscourt Lakes and on the Strule and Fairy Water Rivers. The necessary permits, equipment, and good advice are available from **C. A. Anderson & Co.,** 64 Market St., Omagh (ℂ 028/8224-2311); **Mourne Valley Tackle,** 50 Main St., Newtownstewart (ℂ 028/8166-1543); and **Floyd's Fish and Tackle,** 28 Melmount Villas, Strabane (ℂ 028/7188-3981). In fact, if you're in the market for an experienced *ghillie* (guide), ask at Floyd's for Martin Floyd.

GOLF   There are several 18-hole courses in county Tyrone within a modest drive from the heart of the Sperrins: **Strabane Golf Club,** 33 Ballycolman Rd., Strabane (✆ **028/7138-2007**), with greens fees of £17 ($24) weekdays, £20 ($28) on weekends; **Newtownstewart Golf Club,** 38 Golf Course Rd., Newtownstewart (✆ **028/8166-1466**), with greens fees of £14 ($20) weekdays, £19 ($27) weekends; **Omagh Golf Club,** 83a Dublin Rd., Omagh (✆ **028/8164-1442**), with greens fees of £14 ($20) weekdays, £20 ($28) weekends; and **Killymoon Golf Club,** 200 Killymoon Rd., Cookstown (✆ **028/8676-3762**), with greens fees of £20 ($28) weekdays, £25 ($36) weekends.

HORSEBACK RIDING   To rent by the hour or take a multiday journey through the mountains, contact the **Edergole Riding Centre,** 7 Moneymore Rd., Cookstown (✆ **028/8676-2924**).

WALKING   Whether you're on foot, wheels, or horseback, be sure to traverse the **Glenshane Pass** between Mullaghmore (545m/1,818 ft.) and Carntogher (455m/1,516 ft.), and the **Sawel Mountain Drive** along the east face of the mountain. The vistas along these routes through the Sperrins will remind you of why you've gone out of your way to spend time in Tyrone.

WHERE TO STAY
MODERATE
Grange Lodge ⭐⭐   Norah and Ralph Brown are the gracious hosts of this handsome Georgian guesthouse, which began life as a 17th-century settler's hall. Set high on a hill atop a 8-hectare (20-acre) estate, it's a classy, tranquil retreat and a good base for day trips throughout county Tyrone. Guest rooms are attractive and comfortable, but the best reason for staying here is the food. Norah has won all sorts of culinary awards, and her lovingly-prepared, home-style meals have achieved almost cult status in this otherwise gastronomically-challenged part of the North. At breakfast, don't miss the house specialty: Porridge infused with Bushmills Whiskey and cream. And do book for dinner, too (£25/$36), for you'll eat better here than anywhere else in the Sperrins. Unfortunately for nonguests, Norah only cooks for residents of Grange Lodge.

7 Grange Rd. (signposted 1.6km/1 mile south of M1, Junction 15), Moy, Dungannon, county Tyrone. ✆ **028/8778-4212.** Fax 028/8778-4313. 5 units. £78 ($111) double. Rates include full breakfast. MC, V. Closed Jan. **Amenities:** Nonsmoking rooms; sitting room. *In room:* TV.

INEXPENSIVE
The Grange ⭐ *(Kids)*   There's loads of character in this charming little cottage near the Ballygawley roundabout and the Folk Park. It dates from 1720, but has been thoroughly modernized. Mrs. Lyttle is the hostess, and her rooms (two doubles and one single) are done up nicely with sturdy farmhouse furniture and homey bedspreads. Mrs. Lyttle welcomes small children.

15 Grange Rd., Ballygawley, county Tyrone. ✆ **028/8556-8053.** 3 units. £36 ($51) double. Children's discount available. Rates include full breakfast. No credit cards. Closed Dec. **Amenities:** Laundry facilities; sitting room. *In room:* TV.

Greenmount Lodge ⭐ *(Kids)*   This large, first-rate guesthouse is set on a 60-hectare (150-acre) farm. All the bedrooms were refurbished a few years back and are nicely appointed; four are family units. Mrs. Frances Reid, the friendly hostess, is a superb cook; both breakfasts and evening meals are a home-style delight.

58 Greenmount Rd. (13km/8 miles southeast of Omagh on A5), Gortaclare, Omagh, county Tyrone. ✆ **028/8284-1325.** Fax 028/8284-0019. 8 units. £42 ($60) double. Children's discount available. Rates include full breakfast. Dinner £16 ($23). MC, V. **Amenities:** Sitting room. *In room:* TV.

SELF-CATERING

Sperrin Clachan ★★ This restored *clachan,* or family cottage compound, sits beside the Sperrin Heritage Centre in the beautiful Glenelly Valley. It makes an ideal base for exploring the natural riches and cultural legacy of the Sperrin region, as well as the city of Derry, only 40km (25 miles) to the north. Each cottage has everything you'll need to set up house, including central heating and an open fireplace. There are four cottages in all; each sleeps two to five people. In addition to these, Rural Cottage Holidays offers a wide array of other traditional cottages in the region, including the award-winning, four-star Glenelly Cottages.

Glenelly Valley, Cranagh, county Tyrone. Contact RCH at ℂ **028/9024-1100.** Fax 028/9024-1198. www. cottagesinireland.com. 4 cottages. £110–£330 ($156–$469) per week. Also available for 2- or 3-day stays. No credit cards. Free parking. **Amenities:** Kitchen; fridge; oven/stove; microwave; dishwasher; washing machine. *In room:* TV.

WHERE TO DINE

Mellon Country Inn ★ INTERNATIONAL Located 1.6km (1 mile) north of the Ulster-American Folk Park, this old-world country inn combines an Irish theme with a connection to the Mellons of Pennsylvania. The menu includes simple fare—burgers, soup, salads, and ploughman's platters—as well as elegant dishes such as lobster Newburg, beef Stroganoff, coquilles St.-Jacques, and sole *bonne femme.* The house specialty is Tyrone black steak, a locally bred hormone-free beef. Food is available all day on a hot and cold buffet, and you can also order a late breakfast or afternoon tea.

134 Beltany Rd., Omagh, county Tyrone. ℂ **028/8166-1244.** Fax 028/8166-2245. Dinner main courses £9–£17 ($13–$24). AE, MC, V. Daily 10:30am–10pm.

8 The Fermanagh Lakelands

Enniskillen, in the heart of the Fermanagh Lakelands, is 134km (83 miles) SW of Belfast, 98km (61 miles) SW of Derry, 84km (52 miles) W of Armagh, 44km (27 miles) SW of Omagh, 174km (108 miles) NW of Dublin, and 271km (168 miles) NE of Shannon

Tucked in the extreme southwest corner of Northern Ireland, county Fermanagh is a premier resort area dominated by **Lough Erne,** a long lake dotted with 154 islands and rimmed by countless alcoves and inlets. It has 81km (50 miles) of cruising waters—the least congested in Europe—ranging from a shallow channel in some places to a 8km (5-mile) width in others. The total signposted driving circuit around the lake is 105km (65 miles).

The 1994 reopening of the **Shannon-Erne Waterway,** linking the lough to the Shannon system, greatly enhanced the lure of Lough Erne as a cruising destination. The 65km (40-mile) waterway between the cross-border village of Leitrim and Lough Erne consists of a series of 16 lochs, three lakes, and the Woodford River.

The hub of this lakeland paradise, wedged between the upper and lower branches of Lough Erne, is **Enniskillen,** a delightful resort town that was the medieval seat of the Maguire clan and a major crossroads between Ulster and Connaught. Both Oscar Wilde and Samuel Beckett were once students here, at the royal school.

At the northern tip of the lake is **Belleek,** sitting right on the border with the Republic of Ireland, and known the world over for delicate bone chinaware. At the southern end of the lake is county Cavan and another slice of border with the Irish Republic. The surrounding countryside holds diverse attractions, from stately homes at Florence Court and Castle Coole to the unique Marble Arch Caves. In the waters lie myriad islands, Devenish and Boa being two of the most interesting.

In medieval times, a chain of island monasteries stretched across the waters of Lough Erne, establishing it as a haven for contemplatives. Making certain allowances for less lofty minds, the Fermanagh Lakelands remain a great place to get away from it all and to gaze, in a phrase from Hopkins, at the "pied beauty" of it all.

VISITOR INFORMATION   Contact the **Fermanagh Tourist Information Centre,** Wellington Road, Enniskillen, county Fermanagh (© **028/7032-3110**). It's open weekdays, year-round, from 9am to 5:30pm (7pm July–Aug). From Easter to September it's also open on weekends, Saturday 10am to 6pm and Sunday 11am to 5pm. For an introduction to the Fermanagh Lakelands on the Web, take a look at **www.fermanagh-online.com**.

EXPLORING THE LAKELANDS
TOURING THE LAKES & ISLANDS

Erne Tours Ltd., Enniskillen (© **028/6632-2882**), operates cruises on Lower Lough Erne. The M.V. *Kestrel,* a 63-seat cruiser, departs from the Round "O" Jetty, Brook Park, Enniskillen. Trips, including a stop at Devenish Island, last just under 2 hours. They operate daily in July and August at 10:30am, 2:15, and 4:15pm; in May and June on Sunday at 2:30pm; and in September on Tuesday, Saturday, and Sunday at 2:30pm. Call for reservations and to confirm times. The fare is £5 ($7.10) for adults, £2.50 ($3.55) for children under 14.

The **Share Holiday Village,** Smith's Strand, Lisnaskea (© **028/6772-2122**), operates cruises on Upper Lough Erne. These 1½-hour trips are conducted on board the *Inishcruiser,* a 57-passenger ship. Sailings are scheduled Easter through September on Sunday at 2:30pm (July–Aug also Thurs–Sun at 2:30pm). The fare is £7 ($9.95) for adults, and £6 ($8.50) for seniors and children under 18. Share Centre also offers other watersports activities and self-catering chalets.

Independent boatmen offer ferry crossings to some of the many islands in Lough Erne. White Island, Devinish Island, and Boa Island are particularly rich in archaeological and early-Christian remains. Devenish Island boasts Lough Erne's most important island monastery, founded in the 6th century by St. Molaise. The extensive remains include a 12th-century round tower that can be climbed. From April to September, a ferry runs to Devenish Island from Trory Point, 6.5km (4 miles) from Enniskillen on A32; journey time is about 12 minutes. On White Island, there remain seven stone figures from a vanished 10th-century monastery inside a ruined 12th-century church. From April through August, a ferry runs to White Island, departing from Castle Archdale Marina, (© **028/6862-1333** or mobile 0836/787123), 16km (10 miles) from Enniskillen on the Kesh road; journey time is about 18 minutes. Departures April through June are on Sunday only, every hour on the hour from 11am to 6pm with the exception of 1pm. July and August the ferry runs daily, with the same sailing times. The round-trip fare is £3 ($4.25) for adults and £2 ($2.85) for children. In the cemetery at the west end of Boa Island, there are two ancient Janus (looking both ways) idols, which are thought to date from the 1st century. Boa Island is connected to the shore by bridges. Though it's possible to visit all three islands in a single day, it's a bit ambitious. Begin with Devinish, then visit White, and, if time permits, finish up with Boa.

SEEING THE SIGHTS

Belleek Pottery ★★   With the exception of Waterford crystal, Belleek china is the name most readily identified throughout the world as a symbol of the finest Irish craftsmanship. Established in 1857, this pottery enterprise produces distinctive, delicate porcelain china, made into tableware, vases, ornaments, and other pieces. The visitor center has a museum showing the product from its earliest days to the present. Tours are conducted weekdays every 20 minutes, with the last tour at 3:30pm. The coffee shop serves tea, coffee, snacks, and a hot lunch.

Belleek, county Fermanagh. ☎ 028/6865-8501. www.belleek.ie. Free admission; tours £2.50 ($3.55) adults and children over 12. Apr–June and Sept, Mon–Fri 9am–6pm, Sat 10am–6pm, Sun 2–6pm; July–Aug Mon–Fri 9am–6pm, Sat 10am–6pm, Sun 11am–6pm; Oct Mon–Fri 9am–5:30pm, Sat 10am–5:30pm, Sun 2–6pm; Nov Mon–Fri 9am–5:30pm, Sat 10am–5:30pm; Dec–Mar Mon–Fri 9am–5:30pm.

Castle Coole ★   On the east bank of Lower Lough Erne, this quintessential neoclassical mansion was designed by James Wyatt for the earl of Belmore and completed in 1796. Its rooms include a lavish state bedroom hung with crimson silk, said to have been prepared for George IV. Other features include a Chinese-style sitting room, magnificent woodwork, fireplaces, and furniture dating from the 1830s. A nearly 600-hectare (1,500-acre) woodland estate surrounds the house. A classical music series runs from May to October.

2.4km (1½ miles) southeast of Enniskillen on the main Belfast-Enniskillen rd. (A4), county Fermanagh. ☎ 028/6632-2690. House admission £3 ($4.25) adults, £1.50 ($2.15) children, £8 ($11) family; grounds £2 ($2.85) per car. Easter–May and Sept Sat–Sun 1–6pm; June–Aug Fri–Wed 1–6pm (last tour 5:15pm).

Crom Estate ★★   This nearly 800-hectare (2,000-acre) nature reserve is a splendid National Trust property, with forest, parks, wetlands, fen meadows, and an award-winning lakeshore visitor center. There are numerous trails, with hides for observing birds and wildlife, as well as a heronry and boat rental. The estate is also a great place to fish for bream and roach. Permits and day tickets are available at the gate lodge. During the summer, there are frequently special programs and guided nature walks on weekends.

Newtownbutler, county Fermanagh. ☎ 028/6773-8118. Admission £3 ($4.25) per car or boat. Apr–Sept Mon–Sat 10am–6pm, Sun noon–6pm. 34km (21 miles) south of Enniskillen. Take A4 and A34 from Enniskillen to Newtownbutler, then take the signposted right turn onto a minor road.

Devenish Island ★★   This is the most extensive of the ancient Christian sites in Lough Erne. In the 6th century, St. Molaise founded a monastic community here, to which the Augustinian Abbey of St. Mary was added in the 12th century. In other words, this is hallowed ground, hallowed all the more by the legend that the prophet Jeremiah is buried somewhere nearby—if you can figure that one out. The intact 12th-century round tower was erected with Vikings in mind. The island is a marvelous mélange of remnants and ruins, providing a glimpse into the lake's mystical past. While you're in the spirit, be sure to explore Boa and White islands, with their extraordinary carved stone figures, and bring your camera (see the introduction to this section for details on island hopping).

2.4km (1½ miles) downstream from Enniskillen. Admission £1.50 ($2.15). Ferry from Trory Point (6.5km/4 miles from Enniskillen on A32). Apr–Sept every 20–30 min. Round-trip fare £2.50 ($3.55) adults, £1.50 ($2.15) children.

Enniskillen Castle ★★   Dating from the 15th century, this magnificent stone fortress sits overlooking Lough Erne on the western edge of town. It incorporates three museums: the medieval castle, with its unique twin-turreted Watergate tower, once the seat of the Maguires, chieftains of Fermanagh; the county museum, with exhibits on the area's history, wildlife, and landscape; and

---

Tips **Arts & Crafts**

If you'd rather sketch a trout than snag it, you might want to contact the **Ardess Craft Centre,** near Kesh (⌀ **028/6863-1267**). It offers a range of courses, from drawing and painting to stone walling and weaving. Room and board are available and optional. For a complete guide to crafts in the Fermanagh region, go to **www.fermanaghcraft.com**.

---

the museum of the famous Royal Inniskilling Fusiliers, with a collection of uniforms, weapons, and medals dating from the 17th century. Other exhibits include life-size figurines and 3-D models of old-time castle life.

Castle Barracks, Enniskillen, county Fermanagh. ⌀ **028/6632-5000.** Admission £2 ($2.85) adults, £1.50 ($2.15) seniors and students, £1 ($1.40) children, £5 ($7.10) family. May–June and Sept Mon 2–5pm, Tues–Fri 10am–5pm, Sat 2–5pm; July–Aug Tues–Fri 10am–5pm, Sat–Mon 2–5pm; Oct–Apr Mon 2–5pm, Tues–Fri 10am–5pm.

ExplorErne ⚑   Just outside Belleek village, this exhibition offers an engaging multimedia introduction to Lough Erne. It covers its geologic formation and the lives, ancient and modern, lived along its reedy banks. Science, myth, and history blend to tell the story of this legendary, alluring lake.

Erne Gateway Centre, off main Enniskillen-Belleek rd., Corry, Belleek, county Fermanagh. ⌀ **028/6865-8866.** Admission £1 ($1.40) adults, 50p (70¢) seniors and children, £2.50 ($3.55) family. Mid-Mar to Oct daily 10am–6pm.

Florence Court ⚑⚑   One of the most beautifully situated houses in Northern Ireland, this 18th-century Palladian mansion is set among dramatic hills, 13km (8 miles) southwest of Upper Lough Erne and Enniskillen. Originally the seat of the earls of Enniskillen, its interior is rich in rococo plasterwork and antique Irish furniture, while its exterior has a fine walled garden, an icehouse, and a water wheel–driven sawmill. The forest park offers a number of trails, one leading to the top of Mount Cuilcagh (nearly 660m/2,200 ft.). There's also a tearoom.

Florence Court, off A32, county Fermanagh. ⌀ **028/6634-8249.** Admission £3 ($4.25) adults, £1.50 ($3.55) children, £8 ($11) family. Apr and Sept Sat–Sun 1–6pm; May–Aug Wed–Mon 1–6pm.

Marble Arch Caves ⚑⚑⚑ *Kids*   Located west of Upper Lough Erne and 19km (12 miles) from Enniskillen near the Florence Court estate, these caves are among the finest in Europe for exploring underground rivers, winding passages, and hidden chambers. Electrically powered boat tours take visitors underground, and knowledgeable guides explain the origins of the amazing stalactites and stalagmites. Tours last 75 minutes and leave at 15-minute intervals. The caves are occasionally closed after heavy rains, so phone ahead before making the trip.

Marlbank, Florence Court, off A32, county Fermanagh. ⌀ **028/6634-8855.** Admission £6 ($8.50) adults, £4 ($5.70) seniors and students, £3 ($4.25) children under 18, £14 ($20) family. Reservations recommended. Late Mar–June and Sept, daily 10am–4:30pm (last tour at 4:30pm); July–Aug daily 10am–5pm (last tour at 5pm).

SHOPPING

Enniskillen has fine shops along its main street, which changes its name six times (East Bridge, Townhall, High, Church, Darling, Ann) as it runs the length of the town. Most shops are open Monday to Saturday 9:30am to 5:30pm.

The largest shopping complex in Enniskillen is the **Erneside Shopping Center,** a modern bilevel mall on Shore Road, just off Wellington Road. It stays open until 9pm on Thursday and Friday. The other principal towns for shopping in the area are **Irvinestown** and **Lisnaskea.**

The town's former Butter Market offers a nifty shopping experience. Dating from 1835, it has been restored and transformed into **The Buttermarket, The Enniskillen Craft and Design Centre,** Down Street (© **028/6632-3837**). It offers craft workshops and retail outlets, with occasional traditional music, craft fairs, and street theater to enliven the atmosphere.

SPORTS & OUTDOOR PURSUITS

BICYCLING   Several of the watersports and activity centers in the area, such as **Erne Tours** and **Lakeland Canoe Center** (see "Watersports," below), also rent bicycles. Bicycles are also available from **Corralea Activity Centre,** Belcoo (© **028/6638-6668**); **Out & Out Activities,** 501 Rosscor, Belleek (© **028/6865-8105**); and **Marble Arch Cycle Hire,** 69 Marlbank Rd., Florencecourt (© **028/6634-8320**). Daily bike rental runs £7 to £10 ($9.95–$14). For cycle tours with **Kingfisher Cycle Trail,** contact Pat Collum at the Tourist Information Centre, Wellington Road, Enniskillen (© **028/6632-0121;** www.cycle ireland.com).

BIRD-WATCHING   These lakelands are prime bird-watching territory. To mention a few, you'll find whooper swans, great-crested grebes, golden plovers, curlews, corncrakes, kingfishers, herons, merlins, peregrines, kestrels, and sparrow hawks. On Upper Lough Erne, the primary habitats are the reed swamps, flooded drumlins, and fen; on the lower lake, the habitats of choice are the less-visited islands and the hay meadows. Two important preserves are at the Crom Estate (see "Seeing the Sights," above) and the Castlecaldwell Forest and Islands.

BOATING   Lough Erne is an explorer's dream, and you can take that dream all the way to the Atlantic if you want. The price range for fully equipped two- to eight-berth cruisers is £460 to £1,300 ($653–$1,846) per week, including VAT, depending on the season and the size of the boat. The many local cruiser-hire companies include **Belleek Charter Cruising,** Belleek (© **028/6865-8027;** www.angelfire.com/co/belleekcruising); **Erne Marine,** Bellanaleck (© **028/6634-8267**); and **Erincurrach Cruising,** Blaney (© **028/6864-1737;** www.ernemarine.com). Erincurrach has a cruiser that's specially adapted for travelers with disabilities.

On Lower Lough Erne, north of town, you can hire motorboats from **Manor House Marine,** Killadeas (© **028/6862-8100**). Charges average £45 ($64) for a half day, and £65 ($92) for a full day.

FISHING   The **Fermanagh Lakes** are an angler's heaven. If you can't catch a fish here, you must have been one in a past life. The best time for salmon is February to mid-June; for trout, mid-March to June or mid-August until late September. As for coarse fishing, about a dozen species await your line in the area's lakes and rivers. If you've left time for advance planning and consultation, contact the **Fisheries Conservancy Board,** 1 Mahon Rd., Portadown BT62 3EE (© **028/3833-4666**). For on-the-spot info, tackle, and bait, try **Trevor Kingston,** 18 Church St., Enniskillen (© **028/6632-2114**). For locally arranged game fishing, call or drop in on **Melvin Tackle,** Main Street, Garrison, county Fermanagh (© **028/6865-8194**). All necessary permits and licenses are available at the **Fermanagh Tourist Information Centre** (see "Visitor Information," above).

GOLF There are two 18-hole courses in the Lakelands, both in Enniskillen. The **Enniskillen Golf Club,** in the Castle Coole estate (② **028/6632-5250**), charges greens fees of £17 ($24) weekdays, £20 ($28) weekends. The **Castle Hume Golf Club,** Castle Hume (② **028/6632-7077**; www.castlehumegolf. com), is 5.6km (3½ miles) north of Enniskillen, with greens fees of £18 ($26) weekdays, £23 ($33) weekends.

HORSEBACK RIDING The **Ulster Lakeland Equestrian Centre,** Necarne Castle, Irvinestown (② **028/6862-1919**), is an international center that offers full equestrian holidays. Pony trekking and riding lessons are available from **Drumhoney Stables,** Lisnarick (② **028/6862-1892**), and **Lakeview Riding Centre,** Leggs, Belleek (② **028/6865-8163**).

WALKING The southwestern branch of the **Ulster Way** follows the western shores of Lough Erne, between the lake and the border. The area is full of great walks. One excellent 11km (7-mile, 3- to 7-hr.) hike is from a starting point near Florence Court and the Marble Arch Caves (see "Seeing the Sights," above) to the summit of **Mount Cuilagh** (656m/2,188 ft.). A trail map is included in the Northern Ireland Tourist Board's *Information Guide to Walking*.

WATERSPORTS The **Lakeland Canoe Center,** Castle Island, Enniskillen (② **028/6632-4250**), is a watersports center based on an island west of downtown. For a full day of canoeing and other sports, including archery, cycling, dinghy sailing, and windsurfing, prices start roughly at £12 ($17) per day. Camping and simple accommodations are also available at a modest cost. The **Share Holiday Village,** Smith's Strand, Lisnaskea (② **028/6772-2122**; www.sharevillage.org), offers sailing, canoeing, windsurfing, and banana skiing. A single 2½-hour session, including instruction and equipment, costs £5 ($7.10) per person. Other watersports centers include the **Boa Island Activity Centre,** Tudor Farm, Kesh (② **028/6863-1943**; www.tudorfarm.com); and the **Drumrush Watersports Centre,** Kesh (② **028/6863-1035**; www.drumrush. co.uk).

WHERE TO STAY
EXPENSIVE

Castle Leslie ★★★ *(Finds)* This majestic place is where ex-Beatle Paul McCartney wed Heather Mills in June 2002. W. B. Yeats, Winston Churchill, and Mick Jagger also loved Castle Leslie, a quintessential Victorian retreat just across the border in county Monaghan. A stay here is one of Ireland's unique surprises, an experience well worth whatever detour it takes. The 400-hectare (1,000-acre) estate, with its three lakes (famous for pike) and ancient hardwood forests, casts a relaxing spell, and the great house—about 2,500 sq. m (27,000 sq. ft.) of history—is as comfortable as an old slipper. This is a place of astounding treasures—the bridle worn by Wellington's horse Copenhagen at Waterloo, Wordsworth's harp, the Bechstein grand on which Wagner composed *Tristan and Isolde,* and Winston Churchill's baby clothes, to mention only a few. The greatest treasures are the stories you will take away with you. Each unique, anecdote-rich guest room has its own special feature—a claw-foot tub in an alcove near the bed, a spectacular view in a bay window, or perhaps a beefy four-poster bed. (The hotel's website has photos of each room, so you can book your favorite in advance). The meals alone (see "Where to Dine," below) are worth the drive.

Glasslough, county Monaghan. ② **047/88109.** Fax 047/88256. www.castleleslie.com. 14 units, 4 with shower only. £154–£206 ($219–$293) double. Rates include full Irish breakfast and service charge. Packages available. MC, V. **Amenities:** Restaurant (Continental); tennis courts; drawing room. *In room:* TV, hair dryer.

MODERATE

Manor House Country Hotel ★★ *Kids*   Dating from 1860, this splendid three-story Victorian mansion has a varied history that includes its use by American forces as a base during World War II. The public areas are full of antiques and ornate plasterwork, and the windows look out to Lough Erne. Rooms are furnished in traditional style, with dark woods, frilly fabrics, and decorative wallpaper; some have four-posters or half-canopy beds. The hotel sits on the shores of Lower Lough Erne, 8.9km (5½ miles) north of Enniskillen. For those traveling with kids and sick of sacrificing character for convenience, this place offers luxurious charm in spades. Kid-friendly facilities include a swimming pool, minigolf, and a supervised playroom.

Killadeas, Irvinestown, Enniskillen, county Fermanagh. © 028/6862-1561. Fax 028/6862-1545. www.manor-house-hotel.com. 46 units. £116 ($165) double. Rates include full breakfast. AE, MC, V. **Amenities:** Restaurant (Continental); 2 bars; indoor swimming pool; miniature golf; tennis court; gym; sauna/steam room; marina; supervised children's playroom; beauty treatments. *In room:* TV, tea/coffeemaker, garment press.

INEXPENSIVE

Belmore Court Motel ★ *Value*   If you're just looking for a bed on which to crash, this three-story motel offers a variety of accommodations, from single rooms to family rooms, at rock bottom prices. It's the same motel principle as in the United States: bland decor, no amenities, but rates that you really can't beat. Most rooms have kitchenettes, and about a third of the units have two bedrooms or a suite setup of bedroom and sitting room. Guest rooms are nondescript but inoffensive, done up with pastel colors, standard furnishings in light woods, floral fabrics, down comforters, and writing desks. The motel is on the east edge of town, within walking distance of all the major sights and shops.

Temp Rd., Enniskillen, county Fermanagh. © 028/6632-6633. Fax 028/6632-6362. www.motel.co.uk. 30 units. £44 ($62) double; £48 ($68) double with minikitchen. Continental breakfast £4 ($5.70). AE, MC, V. *In room:* TV, kitchenette or tea/coffeemaker.

SELF-CATERING

Corraquil Country Cottages ★★   These comfortable traditional cottages, on the banks of the Shannon-Erne Waterway, are ideal for couples or families wanting to take full advantage of the splendid fishing, walking, boating, bird-watching, and exploring opportunities that the Lakelands offer. The cottages sleep four, five, and six. What's more, taking to the waterways could not be more convenient—a small fleet of day cruisers moors just beyond the front yard. You'll find everything you need, including washing machines. All cottages have an open fire as well as central heating.

   In addition to these six cottages, Lakeland Country Breaks (LCB) offers a surprisingly diverse and attractive selection of self-catering cottages, lodges, and estates throughout the Lakelands region.

Teemore, county Fermanagh. Contact LCB at © 01365/327205. Fax 01365/325511. www.lakelandbreaks. ie. 6 cottages. £250–£385 ($355–$547) per week. Also available for 2- or 3-day stays. Additional charge for heat and electricity. MC, V. **Amenities:** TV; kitchen; fridge; oven/stove; dishwasher; washing machine.

WHERE TO DINE

Castle Leslie ★★★ CONTINENTAL   Dinner at Castle Leslie (see "Where to Stay," above) offers all the relaxed graciousness—and drama—of a prewar dinner party. The dining rooms in the great house look out on one of the estate's lovely lakes and on ancient hardwood forests. The view alone is a perfect appetizer. Sammy Leslie, trained at a fine Swiss culinary school, is largely responsible for the wizardry in the kitchen. The cuisine is classic and French-influenced, with a well-chosen wine list. The menu changes to embrace what is freshest and most enticing to the chef; imagine starting with roast goat's-cheese salad with beets and hazelnuts; proceeding to honey roast quail, filet of salmon, or grilled filet of beef with Madeira sauce; and finishing with white chocolate crème brûlée.

Glaslough, county Monaghan. Drive through the center of Glaslough to castle gates. ℂ **047/88109**. Reservations required. Fixed-price dinner £36 ($51); a la carte menu available. MC, V. Daily 7–9:30pm. Closed 2 weeks Jan.

Franco's ✿ INTERNATIONAL Next to the Butter Market in three converted and restored buildings that were once part of Enniskillen's working waterfront, this pleasant, casual restaurant blends old-world ambience and the legacy of the sea with contemporary recipes and fresh local ingredients. Choices might include filet of beef en croûte, black sole and salmon with sorrel sauce, lobster thermidor, Lough Melvin salmon on a bed of spinach in pastry and saffron sauce, or duck breast in plum sauce. There's a variety of specialty pastas and pizzas too. Wednesday to Sunday, traditional music starts at 9pm.

Queen Elizabeth Rd., Enniskillen, county Fermanagh. ℂ **028/6632-4424**. Reservations not accepted. Dinner main courses £9–£18 ($13–$26). AE, MC, V. Daily noon–11pm.

ENNISKILLEN AFTER DARK

Many or even most of the pubs and hotels in the area offer live entertainment, especially in the summer and on weekends.

The area's outstanding public house is **Blakes of the Hollow** ✿, 6 Church St., Enniskillen (ℂ **028/6632-2143**). Opened in 1887, the pub has been in the Blake family ever since, retaining its original Victorian decor and ambience, with a long marble-topped mahogany bar and pinewood alcoves.

Check out what's on at the **Ardhowen Theatre,** Dublin Road, Enniskillen (ℂ **028/6632-5440**). Also known as the Theatre by the Lakes because of its enviable position overlooking Upper Lough Erne, this 300-seat theater presents a varied program of concerts, drama, cabarets, jazz, gospel, blues, and other modern music. Tickets run from £5 to £12 ($7.10–$17) for most performances; curtain time is usually 8pm.

Appendix:
Ireland in Depth

1 History 101

So how do we know about the prehistoric past? Except for some monuments still staring us in the face, prehistoric Ireland has to be dug up like a grave rather than opened up like a book. Indeed, Ireland has richly rewarded the archaeologist's shovel, and the farmer's plow, for that matter. Many treasures have been unearthed by chance in the course of other chores. To be found underfoot or under bog are the remains of houses, forts, tombs, tools, weapons, ornaments—all the whatnots of earlier lives—offering wordless clues to the past. It's said that ancient stones speak. Actually, they mumble at best. It's up to archaeologists and prehistorians, using both science and intuition, to turn those mumblings into a confession.

The first Irish antiquaries, the earliest writings of the Irish about their own past, characterize that past as a series of "invasions" beginning before the deluge and continuing into the present. That, too, is mostly how modern historians tell the story of the Irish past, which I'll retell briefly here.

IRISH PREHISTORY
THE FIRST SETTLERS At the end of its last ice age, around the year 8000 B.C., Ireland warmed up to agreeable, even attractive, temperatures. With some degree of confidence, we can place the date of the first human habitation of the island somewhere between the late 8000s and the early 6000s B.C. Regardless of where in that span the date actually fell, Ireland seems to have been among

Dateline

- 8000 B.C. Earliest human immigration to Ireland.
- 3500 B.C. Farmers and megalithic builders reach Ireland.
- 2000 B.C. First metalworkers come to Ireland.
- 700 B.C. Celtic settlement of Ireland begins.
- A.D. 432 Traditional date of Patrick's return to Ireland.
- 500–800 Ireland's "golden age."
- 795 First Viking invasion.
- 841 The Norse build a sea fort on the River Liffey.
- 853 Danes take possession of the Norse settlement.
- 988 Dublin officially recognized as an Irish city.
- 1014 Battle of Clontarf. Brian Boru defeats the Vikings.
- 1167–69 Norman invasion of Ireland.
- 1171 Henry II visits Ireland and claims feudal lordship.
- 1204 Dublin Castle becomes base of British power.
- 1297 First parliamentary sessions in Dublin.
- 1541 Henry III proclaims himself king of Ireland.
- 1534–52 Henry VIII begins suppression of Catholic Church in Ireland.
- 1558–1603 Reign of Elizabeth I. Elizabeth conducts several Irish wars, initiates the "plantation" of Munster, divides Ireland into counties, and in 1591 founds Trinity College, Dublin.
- 1601 Mountjoy defeats combined Spanish and Irish forces at Kinsale.
- 1603 Articles of Confederation introduced. "Plantation" of Ulster commences.

continues

the last lands in Europe to have felt the human footprint.

Ireland's first colonizers, Mesolithic Homo sapiens, walked, waded, or floated—depending on the status of the early land bridges—across the narrow strait from Britain in search of flint and, of course, food. They found both and stayed on, more or less uneventfully (from our perspective, at least), for a good 4,000 to 5,000 years. Their contribution to the future of Ireland may seem minimal, but most beginnings are. And they did, after all, begin the gene pool.

THE NEOLITHIC AGE   The next momentous prehistoric event was the arrival of Neolithic farmers and herders, sometime around 3500 B.C. The Neolithic "revolution" was the first of many to come to Ireland a bit late, at least 5,000 years after its inception in the ancient Near East. The domestication of the human species— settled life, agriculture, animal husbandry—brought with it a radically increased population, enhanced skills, stability, and all the implications of leisure. Unlike Ireland's Mesolithic hunters, who barely left a trace, this second wave of colonizers began at once to transform the island. They came with stone axes that could fell a good-sized elm in less than an hour. Ireland's hardwood forests began to recede to make room for tilled fields and pastureland. Villages sprang up, like those discovered and reconstructed at Lough Gur, county Limerick. Larger, more permanent homes, planked with split oak, appeared roughly at this time.

Far more startling, however, is the appearance of massive megalithic monuments, including court cairns, dolmens, passage tombs, and wedge tombs, only a small percentage of which have been excavated. The more than 1,000 megalithic monuments that have been unearthed mumble symphonically about beliefs, cults,

- 1607 The flight of the Irish earls, marking the demise of the old Gaelic order.
- 1641 Irish Catholic revolt in Ulster led by Sir Phelim O'Neill ends in defeat.
- 1649 Oliver Cromwell invades and begins the reconquest of Ireland.
- 1690 The forces of James II, a Catholic, are defeated at the Battle of the Boyne, assuring British control of Ireland.
- 1691 Patrick Sarsfield surrenders Limerick. He and some 14,000 Irish troops, the "Wild Geese," flee to the Continent.
- 1704 Enactment of first Penal Laws. Apartheid comes to Ireland.
- 1778 The Penal Laws are progressively repealed.
- 1782 The Irish Parliament is granted independence.
- 1791 Wolfe Tone founds the Society of the United Irishmen.
- 1796–97 Wolfe Tone launches an invasion from France, fails, is taken captive, and commits suicide.
- 1798 "The Year of the French." A French invasion force is defeated at Killala Bay. General Humbert surrenders to Cornwallis.
- 1800 The Irish Parliament is induced to dissolve itself.
- 1803 In Dublin, Robert Emmet leads a rising of less than 100 men and is hanged.
- 1829 Daniel O'Connell secures passage of the Catholic Emancipation Act.
- 1841 Daniel O'Connell is named lord mayor of Dublin.
- 1845–48 The Great Famine. Two million Irish die or emigrate.
- 1848 The revolt of the Young Irelanders ends in failure.
- 1858 The Irish Republican Brotherhood, a secret society known as the Fenians, is founded in New York.
- 1867 A Fenian uprising is easily crushed.
- 1879 Michael Davitt founds the National Land League to support the claims of tenant farmers.

and aspirations as profound as any we might imagine. A visit to Newgrange and Knowth in the Boyne Valley and to Carrowmore in county Sligo will both dazzle and deepen anyone's understanding of the human past. It certainly did so for the later Celtic inhabitants of the island, who wondered and told stories about the tremendous stones and mounds raised by what, they assumed, must have been giants—their ancestors, whom they imagined to inhabit them still. They called them the people of the *sí*, who eventually became the *Tuatha Dí Danann*, then the faeries. The once-great and now-little people lived a quite magical life, mostly underground, in the thousands of *raths*, or earthwork structures, coursing the island like giant mole works.

In the ensuing millennia of the pre-historic period, the first farmers were followed by others, skilled in prospecting and metallurgy. Bronze implements and ornaments, and some jewelry wrought in gold, were now added to the pots and woven fabrics already being produced on the island. A still later wave of farmers and craftsmen moved their settlements from the edges of lakes to the center, where they constructed artificial islands surrounded by palisades. An example of these curious creations, called *crannógs*, has been reconstructed at the Craggaunowen Project, county Clare. A visit there—as well as to Lough Gur in county Limerick and to the Irish National Heritage Park at Ferrycarrig, county Wexford—would reward anyone interested in learning more about life in prehistoric Ireland. Although the Bronze Age Irish (like the Stone Age Irish who preceded them) left no written records, they did bequeath to their dead, and so to us, works of exquisite beauty. Examples may be seen in the National Museum in Dublin.

THE CELTS The first "invasion" of Ireland that can be traced with

- **1879–82** The "land war" forces the enactment of reform. The tenant system unravels; land returns to those who work it.
- **1884** Gaelic Athletic Association is formed to preserve native sports.
- **1886 and 1894** Bills for Home Rule are defeated in Parliament.
- **1893** The Gaelic League is founded to revive the Irish language.
- **1904** Establishment of the Abbey Theatre.
- **1905–08** Founding of Sinn Fein, "we ourselves," with close links to the Irish Republican Brotherhood.
- **1912** Third Home Rule bill passes in the House of Commons and is defeated by the House of Lords.
- **1913** Founding of the Irish Citizens Army.
- **1916** Patrick Pearse and James Connolly lead an armed uprising on Easter Monday to proclaim the Irish Republic. Defeat is followed by the execution of 15 leaders of the revolt.
- **1918** Sinn Fein wins a landslide election victory against the Irish Parliamentary Party.
- **1919** Sinn Fein, led by Eamon de Valera, constitutes itself as the first Irish áil and declares independence.
- **1919–21** The Irish War of Independence. Michael Collins commands the Irish forces.
- **1921** Anglo-Irish Treaty. Ireland is partitioned. Twenty-six counties form the Free State. William Cosgrave becomes the first president. His party, Cumann na nGaedheal, later becomes Fine Gael.
- **1922** The Free State adopts its first constitution.
- **1922–23** The Irish civil war, between the government of the Free State and those who opposed the treaty. Michael Collins is assassinated.
- **1932** Eamon de Valera leads Fianna Fáil to victory and becomes head of government.
- **1932–38** Economic war with Britain brings great hardship.
- **1937** Ireland's 26 counties adopt a new constitution, abandoning membership in British Commonwealth.

continues

historical confidence is that of the Celts, cousins of the *Celtae* who sacked Rome and the *Keltoi* who did the same to Delphi. Indeed, Irish history before the modern period may be sketched in terms of four invasions: those of the Celts, the Vikings, the Normans, and the English. Each left an indelible imprint on the landscape and the psyche of the island. Ireland and the Irish people today are the heirs, culturally and genetically, of their prehistoric and historic invaders.

Of all of Ireland's uninvited guests, the Celts made the greatest impact. They came in waves, the first perhaps as early as the 6th century B.C. and continuing until the end of the millennium. In time, they controlled the island and absorbed into their culture everyone they found there. Their ways and their genes were, in a word, dominant. They brought iron weapons, war chariots, codes of combat and honor, cults and contests, poetic and artistic genius, music and mania, all of which took root and flourished in Irish soil as if they were native plants. The Celts, however, were dismally disorganized in comparison with the kingdoms and empires of Europe. They divided the island among as many as 150 tribes, or *tuatha,* grouped under alliances with allegiance to one of five provincial kings. The provinces of Munster, Leinster, Ulster, and Connaught date from this period. They fought among themselves, fiercely, over cattle (their "currency" and standard of wealth), land, and women. None among them ever achieved high kingship of the island, though not for lack of trying. One of the most impressive monuments from the time of the warring Celtic chiefs is the stone fortress of Dún Aengus on the Aran Islands.

IRISH HISTORY
THE COMING OF CHRISTIANITY
The Celtic powers-that-be neither warmly welcomed nor violently

- 1938 Douglas Hyde inaugurated as Eire's first president.
- 1939 Dublin is bombed by Germany at start of World War II, but Ireland remains neutral.
- 1948 The Republic of Ireland Act. Ireland severs its last constitutional links with Britain.
- 1955 Ireland is admitted into the United Nations.
- 1959 Eamon de Valera becomes president of Ireland.
- 1963 U.S. Pres. John F. Kennedy visits Dublin.
- 1969 Violence breaks out in Northern Ireland. British troops are called in.
- 1972 In Derry, a peaceful rally turns into "Bloody Sunday." The Northern Irish Parliament is dissolved, and the North is ruled directly from Britain.
- 1973 Ireland joins the European Community.
- 1986 Ireland signs the Anglo-Irish Agreement.
- 1990 Ireland elects Mary Robinson, its first woman president. Sir Peter Brooke, British secretary of state for Northern Ireland, declares that Britain no longer has any selfish economic or strategic interest in Northern Ireland.
- 1992 Ireland approves the European Union.
- 1993 The Joint Declaration on Northern Ireland, written by John Hume and Gerry Adams, establishes the principles and framework for a peaceful, democratic resolution of issues regarding the political status of the North.
- 1994 The IRA announces a cease-fire, and the Protestant paramilitaries follow suit. Commencement of peace talks.
- 1995 The British and Irish governments issue "A New Framework for Agreement," and U.S. Pres. Bill Clinton makes a historic visit to Ireland, speaking to large crowds in Belfast and Derry. Received with great enthusiasm in the Republic, he is made a "freeman" of the City of Dublin.
- 1996 The IRA resumes its campaign of violence. New disturbances in the North lead to the worst rioting in 15 years. The cease-fire is over, and the peace process is in tatters.

resisted the Christians who, beginning in the 5th century A.D., came ashore and walked the island with a new message. Although threatened to the core, the Celtic kings and bards settled for a bloodless rivalry and made no Christians martyrs.

Not the first, but eventually the most famous, of these Christian newcomers was Patrick, a young Roman citizen torn from his British homeland in a Celtic raid and brought to Ireland as a slave. In time, he escaped slavery but not Ireland, to which he felt called. Ordained a priest and consecrated a bishop, Patrick made his own raid on Ireland and took its people by storm. He abhorred slavery, which he had known firsthand, and he preached it off the island. Within 30 years, the Christian church, like a young forest, was well rooted and spreading in every direction. By the time of his death, around A.D. 461, the Roman Empire was in near collapse while Ireland was on the brink of its golden age.

The truth of Ireland's conversion to Christianity was that it was mutual. The church of Patrick was, like the man who brought it, Roman, something Ireland never was and never would be. Roman Catholicism didn't "take" in Ireland. Instead, it "went native" and became uniquely Celtic. Patrick's eminent successors, Columcille, Bridgit, and Columbanus, were Irish in a way that Patrick could never be—and so was their church. Although orthodox on most points of doctrine, the Irish church was Celtic in structure, tribal and unruly by Roman standards. To Ireland, an island without towns or cities, the Roman system of dioceses and archdioceses was beside the point. Instead, the Irish built monasteries with extended monastic families, each more or less autonomous and regional. The pope, like an Irish high king, was essentially a peer. He had to defend his title with every challenge, like a prizefighter. Besides, the pope reigned

- **1997** The IRA declares a new ceasefire. On October 7, Sinn Fein enters inclusive all-party peace talks designed to bring about a comprehensive settlement in the North.

- **1998** The all-party peace talks conclude with the Belfast Agreement, affirmed by all participating parties and strongly supported in referendums held on the same day in the Republic and in the North. The North elects its new assembly. The strength and resolve of the new government, however, is put to a bitter test in July by the standoff at Drumcree and the eruption of violence across the North, culminating in the unspeakable massacre at Omagh. The response across Ireland is horror, accompanied by a resonant appeal for a final end to all sectarian violence. John Hume and David Trimble are awarded the Nobel Peace Prize for their key roles in bringing about this agreement.

- **1999** The implementation of the Belfast Agreement is blocked by the Unionist demand—"in the spirit" but contrary to the letter of the Good Friday Agreement—that IRA decommissioning precede the appointment of a New Northern Ireland executive. The peace process stalls and threatens to unravel, until late in November, when the deadlock is broken and the new power-sharing Northern Ireland Executive is established.

- **2000** Peter Mandelson, the Northern Ireland Secretary, suspends the Northern Ireland Executive and Assembly less than 4 months after they were up and running. Direct British rule is restored, and the peace process is in freefall. The IRA issues a statement saying it will decommission its arms. In May, power is restored to the institutions established by the Belfast Agreement, and the cloud cover over the peace begins to break up.

- **2001** In June, Irish voters reject the Nice Treaty in a referendum, which would pave the way for enlargement of the EU. David Trimble threatens to resign as Ulster Unionist party leader if the IRA does not live up to its

continues

in "a place out of mind," a place that was in a shambles at the time.

IRELAND OF THE SAINTED MISSIONARIES

Meanwhile, Ireland flourished for several centuries as a land of saints and scholars. Its monasteries were centers of learning and culture—some of the few left in post-Roman Europe—where literacy itself was effectively kept alive through the voluminous and imaginative work of scholars and scribes. Moreover, some of these monasteries—Bridgit's own, for instance—were models of sexual equality, populated by both men and women and sometimes presided over by a woman, a high abbess, who was likely to have a handful of bishops under her jurisdiction.

Not only were monks and scholars drawn to Ireland in great numbers, but they were sent out in great numbers as well, to Britain and the Continent, bearing with them all the otherwise-forgotten knowledge of Europe. As historian Thomas Cahill wrote in his *How the Irish Saved Civilization,* "Wherever they went the Irish brought with them their books, many unseen in Europe for centuries and tied to their waists as signs of triumph, just as Irish heroes had once tied to their waists their enemies' heads." The influence of these monks cannot be underestimated. They went everywhere; it's likely that some of them even reached North America. And they worked with a fervor, so much so that the Irish penned more than half the biblical commentaries written between 650 and 850.

The prime legacy of these monks lies in knowledge perpetuated, but like their megalithic ancestors, they too left some enduring monuments to their profound spirituality. With the help of a little imagination, visits to the early monastic sites—Glendalough in county Wicklow, Clonmacnois in county Offaly, and Skellig Michael off the Kerry coast—together with a stop at Trinity College Dublin to see the Book of Kells, will bring to life Ireland's lost age of splendor.

THE VIKING INVASIONS

The monastic city-states of early medieval Ireland died no natural death. After several centuries of dazzling peace, the sea brought new invaders, this time the Vikings. By assaulting Ireland's monasteries, these seagoing berserkers from Scandinavia went straight for the jugular of Irish civilization. Regardless of their Celtic blood, the monks were not warriors, and the round towers to which they retreated were neither high enough nor strong enough to protect them and their treasures from the Scandinavian pirates. The Vikings knew a soft touch when they saw one and just kept coming, from around 800 into the 10th century. The Vikings knew how to pillage and plunder, but, thankfully, they didn't know how to read. Therefore, they didn't much bother with the books they came across, allowing the monks some means besides their memories of preserving their knowledge and of passing their history down to us.

Belfast Agreement promise to decommission its weapons. The IRA doesn't bite; Trimble resigns in June. Following a surge of feeling in the wake of the September 11 terrorist attacks on the USA, IRA decommissioning is confirmed to have taken place by General de Chastelain.

- 2002 In March, Irish voters defeated a referendum that would have further restricted the availability of abortion in Ireland. The peace process continues to be fraught by sectarian violence on both sides. The Irish past, like that of every other people, may be divided into two parts: prehistory and history. This is a distinction we make, looking back at them. History here means written history: texts, not stories; words, not pictures. Prehistoric has a hunched-over, savage ring to it, but that's our problem. People who didn't write about themselves were still people.

For better or worse, the Vikings did more than hit and run. They settled as well, securing every major harbor on Ireland's east coast with a fortified town. These were the first towns in Ireland: Dublin, Cork, Waterford, and the river city of Limerick. Eventually, the Irish, though disinclined to unite, did so anyway. This led to decisive Viking defeats by the armies of Brian Boru in 999 and 1014. When the Vikings left, they left their towns behind, forever altering the Irish way of life. The legacy of the Vikings in Ireland is complex, and a visit to Dublin's Wood Quay and the city walls of Waterford may put those interested on the scent.

With the Vikings gone, Ireland enjoyed something of a renaissance in the 11th and 12th centuries. Meanwhile, its towns grew, its regional kings made their bids for high kingship, and its church came under concerted pressure to conform with the Vatican. All of these, in fact, played their part in ripening Ireland for its next invasion. Prosperous and factionalized, Ireland made attractive prey, and it was, tragically, an Irish king who opened the door to the predator. Diarmait Mac Murchada, king of Leinster, whose ambition was to be king of all of Ireland, decided he needed outside help and called on a Welsh Norman, Richard de Clare, better known as Strongbow. Strongbow and his army, in turn, acted on behalf of Henry II of England, who had taken the pious and political precaution of securing a papal blessing for the invasion of Catholic Ireland. The accommodating pope was Adrian IV, who must have envisioned not only a more papal Ireland but also a more British one. After all, he was the first and only Briton ever to ascend to the papacy.

THE NORMAN INVASION   In successive expeditions from 1167 to 1169, the Normans crossed the Irish Sea with crushing force. When you see the massive Norman fortifications at Trim, you'll realize the clout the invaders brought with them. In 1171, Henry II of England made a royal visit to what was now one of his domains. Across the next century, the Normans settled in, consolidated their power, developed Irish towns and cities, and grew terribly fond of the island. They became as Irish as the Irish themselves.

In 1314, Scotland's Robert the Bruce defeated the English at Bannockburn and set out to fulfill his dream of a united Celtic kingdom. He installed his brother Edward on the Irish throne, but the constant state of war took a heavy toll. Within 2 years, famine and economic disorder had eroded any public support Edward might have enjoyed. By the time he was defeated and killed at Dundalk in 1317, few were prepared to mourn him. Over the next 2 centuries, attempts to rid Ireland of its Norman overlords were laudable but fell short. Independent Gaelic lords in the north and west continued to maintain their territories. By the close of the 15th century, British control of the island was effectively limited to the Pale, a walled and fortified cordon around what might have been called "greater Dublin." The Normans themselves became more and more Irish and less and less British in their loyalties. Ireland was becoming British in name only.

ENGLISH POWER & THE FLIGHT OF THE EARLS   In the 16th century, under the Tudors, the brutal reconquest of Ireland was set in motion. In mid-century, Henry VIII proclaimed himself king of Ireland, something his predecessors had never done. However, it wasn't until late in the century that the claim was backed up by force. Elizabeth I, Henry's daughter, declared that all Gaelic lords in Ireland must surrender their lands to her, with the altruistic pronouncement that she would immediately regrant them—a proposition met with no great joy, to say the least. The Irish, under Ulster's Hugh O'Neill and Red

Hugh O'Donnell, struck out, defeating the Earl of Essex, whom Elizabeth had personally sent to subdue them. In 1600, a massive force commanded by Lord Mountjoy landed and set about subduing the country. By 1603 O'Neill was left with few allies and no option but to surrender, which he did on March 23, the day before Elizabeth died. Had he waited, who knows how history would have differed? As it was, O'Neill had his lands returned, but constant harassment by the English prompted him, along with many of Ireland's other Gaelic lords, to sail for the continent on September 14, 1607, abandoning their lands and their aspirations.

THE COMING OF CROMWELL   By the 1640s, Ireland was effectively an English plantation. Family estates had been seized and foreign (Scottish) labor brought in to work them. The persecution of Catholics, begun with Henry VIII's split from Rome, barred them from practicing their faith. Resentment led to uprisings in Ulster and Leinster in 1641, and by early 1642 most of Ireland was again under Irish control. Any hope of extending the victories was destroyed by internal disunion and by the eventual decision to support the Royalist side in the English civil war. In 1648, English King Charles I was beheaded, and the following year the Royalist forces in Ireland were defeated at Rathmines. The stage was set for disaster.

In 1649, Oliver Cromwell arrived in Dublin as commander in chief and lord lieutenant of Ireland, and set about destroying all opposition. One of the most brutal and effective butchers any empire has ever enlisted, Cromwell simply devastated Ireland, which still bears the scars of his savagery. To this day, some Irish spit when they say his name. Cromwell left no doubt about who was in charge. His campaign lasted only 7 months, but his brutal, bloodthirsty methods broke the back of all resistance. In his siege of the town of Drogheda alone, 3,552 Irish were killed, while Cromwell lost only 64 men. After subduing all but Galway and Waterford, Cromwell left Ireland and its administration in the care of his lieutenants and returned to England. His stamp lingered for centuries, and the memory of it still burns.

The Irish were offered a choice after the massacres: Anyone suspected of resisting the English forces could leave the country, give up his lands, and resettle in Connaught or county Clare; or die. With this expropriation, the English gained control over most of the country's arable land, and cemented their power.

After the restoration of the British monarchy in 1660, and especially after the succession to the throne of the Catholic King James II in 1685, Irish Catholics began to sense hope in the air. By 1688, Protestant power in the country was seriously diminished, but William of Orange's seizure of the English throne in November of that year reversed the trend. James fled to France to regroup, then sailed to Ireland to launch his counterattack. He struck first at Londonderry, to which he laid siege for 15 weeks before being defeated by William's forces at the Battle of the Boyne. The battle effectively ended James's cause and the last Irish hope of freedom in Ireland. Soon after, the Treaty of Limerick sealed the defeat, and many Irish patriots sailed for America to fight the British Empire in a war that could be won.

THE PENAL LAWS   After James's defeat, the boot of English power sat heavier than ever on Ireland's neck. Protestant lords were granted total political power and control of the land, and laws were enacted to effectively impoverish the Catholic population. Catholics could not purchase land; Catholic landholdings were split up unless the family who held them converted; Catholic schools and priests were banned; and Catholics were barred from professions or commissions in the army and were forced to pay a tax to the Anglican church. The laws had an unintended consequence, though. As happens whenever unjust laws are inflicted on a people, they institutionalized civil disobedience and inspired creative sedition.

Meanwhile, the new British lords and landlords of Ireland settled in, sunk their own roots, planted crops, made laws, and sowed their own seed. Inevitably, over time, the "Angles" became the Anglo-Irish. Hyphenated or not, they were Irish, and their loyalties were increasingly unpredictable. Colonialism only works effectively for one generation, after all—the very next generation is native to the new country, not the old. As this process played out in Ireland, history settled into one of its periodic states of inactivity, and little of note transpired. Prosperity remained on the Protestant side of the fence, and deprivation on the Catholic side. The Penal Laws remained in effect for a century. The first were relaxed in 1770, and the bulk of them repealed with England's 1783 acknowledgment of the Irish Parliament's right, along with the king, to determine the laws by which Ireland should be governed.

WOLFE TONE, THE UNITED IRISHMEN & THE 1798 REBELLION

England's difficulty is Ireland's opportunity, or so the saying goes, so when war broke out between the British and French in the 1790s, the United Irishmen— a nonviolent society formed to lobby for admission of Catholic and landless Irishmen to the Irish parliament—went underground to try to persuade the French to intervene on Ireland's behalf against the British. Their emissary in this venture was a Dublin lawyer named Wolfe Tone. In 1796, Tone sailed with a French invasion force bound for Ireland, but was turned back by storms.

Come 1798, Ireland was embroiled in insurrection. Wexford and Ulster teetered, with the United Irishmen proving they hadn't united enough of their countrymen to mount a credible, sustainable campaign. The nadir of the rebellion came when Wolfe Tone, having raised another French invasion force, sailed into Lough Swilley in Donegal and was promptly captured by the British. At his trial, wearing a French uniform, Tone requested that he be shot. When the request was refused, he slit his own throat. The rebellion was over. In the space of 3 weeks, more than 30,000 Irish had been killed. In the aftermath of "The Year of the French," as it came to be known, the British induced the Irish parliament to dissolve itself, and Ireland reverted to strict British rule.

DANIEL O'CONNELL

In 1828, a Catholic lawyer named Daniel O'Connell, who had earlier formed the Catholic Association to represent the interests of tenant farmers, was elected to the British parliament to represent Ireland. Public opinion was so solidly behind him that he was able to persuade the Duke of Wellington, Britain's prime minister, that the only way to avoid an Irish civil war was to force the Catholic Emancipation Act through parliament. Once this was secured, O'Connell accepted the position as Ireland's MP (Member of Parliament). For 12 years he served in the post, winning concessions and fighting against unpopular leftovers of the Penal Laws. In 1841 he left parliament and was elected lord mayor of Dublin, and began his push for repeal of the Irish-British union imposed after the 1798 rebellion. Toward this end, he organized enormous meetings that often reached the hundreds of thousands, but succeeded in provoking an unresponsive conservative government to such an extent that it eventually arrested O'Connell on charges of seditious conspiracy. The charges were dropped, but the incident—coupled with dissension among the Irish, criticism by a group known as the Young Irelanders, and distress from the incipient famine—led to the breaking of his power base. "The Liberator," as he had been known, faded, his health failed, and he eventually died on a trip to Rome. The Young Irelanders, led by "Meagher of the Sword," went on to stage a pathetic revolt in 1848. The English authorities easily put it down.

THE GREAT HUNGER   As the efforts of Ireland's hoped-for liberators failed, the Irish were faced with something they could barely imagine: a worse state of affairs.

In the years 1845 through 1848, famine struck. The majority of Ireland owned by the Irish was harsh, difficult land, unsuitable for most farming. For this reason the Irish had come to depend on the potato, one of the hardiest of crops, as the staple of their diet. When blight struck, they were left with nothing to keep body and soul together.

It has often been said that colonialism can succeed only when it's paired with genocide, and in the "Great Hunger," as it's called, that collusion nearly came to pass. Whether the famine was an act of God, the British, or bad farming practices on the part of the Irish peasantry remains unresolved. The fact stands that it claimed a million Irish lives and dispatched another million to the sea on death ships, most pointed toward the United States. Those who remained faced only continued hardship, and in the years to follow emigration reached flood level. Within a century, the population of Ireland was less than half of what it had been in 1841.

THE STRUGGLE FOR HOME RULE   Fewer Irish did not mean more manageable Irish, however. On multiple fronts, violent and nonviolent, the Irish people kept up the pressure on Britain. They won some partial concessions, but gratitude was minimal. The return of selected stolen goods appears generous only to thieves. What the Irish wanted back was Ireland, intact: land, religion, language, and law. In the 1870s and 1880s, Ireland's Member of Parliament, Charles Stewart Parnell, was able to unite various factions of Irish nationalists, including the Fenian Brotherhood in America and the Land League, to fight for home rule. In a tumultuous decade of legislation, he came close, but revelations about his long affair with Kitty O'Shea, wife of a former follower, brought about his downfall, and an end to the legislative quest for home rule.

THE EASTER REBELLION & THE WAR OF INDEPENDENCE   Coming close counts for nothing in revolution, and near-misses on the negotiation front opened the way to violence. The 1912 defeat of the third Home Rule Bill in the House of Lords, after it had passed in the House of Commons, was followed in 1913 by the founding of the Irish Citizens Army and the Irish Volunteers. Revolution was imminent. The motive had been there for centuries, the ability was in development, and the opportunity was around the corner. In 1916, the Irish celebrated Easter, the feast of the Resurrection, in unique fashion.

On Easter Monday 1916, the Irish tricolor flag was raised over the General Post Office in the heart of Dublin. Inside were 1,500 fighters, led by the Gaelic League's Patrick Pearse and Socialist leader James Connolly. Pearse read the newly written Proclamation of the Irish Republic, and his men fought off the British for 6 days before being captured. Pearse, Connolly, and 12 other leaders were imprisoned, secretly tried, and speedily executed.

In looking back over Irish history for those turning points that cumulatively led to the violence of 1916, the War of Independence, and the Irish civil war, William Butler Yeats wrote of four bells that tolled for Ireland. One sounded at each of its irreversibly decisive moments: the Flight of the Earls, the Battle of the Boyne, the spread of French revolutionary ideas under the United Irishmen, and the fall of Parnell. However it is that we trace the path to violence, the 1916 rising, compounded by the savage stupidity of the British response, all but guaranteed that Ireland's future would be decided by the gun. Like the religious faith the people had strained for centuries to preserve, the Irish faith in revolution was seeded and nourished by the blood of martyrs—martyrs the British had been fools enough to provide.

The last straw for the British was Sinn Fein's landslide victory in the general election of 1918 and its subsequent proclamation of the first Dáil, or independent parliament. The declaration of independence issued 2 years earlier from the General Post Office now seemed a good deal more real. When the British attempted to smash the new parliament, the result was the War of Independence, in which the Irish forces, led by Michael Collins, eventually forced the British to the negotiating table.

The Anglo-Irish Treaty of 1921 gave independence to only 26 of 32 Irish counties. The fate of the remaining six counties in Ulster was yet to be decided. In the meantime, they would remain within the United Kingdom. Some of the Irish, weary of war, accepted compromise as close enough to victory and embraced the Free State of Ireland. Others, led by Eamon de Valera, shouted betrayal and declared the Free State their latest enemy. The ensuing civil war claimed many casualties, including Michael Collins and Cathal Brugha, two of the revolution's shining heroes.

Victory—if civil wars have winners—went to de Valera and those who opposed the treaty. They did not overturn it, though, and their successors have yet to do so. Instead, they reformed the government and led the new Free State of Ireland out of the ravages of war and into the rigors of peace. The Free State, in passing the Republic of Ireland Act in 1948, severed its last constitutional ties to Britain. Only 25 years later did it join the European Community, pursuing its ties to Europe where the Irish people had for centuries looked for friendship and support.

Ireland was the first colony acquired by the British Empire and nearly the last to be relinquished, but regrettably, this story still has no proper ending. The "troubles" spawned by the partitioning of Ireland in 1921 have lived on to the end of the century, a wound that until very recently has shown little promise of healing. There remain two Irelands, fewer than there have been in the past and yet, for some, still one too many.

2 Ireland Today

The Irish landscape remains breathtaking, its natural beauty intact, its rivers and lakes still largely pollution free, and its people disarmingly gracious. For a decade up through 2000, Ireland welcomed roughly 6.5 million visitors annually to its shores. In the wake of the September 11 tragedy in the United States, 2001 was a dismal year for tourism, and yet the Emerald Isle still welcomed over six million visitors, a number that far surpasses Ireland's population of 3.9 million (the highest it's been since 1881). Irish hospitality is legendary, and deservedly so.

Included in that hospitality, however, can be a misleading sense of tranquillity, continuity, and cohesion. Like an overgrown family, Ireland is mostly inclined to keep its turmoil to itself and to offer its guests the vacation of their lives, which is what its guests are mostly looking for.

What is easy for any visitor to miss or to underestimate is the depth and pace of the change occurring in Ireland today. Ireland has long been a land of profound conflicts, and never more so than at present. To mention one, *Irish* and

Roman Catholic are assumed by many to be synonymous. The truth is that they have never meant the same thing, nor made lasting peace with each other. The Roman Catholicism preached by Patrick was transformed as fast as it was embraced by the Celts of Ireland. The Vatican, like the British royalty, found the Irish unruly and bent on taking their own road. For all their faith and devotion, Irish Catholics have never finally decided whether to trust or mistrust their hierarchy, appointed from Rome. Recent public scandals in the Church, followed not by candor but by coverup, have served only to widen ancient misgivings. The 1996 referendum to permit legal divorce—as well as the decriminalizing of homosexuality and the passing of the abortion information law—all urged and supported by Ireland's first female president, Mary Robinson, point to an Ireland where Rome's iron grip is being pried away a finger at a time.

The Ireland of today, which may present a traditional face to the tourist, is increasingly defined and determined by its youth, whose sheer numbers and unconventional ways are creating a generation gap of seismic proportions. For one thing, they aren't marrying and having children with anything approximating the regularity of their parents. Young people are taking their time before approaching the altar, and taking even longer before starting a family. Although it has since recovered somewhat, the Irish birthrate fell in 1993, for the first time in recorded history, below the minimum population replacement rate of 2.1 children per woman of child-bearing age. This is not to say that the Irish are endangered. What is endangered, however, are the stereotypes visitors might have of them.

Another gap dividing the Irish people is a product of Ireland's sudden and dramatic economic boom. In 1998 the economy ran in the black for the first time in 30 years, and the following year clocked in as the world's fourth fastest-growing economy, beating out all of its European rivals. In fact, the current growth rate of the Irish economy (8.4%) is four times the EU average, and Ireland is Europe's number one exporter of computer software. Nicknamed the Celtic or emerald tiger, Ireland has emerged as Europe's unlikely and unrivaled wunderkind. Partly, it's a matter of Ireland's having received more than $17 billion from the European Union over the past dozen years, but it's also a matter of Ireland's own policies and initiatives having paid off. The bottom line is that some people in Ireland are getting very rich, but most only work and watch. The paradoxical situation—wealth accompanied by rising crime, rural poverty, teen violence and suicide, and urban homelessness—is familiar to many nations, but new to Ireland.

Although Ireland today is increasingly prosperous, European, and committed to pluralistic human values, it is at the same time determined to preserve its rich legacy and distinct character. Irish-speaking and -reading citizens represent a minority of the population, but Irish writers, especially poets, continue to create new work. In fact, Ireland has an Irish-language television channel. Helping to fire the renaissance is the fact that the Irish, including some of their most talented artists and writers, are staying or coming home in large numbers. According to the 2002 census, net migration to Ireland is at a historic high, with "returnees" accounting for more than half of recent immigration figures.

Finally, it must be said that the cry for peace in and with the North has never been more desperate or determined. The peace process has been turbulent and uncertain, with negotiators hesitant to move forward, yet dreading any return to the chaos that preceded it. The majority of the Irish people, North and South, want peace above all else, but murderous factions on both sides—defying

> **Fun Fact** **Did You Know?**
>
> - The Irish per capita consumption of poetry surpasses that of any other English-speaking country. Not surprisingly, they also produce their fair share.
> - For certain scenic areas in Ireland, mobile phone "masts," as they're known, have been designed in the shape of trees, to minimize the visual blight on the Irish landscape caused by the cellular revolution.
> - Katherine Kelly, one of Ireland's authenticated little people, was 34 inches tall and weighed 28 pounds when she died in 1735.
> - The newt (Triturus vulgaris) is Ireland's only indigenous reptile.
> - Robert Emmet is said to have been able to rattle off the English alphabet backward without taking a breath. This was not how or why he died.
> - Little John, Robin Hood's "main man," met his end not in Sherwood Forest, but in Arbour Hill in Dublin, where he was hanged.
> - Under Cromwell, it became law that the same bounty was offered for the head of a wolf and the head of a priest—£5.
> - The longest formal debate on record anywhere in the world was conducted at University College Galway in 1995. The motion debated—for 28 days—read as follows: "This house has all the time in the world."
> - In January 1997, the Irish government granted its first-ever divorce. The recipient was a terminally ill man, long separated from his wife, who sought to marry his current partner before he died. They did marry, and he died shortly afterward.
> - When the Censorship of Films Act was passed in 1923, the first appointed censor was James Montgomery, who confessed to knowing little to nothing about films. He was quite clear, however, about his job, which, in his own words, was "to prevent the Californication of Ireland."

common sense and common decency—simply ignore them. One day a lasting peace will break out, as miraculous and inevitable as springtime, no matter how long and dark the winter has been.

3 Language

Ireland has two official languages, Irish Gaelic and English. Today, English is the first and most commonly spoken language for the vast majority of the Irish people, although Irish instruction is compulsory in the public schools. Every public school teacher must pass a proficiency examination in Irish in order to be certified. All Irish citizens are entitled by law to conduct any official business with the state (legal proceedings, university interviews, and filing taxes, for example) in the Irish language. In 1835, the Irish-speaking population of Ireland was reckoned at four million. According to the 2002 census, the Irish-speaking population of the Gaeltacht, those scattered regions of the country where Irish is the first and, in some cases, only language spoken, is just under 60,000. Irish speakers, however, are not confined to the Gaeltacht. Dublin, for instance, has a significant number of Irish-speaking individuals and families. When you consider how many people use Irish Gaelic habitually in their speech, the number is more like 100,000. And over a million Irish people claim to speak at least some Irish Gaelic.

Irish, a Celtic language, belongs to the same Indo-European family as most European tongues. Modern Irish descends from Old Irish, the language of Ireland's golden age and the earliest variant of the Celtic languages. Despite the language's decline, poets and playwrights continue to write in Ireland's mother tongue, and Irish-language programs hold their own on television and radio.

Index

HIT THE ROAD WITH FROMMER'S DRIVING TOURS!

Frommer's
Portable Guides
Complete Guides for the
Short-Term Traveler

Portable Acapulco, Ixtapa & Zihuatanejo
Portable Amsterdam
Portable Aruba
Portable Australia's Great Barrier Reef
Portable Bahamas
Portable Berlin
Portable Big Island of Hawaii
Portable Boston
Portable California Wine Country
Portable Cancún
Portable Charleston & Savannah
Portable Chicago
Portable Disneyland®
Portable Dublin
Portable Florence
Portable Frankfurt
Portable Hong Kong
Portable Houston
Portable Las Vegas
Portable London
Portable Los Angeles
Portable Los Cabos & Baja

Portable Maine Coast
Portable Maui
Portable Miami
Portable New Orleans
Portable New York City
Portable Paris
Portable Phoenix & Scottsdale
Portable Portland
Portable Puerto Rico
Portable Puerto Vallarta, Manzanillo &
    Guadalajara
Portable Rio de Janeiro
Portable San Diego
Portable San Francisco
Portable Seattle
Portable Sydney
Portable Tampa & St. Petersburg
Portable Vancouver
Portable Venice
Portable Virgin Islands
Portable Washington, D.C.

Available at bookstores everywhere.

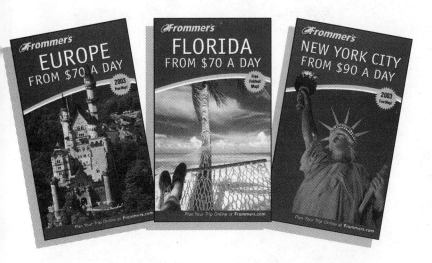

FROMMER'S® COMPLETE TRAVEL GUIDES

Alaska
Alaska Cruises & Ports of Call
Amsterdam
Argentina & Chile
Arizona
Atlanta
Australia
Austria
Bahamas
Barcelona, Madrid & Seville
Beijing
Belgium, Holland & Luxembourg
Bermuda
Boston
Brazil
British Columbia & the Canadian
  Rockies
Budapest & the Best of Hungary
California
Canada
Cancún, Cozumel & the Yucatán
Cape Cod, Nantucket & Martha's
  Vineyard
Caribbean
Caribbean Cruises & Ports of Call
Caribbean Ports of Call
Carolinas & Georgia
Chicago
China
Colorado
Costa Rica
Denmark
Denver, Boulder & Colorado
  Springs
England
Europe
European Cruises & Ports of Call
Florida

France
Germany
Great Britain
Greece
Greek Islands
Hawaii
Hong Kong
Honolulu, Waikiki & Oahu
Ireland
Israel
Italy
Jamaica
Japan
Las Vegas
London
Los Angeles
Maryland & Delaware
Maui
Mexico
Montana & Wyoming
Montréal & Québec City
Munich & the Bavarian Alps
Nashville & Memphis
Nepal
New England
New Mexico
New Orleans
New York City
New Zealand
Northern Italy
Nova Scotia, New Brunswick &
  Prince Edward Island
Oregon
Paris
Philadelphia & the Amish Country
Portugal
Prague & the Best of the Czech
  Republic

Provence & the Riviera
Puerto Rico
Rome
San Antonio & Austin
San Diego
San Francisco
Santa Fe, Taos & Albuquerque
Scandinavia
Scotland
Seattle & Portland
Shanghai
Singapore & Malaysia
South Africa
South America
South Florida
South Pacific
Southeast Asia
Spain
Sweden
Switzerland
Texas
Thailand
Tokyo
Toronto
Tuscany & Umbria
USA
Utah
Vancouver & Victoria
Vermont, New Hampshire &
  Maine
Vienna & the Danube Valley
Virgin Islands
Virginia
Walt Disney World® & Orlando
Washington, D.C.
Washington State

FROMMER'S® DOLLAR-A-DAY GUIDES

Australia from $50 a Day
California from $70 a Day
Caribbean from $70 a Day
England from $75 a Day
Europe from $70 a Day

Florida from $70 a Day
Hawaii from $80 a Day
Ireland from $60 a Day
Italy from $70 a Day
London from $85 a Day

New York from $90 a Day
Paris from $80 a Day
San Francisco from $70 a Day
Washington, D.C. from $80 a Day

FROMMER'S® PORTABLE GUIDES

Acapulco, Ixtapa & Zihuatanejo
Amsterdam
Aruba
Australia's Great Barrier Reef
Bahamas
Berlin
Big Island of Hawaii
Boston
California Wine Country
Cancún
Charleston & Savannah
Chicago
Disneyland®
Dublin
Florence

Frankfurt
Hong Kong
Houston
Las Vegas
London
Los Angeles
Los Cabos & Baja
Maine Coast
Maui
Miami
New Orleans
New York City
Paris
Phoenix & Scottsdale

Portland
Puerto Rico
Puerto Vallarta, Manzanillo &
  Guadalajara
Rio de Janeiro
San Diego
San Francisco
Seattle
Sydney
Tampa & St. Petersburg
Vancouver
Venice
Virgin Islands
Washington, D.C.

FROMMER'S® NATIONAL PARK GUIDES

Banff & Jasper
Family Vacations in the National
  Parks
Grand Canyon

National Parks of the American
  West
Rocky Mountain

Yellowstone & Grand Teton
Yosemite & Sequoia/ Kings Canyon
Zion & Bryce Canyon

FROMMER'S® MEMORABLE WALKS

Chicago	New York	San Francisco
London	Paris	Washington, D.C.

FROMMER'S® GREAT OUTDOOR GUIDES

Arizona & New Mexico	Northern California	Vermont & New Hampshire
New England	Southern New England	

SUZY GERSHMAN'S BORN TO SHOP GUIDES

Born to Shop: France	Born to Shop: Italy	Born to Shop: New York
Born to Shop: Hong Kong, Shanghai & Beijing	Born to Shop: London	Born to Shop: Paris

FROMMER'S® IRREVERENT GUIDES

Amsterdam	Los Angeles	San Francisco
Boston	Manhattan	Seattle & Portland
Chicago	New Orleans	Vancouver
Las Vegas	Paris	Walt Disney World®
London	Rome	Washington, D.C.

FROMMER'S® BEST-LOVED DRIVING TOURS

Britain	Germany	Northern Italy
California	Ireland	Scotland
Florida	Italy	Spain
France	New England	Tuscany & Umbria

HANGING OUT™ GUIDES

Hanging Out in England	Hanging Out in France	Hanging Out in Italy
Hanging Out in Europe	Hanging Out in Ireland	Hanging Out in Spain

THE UNOFFICIAL GUIDES®

Bed & Breakfasts and Country Inns in:	Southwest & South Central Plains	Mid-Atlantic with Kids
California	U.S.A.	Mini Las Vegas
Great Lakes States	Beyond Disney	Mini-Mickey
Mid-Atlantic	Branson, Missouri	New England and New York with Kids
New England	California with Kids	New Orleans
Northwest	Chicago	New York City
Rockies	Cruises	Paris
Southeast	Disneyland®	San Francisco
Southwest	Florida with Kids	Skiing in the West
Best RV & Tent Campgrounds in:	Golf Vacations in the Eastern U.S.	Southeast with Kids
California & the West	Great Smoky & Blue Ridge Region	Walt Disney World®
Florida & the Southeast	Inside Disney	Walt Disney World® for Grown-ups
Great Lakes States	Hawaii	Walt Disney World® with Kids
Mid-Atlantic	Las Vegas	Washington, D.C.
Northeast	London	World's Best Diving Vacations
Northwest & Central Plains		

SPECIAL-INTEREST TITLES

Frommer's Adventure Guide to Australia & New Zealand	Frommer's Italy's Best Bed & Breakfasts and Country Inns
Frommer's Adventure Guide to Central America	Frommer's New York City with Kids
Frommer's Adventure Guide to India & Pakistan	Frommer's Ottawa with Kids
Frommer's Adventure Guide to South America	Frommer's Road Atlas Britain
Frommer's Adventure Guide to Southeast Asia	Frommer's Road Atlas Europe
Frommer's Adventure Guide to Southern Africa	Frommer's Road Atlas France
Frommer's Britain's Best Bed & Breakfasts and Country Inns	Frommer's Toronto with Kids
Frommer's Caribbean Hideaways	Frommer's Vancouver with Kids
Frommer's Exploring America by RV	Frommer's Washington, D.C., with Kids
Frommer's Fly Safe, Fly Smart	Israel Past & Present
Frommer's France's Best Bed & Breakfasts and Country Inns	The New York Times' Guide to Unforgettable Weekends
Frommer's Gay & Lesbian Europe	Places Rated Almanac
	Retirement Places Rated

Booked seat 6A, open return.

Rented red 4-wheel drive.

Reserved cabin, no running water.

Discovered space.

With over 700 airlines, 50,000 hotels, 50 rental car companies and ,000 cruise and vacation packages, you can create the perfect get-way for you. Choose the car, the room, even the ground you walk on.

Travelocity.com
A Sabre Company
Go Virtually Anywhere.